American
Public School
Law

Second Edition

American Public School Law

Kern Alexander
University of Florida

M. David Alexander
Virginia Tech University

West Publishing Company
St. Paul   New York   Los Angeles   San Francisco

COPYRIGHT © 1980 BY WEST PUBLISHING CO.

COPYRIGHT © 1985 By WEST PUBLISHING CO.
50 West Kellogg Boulevard
P.O. Box 64526
St. Paul, Minnesota 55164–1003

Library of Congress Cataloging in Publication Data

Alexander, Kern.
  American public school law.

  Includes index.
  1. Educational law and legislation—United States—
Cases. I. Alexander, M. David. II. Title.
KF4118.A39 1985   344.73'071   84–21993
ISBN 0–314–85213–1   347.30471

Formerly SCHOOL LAW

Dedicated to our sisters, Harriet Alexander Hall
and Hannah Alexander Crume.

Contents in Brief

Contents

3

Role of the Federal Government   55

4

State Governance of Public Schools   85

5

Church and State   129

6

School Attendance   207

7

The Instructional Program   247

8

Student Rights   291

9

Rights of Handicapped Children   365

Burlington

10

Desegregation   405

11

Torts   453

12

Terms and Conditions of
Teacher Employment   529

13

Teacher Freedoms   565

14

Teacher Dismissal: Procedural
Due Process and Tenure   597

15

Discrimination in Employment   625

18

Property   755

Appendices   785

Table of Cases

Preface

This book is designed for graduate students in education or law school students who desire a comprehensive view of the law that governs the state school systems of America. The legal precedents discussed and presented deal with many of the multitude of issues which occur in a country that has developed an extraordinary reliance on the public schools as a mechanism for societal and cultural improvement. The desire to educate the masses to a high degree of competency has made the public schools emerge as the common ground of learning for persons of all backgrounds and persuasions. An undertaking of this scope and breadth, involving such an amalgam of people, is naturally fertile ground for human differences and perceptions that cause conflict. This book is about those conflicts which were not resolvable through the normal political processes and resort to court resolution was necessary. What the courts have said in enunciating precedents and the rules of law they have established provide a basis of knowledge valuable to all those involved with the public schools.

Education in America is large and diverse and, unlike most European systems of education, is truly federalistic in nature with each of the fifty states having a certain uniqueness of educational origin which adds strength and vitality to the whole. Because of the decentralized nature of our educational structure, it is many times difficult to identify any one, single rule of law which prevails in all states. Even with the great sweep of constitutional precedents which the Supreme Court of the United States, from time to time delivers, the law governing our schools can often be difficult to accurately assess and summarize. Beyond constitutional law, which is sometimes tighter knit because the Supreme Court can give the final word, we have a great mass of law pertaining to contracts, property, torts, general administrative law, et cetera which all bear on the administration of the schools. Too, substantial variation may be found from state to state, not merely because of the differing statutory bases, but also because of widely varying perspectives and philosophies of education which the judges, themselves, may have in viewing particular school litigation. Certainly, the social context from which the cases emanate may have strong influence on the outcome of particular disputes.

The reader of this book should, therefore, keep fully in mind that the authors, of necessity, have had to select from the great mass of case law among the hundreds of jurisdictions in this country which appear to best exemplify the prevailing view of the courts in the various areas of law. The precedents identified by the authors may not neatly fit the multitude of situations and conditions which can exist in all the local school districts across the nation. For this reason, the reader will be well advised to carefully compare the precedents of the book with the rule of law in his or her own locality before drawing hard and fast conclusions. Also, as explained in the first chapter of the text, the reader should, at all times, realize that the facts of the case are of utmost importance and small variations in facts may result in very large differences in rules of law.

This book employs the "case" or "discussion" method of teaching the law. Over the years, this method of instruction has been tried and tested largely in business schools and law schools and has been found to be a very effective approach to involve the student in the learning process. Case or discussion teaching enables the instructor to depart from merely lecturing or "telling" about the law to becoming a facilitator of classroom discussion. With this approach the instructor will circumscribe the issue for the students and then by questioning, probing, and challenging bring out the rules of law. This technique allows each student to relate one rule of law to a particular set of facts which will clarify or distinguish the educational dispute in question. By relating concrete factual situations to the law the student will be better able to recognize similar experiences when they encounter them as practicing teachers or school administrators. For the fledgling educator the study of actual cases may well prevent costly repetition. In most instances a better knowledge of both education and the law could have prevented resorting to the courts for redress of an issue. Employment of the case approach relates the student to actual experiences in a setting where the consequences of misjudgment are not so great. Learning by discussing and examining the experiences of others is of course not new; Roger Ascham in 1570 in his dissertation entitled *The Schoolmaster* observed that "Learning teacheth more in one year than experience in twenty; and learning teacheth safely, when experience maketh more miserable than wise. He hasardeth sore that waxeth wise by experience. . . . It is costly wisdom that is brought by experience." The case method in conveying not only the rule of law but the litigious factual experiences of earlier educators provides inexpensive lessons to be learned.

An effort is made, herein, to present an encompassing book, ranging across civil, criminal, and constitutional law as they touch the student, teacher, and administrator. Several chapters in the book may be of primary interest to teachers who are concerned with such matters as control over the curriculum, teacher tenure, contracts, student rights, and collective bargaining. While these too are essential information for the administrator, additional administrative legal problems are addressed in chapters on financing, property law, desegregation and intergovernmental relations. Because of the profusion of litigation that has emanated in recent years from several federal statutes, separate chapters are provided for issues concerning the education of the handicapped and employment discrimination. In totality, the book represents an attempt to convey to the educator a fully comprehensive treatment of the law, whether emanating from common law, statute or constitutional law.

We are greatly indebted to several wonderful persons who contributed to this effort in many different ways. Because this is a second edition, all those persons who were so intimately involved in the original edition are to a large measure responsible for this book as well. This particular edition, however, would not have come to fruition without the dedicated and timely assistance of Mary Jane Connelly, Patricia Anthony, Pamela Zimpfer and Lisa Spinella. First and foremost we want to express appreciation to Professor Connelly of Glassboro State College, New Jersey, who pitched in and devoted her substantial academic talents at a critical point in the preparation of the manuscript. Her editorial and substantive work in shaping material in several parts of the book were instrumental, indeed essential, to the final production of the manuscript. Dr. Anthony, University of Florida, provided the authors with the expert assistance needed to expand and round out the treatment of the law as it affects the education of the handicapped. Pam Zimpfer, now working in the Executive Office of the Governor of Florida, spent many hours in assembling and coordinating the flow of information for this project. We, also, wish to acknowledge Lynne Crist and Sharon Walrath of West Publishing Company whose efficiency of style and cordiality of manner made progress from the manuscript stage to the final product a most pleasurable experience for the authors.

Gainesville, Florida   Kern Alexander
January, 1985   M. David Alexander

1

The Legal System

INTRODUCTION

The law of the school includes all those areas of jurisprudence that bear on the operation of public elementary and secondary schools in the United States. School law as a field of study is a generic term covering a wide range of legal subject matter including the basic fields of contracts, property, torts, constitutional law, and other areas of law that directly affect the educational and administrative processes of the educational system. Because of the breadth of the subject matter involved it is necessary for the school law student to be versed in certain fundamental concepts of the American legal system and to be able to apply this knowledge to situations that daily affect school operation.

Since public schools are in fact, governmental agencies their conduct is circumscribed by legal concepts of general administrative law supplemented by those necessary legal doctrines that have uniquely evolved from the historical traditions surrounding an educational organization that is state established, yet locally administered. In this setting, legal and educational structural issues must be considered, the most important of which is the basis for the power to operate, control, and manage the schools. In analyzing the American educational system and comparing it to state systems of education in foreign countries one is struck by the diversity of power and authority under which the American public schools are governed. American federalism is nowhere more pronounced or obvious than in the public school system where there are not only fifty separate state systems but several thousand local school districts. Through all of this organizational multiformity and, indeed, complexity runs the legal basis on which the entire system is founded. The fundamental principles of legal control are quite simply those generally prescribed by our constitutional system, from which the basic organic law of the land emanates, the written constitutions of the fifty states and the federal government. Constitutions at both levels of government are basic since the positive power to create public education systems is assumed by state constitutions, and provisions of both the state and federal constitutions serve as restraints to protect the people from unwarranted denial of basic constitutional rights and freedoms.

The power of operation of the public educational system, therefore, originates with a constitutional delegation to the legislature to provide for a system of education. With legislative enactments providing the basis for public school law, it then becomes the role of the courts, through litigation, to interpret the will of the legislature. The combination of constitutions, statutes, and court or case law form the primary legal foundation on which the public schools are based.

Constitutions

A constitution is a body of precepts that provides a framework of law within which orderly governmental processes may operate. The constitutions of this country are characterized by their provisions for securing fundamental personal, property, and political rights. One of the primary precepts embodied in a constitution is the provision for authorized modification of the document. Experience in human and governmental relations teaches that to be effective a constitution must be flexible and provide for systematic change processes. The Constitution of the United States expressly provides in Article V a process for proposing amendments by a two-thirds vote of each house of Congress or by a convention that shall be called by Congress upon application by two-thirds of the state legislatures. Amendments must be ratified by the legislatures of three-fourths of the states or by conventions in three-fourths of the states.

Another precept reflected in the state and federal constitutions of this country is the importance of a government of separated powers. While all state constitutions do not expressly provide for a separation of all legislative, executive, and judicial departments, in actual practice, all states have governments of separated powers. There is no requirement in the federal constitution that the states have constitutions that require a separation of powers. Theoretically, if a state so desired, it could clothe an officer or an agency with not only executive but plenary judicial and legislative powers. However, as indicated previously, this is not the case and all states have governments with separate branches, each of which exercises checks and balances on the powers of other branches.

All state constitutions make provision for a system of free public schools. Such provisions range from very specific educational provisions to broad mandates that the legislature of the state shall provide funds for the support of a public school system.

Statutes

A statute is an act of the legislative department of government expressing its will and constituting a law of the state. Statute is a word derived from the Latin term *statutum,* which means "it is decided." Statutes, in our American form of government, are the most viable and effective means of making new law or changing old law. Statutes enacted at the state or federal level may either follow custom or forge ahead and establish new laws that shape the future.

Statutes in this country are subject to review by the judiciary to determine their constitutionality. This procedure is different from England's where the legislature has ultimate authority and there is no means by which the courts can hold legislation unconstitutional. This is true primarily because in England the constitution, for the most part, is unwritten and the legislature, Parliament, may amend the constitution when it so desires.

The public schools of the United States are governed by statutes enacted by state legislatures. The schools have no inherent powers and the authority to operate them must be found in either express or implied terms of statute. The specificity of statutes in governing the operation of public schools varies from state to state and from subject to subject. For example, one state may only generally require appropriate measures to be followed in budgeting and accounting for public funds, while in another state the legislature may actually specify each line item of the budget for school systems and lay down intricate details for accounting for these funds.

Rules and regulations of both state and local boards of education fall within the category of statutory sources of school law. As a general rule, the legislature cannot delegate its legislative powers to govern the schools to a subordinate agency or official. Boards of education must, in devising rules and regulations for the administration of the schools, do so within the limits defined by the legislature and cannot exercise legislative authority. However, the legislature may through statute expressly or impliedly confer administrative duties upon an agency or official. These administrative powers must be well defined and "canalized" within definitely circumscribed channels.

Court or Case Law

The third source of school law is judge-made or case law, sometimes called common law. The terms case law or common law are used to distinguish rules of law that are enunciated by the courts from those that have originated in legislative bodies. The term common law, in its broadest sense, may sometimes be used to contrast the entire system of Anglo-American law with the law of non-English speaking countries sometimes referred to as having systems of civil law. Civil law is a system of statutes where there is no reliance on precedent. Common law originated in England where the word "common" was derived as customs of the various parts of the country became common to the entire country. The customs of various parts of the country became crystalized into legal principles that were applied and used as precedent throughout England.

POWERS AND FUNCTIONS OF THE COURTS

The question of what powers may be exercised by the judiciary in reviewing decisions or enactments by the other two branches of government is essential to our system of government. The courts have traditionally maintained and enforced the concept of "separation of powers" when confronted with cases involving education. They will not usually question the judgment of either the administrative agencies of the executive branch or the legislative branch. This is true at the federal level as well as the state.

One court, in describing the hesitancy of the courts to interfere with the other two branches of government, said:

> This reluctance is due, in part, to an awareness of the sometimes awesome responsibility of having to circumscribe the limits of their authority. Even more persuasive is an appreciation of the importance in our system of the concept of separation of powers so that each division of government may function freely within the area of its responsibility. This safeguarding of the separate powers is essential to preserve the balance which has always been regarded as one of the advantages of our system.[1]

In accordance with this reasoning, the courts presume that legislation or administrative actions were enacted conscientiously with due deliberation and are not arbitrary or capricious.[2] When the courts do intervene they perform three types of judicial functions: (a) settle controversies by applying principles of law to a specific set of facts, (b) construe or interpret enactments of the legislature, and (c) determine the constitutionality of legislative or administrative actions.

Applying Principles

In applying principles of law to factual situations, the court may find the disputants to be either school districts, individuals, or both. Although school law cases will generally involve the school district itself, they may, in some instances, concern litigation between individuals, for example, a teacher and a student. In many cases, the principles of law governing the situation are vague, and statutory and constitutional guidance are difficult to find or virtually nonexistent. In such instances, the judges must look to judicial law precedent for guidance. Cardoza related the process in this manner:

> Where does the judge find the law he embodies in his judgment? There are times when the source is obvious. The rule that fits the case may be supplied by the constitution or by statute. If that is so, the judge looks no further. The correspondence ascertained, his duty is to obey. The constitution overrides a statute, but a statute, if consistent with the constitution, overrides the law of judges. In this sense, judge-made law is secondary and subordinate to the law that is made by legislators . . . . We reach the land of mystery when constitution and statute are silent, and the judge must look to the common law for the rule that fits the case. He is the "living oracle of the law" in Blackstone's vivid phrase.[3]

Interpreting Statutes

The second function of the courts, the task of construing and interpreting statutes, is the most common litigation involving public school operation. Since statutes are merely words, to which many definitions and interpretations may be applied, courts may actually affect the meaning of the legislation. Pound conceives of four ways with which legislation may be dealt by the courts once litigation arises:

1. They might receive it fully into the body of the law as affording not only a rule to be applied but a principle from which to reason, and hold it, as a later and more direct expression of the general will, of superior authority to judge-made rules on the same general subject; and so reason from it by analogy in preference to them.

2. They might receive it fully into the body of the law to be reasoned from by analogy the same as any other rule of law, regarding it, however, as of equal or coordinate authority in this respect with judge-made rules upon the same general subject.

3. They might refuse to receive it fully into the body of the law and give effect to it directly only; refusing to reason from it by analogy but giving it, nevertheless, a liberal interpretation to cover the whole field it was intended to cover.

4. They might not only refuse to reason from it by analogy and apply it directly only, but also give to it a strict and narrow interpretation, holding it down rigidly to those cases which it covers expressly.[4]

The last hypothesis is probably the orthodox, traditional approach; however, the courts today, in interpreting statutes, tend to adhere more and more to the second and third hypotheses.

The philosophy of the courts toward statutory interpretation varies not only among judges and courts but also in the content of the legislation being interpreted. The courts are generally more willing to grant implied authority to perform educational programs where large sums of public monies are not involved. In cases in which taxing authority is in question or in which large capital outlay programs are at issue, the courts tend to require very specific and express statutory authority in order for a school board to perform.[5]

Another, and possibly clearer, explanation of how courts construe statutes may be found in rules of law laid down by several judicial precedents. These rules—the Mischief Rule, The Golden Rule, The Literal Rule, and The Plain Meaning Rule—are useful in delineating the judiciary's options in dealing with statutory construction.[6]

The Mischief Rule ". . . for the sure and true interpretation of all statutes in general (be they penal or beneficial, restrictive or enlarging of the common law,) four things are to be discerned and considered:

1. What was the common law before the making of the Act.

2. What was the mischief and defect for which the common law did not provide.

3. What remedy the Parliament hath resolved and appointed to cure the disease of the commonwealth.

4. The true reason of the remedy; and then the office of all the Judges is always to make sure construction as shall suppress the mischief, and advance the remedy, and to suppress subtle inventions and evasions for continuance of the mischief, and *pro privato commodo,* and to add force and life to the cure and remedy, according to the true intent of the makers of the Act, *pro bono publico.*[7]

The "Golden" Rule   But it is to be borne in mind that the office of the judges is not to legislate, but to declare the expressed intention of the Legislature, even if that intention appears to the court injudicious; and I believe that it is not disputed that what Lord Wensleydale used to say is right, namely that we are to take the whole statute together, and construe it all together, giving the words their ordinary signification, unless when so applied they produce an inconsistency, or an absurdity or inconvenience so great as to convince the court that the intention could not have been to use them in their ordinary signification, and to justify the court in putting on them some other signification, which, though less proper, is one which the court thinks the words will bear.[8]

The Literal Rule   If the language of a statute be plain, admitting of only one meaning, the Legislature must be taken to have meant and intended what it has plainly expressed, and whatever it has in clear terms enacted must be enforced though it should lead to absurd or mischievous results.   If the language of this subsection be not controlled by some of the other provisions of the statute, it must, since its language is plain and unambiguous, be enforced, and your lordships' House sitting judicially is not concerned with the question whether the policy it embodies is wise or unwise, or whether it leads to consequences just or unjust, beneficial or mischievous.[9]

I should like to have a good definition of what is such an absurdity that you are to disregard the plain words of an Act of Parliament.   It is to be remembered that what seems absurd to one man does not seem absurd to another . . .   I think it is infinitely better, although an absurdity or an injustice or other objectionable result may be evolved as the consequence of your construction, to adhere to the words of an Act of Parliament and leave the legislature to set it right than to alter those words according to one's notion of an absurdity.[10]

The Plain Meaning Rule   It is elementary that the meaning of a statute must, in the first instance, be sought in the language in which the act is framed, and if that is plain, and if the law is within the constitutional authority of the lawmaking body which passed it, the sole function of the courts is to enforce it according to its terms.   . . .

Where the language is plain and admits of no more than one meaning the duty of interpretation does not arise and the rules which are to aid doubtful meanings need no discussion.   . . .

Statutory words are uniformly presumed, unless the contrary appears to be used in their ordinary and usual sense, and with the meaning commonly attributed to them.[11]

The general rule is perfectly well settled that, where a statute is of doubtful meaning and susceptible upon its face of two constructions, the court may look into prior and contemporaneous acts, the reasons which induced the act in question, the mischiefs intended to be remedied, the extraneous circumstances, and the purpose intended to be accomplished by it to determine its proper construction.   But when the act is clear upon its face, and when standing alone it is fairly susceptible of but one construction, that construction must be given to it.   . . .

The whole doctrine applicable to the subject may be summed up in the single observation that prior acts may be resorted to, to *solve,* but not to *create* an ambiguity.[12]

Constitutionality

The functions and responsibility of the judiciary in determining the constitutionality of legislation were set out early in *Marbury* v. *Madison*[13] in prescribing the power of the United States Supreme Court. This case shaped the American view of the role of the judiciary. Chief Justice Marshall's landmark opinion stated:

> It is emphatically the province and duty of the judicial department to say what the law is. Those who apply the rule to particular cases, must of necessity expound and interpret that rule. If two laws conflict with each other, the courts must decide on the operation of each. So, if a law be in opposition to the constitution; if both the law and the constitution apply to a particular case, so that the court must either decide that case, conformably to the law, disregarding the constitution; or conformably to the constitution, disregarding the law; the court must determine which of these conflicting rules governs the case. This is of the very essence of judicial duty. If then the courts are to regard the constitution, and the constitution is superior to any ordinary act of the legislature; the constitution, and not such ordinary act, must govern the case to which they both apply.

In determining the constitutionality of statutes the courts first presume the act to be constitutional and anyone maintaining the contrary must bear the burden of proof. The Florida Supreme Court has related the principle in this manner: "We have held that acts of the legislature carry such a strong presumption of validity that they should be held constitutional if there is any reasonable theory to that end . . . . Moreover, unconstitutionality must appear beyond all reasonable doubt before an Act is condemned . . . ." [14] If a statute can be interpreted in two different ways, one by which it will be constitutional, the courts will adopt the constitutional interpretation.[15]

With specific regard to the United States Supreme Court's review of legislation, either state or federal, the judicial duty in the eyes of Justice Brandeis was that "It must be evident that the power to declare legislative enactment void is one which the judge, conscious of the fallibility of human judgment, will shrink from exercising in any case where he can conscientiously and with due regard to duty and official oath decline the responsibility." [16] Using this basic philosophy, Justice Brandeis, in 1936, set out certain criteria for judicial review that are still generally referred to today in considering the standing of litigants before the Supreme Court.

1. The Court will not pass upon the constitutionality of legislation in a friendly, nonadversary proceeding, declining because to decide such questions is legitimate only in the last resort, and as a necessity in the determination of real, earnest, and vital controversy between individuals.

2. The Court will not anticipate a question of constitutional law in advance of the necessity of deciding it. It is not the habit of the Court to decide questions of a constitutional nature unless absolutely necessary to a decision of the case.

3. The Court will not formulate a rule of constitutional law broader than is required by the precise facts to which it is to be applied.

4. The Court will not pass upon a constitutional question although properly presented by the record, if there is also present some other ground upon which the case may be disposed of. This rule has found most varied application. Thus, if a case can be decided on either of two grounds, one

involving a constitutional question, the other a question of statutory construction or general law, the Court will decide only the latter.

5. The Court will not pass upon the validity of a statute upon complaint of one who fails to show that he or she is injured by its operation. Among the many applications of this rule, none is more striking than the denial of the right of challenge to one who lacks a personal or property right. Thus, the challenge by public officials interested only in the performance of their official duty will not be entertained.

6. The Court will not pass upon the constitutionality of a statute at the instance of one who has availed himself or herself of its benefits.

7. When the validity of an act of Congress is drawn in question, and even if a serious doubt of constitutionality is raised, it is a cardinal principle that this Court will first ascertain whether the construction of the statute is fairly possible by which the question may be avoided.[17]

STARE DECISIS

Implicit in the concept of common or case law is the reliance on past court decisions that reflect the historical development of legal controversies. Precedents established in past cases form the groundwork for decisions in the future. In the United States, the doctrine of precedent or the rule of *stare decisis,* "let the decision stand," prevails and past decisions are generally considered to be binding on subsequent cases that have the same or substantially the same factual situations. The rule of *stare decisis* is rigidly adhered to by lower courts when following decisions by higher courts in the same jurisdiction. Courts can limit the impact of the doctrine of precedent by carefully distinguishing the facts of the case from those of the previous case that established the rule of law. Aside from distinguishing factual situations, courts of last resort can reverse their own previous decisions and change a rule of law that they themselves established.

Stare decisis in American law does not constitute the strict adherence to older decisions that is found in English courts. The American rule of today is probably best stated by Justice Brandeis when he said that "stare decisis is usually the wise policy . . .[18] and Justice Cardoza observed that "I think adherence to precedent should be the rule and not the exception."[19]

THE HISTORICAL
DEVELOPMENT OF THE
DOCTRINE OF PRECEDENT

(Reprinted with permission, Harold J.
Berman and William R. Greiner, *The
Nature and Functions of Law,* The
Foundation Press, 1966, pp. 491–494.)

If we go back to the early history of modern English law, we find that by the end of the twelfth century, virtually as soon as records of court proceedings were kept, there developed an interest in judicial decisions as guides to what the law is. Bracton in his treatise on English law, written in the middle of the thirteenth century, referred to about 500 decided cases; he also wrote a Notebook containing digests of 2000 cases. The word "precedent," however, is entirely absent from Bracton's vocabulary; cases for him and for his contemporaries were not binding authorities but merely illustrations of legal principles.

In the fourteenth, fifteenth, and early sixteenth centuries law students kept notes of oral arguments in court cases. These notes, preserved in the so-called Yearbooks, show that not only the students but also the courts were concerned with analogizing and distinguishing cases. Again, however, the decisions were not treated as authorities in any sense, and if a judge did not approve of a decision he would just say it was wrong.

In the sixteenth and seventeeth centuries we get the first systematic reports of cases and the first mention of precedent. Judges then began to say that they are bound by precedents in matters of procedure, and especially in matters of pleading, and the practice of citing previous cases became firmly established. It is interesting to note, however, that in the first known use of the word precedent, in 1557, it is stated that a decision was given "notwithstanding two precedents." Indeed, the doctrine of precedent which developed in those centuries did not provide that a single decision was binding but rather that a line of decisions would not be overturned. Lord Mansfield could still say, in the latter part of the eighteenth century, "The reason and spirit of cases make law; not the letter of particular precedents."

Nevertheless, with the development in the seventeenth century of the distinction between dictum and holding, the way was paved for the modern doctrine. It should be noted that the seventeenth century in England was a time when analogical reasoning also became prevalent in fields other than law.

In the later nineteenth century for the first time there developed the rule that a holding by a court in a previous case is binding on the same court (or on an inferior court) in a similar case. The doctrine was called *stare decisis*—"to stand by the decisions." It was never absolute. The court is only bound "in the absence of weighty reasons." . . .

In the heyday of the doctrine of *stare decisis,* that is, in the last quarter of the nineteenth and the first quarter of the twentieth century, belief was prevalent that certainty in law could be obtained by a scientific use of precedent. The legislature alone was thought to have the function of changing the law; the court's function was "merely" to apply the law, and to apply it in accordance with the holdings of previous decisions. The common law as an organically growing body of experience and doctrine was supposed, in effect, to have been superseded by a body of fixed rules which could be mechanically applied.

The idea that the common law is a body of fixed rules vanished in the second quarter of the twentieth century, and perhaps earlier, in the face of overwhelming changes in social, economic, and political life. The mathematical or mechanical jurisprudence of the late nineteenth century which denied that there is an ethical element in the analogizing and distinguishing of cases can seldom be found today among leaders of legal thought, at least in the United States. This does not mean, however, that the doctrine of precedent has been repudiated. It means, rather, that there has been a return to an older concept of precedent.   Precedent is seen as a means of marshalling past experience, of providing a historical context, for making the choice at hand.   While condemning the hocus-pocus aspects of the strict nineteenth century doctrine, many American thinkers about law would agree with Lord Mansfield that "the common law works itself pure."

HENRY CAMPBELL BLACK, NATURE AND AUTHORITY OF JUDICIAL PRECEDENTS
H. Black, The Law of Judicial Precedents
10–11 (1912).

Not as a classification, but as exhibiting the chief aspects or applications of the doctrine of precedents, the subject might be broadly divided into five branches, in each of which there is to be noted one general rule or governing principle, as follows:

First.   Inferior courts are absolutely bound to follow the decisions of the courts having appellate or revisory jurisdiction over them.   In this aspect, precedents set by the higher courts are imperative in the strictest sense. They are conclusive on the lower courts, and leave to the latter no scope for independent judgment or discretion.

Second.   The judgments of the highest court in any judicial system—state or national—are binding on all other courts when they deal with matters committed to the peculiar or exclusive jurisdiction of the court making the precedent.   Thus, when the Supreme Court of the United States renders a decision construing the federal constitution or an act of Congress, that decision must be accepted by all state courts, as well as the inferior federal courts, as not merely persuasive, but of absolutely conclusive authority.   In the same way, when the supreme court of a state pronounces judgment upon the interpretation of a statute of the state, its decision has imperative force in the courts of the United States, as well as in the courts of another state.

Third.   It is the duty of a court of last resort to abide by its own former decisions, and not to depart from or vary them unless entirely satisfied, in the first place, that they were wrongly decided, and, in the second place, that less mischief will result from their overthrow than from their perpetuation. This is the proper application of the maxim, "stare decisis."

Fourth.   When a case is presented to any court for which there is no precedent, either in its own former decisions or in the decisions of any court whose rulings, in the particular matter, it is bound to follow, it may consult and be guided by the applicable decisions by any other court, domestic or foreign.   In this case, such decisions possess no constraining force, but should be accorded such a measure of weight and influence as they may be intrinsically entitled to receive, the duty of the court being to conform its decision to what is called the "general current of authority" or the "preponderance of authority," if such a standard can be ascertained to exist with reference to the particular question involved.

Fifth.   On the principle of judicial comity, a court which is entirely free to exercise its independent judgment upon the matter at issue, and under no legal obligation to follow the decision of another court on the same question, will nevertheless accept and conform to that decision, as a correct statement of the law, when such a course is necessary to secure the harmonious and consistent administration of the law or to avoid unseemly conflicts of judicial authority. But comity does not require any court to do violence to its own settled convictions as to what the law is.

BLACKSTONE, COMMENTARIES

1 W. Blackstone, Commentaries *69–70.

For it is an established rule to abide by former precedents, where the same points come again in litigation: as well to keep the scale of justice even and steady, and not liable to waver with every new judge's opinion; as also because the law in that case being solemnly declared and determined, what before was uncertain, and perhaps indifferent, is now become a permanent rule, which it is not in the breast of any subsequent judge to alter or vary from according to his private sentiments: he being sworn to determine, not according to his own private judgment; but according to the known laws and customs of the land; not delegated to pronounce a new law, but to maintain and expound the old one. Yet this rule admits of exception, where the former determination is most evidently contrary to reason; much more if it be clearly contrary to the divine law. But even in such cases the subsequent judges do not pretend to make a new law, but to vindicate the old one from misrepresentation. For if it be found that the former decision is manifestly absurd or unjust, it is declared, not that such a sentence was *bad law,* but that it was *not law;* that is, that it is not the established custom of the realm, as has been erroneously determined. And hence it is that our lawyers are with justice so copious in their encomiums on the reason of the common law; that they tell us, that the law is the perfection of reason, that it always intends to conform thereto, and that what is not reason is not law. Not that the particular reason of every rule in the law can at this distance of time be always precisely assigned; but it is sufficient that there be nothing in the rule flatly contradictory to reason, and then the law will presume it to be well founded.

JOHN HANNA, THE ROLE OF PRECEDENT IN JUDICIAL DECISION

Reprinted with permission from Villanova Law Review Volume 2, No. 3, pp. 367–368 Copyright 1957, by Villanova University.

Stare decisis or, in its complete form, *stare decisis et non quieta movere* is usually translated "to stand by (or adhere to) decisions and not to disturb what is settled." The classic English version is by Coke: "They said that those things which have been so often adjudged ought to rest in peace." Blackstone says: "The doctrine of the law then is this: that precedents and rules be followed, unless flatly absurd or unjust; for though their reason be not obvious at first view, yet we owe such a deference to former times as not to suppose that they acted wholly without consideration." The general American doctrine as applied to courts of last resort is that a court is not inexorably bound by its own precedents but will follow the rule of law which it has established in earlier cases, unless clearly convinced that the rule was originally erroneous or is no longer sound because of changing conditions and that more good than harm will come by departing from precedent. The alternative to stare decisis as popularly defined would be (1) absolute discretion on the part of a court to decide each case without reference to any precedent; or (2) complete codification of our law, with a requirement that each court look independently to the code for a basis of decision. A more limited reform would be to bar the courts from following precedents of decisions on statutory and constitutional law. None of these alternatives is a matter of much contemporary debate in America. If we define stare decisis in terms of its proper limitations, it should always be applied. We shall stay closer to the points of controversy if we appreciate that our real subject is the theory of judicial precedent.

UNDERSTANDING JUDICIAL DECISIONS

In order to determine the rule of a case, it is necessary to find the *ratio decidendi* or the point on which the judgment balances. This is done primarily by carefully analyzing the facts of the case that are treated by the judge as being material. Only the material facts are relevant to the identification of the *ratio decidendi* of a case. Conclusions of a judge departing from the *ratio* are not binding as precedent and are considered to be *obiter dicta*. Essentially there are two types. First, a statement of law is *obiter* if it is based on facts that were not found to exist, or if the facts are present they are immaterial. Second, it may also be a statement of law that, although based on established facts of the case, does not form the rationale for the decision. A statement of law supporting a dissenting opinion is one example. Another instance of *obiter* may be where a court makes a statement of law leading to one conclusion but then reaches a contrary decision on the facts for a different reason.[20]

Karl N. Llewellyn,[21] late Professor of Law, University of Chicago, in his work *The Bramble Bush* probably offers the best and most concise explanation of what to look for when reading case law. Since the case method is employed in presenting most of the materials in this book it seems appropriate to quote a portion of Llewellyn's comments on reading and analyzing judicial opinions.

> The first thing to do with an opinion, then, is read it. The next thing is to get clear the actual decision, the judgment rendered. Who won, the plaintiff or defendant? And watch your step here. You are after in first instance the plaintiff and defendant below, in the trial court. In order to follow through what happened you must therefore first know the outcome below; else you do not see what was appealed from, nor by whom. You now follow through in order to see exactly what further judgment has been rendered on appeal. The stage is then cleared of form—although of course you do not yet know all that these forms mean, that they imply. You can turn now to what you peculiarly do know. Given the actual judgments below and above as your indispensable

framework—what has the case decided, and what can you derive from it as to what will be decided later?

You will be looking, in the opinion, or in the preliminary matter plus the opinion, for the following: a statement of the facts the court assumes; a statement of the precise way the question has come before the court—which includes what the plaintiff wanted below, and what the defendant did about it, the judgment below, and what the trial court did that is complained of; then the outcome on appeal, the judgment; and finally the reasons this court gives for doing what it did. This does not look so bad. But it is much worse than it looks. For all our cases are decided, all our opinions are written, all our predictions, all our arguments are made, on certain four assumptions. . . . (1) *The court must decide the dispute that is before it.* It cannot refuse because the job is hard, or dubious, or dangerous. (2) *The court can decide only the particular dispute which is before it.* When it speaks to that question it speaks *ex cathedra*, with authority, with finality, with an almost magic power. When it speaks to the question before it, it announces law, and if what it announces is new, it legislates, it makes the law. But when it speaks to any other question at all, it says mere words, which no man needs to follow. Are such words worthless? They are not. We know them as judicial *dicta;* when they are wholly off the point at issue we call them *obiter dicta* —words dropped along the road, wayside remarks. Yet even wayside remarks shed light on the remarker. They may be very useful in the future to him, or to us. But he will not feel bound to them, as to his *ex cathedra* utterance. They came not hallowed by a Delphic frenzy. He may be slow to change them; but not so slow as in the other case. (3) *The court can decide the particular dispute only according to a general rule which covers a whole class of like disputes.* Our legal theory does not admit of single decisions standing on their own. If judges are free, are indeed forced, to decide new cases for which there is no rule, they must at least make a new rule as they decide. So far, good. But how wide or how narrow, is the general rule in this particular case? That is a troublesome matter. The practice of our case-law, however, is I think, fairly stated thus: It pays to be suspicious of general rules which look too wide; it pays to go slow in feeling certain that a wide rule has been laid down at all, or that, if seemingly laid down, it will be followed. For there is a fourth accepted canon: (4) *Everything, everything, everything, big or small, a judge may say in an opinion, is to be read with primary reference to the particular dispute, the particular question before him.* You are not to think that the words mean what they might if they stood alone. You are to have your eye on the case in hand, and to learn how to interpret all that has been said merely as a reason for deciding that case that way. . . .

CASE OR CONTROVERSY

Article III of the Constitution of the United States limits the power of the judiciary to "decide and pronounce a judgment and carry it into effect between persons and parties who bring a case before it for decision." [22] The judicial branch may settle conflicts that involve only actual "cases" and "controversies." [23] The determination of what constitutes a "case" and "controversy" is left to the judgment of the Supreme Court.

The courts of the United States do not sit to decide questions of law presented in a vacuum, but only such questions as arise in a "case or controversy." [24] The two terms can be used interchangeably, for, we are authoritatively told, a "controversy," if distinguishable at all from a "case," is distinguishable only in that it is a less comprehensive term, and includes only suits of a civil nature. [25]

That which is a "case or controversy"—justiciable in the federal courts—was defined by Chief Justice Hughes in a classic and cryptic statement. He said: "A 'controversy' in this sense must be one that is appropriate for judicial determination. A justiciable controversy is thus distinguished from a difference or dispute of a hypothetical character; from one that is academic or moot. The controversy must be definite and concrete, touching the legal relations of parties having adverse legal interests. It must be a real and substantial controversy admitting of specific relief through a decree of a conclusive character, as distinguished from an opinion advising what the law would be upon a hypothetical state of facts." [26]

Later, Chief Justice Warren said of the "case or controversy" requirement that "those two words have an iceberg quality, containing beneath their surface simplicity submerged complexities which go to the very heart of our constitutional form of government. Embodied in the words 'cases' and 'controversies' are two complementary but somewhat different limitations. In part those words limit the business of federal courts to questions presented in an adversary context and in a form historically viewed as capable of resolution through the judicial process. And in part those words define the role assigned to the judiciary in a tripartite allocation of power to assure that the federal courts will not intrude into areas committed to the other branches of government. Justiciability is the term of art employed to give expression to this dual limitation placed upon federal courts by the case and controversy doctrine." [27]

It should also be noted that the limitation to "case or controversy" is intimately related to the doctrine of judicial review. In *Marbury* v. *Madison* [28] it was central to Marshall's argument that a court has power to declare a statute unconstitutional only as a consequence of the power of the court to decide a case properly before it. Unconstitutional statutes there may be, but unless they are involved in a case properly susceptible of judicial determination, the courts have no power to pronounce that they are unconstitutional. The reluctance of courts to pass on constitutional issues unless absolutely necessary has led to a rigorous set of rules as to what constitutes a justiciable "case or controversy."

THE AMERICAN COURT SYSTEM

In our federal form of government it is necessary to have a dual judicial system, state and federal. Cases involving public schools may be litigated at either level and while most actions involve nonfederal questions and are decided by state courts, recent years have brought on a substantial increase in the number of school cases handed down by federal courts.

State Courts

State constitutions will generally prescribe the powers and the jurisdiction of the primary or main state courts. The legislature, through power granted in the constitution, provides for the specific operation of the constitutional courts and it may create new and additional courts if so authorized by the constitution.

The types of state courts may be classified into four categories: those of general jurisdiction, special jurisdiction, small claims, and appeals.[29]

Courts of general jurisdiction are usually called district or circuit courts. The jurisdiction of these courts covers all cases except those reserved for special courts. The subject matter of cases of general jurisdiction sometimes overlaps with that of courts of special jurisdiction.

Courts of special jurisdiction are set up to handle cases involving litigation in special subject matter areas that generally involve large numbers of cases. Probate courts, domestic relations courts, and juvenile courts are common types of courts of special jurisdiction.

Small claims courts are established to handle lawsuits involving small amounts of money. Justice of the peace courts are usually classified as small claims courts, although some states may classify small claims courts and justice of the peace courts as having separate jurisdictions; for example, in Florida small claims courts have civil jurisdiction in cases at law in which the demand or value of the property does not exceed two hundred and fifty dollars [30] while the justice of the peace courts have jurisdiction over disputes involving actions for not more than one hundred dollars.[31]

Appellate courts are found in all states and in most are the only courts to which appeals may be made involving decisions of trial courts of general jurisdiction. These courts are usually called Supreme Courts or Courts of Appeals. Some states, because of the sheer volume of cases, have established intermediate appellate courts. For example, New York and California have intermediate appellate courts, and Indiana has both a Court of Appeals and a Supreme Court. In states with intermediate courts of appeals, certain cases on appeal may terminate at the intermediate appellate court while other cases can be appealed to the state's highest court.

Federal Courts

Article III of the Constitution of the United States provides in part: "The judicial power of the United States, shall be vested in one supreme court, and in such inferior courts as the Congress may from time to time ordain and establish."[32] Pursuant to this provision Congress has created a network of courts.

Today, the federal court system in the United States includes District Courts, Courts of Appeals, Special Federal Courts, and the Supreme Court.

There is at least one district court in each state and usually more than two. Cases litigated before federal district courts may largely be classified into two types: (1) cases between citizens of different states and (2) cases involving litigation of federal statutes or the federal constitution. Cases before district courts are usually presided over by one judge. However, in limited situations, involving challenges to apportionment of statewide legislative bodies or apportionment of Congressional districts or otherwise required by Congress, a three-judge court made up of a circuit judge and two district judges may be appointed to hear a case. Decisions of district courts may be appealed to the federal courts of appeals and, in some instances, directly to the Supreme Court of the United States. There are thirteen courts of appeals, each in one of the thirteen federal judicial circuits. (See Figures 1–3).

In addition, federal courts have been established by the Congress to handle special problems or to cover special jurisdictions. These courts are the courts of the District of Columbia, the Court of Claims, the Tax Court, the Customs Courts, the Courts of Customs and Patent Appeals, the Emergency Court of Appeals, and the territorial courts.

The Supreme Court of the United States is the highest court in the land beyond which there is no redress. Cases may be brought before the Supreme Court by appeal, *writ of certiorari*, or through the original jurisdiction of the Court.

Most school cases that go to the Supreme Court are taken on *writs of certiorari*, certiorari being an original action whereby a case is removed from an inferior to a superior court for trial. Cases may be taken to the Supreme Court from state courts by *writ of certiorari* where a state statute or federal statute is questioned as to its validity under the federal Constitution or where any title, right, privilege, or immunity is claimed under the Constitution. Since most school law cases fall within this category, the *writ of certiorari* is the most common means of getting a case before the Supreme Court.

ARCHIBALD COX, THE ROLE OF THE SUPREME COURT IN AMERICAN SOCIETY

Reprinted by permission, 50 Marq.L.Rev.
575, 582–84 (1967).

The task of protecting the individual against the aggressions of government, which under our system usually means aggressions willed by representatives of a majority of the people, often conflicts with the Court's special duty of maintaining the frame of government, which includes the separation of legislative and judicial power. Judicial review calls upon the Court to go over the very social, political and economic questions committed to the Congress and State legislatures, yet it can scarcely do so without usurping in some degree the legislative function of weighing and balancing competing interests. . . .

The conventional escape from this dilemma is to say that the conclusions of Congress will stand unless they are so wrong, upon any state of facts that might rationally be supposed to exist, as to be irrational, arbitrary or capricious, fundamentally unfair or shocking to the conscience of a free people. The formula has substance to command it but the difference between saying that an important law is foolish and saying that it is arbitrary or violates fundamental rights lies chiefly in the strength of the speaker's conviction. Any weighing and balancing of the very same interests appraised by the legislature inescapably evokes personal judgments upon the relative importance of imponderable elements.

Whatever the answer to these questions the Court's responsibility for the framework of government does less to check the Court's reviewing of laws affecting personal liberty than its scrutiny of statutes regulating business and economic practices. This position has strong roots in constitutional history. The Bill of Rights is the chief express constitutional limitation upon legislative power. It is concerned not with the physical safety of society, jobs or economic activity and security—the bricks and mortar of the community—but with the realm of the spirit. The Framers dreamed that if their hopes for civil liberty were codified, man's energies of mind and spirit, released from fear, would flourish. They also knew that society's respect for the freedom of a man to grow and choose the best he can discern must be founded upon the protection of privacy and just and humane criminal procedure. . . .

NOTES

United States Circuit Court of Appeals, 42 U.S.C.A. § 41.

Number and composition of circuits

The thirteen judicial circuits of the United States are constituted as follows:

Circuits	Composition
District of Columbia	District of Columbia.
First	Maine, Massachusetts, New Hampshire, Puerto Rico, Rhode Island.
Second	Connecticut, New York, Vermont.
Third	Delaware, New Jersey, Pennsylvania, Virgin Islands.
Fourth	Maryland, North Carolina, South Carolina, Virginia, West Virginia.
Fifth	District of the Canal Zone, Louisiana, Mississippi, Texas.
Sixth	Kentucky, Michigan, Ohio, Tennessee.
Seventh	Illinois, Indiana, Wisconsin.
Eighth	Arkansas, Iowa, Minnesota, Missouri, Nebraska, North Dakota, South Dakota.
Ninth	Alaska, Arizona, California, Idaho, Montana, Nevada, Oregon, Washington, Guam, Hawaii.
Tenth	Colorado, Kansas, New Mexico, Oklahoma, Utah, Wyoming.
Eleventh	Alabama, Florida, Georgia.
Federal	All federal judicial districts.

FIGURE 1 THE UNITED STATES COURT SYSTEM

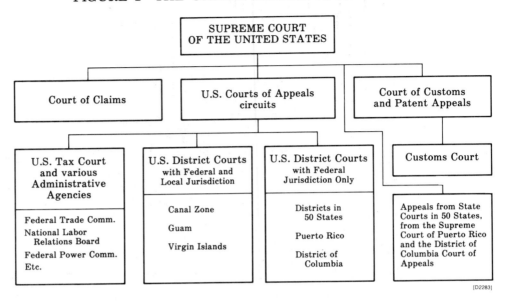

FIGURE 2 A TYPICAL STATE COURT SYSTEM

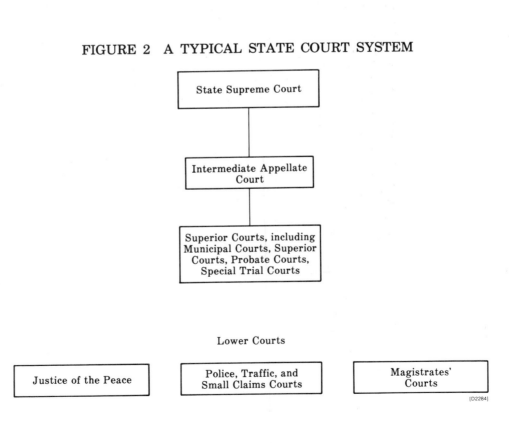

FIGURE 3 THE THIRTEEN FEDERAL JUDICIAL CIRCUITS

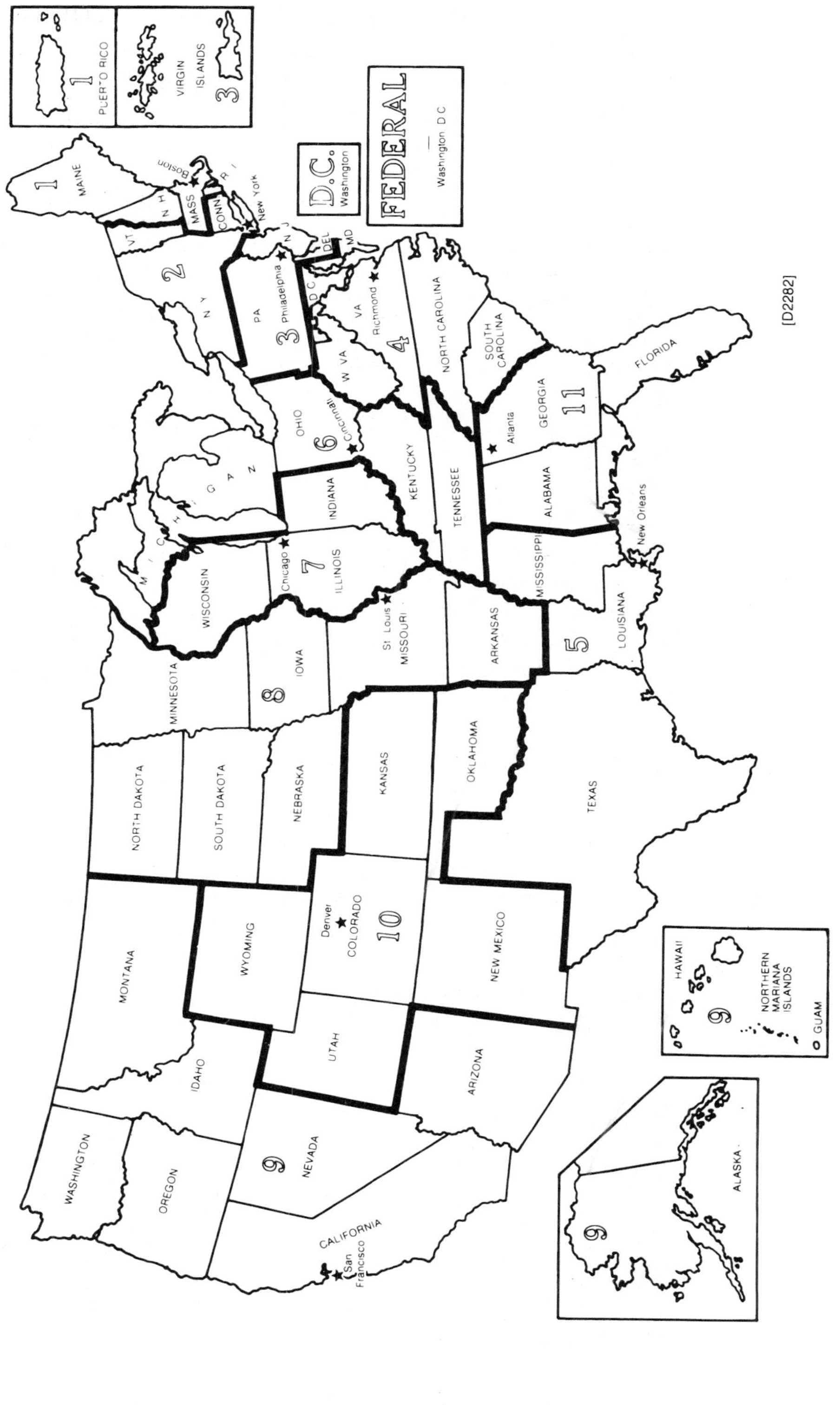

[D2282]

Footnotes

1. Ricker v. Board of Education of Millard County School District, 16 Utah 2d 106, 396 P.2d 416 (1964).

2. Latham v. Board of Education of City of Chicago, 31 Ill.2d 178, 201 N.E.2d 111 (1965).

3. Cardoza, Benjamin N., *The Nature of the Judicial Process* (New Haven and London: Yale University Press, 1962), pp. 18–19.

4. Pound, Roscoe, "Common Law and Legislation," 21 *Harvard Law Review,* pp. 383, 385 (1908). Copyright © 1908 by The Harvard Law Review Association.

5. Marion & McPherson Railway Co. v. Alexander, 63 Kan. 72, 64 P. 978 (1901).

6. See H. Hart and A. Sacks, *The Legal Process: Basic Problems in the Making and Application of Law* (Cambridge, 10th ed. 1958) pp. 1144–46. Reprinted by permission of Dean Albert M. Sacks.

7. Heydon's Case, Exchequer, 30 Co. 7a, 76 Eng.Rep. 637 (1584).

8. Lord Blackburn in River Wear Commissioners v. Adamson, 2 App.Cas. 742, 746 (House of Lords, 1877).

9. Lord Atkinson, in Vacher & Sons, Limited v. London Society of Compositers, 107 L.T.Rep. 722 (House of Lords 1913).

10. Lord Bramwell, in Hill v. East and West India Dock Co., 9 A.C. 448, 464–65 (House of Lords, 1884).

11. Mr. Justice Day, in Caminetti v. United States, 242 U.S. 468, 485–486, 37 S.Ct. 192, 194 (1917).

12. Mr. Justice Brown, in Hamilton v. Rathbone, 175 U.S. 414, 419, 421, 20 S.Ct. 155, 157 (1899).

13. 5 U.S. (1 Cranch) 137 (1803).

14. Bonvento v. Board of Public Instruction of Palm Beach County, 194 So.2d 605 (Fla.1967).

15. Hobbs v. County of Moore, 267 N.C. 665, 149 S.E.2d 1 (1966).

16. Ashwander v. Tennessee Valley Authority, 297 U.S. 288, 56 S.Ct. 466 (1936).

17. Supra.

18. Burnet v. Coronado Oil & Gas Co., 285 U.S. 393, 52 S.Ct. 443 (1932).

19. Supra, p. 449.

20. R.J. Walker & M.G. Walker, *The English Legal System* (London: Butterworths, 1972), p. 124.

21. K.N. Llewellyn, *The Bramble Bush, On Our Law and Its Study* (New York: Oceana Publications, 1960) pp. 41–43.

22. Muskrat v. United States, 219 U.S. 346, 31 S.Ct. 250 (1911).

23. Constitution of the United States, Art. III, § 2.

24. Charles Alan Wright, *Law of Federal Courts* (St. Paul, MN: West Publishing Co., 1970).

25. Aetna Life Insurance Co. v. Haworth, 300 U.S. 227, 229, 57 S.Ct. 461, 463, 108 A.L.R. 1000, 1937, quoting from In re Pacific Railway Commission, 32 F. 241, 255 (C.C.D.Cal.1887).

26. Id.

27. Flast v. Cohen, 392 U.S. 83, 94–95, 88 S.Ct. 1942, 1949–50 (1968).

28. 5 U.S. (1 Cranch) 137, (1803).

29. Carl A. Auerbach, Lloyd K. Garrison, Willard Hurst, and Samuel Mermin, *The Legal Process* (San Francisco: Chandler Publishing Company, 1961) pp. 3–4.

30. West's Ann.Fla.S.A. 42.03.

31. West's Ann.Fla.S.A. 37.01(1).

32. Constitution of the United States, Art. III, § 1.

2

Historical
Perspective

The law of public education is shaped by the philosophical, political, and social traditions of the United States. In the early years, the colonies quite naturally assumed the pattern of the class-oriented English educational system in which free and universal education was far beyond the eye of the most progressive leaders. Children of poor and lower-class families received no education at all or were attached as apprentices to learn a trade and develop manual skills.

Even though there was some governmental recognition of the benefits of education, as evidenced by a 1642 statute in Massachusetts in which all parents were charged with seeing to the education of their children and later in 1647 when the legislature required certain towns to appoint a teacher and permitted taxes for education, by and large early colonial legislatures tended to ignore education. The law of 1647 was promulgated to teach all to read the scriptures in order to avoid falling prey to "the old deluder, Satan." What efforts were made to educate were through pauper school laws that provided that if indigent parents would declare themselves paupers their children could be sent to specified private or pay schools for a free education.[1] A vestige of the English system that was used in some colonies was the "rate bill," which required the parent to pay an amount for each child to supplement inadequate school revenues. The amount assessed was collected from the parents through ordinary tax bills. Such rate bills were still in effect in New York State as late as 1867.[2]

It was not until the eighteenth century that a new political philosophy developed that conceived of education as essential to the welfare of the state. Until then, the benefits of education were viewed as largely personal; the external value of education to society had not yet been realized. As the colonies began to struggle for independence from England, the concept of free public education gained momentum. Americans became obsessed with freedom and schools were viewed as the primary means by which freedom could be obtained and maintained.

During the 1760s and 1770s the idea developed that there should be a free system of education that would provide for a general diffusion of knowledge, cultivate new learning, and nurture the democratic ideals of government. A "system" of education implied at least three attributes. First, there should be some uniformity of access so that the general population would have the opportunity to acquire some appropriate level of learning. Second, there should be some method by which one could pursue a particular curriculum. Third, there should be some institutional organization whereby a person could progress from primary, to secondary, to college or university.[3] This view was especially well enunciated by Benjamin Rush who called for the state to be "tied together by one system of education." "The university," he said, "will in time furnish masters for the colleges, and colleges will furnish masters for the free schools, while the free schools, in their turns, will supply the colleges and the universities with scholars, students and pupils. The same systems of grammar, oratory and philosophy, will be taught in every part of the state, and the literary features of Pennsylvania will thus designate one great, and equally enlightened family."[4]

Rush emphasized the need to have a free and uniform system of education that would "render the mass of the people more homogeneous, and thereby fit them more easily for uniform and peaceable government."[5]

As Butts observed, "the really important reason for believing in the value of education is that it can be the foundation of freedom. In the first place, a truly democratic society must rest upon the knowledge, intelligence, and wisdom of all the people."[6] Americans generally embraced the words of Jefferson, that "a people who mean to be their own Governors must arm themselves with the power which knowledge gives." More than any other, Jefferson's words redounded the public or common school philosophy that was to sweep the young nation in generations to come. Typical of Jefferson's position was his letter from Paris in 1786 to his old professor George Wythe written in support of a bill for general education:

> I think by far the most important bill in our whole code is that for the diffusion of knowledge among the people. No other sure foundation can be devised for the preservation of freedom and happiness. . . . Preach, my dear sir, a crusade against ignorance; establish and improve the law for educating the common people. Let our countrymen know . . . that the tax which will be paid for this purpose is not more than the thousandth part of what will be paid to kings, priests, and nobles who will rise up among us if we leave the people in ignorance.[7]

In this new era, not only was universal education in greater demand but a discernible shift toward more practical studies was in evidence and the old Latin grammar school began to deteriorate as the major source of learning. After 1750 the enthusiasm for schools based on religious motivations began to die down and the European traditions for both types and methods of education no longer satisfied the American appetite for knowledge.[8] A concept of public education evolved that was uniquely American. During this period general school laws in older states, which marked the progression of public education, required maintenance of schools by towns for a definite term each year, imposed taxation, and generally statutorily sanctioned the public school movement that had evolved over a century and a half.[9]

A clearly defined role of the state in education, however, had not emerged by 1796 when George Washington, in his Farewell Address, called for the American people to:

> Promote, then, as an object of primary importance, institutions for the general diffusion of knowledge. In proportion as the structure of a government gives force to public opinion, it is essential that public opinion be enlightened.[10]

To progress from the sporadic and inadequate early general school laws to uniform state systems of free public education was a laborious journey with battles over tax support and sectarianism marking the way. By 1825, it had become commonly recognized that a state system of education would require general and direct taxation of a major source of revenue such as real property. A broad base of taxation became the watchword; "The wealth of the State must educate the children of the State" aptly described the principle of taxation for education that was to eventually emerge.[11]

Established traditions were not easily overcome and it was difficult to convince many of the citizens that pauper schools were not the appropriate educational concept since it was believed to be merely the poor and poverty stricken who would benefit from free public schools.

A major impetus for education had come from the churches that sought to advance Christianity through knowledge of the Bible. Early states generally recognized and supported these efforts and several states set aside lands to help church schools. As the new philosophy of public education became entrenched and people started to grasp its benefits, new advocates for state education emerged and conflict with church leaders developed. The inherent discord between sectarian education and free state education were soon manifested in bitter struggles in several states, the story of which is more fully developed in a later chapter of this book.

Into the vortex of these conflicts stepped public education advocates such as Horace Mann of Massachusetts,[12] who preached an educational awakening that was ultimately to form the basis for state systems of public education as we know them today—free secular public schools supported by both local and state general taxation.

The early nineteenth century saw an extraordinary group of dedicated and effective leaders who were "public school men" emerge in several states. They argued against tuition in any shape or form and most importantly they maintained that the term "free school" should no longer mean merely a place where the poor were given a free education and all others paid tuition. Class distinctions, they argued, would be reduced if all children could be given a free education financed with revenues from taxes levied on everyone.[13]

This view was reflected in an 1822 report to the Kentucky legislature that advocated free common schools and specifically rejected the pauper school approach:

> To be separated from the rest of the community as a distinct and inferior caste, and held out to the world as the objects of public charity, is a degradation too humiliating for the pride of freemen.[14]

In this same state in 1819, the Governor, in an eloquent plea to the legislature for creation of a free system of common schools, asserted both the value of education for the welfare of the state and for the equality and livelihood of the people. Although his message fell on deaf legislative ears at that particular time, his statement is worth repeating because this is the philosophy on which the free common schools of the United States were founded:

> Our government depends for its perpetuity upon the virtue and wisdom of the people; virtue is the offspring of wisdom. To be virtuous, the people must be wise. But how shall they be wise, unless the appropriate means are employed? And how shall the appropriate means be extended to the bereaved and destitute, otherwise than by legislative provision? Education is more vitally important in a republican than in any other form of government; for there the right to administer the government is common to all, and when they have the opportunity of administering the government, the means of obtaining the wisdom requisite for its administration should be accessible to all. The wealthy are never without the means of obtaining education; the poor never, or rarely possess them. But the capacity for the acquisition of knowledge, and the display of virtue, is not confined to the wealthy. It is often, and perhaps more frequently found amongst the poor. Instances are not rare in which genius has emerged from poverty, surmounted the difficulties and privations inseparable from that condition, and like the sun burst through a cloud, illumined the social and political horizon by its benignant irradiations. The ornaments and benefactors of society have not unfrequently arisen when but very slight helps were afforded, from the humblest walks of life.[15]

During this period, struggles over public schools were fought with conviction by those on both sides. Cubberley described this era when public, free, nonsectarian, tax-supported schools were first given serious consideration and there was much public debate between church and private school advocates and public school proponents.

> The second quarter of the nineteenth century may be said to have witnessed the battle for tax-supported, publicly controlled and directed, and nonsectarian common schools. In 1825 such schools were the distant hope of statesmen and reformers; in 1850 they were becoming an actuality in almost every Northern State. The twenty-five years intervening marked a period of public agitation and educational propaganda; of many hard legislative fights; of a struggle to secure desired legislation, and then to hold what had been secured; of many bitter contests with church and private-school interests, which felt that their "vested rights" were being taken from them; and of occasional referenda in which the people were asked, at the next election, to advise the legislature as to what to do. Excepting the battle for the abolition of slavery, perhaps no question has ever been before the American people for settlement which caused so much feeling or aroused such bitter antagonisms. Old friends and business associates parted company over the question, lodges were forced to taboo the subject to avoid disruption, ministers and their congregations often quarreled over the question of free schools, and politicians avoided the issue. The friends of free schools were at first commonly regarded as fanatics, dangerous to the State, and the opponents of free schools were considered by them as old-time conservatives or as selfish members of society. . . .
>
> Many thought that tax-supported schools would be dangerous for the State, harmful to individual good, and thoroughly undemocratic. There was

danger, too, of making education too common. Schools of any kind were, or should be, for the few, and chiefly for those who could afford private instruction. It was argued that education demands a leisure class and that the poor do not have the necessary leisure, that it was not possible for the government to provide a general educational system, and that all such proposals represented the deliberate confiscation of the property of one class in society for the benefit of another class. These and other arguments were well answered some years later by Horace Mann when he stated, at some length, the political and economic "Ground of the Free School System." Others were afraid that free schools were only a bait, the real purpose being to "religiously traditionalize the children," and then later unite Church and State. Many did not see the need for schools at all, and many more were in the frame of mind of the practical New England farmer who declared that "the Bible and figgers is all I want my boys to know." Strangely enough, the most vigorous opposition often came from the ignorant, improvident, hand-to-mouth laborers, who most needed schools, and free schools at that. Often those in favor of taxation were bitterly assailed, and even at times threatened with personal violence. Henry Barnard, who rendered such useful service in awakening Connecticut and Rhode Island, between 1837 and 1845, to the need for better schools, tells us that a member of the Rhode Island legislature told him that a bill providing a small state tax for schools, which he was then advocating, even if passed by the legislature, could not be enforced in Rhode Island at the point of the bayonet.[16]

Legislatures gradually accepted the idea of free or common schools for all and by statute began to require local school districts to tax themselves to support the public schools. In this early period, it became clear that the states must require rather than permit localities to establish free schools. Local control of education gradually became limited by state constitutions and by actions of state legislatures. Uniformity of education across states, it was decided, would be better brought to fruition by a degree of central state planning rather than through completely decentralized local school control.[17]

By 1852, when Massachusetts enacted the first compulsory attendance law, the responsibility for public education was firmly lodged at the state level. The idea of free common schools was well established but the implementation of the concept developed slowly. It remained for succeeding generations to deal with the pervasive issues of "uniformity" and "equality," which have grown to be as vital to the public school movement as the word "freedom" was originally.

As a major governmental enterprise the development of the public school system was accompanied by a continuous string of legal controversies in every state in the nation. As a result, court decisions have to a great extent given form and substance to the philosophical base on which the public schools are founded. The courts have made it quite clear that "Public education is not merely a function of government; it is of government." [18] In legal theory, public schools exist not only to confer benefits on the individual but just as importantly they are necessary, indeed essential, to the advancement of civil society.[19] Of such importance is the public education function that the state can, under certain conditions, limit parental control in order to advance the common weal.[20]

The rationale for the creation of a system of free public schools has been reiterated may times by the courts expounding the importance of an educated citizenry for the general welfare of the people and for the protection of the state.[21]

Recognition of the role and importance of public schools to the well-being of the people and the state was expressed by the Supreme Court of Illinois in 1914. This court declared that public schools were created not out of philanthropic motives, but out of a consideration of the essentials of good government. The conduct and maintenance of schools is no less an "exercise of the functions vested in those charged with the conduct of government," is no less a part of "the science and art of government," and deals no less with the "organization, regulation and administration of a State" in its internal affairs, than the construction and maintenance of roads by the commissioners of highways; the conduct and maintenance of the charitable institutions of the state by the board of administration; the inspection of factories, and the enforcement of the laws for the protection of workers and in regard to the employment of women and children by the factory inspectors; the performance of the industrial board of the duties imposed upon it by law, and the performance of many other duties by public officials that, however beneficial to individuals, are not undertaken from philanthropic or charitable motives, but for the protection, safety, and welfare of the citizens of the state in the interest of good government." [22]

Similarly, it was said by the Supreme Court of New Hampshire:

> The primary purpose of the maintenance of the common school system is the promotion of the general intelligence of the people constituting the body politic and thereby to increase the usefulness and efficiency of the citizens, upon which the government of society depends. Free schooling furnished by the state is not so much a right granted to pupils as a duty imposed upon them for the public good. If they do not voluntarily attend the schools provided for them, they may be compelled to do so. While most people regard the public schools as the means of great personal advantage to the pupils, the fact is too often overlooked that they are governmental means of protecting the state from the consequences of an ignorant and incompetent citizenship.[23]

This judicial philosophy is stated in various ways by the decisions in other state supreme courts. The high court for Tennessee, for example, saw a need for a uniform system of public schools to promote the general welfare "by educating the people, and thus, by providing and securing a higher state of intelligence and morals, conserve the peace, good order, and well-being of society." [24]

MASSACHUSETTS SCHOOL
LAW OF 1647

Sec. 1. It being one chief project of the old deluder, Satan, to keep men from the knowledge of the Scriptures, as in former times by keeping them in an unknown tongue, so in these latter times by persuading them from the use of tongues that so at least the true sense and meaning of the original might be clouded by false glosses of saint-seeming deceivers, that learning may not be buried in the grave of our fathers in the church and commonwealth, the Lord assisting our endeavors . . . .

It is therefore ordered by this court and authority thereof, that every township in this jurisdiction, after the Lord hath increased them to the number of fifty householders, shall then forthwith appoint one within their town to teach all such children as shall resort to him to write and read, whose wages shall be paid either by the parents or masters of such children, or by the inhabitants in general, by way of supply, as the major part of those that order the prudentials of the town shall appoint; provided, those that sent their children be not oppressed by paying much more than they can have them taught for in other towns.

Sec. 2. It is further ordered, that where any town shall increase to the number of one hundred families or householders they shall set up a grammar school, the master thereof being able to instruct youth so far as they may be fitted for the university; and if any town neglect the performance hereof above one year, every such town shall pay five pounds per annum to the such school till they shall perform this order. . . .

PREAMBLE TO A BILL FOR THE MORE GENERAL DIFFUSION OF KNOWLEDGE
(1779)

From *The Works of Thomas Jefferson*, collected and edited by Paul Leicester Ford, Volume II, Federal Edition (New York: G. P. Putnam's Sons, 1904), pp. 414–426, abridged.

Whereas it appeareth that however certain forms of government are better calculated than others to protect individuals in the free exercise of their natural rights, and are at the same time themselves better guarded against degeneracy, yet experience hath shown, that even under the best forms, those entrusted with power have, in time, and by slow operations, perverted it into tyranny; and it is believed that the most effectual means of preventing this would be, to illuminate, as far as practicable, the minds of the people at large, and more especially to give them knowledge of those facts, which history exhibiteth, that, possessed thereby of the experience of other ages and countries, they may be enabled to know ambition under all its shapes, and prompt to exert their natural powers to defeat its purposes. And whereas, it is generally true that people will be happiest whose laws are best, and are best administered, and that laws will be wisely formed, and honestly administered, in proportion as those who form and administer them are wise and honest; whence it becomes expedient for promoting the publick happiness that those persons, whom nature hath endowed with genius and virtue, should be rendered by liberal education worthy to receive, and able to guard the sacred deposit of the rights and liberties of their fellow citizens, and that they should be called to that charge without regard to wealth, birth or other accidental condition or circumstance; but the indigence of the greater number disabling them from so educating, at their own expense, those of their children whom nature hath fitly formed and disposed to become useful instruments for the public, it is better that such should be sought for and educated at the common expence of all, than that the happiness of all should be confided to the weak or wicked. . . .

HORACE MANN'S TENTH and TWELFTH ANNUAL REPORTS TO THE MASSACHUSETTS BOARD OF EDUCATION

From the 10th Annual Report, published in *The Common School Journal*, Vol. IX, No. 9, edited by Horace Mann (Boston: William B. Fowle, 1847); the 12th Annual Report, published separately from the *Journal* by Fowle in 1849.

From the Tenth Report (1846):

I believe in the existence of a great, immutable principle of natural law, or natural ethics, a principle antecedent to all human institutions and incapable of being abrogated by any ordinances of man, a principle of divine origin, clearly legible in the ways of Providence as those ways are manifested in the order of nature and in the history of the race, which proves the *absolute right* of every human being that comes into the world to an education; and which, of course, proves the correlative duty of every government to see that the means of that education are provided for all.

In regard to the application of this principle of natural law, that is, in regard to the extent of the education to be provided for all, at the public expense, some differences of opinion may fairly exist, under different political organizations; but under a republican government, it seems clear that the minimum of this education can never be less than such as is sufficient to qualify each citizen for the civil and social duties he will be called to discharge; such an education as teaches the individual the great laws of bodily health; as qualifies for the fulfilment of parental duties; as is indispensable for the civil functions of a witness or a juror; as is necessary for the voter in municipal affairs; and finally, for the faithful and conscientious discharge of all those duties which devolve upon the inheritor of a portion of the sovereignty of this great republic.

From the Twelfth Report (1848):

The Capacities of Our Present School System to Improve the Pecuniary Condition and to Elevate the Intellectual and Moral Character of the Commonwealth

Under the Providence of God, our means of education are the grand machinery by which the "raw material" of human nature can be worked up into inventors and discoverers, into skilled artisans and scientific farmers, into scholars and jurists, into the founders of benevolent institutions, and the great expounders of ethical and theological science. By means of early education, those embryos of talent may be quickened, which will solve the difficult problems of political and economical law; and by them, too, the genius may be kindled which will blaze forth in the Poets of Humanity. Our schools, far more than they have done, may supply the Presidents and Professors of Colleges, and Superintendents of Public Instruction, all over the land; and send, not only into our sister states, but across the Atlantic, the man of practical science, to superintend the construction of the great works of art. Here, too, may those judicial powers be developed and invigorated, which will make legal principles so clear and convincing as to prevent appeals to force; and, should the clouds of war ever lower over our country, some hero may be found, the nursling of our schools, and ready to become the leader of our armies, the best of all heroes, who will secure the glories of a peace, unstained by the magnificent murders of the battle-field. . . .

Without undervaluing any other human agency, it may be safely affirmed that the Common School, improved and energized, as it can easily be, may become the most effective and benignant of all the forces of civilization. Two reasons sustain this position. In the first place, there is a universality in its operation, which can be affirmed of no other institution whatever. If administered in the spirit of justice and conciliaton, all the rising generation may be brought within the circle of its reformatory and elevating influences. And, in the second place, the materials upon which it operates are so pliant and ductile as to be susceptible of assuming a greater variety of forms than any other earthly work of the Creator. . . .

I proceed, then, in endeavoring to show how the true business of the schoolroom connects itself, and becomes identical, with the great interests of society. The former is the infant, immature state of those interests; the latter, their developed, adult state. As "the child is father to the man," so may the training of the schoolroom expand into the institutions and fortunes of the State.

According to the European theory, men are divided into classes—some to toil and earn, others to seize and enjoy. According to the Massachusetts theory, all are to have an equal chance for earning, and equal security in the enjoyment of what they earn. The latter tends to equality of condition; the former to the grossest inequalities. Tried by any Christian standard of morals, or even by any of the better sort of heathen standards, can any one hesitate, for a moment, in declaring which of the two will produce the greater amount of human welfare; and which, therefore, is the more conformable to the Divine will? . . .

I suppose it to be the universal sentiment of all those who mingle any ingredient of benevolence with their notions on Political Economy, that vast and overshadowing private fortunes are among the greatest dangers to which the happiness of the people in a republic can be subjected. Such fortunes would create a feudalism of a new kind; but one more oppressive and unrelenting than that of the Middle Ages. The feudal lords in England, and on the continent, never held their retainers in a more abject condition of servitude, than the great majority of foreign manufacturers and capitalists hold their operatives and laborers at the present day. The means employed are different, but the similarity in results is striking. What force did then, money does now. . . . The baron prescribed his own terms to his retainers; those terms were peremptory, and the serf must submit or perish. . . .

Now, surely, nothing but Universal Education can counter-work this tendency to the domination of capital and the servility of labor. If one class possesses all the wealth and the education, while the residue of society is ignorant and poor, it matters not by what name the relation between them may be called; the latter, in fact and in truth, will be the servile dependents and subjects of the former. But if education be equably diffused, it will draw property after it, by the strongest of all attractions; for such a thing never did happen, and never can happen, as that an intelligent and practical body of men should be permanently poor. . . .

Education, then, beyond all other devices of human origin, is the great equalizer of the conditions of men—the balance-wheel of the social machinery. I do not here mean that it so elevates the moral nature as to make men disdain and abhor the oppression of their fellow-men. This idea pertains to another of its attributes. But I mean that it gives each man the independence and the means, by which he can resist the selfishness of other men. . . .

For the creation of wealth, then—for the existence of a wealthy people and a wealthy nation—intelligence is the grand condition. The number of improvers will increase, as the intellectual constituency, if I may so call it, increases. In former times, and in most parts of the world even at the present day, not one man in a million has ever had such a development of mind, as made it possible for him to become a contributor to art or science. Let this development precede, and contributions, numberless, and of inestimable value, will be sure to follow. That Political Economy, therefore, which busies itself about capital and labor, supply and demand, interest and rents, favorable and unfavorable balances of trade; but leaves out of account the element of a wide-spread mental development, is nought but stupendous folly. The greatest of all the arts in political economy is to change a consumer into a producer; and the next greatest is to increase the producing power—an end to be directly attained, by increasing his intelligence. . . .

JUDICIAL APPROVAL OF COMMON SCHOOLS

The egalitarian motivation for the common school necessitated the enrollment of all children of all social and economic backgrounds. To enlarge public schools from a system of limited free education for poor children—pauper schools—to common schools at the elementary and high school levels required an ever-increasing commitment of public funds.[25]

The transformation to truly *common* schools required that the public schools be of such quality that they could attract the children of the more affluent in addition to the children of the poor. Ravitch points out that this movement toward common schools was a logical extension of the Jacksonian philosophy of 1828 that heralded the frontier philosophy of equality and the decline of social class based on wealth and position. "Political equality forced the emergence of new political patterns, and the schools, like other social institutions, began to adjust to the demands of the rising middle class."[26]

Opposition to this movement was expressed both politically and in the courts. An early example of such litigation is found in the *Hartman* [27] case in Pennsylvania decided in 1851 wherein school directors refused to comply with a statute requiring them to create a system of common schools for all children, not just the poor. The school directors defended their position by maintaining that the Pennsylvania Constitution did not permit the legislature to expand the public schools from pauper schools to common schools. The court disagreed.

Legislature Is Not Prohibited from
Creating a System of Common Schools
by Expanding on the Pauper School
Provision in State Constitution

COMMONWEALTH v. HARTMAN

Supreme Court of Pennsylvania, 1851.
17 Pa. 118.

The appellants, Hartman and five others, had been elected school directors of Lowhill township, Lehigh county. They organized by electing the officers required by the common school law, and made provision for the education of the poor children in that township, but refused to comply with the provisions of the Acts of Assembly of 1848 and 1849, requiring them to provide for the establishment of common schools in that township: and they refused to resign. A petition was presented to the Court of Quarter Sessions, on April 30, 1849, praying the court to declare their offices vacant, and to appoint substitutes. The court granted a rule upon them to appear and answer; and on May 5, 1849, JONES, J., vacated their office and appointed others in their stead to act until the next annual election for directors. The objection made on the part of Hartman and others was that the school laws of 1848 and 1849 *were unconstitutional*, as being at variance with the provision in the first section of the 7th article of the Constitution of Pennsylvania, which is as follows: Sect. 1. "The legislature shall, as soon as conveniently may be, provide by law for the establishment of schools throughout the state, in such manner that the poor may be taught *gratis*." It was provided in the Act of Assembly of 11th April, 1848, "That the common school system, from and after the passage of this Act, shall be deemed, held, and taken to be adopted by the several school districts in this Commonwealth," . . . .

In the Act of 7th April 1849, it is provided, "That a system of common school education be and the same is hereby deemed, held, and taken to be adopted, according to the provisions of this Act, in all the counties in this Commonwealth," . . . .

The Act points out the mode of electing directors, and defines their "general powers and duties." It provided that "They shall establish a sufficient number of *common schools* for the education of every individual between the ages of five and twenty-one years, in the districts, who may apply for admission and instruction, either in person, or by parent, guardian, or next friend." [italics added]

The opinion of the court was delivered Dec. 29, 1851, by

BLACK, C.J.—The only ground on which this court has been urged to reverse the order of the Quarter Sessions, is, that the school law is unconstitutional. We are of opinion that there is nothing in that law, certainly nothing in that part of it to which our attention has been particularly called, which, in the slightest degree, contravenes the constitution. It is to be remembered, that the rule of interpretation for the state constitution differs totally from that which is applicable to the constitution of the United States. The latter instrument must have a strict construction; the former a liberal one. Congress can pass no laws but those which the constitution authorizes either expressly or by clear implication; while the Assembly has jurisdiction of all subjects on which its legislation is not prohibited. The powers, not granted to the government of the Union, are withheld; but the state retains every attribute of sovereignty which is not taken away. In applying this principle to the present case, it is enough to say, that there is no syllable in the constitution which forbids the legislature to provide for a system of general education in any way which they, in their own wisdom, may think best. But it is argued, that for the purpose of promoting education, and carrying out the system of common schools, laws may be passed which will work intolerable wrong, and produce grievous hardship. The answer to this is, that a decent respect for a coordinate branch of the government, compels us to deny that any such danger can ever exist. But if a law, unjust in its operation, and nevertheless not forbidden by the constitution, should be enacted, the remedy lies, not in an appeal to the judiciary, but to the people, who must apply the corrective themselves, since they have not intrusted the power to us.

The constitution, in sect. 1 of article VII, provides that "the legislature shall, as soon as conveniently may be, provide by law for the establishment of schools throughout the state *in such manner that the poor may be taught gratis.*" It seems to be believed that the last clause of this section is a limitation to the power of the legislature, and that no law can be constitutional which looks to any other object than that of teaching the poor gratis. The error consists in supposing this to define the *maximum* of the legislative power, while in truth it only fixes the minimum. It enjoins them to do thus much, but does not forbid them to do more. If they stop short of that point, they fail in their duty; but it does not result from this that they have no authority to go beyond it.

Order affirmed.

EXPANSION OF FREE PUBLIC SCHOOLS

Earlier, education above the elementary school level had to be acquired at private academies for which a tuition fee was charged and few, if any, poor children attended. Common schools were generally looked upon as being for the elementary grades only. Yet, free public high schools soon became a democratic necessity. Cubberley observed that "the rising democracy of the second quarter of the nineteenth century now demanded and obtained the democratic high school." [28]   Gradually the high school became an integral part of the free public school system.

The academy had succeeded the old Latin schools with a more practical curriculum designed to more adequately meet the needs of the older youths beyond preparation for college. These academies spread rapidly and were variously known as institutes, seminaries, collegiate institutes, and sometimes colleges. By the early 1800s, Massachusetts had thirty-six academies, New York nineteen, Georgia ten, and some states, including Kentucky and Indiana, by the early 1800s had systems of county academies. [29] The greatest growth of the academies was during the period from 1820 to 1840. Most of these academies were residential schools and charged fees for room and board as well as for tuition. Some were financed by local taxation and a few even had state assistance. The academies, however, were inadequate to meet the burgeoning need for extended educational opportunity. The tuition and fees made accessibility difficult for the poor and, even though their numbers were substantial, they were not numerous enough to be within reasonable walking, wagon, or horseback distance from rural homes to be nonresidential.

The solution was the genesis of the American high school. The American high school had no forerunners and was distinguished from previous European models by its close relationship to the common schools. The high school was an extension of the common elementary school making it, from the beginning, a higher common school.

The first American high school was established in Boston in 1821 and the increase in the number of high schools was slow, but methodical, for the next thirty years. Skepticism as to the viability of the high school was expressed by many who were imbued with the tradition of the academy. As late as 1874, President Porter of Yale University observed that "the expenditure of money for high schools to prepare boys and girls for college was a doubtful experiment." By 1872, 70 percent of the students entering colleges in the east were graduates of academies, but by 1920, 90 percent of the entering freshmen were graduates of high schools.

Opposition to the high school as an extension of the common school generally came from taxpayers who did not want to bear the increased financial burden, as well as from those advocates of the academies and private sectarian schools who thought that creation of high schools would further diminish the public's reliance on their respective schools.

The court decision generally credited with opening the doors to the public high school as we know it today was the famous *Kalamazoo* case in 1872. [30] No constitutional or legislative provisions in Michigan had previously explicitly established a system of high schools. The legal basis for education was found in legislation in 1817 that contained a provision for public academies and in the constitution of 1835, which provided for free primary schooling, but neither established a pathway between the primary schooling and the university. Local students aspiring to a university education had entered the preparatory department of the private Kalamazoo College (chartered in 1855). No public accommodation had been made for students' preparation for college until 1858 when the local school superintendent created the union high school at a time when several of these union high schools had been created elsewhere in Michigan. This particular school thrived amid local controversy created by both taxpayers, who objected to paying for the school, and the proprietors of Kalamazoo College, who had lost students to the union high school. Finally, in 1873 a group of prominent citizens filed suit to restrain the school board from expending public funds to support the high school. Ultimately, the case was appealed to the Supreme Court of Michigan where Judge Thomas M. Cooley rendered a landmark decision.

Even though there was other litigation of this nature during this period, this case was particularly important because of the stature of the court and the judicial rationale by which the high school was justified. Courts are generally reticent, in the absence of express statutory language, to imply authority to perform some public function if the expenditure of funds is involved, but here the court did not hesitate to do so.

This judicial recognition of the importance of public schools provided a philosophical basis for both legislatures and courts to broaden educational opportunity by extending the school system not only upward, but also downward to kindergartens as well as to expand the scope of education to areas such as vocational education, special education for the handicapped, and compensatory education.

*Taxes May be Levied on the General
Public to Expand Common School
Program Through High School*

STUART v. SCHOOL DISTRICT NO. 1 OF THE VILLAGE OF KALAMAZOO

Supreme Court of Michigan, 1874.
30 Mich. 69.

COOLEY, J.: The bill in this case is filed to restrain the collection of such portion of the school taxes assessed against complainants for the year 1872, as have been voted for the support of the high school in that village, and for the payment of the salary of the superintendent. While, nominally, this is the end sought to be attained by the bill, the real purpose of the suit is wider and vastly more comprehensive than this brief statement would indicate, inasmuch as it seeks a judicial determination of the right of school authorities, in what are called union school districts of the state, to levy taxes upon the general public for the support of what in this state are known as high schools, and to make free by such taxation the instruction of children in other languages than the English. The bill is, consequently, of no small interest to all the people of the state; and to a large number of very flourishing schools, it is of the very highest interest, as their prosperity and usefulness, in a large degree, depend upon the method in which they are supported, so that a blow at this method seems a blow at the schools themselves. . . .

The more general question which the record presents we shall endeavor to state in our own language, but so as to make it stand out distinctly as a naked question of law, disconnected form all considerations of policy or expediency; in which light alone are we at liberty to consider it. It is, as we understand it, that there is no authority in this state to make the high schools free by taxation levied on the people at large. The argument is that while there may be no constitutional provision expressly prohibiting such taxation, the general course of legislation in the state and the general understanding of the people have been such as to require us to regard the instruction in the classics and in living modern languages in these schools as in the nature not of practical and therefore necessary instruction for the benefit of the people at large, but rather as accomplishments for the few, to be sought after in the main by those best able to pay for them, and to be paid for by those who seek them, and not by general tax. And not only has this been the general state policy, but this higher learning of itself, when supplied by the state, is so far a matter of private concern to those who receive it that the courts ought to declare it incompetent to supply it wholly at the public expense. This is in substance, as we understand it, the position of the complainants in this suit. . . .

It is not disputed that the dissemination of knowledge by means of schools has been a prominent object from the first, and we allude to the provision of the ordinance of 1787 on that subject, and to the donation of lands by congress for the purpose. . . .

Thus stood the law when the constitution of 1835 was adopted. The article on education in that instrument contained the following provisions:

"2.   The legislature shall encourage by all suitable means the promotion of intellectual, scientical and argicultural improvement. . . .

"3.   The legislature shall provide for a system of common schools . . . ."

. . . Two things are specially noticeable in these provisions: *first,* that they contemplated provision by the state for a complete system of instruction, beginning with that of the primary school and ending with that of the university; *second,* that while the legislature was required to make provision for district schools for at least three months in each year, no restriction was imposed upon its power to establish schools intermediate the common district school and the university, and we find nothing to indicate an intent to limit their discretion as to the class or grade of schools to which the proceeds of school lands might be devoted, or as to the range of studies or grade of instruction which might be provided for in the district schools. . . .

The system adopted by the legislature, and which embraced a university and branches, and a common or primary school in every school district of the state, was put into successful operation, and so continued, with one important exception, until the adoption of the constitution of 1850. The exception relates to the branches of the university, which the funds of the university did not warrant keeping up, and which were consequently abandoned. Private schools to some extent took their place; but when the convention met to frame a constitution in 1850, there were already in existence, in a number of the leading towns, schools belonging to the general public system, which were furnishing instruction which fitted young men for the university. These schools for the most part had been organized under special laws, which, while leaving the primary school laws in general applicable, gave the districts a larger board of officers and larger powers of taxation for buildings and the payment of teachers. As the establishment and support of such schools were optional with the people, they encountered in some localities considerable opposition, which, however, is believed to have been always overcome, and the authority of the districts to provide instruction in the languages in these union schools was not, so far as we are aware, seriously contested. . . .

It now becomes important to see whether the constitutional convention and the people, in 1850, did any thing to undo what previously had been accomplished towards furnishing high schools as a part of the primary school system. The convention certainly did nothing to that end. On the contrary, they demonstrated in the most unmistakable manner that they cherished no such desire or purpose. . . .

The instrument submitted by the convention to the people and adopted by them provided for the establishment of free schools in every school district for at least three months in each year, and for the university. By the aid of these we have every reason to believe the people expected a complete collegiate education might be obtained. The branches of the university had ceased to exist; the university had no prepatory department, and it must either have been understood that young men were to be prepared for the university in the common schools, or else that they should go abroad for the purpose, or be prepared in private schools. Private schools adapted to the purpose were almost unknown in the state, and comparatively a very few persons were at that time of sufficient pecuniary ability to educate their children abroad. The inference seems irresistible that the people expected the tendency towards the establishment of high schools in the primary school districts would continue until every locality capable of supporting one was supplied. . . .

If these facts do not demonstrate clearly and conclusively a general state policy, beginning in 1817 and continuing until after the adoption of the present constitution, in the direction of free schools in which education, and at their option the elements of classical education, might be brought within the reach of all the children of the state, then, as it seems to us, nothing can demonstrate it. We might follow the subject further, and show that the subsequent legislation has all concurred with this policy, but it would be a waste of time and labor. We content ourselves with the statement that neither in our state policy, in our constitution, or in our laws, do we find the primary school districts restricted in the branches of knowledge which their officers may cause to be taught, or the grade of instruction that may be given, if their voters consent in regular form to bear the expense and raise the taxes for the purpose.

It follows that the decree dismissing the bill was right, and should be affirmed.

The other justices concurred.

NOTES

1. Constitutional provisions requiring an "efficient" system of schools is a command to the legislature to provide a fair and efficient system open to all children. People ex rel. Tuohy v. Barrington Consol. High School

Dist. No. 224, 396 Ill. 129, 71 N.E.2d 86 (1947); Fiedler v. Eckfeldt, 335 Ill. 11, 166 N.E. 504 (1929). (See also school of finance cases in Chapter 17).

2. The efficiency and fairness of a state school system is for the determination of the legislature. McLain v. Phelps, 409 Ill. 393, 100 N.E.2d 753 (1951).

3. Constitutional requirements of a "uniform" system of free public schools are distinguished from other state educational institutions in determination of the uniformity of the system. State ex rel. Clark v. Henderson, 137 Fla. 666, 188 So. 351 (1939).

4. The requirement of uniformity does not mean that all schools have a uniform school government nor that all children be provided the same means of instruction. It simply means that all areas of the state may enjoy the same sort of school based on a particular class or grade, Landis v. Ashworth, 57 N.J. Law 509, 31 A. 1017 (1895); Smith v. Simmons, 129 Ky. 93, 110 S.W. 336 (1908).

5. Because of the public concern for education, the legislature can require compulsory attendance, provided such requirement does not violate constitutional limitations. See Everson v. Board of Educ. of Ewing Twp., 330 U.S. 1, 67 S.Ct. 504 (1947), and Pierce v. Society of the Sisters of the Holy Names of Jesus and Mary, 268 U.S. 510, 45 S.Ct. 571 (1925) in later chapters.

6. In an early Virginia decision the court explained the power of the state to enact legislation governing the public schools. The court said:

> While the Constitution of the state provides in mandatory terms that the Legislature shall establish and maintain public free schools, there is neither mandate nor inhibition in the provisions as to the regulation thereof. The Legislature, therefore, has the power to enact any legislation in regard to the conduct, control, and regulation of the public free schools, which does not deny to the citizen the Constitutional right to enjoy life and liberty, to pursue happiness and to acquire property. Flory v. Smith, 145 Va. 164, 134 S.E. 360 (1926).

TUITION AND FEES IN PUBLIC SCHOOLS

Courts have generally held that tuition fees, "matriculation" or "registration" fees, and fees for materials, activities, or privileges cannot be levied in public schools.[31] In most cases invalidating fees, the courts have reasoned that the fee was charged as a condition of attendance, which violated the state's constitutional or statutory provisions establishing "free" public schools. Another reason often given by the courts for invalidating fees is the lack of statutory authority to exact the fee. Courts have usually held fees invalid when the fees have been charged for an essential element of a school's activity. When fees have been upheld, the courts have found that there was statutory authorization for the fee, that the purpose for the fee was a reasonable one, or that the term "free schools" did not include furnishing textbooks.[32]

Courts have on occasion distinguished tuition fees from incidental fees, and, in at least one jurisdiction, a court has upheld an incidental fee of twenty-five cents per pupil per month to be used for raising funds to pay for fuel to heat the schoolroom, for brooms to sweep the schoolroom, and for water buckets to contain water.[33] In the same jurisdiction, an incidental fee for improvement of grounds, insurance, and other incidental expenses did not violate the state constitution.[34]

However, in other jurisdictions incidental fees have been held invalid. In Georgia,[35] a very early decision held that a state statute requiring each child upon entering municipal public schools to pay the board of education an "incidental fee" was "clearly unconstitutional." However, a court in Illinois ruled that the state constitutional provision requiring the establishment of a thorough and efficient system of free schools did not prevent the state legislature from authorizing school boards to purchase textbooks and rent them to pupils.[36]

In most cases, fees for activities, materials, or privileges have been held invalid.[37] A $25 annual fee required by one school district as a condition to furnishing each high school student a transcript of courses studied and grades achieved was held to be unconstitutional in Idaho.[38] The fee consisted of $12.50 for school activity fees and $12.50 for textbook fees, and had to be paid before a student could receive a transcript. Responding to each of these separately, the court reasoned that the student activity fee was imposed on all students whether they participated in extra-curricular activities or not. Therefore, the fee was on attendance not on activities and as such contravened the state constitutional mandate that public schools be free. The court did note that since social and extracurricular activities were not necessarily principal elements of a high school career, the state constitution did not prohibit the school district from setting activity fees for students who voluntarily participated. With regard to the textbook fee, the court observed that since textbooks were necessary to the school, they were indistinguishable from other fixed educational expense items such as building maintenance and teachers' salaries, all for which fees could not be charged.[39]

The requirement that pupils purchase textbooks and school supplies has been held invalid in Michigan.[40] In this case, the school district maintained the word "free" in the state constitution did not include textbooks and supplies. The Supreme Court of Michigan held that books and supplies were necessary elements of any school's activity and an integral and fundamental part of elementary and secondary education.

Textbook Fee in Elementary Grades
Violates State Constitution

CARDIFF v. BISMARCK
PUBLIC SCHOOL DISTRICT
Supreme Court of North Dakota, 1978.
263 N.W.2d 105.

SAND, Justice. . . .

Gary Cardiff and other parents of school children attending elementary schools in the Bismarck Public School District brought an action in Burleigh County district court challenging the authority of the school district to charge rental fees for the use of necessary school textbooks. . . .

The basic issue for our resolution is whether or not § 148 of the North Dakota Constitution provides for free textbooks and prohibits the Legislature from authorizing school districts to charge for textbooks. The parents contend the constitutional provision prohibits charging for textbooks, and the school district contends it merely prohibits charging tuition. . . .

To resolve the first issue we must examine and construe the provisions of § 148 of the North Dakota Constitution, which provides as follows:

> The legislative assembly shall provide at their first session after the adoption of this constitution, for a uniform system of free public schools throughout the state, beginning with the primary and extending through all grades up to and including the normal and collegiate course.

In 1968 this section was amended, as follows:

> The legislative assembly shall provide for a uniform system of free public schools throughout the state, beginning with the primary and extending through all grades up to and including schools of higher education, except that the legislative assembly may authorize tuition, fees and service charges to assist in the financing of public schools of higher education.

In construing a written constitution we must make every effort to determine the intent of the people adopting it. . . .

We must examine the whole instrument in order to determine the true intention of every part so as to give effect to each section and clause. If different portions seem to be in conflict, we must make a true effort to harmonize them if practicable.

In interpreting clauses in a constitution we must presume that words have been employed in their natural and ordinary meaning.

Both parties contended that contemporaneous construction, as an aid in construction and interpretation of the constitution, . . . favored its point of view on the construction of § 148 of the North Dakota Constitution. . . .

From this examination we are left with a firm conviction that the legislative acts referred to do not lend any significant comfort or aid to the resolution of the basic question under consideration, namely, what does the term "uniform system of free public schools" mean? Contemporaneous construction in this instance is not helpful to either party. The Journal entries of the constitutional convention are not very helpful in determining the meaning of the language, "free public schools."

The first item relating to public schools introduced at the North Dakota Constitutional Convention, as found in the Journal, was File No. 47, § 2, which provided, in part:

> It shall be the duty of the Legislature to establish and maintain a system of free public schools, adequate for education of all children in the state, between the ages of six and eighteen years, inclusive, in the common branches of knowledge, and in virtue and christian morality. . . .

From this brief review it is clear that the framers consistently had in mind a free public school.

A short survey of the constitutional provisions of other states and their case law will shed some light on our question.

ARIZONA:
> The Legislature shall provide for a system of common schools by which a free school shall be established . . . Constitution, Article XI, § 6.

In Carpio v. Tucson High School District No. 1 of Pima County, 111 Ariz. 127, 524 P.2d 948 (1974), cert. denied 420 U.S. 982, 95 S.Ct. 1412, 43 L.Ed.2d 664, the court had under consideration Article XI, § 6, of the Arizona Constitution. The court held that textbooks were not required to be furnished to high school students. However, the court referred to an earlier decision, Shoftstall v. Hollins, 110 Ariz. 88, 515 P.2d 590 (1973), where the court held that these constitutional provisions had been satisfied when the legislature provided for the means of establishing required courses, qualifications of teachers, textbooks to be used in common schools, etc. Considering this statement and the statement in *Carpio* that "textbooks have not been provided free in high schools as they have been in the common schools" leaves the impression that under the constitutional provisions of Arizona textbooks in common schools were provided free of charge.

COLORADO:
> The general assembly shall . . . provide for the establishment and maintenance of a thorough and uniform system of free public schools . . . Constitution, Art. IX, § 2.

In Marshall v. School District RE # 3 Morgan County, 553 P.2d 784 (Colo.1976), the court held that the school district was not required to furnish books free of charge to all students.

INDIANA:
> . . . it shall be the duty of the General Assembly . . . to provide, by law, for a general and uniform system of Common Schools, wherein tuition shall be without charge, and equally open to all. Constitution, Article 8, Section 1.

In Chandler v. South Bend Community School Corporation, 160 Ind.App. 592, 312 N.E.2d 915 (1974), the court held that this constitutional provision did not require textbooks to be provided free, but merely to provide a system of common schools where tuition would be without charge.

ILLINOIS:

Education in public schools through the secondary level shall be free. Constitution, Article X, section 1.

In Beck v. Board of Education of Harlem Consolidated School District No. 122, 63 Ill.2d 10, 344 N.E.2d 440 (1976), the court held that workbooks, and other educational material, were not textbooks so as to come within the statutory provision of free textbooks, and as such it did not preclude the school board from charging the parents a fee for supplying the students with such material.

Earlier, in Hamer v. Board of Education of School District No. 109, 47 Ill. 2d 480, 265 N.E.2d 616 (1970), the court was specifically concerned with the constitutional provision and held that under its provisions the school board was not prohibited from purchasing textbooks and renting them to pupils. It further held that the legislature had the power to direct the district school boards to issue textbooks to students free of charge but the constitution did not require it. In a related case entitled Hamer v. Board of Education of School District No. 109, County of Lake, 9 Ill.App.3d 663, 292 N.E.2d 569 (1973), the court in effect re-affirmed its earlier decision in the *Hamer* case.

WISCONSIN:

The legislature shall provide . . . for . . . district schools . . . and such schools shall be free and without charge for tuition . . . Constitution, Article X, section 3.

The court in Board of Education v. Sinclair, 65 Wis.2d 179, 222 N.W.2d 143 (1974), held that the schools may charge a fee for the use of textbooks and items of similar nature authorized by statute and that such did not violate the constitutional provision commanding that schools shall be free without charge for tuition for all children. It basically held that the term "free" referred to school buildings and equipment and what is normally understood by the term "tuition."

IDAHO:

. . . . it shall be the duty of the legislature of Idaho, to establish and maintain a general, uniform and thorough system of public, free common schools. Constitution, Art. 9, sec. 1.

In Paulson v. Minidoka County School District No. 331, 93 Idaho 469, 463 P.2d 935 (1970), the court held that school districts could not charge students for textbooks under the state constitutional provision. It also held that public high schools in Idaho are "common schools."

MICHIGAN:

The legislature shall maintain and support a system of free public elementary and secondary schools . . . Constitution, Article 8, § 2.

In 1908 the Michigan Constitution, Article 11, § 9, in part provided:

The legislature shall continue a system of primary schools, whereby every school district in the state shall provide for the education of its pupils without charge for tuition .

The Michigan court in Bond v. Public Schools of Ann Arbor, School District, 383 Mich. 693, 178 N.W.2d 484 (1970), held that the 1963 constitutional provision meant that books and school supplies were an essential part of the system of free public elementary and secondary schools and that the schools should not charge for such items. We note that the 1908 Constitution provided "without charge for tuition," whereas the 1963 Constitution provides for a system of "free public elementary and secondary schools."

MONTANA:

> It shall be the duty of the legislative assembly of Montana to establish and maintain a general, uniform and thorough system of public, free, common schools. Constitution, Article XI, Section 1.

In Granger v. Cascade County School District No. 1, 159 Mont. 516, 499 P.2d 780 (1972), the school district, as the school district here, contended that the pertinent language simply meant "tuition-free" as far as required courses were concerned and did not prohibit fees and charges for optional extracurricular or elective courses and activities. The Montana parents, however, contended that the schools could not impose fees or charges for anything, whether elective or required, that is encompassed in the constitutional requirement of a "thorough system of public, free, common schools." The fees involved more than just charges for workbooks and textbooks, as in this case. The Montana Supreme Court answered the question in the following manner:

> We believe that the controlling principle or test should be stated in this manner: Is a given course or activity reasonably related to a recognized academic and educational goal of a particular school system? If it is, it constitutes part of the free, public school system commanded by Art. XI, Sec. 1 of the Montana Constitution and additional fees or charges cannot be levied, directly or indirectly, against the student or his parents. If it is not, reasonable fees or charges may be imposed.

The court, however, pointed out that its decision does not apply to supplementary instruction offered by the school district on a private basis during the summer recess or at special times. It should be observed that the school district in the *Granger* case, as well as in the instant case, argued that they had a system of waivers and charges for welfare recipients and other cases of economic hardship. The court rejected this argument.

NEW MEXICO:

> A uniform system of free public schools sufficient for the education of, and open to, all children of school age in the state shall be established and maintained. Constitution, Article XII, § 1.

The court, in Norton v. Board of Education of School District No. 16, 89 N.M. 470, 553 P.2d 1277 (1976), held that under this constitutional provision courses required of every student shall be without charge to the student. However, reasonable fees may be charged for elective courses. The court also recognized that the board of education shall define what are required or elective courses in the educational system of New Mexico.

SOUTH DAKOTA:

> . . . it shall be the duty of the legislature to establish and maintain a general and uniform system of public schools wherein tuition shall be without charge. Constitution adopted 1889, Article VIII, § 1.

We have found no South Dakota case law on the question of tuition or textbooks.

WEST VIRGINIA:
> The legislature shall provide by general law, for a thorough and efficient system of free schools. Constitution, Article XII, Section 1.

The court in Vandevender v. Cassell, 208 S.E.2d 436 (W.Va.1974), held that furnishing textbooks free to needy students satisfied the constitutional requirement. But two of the five judges, in a concurring opinion, stated that they did not interpret "free" as pertaining only to indigent pupils. They further stated:

> It is clear to me [us], however, that where state constitutions contain language providing for free schools, such as Article XII, Section 1 of the West Virginia Constitution, that this means free schools for students of all economic classes.

MISSOURI:
> . . . schools and the means of education shall forever be encouraged in this state. [The legislature was required to establish schools] as soon as practicable and necessary, where the poor shall be taught gratis. Constitution of 1820, art. VI, § 1.
>
> A general diffusion of knowledge and intelligence being essential to the preservation of the rights and liberties of the people, the general assembly shall establish and maintain free public schools for the gratuitous instruction of all persons in this state within ages not in excess of twenty-one years as prescribed by law. . . . Constitution, Art. IX, § 1(a), source Constitution of 1875, Art. XI, §§ 1 and 3.

The court held in Concerned Parents v. Caruthersville School District No. 18, 548 S.W.2d 554 (Mo.1977), that under this constitutional provision school districts were prohibited from charging registration fees or course fees in connection with courses for which academic credit was given.

WASHINGTON:
> The Legislature shall provide for a general and uniform system of public schools. The public school system shall include common schools, and such high schools, normal schools, and technical schools as may hereafter be established. Constitution, art. 9, sec. 2.

The Supreme Court of the State of Washington, in Litchman v. Shannon, 90 Wash. 186, 155 P. 783 (1916), said:

> Public schools are usually defined as schools established under the laws of the state, usually regulated in matters of detail by local authorities in the various districts, towns, or counties, and maintained at the public expense by taxation, and open without charge to the children of all the residents of the town or other district.

Earlier, the Supreme Court of Washington, in School District No. 20, Spokane County v. Bryan, 51 Wash. 498, 99 P. 28 (1909), defined "common school" as found in its constitution as "one that is common to all children of proper age and capacity, free and subject to, and under the control of, the qualified voters of the school district."

From this study we have concluded that the courts have consistently construed the language "without payment of tuition" or "wherein tuition shall be without charge" or such similar language to mean that a school is prohibited from charging a fee for a pupil attending school. This language has also been construed as not prohibiting the charging of fees for textbooks.

However, as to constitutions containing language such as "free public schools" or "free common schools" or similar language, the courts have generally held, with a few exceptions, that this language contemplates furnishing textbooks free of charge, at least to the elementary schools. The exceptions have generally relied upon extrinsic material such as contemporary construction, history, or practices, as well as the language itself. Although the cases involving language similar to that contained in the North Dakota Constitution are not in themselves conclusive, they nevertheless are helpful, if not persuasive.

A comparison of the key constitutional provisions and existing case law of states which entered the Union at the same time and under similar conditions as North Dakota will be very helpful and valuable in determining the intent of the people of North Dakota in adopting § 148 of the North Dakota Constitution.

At the time North Dakota formulated and adopted its Constitution, three other States—Montana, South Dakota, and Washington—were going through a similar process. All four States were included in the same Enabling Act, Chapter 180, 25 Statutes at Large, 676, and were required to meet the conditions in § 4, which provided:

> That provision shall be made for the establishment and maintenance of systems of public schools, which shall be open to all the children of said states, and free from sectarian control.

The key language in the constitutional provisions of the four States is as follows:

Montana: ". . . thorough system of public, free common schools."

South Dakota: ". . . uniform system of public schools wherein tuition shall be without charge."

North Dakota: ". . . uniform system of free public schools throughout the state . . . ."

Washington: ". . . uniform system of public schools . . . ."

We are impressed with the different language employed in the constitutions of the four states, Montana, South Dakota, North Dakota, and Washington, which came into the Union at the same time and under the same Enabling Act. We must assume that each state had available the same information as the other states and was free to choose its constitutional provisions, provided they met the requirements of the Enabling Act. It is significant to note that Montana and North Dakota adopted the "free common schools" and the "free public schools" concept, whereas South Dakota adopted the "public schools wherein tuition shall be without charge" concept, and Washington merely provided for a "uniform system of public schools."

We also note that the Washington Supreme Court in the *Bryan* case, supra, under the Washington Constitution held that a common school district is free for all children of proper age even though its Constitution merely required a uniform system of public schools. Therefore, if the term "common schools" implies a school for which no tuition may be charged, then the expression "free public schools" should mean something more than merely not permitting the charging of tuition. This position becomes persuasive when we recognize that other states specifically provided that no charge for "tuition" would be allowed.

If the framers of the North Dakota Constitution and the people of North Dakota had in mind only to provide public schools without charging tuition they could have, and probably would have, used the language "without payment of tuition" or "wherein tuition shall be without charge," rather than the language "free public schools." We must assume that the framers of the constitution made a deliberate choice of words which reflected or expressed their thoughts. The term "free public schools" without any other modification must necessarily mean and include those items which are essential to education.

It is difficult to envision a meaningful educational system without textbooks. No education of any value is possible without school books. . . .

We cannot overlook the fact that attendance at school between certain ages was compulsory from the very beginning under penalty of law. This lends support to the contention that textbooks were to be included in the phrase "free public schools." . . .

The word "free" takes on its true and full meaning from the context in which it is used. There can be no doubt that the term means "without charge or cost." In the absence of any other showing we must conclude that the term was commonly understood by the people to mean "without charge or cost." Books and school supplies are a part of the education system. This is true whether we apply the necessary elements of the school's activities test or the integral part of the educational system test.

After a review of the case law and constitutional provisions of other states, and after a careful analysis of the key language of the four states which were admitted under the same Enabling Act, we have come to the conclusion that the term "free public schools" means and includes textbooks, and not merely "free from tuition."

However, our conclusion must necessarily apply only to the elementary schools, as they are the only ones covered in this action. The action in district court was not a class action and factually involved only students enrolled in the elementary schools. . . . This opinion therefore is limited to textbooks used in elementary schools in the required subjects, as set out in [statute]. . . .

. . . to the extent that they apply to elementary textbooks [they] are in conflict with § 148 of the North Dakota Constitution and are therefore invalid and unconstitutional as to elementary school textbooks. . . .

The judgment and order of the district court are both affirmed.

State Constitutional Provision for Free
Public Schooling Prohibits Fees for
Either Regular or Extracurricular
Programs

HARTZELL v. CONNELL

Supreme Court of California,
In Bank, 1984.
35 Cal.3d 899, 201 Cal.Rptr. 601,
679 P.2d 35.

BIRD, Chief Justice.

May a public high school district charge fees for educational programs simply because they have been denominated "extracurricular"?

The Santa Barbara High School District (District) offers a wide variety of extracurricular activities, ranging from cheerleading to madrigal singing, and from archery to football. Many of these activities are of relatively recent origin. For example, in 1956, Santa Barbara High School fielded six athletic teams while today there are thirty-eight.

Prior to the 1980–1981 school year, any student could participate in these activities free of charge. The programs were financed by a combination of District contributions (mostly state aid and local tax revenues), ticket sales, and fundraising activities conducted by the constituent high schools.

In the spring of 1980, the District school board (Board) decided to cut its budget by $1.1 million. This decision reflected a drop in revenues due to the combined effects of inflation, declining enrollment, and the adoption of Proposition 13. Among the items to be reduced was the District's contribution to the high school extracurricular programs.

The Board considered two plans for adapting the programs to fit its reduced budget. The first plan called for a major cut in interscholastic athletic competition, including the reduction of the high school program from over thirty teams to only eight and the elimination of interscholastic competition at the ninth-grade level. Under this plan, the surviving programs were to remain open to all students free of charge.

The second plan provided for a less extensive cut in athletic competition—elimination of the ninth-grade program only. To make up the difference, it proposed to raise money by charging students fees for participation in dramatic productions, musical performances, and athletic competition.

The Board chose the second option. Under the plan finally adopted, students are required to pay $25 for *each* athletic team in which they wish to participate, and $25 per category for any or all activities in *each* of the following four categories: (1) dramatic productions (e.g., plays, dance performances, and musicals); (2) vocal music groups (e.g., choir and madrigal groups); (3) instrumental groups (e.g., orchestra, marching band, and related groups such as the drill team and flag twirlers); and (4) cheerleading groups.

Thus, a student who desires to play football in the fall and tennis in the spring, in addition to participating in a dramatic production, must pay $75. A more musically inclined student, who plays an instrument, sings in a group, and performs in a musical, also pays $75.

None of the affected activities yield any credit toward graduation. . . .

The teachers of the credit courses also supervise the noncredit performances. . . .

In an attempt to ensure that the fees would not prevent any students from participating, the District has implemented a fee-waiver program. Upon a showing of financial need, a student may obtain a "scholarship" to participate without paying the fee. The standard of need is similar to that of the free lunch program. . . .

The District's three high schools granted a total of seventy-seven waivers. . . .

Shortly before the start of the 1980–1981 school year, Barbara Hartzell, a taxpayer with two children in the public schools, and the Coalition Opposing Student Fees, a grouping of community organizations, filed this taxpayers' action against the District, various school officials, and the members of the Board. . . .

The California Constitution requires the Legislature to "provide for a system of common schools by which a *free school* shall be kept up and supported in each district . . . ." (Cal. Const., art. IX, § 5, emphasis added.) This provision entitled "the youth of the State . . . to be educated at the public expense." (*Ward v. Flood* (1874) 48 Cal. 36, 51.)

Plaintiffs assert that the imposition of fees for educational extracurricular activities violates the free school guarantee. They are correct.

The first question raised by plaintiffs' challenge is whether extracurricular activities fall within the free education guaranteed by section 5. California courts have not yet addressed this issue. The reported decisions from other jurisdictions reveal two distinct approaches.

One approach restricts the free school guarantee to programs that are "essential to the prescribed curriculum." . . . Under this view, the right to an education does not extend to activities that are "outside of or in addition to the regular academic courses or curriculum of a school." . . . Accordingly, it has been held that students have no right to participate in extracurricular activities. . . .

The second approach holds that the free school guarantee extends to all activities which constitute an "integral fundamental part of the elementary and secondary education" or which amount to " 'necessary elements of any school's activity.' " . . . Courts applying this approach have held that "the right to attend school includes the right to participate in extracurricular activities." In particular, courts have struck down extracurricular activities fees as unconstitutional. . . .

To determine which, if either, of these approaches is consistent with California's free school guarantee, this court must examine the role played by education in the overall constitutional scheme. Because the nature of the free school concept has rarely been addressed by the courts, it will be necessary to explore its underpinnings in some depth.

The free school guarantee was enacted at the Constitutional Convention of 1878–1879. Also adopted was article IX, section 1, which proclaims that "[a] general diffusion of knowledge and intelligence [is] essential *to the preservation of the rights and liberties of the people* . . . ." (Emphasis added.) Joseph W. Winans, chairperson for the convention's Committee on Education, elaborated: "Public education forms the basis of self-government and constitutes the very corner stone of republican institutions." (Debates and Proceedings, Cal. Const. Convention 1878–1879, p. 1087 [hereafter Proceedings].) In support of section 1, delegate John T. Wickes argued that "a liberal education . . . breaks down aristocratic caste; for the man who has a liberal education, if he has no money, if he has no wealth, he can stand in the presence of his fellow-men with the stamp of divinity upon his brow, and shape the laws of the people . . . ." (Proceedings, at p. 1088.)

This theme runs like a unifying thread through the writings of our forefathers. In 1786, Thomas Jefferson wrote from France, then a monarchy: "I think by far the most important bill in our whole code is that for the diffusion of knowledge among the people. No other sure foundation can be devised for the preservation of freedom, and happiness . . . ." (Jefferson, *Letter to George Wythe,* in The Portable Thomas Jefferson (Peterson edit. 1979) pp. 399–400.)

John Swett, California's most prominent free school advocate at the time section 5 was adopted, warned: "Our destruction, should it come at all, will be . . . [f]rom the inattention of the people to the concerns of their government . . . . I fear that they may place too implicit confidence in their public servants and fail properly to scrutinize their conduct . . . . Make them intelligent, and they will be vigilant; give them the means of detecting the wrong, and they will apply the remedy." (Quoted in Cloud, The Story of California's Schools (194–) p. 20.) Without education for all, a majority of the people would be—in the words of Horace Mann—"the vassals of as severe a tyranny, in the form of capital, as the lower classes of Europe are bound to in the form of brute force." (Mann, *Twelfth Annual Report,* in Educational Ideas in America: A Documentary History (Rippa edit.1969) p. 199.)

Perhaps the most eloquent expression of the free school idea came not from a political leader or educator, but from the poet, Ralph Waldo Emerson: "We have already taken, at the planting of the Colonies, . . . the initial step, which for its importance, might have been resisted as the most radical of revolutions, thus deciding at the start the destiny of this country,—this, namely, that the poor man, whom the law does not allow to take an ear of corn when starving, nor a pair of shoes for his freezing feet, is allowed to put his hand into the pocket of the rich, and say, You shall educate me, not as you will, but as I will: not alone in the elements, but, by further provision, in the languages, in sciences, in the useful and in elegant arts." (Emerson, *Education,* in Educational Ideas in America: A Documentary History, supra, at p. 176.)

The contribution of education to democracy has a political, an economic, and a social dimension.

As this court has previously noted, education prepares students for active involvement in political affairs. . . . Education stimulates an interest in the political process and provides the intellectual and practical tools necessary for political action. Indeed, education may well be "the dominant factor in influencing political participation and awareness." . . . Without high quality education, the populace will lack the knowledge, self-confidence, and critical skills to evaluate independently the pronouncements of pundits and political leaders. . . .

Not only does education provide skills useful in political activity, it also prepares individuals to participate in the institutional structures—such as labor unions and business enterprises—that distribute economic opportunities and exercise economic power. Education holds out a "bright hope" for the "poor and oppressed" to participate fully in the economic life of American society. . . .

Finally, education serves as a "unifying social force" among our varied population, promoting cohesion based upon democratic values. . . . The public schools bring together members of different racial and cultural groups and, hopefully, help them to live together " 'in harmony and mutual respect.' " . . .

Viewed in light of these constitutionally recognized purposes, the first of the two tests described above is insufficient to ensure compliance with California's free school guarantee. That approach determines whether a given program falls within the guarantee not by assessing its actual educational value, but by deferring to a school board's decision on whether or not to offer it for formal, academic credit. Under this test, a for-credit program would fall within the guarantee, while a noncredit program with identical content—and equal value in fulfilling the constitutionally recognized purposes of education—could be offered for a fee.

The second approach, on the other hand, does not sever the concept of education from its purposes. It focuses not upon the formalities of credit, but upon the educational character of the activities in question.

It can no longer be denied that extracurricular activities constitute an integral component of public education. Such activities are " 'generally recognized as a fundamental ingredient of the educational process.' " . . . They are "[no] less fitted for the ultimate purpose of our public schools, to wit, the making of good citizens physically, mentally, and morally, than the study of algebra and Latin . . . ." . . .

In a variety of legal contexts, courts have emphasized the vital importance of student participation in educational extracurricular programs. . . .

In addition to the particular skills taught, group activities encourage active participation in community affairs, promote the development of leadership qualities, and instill a spirit of collective endeavor. These results are directly linked to the constitutional role of education in preserving democracy, as set forth in article IX, section 1, and elaborated in *Serrano I,* 96 Cal. Rptr. 601, 487 P.2d 1241.

Accordingly, this court holds that all educational activities—curricular or "extracurricular"—offered to students by school districts fall within the free school guarantee of article IX, section 5. Since it is not disputed that the programs involved in this case are "educational" in character, they fall within that guarantee.

Defendants argue, however, that the fee-waiver policy for needy students satisfies the requirements of the free school guarantee. They suggest that the right "to be educated at the public expense" . . . amounts merely to a right *not to be financially prevented* from enjoying educational opportunities. This argument contradicts the plain language of the Constitution.

In guaranteeing "free" public schools, article IX, section 5 fixes the precise extent of the financial burden which may be imposed on the right to an education—none. . . . A school which conditions a student's participation in educational activities upon the payment of a fee clearly is *not* a "free school."

The free school guarantee reflects the people's judgment that a child's public education is too important to be left to the budgetary circumstances and decisions of individual families. It makes no distinction between needy and nonneedy families. Individual families, needy or not, may value education more or less depending upon conflicting budget priorities. As John Swett, the "father of the California public school system," recognized in 1863, "[i]f left to their own unaided efforts, a great majority of the people will fail through want of means to properly educate their children; *another class, with means at command, will fail through want of interest.* The people then, can be educated only by a system of Free Schools, supported by taxation, and controlled directly by the people." (Swett, *Duties of the State to Public Schools,* reprinted in Swett, History of the Public School System of California (1876) p. 110, emphasis added.)

The free school guarantee lifts budgetary decisions concerning public education out of the individual family setting and requires that such decisions be made by the community as a whole. Once the community has decided that a particular educational program is important enough to be offered by its public schools, a student's participation in that program cannot be made to depend upon his or her family's decision whether to pay a fee or buy a toaster.

Nor may a student's participation be conditioned upon application for a special waiver. The stigma that results from recording some students as needy was recognized early in the struggle for free schools. Thaddeus Stevens once declared, in response to an 1835 proposal that teachers keep a list of "poor scholars": "Sir, hereditary distinctions of rank are sufficiently odious; but that which is founded on poverty is infinitely more so. Such a law should be entitled 'an act for branding and marking the poor, so that they may be known from the rich and proud.'" (Stevens, *A Plea for Free Schools,* in Educational Ideas in America: A Documentary History, supra, at p. 188.) Defendants' extracurricular programs are not truly "free" even to those students who are eligible for waivers. "[T]o a child or his parents financially unable to pay the additional fees and charges imposed by a *free, public school system* any waiver procedure is a degrading experience." . . .

Finally, defendants warn that, if the fees are invalidated, many school districts may be forced to drop some extracurricular activities. They argue that invalidation would—in the name of the free school guarantee—produce the anomalous result of reducing the number of educational opportunities available to students.

This court recognizes that, due to legal limitations on taxation and spending, school districts do indeed operate under difficult financial constraints. However, financial hardship is no defense to a violation of the free school guarantee. . . .

Perhaps, in the view of some, public education could be more efficiently financed by peddling it on the open market. Under the California Constitution, however, access to public education is a right enjoyed by all—not a commodity for sale. Educational opportunities must be provided to all students without regard to their families' ability or willingness to pay fees or request special waivers. This fundamental feature of public education is not contingent upon the inevitably fluctuating financial health of local school districts. A solution to those financial difficulties must be found elsewhere—for example, through the political process.

In conclusion, this court holds that the imposition of fees for educational activities offered by public high school districts violates the free school guarantee. The constitutional defect in such fees can neither be corrected by providing waivers to indigent students, nor justified by pleading financial hardship. . . .

In conclusion, the imposition of fees as a precondition for participation in educational programs offered by public high schools on a noncredit basis violates the free school guarantee of the California Constitution and the prohibition against school fees contained in title 5, section 350 of the California Administrative Code.

The judgment is reversed.

NOTES

1. Constitutional or statutory provisions using the term "common schools" have caused the courts to interpret and delineate precisely what is meant by the term. In interpreting that community junior colleges are not "common schools" the Supreme Court of Kansas referred to the following definitions:

> A common school is one which is open to all within the school boundaries and is supported at public expense through taxation, free of any charge to the attending students. C.J.S. Schools and School Districts § 1, p. 606; 47 Am. Jur., Schools § 3, p. 298.
> "Common schools," as that term is used in the Kansas Constitution, means free schools common or accessible to all. Board of Education of City of Lawrence v. Dick, 70 Kan. 434, 78 P. 812 (1904).

   The Kansas Court held that community junior colleges were not "common schools" primarily because they were not free, and part of the operating expenses of such schools came from student tuition. State ex rel. Londerholm v. Hayden, 197 Kan. 199, 416 P.2d 61 (1966).

2. Courts have generally held that schools for adults do not fall within the system of public schools as described by constitutional provision.

3. Neither legislative assertions nor court pronouncements can make an institution part of the state common school system contrary to constitutional mandate. Hodgkin v. Board for Louisville & Jefferson County Children's Home, 242 S.W.2d 1008 (Ky.1951).

4. A school for the blind is not a part of the public or common school system. Walls v. State Board of Education, 195 Ark. 955, 116 S.W.2d 354 (1938).

5. The authority of the legislature is not limited to certain common branches of education but extends to higher branches of education. State Bank of Commerce of Brockport v. Stone, 261 N.Y. 175, 184 N.E. 750 (1933).

6. A high school is within the definition of public, free common schools as described by state constitution. Young v. Board of Trustees of Broadwater County High School, 90 Mont. 576, 4 P.2d 725 (1931). See also People ex rel. Board of Education of Deerfield-Shields Township High School District No. 113, Lake County v. Read, 344 Ill. 397, 176 N.E. 284 (1931).

7. In the absence of constitutional restrictions, the state legislature may establish normal schools or other higher education. Briggs v. Johnson County, C.C.Mo., F.Cas. No. 1,872, 4 Dill. 148 (1930).

8. Power of legislature to expand educational programs is limited only by direct state constitutional limitation. In re Kindergarten Schools, 18 Colo. 234, 32 P. 422 (1893).

Footnotes

1. Ellwood P. Cubberley, *A Brief History of Education*, (Boston: Houghton Mifflin Company, 1922) p. 374.

2. Id., p. 376.

3. Lawrence A. Cremin, *American Education: The National Experience 1783–1876* (New York: Harper & Row Publishers, 1980) p. 125.

4. Benjamin Rush, *Essays, Moral and Philosophical*, (2nd ed., Thomas and William Bradford, 1806) pp. 4, 6–7.

5. *Id.*, p. 7–8.

6. R. Freeman Butts, "Search for Freedom: The Story of American Education", *NEA Journal* (March 1960): 33–48.

7. Letter from Thomas Jefferson to George Wythe, Paris, August 14, 1786, Bernard Mayo, *Jefferson Himself* (Charlottesville: University Press of Virginia, 1942) p. 89.

8. Cubberley, Id., p. 286.

9. Id. General school laws were enacted in: Connecticut in 1700, 1712, and 1714, Vermont in 1782, in addition to earlier statutes in Massachusetts (1647), and New Hampshire (1680). Georgia created a state system of academies in 1783. In 1795, New York provided for a state system of elementary education. Delaware established a state school fund in 1796 and Virginia enacted an optional school law in 1796.

10. Id., p. 288.

11. Id., p. 371.

12. Horace Mann.

13. *Butts*, supra.

14. *House Journal 1822*, Commonwealth of Kentucky, p. 236.

15. *House Journal 1818–1819*, Commonwealth of Kentucky, p. 13.

16. Ellwood P. Cubberley, *Public Education in the United States*, pp. 164–166. Copyright © 1934, renewed 1962 by Ira S. Lillick, adapted by permission of Houghton Mifflin Company.

17. *Butts*, supra.

18. Newton Edwards, *The Courts and The Public Schools*, (The University of Chicago Press, 1955) p. 23.

19. Id., p. 24.

20. Meyer v. State of Nebraska, 262 U.S. 390, 43 S.Ct. 625 (1923).

21. Fogg v. Board of Education, 76 N.H. 296, 82 A. 173 (1912).

22. Scown v. Czarnecki, 264 Ill. 305 (1914).

23. Fogg v. Board of Education, 76 N.H. 296, 82 A. 173, at 174–175 (1912).

24. Leeper v. State, 103 Tenn. 500, 53 S.W. 962 (1899).

25. Cubberley, *Public Education in the United States,* p. 260.

26. Diane Ravich, *The Great School Wars,* New York City, 1805–1973 (New York: Basic Books, Inc. Harper, 1974) p. 23.

27. Commonwealth v. Hartman, 17 Pa. 118 (1851).

28. Cubberley, supra, p. 386.

29. Cubberley, supra, p. 247.

30. Stuart v. School District No. 1 of the Village of Kalamazoo, 30 Mich. 69 (1874).

31. 41 A.L.R.3rd 755.

32. Id.

33. Kennedy v. County Board of Education, 214 Ala. 349, 107 So. 907 (1926).

34. Vincent v. County Board of Education, 222 Ala. 216, 131 So. 898 (1931).

35. Irvin v. Gregory, 86 Ga. 605, 13 S.E. 120 (1891).

36. Hamer v. Board of Education, 47 Ill.2d 480, 265 N.E.2d 616 (1970).

37. Mathis v. Gordy, 119 Ga. 817, 47 S.E. 171 (1904).

38. Paulson v. Minidoka County School District, 93 Idaho 469, 463 P.2d 935 (1970).

39. Id.

40. Bond v. Public Schools of Ann Arbor School District, 383 Mich. 693, 178 N.W.2d 484 (1970). See also: Board of Education of Freeport v. Nyquist, 92 Misc.2d 43, 399 N.Y.S.2d 844 (1977).

3

Role of the Federal Government

Historically, the federal government has exhibited an active interest in education. Even before the adoption of the Constitution, The Ordinance of 1785 included the provision that "there shall be reserved the lot number 16 of every township for the maintenance of public schools in each township." Two years later, the policies set forth in 1785 were put into effect in The Ordinance of 1787 with the sale of lands to the Ohio Company. The Ordinance of 1787 enunciated the federal government's policy toward education in the often quoted statement: "Religion, morality and knowledge being necessary to good government and the happiness of mankind, schools and the means of education shall be forever encouraged." These federal land grants served to stimulate interest in public schools and, as the funds derived from the land grants became insufficient, the states began to supplement the funding. In this way, the federal policy toward education established a precedent that the states followed and have so fully developed in our present state systems of public education. This early method of federal land grants for education was notable in two particular aspects. First, the grants were made for the purpose of creating and aiding public schools directly, thus espousing a federal interest in mass general common school education for everyone, and, second, the federal government exercised no control over education as a condition for receiving the grants.[1] From these beginnings, it was established that the federal government was to play an indirect role in the development of public education, to serve a stimulus function without direct control of educational policy and operation.

Over the years, the federal government's role has remained one of indirect support of education; never directly controlling education, but generally in a positive and affirmative manner, the Congress has, from time to time, fashioned educational policy to address certain perceived national interests. The first Morrill Act passed by Congress in 1862, like the early land grants, shaped American education policy by providing a grant of land to each state to be sold with the proceeds to be used for the "endowment, maintenance and support of at least one college where the leading object shall be, without excluding other scientific and classical studies and including military tactics, to teach such branches of learning as are related to agriculture and mechanic arts in such manner as the legislatures of the states may respectively prescribe." [2] In relying on this Act, the great land grant colleges were established and supported. Herein, Congress advanced a role of higher education that transcended the traditional, narrow European model by expanding and giving credibility to the study of agriculture and engineering, disciplines that a new and developing nation so badly needed. Subsequent legislation, the second Morrill Act of 1890 and the Hatch Act of 1887, the Adams Act of 1906, and other provisions, expanded the activities of the land-grant colleges and introduced grants-in-aid as another type of federal support.

Following these initial steps the federal government has continued to provide assistance to various phases of education. Categorical grants that were geared toward bringing about a particular educational emphasis became the method of allocation most relied upon. Federal grants of particular importance have been: The Smith-Lever Act of 1914, which was quite specific in purpose prescribing the expenditure of grant funds for, among other things, extension services by county agents for agriculture and homemaking and for training of teachers in these areas; the Smith-Hughes Act of 1917, which provided for funds for vocational education below college level; the National Defense Education Act of 1958, the response to Sputnik I, which instituted several types of programs at the elementary, secondary, and higher education levels to give impetus to scientific training and research; the Higher Education Facilities Act of 1963, creating financial assistance for construction at all levels of higher education; the Vocational Education Act of 1963, substantially increasing federal appropriations for vocational education; and the Elementary and Secondary Education Act of 1965, the most important elementary and secondary program ever enacted by Congress, which provided funding primarily for the educations of culturally disadvantaged children. [3]

In each of these acts, the role of the federal government is conveyed by Congress to be one of supplementary assistance to the state systems of education. The Congress has sought to shape educational policy through the indirect means of categorical grants giving direction to certain educational programs once states accept the funds. In each instance, the states have the option of accepting or rejecting the funds, but once they are accepted, the states must abide by the federal guidelines for use of the resources. As states have accepted the conditions of these categorical grants over the years, the role of the federal government in guiding educational choices has become more predominant and some commentators have maintained that too much control is today vested in the federal government. As a result, even though the federal government's role in education is said to be indirect and secondary, myriad regulations and conditions bear down quite heavily on the public schools and have led some to question the legal scope of federal powers. Unfortunately, legal definition of the role of the federal government in education is as hazy and uncertain as the legal parameters of our federal system of government itself. Courts continue today to ponder the nature of the states' relationship to the central government not only in education, but in all areas of domestic activity.

RESERVED STATE POWERS

The powers of the federal government are circumscribed by delegation within the Constitution and are specifically limited by the Tenth Amendment of the Constitution, which provides that "The powers not delegated to the United States by the Constitution, nor prohibited by it to the States, are reserved to the States respectively or to the people." Education is not mentioned in the Constitution and is, therefore, presumably reserved "to the states or to the people". The Tenth Amendment was intended to reconfirm the implicit understanding at the time of the Constitution's adoption that powers not granted to the central government were reserved.[4] James Madison at the urging of Jefferson sponsored the Tenth Amendment. In the course of debate that took place while the Amendment was still pending Madison declared: "Interference with the power of the States was no constitutional criterion of the power of Congress. If the power was not given, Congress could not excercise it; if given, they might exercise it, although it should interfere with the laws, or even the Constitutions of the States".[5]

A discrete boundary line between federal and state power was not to evolve, however, in spite of Madison's apparently clear conception of the doctrine. Chief Justice Marshall in the famous case of *McCulloch* v. *Maryland*[6] added ambiguity by noting that the word "expressly" was not included in the Tenth Amendment as it had been in the Articles of Confederation, effectively leaving the issue "whether the particular power which may become the subject of contest has been delegated to the one government, or prohibited to the other" to depend upon a fair construction of the whole instrument.[7] Justice Marshall's view of the Tenth Amendment was merely a restatement of the already presumed and established relationship that is delineated in other parts of the Constitution. In *Darby* the Court said:

> The Amendment states but a truism that all is retained which has not been surrendered. There is nothing in the history of its adoption to suggest that it was more than declaratory of the relationship between the national and state governments as it had been established by the Constitution before the amendment or that its purpose was other than to allay fears that the new national government might seek to exercise powers not granted, and that the states might not be able to exercise fully their reserved powers.[8]

Standing alone the Tenth Amendment does little more than bear witness to the fact that our system of government assumes some separation of powers and prevents federal activity without express or implied constitutional authority. As such, there is a presumption of state power, which effectively places the burden on the federal government to justify in court its involvement in affairs that may have been presumed to be left to the states. As Justice Cardoza declared, the Tenth Amendment voices an assumption of "quasi-sovereignty . . . which the state is privileged to redress as a suitor in the courts".[9] This presumption on behalf of the states provides a constitutional basis through which a state can seek legal redress in challenging a federal statute. Without the Tenth Amendment, no such action would be possible. In the face of such challenges, the federal government has been forced, on many occasions, to identify other constitutional provisions that justify its activity in regulation of functions that states have assumed to be within their prerogative. In this light, the federal government does not possess general police powers, as such, and in justifying its many activities has invoked implied powers of the general welfare and commerce clauses of the Constitution.

FEDERAL CONTROL OF EDUCATION

By virtue of the Tenth Amendment, federal control over education is secondary to the power exercised by the states. While a state can create, organize, and reorganize school districts, employ and dismiss personnel, prescribe curriculum, establish and enforce accreditation standards and govern all management and operation functions of the public schools directly, the federal government can intervene only in a peripheral and oblique way. Federal controls emanate from three sources: (1) acquiescence by states in accepting federal grants that are provided under the authority given the Congress by the General Welfare Clause; (2) standards or regulations that the Congress has authorized within the Commerce Clause; and (3) courts may constrain actions when they come in conflict with federal constitutional provisions protecting individual rights and freedoms.

Education and General Welfare

Two major questions concern education and general welfare—first, does education come under the definition of general welfare and, second, how can Congress provide for education if it does come within the definition? Section 8 of Article I gives Congress the power to tax and spend: "The Congress shall have Power to lay and collect Taxes, Duties, Imports and Excises, to pay the Debts and provide for the common Defense and General Welfare of the United States . . .." [10]

The interpretation of the meaning of the general welfare clause has been the subject of much debate and controversy. James Madison contended that the clause "amounted to no more than a reference to other powers enumerated in subsequent clauses of the same section; that, as the United States is a government of limited and enumerated powers, the grant of power to tax and spend for the general welfare must be confined to the enumerated legislative fields committed to the Congress". [11] Madison pointed out that the framers of the Constitution borrowed the phrase from the Articles of Confederation, and it was not looked upon as a phrase to extend the parameters of federal authority. In taking an opposing point of view, Hamilton maintained that this Article conferred upon the Congress a substantive power to tax and spend for purposes that would provide for the general welfare of the United States.

The Supreme Court adopted the Hamiltonian philosophy in a 1936 case that tested the constitutionality of the Agriculture Adjustment Act.[12] The Court stated that Congress was not limited in the expenditure of public monies to the direct or express grants of legislative power found in the Constitution.

In a later case, *Helvering* v. *Davis,*[13] the Supreme Court upheld the Social Security Act and in so doing ruled conclusively that Congress can tax and spend under the general welfare clause. In this case, the Court said that the general welfare concept is not static but is flexible, and Congress may tax and expend public money for general welfare purposes so long as it does not demonstrate a display of arbitrary power. With this elastic definition of general welfare, the Congress is free to define education as general welfare and to tax and appropriate funds for educational purposes.

With the prerogative to broadly define general welfare as inclusive of education, Congress then looks to the taxing power of the clause for the instrumentality to "provide" for education. Jefferson explained the power and purpose of the clause in this manner: the laying of taxes is the *power* and the general welfare the *purpose* for which the power is to be exercised. They [Congress] are not to lay taxes *ad libitum for any purpose they please*, but only *to pay the debts or provide for the welfare of the Union*. In like manner, they are not *to do anything they please* to provide for the general welfare, but only to *lay taxes* for that purpose [italics added]." [14] This clause therefore expresses not an unlimited power but only a qualified one. Congress has never acted to assert an unlimited power to tax and the Court has therefore never been compelled to decide the point.[15]

The last sentence in Jefferson's statement raises the point quite clearly that Congress cannot provide for the general welfare in any manner other than through its taxing and appropriation power. With regard to education, this means that Congress can only involve itself in educational matters through the indirect means of appropriation of funds and does not have the power to directly legislate changes in education. It is for this reason that Congress has so consistently used the categorical aid approach to bring about change in education. Constitutionally, regulation of educational functions can be acquired only through conditional grants.

The federal government cannot, therefore, affirmatively and directly require that states alter educational policy; this would be an affront to state autonomy. Constitutionally, the issue is really one of inducement versus compulsion, as one commentator has observed:

> The Constitution counts upon the necessary participation of the states . . . not by direct command but by incentive of not losing the opportunity of participation.[16]

In matters of education, then, the Congress can only effect change through persuasion or by giving the states an option that allows a state to act of its own volition. Welch says:

> The volitional nature of the state's acquiescence to conditional spending programs touches the very core of political autonomy. . . . Undoubtedly, economic necessity often forces states to alter governmental operations to qualify for federal funds; yet, the conditioning of needed funds does not

preempt the state's decision-making process. Although the distinction may often be one of form rather than substance, the Court treats it as a critically important question of form. Such observance of form is more than a ritualistic bow to the founders' respect for the states. Apparently, the Court considers the sanctity of a state's decision-making process a necessary component of the Constitution's structure which endows the states with at least a degree of autonomous, volitional control.[17]

A choice of accepting the grant and the conditions attached thereto must be provided the state. Under the General Welfare Clause, then, a state may elect not to participate in a federal program if the conditions are educationally, financially, or legally offensive.[18]

Education and Commerce

Increasingly, Congress has relied on the Commerce Clause to require affirmative action by states. Quite beyond the limitations governing general welfare, the Congress has power under this Clause to "regulate Commerce with foreign Nations, and among the several States, and with the Indian Tribes".[19] Education can be affected by congressional action pursuant to this clause in many different ways, but most notably safety, transportation, and labor regulations have touched education. While one would naturally assume that the term commerce included commercial activity, to buy, sell, and trade goods to and fro among states, the definition, as applied by the Supreme Court, has been given broader meaning. In *Gibbons* v. *Ogden*,[20] Chief Justice Marshall rejected the narrow "trading" definition and maintained that it was "something more—intercourse." Commerce as intercourse was defined in *Gibbons* as not merely an exchange of goods but as a means for "advancement of society, labor, transportation, *intelligence,* care, and various mediums of exchange [italics added] . . ."

As a mere limitation on states to prevent interference with interstate commerce such a definition has little practical effect on education, but when read in its larger context in relation to the "necessary and proper clause"[21] then Congress may act to improve commerce in an affirmative way rather than merely act to prevent state impediments. This, coupled with the fact that commerce regulation is not limited to interstate but may also, under certain conditions, include intrastate activities, brings public education within the purview of the clause.[22] In this broad context, education could conceivably be brought within the scope of commerce in that the movement of an intelligent citizenry among the states is vital to the growth and prosperity of the nation.

With this definition the courts are presented with a difficult dilemma of weighing the state powers under the Tenth Amendment against the apparent boundless scope of "commerce." Until recently, few decisions were rendered in favor of state prerogative; in expounding the philosophy that the "political process", in which each state has representation in the Congress and this representation will protect state interests, the Supreme Court largely exhibited a hands-off attitude toward the expansion of the federal role through the Commerce Clause.[23]

The expansive view of the Commerce Clause was expounded by the Supreme Court in 1941 in upholding Congress' Fair Labor Standards Act of 1938, which established a national minimum wage and prohibited the shipment in interstate commerce of goods produced by child labor. The Court said:

The power of Congress over interstate commerce is not confined to the regulation of commerce among the states. It extends to those activities intrastate which so affect interstate commerce or the exercise of the power of Congress as to make regulation of them appropriate means to the attainment of a legitimate end, the exercise of the granted power of Congress to regulate interstate commerce . . . .[24]

By 1942, Congress' economic regulatory power was viewed by the Supreme Court as being virtually unlimited. In that year, Justice Jackson, Roosevelt's latest appointee, delivered the opinion of the Court:

Whether the subject of the regulation in question was "production," "consumption," or "marketing" is . . . not material for purposes of deciding the question of federal power before us. That an activity is of a local character may help in a doubtful case to determine whether Congress intended to reach it. The same consideration might help in determining whether in the absence of Congressional action it would be permissible for the state to exert its power on the subject matter, even though in so doing it to some degree affected interstate commerce. But even if appellee's activity be local and though it may not be regarded as commerce, it may still, whatever its nature, be reached by Congress if it exerts a substantial economic effect on interstate commerce, and this irrespective of whether such effect is what might at some earlier time have been defined as "direct" or "indirect." [25]

Later, in 1946, the Court said that the commerce power is "as broad as the economic needs of the nation." [26] At this time, the national prerogative, through the Commerce Clause, attained its broadest scope.

This expansive view, though, was apparently changed, if not reversed, in *National League of Cities* v. *Usery* [27] handed down by the Supreme Court in 1976. Under litigation was the 1974 Amendments to the Fair Labor Standards Act, which extended wage and hour standards to almost all public employment, including local school districts. In this case, the Court, while admitting that the Amendments were within the scope of the Commerce Clause, nevertheless held that the Tenth Amendment was violated. The decision enunciated a more restricted view of the Commerce Clause and interpreted the Tenth Amendment as an affirmative limitation upon the power of Congress to regulate activities of state and local governments.[28] Justice Rehnquist, writing for the majority, maintained that the state's power to determine wages of its own employees is an "undoubted attribute of state sovereignty" and that the functions performed by the affected state employees were "essential to the separate and independent existence" of the state.[29]

Usery, however, was reversed by the Supreme Court on February 19, 1985 in *Garcia* v. *San Antonio Metropolitan Transit Authority.*[30] In this 5–4 decision, Justice Blackmun, writing for the majority, said that judicial restraint and assuring state sovereignty is unnecessary in our federal system. Blackmun said that the *Usery* test, "inevitably invites an unelected federal judiciary to make decisions about state policies it favors and those it dislikes." Blackmun was of the opinion that the balance in the federal system is sufficiently insured by the political processes and constant intervention by the courts is unnecessary. He further stated, "state sovereign interests, then, are more properly protected by procedural safeguards inherent in the structure of the federal system than by judicially created limitations on federal power."

The *Usery* view was, in fact, followed in the *Pennhurst* case in 1981 when the Supreme Court reasserted that states must voluntarily and knowingly agree to financial obligations that may be imposed through mutual agreement and that the terms of the agreement must be clear and unambiguous.[31] On the other hand, when states do voluntarily agree to conditions of a contract, they must perform as agreed or the federal government may have legal redress for financial obligations.[32]

Constitutional Rights and Freedoms of Individuals

Under our system of government, state laws that violate or deny individual rights or freedoms may be invalidated by the courts through application of the United States Constitution. Many of the restraints that educators refer to as "federal control" emanate from the application of federal constitutional provisions to state statutes, regulations, or actions by agents of the public school system. Virtually all the cases that have held state actions unconstitutional have been based on either the First or the Fourteenth Amendments to the Constitution, with a scattering involving the Fourth, Fifth, Sixth, and even the Eighth Amendments. Outside the Amendments proper, some early litigation was directed toward the impairment of contracts provision of the Constitution, Article I, Section 10, which prohibits unilateral abrogation of contracts by government. (These cases will be discussed in a later chapter of this text.)

Judicial action through injunctive relief on behalf of a student, teacher, or parent may well serve to limit state options in educational policy issues. Most notable among these has been the pervasive impact of the federal courts in shaping educational policy to effect racial integration in the public schools. Each of these actions is taken by the courts, though, on a case by case basis and judicial control is imposed only where past state action has denied individual constitutional rights.

Suppression of individual freedoms that are given constitutional status in the First Amendment also serves as the basis for frequent litigation and many times subsequent judicial control of educational activity. Personal freedoms and civil rights found in the First Amendment pertain to religion, speech, association, press, and assembly. Each of these has been brought into play as restraints on objectionable activities by state school systems.

Each of these constitutional issues will be fully discussed in subsequent chapters of this book, but it is important to note here that it is these legitimate constitutional concerns involving personal freedoms and rights that are primarily responsibile for the "federal involvement in education."

ROLE OF THE FEDERAL GOVERNMENT

Such activity by the federal courts in no way violates the sovereign power of the states to operate the public schools.

Beyond these direct judicial controls, whereby the court normally enjoins or mandates, the Congress has evolved certain power from the Fourteenth Amendment to bring about and enforce constitutional purposes. Federal regulation of state employment practices, as justified under the Fourteenth Amendment, have been upheld by the Supreme Court. In *Fitzpatrick* v. *Bitzer*,[33] Justice Rehnquist appeared to distinguish between Congress' Fourteenth Amendment and Commerce Clause powers by maintaining that the Fourteenth Amendment "clearly contemplates limitations on [the states'] authority". From such precedents, then, it appears that the federal role in education extends to both judicial action to prevent unconstitutional state action and to affirmative Congressional action to effectuate equality through the Fourteenth Amendment.

*The Scope of the Commerce Clause is
Defined By Political Process*

GARCIA v. SAN ANTONIO METROPOLITAN TRANSIT AUTHORITY

Supreme Court of the United States, 1985.
___ U.S. ___, ___ S.Ct. ___ (1985).

Justice BLACKMUN delivered the opinion of the Court.

We revisit in these cases an issue raised in *National League of Cities* v. *Usery,* 426 U.S. 833 (1976). In that litigation, this Court, by a sharply divided vote, ruled that the Commerce Clause does not empower Congress to enforce the minimum-wage and overtime provisions of the Fair Labor Standards Act (FLSA) against the States "in areas of traditional governmental functions." . . .

The present controversy concerns the extent to which SAMTA (San Antonio Metropolitan Transit Authority) may be subjected to the minimum-wage and overtime requirements of the FLSA. . . .

. . . *National League of Cities, supra,* overruled *Maryland* v. *Wirtz,* and held that the FLSA could not be applied constitutionally to the "traditional governmental functions" of state and local governments. . . .

Appellees have not argued that SAMTA is immune from regulation under the FLSA on the ground that it is a local transit system engaged in intrastate commercial activity. In a practical sense, SAMTA's operations might well be characterized as "local." Nonetheless, it long has been settled that Congress' authority under the Commerce Clause extends to intrastate economic activities that affect interstate commerce. . . . Were SAMTA a privately owned and operated enterprise, it could not credibly argue that Congress exceeded the bounds of its Commerce Clause powers in prescribing minimum wages and overtime rates for SAMTA's employees. . . .

. . . four conditions must be satisfied before a state activity may be deemed immune from a particular federal regulation under the Commerce Clause. First, it is said that the federal statute at issue must regulate "the

'States as States.' " Second, the statute must "address matters that are indisputably 'attribute[s] of state sovereignty.' " Third, state compliance with the federal obligation must "directly impair [the States'] ability 'to structure integral operations in areas of traditional governmental functions.' " Finally, the relation of state and federal interests must not be such that "the nature of the federal interest . . . justifies state submission." . . .

The controversy in the present cases has focused on the third . . . requirement—that the challenged federal statute trench on "traditional governmental functions." . . .

The central theme of *National League of Cities* was that the States occupy a special position in our constitutional system and that the scope of Congress' authority under the Commerce Clause must reflect that position. Of course, the Commerce Clause by its specific language does not provide any special limitation on Congress' actions with respect to the States. . . . It is equally true, however, that the text of the Constitution provides the beginning rather than the final answer to every inquiry into questions of federalism, for "[b]ehind the words of the constitutional provisions are postulates which limit and control." . . . In order to be faithful to the underlying federal premises of the Constitution, courts must look for the "postulates which limit and control."

What has proved problematic is not the perception that the Constitution's federal structure imposes limitations on the Commerce Clause, but rather the nature and content of those limitations. One approach to defining the limits on Congress' authority to regulate the States under the Commerce Clause is to identify certain underlying elements of political sovereignty that are deemed essential to the States' "separate and independent existence." . . . This approach obviously underlay the Court's use of the "traditional governmental function" concept in *National League of Cities*. It also has led to the separate requirement that the challenged federal statute "address matters that are indisputably 'attribute[s] of state sovereignty.' " . . . In *National League of Cities* itself, for example, the Court concluded that decisions by a State concerning the wages and hours of its employees are an "undoubted attribute of state sovereignty." . . . The opinion did not explain what aspects of such decisions made them such an "undoubted attribute," and the Court since then has remarked on the uncertain scope of the concept. . . . The point of the inquiry, however, has remained to single out particular features of a State's internal governance that are deemed to be intrinsic parts of state sovereignty.

We doubt that courts ultimately can identify principled constitutional limitations on the scope of Congress' Commerce Clause powers over the States merely by relying on *a priori* definitions of state sovereignty. In part, this is because of the elusiveness of objective criteria for "fundamental" elements of state sovereignty, a problem we have witnessed in the search for "traditional governmental functions." There is, however, a more fundamental reason: the sovereignty of the States is limited by the Constitution itself. A variety of sovereign powers, for example, are withdrawn from the States by Article I, § 10. Section 8 of the same Article works an equally sharp contraction of state sovereignty by authorizing Congress to exercise a wide range of legislative powers and (in conjunction with the Supremacy Clause of Article VI) to displace contrary state legislation. . . . By providing for final review of questions of federal law in this Court, Article III curtails the sovereign power of the States' judiciaries to make authoritative determinations of law. . . . Finally, the developed application, through the Fourteenth Amendment, of the greater part of the Bill of Rights to the States limits the sovereign authority that States otherwise would possess to legislate with respect to their citizens and to conduct their own affairs.

The States unquestionably do "retai[n] a significant measure of sovereign authority." . . . They do so, however, only to the extent that the Constitution has not divested them of their original powers and transferred those powers to the Federal Government. . . . If the power was not given, Congress could not exercise it; if given, they might exercise it, although it should interfere with the laws, or even the Constitution of the States. . . .

. . . The power of the Federal Government is a "power to be respected" as well, and the fact that the States remain sovereign as to all powers not vested in Congress or denied them by the Constitution offers no guidance about where the frontier between state and federal power lies. In short, we have no license to employ freestanding conceptions of state sovereignty when measuring congressional authority under the Commerce Clause.

When we look for the States' "residuary and inviolable sovereignty," The Federalist No. 39, p. 285 (B. Wright ed. 1961) (J. Madison), in the shape of the constitutional scheme rather than in predetermined notions of sovereign power, a different measure of state sovereignty emerges. Apart from the limitation on federal authority inherent in the delegated nature of Congress' Article I powers, the principal means chosen by the Framers to ensure the role of the States in the federal system lies in the structure of the Federal Government itself. It is no novelty to observe that the composition of the Federal Government was designed in large part to protect the States from overreaching by Congress. The Framers thus gave the States a role in the selection both of the Executive and the Legislative Branches of the Federal Government. The States were vested with indirect influence over the House of Representatives and the Presidency by their control of electoral qualifications and their role in presidential elections. U.S. Const., Art. I, § 2, and Art. II, § 1. . . .

. . . In short, the Framers chose to rely on a federal system in which special restraints on federal power over the States inhered principally in the workings of the National Government itself, rather than in discrete limitations on the objects of federal authority. State sovereign interests, then, are more properly protected by procedural safeguards inherent in the structure of the federal system than by judicially created limitations on federal power.

. . . The fact that some federal statutes such as the FLSA extend general obligations to the States cannot obscure the extent to which the political position of the States in the federal system has served to minimize the burdens that the States bear under the Commerce Clause.

We realize that changes in the structure of the Federal Government have taken place since 1789, ... Nonetheless, against this background, we are convinced that the fundamental limitation that the constitutional scheme imposes on the Commerce Clause to protect the "States as States" is one of process rather than one of result. Any substantive restraint on the exercise of Commerce Clause powers must find its justification in the procedural nature of this basic limitation, and it must be tailored to compensate for possible failings in the national political process rather than to dictate a "sacred province of state autonomy." . . .

Insofar as the present cases are concerned, then, we need go no further than to state that we perceive nothing in the overtime and minimum-wage requirements of the FLSA, as applied to SAMTA, that is destructive of state sovereignty or violative of any constitutional provision. . . .

. . . Congress' treatment of public mass transit reinforces our conviction that the national political process systematically protects States from the risk of having their functions in that area handicapped by Commerce Clause regulation.

This analysis makes clear that Congress' action in affording SAMTA employees the protections of the wage and hour provisions of the FLSA contravened no affirmative limit on Congress' power under the Commerce Clause. . . .

Of course, we continue to recognize that the States occupy a special and specific position in our constitutional system and that the scope of Congress' authority under the Commerce Clause must reflect that position. But the principal and basic limit on the federal commerce power is that inherent in all congressional action—the built-in restraints that our system provides through state participation in federal governmental action. The political process ensures that laws that unduly burden the States will not be promulgated. In the factual setting of these cases the internal safeguards of the political process have performed as intended.

These cases do not require us to identify or define what affirmative limits the constitutional structure might impose on federal action affecting the States under the Commerce Clause. . . . We note and accept Justice Frankfurter's observation in *New York* v. *United States*, 326 U.S. 572, 583 (1946):

> "The process of Constitutional adjudication does not thrive on conjuring up horrible possibilities that never happen in the real world and devising doctrines sufficiently comprehensive in detail to cover the remotest contingency. Nor need we go beyond what is required for a reasoned disposition of the kind of controversy now before the Court."

. . . *National League of Cities* v. *Usery,* 426 U.S. 833 (1976), is overruled. . . .

NOTES

1. Even though the Supreme Court struck down the Agricultural Adjustment Act in 1936, in United States v. Butler, 297 U.S. 1, 56 S.Ct. 312 (1936), the Court interpreted the General Welfare Clause as giving Congress broad powers. In so doing, the Court adopted the Hamilton expansive viewpoint and rejected Madison's more restrictive view. The Court said "Congress is expressly empowered to lay taxes to provide for

the general welfare. Funds in the Treasury as a result of taxation may be expended only through appropriation, Article 1, § 9, cl. 7. They can never accomplish the objects for which they were collected, unless the power to appropriate is as broad as the power to tax. The necessary implication is that public funds may be appropriated 'to provide for the general welfare of the United States'."

2. In the case of Helvering v. Davis, 301 U.S. 619, 57 S.Ct. 904 (1937), the Supreme Court of the United States was called upon to determine the constitutionality of the Social Security Act of 1935. Although this case does not directly involve education, it provides precedent for interpreting the meaning of the "general welfare clause." In this case, the Court makes two especially important determinations: (a) In drawing the line between what is "general" welfare, and what is "particular," the determination of Congress must be respected by the courts, unless it be plainly arbitrary; (b) The concept of "general welfare" is not static but adapts itself to the crises and necessities of the times. The Court said:

Congress may spend money in aid of the "general welfare" . . . . There have been great statesmen in our history who have stood for other views. We will not resurrect the contest. It is now settled by decision. . . . The conception of the spending power advocated by Hamilton and strongly reinforced by Story has prevailed over that of Madison, which has not been lacking in adherents. Yet difficulties are left when the power is conceded. The line must still be drawn between one welfare and another, between particular and general. Where this shall be placed cannot be shown through a formula in advance of the event. There is a middle ground or certainly a penumbra in which discretion is at large. The discretion, however, is not confined to the courts. The discretion belongs to Congress, unless the choice is clearly wrong, a display of arbitrary power, not an exercise of judgment. This is now familiar law. . . .

When such a contention comes here we naturally require a showing that by no reasonable possibility can the challenged legislation fall within the wide range of discretion permitted to the Congress. . . . Nor is the concept of the general welfare static. Needs that were narrow or parochial a century ago may be interwoven in our day with the well-being of the Nation. What is critical or urgent changes with the times.

3. Powers not expressly or impliedly conferred by the Constitution to the federal government are reserved to the "States respectively or to the people." (Amendment X, Constitution of the United States of America). James Madison, in debate concerning the pending Tenth Amendment, declared that: "Interference with the power of the States was no constitutional criterion of the power of Congress. If the power was not given, Congress could not exercise it; if given, they might exercise it, although it should interfere with the laws, or even the constitutions of the States." (Annals of Congress, 1897, 1791).

4. It is interesting to note that in 1788, before the Tenth Amendment was enacted, Madison described the federal government relationship to the states in the new Constitution thusly:

The powers delegated by the proposed Constitution to the Federal Government, are few and defined. Those which are to remain in the State Governments are numerous and indefinite. The former will be exercised principally on external objects, as war, peace, negotiation, and foreign commerce; with which the power of taxation will for the most part be connected. The powers reserved to the several States will extend to all the objects, which, in the ordinary course of affairs, concern the lives, liberties and properties of the people; and the internal order, improvement, and prosperity of the State. (The Federalist, No. 45, January 26, 1788)

5. The United States Supreme Court has summarily rejected doctrines of nullification and interposition. The doctrine of interposition being a

concept based on the proposition that the United States is a compact of States, any one of which may interpose its sovereignty against the enforcement within its borders of any decision of the Supreme Court or act of Congress, irrespective of the fact that the constitutionality of the act has been established by decision of the Supreme Court . . .. interposition is not a constitutional doctrine . . . [and] if taken seriously, it is illegal defiance of constitutional authority. (Bush v. Orlean School Bd., 364 U.S. 500, 81 S.Ct. 260 (1960); 188 F.Supp. 916 (E.D.La.1960).)

The Supreme Court had this to say about interposition as it concerns education. Although "the responsibility of public education is primarily the concern of the States . . . such responsibilities . . . must be exercised consistently with federal constitutional requirements as they apply to state action." Cooper v. Aaron, 358 U.S. 1, 78 S.Ct. 1401 (1958).

6. In an early case, the Kentucky Court of Appeals described the relationship of the federal government to the states: "The power of the states to establish and maintain systems of common schools, to raise money for that purpose by taxation, and to govern, control, and regulate such schools when established, is one of 'the powers not delegated to the United States by the Constitution, nor prohibited by it to the states,' and consequently it is reserved to the states respectively or to their people." Marshall v. Donovan, 10 Bush 681 (1874).

*Congress' Authority to Spend Rests on
Whether State Voluntarily and
Knowingly Accepts the Terms
of the Contract*

PENNHURST STATE SCHOOL AND HOSPITAL v. HALDERMAN

Supreme Court of the United States, 1981.
451 U.S. 1, 101 S.Ct. 1531.

MR. JUSTICE REHNQUIST delivered the opinion of the Court.

At issue in this case is the scope and meaning of the Developmentally Disabled Assistance and Bill of Rights Act of 1975, 42 U.S.C. § 6000 et seq. The Court of Appeals for the Third Circuit held that the Act created substantive rights in favor of the mentally retarded, that those rights were judicially enforceable, and that conditions at the Pennhurst State School and Hospital (Pennhurst), a facility for the care and treatment of the mentally retarded, violated those rights. For the reasons stated below, we reverse the decision of the Court of Appeals and remand the case for further proceedings.

The Commonwealth of Pennsylvania owns and operates Pennhurst. Pennhurst is a large institution, housing approximately 1,200 residents. Seventy-five percent of the residents are either "severely" or "profoundly" retarded—that is, with an IQ of less than 35—and a number of the residents are also physically handicapped. About half of its residents were committed there by court order and half by a parent or other guardian.

In 1974, respondent Terri Lee Halderman, a minor retarded resident of Pennhurst, filed suit in the District Court for the Eastern District of Pennsylvania on behalf of herself and all other Pennhurst residents against Pennhurst, its superintendent, and various officials of the Commonwealth of Pennsylvania responsible for the operation of Pennhurst. The additional respondents in this case—other mentally retarded persons, the United States, and the Pennsylvania Association for Retarded Citizens (PARC)—subsequently intervened as plaintiffs. PARC added several surrounding counties as defendants, alleging that they were responsible for the commitment of persons to Pennhurst.

As amended in 1975, the complaint alleged *inter alia* that conditions at Pennhurst were unsanitary, inhumane and dangerous. Specifically, the complaint averred that these conditions denied the class members due process and equal protection of the law in violation of the Fourteenth Amendment, inflicted on them cruel and unusual punishment in violation of the Eighth and Fourteenth Amendments, and denied them certain rights conferred by the Rehabilitation Act of 1973. 29 U.S.C. § 700 et seq., the Developmentally Disabled Assistance and Bill of Rights Act, 42 U.S.C. §§ 6001–6080, and the Pennsylvania Mental Health and Mental Retardation Act of 1966, Pa. Stat. Ann., Tit. 50, §§ 4101–4704. In addition to seeking injunctive and monetary relief, the complaint urged that Pennhurst be closed and that "community living arrangements" be established for its residents. . . .

We turn first to a brief review of the general structure of the Act. It is a federal-state grant program whereby the Federal Government provides financial assistance to participating States to aid them in creating programs to care for and treat the developmentally disabled. Like other federal-state cooperative programs, the Act is voluntary and the States are given the choice of complying with the conditions set forth in the Act or foregoing the benefits of federal funding. The Commonwealth of Pennsylvania has elected to participate in the program. The Secretary of Health and Human Services, the agency responsible for administering the Act, has approved Pennsylvania's state plan and in 1976 disbursed to Pennsylvania approximately $1.6 million. Pennhurst itself receives no federal funds from Pennsylvania's allotment under the Act, though it does receive approximately $6 million per year in Medicaid funds.

The Act begins with an exhaustive statement of purposes. 42 U.S.C. § 6000(b)(1). The "overall purpose" of the Act, as amended in 1978, is:

To assist the states to ensure that persons with developmental disabilities receive the care, treatment, and other services necessary to enable them to achieve their maximum potential through a system which coordinates, monitors, and plans and evaluates those services and which ensures the protection of the legal and human rights of persons with developmental disabilities. (Emphasis supplied.)

As set forth in the margin, the "specific purposes" of the Act are to "assist" and financially "support" various activities necessary to the provision of comprehensive services to the developmentally disabled. § 6000(b)(2).

The Act next lists a variety of conditions for the receipt of federal funds. Under § 6005, for example, the Secretary "as a condition of providing assistance" shall require that "each recipient of such assistance take affirmative action" to hire qualified handicapped individuals. Each State, in turn, shall "as a condition" of receiving assistance submit to the Secretary a plan to evaluate the services provided under the Act. § 6009. Each State shall also "as a condition" of receiving assistance "provide the Secretary satisfactory assurances that each program . . . which receives funds from the State's allotment . . . has in effect for each developmentally disabled person who receives services from or under the program a habilitation plan." § 6011. And § 6012 conditions aid on a state's promise to "have in effect a system to protect and advocate the rights of persons with developmental disabilities."

At issue here, of course, is § 6010, the "bill of rights" provision. It states in relevant part that:

> Congress makes the following findings respecting the rights of persons with developmental disabilities:
> (1) Persons with developmental disabilities have a right to appropriate treatment, services, and habilitation for such disabilities.
> (2) The treatment, services, and habilitation for a person with developmental disabilities should be designed to maximize the developmental potential of the person and should be provided in the setting that is least restrictive of the person's liberty.
> (3) The Federal Government and the States both have an obligation to assure that public funds are not provided to any institution . . . that (A) does not provide treatment, services, and habilitation which are not appropriate to the needs of such person; or (B) does not meet the following minimum standards. . . .

Noticeably absent from § 6010 is any language suggesting that § 6010 is a "condition" for the receipt of federal funding under the Act. Section 6010 thus stands in sharp contrast to §§ 6005, 6009, 6011 and 6012. . . .

As support for its broad remedial order, the Court of Appeals found that § 6010 of the Act created substantive rights in favor of the disabled and imposed an obligation on the States to provide, at their own expense, certain kinds of treatment. The initial question before us, then, is one of statutory construction: Did Congress intend in § 6010 to create enforceable rights and obligations?

In discerning congressional intent, we necessarily turn to the possible sources of Congress' power to legislate, namely Congress' power to enforce the Fourteenth Amendment and its power under the Spending Clause to place conditions on the grant of federal funds. Although the court below held that Congress acted under both powers, the respondents themselves disagree on this point. The Halderman respondents argue that § 6010 was enacted pursuant to § 5 of the Fourteenth Amendment. Accordingly, they assert that § 6010 is mandatory on the States, regardless of their receipt of federal funds. The Solicitor General, in contrast, concedes that Congress acted pursuant to its Spending Power alone. Tr. of Oral Arg., at 54. Thus, in his view, § 6010 only applies to those States which accept federal funds.

Although this Court has previously addressed issues going to Congress' power to secure the guarantees of the Fourteenth Amendment . . . we have had little occasion to consider the appropriate test for determining when Congress intends to enforce those guarantees. Because such legislation imposes congressional policy on a State involuntarily, and because it often intrudes on traditional state authority, we should not quickly attribute to Congress an unstated intent to act under its authority to enforce the Fourteenth Amendment. Our previous cases are wholly consistent with that view, since Congress in those cases expressly articulated its intent to legislate pursuant to § 5. . . . Those cases, moreover, involved statutes which simply prohibited certain kinds of state conduct. The case for inferring intent is at its weakest where, as here, the rights asserted impose *affirmative* obligations on the States to fund certain services, since we may assume that Congress will not implicitly attempt to impose massive financial obligations on the States.

Turning to Congress' power to legislate pursuant to the Spending Power, our cases have long recognized that Congress may fix the terms on which it shall disburse federal money to the States. Unlike legislation enacted under § 5, however, legislation enacted pursuant to the Spending Power is much in the nature of a contract; in return for federal funds, the States agree to comply with federally imposed conditions. The legitimacy of Congress' power to legislate under the Spending Power thus rests on whether the State voluntarily and knowingly accepts the terms of the "contract." There can, of course, be no knowing acceptance if a State is unaware of the conditions or is unable to ascertain what is expected of it. Accordingly, if Congress intends to impose a condition on the grant of federal moneys, it must do so unambiguously. By insisting that Congress speak with a clear voice, we enable the States to exercise their choice knowingly, cognizant of the consequences of their participation.

Indeed, in those instances where Congress has intended the States to fund certain entitlements as a condition of receiving federal funds, it has proved capable of saying so explicitly. We must carefully inquire, then, whether Congress in § 6010 imposed an obligation on the States to spend state money to fund certain rights as a condition of receiving federal moneys under the Act or whether it spoke merely in precatory terms.

Applying those principles to this case, we find nothing in the Act or its legislative history to suggest that Congress intended to require the States to assume the high cost of providing "appropriate treatment" in the "least restrictive environment" to their mentally retarded citizens.

There is virtually no support for the lower court's conclusion that Congress created rights and obligations pursuant to its power to enforce the Fourteenth Amendment. The Act nowhere states that that is its purpose. Quite the contrary, the Act's language and structure demonstrate that it is a mere federal-state funding statute. The explicit purposes of the Act are simply "to assist" the States through the use of federal grants to improve the care and treatment of the mentally retarded. § 6000(b). Nothing in either the "overall" or "specific" purposes of the Act reveals an intent to require the States to fund new, substantive rights. Surely Congress would not have established such elaborate funding incentives had it simply intended to impose absolute obligations on the States.

Respondents nonetheless insist that the fact that § 6010 speaks in terms of "rights" supports their view. Their reliance is misplaced. "In expounding a statute, we must not be guided by a single sentence or member of a sentence, but look to the provisions of the whole law, and to its object and policy." Contrary to respondents' assertion, the specific language and the legislative history of § 6010 are ambiguous. We are persuaded that § 6010, when read in the context of other more specific provisions of the Act, does no more than express a congressional preference for certain kinds of treatment. . . .

In sum, nothing suggests that Congress intended the Act to be something other than a typical funding statute. Far from requiring the States to fund newly declared individual rights, the Act has a systematic focus, seeking to improve care to individuals by encouraging better state planning, coordination and demonstration projects. Much like the Medicaid statute considered in *Harris v. McRae* 448 U.S. 297 (1980), the Act at issue here "was designed as a cooperative program of shared responsibilities, not as a device for the Federal Government to compel a State to provide services that Congress itself is unwilling to fund."

There remains the contention of the Solicitor General that Congress, acting pursuant to its Spending Power, conditioned the grant of federal money on the State's agreeing to underwrite the obligations the Court of Appeals read into § 6010. We find that contention wholly without merit. As amply demonstrated above, the "findings" in § 6010, when viewed in the context of the more specific provisions of the Act, represent general statements of federal policy, not newly created legal duties. . . .

Our conclusion is also buttressed by the rule of statutory construction established above, that Congress must express clearly its intent to impose conditions on the grant of federal funds so that the States can knowingly decide whether or not to accept those funds. That canon applies with greatest force where, as here, a State's potential obligations under the Act are largely indeterminate. It is difficult to know what is meant by providing "appropriate treatment" in the "least restrictive" setting and it is unlikely that a State would have accepted federal funds had it known it would be bound to provide such treatment. The crucial inquiry, however, is not whether a State would knowingly undertake that obligation, but whether Congress spoke so clearly that we can fairly say that the State could make an informed choice. In this case, Congress fell well short of providing clear notice to the States that they, by accepting funds under the Act, would indeed be obligated to comply with § 6010. Not only does § 6010 lack conditional language, but it strains credulity to argue that participating States should have known of their "obligations" under § 6010 when the Secretary of HHS, the governmental agency responsible for the administration of the Act and the agency with which the participating States have the most contact, has never understood § 6010 to impose conditions on participating States. Though Congress' power to legislate under the Spending Power is broad, it does not include surprising participating States with post-acceptance or "retroactive" conditions. . . .

In sum, the court below failed to recognize the well-settled distinction between Congressional "encouragement" of state programs and the imposition of binding obligations on the States. Relying on that distinction, this Court in Southeastern Community College v. Davis, 442 U.S. 397, 99 S.Ct. 2361 (1979), rejected a claim that § 504 of the Rehabilitation Act of 1973, which bars discrimination against handicapped persons in federally funded programs, obligates schools to take affirmative steps to eliminate problems raised by an applicant's hearing disability. Finding that "state agencies such as Southeastern are only 'encouraged' . . . to adopt such policies and procedures,'" Id., at 410, 99 S.Ct. at 2369 (quoting the Act), we stressed that "Congress understood that accommodation of the needs of handicapped individuals may require affirmative action and knew how to provide for it in those instances where it wished to do so." Id., at 411, 99 S.Ct. at 2369. Likewise in this case, Congress was aware of the need of developmentally disabled persons and plainly understood the difference, financial and otherwise, between encouraging a specified type of treatment and mandating it. . . .

Congress in recent years has enacted several laws designed to improve the way in which this Nation treats the mentally retarded. The Developmentally Disabled Assistance and Bill of Rights Act is one such law. It establishes a national policy to provide better care and treatment to the retarded and creates funding incentives to induce the States to do so. But the Act does no more than that. We would be attributing far too much to Congress if we held that it required the States, at their own expense, to provide certain kinds of treatment. Accordingly, we reverse the principal holding of the Court of Appeals and remand for further proceedings consistent with this opinion.

Reversed.

State Statute Impeding Intent of
Federal Statute Violates
Supremacy Clause

SHEPHEARD v. GODWIN

U.S. Dist. Ct. of Eastern Virginia, 1968.
280 F.Supp. 869.

ALBERT V. BRYAN, Circuit Judge:
"Impacted" school areas are those whose school populations have been substantially enlarged by the attendance of Federal employees' children, but at the same time are losing school tax revenues because of the United States government's immunity from land taxes, both factors arising from increased Federal activities in the area. These conditions prompted Congress to provide financial aid for operation of the local educational facilities, P.L. 874.

In applying a State formula for State assistance to local school districts, Virginia has deducted from the share otherwise allocable to the district a sum equal to a substantial percentage of any Federal "impact" funds receivable by the district.

Residents, real estate owners and taxpayers of the City of Norfolk, later joined by those of the County of Fairfax, Virginia, in behalf of themselves and others similarly situated, here attack this deduction . . . as violative of the purpose and intent of the act of Congress and as transgressing the Fourteenth Amendment. We uphold their contention. . . .

The theory of the deduction in toto was that the Federal moneys were substituting for the taxes lost to the district by reason of the immunity of the Government property, and hence should be charged to the locality, just as the taxes would have been, in fixing the State supplementary aid. . . .

The grievance of the plaintiffs is obvious: any deduction whatsoever of the Federal supplement in apportioning State aid, pro tanto burdens them as taxpayers, for they and the other property owners in Norfolk and Fairfax have to make up the unindemnified portion of the impact costs. They contend that any deduction is prohibited by the purpose and plan of the Federal act.

The rejoinder of the defendant officials is, first, that the impact pupils are counted by the State in computing the minimum program cost in the district, and in accounting with the district for the State's supplementary aid it is not inequitable to insist upon a deduction of a commensurate amount of the impact moneys. At first appealing, this argument ignores the fact that the Federal children are to a large extent paying their own way so far as the *State* is concerned. Quite soundly, the Congressional Committee on Education and Labor in recommending passage of P.L. 874, observed that the influx of Federal employees, and the withdrawal of real estate from taxes, did not diminish the tax sources of the State or otherwise burden the State.

. . .

Our conclusion is that the State formula wrenches from the impacted localities the very benefaction the act was intended to bestow. The State plan must fall as violative of the supremacy clause of the Constitution. Our decision rests entirely on the terms, pattern and policy of the act.

The act makes these propositions clear: (1) the Federal funds are exclusively for supplementation of the local sources of revenues for school purposes; and (2) the act was not intended to lessen the efforts of the State. Those postulates are manifested in the statute by these provisions, especially: that the Federal contribution be paid directly to the local school agency on reports of the local agency, and that the contribution be computed by reference to the expenditures "made from revenues derived from local sources" in comparable school districts.

But the State formula at once sets these precepts at naught. It uses the impact funds to account in part for fulfillment of the State's pledge of supplementary aid to the community; and the State moneys thus saved are available for State retention or such use as Virginia determines. Without the inclusion of the Federal sums the State's annual payments towards supplementary aid would be increased, it is estimated, by more than $10,000,000.

This commandeering of credit for the Federal moneys severely injures both the community and the pupil. First and foremost, it does not relieve the local taxpayers to the extent Congress contemplated. Next, without the exclusive application of the funds to the areas where the need arose and remains, the result may be to lower the standard of education provided in an impacted district. Instead of maintaining the previous standards for the additional pupils, the impact money when thinned by the State would obviously be inadequate to continue that level for the increased school attendance, a result certainly thwarting the aim of the Federal law.

The construction and the implications we put upon the act find confirmation in its legislative history. . . . The exposition underscores the Congressional mandate that the impact payments are for local use and are not to be applied to compensate the State in any respect. Thus, at p. 13, it is stated:

> The effect of the payments provided for in this section is to compensate the local educational agency for loss in its *local* revenues. *There is no compensation for any loss in States revenues.* . . . (Accent added.)

Since its explanation in 1950 when P.L. 874 was passed that no compensation was intended for the State, Congress has reiterated this intention. In this repetition it definitely disapproves the accounting use Virginia's formula makes of the impact moneys. The House of Representatives Committee Report No. 1814, dated August 5, 1966, in proposing an amendment to P.L. 874 stated:

> Fifteen States offset the amount of Public Law 874 funds received by their school districts by reducing part of their State aid to those districts. *This is in direct contravention to congressional intent.* Impact aid funds are intended to compensate districts for loss of tax revenues due to Federal connection, not to substitute for State funds the districts would otherwise receive.

The committee report and the amendment are cited merely as evidence of Congressional intendment. The amendment provides only an administrative remedy of the Government and does not deprive the plaintiffs of standing to prevent future State infringement of their Constitutional right to the benefits of the aid proposed by Congress. Necessarily, then, the upshot is that the defendants must be enjoined from hereafter in any way denying to the impacted area the exclusive use and enjoyment of the impact funds. . . .

An order implementing this opinion is filed herewith. . . .

State Is Not Obligated to Expend
Federal Funds for Purposes That
Violate the State Constitution

WHEELER v. BARRERA

Supreme Court of the United States, 1974.
417 U.S. 402, 94 S.Ct. 2274.

Mr. Justice BLACKMUN delivered the opinion of the Court.

Title I of the Elementary and Secondary Education Act of 1965, as amended, 20 U.S.C.A. § 241a et seq., provides for federal funding of special programs for educationally deprived children in both public and private schools.

This suit was instituted on behalf of parochial school students who were eligible for Title I benefits and who claimed that the public school authorities in their area, in violation of the Act, failed to provide adequate Title I programs for private school children as compared with those programs provided for public school children. The defendants answered that the extensive aid sought by the plaintiffs exceeded the requirements of Title I and contravened the State's Constitution and state law and public policy. First Amendment rights were also raised by the parties. The District Court, concluding that the State had fulfilled its Title I obligations, denied relief. The United States Court of Appeals for the Eighth Circuit, by a divided vote, reversed. We granted certiorari to examine serious questions that appeared to be present as to the scope and constitutionality of Title I. . . .

The questions that arise in this case concern the scope of the State's duty to insure that a program submitted by a local agency under Title I provides "comparable" services for eligible private school children.

Plaintiff-respondents are parents of minor children attending elementary and secondary nonpublic schools in the inner city area of Kansas City, Missouri. They instituted this class action in the United States District Court for the Western District of Missouri on behalf of themselves and their children, and others similarly situated, alleging that the defendant-petitioners, the then State Commissioner of Education and the members of the Missouri Board of Education, arbitrarily and illegally were approving Title I programs that deprived eligible nonpublic school children of services comparable to those offered eligible public school children. The complaint sought an injunction restraining continued violations of the Act and an accounting and restoration of some $13,000,000 in Title I funds allegedly misapplied from 1966 to 1969. . . .

In what perhaps may be described as something less than full cooperation by both sides, the possibility of providing "comparable" services was apparently frustrated by the fact that many parochial schools would accept only services in the form of assignment of federally funded Title I teachers to teach in those schools during regular school hours. At the same time, the petitioners refused to approve any program providing for on-the-premises instruction on the grounds that it was forbidden under both Missouri law and the First Amendment and, furthermore, that Title I did not require it. Since the larger portion (over 65%) of Title I funds allocated to Missouri has been used to provide personnel for remedial instruction, the effect of this stalemate is that substantially less money per pupil has been expended for eligible students in private schools, and that the services provided in those schools in no sense can be considered "comparable." . . .

In response to petitioners' argument that Missouri law forbids sending public school teachers into private schools, the court held that the state constitutional provision barring use of "public" school funds in private schools had no application to Title I funds. The court reasoned that although the Act was generally to be accommodated to state law, the question whether Title I funds were "public," within the meaning of the Missouri Constitution, must necessarily be decided by federal law. . . .

In this Court the parties are at odds over two issues: First, whether on this record Title I requires the assignment of publicly employed teachers to provide remedial instruction during regular school hours on the premises of private schools attended by Title I eligible students, and, second, whether that requirement, if it exists, contravenes the First Amendment. We conclude that we cannot reach and decide either issue at this stage of the proceedings.

A. *Title I requirements.* As the case was presented to the District Court, petitioners clearly had failed to meet their statutory commitment to provide comparable services to children in nonpublic schools. The services provided to the class of children represented by respondents were plainly inferior, both qualitatively and quantitatively, and the Court of Appeals was correct in ruling that the District Court erred in refusing to order relief. But the opinion of the Court of Appeals is not to be read to the effect that petitioners *must* submit and approve plans that employ the use of Title I teachers on private school premises during regular school hours.

The legislative history, the language of the Act, and the regulations clearly reveal the intent of Congress to place plenary responsibility in local and state agencies for the formulation of suitable programs under the Act. There was a pronounced aversion in Congress to "federalization" of local educational decisions. . . . Although this concern was directed primarily at the possibility of HEW's assuming the role of a national school board, it has equal application to the possibility of a federal court's playing an overly active role in supervising the manner of Title I expenditures.

At the outset, we believe that the Court of Appeals erred in holding that federal law governed the question whether on-the-premises private school instruction is permissible under Missouri law. Whatever the case might be if there were no expression of specific congressional intent, Title I evinces a clear intention that state constitutional spending proscriptions not be preempted as a condition of accepting federal funds. The key issue, namely, whether federal aid is money "donated to any state fund for public school purposes," within the meaning of the Missouri Constitution, Art. 9, § 5, is purely a question of state and not federal law. By characterizing the problem as one involving "federal" and not "state" funds, and then concluding that federal law governs, the Court of Appeals, we feel, in effect nullified the Act's policy of accommodating state law. The correct rule is that the "federal law" under Title I is to the effect that state law should not be disturbed. If it is determined, ultimately, that the petitioners' position is a correct exposition of Missouri law, Title I requires, not that that law be preempted, but, rather, that it be accommodated by the use of services not proscribed under state law. The question whether Missouri law prohibits the use of Title I funds for on-the-premises private school instruction is still unresolved.

Furthermore, in the present posture of this case, it was unnecessary for the federal court even to reach the issue whether on-the-premises parochial school instruction is permissible under state law. The state-law question appeared in the case by way of petitioners' defense that it could not provide on-the-premises services because it was prohibited by the State's Constitution. But, as is discussed more fully below, the State is not obligated by

Title I to provide on-the-premises instruction. The mandate is to provide "comparable" services. Assuming, *arguendo*, that state law does prohibit on-the-premises instruction, this would not provide a defense to respondents' complaint that comparable services are not being provided. The choice of programs is left to the State with the proviso that comparable (not identical) programs are also made available to eligible private school children. If one form of services to parochial school children is rendered unavailable because of state constitutional proscriptions, the solution is to employ an acceptable alternative form. In short, since the illegality under state law of on-the-premises instruction would not provide a defense to respondents' charge of noncompliance with Title I, there was no reason for the Court of Appeals to reach this issue. By deciding that on-the-premises instruction was not barred by state law, the court in effect issued an advisory opinion. Even apart from traditional policies of abstention and comity, it was unnecessary to decide this question in the current posture of the case.

The Court of Appeals properly recognized, as we have noted, that petitioners failed to meet their broad obligation and commitment under the Act to provide comparable programs. "Comparable," however, does not mean "identical," and, contrary to the assertions of both sides, we do not read the Court of Appeals' opinion or, for that matter, the Act itself, as ever requiring that identical services be provided in nonpublic schools. Congress recognized that the needs of educationally deprived children attending nonpublic schools might be different from those of similar children in public schools; it was also recognized that in some States certain programs for private and parochial schools would be legally impossible because of state constitutional restrictions, most notably in the church-state area. Title I was not intended to override these individualized state restrictions. Rather, there was a clear intention that the assistance programs be designed on local levels so as to accommodate the restrictions.

Inasmuch as comparable, and not identical, services are required, the mere fact that public school children are provided on-the-premises Title I instruction does not necessarily create an obligation to make identical provision for private school children. Congress expressly recognized that different and unique problems and needs might make it appropriate to utilize different programs in the private schools. A requirement of identity would run directly counter to this recognition. It was anticipated, to be sure, that one of the options open to the local agency in designing a suitable program for private school children was the provision of on-the-premises instruction, and on remand this is an option open to these petitioners and the local agency. If, however, petitioners choose not to pursue this method, or if it turns out that state law prevents its use, three broad options still remain:

First, the State may approve plans that do not utilize on-the-premises private school Title I instruction but, nonetheless, still measure up to the requirement of comparability. . . . In essence, respondents are asking this Court to hold, as a matter of federal law, that one mode of delivering remedial Title I services is superior to others. To place on this Court, or on any federal court, the responsibility of ruling on the relative merits of various possible Title I programs seriously misreads the clear intent of

Congress to leave decisions of that kind to the local and state agencies. It is unthinkable, both in terms of the legislative history and the basic structure of the federal judiciary, that the courts be given the function of measuring the comparative desirability of various pedagogical methods contemplated by the Act.

In light of the uncontested statutory proscription in Missouri against dual enrollment, it may well be a significant challenge to these petitioners and the local agencies in their State to devise plans that utilize on-the-premises public school instruction and, at the same time, forgo on-the-premises private school instruction. . . .

Of course, the cooperation and assistance of the officials of the private school are obviously expected and required in order to design a program that is suitable for the private school. It is clear, however, that the Act places ultimate responsibility and control with the public agency, and the overall program is not to be defeated simply because the private school refuses to participate unless the aid is offered in the particular form it requests. The private school may refuse to participate if the local program does not meet with its approval. But the result of this would then be that the private school's eligible children, the direct and intended beneficiaries of the Act, would lose. The Act, however, does not give the private school a veto power over the program selected by the local agency.

In sum, although it may be difficult, it is not impossible under the Act to devise and implement a legal local Title I program with comparable services despite the use of on-the-premises instruction in the public schools but not in the private schools. On the facts of this case, petitioners have been approving plans that do not meet this requirement, and certainly, if public school children continue to receive on-the-premises Title I instruction, petitioners should not approve plans that fail to make a genuine effort to employ comparable alternative programs that make up for the lack of on-the-premises instruction for the nonpublic school children. A program which provides instruction and equipment to the public school children and the same equipment but no instruction to the private school children cannot, on its face, be comparable. In order to equalize the level and quality of services offered, something must be substituted for the private school children. The alternatives are numerous. Providing nothing to fill the gap, however, is not among the acceptable alternatives.

Second, if the State is unwilling or unable to develop a plan which is comparable, while using Title I teachers in public but not in private schools, it may develop and submit an acceptable plan which eliminates the use of on-the-premises instruction in the public schools and, instead, resorts to other means, such as neutral sites or summer programs that are less likely to give rise to the gross disparity present in this case.

Third, and undoubtedly least attractive for the educationally deprived children, is nonparticipation in the program. Indeed, under the Act, the Commissioner, subject to judicial review, 20 U.S.C.A. § 241k, may refuse to provide funds if the State does not make a bona fide effort to formulate programs with comparable services. 20 U.S.C.A. § 241j.

B. *First Amendment.* The second major issue is whether the Establishment Clause of the First Amendment prohibits Missouri from sending public school teachers paid with Title I funds into parochial schools to teach remedial courses. The Court of Appeals declined to pass on this significant issue, noting that since no order had been entered requiring on-the-premises parochial school instruction, the matter was not ripe for review. We agree. As has been pointed out above, it is possible for the petitioners to comply with Title I without utilizing on-the-premises parochial school instruction. Moreover, even if, on remand, the state and local agencies do exercise their discretion in favor of such instruction, the range of possibilities is a broad one and the First Amendment implications may vary according to the precise contours of the plan that is formulated. . . .

It would be wholly inappropriate for us to attempt to render an opinion on the First Amendment issue when no specific plan is before us. A federal court does not sit to render a decision on hypothetical facts, and the Court of Appeals was correct in so concluding.

. . . The comparability mandate is a broad one, and in order to implement the overriding concern with localized control of Title I programs, the District Court should make every effort to defer to the judgment of the petitioners and of the local agency. Under the Act, respondents are entitled to comparable services, and they are, therefore, entitled to relief. As we have stated repeatedly herein, they are not entitled to any particular form of service, and it is the role of the state and local agencies, and not of the federal courts, at least at this stage, to formulate a suitable plan.

On this basis, the judgment of the Court of Appeals is affirmed.

*Federal Government May Recover
Misused Funds From States*

BELL v. NEW JERSEY AND PENNSYLVANIA

Supreme Court of the United States, 1983.
461 U.S. 773, 103 S.Ct. 2187.

JUSTICE O'CONNOR delivered the opinion of the Court.

In this case we consider both the rights of the Federal Government when a State misuses funds advanced as part of a federal grant-in-aid program under Title I of the Elementary and Secondary Education Act and the manner in which the Government may assert those rights. We hold that the Federal Government may recover misused funds, that the Department of Education may determine administratively the amount of the debt, and that the State may seek judicial review of the agency's determination.

The respondents, New Jersey and Pennsylvania, received grants from the Federal Government under Title I of the Elementary and Secondary Education Act of 1965 (ESEA), Pub. 89–10, 79 Stat. 27, as amended, 20 U.S.C. § 2701 et seq. (1976 ed. Supp. V). Title I created a program designed to improve the educational opportunities available to disadvantaged children. § 102, 20 U.S.C. § 2701 (1976 ed. Supp. V). Local educational agencies obtain federal grants through state educational agencies, which in turn obtain grants from the Department of Education upon providing assurances to the Secretary that the local educational agencies will spend the funds only on qualifying programs. § 182(a), 20 U.S.C. § 2734 (1976 ed. Supp. V). In auditing New Jersey for the period September 1, 1970, through August 1973, and Pennsylvania for the period July 1, 1967, through June 30, 1973, to ensure compliance with ESEA and the regulations promulgated under ESEA, federal auditors determined that each State had misapplied funds. After review requested by the States, the Education Appeal Board (the Board) modified the findings of the auditors and assessed a deficiency of $1,031,304 against New Jersey and a deficiency of $422,424.29 against Pennsylvania. The Secretary declined to review the orders establishing the deficiencies, and, after a period for comment, the orders became final. Both States filed timely petitions for review in the United States Court of Appeals for the Third Circuit, which consolidated the cases and held that the Department did not have the authority to issue the orders. It therefore did not reach New Jersey's arguments that the State had not in fact misapplied the funds, App. to Pet. for Cert. 3a, or Pennsylvania's arguments challenging the agency's rulemaking procedures and its application of ESEA's limitations provision, ibid. . . .

Turning to the merits, the States first challenge the Secretary's order by asserting that, even if the Board properly determined that they misused the funds, the Federal Government cannot recover the amount misused. Thus, we must decide whether, assuming that a State has misused funds granted to it under Title I of ESEA, it becomes liable to the Federal Government for those funds. The Education Amendments of 1978 (1978 amendments), Pub. 95–561, 92 Stat. 2143, 20 U.S.C. §§ 2701 et seq. (1976 ed. Supp. V), rendered explicit the authority of the Secretary to recover funds misspent by a recipient. § 185, 92 Stat. 2190, 20 U.S.C. § 2835(b) (1976 ed. Supp. V). Although the final determination of the Board in each of these appeals occurred after the enactment of the 1978 amendments, the audits reviewed periods before 1978. Both States take the position that, before the 1978 amendments, the Secretary's sole remedy for noncompliance was prospective: he could withhold funds from a State that did not comply, until the State brought its program into compliance, § 146, 20 U.S.C. § 241j, or he could deny applications for funds for noncomplying programs, § 142, 20 U.S.C. § 241f. Further, they contend that the 1978 amendments operated prospectively only. The Secretary has argued both that the 1978 amendments had retroactive effect and that the right of recovery existed in the pre-1978 version of ESEA. Since we are persuaded that the pre-1978 version contemplated that States misusing federal funds would incur a debt to the Federal Government for the amount misused, we need not address the possible retroactive effect of the 1978 amendments.

Section 207(a)(1) of ESEA, Pub. 89–10, 79 Stat. 27, 32, originally provided:

> The Commissioner shall, subject to the provisions of § 208 [dealing with inadequate appropriations], from time to time pay to each State, in advance or otherwise, the amount which the local educational agencies of that State are eligible to receive under this part. Such payments shall take into account the extent (if any) to which any previous payment to such State educational agency under this title (whether or not in the same fiscal year) was greater or less than the amount which should have been paid to it.

This provision, which remained substantially unchanged as part of Title I until 1970, in our view, gives the Federal Government a right to the amount of any funds overpaid. The plain language of the statute recognizes the right, and the legislative history supports that natural reading. The Senate Report explained, "Since the State is given no authority to retain excess sums paid to it under the title, any excess paid to a State would have to be returned or taken into account in making subsequent payments to the State." S.Rep. No. 146, 89th Cong, 1st Sess., 14 (1965). Indeed, the Committee obtained assurances from the Department that it would recapture these payments, and the debate on the floor termed those assurances "an essential condition for enacting the proposed legislation." 111 Cong.Rec. 7690 (1965).
. . . In sum, not only does our conclusion give meaning to the efforts of the 95th Congress, it gives meaning to their understanding of the law that they were amending. Accordingly, we adhere to our view that the pre-1978 version of ESEA requires that recipients be held liable for funds that they misuse.

New Jersey, relying on our decision in National League of Cities v. Usery, 426 U.S. 833, 96 S.Ct. 2465, 49 L.Ed.2d 245 (1976), also urges that the imposition of liability for misused funds interferes with state sovereignty, in violation of the Tenth Amendment. It views our construction of the statute as presenting it with "unpalatable" alternatives: making a special appropriation to repay the misused funds, or cutting back its budget for education by the amount owed to the Federal Government. . . . Either alternative, it asserts, infringes its sovereignty.

We cannot agree. Requiring States to honor the obligations voluntarily assumed as a condition of federal funding before recognizing their ownership of funds simply does not intrude on their sovereignty. The State chose to participate in the Title I program and, as a condition of receiving the grant, freely gave its assurances that it would abide by the conditions of Title I.
. . . As we must assume at this stage of the litigation, the State failed to fulfill those assurances, and it therefore became liable for the funds misused, as the grant specified. New Jersey has not challenged the program itself as intruding unduly on its sovereignty . . . but challenges only the requirement that it account for funds that it accepted under admittedly valid conditions with which it failed to comply. If the conditions were valid, the State had no sovereign right to retain funds without complying with those conditions. . . .

In these cases, then, we conclude that the Secretary has followed the proper procedures. He has administratively determined the amount of the debt owed by each State to the Federal Government as he is empowered to do. Whether that determination is supported by substantial evidence and by the application of the proper legal standards is a question for the courts, if the affected parties seek judicial review. Here, New Jersey and Pennsylvania sought that review, and we remand to the Court of Appeals to permit it to undertake to review the challenges raised by each State to the Secretary's determination. Accordingly, the case is reversed and remanded for further proceedings consistent with this opinion.

It is so ordered.

Footnotes

1. Roe L. Johns, Edgar L. Morphet, and Kern Alexander, The Economics and Financing of Education, 4th ed. (Englewood Cliffs, N.J.: Prentice-Hall, Inc., 1983) p. 332.

2. U.S.C.A., Title 20, Education 81 to 1686.

3. Id.

4. United States v. Sprague, 282 U.S. 716, 51 S.Ct. 220 (1931).

5. Annals of Congress, 1897 (1791). See: Edward S. Corwin (ed.), *The Constitution of the United States of America,* (United States Government Printing Office, Wash. D.C., 1964) pp. 1035–1036.

6. Wheat 316 (1819).

7. Id. p. 406.

8. United States v. Darby, 312 U.S. 100 at 124, 61 S.Ct. 451, at 453 (1941).

9. Hopkins Federal Sav. and Loan Ass'n v. Cleary, 296 U.S. 315, 56 S.Ct. 235 (1935).

10. Article I, Sec. 8, cl. 1.

11. United States v. Butler, 297 U.S. 1, 56 S.Ct. 312 (1936).

12. Id.

13. 301 U.S. 619, 57 S.Ct. 904 (1937).

14. 3 Writings of Thomas Jefferson, pp. 147–149 (Library Edition, 1904).

15. Edward S. Corwin, *The Constitution,* rev. by Harold W. Chose and Craig R. Ducet (Princeton University Press, 1978), pp. 139–144.

16. Henry Hart, "The Relations Between State and Federal Law", 54 *Columbia Law Review* 489 (1954).

17. Richard E. Welch III, "At Federalism's Crossroads: National League of Cities v. Usery," *Boston University Law Review* 178 (1977).

18. Wheeler v. Barrera, 417 U.S. 402, 94 S.Ct. 2274 (1974).

19. Article 1, Sec. 8, cl. 3.

20. 22 U.S. (9 Wheat) 1 (1924).

21. The power of Congress "To make all Laws which shall be necessary and proper for carrying into Execution the foregoing Powers. . . . " Article I, Sec. 8, cl. 18.

22. Justice Marshall in Gibbons stated: "the power of Congress does not stop at the jurisdictional lines of the several States", but "must be exercised whenever [and wherever] the subject exists. . . . Commerce among the States must, of necessity, be commerce [within] the States." Gibbons v. Ogden, 22 U.S. (9 Wheat) 1 (1924).

23. "[T]he power over commerce . . . is vested in Congress as absolutely as it would be in a single government, having in its constitution the same restrictions on the exercise of the power as are found in the constitution of the United States. The wisdom and the discretion of Congress, their identity with the people, and the influence which their constituents possess at elections, are . . . the sole restraints on which they have relied, to secure them from its abuse. They are the restraints on which the people must often rely solely, in all representative governments." Gibbons v. Ogden, 22 U S. (9 Wheat) 1 (1924).

24. United States v. Darby Lumber Co., 312 U.S. 100, 61 S.Ct. 451 (1941).

25. Wickard v. Filburn, 317 U.S. 111, 63 S.Ct. 82 (1942).

26. American Power and Light Co. v. Securities and Exchange Commission, 329 U.S. 90, 67 S.Ct. 133 (1946).

27. 426 U.S. 833, 96 S.Ct. 2465 (1976).

28. Welch, op. cit. pp. 178–179.

29. National League of Cities v. Usery, 426 U.S. 833, 96 S.Ct. 2465 (1976).

30. Garcia v. San Antonio Metro Transit Auth., __ U.S. __, __ S.Ct. __ (1985).

31. Pennhurst State School and Hospital v. Halderman, 451 U.S. 1, 101 S.Ct. 1531 (1981).

32. Bell v. New Jersey and Pennsylvania, 461 U.S. 773, 103 S.Ct. 2187 (1983).

33. 427 U.S. 445, 96 S.Ct. 2666 (1976).

4

State Governance
of Public Schools

State government, through statute, regulates and controls education subject
only to limitations placed on it by the state and federal constitutions. The
courts have consistently held that the power over education is an essential
attribute of state sovereignty of the same order as the power to tax, exercise
of police power, and to provide for the welfare of the citizenry. In the
exercise of this pervasive function, states have established systems of public
schools that are operated as administrative arms of the state government.

The broad power of the state extends to provision for education generally
within its boundaries and not merely to the public schools alone. Education
in this broader context encompasses educational purposes and pursuits of
the populace and the schools, both public and private. The interest in an
educated citizenry is such an important part of state sovereignty that a
certain minimal quality of education for all children is guaranteed whether
their education is acquired in public or private schools.

Court decisions abundantly support the preeminence of the state in
control of education. Interestingly, most precedents indicate that the legislature has the prerogative to govern education, when what they actually
mean is that education is governed by the democratic legislative process,
which requires action by both the legislative and executive branches of
government. The legal principles controlling education have been stated
many times in different ways by state courts; for example; the legislature
has plenary power to set up public schools,[1] the maintenance of common
schools is a concern of the state and legislature,[2] or a uniform system of
public schools is exclusively within the province of the legislature.[3] The
pervasiveness of this power is adequately illustrated by a Michigan decision
which states that, "The legislature has entire control over the schools of the
state . . . . The division of the territory of the state into districts, the
conduct of the schools, the qualifications of teachers, the subjects to be
taught therein, are all within its (the state's) control."[4]

An Ohio court has briefly encapsulated this power as follows:

. . . that the control of schools, be they public or private, providing elementary and secondary education for the youth of Ohio, reposes in the Legislature
of our state. When the General Assembly speaks on matters concerning

education it is exercising *plenary* power and its action is subject only to the limitations contained in the Constitution. . . . We can, therefore, indulge in generalities and make a broad statement to the effect that the Legislature of Ohio, in passing laws concerning elementary and secondary schools, is restrained only by its own conscience, [and] fear of the electorate. . . .[5]

The power of the state to control education has sometimes been characterized as emanating from the state's police power.[6] Although police power has not been fully defined by the courts, it is clear that the term encompasses all the elements vested in state sovereignty including those powers necessary to preserve the peace, morals, good order, and well-being of society.[7] It embraces the broad prerogatives of general welfare. The United States Supreme Court has said: "The police power of a state extends to the protection of the lives, limbs, health, comfort, and quiet of all persons, and to the protection of all property, within the state, and hence to the making of all regulations promotive of domestic order, morals, health, and safety."[8] Within this framework is the power of the state to protect the individual and society through provision for a system of education.

In holding that education is a state function, the courts maintain that the state's authority over education is not a distributive one to be exercised by local government but is a central power residing in the state. The legislature has the unrestricted prerogative to prescribe the methods of education, and the courts will not intervene unless the legislation is contrary to constitutional provisions.

The state legislature holds plenary power for purposes of education and civil government. In matters of education as in all other functions of state government, the state constitution is fundamental and is determinative of the broad scope within which the legislature can operate. The fact that the legislature is created by the constitution and given law making authority, in conjunction with the executive branch, is in and of itself a pervasive and general delegation that is not limited to special conditions or situations. By way of explaining this prerogative, the Court of Appeals of New York has said: "The people, in framing the constitution, committed to the legislature the whole law making power of the state, which they did not expressly or impliedly withhold. Plenary power in the legislature of all purposes of civil government is the rule."[9] Unlike the Congress of the United States, which has only those powers delegated to it by the Constitution, state legislatures have plenary power and may pass any act that is not expressly or impliedly forbidden by the state constitution.[10] A constitutional mandate that the legislature provide education for a certain class of the population is not, as a rule, considered to be a limitation on the educational opportunities that may be made available to other classes. According to Edwards, "The legislature must do so much; it may do more."[11]

STATE AND LOCAL EDUCATION AGENCIES

All states and the federal government have networks of administrative agencies usually called boards, commissions, bureaus, or offices that have been created to implement and administer statutes. State legislatures and the United States Congress have not seen fit historically to actually administer legislative enactments themselves even though the legislative branch of government could conceivably assume the role of program administration. Traditionally, the view has been that the legislature should not perform the multi-duties of enacting legislation, appropriating funds, and then administering the funds, thereby invading the gray area of executive responsibility. In education, for example, it would be tedious and legislatively cumbersome for a state legislature to attempt to establish by statute rules and regulations governing specific certification requirements for teachers. Jaffe has suggested the reasoning for such delegation of regulatory power by saying:

> Power should be delegated where there is agreement that a task must be performed and it cannot be effectively performed by the legislature without the assistance of a delegate or without an expenditure of time so great as to lead to the neglect of equally important business.[12]

The result has been for the state legislature to create agencies that handle the administrative functions necessary to properly implement legislation. In most states, this delegation by the legislature manifests itself in a state board of education, which may be either elected or appointed and has authority to perform administrative and supervisory functions. An alternative to this approach is to vest officials of the executive branch with regulatory and attendant authority to administer the school system of the state; such officers are generally referred to as chief state school officers. Legislatures may also delegate powers to local school districts.

It is well established that the local school district is a state agency that simply operates at the local level. The Supreme Court of Michigan has said the school district is a legislative creation. "It is true that it was provided for in obedience to a constitutional requirement; and whatever we may think . . . we cannot doubt that such management must be in conformity to the provisions of such laws of a general character as may from time to time be passed, and that the property of the district is in no sense private property, but is public property devoted to the purposes of the state, for the general good, just as almshouses and courthouses are, although confided to local management, and applied to uses which are in a sense local, though in another sense general." [13]

Another Michigan decision described the legal relationship between the state and local school districts in this way:

> Fundamentally, provision for and control of our public school system is a state matter, delegated and lodged in the state legislature by the Constitution in a separate article entirely distinct from that relating to local government. The general policy of the state has been to retain control of its school system, to be administered throughout the state under state laws by local state agencies organized with plenary powers independent of the local government with which, by location and geographical boundaries, they are necessarily closely associated and to a greater or lesser extent authorized to co-operate. "Education belongs to the state." [14]

Since local school boards are state bodies, it follows that school board members are state, not local officials.[15] Local school boards are vested with a portion of the sovereignty of the state through delegation by which they acquire certain administrative functions having attributes of all three branches of government, executive, quasi-judicial, and regulatory or quasi-legislative. As creatures of the legislature or constitution, local school districts abide within their legal prerogatives and cannot give away or re-delegate their judgmental powers to other agencies or individuals.

The courts commonly divide the administrative functions of the local school board into two categories, discretionary and ministerial. The meaning of discretionary powers here is those acts that require judgment on the part of the board. Examples of such responsibilities could be the location of a school building site, the employment of a particular teacher, or the purchase of a certain type of school bus. The greatest portion of a board's powers may be classified as discretionary. In exercising these discretionary powers, a board of education is limited only by the requirements and restrictions of the law. As has been pointed out in the case of state education agencies, the courts will not interfere with a board's exercise of discretion even though the judgment is unwise except where the board's action violates the law, abuses authority, or is *ultra vires*.

The operation of school districts is based upon the express or implied authority of statute. The courts in circumscribing the authority of school boards from statutory implication have held that in the absence of statute, travel expenses can be paid for the recruitment of teachers outside the state,[16] a school district can establish a cafeteria,[17] and a school board can establish a school health inspection department made up of doctors, dentists, and nurses.[18] On the other hand, authority has been denied for a school district to pay for surgical and dental operations for pupils,[19] for medical care for pupils injured in athletic contests,[20] and for purchase of basketball uniforms to be used on land not under school control.[21]

Functions of Education Agencies

Functions of public agencies can generally be classified as (1) legislative, (2) executive, and (3) judicial (or quasi-judicial). As agencies of government, both state and local education authorities have these basic powers.

Administration encompasses the rule-making and adjudication processes and incidental powers such as coordinating, supervising, investigating, prosecuting, advising, and declaring.[22] The exercise of administrative functions may be reviewed by the courts to determine if duties have been carried forth within the scope of law and whether proper procedures have been followed.

Delegation of Legislative Powers

Legislative functions of the state agency include the promulgation of rules and regulations made pursuant to and within the scope of statute. The legislative function performed by state agencies has been justified on the grounds that the agency was merely "filling in the details" within the meaning of general statute.[23] In the public interest, it is said the state agency should not have legislative powers since agency officials are not direct representatives of the people with constitutionally sanctioned law-making prerogative. This is a basic tenet of representative government recognized early by John Locke. In his treatises on civil government, he said:

> The legislature cannot transfer the power of making laws to any other hands, for it being but a delegated power from the people, they who have it cannot pass it over to others. . . . nobody else can say other men shall make laws for them; nor can they be bound by any laws but such as are enacted by those whom they have chosen and authorized to make laws for them.[24]

Exclusive powers of the legislature should not therefore be delegated away to subordinate agencies. In way of clarification of this theory of government, a Michigan court has said:

> This is not to say, however, that a subordinate body or official may not be clothed with authority to say when the law shall operate, or to whom, or upon what occasion, provided, however, that the standards prescribed for guidance are as reasonably precise as the subject matter requires or permits.[25]

Davis maintains, though, that formulations by state courts that attempt to circumscribe the legislative function of subordinate agencies are largely without substance.[26] While generally it appears that most courts seek to restrain too broad a delegation in order to prevent arbitrary use of uncontrolled power by subordinate officials, the actual legal theory and its implementation by the courts is sometimes difficult to follow. Basically, the theory of delegation appears to have been justified on the grounds of "adequacy of standards." Does the statute provide sufficient delineation of the particular requirement or prohibition so that in light of the surrounding facts and circumstances the agency can ascertain, interpret, and implement the true purpose of the act? The legislature must prescribe a "reasonably adequate standard." [27] Some courts maintain that "definite standards are indispensable, not only to avoid a delegation of the essential legislative power, but to guard against an arbitrary use of the delegated administrative authority." [28] Limitations on legislative delegation to subordinate agencies may have been best described by a Washington court that said:

> The legislature may delegate these legislative controls to an administrative agency of the state; provided, in so doing, it defines what is to be done; the instrumentality which is to accomplish it; and the scope of the instrumentality's authority in so doing, by prescribing reasonable administrative standards.[29]

This statement probably represents the prevailing view of the courts but the doctrine of delegation is one which must be treated as highly flexible. Courts, for example, will tend to restrict agency prerogatives in the area of taxation, property rights, or individual civil rights. On the other hand, state education agencies may have broad latitude in dealing with regulation of purely educational matters such as school district organization. For example, a Wisconsin statute was contested as being unconstitutional because it authorized the state superintendent to merge certain school districts of low assessed valuation with contiguous school districts. The Wisconsin Supreme Court said that "the power to exercise discretion in determining whether such districts shall be altered . . . may be delegated without any standard whatsoever to guide in the exercise of the power delegated." [30]

The tendency has been in recent years for the courts to follow a much more lenient policy toward delegation of legislative power.[31] Changes in the nature of modern government and the increasing complexity of society necessitates that public agencies have more general authority to assume broader prerogatives. As it now stands, the delegation principle is still applicable to the state educational process and it remains in use to prevent unconstitutional usurpation of unauthorized powers, but it is much less pervasive than before. The rule today as expounded by state courts is best exemplified by a New York court [32] that quoted with approval the standard established by the United States Supreme Court, which said that a legislative body

> . . . does not abdicate its functions when it describes what job must be done, who must do it, and what is the scope of his authority. In our complex economy that indeed is frequently the only way in which the legislative process can go forward.[33]

Although the rationale of the courts continues to follow the delegation doctrine, it should be observed that proper delegation and guarantee against arbitrary action by agencies cannot be assured through the specification of standards in legislative declarations. Protection against inappropriate action and injustice in education are to be found more in procedural safeguards and various checks and balances, the most effective of which is, of course, justification of the action to the voters and taxpayers.

Executive Functions

Although functions of education agencies are difficult to compartmentalize it is possible to identify certain ones that may be more readily described as executive rather than legislative or judicial. In fact, the organizational structures of state education agencies tend to adhere to such definition in that the legislative functions are usually vested in a state board of education, the executive functions in a chief state school officer and his staff, the state department of education, while the quasi-judicial functions may be found within the prerogatives of either or both. A similar situation exists at the local level where the board makes policy and the superintendent implements it with both sometimes exercising quasi-judicial functions.

The distinction between legislative and executive acts can be expressed as the difference between the general and the particular. "A legislative act is the creation and promulgation of a general rule of conduct without reference to particular cases; an administrative act cannot be exactly defined, but it includes the adoption of policy, the making and issue of specific direction, and the application of a general rule to a particular case in accordance with the requirements of policy or expediency or administrative practice." [34]

Activities of the education agency that may be classified as purely executive are declaring and enforcing policy as well as advising and supervising implementation of policy. One can easily identify such activities as they are performed daily in state agencies; for example, when a policy is established it must be properly interpreted and conveyed to the local school district administrators, then advice may be given and certain supervisory activities may be followed to assist in implementation. Should problems arise, steps must be taken to assure enforcement of the particular policy.

Executive actions can also be viewed in the more commonly used legislative categories of ministerial and discretionary functions. Ministerial refers to those required duties performed by the administrator and no exercise of judgment is permitted. Discretionary functions, on the other hand, are judgmental and represent exercise of substantial administrative prerogative. An administrator can pass on to a subordinate ministerial functions, but cannot delegate duties that are discretionary in nature. Discretionary functions, of course, represent an area of major overlap with the broader quasi-judicial functions of agencies. The maxim *delegatus non protest delegare* has, on the whole, been more strictly enforced when applied to sub-delegation than at the primary or legislative level of delegation. In other words, courts tend to examine more critically the internal delegation of a discretionary function from the state superintendent down to an assistant than from the legislature to the agency itself. For example, where statute vests a specific discretionary power in a state board, the board cannot sub-delegate to one board member or to some other officer such as the state superintendent. Similarly, statutory discretion vested in the state superintendent cannot be re-delegated to a deputy or assistant. Ministerial functions, on the other hand, can be sub-delegated.

Will[35] has pointed out that there is a discernible trend toward the separation of the legislative function and the executive powers in state educational administration. He describes the pattern in this way:

> Students of state educational administration commonly hold that the central education agency should consist of a state board of education, a chief state school officer, and the necessary staff. The state board of education is looked upon as the agency's legislative policy-making body, the chief state school officer as the agency's executive officer, and the organized staff as the agency's work force. A virtually complete separation of legislative and executive powers at the administrative level is intended under this pattern.[36]

The powers and duties of the state board of education, the chief state school officer, and the state department of education vary from state to state; however, general rules governing the delegation of legislative powers, the exercises of discretionary authority, and the quasi-judicial role of central state agencies are carefully circumscribed by court decisions.

Quasi-Judicial Functions

In their tripartite capacity, administrative agencies hand down many more decisions affecting individuals than do the formal courts of this country. Decisions by educational tribunals form an important source of law under which education operates. Authority for decisions by educational tribunals may be found at federal, state, and local levels. At the federal level, statute often vests the United States Commissioner of Education with quasi-judicial authority to render decisions in disputes over federal grant processes and procedures that may have direct impact on individuals or states. At the state level, quasi-judicial authority may be given to state boards of education, to state superintendents, or, in some cases, to other legislatively authorized bodies. New Jersey and New York are good examples of such powers being vested in the chief state school officer.

The state commissioner of education in New Jersey has the authority to decide cases involving internal administrative operations of the public schools of that state. A New Jersey court has said that a statute providing that the state commissioner shall decide all controversies under the school laws of the state is evidence of legislative purpose to set up a comprehensive system of internal appeals with broad powers. Such an authority invested in administrative tribunals assures that controversies are justly disposed of in accordance with the law.[37]

In another New Jersey case illustrating the judicial function of the state commissioner of education, the court said that the commissioner must enforce all rules and regulations prescribed by the state board and decide all questions arising under rules and regulations of the state board.[38]

Determinations by these tribunals are binding on the parties involved and serve additionally to establish a type of quasi-judicial *stare decisis* within the agencies' jurisdiction. Agencies, in exercise of their judicial powers, are required generally to merely provide fair treatment to the parties involved. Some states, through administrative procedure acts, may provide specific definition of the requirements of fairness, and, when administrative tribunals are dealing with disputes involving constitutional interests, more elaborate procedures are necessary. In the absence, though, of statutory or constitutional restraints, the courts have been very liberal in allowing educational tribunals to establish their own procedures. In so doing, courts more or less adhere to a requirement similar to the English doctrine of *audi alteram partem,* of natural justice that requires tribunals to adjudicate fairly. Fairness is not always easily defined but may be roughly equated to reasonableness and good faith. These two standards are not the same but may be viewed as complementary. It has been said that "some of the most honest people are the most unreasonable; and some excesses may be sincerely believed in but yet be quite beyond the limits of reasonableness."[39] It is true, however, that the actions of one conducting a hearing could be so unreasonable as to be arbitrary and capricious and as such appear to be taken in bad faith.

To ensure fairness, members of tribunals should not have special interests in the outcome of a particular issue. A personal conflict of interest on the part of the adjudicator will invalidate a decision. However, the mere fact that the public agency is, as a body, a party to the dispute is not alone an indication of bias.[40]

Judicial Review of Education Agency Actions

Whether the administrative actions be legislative or executive or judicial, the courts agree that school boards or officials may exercise those powers expressly granted by statute, and those fairly and necessarily implied.

> The rule respecting such powers is that, in addition to the powers expressly given by statute to an officer or board of officers, he or it has by implication such additional powers as are necessary for the due and efficient exercise of the powers expressly granted or which may be fairly implied from the statute granting the express powers.[41]

While some flexibility in discretion is necessary, indeed indispensable for the schools to operate efficiently, the courts cannot usurp the legislative function by too broad an interpretation of administrative powers.[42]

In challenging the exercise of administrative powers by an educational agency, be they express or implied, the aggrieved parties are required by the courts to exhaust their administrative remedies before they are allowed to bring an action before the courts. Such a rule assures the courts that issues have been properly treated at lower levels, within the realm of administrative authority, thus preventing continuous involvement of the courts in educational disputes where legitimate legal controversy is not present. Examples of the hesitancy of courts to intervene until administrative remedies are exhausted may be found in many instances.[43]

In New York, the state administrative decisions are considered to have substantial weight owing largely to a statute that provides that decisions of the commissioner of education "shall be final and conclusive, and not subject to question or review in any place or court whatsoever." While this provision on its face would appear to preclude any judicial intervention, the true "intent" has been interpreted to mean that the decisions of the commissioner would stand so long as they were not arbitrary.[44]

The general rule of law is probably best expounded by an Illinois court, which stated:

> . . . A court of review cannot substitute its judgment for the judgment of the administrative tribunal. The question is not simply whether the court of review agrees or disagrees with the finding below. It has been said that courts should not disturb administrative findings unless such findings are arbitrary, or constitute an abuse of discretion, or are without substantial foundation in evidence, or are obviously and clearly wrong, or unless an opposite conclusion is clearly evident.[45]

While this rule governing judicial review of administrative actions is generally followed by courts across the country, the individual interpretations of the rule are widely variant ranging from rather strict adherence to what some would consider to be relative disregard. As a matter of fact, courts may exercise their prerogatives to intervene and alter administrative action with several different legal bases. Ministerial actions of government agencies have been successfully challenged under the ancient legal doctrines of nonfeasance, misfeasance, or malfeasance. Failure to perform properly may be remedied by the courts by use of the common law remedy, writ of *mandamus.* If the aggrieved party is seeking to prevent an inappropriate action, then an *injunction* may be the appropriate legal remedy.

On the other hand, if discretionary actions are in question, then the person challenging the action may proceed from a broader legal basis. As mentioned above, fairness and reasonableness of action are requisite to appropriate use of the quasi-judicial authority of an agency. More directly, discretionary powers may be viewed quite broadly and if an agency acts beyond the scope of its powers it may well be *ultra vires*. A discretionary power may be abused in either good faith or in bad faith, but in both instances the action may be voided by the courts.[46] Beyond inquiry into *vires,* judicial intervention may be justifiable if: (1) A power granted to an agency is not properly applied. Here the courts will seek to determine whether the agency had either express or implied statutory power to perform as it did and if the statute was broad enough with possibly a plurality of purposes sufficient to support the action. The court will generally apply certain tests including seeking to ascertain (a) the true purpose for the action, (b) the dominant purpose, and (c) if there was an unauthorized or illicit purpose,[47] or if the action was taken in bad faith. (2) Exercise of discretionary power may also be challenged if the agency, official, or tribunal was influenced by considerations that could not have been lawfully taken into account or if it ignored obviously relevant considerations. Plaintiff, though, must show that irrelevant considerations were actually relied upon in the decision. Certainly if extraneous or irrelevant matters are set out as reasons in support of the decision, then courts may consider the result to be invalid. (3) Prescription of law is not followed in effecting administrative actions. While most instances that come to mind here involve ministerial functions, e.g., following election procedures or budgetary submission processes, the educational agency's action may also be challenged if it fails to recognize or appreciate the amplitude of its discretion.[48] For example, a state authority may have the statutory power to grant salary increases or increase fringe benefits but misconstrues and through misunderstanding fails to recognize the discretion. Here it is not the reasonableness of the decision made by the agency but the failure of the agency to recognize its power that is judicially questionable. (4) A public education board binds itself through its own regulation in such a way as to constrict or disable itself from fulfilling the primary purposes for which it was created. Where a public body is entrusted by the legislature with certain powers and duties either express or implied for public purposes, the body cannot divest itself of such powers and duties. Regulations or by-laws that effectively thwart statutory intent, for example, by contracting away a power or requiring the exercise of a broad power in a restrictive way, may be unreasonable and incompatible with public purpose.

Courts will not penalize a state agency for possible error in the exercise of discretion where judgment or opinion of the public officials is in contest. If there are reasonable grounds the judge has no further duty to inquire. The criterion of reasonableness is not subjective, but objective in the sense that it must be weighed in light of surrounding facts and circumstances.

Regulation of Common Schools Is
Within the Power of the Legislature

STATE EX REL. CLARK v.
HAWORTH

Supreme Court of Indiana, 1890.
122 Ind. 462, 23 N.E. 946.

ELLIOTT, J. . . . It is sufficient, to bring the question clearly enough before the mind for investigation and consideration, to say that the relator petitioned for a writ of mandate to compel the appellee, as school trustee of Monroe township, in the county of Howard, to certify to the county superintendent of schools the number of text-books required by the children of the township for use in the public schools, and to procure and furnish such books as the law requires . . . Elliott's Supp. § 1289 (Acts 1889, p. 74.)

The act assailed does not impinge in the slightest degree upon the right of local self-government. The right of local self-government is an inherent, and not a derivative, one. Individualized, it is the right which a man possesses in virtue of his character as a free man. It is not bestowed by legislatures, nor derived from statutes. But the courts which have carried to its utmost extent the doctrine of local self-government have never so much as intimated that it exists as to a matter over which the constitution has given the law-making power supreme control; nor have they gone beyond the line which separates matters of purely local concern from those of state control. Essentially and intrinsically, the schools in which are educated and trained the children who are to become the rulers of the commonwealth are matters of state, and not of local, jurisdiction. In such matters the state is a unit, and the legislature the source of power. The authority over schools and school affairs is not necessarily a distributive one, to be exercised by local instrumentalities; but, on the contrary, it is a central power, residing in the legislature of the state. It is for the law-making power to determine whether the authority shall be exercised by a state board of education, or distributed to county, township, or city organizations throughout the state. With that determination the judiciary can no more rightfully interfere than can the legislature with a decree or judgment pronounced by a judicial tribunal. The decision is as conclusive and inviolable in the one case as in the other; and an interference with the legislative judgment would be a breach of the constitution which no principle would justify, nor any precedent excuse.

. . . Judge Cooley has examined the question with care, and discussed it with ability; and he declares that the legislature has plenary power over the subject of the public schools. He says, in the course of his discussion, that "to what degree the legislature shall provide for the education of the people at the cost of the state, or of its municipalities, is a question which, except as regulated by the constitution, addresses itself to the legislative judgment exclusively." Again, he says, "The governing school boards derive all their authority from the statute, and can exercise no powers except those expressly granted, and those which result by necessary implication from the grant." Const.Lim. (5th Ed.) p. 225, note 1. No case has been cited by

counsel, and none has been discovered by us,—although we have searched
the reports with care,—which denies the doctrine that the regulation of the
public schools is a state matter, exclusively within the dominion of the
legislature. . . .

As the power over schools is a legislative one, it is not exhausted by
exercise. The legislature, having tried one plan, is not precluded from
trying another. It has a choice of methods, and may change its plans as
often as it deems necessary or expedient; and for mistakes or abuses it is
answerable to the people, but not to the courts. It is clear, therefore, that,
even if it were true that the legislature had uniformly intrusted the
management of school affairs to local organizations, it would not authorize
the conclusion that it might not change the system. To deny the power to
change, is to affirm that progress is impossible, and that we must move
forever "in the dim footsteps of antiquity." But the legislative power moves
in a constant stream, and is not exhausted by its exercise in any number of
instances, however great. It is not true, however, that the authority over
schools was originally regarded as a local one. On the contrary, the earlier
cases asserted that the legislature could not delegate the power to levy taxes
for school purposes to local organizations, but must itself directly exercise
the power; thus denying, in the strongest possible form, the theory of local
control. . . . All the public schools have been established under legislative enactments, and all rules and regulations have been made pursuant to
statutory authority. Every school that has been established owes its existence to legislation, and every school officer owes his authority to the
statute.

It is impossible to conceive of the existence of a uniform system of
common schools without power lodged somewhere to make it uniform; and,
even in the absence of express constitutional provisions, that power must
necessarily reside in the legislature. If it does reside there, then that body
must have, as an incident of the principal power, the authority to prescribe
the course of study, and the system of instruction, that shall be pursued and
adopted, as well as the books which shall be used. This general doctrine is
well entrenched by authority. Hovey v. State, 119 Ind. 395, 21 N.E.Rep. 21;
Hovey v. Riley, 119 Ind. 386, 21 N.E.Rep. 890; State v. Hawkins, 44 Ohio St.
98, 5 N.E.Rep. 228; State v. Harmon, 31 Ohio St. 250. Having this
authority, the legislature may not only prescribe regulations for using such
books, but it may also declare how the books shall be obtained and distributed. If it may do this, then it may provide that they shall be obtained
through the medium of a contract awarded to the best or lowest bidder,
since, if it be true, as it unquestionably is, that the power is legislative, it
must also be true that the legislature has an unrestricted discretion, and an
unfettered choice of methods. It cannot be possible that the courts can
interfere with this legislative power, and adjudge that the legislature shall
not adopt this method or that method; for, if the question is at all legislative, it is so in its whole length and breadth. . . .

Either the state has power to regulate and control the schools it owns, or
it has not. That it does not have the power, we venture to say, no one will
affirm. If it does have the power, it must reside in the law-making
department, for it is impossible for it to exist elsewhere. If the power does

reside in the law-making department, then that department must exercise its discretion, and adopt such measures as it deems best; and, if the measures adopted lead to the exclusion of some book-owners, it is an incident that no ingenuity can escape, nor any system avoid. The denial of the right to select the books is the denial of the right of regulation and control, and we cannot conceive it possible to deny this right. If the right of regulation and control exists, then the fact that the exercise of the right does not exclude some publisher is an inseparable and unavoidable condition of the exercise of the right. Without it, the right is annihilated. If a clear and manifest legislative right cannot be exercised without conferring privileges in the nature of a monopoly, then, as the authorities all agree, a monopoly may be created; for a denial of the right will not be suffered. This doctrine is discussed by Judge Cooley in his work on Torts, and by Mr. Tiedeman in his work on the Police Power, to which we refer without comment. Cooley, Torts, 277; Tied.Lim. 315 *et seq.* But we need not enter the field traveled by those authors, for here there is no denial of a right to sell books to a community. All that is here done is to provide that the person who receives, after fair and open competition, the contract for supplying books to the school children, shall enjoy an exclusive privilege for the period prescribed by the statute. Judge Cooley says that "it is held competent for the state to contract with a publisher to supply all the schools of the state with text-books of a uniform character and price." Const.Lim. (5th Ed.) p. 225, note 1. . . .

Judgment reversed, with instructions to proceed in accordance with this opinion. . . .

NOTES

1. The Supreme Court of New York has held that the requirement of the New York State Constitution stating that "the legislature shall provide for the maintenance and support of a system of free common schools, wherein all the children of this state may be educated" gave the legislature plenary power over the educational system of the state. Cohen v. State, 52 Misc.2d 324, 275 N.Y.S.2d 719 (1966). Such power allows the legislature to create school districts and to establish different types and structures of school boards to govern and regulate the local school districts.

2. The Supreme Court of Tennessee early explained the role of the state in exercising police power over public education:

   We are of the opinion that the legislature, under the constitutional provision, may as well establish a uniform system of schools and a uniform administration of them, as it may establish a uniform system of criminal laws and of courts to execute them. The object of the criminal laws is, by punishment, to deter others from the commission of crimes, and thus preserve the peace, morals, good order and well-being of society; and the object of the public-school system is to prevent crime, by educating the people, and thus, by providing and securing a higher state of intelligence and morals, conserve the peace, good order, and well-being of society. The prevention of crime, and preservation of good order and peace, is the highest exercise of the police power of the state, whether done by punishing offenders or educating the children. What is the scope and meaning of the term "police power" has never been defined. The supreme court of the United States has expressly declined to define its limits. Stone v. Mississippi, 101 U.S. 814 (1879). In Mayor, etc., v. Miln, 36 U.S. 102, 11 Pet. 102 (1835), it is said: "It embraces every law which concerns the welfare of the whole people, of the state or any individual within it, whether it relates to their rights or duties, whether it respects them as men or citizens of the state, whether in their public or private relations, whether it relates to the rights of persons or property of the whole people of the state or of any individual within it." In Railroad Co. v. Husen, 95 U.S. 465 (1877), it is said: "The police power of a state extends to the protection of the lives, limbs, health, comfort, and quiet of all persons, and to the protection of all property, within the state, and hence to the making of all regulations promotive of domestic order, morals, health, and safety." In Smith v. State, 100 Tenn. 494, 46 S.W. 566, it is said, in substance, that it extends to all questions of health, morals, safety, order, comfort, and well-being of the public, and that this enumeration does not make the list complete. Similar language has but recently been used in the case of Harbison v. Iron Co., [103 Tenn. 421] 53 S.W. 955, and this is no new doctrine, either in this state or in the United States. Leeper v. State, 103 Tenn. 500, 53 S.W. 962 (1899).

School Districts Can Exercise Only
Those Powers Fairly Implied or
Expressly Granted By Statute

McGILVRA v. SEATTLE SCHOOL DISTRICT NO. 1

Supreme Court of Washington, 1921.
113 Wash. 619, 194 P.2d 817.

PARKER, J. The plaintiffs, McGilvra and others, residents and taxpayers of Seattle school district No. 1, of King county, suing for themselves and in behalf of all others similarly situated, commenced this action in the superior court for that county seeking an injunction to restrain the school district and its officers from maintaining in one of its school buildings and expending funds of the school district for the maintenance therein of a so-called "clinic," which, as we proceed we think it will appear would be more properly designated as a "hospital," for the medical, surgical, and dental treatment of the physical ailments of pupils of the schools of the district, whose parents or guardians are financially unable to furnish such treatment. Trial in the superior court upon the merits resulted in findings and judgment denying the relief prayed for, from which the plaintiffs have appealed to this court. . . .

The question to be here answered is: Have the school district and its officers legal authority for so furnishing the use of, and equipping rooms in its buildings and the maintenance therein of such clinic, by the expenditure of the taxpayers' funds collected and placed at their disposal, for the sole purpose of maintaining the public schools of the district? At the outset let us be reminded in the language of Judge Dillon, in his work on Municipal Corporations, quoted with approval by this court in State ex rel. Winsor v. Mayor and Council, 10 Wash. 4, 37 Pac. 761, that

It is a general and undisputed proposition of law that a municipal corporation possesses and can exercise the following powers, and no others:

First, those granted in express words; second, those necessarily or fairly implied in or incident to the powers expressly granted; third, those essential to the declared objects and purposes of the corporation—not simply convenient but indispensable. Any fair or reasonable doubt concerning the existence of power is resolved by the courts against the corporation, and the power is denied.

This view of the law is of added weight when applied to school districts, because they are municipal corporations with powers of a much more limited character than are cities, or towns, or even than counties. . . .

We are quite unable to find in . . . statutory provisions any power given to the school district officers, other than the power to cause inspection of the buildings and premises of the district to be made with a view to making them sanitary and healthful, and to cause inspection of persons with a view to the exclusion from the school premises of all persons afflicted with contagious diseases, to the end that such diseases shall not obtain a foothold among the pupils and other persons whose duties require them to be upon the school premises.

Counsel for the school district officers call our attention to, and rely upon, our decision in State ex rel. School District No. 56 v. Superior Court, 69 Wash. 189, 124 Pac. 484, and Sorenson v. Perkins & Co., 72 Wash. 16, 129 Pac. 577, commonly known as the "playground" and "gymnasium" cases, wherein it was held that a school district has the power to acquire, by expenditure of the funds of the district, additional land for playgrounds for the pupils, and also at the expense of the district to construct and equip gymnasiums. We do not think these cases are of any controlling force touching the present inquiry. Playgrounds in connection with public schools have for generations been so common that it must be presumed that the Legislature by giving the general power to maintain public schools incidentally intended to also give the authority to provide such playgrounds in connection therewith; and, while gymnasiums in connection with public schools have not been so common, the work and exercise of the students carried on therein is manifestly so intimately connected with the education of the pupil as to warrant the assumption that the Legislature intended the school districts and their officers to possess the power of providing the same as a proper public school equipment. The rendering of medical, surgical, and dental services to the pupils, however, is, and always has been, we think, so foreign to the powers to be exercised by a school district or its officers, that such power cannot be held to exist in the absence of express legislative language so providing. . . .

The specific legislative enumeration of these powers which it seems could with much sounder reason be considered as implied powers in the absence of express language in the statute than the claimed powers here in question, argues, in the light of well-settled rules of statutory construction, that the Legislature has not intended that there should be an exercise of such claimed powers. We see no argument lending any substantial support, in a legal way, to the view that a school district and its officers possess the powers they are seeking to exercise and threatening to continue to exercise. There is much in the argument of counsel for the school officers which might be considered as lending support to the view that such powers ought to be possessed by the school district and its officers, and it is probable that counsel has many well meaning people upon his side of that question. The Legislature may give heed to such arguments, but the courts cannot do so.

The judgment of the trial court is reversed, and the case remanded to that court, with directions to render a judgment enjoining the school district and its officers from furnishing or equipping upon the school premises, or elsewhere, appliances for the medical, surgical, or dental treatment of the physical ailments of the pupils of the schools at the expense of the district, and from employing physicians, dentists, or nurses for the rendering of such medical, surgical, or dental treatment; it being understood, however, that such injunction shall not restrain the school district or its officers from the doing of these things at the expense of the district in connection with, and as may be necessary in, the maintenance of the parental schools of the district and the proper care of the pupils committed to such schools.

County Board of Education Has
Implied Authority to Establish Day
Care Centers

CLARK v. JEFFERSON COUNTY BOARD OF EDUCATION

Supreme Court of Alabama, 1982.
410 So.2d 23.

MADDOX, Justice. Does a county board of education have legal authority to operate a child care center? That is the sole question presented by this appeal.

The Jefferson County Board of Education offers child care services as an adjunct to its regular academic program. . . .

Participation in these programs is voluntary and on a fee basis. The community education program of the Board and the child care program, in particular, are "self-sufficient" in that all expenses are met by fees generated from the programs. All programs are conducted within existing school facilities.

Appellant Clara Clark owns two day care centers in Jefferson County and one in Shelby County under the name of Happy House Day Care Center, Inc. The Jefferson County facilities owned and operated by Clark are in Irondale and Hoover. Clark identified several facilities which she contends are in competition with her Irondale facility, including at least one child care program operated by the Jefferson County Board of Education. . . .

The trial judge held that the operation of a child care center was an activity within the broad powers granted to county boards of education. . . .

We first state, in summary form, Clark's argument that the Board has no authority to operate a child care program. She says that county boards of education, creatures of statute, can exercise only those powers which are expressly conferred upon them, that the powers granted to county boards by Code 1975, §§ 16–8–8, and 16–8–9, to administer and supervise is limited to *public schools,* and that a day care program is not a part of a *public school* because "public schools" are those established and maintained for persons between the ages of 7 and 21. . . . Clark's position is aptly stated by this quote from her brief: "No statute authorizes the education of children between one day and 5 years old."

The County Board contends that "the curricular and extracurricular offerings of the public school systems within this state, as in all states, are established by local boards of education in the exercise of their broad discretionary authority conferred by statute" and that in Alabama, this grant of authority is manifested throughout Chapter 8 of Title 16 of the Alabama Code. . . .

The Board, therefore, says that where there is a broad grant of statutory authority, no specific grant of authority to operate a child care program is required. . . .

The Board also calls our attention to evidence introduced during the trial which shows that the State Board of Education has actively and officially supported the implementation and development of Community Education in local school systems. Illustrative of this evidence is a position statement adopted by the Alabama State Board of Education on March 23, 1977, which reads as follows:

> The State Board of Education in its efforts to provide the highest quality education for the citizens of Alabama recognizes the components of community education as a most positive influence on the lifelong learning process and the democratic way of life. . . .

Other exhibits included a publication which showed that the Alabama State Department of Education defines "community education" as follows:

WHAT IS COMMUNITY EDUCATION?
> Community education is a concept that stresses an expanded role for public education and provides a dynamic approach to individual and community improvement. . . .

The publication includes a page which shows that "day care" is one of the activities under the umbrella of "people of all ages together using a community school and community resources."

The concept of community education is probably best expressed in a publication entitled "Community Education: A Position Statement," which was adopted by the Alabama State Board of Education in March, 1977, and which is included in the record. . . . The publication states that "the State Board of Education, recognizing the importance of and supporting the concepts involved in Community Education, adopted a resolution in March, 1975, urging all local school systems 'to actively pursue the community education concept.'" . . .

Based on the foregoing facts, and applying the law to those facts, we conclude that the judgment of the trial court is due to be affirmed.

The legislature has made broad grants of authority to the Alabama State Board of Education, the Alabama State Department of Education and to the individual county boards of education to administer and supervise the public schools. It is apparent that the Alabama State Board of Education, pursuant to authority granted it by law, has encouraged the development of "community education," of which "day care" is a part, and has determined that community education is in the best interest of the public schools in Alabama. . . .

We have carefully considered Clark's argument that a public body, without statutory authority, is encroaching upon an area of private enterprise.

Upon consideration of the facts and the law, we hold that while there is no specific statutory grant of authority to local boards of education to operate day care centers, there is authority for such activity under the broad grants of power which we have evaluated and discussed in this opinion. We, therefore, affirm the judgment of the trial court.

Affirmed.

School Board Regulations Must Be
Reasonable

HENNESSEY v. INDEPENDENT SCHOOL DISTRICT NO. 4, LINCOLN COUNTY, 1976.

Supreme Court of Oklahoma, 1976.
552 P.2d 1141.

DOOLIN, Justice. This is an action filed in the district court by the Wellston Parent Teacher Association (PTA) seeking a writ of mandamus to require Independent School District No. 4, Lincoln County School Board (Board) to allow PTA use of school facilities for its meetings. . . .

Board has uniformly permitted outside organizations such as Lions Club, Young Homemakers' Organization, Booster Club, 4H Club, Boy Scouts, Bible Lovers' League and Vocational Agriculture Teachers to use the building as authorized by 70 O.S.1971 § 5–130. . . .

At some time after PTA's first request was denied, Board adopted rules for use of school property by outside organizations. These rules, in addition to general platitudes, contained the following provisions:

The Wellston School Board will not tolerate nor continue affiliation with any organization that it determines to be disruptive to or *unsupportive* of the school board or any part of the school system. . . .

Board's refusal to allow PTA to use its building fails for the following reasons:

First, there is no evidence any of Board's stated rules, constitutional or otherwise, have been violated. The record is absolutely void of any testimony as to any legitimate reason why PTA should be forbidden use of the building, or that PTA is not supportive of the school system. The Superintendent of Schools testified he had no personal knowledge of any past action of PTA that would be considered a violation of Board's regulations.

The general statement in the minutes of the Board that use by PTA of school facilities would not be in best interests of community is unsupported by *any* evidence. To the contrary, it was shown that in the past PTA has sponsored many admittedly worthwhile activities for the community children. The superintendent admitted the guidelines and objectives of PTA are all worthwhile. He indicated PTA's request was refused because a vote of the teachers showed a majority of them were not interested in becoming members of PTA. PTA is chartered and supported by both the state and national Parent-Teacher Association. There is nothing in either organization's rules or guidelines requiring teachers to be members in order to be recognized.

Board's reasoning is *circulus in probanda;* PTA is not comparable to other organizations, because the Board does not officially recognize it, since it is not comparable to other organizations. 70 O.S.1971 § 5–130 was certainly not intended to omit PTA objectives from its list of permitted purposes and it cannot be successfully argued PTA is not comparable to the acceptable organizations.

The other grounds for reversal are constitutional. Board's rules and regulations as set forth above and their implementation violate the first and fourteenth amendments to the Constitution of the United States as an abridgment of freedom of speech, and a denial of equal protection and further are a violation of the Constitution of Oklahoma Art. 2, § 22. A regulation by a governmental body such as a school board which permits a public official or body to determine what expressions or views will be permitted or allows the board to engage in invidious discrimination among groups by use of a statute granting discretionary powers and by a system of selective enforcement cannot stand. . . .

There is no doubt 70 O.S.1971 § 5–130 gives Board absolute discretionary authority as to whether or not to open a school building to activities and meetings of outside organizations. The only absolute discretion exercised however is whether to open the building to outside organizations or not to open it. Once this discretion has been exercised and the decision has been made to permit use of property for any of the enumerated purposes, then it must not adopt a discriminatory and unconstitutional policy as to who will be allowed access to its facilities. Its classifications must be reasonable. Discretion of an administrative body must not be used in a discriminatory matter. Administrative action must have a reasonable or rational basis if it is to avoid the stigma of arbitrariness. All governmental bodies must remain within bounds of the Constitution.

A school board may withhold school facilities altogether from use by non-scholastic groups or may make *reasonable* classifications in determining availability. The state may control the use made of its premises but not without regard to the Constitution. The equal protection clause precludes a school from censoring expressions because it does not like its content or message, and it requires a state authority to deal with similarly situated organizations in an even-handed manner. The privilege of using a school should be available on a reasonable basis.

A state is under no duty to make school buildings available for public gatherings and a school board is not prevented from barring its use for unlawful purposes. But where a school district allows a number of organizations to use its facilities for non-academic purposes, a board must not unconstitutionally discriminate against any comparable applicant in deciding who will and who will not be permitted its use.

Reversed.

NOTES

1. The decision of the Commissioner of Education of New York in interpreting a statute is to be given great weight by the courts and unless irrational or unreasonable it will be upheld. Board of Education of Roslyn Union Free School District v. Nyquist, 90 Misc.2d 955, 396 N.Y.S.2d 567 (1977).

2. Administrative agencies in quasi-judicial hearings have traditionally not been held to the intricate procedural requirement of the courts. However, there are fundamental requirements of fairness which must be observed. A West Virginia court had this to say concerning the conduct of hearings by administrative agencies.

> An administrative body, clothed by law with quasi-judicial powers, must never depart from those elemental principles of discreetness and circumspection which our system of law requires in all tribunals which purport to conduct trials. . . . There was a time in the history of English jurisprudence when a felon was not entitled to have the assistance of an attorney at law, but in America, the very word "hearing," both in common and legal parlance, implies some kind of trial, formal or informal, and presupposes permission to have legal aid if desired. State ex rel. Rogers v. Board of Education of Lewis County, 125 W.Va. 579, 25 S.E.2d 537 (1943).

3. Legislation in Texas has been interpreted to mean that all administrative steps should be taken to resolve a dispute before appeal can be taken to the courts. Exception to this rule is only found where an action involves a question of taxation, City of Dallas v. Mosely, 286 S.W. 497 (Texas 1926), if the facts are undisputed and the issue is one purely of law and not of education; in such instances, direct access to the courts is available. Alvin Independent School District v. Cooper, 404 S.W.2d 76 (Texas 1966).

4. A Maryland court has held that the State Board of Education has the last word on any matter concerning educational policy or administration of the system of public instruction; however, it cannot finally decide pure questions of law nor exercise its visitatorial power fraudulently, in bad faith or in breach of trust. Where the State Board of Education of Maryland set a rule of a county board of education requiring fingerprint cards of all employees to be submitted to local police, the court upheld the action of the State Board as being a valid exercise of its authority. Wilson v. Board of Education of Montgomery County, 234 Md. 561, 200 A.2d 67 (1964).

5. A Missouri court has held that, where four local school districts were unable to reorganize because of refusal of one to discuss the matter, the state board of education was vested with exclusive jurisdiction to make the decision for the board and once this decision by the state board was approved by the voters, the school district became officially and legally

organized. Eagleton ex rel. Reorganized School District R–I of Miller County v. Van Landuyt, 359 S.W.2d 773 (Mo.1962).

School Board Cannot Re-delegate Its
Rule-making Power

BUNGER v. IOWA HIGH SCHOOL ATHLETIC ASSOCIATION

Supreme Court of Iowa, 1972.
197 N.W.2d 555.

UHLENHOPP, Justice. This case involves the validity of a rule of the Iowa High School Athletic Association (which we will refer to as IHSAA or the association).

IHSAA is an unincorporated association in charge of boys' interscholastic athletic events in Iowa, including tournaments. Waverly-Shell Rock Community School District is a member of IHSAA, as are all other high schools in Iowa except the school at Kalona. Member schools agree to abide by the constitution and bylaws of IHSAA, which may be amended by referendum of the members. . . .

Under the constitution and bylaws, a member school cannot allow an athlete who is known to be ineligible to engage in interscholastic athletic events. Nor can a member school engage in such events with a nonmember school. A member school violating the constitution or bylaws is subject to probation, suspension, or expulsion. One portion of the constitution and bylaws deals with eligibility of athletes to participate in interscholastic events.

The member schools strongly oppose the use of alcoholic beverages by athletes. In recent years, the drinking problem has increased, particularly the drinking of beer. Attempts by individual school boards to deal with the problem proved unsatisfactory. School boards and administrators were sometimes under local pressure to play outstanding athletes notwithstanding infractions, and different boards had varying rules relating to similar violations.

Largely at the behest of the schools themselves, a committee of IHSAA studied the problem and proposed rules which were adopted by a substantial majority vote of the membership. . . .

> Item 2: In the event a boy pleads guilty or is found guilty of using alcoholic beverages or pleads guilty or is found guilty of the use of dangerous drugs, or the transportation of either such beverages or drugs, he shall be declared ineligible for participation in interscholastic athletic competition for a minimum of six weeks for the first offense. (Individual member schools may exclude a boy for more than six weeks.) . . .

The State Department of Public Instruction approved the Good Conduct Rule and the interpretation of it and IHSAA disseminated that Rule and the interpretation among its members. The members made the Rule and interpretation known to athletes, including plaintiff William Hal Bunger.

William is a 16-year-old football player of ability on the outstanding Waverly-Shell Rock team.

On the evening of June 7, 1971, William and three other minors were riding in a car containing a case of beer. William knew the beer was in the car. An Iowa highway patrolman stopped the four minors, discovered the beer, and issued summonses to all four for possession of beer as minors. Three pleaded guilty. William pleaded not guilty, and the charges against him were subsequently dismissed by the county attorney.

On June 10, 1971, William reported the beer incident to his school athletic director and stated he knew at the time that the beer was in the car. Thereupon, the school officials declared William ineligible for six weeks commencing with the opening of the fall football season.

William brought the present suit to enjoin enforcement of the rule. The trial court upheld the rule, and William appealed.

William levels a number of charges against the rule. We think, however, that we need not consider all of his claims, for two basic questions control the case. First, does IHSAA have authority to promulgate the rule in question? Second, is the rule valid on its merits? We confine ourselves to the rule before us rendering ineligible an athlete who occupies a car with knowledge of the presence of beer which is found by a law officer. . . .

The rules are actually association rules. A rule is initially adopted by majority vote of the association members. Bearing in mind that a school board cannot re-delegate its rule-making power, how can we say that a school which votes against a proposed rule has itself promulgated that rule? Again, a school which joins IHSAA after a number of rules have been adopted has no choice as to the rules it will accept. It must take them all and abdicate its nondelegable responsibility to select the rules it wishes to have. Then what about a member school which becomes dissatisfied with a rule? It has no power to repeal the rule. To say the school can withdraw from IHSAA is no answer. If it leaves IHSAA voluntarily, or involuntarily for violating the rule, its boys' interscholastic athletic program is at an end—except for playing Kalona. Its hands are tied. The power is actually in the association, not in each school board where the statute places it. . . .

IHSAA also contends that a statute has been enacted which makes the rule valid in two separate ways—by authorizing schools to delegate their rule-making power to an association, and by authorizing the association itself to make rules subject to the approval of the State Board of Public Instruction. The statute is § 257.25(10), Code, 1971. . . .

Enactment of § 257.25(10) probably resulted in part from a desire on the part of schools to obtain interscholastic activity rules of statewide uniformity.

Our statutes also provide that if a state agency promulgates a rule of general application, as distinguished from a rule relating solely to the internal operation of the agency, the agency must submit the rule to the Attorney General and the Legislative Departmental Rules Committee for a prescribed procedure. Code, 1971, ch. 17A.

In accordance with § 257.25(10), the State Board of Public Instruction in 1966 promulgated several rules regarding athletic associations and interscholastic athletic events, and complied with the procedure prescribed by chapter 17A. But none of the rules related to the subject matter of the rule before us.

In 1968 IHSAA adopted the Good Conduct Rule and the interpretation of it and reported them to the State Department of Public Instruction, which approved them. But the State Board did not promulgate them as its own rules or put them through chapter 17A procedure.

IHSAA's first contention, that § 257.25(10) authorizes school boards to redelegate to it their rule-making authority, overextends the statute. The language of § 257.25(10) is that public schools shall not allow students to participate in an interscholastic contest or competition "which is sponsored or administered by an organization as defined in this subsection" unless the organization registers and files financial statements with the State Department of Public Instruction and complies with the Board's rules. An "organization" is defined to include an association such as IHSAA.

This language of § 257.25(10) clearly means that schools may participate in interscholastic events sponsored by qualifying organizations, and we think it also means, inferentially, that schools may belong to such organizations. But the language cannot be stretched to mean that schools may turn over their statutory rule-making authority to such organizations.

IHSAA's second contention, that § 257.25(10) authorizes IHSAA itself to promulgate rules if approved by the State Department of Public Instruction is contrary to the language of the statute. Subsection 10 permits schools to allow students to participate in interscholastic events sponsored by organizations that are, among other things, "in compliance with rules and regulations which the *state board of public instruction shall adopt* for the proper administration, supervision, operation, *eligibility requirements,* and scheduling of such extracurricular interscholastic contests and competitions. . . ." (Italics added.) Thus the eligibility rule-making authority, so far as § 257.25(10) is concerned, is in the State Board, not in IHSAA. Moreover, since promulgation of eligibility rules involves judgment and discretion, we think the State Board cannot re-delegate its rule-making authority under § 257.25(10) any more than a school board can re-delegate its rule-making authority under § 279.8. . . .

The rule before us is, in fact, a rule of IHSAA and not of the Waverly-Shell Rock Board of Education or of the State Board. Neither of the latter public bodies could re-delegate its rule-making authority. We hold that the rule is invalid for want of authority in IHSAA to promulgate it. . . .

NOTES

1. The validity of athletic association rules has been challenged on both the "delegation" grounds of *Bunger* and on the grounds of "reasonableness" as in Robinson v. Illinois High School Association, 45 Ill.App.2d 277, 195 N.E.2d 38 (1963), certiorari denied 379 U.S. 960, 85 S.Ct. 647 (1965). The South Carolina Supreme Court upheld a rule of the state high school athletic association that excluded a transfer student from high school athletic competition for a period of one year. The court said the rule was reasonable because it prevented interschool recruitment of high school athletes. The issue of illegal delegation was apparently not tested in this

case. Bruce v. South Carolina High School League, 258 S.C. 546, 189
S.E.2d 817 (1972).

In line with *Bunger,* a California court held that educational institutions can delegate to athletic associations only as much power as they themselves are given to delegate by the legislature. Cabrillo Community College Dist. of Santa Cruz County v. California Junior College Association, 44 Cal.App.3d 367, 118 Cal.Rptr. 708 (1975).

2. The Supreme Court of Nebraska has defined the Legislature's power to delegate authority as follows:

> The law appears to be well settled that the Legislature may properly delegate authority to an executive or administrative agency to formulate rules and regulations to carry out the expressed legislative purpose, or to implement such expressed purpose in order to provide for the complete operation and enforcement of the statute. The purpose of the delegation of authority ordinarily must be limited by express standards which have the effect of restricting the actions of the agency to the expressed legislative intent. In State ex rel. Martin v. Howard, 96 Neb. 278, 147 N.W. 689, this court approved the following: "In order to justify the courts in declaring invalid as a delegation of legislative power a statute conferring particular duties or authority upon administrative officers, it must clearly appear beyond a reasonable doubt that the duty or authority so conferred is a power that appertains exclusively to the legislative department, and the conferring of it is not warranted by the provisions of the Constitution. . . . Authority to make rules and regulations to carry out an expressed legislative purpose, or for the complete operation and enforcement of a law within designated limitations, is not an exclusively legislative power. Such authority is administrative in its nature and its use by administrative officers is essential to the complete exercise of the powers of all the departments." . . .
>
> The difference between a delegation of legislative power and the delegation of authority to an administrative agency to carry out the expressed intent of the Legislature and the details involved has long been a difficult and important question. Increased complexity of our social order, and the multitude of details that necessarily follow, has led to a relaxation of the specific standards in the delegating statute in favor of more general ones where a specialized state agency is concerned. It is almost impossible for a legislature to prescribe all the rules and regulations necessary for a specialized agency to accomplish the legislative purpose. The delegation of authority to a specialized department under more generalized standards has been the natural trend as the need for regulation has become more evident and complex. . . .
> School District No. 8 of Sherman County v. State Board of Education, 176 Neb. 722, 127 N.W.2d 458 (1964).

3. The courts have held that discretionary administrative powers may be delegated while legislative powers cannot. It this regard, the Supreme Court of Nebraska has said:

> The legislature cannot delegate legislative authority to an individual. It can prescribe the terms and conditions which may bring into operation a dissolution or consolidation of school districts. This is the legislative act. It then can authorize the county superintendent to determine if the facts exist which call the law into operation. Bierman v. Campbell, 175 Neb. 877, 124 N.W.2d 918 (1963).

An Illinois court has said that the legislature may not delegate legislative authority but it may "give an administrative body discretionary powers to decide an issue if it establishes standards under which that discretion may be exercised." People ex rel. Community Unit School District No. 1 v. Decatur School District No. 61, 45 Ill.App.2d 33, 194 N.E.2d 659 (1963).

4. The courts have held that the Superintendent of Public Instruction of Illinois is the head of the public school system of that state and has been vested by the General Assembly with the duty of establishing standards in education, along the lines delineated by statute. Games v. County Board of School Trustees of McDonough County, 13 Ill.2d 78, 147 N.E.2d 306 (1958).

5. A Massachusetts court has held that the state Commissioner of Education has the power to compel local school officials to produce information by racial census. The court said that the Commissioner had the implied authority to do in an ordinary and reasonable manner those things required for the efficient exercise of powers and satisfactory performance of duties. School Committee of New Bedford v. Commissioner of Education, 349 Mass. 410, 208 N.E.2d 814 (1965).

6. In a Kentucky case concerning the constitutionality of delegation of legislative power to agencies in general and county boards of education in particular, the court said:

It has been suggested that the statute in this respect . . . is unconstitutional as being a delegation of legislative power to the several county boards of education. Such bodies may and do have conferred upon them legislative authority in a degree, for rules and regulations partake of that function. But delegation of legislative power in relation to constitutional limitations means delegation of discretion as to what the law shall be, and does not mean that the legislature may not confer discretion in the administration of the law itself. . . . Many are the instances where powers more nearly approaching the legislative prerogative than this have been vested in executive or administrative agencies and sustained as valid. This authority given the school boards is administrative and not legislative, and the act does not offend the Constitution in this regard. Board of Education of Bath County v. Goodpaster, 260 Ky. 198, 84 S.W.2d 55 (1935).

7. A decision by the Commissioner of Education of New York requiring school boards to furnish transportation to nonpublic school children was held not to be arbitrary even though the decision was rendered under two "somewhat inconsistent rules". Board of Education of Cornwall v. Nyquist, 61 A.D.2d 132, 401 N.Y.S.2d 589 (1978).

SCHOOL OFFICERS

A school officer, as opposed to a school employee, is one who holds public office by virtue of which he or she possesses a delegation of sovereign power. An Indiana court[49] has defined a public office as "a position to which a portion of the sovereignty of the state attaches for the time being, and which is exercised for the benefit of the public." The most important characteristic that may be said to distinguish an office from an employment is that the duties of an office must involve an exercise of some portion of the sovereignty; there are powers and duties conferred by the legislature or the constitution. The duties must be performed independently, without the control of a superior power, unless statute provides for a subordinate office. Other characteristics that typically identify the office are a permanency or continuity of office, a required oath of office, and a procedure for removal that is usually fixed by statute. In addition, employees may exercise only ministerial powers and have no authority to exercise discretionary powers.

A superintendent of a local school district is, in most states, considered an employee. A case in point is that of a local superintendent in California who was discharged by the board of education and claimed he could be discharged only by the grand jury since he was a school officer. The school code provided that the school board shall "elect" a superintendent for a four-year term. Other provisions of the code said the school board may "employ" a superintendent. The superintendent in this case asserted that the term "elect" was indicative of public office. The court, however, held that the terms "elect" and "employ" in this case meant the same thing. The court further pointed out that the position of superintendent did not exercise a sovereign power, was not created by the constitution or statute, and statutes did not impose independent police power duties upon the individual.[50]

Public officers are not allowed to hold two offices that are in conflict. Offices may be incompatible when one exercises control over the other, one office is subordinate to another, or the offices are held in more than one branch of the government at the same time. For example, a judge cannot also be a prosecuting attorney, a legislator cannot also be school board member, and a governor cannot also be a legislator. Extending this principle further, it has been held that teachers, even though they are only employees, cannot also serve as board members in the same school district.[51]

Some state constitutions may say that a person cannot hold two lucrative offices regardless of whether one is subordinate to the other. The Indiana Constitution provides, "No person holding a lucrative office or appointment under the United States or under this State, shall be eligible to a seat in the General Assembly; nor shall any person hold more than one lucrative office at the same time, except as in this Constitution expressly prohibited . . . ."[52] Such "lucrative offices" have been held to prevent a person from serving both as a justice of the peace and a school board member, or to be sheriff while serving as a school board member.

Nearly all states have statutes that prevent public officers from having an interest in contracts made with the agencies they administer. A case illustrating a conflict of interest occurred when a board member with an interest in an insurance company wrote a policy for his own school district. The court held that this board member could be removed because he had wrongfully gained advantage through his public position.[53]

A public office, theoretically, is a public duty and an officer must have the consent of the governing power before he can resign. In other words, a public office is held at the will of both parties, and the public has a right to the services of its citizens. Therefore, to be valid a resignation must be accepted. Without acceptance, the resignation is of no effect and the officer remains in office.[54] Although this is one theory of vacation of a public office, some states provide for an "absolute" right to resign.[55] In states in which the officer has an "absolute" right to resign, if he tenders a resignation, he cannot withdraw it. There is immediate unconditional acceptance. In states that follow the "public duty" theory, a resignation probably can be withdrawn prior to acceptance or prior to an effective date if resignation specifies such a date. An Illinois court has held that resignations in advance are not legal. In a case in which a mayor required board members to put resignations in writing at the time of appointment, and the mayor later accepted, the court said that such resignations were invalid as they were not contemplated by the law.[56]

Statutes provide the procedure to be used for the removal of public officers. In the absence of statute, removal is an incidental power of the appointing agency. For removal for cause only a notice and a hearing are generally required. Cause may be malfeasance, improper or illegal performance of duties or breach of good faith, inefficiency, and incapacity. A public officer cannot be removed during a term of office, when the term is fixed by statute, unless for cause. In a case in which school board members took "kickbacks" from a contractor for violation of competitive bid law, the court removed the board. The court held that even in the absence of statute, the board members could be punished under common law for wilful misconduct in office.[57]

SCHOOL ELECTIONS

Legal issues relating to school elections are nearly as diverse as the general election laws of a state. No attempt is made here to fully encompass this wide body of law, but it is necessary to generally examine election law with regard to reapportionment precedents and to those legal requirements pertaining to compliance with election statutes.

Until 1962, the view of the courts prevailed that legislative representation and how it was apportioned throughout a state was a matter for only the legislature to determine. Malapportionment and rottenboroughs were of grave concern to many and the problems became more acute as population mobility left some voters with very little legislative power, while others reaped disproportionately great political muscle. Judicial precedent, which permitted this to transpire, was found in Colegrove v. Green,[58] in which case Justice Frankfurter, writing for the Supreme Court, opted to keep the courts out of the "political thicket." Frankfurter said:

> To maintain this action would cut very deep into the very being of Congress. Courts ought not to enter this political thicket. The remedy for unfairness in distributing is to secure state legislatures that will apportion properly, or to invoke the ample powers of Congress. . . . The Constitution has left the performance of many duties in our governmental scheme to depend on the fidelity of the executive and legislative action and, ultimately, in the vigilance of the people in exercising their political rights.[59]

After this decision, it soon became clear that the problems of apportionment would not be corrected by the legislators themselves, and the people were powerless to fully exercise their political rights. In reevaluation of its position, the Supreme Court handed down a new precedent in Baker v. Carr[60] in 1962. In so doing, the court found that the Equal Protection Clause was violated by the resulting discrimination against some voters, which was not reasonable or rational but instead was arbitrary and capricious.

This case has had bearing on school district elections in the same manner as it has influenced state-wide elections; if officials are elected by popular vote, then the Constitution assures "that each person's vote counts as much, insofar as it is practicable, as any other person's." [61]

*Constitutionality of One-Person One-
Vote Is Not Applicable to
Appointive Boards*

SAILORS v. BOARD OF
EDUCATION OF COUNTY OF
KENT

Supreme Court of the United States, 1967.
387 U.S. 105, 87 S.Ct. 1549.

Mr. Justice DOUGLAS delivered the opinion of the Court.

Appellants, qualified and registered electors of Kent County, Michigan, brought this suit in the Federal District Court to enjoin the Board of Education of Kent County from detaching certain schools from the city of Grand Rapids and attaching them to Kent County, to declare the county board to be unconstitutionally constituted, and to enjoin further elections until the electoral system is redesigned. Attack is also made on the adequacy of the statutory standards governing decisions of the county board in light of the requirements of due process. We need not bother with the intricate problems of state law involved in the dispute. For the federal posture of the case is a very limited one. The people of Michigan (qualified school electors) elect the local school boards. No constitutional question is presented as respects those elections. The alleged constitutional questions arise when it comes to the county school board. It is chosen, not by the electors of the county, but by delegates from the local boards. Each board sends a delegate to a biennial meeting and those delegates elect a county board of five members, who need not be members of the local boards, from candidates nominated by school electors. It is argued that this system of choosing county board members . . . violates the principle of "one man, one vote," which we held . . . in Reynolds v. Sims, 377 U.S. 533, 84 S.Ct. 1362, 12 L.Ed.2d 506, was constitutionally required in state elections. A vast array of facts is assembled showing alleged inequities in a system which gives one vote to every local school board (irrespective of population, wealth, etc.) in the selection of the county board. . . .

We start with what we said in Reynolds v. Sims, supra, at 575, 84 S.Ct. at 1388:

> Political subdivisions of States—counties, cities or whatever—never were and never have been considered as sovereign entities. Rather, they have been traditionally regarded as subordinate governmental instrumentalities created by the State to assist in the carrying out of state governmental functions. As stated by the Court in Hunter v. City of Pittsburgh, 207 U.S. 161, 168 [28 S.Ct. 40, 52 L.Ed. 151,] these governmental units are "created as convenient agencies for exercising such of the governmental powers of the state, as may

be entrusted to them," and the "number, nature and duration of the powers conferred upon [them] . . . and the territory over which they shall be exercised rests in the absolute discretion of the state."

We find no constitutional reason why state or local officers of the nonlegislative character involved here may not be chosen by the governor, by the legislature, or by some other appointive means rather than by an election. . . .

A State cannot of course manipulate its political subdivisions so as to defeat a federally protected right, as for example, by realigning political subdivisions so as to deny a person his vote because of race. . . .

The Michigan system for selecting members of the county school board is basically appointive rather than elective. We need not decide at the present time whether a State may constitute a local legislative body through the appointive rather than the elective process. . . . We do not have that question here, as the County Board of Education performs essentially administrative functions; and while they are important, they are not legislative in the classical sense.

Viable local governments may need many innovations, numerous combinations of old and new devices, great flexibility in municipal arrangements to meet changing urban conditions. We see nothing in the Constitution to prevent experimentation. At least as respects nonlegislative officers, a State can appoint local officials or elect them or combine the elective and appointive systems as was done here. If we assume *arguendo* that where a State provides for an election of a local official or agency—whether administrative, legislative, or judicial—the requirements of . . . Reynolds v. Sims must be met, no question of that character is presented. For while there was an election here for the local school board, no constitutional complaint is raised respecting that election. Since the choice of members of the county school board did not involve an election and since none was required for these nonlegislative offices, the principle of "one man, one vote" has no relevancy.

Affirmed.

NOTES

1. A statute limiting the franchise in school elections to parents of children enrolled in the public schools and owners and leasees of taxable real property denies equal protection. Kramer v. Union Free School District, No. 15, 395 U.S. 621, 89 S.Ct. 1886 (1969).

Similarly, the Supreme Court has held unconstitutional a statute that limited electors in a public utility bond election to only "property taxpayers." Cipriano v. City of Houma, 395 U.S. 701, 89 S.Ct. 1897 (1969).

2. The Civil Rights Acts of 1957 and 1960 protect voters in federal elections from intimidation amd interference and requires State election officials to preserve federal election records. 42 U.S.C. 1971(b), 1974–1974(b). Also, state laws requiring literacy to vote cannot be ambiguous and vague violating the Fifteenth Amendment. Smith v. Allwright, 321 U.S. 649 (1944).

Equality of Voting Power Is Required
in Local District Elections

HADLEY v. JUNIOR COLLEGE DISTRICT OF METROPOLITAN KANSAS CITY, MO.

Supreme Court of the United States, 1970.
397 U.S. 50, 90 S.Ct. 791.

Mr. Justice BLACK delivered the opinion of the Court.

This case involves the extent to which the Fourteenth Amendment and the "one man, one vote" principle apply in the election of local governmental officials. Appellants are residents and taxpayers of the Kansas City School District, one of eight separate school districts that have combined to form the Junior College District of Metropolitan Kansas City. Under Missouri law separate school districts may vote by referendum to establish a consolidated junior college district and elect six trustees to conduct and manage the necessary affairs of that district. The state law also provides that these trustees shall be apportioned among the separate school districts on the basis of "school enumeration," defined as the number of persons between the ages of six and twenty years, who reside in each district. In the case of the Kansas City School District this apportionment plan results in the election of three trustees, or 50 percent of the total number from that district. Since that district contains approximately 60 percent of the total school enumeration in the junior college district, appellants brought suit claiming that their right to vote for trustees was being unconstitutionally diluted in violation of the Equal Protection Clause of the Fourteenth Amendment. The Missouri Supreme Court upheld the trial court's dismissal of the suit, stating that the "one man, one vote" principle was not applicable in this case. . . . [F]or the reasons set forth below we reverse and hold that the Fourteenth Amendment requires that the trustees of this junior college district be apportioned in a manner that does not deprive any voter of his right to have his own vote given as much weight, as far as is practicable, as that of any other voter in the junior college district. . . .

This Court has consistently held in a long series of cases that in situations involving elections, the States are required to insure that each person's vote counts as much, insofar as it is practicable, as any other person's. We have applied this principle in congressional elections, state legislative elections, and local elections. The consistent theme of those decisions is that the right to vote in an election is protected by the United States Constitution against dilution or debasement. While the particular offices involved in these cases have varied, in each case a constant factor is the decision of the government to have citizens participate individually by ballot in the selection of certain people who carry out governmental functions. Thus in the case now before us, while the office of junior college trustee differs in certain respects from those offices considered in prior cases, it is exactly the same in the one crucial factor—these officials are elected by popular vote. . . . While there are differences in the powers of different officials, the crucial consideration is the right of each qualified voter to participate on an equal footing in the election process. It should be remembered that in cases like this one we are asked by voters to insure that they are given equal treatment, and from their perspective the harm from unequal treatment is the same in any election, regardless of the officials selected. . . .

It has also been urged that we distinguish for apportionment purposes between elections for "legislative" officials and those for "administrative" officers. Such a suggestion would leave courts with an . . . unmanageable principle since governmental activities "cannot easily be classified in the neat categories favored by civics texts," . . . and it must also be rejected. We therefore hold today that as a general rule, whenever a state or local government decides to select persons by popular election to perform governmental functions, the Equal Protection Clause of the Fourteenth Amendment requires that each qualified voter must be given an equal opportunity to participate in that election, and when members of an elected body are chosen from separate districts, each district must be established on a basis that will insure, as far as is practicable, that equal numbers of voters can vote for proportionally equal numbers of officials. . . .

Although the statutory scheme reflects to some extent a principle of equal voting power, it does so in a way that does not comport with constitutional requirements. This is so because the Act necessarily results in a systematic discrimination against voters in the more populous school districts. This discrimination occurs because whenever a large district's percentage of the total enumeration falls within a certain percentage range it is always allocated the number of trustees corresponding to the bottom of that range. Unless a particularly large district has exactly 33⅓ percent, 50 percent or 66⅔ percent of the total enumeration it will always have proportionally fewer trustees than the small districts. As has been pointed out, in the case of the Kansas City School District, approximately 60 percent of the total enumeration entitles that district to only 50 percent of the trustees. Thus while voters in large school districts may frequently have less effective voting power than residents of small districts, they can never have more. Such built-in discrimination against voters in large districts cannot be sustained as a sufficient compliance with the constitutional mandate that each person's vote count as much as another's, as far as practicable. . . . We have said before that mathematical exactitude is not required . . . but a plan that does not automatically discriminate in favor of certain districts is.

In holding that the guarantee of equal voting strength for each voter applies in all elections of governmental officials, we do not feel that the States will be inhibited in finding ways to insure that legitimate political goals of representation are achieved. We have previously upheld against constitutional challenge an election scheme that required that candidates be residents of certain districts that did not contain equal numbers of people. . . . Since all the officials in that case were elected at large, the right of each voter was given equal treatment. We have also held that where a State chooses to select members of an official body by appointment rather than election, and that choice does not itself offend the Constitution, the fact that each official does not "represent" the same number of people does not deny those people equal protection of the laws. . . . And a State may, in certain cases, limit the right to vote to a particular group or class of people. . . . But once a State has decided to use the process of popular election and "once the class of voters is chosen and their qualifications specified, we see no constitutional way by which equality of voting power may be evaded." . . .

NOTES

1. Where there is no fraud, bad faith, or misleading of the voters, it is a well settled rule that statutory provisions that are treated as mandatory before an election will be construed as directory after the election. Lindahl v. Independent School District No. 306, 270 Minn. 164, 133 N.W.2d 23 (1965).

2. A Minnesota court, in Bakken v. Schroeder, 269 Minn. 381, 130 N.W.2d 579 (1964), stated that challenges to consolidation proceedings will not serve to invalidate the election unless there is proof of prejudice and that statutory requirements are treated as directory rather than mandatory when election proceedings are contested following the election. In a case involving a challenge, the court quoted an earlier decision, Erickson v. Sammons, 242 Minn. 345, 65 N.W.2d 198, and said:

It is the general rule that, before an election is held, statutory provisions regulating the conduct of the election will usually be treated as mandatory and their observance may be insisted upon and enforced. After an election has been held, the statutory regulations are generally construed as directory and such rule of construction is in accord with the policy of this state, which from its beginning has been that, in the absence of fraud or bad faith or constitutional violation, an election which has resulted in a fair and free expression of the will of the legal voters upon the merits will not be invalidated because of a departure from the statutory regulations governing the conduct of the election except in those cases where the legislature has clearly and unequivocally expressed an intent that a specific statutory provision is an essential jurisdictional prerequisite and that a departure therefrom shall have the drastic consequence of invalidity. . . .

3. Where a statute requires a resolution by the board of education for the initiation of a bond election the courts have held that the resolution need not be formal, "Be it resolved," nor need it even be in writing. The statute is fulfilled by any official action by the board. Lindahl v. Independent School District No. 306, 270 Minn. 164, 133 N.W.2d 23 (1965).

4. The Supreme Court of Texas in McKinney v. O'Conner, 26 Tex. 5 (1861), has stated the rule for elections as:

rules prescribing the manner in which the qualified electors shall hold the election, at the time and place designated, and those prescribing the manner in which their act, when done, shall be authenticated, so as to import verity on its face, are directory. Irregularities in their observance will not vitiate an election, unless they be such that the true result of the ballot cannot be arrived at with reasonable certainty. The ultimate test of the validity of an election is involved in the questions: *Did the qualified electors, at the time and place designated, acting in concert, either actively or by acquiescence, hold an election and cast their votes in the ballot box; and has it been done in a manner sufficiently conformable to the directions of the law, as that the true result can be arrived at with reasonable certainty?* (Emphasis supplied.)

5. Judicial reluctance to overthrow an election was illustrated in Stafford v. Stegle, 271 S.W.2d 833 (Tex.Civ.App.1954), wherein the court said:

> While those charged with conducting elections would use every precaution possible to see that elections are conducted strictly in accordance with the provisions of the Election Code, nevertheless, after an election has been held and it appears that it has been fairly conducted and the result correctly declared and there [are] no charges of fraud, misconduct or illegality, the entire election will not be set aside for irregularities in the manner of conducting the election, unless the statutes governing such matters state that the election must be vitiated.

6. In a case contending a lack of sufficiency of notice for a special election, a Missouri court said that: "Generally, statutory provisions as to notice of special elections are mandatory, must be strictly followed, the failure to properly call a special election will invalidate it. . . . A special election, however, will not be vitiated by failure to comply strictly with the statutory requirements with respect to the giving of notice where the electors were in fact informed of the time, place, and purpose of the election and generally voted on the question submitted; where it is not shown that the electors did not participate in the election because of lack of notice or knowledge or that a different result would have obtained if the full statutory notice had been given. State v. Whittle, 401 S.W.2d 401 (Mo.1966).

SCHOOL BOARD MEETINGS

A fundamental rule of school board meetings is that the meeting must be held within the geographic boundaries of the school district. A Missouri court has explained the reasons for this requirement in this manner:

> . . . it is obvious that considerations of public policy demand that the official meetings of public bodies be held within the limits of their territorial jurisdictions; otherwise, public servants might do in secret that which they would not attempt to do under public scrutiny, and thereby much injury might be done the public welfare . . . . It would be just as proper for the state legislature to hold its sessions outside the state or for a county court to transact business in another county . . . .

The courts have traditionally been rather lenient concerning the procedure used by boards of education in meetings. Unless the rules of procedure are prescribed by statute, a board of education may establish its own rules of procedure. Where neither statutes nor adopted board procedures are used, the generally accepted rules of parliamentary procedure will control. As indicated, the courts are indulgent concerning procedure and will not insist on a specific set of rules. The court is primarily concerned that every board member has been given a right to be heard and to vote.

The actual board meeting is an important prerequisite to an action by a board of education. Action taken separately or individually, by board members outside a board meeting, has no validity. Likewise, promises made by individual board members outside official meetings have no legal validity. However, a board of education, if it chooses, may ratify a previous individual commitment made by a board member. Official action at a later meeting is necessary for ratification.

*School Records Are Open to Public
and May Be Photographed*

PEOPLE EX REL. GIBSON v.
PELLER

Appellate Court of Illinois, 1962.
34 Ill.App.2d 372, 181 N.E.2d 376.

BURKE, Justice. Plaintiffs are residents and taxpayers of the area comprising School District 89 and have children who attend a school of the district. Defendants are members of the Board of Education of the district and govern and administer the schools within the district. On April 4, 1960, at a designated time and place previously consented to by the defendants for the inspection of the financial records of the Board of Education of the district for the years 1955 through 1960, the plaintiffs were refused the right to make photographic reproduction thereof. They had brought a professional photographer with them to enable them to photographically reproduce the records. In their pleadings plaintiffs allege the right to photograph the records under the common law as well as pursuant to the State Records Act, Sec. 43.7, Ch. 116, Ill.Rev.Stat.1959. The pleadings present the issue whether relators have the right to photograph the records. From the judgment that a writ of mandamus issue commanding the defendants to permit relators to examine and reproduce by photographic means the financial records of expenditures and receipts of the Board for the years 1955 to 1960, inclusive, the defendants appeal.

Defendants insist that the State Records Act does not apply to them. They concede the right of relators to inspect the records and take copies thereof when necessary to the attainment of justice. They deny the right of relators to photograph the records for the period mentioned. We are of the opinion that the State Records Act applies to members of a Board of Education and to the public records in custody of the members and the Board. A Board of Education is an agency of the state government. . . . The Board of Education is an executive administrative agency of the state. Inasmuch as it is an agency of the state government and its members public officers of the state government, Sec. 43.7 of the State Records Act applies to permit the relators to photograph the records of the Board of Education.

The right of relators to reproduce the public records is not solely dependent upon statutory authority. There exists at common law the right to reproduce, copy and photograph public records as an incident to the common law right to inspect and use public records. Good public policy requires liberality in the right to examine public records. In C.J.S. Records § 35, p. 133, the author states: "The right of access to, and inspection of, public records is not entirely a matter of statute. The right exists at common law. . . . all authorities are agreed that at common law a person may inspect public records . . . or make copies or memoranda thereof." In Clay v.

Ballard, 87 Va. 787, 790, 13 S.E. 262, 263, the court said that at common law the right to inspect includes the right to copy. . . .

Defendants say that relators have the right to look, examine and inspect with the naked eye the public records and copy by hand these public records, but that they have no right to photograph the records. This argument cannot be sustained by logic or common knowledge. Modern photography is accurate, harmless, noiseless and time saving. It does nothing more than capture that which is seen with the naked eye. Neither defendants nor the public can be harmed by the reproduction of the records exactly as they exist. The fact that more modern methods of copying are devised should not lessen the basic right given under the common law. The State Records Act declares the public policy relating to public records in the State of Illinois. It does not abrogate the common law.

The trial judge was right in entering judgment for the relators, and the judgment is affirmed.

Judgment affirmed.

NOTES

1. A teacher's association can videotape proceedings of a school board meeting. A court in New Jersey, in upholding videotaping of a board meeting, reasoned that video cameras and recorders are so commonplace today that one would have great difficulty showing that their use would in some manner impede the deliberations or harm the public interest. On the school board's behalf, the court did say that the videotaping equipment could not be used in such a manner as to disrupt the meeting. The court, though, was not sympathetic with school board members who wanted to ban the cameras merely because the cameras' presence made the members feel uncomfortable or inhibited. Maurice River Board of Education v. Maurice River Teachers, 193 N.J.Super. 488, 475 A.2d 59 (1984). See also: Sony Corp. of America v. Universal City Studios, Inc., ___ U.S. ___, 104 S.Ct. 774 (1984).

2. *Open Meetings.* Some states require open school board meetings by statute (Sunshine Laws), but, even in the absence of statute, board meetings are required to be open by the courts. The primary difference lies in that, by common law, boards can adjourn to executive session to consider any issue, but can only act in public. Most sunshine statutes require both deliberations and actions to be taken in public; the exception being only for sensitive matters that would, if aired in public, be personally detrimental to some party or would harm the public interest. See chart on p. 000.

In New Jersey a statute requires open meetings. A board meeting was called for 8:00 p.m. to consider the appointment of a superintendent of schools. Three members (of the five) met at 7:00 p.m. and, without notifying the other two members, privately agreed to appoint a certain individual as superintendent. At 8:00 p.m. the "resolution" was announced; the remainder of the board objected. The court held the appointment was void and said that for a public meeting to be valid there must be a fair opportunity for discussion. This did not prevent "advance" meetings of the board for "tentative" discussion, but it did preclude final action as was taken in this case. Cullum v. Board of Education, 27 N.J.Super. 243, 99 A.2d 323 (1953).

In a Utah case the court held that "unless matters [are] . . . of such a delicate nature or of the type where public policy dictates non-dissemination, the meeting itself should be open to the public and press . . . . The truth about official acts of public servants always should be displayed in the public market place, subject to public appraisal." Conover v. Board of Education, 1 Utah 2d 375, 267 P.2d 768 (1954).

A New York court has held that "All official action (of a school board) must be taken at a public meeting, and not at a closed one which only certain members of the public are permitted to attend." Application of Flinn, 154 N.Y.S.2d 124 (1956).

3. *Executive Sessions.* Executive sessions, where the board retires to privacy, may be used for discussion, but not for action. Where a board met in open session, adjourned for an hour or so, reconvened in executive session, and then met again in open session, and teachers' contracts were terminated in the open session after discussion in the executive session, the teachers sued, questioning the validity of the action. The court said the meeting was a legal one, despite the fact that the contracts were discussed in the executive session. The requirements of the law were met when the official action of the board was taken in open session. Alva v. Sequoia Union High School District, 98 Cal.App.2d 656, 220 P.2d 788 (1950); Dryden v. Marcelluse Community Schools, 401 Mich. 76, 257 N.W. 2d 79 (1977).

In a later case, in Illinois, the board of education voted in an executive session to condemn land. Action was later ratified in an open meeting. The action was challenged and the court held that the action in the executive session was "not an effective exercise of the power of the board to commence condemnation. The original petition was, thus, insufficient." However, since the board had later ratified the action in an official meeting, the condemnation proceedings were legal. Goldman v. Zimmer, 64 Ill.App.2d 277, 212 N.E.2d 132 (1965).

4. *Procedure.* As pointed out earlier, courts are rather flexible as to the procedure used by local school boards.

In 1960, a New Hampshire court upheld action by a school board when there was considerable irregularity in parliamentary procedure. The court said that a board's action could not be voided so long as no statutes were violated. If the machinery of government were not allowed a little play in its joints it would not work. Lamb v. Danville School Board, 102 N.H. 569, 162 A.2d 614 (1960).

However, the courts will not go too far in upholding flimsy procedure. In a Missouri case, two board members, without notifying a third, got together informally at home and decided to call a special school election. No minutes were kept. The court said that school elections called as a result of the meeting were invalid. The board meeting was not a legal one: "While there is no question but that the motives of the (board members) . . . were of the highest, we think their manner of getting together had no more dignity than any ordinary fence-row conference."

State ex rel. Stewart v. Consolidated School District, 281 S.W.2d 511 (Mo. 1955).

Boards of education should adopt rules of procedure. However, when they do, they are bound by their own rules. In an early Kentucky case, illustrating the binding force of a board rule, a board made a rule that purchases of supplies and materials of $500 or less could be made without bid. Pianos were purchased in an amount of $2,500 without bids. The membership of the board changed and the new board refused to pay for the pianos. The vendor sued. The action of the vendor was unsuccessful. The court held that the school board rules had the force of law upon the board itself, which the board could not disregard. Montenegro-Riehm Music Co. v. Board of Education of Louisville, 147 Ky. 720, 145 S.W. 740 (1912).

An Ohio school board passed a rule that provided that bus drivers involved in five accidents causing police investigation shall be dismissed. A bus driver arrived home from a vacation trip at three in the morning, arose four hours later to drive a school bus. The bus left the road and struck an embankment seventeen feet from the highway. No one was injured. The board dismissed the driver and the driver sued. The court held for the driver saying that the rule of five accidents of the board was "unfortunate." Since there was evidence of only one accident and even though the discharge of the driver was desirable, the board could not discharge him because of its own regulation. State ex rel. Edmundson v. Board of Education, 2 Ohio Misc. 137, 201 N.E.2d 729 (1964).

5. *Quorum.* A quorum under common law is a simple majority of the total membership. In the absence of statute, the common law rule will be applied. Gunnip v. Lautenklos, 33 Del. 415, 94 A.2d 712 (1953).

A Kentucky court has held that where there was one vacancy on a five-member board the four remaining members represented a quorum. Trustees v. Brooks, 163 Ky. 200, 173 S.W. 305 (1915). The number required for a quorum is not reduced by a reduction in the membership due to vacancies. This means that in the case of a five-member board, which has three vacancies, the two remaining board members cannot take action.

6. *Voting.* Boards, in the absence of statute, may establish voting procedures (voice vote, show of hands, secret ballot). There is no authority for a board member to allow someone else to vote for him.

When a board member refuses to vote, the general rule is that this vote is considered as an assent to the will of the majority. Mullins v. Eveland, 234 S.W.2d 639 (Mo.1950). In a Tennessee case, in which a board of seven members considered a motion to execute a contract, three voted in favor, two opposed, and two did not vote. The court said the motion carried by a vote of five to two. Those not voting were considered as assenting to the majority. Collins v. Janey, 147 Tenn. 477, 249 S.W. 801 (1923).

Common law does not require that individual votes be recorded in the board minutes so long as the totals are made a part of the record. Diefenderfer v. Budd, 563 P.2d 1355 (Wyo.1977).

7. *Minutes and Records.* Courts hold that the school boards can act only through their minutes. The minutes of a board member are the only legal evidence of what has transpired during the meeting. An Illinois court has said that: "Proper minutes and records should be kept by a board of education to the end that the persons who are carrying the tax load may make reference thereto and the future boards may be advised of the manner of disposition of questions that have arisen." Hankenson v. Board of Education, 10 Ill.App.2d 79, 134 N.E.2d 356 (1956).

A board secretary may record minutes after the meeting has adjourned. Kent v. School District, 166 Okl. 30, 233 P. 431 (1925).

Memoranda kept by the board secretary cannot be examined by the public prior to transcribing the minutes. In a 1954 case, on the day after a board meeting, citizens requested permission to examine the minutes. The school board secretary had not as yet transcribed his notes and refused permission to the group. The court upheld the board and said "the clerk's untranscribed notes reasonably are not classifiable as a public writing . . . whereas the transcribed minutes, in final form, but awaiting only approval and placement in the journal, are a public writing . . . ." Conover v. Board of Education, 1 Utah 2d 375, 267 P.2d 768 (1954).

The form and wordage used in school board minutes are looked upon with indulgence by the court. "Although they may be unskillfully drawn, if by fair and reasonable interpretation their meaning can be ascertained, they will be sufficient to answer the requirements of law." Noxubee Co. v. Long, 141 Miss. 72, 106 So. 83 (1925).

A public records law may require that names of applicants screened for a superintendent's position be released to the press. Attorney General v. School Committee of Northampton, 375 Mass. 127, 375 N.E.2d 1188 (1978).

8. *Notice of Meetings.* In order for a board meeting to be legal, proper notice must be given and all members must be notified in time to be given an opportunity to participate. A reasonable time in advance of a meeting for notice to be given is "sufficient time to the party notified for preparation and attendance at the time and place of such meeting." Green v. Jones, 144 W.Va. 276, 108 S.E.2d 1 (1959).

When a board meeting was called with a few minutes' notice, the chairman was unable to attend, and the board employed a teacher, the court held the employment invalid. "(The chairman) was hardly bound to quit the work he had started to do and rush over to attend a suddenly called meeting of the board. The notice should have given him reasonable opportunity to attend. It did not." Wood v. School District, 137 Minn. 138, 162 N.W. 1081 (1917).

Notice should include the time and the place of the meeting. Members should be notified of any changes.

When a meeting is held without notice, and all members are present and consent to act, the requirement of notice is waived.

Notice is not required for regular board meetings because members have constructive notice. For example, boards usually establish a regular meeting date each month for which special notice is not required. Notice is only required for special board meetings.

9. *Special Board Meetings.* Notice of a special board meeting must include the purpose for the meeting. If a purpose is specified, actions taken by the board on other subjects are null and void. When a special board meeting was called to consider the budget, "and all other matters to come before the board," and during the meeting a tenure teacher submitted her resignation and later attempted to rescind it, the court held that the board had acted within the law since it had included the "catchall" phrase "and other matters" in the notice. Evaul v. Board of Education, 65 N.J.Super. 68, 167 A.2d 39 (1961).

Characteristics of 'Sunshine' Laws in the 50 States

1. A policy statement says the sunshine law should be liberally construed.
2. No governmental bodies are explicitly exempted.
3. Where closed (executive) sessions are allowed, all final action must be taken in open meetings.
4. Discussions, in addition to actual decision making, must be held in open meetings.
5. Information gathering must be held in the open.
6. Committee meetings must be open.
7. Advisory-board meetings must be open.
8. Informal meetings (including, in some states, telephonic or other electronic communication) must be open.
9. Quasi-judicial meetings must be open.
10. Meetings of local entities must be open.
11. Meetings must be open even if there is no quorum.
12. When the law permits closed meetings, the parties involved may request that they be open.
13. Minutes of closed meetings must be kept, although in most cases the records may remain confidential.
14. Injunctive relief or other remedial action is provided if the law is violated.
15. Criminal penalties—usually including a fine, a jail term, or both—may be levied if the law is violated.
16. No exemptions to open-meeting provisions are allowed unless they are specified in the law.
17. Discussions that may affect a person's character or reputation must be open.
18. Discussions on general personnel matters, including employment or appointment, must be open.
19. Discussions surrounding property transactions must be open.
20. There is no provision for discussing investments, donations, or other financial matters in executive session.
21. Discussions of a public body with its legal counsel must be open.
22. Strategy sessions to prepare for labor negotiations must be open.
23. Labor negotiations must be open.

Provision number:	1	2	3	4	5	6	7	8	9	10	11	12	13	14	15	16	17	18	19	20	21	22	23	Total
Alabama	✓	✓	✓	✓	✓	✓		✓	✓	✓				✓	✓	✓		✓	✓	✓	✓	✓	✓	18
Alaska	✓		✓	✓		✓	✓					✓		✓		✓		✓	✓		✓	✓	✓	13
Arizona	✓		✓	✓		✓	✓		✓	✓		✓		✓	✓	✓			✓	✓				13
Arkansas	✓	✓	✓			✓		✓	✓	✓				✓	✓	✓		✓	✓			✓	✓	14
California	✓		✓			✓	✓		✓			✓	✓	✓	✓	✓		✓						11
Colorado	✓	✓	✓	✓				✓	✓		✓			✓	✓	✓			✓				✓	12
Connecticut	✓					✓		✓	✓		✓	✓	✓	✓	✓	✓			✓					10
Delaware				✓		✓	✓		✓	✓		✓	✓	✓		✓							✓	10
Florida		✓	✓	✓	✓	✓	✓	✓		✓		✓	✓	✓	✓	✓	✓	✓	✓	✓	✓	✓	✓	20
Georgia		✓	✓				✓	✓		✓				✓		✓						✓	✓	9
Hawaii	✓		✓	✓		✓				✓		✓		✓		✓			✓					9
Idaho	✓		✓	✓		✓				✓			✓	✓		✓								8
Illinois	✓		✓	✓	✓	✓	✓	✓	✓	✓	✓			✓	✓	✓								13
Indiana	✓	✓	✓	✓	✓	✓	✓	✓		✓	✓			✓		✓								11
Iowa	✓	✓		✓		✓		✓		✓		✓	✓	✓		✓						✓		11
Kansas	✓		✓	✓		✓	✓	✓		✓	✓	✓		✓		✓						✓		12
Kentucky		✓	✓	✓	✓	✓	✓		✓		✓	✓	✓	✓	✓									12
Louisiana	✓		✓	✓		✓	✓		✓	✓		✓		✓		✓		✓						11
Maine	✓	✓	✓			✓			✓	✓		✓		✓		✓	✓	✓		✓				11
Maryland	✓		✓	✓		✓	✓	✓		✓				✓	✓		✓							10
Massachusetts		✓	✓		✓								✓	✓	✓		✓		✓		✓			9
Michigan		✓	✓	✓	✓		✓	✓	✓					✓	✓	✓		✓		✓				12
Minnesota		✓	✓	✓		✓			✓	✓	✓		✓		✓		✓	✓	✓					12

Provision number:	1	2	3	4	5	6	7	8	9	10	11	12	13	14	15	16	17	18	19	20	21	22	23	Total
Mississippi	✓					✓			✓	✓		✓	✓			✓						✓	✓	9
Missouri		✓	✓	✓	✓	✓	✓	✓	✓					✓						✓			✓	11
Montana	✓	✓		✓	✓	✓	✓		✓	✓		✓		✓		✓		✓	✓	✓	✓		✓	16
Nebraska	✓		✓	✓	✓	✓	✓	✓	✓	✓		✓	✓	✓	✓		✓		✓				✓	16
Nevada	✓		✓	✓		✓	✓		✓	✓			✓	✓	✓	✓		✓	✓	✓	✓	✓	✓	17
New Hampshire	✓		✓		✓	✓			✓	✓		✓	✓	✓						✓	✓	✓	✓	13
New Jersey	✓		✓	✓	✓				✓	✓		✓	✓	✓		✓								10
New Mexico	✓	✓	✓	✓	✓	✓			✓	✓		✓		✓	✓	✓								12
New York	✓		✓	✓	✓	✓	✓		✓					✓		✓								9
North Carolina	✓		✓	✓	✓	✓	✓		✓			✓	✓										✓	10
North Dakota		✓	✓	✓	✓		✓	✓	✓				✓	✓				✓	✓			✓	✓	13
Ohio	✓	✓	✓	✓		✓			✓	✓	✓	✓		✓		✓								11
Oklahoma	✓		✓	✓	✓	✓	✓	✓	✓	✓				✓	✓	✓			✓	✓				14
Oregon	✓		✓	✓	✓	✓	✓	✓	✓	✓			✓	✓	✓		✓							13
Pennsylvania		✓				✓			✓	✓														4
Rhode Island	✓		✓		✓				✓	✓		✓	✓	✓		✓		✓						10
South Carolina		✓	✓	✓			✓	✓	✓		✓		✓	✓						✓			✓	11
South Dakota		✓	✓	✓				✓	✓						✓			✓	✓				✓	9
Tennessee	✓	✓	✓	✓	✓	✓		✓	✓	✓	✓	✓	✓	✓		✓	✓	✓	✓	✓	✓	✓	✓	21
Texas		✓	✓		✓				✓	✓			✓	✓	✓								✓	9
Utah	✓	✓	✓	✓		✓	✓		✓	✓			✓		✓			✓		✓			✓	13
Vermont	✓		✓	✓	✓	✓			✓				✓	✓				✓	✓					10
Virginia	✓	✓	✓	✓		✓		✓	✓	✓			✓			✓						✓	✓	12
Washington	✓		✓			✓			✓		✓		✓					✓	✓				✓	9
West Virginia	✓		✓	✓		✓	✓		✓	✓		✓		✓	✓	✓					✓	✓	✓	14
Wisconsin	✓		✓	✓		✓			✓	✓		✓		✓										8
Wyoming	✓		✓			✓			✓		✓		✓		✓					✓				8
TOTAL	37	16	37	42	19	46	22	21	34	46	8	29	18	47	21	40	2	13	13	25	10	12	25	

FULL REPORT AVAILABLE FROM: THE ASSOCIATION OF GOVERNING BOARDS OF UNIVERSITIES AND COLLEGES, 1 DUPONT CIRCLE, WASHINGTON, D.C.

Footnotes

1. State Tax Commission v. Board of Education of Jefferson County, 235 Ala. 388, 179 So. 197 (1938).

2. Board of Education v. Stoddard, 294 N.Y. 667, 60 N.E.2d 757 (1945).

3. Moore v. Board of Education, 212 N.C. 499, 193 S.E. 732 (1937).

4. Child Welfare Society of Flint v. Kennedy School District, 220 Mich. 290, 189 N.W. 1002 (1922).

5. Board of Education of Aberdeen-Huntington Local School District v. State Board of Education, 116 Ohio App. 515, 189 N.E.2d 81 (1962).

6. Campbell v. Aldrich, 159 Or. 208, 79 P.2d 257, appeal dismissed, 305 U.S. 559, 59 S.Ct. 87 (1938).

7. Leeper v. State, 103 Tenn. 500, 53 S.W. 962 (1899).

8. Railroad Co. v. Husen, 95 U.S. 465 (1877).

9. People v. Draper, 15 N.Y. 532 (1857).

10. See Newton Edwards, The Courts and the Public Schools (University of Chicago Press, 1955) p. 27; Also, Commonwealth v. Hartman, 17 Pa. 118 (1851); Moseley v. Welch, 209 S.C. 19, 39 S.E.2d 133 (1946); Board of Education of Chicago v. Upham, 357 Ill. 263, 191 N.E. 876 (1934); Board of Education v. State Board of Education, 116 Ohio App. 515, 189 N.E.2d 81 (1962); Associated Schools of Independent District No. 63 v. School District No. 83 of Renville County, 122 Minn. 254, 142 N.W. 325 (1913).

11. Edwards, p. 28.

12. Jaffe, Louis L., Essay on Delegation of Legislative Power 47 Col.L.Rev. 359, 361 (1947).

13. Attorney General v. Lowrey, 131 Mich. 639, 92 N.W. 289 (1902).

14. MacQueen v. City Comm. of City of Port Huron, 194 Mich. 328, 160 N.W. 627 (1916).

15. Board of Educ. Louisville v. Society of Alumni of Louisville Male High School, 239 S.W.2d 931 (Ky.1951).

16. School District No. 1, Multnomah County v. Bruck, 225 Or. 496, 358 P.2d 283 (1960).

17. Goodman v. School District, 32 F.2d 586 (C.C.A.Colo.1929).

18. Hallett v. Post Printing & Publishing Co., 68 Colo. 573, 192 P. 658 (1920).

19. McGilvra v. Seattle School District No. 1, 113 Wash. 619, 194 P. 817 (1921).

20. Jarrett v. Goodall, 113 W.Va. 478, 168 S.E. 763 (1933).

21. Brine v. City of Cambridge, 265 Mass. 452, 164 N.E. 619 (1929).

22. Kenneth Culp Davis, Administrative Law Treatise, vol. 1 (St. Paul, MN: West Publishing Company, 1958), p. 5.

23. Id., p. 102.

24. John Locke, Two Treatises of Civil Government, Book II, Ch. XI, Sec. 141.

25. Osius v. City of St. Clair Shores, 344 Mich. 693, 75 N.W.2d 25 (1956).

26. Davis, op. cit. p. 103.

27. Ward v. Scott, 11 N.J. 117, 93 A.2d 385 (1952).

28. Id.

29. State v. Kinnear, 70 Wash.2d 482, 423 P.2d 937 (1967).

30. School District No. 3 of Town of Adams v. Callahan, 237 Wis. 560, 297 N.W. 407 (1941).

31. Schinck v. Board of Education of Westwood Consolidated School Dist., 60 N.J.Super. 448, 159 A.2d 396 (1960).

32. Jokinen v. Allen, 15 Misc.2d 124, 182 N.Y.S.2d 166 (1958).

33. Bowles v. Willingham, 321 U.S. 503, 64 S.Ct. 641 (1944).

34. S.A. de Smith, Judicial Review of Administrative Action, (London: Stevens & Sons, 1973) p. 60.

35. Will, Robert F., State Education, Structure and Organization (United States Department of Health, Education and Welfare, United States Office of Education, 1964) pp. 8–10.

36. Id.

37. Laba v. Board of Education of Newark, 23 N.J. 364, 129 A.2d 273 (1966).

38. In re Masiello, 25 N.J. 590, 138 A.2d 393 (1966).

39. R. v. Roberts, 2 K.B. 695 (1924). See also, Kern Alexander, "Administrative Prerogative: Restraints of Natural Justice on Student Discipline," *Journal of Law and Education,* vol. 7, no. 3 (July 1978): 331–58.

40. Hortonville Joint School District No. 1 v. Hortonville Education Association, 426 U.S. 482, 96 S.Ct. 2308 (1976).

41. A. H. Andrews Co. v. Delight Special School District, 95 Ark. 26, 128 S.W. 361 (1910).

42. Edwards, op. cit. p. 147.

43. Knox County Board of Education v. Fultz, 241 Ky. 265, 43 S.W.2d 707 (1931); Lyerley v. Manila School District, 214 Ark. 245, 215 S.W.2d 733 (1948); Board of Education v. County Board of School Trustees, 25 Ill.App.2d 390, 166 N.E.2d 472 (1960); Detroit Edison Co. v. East China Township School District, 366 Mich. 638, 115 N.W.2d 298 (1962); School District No. 12, Phillips County v. Hughes, 170 Mont. 267, 552 P.2d 328 (1976).

44. Board of Education of City of New York v. Allen, 6 N.Y.2d 127, 188 N.Y.S.2d 515, 160 N.E.2d 60 (1959).

45. Board of Education v. County Board of School Trustees, 32 Ill.App.2d 1, 176 N.E.2d 633 (Ill. 1961).

46. de Smith, op. cit. p. 283.

47. Id., pp. 288, 289.

48. Id., p. 279.

49. Shelmadine v. City of Elkhart, 75 Ind.App. 493, 129 N.E. 878 (1921).

50. Main v. Claremont Unified School District, 161 Cal.App.2d 189, 326 P.2d 573 (1958).

51. Maddox v. State, 220 Ark. 762, 249 S.W.2d 972 (1952).

52. Constitution of Indiana, Art. 2, § 9.

53. People v. Becker, 112 Cal.App.2d 324, 246 P.2d 103 (1952).

54. Green v. Jones, 144 W.Va. 276, 108 S.E.2d 1 (1959).

55. Leech v. State, 78 Ind. 570 (1881).

56. People v. Reinberg, 263 Ill. 536, 105 N.E. 715 (1914).

57. Commonwealth v. Fahey, 156 Pa.Super. 254, 40 A.2d 167 (1944).

58. 328 U.S. 549, 66 S.Ct. 1198 (1946).

59. Id.

60. 369 U.S. 186, 82 S.Ct. 691 (1962).

61. Hadley v. Junior College District of Metropolitan Kansas City, Mo., 397 U.S. 50, 90 S.Ct. 791 (1970).

5

Church and State

During the first half of the decade of the 1980s religion emerged as an important political issue in the United States. Religious considerations began to have an important effect on governmental policy resulting in both church leaders and governmental officials taking sides on abortion, prayer in public schools, and tuition tax credits for parochial schools. Other issues, including President Reagan's reopening of diplomatic ties with the Vatican and his designation of 1983 as the "Year of the Bible," have created much public discussion and concern. Also, much criticism has been launched questioning the influence of Protestant Fundamentalist and Catholic opinion on governmental policy at the national level and, in particular, the effect of such groups on the formulation of the platforms of the two major political parties during the presidential campaign of 1984.

Polls indicated the average American's skepticism toward this new insertion of religion into the nation's political processes, and some existing evidence suggests that many politicians themselves are having second thoughts about such involvement.[1] The feeling that religion and politics cause uneasy and undesirable alliances is borne out by a long history of church and state conflicts in western civilization.

Centuries of religious strife in Europe left an indelible mark on the minds of the fathers of the American Constitution. Diversity of religious background among the American colonies was so great and religious sentiments so deep that representatives at the Convention in Philadelphia in 1787 were loath to address the issue lest the Convention founder on the shoals of religious dissension. Avoidance was implicitly agreed upon by all, and everyone more or less adopted the position of John Adams who assumed that if the issue was not mentioned both the state and religion would be best served. Adams expressed the hope that "Congress will never meddle with religion further than to say their own prayers, and to fast and to give thanks once a year."[2] Some believed that simple omission was not the appropriate solution to the religious dilemma and although it was not acted upon by the Convention, Pinckney of South Carolina sought to make the absence of congressional power in religion explicit by proposing that the new Constitution provide that "the Legislature of the United States shall pass no law on the subject of religion."[3] Even though no general religious provision was acted upon, there is little doubt that the failure resulted from the delegates' firm belief that such a provision was not necessary to preserve religious liberty. While no general religious separation provision was thought to be needed, the Convention did decide to specifically prohibit states from imposing religious tests for federal office. Madison explained that it might be implied that "without [an] exception, a power would have been given to impose an oath involving religious test as a qualification for office." [4] Obviously, it was in the interest of the central government to prevent states with different religious ties to require religious tests for federal office. With cognizance of this the Convention adopted Pinckney's motion that "no religious test shall ever be required as a qualification to any office or public trust under the United States"; this became the last clause of Article VI in the Constitution.

Thus, when the Constitution was ratified by the states only the "religious test" of office provision was included and no other reference was made regarding religious toleration. This omission was not taken lightly when the states were called upon to ratify the document. Six states ratified but proposed amendments guaranteeing religious liberty and two other states, North Carolina and Rhode Island, refused to ratify until a bill of rights including religious freedom was promulgated.[5] Although Madison defended the omission saying, "the government has no jurisdiction over it [religion]," [6] it was argued by others that there was no security for the rights of conscience. Jefferson ultimately convinced Madison that a religious provision in a bill of rights was necessary. Commenting on the proposed constitution in a letter to Madison from Paris where Jefferson was serving as ambassador, he said:

> I will now add what I do not like. First, the omission of a bill of rights providing clearly and without the aid of sophisms for freedom of religion, freedom of the press, protection against monopolies, the eternal and unremitting force of the habeas corpus laws, and trials by juries. . . . [A] bill of rights is what the people are entitled to against every government on earth, general or particular, and what no just government should refuse or rest on inference.[7]

The very uncertainty itself of whether such rights were implied in the Constitution was evidence enough that a bill of rights protecting religious freedom and assuring disestablishment was necessary. Madison, with Jefferson's urging and his own experience in persuading the states to ratify only after promising amendments as specific affirmation of individual rights and freedoms, stated that he now favored amendments to provide for "all essential rights, particularly the rights of Conscience in the fullest latitude, the freedom of the press, trial by jury, etc." [8] In accordance with this position, Madison introduced to the House of Representatives, in 1789, a compilation of proposals for amendments that he maintained would prevent encroachments by the sovereign power into individual rights and liberties. Madison's proposals before the House were to finally become the Bill of Rights, which were approved by the requisite number of states in 1791. Prominent among these rights was the separation of church and state provision, which guaranteed religious freedom and prohibited establishment of religion by government. The First Amendment states:

> Congress shall make no law respecting an establishment of religion, or prohibiting the free exercise thereof; or abridging the freedom of speech, or of

the press; or the right of the people peaceably to assembly and to petition the Government for a redress of grievances.

ANTECEDENTS OF THE FIRST AMENDMENT

Much of the history of western civilization has had its basis in religious controversy. Disputes between tribal chiefs and priests were fertile ground for discord that materially affected both church and state. In more primitive eras, the state did not attempt to delineate religious from secular activities, with some polytheistic societies merely cataloguing and assigning gods to a particular divine hierarchy, as in the Code of Hammurabi.[9] In most instances, the state and religion were entwined in the interests and affairs of the day, but it was very clear that of the two forces, the state was supreme. In ancient Greece, the head of state was also chief priest and served as the supreme guardian of religion. As the Athenian republic became well established, the unity of religion with state continued.[10]

Rome, too, was originally a state of many gods with the innovation that great heads of state, upon death, were placed among the ranks of the gods.[11] So long as there were many gods to worship and everyone recognized the state was supreme, little conflict developed; however, with the advent of Christianity, full-fledged discord became apparent. Christians ascribed to a dogmatic exclusiveness that was not tolerated by the Romans. Religious persecution of Christians began with Nero, with the justification that they were "enemies of mankind" and "arsonists," conveniently serving as scapegoats for the burning of Rome.[12] Persecution continued until Constantine when he and his two co-rulers of the empire issued the Edict of Milan in 312 or 313 A.D., a document of great importance in religious history, providing "that liberty of worship shall not be denied to any, but that the mind and will of every individual shall be free to manage divine affairs according to his own choice."[13] From this point on, the Christian religion became dominant as Constantine adopted it as a primary means of consolidating his empire.[14]

In the centuries that followed, the Christian Church gained power and authority, to the point that it became quite clear that the church was supreme over any head of state. Strength of the Church was demonstrated by Pope Gelasius I in 496 when he proclaimed to the emperor:

> There are two things, most august emperor, by which this world is chiefly ruled: the sacred authority of the priesthood and the royal power. Of these two the priests carry the greater weight, because they will have to render account in the divine judgment even for the kings of men.[15]

Although Christianity had, under the Romans, been the oppressed, when it gained dominion it became the oppressor and little tolerance was exhibited. St. Augustine strongly advanced the conviction that the civil power of the state should be used to suppress dissidents of the Church. Compulsion was the watchword and St. Augustine espoused the belief that "freedom to err" was the worst killer of the soul. In keeping with that philosophy, "the Medieval Church was intolerant, was the source and author of persecution, justified and defended the most violent measures which could be taken against those who differed from it."[16]

From this basis, the development of medieval Europe was almost solely that of continual struggle between church and state, with kings rebelling against the Church, and the sword of the state being alternatively put to use to stamp out heretics and nonconformists.

While most people are aware of the centuries of intolerance on the European continent, the most extreme example of which is probably the Spanish Inquisition, our more direct church-state antecedents derive from English origins. With the Reformation, problems of church and state were compounded as new religious doctrines were advanced and various ideologies began to emerge as separate and viable religions. Intolerance prevailed, whether Catholics or Protestants were in power. Henry VIII's conflict with Rome blossomed into bloody internal strife as Edward VI, Mary, and Elizabeth took the throne and in succession persecuted religious opponents. For her deeds, Mary was remembered in history as "Bloody Mary." During Elizabeth's long reign, the Church of England was firmly established as the state religion and the supremacy of the state over the church was complete. Ecclesiastical offices were regulated by her proclamations and opposing religious viewpoints were not tolerated. From this point in England, there existed a church that was Protestant in nature and entirely subject to state authority and control. Intra-Protestant struggles developed, and internal Protestant religious peace was not actually achieved in England until 1689 with the act of Toleration.

Even though the great religious wars of Europe were not of the same era with the lifespan of the constitutional forefathers of the United States, the strife of the Old World was still much in their minds. The Supreme Court of the United States has best expressed the situation:

> The centuries immediately before and contemporaneous with the colonization of America had been filled with turmoil, civil strife, and persecution, generated in large part by established sects determined to maintain their absolute political and religious supremacy. With the power of government to support them, at various times and places, Catholics had persecuted Protestants, Protestants had persecuted Catholics, Protestant sects had persecuted other Protestant sects, Catholics of one shade of belief had persecuted Catholics of another shade of belief, and all of these had from time to time persecuted Jews.[17]

When the matter of religion was to be considered in 1787, there were essentially three rationalizations for church-state relationships that had arisen out of the Reformation: the Erastian (named after the German philosopher Erastus), the theocratic, and the separatist. Dominate among these was the Erastian view, which assumed that state superiority over ecclesiastical affairs and religion was used to further the interests of the state. It was during the Elizabethan era in England that the Erastian philosophy was fully implemented. The second, the theocratic, was founded in the idea that the church is supreme and the state should be used to further ecclesiastical policy. Third, complete separation, was advanced as the proper course by minority dissident groups in Europe but did not find full expression until 1791 in America.[18] It was, however, John Locke on whom both Madison and Jefferson relied for their basic philosophical ideas concerning separation. In his *Letter Concerning Toleration,* Locke maintained that, "The care of souls cannot belong to the civil magistrate because his power consists only in outward force, but true and saving religion consists in the inward persuasion of the mind . . . ." [19]

Locke's ideas were developed and expanded under fire in the great dispute in Virginia over established religion that had been carefully protected by statutes promulgated by the Anglican Church until the Revolution. These laws provided for religious services according to the laws and orders of the Church of England: compulsory attendance at religious services, regulation of nonconformists, glebe lands for support of the clergy, and a system of governmentally sanctioned vestries empowered to levy tithes for upkeep of the Church and ministers' salaries.

Jefferson, more than any other individual, led in enunciating and implementing the separation principle. In 1776, while he was in Philadelphia writing the *Declaration of Independence,* he drafted a proposed constitution for Virginia that stated: "All persons shall have full and free liberty of religious opinion; nor shall any be compelled to frequent or maintain any religious institution." [20] Although this particular measure was not passed, it nevertheless set the tone for religious freedom for Virginia in the era to come. In spite of Jefferson's position, however, in 1779, a bill was introduced in the Virginia legislature that declared that "the Christian Religion shall in all times coming be deemed and held to be the established Religion of the Commonwealth." [21] It required every person to enroll his name with the county clerk and designate the society that he intended to support, whereupon the clerk would present the roll and the appropriate religious group to determine assessment rates; these were then collected by the sheriff and the proceeds were turned over to the church. Taxes obtained from persons failing to enroll in a religious society had their payments spread across all religious groups. [22]

In 1784, the bill was called up for a vote; entitled a "Bill Establishing a Provision for Teachers of the Christian Religion," it was sponsored by Patrick Henry. Although the bill was defeated, from the preceding and ensuing debate, two of the most important documents in religious freedom were written, Jefferson's *Bill for Establishing Religious Freedom* and Madison's *Memorial and Remonstrance against Religious Assessments.* When Jefferson's bill was finally enacted into law in 1786 it set forth among other provisions

> that no man shall be compelled to frequent or support any religious worship, place or ministry whatsoever, nor shall be enforced, restrained, molested or burdened in his body or goods, nor shall otherwise suffer on account of his religious opinions or beliefs, but that all men shall be free to profess, and by argument to maintain, their opinions in matters of religion, and that the same shall in no wise diminish, enlarge or affect their civil capacities.

Madison's *Memorial,* in opposition to Henry's bill for religious assessments, was of great historical significance. The philosophy stated therein has often been referred to by the United States Supreme Court in support of its opinions. The *Memorial* presents several arguments against the religious assessment bill but more importantly it conveys a philosophy of separation that, along with Jefferson's, provided the logic and rationale for the "wall of separation" provisions of the First Amendment in 1791.

AN ACT FOR ESTABLISHING
RELIGIOUS FREEDOM
by Thomas Jefferson (1786)

Well aware that Almighty God hath created the mind free; that all attempts to influence it by temporal punishments or burdens, or by civil incapacitations, tend only to beget habits of hypocrisy and meanness, and are a departure from the plan of the Holy Author of our religion, who being Lord both of body and mind, yet chose not to propagate it by coercions on either, as was in his Almighty power to do;

That the impious presumption of legislators and rulers, civil as well as ecclesiastical, who, being themselves but fallible and uninspired men, have assumed dominion over the faith of others, setting up their own opinions and modes of thinking as the only true and infallible, and as such endeavoring to impose them on others, hath established and maintained false religions over the greatest part of the world, and through all time;

That to compel a man to furnish contributions of money for the propagation of opinions which he disbelieves, is sinful and tyrannical; that even the forcing him to support this or that teacher of his own religious persuasion, is depriving him of the comfortable liberty of giving his contributions to the particular pastor whose morals he would make his pattern, and whose power he feels most persuasive to righteousness, and is withdrawing from the ministry those temporal rewards, which proceeding from an approbation of their personal conduct, are an additional incitement to earnest and unremitting labors for the instruction of mankind;

That our civil rights have no dependence on our religious opinions, any more than our opinions in physics or geometry; that, therefore, the proscribing any citizen as unworthy the public confidence by laying upon him an incapacity of being called to the offices of trust and emolument, unless he profess or renounce this or that religious opinion, is depriving him injuriously of those privileges and advantages to which in common with his fellow citizens he has a natural right;

That it tends also to corrupt the principles of that very religion it is meant to encourage, by bribing, with a monopoly of worldly honors and emoluments, those who will externally profess and conform to it; that though indeed these are criminal who do not withstand such temptation, yet neither are those innocent who lay the bait in their way;

That to suffer the civil magistrate to intrude his powers into the field of opinion and to restrain the profession or propagation of principles, on the supposition of their ill tendency, is a dangerous fallacy, which at once destroys all religious liberty, because he being of course judge of that tendency, will make his opinions the rule of judgment, and approve or condemn the sentiments of others only as they shall square with or differ from his own;

That it is time enough for the rightful purposes of civil government, for its officers to interfere when principles break out into overt acts against peace and good order;

And finally, that truth is great and will prevail if left to herself, that she is the proper and sufficient antagonist to error, and has nothing to fear from the conflict, unless by human interposition disarmed of her natural weapons, free argument and debate, errors ceasing to be dangerous when it is permitted freely to contradict them.

Be it therefore enacted by the General Assembly, That no man shall be compelled to frequent or support any religious worship, place or ministry whatsoever, nor shall be enforced, restrained, molested, or burthened in his body or goods, nor shall otherwise suffer on account of his religious opinions or belief; but that all men shall be free to profess, and by argument to maintain, their opinions in matters of religion, and that the same shall in nowise diminish, enlarge, or affect their civil capacities.

And though we well know this Assembly, elected by the people for the ordinary purposes of legislation only, have no power to restrain the acts of succeeding assemblies, constituted with the powers equal to our own, and that therefore to declare this act irrevocable, would be of no effect in law, yet we are free to declare, and do declare, that the rights hereby asserted are of the natural rights of mankind, and that if any act shall be hereafter passed to repeal the present or to narrow its operation, such act will be an infringement of natural right.

MEMORIAL AND
REMONSTRANCE AGAINST
RELIGIOUS ASSESSMENTS
by James Madison

To the Honorable General Assembly of the Commonwealth of Virginia. A Memorial and Remonstrance.

We, the subscribers, citizens of the said Commonwealth, having taken into serious consideration, a Bill printed by order of the last Session of General Assembly, entitled "A Bill establishing a provision for teachers of the Christian Religion," and conceiving that the same, if finally armed with the sanctions of a law, will be a dangerous abuse of power, are bound as faithful members of a free State, to remonstrate against it, and to declare the reasons by which we are determined. We remonstrate against the said Bill,

Because we hold it for a fundamental and undeniable truth, "that religion, or the duty which we owe to our Creator, and the manner of discharging it, can be directed only by reason and conviction, not by force or violence." [23] The Religion then of every man must be left to the conviction and conscience of every man; and it is the right of every man to exercise it as these may dictate. This right is in its nature an unalienable right. . . .

Because, it is proper to take alarm at the first experiment on our liberties. We hold this prudent jealousy to be the first duty of citizens, and one of [the] noblest characteristics of the late Revolution. The freemen of America did not wait till usurped power had strengthened itself by exercise, and entangled the question in precedents. They saw all the consequences in the principle, and they avoided the consequences by denying the principle. We reverse this lesson too much, soon to forget it. Who does not see that the same authority which can establish Christianity, in exclusion of all other Religions, may establish with the same ease any particular sect of Christians, in exclusion of all other Sects? That the same authority which can force a citizen to contribute three pence only of his property for the support of any one establishment, may force him to conform to any other establishment in all cases whatsoever?

Because, the bill violates that equality which ought to be the basis of every law, and which is more indispensable, in proportion as the validity or expediency of any law is more liable to be impeached. If "all men are by nature equally free and independent," [24] all men are to be considered as entering into Society on equal conditions; as relinquishing no more, and therefore retaining no less, one than another, of their natural rights. Above all are they to be considered as retaining an "equal title to the free exercise of Religion according to the dictates of conscience." [25] Whilst we assert for ourselves a freedom to embrace, to profess and to observe the Religion which we believe to be of divine origin, we cannot deny an equal freedom to those whose minds have not yet yielded to the evidence which has convinced us. If this freedom be abused, it is an offense against God, not against man: To God, therefore, not to men, must an account of it be rendered. As the Bill violates equality by subjecting some to peculiar burdens; so it violates the same principle, by granting to others peculiar exemptions. Are the Quakers and Menonists the only sects who think a compulsive support of their religions unnecessary and unwarrantable? Can their piety alone be entrusted with the care of public worship? Ought their Religions to be endowed above all others, with extraordinary privileges, by which proselytes may be enticed from all others? We think too favorably of the justice and good sense of these denominations, to believe that they either covet preeminencies over their fellow citizens, or that they will be seduced by them, from the common opposition to the measure. . . .

What influence in fact have ecclesiastical establishments had on Civil Society? In some instances they have been seen to erect a spiritual tyranny on the ruins of Civil authority; in many instances they have been seen upholding the thrones of political tyranny; in no instance have they been seen the guardians of the liberties of the people. Rulers who wished to subvert the public liberties, may have found an established clergy convenient auxiliaries. A just government, instituted to secure and perpetuate it, needs them not. Such a government will be best supported by protecting every citizen in the enjoyment of his Religion with the same equal hand which protects his person and his property; by neither invading the equal rights by any Sect, nor suffering any Sect to invade those of another.

Because the proposed establishment is a departure from that generous policy, which offering an asylum to the persecuted and oppressed of every Nation and Religion, promised a lustre to our country, an accession to the number of its citizens. What a melancholy mark is the Bill of sudden degeneracy? Instead of holding forth an asylum to the persecuted, it is itself a signal of persecution. It degrades from the equal rank of citizens all those whose opinions in Religion do not bend to those of the Legislative authority. Distant as it may be, in its present form, from the Inquisition it differs from it only in degree. The one is the first step, the other the last in the career of intolerance. . . .

Because, it will destroy that moderation and harmony which the forbearance of our laws to intermeddle with Religion, has produced amongst its several sects. Torrents of blood have been spilt in the old World, by vain attempts of the secular arm to extinguish Religious discord, by proscribing all difference in Religious opinions. Time has at length revealed the true remedy. Every relaxation of narrow and rigorous policy, wherever it has been tried, has been found to assuage the disease. The American Theatre has exhibited proofs, that equal and complete liberty, if it does not wholly eradicate it, sufficiently destroys its malignant influence on the health and prosperity of the State. If with the salutary effects of this system under our own eyes, we begin to contract the bonds of Religious freedom, we know no name that will too severely reproach our folly. At least let warning be taken at the first fruit of the threatened innovation. The very appearance of the Bill has transformed that "Christian forbearance,[26] love and charity," which of late mutually prevailed, into animosities and jealousies, which may not soon be appeased. What mischiefs may not be dreaded should this enemy to the public quiet be armed with the force of a law? . . .

Because, finally, "the equal right of every citizen to the free exercise of his Religion according to the dictates of conscience" is held by the same tenure with all our other rights. If we recur to its origin, it is equally the gift of nature; if we weigh its importance, it cannot be less dear to us; if we consult the Declaration of those rights which pertain to the good people of Virginia, as the "basis and foundation of Government," [27] it is enumerated with equal solemnity, or rather studied emphasis. Either then, we must say, that the will of the Legislature is the only measure of their authority; and that in the plentitude of this authority, they may sweep away all our fundamental rights; or, that they are bound to leave this particular right untouched and sacred: Either we must say, that they may control the freedom of the press, may abolish the trial by jury, may swallow up the Executive and Judiciary powers of the State; nay that they may despoil us of our very right of suffrage, and erect themselves into an independent and hereditary assembly: or we must say, that they have no authority to enact into law the Bill under consideration. We, the subscribers, say, that the General Assembly of this Commonwealth have no such authority: And that no effort may be omitted on our part against so dangerous an usurpation, we oppose to it, this remonstrance; earnestly praying, as we are in duty bound, that the Supreme Lawgiver of the Universe, by illuminating those to whom it is addressed, may on the one hand turn their councils from every act which would affront his holy prerogative, or violate the trust committed to them: and on the other, guide them into every measure which may be worthy of his [blessing, may re] dound to their own praise, and may establish more firmly the liberties, the prosperity, and the Happiness of the Commonwealth.

THE PUBLIC SCHOOL AND RELIGION

Public education is founded on three fundamental assumptions that relate either directly or indirectly to the issue of church and state. First, education is a benefit to the entire society and the legislature has the power to tax all for support. Essential to this concept is that general taxation is used for support and that taxation is not levied merely on those who use the public schools—the childless and those who sent their children to private schools must all pay their fair share. Thaddeus Stevens in 1835, in dramatically defeating a legislative proposal to repeal general taxation for education, enunciated the principle of universal responsibility for universal education in Pennsylvania. It was claimed that it was unjust to tax people to educate children of others; Stevens responded thusly:

> It is for their own benefit, inasmuch as it perpetrates the government and ensures the due administration of the laws under which they live, and by which their lives and property are protected. Why do they not urge the same objection against all other taxes? The industrious, thrifty, rich farmer pays a heavy county tax to support criminal courts, build jails, and pay sheriffs and jail keepers, and yet probably he never has had and probably never will have any direct personal use for them. . . . He cheerfully pays burdensome taxes which are necessarily levied to support and punish convicts, but loudly complains of that which goes to prevent his fellowbeing from becoming a criminal and to obviate the necessity of those humiliating institutions.[28]

To Stevens, education was a public obligation that must be nurtured to develop the entire civic intelligence to better govern through an elective republic. Those who do not directly benefit from public education certainly gain indirectly through association with an enlightened citizenry.

Second, education provided by the state must be secular and individual religious beliefs should not be inhibited. An important element of the secular state envisioned by Jefferson was a system of public schools that could convey all necessary temporal knowledge and yet not impede religious freedom. The power of the state could not be used to inculcate religious beliefs nor could the authority of the state to tax be used to assist religious training.

The First Amendment has two religious clauses that protect the individual's religious liberty, "the establishment" clause and the "free exercise" clause. These two combined prevent the use of public schools to proselytize and, correspondingly, forbid the expenditure of public tax funds to support religion. An extract from an opinion by the Supreme Court of Iowa forcefully illuminates this:

> If there is any one thing which is well settled in the policies and purposes of the American people as a whole, it is the fixed and unalterable determination that there shall be an absolute and unequivocal separation of church and state, and that our public school system, supported by the taxation of the property of all alike—Catholic, Protestant, Jew, Gentile, believer and infidel— shall not be used directly or indirectly for religious instruction, and above all that it shall not be made an instrumentality of proselyting influence, in favor of any religious organization, sect, creed, or belief.[29]

The third assumption, that the state can compel all parents to provide their children with a minimum secular education, is essential to the concept of general mass education. Every government has as a goal its own continuation and preservation, and in a republic an educated electorate is fundamental. As such, the state must be conceived as *parens patriae* in enforcing minimum educational and welfare requirements. The validity of the state's interest was established several years ago in *Prince* v. *Massachusetts*. [30]

The primary issue emanates from placing the force and power of the state, whether it be through taxation or other public policy decision, in a position to either enhance or inhibit religion. This was one of the most obstinate problems that Horace Mann was forced to overcome in his great crusade to found free common schools in Massachusetts. Mann vigorously maintained that the only purpose of religious education in the schools was to convey to each child the idea and respect of religious liberty. According to him the child should be able

> to judge for himself according to the dictates of his own reason and conscience, what his religious obligations are and whither they lead. But if a man is taxed to support a school where religious doctrines are inculcated which he believes to be false, and which he believes that God condemns, then he is excluded from the school by the divine law, at the same time that he is compelled to support it by the human law. This is a double wrong. [31]

Today the public schools of America are secular and not merely nonsectarian; this is necessary if separation of church and state is to be complete. The important position of education in the governmental process is the key to maintaining religious liberty. Pfeffer observes that to be secular does not mean to be "Godless"; it is merely a guarantee that the state will not dictate or encroach on religious beliefs of the individual. He says:

> A secular state requires a secular state school; but the secularization of the state does not mean the secularization of society. Only by accepting a totalitarian philosophy, either in religion or politics or both, can the state be equated with society. We are a religious people even though our government is secular. Our democratic state must be secular, for it does not purport or seek to pre-empt all of societal life. Similarly the public school need not and should not be the totality of the education process. [32]

In this regard, our Constitution precludes religious indoctrination in the public schools and prohibits use of public funds in supporting religion in parochial schools and it also proscribes the state from pre-empting all the child's time, thereby allowing substantial opportunity for religious training outside the school by parents and churches. [33]

TEXTBOOKS AND TRANSPORTATION FOR PAROCHIAL SCHOOL PUPILS

The United States Supreme Court, in the case of *Cochran* v. *Louisiana,* ruled that a state plan to provide textbooks to parochial school students does not violate the Fourteenth Amendment. [34] The Court in this decision was not asked to determine whether the First Amendment was violated. The decision in the *Cochran* case was rendered in 1930, ten years before the Court decided in the *Cantwell* case that the religious liberties of the First Amendment not only provided protection against actions by the Congress but, when applied through the Fourteenth Amendment, protected the individual from arbitrary acts of the states.[35] However, the Court in this case did identify and adopt the "child benefit" concept that has subsequently been used in many instances to defend the appropriation of public funds for private and parochial school use.

The Supreme Court in the Everson case, a 1947 decision, held that the use of public funds for transportation of parochial school children does not violate the First Amendment. However, many state constitutions impose stricter regulations concerning separation of church and state than does the United States Constitution and, as a result, the highest courts in several states have ruled that their state constitutions would be violated if public funds were used to provide transportation for parochial school pupils.

In the Everson case, the legislature of New Jersey enacted a law that allowed boards of education to provide transportation for parochial school children at public expense. A school board, acting under this statute, authorized reimbursement of parents for bus fares spent in sending their children to parochial schools. The plaintiff attacked the statute on the grounds that it violated the First and Fourteenth Amendments of the federal Constitution. The Court, in a 5–4 decision, ruled that that statute did not violate the Constitution. The Court adopted the "child benefit" doctrine and reasoned that the funds were expended for the benefit of the individual child and not for religious purposes. The transportation law was a general program that provided assistance in getting children safely to and from school regardless of their religion.

In 1968, the Supreme Court applied the reasoning of the *Cochran* and *Everson* cases in upholding as constitutional a New York statute that provided textbooks distributed free of charge to students attending parochial schools. The court stated that there was no indication that the books were being used to teach religion and that since private schools serve a public purpose and perform a secular as well as a sectarian function, such an expenditure of public funds is not unconstitutional.[36]

*Establishment Clause Does Not
Prohibit Spending Tax Funds to Pay
Bus Fares for Parochial School
Students*

EVERSON v. BOARD OF EDUCATION

Supreme Court of the United States, 1947.
330 U.S. 1, 67 S.Ct. 504.

Mr. Justice BLACK delivered the opinion of the Court.

A New Jersey statute authorizes its local school districts to make rules and contracts for the transportation of children to and from schools. The appellee, a township board of education, acting pursuant to this statute authorized reimbursement to parents of money expended by them for the bus transportation of their children on regular buses operated by the public transportation system. Part of this money was for the payment of transportation of some children in the community to Catholic parochial schools. These church schools give their students, in addition to secular education, regular religious instruction conforming to the religious tenets and modes of worship of the Catholic Faith. The superintendent of these schools is a Catholic priest.

The appellant, in his capacity as a district taxpayer, filed suit in a State court challenging the right of the Board to reimburse parents of parochial school students. He contended that the statute and the resolution passed pursuant to it violated both the State and the Federal Constitutions. That court held that the legislature was without power to authorize such payment under the State constitution. 132 N.J.L. 98, 39 A.2d 75. The New Jersey Court of Errors and Appeals reversed, holding that neither the statute nor the resolution passed pursuant to it was in conflict with the State constitution or the provisions of the Federal Constitution in issue. 133 N.J.L. 350, 44 A.2d 333. The case is here on appeal under 28 U.S.C. § 344(a), 28 U.S.C.A. § 344(a). . . .

The only contention here is that the State statute and the resolution, in so far as they authorized reimbursement to parents of children attending parochial schools, violate the Federal Constitution in these two respects, which to some extent, overlap. First. They authorize the State to take by taxation the private property of some and bestow it upon others, to be used for their own private purposes. This, it is alleged, violates the due process clause of the Fourteenth Amendment. Second. The statute and the resolution forced inhabitants to pay taxes to help support and maintain schools which are dedicated to, and which regularly teach, the Catholic Faith. This is alleged to be a use of State power to support church schools contrary to the prohibition of the First Amendment which the Fourteenth Amendment made applicable to the states.

First. The due process argument that the State law taxes some people to help others carry out their private purposes is framed in two phases. The first phase is that a state cannot tax A to reimburse B for the cost of transporting his children to church schools. This is said to violate the due process clause because the children are sent to these church schools to satisfy the personal desires of their parents, rather than the public's interest in the general education of all children. This argument, if valid, would apply equally to prohibit state payment for the transportation of children to any non-public school, whether operated by a church, or any other non-government individual or group. But, the New Jersey legislature has decided that a public purpose will be served by using tax-raised funds to pay the bus fares of all school children, including those who attend parochial schools. The New Jersey Court of Errors and Appeals has reached the same conclusion. The fact that a state law, passed to satisfy a public need, coincides with the personal desires of the individuals most directly affected is certainly an inadequate reason for us to say that a legislature has erroneously appraised the public need. . . .

It is much too late to argue that legislation intended to facilitate the opportunity of children to get a secular education serves no public purpose. Cochran v. Louisiana State Board of Education, 281 U.S. 370, 50 S.Ct. 335, 74 L.Ed. 913 . . . . The same thing is no less true of legislation to reimburse needy parents, or all parents, for payment of the fares of their children so that they can ride in public buses to and from schools rather than run the risk of traffic and other hazards incident to walking or "hitchhiking." See Barbier v. Connolly, 113 U.S. at page 31, 5 S.Ct. at page 359. . . . Nor does it follow that a law has a private rather than a public purpose because it provides that tax-raised funds will be paid to reimburse individuals on account of money spent by them in a way which furthers a public program. See Carmichael v. Southern Coal & Coke Co., 301 U.S. 495, 518, 57 S.Ct. 868, 876 . . . . Subsidies and loans to individuals such as farmers and home owners, and to privately owned transportation systems, as well as many other kinds of businesses, have been commonplace practices in our state and national history.

Insofar as the second phase of the due process argument may differ from the first, it is by suggesting that taxation for transportation of children to church schools constitutes support of a religion by the State. But if the law is invalid for this reason, it is because it violates the First Amendment's prohibition against the establishment of religion by law. This is the exact question raised by appellant's second contention, to consideration of which we now turn.

Second. The New Jersey statute is challenged as a "law respecting an establishment of religion." The First Amendment, as made applicable to the states by the Fourteenth, Murdock v. Commonwealth of Pennsylvania, 319 U.S. 105, 63 S.Ct. 870, 872 . . . commands that a state "shall make no law respecting an establishment of religion, or prohibiting the free exercise thereof." These words of the First Amendment reflected in the minds of early Americans a vivid mental picture of conditions and practices which they fervently wished to stamp out in order to preserve liberty for themselves and for their posterity. Doubtless their goal has not been entirely reached; but so far has the Nation moved toward it that the expression "law respecting an establishment of religion," probably does not so vividly remind present-day Americans of the evils, fears, and political problems that caused that expression to be written into our Bill of Rights. . . .

The "establishment of religion" clause of the First Amendment means at least this: Neither a state nor the Federal Government can set up a church. Neither can pass laws which aid one religion, aid all religions, or prefer one religion over another. Neither can force nor influence a person to go to or to remain away from church against his will or force him to profess a belief or disbelief in any religion. No person can be punished for entertaining or professing religious beliefs or disbeliefs, for church attendance or non-attendance. No tax in any amount, large or small, can be levied to support any religious activities or institutions, whatever they may be called, or whatever form they may adopt to teach or practice religion. Neither a state nor the Federal Government can, openly or secretly, participate in the affairs of any religious organizations or groups and vice versa. In the words of Jefferson, the clause against establishment of religion by law was intended to erect "a wall of separation between Church and State." Reynolds v. United States, 98 U.S. at page 164, 25 L.Ed. 244.

We must consider the New Jersey statute in accordance with the foregoing limitations imposed by the First Amendment. But we must not strike that state statute down if it is within the state's constitutional power even though it approaches the verge of that power. . . . New Jersey cannot consistently with the "establishment of religion" clause of the First Amendment contribute tax-raised funds to the support of an institution which teaches the tenets and faith of any church. On the other hand, other language of the amendment commands that New Jersey cannot hamper its citizens in the free exercise of their own religion. Consequently, it cannot exclude individual Catholics, Lutherans, Mohammedans, Baptists, Jews, Methodists, Non-believers, Presbyterians, or the members of any other faith, *because of their faith, or lack of it,* from receiving the benefits of public welfare legislation. While we do not mean to intimate that a state could not provide transportation only to children attending public schools, we must be careful, in protecting the citizens of New Jersey against state-established churches, to be sure that we do not inadvertently prohibit New Jersey from extending its general State law benefits to all its citizens without regard to their religious belief.

Measured by these standards, we cannot say that the First Amendment prohibits New Jersey from spending tax-raised funds to pay the bus fares of parochial school pupils as a part of a general program under which it pays the fares of pupils attending public and other schools. It is undoubtedly true that children are helped to get to church schools. There is even a possibility that some of the children might not be sent to the church schools if the parents were compelled to pay their children's bus fares out of their own pockets when transportation to a public school would have been paid for by the State. The same possibility exists where the state requires a local transit company to provide reduced fares to school children including those attending parochial schools, or where a municipally owned transportation system undertakes to carry all school children free of charge. Moreover, state-paid policemen, detailed to protect children going to and from church schools from the very real hazards of traffic, would serve much the same purpose and accomplish much the same result as state provisions intended to guarantee free transportation of a kind which the state deems to be best for the school children's welfare. And parents might refuse to risk their children to the serious danger of traffic accidents going to and from parochial schools, the approaches to which were not protected by policemen. Similarly, parents might be reluctant to permit their children to attend schools which the state had cut off from such general government services as ordinary police and fire protection, connections for sewage disposal, public highways and sidewalks. Of course, cutting off church schools from these services, so separate and so indisputably marked off from the religious function, would make it far more difficult for the schools to operate. But such is obviously not the purpose of the First Amendment. That Amendment requires the state to be a neutral in its relations with groups of religious believers and non-believers; it does not require the state to be their adversary. State power is no more to be used so as to handicap religions, than it is to favor them. . . .

The First Amendment has erected a wall between church and state. That wall must be kept high and impregnable. We could not approve the slightest breach. New Jersey has not breached it here.

Affirmed.

NOTES

1. In 1982, twenty-eight states provided public funds to transport private school children to and from school (Alaska, Arizona, California, Delaware, Illinois, Indiana, Iowa, Kansas, Kentucky, Louisiana, Maryland, Massachusetts, Michigan, Minnesota, Nebraska, New Hampshire, New Jersey, New Mexico, New York, Ohio, Oregon, Pennsylvania, Rhode Island, South Dakota, Washington, West Virginia, Wisconsin, and Wyoming). The funding of nonpublic school children's transportation takes many forms. Maryland statutory authority requires funding from local sources only, with none authorized from state sources. In Washington, the local district private school children may ride the buses, but parents must reimburse the school on an actual cost per seat. Although in Wyoming there is no actual statutory authority, the State Board of Education allows local boards to provide services. (See: *Public Aid for the Transportation of Private Elementary and Secondary School Pupils in the United States,* Susan E. Mittereder, unpublished doctoral dissertation, Virginia Tech University, 1984.)

2. A Pennsylvania statute that allowed the transportation of private school children beyond school district boundary lines was ruled constitutional. School District of Pittsburgh v. Commonwealth Department of Education, 33 Pa.Cmwlth. 535, 382 A.2d 772 (1978), appeal dismissed 443 U.S. 901, 99 S.Ct. 3091 (1979). See also Springfield School District v. Department of Education, 483 Pa. 539, 397 A.2d 1154 (1979), appeal dismissed 443 U.S. 901, 99 S.Ct. 3091 (1979).

3. What is the reasoning of the court in the majority opinion in ruling that the New Jersey statute does not violate the "establishment of religion" clause?

4. Relate the historical background and rationale of Jefferson's *Bill for Establishing Religious Freedom* and *Madison's Memorial and Remonstrance Against Religious Assessments* to *Everson.*

5. Is the state's contribution under the New Jersey law in defraying the cost of conveying pupils to a place where they will receive primarily religious instruction in fact a substitution of resources for parents and an encouragement to aid religion?

6. Do you believe that the "child benefit" or "public purpose" theory contradicts the meaning of the First Amendment?

7. Statutes that authorize public transportation for parochial school children to travel to and from the private schools do not constitute mandatory authority for the public schools to also transport such children for

educational field trips. Cook v. Griffin, 47 A.D.2d 23, 364 N.Y.S.2d 632 (1975). See also: Wolman v. Walter, 433 U.S. 229, 97 S.Ct. 2593 (1977).

8. A statute that provides bus transportation to public school students only does not deny nonpublic students equal protection or due process. Luetkemeyer v. Kaufmann, 364 F.Supp. 376 (W.D. Mo.1973), *affirmed* 419 U.S. 888, 95 S.Ct. 167 (1974).

Loan of Textbooks to Parochial
School Students Does Not Violate
Establishment Clause

BOARD OF EDUCATION OF CENTRAL SCHOOL DISTRICT NO. 1 v. ALLEN

Supreme Court of the United States, 1968.
392 U.S. 236, 88 S.Ct. 1923.

Mr. Justice WHITE delivered the opinion of the Court.

A law of the State of New York requires local public school authorities to lend textbooks free of charge to all students in grades seven through twelve; students attending private schools are included. This case presents the question whether this statute is a "law respecting an establishment of religion, or prohibiting the free exercise thereof," and so in conflict with the First and Fourteenth Amendments to the Constitution, because it authorizes the loan of textbooks to students attending parochial schools. We hold that the law is not in violation of the Constitution. . . .

Beginning with the 1966–1967 school year, local school boards were required to purchase textbooks and lend them without charge "to all children residing in such district who are enrolled in grades seven to twelve of a public or private school which complies with the compulsory education law." [37] The books now loaned are "text-books which are designated for use in any public, elementary or secondary schools of the state or are approved by any boards of education," and which—according to a 1966 amendment—"a pupil is required to use as a text for a semester or more in a particular class in the school he legally attends."

Appellant Board of Education of Central School District No. 1 in Rensselaer and Columbia Counties brought suit in the New York courts against appellee James Allen. The complaint alleged that § 701 violated both the State and Federal Constitutions; that if appellants, in reliance on their interpretation of the Constitution, failed to lend books to parochial school students within their counties appellee Allen would remove appellants from office; and that to prevent this, appellants were complying with the law and submitting to their constituents a school budget including funds for books to be lent to parochial school pupils. Appellants therefore sought a declaration that § 701 was invalid, an order barring appellee Allen from removing appellants from office for failing to comply with it, and another order restraining him from apportioning state funds to school districts for the purchase of textbooks to be lent to parochial students. . . .

Everson and later cases have shown that the line between state neutrality to religion and state support of religion is not easy to locate. "The constitutional standard is the separation of Church and State. The problem, like many problems in constitutional law, is one of degree." Zorach v. Clauson, 343 U.S. 306, 314, 72 S.Ct. 679, 684, 96 L.Ed. 954 (1952). . . . Based on *Everson, Zorach, McGowan,* and other cases, Abington Tp. School District v. Schempp, 374 U.S. 203, 83 S.Ct. 1560, 10 L.Ed.2d 844 (1963), fashioned a test subscribed to by eight Justices for distinguishing between forbidden involvements of the State with religion and those contacts which the Establishment Clause permits:

> The test may be stated as follows: what are the purpose and the primary effect of the enactment? If either is the advancement or inhibition of religion then the enactment exceeds the scope of legislative power as circumscribed by the Constitution. That is to say that to withstand the strictures of the Establishment Clause there must be a secular legislative purpose and a primary effect that neither advances nor inhibits religion. Everson v. Board of Education . . . . 374 U.S. at 222, 83 S.Ct., at 1571.

This test is not easy to apply, but the citation of *Everson* by the *Schempp* Court to support its general standard made clear how the *Schempp* rule would be applied to the facts of *Everson*. The statute upheld in *Everson* would be considered a law having "a secular legislative purpose and a primary effect that neither advances nor inhibits religion." We reach the same result with respect to the New York law requiring school books to be loaned free of charge to all students in specified grades. The express purpose of § 701 was stated by the New York Legislature to be furtherance of the educational opportunities available to the young. Appellants have shown us nothing about the necessary effects of the statute that is contrary to its stated purpose. The law merely makes available to all children the benefits of a general program to lend school books free of charge. Books are furnished at the request of the pupil and ownership remains, at least technically, in the State. Thus no funds or books are furnished to parochial schools, and the financial benefit is to parents and children, not to schools. Perhaps free books make it more likely that some children choose to attend a sectarian school, but that was true of the state-paid bus fares in *Everson* and does not alone demonstrate an unconstitutional degree of support for a religious institution. . . .

The major reason offered by appellants for distinguishing free textbooks from free bus fares is that books, but not buses, are critical to the teaching process, and in a sectarian school that process is employed to teach religion. However this Court has long recognized that religious schools pursue two goals, religious instruction and secular education. In the leading case of Pierce v. Society of Sisters, 268 U.S. 510, 45 S.Ct. 571, 69 L.Ed. 1070 (1925), the Court held that although it would not question Oregon's power to compel school attendance or require that the attendance be at an institution meeting State-imposed requirements as to quality and nature of curriculum, Oregon had not shown that its interest in secular education required that all children attend publicly operated schools. A premise of this holding was the view that the State's interest in education would be served sufficiently by reliance on the secular teaching that accompanied religious training in the schools maintained by the Society of Sisters. Since *Pierce,* a substantial body of case law has confirmed the power of the States to insist that attendance at private schools, if it is to satisfy state compulsory-attendance laws, be at institutions which provide minimum hours of instruction, employ teachers of specified training, and cover prescribed subjects of instruction. Indeed, the State's interest in assuring that these standards are being met has been considered a sufficient reason for refusing to accept instruction at home as compliance with compulsory education statutes. These cases were a sensible corollary of *Pierce* v. *Society of Sisters* : if the State must satisfy its interest in secular education through the instrument of private schools, it has a proper interest in the manner in which those schools perform their secular educational function. Another corollary was Cochran v. Louisiana State Board of Education, 281 U.S. 370, 50 S.Ct. 335, 74 L.Ed. 913 (1930), where appellants said that a statute requiring school books to be furnished without charge to all students, whether they attended public or private schools, did not serve a "public purpose," and so offended the Fourteenth Amendment. Speaking through Chief Justice Hughes, the Court summarized as follows its conclusion that Louisiana's interest in the secular education being provided by private schools made provision of textbooks to students in those schools a properly public concern: "[The State's] interest is education, broadly; its method, comprehensive. Individual interests are aided only as the common interest is safeguarded." 281 U.S., at 375, 50 S.Ct., at 336.

Underlying these cases, and underlying also the legislative judgments that have preceded the court decisions, has been a recognition that private education has played and is playing a significant and valuable role in raising national levels of knowledge, competence, and experience. Americans care about the quality of the secular education available to their children. They have considered high quality education to be an indispensable ingredient for achieving the kind of nation, and the kind of citizenry, that they have desired to create. Considering this attitude, the continued willingness to rely on private school systems, including parochial systems, strongly suggests that a wide segment of informed opinion, legislative and otherwise, has found that those schools do an acceptable job of providing secular education to their students. This judgment is further evidence that parochial schools are performing, in addition to their sectarian function, the task of secular education.

Against this background of judgment and experience, unchallenged in the meager record before us in this case, we cannot agree with appellants either that all teaching in a sectarian school is religious or that the processes of secular and religious training are so intertwined that secular textbooks furnished to students by the public are in fact instrumental in the teaching of religion. This case comes to us after summary judgment entered on the pleadings. Nothing in this record supports the proposition that all textbooks, whether they deal with mathematics, physics, foreign languages, history, or literature, are used by the parochial schools to teach religion. No evidence has been offered about particular schools, particular courses, particular teachers, or particular books. We are unable to hold, based solely on judicial notice, that this statute results in unconstitutional involvement of the State with religious instruction or that § 701, for this or the other reasons urged, is a law respecting the establishment of religion within the meaning of the First Amendment. . . .

Mr. Justice BLACK, dissenting.

. . . I believe the New York law held valid is a flat, flagrant, open violation of the First and Fourteenth Amendments which together forbid Congress or state legislatures to enact any law "respecting an establishment of religion." For that reason I would reverse the New York Court of Appeals' judgment. . . .

The *Everson* and *McCollum* cases plainly interpret the First and Fourteenth Amendments as protecting the taxpayers of a State from being compelled to pay taxes to their government to support the agencies of private religious organizations the taxpayers oppose. To authorize a State to tax its residents for such church purposes is to put the State squarely in the religious activities of certain religious groups that happen to be strong enough politically to write their own religious preferences and prejudices into the laws. This links state and churches together in controlling the lives and destinies of our citizenship—a citizenship composed of people of myriad religious faiths, some of them bitterly hostile to and completely intolerant of the others. It was to escape laws precisely like this that a large part of the Nation's early immigrants fled to this country. It was also to escape such laws and such consequences that the First Amendment was written in language strong and clear barring passage of any law "respecting an establishment of religion."

It is true, of course, that the New York law does not as yet formally adopt or establish a state religion. But it takes a great stride in that direction and coming events cast their shadows before them. The same powerful sectarian religious propagandists who have succeeded in securing passage of the present law to help religious schools carry on their sectarian religious purposes can and doubtless will continue their propaganda, looking toward complete domination and supremacy of their particular brand of religion.[38] And it nearly always is by insidious approaches that the citadels of liberty are most successfully attacked.[39]

I know of no prior opinion of this Court upon which the majority here can rightfully rely to support its holding this New York law constitutional. In saying this, I am not unmindful of the fact that the New York Court of Appeals purported to follow *Everson* v. *Board of Education,* in which this Court, in an opinion written by me, upheld a New Jersey law authorizing reimbursement to parents for the transportation of children attending sectarian schools. That law did not attempt to deny the benefit of its general terms to children of any faith going to any legally authorized school. Thus, it was treated in the same way as a general law paying the streetcar fare *of all school children,* or a law providing midday lunches for all children or all school children, or a law to provide police protection for children going to and from school, or general laws to provide police and fire protection for buildings, including, of course, churches and church school buildings as well as others.

As my Brother DOUGLAS so forcefully shows, in an argument with which I fully agree, upholding a State's power to pay bus or streetcar fares for school children cannot provide support for the validity of a state law using tax-raised funds to buy school books for a religious school. The First Amendment's bar to establishment of religion must preclude a State from using funds levied from all of its citizens to purchase books for use by sectarian schools, which, although "secular," realistically will in some way inevitably tend to propagate the religious views of the favored sect. Books are the most essential tool of education since they contain the resources of knowledge which the educational process is designed to exploit. In this sense it is not difficult to distinguish books, which are the heart of any school, from bus fares, which provide a convenient and helpful general public transportation service. With respect to the former, state financial support actively and directly assists the teaching and propagation of sectarian religious viewpoints in clear conflict with the First Amendment's establishment bar; with respect to the latter, the State merely provides a general and nondiscriminatory transportation service in no way related to substantive religious views and beliefs.

This New York law, it may be said by some, makes but a small inroad and does not amount to complete state establishment of religion. But that is no excuse for upholding it. It requires no prophet to foresee that on the argument used to support this law others could be upheld providing for state or federal government funds to buy property on which to erect religious school buildings or to erect the buildings themselves, to pay the salaries of the religious school teachers, and finally to have the sectarian religious groups cease to rely on voluntary contributions of members of their sects while waiting for the Government to pick up all the bills for the religious schools. Arguments made in favor of this New York law point squarely in this direction, namely, that the fact that government has not heretofore aided religious schools with tax-raised funds amounts to a discrimination against those schools and against religion. And that there are already efforts to have government supply the money to erect buildings for sectarian religious schools is shown by a recent Act of Congress which apparently allows for precisely that. See Higher Education Facilities Act of 1963, 77 Stat. 363, 20 U.S.C.A. § 701 et seq.

I still subscribe to the belief that tax-raised funds cannot constitutionally be used to support religious schools, buy their school books, erect their buildings, pay their teachers, or pay any other of their maintenance expenses, even to the extent of one penny. The First Amendment's prohibition against governmental establishment of religion was written on the assumption that state aid to religion and religious schools generates discord, disharmony, hatred, and strife among our people, and that any government that supplies such aids is to that extent a tyranny. And I still believe that the only way to protect minority religious groups from majority groups in this country is to keep the wall of separation between church and state high and impregnable as the First and Fourteenth Amendments provide. The Court's affirmance here bodes nothing but evil to religious peace in this country. . . .

NOTES

1. Observe that Justice Black wrote the majority opinion in *Everson* and dissented in *Allen*. This is particularly interesting since the majority opinion by Justice White relied heavily on the interpretation and meaning of the majority in *Everson*.

2. The *Cochran* case in Louisiana was preceded by Borden v. Louisiana State Board of Education, 168 La. 1005, 123 So. 655 (1929), which held that the Acts of 1928, Nos. 100 and 143, the same acts contested in *Cochran*, were not violative of religious constitutional prohibitions, nor did the acts violate constitutional provisions prohibiting public funds for private or benevolent purposes and were not adverse to due process requirements.

3. A South Dakota statute providing for free textbooks to "pupils" without designation as to whether the pupils were to be in public or private schools, or both, was held to exclude pupils in private, sectarian, and parochial schools. Haas v. Independent School District No. 1 of Yankton, 69 S.D. 303, 9 N.W.2d 707 (1943).

   In an Oregon case, the court held that distribution of free textbooks to parochial schools violated state constitutional prohibitions against public aid to religious institutions. Dickman v. School District No. 62C, Oregon City, 232 Or. 238, 366 P.2d 533 (1961), cert. denied 371 U.S. 823, 83 S.Ct. 41 (1962).

4. Appellants in *Allen* argue that transportation of parochial pupils may be constitutional while providing textbooks is not. How does the Court react to this argument? Compare the Court's opinion to the dissenting opinion of Justice Jackson in the *Everson* case.

5. What is the implication of Justice White's statement that "parochial schools are performing, in addition to their sectarian function, the task of secular education?"

6. How does Justice Black, in dissent in *Allen*, distinguish textbooks from transportation in *Everson* in which he wrote the majority opinion?

7. In an advisory opinion to the state senate, the Supreme Court of Michigan held that provision of textbooks and supplies to religious schools violated the Michigan Constitution. The court reasoned that both textbooks and supplies were primary elements necessary for schools to exist and it therefore constituted aid to religion. In re Advisory Opinion re Constitutionality of 1974, P.A. 242, 394 Mich. 41, 228 N.W.2d 772 (1975).

STATE FINANCIAL AID TO PAROCHIAL SCHOOLS

The decision by the Supreme Court in the *Allen* case[40] created many questions on the part of both public and parochial school leaders throughout the country. The language of Justice White, speaking for the majority, was unclear, failing to delineate First Amendment restrictions in providing state aid to parochial schools. White applied the public purpose theory and apparently reasoned that the state could give assistance to religious schools so long as the aid was provided for only secular services in the operation of parochial schools. He said

> a wide segment of informed opinion, legislative and otherwise, has found that those schools [parochial] do an acceptable job of providing secular education to their students. *This judgment is further evidence that parochial schools are performing, in addition to their sectarian function, the task of secular education.*

This statement was taken by many parochial school educators to mean that a state could permissibly provide funds to parochial schools for such things as teachers' salaries, operation, building, et cetera, so long as the funds were used by the parochial school only for "public secular purposes." State legislatures were suddenly flooded with hundreds of bills to provide state support to parochial schools; some were passed and others, for various reasons, failed.

It was into this fertile area of conjecture that the Supreme Court of the United States walked in 1971 when it was asked to rule on the constitutionality of two such state acts from Pennsylvania and Rhode Island. Both states, relying on the vagueness of *Allen*, were attempting to aid parochial schools. The Supreme Court struck down the statutes of both states. The court found the "secular purpose" standard alone to be inadequate and added its own standard of "excessive entanglement." This new standard seeks to prevent the state from infringing on the separate rights of religion by becoming too intermingled with the process of religion. The Supreme Court summarized three tests for determining constitutionality of a state statute and applied and discussed each of these in *Lemon v. Kurtzman.* The tests are: (1) the statute must have a secular legislative purpose, (2) its principal or primary effect must be one that neither advances nor inhibits religion, and (3) it must not foster excessive government entanglement with religion. Subsequent Supreme Court cases have explained the law as prescribed by these tests.[41]

In a series of cases the Supreme Court held that reimbursement to parents for tuition expense,[42] auxiliary services including counseling, testing, and psychological services, and therapy for exceptional children,[43] loans spending state money for instructional materials and equipment in parochial schools, and permitting parochial school students to take field trips to museums and other points of interest at public expense[44] were all unconstitutional.

On the other hand, state-financed activities, such as the loaning of textbooks, administering standardized tests to parochial school students, treatment for speech and hearing problems, and taking care of students' dental needs, have been held constitutional.[45]

Significantly, in the *Nyquist* case,[46] the Supreme Court held that New York's income tax deduction for low-income parents of nonpublic school children violated the Establishment Clause. The Court said that "Special tax benefits, however, cannot be squared with the principle of neutrality established by the decisions of this Court. To the contrary, insofar as such benefits render assistance to parents who send their children to sectarian schools, their purpose and inevitable effect are to aid and advance those religious institutions."

Since *Nyquist,* the view of the Court toward tax benefits has apparently shifted considerably. In *Mueller* v. *Allen,*[47] a case that could prove to be a major watershed in church-state relations in this country, the Supreme Court allowed tax benefits that would surely have the "inevitable effect" of aiding religious institutions. Here, the Court upheld tax deductions for tuition, textbooks, and transportation costs incurred by parents of children in either nonpublic or public schools. This ruling may allow states and the federal government to enact laws that would give tax benefits to parents of children in religious schools.

This decision could result in very important structural changes in the educational system of this country, tending conceivably to shift tax resources from public schools to private and parochial schools. After the *Mueller* decision, over thirty state legislatures, in 1984, entertained tax benefit legislation to aid nonpublic schools and President Reagan advanced bills in the Congress providing for tuition tax credits. Undoubtedly, as many such bills become law, and depending on their magnitude, substantial amounts of public tax funds could be redirected away from public schools. Thus, this case may represent a significant break in the wall of separation.

In explaining its decision in *Mueller,* the Court distinguished *Nyquist* by saying that in *Nyquist* tax assistance was provided only to parents of nonpublic school children, whereas in *Mueller* the law was so constructed as to allow deductions for tuition and costs to parents with children in public schools as well. The Court ignored the obvious rejoinder that public schools are by definition free and have few, if any, costs that could be deducted by a parent.

State Aid to Parochial Schools
Through Salary Supplements and
Purchase of Services Constitutes
Impermissible Entanglement Between
Church and State

LEMON v. KURTZMAN
Supreme Court of the United States, 1971.
403 U.S. 602, 91 S.Ct. 2105.

Mr. Chief Justice BURGER delivered the opinion of the Court.

These two appeals raise questions as to Pennsylvania and Rhode Island statutes prcviding state aid to church-related elementary and secondary schools. Both statutes are challenged as violative of the Establishment and Free Exercise Clauses of the First Amendment and the Due Process Clause of the Fourteenth Amendment.

Pennsylvania has adopted a statutory program that provides financial support to nonpublic elementary and secondary schools by way of reimbursement for the cost of teachers' salaries, textbooks, and instructional materials in specified secular subjects. Rhode Island has adopted a statute under which the State pays directly to teachers in nonpublic elementary schools a supplement of 15 percent of their annual salary. Under each statute state aid has been given to church-related educational institutions. We hold that both statutes are unconstitutional.

The Rhode Island Statute   The Rhode Island Salary Supplement Act[48] was enacted in 1969. It rests on the legislative finding that the quality of education available in nonpublic elementary schools has been jeopardized by the rapidly rising salaries needed to attract competent and dedicated teachers. The Act authorizes state officials to supplement the salaries of teachers of secular subjects in nonpublic elementary schools by paying directly to a teacher an amount not in excess of 15 percent of his current annual salary. As supplemented, however, a nonpublic school teacher's salary cannot exceed the maximum paid to teachers in the State's public schools, and the recipient must be certified by the state board of education in substantially the same manner as public school teachers.

In order to be eligible for the Rhode Island salary supplement, the recipient must teach in a nonpublic school at which the average per-pupil expenditure on secular education is less than the average in the State's public schools during a specified period. Appellant State Commissioner of Education also requires eligible schools to submit financial data. If this information indicates a per-pupil expenditure in excess of the statutory limitation, the records of the school in question must be examined in order to assess how much of the expenditure is attributable to secular education and how much to religious activity.

The Act also requires that teachers eligible for salary supplements must teach only those subjects that are offered in the State's public schools. They must use "only teaching materials which are used in the public schools." Finally, any teacher applying for a salary supplement must first agree in writing "not to teach a course in religion for so long as or during such time as he or she receives any salary supplements" under the Act.

Appellees are citizens and taxpayers of Rhode Island. . . . Appellants are state officials charged with administration of the Act, teachers eligible for salary supplements under the Act, and parents of children in church-related elementary schools whose teachers would receive state salary assistance.

A three-judge federal court was convened pursuant to 28 U.S.C.A. §§ 2281, 2284. It found that Rhode Island's non-public elementary schools accommodated approximately 25 percent of the State's pupils. About 95 percent of these pupils attended schools affiliated with the Roman Catholic church. To date some 250 teachers have applied for benefits under the Act. All of them are employed by Roman Catholic schools.

The court held a hearing at which extensive evidence was introduced concerning the nature of the secular instruction offered in the Roman Catholic schools whose teachers would be eligible for salary assistance under the Act. Although the court found that concern for religious values does not necessarily affect the content of secular subjects, it also found that the parochial school system was "an integral part of the religious mission of the Catholic Church."

The District Court concluded that the Act violated the Establishment Clause, holding that it fostered "excessive entanglement" between government and religion. In addition two judges thought that the Act had the impermissible effect of giving "significant aid to a religious enterprise." 316 F.Supp. 112. We affirm.

The Pennsylvania Statute Pennsylvania has adopted a program that has some but not all of the features of the Rhode Island program. The Pennsylvania Nonpublic Elementary and Secondary Education Act[49] was passed in 1968 in response to a crisis that the Pennsylvania Legislature found existed in the State's nonpublic schools due to rapidly rising costs. The statute affirmatively reflects the legislative conclusion that the State's educational goals could appropriately be fulfilled by government support of "those purely secular educational objectives achieved through nonpublic education . . . ."

The statute authorizes appellee state Superintendent of Public Instruction to "purchase" specified "secular educational services" from nonpublic schools. Under the "contracts" authorized by the statute, the State directly reimburses nonpublic schools solely for their actual expenditures for teachers' salaries, textbooks, and instructional materials. A school seeking reimbursement must maintain prescribed accounting procedures that identify the "separate" cost of the "secular educational service." These accounts are subject to state audit. The funds for this program were originally derived from a new tax on horse and harness racing, but the Act is now financed by a portion of the state tax on cigarettes.

There are several significant statutory restrictions on state aid. Reimbursement is limited to courses "presented in the curricula of the public schools." It is further limited "solely" to courses in the following "secular" subjects: mathematics, modern foreign languages,[50] physical science, and physical education. Textbooks and instructional materials included in the program must be approved by the state Superintendent of Public Instruction. Finally, the statute prohibits reimbursement for any course that contains "any subject matter expressing religious teaching, or the morals or forms of worship of any sect."

The Act went into effect on July 1, 1968, and the first reimbursement payments to schools were made on September 2, 1969. It appears that some $5 million has been expended annually under the Act. The State has now entered into contracts with some 1,181 nonpublic elementary and secondary schools with a student population of some 535,215 pupils—more than 20 percent of the total number of students in the State. More than 96 percent of these pupils attend church-related schools, and most of these schools are affiliated with the Roman Catholic church.

Appellants brought this action in the District Court to challenge the constitutionality of the Pennsylvania statute. The organizational plaintiffs-appellants are associations of persons resident in Pennsylvania declaring belief in the separation of church and state; individual plaintiffs-appellants are citizens and taxpayers of Pennsylvania. Appellant Lemon, in addition to being a citizen and a taxpayer, is a parent of a child attending public school in Pennsylvania. Lemon also alleges that he purchased a ticket at a race track and thus had paid the specific tax that supports the expenditures under the Act. . . . The District Court held that the individual plaintiffs-appellants had standing to challenge the Act, 310 F.Supp. 42. . . .

The court granted appellees' motion to dismiss the complaint for failure to state a claim for relief. 310 F.Supp. 35. It held that the Act violated neither the Establishment nor the Free Exercise Clause, Chief Judge Hastie dissenting. We reverse.

In Everson v. Board of Education, 330 U.S. 1, 67 S.Ct. 504, 91 L.Ed. 711 (1947), this Court upheld a state statute that reimbursed the parents of parochial school children for bus transportation expenses. There Mr. Justice Black, writing for the majority, suggested that the decision carried to "the verge" of forbidden territory under the Religion Clauses. Id., at 16, 67 S.Ct., at 511. Candor compels acknowledgment, moreover, that we can only dimly perceive the lines of demarcation in this extraordinarily sensitive area of constitutional law.

The language of the Religion Clauses of the First Amendment is at best opaque, particularly when compared with other portions of the Amendment. Its authors did not simply prohibit the establishment of a state church or a state religion, an area history shows they regarded as very important and fraught with great dangers. Instead they commanded that there should be "no law *respecting* an establishment of religion." A law may be one "respecting" the forbidden objective while falling short of its total realization. A law "respecting" the proscribed result, that is, the establishment of religion, is not always easily identifiable as one violative of the Clause. A given law might not *establish* a state religion but nevertheless be one "respecting" that end in the sense of being a step that could lead to such establishment and hence offend the First Amendment.

In the absence of precisely stated constitutional prohibitions, we must draw lines with reference to the three main evils against which the Establishment Clause was intended to afford protection: "sponsorship, financial support, and active involvement of the sovereign in religious activity." Walz v. Tax Commission, 397 U.S. 664, 668, 90 S.Ct. 1409, 1411, 25 L.Ed.2d 697 (1970).

Every analysis in this area must begin with consideration of the cumulative criteria developed by the Court over many years. Three such tests may be gleaned from our cases. First, the statute must have a secular legislative purpose; second, its principal or primary effect must be one that neither advances nor inhibits religion, Board of Education v. Allen, 392 U.S. 236, 243, 88 S.Ct. 1923, 1926, 20 L.Ed.2d 1060 (1968); finally, the statute must not foster "an excessive government entanglement with religion." Walz, supra, at 674, 90 S.Ct. at 1414.

Inquiry into the legislative purposes of the Pennsylvania and Rhode Island statutes affords no basis for a conclusion that the legislative intent was to advance religion. On the contrary, the statutes themselves clearly state that they are intended to enhance the quality of the secular education in all schools covered by the compulsory attendance laws. There is no reason to believe the legislatures meant anything else. A State always has a legitimate concern for maintaining minimum standards in all schools it allows to operate. As in *Allen,* we find nothing here that undermines the stated legislative intent; it must therefore be accorded appropriate deference.

In *Allen* the Court acknowledged that secular and religious teachings were not necessarily so intertwined that secular textbooks furnished to students by the State were in fact instrumental in the teaching of religion. 392 U.S., at 248, 88 S.Ct., at 1929. The legislatures of Rhode Island and Pennsylvania have concluded that secular and religious education are identifiable and separable. In the abstract we have no quarrel with this conclusion.

The two legislatures, however, have also recognized that church-related elementary and secondary schools have a significant religious mission and that a substantial portion of their activities is religiously oriented. They have therefore sought to create statutory restrictions designed to guarantee the separation between secular and religious educational functions and to ensure that State financial aid supports only the former. All these provisions are precautions taken in candid recognition that these programs approached, even if they did not intrude upon, the forbidden areas under the Religion Clauses. We need not decide whether these legislative precautions restrict the principal or primary effect of the programs to the point where they do not offend the Religion Clauses, for we conclude that the cumulative impact of the entire relationship arising under the statutes in each State involves excessive entanglement between government and religion. . . .

(a) Rhode Island program The District Court made extensive findings on the grave potential for excessive entanglement that inheres in the religious character and purpose of the Roman Catholic elementary schools of Rhode Island, to date the sole beneficiaries of the Rhode Island Salary Supplement Act.

The church schools involved in the program are located close to parish churches. This understandably permits convenient access for religious exercises since instruction in faith and morals is part of the total educational process. The school buildings contain identifying religious symbols such as crosses on the exterior and crucifixes, and religious paintings and statues either in the classrooms or hallways. Although only approximately thirty minutes a day are devoted to direct religious instruction, there are religiously oriented extracurricular activities. Approximately two-thirds of the teachers in these schools are nuns of various religious orders. Their dedicated efforts provide an atmosphere in which religious instruction and religious vocations are natural and proper parts of life in such schools. Indeed, as the District Court found, the role of teaching nuns in enhancing the religious atmosphere has led the parochial school authorities to attempt to maintain a one-to-one ratio between nuns and lay teachers in all schools rather than to permit some to be staffed almost entirely by lay teachers.

On the basis of these findings the District Court concluded that the parochial schools constituted "an integral part of the religious mission of the Catholic Church." The various characteristics of the schools make them "a powerful vehicle for transmitting the Catholic faith to the next generation." This process of inculcating religious doctrine is, of course, enhanced by the impressionable age of the pupils, in primary schools particularly. In short, parochial schools involve substantial religious activity and purpose.

The substantial religious character of these church-related schools gives rise to entangling church-state relationships of the kind the Religion Clauses sought to avoid. Although the District Court found that concern for religious values did not inevitably or necessarily intrude into the content of secular subjects, the considerable religious activities of these schools led the legislature to provide for careful governmental controls and surveillance by state authorities in order to ensure that state aid supports only secular education. . . .

The Rhode Island Legislature has not, and could not, provide state aid on the basis of a mere assumption that secular teachers under religious discipline can avoid conflicts. The State must be certain, given the Religion Clauses, that subsidized teachers do not inculcate religion—indeed the State here has undertaken to do so. To ensure that no trespass occurs, the State has therefore carefully conditioned its aid with pervasive restrictions. An eligible recipient must teach only those courses that are offered in the public schools and use only those texts and materials that are found in the public schools. In addition the teacher must not engage in teaching any course in religion.

A comprehensive, discriminating, and continuing state surveillance will inevitably be required to ensure that these restrictions are obeyed and the First Amendment otherwise respected. Unlike a book, a teacher cannot be inspected once so as to determine the extent and intent of his or her personal beliefs and subjective acceptance of the limitations imposed by the First Amendment. These prophylactic contacts will involve excessive and enduring entanglement between state and church.

There is another area of entanglement in the Rhode Island program that gives concern. The statute excludes teachers employed by nonpublic schools whose average per-pupil expenditures on secular education equal or exceed the comparable figures for public schools. In the event that the total expenditures of an otherwise eligible school exceed this norm, the program requires the government to examine the school's records in order to determine how much of the total expenditures is attributable to secular education and how much to religious activity. This kind of state inspection and evaluation of the religious content of a religious organization is fraught with the sort of entanglement that the Constitution forbids. It is a relationship pregnant with dangers of excessive government direction of church schools and hence of churches. The Court noted "the hazards of government supporting churches" in Walz v. Tax Commission, supra, 397 U.S., at 675, 90 S.Ct., at 1414, and we cannot ignore here the danger that pervasive modern governmental power will ultimately intrude on religion and thus conflict with the Religion Clauses.

(b) Pennsylvania program The Pennsylvania statute also provides state aid to church-related schools for teachers' salaries. The complaint describes an educational system that is very similar to the one existing in Rhode Island. According to the allegations, the church-related elementary and secondary schools are controlled by religious organizations, have the purpose of propa-

gating and promoting a particular religious faith, and conduct their operations to fulfill that purpose. Since this complaint was dismissed for failure to state a claim for relief, we must accept these allegations as true for purposes of our review.

As we noted earlier, the very restrictions and surveillance necessary to ensure that teachers play a strictly nonideological role give rise to entanglements between church and state. The Pennsylvania statute, like that of Rhode Island, fosters this kind of relationship. Reimbursement is not only limited to courses offered in the public schools and materials approved by state officials, but the statute excludes "any subject matter expressing religious teaching, or the morals or forms of worship of any sect." In addition, schools seeking reimbursement must maintain accounting procedures that require the State to establish the cost of the secular as distinguished from the religious instruction.

The Pennsylvania statute, moreover, has the further defect of providing state financial aid directly to the church-related schools. This factor distinguishes both *Everson* and *Allen,* for in both those cases the Court was careful to point out that state aid was provided to the student and his parents—not to the church-related school. . . . In Walz v. Tax Commission, supra, 397 U.S., at 675, 90 S.Ct., at 1414, the Court warned of the dangers of direct payments to religious organizations:

> Obviously a direct money subsidy would be a relationship pregnant with involvement and, as with most governmental grant programs, could encompass sustained and detailed administrative relationships for enforcement of statutory or administrative standards . . . .

The history of government grants of a continuing cash subsidy indicates that such programs have almost always been accompanied by varying measures of control and surveillance. The government cash grants before us now provide no basis for predicting that comprehensive measures of surveillance and controls will not follow. In particular the government's post-audit power to inspect and evaluate a church-related school's financial records and to determine which expenditures are religious and which are secular creates an intimate and continuing relationship between church and state.

A broader base of entanglement of yet a different character is presented by the divisive political potential of these state programs. In a community where such a large number of pupils are served by church-related schools, it can be assumed that state assistance will entail considerable political activity. Partisans of parochial schools, understandably concerned with rising costs and sincerely dedicated to both the religious and secular educational missions of their schools, will inevitably champion this cause and promote political action to achieve their goals. Those who oppose state aid, whether for constitutional, religious, or fiscal reasons, will inevitably respond and employ all of the usual political campaign techniques to prevail. Candidates will be forced to declare and voters to choose. It would be unrealistic to ignore the fact that many people confronted with issues of this kind will find their votes aligned with their faith.

Ordinarily political debate and division, however vigorous or even partisan, are normal and healthy manifestations of our democratic system of government, but political division along religious lines was one of the principal evils against which the First Amendment was intended to protect. . . . The potential divisiveness of such conflict is a threat to the normal political process. . . .

The potential for political divisiveness related to religious belief and practice is aggravated in these two statutory programs by the need for continuing annual appropriations and the likelihood of larger and larger demands as costs and populations grow. . . .

In *Walz* it was argued that a tax exemption for places of religious worship would prove to be the first step in an inevitable progression leading to the establishment of state churches and state religion. That claim could not stand up against more than 200 years of virtually universal practice imbedded in our colonial experience and continuing into the present.

The progression argument, however, is more persuasive here. We have no long history of state aid to church-related educational institutions comparable to 200 years of tax exemption for churches. Indeed, the state programs before us today represent something of an innovation. We have already noted that modern governmental programs have self-perpetuating and self-expanding propensities. These internal pressures are only enhanced when the schemes involve institutions whose legitimate needs are growing and whose interests have substantial political support. Nor can we fail to see that in constitutional adjudication some steps, which when taken were thought to approach "the verge," have become the platform for yet further steps. A certain momentum develops in constitutional theory and it can be a "downhill thrust" easily set in motion but difficult to retard or stop. Development by momentum is not invariably bad; indeed, it is the way the common law has grown, but it is a force to be recognized and reckoned with. The dangers are increased by the difficulty of perceiving in advance exactly where the "verge" of the precipice lies. As well as constituting an independent evil against which the Religion Clauses were intended to protect, involvement or entanglement between government and religion serves as a warning signal.

Finally, nothing we have said can be construed to disparage the role of church-related elementary and secondary schools in our national life. Their contribution has been and is enormous. Nor do we ignore their economic plight in a period of rising costs and expanding need. Taxpayers generally have been spared vast sums by the maintenance of these educational institutions by religious organizations, largely by the gifts of faithful adherents.

The merit and benefits of these schools, however, are not the issue before us in these cases. The sole question is whether state aid to these schools can be squared with the dictates of the Religion Clauses. Under our system the choice has been made that government is to be entirely excluded from the area of religious instruction and churches excluded from the affairs of government. The Constitution decrees that religion must be a private matter for the individual, the family, and the institutions of private chioce, and that while some involvement and entanglement are inevitable, lines must be drawn.

The judgment of the Rhode Island District Court in No. 569 and No. 570 is affirmed. The judgment of the Pennsylvania District Court in No. 89 is reversed, and the case is remanded for further proceedings consistent with this opinion. . . .

NOTES

1. In *Earley* v. *DiCenso,* a companion case to *Lemon* v. *Kurtzman,* the Supreme Court invalidated a Rhode Island statute authorizing salary supplements for teachers of secular subjects in nonpublic schools. 403 U.S. 602, 91 S.Ct. 2105 (1971).

2. *Lemon* prohibited aid to sectarian schools but did not proscribe state assistance to private nonsectarian schools.

3. Lease of classroom space from a parochial school by the public school system was held to be constitutional where the public schools actually faced a severe classroom shortage and the classrooms were in a separable part of the parochial school where no religious impediments were present. A significant effort had been made by the public schools, it was found, to prevent intermingling of the two school programs. Thomas v. Schmidt, 397 F.Supp. 203 (D.C.R.I.1975).

4. Lease of public school facilities for religious activities is unconstitutional where the rental charge covered only the cost of janitorial services and the lease extended for an indefinite period of time. The court found that such nominal rent is functionally a subsidy to the church. Resnick v. East Brunswick Township Board of Education, 135 N.J.Super. 257, 343 A.2d 127 (1975).

*Maintenance and Repair Grants for
Parochial Schools as Well as Tuition
Reimbursement and Income Tax
Benefits to Parents of Parochial
School Children Are Unconstitutional*

COMMITTEE FOR PUBLIC EDUCATION AND RELIGIOUS LIBERTY v. NYQUIST

Supreme Court of the United States, 1973.
413 U.S. 756, 93 S.Ct. 2955.

Mr. Justice POWELL delivered the opinion of the Court.

These cases raise a challenge under the Establishment Clause of the First Amendment to the constitutionality of a recently enacted New York law which provides financial assistance, in several ways to nonpublic elementary and secondary schools in that State. The cases involve an intertwining of societal and constitutional issues of the greatest importance.

In May 1972, the Governor of New York signed into law several amendments to the State's Education and Tax Laws. The first five sections of these amendments established three distinct financial aid programs for nonpublic elementary and secondary schools. . . .

The first section of the challenged enactment, entitled "Health and Safety Grants for Nonpublic School Children," provides for direct money grants from the State to "qualifying" nonpublic schools to be used for the "maintenance and repair of . . . school facilities and equipment to ensure the health, welfare and safety of enrolled pupils." A "qualifying" school is any nonpublic, nonprofit elementary or secondary school which "has been designated during the [immediately preceding] year as serving a high concentration of pupils from low-income families for purposes of Title IV of the Federal Higher Education Act of nineteen hundred sixty-five (20 U.S.C.A. § 425)." Such schools are entitled to receive a grant of $30 per pupil per year, or $40 per pupil per year if the facilities are more than twenty-five years old. . . .

"Maintenance and repair" is defined by the statute to include "the provision of heat, light, water, ventilation and sanitary facilities; cleaning, janitorial and custodial services; snow removal; necessary upkeep and renovation of buildings, grounds and equipment; fire and accident protection; and such other items as the commissioner may deem necessary to ensure the health, welfare and safety of enrolled pupils." . . .

The remainder of the challenged legislation—§§ 2 through 5—is a single package captioned the "Elementary and Secondary Education Opportunity Program." It is composed, essentially, of two parts, a tuition grant program and a tax benefit program. Section 2 establishes a limited plan providing tuition reimbursements to parents of children attending elementary or secondary nonpublic schools. . . .

The remainder of the "Elementary and Secondary Education Opportunity Program," contained in §§ 3, 4, and 5 of the challenged law, is designed to provide a form of tax relief to those who fail to qualify for tuition reimbursement. Under these sections parents may subtract from their adjusted gross income for state income tax purposes a designated amount for each dependent for whom they have paid at least $50 in nonpublic school tuition. . . .

Plaintiffs argued below that because of the substantially religious character of the intended beneficiaries, each of the State's three enactments offended the Establishment Clause. The District Court, in an opinion carefully canvassing this Court's recent precedents, held unanimously that § 1 (maintenance and repair grants) and § 2 (tuition reimbursement grants) were invalid. As to the income tax provisions of §§ 3, 4, and 5, however, a majority of the District Court, over the dissent of Circuit Judge Hays, held that the Establishment Clause had not been violated. . . . We affirm the District Court insofar as it struck down §§ 1 and 2 and reverse its determination regarding §§ 3, 4, and 5.

The history of the Establishment Clause has been recounted frequently and need not be repeated here. . . . It is enough to note that it is now firmly established that a law may be one "respecting an establishment of religion" even though its consequence is not to promote a "state religion," . . . and even though it does not aid one religion more than another but merely benefits all religions alike. . . . It is equally well established, however, that not every law that confers an "indirect," "remote," or "inci-

dental" benefit upon religious institutions is, for that reason alone, constitutionally invalid. . . .

Most of the cases coming to this Court raising Establishment Clause
questions have involved the relationship between religion and education.
Among these religion-education precedents, two general categories of cases
may be identified: those dealing with religious activities within the public
schools, and those involving public aid in varying forms to sectarian educational institutions. While the New York legislation places this case in the
latter category, its resolution requires consideration, not only of the several
aid-to-sectarian-education cases, but also of our other education precedents
and of several important noneducation cases. For the now well-defined
three-part test that has emerged from our decisions is a product of considerations derived from the full sweep of the Establishment Clause cases. Taken
together, these decisions dictate that to pass muster under the Establishment Clause the law in question first must reflect a clearly secular legislative purpose . . . second, must have a primary effect that neither advances
nor inhibits religion . . . and, third, must avoid excessive government
entanglement with religion. . . .

In applying these criteria to the three distinct forms of aid involved in
this case, we need touch only briefly on the requirement of a "secular
legislative purpose." As the recitation of legislative purposes appended to
New York's law indicates, each measure is adequately supported by legitimate, nonsectarian state interests. We do not question the propriety, and
fully secular content, of New York's interest in preserving a healthy and
safe educational environment for all of its schoolchildren. And we do not
doubt—indeed, we fully recognize—the validity of the State's interest in
promoting pluralism and diversity among its public and nonpublic schools.
Nor do we hesitate to acknowledge the reality of its concern for an already
overburdened public school system that might suffer in the event that a
significant percentage of children presently attending nonpublic schools
should abandon those schools in favor of the public schools.

But the propriety of a legislature's purposes may not immunize from
further scrutiny a law which either has a primary effect that advances
religion, or which fosters excessive entanglements between Church and
State. Accordingly, we must weigh each of the three aid provisions challenged here against these criteria of effect and entanglement.

The "maintenance and repair" provisions of § 1 authorize direct payments to nonpublic schools, virtually all of which are Roman Catholic
schools in low-income areas. The grants, totaling $30 or $40 per pupil
depending on the age of the institution, are given largely without restriction
on usage. So long as expenditures do not exceed 50% of comparable
expenses in the public school system, it is possible for a sectarian elementary
or secondary school to finance its entire "maintenance and repair" budget
from state tax-raised funds. No attempt is made to restrict payments to
those expenditures related to the upkeep of facilities used exclusively for
secular purposes, nor do we think it possible within the context of these
religion-oriented institutions to impose such restrictions. Nothing in the
statute, for instance, bars a qualifying school from paying out of state funds
the salaries of employees who maintain the school chapel, or the cost of

renovating classrooms in which religion is taught, or the cost of heating and lighting those same facilities. Absent appropriate restrictions on expenditures for these and similar purposes, it simply cannot be denied that this section has a primary effect that advances religion in that it subsidizes directly the religious activities of sectarian elementary and secondary schools. . . .

It might be argued, however, that while the New York "maintenance and repair" grants lack specifically articulated secular restrictions, the statute does provide a sort of statistical guarantee of separation by limiting grants to 50% of the amount expended for comparable services in the public schools. . . . Quite apart from the language of the statute, our cases make clear that a mere statistical judgment will not suffice as a guarantee that state funds will not be used to finance religious education. . . .

What we have said demonstrates that New York's maintenance and repair provisions violate the Establishment Clause because their effect, inevitably, is to subsidize and advance the religious mission of sectarian schools. We have no occasion, therefore, to consider the further question whether those provisions as presently written would also fail to survive scrutiny under the administrative entanglement aspect of the three-part test because assuring the secular use of all funds requires too intrusive and continuing a relationship between Church and State, *Lemon* v. *Kurtzman,* supra.

New York's tuition reimbursement program also fails the "effect" test for much the same reasons that govern its maintenance and repair grants. The state program is designed to allow direct, unrestricted grants of $50 to $100 per child (but no more than 50% of tuition actually paid) as reimbursement to parents in low-income brackets who send their children to non-public schools, the bulk of which is concededly sectarian in orientation. . . .

The controlling question here, then, is whether the fact that the grants are delivered to parents rather than schools is of such significance as to compel a contrary result. The State and intervenor-appellees rely on *Everson* and *Allen* for their claim that grants to parents, unlike grants to institutions, respect the "wall of separation" required by the Constitution. It is true that in those cases the Court upheld laws that provided benefits to children attending religious schools and to their parents: As noted above, in *Everson* parents were reimbursed for bus fares paid to send children to parochial schools, and in *Allen* textbooks were loaned directly to the children. But those decisions make clear that, far from providing a per se immunity from examination of the substance of the State's program, the fact that aid is disbursed to parents rather than to the schools is only one among many factors to be considered.

In *Everson,* the Court found the bus fare program analogous to the provision of services such as police and fire protection, sewage disposal, highways, and sidewalks for parochial schools. 330 U.S., at 17–18, 67 S.Ct., at 512–513. Such services, provided in common to all citizens, are "so separate and so indisputably marked off from the religious function," ibid., at 18, 67 S.Ct., at 513 that they may fairly be viewed as reflections of a neutral posture toward religious institutions. *Allen* is founded upon a similar principle. The Court there repeatedly emphasized that upon the record in that case there was no indication that textbooks would be provided for anything other than purely secular courses. "Of course books are different from buses. Most bus rides have no inherent religious significance, while religious books are common. However, the language of [the law under consideration] does not authorize the loan of religious books, and the State claims no right to distribute religious literature. . . . Absent evidence, we cannot assume that school authorities . . . are unable to distinguish between secular and religious books or that they will not honestly discharge their duties under the law." . . .

The tuition grants here are subject to no such restrictions. There has been no endeavor "to guarantee the separation between secular and religious educational functions and to ensure that State financial aid supports only the former." . . . Indeed, it is precisely the function of New York's law to provide assistance to private schools, the great majority of which are sectarian. By reimbursing parents for a portion of their tuition bill, the State seeks to relieve their financial burdens sufficiently to assure that they continue to have the option to send their children to religion-oriented schools. And while the other purposes for that aid—to perpetuate a pluralistic educational environment and to protect the fiscal integrity of overburdened public schools—are certainly unexceptionable, the effect of the aid is unmistakably to provide desired financial support for nonpublic, sectarian institutions. . . .

Although we think it clear, for the reasons above stated, that New York's tuition grant program fares no better under the "effect" test than its maintenance and repair program, in view of the novelty of the question we will address briefly the subsidiary arguments made by the state officials and intervenors in its defense.

First, it has been suggested that it is of controlling significance that New York's program calls for *reimbursement* for tuition already paid rather than for direct contributions which are merely routed through the parents to the schools, in advance of or in lieu of payment by the parents. The parent is not a mere conduit, we are told, but is absolutely free to spend the money he receives in any manner he wishes. There is no element of coercion attached to the reimbursement, and no assurance that the money will eventually end up in the hands of religious schools. The absence of any element of coercion, however, is irrelevant to questions arising under the Establishment Clause. . . . [I]f the grants are offered as an incentive to parents to send their children to sectarian schools by making unrestricted cash payments to them, the Establishment Clause is violated whether or not the actual dollars given eventually find their way into the sectarian institutions. Whether the grant is labeled a reimbursement, a reward, or a subsidy, its substantive impact is still the same. In sum, we agree with the conclusion of the District Court that "[w]hether he gets it during the current year, or as reimbursement for the past year, is of no constitutional importance." . . .

Finally, the State argues that its program of tuition grants should survive scrutiny because it is designed to promote the free exercise of religion. The State notes that only "low-income parents" are aided by this law, and without state assistance their right to have their children educated in a religious environment "is diminished or even denied." It is true, of course, that this Court has long recognized and maintained the right to choose nonpublic over public education. . . . It is also true that a state law interfering with a parent's right to have his child educated in a sectarian school would run afoul of the Free Exercise Clause. But this Court repeatedly has recognized that tension inevitably exists between the Free Exercise and the Establishment Clauses . . . and that it may often not be possible to promote the former without offending the latter. As a result of this tension, our cases require the State to maintain an attitude of "neutrality," neither "advancing" nor "inhibiting" religion. In its attempt to enhance the opportunities of the poor to choose between public and nonpublic education, the State has taken a step which can only be regarded as one "advancing" religion. However great our sympathy . . . for the burdens experienced by those who must pay public school taxes at the same time that they support other schools because of the constraints of "conscience and discipline," ibid., and notwithstanding the "high social importance" of the State's purposes . . . neither may justify an eroding of the limitations of the Establishment Clause now firmly emplanted.

Sections 3, 4, and 5 establish a system for providing income tax benefits to parents of children attending New York's nonpublic schools. . . .

These sections allow parents of children attending nonpublic elementary and secondary schools to subtract from adjusted gross income a specified amount if they do not receive a tuition reimbursement under § 2, and if they have an adjusted gross income of less than $25,000. . . .

In practical terms there would appear to be little difference, for purposes of determining whether such aid has the effect of advancing religion, between the tax benefit allowed here and the tuition grant allowed under § 2. The qualifying parent under either program receives the same form of encouragement and reward for sending his children to nonpublic schools. The only difference is that one parent receives an actual cash payment while the other is allowed to reduce by an arbitrary amount the sum he would otherwise be obliged to pay over to the State. . . .

Appellees defend the tax portion of New York's legislative package on two grounds. First, they contend that it is of controlling significance that the grants or credits are directed to the parents rather than to the schools. This is the same argument made in support of the tuition reimbursements and rests on the same reading of the same precedents of this Court, primarily *Everson* and *Allen.* Our treatment of this issue in Part II–B is applicable here and requires rejection of this claim. Second, appellees place their strongest reliance on *Walz* v. *Tax Commission,* in which New York's property tax exemption for religious organizations was upheld. We think that *Walz* provides no support for appellees' position. Indeed, its rationale plainly compels the conclusion that New York's tax package violates the Establishment Clause.

Tax exemptions for church property enjoyed an apparently universal approval in this country both before and after the adoption of the First Amendment. The Court in *Walz* surveyed the history of tax exemptions and found that each of the fifty States has long provided for tax exemptions for places of worship, that Congress has exempted religious organizations from taxation for over three-quarters of a century, and that congressional enactments in 1802, 1813, and 1870 specifically exempted church property from taxation. In sum, the Court concluded that "[f]ew concepts are more deeply embedded in the fabric of our national life, beginning with pre-Revolutionary colonial times, than for the government to exercise at the very least this kind of benevolent neutrality toward churches and religious exercise generally." . . . We know of no historical precedent for New York's recently promulgated tax relief program. Indeed, it seems clear that tax benefits for parents whose children attend parochial schools are a recent innovation, occasioned by the growing financial plight of such nonpublic institutions and designed, albeit unsuccessfully, to tailor state aid in a manner not incompatible with the recent decisions of this Court. . . .

But historical acceptance without more would not alone have sufficed, as "no one acquires a vested or protected right in violation of the Constitution by long use." . . . It was the reason underlying that long history of tolerance of tax exemptions for religion that proved controlling. A proper respect for both the Free Exercise and the Establishment Clauses compels the State to pursue a course of "neutrality" toward religion. Yet governments have not always pursued such a course, and oppression has taken many forms, one of which has been taxation of religion. Thus, if taxation was regarded as a form of "hostility" toward religion, "exemption constitute[d] a reasonable and balanced attempt to guard against those dangers." . . . Special tax benefits, however, cannot be squared with the principle of neutrality established by the decisions of this Court. To the contrary, insofar as such benefits render assistance to parents who send their children to sectarian schools, their purpose and inevitable effect are to aid and advance those religious institutions. . . .

One further difference between tax exemption for church property and tax benefits for parents should be noted. The exemption challenged in *Walz* was not restricted to a class composed exclusively or even predominantly of religious institutions. Instead, the exemption covered all property devoted to religious, educational, or charitable purposes. As the parties here must concede, tax reductions authorized by this law flow primarily to the parents of children attending sectarian, nonpublic schools. Without intimating whether this factor alone might have controlling significance in another context in some future case, it should be apparent that in terms of the potential divisiveness of any legislative measure the narrowness of the benefited class would be an important factor.

In conclusion, we find the *Walz* analogy unpersuasive, and in light of the practical similarity between New York's tax and tuition reimbursement programs, we hold that neither form of aid is sufficiently restricted to assure that it will not have the impermissible effect of advancing the sectarian activities of religious schools.

Because we have found that the challenged sections have the impermissible effect of advancing religion, we need not consider whether such aid would result in entanglement of the State with religion in the sense of "[a] comprehensive, discriminating, and continuing state surveillance." . . . But the importance of the competing societal interests implicated here prompts us to make the further observation that, apart from any specific entanglement of the State in particular religious programs, assistance of the sort here involved carries grave potential for entanglement in the broader sense of continuing political strife over aid to religion. . . .

All three of these programs start out at modest levels: the maintenance grant is not to exceed $40 per pupil per year in approved schools; the tuition grant provides parents not more than $50 a year for each child in the first eight grades and $100 for each child in the high school grades; and the tax benefit, though more difficult to compute, is equally modest. But we know from long experience with both Federal and State Governments that aid programs of any kind tend to become entrenched, to escalate in cost, and to generate their own aggressive constituencies. And the larger the class of recipients, the greater the pressure for accelerated increases. Moreover, the State itself, concededly anxious to avoid assuming the burden of educating children now in private and parochial schools, has a strong motivation for increasing this aid as public school costs rise and population increases. In this situation, where the underlying issue is the deeply emotional one of Church-State relationships, the potential for seriously divisive political consequences needs no elaboration. And while the prospect of such divisiveness may not alone warrant the invalidation of state laws that otherwise survive the careful scrutiny required by the decisions of this Court, it is certainly a "warning signal" not to be ignored. . . .

Our examination of New York's aid provisions, in light of all relevant considerations, compels the judgment that each, as written, has a "primary effect that advances religion" and offends the constitutional prohibition against laws "respecting an establishment of religion." We therefore affirm the three-judge court's holding as to §§ 1 and 2, and reverse as to §§ 3, 4, and 5.

It is so ordered.

Affirmed in part and reversed in part.

NOTES

1. Following the precedent established by the United States Supreme Court in *Nyquist,* the United States Court of Appeals for the Third Circuit struck down a $4.4 million tax deduction plan that would have assisted parents with children in parochial schools. The statute enacted in 1976 provided for a personal income tax deduction of $1000 for each child attending a nonpublic elementary and secondary school on a full-time basis. The federal court found that the statute had a secular purpose, but failed to meet the primary effect test and thus was constitutionally deficient because it advanced religion. Since the act violated the primary effect standard the court saw no need to evaluate it under the excessive entanglement criterion. The United States Supreme Court in a vote of 6 to 3 upheld without a hearing the lower court's decision. Public Funds for Public Schools of New Jersey v. Byrne, 590 F.2d 514 (1979).

2. In 1973, in a companion case to *Lemon* v. *Kurtzman,* the Supreme Court of the United States struck down a Pennsylvania law entitled "Parent Reimbursement Act for Nonpublic Education" that provided for reimbursement to parents who pay tuition for their children to attend the state's nonpublic elementary and secondary schools. In holding the act violative of the Establishment Clause the Court observed that "Whether

that benefit (tuition reimbursement to parents) be viewed as a simple tuition subsidy, as an incentive to parents to send their children to sectarian schools, or as a reward for having done so, at bottom its intended consequence is to preserve and support religion-oriented institutions." Sloan v. Lemon, 413 U.S. 825, 93 S.Ct. 2982 (1973).

State Financing of Auxiliary Services
and Direct Loans for Instructional
Materials and Equipment for
Parochial Schools Is Unconstitutional

MEEK v. PITTENGER

Supreme Court of the United States, 1975.
421 U.S. 350, 95 S.Ct. 1753.

Mr. Justice STEWART announced the judgment of the Court and delivered the opinion of the Court (Parts I, II, IV, and V), together with an opinion (Part III), in which Mr. Justice BLACKMUN and Mr. Justice POWELL, joined.

This case requires us to determine once again whether a state law providing assistance to nonpublic, church-related, elementary and secondary schools is constitutional under the Establishment Clause of the First Amendment, made applicable to the States by the Fourteenth Amendment. . . .

With the stated purpose of assuring that every schoolchild in the Commonwealth will equitably share in the benefits of auxiliary services, textbooks, and instructional material provided free of charge to children attending public schools, the Pennsylvania General Assembly in 1972 added Acts 194 and 195, July 12, 1972, Pa.Stat.Ann., Tit. 24, § 9–972, to the Pennsylvania Public School Code of 1949, Pa.Stat.Ann., Tit. 24, §§ 1–101 to 27–2702.

Act 194 authorizes the Commonwealth to provide "auxiliary services" to all children enrolled in nonpublic elementary and secondary schools meeting Pennsylvania's compulsory-attendance requirements. "Auxiliary services" include counseling, testing, and psychological services, speech and hearing therapy, teaching and related services for exceptional children, for remedial students, and for the educationally disadvantaged, "and such other secular, neutral, nonideological services as are of benefit to nonpublic school children and are presently or hereafter provided for public school children of the Commonwealth." Act 194 specifies that the teaching and services are to be provided in the nonpublic schools themselves by personnel drawn from the appropriate "intermediate unit," part of the public school system of the Commonwealth established to provide special services to local school districts.

Act 195 authorizes the State Secretary of Education, either directly or through the intermediate units, to lend textbooks without charge to children attending nonpublic elementary and secondary schools that meet the Commonwealth's compulsory-attendance requirements. The books that may be lent are limited to those "which are acceptable for use in any public, elementary, or secondary school of the Commonwealth."

Act 195 also authorizes the Secretary of Education, pursuant to requests from the appropriate nonpublic school officials, to lend directly to the nonpublic schools "instructional materials and equipment, useful to the education" of nonpublic school children. "Instructional materials" are defined to include periodicals, photographs, maps, charts, sound recordings, films, "or any other printed and published materials of a similar nature." "Instructional equipment," as defined by the Act, includes projection equipment, recording equipment, and laboratory equipment. . . .

In judging the constitutionality of the various forms of assistance authorized by Acts 194 and 195, the District Court applied the three-part test that has been clearly stated, if not easily applied, by this Court in recent Establishment Clause cases. . . . First, the statute must have a secular legislative purpose. . . . Second, it must have a "primary effect" that neither advances nor inhibits religion. . . . Third, the statute and its administration must avoid excessive government entanglement with religion. . . .

These tests constitute a convenient, accurate distillation of this Court's efforts over the past decades to evaluate a wide range of governmental action challenged as violative of the constitutional prohibition against laws "respecting an establishment of religion," and thus provide the proper framework of analysis for the issues presented in the case before us. It is well to emphasize, however, that the tests must not be viewed as setting the precise limits to the necessary constitutional inquiry, but serve only as guidelines with which to identify instances in which the objectives of the Establishment Clause have been impaired. . . .

The District Court held that the textbook loan provisions of Act 195 are constitutionally indistinguishable from the New York textbook loan program upheld in Board of Education v. Allen, 392 U.S. 236, 88 S.Ct. 1923, 20 L.Ed. 2d 1060. We agree. . . .

Like the New York program, the textbook provisions of Act 195 extend to all schoolchildren the benefits of Pennsylvania's well-established policy of lending textbooks free of charge to elementary and secondary school students. As in *Allen,* Act 195 provides that the textbooks are to be lent directly to the student, not to the nonpublic school itself, although, again as in *Allen,* the administrative practice is to have student requests for the books filed initially with the nonpublic school and to have the school authorities prepare collective summaries of these requests which they forward to the appropriate public officials. Thus, the financial benefit of Pennsylvania's textbook program, like New York's, is to parents and children, not to the nonpublic schools. . . . Moreover, the record in the case before us, like the record in *Allen* . . . contains no suggestion that religious textbooks will be lent or that the books provided will be used for anything other than purely secular purposes.

In sum, the textbook loan provisions of Act 195 are in every material respect identical to the loan program approved in *Allen.* Pennsylvania, like New York, "merely makes available to all children the benefits of a general program to lend school books free of charge." As such, those provisions of Act 195 do not offend the constitutional prohibition against laws "respecting an establishment of religion."

Although textbooks are lent only to students, Act 195 authorizes the loan of instructional material and equipment directly to qualifying nonpublic elementary and secondary schools in the Commonwealth. The appellants assert that such direct aid to Pennsylvania's nonpublic schools, including church-related institutions, constitutes an impermissible establishment of religion. . . .

The only requirement imposed on nonpublic schools to qualify for loans of instructional material and equipment is that they satisfy the Commonwealth's compulsory-attendance law by providing, in the English language, the subjects and activities prescribed by the standards of the State Board of Education. Commonwealth officials, as a matter of state policy, do not inquire into the religious characteristics, if any, of the nonpublic schools requesting aid pursuant to Act 195. The Coordinator of Nonpublic School Services, the chief administrator of Acts 194 and 195, testified that a school would not be barred from receiving loans of instructional material and equipment even though its dominant purpose was the inculcation of religious values, even if it imposed religious restrictions on admissions or on faculty appointments, and even if it required attendance at classes in theology or at religious services. In fact, of the 1,320 nonpublic schools in Pennsylvania that comply with the requirements of the compulsory-attendance law and thus qualify for aid under Act 195, more than 75% are church-related or religiously affiliated educational institutions. Thus, the primary beneficiaries of Act 195's instructional material and equipment loan provisions, like the beneficiaries of the "secular educational services" reimbursement program considered in *Lemon* v. *Kurtzman,* and the parent tuition-reimbursement plan considered in *Sloan* v. *Lemon,* are nonpublic schools with a predominant sectarian character. . . .

The church-related elementary and secondary schools that are the primary beneficiaries of Act 195's instructional material and equipment loans typify such religion-pervasive institutions. The very purpose of many of those schools is to provide an integrated secular and religious education; the teaching process is, to a large extent, devoted to the inculcation of religious values and belief. . . . Substantial aid to the educational function of such schools, accordingly, necessarily results in aid to the sectarian school enterprise as a whole. "[T]he secular education those schools provide goes hand in hand with the religious mission that is the only reason for the schools' existence. Within the institution, the two are inextricably intertwined." . . . For this reason, Act 195's direct aid to Pennsylvania's predominantly church-related, nonpublic elementary and secondary schools, even though ostensibly limited to wholly neutral, secular instructional material and equipment, inescapably results in the direct and substantial advancement of religious activity . . . and thus constitutes an impermissible establishment of religion.

Unlike Act 195, which provides only for the loan of teaching material and equipment, Act 194 authorizes the Secretary of Education, through the intermediate units, to supply professional staff, as well as supportive materials, equipment, and personnel, to the nonpublic schools of the Commonwealth. The "auxiliary services" authorized by Act 194—remedial and accelerated instruction, guidance counseling and testing, speech and hearing services—are provided directly to nonpublic school children with the appropriate special need. But the services are provided only on the nonpublic school premises, and only when "requested by nonpublic school representatives." . . . The appellants concede the validity of this secular legislative purpose. Nonetheless, they argue that Act 194 constitutes an impermissible establishment of religion because the auxiliary services are provided on the premises of predominantly church-related schools. . . .

We need not decide whether substantial state expenditures to enrich the curricula of church-related elementary and secondary schools, like the expenditure of state funds to support the basic educational program of those schools, necessarily result in the direct and substantial advancement of religious activity. For decisions of this Court make clear that the District Court erred in relying entirely on the good faith and professionalism of the secular teachers and counselors functioning in church-related schools to ensure that a strictly nonideological posture is maintained.

In *Earley* v. *DiCenso,* a companion case to *Lemon* v. *Kurtzman,* the Court invalidated a Rhode Island statute authorizing salary supplements for teachers of secular subjects in nonpublic schools. The Court expressly rejected the proposition, relied upon by the District Court in the case before us, that it was sufficient for the State to assume that teachers in church-related schools would succeed in segregating their religious beliefs from their secular educational duties. . . .

The prophylactic contacts required to ensure that teachers play a strictly nonideological role, the Court held, necessarily give rise to a constitutionally intolerable degree of entanglement between church and state. . . . The same excessive entanglement would be required for Pennsylvania to be "certain," as it must be, that Act 194 personnel do not advance the religious mission of the church-related schools in which they serve. . . .

That Act 194 authorizes state funding of teachers only for remedial and exceptional students, and not for normal students participating in the core curriculum, does not distinguish this case from *Earley* v. *DiCenso* and *Lemon* v. *Kurtzman.* Whether the subject is "remedial reading," "advanced reading," or simply "reading," a teacher remains a teacher, and the danger that religious doctrine will become intertwined with secular instruction persists. The likelihood of inadvertent fostering of religion may be less in a remedial arithmetic class than in a medieval history seminar, but a diminished probability of impermissible conduct is not sufficient: "The State must be certain, given the Religion Clauses, that subsidized teachers do not inculcate religion." . . . And a state-subsidized guidance counselor is surely as likely as a state-subsidized chemistry teacher to fail on occasion to separate religious instruction and the advancement of religious beliefs from his secular educational responsibilities.

The fact that the teachers and counselors providing auxiliary services are employees of the public intermediate unit, rather than of the church-related schools in which they work, does not substantially eliminate the need for continuing surveillance. To be sure, auxiliary-services personnel, because not employed by the nonpublic schools, are not directly subject to the discipline of a religious authority. . . . But they are performing important educational services in schools in which education is an integral part of the dominant sectarian mission and in which an atmosphere dedicated to the advancement of religious belief is constantly maintained. . . . The potential for impermissible fostering of religion under these circumstances, although somewhat reduced, is nonetheless present. To be certain that auxiliary teachers remain religiously neutral, as the Constitution demands, the State would have to impose limitations on the activities of auxiliary personnel and then engage in some form of continuing surveillance to ensure that those restrictions were being followed.

In addition, Act 194, like the statutes considered in *Lemon* v. *Kurtzman* and *Committee for Public Education & Religious Liberty* v. *Nyquist*, creates a serious potential for divisive conflict over the issue of aid to religion— "entanglement in the broader sense of continuing political strife." . . . The recurrent nature of the appropriation process guarantees annual reconsideration of Act 194 and the prospect of repeated confrontation between proponents and opponents of the auxiliary services program. The Act thus provides successive opportunities for political fragmentation and division along religious lines, one of the principal evils against which the Establishment Clause was intended to protect. . . . This potential for political entanglement, together with the administrative entanglement which would be necessary to ensure that auxiliary-services personnel remain strictly neutral and nonideological when functioning in church-related schools, compels the conclusion that Act 194 violates the constitutional prohibition against laws "respecting an establishment of religion."

The judgment of the District Court as to Act 194 is reversed; its judgment as to the textbook provisions of Act 195 is affirmed, but as to that Act's other provisions now before us its judgment is reversed.

It is so ordered.

Judgment reversed in part and affirmed in part.

NOTES

1. Meetings by students Youth For Christ group after school hours on school property supervised by a faculty sponsor were held to violate the Establishment Clause. Viewed in light of the circumstances in which the school supported religious assemblies by posting religious signs on bulletin boards and making announcements on the school's public address system, the court found both enhancement of religion and excessive entanglement. Nartowicz v. Clayton County School Dist., 736 F.2d 646 (11th Cir. 1984).

2. District policy allowing only two days paid "special leave" did not constitute discrimination against a Jewish teacher under either Title VII of the Civil Rights Act or the Free Exercise Clause. Pinsker v. Joint District, 735 F.2d 388 (10th Cir. 1984).

3. A New York law permitting the state to reimburse parochial schools for state-required record keeping and testing services was held unconstitutional by the United States Supreme Court. The law was found to constitute both direct aid to religion and to involve excessive entanglement. Levitt v. Committee for Public Education and Religious Liberty,

413 U.S. 472, 93 S.Ct. 2814 (1973). After the *Levitt* decision, New York legislated payment for teacher-made tests but required a fiscal audit of funds that *Levitt* did not. The Supreme Court ruled the reimbursement for teacher-made tests now met all constitutional standards because the funds were audited by the State. Committee for Public Education v. Regan, 444 U.S. 646, 100 S.Ct. 840 (1980).

4. In a Vermont suit by a taxpayer against a town school district the question was presented: does the payment of tuition for attendance of students at a religious school by a public entity create a fusion of secular and sectarian education? The court held the payment of students' tuition to the religious denominational high school violates the Federal Constitution. The court quoted the United States Supreme Court in Zorach v. Clauson, 343 U.S. 306, 72 S.Ct. 679 (1952) stating: "Government may not finance religious groups nor undertake religious instruction nor blend secular and sectarian education nor use secular institutions to force one or some religion on any person." Swart v. South Burlington Town School District, 122 Vt. 177, 167 A.2d 514 (1961).

5. In Virginia an Appropriation Act providing money for education of orphans of soldiers, sailors, and marines for tuition, institutional fees, etc., at any educational institution whether public or nonpublic was held to violate the First Amendment and Virginia constitutional prohibitions against public appropriations to schools not under public control. Almond v. Day, 197 Va. 419, 89 S.E.2d 851 (1955).

Tax Deductions Benefiting Parents of Parochial School Children Do Not Violate the Establishment Clause

MUELLER v. ALLEN
Supreme Court of the United States, 1983.
463 U.S. 388, 103 S.Ct. 3062.

Justice REHNQUIST delivered the opinion of the Court.

Minnesota allows taxpayers, in computing their state income tax, to deduct certain expenses incurred in providing for education of their children. . . .

Minnesota, like every other state, provides its citizens with free elementary and secondary schooling. It seems to be agreed that about 820,000 students attended this school system in the most recent school year. During the same year, approximately 91,000 elementary and secondary students attended some 500 privately supported schools located in Minnesota, and about 95% of these students attended schools considering themselves to be sectarian.

Minnesota, by a law originally enacted in 1955 and revised in 1976 and again in 1978, permits state taxpayers to claim a deduction from gross income for certain expenses incurred in educating their children. The deduction is limited to actual expenses incurred for the "tuition, textbooks and transportation" of dependents attending elementary or secondary schools. A deduction may not exceed $500 per dependent in grades K through six and $700 per dependent in grades seven through twelve. . . .

Today's case is no exception to our oft-repeated statement that the Establishment Clause presents especially difficult questions of interpretation and application. It is easy enough to quote the few words comprising that clause—"Congress shall make no law respecting an establishment of religion." It is not at all easy, however, to apply this Court's various decisions construing the Clause to governmental programs of financial assistance to sectarian schools and the parents of children attending those schools. Indeed, in many of these decisions "we have expressly or implicitly acknowledged that 'we can only dimly perceive the lines of demarcation in this extraordinarily sensitive area of constitutional law.'" Lemon v. Kurtzman, 403 U.S. 602, 609, 612, 91 S.Ct 2105, 2109, 2111, 29 L.Ed.2d 745 (1971), quoted with approval in Nyquist, 413 U.S., at 761, 93 S.Ct. at 2959.

One fixed principle in this field is our consistent rejection of the argument that "any program which in some manner aids an institution with a religious affiliation" violates the Establishment Clause. . . .

Petitioners place particular reliance on our decision in Committee for Public Education v. Nyquist, supra, where we held invalid a New York statute providing public funds for the maintenance and repair of the physical facilities of private schools and granting thinly disguised "tax benefits," actually amounting to tuition grants, to the parents of children attending private schools. As explained below, we conclude that § 290.09(22) bears less resemblance to the arrangement struck down in Nyquist than it does to assistance programs upheld in our prior decisions and those discussed with approval in Nyquist.

The general nature of our inquiry in this area has been guided, since the decision in Lemon v. Kurtzman, 403 U.S. 602, 91 S.Ct. 2105, 29 L.Ed.2d 745 (1971), by the "three-part" test laid down in that case:

> First, the statute must have a secular legislative purpose; second, its principal or primary effect must be one that neither advances nor inhibits religion . . . ; finally, the statute must not foster "an excessive government entanglement with religion." Ibid., at 612–613, 91 S.Ct., at 2111.

While this principle is well settled, our cases have also emphasized that it provides "no more than [a] helpful signpost" in dealing with Establishment Clause challenges. Hunt v. McNair, 413 U.S., at 741, 93 S.Ct., at 2873. With this caveat in mind, we turn to the specific challenges raised against § 290.09(22) under the Lemon framework.

Little time need be spent on the question of whether the Minnesota tax deduction has a secular purpose. Under our prior decisions, governmental assistance programs have consistently survived this inquiry even when they have run afoul of other aspects of the Lemon framework. See, e.g., Lemon v. Kurtzman, supra; Meek v. Pittenger, 421 U.S., at 363, 95 S.Ct., at 1762; Wolman v. Walter, 433 U.S., at 236, 97 S.Ct., at 2599. This reflects, at least in part, our reluctance to attribute unconstitutional motives to the states, particularly when a plausible secular purpose for the state's program may be discerned from the face of the statute.

A state's decision to defray the cost of educational expenses incurred by parents—regardless of the type of schools their children attend—evidences a purpose that is both secular and understandable. . . .

We turn therefore to the more difficult but related question whether the Minnesota statute has "the primary effect of advancing the sectarian aims of the nonpublic schools." In concluding that it does not, we find several features of the Minnesota tax deduction particularly significant. First, an essential feature of Minnesota's arrangement is the fact that § 290.09(22) is only one among many deductions—such as those for medical expenses, Minn. Stat. § 290.09(10) and charitable contributions, Minn.Stat. § 290.21—available under the Minnesota tax laws. . . . . Under our prior decisions, the Minnesota legislature's judgment that a deduction for educational expenses fairly equalizes the tax burden of its citizens and encourages desirable expenditures for educational purposes is entitled to substantial deference.

Other characteristics of § 290.09(22) argue equally strongly for the provision's constitutionality. Most importantly, the deduction is available for educational expenses incurred by *all* parents, including those whose children attend public schools and those whose children attend nonsectarian private schools or sectarian private schools. . . .

In this respect, as well as others, this case is vitally different from the scheme struck down in *Nyquist*. There, public assistance amounting to tuition grants, was provided only to parents of children in *nonpublic* schools. This fact had considerable bearing on our decision striking down the New York statute at issue; we explicitly distinguished both *Allen* and *Everson* on the grounds that "In both cases the class of beneficiaries included *all* schoolchildren, those in public as well as those in private schools." Moreover, we intimated that "public assistance (e.g., scholarships) made available generally without regard to the sectarian-nonsectarian or public-nonpublic nature of the institution benefited," might not offend the Establishment Clause. We think the tax deduction adopted by Minnesota is more similar to this latter type of program than it is to the arrangement struck down in *Nyquist*. . . .

We also agree with the Court of Appeals that, by channeling whatever assistance it may provide to parochial schools through individual parents, Minnesota has reduced the Establishment Clause objections to which its action is subject. It is true, of course, that financial assistance provided to parents ultimately has an economic effect comparable to that of aid given directly to the schools attended by their children. It is also true, however, that under Minnesota's arrangement public funds become available only as a result of numerous, private choices of individual parents of school-age children. For these reasons, we recognized in *Nyquist* that the means by which state assistance flows to private schools is of some importance: we said that "the fact that aid is disbursed to parents rather than to . . . schools" is a material consideration in Establishment Clause analysis, albeit "only one among many to be considered." . . .

We find it useful, in the light of the foregoing characteristics of § 290.09(22), to compare the attenuated financial benefits flowing to parochial schools from the section to the evils against which the Establishment Clause was designed to protect. These dangers are well-described by our statement that "what is at stake as a matter of policy [in Establishment Clause cases] is preventing that kind and degree of government involvement in religious life that, as history teaches us, is apt to lead to strife and frequently strain a political system to the breaking point." It is important, however, to "keep these issues in perspective.":

> At this point in the 20th century we are quite far removed from the dangers that prompted the Framers to include the Establishment Clause in the Bill of Rights. The risk of significant religious or denominational control over our democratic processes—or even of deep political division along religious lines— is remote, and when viewed against the positive contributions of sectarian schools and such risk seems entirely tolerable in light of the continuing oversight of this Court. *Wolman,* 433 U.S., at 263, 97 S.Ct., at 2613.

The Establishment Clause of course extends beyond prohibition of a state church or payment of state funds to one or more churches. We do not think, however, that its prohibition extends to the type of tax deduction established by Minnesota. The historic purposes of the clause simply do not encompass the sort of attenuated financial benefit, ultimately controlled by the private choices of individual parents, that eventually flows to parochial schools from the neutrally available tax benefit at issue in this case.

Petitioners argue that, notwithstanding the facial neutrality of § 290.09(22), in application the statute primarily benefits religious institutions. Petitioners rely, as they did below, on a statistical analysis of the type of persons claiming the tax deduction. They contend that most parents of public school children incur no tuition expenses, and that other expenses deductible under § 290.09(22) are negligible in value; moreover, they claim that 96% of the children in private schools in 1978–1979 attended religiously-affiliated institutions. Because of all this, they reason, the bulk of deductions taken under § 290.09(22) will be claimed by parents of children in sectarian schools. Respondents reply that petitioners have failed to consider the impact of deductions for items such as transportation, summer school tuition, tuition paid by parents whose children attended schools outside the school districts in which they resided, rental or purchase costs for a variety of equipment, and tuition for certain types of instruction not ordinarily provided in public schools.

We need not consider these contentions in detail. We would be loath to adopt a rule grounding the constitutionality of a facially neutral law on annual reports reciting the extent to which various classes of private citizens claimed benefits under the law. Such an approach would scarcely provide the certainty that this field stands in need of, nor can we perceive principled standards by which such statistical evidence might be evaluated. Moreover, the fact that private persons fail in a particular year to claim the tax relief to which they are entitled—under a facially neutral statute—should be of little importance in determining the constitutionality of the statute permitting such relief.

Finally, private educational institutions, and parents paying for their children to attend these schools, make special contributions to the areas in which they operate. "Parochial schools, quite apart from their sectarian purpose, have provided an educational alternative for millions of young Americans; they often afford wholesome competition with our public schools; and in some States they relieve substantially the tax burden incident to the operation of public schools." *Wolman,* at 262, 97 S.Ct., at 2613 (POWELL, J., concurring and dissenting). If parents of children in private schools choose to take especial advantage of the relief provided by § 290.09(22), it is no doubt due to the fact that they bear a particularly great financial burden in educating their children. More fundamentally, whatever unequal effect may be attributed to the statutory classification can fairly be regarded as a rough return for the benefits, discussed above, provided to the state and all taxpayers by parents sending their children to parochial schools. In the light of all this, we believe it wiser to decline to engage in the type of empirical inquiry into those persons benefited by state law which petitioners urge.

Thus, we hold that the Minnesota tax deduction for educational expenses satisfies the primary effect inquiry of our Establishment Clause cases.

Turning to the third part of the *Lemon* inquiry, we have no difficulty in concluding that the Minnesota statute does not "excessively entangle" the state in religion. The only plausible source of the "comprehensive, discriminating, and continuing state surveillance" necessary to run afoul of this standard would lie in the fact that state officials must determine whether particular textbooks qualify for a deduction. In making this decision, state officials must disallow deductions taken from "instructional books and materials used in the teaching of religious tenets, doctrines or worship, the purpose of which is to inculcate such tenets, doctrines or worship." Making decisions such as this does not differ substantially from making the types of decisions approved in earlier opinions of this Court. In Board of Education v. Allen, 392 U.S. 236, 88 S.Ct. 1923, 20 L.Ed.2d 1060 (1968), for example, the Court upheld the loan of secular textbooks to parents or children attending nonpublic schools; though state officials were required to determine whether particular books were or were not secular, the system was held not to violate the Establishment Clause. See also *Wolman* v. *Walter; Meek* v. *Pittenger.* The same result follows in this case.

For the foregoing reasons, the judgment of the Court of Appeals is Affirmed.

NOTES

1. Justice Marshall, in writing the dissenting opinion in *Mueller,* in which Justices Brennan, Blackmun, and Stevens joined, maintained that the Minnesota law was, in fact, aid to parochial schools disguised as a tax deduction to *all* parents of school children. The Justice said:

   The majority first attempts to distinguish *Nyquist* on the ground that Minnesota makes all parents eligible to deduct up to $500 or $700 for each dependent, whereas the New York law allowed a deduction only for parents whose children attended nonpublic schools. Although Minnesota taxpayers who send their children to local public schools may not deduct tuition expenses because they incur none, they may deduct other expenses, such as the cost of gym clothes, pencils, and notebooks, which are shared by all parents of school-age children. This, in the majority's view, distinguishes the Minnesota scheme from the law at issue in *Nyquist*.

That the Minnesota statute makes some small benefit available to all parents cannot alter the fact that the most substantial benefit provided by the statute is available only to those parents who send their children to schools that charge tuition. It is simply undeniable that the single largest expense that may be deducted under the Minnesota statute is tuition. The statute is little more than a subsidy of tuition masquerading as a subsidy of general educational expenses. The other deductible expenses are *de minimis* in comparison to tuition expenses.

Contrary to the majority's suggestion, . . ., the bulk of the tax benefits afforded by the Minnesota scheme are enjoyed by parents of parochial school children not because parents of public school children fail to claim deductions to which they are entitled, but because the latter are simply *unable* to claim the largest tax deduction that Minnesota authorizes. Fewer than 100 of more than 900,000 school-age children in Minnesota attend public schools that charge a general tuition. Of the total number of taxpayers who are eligible for the tuition deduction, approximately 96% send their children to religious schools. Parents who send their children to free public schools are simply ineligible to obtain the full benefit of the deduction except in the unlikely event that they buy $700 worth of pencils, notebooks, and bus rides for their school-age children. Yet parents who pay at least $700 in tuition to nonpublic, sectarian schools can claim the full deduction even if they incur no other educational expenses. . . .

In this case, it is undisputed that well over 90% of the children attending tuition-charging schools in Minnesota are enrolled in sectarian schools. History and experience likewise instruct us that any generally available financial assistance for elementary and secondary school tuition expenses mainly will further religious education because the majority of the schools which charge tuition are sectarian. Because Minnesota, like every other State, is committed to providing free public education, tax assistance for tuition payments inevitably redounds to the benefit of nonpublic, sectarian schools and parents who send their children to those schools. . . .

There can be little doubt that the State of Minnesota intended to provide, and has provided, "[s]ubstantial aid to the educational function of [church-related] schools," and that the tax deduction for tuition and other educational expenses "necessarily results in aid to the sectarian school enterprise as a whole." Meek v. Pittenger, 421 U.S., at 366, 95 S.Ct., at 1763. It is beside the point that the State may have legitimate secular reasons for providing such aid. In focusing upon the contributions made by church-related schools, the majority has lost sight of the issue before us in this case.

> "The sole question is whether state aid to these schools can be squared with the dictates of the Religion Clauses. Under our system the choice has been made that government is to be entirely excluded from the area of religious instruction. . . . The Constitution decrees that religion must be a private matter for the individual, the family, and the institutions of private choice, and that while some involvement and entanglement are inevitable, lines must be drawn." Lemon v. Kurtzman, 403 U.S. 602, 625, 91 S.Ct. 2105, 2117, 29 L.Ed.2d 745 (1971).

2. Separation of church and state requirement prohibits courts from intervening in religious disputes involving matters of doctrine. Reardon v. Lemoyne, 122 N.H. 1042, 454 A.2d 428 (1982).

State Funding of Certain Services to
Parochial School Students is
Constitutional

WOLMAN v. WALTER

Supreme Court of the United States, 1977.
433 U.S. 229, 97 S.Ct. 2593.

Mr. Justice BLACKMUN, delivered the opinion of the Court . . ..

This is still another case presenting the recurrent issue of the limitations imposed by the Establishment Clause of the First Amendment, made applicable to the States by the Fourteenth Amendment, Meek v. Pittenger, on state aid to pupils in church-related elementary and secondary schools.
. . .

Section 3317.06 was enacted after this Court's May 1975 decision in Meek v. Pittenger, supra, and obviously is an attempt to conform to the teachings of that decision. . . . In broad outline, the statute authorizes the State to provide nonpublic school pupils with books, instructional materials and equipment, standardized testing and scoring, diagnostic services, therapeutic services, and field trip transportation.

The initial biennial appropriation by the Ohio Legislature for implementation of the statute was the sum of $88,800,000. Funds so appropriated are paid to the State's public school districts and are then expended by them. All disbursements made with respect to nonpublic schools have their equivalents in disbursements for public schools, and the amount expended per pupil in nonpublic schools may not exceed the amount expended per pupil in the public schools.

The parties stipulated that during the 1974–1975 school year there were 720 chartered nonpublic schools in Ohio. Of these, all but 29 were sectarian. More than 96% of the nonpublic enrollment attended sectarian schools, and more than 92% attended Catholic schools. . . .

The mode of analysis for Establishment Clause questions is defined by the three-part test that has emerged from the Court's decisions. . . .

In the present case we have no difficulty with the first prong of this three-part test. We are satisfied that the challenged statute reflects Ohio's legitimate interest in protecting the health of its youth and in providing a fertile educational environment for all the school children of the State. As is usual in our cases, the analytical difficulty has to do with the effect and entanglement criteria.

We have acknowledged before, and we do so again here, that the wall of separation that must be maintained between church and state "is a blurred, indistinct, and variable barrier depending on all the circumstances of a particular relationship." . . . Nonetheless, the Court's numerous precedents "have become firmly rooted," . . . and now provide substantial guidance. We therefore turn to the task of applying the rules derived from our decisions to the respective provisions of the statute at issue.

Textbooks

Section 3317.06 authorizes the expenditure of funds:

"(A) To purchase such secular textbooks as have been approved by the superintendent of public instruction for use in public schools in the state and to loan such textbooks to pupils attending nonpublic schools within the district or to their parents. . . .

This system for the loan of textbooks to individual students bears a striking resemblance to the systems approved in Board of Education v. Allen, and in Meek v. Pittenger. . . . As read, the statute provides the same protections against abuse as were provided in the textbook programs under consideration in *Allen* and in *Meek*.

In the alternative, appellants urge that we overrule *Allen* and *Meek*. This we decline to do. Accordingly, we conclude that § 3317.06(A) is constitutional.

Testing and Scoring

Section 3317.06 authorizes expenditure of funds:

"(J) To supply for use by pupils attending nonpublic schools within the district such standardized tests and scoring services as are in use in the public schools of the state."

These tests "are used to measure the progress of students in secular subjects." Nonpublic school personnel are not involved in either the drafting or scoring of the tests. The statute does not authorize any payment to nonpublic school personnel for the costs of administering the tests. . . .

The State may require that schools that are utilized to fulfill the State's compulsory education requirement meet certain standards of instruction, ... The nonpublic school does not control the content of the test or its result. This serves to prevent the use of the test as a part of religious teaching, and thus avoids that kind of direct aid to religion found present in *Levitt*. Similarly, the inability of the school to control the test eliminates the need for the supervision that gives rise to excessive entanglement. We therefore agree with the District Court's conclusion that § 3317.06(J) is constitutional.

Diagnostic Services

Section 3317.06 authorizes expenditures of funds:

"(D) To provide speech and hearing diagnostic services to pupils attending nonpublic schools within the district. Such service shall be provided in the nonpublic school attended by the pupil receiving the service. . . .

"(F) To provide diagnostic psychological services to pupils attending nonpublic schools within the district. Such services shall be provided in the school attended by the pupil receiving the service."

It will be observed that these speech and hearing and psychological diagnostic services are to be provided within the nonpublic school. . . .

The District Court found these dangers so insubstantial as not to render the statute unconstitutional. We agree. This Court's decisions contain a common thread to the effect that the provision of health services to all school children—public and nonpublic—does not have the primary effect of aiding religion. . . .

In *Meek* the Court did hold unconstitutional a portion of a Pennsylvania statute at issue there that authorized certain auxiliary services—"remedial and accelerated instruction, guidance counseling and testing, speech and hearing services"—on nonpublic school premises. . . . The Court in *Meek* explicitly stated, however, that the provision of diagnostic speech and hearing services by Pennsylvania seemed "to fall within that class of general welfare services for children that may be provided by the State regardless of the incidental benefit that accrues to church-related schools." . . .

The reason for considering diagnostic services to be different from teaching or counseling is readily apparent. First, diagnostic services, unlike teaching or counseling, have little or no educational content and are not closely associated with the educational mission of the nonpublic school. . . . Second, the diagnostician has only limited contact with the child, and that contact involves chiefly the use of objective and professional testing methods to detect students in need of treatment. The nature of the relationship between the diagnostician and the pupil does not provide the same opportunity for the transmission of sectarian views as attends the relationship between teacher and student or that between counselor and student.

We conclude that providing diagnostic services on the nonpublic school premises will not create an impermissible risk of the fostering of ideological views. It follows that there is no need for excessive surveillance, and there will not be impermissible entanglement. We therefore hold that §§ 3317.06(D) and (F) are constitutional.

Therapeutic Services

Sections 3317.06(G), (H), (I), and (K) authorize expenditures of funds for certain therapeutic, guidance, and remedial services for students who have been identified as having a need for specialized attention. Personnel providing the services must be employees of the local board of education or under contract with the State Department of Health. The services are to be performed only in public schools, in public centers, or in mobile units located off the nonpublic school premises. . . .

At the outset, we note that in its present posture the case does not properly present any issue concerning the use of a public facility as an adjunct of a sectarian educational enterprise. The District Court construed the statute, as do we, to authorize services only on sites that are "neither physically nor educationally identified with the functions of the nonpublic school." Thus, the services are to be offered under circumstances that reflect their religious neutrality. . . .

The fact that a unit on a neutral site on occasion may serve only sectarian pupils does not provoke the same concerns that troubled the Court in *Meek*. The influence on a therapist's behavior that is exerted by the fact that he serves a sectarian pupil is qualitatively different from the influence of the pervasive atmosphere of a religious institution. The dangers perceived in *Meek* arose from the nature of the institution, not from the nature of the pupils.

Accordingly, we hold that providing therapeutic and remedial services at a neutral site off the premises of the nonpublic schools will not have the impermissible effect of advancing religion. Neither will there be any excessive entanglement arising from supervision of public employees to insure that they maintain a neutral stance. It can hardly be said that the supervision of public employees performing public functions on public property creates an excessive entanglement between church and state. Sections 3317.06(G), (H), (I), and (K) are constitutional.

Instructional Materials and Equipment

Sections 3317.06(B) and (C) authorize expenditures of funds for the purchase and loan to pupils or their parents upon individual request of instructional materials and instructional equipment of the kind in use in the public schools within the district and which is "incapable of diversion to religious use." Section 3717.06 also provides that the materials and equipment may be stored on the premises of a nonpublic school and that publicly hired personnel who administer the lending program may perform their services upon the nonpublic school premises when necessary "for efficient implementation of the lending program." . . .

Appellees seek to avoid *Meek* by emphasizing that it involved a program of direct loans to nonpublic schools. In contrast, the material and equipment at issue under the Ohio statute are loaned to the pupil or his parent. In our view, however, it would exalt form over substance if this distinction were found to justify a result different from that in *Meek*. . . . In view of the impossibility of separating the secular education function from the sectarian, the state aid inevitably flows in part in support of the religious role of the schools.

If a grant in cash to parents is impermissible, we fail to see how a grant in kind of goods furthering the religious enterprise can fare any better. Accordingly, we hold §§ 3317.06(B) and (C) to be unconstitutional.

Field Trips

Section 3317.06 also authorizes expenditures of funds:

"(L) To provide such field trip transportation and services to nonpublic school students as are provided to public school students in the district. . . .

There is no restriction on the timing of field trips; the only restriction on number lies in the parallel the statute draws to field trips provided to public school students in the district. The parties have stipulated that the trips "would consist of visits to governmental, industrial, cultural, and scientific centers designed to enrich the secular studies of students." The choice of destination, however, will be made by the nonpublic school teacher from a wide range of locations.

The District Court, held this feature to be constitutionally indistinguishable from that with which the Court was concerned in Everson v. Board of Education. We do not agree. . . .

The Ohio situation is in sharp contrast. First, the nonpublic school controls the timing of the trips and, within a certain range, their frequency and destinations. Thus, the schools, rather than the children, truly are the recipients of the service and, as this Court has recognized, this fact alone may be sufficient to invalidate the program as impermissible direct aid. . . . Second, although a trip may be to a location that would be of interest to those in public schools, it is the individual teacher who makes a field trip meaningful. . . . The field trips are an integral part of the educational experience, and where the teacher works within and for a sectarian institution, an unacceptable risk of fostering of religion is an inevitable byproduct. . . . Funding of field trips, therefore, must be treated as was the funding of maps and charts in Meek v. Pittenger, supra, the funding of buildings and tuition in Committee for Public Education v. Nyquist, supra, and the funding of teacher-prepared tests in Levitt v. Committee for Public Education; it must be declared an impermissible direct aid to sectarian education.

Moreover, the public school authorities will be unable adequately to insure secular use of the field trip funds without close supervision of the nonpublic teachers. This would create excessive entanglement: . . . .

We hold § 3317.06(L) to be unconstitutional.

In summary, we hold constitutional those portions of the Ohio statute authorizing the State to provide nonpublic school pupils with books, standardized testing and scoring, diagnostic services, and therapeutic and remedial services. We hold unconstitutional those portions relating to instructional materials and equipment and field trip services. . . .

NOTE

A U.S. Court of Appeals has held that Title I, ESEA (now Chapter 1) as applied to parochial schools in New York City violates the Establishment Clause. The program provides funds for itinerate teachers to teach deprived children in nonpublic schools; 84 percent of the nonpublic school students in New York City are in Catholic schools. Felton v. Secretary, U.S.Dept. of Education, 739 F.2d 48 (2nd Cir.1984). This decision has been appealed and was argued before the U.S. Supreme Court on December 5, 1984. In view of the high courts changing philosophy on church-state matters, the *Felton* decision may well be overturned.

RELEASED TIME FOR RELIGIOUS INSTRUCTION

The practice of releasing public school children during regular school hours for religious instruction first began in the United States in Gary, Indiana, in 1914. Since then, the Supreme Court has had before it two cases involving release time. The first was the *McCollum* case in 1948,[51] in which pupils were released to attend religious instruction in the classrooms of the public school building. Students who did not want to participate were not released, but were required to leave their classrooms and go to another part of the building to pursue their secular studies. The Supreme Court held that this "release time" program violated the First Amendment of the Constitution.

In 1952, the Supreme Court was once again called upon to test the constitutionality of "release time." In this case a New York statute permitted pupils to leave the school building and grounds to attend religious centers for religious instruction.[52] Students who did not wish to participate in such services stayed in their classrooms, and no supervision or approval of their activities was required. The Supreme Court found that this statute did not violate the doctrine of separation of church and state. The Court pointed out that while the Constitution forbids the government financing of religious groups and the promotion of religious instruction, the First Amendment does not require governmental hostility toward religion. From this decision it is clear that the Supreme Court does not prohibit some cooperation between schools and churches, but the nature and degree of the cooperation is important; and, if it exceeds certain reasonable limitations, the relationship will violate the Constitution.

*Released Time for Religious
Instruction on Public School Premises
Is Unconstitutional*

PEOPLE OF STATE OF ILLINOIS EX REL. McCOLLUM v. BOARD OF EDUCATION OF SCHOOL DISTRICT NO. 71, CHAMPAIGN COUNTY, ILLINOIS

Supreme Court of the United States, 1948.
333 U.S. 203, 68 S.Ct. 461.

Mr. Justice BLACK delivered the opinion of the Court.

This case relates to the power of a state to utilize its tax-supported public school system in aid of religious instruction insofar as that power may be restricted by the First and Fourteenth Amendments to the Federal Constitution. . . .

Appellant's petition for mandamus alleged that religious teachers, employed by private religious groups, were permitted to come weekly into the school buildings during the regular hours set apart for secular teaching, and then and there for a period of thirty minutes substitute their religious teaching for the secular education provided under the compulsory education law. The petitioner charged that this joint public-school religious-group program violated the First and Fourteenth Amendments to the United States Constitution. The prayer of her petition was that the Board of Education be ordered to "adopt and enforce rules and regulations prohibiting all instruction in and teaching of all religious education in all public schools in Champaign District Number 71 . . . and in all public school houses and buildings in said district when occupied by public schools." . . .

Although there are disputes between the parties as to various inferences that may or may not properly be drawn from the evidence concerning the religious program, the following facts are shown by the record without dispute. In 1940 interested members of the Jewish, Roman Catholic, and a few of the Protestant faiths formed a voluntary association called the Champaign Council on Religious Education. They obtained permission from the Board of Education to offer classes in religious instruction to public school pupils in grades four to nine inclusive. Classes were made up of pupils whose parents signed printed cards requesting that their children be permitted to attend; they were held weekly, thirty minutes for the lower grades, forty-five minutes for the higher. The council employed the religious teachers at no expense to the school authorities, but the instructors were subject to the approval and supervision of the superintendent of schools. The classes were taught in three separate religious groups by Protestant teachers, Catholic priests, and a Jewish rabbi, although for the past several years there have apparently been no classes instructed in the Jewish religion. Classes were conducted in the regular classrooms of the school building. Students who did not choose to take the religious instruction were not released from public school duties; they were required to leave their classrooms and go to some other place in the school building for pursuit of their secular studies. On the other hand, students who were released from secular study for the religious instructions were required to be present at the religious classes. Reports of their presence or absence were to be made to their secular teachers.

The foregoing facts, without reference to others that appear in the record, show the use of tax-supported property for religious instruction and the close cooperation between the school authorities and the religious council in promoting religious education. The operation of the state's compulsory education system thus assists and is integrated with the program of religious instruction carried on by separate religious sects. Pupils compelled by law to go to school for secular education are released in part from their legal duty upon the condition that they attend the religious classes. This is beyond all question a utilization of the tax-established and tax-supported public school system to aid religious groups to spread their faith. And it falls squarely under the ban of the First Amendment (made applicable to the States by the Fourteenth) as we interpreted it in Everson v. Board of Education, 330 U.S. 1, 67 S.Ct. 504. . . .

To hold that a state cannot consistently with the First and Fourteenth Amendments utilize its public school system to aid any or all religious faiths or sects in the dissemination of their doctrines and ideals does not, as counsel urge, manifest a governmental hostility to religion or religious teachings. A manifestation of such hostility would be at war with our national tradition as embodied in the First Amendment's guaranty of the free exercise of religion. For the First Amendment rests upon the premise that both religion and government can best work to achieve their lofty aims if each is left free from the other within its respective sphere. Or, as we said in the *Everson* case, the First Amendment has erected a wall between Church and State which must be kept high and impregnable.

Here not only are the state's tax-supported public school buildings used for the dissemination of religious doctrines. The State also affords sectarian groups an invaluable aid in that it helps to provide pupils for their religious classes through use of the state's compulsory public school machinery. This is not separation of Church and State.

The cause is reversed and remanded to the State Supreme Court for proceedings not inconsistent with this opinion.

Reversed and remanded.

NOTE

Released Time. Courts upholding discretionary power of boards of education to provide released time programs: People ex rel. Lewis v. Graves, 245 N.Y. 195, 156 N.E. 663 (1927); People ex rel. Latimer v. Board of Education of City of Chicago, 394 Ill. 228, 68 N.E.2d 305 (1946); Dilger v. School District, 222 Or. 108, 352 P.2d 564 (1960). Some decisions indicated parents had the right to have children excused or released from school for religious purposes: Lewis v. Spaulding, 193 Misc. 66, 85 N.Y.S.2d 682 (1948), appeal dismissed 299 N.Y. 564, 85 N.E.2d 791 (1949); Gordon v. Board of Education of City of Los Angeles, 78 Cal.App.2d 464, 178 P.2d 488 (1947); Perry v. School District No. 61, Spokane, 54 Wa.2d 886, 344 P.2d 1036 (1959).

*Released Time for Public School
Students to Attend Religious Classes
Off Public School Grounds Is
Constitutional*

ZORACH v. CLAUSON

Supreme Court of the United States, 1952.
343 U.S. 306, 72 S.Ct. 679.

Mr. Justice DOUGLAS delivered the opinion of the Court.

New York City has a program which permits its public schools to release students during the school day so that they may leave the school buildings and school grounds and go to religious centers for religious instruction or devotional exercises. A student is released on written request of his parents. Those not released stay in the classrooms. The churches make weekly reports to the schools, sending a list of children who have been released from public school but who have not reported for religious instruction.

This "released time" program involves neither religious instruction in public school classrooms nor the expenditure of public funds. All costs, including the application blanks, are paid by the religious organizations. The case is therefore unlike McCollum v. Board of Education, 333 U.S. 203, 68 S.Ct. 461, 92 L.Ed. 249, which involved a "released time" program from Illinois. In that case the classrooms were turned over to religious instructors. We accordingly held that the program violated the First Amendment which (by reason of the Fourteenth Amendment) prohibits the states from establishing religion or prohibiting its free exercise.

Appellants, who are taxpayers and residents of New York City and whose children attend its public schools, challenge the present law, contending it is in essence not different from the one involved in the *McCollum* case. Their argument, stated elaborately in various ways, reduces itself to this: the weight and influence of the school is put behind a program for religious instruction; public school teachers police it, keeping tab on students who are released; the classroom activities come to a halt while the students who are released for religious instruction are on leave; the school is a crutch on which the churches are leaning for support in their religious training; without the cooperation of the schools this "released time" program, like the one in the *McCollum* case, would be futile and ineffective. The New York Court of Appeals sustained the law against this claim of unconstitutionality. . . .

It takes obtuse reasoning to inject any issue of the "free exercise" of religion into the present case. No one is forced to go to the religious classroom and no religious exercise or instruction is brought to the classrooms of the public schools. A student need not take religious instruction. He is left to his own desires as to the manner or time of his religious devotions, if any.

There is a suggestion that the system involves the use of coercion to get public school students into religious classrooms. There is no evidence in the record before us that supports that conclusion. The present record indeed tells us that the school authorities are neutral in this regard and do no more than release students whose parents so request. If in fact coercion were used, if it were established that any one or more teachers were using their office to persuade or force students to take the religious instruction a wholly different case would be presented. Hence we put aside that claim of coercion both as respects the "free exercise" of religion and "an establishment of religion" within the meaning of the First Amendment. . . .

We would have to press the concept of separation of Church and State to these extremes to condemn the present law on constitutional grounds. . . .

We are a religious people whose institutions presuppose a Supreme Being. We guarantee the freedom to worship as one chooses. We make room for as wide a variety of beliefs and creeds as the spiritual needs of man deem necessary. We sponsor an attitude on the part of government that shows no partiality to any one group and that lets each flourish according to the zeal of its adherents and the appeal of its dogma. When the state encourages religious instruction or cooperates with religious authorities by adjusting the schedule of public events to sectarian needs, it follows the best of our traditions. For it then respects the religious nature of our people and accommodates the public service to their spiritual needs. To hold that it may not would be to find in the Constitution a requirement that the government show a callous indifference to religious groups. That would be preferring those who believe in no religion over those who do believe. Government may not finance religious groups nor undertake religious instruction nor blend secular and sectarian education nor use secular institutions to force one or some religion on any person. But we find no constitutional requirement which makes it necessary for government to be hostile to religion and to throw its weight against efforts to widen the effective scope of religious influence. The government must be neutral when it comes to competition between sects. It may not thrust any sect on any person. It may not make a religious observance compulsory. It may not coerce anyone to attend church, to observe a religious holiday, or to take religious instruction. But it can close its doors or suspend its operations as to those who want to repair to their religious sanctuary for worship or instruction. No more than that is undertaken here. . . .

In the *McCollum* case the classrooms were used for religious instruction and the force of the public school was used to promote that instruction. Here, as we have said, the public schools do no more than accommodate their schedules to a program of outside religious instruction. We follow the *McCollum* case. But we cannot expand it to cover the present released time program unless separation of Church and State means that public institutions can make no adjustments of their schedules to accommodate the religious needs of the people. We cannot read into the Bill of Rights such a philosophy of hostility to religion.

Affirmed.

NOTES

1. *Shared Time.* "Dual Enrollment" or "shared time" is an arrangement between a public school and a private school by which the shared use of the public school facilities is provided for private school teachers or students. A pupil may be a part-time student in a public school while concurrently attending a nonpublic school part-time.

2. Shared time and community education programs in leased parochial school facilities have been held to be unconstitutional. The classes were taught and controlled by religious schools, the majority of board administrators and teachers were adherents to a particular religious faith, over $6 million in tax funds had been expended, and a substantial number of the teachers employed in the Shared Time program had previously been employed at the same parochial school. Americans United for Separation of Church and State v. School District, 718 F.2d 1389 (6th Cir.1983).

3. The United States Court of Appeals, Tenth Circuit, has held that provisions in a released time program, in which students attended church-related seminaries and received public school credit for classes that were "mainly denominational" in content, was unconstitutional. Unconstitutional, also was a procedure whereby the public school bore the burden of gathering the seminary's attendance slips. Lanner v. Wimmer, 662 F.2d 1349 (10th Cir.1981).

4. In a case involving "shared time" the Supreme Court of Missouri held that use of public moneys to send speech teachers of a school district into parochial schools for speech therapy was not for the purpose of maintaining free public schools and was therefore unconstitutional (Section 5 of Article IX, Missouri Constitution). Also, when the school district provided speech therapy for parochial school children in buildings maintained by the school district and parochial children who desired such therapy were released from school for part of their regular six-hour day, such practice violated compulsory attendance laws that required each school

child to attend school regularly for six hours a school day. Special District for the Education and Training of Handicapped Children of St. Louis County v. Wheeler, 408 S.W.2d 60 (Mo.1966).

5. An Illinois court reached a conclusion different from that of the Missouri court concerning shared time. Plaintiffs in this case sought to enjoin the Board of Education from maintaining a dual enrollment program where children were enrolled part-time in a public school and part-time in a nonpublic school, on the grounds that the program violated statutory and constitutional provisions. The court held that the dual enrollment program did not violate either statutory or constitutional provisions.

The object of compulsory attendance law is that all children be educated and not that they be educated in any particular manner or place, and part-time enrollment in a public school and part-time enrollment in a nonpublic school under a dual enrollment program is permitted so long as the child receives a complete education. Morton v. Board of Education of City of Chicago, 69 Ill. App.2d 38, 216 N.E.2d 305 (1966).

6. How does the released time program of the *Zorach* case differ from the program in the *McCollum* case?

7. What does the court say about the relationship between church and state? What is the role of the state in dealing with religion?

8. Relate the reasoning in the decisions by the Supreme Court in *McCollum* and *Zorach* to the concept of dual enrollment. What legal principles of the cases may be applied in a case involving dual enrollment?

9. In regard to a shared time program where the school district leased parochial school facilities and public school teachers taught classes therein, the court held that neither the state nor federal constitutions were violated. This was true even in light of the fact that classes were conducted in the same building. Citizens to Advance Public Education v. Porter, 65 Mich.App. 168, 237 N.W.2d 232 (1975).

10. Public school policy denying admission to courses of all but full-time public school students does not violate nonpublic students' constitutional rights. When a girl enrolled in a private school sought to take band at the public school and was excluded, the court said that the school's rationale—that the admission of part-time students would cause dilution of the school program for full-time students and that permitting part-time admission would cause an overall decline in full-time student enrollment, resulting in a loss of state aid—was reasonable and rationally related to the operation of a public school district. Snyder v. Charlotte Public School District, 123 Mich.App. 56, 333 N.W.2d 542 (1983).

PRAYER AND BIBLE READING IN THE PUBLIC SCHOOLS

Prayer and Bible reading in the public schools have been the source of much judicial controversy. Over half the states have, at some point, permitted or required prayer and Bible reading in public schools. Prior to 1962, at least twelve states and the District of Columbia required Bible reading. The typical attitude of the courts was that the Bible and general prayer were not sectarian in nature, and their use did not violate constitutional religious guarantees.[53] That the Bible was not sectarian was even reflected in statute; the North Dakota legislature had provided:

> The Bible shall not be deemed a sectarian book. It shall not be excluded from any public school. It may at the option of the teacher be read in school without sectarian comment, not to exceed ten minutes daily. No pupil shall be required to read it nor be present in the schoolroom during the reading thereof contrary to the wishes of his parents or guardian or other person having him in charge.[54]

Voluntariness of the exercise, whether it was Bible reading or prayer, was thought to be an important factor as evidenced by this type of legislation. Proponents of religious exercises generally relied upon this, tradition, and nonsectarianism of the Bible as the primary defense of the practice. In 1962, however, the United States Supreme Court, in *Engel* v. *Vitale*, found a New York Regents prayer unconstitutional, and a year later held both prayer and Bible reading offensive to the First Amendment even though the defendants claimed that the exercises were voluntary and the Bible was nondenominational. This result could probably have been anticipated since the position established by the Court in *McCollum* in 1948 indicated that neither the nature of the religious instruction nor the voluntariness of the exercise were valid defenses. In *McCollum*, Justice Frankfurter stated:

> That a child is offered an alternative may reduce the constraint; it does not eliminate the operation of influence by the school in matters sacred to conscience and outside the school's domain. The law of imitation operates, and nonconformity is not an outstanding characteristic of children. The result is an obvious pressure upon children to attend. . . .[55]

Likewise, the nondenominational nature of a prayer was found to be no defense when the issue was raised in *Engel*. The Court explained that neither the fact that a prayer is denominationally neutral nor that it is voluntary can serve to free it from the limitations of the Establishment Clause of the First Amendment. According to the Court:

> The Establishment Clause, unlike the Free Exercise Clause, does not depend upon any showing of direct governmental compulsion and is violated by the enactment of laws which establish an official religion whether those laws operate directly to coerce non-observing individuals or not. . . .[56]

The result of both the *Engel*, the *Schempp*, and its companion case, *Murray*,[57] in 1963, was that religious exercises in the public schools are clearly unconstitutional. Neither state, nor school, nor teacher can hold religious services of any type in the public schools. The Court did point out, however, that the study of the Bible and religion, as a part of a secular program of education for their literary and historic values would not be unconstitutional.

In 1980, the Supreme Court, in *Stone v. Graham*,[58] followed the precedents of *Schempp* and *Murray* in holding a Kentucky statute unconstitutional that required the posting of the Ten Commandments on the walls of each public school classroom. In spite of an avowal by the state that the posting was premised on a secular legislative purpose, the High Court said that no legislative recitation of a supposed secular purpose could deny that the Ten Commandments are a sacred text of the Jewish and Christian faiths.

More recently, there has been some evidence of a tendency on the part of the United States Supreme Court [59] to lower the "wall of separation" somewhat. In 1984, the Court approved, by a 5 to 4 vote, a city's financing and sponsorship of a nativity scene at Christmas. In writing for the majority, Chief Justice Burger called the crèche a "passive" symbol only remotely benefiting religion. The opinion also observed that the nativity scene was not exclusively religious since it was accompanied by reindeer, clowns, and a life-sized teddy bear.

With the impetus from President Ronald Reagan and several highly visible religious groups, the prayer issue again became a source of major political controversy in 1983 and 1984. The Reagan Administration proposed to amend the United States Constitution, effectively changing the First Amendment, to allow prayer in public schools. The proposed amendment, after some modification in the United States Senate, finally read as follows:

> Nothing in this Constitution shall be construed to prohibit individual or group prayer in public schools or other public institutions. Neither the United States nor any state shall compose the words of prayers to be said in public schools.

Opposition to the proposed amendment was led by Senator Lowell Weicker of Connecticut and the leadership of Methodist, Presbyterian, Episcopalian, Lutheran, Unitarian, and Jewish groups. On March 20, 1984, the United States Senate voted and the proposed amendment failed, by eleven votes, to gain the two-thirds majority needed for approval. Had it passed and subsequently been approved by the people, the measure would have nullified *McCollum, Schempp,* and *Murray,* but would have left *Engel* intact. Under the proposed amendment, teachers or school administrators or clergy could have led the student body in prayer, but could not have actually composed a written prayer and mandated that all students use it.

Later, in 1984, at the urging of President Reagan, the United States Congress enacted a new law designed to open public schools to organized prayer and religious worship. President Reagan and many members of Congress openly disagreed with the Supreme Court's religion interpretations and sought to mitigate their effect by enacting a new statute called the "Equal Access" Amendment, to allow student groups to organize and hold religious meetings in public school facilities. The bill was passed and sent to the President on July 25, 1984. The original bill simply assured that religious services could be held in public schools but before it could gain sufficient votes to assure passage, the scope was broadened by amendments that assured that meetings for political and philosophical purposes could also be held. (The text of the Equal Access Amendment follows the *Schempp* and *Murray* cases below.)

The effect of the law will probably not be clearly understood until it is implemented in the schools; however, an indication of some points of contention have emerged. Some constitutional scholars maintain that in view of other judicial precedents the Act may be held unconstitutional under any of the three tests of purpose, effect, and entanglement. The congressional debates and public reports on the history of the legislation suggest that the purpose of the law may well exceed neutrality and is designed to assist religion in a state-sanctioned environment.

Too, on its face it appears the law may be difficult to implement without running afoul of the effect test. The religious services may require too great administrative and/or faculty participation constituting entanglement. The constitutionality of the Act is drawn directly into question by a three-judge Federal Court of Appeals decision, rendered the same month the Act was passed by Congress, which held that a Protestant student club could not meet during the school day, from 7:45 A.M. to 7:57 A.M., a time set aside for student activities. The students had claimed that their rights of free speech overcame the religious prohibitions, but the court disagreed maintaining that the "primary effect" was to advance religion and, too, that such a program would involve schools in "excessive entanglement" with religion.[60]

A similar conclusion was reached by the United States Court of Appeals for the Second Circuit in 1980 when it upheld a school board's refusal to permit a student-initiated prayer group to hold voluntary prayer meetings in school immediately before the school day began. Here again the court found that the board's refusal to permit such religious services did not constitute an infringement on the students' First Amendment rights of freedom of speech.[61] In each of these cases the schools' involvement was minimal, similar to that prescribed by the Equal Access Act, yet the courts felt that the use of the school for such religious purposes still represented too great a cooperation between the state and church.

In other instances in which school encouragement and participation were admittedly much more overt, as in a Clayton County, Georgia, case,[62] where the school district permitted religious groups to meet on school grounds under faculty supervision, and in a Lubbock, Texas, case,[63] where the school board's policy permitted and encouraged groups to gather voluntarily for religious purposes before and after regular school hours, the federal courts of appeals have acted uniformly in holding the activities unconstitutional.

In spite of these cases, some commentators believe that recent shifts in the philosophy of the United States Supreme Court on church-state matters may well result in the Equal Access Act's being held to be constitutional under the First Amendment. In any case, the Equal Access Act will undoubtedly fuel new and protracted legal controversy over school and religious affairs.

State Enforced Bible Reading and
Prayer in the Public Schools Is
Unconstitutional

SCHOOL DISTRICT OF
ABINGTON TOWNSHIP v.
SCHEMPP AND MURRAY v.
CURLETT

Supreme Court of the United States, 1963.
374 U.S. 203, 83 S.Ct. 1560.

Mr. Justice CLARK delivered the opinion of the Court.

Once again we are called upon to consider the scope of the provision of the First Amendment to the United States Constitution which declares that "Congress shall make no law respecting an establishment of religion, or prohibiting the free exercise thereof . . . ." These companion cases present the issues in the context of state action requiring that schools begin each day with readings from the Bible. While raising the basic questions under slightly different factual situations, the cases permit of joint treatment. In light of the history of the First Amendment and of our cases interpreting and applying its requirements, we hold that the practices at issue and the laws requiring them are unconstitutional under the Establishment Clause, as applied to the States through the Fourteenth Amendment.

The Facts in Each Case: No. 142. The Commonwealth of Pennsylvania by law, 24 Pa.Stat. § 15–1516, as amended, Pub.Law 1928 (Supp.1960) Dec. 17, 1959, requires that "At least ten verses from the Holy Bible shall be read, without comment, at the opening of each public school on each school day. Any child shall be excused from such Bible reading, or attending such Bible reading, upon the written request of his parent or guardian." The Schempp family, husband and wife and two of their three children, brought suit to enjoin enforcement of the statute, contending that their rights under the Fourteenth Amendment to the Constitution of the United States are, have been, and will continue to be violated unless this statute be declared unconstitutional as violative of these provisions of the First Amendment. They sought to enjoin the appellant school district, wherein the Schempp children attend school, and its officers and the Superintendent of Public Instruction of the Commonwealth from continuing to conduct such readings and recitation of the Lord's Prayer in the public schools of the district pursuant to the statute. . . .

No. 119. In 1905 the Board of School Commissioners of Baltimore City adopted a rule pursuant to Art. 77, § 202 of the Annotated Code of Maryland. The rule provided for the holding of opening exercises in the schools of the city, consisting primarily of the "reading, without comment, of a chapter in the Holy Bible and/or the use of the Lord's Prayer." The petitioners, Mrs. Madalyn Murray and her son, William J. Murray III, are both professed atheists. Following unsuccessful attempts to have the respondent school board rescind the rule, this suit was filed for mandamus to compel its rescission and cancellation. It was alleged that William was a student in a public school of the city and Mrs. Murray, his mother, was a taxpayer therein; that it was the practice under the rule to have a reading on each school morning from the King James version of the Bible; that at petitioners' insistence the rule was amended [64] to permit children to be excused from the exercise on request of the parent and that William had been excused pursuant thereto; that nevertheless the rule as amended was in violation of the petitioners' rights "to freedom of religion under the First and Fourteenth Amendments" and in violation of "the principle of separation between church and state, contained therein. . . ."

Applying the Establishment Clause principles to the cases at bar we find that the States are requiring the selection and reading at the opening of the school day of verses from the Holy Bible and the recitation of the Lord's Prayer by the students in unison. These exercises are prescribed as part of the curricular activities of students who are required by law to attend school. They are held in the school buildings under the supervision and with the participation of teachers employed in those schools. None of these factors, other than compulsory school attendance, was present in the program upheld in *Zorach* v. *Clauson*. The trial court in No. 142 has found that such an opening exercise is a religious ceremony and was intended by the State to be so. We agree with the trial court's finding as to the religious character of the exercises. Given that finding, the exercises and the law requiring them are in violation of the Establishment Clause.

There is no such specific finding as to the religious character of the exercises in No. 119, and the State contends (as does the State in No. 142) that the program is an effort to extend its benefits to all public school children without regard to their religious belief. Included within its secular purposes, it says, are the promotion of moral values, the contradiction to the materialistic trends of our times, the perpetuation of our institutions and the teaching of literature. The case came up on demurrer, of course, to a petition which alleged that the uniform practice under the rule had been to read from the King James version of the Bible and that the exercise was sectarian. The short answer, therefore, is that the religious character of the exercise was admitted by the State. But even if its purpose is not strictly religious, it is sought to be accomplished through readings, without comment, from the Bible. Surely the place of the Bible as an instrument of religion cannot be gainsaid, and the State's recognition of the pervading religious character of the ceremony is evident from the rule's specific permission of the alternative use of the Catholic Douay version as well as the recent amendment permitting nonattendance at the exercises. None of these factors is consistent with the contention that the Bible is here used either as an instrument for nonreligious moral inspiration or as a reference for the teaching of secular subjects.

The conclusion follows that in both cases the laws require religious exercises and such exercises are being conducted in direct violation of the rights of the appellees and petitioners. Nor are these required exercises mitigated by the fact that individual students may absent themselves upon parental request, for that fact furnishes no defense to a claim of unconstitutionality under the Establishment Clause. . . . Further, it is no defense to urge that the religious practices here may be relatively minor encroachments on the First Amendment. The breach of neutrality that is today a trickling stream may all too soon become a raging torrent and, in the words of Madison, "it is proper to take alarm at the first experiment on our liberties." *Memorial and Remonstrance Against Religious Assessments.* . . .

It is insisted that unless these religious exercises are permitted a "religion of secularism" is established in the schools. We agree of course that the State may not establish a "religion of secularism" in the sense of affirmatively opposing or showing hostility to religion, thus "preferring those who believe in no religion over those who do believe." Zorach v. Clauson, 343 U.S., at 314, 72 S.Ct., at 684, 96 L.Ed. 954. We do not agree, however, that this decision in any sense has that effect. In addition, it might well be said that one's education is not complete without a study of comparative religion or the history of religion and its relationship to the advancement of civilization. It certainly may be said that the Bible is worthy of study for its literary and historic qualities. Nothing we have said here indicates that such study of the Bible or of religion, when presented objectively as part of a secular program of education, may not be effected consistently with the First Amendment. But the exercises here do not fall into those categories. They are religious exercises, required by the States in violation of the command of the First Amendment that the Government maintain strict neutrality, neither aiding nor opposing religion.

Finally, we cannot accept that the concept of neutrality, which does not permit a State to require a religious exercise even with the consent of the majority of those affected, collides with the majority's right to free exercise of religion. While the Free Exercise Clause clearly prohibits the use of state action to deny the rights of free exercise to *anyone,* it has never meant that a majority could use the machinery of the State to practice its beliefs. Such a contention was effectively answered by Mr. Justice Jackson for the Court in West Virginia Board of Education v. Barnette, 319 U.S. 624, 638, 63 S.Ct. 1178, 1185, 87 L.Ed. 1628 (1943):

> The very purpose of a Bill of Rights was to withdraw certain subjects from the vicissitudes of political controversy, to place them beyond the reach of majorities and officials and to establish them as legal principles to be applied by the courts. One's right to . . . freedom of worship . . . and other fundamental rights may not be submitted to vote; they depend on the outcome of no elections.

The place of religion in our sociey is an exalted one, achieved through a long tradition of reliance on the home, the church and the inviolable citadel of the individual heart and mind. We have come to recognize through bitter experience that it is not within the power of government to invade that citadel, whether its purpose or effect be to aid or oppose, to advance or retard. In the relationship between man and religion, the State is firmly committed to a position of neutrality. Though the application of that rule requires interpretation of a delicate sort, the rule itself is clearly and concisely stated in the words of the First Amendment. Applying that rule to the facts of these cases, we affirm the judgment in No. 142. In No. 119, the judgment is reversed and the cause remanded to the Maryland Court of Appeals for further proceedings consistent with this opinion.

It is so ordered.

Judgment in No. 142 affirmed; judgment in No. 119 reversed and cause remanded with directions.

NOTES

1. Many decisions were rendered by state courts before the *Engel* and *Schempp* cases, which found that morning religious activities did not violate constitutional or statutory provisions. Some of these were: Hackett v. Brooksville Graded School District, 120 Ky. 608, 87 S.W. 792 (1905); Donahoe v. Richards, 38 Me. 379, 61 Am.Dec. 256 (1854); Moore v. Monroe, 64 Iowa 367, 20 N.W. 475 (1884); Billard v. Board of Education of City of Topeka, 69 Kan. 53, 76 P. 422 (1904); Knowlton v. Baumhover, 182 Iowa 691, 166 N.W. 202 (1918); McCormick v. Burt, 95 Ill. 263 (1880).

   Other state courts listed below found religious exercises offended their constitutions: State ex rel. Weiss v. District Board, 76 Wis. 177, 44 N.W. 967 (1890); State ex rel. Freeman v. Scheve, 65 Neb. 853, 91 N.W. 846 (1902); People ex rel. Ring v. Board of Education of District 24, 245 Ill. 334, 92 N.E. 251 (1910); Herold v. Parish Board of School Directors, 136 La. 1034, 68 So. 116 (1915); State ex rel. Finger v. Weedman, 55 S.D. 343, 226 N.W. 348 (1929).

2. How does the court distinguish the "Establishment" clause from the "Free Exercise" clause?

3. Does prohibition against state laws that require or permit religious services in public schools indicate an hostility to religion? What does the court say?

4. A statute requiring a period of silence for prayer or meditation at the opening of each school day does not violate the Free Exercise Clause. Lack of mandatory direction indicated to the court that the state intended to maintain neutrality. Gaines v. Anderson, 421 F.Supp. 337 (D.Mass. 1976).

5. A school district was held to be acting in aid of religion in violation of the First Amendment when: (1) student council members read the Lord's Prayer and read verses from the Bible over the school's public address system each day, (2) the Gideon society was regularly invited to distribute religious books and give talks, (3) certain teachers required their classes to memorize prayers and conducted Bible-reading sessions during class, and (4) various ministers were invited to address classes during which time students were questioned about their religious beliefs. Plaintiffs, however, failed to meet the burden of proving that another part of the exercises, the conduct of Baccalaureate services on school grounds prior to graduation, was also unconstitutional. The court relied on both *Schempp* and *McCollum* in rendering the decision. Goodwin v. Cross County School District, 394 F.Supp. 417 (E.D.Ark.1973).

6. *Religious Garb in Public Schools.* Whether public school teachers can wear religious garb of any particular religious order or society has been

litigated on several occasions. While there is no precise definition of what constitutes religious garments, some states have sought prohibition of any apparel that showed that the person belonged to a particular sect, denomination, or order. See: Donald E. Boles, *The Two Swords* (Ames, IA: Iowa State University Press, 1967) p. 222.

In 1894, the Supreme Court of Pennsylvania held that the wearing by nuns of garb and insignia of the Sisterhood of St. Joseph while teaching in the public schools did not constitute sectarian teaching. Hysong v. Gallitzin Borough School District, 164 Pa. 629, 30 A. 482 (1894). The court reasoned that to deny wearing of such apparel would violate the teachers' religious liberty. Later, the Legislature of Pennsylvania prohibited the wearing of garb by public school teachers while in performance of their duties. This statute was subsequently upheld by the Pennsylvania Supreme Court. This time the court maintained that the Act was a reasonable exercise of state power in regulating the educational system to prevent sectarian control. The court found that the legislation "is directed against acts, not beliefs, and only against acts of the teacher while engaged in the performance of his or her duties as such teacher." Commonwealth v. Herr, 229 Pa. 132, 78 A. 68 (1910).

Litigation over the years in other states has been split on the issue. A New York Court in 1906 held that "the influence of such apparel is distinctly sectarian." O'Connor v. Hendrick, 184 N.Y. 421, 77 N.E. 612 (1906). Similarly, the Nebraska Supreme Court refused to mandate that the State Superintendent distribute state school trust funds to a school because of the school's religious nature. The school rested on church property, was adorned with religious emblems, and the teachers wore distinctive garb, including the rosary, indicative of the Catholic sisterhood. State ex rel. Public School District No. 6 v. Taylor, 122 Neb. 454, 240 N.W. 573 (1932); see also: Zellers v. Huff, 55 N.M. 501, 236 P.2d 949 (1951).

On the other hand, the wearing of religious garb has been upheld by at least three state supreme courts. In a North Dakota case, the court held that there was no evidence that nuns imparted religious instruction even though they were dressed in religious garb of the Sisterhood of St. Benedict. Gerhardt v. Heid, 66 N.D. 444, 267 N.W. 127 (1936); see also: City of New Haven v. Town of Torrington, 132 Conn. 194, 43 A.2d 455 (1945) and Rawlings v. Butler, 290 S.W.2d 801 (Ky.1956).

Lack of consensus by the courts is due to their legitimate hesitancy to invade either the religious rights of teachers or students. The issue boils down to one of a weighing of interests in view of the particular facts of the case. As the Connecticut Supreme Court said:

> The decisions in these cases, however, are, as is to be expected, based upon a wide diversity of facts. The only definite conclusion that may be drawn from them is that whether sectarian influence connected with a school is such as to affect its public character is ordinarily a question of fact for the trial court. City of New Haven v. Town of Torrington, 132 Conn. 194, 43 A.2d 455 (1945).

7. Students have requested the opportunity to voluntarily study the Bible and have religious exercises before or after school and, occasionally, during periods designated for clubs. The students have claimed this is a basic free exercise right. In Lubbock Civil Liberties Union v. Lubbock Independent School District, 669 F.2d 1038 (5th Cir.1982), the court rejected the free exercise argument of the students since it would be credible only if there were a total foreclosure of a student's right to worship. The court noted "[t]he students attend school only several hours a day, five days a week, nine months during the year. The other hours are effectively open for their attendance at religious activities at places other than state-supported schools." The United States Circuit Court of Appeals, Second Circuit, also ruled that the refusal of a school to allow voluntary prayer meetings before and after school was not a violation of the free exercise clause. Brandon v. Board of Education of Guilderland Central School District, 635 F.2d 971 (2d Cir.1980), cert. denied 454 U.S. 1123, 102 S.Ct. 970 (1981).

8. The United States Supreme Court ruled, in Widmar v. Vincent, 454 U.S. 263, 102 S.Ct. 269 (1981), that a university policy prohibiting students from using university buildings for voluntary religious meetings was unconstitutional. The Court ruled the campus was a public forum and to deny students "equal access" to university buildings was a violation of free speech. In seeking to constitutionally justify religious activities in public schools, the United States Congress seized upon the words "equal access" in enacting a new statute, the Equal Access Amendment.

✳ TEXT OF EQUAL ACCESS AMENDMENT

The following is the text of the Equal Access statute as enacted by Congress and sent to President Reagan on July 25, 1984. 20 U.S.C. 4071

Sec. 802(a). It shall be unlawful for any public secondary school which receives Federal financial assistance and which has a limited open forum to deny equal access or a fair opportunity to, or discriminate against, any students who wish to conduct a meeting within that limited open forum on the basis of the religious, political, philosophical, or other content of the speech at such meetings.

(b) A public secondary school has a limited open forum whenever such school grants an offering to or opportunity for one or more noncurriculum related student groups to meet on school premises during noninstructional time.

(c) Schools shall be deemed to offer a fair opportunity to students who wish to conduct a meeting within its limited open forum if such school uniformly provides that—

(1) the meeting is voluntary and student-initiated;

(2) there is no sponsorship of the meeting by the school, the government, or its agents or employees;

(3) employees or agents of the school or government are present at religious meetings only in a nonparticipatory capacity;

(4) the meeting does not materially and substantially interfere with the orderly conduct of educational activities within the school; and

(5) nonschool persons may not direct, conduct, control, or regularly attend activities of student groups.

(d) Nothing in this title shall be construed to authorize the United States or any State or political subdivision thereof—

(1) to influence the form or content of any prayer or other religious activity;

(2) to require any person to participate in prayer or other religious activity;

(3) to expend public funds beyond the incidental cost of providing the space for student-initiated meetings;

(4) to compel any school agent or employee to attend a school meeting if the content of the speech at the meeting is contrary to the beliefs of the agent or employee;

(5) to sanction meetings that are otherwise unlawful;

(6) to limit the rights of groups of students which are not of a specified numerical size; or

(7) to abridge the constitutional rights of any person.

(e) Notwithstanding the availability of any other remedy under the Constitution or the laws of the United States, nothing in this title shall be construed to authorize the United States to deny or withhold Federal financial assistance in any school.

(f) Nothing in this Act shall be construed to limit the authority of the school, its agents or employees, to maintain order and discipline on school premises, to protect the well-being of students and faculty, and to assure that attendance of students at meetings is voluntary.

Sec. 803. As used in this title—

(1) The term "secondary school" means a public school which provides secondary education as determined by state law.

(2) The term "sponsorship" includes the act of promoting, leading or participating in a meeting. The assignment of a teacher, administrator, or other school employee to a meeting for custodial purposes does not constitute sponsorship of the meeting.

(3) The term "meeting" includes those activities of student groups which are permitted under a school's limited open forum and are not directly related to the school curriculum.

(4) The term "noninstructional time" means time set aside by the school before actual classroom instruction begins or after actual classroom instruction ends.

Sec. 804. If any provision of this title or the application thereof to any person or curcumstances is judicially determined to be invalid, the provisions of the remainder of the title and the application to other persons or circumstances shall not be affected thereby.

Sec. 805. The provisions of this title shall supersede all other provisions of Federal law that are inconsistent with the provisions of this title.

Posting of Ten Commandments in
Public School Classrooms Is
Unconstitutional

STONE v. GRAHAM

Supreme Court of the United States, 1980.
449 U.S. 39, 101 S.Ct. 192.

PER CURIAM.

A Kentucky statute requires the posting of a copy of the Ten Commandments, purchased with private contributions, on the wall of each public classroom in the State. Petitioners, claiming that this statute violates the Establishment and Free Exercise Clauses of the First Amendment, sought an injunction against its enforcement. The state trial court upheld the statute, finding that its "avowed purpose" was "secular and not religious," and that the statute would "neither advance nor inhibit any religion or religious group" nor involve the State excessively in religious matters. The Supreme Court of the Commonwealth of Kentucky affirmed by an equally divided court. Stone v. Graham, 599 S.W.2d 157 (Ky.1980). We reverse. . . .

The Commonwealth insists that the statute in question serves a secular legislative purpose, observing that the legislature required the following notation in small print at the bottom of each display of the Ten Commandments: "The secular application of the Ten Commandments is clearly seen in its adoption as the fundamental legal code of Western Civilization and the Common Law of the United States." Enact. Acts 1978, ch. 436, § 1 (effective June 17, 1978); K.R.S. 158.178 (1980). . . .

The preeminent purpose for posting the Ten Commandments on schoolroom walls is plainly religious in nature. The Ten Commandments is undeniably a sacred text in the Jewish and Christian faiths, and no legislative recitation of a supposed secular purpose can blind us to that fact. The Commandments do not confine themselves to arguably secular matters, such as honoring one's parents, killing or murder, adultery, stealing, false witness, and covetousness. See Exodus 20:12–17; Deuteronomy 5:16–21. Rather, the first part of the Commandments concerns the religious duties of believers: worshipping the Lord God alone, avoiding idolatry, not using the Lord's name in vain, and observing the sabbath day. See Exodus 20:1–11; Deuteronomy 5:6–15.

This is not a case in which the Ten Commandments are integrated into the school curriculum, where the Bible may constitutionally be used in an appropriate study of history, civilization, ethics, comparative religion, or the like. . . . Posting of religious texts on the wall serves no such educational function. If the posted copies of the Ten Commandments are to have any effect at all, it will be to induce the school children to read, meditate upon, perhaps to venerate and obey, the Commandments. However desirable this might be as a matter of private devotion, it is not a permissible state objective under the Establishment Clause.

The petition for a writ of certiorari is granted and the judgment below is reversed.

NOTE

An Alabama statute that provided for a one-minute period of silence "for meditation or voluntary prayer" at the commencement of each day's classes has been held to be unconstitutional by a federal district court. Jaffree v. Board of School Commissioners of Mobile County, 554 F.Supp. 1104 (1983). Later Justice Powell, sitting as a circuit justice, upheld the lower courts' judgment. Jaffree v. Board of School Commissioners of Mobile County, 459 U.S. 1314, 103 S.Ct. 842 (1983). This case has been appealed to the United States Supreme Court, but at the date of publication of this book no opinion had been rendered.

FLAG SALUTE

The flag-salute ceremony in the United States originated in 1892 after a substantial rise in national sentiment to stimulate patriotism in the schools. In 1898, New York passed the first flag-salute statute only one day after the United States declared war on Spain.[65] By 1940, eighteen states had statutes making provision for "some sort of teaching regarding the flag."[66] Even though the statutes did not specifically require individual recitation, the reality of the classroom regimentation tended to make such statutory pronouncement unnecessary.[67] Opposition sprang up on sporadic bases from certain religious groups, the most persistent of which was Jehovah's Witnesses. In early litigation, the Georgia Supreme Court held that the Witnesses' religious freedom was not violated since the flag salute was merely an exercise in patriotism and not a religious rite.[68] Other rulings were unfavorable to the plaintiffs, the most intolerant of which stated that "Those who do not desire to conform with the demands of the statute can seek their school elsewhere."[69] In California, that state's high court upheld the expulsion of pupils for refusing to salute the flag.[70] Similarly, a New York court in 1939 held that "The flag has nothing to do with religion"; therefore, religious freedoms could not be offended.[71]

Nationalistic fervor just before World War II brought on more heated controversy, and the Supreme Court, in 1940, rendered a decision. In this case, Justice Frankfurter, speaking for an eight-to-one majority, held that freedom of religion guaranteed by the First Amendment was not violated by a Pennsylvania statute that required a flag salute and pledge of allegiance. Significantly, the opinion concluded that:

> Conscientious scruples have not, in the course of the long struggle for religious toleration, relieved the individual from obedience to a general law not aimed at the promotion or restriction of religious beliefs. The mere possession of religious convictions which contradict the relevant concerns of a political society does not relieve the citizen from the discharge of political responsibilities.[72]

This decision engendered substantial controversy, and the legal and academic community generally disapproved of the decision as an infringement on individual constitutional rights.[73] Some state courts tended to ignore the federal constitutional implications and held that flag-salute requirements violated their own state constitutions.[74] Other state courts

followed the decision.[75]   Disenchantment with the *Gobitis* decision was so
great and the constitutional foundation so weak that the case was officially
overruled in West Virginia State Board of Education v. Barnette in 1943.[76]
In reconsideration of the issues, Justice Jackson, writing for a six-man
majority, held that a state may require pupils to attend educational exercises
based on American history and civics to teach patriotism, but that ceremo-
nies involving compulsory rituals, such as flag salute, were unconstitutional.
Justices Black, Douglas, and Murphy had changed their minds, and even
though Frankfurter remained steadfast, the precedent of *Gobitis* was overturned.   The swing vote of the three justices was predictable by the announcement a year earlier, in 1942, in *Jones* v. *Opelika*[77] that: "Since we
joined in the opinion in the *Gobitis* case, we think this is an appropriate
occasion to state that we now believe that it was . . . wrongly decided."

Required Participation in Flag Salute
is Unconstitutional

WEST VIRGINIA STATE
BOARD OF EDUCATION v.
BARNETTE

Supreme Court of the United States, 1943.
319 U.S. 624, 63 S.Ct. 1178.

Mr. Justice JACKSON delivered the opinion of the Court.

Following the decision by this Court on June 3, 1940, in Minersville
School District v. Gobitis, 310 U.S. 586, 60 S.Ct. 1010, 84 L.Ed. 1375, 127
A.L.R. 1493, the West Virginia legislature amended its statutes to require all
schools therein to conduct courses of instruction in history, civics, and in the
Constitutions of the United States and of the State "for the purpose of
teaching, fostering and perpetuating the ideals, principles and spirit of
Americanism, and increasing the knowledge of the organization and machinery of the government."   Appellant Board of Education was directed, with
advice of the State Superintendent of Schools, to "prescribe the courses of
study covering these subjects" for public schools.   The Act made it the duty
of private, parochial and denominational schools to prescribe courses of
study "similar to those required for the public schools."

The Board of Education on January 9, 1942, adopted a resolution containing recitals taken largely from the Court's *Gobitis* opinion and ordering that
the salute to the flag become "a regular part of the program of activities in
the public schools," that all teachers and pupils "shall be required to
participate in the salute honoring the Nation represented by the Flag;
provided, however, that refusal to salute the Flag be regarded as an Act of
insubordination, and shall be dealt with accordingly."   . . .

Appellees, citizens of the United States and of West Virginia, brought
suit in the United States District Court for themselves and others similarly
situated asking its injunction to restrain enforcement of these laws and
regulations against Jehovah's Witnesses.   The Witnesses are an unincorporated body teaching that the obligation imposed by law of God is superior to
that of laws enacted by temporal government.   Their religious beliefs in-

clude a literal version of Exodus, Chapter 20, verses 4 and 5, which says: "Thou shalt not make unto thee any graven image, or any likeness of anything that is in heaven above, or that is in the earth beneath, or that is in the water under the earth; thou shalt not bow down thyself to them nor serve them." They consider that the flag is an "image" within this command. For this reason they refuse to salute it. . . .

This case calls upon us to reconsider a precedent decision, as the Court throughout its history often has been required to do. Before turning to the *Gobitis* case, however, it is desirable to notice certain characteristics by which this controversy is distinguished.

The freedom asserted by these appellees does not bring them into collision with rights asserted by any other individual. It is such conflicts which most frequently require intervention of the State to determine where the rights of one end and those of another begin. But the refusal of these persons to participate in the ceremony does not interfere with or deny rights of others to do so. Nor is there any question in this case that their behavior is peaceable and orderly. The sole conflict is between authority and rights of the individual. The State asserts power to condition access to public education on making a prescribed sign and profession and at the same time to coerce attendance by punishing both parent and child. The latter stand on a right of self-determination in matters that touch individual opinion and personal attitude. . . .

Nor does the issue as we see it turn on one's possession of particular religious views or the sincerity with which they are held. While religion supplies appellees' motive for enduring the discomforts of making the issue in this case, many citizens who do not share these religious views hold such a compulsory rite to infringe constitutional liberty of the individual. It is not necessary to inquire whether non-conformist beliefs will exempt from the duty to salute unless we first find power to make the salute a legal duty.

The *Gobitis* decision, however, *assumed,* as did the argument in that case and in this, that power exists in the State to impose the flag salute discipline upon school children in general. The Court only examined and rejected a claim based on religious beliefs of immunity from an unquestioned general rule. The question which underlies the flag salute controversy is whether such a ceremony so touching matters of opinion and political attitude may be imposed upon the individual by official authority under powers committed to any political organization under our Constitution. . . .

The Fourteenth Amendment, as now applied to the States, protects the citizen against the State itself and all of its creatures—Boards of Education not excepted. These have, of course, important, delicate, and highly discretionary functions, but none that they may not perform within the limits of the Bill of Rights. That they are educating the young for citizenship is reason for scrupulous protection of Constitutional freedoms of the individual, if we are not to strangle the free mind at its source and teach youth to discount important principles of our government as mere platitudes. . . .

The very purpose of a Bill of Rights was to withdraw certain subjects from the vicissitudes of political controversy, to place them beyond the reach of majorities and officials and to establish them as legal principles to be applied by the courts. One's right to life, liberty, and property, to free speech, a free press, freedom of worship and assembly, and other fundamental rights may not be submitted to vote; they depend on the outcome of no elections. . . .

National unity as an end which officials may foster by persuasion and example is not in question. The problem is whether under our Constitution compulsion as here employed is a permissible means for its achievement. . . .

If there is any fixed star in our constitutional constellation, it is that no official, high or petty, can prescribe what shall be orthodox in politics, nationalism, religion, or other matters of opinion or force citizens to confess by word or act their faith therein. If there are any circumstances which permit an exception, they do not now occur to us.

We think the action of the local authorities in compelling the flag salute and pledge transcends constitutional limitations on their power and invades the sphere of intellect and spirit which it is the purpose of the First Amendment to our Constitution to reserve from all official control.

The decision of this Court in *Minersville School District* v. *Gobitis* and the holding of those few per curiam decisions which preceded and foreshadowed it are overruled, and the judgment enjoining enforcement of the West Virginia Regulation is affirmed. . . .

NOTE

When a student was offered the option of either leaving the classroom or standing silently during the Pledge of Allegiance, the court held that to leave the classroom is a benign type of punishment for nonparticipation, while to compel the student to stand in silence was to compel an act of acceptance to the Pledge over the student's deeply held contrary convictions. The requirement of the school was therefore unconstitutional regardless of option. Goetz v. Ansell, 477 F.2d 636 (2d Cir.1973).

Footnotes

1. *Religion and Politics: The 1984 Campaign,* The New York Times/CBS News Poll, The New York Times, September 19, 1984, p. 13.

2. Evarts B. Green, *Religion and The State in America* (New York: New York University Press, 1941) p. 83.

3. Jonathan Elliot, *The Debates in the Several State Conventions on the Adoption of the Federal Constitution,* 2d ed., (Philadelphia: J.B. Lippincott & Co., 1888) p. 131.

4. Leo Pfeffer, *Church, State and Freedom* (Boston: Beacon Press 1967) p. 123.

5. R. Freeman Butts, *The American Tradition in Religion and Education* (Boston: Beacon Press, 1950) p. 72.

6. Pfeffer, op. cit. p. 125.

7. Id.

8. Id. p. 126.

9. Leo Pfeffer, op. cit. p. 4.

10. Id.

11. Id.

12. Williston Walker, *A History of the Christian Church* (New York: Charles Scribner's Sons, 1929) p. 464.

13. *History of Christianity in the Light of Modern Knowledge* (London: Blackie and Son, 1929) p. 464.

14. Pfeffer, op. cit. p. 14.

15. M. Searle Bates, *Religious Liberty: An Inquiry* (New York and London: International Missionary Council, 1945) p. 134.

16. Alexander J. Carlyle, *The Christian Church and Liberty* (London: J. Clark, 1924) p. 96.

17. Everson v. Board of Education, 330 U.S. 1, 67 S.Ct. 504 (1947).

18. Pfeffer, op. cit. p. 26.

19. John Locke, *A Letter Concerning Toleration* (Liberal Arts Press, 1955) pp. 17–18.

20. Saul K. Padover, *The Complete Jefferson* (New York: Duell, Sloan & Pearce, 1943).

21. Id.

22. Pfeffer, op. cit. p. 109.

23. Decl.Rights, Art. 16. [Note in the original.]

24. Decl.Rights, Art. 1. [Note in the original.]

25. Art. 16 [Note in the original.]

26. Art. 16. [Note in the original.]

27. Decl.Rights-title [Note in the original.]

28. V.T. Thayer, *The Attack Upon the American Secular School* (Boston: Beacon Press, 1951) pp. 26–27.

29. Knowlton v. Baumhover, 182 Iowa 691, 166 N.W. 202 (1918).

30. 321 U.S. 158, 64 S.Ct. 438 (1944).

31. Joseph L. Blow, *Cornerstones of Religious Freedom in America* (Boston: Beacon Press, 1949) pp. 179–182.

32. Pfeffer, op. cit. p. 338.

33. Wisconsin v. Yoder, 406 U.S. 205, 92 S.Ct. 1526 (1972).

34. Cochran v. Louisiana State Board of Education, 281 U.S. 370, 50 S.Ct. 335 (1930).

35. Cantwell v. Connecticut, 310 U.S. 296, 60 S.Ct. 900 (1940).

36. Board of Education of Central School District v. Allen, 392 U.S. 236, 88 S.Ct. 1923 (1968).

37. New York Education law § 701 (1967 suppl.).

38. See dissenting opinion of Mr. Justice Douglas.

39. See Boyd v. United States, 116 U.S. 616, 6 S.Ct. 524 (1886).

40. Board of Education of Central School District No. 1 v. Allen, 392 U.S. 236, 88 S.Ct. 1923 (1968).

41. Sloan v. Lemon, 413 U.S. 825, 93 S.Ct. 2982 (1973), rehearing denied 414 U.S. 881, 94 S.Ct. 30 (1973); Committee for Public Education and Religious Liberty v. Nyquist, 413 U.S. 756, 93 S.Ct. 2955 (1973).

42. Sloan v. Lemon, 413 U.S. 825, 93 S.Ct. 2982 (1973).

43. Meek v. Pittenger, 421 U.S. 349, 95 S.Ct. 1753 (1975).

44. Wolman v. Walter, 433 U.S. 229, 97 S.Ct. 2593 (1977).

45. Id.

46. Committee for Public Education and Religious Liberty v. Nyquist, 413 U.S. 756, 93 S.Ct. 2955 (1973).

47. 463 U.S. 388, 103 S.Ct. 3062 (1983).

48. R.I.Pen.Laws Ann. § 16–51–1 et seq. (Supp.1970).

49. 24 Pa.Stat. §§ 5601–5609.

50. Latin, Hebrew, and classical Greek are excluded.

51. People of State of Illinois ex rel. McCollum v. Board of Education of School District No. 71, 333 U.S. 203, 68 S.Ct. 461 (1948).

52. Zorach v. Clauson, 343 U.S. 306, 72 S.Ct. 679 (1952).

53. Hackett v. Brooksville Graded School District, 120 Ky. 608, 87 S.W. 792 (1905).

54. North Dakota Compiled Laws, Sec. 1388 (1913).

55. People ex rel. McCollum v. Board of Education, 333 U.S. 203, 68 S.Ct. 461 (1948).

56. Engel v. Vitale, 370 U.S. 421, 82 S.Ct. 1261 (1962).

57. School District of Abington Township v. Schempp and Murray v. Curlett, 374 U.S. 203, 83 S.Ct. 1560 (1963).

58. 449 U.S. 39, 101 S.Ct. 192 (1980).

59. Lynch v. Donnelly, ___ U.S. ___, 104 S.Ct. 1355 (1984).

60. Bender v. Williamsport Area School District, 741 F.2d 538 (3d Cir.1984).

61. Brandon v. Board of Education of Guilderland Central School District, 635 F.2d 971 (2d Cir. 1980).

62. Nartowicz v. Clayton County School District, 736 F.2d 646 (11th Cir.1984).

63. Lubbock Civil Liberties Union v. Lubbock Independent School District, 669 F.2d 1038 (5th Cir.1982).

64. The rule as amended provides as follows:
"Opening Exercises. Each school, either collectively or in classes, shall be opened by the reading, without comment, of a chapter in the Holy Bible and/or the use of the Lord's Prayer. The Douay version may be used by those pupils who prefer it. Appropriate patriotic exercises should be held as a part of the general opening exercise of the school or class. Any child shall be excused from participating in the opening exercises or from attending the opening exercises upon the written request of his parent or guardian."

65. Donald E. Boles, *The Two Swords* (Ames, Iowa: The Iowa State University Press, 1967), p. 139.

66. D.R. Manwaring, *Render Unto Caesar: The Flag-Salute Controversy* (Chicago: University of Chicago Press, 1962).

67. Id.

68. Leoles v. Landers, 184 Ga. 580, 192 S.E. 218 (1937), appeal dismissed 302 U.S. 656, 58 S.Ct. 364 (1937).

69. Hering v. State Board of Education, 117 N.J.L. 455, 189 A. 629 (1937).

70. Gabrielli v. Knickerbocker, 12 Cal.2d 85, 82 P.2d 391 (1938).

71. People ex rel. Fish v. Sandstrom, 279 N.Y. 523, 18 N.E.2d 840 (1839).

72. Minersville School District v. Gobitis, 310 U.S. 586, 60 S.Ct. 1010 (1940).

73. Boles, op. cit. p. 148.

74. State v. Smith, 155 Kan. 588, 127 P.2d 518 (1942); Bolling v. Superior Court, 16 Wash.2d 373, 133 P.2d 803 (1943).

75. Matter of Latrecchia, 128 N.J.L. 472, 26 A.2d 881 (1942); State v. Davis, 58 Ariz. 444, 120 P.2d 808 (1942).

76. 319 U.S. 624, 63 S.Ct. 1178 (1943).

77. 316 U.S. 584, 62 S.Ct. 1231 (1942); see: Bates, op. cit. pp. 151–152.

6

School
Attendance

Operating under constitutional requirements, legislatures have prescribed the admission and residence requirements for attendance in the public schools. Where state constitutions have established the age span within which all have a right to attend public schools, legislatures must provide at least the specified minimum education, but are not restricted from creating additional educational opportunities. For example, the constitutional requirement that a state provide schools for all children between the ages of five and twenty years does not prevent the legislature from establishing a nursery school for four-year-olds. Neither does such a provision prohibit the establishment of institutions for higher education.

When a state establishes a system of public education, it cannot arbitrarily withhold services from a particular class of persons. While a state is not required by the federal constitution to provide public education at all, when it does so provide, it must be open and available to all.[1] In this regard, children whose parents are illegal aliens are entitled to attend public schools so long as they reside in the United States. The United States Supreme Court has said that if a state is to deny the child of illegal alien parents a free public education, then the state must demonstrate the denial enhances a substantial state interest. It is insufficient for the state to claim the denial of a free education is justified on the grounds that the presence of undocumented children requires the state to spread scarce fiscal resources among greater numbers of children.[2]

States, though, can impose restrictions on school attendance provided they are reasonably related to a valid state purpose. Reasonableness may relate to the health, safety, and welfare of other children or may have to do with the orderly organization and administration of school systems. Residence requirements based on geographical boundaries drawn within and between school districts have been upheld by the courts absent intent to unconstitutionally discriminate against a certain class of student. Indeed, the drawing of attendance zones has been upheld as a valid exercise of state prerogative where boundaries were drawn to effectuate integration.

Most state laws require that children be residents of the school district in which they attend school. A school district has the legal authority to challenge the residence of a student.

A student who changes guardianship solely for the purposes of attending a particular school may be denied attendance.[3] The United States Supreme Court has held that an appropriately defined and uniformly applied residence law is constitutionally valid. The state's interest in assuring appropriate educational services to be enjoyed by the residents is rationale enough to support such a requirement.[4]

To establish residence, one must be physically present and intend to remain at that location. The Supreme Court of Maine, in an early decision, held that residence was established "when a person takes up his abode in a given place, without any present intention to remove therefrom . . . ."[5]

*Undocumented Children of Alien
Parents Cannot Be Denied a Public
Education*

PLYLER v. DOE

Supreme Court of the United States, 1982.
457 U.S. 202, 102 S.Ct. 2382.

Mr. Justice BRENNAN delivered the opinion of the Court.

The question presented by these cases is whether, consistent with the Equal Protection Clause of the Fourteenth Amendment, Texas may deny to undocumented school-age children the free public education that it provides to children who are citizens of the United States or legally admitted aliens.

Since the late nineteenth century, the United States has restricted immigration into this country. Unsanctioned entry into the United States is a crime, 8 U.S.C. § 1325, and those who have entered unlawfully are subject to deportation, 8 U.S.C. §§ 1251–1252. But despite the existence of these legal restrictions, a substantial number of persons have succeeded in unlawfully entering the United States, and now live within various States, including the State of Texas.

In May 1975, the Texas legislature revised its education laws to withhold from local school districts any state funds for the education of children who were not "legally admitted" into the United States. The 1975 revision also authorized local school districts to deny enrollment in their public schools to children not "legally admitted" to the country. Tex.Educ.Code Ann. § 21.031 (Vernon Cum.Supp.1981). These cases involve constitutional challenges to those provisions. . . .

The Fourteenth Amendment provides that "No State shall . . . deprive any person of life, liberty, or property, without due process of law; nor deny to *any person within its jurisdiction* the equal protection of the laws." Appellants argue at the outset that undocumented aliens, because of their immigration status, are not "persons within the jurisdiction" of the State of Texas, and that they therefore have no right to the equal protection of Texas law. We reject this argument. Whatever his status under the immigration laws, an alien is surely a "person" in any ordinary sense of that term. Aliens, even aliens whose presence in this country is unlawful, have long been recognized as "persons" guaranteed due process of law by the Fifth and Fourteenth Amendments. Indeed, we have clearly held that the Fifth

Amendment protects aliens whose presence in this country is unlawful from invidious discrimination by the Federal Government.

Appellants seek to distinguish our prior cases, emphasizing that the Equal Protection Clause directs a State to afford its protection to persons *within its jurisdiction* while the Due Process Clauses of the Fifth and Fourteenth Amendments contain no such assertedly limiting phrase. In appellants' view, persons who have entered the United States illegally are not "within the jurisdiction" of a State even if they are present within a State's boundaries and subject to its laws. Neither our cases nor the logic of the Fourteenth Amendment supports that constricting construction of the phrase "within its jurisdiction." We have never suggested that the class of persons who might avail themselves of the equal protection guarantee is less than coextensive with that entitled to due process. To the contrary, we have recognized that both provisions were fashioned to protect an identical class of persons, and to reach every exercise of State authority.

> The Fourteenth Amendment to the Constitution is not confined to the protection of citizens. It says: "Nor shall any state deprive any person of life, liberty or property without due process of law; nor deny to any person within its jurisdiction the equal protection of the laws." *These provisions are universal in their application, to all persons within the territorial jurisdiction,* without regard to any differences of race, color, or of nationality; and the protection of the laws is a pledge of the protection of equal laws. (Emphasis added.)

In concluding that "all persons within the territory of the United States," including aliens unlawfully present, may invoke the Fifth and Sixth Amendment to challenge actions of the Federal Government, we reasoned from the understanding that the Fourteenth Amendment was designed to afford its protection to all within the boundaries of a State. . . .

There is simply no support for appellants' suggestion that "due process" is somehow of greater stature than "equal protection" and therefore available to a larger class of persons. To the contrary, each aspect of the Fourteenth Amendment reflects an elementary limitation on state power. To permit a State to employ the phrase "within its jurisdiction" in order to identify subclasses of persons whom it would define as beyond its jurisdiction, thereby relieving itself of the obligation to assure that its laws are designed and applied equally to those persons, would undermine the principal purpose for which the Equal Protection Clause was incorporated in the Fourteenth Amendment. The Equal Protection Clause was intended to work nothing less than the abolition of all caste- and invidious class-based legislation. That objective is fundamentally at odds with the power the State asserts here to classify persons subject to its laws as nonetheless excepted from its protection. . . .

Use of the phrase "within its jurisdiction" thus does not detract from, but rather confirms, the understanding that the protection of the Fourteenth Amendment extends to anyone, citizen or stranger, who *is* subject to the laws of a State, and reaches into every corner of a State's territory. That a person's initial entry into a State, or into the United States, was unlawful, and that he may for that reason be expelled, cannot negate the simple fact of his presence within the State's territorial perimeter. Given such presence, he is subject to the full range of obligations imposed by the State's civil and criminal laws. And until he leaves the jurisdiction—either voluntarily, or involuntarily in accordance with the Constitution and laws of the United States—he is entitled to the equal protection of the laws that a State may choose to establish.

Our conclusion that the illegal aliens who are plaintiffs in these cases may claim the benefit of the Fourteenth Amendment's guarantee of equal protection only begins the inquiry. The more difficult question is whether the Equal Protection Clause has been violated by the refusal of the State of Texas to reimburse local school boards for the education of children who cannot demonstrate that their presence within the United States is lawful, or by the imposition by those school boards of the burden of tuition on those children. . . .

The Equal Protection Clause directs that "all persons similarly circumstanced shall be treated alike." But so too, "The Constitution does not require things which are different in fact or opinion to be treated in law as though they were the same." The initial discretion to determine what is "different" and what is "the same" resides in the legislatures of the States. A legislature must have substantial latitude to establish classifications that roughly approximate the nature of the problem perceived, that accommodate competing concerns both public and private, and that account for limitations on the practical ability of the State to remedy every ill. In applying the Equal Protection Clause to most forms of state action, we thus seek only the assurance that the classification at issue bears some fair relationship to a legitimate public purpose.

But we would not be faithful to our obligations under the Fourteenth Amendment if we applied so deferential a standard to every classification. The Equal Protection Clause was intended as a restriction on state legislative action inconsistent with elemental constitutional premises. Thus we have treated as presumptively invidious those classifications that disadvantage a "suspect class," or that impinge upon the exercise of a "fundamental right." With respect to such classifications, it is appropriate to enforce the mandate of equal protection by requiring the State to demonstrate that its classification has been precisely tailored to serve a compelling governmental interest. In addition, we have recognized that certain forms of legislative classification, while not facially invidious, nonetheless give rise to recurring constitutional difficulties; in these limited circumstances we have sought the assurance that the classification reflects a reasoned judgment consistent with the ideal of equal protection by inquiring whether it may fairly be viewed as furthering a substantial interest of the State. We turn to a consideration of the standard appropriate for the evaluation of § 21.031.

Sheer incapability or lax enforcement of the laws barring entry into this country, coupled with the failure to establish an effective bar to the employment of undocumented aliens, has resulted in the creation of a substantial "shadow population" of illegal migrants—numbering in the millions—within our borders. This situation raises the specter of a permanent caste of undocumented resident aliens, encouraged by some to remain here as a source of cheap labor, but nevertheless denied the benefits that our society makes available to citizens and lawful residents. The existence of such an underclass presents most difficult problems for a Nation that prides itself on adherence to principles of equality under law.

The children who are plaintiffs in these cases are special members of this underclass. Persuasive arguments support the view that a State may withhold its beneficence from those whose very presence within the United States is the product of their own unlawful conduct. These arguments do not apply with the same force to classifications imposing disabilities on the minor *children* of such illegal entrants. At the least, those who elect to enter our territory by stealth and in violation of our law should be prepared to bear the consequences, including, but not limited to, deportation. But the children of those illegal entrants are not comparably situated. Their "parents have the ability to conform their conduct to societal norms," and presumably the ability to remove themselves from the State's jurisdiction; but the children who are plaintiffs in these cases "can affect neither their parents' conduct nor their own status." Even if the State found it expedient to control the conduct of adults by acting against their children, legislation directing the onus of a parent's misconduct against his children does not comport with fundamental conceptions of justice. . . .

Of course, undocumented status is not irrelevant to any proper legislative goal. Nor is undocumented status an absolutely immutable characteristic since it is the product of conscious, indeed unlawful, action. But § 21.031 is directed against children, and imposes its discriminatory burden on the basis of a legal characteristic over which children can have little control. It is thus difficult to conceive of a rational justification for penalizing these children for their presence within the United States. Yet that appears to be precisely the effect of § 21.031.

Public education is not a "right" granted to individuals by the Constitution. But neither is it merely some governmental "benefit" indistinguishable from other forms of social welfare legislation. Both the importance of education in maintaining our basic institutions, and the lasting impact of its deprivation on the life of the child, mark the distinction. . . .

In sum, education has a fundamental role in maintaining the fabric of our society. We cannot ignore the significant social costs borne by our Nation when select groups are denied the means to absorb the values and skills upon which our social order rests. . . .

Paradoxically, by depriving the children of any disfavored group of an education, we foreclose the means by which that group might raise the level of esteem in which it is held by the majority. But more directly, "education prepares individuals to be self-reliant and self-sufficient participants in society." Illiteracy is an enduring disability. The inability to read and write will handicap the individual deprived of a basic education each and every day of his life. The inestimable toll of that deprivation on the social, economic, intellectual and psychological well-being of the individual, and the obstacle it poses to individual achievement, makes it most difficult to reconcile the cost or the principle of a status-based denial of basic education with the framework of equality embodied in the Equal Protection Clause. . . .

These well-settled principles allow us to determine the proper level of deference to be afforded § 21.031. Undocumented aliens cannot be treated as a suspect class because their presence in this country in violation of federal law is not a "constitutional irrelevancy." Nor is education a fundamental right; a State need not justify by compelling necessity every variation in the manner in which education is provided to its population. But more is involved in this case than the abstract question whether § 21.031 discriminates against a suspect class, or whether education is a fundamental right. Section 21.031 imposes a lifetime hardship on a discrete class of children not accountable for their disabling status. The stigma of illiteracy will mark them for the rest of their lives. By denying these children a basic education, we deny them the ability to live within the structure of our civic institutions, and foreclose any realistic possibility that they will contribute in even the smallest way to the progress of our Nation. In determining the rationality of § 21.031, we may appropriately take into account its costs to the Nation and to the innocent children who are its victims. In light of these countervailing costs, the discrimination contained in § 21.031 can hardly be considered rational unless it furthers some substantial goal of the State. . . .

To be sure, like all persons who have entered the United States unlawfully, these children are subject to deportation. 8 U.S.C. §§ 1251–1252. But there is no assurance that a child subject to deportation will ever be deported. An illegal entrant might be granted federal permission to continue to reside in this country, or even to become a citizen. See, e.g., 8 U.S.C. §§ 1252, 1253(h), 1254. In light of the discretionary federal power to grant relief from deportation, a State cannot realistically determine that any particular undocumented child will in fact be deported until after deportation proceedings have been completed. It would of course be most difficult for the State to justify a denial of education to a child enjoying an inchoate federal permission to remain. . . .

Appellants argue that the classification at issue furthers an interest in the "preservation of the state's limited resources for the education of its lawful residents." . . . Apart from the asserted state prerogative to act against undocumented children solely on the basis of their undocumented status—an asserted prerogative that carries only minimal force in the circumstances of this case—we discern three colorable state interests that might support § 21.031.

First, appellants appear to suggest that the State may seek to protect the State from an influx of illegal immigrants. While a State might have an interest in mitigating the potentially harsh economic effects of sudden shifts in population, § 21.031 hardly offers an effective method of dealing with an urgent demographic or economic problem. There is no evidence in the record suggesting that illegal entrants impose any significant burden on the State's economy. . . .

Second, while it is apparent that a state may "not . . . reduce expenditures for education by barring [some arbitrarily chosen class of] children from its schools," appellants suggest that undocumented children are appropriately singled out for exclusion because of the special burdens they impose on the State's ability to provide high quality public education. But the record in no way supports the claim that exclusion of undocumented children is likely to improve the overall quality of education in the State. . . .

In terms of educational cost and need, however, undocumented children are "basically indistinguishable" from legally resident alien children.

Finally, appellants suggest that undocumented children are appropriately singled out because their unlawful presence within the United States renders them less likely than other children to remain within the boundaries of the State, and to put their education to productive social or political use within the State. Even assuming that such an interest is legitimate, it is an interest that is most difficult to quantify. The State has no assurance that any child, citizen or not, will employ the education provided by the State within the confines of the State's borders. In any event, the record is clear that many of the undocumented children disabled by this classification will remain in this country indefinitely, and that some will become lawful residents or citizens of the United States. It is difficult to understand precisely what the State hopes to achieve by promoting the creation and perpetuation of a subclass of illiterates within our boundaries, surely adding to the problems and costs of unemployment, welfare, and crime. It is thus clear that whatever savings might be achieved by denying these children an education, they are wholly insubstantial in light of the costs involved to these children, the State, and the Nation.

If the State is to deny a discrete group of innocent children the free public education that it offers to other children residing within its borders, that denial must be justified by a showing that it furthers some substantial state interest. No such showing was made here. Accordingly, the judgment of the Court of Appeals in each of these cases is

Affirmed.

Bona Fide Residence Requirement
That Furthers State Interest Is
Constitutional

MARTINEZ v. BYNUM

Supreme Court of the United States, 1983.
461 U.S. 321, 103 S.Ct. 1838.

Justice POWELL delivered the opinion of the Court.

This case involves a facial challenge to the constitutionality of the Texas residency requirement governing minors who wish to attend public free schools while living apart from their parents or guardians.

Roberto Morales was born in 1969 in McAllen, Texas, and is thus a United States citizen by birth. His parents are Mexican citizens who reside in Reynosa, Mexico. He left Reynosa in 1977 and returned to McAllen to live with his sister, petitioner Oralia Martinez, for the primary purpose of attending school in the McAllen Independent School District. Although Martinez is now Morales's custodian, she is not—and does not desire to become—his guardian. As a result, Morales is not entitled to tuition-free admission to the McAllen schools. Section 21.031(b) and (c) of the Texas Education Code would require the local school authorities to admit him if he or "his parent, guardian, or the person having lawful control of him" resided in the school district, Tex.Educ.Code Ann. § 21.031(b) and (c) (Supp.1982), but § 21.031(d) denies tuition-free admission for a minor who lives apart from a "parent, guardian, or other person having lawful control of him under an order of a court" if his presence in the school district is "for the primary purpose of attending the public free schools." Respondent McAllen Independent School District therefore denied Morales's application for admission in the fall of 1977. . . .

This Court frequently has considered constitutional challenges to residence requirements. On several occasions the Court has invalidated requirements that condition receipt of a benefit on a minimum period of residence within a jurisdiction, but it always has been careful to distinguish such durational residence requirements from bona fide residence requirements. . . .

We specifically have approved bona fide residence requirements in the field of public education. The Connecticut statute before us in Vlandis v. Kline, 412 U.S. 441, 93 S.Ct. 2230, 37 L.Ed.2d 63 (1973), for example, was unconstitutional because it created an irrebuttable presumption of nonresidency for state university students whose legal addresses were outside of the State before they applied for admission. The statute violated the Due Process Clause because it in effect classified some bona fide state residents as nonresidents for tuition purposes. But we "fully recognize[d] that a State has a legitimate interest in protecting and preserving . . . the right of its own bona fide residents to attend [its colleges and universities] on a preferential tuition basis." This "legitimate interest" permits a "State [to] establish such reasonable criteria for in-state status as to make virtually certain that students who are not, in fact, bona fide residents of the State, but who have come there solely for educational purposes, cannot take advantage of the in-state rates." Last Term, in Plyler v. Doe, 457 U.S. 202, 102 S.Ct. 2382, 72 L.Ed.2d 786 (1982), we reviewed an aspect of Tex.Educ.Code Ann. § 21.031— the statute at issue in this case. Although we invalidated the portion of the statute that excluded undocumented alien children from the public free schools, we recognized the school districts' right "to apply . . . established criteria for determining residence." . . .

A bona fide residence requirement, appropriately defined and uniformly applied, furthers the substantial state interest in assuring that services provided for its residents are enjoyed only by residents. Such a requirement with respect to attendance in public free schools does not violate the Equal Protection Clause of the Fourteenth Amendment. It does not burden or penalize the constitutional right of interstate travel, for any person is free to move to a State and to establish residence there. A bona fide residence requirement simply requires that the person *does* establish residence before demanding the services that are restricted to residents. . . .

The provision of primary and secondary education, of course, is one of the most important functions of local government. Absent residence requirements, there can be little doubt that the proper planning and operation of the schools would suffer significantly. The State thus has a substantial interest in imposing bona fide residence requirements to maintain the quality of local public schools.

The central question we must decide here is whether § 21.031(d) is a bona fide residence requirement. Although the meaning may vary according to context, "residence" generally requires both physical presence and an intention to remain. As the Supreme Court of Maine explained over a century ago,

> When . . . a person voluntarily takes up his abode in a given place, with intention to remain permanently, or for an indefinite period of time; or, to speak more accurately, when a person takes up his abode in a given place, without any present intention to remove therefrom, such place of abode becomes his residence. . . . " Inhabitants of Warren v. Inhabitants of Thomaston, 43 Me. 406, 418 (1857).

This classic two-part definition of residence has been recognized as a minimum standard in a wide range of contexts time and time again. . . . But at the very least, a school district generally would be justified in requiring school-age children or their parents to satisfy the traditional, basic residence criteria—i.e., to live in the district with a bona fide intention of remaining there—before it treated them as residents.

Section 21.031 is far more generous than this traditional standard. It compels a school district to permit a child such as Morales to attend school without paying tuition if he has a bona fide intention to remain in the school district indefinitely, for he then would have a reason for being there other than his desire to attend school: his intention to make his home in the district. Thus § 21.031 grants the benefits of residency to all who satisfy the traditional requirements. The statute goes further and extends these benefits to many children even if they (or their families) do not intend to remain in the district indefinitely. As long as the child is not living in the district for the sole purpose of attending school, he satisfies the statutory test. . . .

The Constitution permits a State to restrict eligibility for tuition-free education to its bona fide residents. We hold that § 21.031 is a bona fide residence requirement that satisfies constitutional standards. The judgment of the Court of Appeals accordingly is

Affirmed.

NOTES

1. School districts may inquire as to the reason for the change in the custody of a child and may deny admission if the parent's purpose is to circumvent the school district's zoning requirements. Matter of Curry, 113 Mich.App. 821, 318 N.W.2d 567 (1982).

2. A change in student residence simply to participate in an athletic program may be denied by athletic association rules without violating a student's property rights. Pennsylvania Interscholastic Athletic Association v. Greater Johnstown School District, 76 Pa.Cmwlth. 65, 463 A.2d 1198 (1983).

3. The Supreme Court of Arkansas has held that children residing in one school district could pay tuition and attend school in another school district, but only if both school districts agree to the arrangement. Delta Special School District # 5 v. McGehee Special School District # 17, 280 Ark. 489, 659 S.W.2d 508 (1983).

4. The word "domicile" is derived from the Latin "domus" meaning home or dwelling house. The word may be defined, by law, as the true place of habitation. A Washington statute was upheld as constitutional by the United States Supreme Court when it defined "domicile" as "a person's true, fixed and permanent home and place of habitation. It is the place where he intends to remain, and to which he expects to return when he leaves without intending to establish a new domicile elsewhere." Sturgis v. Washington, 414 U.S. 1057, 94 S.Ct. 563 (1973). A bona fide residence requirement may have the same legal connotation as domicile. Domicile and residence are usually in the same place, but the terms are not identical. A person may have two residences, but can have only one domicile. Whether the term "residence" or "domicile" is used, the key is the "intention to remain."

COMPULSORY ATTENDANCE

Legal authority for the state to require that all attend school is found in the common law doctrine of *parens patriae,* which maintains, essentially, that as a father to all persons, the state has the inherent prerogative to provide for the commonwealth and individual welfare. It can through the exercise of the police power of the legislature establish reasonable laws, not repugnant to the constitution, as it may judge for the good of the state. As guardian over everyone, the state has the authority to protect those who are not legally competent to act in their own behalf, *non sui juris* (literally, "not his own master"). This protection was quite naturally interpreted to apply to minor children who, because of their age, were unable to take care of themselves. Unavoidably, the state's interest in the child was to collide with parental interest and this, today, still forms the framework on which most compulsory education and curriculum controversies are litigated. It is well established, going back into English law, that the state's or the King's prerogative is superior to that of the parent when the parent's natural right is improperly exercised. Authority for the power of the state was clearly stated in English precedent and *parens patriae* was adopted throughout the United States "to the end that the health, patriotism, morality, efficiency, industry, and integrity of its citizenship may be preserved and protected, looking to the preservation and stability of the state."[6] In this country, the desirability of the doctrine as a rudiment of governmental responsibility was well expressed in an 1882 Illinois case, wherein the court said:

> It is the unquestioned right and imperative duty of every enlightened government, in its character of *parens patriae,* to protect and provide for the comfort and well-being of such of its citizens as by reason of infancy . . . were unable to take care of themselves. The performance of these duties is justly regarded as one of the most important of governmental functions, and all constitutional limitations must be so understood and construed as not to interfere with its proper and legitimate exercise.[7]

A child has a right to be protected not only from the patent abuses of his parents but also against the ignorance of his parents. The state has recognized more truth than fiction in the adage, "There are no delinquent children, only delinquent parents." In support of this view, juvenile courts and welfare agencies of the state have traditionally intervened between parent and child in cases of parental abuse. Public education may thus serve as a mechanism to free the child from the shackles of unfit parents.

To protect the child from the parent requires affirmative state action. A child has no constitutional protection from the parent; such protection must come in the form of statutory action by the state to protect the child, examples of which are compulsory attendance laws and requirements that children be exposed to certain kinds of educational curricula. On the other hand, the state's action must be supported by a compelling or, at least, a rational state interest before either the child's or the parent's rights can be restricted or infringed upon.

In the United States today, a dual set of precedents have emerged. One tends to limit *parens patriae*, as is evidenced by court-imposed limitations on state handling of juvenile cases.[8] This was illustrated by the exception from state compulsory attendance laws in *Yoder*.[9] The second precedent is a tendency of the courts to allow the state to protect the infant from parental abuse as was reflected by the United States Supreme Court in *Ford* v. *Ford* [10] in 1962:

> Unfortunately, experience has shown that the question of custody, so vital to a child's happiness and well-being, frequently cannot be left to the discretion of the parents. This is particularly true where, as here, the estrangement of husband and wife beclouds parental judgment with emotion and prejudices.

The language of the Supreme Court in *Pierce* v. *Society of Sisters* [11] indicated that only limited tolerance would be given the state in interfering with the parent's control of the child:

> In this day and under our civilization, the child of man is his parent's child and not the state's. . . . It is not seriously debatable that the parental right to guide one's child intellectually and religiously is a most substantial part of the liberty and freedom of the parent.

This does not mean that parental rights fully preempt those of the state. On the contrary, it would appear that a parent may forfeit his right to control his child by either omission or commission. In such case, the parent has no immunity from state intervention.

Nearly twenty years after *Pierce,* in 1943, the Supreme Court more clearly defined its position toward state intervention in *Prince* v. *Massachusetts*.[12] Here, a legal guardian was found guilty of contributing to the delinquence of a minor by permitting her nine-year-old ward to sell Jehovah's Witnesses publications on a public street. The act was found to be in violation of Massachusetts' child labor laws. The Supreme Court addressed the conflicting claims of parent and state saying:

> [T]he family itself is not beyond regulation in the public interest . . . acting to guard the general interest in youth's well being, the state as *parens patriae* may restrict the parent's control by requiring school attendance, regulating or prohibiting the child's labor and in many other ways.

In *Yoder,* the court said that the power of the parent, even when linked to free exercise of religion, may be subject to limitation if it appears that parental decisions will jeopardize the health or safety of the children or have "potential for significant social burdens."

A common thread running through these precedents is a renewed judicial concern for the child, with the parental interest and the state interest secondary. However, the general welfare is always a concern of the state and the maxim *salus populi suprema lex esto,* let the welfare of the people be the supreme law, is sufficient justification for the exercise of the *parens patriae* doctrine.

State intervention to compel attendance includes distinguishable premises: the state may provide education for all who cannot appropriately educate themselves, protect infants from those who would deny them education, and compel all citizens to act in ways most beneficial to the child and society.[13] Reflecting state concern in these areas, compulsory attendance laws both require schooling and provide enforcement to protect the child from undesirable parental conduct.[14]

Cases involving challenges to compulsory attendance laws generally emanate from disputes between parents and officials. This may be due, in part, to the old notion that "the basic right of a juvenile is not to liberty but to custody."[15] It may also result directly from enforcement provisions in compulsory attendance laws that penalize the parent, rather than the child.

Confrontation between state and parent instead of between state and child is probably the result of two subtle theories suggested by Kleinfeld.[16] One is that parents have a duty to a child to educate him, and the state may compel fulfillment of this duty. The other is that parents have a duty to the state to educate their children, which the state may compel them to perform.

Whether the judgment of the parent should prevail over the collective judgment of the state in educational matters is a much broader question, however, than may be evidenced by simple challenges to compulsory attendance laws. In a dispute between parent and state regarding an educational matter, parents may be pictured as intelligent, well-meaning, and motivated for the betterment of the child. This is not always the case. The invocation of the doctrine of *parens patriae* in matters of education may result from broken homes where parents will not assist or support the child in obtaining an education. Where children have sought financial assistance from parents toward a common school education, the courts have uniformly termed such education as "necessary" and granted the support. Common school education is a "necessary," just as food, lodging, clothing, and medicine are.[17]

In the courts' view, education has traditionally been of such importance that even items assisting school attendance have been considered necessary for child support purposes. For example, one early Texas court held that a buggy may be a "necessary" if it is needed to convey a child to and from school.[18] In some states, the courts have given alimony in divorce decrees that considers education to be a "necessary" over and beyond the normal public school education.[19]

Exercise of *parens patriae* by the state may result in more severe action than that of requiring a child to attend school or mandating that a parent furnish resources for attendance in school or college. The child-parent relationship can be partly or totally severed by judicial enforcement of divorce, neglect,[20] or child abuse statutes.[21] The concept of *parens patriae* extends to compulsory medical care over the objection of parents. Some states have explicit statutory language declaring a parent neglectful if he fails to provide medical care for his child. Under a finding of neglect, the court is empowered to provide the necessary medical care.[22] Courts have made children the wards of the state and required medical care, acting in *parens patriae*, in the absence of statute and under common law.[23]

It should be noted that the invocation of *parens patriae* by the state does not restrict parental authority in all cases. In some instances, such action may even strengthen it. In cases in which parents are unable to control their own children, the child's action produces not only disharmony within the family but sometimes becomes a nuisance to the public generally. For such situations, some states have enacted "stubborn child laws"[24] that protect the public from children who are "runaways, night walkers, common railers and brawlers."

EXCEPTIONS TO COMPULSORY ATTENDANCE

When compulsory attendance laws are mentioned, one usually thinks of children being compelled to attend only public schools. However, many alternatives and exceptions exist. A child may have the prerogative of home instruction or attendance at private, profit, nonprofit, sectarian, or secular schools. A child may also be exempt from required attendance because of religion, marriage, physical or mental incapacity, distance of travel, and so on. Courts have established many precedents that even today are in a state of transition.

Instruction in Private Schools

Few cases have defined "private school" as used in compulsory attendance laws.[25] Precise definition is lacking perhaps partly because in several jurisdictions children are not required to attend either public or private schools but must obtain "equivalent instruction."[26] Although vaguely defining the term "equivalent" as meaning "equal," the court generally refers to the qualifications of the instructor and the available teaching materials as the primary criteria for determining equivalency of instruction.

The state cannot impose too many regulations on private schools. In holding Ohio's regulation of private schools overly restrictive, tending to make private schools the images of public schools, the court said that the over-regulation of the private schools emanated from state education agency regulations that governed "the content of the curriculum that [was] taught, the manner in which it [was] taught, the person or persons who [taught] it, the physical layout of the building in which the students [were] taught, the hours of instruction, and the educational policies intended to be achieved through the instruction offered."[27]

Most courts have held that to be "recognized," a private school must provide instruction equivalent to the free instruction furnished in public schools. To have equivalent instruction, it is also necessary for the private school to comply with the statutory period of attendance.[28]

Although the state can require instruction equivalent to that of a public school, it cannot deny the parent the right to send his child to a private school. In a 1925 case, a private school itself, as a corporation, claimed denial of due process of law because an Oregon compulsory attendance statute required all children ages eight to sixteen to attend public schools.[29] The appellees in the case were the Society of Sisters and Hill Military Academy, both private, profit-making corporations. The schools claimed that enforcement of the compulsory attendance law would deprive them of students, destroy the profitable features of their businesses, and diminish the value of their property.

No question was raised challenging the power of the state to reasonably regulate, inspect, supervise, and examine all schools, teachers, and pupils and to see that nothing was taught that was inimical to the public welfare. Apparently, the law was originally enacted to combat Bolshevism, syndicalism, and communism. Supporters of the law sought to place all education more directly under the control of the state to prevent the teaching of certain economic doctrines.

In ruling in the plaintiffs' favor, in *Pierce,* the United States Supreme Court decided the case on the grounds that the state cannot, through improper regulation, deprive a business corporation of its patrons or customers. The law deprived the corporations of a liberty protected by the Fourteenth Amendment, according to the Court.

In a statement that must be considered *dictum,* since neither parents or children were appellants, the Court remarked on the rights of both parent and child:

> The fundamental theory of liberty upon which all governments in this union repose excludes any general power of the state to standardize its children by forcing them to accept instruction from public teachers only. The child is not the mere creature of the state; those who nurture him and direct his destiny have the right, coupled with the high duty, to recognize and prepare him for additional obligations.[30]

Religious interests may be used as rationale by private school operators to maintain that their schools should remain open regardless of adherence to state curriculum regulations. Courts will weigh religious interests against state interests and the result may hang in balance on the facts involved. For example, even a church itself may be closed if worship services are held in a residential area of a city and the religious chanting during worship services disturbs the neighborhood.[31] With private religious schools, though, the facts and the interests involved may concern more esoteric questions, such as whether accommodation of minimal state educational requirements is, in and of itself, an encroachment on religious interests. In Nebraska, a lengthy and highly publicized conflict developed when the state closed a private religious school because it did not adhere to state requirements for private schools. The Supreme Court of Nebraska held that the state interests prevailed over the religious interests of the private school proprietors and parents.[32] Religious convictions do not exempt operators of private schools from compliance with reasonable state school laws.[33] In this regard an appeals court in Michigan has held that parochial schools can be required to submit to the state records of enrollment of pupils attending the schools and the qualifications of teachers. Similarly, the state can enforce curriculum and teacher certification requirements.[34]

Compulsory Education Law Requiring
All Children to Attend Public Schools
Violates Due Process Clause

PIERCE v. SOCIETY OF THE SISTERS OF THE HOLY NAMES OF JESUS AND MARY

Supreme Court of the United States, 1925.
268 U.S. 510, 45 S.Ct. 571.

Mr. Justice McREYNOLDS delivered the opinion of the Court.

These appeals are from decrees, based upon undenied allegations, which granted preliminary orders restraining appellants from threatening or attempting to enforce the Compulsory Education Act adopted November 7, 1922 (Laws Or.1923, p. 9), under the initiative provision of her Constitution by the voters of Oregon. Judicial Code, § 266 (Comp.St. § 1243). . . .

The challenged act, effective September 1, 1926, requires every parent, guardian, or other person having control or charge or custody of a child between eight and sixteen years to send him "to a public school for the period of time a public school shall be held during the current year" in the district where the child resides; and failure so to do is declared a misdemeanor. There are exemptions—not specially important here—for children who are not normal, or who have completed the eighth grade, or whose parents or private teachers reside at considerable distances from any public school, or who hold special permits from the county superintendent. The manifest purpose is to compel general attendance at public schools by normal children, between eight and sixteen, who have not completed the eighth grade. And without doubt enforcement of the statute would seriously impair, perhaps destroy, the profitable features of appellees' business and greatly diminish the value of their property.

Appellee the Society of Sisters is an Oregon corporation, organized in 1880, with power to care for orphans, educate and instruct the youth, establish and maintain academies or schools, and acquire necessary real and personal property. It has long devoted its property and effort to the secular and religious education and care of children, and has acquired the valuable good will of many parents and guardians. . . . It owns valuable buildings, especially constructed and equipped for school purposes. The business is remunerative—the annual income from primary schools exceeds $30,000—and the successful conduct of this requires long time contracts with teachers and parents. The Compulsory Education Act of 1922 has already caused the withdrawal from its schools of children who would otherwise continue, and their income has steadily declined. The appellants, public officers, have proclaimed their purpose strictly to enforce the statute.

After setting out the above facts, the Society's bill alleges that the enactment conflicts with the right of parents to choose schools where their children will receive appropriate mental and religious training, the right of the child to influence the parents' choice of a school, the right of schools and teachers therein to engage in a useful business or profession, and is accordingly repugnant to the Constitution and void. And, further, that unless enforcement of the measure is enjoined the corporation's business and property will suffer irreparable injury.

Appellee Hill Military Academy is a private corporation organized in 1908 under the laws of Oregon, engaged in owning, operating, and conducting for profit an elementary, college preparatory, and military training school for boys between the ages of five and twenty-one years. . . . It owns considerable real and personal property, some useful only for school purposes. The business and incident good will are very valuable. . . .

The Academy's bill states the foregoing facts and then alleges that the challenged act contravenes the corporation's rights guaranteed by the Fourteenth Amendment and that unless appellants are restrained from proclaiming its validity and threatening to enforce it irreparable injury will result. The prayer is for an appropriate injunction.

. . . The court ruled that the Fourteenth Amendment guaranteed appellees against the deprivation of their property without due process of law consequent upon the unlawful interference by appellants with the free choice of patrons, present and prospective. It declared the right to conduct schools was property and that parents and guardians, as a part of their liberty, might direct the education of children by selecting reputable teachers and places. . . .

No question is raised concerning the power of the state reasonably to regulate all schools, to inspect, supervise and examine them, their teachers and pupils; to require that all children of proper age attend some school, that teachers shall be of good moral character and patriotic disposition, that certain studies plainly essential to good citizenship must be taught, and that nothing be taught which is manifestly inimical to the public welfare.

The inevitable practical result of enforcing the act under consideration would be destruction of appellees' primary schools, and perhaps all other private primary schools for normal children within the state of Oregon. Appellees are engaged in a kind of undertaking not inherently harmful, but long regarded as useful and meritorious. Certainly there is nothing in the present records to indicate that they have failed to discharge their obligations to patrons, students or the state. And there are no peculiar circumstances or present emergencies which demand extraordinary measures relative to primary education.

Under the doctrine of *Meyer* v. *Nebraska*, we think it entirely plain that the Act of 1922 unreasonably interferes with the liberty of parents and guardians to direct the upbringing and education of children under their control. As often heretofore pointed out, rights guaranteed by the Constitution may not be abridged by legislation which has no reasonable relation to some purpose within the competency of the state. The fundamental theory of liberty upon which all governments in this Union repose excludes any general power of the state to standardize its children by forcing them to accept instruction from public teachers only. The child is not the mere creature of the state; those who nurture him and direct his destiny have the right, coupled with the high duty, to recognize and prepare him for addition-al obligations.

Appellees are corporations, and therefore, it is said, they cannot claim for themselves the liberty which the Fourteenth Amendment guarantees. Accepted in the proper sense, this is true. . . . But they have business and property for which they claim protection. These are threatened with destruction through the unwarranted compulsion which appellants are exercising over present and prospective patrons of their schools. And this court has gone very far to protect against loss threatened by such action. . . .

Generally, it is entirely true, as urged by counsel, that no person in any business has such an interest in possible customers as to enable him to restrain exercise of proper power of the state upon the ground that he will be deprived of patronage. But the injunctions here sought are not against the exercise of any proper power. Appellees asked protection against arbitrary, unreasonable, and unlawful interference with their patrons and the consequent destruction of their business and property. Their interest is clear and immediate . . . .

The decrees below are affirmed.

Instruction at Home

The substantive due process right of children to attend private schools as guaranteed by *Pierce* does not extend to home instruction. State statutes may or may not provide for home instruction as an exemption from public school attendance.

Several states refuse to allow home instruction because it is believed that the sequestration of children in the home, insulated from society and other children, will inhibit social consciousness and prevent the child from living a normal and productive life. A New Jersey court has said that "Cloister and shelter have their place, but not in the everyday give and take of life."[35]

Neither does denial of home instruction, as a valid exemption to compulsory attendance, violate equal protection of the Fourteenth Amendment. A New Mexico court has held that the state need only to show that such denial is rationally related to a legitimate state purpose. The state's desire to have children attend school with other children of their age is an appropriate and defensible state interest. The court said, "By bringing children into contact with some person, other than those in the excluded group, those children are exposed to at least one other set of attitudes, values, morals, lifestyles and intellectual abilities."[36]

An Oregon appellate court has held that the state does not violate equal protection when it distinguishes between children taught by parents or a private teacher in home instruction, and those taught in a private school. The state may clearly have a rational basis for such distinctions.[37]

In states that permit home instruction, the key elements in determining the validity of home instruction are generally the educational level of the parents and the regularity and time of instruction. Obviously, states permitting home instruction must prescribe certain minimal standards for such instruction or their compulsory attendance laws would be nullified.

Courts will uphold reasonable state criteria to qualify for exemption from compulsory attendance. Where a statute provided that parents show a "manifest educational hardship," it was not sufficient that parents show merely the one criterion of "manifest educational hardship" to validly qualify for exemption from compulsory attendance. A state board of education may require adherence to one or more of the criteria, such as the competency of parents to teach, the scope of the subject matter, the child's potential for interaction with peers and adults, and the teaching methods to be employed, before the exemption is considered valid.[38]

The Supreme Court of Virginia has held that parents who were not qualified tutors or teachers as prescribed by state board rule could not gain exemption from compulsory attendance laws by claiming that their home instruction constituted a private school. In this instance, one parent was a high school graduate with an Associate's Degree in Industrial Technology and the other parent had obtained a high school diploma from a correspondence school.[39] In 1984, this board rule was negated by statute.

An early Washington case rejected the home as a private school. In that case, the parent claimed his home instruction was authorized by a statute providing that children must attend "the public school of the district in which the child resides, for the full time such school may be in session, or . . . attend a private school for the same time." The parent further claimed that he was a qualified and competent teacher giving home instruction within the definition to the statute. This claim was rejected by the court, which explained:

> We do not think that the giving of instruction by a parent to a child, conceding the competency of the parent to fully instruct the child in all that is taught in the public schools, is within the meaning of the law "to attend a private school." Such a requirement means more than home instruction; it means that the same character of school as the public school, a regular, organized and existing institution making a business of instructing children of school age in the required studies and for the full time required by the laws of this state. . . . There may be a difference in institution and government, but the purpose and end of both public and private schools must be the same—the education of children of school age. The parent who teaches his children at home, whatever be his reason for desiring to do so, does not maintain such a school.[40]

Home instruction has been rejected because of difficulty of supervision. The state bears the responsibility of reasonable supervision to guarantee that students obtain an adequate education. If home instruction imposes an unreasonable burden on the state's performance of its duties, the instruction is not allowed. For example, a situation may exist where parents use education units so small or facilities of such doubtful quality that supervision creates an unusual expense for the state. The state requires that proper educational facilities be provided for the child and supplied in a way that the state can ascertain facts about the instructional program and maintain proper direction without undue cost.[41]

Critics have charged that home instruction does not comply with statutory requirements that a child attend a public, private, denominational, or parochial school and be taught by a competent instructor. In Kansas, the legislature reenacted a compulsory attendance law, leaving out a former provision for home instruction as a valid exemption from compulsory attendance. A court said that exclusion of home instruction, while including private, denominational, and parochial instruction as valid, indicated legislative intent to disallow home instruction as an excuse for nonattendance.[42]

Another Kansas case distinguished between a "private school" and "scheduled home instruction." Here parents operated a "school," serving as tutors themselves, with only their own children in attendance. The only grades taught were those in which their own children were enrolled. The court interpreted this as falling short of the definition of a private school, and ruled that the instruction given did not meet statutory requirements. In the view of the court, the program was nothing more than "home instruction."[43]

Where reference to home instruction was excluded from the statute, a California court refused to officially regard home instruction programs as qualified "private schools."[44]

Other cases, however, have established that home instruction may constitute "private school" instruction in contemplation of the law. For example, a parent who employs a competent, noncertified school teacher to instruct his child in the same curriculum and for the same period of time as the public schools is complying with the law, which requires instruction in a public, private, or parochial school.[45] The court said:

> The law was made for the parent who does not educate his child, and not for the parent who employs a teacher and pays him out of his private purse, and so places within the reach of the child the opportunity and means of acquiring an education equal to that obtainable in the public schools of the State.

In summary, if a state statute allows for home instruction as an alternative to compulsory attendance, the burden falls on the state to show that the parent is not, in fact, providing such instruction. If the state has set out few standards governing home instruction, the inadequacy of such instruction may be difficult to prove. The state must produce evidence documenting the parent's failure to furnish adequate home instruction and the parent must respond to such evidence.[46] However, the final burden of proof rests on the state to show that the instruction failed to meet state requirements.[47]

Other Exemptions from Compulsory Attendance

While private schools and home instruction provide alternatives to attendance in public schools, the child nevertheless is compelled to attend some school. Another kind of litigation that has arisen over the years has sought exemption from attending any school at all. The claims for exemption have generally been based on illness, marriage, or religion, with religious objection by far the most common.

Illness Parents who claim that their child is ill and cannot attend school must show valid medical proof of illness. An Illinois case illustrates how a claim of illness may well result in a charge of truancy. Under Illinois law, a child is considered to be truant if absent without "valid cause," which is defined as illness, death in the immediate family, a family emergency, or other circumstances that cause concern to the parent for the child's health or safety. In this case, the student was absent from school for 339½ days during a two-year period. Testimony from the student's doctor indicated that he had conducted tests and found that the child had certain allergies, but these were not of such magnitude to warrant absences from school. Having no other proof of illness to justify the noncompliance with the law, the parents' conviction was upheld.[48]

Marriage Exemption from compulsory attendance is a dubious benefit of marriage. Courts have uniformly agreed that when a minor of less than sixteen years (otherwise required to attend school) is married, he or she is exempt from further compulsory attendance.

One of the precedents in this area was derived by the Supreme Court of Louisiana. A fifteen-year-old girl and her husband sought to set aside a judgment of a lower court committing her to the State Industrial School for Girls as a result of her truancy and alleged juvenile delinquency.[49] The girl did not deny truancy but claimed that her legal marriage exempted her from attendance. Although the marriage of a female under sixteen years of age was prohibited by law, the court ruled that once a girl is married, she enjoys the status of wife and has a right to live as such, emancipated from both school and parents. The court stated:

> The marriage relationship, regardless of the age of the persons involved, creates conditions and imposes obligations upon the parties that are obviously inconsistent with compulsory school attendance or with either the husband or wife remaining under the legal control of parents or other persons.

In another Louisiana case, a girl was truant and, in the lower court's opinion, a neglected child.[50] The girl, fourteen years of age, was married only a few days after the truant officer had taken her into custody. The lower court judge ignored the previous case (*Priest*) and committed the girl for an indefinite period to a state girls' school. The judge, exercising *parens patriae,* was of the opinion that the girl needed the care and protection of the state. The Supreme Court of Louisiana, while sympathetically viewing the judge's concern for the girl's welfare, held that the lower juvenile court could not commit her to the girls' school or prevent her from assuming the responsibilities of a married woman. The court stated that the power of such public policy determinations rested with the legislature and not the court.

A New York court followed the rationale of these two cases. A girl had not been committed to a state school or been determined to be a delinquent, but she had resisted attempts to force her to attend school because she was married and wanted to be a housewife and homemaker.[51] The court, while recognizing the state's sovereignty concerning compulsory attendance, decided for the girl, observing that times and mores had changed since the compulsory attendance law was passed. The court also expressed doubt that the legislature had anticipated the question of such youthful marriage in passing the law.

In the eyes of the law, then, youthful marriage is another valid exemption from compulsory attendance laws. This determination, in the absence of specific statutory exemption, is predicated on the assumption that the responsibility of the minor, once married, is to be a productive member of society and that this is better achieved by establishing and supporting a home. The net effect of this reasoning is to remove both state and parental control over the alternatives available to minors. Consequently, they have the choice and the right to decide on their own further education.

Religion Following *Pierce* v. *Society of Sisters*,[52] it was rather uniformly assumed that children could be compelled to attend a public, private, or parochial school, but that no child had a right *not* to attend school at all.

Early cases established that the child's and the parents' rights of religious freedom, as protected by the First Amendment of the United States Constitution, were not sufficient to diminish the state's power to compel compulsory attendance. Justice Cardozo, in a concurring opinion in *Hamilton* v. *Regents*[53] (a case dealing with the rights of a conscientious objector), maintained that undesirable results may evolve where religious scruples predominate over reasonable state laws. In delivering the opinion Cardozo said:

> Manifestly a different doctrine would carry us to lengths that have never yet been dreamed of. The conscientious objector, if his liberties were to be thus extended, might refuse to contribute taxes in furtherance of any other end condemned by his conscience as irreligious or immoral. The right of private judgment has never yet been so exalted above the powers and the compulsion of the agencies of government. One who is a martyr to a principle—which may turn out in the end to be a delusion or an error—does not prove by his martyrdom that he has kept within the law.[54]

Following this rationale, other courts have concluded that the individual cannot be permitted, on religious grounds, to be the judge of his duty to obey reasonable civil requirements enacted in the interest of public welfare.

In a 1945 Virginia case, the parents of three families sought to prevent the enforcement of compulsory attendance laws on religious grounds. These parents interpreted the Bible as commanding parents to teach and train their own children. They believed that sending their children to public schools was incompatible with the primary religious obligation they felt they owed their Maker. Their willful intent to violate the law was solely because of sincere religious convictions. The court, in deciding against the parents, declared:

> No amount of religious fervor he [parent] may entertain in opposition to adequate instruction should be allowed to work a lifelong injury to his child. Nor should he, for this religious reason, be suffered to inflict another illiterate citizen on his community or his state.[55]

Although the religious issue was the *ratio decidendi* in this case, the court ruled that the parents were not capable of adequately educating the children themselves.

Religious grounds have been ruled insufficient to limit the number of days a child attends school. A Moslem parent claimed that his religion prevented him from sending his children to school on Fridays. Regardless of the validity of his religious motives, the court said the state allowed parental choice among public, private, and parochial schools. The parent and child did not, however, have the option of nonattendance on Fridays.[56]

Until recently, the prevailing view of the courts was that religious beliefs cannot impair achievement of the state's objective—universal compulsory education. The precedent-setting case that has radically altered this view is *Wisconsin* v. *Yoder*.[57] This case contested the power of the state to require the school attendance of Amish children after the eighth grade. Although the issue in this case is limited to the compulsory attendance of Amish children between the time they complete the eighth grade and the time they reach sixteen years of age, it nevertheless has profound implications for all future cases involving compulsory attendance.

The decision of the Court in this case can be summarized in three points. First, although the state has power to impose reasonable regulation, this power must be balanced against fundamental rights and interests of individuals. Second, beliefs that are philosophical rather than personal are not sufficient to invoke free exercise of religion. Third, where parents show that enforcement of compulsory education will endanger their religious beliefs, the *parens patriae* power of the state must give way to the free exercise clause of the First Amendment.

Two dramatic limitations on the general applicability of *Yoder* are the objection of the Amish only to post-eighth-grade compulsory attendance of fourteen- and fifteen-year-olds and the well-established Amish customs of living near the soil and shunning modern society generally. These features of the case tend to diminish the compelling interest of the state; they eliminate the possibility of illiteracy by providing at least eight years of schooling and negate the chance of these children becoming unproductive members of society.

The ultimate question of who will determine the child's destiny is not answered by the case. The court is content, instead, to speak rather vaguely of balancing the fundamental religious freedom of the parents against the interest of the state.

State Cannot Compel Amish Children
to Attend Public High School

STATE OF WISCONSIN v. YODER

Supreme Court of the United States, 1972.
406 U.S. 205, 92 S.Ct. 1526.

. . . Respondents Jonas Yoder and Wallace Miller are members of the Old Order Amish religion, and respondent Adin Yutzy is a member of the Conservative Amish Mennonite Church. They and their families are residents of Green County, Wisconsin. Wisconsin's compulsory school-attendance law required them to cause their children to attend public or private school until reaching age sixteen but the respondents declined to send their children, ages fourteen and fifteen, to public school after they completed the eighth grade. The children were not enrolled in any private school, or within any recognized exception to the compulsory-attendance law, and they are conceded to be subject to the Wisconsin statute.

On complaint of the school district administrator for the public schools, respondents were charged, tried, and convicted of violating the compulsory-attendance law in Green County Court and were fined the sum of $5 each. Respondents defended on the ground that the application of the compulsory-attendance law violated their rights under the First and Fourteenth Amendments. . . .

The history of the Amish sect was given in some detail, beginning with the Swiss Anabaptists of the sixteenth century who rejected institutionalized churches and sought to return to the early, simple, Christian life de-emphasizing material success, rejecting the competitive spirit, and seeking to insulate themselves from the modern world. As a result of their common heritage, Old Order Amish communities today are characterized by a fundamental belief that salvation requires life in a church community separate and apart from the world and worldly influence. This concept of life aloof from the world and its values is central to their faith. . . .

Formal high school education beyond the eighth grade is contrary to Amish beliefs, not only because it places Amish children in an environment hostile to Amish beliefs with increasing emphasis on competition in class work and sports and with pressure to conform to the styles, manners, and ways of the peer group, but also because it takes them away from their community, physically and emotionally, during the crucial and formative adolescent period of life. . . .

The Amish do not object to elementary education through the first eight grades as a general proposition because they agree that their children must have basic skills in the "three R's" in order to read the Bible, to be good farmers and citizens, and to be able to deal with non-Amish people when necessary in the course of daily affairs. They view such a basic education as acceptable because it does not significantly expose their children to worldly values or interfere with their development in the Amish community during the crucial adolescent period. While Amish accept compulsory elementary education generally, wherever possible they have established their own elementary schools in many respects like the small local schools of the past. In the Amish belief higher learning tends to develop values they reject as influences that alienate man from God. . . .

There is no doubt as to the power of a State, having a high responsibility for education of its citizens, to impose reasonable regulations for the control and duration of basic education. See, e.g., Pierce v. Society of Sisters, 268 U.S. 510, 534, 45 S.Ct. 571, 573, 69 L.Ed. 1070 (1925). Providing public schools ranks at the very apex of the function of a State. Yet even this paramount responsibility was, in *Pierce,* made to yield to the right of parents to provide an equivalent education in a privately operated system. There the Court held that Oregon's statute compelling attendance in a public school from age eight to age sixteen unreasonably interfered with the interest of parents in directing the rearing of their offspring, including their education in church-operated schools. As that case suggests, the values of parental direction of the religious upbringing and education of their children in their early and formative years have a high place in our society. . . .

Thus, a State's interest in universal education, however highly we rank it, is not totally free from a balancing process when it impinges on fundamental rights and interests, such as those specifically protected by the Free Exercise Clause of the First Amendment, and the traditional interest of parents with respect to the religious upbringing of their children so long as they, in the words of *Pierce*, "prepare [them] for additional obligations." 268 U.S., at 535, 45 S.Ct., at 573.

It follows that in order for Wisconsin to compel school attendance beyond the eighth grade against a claim that such attendance interferes with the practice of a legitimate religious belief, it must appear either that the State does not deny the free exercise of religious belief by its requirement, or that there is a state interest of sufficient magnitude to override the interest claiming protection under the Free Exercise Clause. . . .

The essence of all that has been said and written on the subject is that only those interests of the highest order and those not otherwise served can overbalance legitimate claims to the free exercise of religion. We can accept it as settled, therefore, that, however strong the State's interest in universal compulsory education, it is by no means absolute to the exclusion or subordination of all other interests. . . .

We come then to the quality of the claims of the respondents concerning the alleged encroachment of Wisconsin's compulsory school-attendance statute on their rights and the rights of their children to the free exercise of the religious beliefs they and their forbears have adhered to for almost three centuries. In evaluating those claims we must be careful to determine whether the Amish religious faith and their mode of life are, as they claim, inseparable and interdependent. A way of life, however virtuous and admirable, may not be interposed as a barrier to reasonable state regulation of education if it is based on purely secular considerations; to have the protection of the Religion Clauses, the claims must be rooted in religious belief. Although a determination of what is a "religious" belief or practice entitled to constitutional protection may present a most delicate question, the very concept of ordered liberty precludes allowing every person to make his own standards on matters of conduct in which society as a whole has important interests. Thus, if the Amish asserted their claims because of their subjective evaluation and rejection of the contemporary secular values accepted by the majority, much as Thoreau rejected the social values of his time and isolated himself at Walden Pond, their claims would not rest on a religious basis. Thoreau's choice was philosophical and personal rather than religious, and such belief does not rise to the demands of the Religion Clauses.

Giving no weight to such secular considerations, however, we see that the record in this case abundantly supports the claim that the traditional way of life of the Amish is not merely a matter of personal preference, but one of deep religious conviction, shared by an organized group, and intimately related to daily living. . . .

As the society around the Amish has become more populous, urban, industrialized, and complex, particularly in this century, government regulation of human affairs has correspondingly become more detailed and pervasive. The Amish mode of life has thus come into conflict increasingly with requirements of contemporary society exerting a hydraulic insistence on conformity to majoritarian standards. So long as compulsory education laws were confined to eight grades of elementary basic education imparted in a nearby rural schoolhouse, with a large proportion of students of the Amish faith, the Old Order Amish had little basis to fear that school attendance would expose their children to the worldly influence they reject. But modern compulsory secondary education in rural areas is now largely carried on in a consolidated school, often remote from the student's home and alien to his daily home life. As the record so strongly shows, the values and programs of the modern secondary school are in sharp conflict with the fundamental mode of life mandated by the Amish religion; modern laws requiring compulsory secondary education have accordingly engendered great concern and conflict. The conclusion is inescapable that secondary schooling, by exposing Amish children to worldly influences in terms of attitudes, goals, and values contrary to beliefs, and by substantially interfering with the religious development of the Amish child and his integration into the way of life of the Amish faith community at the crucial adolescent stage of development, contravenes the basic religious tenets and practice of the Amish faith, both as to the parent and the child.

The impact of the compulsory-attendance law on respondents' practice of the Amish religion is not only severe, but inescapable, for the Wisconsin law affirmatively compels them, under threat of criminal sanction, to perform acts undeniably at odds with fundamental tenets of their religious beliefs. . . .

In sum, the unchallenged testimony of acknowledged experts in education and religious history, almost 300 years of consistent practice, and strong evidence of a sustained faith pervading and regulating respondents' entire mode of life support the claim that enforcement of the State's requirement of compulsory formal education after the eighth grade would gravely endanger if not destroy the free exercise of respondents' religious beliefs. . . .

The State advances two primary arguments in support of its system of compulsory education. It notes, as Thomas Jefferson pointed out early in our history, that some degree of education is necessary to prepare citizens to participate effectively and intelligently in our open political system if we are to preserve freedom and independence. Further, education prepares individuals to be self-reliant and self-sufficient participants in society. We accept these propositions.

However, the evidence adduced by the Amish in this case is persuasively to the effect that an additional one or two years of formal high school for Amish children in place of their long-established program of informal vocational education would do little to serve those interests. Respondents' experts testified at trial, without challenge, that the value of all education must be assessed in terms of its capacity to prepare the child for life. It is one thing to say that compulsory education for a year or two beyond the eighth grade may be necessary when its goal is the preparation of the child for life in modern society as the majority live, but it is quite another if the goal of education be viewed as the preparation of the child for life in the separated agrarian community that is the keystone of the Amish faith. . . .

The State attacks respondents' position as one fostering "ignorance" from which the child must be protected by the State. No one can question the State's duty to protect children from ignorance but this argument does not square with the facts disclosed in the record. Whatever their idiosyncrasies as seen by the majority, this record strongly shows that the Amish community has been a highly successful social unit within our society, even if apart from the conventional "mainstream." Its members are productive and very law-abiding members of society; they reject public welfare in any of its usual modern forms. The Congress itself recognized their self-sufficiency by authorizing exemption of such groups as the Amish from the obligation to pay social security taxes. . . .

Insofar as the State's claim rests on the view that a brief additional period of formal education is imperative to enable the Amish to participate effectively and intelligently in our democratic process it must fall. The Amish alternative to formal secondary school education has enabled them to function effectively in their day-to-day life under self-imposed limitations on relations with the world, and to survive and prosper in contemporary society as a separate, sharply identifiable and highly self-sufficient community for more than 200 years in this country. In itself this is strong evidence that they are capable of fulfilling the social and political responsibilities of citizenship without compelled attendance beyond the eighth grade at the price of jeopardizing their free exercise of religious belief. When Thomas Jefferson emphasized the need for education as a bulwark of a free people against tyranny, there is nothing to indicate he had in mind compulsory education through any fixed age beyond a basic education. Indeed, the Amish communities singularly parallel and reflect may of the virtues of Jefferson's ideal of the "sturdy yeoman" who would form the basis of what he considered as the ideal of a democratic society. Even their idiosyncratic separateness exemplifies the diversity we profess to admire and encourage.

The requirement for compulsory education beyond the eighth grade is a relatively recent development in our history. Less than sixty years ago, the educational requirements of almost all of the States were satisfied by completion of the elementary grades, at least where the child was regularly and lawfully employed. The independence and successful social functioning of the Amish community for a period approaching almost three centuries and more than 200 years in this country are strong evidence that there is at best a speculative gain, in terms of meeting the duties of citizenship, from an additional one or two years of compulsory formal education. Against this background it would require a more particularized showing from the State on this point to justify the severe interference with religious freedom such additional compulsory attendance would entail. . . . There is no intimation that the Amish employment of their children on family farms is in any way deleterious to their health or that Amish parents exploit children at tender years. Any such inference would be contrary to the record before us. Moreover, employment of Amish children on the family farm does not present the undesirable economic aspects of eliminating jobs that might otherwise be held by adults.

Finally, the State, on authority of *Prince* v. *Massachusetts*, argues that a decision exempting Amish children from the State's requirement fails to recognize the substantive right of the Amish child to a secondary education, and fails to give due regard to the power of the State as *parens patriae* to extend the benefit of secondary education to children regardless of the wishes of their parents. Taken at its broadest sweep, the Court's language in *Prince* might be read to give support to the State's position. However, the Court was not confronted in *Prince* with a situation comparable to that of the Amish as revealed in this record; this is shown by the Court's severe characterization of the evils that it thought the legislature could legitimately associate with child labor, even when performed in the company of an adult. 321 U.S., at 169–170, 64 S.Ct., at 443–444. The Court later took great care to confine *Prince* to a narrow scope in *Sherbert* v. *Verner,* when it stated:

> On the other hand, the Court has rejected challenges under the Free Exercise Clause to governmental regulation of certain overt acts prompted by religious beliefs or principles, for "even when the action is in accord with one's religious convictions, [it] is not totally free from legislative restrictions." Braunfeld v. Brown, 366 U.S. 599, 603, 81 S.Ct. 1144, 1146, 6 L.Ed.2d 563. The conduct or actions so regulated have invariably posed some substantial threat to public safety, peace or order. See, e.g., Reynolds v. United States, 98 U.S. 145, 25 L.Ed. 244; Jacobson v. Massachusetts, 197 U.S. 11, 25 S.Ct. 358, 49 L.Ed. 643; Prince v. Massachusetts, 321 U.S. 158, 64 S.Ct. 438, 88 L.Ed. 645. . . . 374 U.S., at 402–403, 83 S.Ct., at 1793.

This case, of course, is not one in which any harm to the physical or mental health of the child or to the public safety, peace, order, or welfare has been demonstrated or may be properly inferred. The record is to the contrary, and any reliance on that theory would find no support in the evidence. . . .

Our holding in no way determines the proper resolution of possible competing interests of parents, children, and the State in an appropriate state court proceeding in which the power of the State is asserted on the theory that Amish parents are preventing their minor children from attending high school despite their expressed desires to the contrary. Recognition of the claim of the State in such a proceeding would, of course, call into question traditional concepts of parental control over the religious upbringing and education of their minor children recognized in this Court's past decisions. It is clear that such an intrusion by a State into family decisions in the area of religious training would give rise to grave questions of religious freedom comparable to those raised here and those presented in Pierce v. Society of Sisters, 268 U.S. 510, 45 S.Ct. 571, 69 L.Ed. 1070 (1925). On this record we neither reach nor decide those issues.

The State's argument proceeds without reliance on any actual conflict between the wishes of parents and children. It appears to rest on the potential that exemption of Amish parents from the requirements of the compulsory-education law might allow some parents to act contrary to the best interests of their children by foreclosing their opportunity to make an intelligent choice between the Amish way of life and that of the outside world. The same argument could, of course, be made with respect to all church schools short of college. There is nothing in the record or in the ordinary course of human experience to suggest that non-Amish parents generally consult with children of ages fourteen to sixteen if they are placed in a church school of the parents' faith.

Indeed it seems clear that if the State is empowered, as *parens patriae,* to "save" a child from himself or his Amish parents by requiring an additional two years of compulsory formal high school education, the State will in large measure influence, if not determine, the religious future of the child. Even more markedly than in *Prince,* therefore, this case involves the fundamental interest of parents, as contrasted with that of the State, to guide the religious future and education of their children. The history and culture of Western civilization reflect a strong tradition of parental concern for the nurture and upbringing of their children. This primary role of the parents in the upbringing of their children is now established beyond debate as an enduring American tradition. . . . The record strongly indicates that accommodating the religious objections of the Amish by forgoing one, or at most two, additional years of compulsory education will not impair the physical or mental health of the child, or result in an inability to be self-supporting or to discharge the duties and responsibilities of citizenship, or in any other way materially detract from the welfare of society.

In the fact of our consistent emphasis on the central values underlying the Religion Clauses in our constitutional scheme of government, we cannot accept a *parens patriae* claim of such all-encompassing scope and with such sweeping potential for broad and unforeseeable application as that urged by the State.

For the reasons stated we hold, with the Supreme Court of Wisconsin, that the First and Fourteenth Amendments prevent the State from compelling respondents to cause their children to attend formal high school to age sixteen. Our disposition of this case, however, in no way alters our recognition of the obvious fact that courts are not school boards or legislatures, and are ill-equipped to determine the "necessity" of discrete aspects of a State's program of compulsory education. This should suggest that courts must move with great circumspection in performing the sensitive and delicate task of weighing a State's legitimate social concern when faced with religious claims for exemption from generally applicable educational requirements. It cannot be overemphasized that we are not dealing with a way of life and mode of education by a group claiming to have recently discovered some "progressive" or more enlightened process for rearing children for modern life.

Aided by a history of three centuries as an identifiable religious sect and a long history as a successful and self-sufficient segment of American society, the Amish in this case have convincingly demonstrated the sincerity of their religious beliefs, the interrelationship of belief with their mode of life, the vital role that belief and daily conduct play in the continued survival of Old Order Amish communities and their religious organization, and the hazards presented by the State's enforcement of a statute generally valid as to others. Beyond this, they have carried the even more difficult burden of demonstrating the adequacy of their alternative mode of continuing informal vocational education in terms of precisely those overall interests that the State advances in support of its program of compulsory high school education. In light of this convincing showing, one that probably few other religious groups or sects could make, and weighing the minimal difference between what the State would require and what the Amish already accept, it was incumbent on the State to show with more particularity how its admittedly strong interest in compulsory education would be adversely affected by granting an exemption to the Amish. . . .

Nothing we hold is intended to undermine the general applicability of the State's compulsory school-attendance statutes or to limit the power of the State to promulgate reasonable standards that, while not impairing the free exercise of religion, provide for continuing agricultural vocational education under parental and church guidance by the Old Order Amish or others similarly situated. The States have had a long history of amicable and effective relationships with church-sponsored schools, and there is no basis for assuming that, in this related context, reasonable standards cannot be established concerning the content of the continuing vocational education of Amish children under parental guidance, provided always that state regulations are not inconsistent with what we have said in this opinion.

Affirmed.

State's Interest in Protecting Children
Extends to Home Instruction

STATE OF WEST VIRGINIA v. RIDDLE

Supreme Court of Appeals of West
Virginia, 1981.
285 S.E.2d 359.

NEELY, Justice:

This is a test-case criminal appeal from a conviction of appellants in the Circuit Court of Harrison County for failure to obey the Compulsory School Attendance Law, W.Va.Code, 18–8–1 [1951] and from fines of ten dollars ($10) each.

On an information given by Florence Hunt, School Attendance Officer, appellants were arrested for failing to send their two children to the public schools. Trial before Magistrate Geraldine Floyd resulted in a conviction and a fine of ten dollars ($10) each. Appellants appealed to the Circuit Court of Harrison County where a trial *de novo* involving extensive expert testimony was held on 27 July 1979, and resulted again in conviction. The appellants now appeal to this Court on the grounds that W.Va.Code, 18–8–1 [1951], the Compulsory School Attendance Law, is unconstitutional as a violation of their rights under the first and fourteenth amendments to the Constitution of the United States because it abridges the free exercise of appellants' religion. Appellants rely upon Wisconsin v. Yoder, 406 U.S. 205, 92 S.Ct. 1526, 32 L.Ed.2d 15 (1972) as authority for their position that the free exercise clause of the first amendment entitles them completely to disregard the West Virginia Compulsory School Attendance Law with impunity. We disagree and affirm the convictions.

Bobby and Esther Riddle are "Biblical Christians" who belong to a Methodist sect, the Wesley, which separated from the mainstream Methodist communion before the war between the states and remained resolutely unchanging. By "Biblical Christian" they mean one who "believes in the Bible as God's holy word." They dress modestly, and do not wear makeup or jewelry. A very important tenet of their belief is that one who sins after being saved loses his or her salvation. In short, they find themselves separated from, and at odds with, the values of the world.

Bobby and Esther Riddle have two children, Tim and Jill, both of compulsory school age. For a while they enrolled the children in a school called Emmanuel Christian Academy; however, they disagreed with that school's teaching of the reassuring doctrine that once a sinner is saved, he remains saved even if he accidently sins again. The Riddles strongly believe that a person may be saved once, but if he ever sins again, he "will be lost." Bobby and Esther Riddle are determined to have their children totally indoctrinated and educated in their religious beliefs, with no smattering of heresy. They perceive public school, like television, as a pernicious influence on the young; thus to preserve their children from any false sense of spiritual security, the Riddles began teaching their children at home.

By all accounts in the record below, the Riddles did an excellent job—possibly better than the public schools could do. The Reverend Paul W. Lindstrom, head of the Christian Liberty Academy, which furnishes teaching aids and undertakes to set up schools in homes like the Riddles' as "satellite schools" extolled the Riddles' work. Dr. George Leonard Hopkins of the Jupiter Christian School in Florida testified that the achievements of the two children as measured on tests were excellent.

The case before us is readily distinguishable from *Wisconsin* v. *Yoder,* supra. . . .

While the case before us and *Yoder,* supra, are similar in that in both cases the parents had sincere religious convictions which they thought would be endangered by sending their children to public schools, the similarity ends at that point. In *Yoder* the Supreme Court was confronted with an ancient religious community which the record demonstrated had its own system of vocational and technical training designed to prepare its children for life in a pastoral, relatively self-contained society. . . .

In cases of this type there are actually two issues to be considered. The first, obviously, is the legitimacy of the first amendment, free exercise, objection to a public school education. The second, however, and the more important for the case before us, is the manner in which that free exercise claim is asserted. In *Yoder,* supra, the free exercise claim was compelling on the facts because of the long-established success of Amish culture. The Supreme Court obviously felt it unnecessary to address the manner in which the Amish raised their free exercise objection to compulsory school attendance, namely by a first amendment defense to a criminal prosecution. The case before us, however, is so entirely different from *Yoder* on the facts that we conclude that we are not at odds with the Supreme Court of the United States when we hold that the appellants before us have used an entirely inappropriate vehicle for presenting their first amendment claims.

The relevant portion of W.Va.Code, 18–8–1 [1951] under consideration in this case is as follows:

> Compulsory school attendance shall begin with the seventh birthday and continue to the sixteenth birthday.
>
> Exemption from the foregoing requirements of compulsory public school attendance shall be made on behalf of any child for the following causes or conditions, each such cause or condition being subject to confirmation by the attendance authority of the county:

> Exemption B. Instruction in home or other approved place.—Such instruction shall be in the home of such child or children or at some other place approved by the county board of education and for a time equal to the school term of the county. The instruction in such cases shall be conducted by a person or persons who, in the judgment of the county superintendent and county board of education, are qualified to give instruction in subjects required to be taught in the free elementary schools of the State. It shall be the duty of the person or persons giving the instruction, upon request of the county superintendent, to furnish to the county board of education, such information and records as may be required from time to time with respect to attendance, instruction, and progress of pupils enrolled between the ages of seven and sixteen years receiving such instruction.

. . . Esther Riddle is formally educated through the twelfth grade. She is not certified to teach in the State of West Virginia but standard tests indicate that she is quite intelligent. The textbooks and other educational materials used by the Riddle children are part of a formalized curriculum purchased by the appellants. This curriculum is prepared and distributed by certified professional educators located in Prospect Heights, Illinois. The record indicates that the correspondence school in Illinois prepares and corrects homework and tests, provides lesson plans, assists Esther Riddle with pedagogical problems, and otherwise monitors the educational progress of Tim and Jill Riddle. The children are taught in a formal classroom setting from 8:30 A.M. to 3:00 P.M. daily, as well as in the evenings, five days per week, at least 180 days per school year. Esther Riddle instructs her pupils in all subjects required to be taught in the free elementary schools of West Virginia. However, all subject material is intertwined, integrated and saturated with religious doctrine. Tim and Jill have scored average or above on standardized achievement tests.

Even, however, assuming all of these facts developed by the record to be correct, is the State of West Virginia required to forebear in the enforcement of the compulsory school attendance law upon the suggestion of any parent who wishes to keep his child home from school that there is a conflict between school attendance and freedom of religion? Emphatically we answer this question in the negative. . . .

There can be little doubt that on occasion the state's interest will override even the most sincerely held religious convictions. For example, there is no question that a religious sect which incorporates human sacrifice as an integral part of its ritual will be forbidden to engage in such a ritual even if the victims are consenting adults. Even religious practices which merely expose people to danger have been prohibited. . . . Furthermore, a religious injunction to ploygamy in this country has never been a bar to a prosecution for bigamy. . . . In numerous instances courts have required life-saving medical treatment for children in the face of parental objections grounded in sincerely held religious convictions. . . .

Consequently, notwithstanding the strong language of *Yoder,* since that case arose out of an entirely different factual context, this Court holds that sincerely held religious convictions are never a defense to total noncompliance with the compulsory school attendance law. Exemption B in Code, 18–8–1 [1951] itself provides a constitutionally sound vehicle for balancing and reconciling all divergent constitutional interests. . . .

The language "qualified to give instruction in subjects required to be taught in free elementary schools" is sufficiently definite that an arbitrary and capricious refusal by the county superintendent and county board of education to grant approval to qualified instructors can be corrected either by an action for declaratory judgment or in action in mandamus.

In *Yoder,* we reiterate for emphasis, the Supreme Court was not confronted by a threat to the *basic literacy* of children living in the State of Wisconsin; rather, they were confronted with an organized community's efforts to integrate their children into traditional agricultural life during the last two years of compulsory school attendance. In the test-case before us we are confronted with a potential challenge to basic literacy. If we reverse the convictions below our holding will imply that parents are not required to solicit the approval of the county board of education for home instruction, thereby freeing parents from supervision concerning curriculum, qualification of instructors, and duration of attendance which supervised, approved and regulated home instruction under Exemption B will guarantee.

Since there is no evidence in the record that the county superintendent interpreted the phrase "qualified to give instruction" in Exemption B as requiring a West Virginia teacher's certificate we need not reach that issue. Nonetheless, we do note that the statute requires a *person* who is "qualified to give instruction" and not a correspondence school. Regardless of the quality of prepared instructional material there is no substitute for an educated teacher who is capable of answering questions and guiding inquiring minds into the new and uncontemplated directions to which any well-prepared material should inevitably lead.

Furthermore, as this Court pointed out in *Pauley* v. *Kelly,* the purpose of education is not limited to the fundamentals of reading, writing, and arithmetic. Implicit in the concept of "persons qualified to give instruction" is an instructor's ability to afford students diverse forms of cultural enrichment ranging from organized athletics, art, music, and literature, to an understanding of the multiple possibilities for careers which this society offers. It is obvious under the strong language of *Yoder,* supra, that a child may be foreclosed from the opportunity of pursuing certain subjects (such as evolution) by virtue of the free exercise clause of the first amendment, but it must be demonstrated that there is an *actual* conflict between pursuing a *particular* subject and a sincerely held religious tenet.

We find it inconceivable that in the twentieth century the free exercise clause of the first amendment implies that children can lawfully be sequestered on a rural homestead during all of their formative years to be released upon the world only after their opportunities to acquire basic skills have been foreclosed and their capacity to cope with modern society has been so undermined as to prohibit useful, happy or productive lives. . . .

While the appellants in the case before us are sincere, dedicated, and competent parents, the principle which they are urging, namely the legitimacy of ad hoc non-compliance with our school attendance laws, leads ineluctably to a hideous result. If we were to accept their reasoning, our holding would imply that parents have the right to keep their children in medieval ignorance, quarter them in Dickensian squalor beyond the reach of the ameliorating influence of the social welfare agencies, and so to separate their children from organized society in an environment of indoctrination and deprivation that the children become mindless automatons incapable of coping with life outside of their own families. We hold that the first and fourteenth amendments to the Constitution of the United States do not contemplate such a result.

Accordingly, for the reasons set forth above the judgment of the Circuit Court of Harrison County is affirmed.

Affirmed.

*State's Interest in Compulsory
Attendance Is of Sufficient
Magnitude to Override
Religious Interest of
Parent*

DURO v. DISTRICT ATTORNEY, SECOND JUDICIAL DISTRICT OF NORTH CAROLINA

United States Court of Appeals, Fourth
Circuit, 1983.
712 F.2d 96.

K.K. Hall, Circuit Judge:

Peter Duro (Duro) initiated this action against the District Attorney of the Second Judicial District of North Carolina (D.A.) alleging that his religious beliefs were infringed by the North Carolina compulsory school attendance law, N.C.G.S. § 115C–378. The district court entered summary judgment for Duro, from which the D.A. appeals. We find that North Carolina has demonstrated an interest in compulsory education which is of sufficient magnitude to override the religious interest claimed by Duro. Therefore, we reverse.

Duro, his wife and six children, five of whom are now of school age, have resided in Tyrrell County, North Carolina, since January, 1981. Duro and his wife are Pentecostalists. This religion does not require that children be taught at home; in fact, the majority of children whose parents are members of the Pentecostal Church which the Duros attend, are enrolled in a public school. Notwithstanding this, Duro refuses to enroll his children in a public school or the only available nonpublic school, Cabin Swamp Christian School, operated by the Church of Christ.

According to Duro, exposing his children to others who do not share his religious beliefs would corrupt them. In particular, Duro is opposed to what he terms the "unisex movement where you can't tell the difference between boys and girls and the promotion of secular humanism. . . . " Furthermore, Duro objects to the use of physicians and refuses medical attention for all physical ailments because he believes the Lord will heal any problem. Because of these beliefs, the Duro children are taught in their home away from any "non-Christian beliefs and actions." However, despite Duro's concern that his children be sheltered from corrupting influences, he admits that when they reach eighteen years of age, he expects them to "go out and work . . . in the world."

Although Mrs. Duro has assumed the responsibility for teaching the children, she does not possess a teaching certificate and has never been trained as a teacher. She implements a "self-teaching" program, the Alpha Omega Christian Curriculum, which is the same method of instruction used at Cabin Swamp Christian School. Duro himself does not participate in the instruction of the children.

On February 10, 1981, Duro was charged with four counts of violation of the North Carolina compulsory school attendance law, which requires that children between the ages of seven and sixteen must attend school. N.C.G.S. § 115C–378. . . .

The district court relied heavily upon *Wisconsin* v. *Yoder* . . . in holding that North Carolina's compulsory school attendance law was unconstitutional, as it applied to Duro. . . . We find, however, that the district court, in reaching its conclusion incorrectly interpreted and applied *Yoder,* because it arose in an entirely different factual context from the present case. . . .

The facts in the present case are readily distinguishable from the situation in *Yoder.* In that case, Amish parents were convicted of violating Wisconsin's compulsory school attendance law by refusing to send their children to public or private school after they had graduated from the eighth grade. The Court, in reversing the parents' convictions and holding that they had a valid First Amendment defense to the prosecution, closely examined and scrutinized the unique nature of the Amish community. The evidence in *Yoder* revealed that the Amish children attended public schools for the first eight grades, following which the Amish provided informal vocational education to prepare their children for life in their rural self-sufficient community. The Court stressed the fact that for almost 300 years the Amish society had not altered their lifestyle, which was centered around a separate agrarian community away from "worldly" influence. Because the Court found that secondary school education emphasizes "intellectual and scientific accomplishments, self-distinction, competitiveness, worldly success and social life with other students," it was held to be contrary to the Amish beliefs and way of life. Thus, the Court concluded that requiring Amish children to be exposed to such influence would pose a threat of undermining the entire Amish community and religion. Therefore, in view of the unique facts and circumstances associated with the Amish community, the Court held that Wisconsin's interest in education was not so compelling as to override the sincere religious beliefs of the Amish.

The Duros, unlike their Amish counterparts, are not members of a community which has existed for three centuries and has a long history of being a successful, self-sufficient, segment of American society. Furthermore, in *Yoder,* the Amish children attended public school through the eighth grade and then obtained informal vocational training to enable them to assimilate into the self-contained Amish community. However, in the present case, Duro refuses to enroll his children in any public or nonpublic school for any length of time, but still expects them to be fully integrated and live normally in the modern world upon reaching the age of eighteen.

Despite North Carolina's deregulation of nonpublic education, we disagree with the district court that the state has abdicated its interest in the quality of education received by students in nonpublic schools. North Carolina continues to impose compulsory attendance requirements on all religious and nonpublic schools and further, requires that attendance and disease immunization records be maintained for all pupils. The schools are also subject to reasonable fire, health and safety inspections by public authorities. Moreover, each religious and nonpublic school is required to administer to all students enrolled in grades one, two, three, six, nine and eleven, a nationally standardized test whereby the state can monitor competency levels.

Duro has not demonstrated that home instruction will prepare his children to be self-sufficient participants in our modern society or enable them to participate intelligently in our political system, which, as the Supreme Court stated, is a compelling interest of the state. Therefore, based on all the regulations imposed on religious and nonpublic schools, we find that North Carolina has maintained a compelling interest in compulsory education for the children of the state.

We find, therefore, that this case is factually distinguishable from *Yoder*. Despite Duro's sincere religious belief, we hold that the welfare of the children is paramount and that their future well-being mandates attendance at a public or nonpublic school. Furthermore, we conclude that North Carolina has demonstrated an interest in compulsory education which is of sufficient magnitude to override Duro's religious interest. Accordingly, the judgment of the district court is reversed.

Reversed.

NOTE
Alabama compulsory attendance law does not violate constitutional guarantees of religious freedom. Hill v. State, 410 So.2d 431 (Ala.Cr.App.1981).

VACCINATION

To protect the health and welfare of citizens, states have required school children to be vaccinated. Children going unvaccinated are not allowed to attend school. Courts have generally held that, if a parent violates a statute requiring vaccination, the parent is subject to arrest or fine, even if he claims religious, conscientious, or scientific objections.

In 1905, the United States Supreme Court held that a board of health requirement that all persons in Cambridge, Massachusetts, be vaccinated did not violate personal liberties secured under the Fourteenth Amendment. In this case, the Court noted that "the liberty secured by the Constitution of the United States to every person within its jurisdiction does not impart an absolute right on each person to be, at all times and in all circumstances, wholly freed from restraint. There are manifold restraints to which every person is necessarily subject for the common good."[58]

Although this particular decision directly challenged the vaccination regulation rather than compulsory attendance, the Supreme Court [59] nevertheless cited several state court decisions approving state statutes and making vaccination of children a condition of the right to attend public schools.[60]

In *Viemeister* v. *White*, [61] a turn-of-the-century New York decision, the appellant argued that vaccination not only did not prevent smallpox but tended instead to bring on other harmful diseases. The court, while not ruling that vaccination was a smallpox preventative, nevertheless maintained that laymen and physicians alike commonly believed that it did prevent smallpox. Acknowledging the difference between universal and common belief, the court observed that few beliefs are accepted by everyone. The court then concluded that, even if it could not be conclusively proved that the vaccination was a preventative, in our republican form of government the legislature has the right to pass laws based on common belief and the will of the people to promote health and welfare.

Is a parent guilty of violating the compulsory attendance law, then, if he sends his child to school without vaccination and the child is sent home by school authorities? Answering this question in the affirmative, a New York court said that attendance at a public school imposes certain conditions on a child. These requirements must be met in order for him to attend. However, the 1915 decision went on to say that under the public health law, vaccination was only required for children attending public schools. The parent could offer private equivalent education to the child and avoid vaccination. Here, however, the parent had not provided equivalent education and was, therefore, subject to penalty under the compulsory attendance law.[62]

In an earlier New York case, little tolerance was illustrated for parents who used vaccination as an excuse to prevent their children's attendance in public schools.

> It is obvious that a parent should not be allowed to escape his duty to send his children to school as provided by law on any excuse which is not an ample justification for such course. Our public school system has been developed with great pains and solicitude, and its maintenance and support have been recognized as so important for the welfare of the state that they have been provided for and safeguarded in the Constitution itself. As a part of this system a statute has been passed requiring attendance at school of children within certain limits. If indifferent or selfish parents, for ulterior purposes, such as the desire to place young children at labor, instead of school, or from capricious or recalcitrant motives, may be allowed to manufacture easy excuses for not sending their children to school, a ready method will have been developed for evading the statute compelling such attendance, and, if the statute requires parents to see to it that their children attend and take advantage of this school system may be lightly and easily evaded, the purposes of the state in providing and insisting on education will be frustrated and impaired. Failure to comply with the statute ought not to be excused, except for some good reason.[63]

The earlier cases concerning school vaccinations were not generally related to First Amendment religious protections. As observed above, the Supreme Court did not clarify the application of the "no state" provision of the Fourteenth Amendment until 1940, in *Cantwell* v. *Connecticut*.[64] The precedent of religious exemption from compulsory attendance, established in *Yoder*,[65] has bold implications for cases involving religious freedom from vaccination. In the past and present, however, the courts have ruled that a statute requiring vaccination does not violate the free exercise of religion.

Parents in *State* v. *Drew* refused to have their child vaccinated, giving reasons as "partly religious and partly because they did not want that poison injected into their child." The Supreme Court of New Hampshire upheld the parents' conviction for violating the compulsory attendance law and said:

> The defendant's individual ideas, whether "conscientious," "religious," or "scientific" do not appear to be more than opinions. . . . The defendant's views cannot affect the validity of the statute or entitle him to be excepted from its provisions. . . . It is for the Legislature, not for him or for us, to determine the question of policy involved in public health regulations.[66]

Another factor that has often emerged in vaccination cases is the extenuating circumstance of an epidemic. Where epidemic is imminent, there is no question concerning the state's power to protect the citizenry by requiring vaccination. However, when there is no evidence of the imminence of an epidemic, how do the courts view the issue? The question revolves around the further question of what is a reasonable state regulation? Can the state's requirement of vaccination be a reasonable and permissible restraint on constitutional rights in the absence of epidemic?

In *Maas* [67] the defendant argued that compulsory vaccination and immunization were not needed in Mountain Lakes because there had been no smallpox or diphtheria for almost a decade. The court disagreed and ruled that the absence of an emergency does not warrant a denial of the exercise of preventive means. The court said, "A local board of education need not await an epidemic, or even a single sickness or death, before it decides to protect the public. To hold otherwise would be to destroy prevention as a means of combating the spread of disease."

Likewise, in *Stull* v. *Reber,* [68] the fact there had been no smallpox in the borough for forty years did not prevent enforcement of the compulsory vaccination regulation. Health authorities were not required to wait until an epidemic existed before acting to prevent one, the court said.[69] Neither would the fact that an epidemic had already started and it was too late to prevent the closing of school have been a reason to prevent compulsory vaccination.[70]

If the state board of health enacts a compulsory vaccination regulation made pursuant to statute, general statutory requirements requiring all pupils to comply with law are sufficient grounds for the board of education to enforce the statute.[71]

All these cases contested duly promulgated board rules that were enacted pursuant to state statutes. However, where no statute exists to empower school or health boards to pass compulsory vaccination regulations, the issues shift quite drastically. First, a board cannot enact regulations unless they are based on existing statutes. Where the board acts regardless of statute, the act is *ultra vires* (in excess of legal authority). Second, a board rule restricting school attendance cannot prevail over a legislative act granting free unlimited admittance to public schools.

Accordingly, two Illinois courts have decided that in the absence of a compulsory vaccination statute, an unvaccinated child cannot be denied a public education.[72] In both of these old cases, however, it appeared the school boards made little effort to draw enabling implications from health or education statutes.

In summary, one can reasonably make several conclusions regarding compulsory attendance and vaccination: (1) The legislature has power to enact a statute providing for vaccination and including a penalty for non-compliance. (2) Neither the parent nor the child has a constitutional right to schooling without complying with the statutory requirement of vaccination. (3) A parent cannot escape conviction for failing to have his child vaccinated by demanding the child be admitted to school unvaccinated. (4) Religious objection has not generally prevented enforcement of compulsory vaccination and attendance requirements.

Footnotes

1. Griffin v. County School Board of Prince Edward County, 377 U.S. 218, 84 S.Ct. 1226 (1964).

2. Plyler v. Doe, 457 U.S. 202, 102 S.Ct. 2382 (1982).

3. In the Matter of Proios, 111 Misc.2d 252, 443 N.Y.S.2d 828 (1981).

4. Martinez v. Bynum, 461 U.S. 321, 103 S.Ct. 1838 (1983).

5. Inhabitants of Warren v. Inhabitants of Thomaston, 43 Me. 406 (1857).

6. Strangway v. Allen, 194 Ky. 681, 240 S.W. 384 (1922).

7. County of McLean v. Humphrey, 104 Ill. 378 (1882).

8. In re Gault, 387 U.S. 1, 87 S.Ct. 1428 (1967).

9. Wisconsin v. Yoder, 406 U.S. 205, 92 S.Ct. 1526 (1972).

10. Ford v. Ford, 371 U.S. 187, 83 S.Ct. 273 (1962).

11. 268 U.S. 510, 45 S.Ct. 571 (1925).

12. 321 U.S. at 166, 64 S.Ct. at 442 (1943).

13. Andrew Jay Kleinfeld, "The Balance of Power Among Infants, Their Parents and the State", *ABA Family Law Quarterly* 5 (1971), p. 107.

14. Salem Community School Corp. v. Easterly, 150 Ind.App. 11, 275 N.E.2d 317 (Ind.1971).

15. Id. p. 92.

16. Id. p. 93.

17. Morris v. Morris, 92 Ind.App. 65, 171 N.E. 386 (1930); Sisson v. Schultz, 251 Mich. 553, 232 N.W. 253 (1930).

18. Heffington v. Jackson and Norton, 43 Tex.Civ.App. 560, 96 S.W. 108 (1906).

19. Luques v. Luques, 127 Me. 356, 143 A. 263 (1928).

20. Hiram D. Gordon, "Terminal Placements of Children and Permanent Termination of Parental Rights: The New York Permanent Neglect Statute," *St. Johns Law Review* 46 (1971): 215.

21. Harvey J. Eger and Anthony J. Popeck, "The Abused Child: Problems and Proposals," *Duquesne Law Review* 8 (1969–70): 136.

22. State v. Perricone, 37 N.J. 463, 181 A.2d 751 (1962); People v. Pierson, 176 N.Y. 201, 68 N.E. 243 (1903).

23. Morrison v. State, 252 S.W.2d 97 (Mo.App.1952).

24. Massachusetts Gen.Laws Ann., ch. 272, § 53 (1958).

25. See Alexander v. Bartlett, 14 Mich.App. 177, 165 N.W.2d 445 (1968).

26. 14 A.L.R.2d 1369; Knox v. O'Brien, 7 N.J.Super. 608, 72 A.2d 389 (1950).

27. *State v. Whisner,* 47 Ohio St.2d 181, 351 N.E.2d 750 (1976).

28. State v. Garber, 197 Kan. 567, 419 P.2d 896 (1966).

29. Pierce v. Society of Sisters of the Holy Names of Jesus and Mary, 268 U.S. 510, 45 S.Ct. 571 (1925).

30. Supra, note 26.

31. Grosz v. City of Miami Beach, Florida, 721 F.2d 729 (11th Cir.1983).

32. State ex rel. Douglas v. Faith Baptist Church, 207 Neb. 802, 301 N.W.2d 571 (1981), *appeal dismissed* 454 U.S. 803, 102 S.Ct. 75 (1981).

33. State ex rel. Douglas v. Calvary Academy, 217 Neb. 450, 348 N.W.2d 898 (1984). See also: McCurry v. Tesch, 738 F.2d 271 (8th Cir.1984).

34. Sheridan Road Baptist Church v. Department of Education, 132 Mich.App., 348 N.W.2d 263 (1984).

35. Knox v. O'Brien, 7 N.J.Super. 608, 72 A.2d 389 (1950).

36. State v. Edgington, 99 N.M. 715, 663 P.2d 374 (1983).

37. State v. Bowman, 60 Or.App. 184, 653 P.2d 254 (1982).

38. Appeal of Peirce, 122 N.H. 762, 451 A.2d 363 (1982).

39. Grigg v. Commonwealth, 224 Va. 356, 297 S.E.2d 799 (Va.1982).

40. State v. Counort, 69 Wash. 361, 124 P. 910 (1912).

41. State v. Hoyt, 84 N.H. 38, 146 A. 170 (1929).

42. State v. Well, 99 Kan. 167, 160 P. 1025 (1916).

43. State v. Lowry, 191 Kan. 701, 383 P.2d 962 (1963).

44. People v. Turner, 121 Cal.App.2d 861, 263 P.2d 685 (1953).

45. State v. Peterman, 32 Ind.App. 665, 70 N.E. 550 (1904).

46. Sheppard v. State, 306 P.2d 346 (Okla.Cr.App.1957).

47. State v. Massa, 95 N.J.Super. 382, 231 A.2d 252 (1967).

48. People v. Berger, 65 Ill.Dec. 600, 441 N.E.2d 915 (1982).

49. State v. Priest, 210 La. 389, 27 So.2d 173 (1946).

50. In re State, 214 La. 1062, 39 So.2d 731 (1949).

51. In re Rogers, 36 Misc.2d 680, 234 N.Y.S.2d 179 (1962).

52. Pierce, supra note 30.

53. 293 U.S. 245, 55 S.Ct. 197 (1934).

54. Rice v. Commonwealth, 49 S.E.2d 342, 3 A.L.R.2d 1392 (1948).

55. Commonwealth v. Bey, 57 York Leg.Rec. (Pa.) 200, 92 Pitts.Leg.J. 84 (1944).

56. See also: In re Currence, 42 Misc.2d 418, 248 N.Y.S.2d 251 (1983). Here religious observance was no defense for withdrawing a boy from school weekly on Wednesday afternoons and Thursday mornings.

57. 406 U.S. 205, 92 S.Ct. 1526 (1972).

58. Jacobson v. Commonwealth of Massachusetts, 197 U.S. 11, 25 S.Ct. 358 (1905).

59. Id. p. 364.

60. Blue v. Beach, 155 Ind. 121, 56 N.E. 89 (1900); Morris v. Columbus, 102 Ga. 792, 30 S.E. 850 (1898); State v. Hay, 126 N.C. 999, 35 S.E. 459; Abeel v. Clark, 84 Cal. 226, 24 P. 383 (1890); Bissell v. Davidson, 65 Conn. 183, 32 A. 348 (1894); Hazen v. Strong, 2 Bt. 427 (1830); Duffield v. Williamsport School District, 162 Pa. 476, 29 A. 742 (1894).

61. 179 N.Y. 235, 72 N.E. 97 (1904).

62. People v. McIlwain, 151 N.Y.S. 366 (1915).

63. People v. Ekerold, 211 N.Y. 386, 105 N.E. 670 (1914).

64. 310 U.S. 296, 60 S.Ct. 900, 128 ALR 1352 (1940).

65. *Yoder,* supra note 9.

66. State v. Drew, 89 N.H. 54, 192 A. 629 (1937).

67. Board of Education of Mountain Lakes v. Maas, 56 N.J.Super. 245, 152 A.2d 394 (1959).

68. 215 Pa. 156, 64 A. 419 (1906).

69. Hill v. Bickers, 171 Ky. 703, 188 S.W. 766 (1916).

70. Board of Trustees v. McMurtry, 169 Ky. 457, 184 S.W. 390 (1916).

71. Mosier v. Barren County Board of Health, 308 Ky. 829, 215 S.W.2d 967 (1948).

72. Potts v. Breen, 167 Ill. 67, 47 N.E. 81 (1897); People ex rel. LaBaugh v. Board of Education of District No. 2, 52 N.E. 850 (1899).

7

The Instructional Program

Upon entering a public school a child becomes subject to state and local administrative regulations, as well as to state laws governing public education. These regulations are an exercise of state police power which is the inherent sovereign power allowing the state to provide for the health, safety, and well being of its citizens. Such provisions establish the framework within which each child is afforded a free public education.

Education may be viewed differently by educators, parents, students, or various special interest groups, but few would argue that a public educational program should not be expansive and broadening of one's perspective and knowledge. The role of education has been quite accurately defined as provision of a "marketplace of ideas."

The critical position of education in a democratic society is self-evident. Over the years, the courts have come to conclude that society is best served by an educational system that teaches "through wide exposure to that robust exchange of ideas which discovers truth 'out of a multitude of tongues [rather] than through any kind of authoritative selection.'"[1] Thus, because of the importance of the schools and because this "robust exchange of ideas" is so vital to the educational process, the perpetuation of that exchange is, at all levels of the educational system, "a special concern of the First Amendment."[2] No school can function as "a marketplace of ideas" unless both students and faculty enjoy an atmosphere conducive to debate and scholarly inquiry.[3] The First Amendment not only creates a marketplace of intellectual ideas for the students but benefits the teacher in the presentation of ideas.

Courts have generally given wide latitude to the state in matters involving the educational program. In one notable case, parents sought a writ of *mandamus* to prevent using the novel *Slaughterhouse-Five* as a part of the instructional program. The parents alleged that the material was obscene, profane, and repugnant to the religious provisions of the First Amendment.

The court, in an exposition on the law, first observed that, although there may have been religious references in the work, the book itself did not violate the students' and parents' religious freedom. To declare otherwise, the court concluded, would censor and prevent the public schools from making use of and reference to many great works of the past.

> If plaintiffs' contention was correct, then public school students could no longer marvel at Sir Galahad's saintly quest for the Holy Grail, nor be introduced to the dangers of Hitler's *Mein Kampf* nor read the mellifluous poetry of John Milton and John Donne. Unhappily, Robin Hood would be forced to forage without Friar Tuck and Shakespeare would have to delete Shylock from *The Merchant of Venice*. Is this to be the state of our law? Our Constitution does not command ignorance; on the contrary, it assures the people that the state may not relegate them to such a status and guarantees to all the precious and unfettered freedom of pursuing one's own intellectual pleasures in one's own personal way.[4]

Even more to the point, the court observed that the judges are not to be the experts in what educational programs are offered in the schools. Citing Justice Brennan's admonition in *Schempp*,[5] the court contended that curriculum determination should be entrusted to the experienced school officials of the nation's public schools and not to the judges. The appellate court reprimanded the lower trial court for imposing its judgment of "right" and "morality" over that of the school authorities. Such action by a court was forbidden by the state constitution and a matter for the lawfully elected school board to determine. The appellate court concluded that the judicial censor was *persona non grata* in the formation of public education curriculum policies.

Parental intervention does not always promote greater freedom and choice for students. In many instances, such intervention may amount to an attempt to restrict knowledge and limit educational prerogative. Similarly, a court, unless it exercises sufficient restraint, could find itself sanctioning restriction rather than protecting freedom.

The school, in this context, is an arm of the state.[6] It is a creature of the legislature over which the legislature has complete control. The actual control of public schools is vested in the school board, which is required by the legislature to conduct the school in the best interest of the pupils. The determination of subject matter and required teaching force are solely within the discretion of the board.[7]

The educational program of the public school has both academic and disciplinary aspects. Courts have been very hesitant to enter into the academic arena. The position of the courts is stated by the United States Supreme Court in a higher education case that has applicability for elementary and secondary school operation. In *Horowitz*, the Court said:

> Academic evaluations of a student, in contrast to disciplinary determinations, bear little resemblance to the judicial and administrative fact-finding proceedings to which we have traditionally attached a full learning requirement. . . . Like the decision of an individual professor as to the proper grade for a student in his course, the determination whether to dismiss a student for academic reasons requires expert evaluation of cumulative information and is not readily adapted to the procedural tools of judicial or administrative decisionmaking. . . . Courts are particularly ill-equipped to evaluate academic performance.[8]

The courts have generally supported the school boards when they have expanded the school program or introduced innovative curricula. Thus far, the courts have agreed that the school has the power to regulate and develop curricula for the well-being of the students. These cases also establish that not all parental discontent is aimed at broadening student knowledge and choice. In many instances, parents seek to restrict or "contract the spectrum of knowledge." As a result, the courts will tend to weigh such grievances very carefully, even when a parent feels that a constitutional right is being offended.

This judicial position has been demonstrated when a school board sought to reduce the length of the school day, thereby restricting the educational program. For lack of funds, the school board decided to hold one-half sessions and to teach certain subjects on a compressed schedule.[9] The Supreme Court of Michigan decided that in the absence of state board regulations limiting local school board authority in this area, the reduction in the school program was valid.

Although the content of the school program itself is an area of concern to parents, an even more direct concern is the placement of their children. Aside from the recent statutory emphasis and litigation dealing with handicapped children, much of the controversy between parent and school has arisen during the child's first few years of schooling. It is at this level that the parent and the child are experiencing the removal of the child from the home and placing him or her in the hands of strangers at school.

In one such New York State case, a mother petitioned the court for an order directing the board of education to admit her son to the first grade.[10] Previously, the boy had established quite a reputation as a "disciplinary problem." The school had demoted the boy from the first grade back to kindergarten, an action the parent maintained was arbitrary, capricious, unreasonable, and in violation of the Fourteenth Amendment and the New York Constitution. The board defended itself by maintaining the school principal had made an "educational decision" based on the boy's inability to perform first-grade work, his test results, and his lack of self-control. The petitioner was unable to rebut the test results. The court held that the placement of the child was within the school's authority to provide rules and regulations for promotion from grade to grade, based not on age but on training, knowledge and ability.[11]

In a similar New York State decision, the parents of a five-year-old child sought to compel the school board to accept the child into the first grade.[12] According to New York law, a five-year-old is entitled to attend public schools, and the boy's parents claimed that kindergarten was not the public schools. The court disagreed with the parent, arguing that when a kindergarten is established it becomes a part of the public school system. Since the boy was already in *public school*, the court maintained, the parents had no right to insist that the boy be admitted to a particular *grade or class* in the public school.

Most precedents indicated that the courts, though sympathetic with the intentions of the parent, generally defer to authorized and trained educational experts in matters of school policy. In recent years, however, there has been a greater tendency by the courts to delve deeper into the justification and rationale supporting educational policy. School authorities, therefore, are well advised to document placement and curriculum decisions with a solid educational rationale.

The collective judgment of the school holds substantial influence with the courts. Courts, therefore, hesitate to substitute their knowledge of children for that of educators. Although the school has generally prevailed in curriculum and placement disputes with parents, the school's power is by no means absolute. Where legitimate constitutional concerns are present, the courts stand ready to invalidate the offending regulations, particularly if the action of the school tends to contract rather than expand knowledge. Such judicial intervention is not uncommon and has been demonstrated in several notable United States Supreme Court cases.

In *Meyer v. State of Nebraska*,[13] the Court ruled that legislative determination of educational matters was subject to supervision by the courts. Nebraska had attempted to contract available knowledge by forbidding the teaching of foreign languages in public and private schools before the eighth grade. The Court rejected the rather elusive notion that the state, in the exercise of its police power, was protecting the child's health by limiting his mental activities.

The Supreme Court has said that the courts should not intervene in conflicts that arise in the daily operation of the schools, so long as the conflicts do not involve basic constitutional values. However, the courts will not "tolerate laws which cast a pall of orthodoxy over the classroom."[14]

The Supreme Court stated in *Sweezy v. New Hampshire*:[15]

> Scholarship cannot flourish in an atmosphere of suspicion and distrust. Teachers and students must always remain free to inquire, to study and to evaluate. . . . [The state cannot] chill that free play of the spirit which all teachers ought especially to cultivate and practice.[16]

Sweezy calls into question state or federal laws, such as a provision in Public Law 98–377, Section 709, August 11, 1984, Education for Economic Security Act, assistance for math and science education, which forbids grants to go to school districts in which teachers teach courses the substance of which is "secular humanism". The intensive scrutiny required to identify and rid schools of secular humanism may result in invasion of academic freedom and force a "pall of orthodoxy" over the classroom.

Other cases, beyond *Sweezy*, firmly establish the precedent for judicial intervention in education matters where constitutional rights and freedoms are at issue. Several Supreme Court decisions have also established that the state cannot compel students to perform rituals that violate their freedom of religion.[17] All these precedents combine to limit somewhat state school power in favor of individual freedom of choice for the teacher and student. However, the state does have a legitimate interest in prescribing a public school curriculum and such will be upheld unless it casts a "pall of orthodoxy" or tends to contract the spectrum of knowledge.

Board Has the Power to Enforce
Reasonable Rules Prescribing
Specific Curriculum

STATE EX REL. ANDREW v. WEBBER

Supreme Court of Indiana, 1886.
108 Ind. 31, 8 N.E. 708.

HOWK, C.J. . . .

The relator . . . said that he was the father and natural guardian of one Abram Andrew, who was a white male child, between the ages of six and twenty-one years, to-wit, of the age of twelve years . . . . The said Abram Andrew being sufficiently advanced in his studies, in accordance with the relator's desire and consent, and in compliance with his legal rights in the premises, was admitted as a pupil in such high school, to receive instruction therein, and thereafter, until his suspension, as hereinafter stated, was regular in his attendance and deportment, and was obedient and respectful to his teachers, and properly subordinate to the rules and regulations of such school; that among the exercises prescribed by such superintendent, with the sanction of such board of trustees, for the pupils of the high school, was a requirement that each of the pupils should, at stated intervals, employ a certain period of time in the study and practice of music, and that they should provide themselves with prescribed books for that purpose; that the relator, believing it was not for the best interest of said Abram Andrew, and not in accordance with the relator's wishes regarding the instruction of his said son, in a respectful manner asked of such superintendent that Abram Andrew might be excused from the study and practice of music at such exercises, and directed Abram Andrew not to participate therein, all in good faith, and in a respectful manner, and with no intention of in any manner interfering with the government, rules, and regulations of such schools, except in so far as he might legally control and direct the education of his said son, which purpose and desire were fully communicated by him to such superintendent.

But the relator said that, notwithstanding his said desire and request so communicated to such superintendent as aforesaid, the superintendent, on or about the fourteenth day of October, 1885, in disregard of the relator's wishes and request, required said Abram Andrew to participate in the practice and study of music, and upon the refusal of said Abram Andrew to participate in such exercises and study, which he did without disrespect to such superintendent, and entirely because of the relator's direction, which was so communicated to such superintendent as aforesaid, the superintendent suspended said Abram Andrew from such school, without assigning any cause therefor. . . .

This action is brought by the father and natural guardian of the suspended pupil, to compel, by mandate, the governing authorities of the school corporation to revoke such suspension, and to readmit such pupil to the high school.

The question for our decision in this case, as it seems to us, may be thus stated: Is the rule or regulation for the government of the pupils of the high school of the school city of La Porte, in relation to the study and practice of music, a valid and reasonable exercise of the discretionary power conferred by law upon the governing authorities of such school corporation? In section 4497, Rev.St.1881, in force since August 16, 1869, it is provided as follows: "The common schools of the state shall be taught in the English language; and the trustee shall provide to have taught in them orthography, reading, writing, arithmetic, geography, English grammer, physiology, history of the United States, and good behavior, and such other branches of learning, and other languages, as the advancement of pupils may require, and the trustees from time to time direct." Under this statutory provision and others of similar purport and effect, to be found in our school laws, it was competent, we think, for the trustees of the school city of La Porte to enact necessary and reasonable rules for the government of the pupils of its high school, directing what branches of learning such pupils should pursue, and regulating the time to be given to any particular study, and prescribing what book or books should be used therein. Such trustees were and are required, by the express provisions of section 4444, Rev.St.1881, in force since March 8, 1873, to "take charge of the educational affairs" of such city of La Porte; "they may also establish graded schools, or such modifications of them as may be practicable, and provide for admitting into the higher departments of the graded school, from the primary schools of their townships, such pupils as are sufficiently advanced for such admission."

The power to establish graded schools carries with it, of course, the power to establish and enforce such reasonable rules as may seem necessary to the trustees, in their discretion, for the government and discipline of such schools, and prescribing the course of instruction therein. Confining our opinion strictly to the case in hand, we will consider and decide these two questions, in the order of their statement, namely: (1) Has the appellant's relator shown, by the averments of his verified complaint, that the rule or regulation for the government of the pupils of the high school, in the school city of La Porte, of which he complains, was or is an unreasonable exercise of the discretionary power conferred by law upon the trustees of such school corporation and the superintendent of its schools? (2) Conceding or assuming such rule or regulation to be reasonable and valid, has the relator shown, in his complaint herein, any sufficient or satisfactory excuse for the non-compliance therewith, and the disobedience thereof, of his son, Abram Andrew, a pupil of such high school, or any sufficient or legal ground for the revocation of the suspension of his son, or for his son's readmission, as a pupil in such high school?

1.   As to the first of these questions . . . we think that the legislature has given the trustees of the public school corporations the discretionary power to direct, from time to time, what branches of learning, in addition to those specified in the statute, shall be taught in the public schools of their respective corporations. Where such trustees may have established a system of graded schools, or such modifications of them as may be practicable, within their respective corporations, they are clothed by law with the discretionary power to prescribe the course of instruction in the different

grades of their public schools. We are of opinion that the rule or regulation of which the relator complains in the case under consideration was within the discretionary power conferred by law upon the governing authorities of the school city of La Porte; that it was not an unreasonable rule; but that it was such a one as each pupil of the high school, in the absence of sufficient excuse, might lawfully be required to obey and comply with. . . .

2. . . . The only cause or reason assigned by the relator for requiring his son to disobey such rule or regulation was that he did not believe it was for the best interest of his son to participate in the musical studies and exercises of the high school, and did not wish him to do so. The relator has assigned no cause or reason, and it may be fairly assumed that he had none, in support either of his belief or his wish. The important question arises, which should govern the public high school of the city of La Porte, as to the branches of learning to be taught and the course of instruction therein,—the school trustees of such city, to whom the law has confided the direction of these matters, or the mere arbitrary will of the relator, without cause or reason in its support? We are of opinion that only one answer can or ought to be given to this question. The arbitrary wishes of the relator in the premises must yield and be subordinated to the governing authorities of the school city of La Porte, and their reasonable rules and regulations for the government of the pupils of its high school. . . .

For the reasons given, our conclusion is that no error was committed by the court below in sustaining appellees' demurrer to the relator's complaint.

The judgment is affirmed, with costs.

Denial of Promotion for Failure to
Complete Requisite Reading Level
Does Not Violate Constitutional
Rights

SANDLIN v. JOHNSON

United States Court of Appeals,
Fourth Circuit, 1981.
643 F.2d 1027.

MURNAGHAN, Circuit Judge:

Four second-grade students filed the case as a class action on behalf of themselves and eighteen other similarly situated second graders against the principal of their school, and the superintendent of schools and school board of Pittsylvania County, Virginia. Plaintiffs attended the Whitmell Elementary School. Only one member of their class was promoted to the third grade at the end of the 1977–1978 school year. The stated and undisputed ground for denial of promotion was the students' failure to complete the requisite level of the Ginn Reading Series. While plaintiffs do not deny that they failed to demonstrate the required reading level, they argue that they are nevertheless capable of reading at the third-grade level. They sued pursuant to 42 U.S.C. § 1983 claiming a denial of equal protection of the law because, as their Complaint had it:

By either the defendants' negligent and careless supervision of the instruction of plaintiffs or by their arbitrary and negligent grading and classification of these plaintiffs, plaintiffs have been effectively denied third-grade educational opportunities commensurate with their abilities and in accord with educational opportunities provided other students similarly situated in the Pittsylvania County School System.

Plaintiffs contended that defendants' actions damaged them by delaying the completion of their education and their obtaining employment, by foreclosing "certain lucrative employment . . . because of a lack of education provided them commensurate with their abilities," and by burdening them with the stigma of failure. . . .

Defendants responded that they had provided equal opportunities to plaintiffs, that while plaintiffs' intelligence was such that they were capable of reading at the third-grade level, they had failed to progress to that level of mastery, and that promoting plaintiffs before they had mastered the requisite reading skills would be counter-productive and would increase plaintiffs' reading deficiencies. . . .

There is no allegation in the case that plaintiffs were classified on the basis of race or any other basis calling for heightened scrutiny, i.e., religious affiliation, alienage, illegitimacy, gender or wealth. Nor is public education a fundamental right which would trigger strict scrutiny of claims of denial of equal protection. Thus, in reviewing the equal protection claim, the only question, as recognized by all parties, is whether the classification by the governmental entity which is at issue here is rationally related to a permissible governmental end.

Defendants here classified plaintiffs according to their attained reading level. The stated purpose for the classification was to enable the school to provide students with the level of instruction most appropriate to their abilities and needs. The objective was to further the education, the preparation for life of the plaintiffs. The governmental end is a permissible one, and defendants' classification scheme is clearly rationally related to achieving it. Defendants, therefore, have not implicated any constitutional right of plaintiffs by classifying them according to their reading level.

Plaintiffs also claim that defendants or the teachers under their supervision negligently and carelessly failed to ensure that plaintiffs were properly and appropriately taught. What appellants denominate a denial of equal educational opportunity sounds rather in tort as a breach of some duty owed by teachers or school boards to their pupils to give them an education. If there is any such cause of action, it does not rise to the level of a constitutional claim and, therefore, is not cognizable in an action pursuant to 42 U.S.C. § 1983. . . .

Decisions by educational authorities which turn on evaluation of the academic performance of a student as it relates to promotion are peculiarly within the expertise of educators and are particularly inappropriate for review in a judicial context. ("We decline to further enlarge the judicial presence in the academic community and thereby risk deterioration of many beneficial aspects of the faculty-student relationship.") We, therefore, affirm the district court's dismissal.

Affirmed. (Held for the school board).

NOTE

Withholding Diploma. It is within the sound judgment of school authorities to determine if and when a pupil has completed the prescribed courses entitling him to a diploma. However, there is no direct relationship between participation in a graduation exercise and the issuance of a diploma. Once the pupil has completed successfully all of the required courses, the issuance of a diploma is a ministerial act that the school officials must perform. Refusal of a pupil to perform some act that is not a part of curriculum nor is required by school regulation prior to graduation will not justify withholding of the diploma.

In a 1921 case in which a student's refusal to wear a cap and gown to graduation resulted in the board's withholding the pupil's diploma, the court mandated that the diploma be granted and stated:

> A diploma, therefore is *prima facie* evidence of educational worth, and is the goal of the matriculate. . . . The issuance of a diploma by the school board to a pupil who satisfactorily completes the prescribed course of study and who is otherwise qualified is mandatory, and, although such duty is not expressly enjoined upon the board by statute, it does arise by necessary and reasonable implication. . . . This Plaintiff . . . having complied with all the rules and regulations precedent to graduation, may not be denied her diploma by the arbitrary action of the school board subsequent to her being made the recipient of the honors of graduation. Valentine v. Independent School Dist. of Casey, 191 Iowa 1100, 183 N.W. 434 (1921).

Statute Prohibiting Teaching of
Foreign Language Violates
Substantive Due Process

MEYER v. NEBRASKA

Supreme Court of the United States, 1923.
262 U.S. 390, 43 S.Ct. 625.

Mr. Justice McREYNOLDS delivered the opinion of the Court.

Plaintiff in error was tried and convicted in the district court for Hamilton county, Nebraska, under an information which charged that on May 25, 1920, while an instructor in Zion Parochial School he unlawfully taught the subject of reading in the German language to Raymond Parpart, a child of ten years, who had not attained and successfully passed the eighth grade. The information is based upon "An act relating to the teaching of foreign languages in the state of Nebraska," approved April 9, 1919 (Laws 1919, c. 249), which follows:

> Section 1. No person, individually or as a teacher, shall, in any private, denominational, parochial or public school, teach any subject to any person in any language than the English language.
> Sec. 2. Languages, other than the English language, may be taught as languages only after a pupil shall have attained and successfully passed the eighth grade as evidenced by a certificate of graduation issued by the county superintendent of the county in which the child resides.

. . . The Supreme Court of the state affirmed the judgment of conviction. It declared the offense charged and established was "the direct and intentional teaching of the German language as a distinct subject to a child who had not passed the eighth grade," in the parochial school maintained by Zion Evangelical Lutheran Congregation, a collection of Biblical stories being used therefor. And it held that the statute forbidding this did not conflict with the Fourteenth Amendment, but was a valid exercise of the police power. The following excerpts from the opinion sufficiently indicate the reasons advanced to support the conclusion.

> The salutary purpose of the statute is clear. The Legislature had seen the baneful effects of permitting foreigners, who had taken residence in this country, to rear and educate their children in the language of their native land. The result of that condition was found to be inimical to our own safety. To allow the children of foreigners, who had emigrated here, to be taught from early childhood the language of the country of their parents was to rear them with that language as their mother tongue. It was to educate them so that they must always think in that language, and, as a consequence, naturally inculcate in them the ideas and sentiments foreign to the best interests of this country. The statute, therefore, was intended not only to require that the education of all children be conducted in the English language, but that, until they had grown into that language and until it had become a part of them, they should not in the schools be taught any other language. The obvious purpose of this statute was that the English language should be and become the mother tongue of all children reared in this state. The enactment of such a statute comes reasonably within the police power of the state. . . .

. . . The problem for our determination is whether the statute as construed and applied unreasonably infringes the liberty guaranteed to the plaintiff in error by the Fourteenth Amendment. "No state . . . shall deprive any person of life, liberty or property without due process of law."

While this court has not attempted to define with exactness the liberty thus guaranteed, the term has received much consideration and some of the included things have been definitely stated. Without doubt, it denotes not merely freedom from bodily restraint but also the right of the individual to contract, to engage in any of the common occupations of life, to acquire useful knowledge, to marry, establish a home and bring up children, to worship God according to the dictates of his own conscience, and generally to enjoy those privileges long recognized at common law as essential to the orderly pursuit of happiness by free men. . . . The established doctrine is that this liberty may not be interfered with, under the guise of protecting the public interest, by legislative action which is arbitrary or without reasonable relation to some purpose within the competency of the state to effect. Determination by the Legislature of what constitutes proper exercise of police power is not final or conclusive but is subject to supervision by the courts. . . .

The American people have always regarded education and acquisition of knowledge as matters of supreme importance which should be diligently promoted. The Ordinance of 1787 declares: "Religion, morality and knowledge being necessary to good government and the happiness of mankind, schools and the means of education shall forever be encouraged." Corresponding to the right of control, it is the natural duty of the parent to give his children education suitable to their station in life; and nearly all the states, including Nebraska, enforce this obligation by compulsory laws.

Practically, education of the young is only possible in schools conducted by especially qualified persons who devote themselves thereto. The calling always has been regarded as useful and honorable, essential, indeed, to the public welfare. Mere knowledge of the German language cannot reasonably be regarded as harmful. Heretofore it has been commonly looked upon as helpful and desirable. Plaintiff in error taught this language in school as part of his occupation. His right thus to teach and the right of parents to engage him so to instruct their children, we think, are within the liberty of the amendment. . . .

That the state may do much, go very far, indeed, in order to improve the quality of its citizens, physically, mentally and morally, is clear; but the individual has certain fundamental rights which must be respected. The protection of the Constitution extends to all, to those who speak other languages as well as to those born with English on the tongue. Perhaps it would be highly advantageous if all had ready understanding of our ordinary speech, but this cannot be coerced by methods which conflict with the Constitution—a desirable end cannot be promoted by prohibited means. . . .

The power of the State to compel attendance at some school and to make reasonable regulations for all schools, including a requirement that they shall give instructions in English, is not questioned. Nor has challenge been made of the state's power to prescribe a curriculum for institutions which it supports. Those matters are not within the present controversy. Our concern is with the prohibition approved by the Supreme Court. Adams v. Tanner, 244 U.S. 594, 37 S.Ct. 662, pointed out that mere abuse incident to an occupation ordinarily useful is not enough to justify its abolition, although regulation may be entirely proper. No emergency has arisen which renders knowledge by a child of some language other than English so clearly harmful as to justify its inhibition with the consequent infringement of rights long freely enjoyed. We are constrained to conclude that the statute as applied is arbitrary and without reasonable relation to any end within the competency of the State.

As the statute undertakes to interfere only with teaching which involves a modern language, leaving complete freedom as to other matters, there seems no adequate foundation for the suggestion that the purpose was to protect the child's health by limiting his mental activities. It is well known that proficiency in a foreign language seldom comes to one not instructed at an early age, and experience shows that this is not injurious to the health, morals or understanding of the ordinary child.

The judgment of the court below must be reversed and the cause remanded for further proceedings not inconsistent with this opinion.

Reversed.

State Can Validly Require a Course
in Sex Education for All Students

CORNWELL v. STATE BOARD OF EDUCATION

United States District Court,
Maryland, 1969.
314 F.Supp. 340 (D.Md.1969), affirmed 428
F.2d 471 (4th Cir.1970), cert. denied 400
U.S. 942, 91 S.Ct. 240 (1970).

HARVEY, District Judge: In this civil action, Baltimore County taxpayers are suing the Maryland State Board of Education seeking to prevent the implementation in the Baltimore County Schools of a program of sex education. In particular, the plaintiffs, who are school children and their parents, seek to have this Court declare unconstitutional a bylaw duly adopted by the State Board. The provision in question is By-Law 720, Section 3, Subsection 4, which provides as follows:

It is the responsibility of the local school system to provide a comprehensive program of family life and sex education in every elementary and secondary school for all students as an integral part of the curriculum including a planned and sequential program of health education.

. . . In determining whether there is here a substantial question of constitutionality, this Court concludes initially that no question whatsoever arises under the Fourteenth Amendment. There is first no denial of substantive due process to the plaintiffs. Under Section 6 of Article 77 of the Maryland Code (as amended and re-codified by Chapter 405 of the Acts of 1969), the State Board is directed to determine the educational policies of the state and to enact bylaws for the administration of the public school system, which when enacted and published shall have the force of law. Assuredly it cannot be said that the bylaw here is an arbitrary or unreasonable exercise of the authority vested in the State Board to determine a teaching curriculum, nor that there is no basis in fact for the legislative policy expressed in the bylaw. Furthermore, it does not appear that the bylaw denies equal protection of the laws, as on its face it applies to all pupils equally.

Plaintiffs allege that the enactment of this bylaw was based on a study made in reference to pregnant pupils. But whatever the genesis of the bylaw, it is not the study that is being attacked here but the bylaw itself, and it is being attacked on its face. It is the provisions of the bylaw then that must be examined in the light of the United States Constitution. The plaintiffs' argument that the bylaw is defective because it applies to non-pregnant as well as to pregnant pupils is difficult to follow. There would appear to be just as much reason for the State Board to provide sex education for the non-pregnant (and, incidentally, for the non-impregnating) as for those students who, because of a lack of information on the subject (or for other reasons), have become pregnant or who have caused pregnancy.

The plaintiffs further assert that they have the exclusive constitutional right to teach their children about sexual matters in their own homes, and that such exclusive right would prohibit the teaching of sex in the schools. No authority is cited in support of this novel proposition, and this Court knows of no such constitutional right. This Court, then, is satisfied that the claims asserted in this complaint under the Fourteenth Amendment are so insubstantial that they do not confer jurisdiction here.

In support of their First Amendment claim, the plaintiffs assert that they have been denied the free exercise of their religious concepts and that the teaching of sex in the Baltimore County Schools will in fact establish religious concepts. . . .

Applying the principles that have been established by the various cases, it is quite clear to this Court that the purpose and primary effect of the bylaw here is not to establish any particular religious dogma or precept, and that the bylaw does not directly or substantially involve the state in religious exercises or in the favoring of religion or any particular religion. The bylaw may be considered quite simply as a public health measure. As the Supreme Court indicated in Prince v. Massachusetts, 321 U.S. 158, 64 S.Ct. 438 (1944), the State's interest in the health of its children outweighs claims based upon religious freedom and the right of parental control. The Court in that particular case said this (at pages 168–169):

> A democratic society rests . . . upon the healthy, well-rounded growth of young people into full maturity as citizens . . . . It is too late now to doubt that legislation appropriately designed to reach such evils is within the state's police power, whether against the parent's claim to control of the child or one that religious scruples dictate contrary action.

In summary, then, the Court concludes that the federal question here is plainly insubstantial. Construing the allegations in a light most favorable to the plaintiffs, as the Court must do on these motions to dismiss, this Court finds that the constitutional questions relied upon are obviously without merit. The unsoundness and insubstantiality of the plaintiffs' position is clearly indicated by the various decisions of the Supreme Court to which I have alluded.

For these reasons then, the two motions to dismiss are granted.

NOTES

1. Sex education does not invade the privacy of school children or parents. Medeiros v. Kiyosaki, 52 Hawaii 436, 478 P.2d 314 (1970).

2. The Supreme Court of New Jersey has upheld a State Board of Education regulation that requires each school district to develop and implement a family life education program in the public elementary and secondary school curricula. The focus of the program was to be on teaching about human sexuality. The regulation included an "excusal clause" establishing procedures by which a parent could withdraw his or her child if the course conflicted with religious belief or conscience. The court held that the regulation did not violate either the Free Exercise or Establishment Clauses of the First Amendment. Concerning free exercise, the court placed emphasis on the fact that the regulation contained an "excusal" provision. In applying the Establishment Clause, the court pointed out that the regulation does not enhance any particular religious viewpoint

nor does it favor a "secular" view over a "religious" one. Smith v. Ricci, 89 N.J. 514, 446 A.2d 501 (1982).

3. The federal circuit court in *Cornwell* dismissed parents' free exercise argument even though there was no provision for the student to be excused. In *Medeiros* in Note 1 and *Smith* in Note 2, above, however, the courts relied on "excusal" provisions in the regulations to offset the free exercise issue.

*Academic Freedom Extends to Protect
Teacher in Use of "Dirty" Word If
Conveyed for Demonstrated
Educational Purpose*

KEEFE v. GEANAKOS

United States Court of Appeals,
First Circuit, 1969.
418 F.2d 359.

ALDRICH, Chief Judge. . . .

Reduced to fundamentals, the substance of plaintiff's position is that as a matter of law his conduct which forms the basis of the charge did not warrant discipline. Accordingly, he argues, there is no ground for any hearing. He divides this position into two parts. The principal one is that his conduct was within his competence as a teacher, as a matter of academic freedom, whether the defendants approved of it or not. The second is that he had been given inadequate prior warning by such regulations as were in force, particularly in the light of the totality of the circumstances known to him, that his actions would be considered improper, so that an ex post facto ruling would, itself, unsettle academic freedom. The defendants, essentially, deny plaintiff's contentions. They accept the existence of a principle of academic freedom to teach, but state that it is limited to proper classroom materials as reasonably determined by the school committee in the light of pertinent conditions, of which they cite in particular the age of the students. Asked by the court whether a teacher has a right to say to the school committee that it is wrong if, in fact, its decision was arbitrary, counsel candidly and commendably (and correctly) responded in the affirmative. This we consider to be the present issue. . . .

On the opening day of school in September 1969 the plaintiff gave to each member of his senior English class a copy of the September 1969 *Atlantic Monthly* magazine, a publication of high reputation, and stated that the reading assignment for that night was the first article therein. September was the educational number, so-called, of the *Atlantic,* and some seventy-five copies had been supplied by the school department. Plaintiff discussed the article, and a particular word that was used therein, and explained the word's origin and context, and the reasons the author had included it. The word, admittedly highly offensive, is a vulgar term for an incestuous son. Plaintiff stated that any student who felt the assignment personally distasteful could have an alternative one.

The next evening the plaintiff was called to a meeting of the school committee and asked to defend his use of the offending word. Following his explanation, a majority of the members of the committee asked him informally if he would agree not to use it again in the classroom. Plaintiff replied that he could not, in good conscience, agree. His counsel states, however, without contradiction, that in point of fact plaintiff has not used it again. No formal action was taken at this meeting. Thereafter plaintiff was suspended, as a matter of discipline, and it is now proposed that he should be discharged.

The Lifton article, which we have read in its entirety, has been described as a valuable discussion of "dissent, protest, radicalism and revolt." It is in no sense pornographic. We need no supporting affidavits to find it scholarly, thoughtful and thought-provoking. The single offending word, although repeated a number of times, is not artificially introduced, but, on the contrary, is important to the development of the thesis and the conclusions of the author. Indeed, we would find it difficult to disagree with plaintiff's assertion that no proper study of the article could avoid consideration of this word. It is not possible to read the article, either in whole or in part, as an incitement to libidinous conduct, or even thoughts. If it raised the concept of incest, it was not to suggest it, but to condemn it; the word was used, by the persons described, as a superlative of opprobrium. We believe not only that the article negatived any other concept, but that an understanding of it would reject, rather than suggest the word's use. . . .

Hence the question in this case is whether a teacher may, for demonstrated educational purposes, quote a "dirty" word currently used in order to give special offense, or whether the shock is too great for high school seniors to stand. If the answer were that the students must be protected from such exposure, we would fear for their future. We do not question the good faith of the defendants in believing that some parents have been offended. With the greatest of respect to such parents, their sensibilities are not the full measure of what is proper education.

We of course agree with defendants that what is to be said or read to students is not to be determined by obscenity standards for adult consumption. . . . At the same time, the issue must be one of degree. A high school senior is not devoid of all discrimination or resistance. Furthermore, as in all other instances, the offensiveness of language and the particular propriety or impropriety is dependent on the circumstances of the utterance. . . . We accept the conclusion of the court below that "some measure of public regulation of classroom speech is inherent in every provision of public education." But when we consider the facts at bar as we have elaborated them, we find it difficult not to think that its application to the present case demeans any proper concept of education. The general chilling effect of permitting such rigorous censorship is even more serious.

We believe it equally probable that the plaintiff will prevail on the issue of lack of any notice that a discussion of this article with the senior class was forbidden conduct. The school regulation upon which defendants rely, although unquestionably worthy, is not apposite. It does not follow that a teacher may not be on notice of impropriety from the circumstances of a case without the necessity of a regulation. In the present case, however, the circumstances would have disclosed that no less than five books, by as many authors, containing the word in question were to be found in the school library. It is hard to think that any student could walk into the library and receive a book, but that his teacher could not subject the content to serious discussion in class.

Such inconsistency on the part of the school has been regarded as fatal. . . . We, too, would probably so regard it. At the same time, we prefer not to place our decision on this ground alone, lest our doing so diminish our principal holding, or lead to a bowdlerization of the school library.

Finally, we are not persuaded by the district court's conclusion that no irreparable injury is involved because the plaintiff, if successful, may recover money damages. Academic freedom is not preserved by compulsory retirement, even at full pay.

The immediate question before us is whether we should grant interlocutory relief pending appeal. This question, as defendants point out, raises the ultimate issue of the appeal itself. The matter has been extensively briefed and argued by both sides. We see no purpose in taking two bites, and believe this a case for action under Local Rule 5. The order of the district court denying an interlocutory injunction pending a decision on the merits is reversed and the case is remanded for further proceedings consistent herewith.

NOTES

1. In a case in which a secondary school teacher wrote on the board and used a four-letter word to illustrate changes in standards of morality, the court held that the teacher must be able to show that the methods used are in keeping with the preponderant opinion of the teaching profession. The court said:

   While secondary schools are not rigid disciplinary institutions, neither are they open forums in which mature adults, already habituated to social restraints, exchange ideas on a level of parity. Moreover, it cannot be accepted as a premise that the student is voluntarily in the classroom and willing to be exposed to a teaching method which, though reasonable, is not approved by the school authorities or by the weight of professional opinion. A secondary school student, unlike most college students, is usually required to attend school classes, and may have no choice as to his teacher.

   Bearing in mind these competing considerations, this court rules that when a secondary school teacher uses a teaching method which he does not prove has the support of the preponderant opinion of the teaching profession or of the part of it to which he belongs, but which he merely proves is relevant to his subject and students, is regarded by experts of significant standing as serving a serious educational purpose, and was used by him in good faith the state may suspend or discharge a teacher for using that method but it may not resort to such drastic sanctions unless the state proves he was put on notice either by a regulation or otherwise that he should not use that method. Mailloux v. Kiley, 323 F.Supp. 1387 (D.Mass.1971).

   On appeal of this case, the higher court cast some doubt on the feasibility of the rule measuring the validity of a teaching method on the preponderant opinion of other educators and noted that each case must be examined on an independent basis, the court considering that "the propriety of regulations or sanctions must depend on such circumstances as the age and sophistication of the students, the closeness of the relation to the specific [teaching] technique used and some concededly valid educational objective, and the context and manner of presentation." Mailloux v. Kiley, 448 F.2d 1242 (1st Cir.1971).

2. In 1973, a group of teachers requested a pilot program, Global Studies, as an alternative to the conventional history course. Students were given a choice between Global Studies and the conventional classes, and most chose the conventional class. Two teachers filed a grievance regarding the student registration procedure because of the decline in students in Global Studies and the fact that they had to teach the traditional class. When they lost the grievance at all levels they filed suit claiming, inter alia, that their academic freedom had been violated and asserted the right of a teacher to select teaching methods and materials. The Supreme Court of Washington ruled that

if Global Studies detracts from the scope of a conventional history course— because it emphasizes small groups, independent reading and writing, and inquiry—discovery techniques—[the teachers] may be compelled to abandon their own preferral techniques and to teach history in a more conventional manner. While teachers should have some measure of freedom in teaching techniques employed, they may not ignore or omit essential course material or disregard the course calendar. Milliken v. Board of Directors of Everett, 93 Wn.2d 522, 611 P.2d 414 (1980)

3. The United States Court of Appeals, Sixth Circuit held that academic freedom

does not encompass the right of a nontenured teacher to have her teaching style insulated from review by her superiors . . . . just because her methods and philosophy are considered acceptable within the teaching profession. Hetrick v. Martin, 480 F.2d 705 at 709 (6th Cir.1973), cert. denied 414 U.S. 1075, 94 S.Ct. 592 (1973). See also: Adams v. Campbell County School District, Campbell County, Wyoming, 511 F.2d 1242 (10th Cir.1975); Saunders v. Reorganized School District No. 2, 520 S.W.2d 29 (Mo.1975); Clark v. Holmes, 474 F.2d 928 (7th Cir.1972), cert denied, 411 U.S. 972, 93 S.Ct. 2148 (1973); Parducci v. Rutland, 316 F.Supp. 352 (M.D.Ala.1970)

Local School Board May Not Remove
Books From School Libraries Simply
Because It Dislikes the Ideas
Contained in the Books

BOARD OF EDUCATION, ISLAND TREES UNION FREE DISTRICT # 26 v. PICO

Supreme Court of the United States, 1982.
457 U.S. 853, 102 S.Ct. 2799.

Justice BRENNAN announced the judgment of the Court, and delivered an opinion in which Justice MARSHALL and Justice STEVENS joined, and in which Justice BLACKMUN joined except for Part II-A-(1).

The principal question presented is whether the First Amendment imposes limitations upon the exercise by a local school board of its discretion to remove library books from high school and junior high school libraries.

Petitioners are the Board of Education of the Island Trees Union Free School District No. 26, in New York, and Richard Ahrens, Frank Martin,

Christina Fasulo, Patrick Hughes, Richard Melchers, Richard Michaels, and Louis Nessim. When this suit was brought, Ahrens was the President of the Board, Martin was the Vice President, and the remaining petitioners were Board members. The Board is a state agency charged with responsibility for the operation and administration of the public schools within the Island Trees School District, including the Island Trees High School and Island Trees Memorial Junior High School. Respondents are Steven Pico, Jacqueline Gold, Glenn Yarris, Russell Rieger, and Paul Sochinski. When this suit was brought, Pico, Gold, Yarris, and Rieger were students at the High School, and Sochinski was a student at the Junior High School.

In September 1975, petitioners Ahrens, Martin, and Hughes attended a conference sponsored by Parents of New York United (PONYU), a politically conservative organization of parents concerned about education legislation in the State of New York. At the conference these petitioners obtained lists of books described by Ahrens as "objectionable," and by Martin as "improper fare for school students." It was later determined that the High School library contained nine of the listed books, and that another listed book was in the Junior High School library. [The nine books in the High School library were: *Slaughterhouse Five*, by Kurt Vonnegut, Jr.; *The Naked Ape*, by Desmond Morris; *Down These Mean Streets*, by Piri Thomas; *Best Short Stories of Negro Writers*, edited by Langston Hughes; *Go Ask Alice*, of anonymous authorship; *Laughing Boy*, by Oliver LaFarge; *Black Boy*, by Richard Wright; *A Hero Ain't Nothin' But A Sandwich*, by Alice Childress; and *Soul On Ice*, by Eldridge Cleaver. The book in the Junior High School library was *A Reader for Writers*, edited by Jerome Archer. Still another listed book, *The Fixer*, by Bernard Malamud, was found to be included in the curriculum of a twelfth grade literature course.] In February 1976, at a meeting with the superintendent of schools and the principals of the High School and Junior High School, the Board gave an "unofficial direction" that the listed books be removed from the library shelves and delivered to the Board's offices, so that Board members could read them. When this directive was carried out, it became publicized, and the Board issued a press release justifying its action. It characterized the removed books as "anti-American, anti-Christian, anti-Semitic, and just plain filthy," and concluded that "It is our duty, our moral obligation, to protect the children in our schools from this moral danger as surely as from physical and medical dangers."

A short time later, the Board appointed a "Book Review Committee," consisting of four Island Trees parents and four members of the Island Trees schools staff, to read the listed books and to recommend to the Board whether the books should be retained, taking into account the books' "educational suitability," "good taste," "relevance," and "appropriateness to age and grade level." In July, the Committee made its final report to the Board, recommending that five of the listed books be retained [*The Fixer, Laughing Boy, Black Boy, Go Ask Alice,* and *Best Short Stories by Negro Writers*] and that two others be removed from the school libraries [*The Naked Ape* and *Down These Mean Streets*]. As for the remaining four books, the Committee could not agree on two, [*Soul on Ice* and *A Hero Ain't Nothin' But A Sandwich*] took no position on one [*A Reader for Writers*. The reason given for this disposition was that all members of the Committee had not been able to read the book], and recommended that the last book be made available to students only with parental approval [*Slaughterhouse Five*]. The Board substantially rejected the Committee's report later that month, deciding that only one book should be returned to the High School library without restriction [*Laughing Boy*], that another should be made available subject to parental approval [*Black Boy*], but that the remaining nine books should "be removed from elementary and secondary libraries and [from] use in the curriculum." [As a result, the nine removed books could not be assigned or suggested to students in connection with school work. However, teachers were not instructed to refrain from discussing the removed books or the ideas and positions expressed in them.] The Board gave no reasons for rejecting the recommendations of the Committee that it had appointed.

Respondents reacted to the Board's decision by bringing the present action. They alleged that petitioners had

> ordered the removal of the books from school libraries and proscribed their use in the curriculum because particular passages in the books offended their social, political and moral tastes and not because the books, taken as a whole, were lacking in educational value.

Respondents claimed that the Board's actions denied them their rights under the First Amendment. They asked the court for a declaration that the Board's actions were unconstitutional. . . .

We emphasize at the outset the limited nature of the substantive question presented by the case before us. Our precedents have long recognized certain constitutional limits upon the power of the State to control even the curriculum and classroom. For example, Meyer v. Nebraska, 262 U.S. 390, 43 S.Ct. 625, 67 L.Ed. 1042 (1923), struck down a state law that forbade the teaching of modern foreign languages in public and private schools, and Epperson v. Arkansas, 393 U.S. 97, 89 S.Ct. 266, 21 L.Ed.2d 228 (1968), declared unconstitutional a state law that prohibited the teaching of the Darwinian theory of evolution in any state-supported school. But the current action does not require us to re-enter this difficult terrain, which *Meyer* and *Epperson* traversed without apparent misgiving. For as this case is presented to us, it does not involve textbooks, or indeed any books that Island Trees students would be required to read. Respondents do not seek in this Court to impose limitations upon their school board's discretion to prescribe the curricula of the Island Trees schools. On the contrary, the only books at issue in this case are *library* books, books that by their nature are optional rather than required reading. Our adjudication of the present case thus does not intrude into the classroom, or into the compulsory courses taught there. Furthermore, even as to library books, the action before us does not involve the *acquisition* of books. Respondents have not sought to compel their school board to add to the school library sheves any books that students desire to read. Rather, the only action challenged in this case is the *removal* from school libraries of books originally placed there by the school authorities, or without objection from them. . . . . [T]he issue before us in this case is a narrow one, both substantively and procedurally. . . . Does the First Amendment impose *any* limitations upon the discretion of petitioners to remove library books from the Island Trees High School and Junior High School? . . .

The Court has long recognized that local school boards have broad discretion in the management of school affairs. . . . [B]y and large, "public education in our Nation is committed to the control of state and local authorities," and . . . federal courts should not ordinarily "intervene in the resolution of conflicts which arise in the daily operation of school systems." Tinker v. Des Moines School Dist., 393 U.S. 503, 507, 89 S.Ct. 733, 736, 21 L.Ed.2d 731 (1969), noted that we have "repeatedly emphasized . . . the comprehensive authority of the States and of school officials . . . to prescribe and control conduct in the schools." We have also acknowledged that public schools are vitally important "in the preparation of individuals for participation as citizens," and as vehicles for "inculcating fundamental values necessary to the maintenance of a democratic political system." We are therefore in full agreement with petitioners that local school boards must be permitted "to establish and apply their curriculum in such a way as to transmit community values," and that "there is a legitimate and substantial community interest in promoting respect for authority and traditional values be they social, moral, or political."

At the same time, however, we have necessarily recognized that the discretion of the States and local school boards in matters of education must be exercised in a manner that comports with the transcendent imperatives of the First Amendment. . . .

In short, "First Amendment rights, applied in light of the special characteristics of the school environment, are available to . . . students."

Of course, courts should not "intervene in the resolution of conflicts which arise in the daily operations of school systems" unless "basic constitutional values" are "directly and sharply implicate[d]" in those conflicts. But we think that the First Amendment rights of students may be directly and sharply implicated by the removal of books from the shelves of a school library. Our precedents have focused "not only on the role of the First Amendment in fostering individual self-expression but also on its role in affording the public access to discussion, debate, and the dissemination of information and ideas." And we have recognized that "The State may not, consistently with the spirit of the First Amendment, contract the spectrum of available knowledge." . . . This [the right to receive information and ideas] is an inherent corollary of the rights of free speech and press that are explicitly guaranteed by the Constitution, in two senses. First, the right to receive ideas follows ineluctably from the *sender's* First Amendment right to send them: "The right of freedom of speech and press . . . embraces the right to distribute literature, . . . and necessarily protects the right to receive it." "The dissemination of ideas can accomplish nothing if otherwise willing addressees are not free to receive and consider them. It would be a barren marketplace of ideas that had only sellers and no buyers."

More importantly, the right to receive ideas is a necessary predicate to the *recipient's* meaningful exercise of his own rights of speech, press, and political freedom. Madison admonished us that

A popular Government, without popular information, or the means of acquiring it, is but a Prologue to a Farce or a Tragedy; or, perhaps both. Knowledge will forever govern ignorance: And a people who mean to be their own Governors, must arm themselves with the power which knowledge gives. . . .

In sum, just as access to ideas makes it possible for citizens generally to exercise their rights of free speech and press in a meaningful manner, such access prepares students for active and effective participation in the pluralistic, often contentious society in which they will soon be adult members. Of course all First Amendment rights accorded to students must be construed "in light of the special characteristics of the school environment." But the special characteristics of the school *library* make that environment especially appropriate for the recognition of the First Amendment rights of students.

A school library, no less than any other public library, is "a place dedicated to quiet, to knowledge, and to beauty." . . . The school library is the principal locus of such freedom. . . .

Petitioners emphasize the inculcative function of secondary education, and argue that they must be allowed *unfettered* discretion to "transmit community values" through the Island Trees schools. But that sweeping claim overlooks the unique role of the school library. It appears from the record that use of the Island Trees school libraries is completely voluntary on the part of students. Their selection of books from these libraries is entirely a matter of free choice; the libraries afford them an opportunity at self-education and individual enrichment that is wholly optional. Petitioners might well defend their claim of absolute discretion in matters of *curriculum* by reliance upon their duty to inculcate community values. But we think that petitioners' reliance upon that duty is misplaced where, as here, they attempt to extend their claim of absolute discretion beyond the compulsory environment of the classroom, into the school library and the regime of voluntary inquiry that there holds sway.

In rejecting petitioners' claim of absolute discretion to remove books from their school libraries, we do not deny that local school boards have a substantial legitimate role to play in the determination of school library content. . . .

Petitioners rightly possess significant discretion to determine the content of their school libraries. But that discretion may not be exercised in a narrowly partisan or political manner. If a Democratic school board, motivated by party affiliation, ordered the removal of all books written by or in favor of Republicans, few would doubt that the order violated the constitutional rights of the students denied access to those books. The same conclusion would surely apply if an all-white school board, motivated by racial animus, decided to remove all books authored by blacks or advocating racial equality and integration. Our Constitution does not permit the official suppression of *ideas*. Thus whether petitioners' removal of books from their school libraries denied respondents their First Amendment rights depends upon the motivation behind petitioners' actions. If petitioners *intended* by their removal decision to deny respondents access to ideas with which petitioners disagreed, and if this intent was the decisive factor in petitioners' decision, then petitioners have exercised their discretion in violation of the Constitution. To permit such intentions to control official actions would be to encourage the precise sort of officially prescribed orthodoxy unequivocally condemned in *Barnette.* On the other hand, respondents implicitly concede that an unconstitutional motivation would *not* be demonstrated if it were shown that petitioners had decided to remove the books at issue because those books were pervasively vulgar. And again, respondents concede that if it were demonstrated that the removal decision was based solely upon the "educational suitability" of the books in question, then their removal would be "perfectly permissible." In other words, in respondents' view such motivations, if decisive of petitioners' actions, would not carry the danger of an official suppression of ideas, and thus would not violate respondents' First Amendment rights.

As noted earlier, nothing in our decision today affects in any way the discretion of a local school board to choose books to *add* to the libraries of their schools. Because we are concerned in this case with the suppression of ideas, our holding today affects only the discretion to *remove* books. In brief, we hold that local school boards may not remove books from school library shelves simply because they dislike the ideas contained in those books and seek by their removal to "prescribe what shall be orthodox in politics, nationalism, religion, or other matters of opinion." . . .

School System's Failure to Provide
English Language Instruction to
Chinese Speaking Children Violates
the Civil Rights Act of 1964

LAU v. NICHOLS
Supreme Court of the United States, 1974.
414 U.S. 563, 94 S.Ct. 786.

Mr. Justice DOUGLAS delivered the opinion of the Court. . . .

This class suit brought by non-English-speaking Chinese students against officials responsible for the operation of the San Francisco Unified School District seeks relief against the unequal educational opportunities, which are alleged to violate the Fourteenth Amendment. No specific remedy is urged upon us. Teaching English to the students of Chinese ancestry who do not speak the language is one choice. Giving instructions to this group in Chinese is another. There may be others. Petitioners ask only that the Board of Education be directed to apply its expertise to the problem and rectify the situation. . . .

The Court of Appeals reasoned that "every student brings to the starting line of his educational career different advantages and disadvantages caused in part by social, economic and cultural background, created and continued completely apart from any contribution by the school system." Yet in our view the case may not be so easily decided. This is a public school system of California and § 71 of the California Education Code states that "English shall be the basic language of instruction in all schools." That section permits a school district to determine "when and under what circumstances instruction may be given bilingually." That section also states as "the policy of the state" to insure "the mastery of English by all pupils in the schools." And bilingual instruction is authorized "to the extent that it does not interfere with the systematic, sequential, and regular instruction of all pupils in the English language."

Moreover, § 8573 of the Education Code provides that no pupil shall receive a diploma of graduation from grade twelve who has not met the standards of proficiency in "English," as well as other prescribed subjects. Moreover, by § 12101 of the Education Code children between the ages of six and sixteen years are (with exceptions not material here) "subject to compulsory full-time education."

Under these state-imposed standards there is no equality of treatment merely by providing students with the same facilities, textbooks, teachers, and curriculum; for students who do not understand English are effectively foreclosed from any meaningful education.

Basic English skills are at the very core of what these public schools teach. Imposition of a requirement that, before a child can effectively participate in the educational program, he must already have acquired those basic skills is to make a mockery of public education. We know that those who do not understand English are certain to find their classroom experiences wholly incomprehensible and in no way meaningful.

We do not reach the Equal Protection Clause argument which has been advanced but rely solely on § 601 of the Civil Rights Act of 1964, 42 U.S.C.A. § 2000d, to reverse the Court of Appeals.

That section bans discrimination based "on the ground of race, color, or national origin," in "any program or activity receiving Federal financial assistance." The school district involved in this litigation receives large amounts of federal financial assistance. HEW, which has authority to promulgate regulations prohibiting discrimination in federally assisted school systems, 42 U.S.C.A. § 2000d–1, in 1968 issued one guideline that "school systems are responsible for assuring that students of a particular race, color, or national origin are not denied the opportunity to obtain the education generally obtained by other students in the system." 33 CFR 4955. In 1970 HEW made the guidelines more specific, requiring school districts that were federally funded "to rectify the language deficiency in order to open" the instruction to students who had "linguistic deficiencies," 35 Fed.Reg. 11595.

By § 602 of the Act HEW is authorized to issue rules, regulations, and orders to make sure that recipients of federal aid under its jurisdiction conduct any federally financed projects consistently with § 601. HEW's regulations, 45 CFR § 80.3(b)(1), specify that the recipients may not

> Provide any service, financial aid, or other benefit to an individual which is different, or is provided in a different manner, from that provided to others under the program. . . .
> Restrict an individual in any way in the enjoyment of any advantage or privilege enjoyed by others receiving any service, financial aid, or other benefit under the program.

Discrimination among students on account of race or national origin that is prohibited includes "discrimination . . . in the availability or use of any academic . . . or other facilities of the grantee or other recipient." Id., § 80.5(b).

Discrimination is barred which has that *effect* even though no purposeful design is present: a recipient "may not . . . utilize criteria or methods of administration which have the effect of subjecting individuals to discrimination" or have "the effect of defeating or substantially impairing accomplishment of the objectives of the program as respect individuals of a particular race, color or national origin." Id., § 80.3(b)(2).

It seems obvious that the Chinese-speaking minority receive fewer benefits than the English-speaking majority from respondents' school system which denies them a meaningful opportunity to participate in the educational program—all earmarks of the discrimination banned by the regulations. In 1970 HEW issued clarifying guidelines (35 Fed.Reg. 11595) which include the following:

> Where inability to speak and understand the English language excludes national origin-minority group children from effective participation in the educational program offered by a school district, the district must take affirmative steps to rectify the language deficiency in order to open its instructional program to these students (Pet.Br.App. 1a).
>
> Any ability grouping or tracking system employed by the school system to deal with the special language skill needs of national origin-minority group children must be designed to meet such language skill needs as soon as possible and must not operate as an educational deadend or permanent track. (Pet.Br. p. 2a).

Respondent school district contractually agreed to "comply with title VI of the Civil Rights Act of 1964 . . . and all requirements imposed by or pursuant to the Regulation" of HEW (45 CFR pt. 80) which are "issued pursuant to that title . . . " and also immediately to "take any measures necessary to effectuate this agreement." The Federal Government has power to fix the terms on which its money allotments to the States shall be disbursed. . . . Whatever may be the limits of that power . . . they have not been reached here. Senator Humphrey, during the floor debates on the Civil Rights Act of 1964, said:

> Simple justice requires that public funds, to which all taxpayers of all races contribute, not be spent in any fashion which encourages, entrenches, subsidizes, or results in racial discrimination.

We accordingly reverse the judgment of the Court of Appeals and remand the case for the fashioning of appropriate relief.

Reversed.

NOTES

1. A school district may admit students who achieve in the top 15 percent to a preferred, college-prepatory high school without violating the Civil Rights Act or the Fourteenth Amendment, even though the percentage of black and Spanish-American is disproportionately low. The court found that the school district's legitimate interest outweighed any harm imagined or suffered by students whose achievement had not qualified them for admission. Berkelman v. San Francisco Unified School District, 501 F.2d 1264 (9th Cir.1974).

2. A federal district court has within its inherent legal prerogative the equitable power to fashion a bilingual-bicultural program that will assure that Spanish-surnamed children receive meaningful education. Serna v. Portales Municipal Schools, 499 F.2d 1147 (10th Cir.1974).

EVOLUTION VERSUS CREATIONISM

The classic argument over Darwin's theory of evolution and the Biblical account of creation has again been debated in legislatures and the courts of the United States. Proponents of teaching "creation science" in the public schools convinced at least two legislatures, those of Arkansas and Louisiana, and the State Board of Texas that the account of creation in the Bible was as scientific as Darwin's theory and it was, therefore, a legitimate scientific theory. Because creationism was viewed by some as a scientific theory, state authorities mandated it be taught alongside evolution. The tenets of creationism are derived from the first two chapters of Genesis in the Bible and include the following judgments: (1) that the earth and universe are relatively young, perhaps only 6,000 to 10,000 years old; (2) that the present physical form of earth is explained by "catastrophism" including a world-wide flood; and (3) that all living things (including humans) were created miraculously, essentially in their present forms.

The National Academy of Sciences and many scientists, individually, have spoken out against the notion that "creation science" is science at all and have opposed its imposition in public school classrooms. The Academy, in an official release on the subject, said:

> . . . the Academy states unequivocally that the tenets of "creation science" are not supported by scientific evidence, that creationism has no place in a *science* curriculum at any level, that its proposed teaching would be impossible in any constructive sense for well-informed and conscientious science teachers, and that its teaching would be contrary to the nation's need for a scientifically literate citizenry and for a large, well-informed pool of scientific and technical personnel.[18]

The Academy further observed that creationism is not a science per se and cannot be characterized as such and to claim that creationism should be given equal time in the classrooms indicates a misunderstanding of the definition of science. Science, according to the Academy, is a systematic organization of knowledge about the universe and its parts. This knowledge is founded on evidence and verifiable consequences of experimentation and observation. Science is a process of formulation of hypotheses, continuous testing, corrections, and new conclusions and findings—it evolves and changes. Creationism, on the other hand, has no foundation in evidence, experimentation, or observation and is, therefore, not a science. Creationism is based on belief and revelation and cannot change regardless of evidence to the contrary.

The effect of the creationism movement was felt by major textbook publishers nationwide who responded to creationists' demands, especially those in Texas, where the State Board of Education adopted textbook guidelines that encouraged censorship. The Texas rule [19] required that all science textbooks identify evolution as only "one of several explanations of the origins of human kind" and that evolution must be treated as a theory rather than fact. As a result, the publishers decreased coverage of evolution in their science textbooks and one even deleted the word "evolution" completely. Finally, after a decade of acrimony, which had a substantial effect on the content of textbooks, the Texas State Board of Education abrogated the rule in April, 1984.

The situation in Texas was merely a modern version of the issues that precipitated the famous "John Scopes monkey trial" in Dayton, Tennessee, which matched the famous lawyer Clarence Darrow against the great politician William Jennings Bryan. A technical victory was won by Bryan for the state, but Darrow won a popular victory in his devastating cross-examination of Bryan. Although the statute that made it a criminal offense to teach evolution in the public school classrooms of Tennessee was not overturned, it was largely ignored and went unenforced after Scopes' conviction.

In 1968, an anti-evolution statute in Arkansas was challenged as violative of the First Amendment.[20] The United States Supreme Court found in the statute an implicit state sanction of the Christian doctrine of creation from the Book of Genesis and the Court declared it unconstitutional.

In a later version of the issue, which coincided with the aforementioned episodes in Texas, the Governor of Arkansas signed into law in 1981 a bill that required balanced treatment for creation science and evolution in the public schools. Proponents of the new statute maintained that not only was creationism a science, but that Darwin's theory of evolution actually constituted a kind of obverse religion, secular humanism, and, as such, its use in the classroom was tantamount to teaching an atheistic religion in public schools.

The statute was promptly challenged as violative of the religion provisions of the First Amendment. The State of Arkansas defended by maintaining that a literal interpretation of Genesis did not necessarily mean that creation science was religious; second, the state's reference to creation did not imply that the creation was caused by a supreme being or God; and, third, to teach in public schools about the concept of a creator was not religious per se.

The federal court in *McLean* v. *Arkansas Board of Education*[21] held against the state on all counts. The judge, in holding the statute unconstitutional, observed that creation science was not a science at all, but, instead, a religious doctrine. For the state to impose such a belief on the youth in public schools violated the First Amendment.

In January 1985, a federal district judge held a Louisiana creation statute, similar to Arkansas', unconstitutional because it "promotes the beliefs of some theistic sects to the detriment of others". According to the judge, the so-called "balanced treatment statute" removed the state from a position of neutrality toward advancing a particular religious belief. Aguillard v. Treen, Governor, —— F.Supp. —— (1985).

*Statute Forbidding the Teaching of
Evolution Is Unconstitutional*

EPPERSON v. STATE OF ARKANSAS

Supreme Court of the United States, 1968.
393 U.S. 97, 89 S.Ct. 266.

Mr. Justice FORTAS delivered the opinion of the Court.

This appeal challenges the constitutionality of the "anti-evolution" statute which the State of Arkansas adopted in 1928 to prohibit the teaching in its public schools and universities of the theory that man evolved from other species of life. . . .

The Arkansas law makes it unlawful for a teacher in any state-supported school or university "to teach the theory or doctrine that mankind ascended or descended from a lower order of animals," or "to adopt or use in any such institution a textbook that teaches" this theory. Violation is a misdemeanor and subjects the violator to dismissal from his position.

The present case concerns the teaching of biology in a high school in Little Rock. According to the testimony, until the events here in litigation, the official textbook furnished for the high school biology course did not have a section on the Darwinian Theory. Then, for the academic year 1965–1966, the school administration, on recommendation of the teachers of biology in the school system, adopted and prescribed a textbook which contained a chapter setting forth "the theory about the origin . . . of man from a lower form of animal."

Susan Epperson, a young woman who graduated from Arkansas' school system and then obtained her master's degree in zoology at the University of Illinois, was employed by the Little Rock school system in the fall of 1964 to teach tenth grade biology at Central High School. At the start of the next academic year, 1965, she was confronted by the new textbook (which one surmises from the record was not unwelcome to her). She faced at least a literal dilemma because she was supposed to use the new textbook for classroom instruction and presumably to teach the statutorily condemned chapter; but to do so would be a criminal offense and subject her to dismissal. . . . Only Arkansas and Mississippi have such "anti-evolution" or "monkey" laws on their books. There is no record of any prosecutions in Arkansas under its statute. It is possible that the statute is presently more of a curiosity than a vital fact of life in these States. Nevertheless, the present case was brought, the appeal as of right is properly here, and it is our duty to decide the issues presented.

At the outset, it is urged upon us that the challenged statute is vague and uncertain and therefore within the condemnation of the Due Process Clause of the Fourteenth Amendment. The contention that the Act is vague and uncertain is supported by language in the brief opinion of Arkansas' Supreme Court. That court, perhaps reflecting the discomfort which the statute's quixotic prohibition necessarily engenders in the modern mind, stated that it "expresses no opinion" as to whether the Act prohibits "explanation" of the theory of evolution or merely forbids "teaching that the theory is true." Regardless of this uncertainty, the court held that the statute is constitutional.

On the other hand, counsel for the State, in oral argument in this Court, candidly stated that, despite the State Supreme Court's equivocation Arkansas would interpret the statute "to mean that to make a student aware of the theory . . . just to teach that there was such a theory" would be grounds for dismissal and for prosecution under the statute; and he said "that the Supreme Court of Arkansas' opinion should be interpreted in that manner." He said: "If Mrs. Epperson would tell her students that 'Here is Darwin's theory, that man ascended or descended from a lower form of being,' then I think she would be under this statute liable for prosecution.

In any event, we do not rest our decision upon the asserted vagueness of the statute. On either interpretation of its language, Arkansas' statute cannot stand. It is of no moment whether the law is deemed to prohibit mention of Darwin's theory, or to forbid any or all of the infinite varieties of communication embraced within the term "teaching." Under either interpretation, the law must be stricken because of its conflict with the constitutional prohibition of state laws respecting an establishment of religion or prohibiting the free exercise thereof. The overriding fact is that Arkansas' law selects from the body of knowledge a particular segment which it proscribes for the sole reason that it is deemed to conflict with a particular religious doctrine; that is, with a particular interpretation of the Book of Genesis by a particular religious group. . . .

Judicial interposition in the operation of the public school system of the Nation raises problems requiring care and restraint. Our courts, however, have not failed to apply the First Amendment's mandate in our educational system where essential to safeguard the fundamental values of freedom of speech and inquiry and of belief. By and large, public education in our Nation is committed to the control of state and local authorities. Courts do not and cannot intervene in the resolution of conflicts which arise in the daily operation of school systems and which do not directly and sharply implicate basic constitutional values. On the other hand, "[t]he vigilant protection of constitutional freedoms is nowhere more vital than in the community of American schools," Shelton v. Tucker, 364 U.S. 479, 487, 81 S.Ct. 247, 251, 5 L.Ed.2d 231 (1960). As this Court said in *Keyishian* v. *Board of Regents,* the First Amendment "does not tolerate laws that cast a pall of orthodoxy over the classroom." 385 U.S. 589, 603, 87 S.Ct. 675, 683, 17 L.Ed.2d 629 (1967). . . .

There is and can be no doubt that the First Amendment does not permit the State to require that teaching and learning must be tailored to the principles or prohibitions of any religious sect or dogma. . . .

In the present case, there can be no doubt that Arkansas has sought to prevent its teachers from discussing the theory of evolution because it is contrary to the belief of some that the Book of Genesis must be the exclusive source of doctrine as to the origin of man. No suggestion has been made that Arkansas' law may be justified by considerations of state policy other than the religious views of some of its citizens. It is clear that fundamentalist sectarian conviction was and is the law's reason for existence. Its antecedent, Tennessee's "monkey law," candidly stated its purpose: to make it unlawful "to teach any theory that denies the story of the Divine Creation of man as taught in the Bible, and to teach instead that man has descended from a lower order of animals." Perhaps the sensational publicity attendant upon the *Scopes* trial induced Arkansas to adopt less explicit language. It eliminated Tennessee's reference to "the story of the Divine Creation of man" as taught in the Bible, but there is no doubt that the motivation for the law was the same: to suppress the teaching of a theory which it was thought "denied" the divine creation of man. . . .

The judgment of the Supreme Court of Arkansas is reversed.

NOTES

The Supreme Court of Mississippi struck down the last of the anti-evolution statutes in Smith v. State, 242 So.2d 692 (Miss.1970).

Tennessee's legislature repealed the anti-evolution statute that had created the Scopes Controversy, Scopes v. State of Tennessee, 154 Tenn. 105, 289 S.W. 363 (1927), and subsequently the use of any textbook that discussed evolution unless the book contained a disclaimer saying that the doctrine was merely a theory and was not based on scientific facts about the origin of man. Further, the statute mandated that the Genesis version of creation be included if any version was treated by the text and, under the statute, the Genesis version needed no disclaimer when included alone. The United States Court of Appeals, Sixth Circuit, held this statute to be unconstitutional because it gave preference to the Biblical version of creation. Daniel v. Walters, 515 F.2d 485 (6th Cir.1975).

*Teaching of "Creation Science" in
Public Schools Violates the
Establishment Clause of the First
Amendment*

McLEAN v. ARKANSAS
BOARD OF EDUCATION

United States District Court, Eastern
District of Arkansas, 1982.
529 F.Supp. 1255.

OVERTON, District Judge.

On March 19, 1981, the Governor of Arkansas signed into law Act 590 of 1981, entitled the "Balanced Treatment for Creation-Science and Evolution-Science Act." The Act is codified as Ark.Stat.Ann. § 80–1663, et seq. (1981 Supp.). Its essential mandate is stated in its first sentence: "Public schools within this State shall give balanced treatment to creation-science and to evolution-science." On May 27, 1981, this suit was filed challenging the constitutional validity of Act 590 on three distinct grounds.

First, it is contended that Act 590 constitutes an establishment of religion prohibited by the First Amendment to the Constitution, which is made applicable to the states by the Fourteenth Amendment. Second, the plaintiffs argue the Act violates a right to academic freedom which they say is guaranteed to students and teachers by the Free Speech Clause of the First Amendment. Third, plaintiffs allege the Act is impermissibly vague and thereby violates the Due Process Clause of the Fourteenth Amendment. . . .

There is no controversy over the legal standards under which the Establishment Clause portion of this case must be judged. The Supreme Court has on a number of occasions expounded on the meaning of the clause, and the pronouncements are clear. . . .

Most recently, the Supreme Court has held that the clause prohibits a state from requiring the posting of the Ten Commandments in public school classrooms for the same reasons that officially imposed daily Bible reading is prohibited. Stone v. Graham, 449 U.S. 39, 101 S.Ct. 192, 66 L.Ed.2d 199 (1980). The opinion in *Stone* relies on the most recent formulation of the Establishment Clause test, that of Lemon v. Kurtzman, 408 U.S. 602, 612–613, 91 S.Ct. 2105, 2111, 29 L.Ed.2d 745 (1971):

> First, the statute must have a secular legislative purpose; second, its principal or primary effect must be one that neither advances nor inhibits religion . . . ; finally, the statute must not foster "an excessive government entanglement with religion."

Stone v. Graham, 449 U.S. at 40, 101 S.Ct. at 193.

It is under this three-part test that the evidence in this case must be judged. Failure on any of these grounds is fatal to the enactment.

The religious movement known as Fundamentalism began in nineteenth century America as part of evangelical Protestantism's response to social changes, new religious thought and Darwinism. Fundamentalists viewed these developments as attacks on the Bible and as responsible for a decline in traditional values.

The various manifestations of Fundamentalism have had a number of common characteristics, but a central premise has always been a literal interpretation of the Bible and a belief in the inerrancy of the Scriptures. Following World War I, there was again a perceived decline in traditional morality, and Fundamentalism focused on evolution as responsible for the decline. One aspect of their efforts, particularly in the South, was the promotion of statutes prohibiting the teaching of evolution in public schools. In Arkansas, this resulted in the adoption of Initiated Act 1 of 1929. . . .

The term "scientific creationism" first gained currency around 1965 following publication of *The Genesis Flood* in 1961 by Whitcomb and Morris. . . .

In the 1960s and early 1970s, several Fundamentalist organizations were formed to promote the idea that the Book of Genesis was supported by scientific data. The terms "creation science" and "scientific creationism" have been adopted by these Fundamentalists as descriptive of their study of creation and the origins of man. . . .

Creationists view evolution as a source of society's ills . . ..

The creationist organizations consider the introduction of creation science into the public schools part of their ministry. . . .

The State of Arkansas, like a number of states whose citizens have relatively homogeneous religious beliefs, has a long history of official opposition to evolution which is motivated by adherence to Fundamentalist beliefs in the inerrancy of the Book of Genesis. This history is documented in

Justice Fortas' opinion in Epperson v. Arkansas, 393 U.S. 97, 89 S.Ct. 266, 21 L.Ed.2d 228 (1968), which struck down Initiated Act 1 of 1929, Ark.Stat.Ann. §§ 80–1627–1628, prohibiting the teaching of the theory of evolution. To this same tradition may be attributed Initiated Act 1 of 1930, Ark.Stat.Ann. § 80–1606 (Repl.1980), requiring "the reverent daily reading of a portion of the English Bible" in every public school classroom in the State. . . .[22]

The unusual circumstances surrounding the passage of Act 590, as well as the substantive law of the First Amendment, warrant an inquiry into the stated legislative purposes. The author of the Act had publicly proclaimed the sectarian purpose of the proposal. The Arkansas residents who sought legislative sponsorship of the bill did so for a purely sectarian purpose. These circumstances alone may not be particularly persuasive, but when considered with the publicly announced motives of the legislative sponsor made contemporaneously with the legislative process; the lack of any legislative investigation, debate or consultation with any educators or scientists; the unprecedented intrusion in school curriculum; and official history of the State of Arkansas on the subject, it is obvious that the statement of purposes has little, if any, support in fact. The State failed to produce any evidence which would warrant an inference or conclusion that at any point in the process anyone considered the legitimate educational value of the Act. It was simply and purely an effort to introduce the Biblical version of creation into the public school curricula. The only inference which can be drawn from these circumstances is that the Act was passed with the specific purpose by the General Assembly of advancing religion. The Act therefore fails the first prong of the three-pronged test, that of secular legislative purpose. . . .

If the defendants are correct and the Court is limited to an examination of the language of the Act, the evidence is overwhelming that both the purpose and effect of Act 590 is the advancement of religion in the public schools. . . .

The evidence establishes that the definition of "creation science" contained in 4(a) has as its unmentioned reference the first eleven chapters of the Book of Genesis. Among the many creation epics in human history, the account of sudden creation from nothing, or *creatio ex nihilo,* and subsequent destruction of the world by flood is unique to Genesis. The concepts of 4(a) are the literal Fundamentalists' view of Genesis. Section 4(a) is unquestionably a statement of religion, with the exception of 4(a)(2) which is a negative thrust aimed at what the creationists understand to be the theory of evolution.

Both the concepts and wording of Section 4(a) convey an inescapable religiosity. Section 4(a)(1) describes "sudden creation of the universe, energy and life from nothing." Every theologian who testified, including defense witnesses, expressed the opinion that the statement referred to a supernatural creation which was performed by God. . . .

The facts that creation science is inspired by the Book of Genesis and that Section 4(a) is consistent with a literal interpretation of Genesis leave no doubt that a major effect of the Act is the advancement of particular religious beliefs. The legal impact of this conclusion will be discussed further at the conclusion of the Court's evaluation of the scientific merit of creation science.

The approach to teaching "creation science" and "evolution science" found in Act 590 is identical to the two-model approach espoused by the Institute for Creation Research and is taken almost verbatim from ICR writings. It is an extension of Fundamentalists' view that one must either accept the literal interpretation of Genesis or else believe in the godless system of evolution.

The two-model approach of the creationists is simply a contrived dualism which has no scientific factual basis or legitimate educational purpose. It assumes only two explanations for the origins of life and existence of man, plants and animals: It was either the work of a creator or it was not. Application of these two models, according to creationists, and the defendants, dictates that all scientific evidence which fails to support the theory of evolution is necessarily scientific evidence in support of creationism and is, therefore, creation science "evidence" in support of Section 4(a).

The emphasis on origins as an aspect of the theory of evolution is peculiar to creationist literature. Although the subject of origins of life is within the province of biology, the scientific community does not consider origins of life a part of evolutionary theory. The theory of evolution assumes the existence of life and is directed to an explanation of *how* life evolved. Evolution does not presuppose the absence of a creator or God and the plain inference conveyed by Section 4 is erroneous.

In addition to the fallacious pedagogy of the two-model approach, Section 4(a) lacks legitimate educational value because "creation science" as defined in that section is simply not science. Several witnesses suggested definitions of science. A descriptive definition was said to be that science is what is "accepted by the scientific community" and is "what scientists do." The obvious implication of this description is that, in a free society, knowledge does not require the imprimatur of legislation in order to become science. . . . .

Creation science, as defined in Section 4(a), not only fails to follow the canons defining scientific theory, it also fails to fit the more general descriptions of "what scientists think" and "what scientists do." The scientific community consists of individuals and groups, nationally and internationally, who work independently in such varied fields as biology, paleontology, geology and astronomy. Their work is published and subject to review and testing by their peers. The journals for publication are both numerous and varied. There is, however, not one recognized scientific journal which has published an article espousing the creation science theory described in Section 4(a). Some of the State's witnesses suggested that the scientific community was "close-minded" on the subject of creationism and that explained the lack of acceptance of the creation science arguments. Yet no witness produced a scientific article for which publication had been refused. Perhaps some members of the scientific community are resistant to new ideas. It is, however, inconceivable that such a loose-knit group of independent thinkers in all the varied fields of science could, or would, so effectively censor new scientific thought.

The creationists have difficulty maintaining among their ranks consistency in the claim that creationism is science. The author of Act 590, Ellwanger, said that neither evolution nor creationism was science. He thinks both are religion. Duane Gish recently responded to an article in *Discover* critical of creationism by stating:

> Stephen Jay Gould states that creationists claim creation is a scientific theory. This is a false accusation. Creationists have repeatedly stated that neither creation nor evolution is a scientific theory (and each is equally religious).

The methodology employed by creationists is another factor which is indicative that their work is not science. A scientific theory must be tentative and always subject to revision or abandonment in light of facts that are inconsistent with, or falsify, the theory. A theory that is by its own terms dogmatic, absolutist and never subject to revision is not a scientific theory.

The creationists' methods do not take data, weigh it against the opposing scientific data, and thereafter reach the conclusions stated in Section 4(a). Instead, they take the literal wording of the Book of Genesis and attempt to find scientific support for it. . . .

While anybody is free to approach a scientific inquiry in any fashion they choose, they cannot properly describe the methodology used as scientific, if they start with a conclusion and refuse to change it regardless of the evidence developed during the course of the investigation. . . .

The proof in support of creation science consisted almost entirely of efforts to discredit the theory of evolution through a rehash of data and theories which have been before the scientific community for decades. The arguments asserted by creationists are not based upon new scientific evidence or laboratory data which has been ignored by the scientific community. . . .

The conclusion that creation science has no scientific merit or educational value as science has legal significance in light of the Court's previous conclusion that creation science has, as one major effect, the advancement of religion. The second part of the three-pronged test for establishment reaches only those statutes having as their *primary* effect the advancement of religion. Secondary effects which advance religion are not constitutionally fatal. Since creation science is not science, the conclusion is inescapable that the *only* real effect of Act 590 is the advancement of religion. The Act therefore fails both the first and second portions of the test in Lemon v. Kurtzman, 403 U.S. 602, 91 S.Ct. 2105, 29 L.Ed.2d 745 (1971).

Act 590 mandates "balanced treatment" for creation science and evolution science. The Act prohibits instruction in any religious doctrine or references to religious writings. The Act is self-contradictory and compliance is impossible unless the public schools elect to forego significant portions of subjects such as biology, world history, geology, zoology, botany, psychology, anthropology, sociology, philosophy, physics and chemistry. Presently, the concepts of evolutionary theory as described in 4(b) permeate the public school textbooks. There is no way teachers can teach the Genesis account of creation in a secular manner.

The State Department of Education, through its textbook selection committee, school boards and school administrators will be required to constantly monitor materials to avoid using religious references. The school boards, administrators and teachers face an impossible task. How is the teacher to respond to questions about a creation suddenly and out of nothing? How will a teacher explain the occurrence of a world-wide flood? How will a teacher explain the concept of a relatively recent age of the earth? The answer is obvious because the only source of this information is ultimately contained in the Book of Genesis. . . .

These conclusions are dispositive of the case and there is no need to reach legal conclusions with respect to the remaining issues. . . .

The application and content of First Amendment principles are not determined by public opinion polls or by a majority vote. Whether the proponents of Act 590 constitute the majority or the minority is quite irrelevant under a constitutional system of government. No group, no matter how large or small, may use the organs of government, of which the public schools are the most conspicuous and influential, to foist its religious beliefs on others.

The Court closes this opinion with a thought expressed eloquently by the great Justice Frankfurter:

> We renew our conviction that "we have staked the very existence of our country on the faith that complete separation between the state and religion is best for the state and best for religion." Everson v. Board of Education, 330 U.S. at 59 [67 S.Ct at 532]. If nowhere else, in the relation between Church and State, "good fences make good neighbors." McCollum v. Board of Education, 333 U.S. 203, 232, 68 S.Ct. 461, 475, 92 L.Ed. 649 (1948).

An injunction will be entered permanently prohibiting enforcement of Act 590.

STUDENT TESTING AND PROMOTION

The state has the authority to establish standards for promotion and graduation. In recent years, states have begun to rely more and more on the standardized test as a criterion to determine students' competencies. So long as such measures of academic attainment are reasonable and nondicriminatory, the courts will not intervene. In fact, courts have traditionally given school officials and teachers wide latitude in deciding on appropriate academic requirements. The United States Supreme Court, in *Horowitz*, pointed out that "Courts are particularly ill-equipped to evaluate academic performance."[23] This judicial position of nonintervention was adopted early by the courts. In a 1913 case in Massachusetts, the court said that "So long as the school committee acts in good faith their conduct in formulating and applying standards and making decisions touching this matter is not subject to review by any other tribunal."[24]

Courts, of course, are not equipped to evaluate the academic standards of the myriad areas of subject matter and to review student performance. The courts confine themselves to determining whether due process is given where discrimination exists, or if a student suffered ill treatment through some arbitrary or capricious action by the school or teacher. In *Gaspar v. Bruton,*[25] the United States Court of Appeals for the Tenth Circuit observed that, "[t]he courts are not equipped to review academic records based upon academic standards within the particular knowledge, experience and expertise of academicians . . . . Thus, when presented with a challenge . . . for failure re academic standards, the court may grant relief, as a practical matter, only in those cases where the student presents positive evidence of ill will or bad motives."

Due Process

Recent years have seen states move to competency tests as minimal criteria for the awarding of high school diplomas. Because of society's great reliance on high school and college diplomas as measures of attainment, the diploma is of special interest to the student. The diploma meets the criteria for a property interest under the Due Process Clause of the Fourteenth Amendment as enunciated in *Board of Regents v. Roth* by the United States Supreme Court where it stated that, "To have a property interest in a benefit, a person clearly must have more than an abstract need or desire for it. He must have more than a unilateral expectation of it. He must, instead, have a legitimate claim of entitlement to it."[26] Certainly, a diploma is a benefit that everyone needs, and when a student progresses academically for twelve years, one may logically assume that the diploma will be forthcoming. The reasonableness of expectation of receipt of a diploma is, of course, contingent on the standards and what is considered by the school to be normal academic progress.

In requiring that students pass minimal competency tests in order to graduate, the states established new criteria to which a student must respond in order to have a reasonable expectation of graduation.

The criteria for graduation, level of test scores, type of questions, and the difficulty of items are all issues requiring subjective academic judgment. Substantive due process, property, and liberty interests do not apply to such subjective standards. It is the objective standards over which the courts will exercise scrutiny. The United States Supreme Court in *Mathews v. Eldridge*[27] enunciated the rationale for invoking due process saying that the dictates of due process are: (1) the nature of the private interest denied by official action, (2) the risk of erroneous deprivation if appropriate procedures are not followed, and (3) the state's interest in imposing the particular requirements or denying the benefit.

Where tests are concerned, "risk of erroneous deprivation" may be caused by tests that do not measure what students are supposed to have been taught; this is known to test experts as predictive validity. Also, tests may not accurately measure what they are intended to measure; educators refer to this as reliability.

These issues of validity and reliability became the foci of the court in the case of *Debra P. v. Turlington* in which the Florida functional literacy examination was challenged. In the original litigation, the plaintiffs prevailed on the due process issues because the state could not show that the school curriculum prepared the students for the items tested.[28]   The United States Court of Appeals for the Fifth Circuit, in addressing test validity as a due process issue, remanded the case back for further findings of fact to determine whether the literacy test covered "material actually taught in Florida's classrooms." To provide this information, the Florida Department of Education went through an elaborate process of surveying teachers to determine the content of courses they were teaching in order to verify that the questions on the literacy test were addressed in the classroom.   On rehearing of the case, the federal district court accepted the evidence submitted by the state indicating validity of the questions and ruled for the state.

Debra P. is an important due process precedent because it expands the judicial view of objective criteria to the extent that test questions come under the scrutiny of the court. This case tends to narrow the state's prerogative in interpreting what has traditionally been a subjective consideration.   By more carefully circumscribing objective criteria in terms of statistical measures of validity and reliability, the court effectively extends the realm of judicial scrutiny into student evaluation processes. In so doing, the court shifts the burden of proof and forces the state to demonstrate that the test was a fair assessment of what was taught.

Debra P. has subsequently been used as precedent by other courts. In *Anderson v. Banks,* a federal district court in Georgia required the school district to show that the questions on the California Achievement Test (CAT) had actually been covered in the high school curriculum before the court would allow the test to be used for an exit examination. The school district sustained this burden by conducting a study that matched objectives measured by the CAT with the school curriculum. Second, the study showed that the textbook content closely paralleled the types of items used and the content measured on the CAT. This was sufficient to meet the court's due process requirements. The court, in quoting *Debra P.*, said that "To require school officials to produce testimony that every teacher finished every lesson and assigned every problem in the curriculum would impose a paralyzing burden on school authorities . . . ."[29]

Equal Protection

Courts are very much aware of the potential for use of tests as a means to justify racial discrimination in violation of equal protection. In 1967, a federal district judge in Washington, D.C. held that the use of tests for tracking students was unconstitutional. The court found that the effect of the tests was to categorize students according to race and little opportunity was afforded to move from one track to another. Similarly, the use of I.Q. tests to evaluate students for placement in classes for the mentally retarded was invalidated by a federal court in California because the state could not show how the I.Q. tests were related to the intellectual capabilities of the students.[30] The effect of these tests was to place an inordinate number of black children in the mentally retarded category.[31]

The "effect" standard required that school officials show a compelling interest to administer such tests if the result was to effectively separate the races in the schools. School officials were uniformly unable to sustain this compelling interest burden and were, thus, virtually foreclosed from using standardized tests for placement or promotion.

Then the United States Supreme Court in *Washington v. Davis*[32] set down a new precedent that required plaintiffs to show not merely that the "effect" of the tests was to racially discriminate, but that the state in adopting the tests had the "intent" to discriminate. In this case, the Court found that to use tests producing racially disparate results was not a violation of equal protection unless it could be shown that there was official intent to discriminate.

Since the *Davis* decision, lower courts have refined the intent standard with a moderating criterion called "institutional intent." This standard requires that officials show a substantial nonracial objective, not a compelling interest if discriminatory results can be reasonably foreseen. This compromise test has been defined this way: "Where the school board adopts policies that foreseeably further an illegitimate objective, and it cannot justify or adequately explain such policies in terms of legitimate educational objectives, one must presume that the school board would not have adopted such a policy but for an illegitimate purpose. Consistent with this perspective, 'institutional segregative intent' may be said to exist where a school board adopts a more, rather than a less, segregative policy and cannot justify its choice in terms of legitimate educational objectives."[33]

The important issue is to determine what is a "compelling" state interest as opposed to what is merely a "reasonable" state interest. There is little doubt that tests can be used as diagnostic instruments even though classifications fall along racial lines. But there may be some legitimate question as to whether such tests can be used as a culling device to weed out those who are not as academically able as others, especially where no opportunity for academic redress is offered the student. Most importantly, though, the "institutional intent" standard shifts the burden of proof to the school district where, with the simple "intent" test, the plaintiff must show evidence that the state had the purpose and intent to discriminate.

Functional Literacy Test May Be
Required as Prerequisite for High
School Diploma, but Test Must Be a
Valid Measure of Instruction

DEBRA P. v. TURLINGTON

United States District Court, Middle
District of Florida, 1983.
564 F.Supp. 177, affirmed 730 F.2d 1405,
1984.

GEORGE C. CARR, District Judge.

In 1978, the Florida Legislature approved an amendment to the Educational Accountability Act of 1976, Fla.Stat. § 229.55 et seq., which required public school students in the State of Florida to pass a functional literacy examination in order to receive a state high school diploma. Fla.Stat. § 232.246(1)(b). Shortly after its enactment, Florida high school students filed a class action challenging the constitutionality of the literacy test requirement. This Court found that the test violated both the equal protection and due process clauses of the Constitution and enjoined its use as a diploma sanction until the 1982–83 school year. Debra P. v. Turlington, 474 F.Supp. 244 (M.D.Fla.1979). On appeal, the Fifth Circuit Court of Appeals affirmed many of this Court's findings. Debra P. v. Turlington, 644 F.2d 397 (5th Cir.1981). However, the appellate court remanded the case for further factual findings on two key issues. Specifically, this Court was directed to make further findings on whether or not the functional literacy test, the Florida Student State Assessment Test, Part II (SSAT–II), covers material actually taught in Florida's classrooms. In addition, the Court of Appeals requested this Court to reexamine the "role and effect of the 'vestiges' of past discrimination" upon twelfth-grade black students.   . . .

The SSAT–II is a test of student's ability to successfully apply basic communications and mathematics skill to everyday life situations. . . . The test covers twenty-four basic skills. Of these, eleven are designated as communications skills and thirteen are designated as mathematics skills. . . .

The Court of Appeals has upheld the denial of a diploma to these students so long as the "test is a fair test of that which was taught." The Court reasoned that "[i]f the test is not fair, it cannot be said to be rationally related to a state interest" and therefore it would be violative of the Equal Protection Clause. In other words, the SSAT–II is only constitutional if it is instructionally valid.

Before determining whether or not the SSAT–II is instructionally valid, it is necessary to define the term and to determine the scope of the appeals court's mandate with regard to this issue. Although professional educators might dispute its meaning, the parties generally agreed that the term, as used by the Court of Appeals, can be summarized in just one question. Put simply, the task assigned to this Court by the Court of Appeals was to find out if Florida is teaching what it is testing. Unfortunately, the answer to this apparently easy question is quite complex.

In an effort to carry its burden of proving that the test is instructionally valid, the defendants commissioned . . . a private consultant firm, to develop a study designed. . . . The survey asked teachers whether they had provided instruction relating to the twenty-four skills tested on the SSAT–II. If they had, the teachers were then asked if they had provided sufficient instruction for a student to master the skills. The teachers were required to answer separately for each individual skill. In addition, although the survey was anonymous, the teachers were asked to identify whether they were an elementary or secondary teacher and, if a secondary teacher, they were to identify their major field of emphasis.

The second part of the study . . . was a survey sent to the sixty-seven school districts and four university laboratory schools in Florida. . . .

The third component of the . . . study consisted of a series of site visits to verify the accuracy of the district reports. . . .

The fourth component of the . . . study was a student survey administered by the site visitors to one or two eleventh-grade social studies and English classes. The survey asked the students to state whether or not they had been taught in school how to answer the types of questions found on the SSAT–II. The sample questions provided to the students included questions on all twenty-four SSAT–II skills.

At trial, the defendant offered three expert witnesses who opined, based on the array of data outlined above, that Florida was teaching what it was testing. . . .

. . . [E]vidence suggests, the resolution of the instructional validity issue depends both on whose experts are believed and on what sort of proof is required. With regard to the former, it is important to understand that the instructional validity issue, and the related concept of minimum competency testing, are relatively new and highly controversial subjects which seem to have polarized the educational community. Thus, in large part, this Court has been called upon to settle not only a legal argument but also a professional dispute. At times, the distinction between these two spheres has blurred. The experts for both sides spoke in terms of "fairness," "adequacy" and "sufficiency." Yet, these terms are not necessarily synonymous with constitutionality. As noted in a law review article cited frequently by the appellate court, any judicial decision on this issue "will reflect only the minimum standards essential to fairness under our legal system. Policymakers must meet, but are not limited to, the minimum standards in pursuing the goal of educational equity for students." . . . In other words, even though the defendants might have implemented a much more equitable program, their actions might still pass constitutional muster.

But, what does the Constitution require in this instance? It may not be fair to expect students with differing interests and abilities to learn the same material at the same rate, but is it unconstitutional? Similarly, it may be inequitable that some students, through random selection, are assigned to mediocre teachers while others are given excellent instructors, but does this inequity rise to the level of a constitutional violation?

These questions lead to other issues concerning the appropriate burden of proof. The plaintiffs argue that the defendants have not carried their burden because they have not attempted to follow students throughout their entire careers. They also assert that there is insufficient evidence of what actually goes on in the classrooms. But, absent viewing a videotape of every student's school career, how can we know what really happened to each child? Even assuming that such videotapes were available, how could this Court decide, in constitutional terms, which students received appropriate instruction and which did not? Suppose that there is one student who never encountered a teacher who taught the SSAT–II skills, or a teacher who taught the skills well, should the entire test be declared invalid? What if the number of students were 3,000 rather than one?

It is necessary to consider these questions in order to appreciate the dilemma confronted by this Court. Instructional validity is an elusive concept. Moreover, unlike some of the other claims made by the plaintiffs at the first trial, the instructional validity issue strikes at the heart of the learning and teaching process. It also lends itself to individualized determinations rather than objective treatment.

Instructional validity is a subpart of content validity which together with curricular validity, insures that a test covers matters actually taught. As the Court of Appeals noted, and as this Court previously found, the SSAT–II is a "good test of what the students *should* know." . . . That is, the subjects tested parallel the curricular goals of the State. To this end, the Department of Education publishes minimum performance standards and also "periodically examine[s] and evaluate[s] procedures, records, and programs in each district to determine compliance with law and rules established by the state board." Thus, although the individual districts are still somewhat autonomous, they no longer have the authority to decide that they will not teach certain minimum skills. In the same vein, the Department of Education, the individual districts, and the separate schools are required to submit annual reports of how well school instructional programs are helping students acquire minimum performance skills. In sum, since at least 1979, school administrators and teachers have been well aware of the minimum performance standards imposed by the State and their duty to teach these skills. . . .

The districts also receive funding from the State to remediate students who need special educational assistance in order to master the basic skills. . . . Each district school board is also required to establish pupil progression plans to insure that students are not promoted without consideration of each student's mastery of basic skills. The State has also established uniform testing standards for grades three, five, eight and eleven to monitor the acquisition of basic skills by students statewide.

These legislative requirements bolster the conclusion that the SSAT–II is, at least, curricularly valid. They lend support to the opinions of the defendants' experts that the SSAT–II is instructionally valid. It is clear from the survey results that the terms of the Educational Accountability Act are not just hollow words found in a statute book. Rather, the district reports, teacher surveys, and site visit audits, as interpreted by the defendants' experts, all indicate that the directives of the Act are a driving force in all of Florida's public schools.

Nevertheless, it is the plaintiffs' position that the instructional validity of the test cannot be established by showing that the skills tested are included in a recognized curriculum. To the contrary, they believe that the only touchstone of the test's validity is proof of what graduating seniors were *actually*, not theoretically, taught. Without such proof, the plaintiffs posit that no one can tell whether the students had a "fair" opportunity to learn. . . .

As noted above, it is impossible to prove conclusively the degree to which every one of the more than 100,000 graduating seniors were exposed to the SSAT–II skills. What is known, is that the districts have reported that these skills are included in their curriculum and that a substantial number of public school teachers have stated that they adhere to this curriculum by including these skills in their course of instruction. In addition, and of even greater significance in determining the constitutionality of the test, it is known that students are given five chances to pass the SSAT–II between the tenth and twelfth grades of school and that, if they fail, they are offered remedial help. They also have the option of staying in school for an additional year in order to "receive special instruction designed to remedy [their] identified deficiencies." Certainly, some remedial programs and teachers will be more effective than others. However, this disparity cannot be said to be unfair in a constitutional sense. While it might be preferable from an educator's standpoint to insure that students learn the requisite skills during their regular courses rather than in remedial sessions, the Constitution clearly does not mandate such a result. What is required is that the skills be included in the official curriculum and that the majority of the teachers recognize them as being something they should teach. Once these basic facts are proven, as they have been in this case, the only logical inference is that the teachers are doing the job they are paid to do and are teaching these skills. It strains credibility to hypothesize that teachers, especially remedial teachers, are uniformly avoiding their responsibilities at the expense of their pupils. . . .

For the reasons stated above, and based on a review of the evidence presented by both sides, the Court finds that the defendants have carried their burden of proving by a preponderance of the evidence that the SSAT–II is instructionally valid and therefore constitutional. Although the instuction offered in all the classrooms of all the districts might not be ideal, students are nevertheless afforded an adequate opportunity to learn the skills tested on the SSAT–II before it is used as a diploma sanction.

As noted earlier, deciding that the SSAT–II is a fair test of that which is taught in the Florida public schools does not end this Court's inquiry. The Court must still decide whether or not the State should be enjoined from imposing the diploma sanction because the vestiges of past purposeful discrimination have an unconstitutional impact on black high school students.

No one disputes the fact that the SSAT–II failure rate among black students is disproportionately high. Of the three thousand twelfth-grade students who have not passed the test, about 57 percent are black even though blacks only constitute about 20 percent of the entire student body. While these statistics are alarming, they do not, standing alone, answer the constitutional question this Court must confront.

In order for this Court to continue to prohibit the State from using the SSAT–II as a diploma sanction, the disproportionate failure rate among today's high school seniors must be found to have been caused by past purposeful segregation or its lingering effects. If the disparate failure of blacks is not due to the present effects of past intentional segregation or if the test is necessary to remedy those effects, then the four-year injunction entered in 1979 can not be extended. . . . .

While it seems clear that some individual teachers, both black and white, carry with them biases which impair their teaching abilities, the Court rejects Dr. McDavis' estimate that as many as 30 percent of the teachers in Florida's public schools are overtly or covertly racist. Similarly, the evidence belies Dr. Akbar's conclusions concerning the causative effect of the problems he identified. For example, the record reveals that more than 90 percent of the black students in Florida's schools have successfully taken the test and that black students in counties where there are black administrators have not done appreciably better on the SSAT–II than black students in counties where there are no black authority figures. As a result, the Court reaffirms its finding that the vestigial problems outlined earlier "do not constitute the denial of an equal educational opportunity . . .." 474 F.Supp. at 252.

The mere fact that black students are not doing as well as white students on the test does not direct a different result. . . . Indeed, as long as past purposeful segregation remains part of our collective memory, its vestiges will, sadly, remain with us, not only in our schools, but in every aspect of our lives. . . .

[T]he plaintiffs seem to argue that the SSAT–II will be invalid as long as any vestiges of discrimination exist.

In the 1979 trial, this Court found, "the most significant burden which accompanied black children into the integrated schools was the existence of years of inferior education." This burden is not shouldered by the Class of 1983. Unlike the Class of 1979, black and white members of the Class of 1983 have had the same textbooks, curricula, libraries and attendance requirements throughout their public school years. Thus, while no two students can have an identical academic experience, their educational opportunities have nonetheless been equal in a constitutional sense. Moreover, to the extent that insidious racism is a problem in the schools, it would seem that a test like the SSAT–II, with objective standards and goals, would lead to its eradication. . . .

Twelve years have passed since the Florida public schools became physically unitary. Since that time, the State of Florida has undertaken massive efforts to improve the education of all of its school children. The SSAT–II is an important part of those efforts. Its use can be enjoined only if it perpetuates the effects of past school segregation or if it is not needed to remedy those effects. Applying this standard to the facts presented at both the 1979 and 1983 trials, the Court finds that the injunction should not be extended. The State of Florida may deny diplomas to the members of the Class of 1983 who have not passed the SSAT–II.

Footnotes

1. Keyishian v. Board of Regents, 385 U.S. 589, 603, 87 S.Ct. 675, 683, 684 (1967), quoting United States v. Associated Press, 52 F.Supp. 362, 372 (S.D.N.Y.1943), affirmed 326 U.S. 1, 65 S.Ct. 1416 (1945); see Weiman v. Updegraff, 344 U.S. 183, 197–198, 73 S.Ct. 215, 221–222 (1952) (Frankfurter, J., concurring).

2. Keyishian v. Board of Regents, 385 U.S. 589, 603, 87 S.Ct. 675, 683, 684 (1967).

3. "Academic Freedom in the Public Schools; The Right to Teach," *New York University Law Review,* vol. 48 (Dec.1973): 1183.

4. Todd v. Rochester Community Schools, 41 Mich.App. 320, 200 N.W.2d 90 (1972).

5. School District of Abington Township v. Schempp, 374 U.S. at 300, 83 S.Ct. at 1612 (1963).

6. Sturgis v. County of Allegan, 343 Mich. 209, 72 N.W.2d 56 (1955).

7. Kelly v. Dickson County School District, 64 Lack.Jur. 13 (1962).

8. Board of Curators of University of Missouri v. Horowitz, 435 U.S. 78, 98 S.Ct. 948 (1978).

9. Welling v. Board of Education, 382 Mich. 620, 171 N.W.2d 545 (1969).

10. Pittman v. Board of Education of Glen Cove, 56 Misc.2d 51, 287 N.Y.S.2d 551 (1967).

11. Id.

12. Isquith v. Levitt, 285 App.Div. 833, 137 N.Y.S.2d 497 (1955).

13. 262 U.S. 390, 43 S.Ct. 625 (1923).

14. Keyishian v. Board of Regents, 385 U.S. 589, 87 S.Ct. 675 (1967).

15. 354 U.S. 234, 77 S.Ct. 1203 (1957).

16. Id. at 1212.

17. McCollum v. Board of Education, 333 U.S. 203, 68 S.Ct. 461 (1948); Engel v. Vitale, 370 U.S. 421, 82 S.Ct. 1261 (1962); School District of Abington Township v. Schempp, 374 U.S. 203, 83 S.Ct. 1560 (1963); West Virginia State Board of Education v. Barnette, 319 U.S. 624, 63 S.Ct. 1178 (1943).

18. *Science and Creationism, A View from the National Academy of Sciences,* Committee on Science and Creationism, National Academy of Sciences (Washington, D.C.: National Academy Press, 1984), pp. 7–8.

19. Rule 81.71(a)(5), *Texas Administrative Code.*

20. Epperson v. State of Arkansas, 393 U.S. 97, 89 S.Ct. 266 (1968).

21. 529 F.Supp. 1255 (E.D.Ark., 1982).

22. This statute is, of course, clearly unconstitutional under the Supreme Court's decision in Abington School Dist. v. Schempp, 374 U.S. 203, 83 S.Ct. 1560, 10 L.Ed.2d 844 (1963).

23. Board of Curators, University of Missouri v. Horowitz, 435 U.S. 78, 98 S.Ct. 948 (1978).

24. Barnard v. Inhabitants of Shelburne, 216 Mass. 19, 102 N.E. 1095 (1913).

25. 513 F.2d 843 at 851 (10th Cir.1975).

26. Board of Regents v. Roth, 408 U.S. 564, 92 S.Ct. 2701 (1972).

27. 424 U.S. 319, 96 S.Ct. 893 (1976).

28. Debra P. v. Turlington, 474 F.Supp. 244 (M.D.Fla.1979) affirmed 644 F.2d 397 (5th Cir.1981).

29. Anderson v. Banks, 540 F.Supp. 761 at 765 (S.D.Ga.1982).

30. Hobson v. Hansen, 269 F.Supp. 401 (D.D.C.1967), affirmed *sub nom.* Smuck v. Hobson, 408 F.2d 175 (D.C.Cir.1969).

31. P. v. Riles, 343 F.Supp. 1306 (N.D.Cal.1972), affirmed 502 F.2d 963 (9th Cir.1974).

32. 426 U.S. 229, 96 S.Ct. 2040 (1976).

33. "Reading the Mind of the School Board: Segregative Intent and the De Facto/De Jure Distinction." 86 Yale L.J. (1976): 317, 335.

8

Student Rights

School authorities are vested with broad powers for the establishment and conduct of the educational program. This prerogative, however, is by no means absolute and school officials must act within the scope of reasonable rules and regulations. Reasonable regulations are those that measurably contribute to the maintenance and advancement of the educational process. Traditionally, courts have given wide discretion in promulgation of regulations governing student conduct but they cannot be so broad or vague as to allow arbitrary or capricious application and administration. School regulations may be held to be sufficiently definitive where they provide students with the adequate information as to what is expected of them and are so stated that persons of common intelligence are not required to guess at their meaning. Reasonable certainty of interpretation requires only the use of ordinary and commonly used terminology. Reasonableness, however, is not predicated on formal adoption and publication of rules before they can have effect, and the absence of a preexisting rule on the books does not prohibit official action. Absence of such formality may, though, make it much more difficult to convince a court that the rule was necessary and that its enforcement was not arbitrary or capricious.

This chapter discusses the power of school boards, in promulgation of rules of student conduct and the reasonableness of the application by school administrators and teachers. Much of the chapter is devoted to limitations that the courts will impose to protect the students where governmental actions have been unreasonable, vague, arbitrary, or direct violations of constitutional rights or freedoms.

IN LOCO PARENTIS

To act to control pupils in the absence of a formal rule is a necessity that has long been recognized under the *in loco parentis* doctrine. Courts are aware that a teacher in the day-to-day activities of working with children must be given considerable supervisory leeway. Immediate classroom control of pupil conduct is put in perspective in an old Wisconsin case:

> While the principal or teacher in charge of a public school is subordinate to the school board or board of education of his district or city, and must enforce rules and regulations adopted by the board for the government of the school,

and execute all its lawful orders in that behalf, he does not derive all his power and authority in the school and over his pupils from affirmative action of the board. He stands for the time being *in loco parentis* to his pupils, and because of that relation he must necessarily exercise authority over them in many things concerning which the board may have remained silent. In the school, as in the family, there exists on the part of the pupils the obligations of obedience to lawful commands, subordination, civil deportment, respect for the rights of other pupils and fidelity to duty. These obligations are inherent in any proper school system, and constitute, so to speak, the common law of the school.[1]

Students have a constitutionally protected interest in attending the public schools that cannot be denied or impaired without due process of law. Within the school setting, students are "persons" and their fundamental rights and freedoms are protected by the United States Constitution. Of course, no child is free to exercise a constitutional right in such a way as to infringe on the rights of other students and to cause disruption of the school. To loudly exercise one's freedom of speech, using a quiet school library as a forum, is naturally not defensible. Unlimited individual freedom in many instances must give way to the rights of other students, the interests of the community, parents, and teachers in conducting a well-run and efficient school system. The courts, therefore, recognizing the importance of discipline and decorum in the schools, attempt to "balance the interests" of the student against the interests of the school in each particular factual situation.

That school teachers have the legal authority to physically punish school children in order to maintain discipline in schools is well documented. For centuries, courts have permitted corporal punishment and continue to do so today. The legality of corporal punishment has been sanctioned by the courts in much the same manner as governmental immunity, that is, in the absence of limiting statutes, the teachers have the power to administer corporal punishment. In the same manner in which governmental immunity is derived from the common law doctrine, "the king can do no wrong," the authority to physically punish children in school is gained from the common law doctrine of "in loco parentis."

While it would not be correct to say that all courts have always upheld corporal punishment, it is certainly true that the vast majority of the courts, and the people for that matter, have generally accepted the idea that the schools must have the authority to physically punish children if classroom decorum and discipline is to be maintained. Consequently, the cases have generally dealt with the degree and reasonableness of the punishment and not whether corporal punishment should be administered at all.

A teacher's right to discipline students within his charge is subject to the same standard of reasonableness that is applicable to parents in disciplining their own children.[2] Courts have advanced two standards governing a teacher's corporal punishment of a child: (1) the reasonableness standard, i.e., "must be exerted within bounds of reason and humanity," [3] and (2) the good faith standard. "The authority of a teacher over his pupil being regarded as a delegation of at least a portion of the parental authority, the presumption is in favor of the correctness of the teacher's action in inflicting corporal punishment upon the pupil. The teacher must not have been activated by malice, nor have inflicted the punishment wantonly. For an error in judgment, although the punishment is unnecessarily excessive, if it is not of a nature to cause lasting injury and he acts in good faith, the teacher is not liable." [4]

Of late, the legality of corporal punishment in the public schools has been drawn into question from several different perspectives. The primary arguments are encompassed in three broad categories: (1) the social and psychological arguments that society has progressed past the physical punishment stage; (2) the idea that legally corporal punishment is "cruel and unusual" punishment as prohibited by the Eighth Amendment; and (3) that corporal punishment should not be administered without first providing the student with procedural due process of law as prescribed in the Fourteenth Amendment.

The first of these arguments is nonlegal but the other two were of sufficient legal consequence to have the United States Supreme Court render an opinion that apparently finally resolved the issues.[5] Prior to the Supreme Court's decision, lower courts had held that corporal punishment was not ipso facto cruel and unusual but it could be if it were immoderate and excessive.

In resolving the question the United States Supreme Court in *Ingraham v. Wright*[6] ruled flatly that corporal punishment as administered in the schools could not be construed to fall within the ambit of the Eighth Amendment. As such, the Court said the prohibition against cruel and unusual punishment did not apply to paddling in schools, but instead was designed to protect those convicted of crimes. The Amendment's intent is threefold: to limit the kinds of punishment that can be imposed on those convicted of crimes, proscribe punishment grossly disproportionate to the severity of the crime, and impose substantive limits on what can be made criminal and punished as such. In this light, it is difficult to conceive of corporal punishment as being circumscribed by the Eighth Amendment and it was not, according to the court, so intended. Regarding due process, the court held that notice and hearing are not required prior to imposition of corporal punishment.

Court Is Not Concerned with Wisdom
of Regulation but Whether It
Is Reasonable

FLORY v. SMITH

Supreme Court of Appeals
of Virginia, 1926.
145 Va. 164, 134 S.E. 360.

CAMPBELL, J. The object of this suit is to test the legality of a rule promulgated by the school board of Gloucester county. This rule is as follows:

"Student Regulation.—Leaving the campus between the hours of 9 A.M. and 3:35 P.M. is strictly prohibited, unless students are accompanied by a teacher." . . .

It was the desire of the appellees that their children be relieved of the restriction placed upon them by the rule stated, supra, and that the children be permitted to eat their midday meal, either in the home, situated about a mile distant from the school, or to eat same with their father at the hotel in the town.

The special privilege was denied by the principal of the school.   .   .   .

The court, on final hearing, overruled the demurrer and entered a decree enjoining and restraining E.D. Flory, principal of the school, from prohibiting and preventing the children of appellees "from eating their midday meals either in the home of their parents or with their father in Botetourt Hotel.   .   .   . "

While the Constitution of the state provides in mandatory terms that the Legislature shall establish and maintain public free schools, there is neither mandate nor inhibition in the provisions as to the regulation thereof. The Legislature, therefore, has the power to enact any legislation in regard to the conduct, control, and regulation of the public free schools, which does not deny to the citizen the constitutional right to enjoy life and liberty, to pursue happiness and to acquire property.

In the conduct of the public schools it is essential that power be vested in some legalized agency in order to maintain discipline and promote efficiency. In considering the exercise of this power, the courts are not concerned with the wisdom or unwisdom of the act done. The only concern of the court is the reasonableness of the regulation promulgated. To hold otherwise would be to substitute judicial opinion for the legislative will.   .   .   .

While appellees allege in their bill "that it is their right to select and provide the best and most suitable food for the nourishment of their children, and to select the mode and manner by which such food shall be received by their children, to the end that their children may be best nourished and their physical development may be best promoted," it is nowhere alleged that the physical condition of the children is such that results detrimental to their physical well-being will follow if the right alleged is denied.

While it may be argued with force that a warm meal at midday is preferable to a cold lunch, it is not conclusive that the latter is destructive of health. It is a matter of common knowledge that in the towns and rural sections the vast majority of school children partake of a cold lunch at midday. In the larger cities, where paternalism is further advanced, children are encouraged to partake of hot food furnished them for a consideration.

Considering the regulation from the viewpoint afforded us by the bill of complaint, demurrer, and answer, we are unable to say that the regulation is an unreasonable one. However, while a rule may be legally reasonable, it should not be without elasticity. In the enforcement of every law there should be brought into play the element of common sense.

We have no serious trouble in disposing of the contention that appellees have a property right in the public schools of the commonwealth.   .   .   .

While it may be a restraint upon liberty and an infringement upon happiness for the Legislature to inhibit a parent from sending his child to any school, it is neither restraint nor infringement for the Legislature to enact laws to debar a child from the mere privilege of acquiring an education at the expense of the state until he is willing to submit himself to all reasonable regulations enacted for the purpose of promoting efficiency and maintaining discipline. There is a marked difference between the inherent right to conduct a private school—that is, to select and pursue a given legitimate vocation—and the right to attend a public school. . . .

The last contention of appellees is that they have been penalized without notice and deprived of their right to seek redress by appeal. . . . Immediately upon the suspension of appellees' child, notice of such suspension was given to the father. We are of the opinion that this was sufficient notice; that upon the receipt thereof he had the absolute right to have the matter reviewed by the county school board within a reasonable time from the date of the receipt of such notice.

For the reasons stated, the decree of the circuit court must be reversed, and this court will enter a decree dismissing the bill of complaint.

Reversed.

NOTES

1. For other related cases on this point, see Bozeman v. Morrow, 34 S.W.2d 654 (Tex.Civ.App.1931); Richardson v. Braham, 125 Neb. 142, 249 N.W. 557 (1933); and Haffner v. Braham, 125 Neb. 147, 249 N.W. 560 (1933).

2. A parent arranged for her daughter to receive private music lessons off campus. The school officials refused to permit the child to leave the school premises during school hours to take the private instruction. When the pupil disobeyed this direction of the school officials, she was suspended. Judgment for whom and why? See Christian v. Jones, 211 Ala. 161, 100 So. 99 (1924).

School Master Has the Power to
Reasonably Punish Pupil for Acts
Detrimental to the Good Order of the
School Whether Committed in School
Hours or After Pupil Has
Returned Home

LANDER v. SEAVER

Supreme Court of Vermont, 1859.
32 Vt. 114, 76 Am.Dec. 156.

Trespass for assault and battery. Defendant pleaded the general issue, and two special pleas in bar. The first special plea alleged that defendant was a school-master; that plaintiff was one of his pupils, and was guilty of misbehavior as such pupil; that for the purpose of punishing him for it, defendant did, in his school, a little beat and bruise the plaintiff, but that no unnecessary injury was done him. This was alleged to be the trespass complained of by plaintiff. The second special plea justified upon the same ground, except that the pupil's offense was stated to have been the use of saucy and disrespectful language towards defendant after the close of the school, but in the presence of other pupils of defendant; that such language tended to degrade the latter in the opinion of such other pupils. The plaintiff replied *de injuria*, etc. The jury rendered a verdict for defendant, and judgment being entered thereon, the plaintiff appealed. The offense of the pupil, a boy eleven years of age, was committed an hour and a half after the close of school, after he had returned home, and while he was driving his father's cow past the teacher's house. Plaintiff, in the presence of some fellow-pupils, and of the master, called the latter "old Jack Seaver." The next morning after school convened, defendant reprimanded the plaintiff for said language, and whipped him with a small rawhide. . . .

Goerge F. Edmunds, for the defendant.

By Court, ALDIS, J. The defendant was a teacher in a public school in Burlington; the plaintiff, his pupil. The first question presented is, Has a school-master the right to punish his pupil for acts of misbehavior committed after the school has been dismissed, and the pupil has returned home and is engaged in his father's service?

I. It is conceded that his right to punish extends to school hours, and there seems to be no reasonable doubt that the supervision and control of the master over the scholar extend from the time he leaves home to go to school till he returns home from school. Most parents would expect and desire that teachers would take care that their children, in going to and returning from school, should not loiter, or seek evil company, or frequent vicious places of resort. But in this case, as appears from the bill of exceptions, the offense was committed an hour and a half after the school was dismissed, and after the boy had returned home, and while he was engaged in his father's service. When the child has returned home, or to his parents' control, then the parental authority is resumed and the control of the teacher ceases, and then, for all ordinary acts of misbehavior, the parent alone has the power to punish. It is claimed, however, that in this case "the boy, while in the presence of other pupils of the same school, used toward the master and in his hearing contemptuous language, with a design to insult him, and which had a direct and immediate tendency to bring the authority of the master over his pupils into contempt and lessen his hold upon them and his control over the school." This, under the charge of the court, must have been found by the jury.

This misbehavior, it is especially to be observed, has a direct and immediate tendency to injure the school, to subvert the master's authority, and to beget disorder and insubordination. It is not misbehavior generally, or towards other persons, or even towards the master in matters in no way connected with or affecting the school; for as to such misconduct, committed by the child after his return home from school, we think the parents, and they alone, have the power of punishment.

But where the offense has a direct and immediate tendency to injure the school and bring the master's authority into contempt, as in this case, when done in the presence of other scholars and of the master, and with a design to insult him, we think he has the right to punish the scholar for such acts if he comes again to school.

The misbehavior must not have merely a remote and indirect tendency to injure the school. All improper conduct or language may perhaps have, by influence and example, a remote tendency of that kind. But the tendency of the acts so done out of the teacher's supervision for which he may punish must be direct and immediate in their bearing upon the welfare of the school, or the authority of the master and the respect due to him. Cases may readily be supposed which lie very near the line, and it will often be difficult to distinguish between the acts which have such an immediate and those which have such a remote tendency. Hence each case must be determined by its peculiar circumstances. . . . By common consent and by the universal custom in our New England schools, the master has always been deemed to have the right to punish such offenses. Such power is essential to the preservation of order, decency, decorum, and good government in schools. Upon this point the charge of the court was substantially correct.

II. The court charged the jury that although the punishment inflicted on the plaintiff was excessive in severity and disproportioned to the offense, still if the master in administering it acted with proper motives, in good faith, and, in his judgment, for the best interests of the school, he would not be liable; that the school-master acts in a judicial capacity, and that the infliction of excessive punishment, when prompted by good intentions and not by malice or wicked motives, or an evil mind, is merely an honest error of opinion, and does not make him liable to the pupil for damages. The plaintiff claims that this was erroneous. . . .

We think the school-master does not belong to the class of public officers vested with such judicial and discretionary powers. He is included rather in the domestic relation of master and servant, and his powers and duties are usually treated of as belonging to that class. . . . .

It is also said that he stands *in loco parentis,* and is invested with all the authority and immunity of the parent. . . .

The parent, unquestionably, is answerable only for malice or wicked motives or an evil heart in punishing his child. This great, and to some extent irresponsible, power of control and correction is invested in the parent by nature and necessity. It springs from the natural relation of parent and child. It is felt rather as a duty than a power. . . . This parental power is little liable to abuse, for it is continually restrained by natural affection, the tenderness which the parent feels for his offspring, an affection ever on the alert, and acting rather by instinct than reasoning.

The school-master has no such natural restraint. Hence he may not safely be trusted with all a parent's authority, for he does not act from the instinct of parental affection. He should be guided and restrained by judgment and wise discretion, and hence is responsible for their reasonable exercise. The limit upon the parental authority transferred to the master is well expressed by Judge Blackstone. He says: "The master is *in loco parentis,* and has such a portion of the powers of the parent committed to his charge as may be necessary to answer the purposes for which he is employed." An English annotator, in a note to the passage, very properly adds: "This power must be temperately exercised, and no school-master should feel himself at liberty to administer chastisement co-extensive with the parent." . . .

The law, as we deem it to exist, is this: A school-master has the right to inflict reasonable corporal punishment. He must exercise reasonable judgment and discretion in determining when to punish, and to what extent. In determining upon what is a reasonable punishment, various considerations must be regarded, the nature of the offense, the apparent motive and disposition of the offender, the influence of his example and conduct upon others, and the sex, age, size, and strength of the pupil to be punished.

Among reasonable persons, much difference prevails as to the circumstances which will justify the infliction of punishment, and the extent to which it may properly be administered. On account of this difference of opinion, and the difficulty which exists in determining what is a reasonable punishment, and the advantage which the master has by being on the spot to know all the circumstances, the manner, look, tone, gestures, and language of the offender (which are not always easily described), and thus to form a correct opinion as to the necessity and extent of the punishment, considerable allowance should be made to the teacher by way of protecting him in the exercise of his discretion. Expecially should he have this indulgence when he appears to have acted from good motives, and not from anger or malice. Hence the teacher is not to be held liable on the ground of excess of punishment, unless the punishment is clearly excessive, and would be held so in the general judgment of reasonable men. If the punishment be thus clearly excessive, then the master should be held liable for such excess, though he acted from good motives in inflicting the punishment; and in his own judgment considered it necessary, and not excessive. But if there is any reasonable doubt whether the punishment was excessive, the master should have the benefit of the doubt. . . .

IV. Whether a rawhide was a proper instrument of punishment, was left to the jury with very suitable instructions.

The evidence to show that the rawhide was used in other schools in the vicinity was properly admitted to rebut the charge of malice, by showing that he did not resort to an unusual instrument of punishment.

The testimony to show the plaintiff did not claim an excess of punishment on the first trial was proper, as tending to prove that that claim on the then pending trial was not well founded.

Judgment reversed.

Teacher Has Authority to Punish
Pupil for Offenses Committed after
Returning Home from School

O'ROURKE v. WALKER

Supreme Court of Errors
of Connecticut, 1925.
102 Conn. 130, 128 A. 25.

KEELER, J. (after stating the facts as above). It is conceded in the brief of the appealing plaintiff that the school board or other proper authority may make reasonable rules concerning the conduct of pupils, and inflict reasonable corporal punishment for the infraction of such rules, and that in the absence of rules so established, the teacher may make all necessary and proper rules for the regulation of the school. We so held in Sheehan v. Sturges, 53 Conn. 481, 2 A. 841. The plaintiff further concedes that—

The conduct of pupils outside of school hours and school property may be regulated by rules established by the school authorities if such conduct directly relates to and affects the management of the school and its efficiency.

This we understand to be the rule abundantly established by authority. 5 C.J. 755. However, plaintiff proceeds to say that this conceded rule of law is qualified in this important particular:

> But no rule can be adopted which attemps to control the conduct of pupils outside of school hours after they have reached their homes.

. . . In Mechem on Public Officers, § 730, the law is summarized in accordance with the decided weight of authority as follows:

> The authority of the teacher is not confined to the school room or grounds, but he may prohibit and punish all acts of his pupils which are detrimental to the good order and best interests of the school, whether such acts are committed in school hours or while the pupil is on his way to or from school or after he has returned home.

Examination of the authorities clearly reveals the true test of the teacher's right and jurisdiction to punish for offenses not committed on the school property or going and returning therefrom, but after the return of the pupil to the parental abode, to be not the time or place of the offense, but its effect upon the morale and efficiency of the school, whether it in fact is detrimental to its good order, and to the welfare and advancement of the pupils therein. If the conduct punished is detrimental to the best interests of the school, it is punishable, and in the instant case, under the rules of the school board, by corporal infliction. The effect of the rule claimed by the plaintiff, if applied, would result in a serious loss of discipline in school, and possible harm to innocent pupils in attendance. Supposing that some strong-armed juvenile bully attending school lived upon the next block and sought for a brief moment the asylum of his home, and thence sallied forth and beat, abused, and terrorized his fellow pupils as they pass by returning home; then by the claim urged by plaintiff he would be immune from punishment by the school authorities, while if he began his assaults before he had passed within the bounds of his own front yard he would be liable to proper punishment for any harm done. Now the harm done to the morale of the school is the same. The injured and frightened pupils are dismayed and discouraged in going to and coming from the school, and demoralized while in attendance. It will not do to say, as plaintiff's counsel argue, that the proper resort to correct such an abuse is the parents of such offenders, or the public prosecutors. Some parents would dismiss the matter by saying that they could give no attention to children's quarrels; many would champion their children as being all right in their conduct. The public authorities would very properly say, unless the offense resulted in quite serious injury, that such affrays were too trifling to deserve their attention. Yet the harm to the school has been done, and its proper conduct and operation seriously harmed, by such acts. Correction will usually be sought in vain at the hands of parents; it can only be successfully applied by the teacher. It is not likely that any milder punishment than corporal infliction would act as a deterrent in cases like the present. The abuse of little girls by young bullies is a base and brutal offense.

In the instant case it will be observed that while the plaintiff had reached his home after school, his victims had not. This is an important fact, even if the rule claimed by plaintiff should be upheld as a general statement. The claim made in argument that the small girls who were abused were trespassers upon the property of plaintiff's mother is of no avail. There is nothing in the record to show that plaintiff was acting under direction of his mother, and even if he were, such conduct as the court has found to exist would not be lawful.

There is no error.

The other Judges concurred.

NOTES

1. As a teacher passed by an automobile in a shopping center on a Sunday evening, a student in the automobile shouted, "There's Stear." Another student in the car then yelled, "He's a prick." On Monday morning the teacher explained the facts to the vice-principal. The vice-principal confronted the student who admitted calling Mr. Stear a prick, whereupon the student was given an in-school suspension, was not allowed to participate in the senior trip, was not permitted to attend any extracurricular activities, and was placed on other restrictions while at school, such as being required to sit at the restricted table in the cafeteria.

   The student challenged the disciplinary action as a violation of his freedom of speech and denial of a property right to an education. The court stated, "It is the opinion of the court that the First Amendment rights of the plaintiff were not violated. His conduct involved an invasion of the right of teacher Stear to be free from being loudly insulted in a public place by 'lewd, lascivious or indecent words or language.' " The court went on to say, "It is our opinion that when a high school student refers to a high school teacher in a public place on a Sunday by a lewd and obscene name in such a loud voice that the teacher and others hear the insult, it may be deemed a matter for discipline in the discretion of the school authorities. To countenance such student conduct even in a public place without imposing sanctions could lead to devastating consequences in the school." Furthermore, since the student continued his education while serving the in-school suspension, he was not deprived of any property right. Fenton v. Stear, 423 F.Supp. 767 (W.D.Pa.1976).

2. Two students, one in a jeep and the other in a pickup truck, impeded the progress of a school bus traveling to school loaded with children. The driver of the jeep positioned his vehicle in front of the bus while the pickup truck was behind, and by alternatively slowing and speeding up obstructed the operation of the bus. Upon arriving at school, the students who had been positively identified were cited by the Wyoming highway patrol and suspended by the school. They challenged the disciplinary action by the school authorities. The court stated, "It matters little that the proscribed conduct occurred on a public highway. It is generally accepted that school authorities may discipline pupils for out-of-school conduct having a direct and immediate effect on the discipline or general welfare of the school. This is particularly true where the discipline is reasonably necessary for the student's physical or emotional safety and well-being of other students." Clements v. Board of

Trustees of Sheridan County, 585 P.2d 197 (Wyo.1978); see also: 53 A.L.R.3d 1124, 68 Am.Jur.2d, Schools, §§ 256 and 266.

3. In the case of Jones v. Cody, 132 Mich. 13, 92 N.W. 495, 62 L.R.A. 160 (1902), a principal enforced a requirement that pupils go directly home after school. A local storekeeper refused to allow the principal to enter her store to send some of the loitering pupils home. The principal then required strict adherence to his rule and the storekeeper sued the principal for loss of profits. The court upheld the rule and indicated that it was not only the right, but the duty of the school to see that children went directly home from school. The court reasoned that if the child did not reach home when scheduled, his parents would be put on notice and would go looking for him, thereby affording greater protection for the safety and well being of the child.

4. A Georgia court refused to enjoin enforcement of a rule prohibiting pupils from attending any movie, show, or social on any night except Friday or Saturday. See Mangum v. Keith, 147 Ga. 603, 95 S.E. 1 (1918).

5. Would a rule prohibiting pupils from attending movies or other social functions on school nights be upheld by courts today? In this regard, what limitations may be imposed on school officials today? Does such a rule grant too much authority to school officials?

6. *In loco parentis* was defined by a Nebraska court as follows: "general education and control of pupils who attend public schools are in the hands of school boards, superintendents, principals and teachers. This control extends to health, proper surroundings, necessary discipline, promotion of morality and other wholesome influences, while parental authority is temporarily superceded." Richardson v. Braham, 125 Neb. 142, 249 N.W. 557 (1933).

7. Courts will not tolerate frivolous suits. In a case in which a student was demoted from first trumpet to second trumpet by the band master, and then refused to go on a band trip and was then dismissed from the band the parents filed suit. The court, in a strongly worded opinion, found for the school authorities and required the child's mother to pay legal fees of $2,250 because of the frivolous, unreasonable, and groundlessness of the action. The court stated, "This complaint is another example of a prevalent disposition by parties and lawyers to litigate over every source of unhappiness to which humankind may be subject. While it might be considered unfortunate that a boy be dismissed from the high school band, it is much more unfortunate that his mother saw fit to take the matter to court and that she was able to find a lawyer willing to do her bidding." Bernstein v. Menard, 557 F.Supp. 90, 557 F.Supp. 92 (E.D.Va. 1983).

8. In another frivolous suit case, a student was expelled from school for one semester for the sale and purchase of drugs. The parents filed suit claiming violation of the due process rights guaranteed in the Fourteenth Amendment and violation of the Fourth Amendment. The court found that no rights had been infringed. The suit was filed after the student was eligible to return to school, but had made no effort to reenter, nor

had his parents made inquiry on his behalf. The court said: "Upon review of the evidence in this case . . . the Court finds that this action was 'frivolous, unreasonable, or without foundation. . . .' Therefore, the Court concludes that the defendants are entitled to recover their reasonable attorney's fees. . . ." Tarter v. Raybuck, 556 F.Supp. 625 (N.D.Ohio 1983).

9. Academic penalties imposed on students are a reasonable exercise of school discretion. When two students were suspended for three days for consuming alcohol on a field trip, the school authorities imposed a scholastic penalty on all graded classwork and three points were deducted from their six-week grade averages for each day of suspension. The students claimed "that imposition of an academic penalty for non-academic disciplinary purposes is constitutionally unreasonable and impermissible because it deprives [the students] of protected property rights and substantive due process." The court concluded, "We hold that reduction of [the students'] six-week grades by three points for each day of suspension has no adverse impact on [the students'] property rights to a public education. Furthermore, the evidence does not show that imposition of the scholastic penalties proposed will have any negative impact on the honor, reputation or name of either [student]." New Braunfels Independent School District v. Armke, 658 S.W.2d 330 (Tex. App., 10 Dist. 1983).

10. In another case involving academic punishment a school district's rules provided that a pupil may miss no more than twelve days, excused or unexcused. A student missed physical science class fourteen times although he only missed four complete days and cut other classes even though he was on school grounds much of the time watching football films. He was expelled from school for excessive absenteeism. The student challenged the expulsion saying he missed only four days, which was not excessive. The Supreme Court of Arkansas upheld the school officials saying, "the decision to dismiss [the student] was one within the power of the board. This court does not have the power to substitute its judgment for that of such a board. We can only determine whether the judgment was arbitrary, capricious, or contrary to law. We cannot so find in this case." Williams v. Board of Education, etc., 274 Ark. 530, 626 S.W.2d 361 (1982).

Cruel and Unusual Punishment Clause of Eighth Amendment Does Not Apply to Corporal Punishment in Schools

INGRAHAM v. WRIGHT

Supreme Court of the United States, 1977.
430 U.S. 651, 97 S.Ct. 1401.

Mr. Justice POWELL delivered the opinion of the Court.

This case presents questions concerning the use of corporal punishment in public schools: first, whether the paddling of students as a means of maintaining school discipline constitutes cruel and unusual punishment in violation of the Eighth Amendment; and second, to the extent that paddling is constitutionally permissible, whether the Due Process Clause of the Fourteenth Amendment requires prior notice and an opportunity to be heard. . . .

Petitioners' evidence may be summarized briefly. In the 1970-1971 school year many of the 237 schools in Dade County used corporal punishment as a means of maintaining discipline pursuant to Florida legislation and a local school board regulation. The statute then in effect authorized limited corporal punishment by negative inference, proscribing punishment which was "degrading or unduly severe" or which was inflicted without prior consultation with the principal or the teacher in charge of the school. The regulation . . . contained explicit directions and limitations. . . .

Petitioners focused on Drew Junior High School, the school in which both Ingraham and Andrews were enrolled in the fall of 1970. In an apparent reference to Drew, the District Court found that "[t]he instances of punishment which could be characterized as severe, accepting the students' testimony as credible, took place in one junior high school." . . .

The District Court made no findings on the credibility of the students' testimony. Rather, assuming their testimony to be credible, the court found no constitutional basis for relief. . . .

A panel of the Court of Appeals voted to reverse. . . . Upon rehearing, the en banc court rejected these conclusions and affirmed the judgment of the District Court. . . .

In addressing the scope of the Eighth Amendment's prohibition on cruel and unusual punishment this Court has found it useful to refer to "[t]raditional common law concepts" . . . and to the "attitude[s] which our society has traditionally taken." . . . So, too, in defining the requirements of procedural due process under the Fifth and Fourteenth Amendments, the Court has been attuned to what "has always been the law of the land" . . . and to "traditional ideas of fair procedure." . . . We therefore begin by examining the way in which our traditions and our laws have responded to the use of corporal punishment in public schools.

The use of corporal punishment in this country as a means of disciplining school children dates back to the colonial period. It has survived the transformation of primary and secondary education from the colonials' reliance on optional private arrangements to our present system of compulsory education and dependence on public schools. Despite the general abandonment of corporal punishment as a means of punishing criminal offenders, the practice continues to play a role in the public education of school children in most parts of the country. Professional and public opinion is sharply divided on the practice, and has been for more than a century. Yet we can discern no trend toward its elimination.

At common law a single principle has governed the use of corporal punishment since before the American Revolution: teachers may impose reasonable but not excessive force to discipline a child. . . . The basic doctrine has not changed. The prevalent rule in this country today privileges such force as a teacher or administrator "reasonably believes to be necessary for [the child's] proper control, training, or education." . . . To the extent that the force is excessive or unreasonable, the educator in virtually all States is subject to possible civil and criminal liability.

Although the early cases viewed the authority of the teacher as deriving from the parents, the concept of parental delegation has been replaced by the view—more consonant with compulsory education laws—that the State itself may impose such corporal punishment as is reasonably necessary "for the proper education of the child and for the maintenance of group discipline." . . . All of the circumstances are to be taken into account in determining whether the punishment is reasonable in a particular case. Among the most important considerations are the seriousness of the offense, the attitude and past behavior of the child, the nature and severity of the punishment, the age and strength of the child, and the availability of less severe but equally effective means of discipline. . . .

Of the twenty-three States that have addressed the problem through legislation, twenty-one have authorized the moderate use of corporal punishment in public schools. Of these States only a few have elaborated on the common law test of reasonableness, typically providing for approval or notification of the child's parents, or for infliction of punishment only by the principal or in the presence of an adult witness. Only two States, Massachusetts and New Jersey, have prohibited all corporal punishment in their public schools. Where the legislatures have not acted, the state courts have uniformly preserved the common law rule permitting teachers to use reasonable force in disciplining children in their charge.

Against this background of historical and contemporary approval of reasonable corporal punishment, we turn to the constitutional questions before us.

The Eighth Amendment provides, "Excessive bail shall not be required, nor excessive fines imposed, nor cruel and unusual punishments inflicted." Bail, fines and punishment traditionally have been associated with the criminal process, and by subjecting the three to parallel limitations the text of the Amendment suggests an intention to limit the power of those entrusted with the criminal law function of government. An examination of the history of the Amendment and the decisions of this Court construing the proscription against cruel and unusual punishment confirms that it was designed to protect those convicted of crimes. We adhere to this longstanding limitation and hold that the Eighth Amendment does not apply to the paddling of children as a means of maintaining discipline in public schools.

The history of the Eighth Amendment is well known. The text was taken, almost verbatim, from a provision of the Virginia Declaration of Rights of 1776, which in turn derived from the English Bill of Rights of 1689. The English version, adopted after the accession of William and Mary, was intended to curb the excesses of English judges under the reign of James II. . . .

At the time of its ratification, the original Constitution was criticized in the Massachusetts and Virginia Conventions for its failure to provide any protection for persons convicted of crimes. This criticism provided the impetus for inclusion of the Eighth Amendment in the Bill of Rights. . . .

In light of this history, it is not surprising to find that every decision of this Court considering whether a punishment is "cruel and unusual" within the meaning of the Eighth and Fourteenth Amendments has dealt with a criminal punishment. . . .

In the few cases where the Court has had occasion to confront claims that impositions outside the criminal process constituted cruel and unusual punishment, it has had no difficulty finding the Eighth Amendment inapplicable. . . .

Petitioners acknowledge that the original design of the Cruel and Unusual Punishments Clause was to limit criminal punishments, but urge nonetheless that the prohibition should be extended to ban the paddling of school children. Observing that the Framers of the Eighth Amendment could not have envisioned our present system of public and compulsory education, with its opportunities for noncriminal punishments, petitioners contend that extension of the prohibition against cruel punishments is necessary lest we afford greater protection to criminals than to school children. It would be anomalous, they say, if schoolchildren could be beaten without constitutional redress, while hardened criminals suffering the same beatings at the hands of their jailors might have a valid claim under the Eighth Amendment. . . . Whatever force this logic may have in other settings, we find it an inadequate basis for wrenching the Eighth Amendment from its historical context and extending it to traditional disciplinary practices in the public schools.

The prisoner and the schoolchild stand in wholly different circumstances, separated by the harsh facts of criminal conviction and incarceration. . . .

The schoolchild has little need for the protection of the Eighth Amendment. Though attendance may not always be voluntary, the public school remains an open institution. Except perhaps when very young, the child is not physically restrained from leaving school during school hours; and at the end of the school day, the child is invariably free to return home. Even while at school, the child brings with him the support of family and friends and is rarely apart from teachers and other pupils who may witness and protest any instances of mistreatment.

The openness of the public school and its supervision by the community afford significant safeguards against the kinds of abuses from which the Eighth Amendment protects the prisoner. In virtually every community where corporal punishment is permitted in the schools, these safeguards are reinforced by the legal constraints of the common law. Public school teachers and administrators are privileged at common law to inflict only such corporal punishment as is reasonably necessary for the proper education and discipline of the child; any punishment going beyond the privilege may result in both civil and criminal liability. . . . As long as the schools are open to public scrutiny, there is no reason to believe that the common law constraints will not effectively remedy and deter excesses such as those alleged in this case.

We conclude that when public school teachers or administrators impose disciplinary corporal punishment, the Eighth Amendment is inapplicable. The pertinent constitutional question is whether the imposition is consonant with the requirements of due process.

The Fourteenth Amendment prohibits any State deprivation of life, liberty or property without due process of law. Application of this prohibition requires the familiar two-stage analysis: we must first ask whether the asserted individual interests are encompassed within the Fourteenth Amendment's protection of "life, liberty or property"; if protected interests are implicated, we then must decide what procedures constitute "due process of law." . . . Following that analysis here, we find that corporal punishment in public school implicates a constitutionally protected liberty interest, but we hold that the traditional common law remedies are fully adequate to afford due process.

"[T]he range of interests protected by procedural due process is not infinite." . . . Among the historic liberties so protected was a right to be free from and to obtain judicial relief, for unjustified intrusions on personal security.

While the contours of this historic liberty interest in the context of our federal system of government have not been defined precisely, they always have been thought to encompass freedom from bodily restraint and punishment. . . . It is fundamental that the state cannot hold and physically punish an individual except in accordance with due process of law.

This constitutionally protected liberty interest is at stake in this case. There is, of course a *de minimis* level of imposition with which the Constitution is not concerned. But at least where school authorities, acting under color of state law, deliberately decide to punish a child for misconduct by restraining the child and inflicting appreciable physical pain, we hold that Fourteenth Amendment liberty interests are implicated.

"[T]he question remains what process is due." . . . Were it not for the common law privilege permitting teachers to inflict reasonable corporal punishment on children in their care, and the availability of the traditional remedies for abuse, the case for requiring advance procedural safeguards would be strong indeed. But here we deal with a punishment—paddling— within that tradition, and the question is whether the common law remedies are adequate to afford due process. . . . Whether in this case the common law remedies for excessive corporal punishment constitute due process of law must turn on an analysis of the competing interests at stake, viewed against the background of "history, reason, [and] the past course of decisions." The analysis requires consideration of three distinct factors: "first, the private interest that will be affected . . . ; second, the risk of an erroneous deprivation of such interest . . . and the probable value, if any, of additional or substitute procedural safeguards; and, finally, the [state] interest, including the function involved and the fiscal and administrative burdens that the additional or substitute procedural requirement would entail." . . .

Because it is rooted in history, the child's liberty interest in avoiding corporal punishment while in the care of public school authorities is subject to historical limitations. . . .

The concept that reasonable corporal punishment in school is justifiable continues to be recognized in the laws of most States. . . . It represents "the balance struck by this country" . . . between the child's interest in personal security and the traditional view that some limited corporal punishment may be necessary in the course of a child's education. Under that longstanding accommodation of interests, there can be no deprivation of substantive rights as long as disciplinary corporal punishment is within the limits of the common law privilege.

This is not to say that the child's interest in procedural safeguards is insubstantial. The school disciplinary process is not "a totally accurate, unerring process, never mistaken and never unfair. . . ." . . . In any deliberate infliction of corporal punishment on a child who is restrained for that purpose, there is some risk that the intrusion on the child's liberty will be unjustified and therefore unlawful. In these circumstances the child has a strong interest in procedural safeguards that minimize the risk of wrongful punishment and provide for the resolution of disputed questions of justification.

We turn now to a consideration of the safeguards that are available under applicable Florida law.

Florida has continued to recognize, and indeed has strengthened by statute, the common law right of a child not to be subjected to excessive corporal punishment in school. Under Florida law the teacher and principal of the school decide in the first instance whether corporal punishment is reasonably necessary under the circumstances in order to discipline a child who has misbehaved. But they must exercise prudence and restraint. For Florida has preserved the traditional judicial proceedings for determining whether the punishment was justified. If the punishment inflicted is later found to have been excessive—not reasonably believed at the time to be necessary for the child's discipline or training—the school authorities inflicting it may be held liable in damages to the child and, if malice is shown, they may be subject to criminal penalties.

Although students have testified in this case to specific instances of abuse, there is every reason to believe that such mistreatment is an aberration. The uncontradicted evidence suggests that corporal punishment in the Dade County schools was, "[w]ith the exception of a few cases . . . unremarkable in physical severity." Moreover, because paddlings are usually inflicted in response to conduct directly observed by teachers in their presence, the risk that a child will be paddled without cause is typically insignificant. In the ordinary case, a disciplinary paddling neither threatens seriously to violate any substantive rights nor condemns the child "to suffer grievous loss of any kind." . . .

In those cases where severe punishment is contemplated, the available civil and criminal sanctions for abuse—considered in light of the openness of the school environment—afford significant protection against unjustified corporal punishment. Teachers and school authorities are unlikely to inflict corporal punishment unnecessarily or excessively when a possible consequence of doing so is the institution of civil or criminal proceedings against them. . . .

But even if the need for advance procedural safeguards were clear, the question would remain whether the incremental benefit could justify the cost. Acceptance of petitioners' claims would work a transformation in the law governing corporal punishment in Florida and most other States. Given the impracticability of formulating a rule or procedural due process that varies with the severity of the particular imposition, the prior hearing petitioners seek would have to precede *any* paddling, however moderate or trivial.

Such a universal constitutional requirement would significantly burden the use of corporal punishment as a disciplinary measure. Hearings—even informal hearings—require time, personnel, and a diversion of attention from normal school pursuits. . . .

Elimination or curtailment of corporal punishment would be welcomed by many as a societal advance. But when such a policy choice may result from this Court's determination of an asserted right to due process, rather than from the normal processes of community debate and legislative action, the societal costs cannot be dismissed as insubstantial. . . . In view of the low incidence of abuse, the openness of our schools, and the common law safeguards that already exist, the risk of error that may result in violation of a schoolchild's substantive rights can only be regarded as minimal. Imposing additional administrative safeguards as a constitutional requirement might reduce that risk marginally, but would also entail a significant intrusion into an area of primary educational responsibility. We conclude that the Due Process Clause does not require notice and a hearing prior to the imposition of corporal punishment in the public schools as that practice is authorized and limited by the common law. . . .

NOTES

1. In cases following *Ingraham* v. *Wright* "substantive due process" has become an important issue. A federal district court in Alabama has said that (1) corporal punishment did not violate the student's "substantive" due process rights; (2) because of the availability of common law remedies, procedural due process is not required, as noted in *Ingraham* v. *Wright*. Hale v. Pringle, 562 F.Supp. 598 (M.D.Ala.1983). On the other hand, the United States Court of Appeals, Fourth Circuit, has ruled that corporal punishment may violate substantive due process. The court concluded that "there may be circumstances under which specific corporal punishment administered by state school officials gives rise to an independent federal cause of action to vindicate substantive due process rights." The standard to be used to determine if a violation has occurred is "whether the force applied caused injury so severe, was so disproportionate to the need presented, and was so inspired by malice or sadism rather than a merely careless or unwise excess of zeal that it amounted to a brutal and inhumane abuse of official power literally shocking to the conscience." Hall v. Tawney, 621 F.2d 607 (4th Cir.1980).

2. Teachers may paddle students in spite of parental opposition. One federal district court upheld the spanking of a child over the parents' protest and said that even though parents generally have control of their children's discipline, ". . . the state has a countervailing interest in the maintenance of order in the school sufficient to sustain the right of teachers and school officials to administer reasonable corporal punishment" over the parent's objections. Baker v. Owen, 395 F.Supp. 294 (D.C. N.C.1975), affirmed without opinion 423 U.S. 907, 96 S.Ct. 210 (1975).

3. In a Texas case, a teacher whipped a pupil with a switch for fighting after school; the court held that the fact that the fighting occurred after school

did not deprive the teacher of his legal right to punish the pupil. Hutton v. State, 23 Tex.App. 386, 5 S.W. 122 (1887). The court stated:

> The authority of the teacher is not confined to the school room or grounds, but he may prohibit and punish all acts of his pupils which are detrimental to the good order and best interests of the school, whether such acts are committed in school hours or while the pupil is on his way to or from school or after he has returned home.

4. In a New York case, a teacher was accused of being malicious in the punishment of a boy. The teacher had been assigned to see that the pupils who were not taking part in class-day assembly should leave the school premises. One boy refused to leave; he had a record of bad behavior and he had been drinking. The boy used profane language when the teacher insisted that he leave. The teacher put his hands on the throat of the boy and either pushed or threw him over a hedge. The boy accused the teacher of assault and battery. The court ruled for the teacher and stated that:

> people will differ as to what force is reasonable in manner and moderate in degree. Taking into consideration the prior conduct of the complainant, the lack of malice on the part of the defendant, the nature of the offense of the pupil, his motive, the effect of his conduct on other pupils, and his size and strength, I find and decide that the guilt of the defendant has not been proved beyond a reasonable doubt. People ex rel. Hogan v. Newton, 185 Misc. 405, 56 N.Y.S.2d 779 (1945).

5. The past behavior of the pupil is an important factor in determining what is reasonable behavior. In a New York case, a pupil was punished by the school principal and the principal was indicted for criminal assault. The boy had dropped a book from a balcony to the seats of an auditorium. The lower court ruled for the pupil but the appellate court reversed the decision saying that reports of the pupil's prior misbehavior should have been considered in deciding the reasonableness of the punishment. People v. Mummert, 183 Misc. 243, 50 N.Y.S.2d 699 (1944).

6. Two cases that demonstrate excessive punishment were decided by courts in Arkansas and Connecticut. In the Arkansas case, a teacher whipped a fifteen-year-old boy twice in the same day, with a paddle made of flooring, against the orders of the school board. The boy was whipped the first time for not repeating a riddle from a newspaper and the second time for throwing a paper wad. The punishment bruised the boy and the court held the punishment was excessive. Berry v. Arnold School District, 199 Ark. 1118, 137 S.W.2d 256 (1940). In a Connecticut case, a principal was accused of using unreasonable force on a small boy who struggled as the principal was dragging him to the school office. The principal threw the boy to the floor and sat on him. The court held that the principal had used unreasonable force and the boy had a right to resist such treatment in self-protection. Calway v. Williamson, 130 Conn. 575, 36 A.2d 377 (1944).

7. An example of excessive and unreasonable punishment by a teacher is also illustrated in an 1872 Kentucky case. In this case, a teacher was taking part in a playground activity with the pupils and one pupil

differed with the opinion of the teacher on a trivial matter. The teacher
in turn beat the boy. The court said:

> The authority of a teacher to hold his pupil to strict accountability in
> school for disorderly behavior did not justify him in assaulting and beating the
> pupil on the playground. Hardy v. James, 5 Ky. 36 (1872).

8. The courts have refused to uphold punishment of children for negligent
or careless destroying of school property. The Supreme Court of Indiana
has held that a "teacher has the right to exact from pupils obedience to
his lawful and reasonable demands and rules, and to punish for disobedience . . . " but the teacher may be found guilty of assault and battery
when he attempts to enforce by chastisement a rule that requires pupils
to "pay for wanton and careless destruction of school property." The
court stated further: "Carelessness on the part of children is one of the
most common, and yet one of the least blameworthy, of their faults. In
simple carelessness there is no purpose to do wrong. To punish a child
for carelessness, in any case, is to punish it when it has no purpose or
intent to do wrong or violate rules. But beyond this no rule is reasonable
which requires of the pupils what they cannot do. The vast majority of
pupils, whether small or large, have no money at their command with
which to pay for school property which they injure or destroy by carelessness or otherwise. If required to pay for such property, they would have
to look to their parents or guardians for the money. If the parent or
guardian should not have the money, or if they should refuse to give it to
the child, the child would be left subject to punishment for not having
done what it had no power to do." State v. Vanderbilt, 116 Ind. 11, 18
N.E. 266 (1888).

CONSTITUTIONAL DUE PROCESS

As pointed out elsewhere in this book, the Fourteenth Amendment to the
Federal Constitution provides that no state shall deprive a person of his life,
liberty, or property without due process of law. Stated positively, a state
may deprive a person of his life, liberty, or property so long as the individual
is given due process.

There are two types of due process. One is called procedural due process.
This means that if an individual is to be deprived of his life, liberty, or
property, a prescribed constitutional procedure must be followed. The
Supreme Court of the United States has said that in order to give an
individual procedural due process as required by the Federal Constitution,
three basic factors must be present. The individual must have proper notice
that he is about to be deprived of his life, liberty, or property; he must be
given an opportunity to be heard; and the hearing must be conducted fairly.

A second type of due process is called substantive due process. To satisfy
this constitutional requirement, if a state is going to deprive a person of his
life, liberty, or property, the state must have a valid objective and the means
used must be reasonably calculated to achieve the objective. Early interpretations by the United States Supreme Court recognized only the procedural
aspects of due process of law.[7] It was not until 1923 that the Supreme Court

defined due process of law as possessing "substantive" protections.[8] Substantive due process was defined by one court as:

> The phrase "due process of law," when applied to substantive rights, as distinguished from procedural rights, means that the state is without power to deprive a person of life, liberty or property by an act having no reasonable relation to any proper governmental purpose, or which is so far beyond the necessity of case as to be an arbitrary exercise of governmental power.[9]

Substantive Due Process

In *Meyer v. Nebraska*,[10] the Supreme Court related substantive protection of the due process clause of the Fourteenth Amendment to education when it held unconstitutional a Nebraska statute forbidding the teaching in public or private schools of foreign languages to pupils below the eighth grade. Since the United States Constitution provided no express relief for offending the statute, the Court extended the due process clause to protect the teacher. The court related the teacher's right to teach to an expanded substantive interpretation of "liberty" and said:

> The problem for our determination is whether the statute as construed and applied unreasonably infringes the liberty guaranteed to the Plaintiff in error by the Fourteenth Amendment. "No state shall . . . deprive any person of life, liberty, or property, without due process of law."
>
> While this court has not attempted to define with exactness the liberty thus guaranteed, the term has received much consideration and some of the included things have been definitely stated. Without doubt, it denotes not merely freedom from bodily restraint but also the right of the individual to contract, to engage in any of the common occupations of life, to acquire useful knowledge, to marry, establish a home and bring up children, to worship God according to the dictates of his own conscience, and generally to enjoy those privileges long recognized at common law as essential to the orderly pursuit of happiness by free men. . . . The established doctrine is that this liberty may not be interfered with, under the guise of protecting the public interest, by legislative action which is arbitrary or without reasonable relation to some purpose within the competency of the State to effect. . . . His [the teacher's] right thus to teach and the right of parents to engage him so to instruct their children, we think, are within the liberty of the Amendment.[11]

With this decision, the Supreme Court not only acknowledged the substantive protections of due process covering life, liberty, and property but clearly extended them to protect a person's right of education,[12] travel,[13] and appearance.[14] Substantive due process rights also generally encompass the First Amendment freedoms of religion, speech, press, and assembly.

Procedural Due Process

Constitutional guarantees of procedural due process were originally assumed to be applicable only to proceedings of the judicial branch of government, i.e., a person's right to a trial by jury. However, in recent years, the courts have made it abundantly clear that procedural due process is not confined to the courts but must also be afforded to individuals by administrative agencies, such as public schools, when the potential loss of a fundamental right is at stake. In other words, when a school district seeks to take action against a student that may permanently impair the student's education, then certain due process procedures must be followed. In *Soglin v. Kauffman,*[15] the court said the point at which disciplinary actions should be subject to constitutional scrutiny is when the action involves suspension "for any period of time substantial enough to prevent one from obtaining credit for a particular term."

Care should be taken by the school administrator to provide the student with fair treatment under any circumstances. The circumstances and the interests of the parties involved are paramount in prescribing the standards of procedural due process.[16] The United States Supreme Court has said:

> Due process unlike some legal rules is not a technical conception with a fixed content, unrelated to time, place and circumstances . . . . It is a delicate process of adjustment inescapably involving the exercise of judgment by those whom the Constitution entrusted the unfolding of its process.[17]

In providing procedural due process, the courts are not uniform in their requirements, but all insist that fundamental fairness must be afforded and "both sides must be given an opportunity to present their sides of the story in detail."[18]

In *Due v. Florida A. & M. University,* the court outlined three minimal due process requirements.

> First, the student should be given adequate notice in writing of the specific ground or grounds and the nature of the evidence on which the disciplinary proceedings are based. Second, the student should be given an opportunity for a hearing in which the disciplinary authority provides a fair opportunity for hearing of the student's position, explanations and evidence. The third requirement is that no disciplinary action be taken on grounds which are not supported by any substantial evidence.[19]

Fundamental fairness prescribed in these early cases for long suspension or expulsion of students has been extended to temporary, short-term suspensions by the United States Supreme Court.[20] The formality and intensity, though, of the procedural process is not fixed, the requirement being only that the process be commensurate with the length of suspension or the detriment that may be imposed on the student.

Procedural Due Process Required for
Students When Expelled

DIXON v. ALABAMA STATE BOARD OF EDUCATION

United States Court of Appeals,
Fifth Circuit, 1961.
294 F.2d 150, cert. denied 368 U.S. 930,
82 S.Ct. 368.

RIVES, Circuit Judge. The question presented by the pleadings and evidence, and decisive of this appeal, is whether due process requires notice and some opportunity for hearing before students at a tax-supported college are expelled for misconduct. We answer that question in the affirmative.

The misconduct for which the students were expelled has never been definitely specified. Defendant Trenholm, the President of the College, testified that he did not know why the plaintiffs and three additional students were expelled and twenty other students were placed on probation. The notice of expulsion which Dr. Trenholm mailed to each of the plaintiffs assigned no specific ground for expulsion, but referred in general terms to "this problem of Alabama State College." . . .

As shown by the findings of the district court . . . the only demonstration which the evidence showed that *all* of the expelled students took part in was that in the lunch grill located in the basement of the Montgomery County Courthouse. The other demonstrations were found to be attended "by several if not all of the plaintiffs." We have carefully read and studied the record, and agree with the district court that the evidence does not affirmatively show that *all* of the plaintiffs were present at any but the one demonstration.

. . . The most elaborate grounds for expulsion were assigned in the testimony of Governor Patterson:

> Q. There is an allegation in the complaint, Governor, that—I believe it is paragraph six, the defendants' action of expulsion was taken without regard to any valid rule or regulation concerning student conduct and merely retaliated against, punished, and sought to intimidate plaintiffs for having lawfully sought service in a publicly owned lunch room with service; is that statement true or false?
>
> A. Well, that is not true; the action taken by the State Board of Education was—was taken to prevent—to prevent incidents happening by students at the College that would bring—bring discredit upon—upon the School and be prejudicial to the School, and the State—as I said before, the State Board of Education took—considered at the time it expelled these students several incidents, one at the Court House at the lunch room demonstration, the one the next day at the trial of this student, the marching on the steps of the State Capitol, and also this rally held at the church, where—where it was reported that—that statements were made against the administration of the School. In addition to that, the—the feeling going around in the community here due to—due to the reports of these incidents of the students, by the students, and due to reports of incidents occurring involving violence in other States, which happened prior to these things starting here in Alabama, all of these things were discussed by the State Board of Education prior to the taking of the action that they did on March 2 and as I was present and acting as Chairman, as a member of the Board, I voted to expel these students and to put these others on probation because I felt that that was what was in the best interest of the College. And the—I felt that the action should be—should be prompt and immediate, because if something—something had not been done, in my opinion, it would have resulted in violence and disorder, and that we wanted to prevent, and we felt that we had a duty to the—to the—to the parents of the students and to the State to require that the students behave themselves while they are attending a State College, and that is [sic] the reasons why we took the action that we did. That is all.

Superintendent of Education Stewart testified that he voted for expulsion because the students had broken rules and regulations pertaining to all of the State institutions . . . .

The evidence clearly shows that the question for decision does not concern the sufficiency of the notice or the adequacy of the hearing, but is

whether the students had a right to any notice or hearing whatever before
being expelled. . . . After careful study and consideration, we find
ourselves unable to agree with the conclusion of the district court that no
notice or opportunity for any kind of hearing was required before these
students were expelled.

It is true, as the district court said, that "there is no statute or rule that
requires formal charges and/or a hearing . . . " but the evidence is
without dispute that the usual practice at Alabama State College had been
to give a hearing and opportunity to offer defenses before expelling a
student. . . .

Whenever a governmental body acts so as to injure an individual, the
Constitution requires that the act be consonant with due process of law. The
minimum procedural requirements necessary to satisfy due process depend
upon the circumstances and the interests of the parties involved. . . .

The precise nature of the private interest involved in this case is the
right to remain at a public institution of higher learning in which the
plaintiffs were students in good standing. It requires no argument to
demonstrate that education is vital and, indeed, basic to civilized society.
Without sufficient education the plaintiffs would not be able to earn an
adequate livelihood, to enjoy life to the fullest, or to fulfill as completely as
possible the duties and responsibilities of good citizens.

There was no offer to prove that other colleges are open to the plaintiffs.
If so, the plaintiffs would nonetheless be injured by the interruption of their
course of studies in mid-term. It is most unlikely that a public college would
accept a student expelled from another public college of the same state.
Indeed, expulsion may well prejudice the student in completing his education at any other institution. Surely no one can question that the right to
remain at the college in which the plaintiffs were students in good standing
is an interest of extremely great value.

Turning then to the nature of the governmental power to expel the
plaintiffs, it must be conceded, as was held by the district court, that that
power is not unlimited and cannot be arbitrarily exercised. Admittedly,
there must be some reasonable and constitutional ground for expulsion or the
courts would have a duty to require reinstatement. The possibility of
arbitrary action is not excluded by the existence of reasonable regulations.
There may be arbitrary application of the rule to the facts of a particular case.
Indeed, that result is well nigh inevitable when the Board hears only one side
of the issue. In the disciplining of college students there are no considerations of immediate danger to the public, or of peril to the national security,
which should prevent the Board from exercising at least the fundamental
principles of fairness by giving the accused students notice of the charges and
an opportunity to be heard in their own defense. Indeed, the example set by
the Board in failing so to do, if not corrected by the courts, can well break the
spirits of the expelled students and of others familiar with the injustice, and
do inestimable harm to their education. . . .

For the guidance of the parties in the event of further proceedings, we
state our views on the nature of the notice and hearing required by due
process prior to expulsion from a state college or university. They should,
we think, comply with the following standards. The notice should contain a

statement of the specific charges and grounds which, if proven, would justify expulsion under the regulations of the Board of Education. The nature of the hearing should vary depending upon the circumstances of the particular case. The case before us requires something more than an informal interview with an administrative authority of the college. By its nature, a charge of misconduct, as opposed to a failure to meet the scholastic standards of the college, depends upon a collection of the facts concerning the charged misconduct, easily colored by the point of view of the witnesses. In such circumstances, a hearing which gives the Board or the administrative authorities of the college an opportunity to hear both sides in considerable detail is best suited to protect the rights of all involved. This is not to imply that a full-dress judicial hearing, with the right to cross-examine witnesses, is required. Such a hearing, with the attending publicity and disturbance of college activities, might be detrimental to the college's educational atmosphere and impractical to carry out. Nevertheless, the rudiments of an adversary proceeding may be preserved without encroaching upon the interests of the college. In the instant case, the student should be given the names of the witnesses against him and an oral or written report on the facts to which each witness testifies. He should also be given the opportunity to present to the Board, or at least to an administrative official of the college, his own defense against the charges and to produce either oral testimony or written affidavits of witnesses in his behalf. If the hearing is not before the Board directly, the results and findings of the hearing should be presented in a report open to the student's inspection. If these rudimentary elements of fair play are followed in a case of misconduct of this particular type, we feel that the requirements of due process of law will have been fulfilled.

The judgment of the district court is reversed and the cause is remanded for further proceedings consistent with this opinion.

Reversed and remanded.

*Temporary Suspension Requires
Procedural Due Process*

GOSS v. LOPEZ

Supreme Court of the United States, 1975.
419 U.S. 565, 95 S.Ct. 729.

Mr. Justice WHITE delivered the opinion of the Court.

This appeal by various administrators of the Columbus, Ohio, Public School System (CPSS) challenges the judgment of a three-judge federal court, declaring that appellees—various high school students in the CPSS—were denied due process of law contrary to the command of the Fourteenth Amendment in that they were temporarily suspended from their high schools without a hearing either prior to suspension or within a reasonable time thereafter, and enjoining the administrators to remove all references to such suspensions from the students' records.

Ohio law, Rev.Code Ann. § 3313.64 (1972), provides for free education to all children between the ages of six and twenty-one. Section 3313.66 of the

Code empowers the principal of an Ohio public school to suspend a pupil for misconduct for up to ten days or to expel him. In either case, he must notify the student's parents within twenty-four hours and state the reasons for his action. A pupil who is expelled, or his parents, may appeal the decision to the Board of Education and in connection therewith shall be permitted to be heard at the board meeting. The Board may reinstate the pupil following the hearing. No similar procedure is provided in § 3313.66 or any other provision of state law for a suspended student. Aside from a regulation tracking the statute, at the time of the imposition of the suspensions in this case the CPSS itself had not issued any written procedure applicable to suspensions. Nor, so far as the record reflects, had any of the individual high schools involved in this case. Each, however, had formally or informally described the conduct for which suspension could be imposed.

The nine named appellees, each of whom alleged that he or she had been suspended from public high school in Columbus for up to ten days without a hearing pursuant to § 3313.66, filed an action under 42 U.S.C.A. § 1983 against the Columbus Board of Education and various administrators of the CPSS. The complaint sought a declaration that § 3313.66 was unconstitutional in that it permitted public school administrators to deprive plaintiffs of their rights to an education without a hearing of any kind, in violation of the procedural due process component of the Fourteenth Amendment. It also sought to enjoin the public school officials from issuing future suspensions pursuant to § 3313.66 and to require them to remove references to the past suspensions from the records of the students in question.

The proof below established that the suspensions arose out of a period of widespread student unrest in the CPSS during February and March 1971. Six of the named plaintiffs, Rudolph Sutton, Tyrone Washington, Susan Cooper, Deborah Fox, Clarence Byars, and Bruce Harris, were students at the Marion-Franklin High School and were each suspended for ten days on account of disruptive or disobedient conduct committed in the presence of the school administrator who ordered the suspension. One of these, Tyrone Washington, was among a group of students demonstrating in the school auditorium while a class was being conducted there. He was ordered by the school principal to leave, refused to do so, and was suspended. Rudolph Sutton, in the presence of the principal, physically attacked a police officer who was attempting to remove Tyrone Washington from the auditorium. He was immediately suspended. The other four Marion-Franklin students were suspended for similar conduct. None was given a hearing to determine the operative facts underlying the suspension, but each, together with his or her parents, was offered the opportunity to attend a conference, subsequent to the effective date of the suspension, to discuss the student's future.

Two named plaintiffs, Dwight Lopez and Betty Crome, were students at the Central High School and McGuffey Junior High School, respectively. The former was suspended in connection with a disturbance in the lunchroom which involved some physical damage to school property. Lopez testified that at least seventy-five other students were suspended from his school on the same day. He also testified below that he was not a party to the destructive conduct but was instead an innocent bystander. Because no one from the school testified with regard to this incident, there is no evidence in the record indicating the official basis for concluding otherwise. Lopez never had a hearing.

Betty Crome was present at a demonstration at a high school other than the one she was attending. There she was arrested together with others, taken to the police station, and released without being formally charged. Before she went to school on the following day, she was notified that she had been suspended for a ten-day period. Because no one from the school testified with respect to this incident, the record does not disclose how the McGuffey Junior High School principal went about making the decision to suspend Crome, nor does it disclose on what information the decision was based. It is clear from the record that no hearing was ever held.

There was no testimony with respect to the suspension of the ninth named plaintiff, Carl Smith. The school files were also silent as to his suspension, although as to some, but not all, of the other named plaintiffs the files contained either direct references to their suspensions or copies of letters sent to their parents advising them of the suspension.

On the basis of this evidence, the three-judge court delcared that plaintiffs were denied due process of law because they were "suspended without hearing prior to suspension or within a reasonable time thereafter," and that Ohio Rev.Code Ann. § 3313.66 (1972) and regulations issued pursuant thereto were unconstitutional in permitting such suspensions. It was ordered that all references to plaintiffs' suspensions be removed from school files.

Although not imposing upon the Ohio school administrators any particular disciplinary procedures and leaving them "free to adopt regulations providing for fair suspension procedures which are consonant with the educational goals of their schools and reflective of the characteristics of their school and locality," the District Court declared that there were "minimum requirements of notice and a hearing prior to suspension, except in emergency situations." In explication, the court stated that relevant case authority would: (1) permit "[i]mmediate removal of a student whose conduct disrupts the academic atmosphere of the school, endangers fellow students, teachers or school officials, or damages property"; (2) require notice of suspension proceedings to be sent to the students' parents within twenty-four hours of the decision to conduct them; and (3) require a hearing to be held, with the student present, within seventy-two hours of his removal. Finally, the court stated that, with respect to the nature of the hearing, the relevant cases required that statements in support of the charge be produced, that the student and others be permitted to make statements in defense or mitigation, and that the school need not permit attendance by counsel.

The defendant school administrators have appealed the three-judge court's decision. Because the order below granted plaintiffs' request for an injunction—ordering defendants to expunge their records—this Court has jurisdiction of the appeal pursuant to 28 U.S.C.A. § 1253. We affirm.

At the outset, appellants contend that because there is no constitutional right to an education at public expense, the Due Process Clause does not protect against expulsions from the public school system. This position misconceives the nature of the issue and is refuted by prior decisions. The Fourteenth Amendment forbids the State to deprive any person of life, liberty, or property without due process of law. Protected interests in property are normally "not created by the Constitution. Rather, they are created and their dimensions are defined" by an independent source such as state statutes or rules entitling the citizen to certain benefits. Board of Regents v. Roth, 408 U.S. 564, 577, 92 S.Ct. 2701, 2709, 33 L.Ed.2d 548 (1972). . . .

The Due Process Clause also forbids arbitrary deprivations of liberty. "Where a person's good name, reputation, honor, or integrity is at stake because of what the government is doing to him," the minimal requirements of the Clause must be satisfied. Wisconsin v. Constantineau, 400 U.S. 433, 437, 91 S.Ct. 507, 510 (1971); Board of Regents v. Roth, supra, 408 U.S. at 573, 92 S.Ct. at 2707. School authorities here suspended appellees from school for periods of up to ten days based on charges of misconduct. If sustained and recorded, those charges could seriously damage the students' standing with their fellow pupils and their teachers as well as interfere with later opportunities for higher education and employment. It is apparent that the claimed right of the State to determine unilaterally and without process whether that misconduct has occurred immediately collides with the requirements of the Constitution.

Appellants proceed to argue that even if there is a right to a public education protected by the Due Process Clause generally, the Clause comes into play only when the State subjects a student to a "severe detriment or grievous loss." The loss of ten days, it is said, is neither severe nor grievous and the Due Process Clause is therefore of no relevance. Appellants' argument is again refuted by our prior decisions; for in determining "whether due process requirements apply in the first place, we must look not to the 'weight' but to the *nature* of the interest at stake." Board of Regents v. Roth, supra, at 570–571, 92 S.Ct. at 2705–2706. Appellees were excluded from school only temporarily, it is true, but the length and consequent severity of a deprivation, while another factor to weigh in determining the appropriate form of hearing, "is not decisive of the basic right" to a hearing of some kind. Fuentes v. Shevin, 407 U.S. 67, 86, 92 S.Ct. 1983, 1997 (1972). The Court's view has been that as long as a property deprivation is not *de minimis,* its gravity is irrelevant to the question whether account must be taken of the Due Process Clause. Sniadach v. Family Finance Corp., 395 U.S. 337, 342, 89 S.Ct. 1820, 1823 (1969) (Harlan, J. concurring); Boddie v. Connecticut, 401 U.S. 371, 378–379, 91 S.Ct. 780, 786 (1971); Board of Regents v. Roth, supra, 408 U.S., at 570 n. 8, 92 S.Ct., at 2705. A ten-day suspension from school is not *de minimis* in our view and may not be imposed in complete disregard of the Due Process Clause.

A short suspension is, of course, a far milder deprivation than expulsion. But, "education is perhaps the most important function of state and local governments," Brown v. Board of Education, 347 U.S. 483, 493, 74 S.Ct. 686, 691 (1954), and the total exclusion from the educational process for more than a trivial period, and certainly if the suspension is for ten days, is a serious event in the life of the suspended child. Neither the property interest in educational benefits temporarily denied nor the liberty interest in reputation, which is also implicated, is so insubstantial that suspensions may constitutionally be imposed by any procedure the school chooses, no matter how arbitrary. . . .

There are certain bench marks to guide us, however. Mullane v. Central Hanover Trust Co., 339 U.S. 306, 70 S.Ct. 652 (1950), a case often invoked by later opinions, said that "[m]any controversies have raged about the cryptic and abstract words of the Due Process Clause but there can be no doubt that at a minimum they require that deprivation of life, liberty or property by adjudication be preceded by notice and opportunity for hearing appropriate to the nature of the case." Id., at 313, 70 S.Ct. at 657. "The fundamental requisite of due process of law is the opportunity to be heard," Grannis v. Ordean, 234 U.S. 385, 394, 34 S.Ct. 779, 783 (1914), a right that "has little reality or worth unless one is informed that the matter is pending and can choose for himself whether to . . . contest." Mullane v. Central Hanover Trust Co., supra, 339 U.S. at 314, 70 S.Ct. at 657. At the very minimum, therefore, students facing suspension and the consequent interference with a protected property interest must be given *some* kind of notice and afforded *some* kind of hearing. "Parties whose rights are to be affected are entitled to be heard; and in order that they may enjoy that right they must first be notified." Baldwin v. Hale, 1 Wall. 223, 233 (1864).

It also appears from our cases that the timing and content of the notice and the nature of the hearing will depend on appropriate accommodation of the competing interests involved. Cafeteria Workers v. McElroy, supra, 367 U.S. at 895, 81 S.Ct. at 1748; Morrissey v. Brewer, supra, 408 U.S. at 481, 92 S.Ct. at 2600. The student's interest is to avoid unfair or mistaken exclusion from the educational process, with all of its unfortunate consequences. The Due Process Clause will not shield him from suspensions properly imposed, but it disserves both his interest and the interest of the State if his suspension is in fact unwarranted. The concern would be mostly academic if the disciplinary process were a totally accurate, unerring process, never mistaken and never unfair. Unfortunately, that is not the case, and no one suggests that it is. Disciplinarians, although proceeding in utmost good faith, frequently act on the reports and advice of others; and the controlling facts and the nature of the conduct under challenge are often disputed. The risk of error is not at all trivial, and it should be guarded against if that may be done without prohibitive cost or interference with the educational process.

The difficulty is that our schools are vast and complex. Some modicum of discipline and order is essential if the educational function is to be performed. Events calling for discipline are frequent occurrences and sometimes require immediate, effective action. Suspension is considered not only to be a necessary tool to maintain order but a valuable educational device. The prospect of imposing elaborate hearing requirements in every suspension case is viewed with great concern, and many school authorities may well prefer the untrammeled power to act unilaterally, unhampered by rules about notice and hearing. But it would be a strange disciplinary system in an educational institution if no communication was sought by the disciplinarian with the student in an effort to inform him of his dereliction and to let him tell his side of the story in order to make sure that an injustice is not done. "[F]airness can rarely be obtained by secret, one-sided determination of facts decisive of rights. . . ." "Secrecy is not congenial to truth-seeking and self-righteousness gives too slender an assurance of rightness. No better instrument has been devised for arriving at truth than to give a person in jeopardy of serious loss notice of the case against him and opportunity to meet it." . . .

We do not believe that school authorities must be totally free from notice and hearing requirements if their schools are to operate with acceptable efficiency. Students facing temporary suspension have interests qualifying for protection of the Due Process Clause and due process requires, in connection with a suspension of ten days or less, that the student be given oral or written notice of the charges against him and, if he denies them, an explanation of the evidence the authorities have and an opportunity to present his side of the story. The Clause requires at least these rudimentary precautions against unfair or mistaken findings of misconduct and arbitrary exclusion from school.

There need be no delay between the time "notice" is given and the time of the hearing. In the great majority of cases the disciplinarian may informally discuss the alleged misconduct with the student minutes after it has occurred. We hold only that, in being given an opportunity to explain his version of the facts at this discussion the student first be told what he is accused of doing and what the basis of the accusation is. Lower courts which have addressed the question of the *nature* of the procedures required in short suspension cases have reached the same conclusion. Tate v. Board of Education, 453 F.2d 975, 979 (CA8 1972); Vail v. Board of Education, 354 F.Supp. 592, 603 (NH 1973). Since the hearing may occur almost immediately following the misconduct, it follows that as a general rule notice and hearing should precede removal of the student from school. We agree with the District Court, however, that there are recurring situations in which prior notice and hearing cannot be insisted upon. Students whose presence poses a continuing danger to persons or property or an ongoing threat of disrupting the academic process may be immediately removed from school. In such cases, the necessary notice and rudimentary hearing should follow as soon as practicable, as the District Court indicated.

In holding as we do, we do not believe that we have imposed procedures on school disciplinarians which are inappropriate in a classroom setting. Instead we have imposed requirements which are, if anything, less than a fair-minded school principal would impose upon himself in order to avoid unfair suspensions. Indeed, according to the testimony of the principal of Marion-Franklin High School, that school had an informal procedure, remarkably similar to that which we now require, applicable to suspensions generally but which was not followed in this case. Similarly, according to the most recent memorandum applicable to the entire CPSS, school principals in the CPSS are now required by local rule to provide at least as much as the constitutional minimum which we have described.

We stop short of construing the Due Process Clause to require, countrywide, that hearings in connection with short suspensions must afford the student the opportunity to secure counsel, to confront and cross-examine witnesses supporting the charge, or to call his own witnesses to verify his version of the incident. Brief disciplinary suspensions are almost countless. To impose in each such case even truncated trial-type procedures might well overwhelm administrative facilities in many places and, by diverting resources, cost more than it would save in educational effectiveness. Moreover, further formalizing the suspension process and escalating its formality and adversary nature may not only make it too costly as a regular disciplinary tool but also destroy its effectiveness as part of the teaching process.

On the other hand, requiring effective notice and informal hearing permitting the student to give his version of the events will provide a meaningful hedge against erroneous action. At least the disciplinarian will be alerted to the existence of disputes about facts and arguments about cause and effect. He may then determine himself to summon the accuser, permit cross-examination, and allow the student to present his own witnesses. In more difficult cases, he may permit counsel. In any event, his discretion will be more informed and we think the risk of error substantially reduced.

Requiring that there be at least an informal give-and-take between student and disciplinarian, preferably prior to the suspension, will add little to the factfinding function where the disciplinarian himself has witnessed the conduct forming the basis for the charge. But things are not always as they seem to be, and the student will at least have the opportunity to characterize his conduct and put it in what he deems the proper context. We should also make it clear that we have addressed ourselves solely to the short suspension, not exceeding ten days. Longer suspensions or expulsions for the remainder of the school term, or permanently, may require more formal procedures. Nor do we put aside the possibility that in unusual situations, although involving only a short suspension, something more than the rudimentary procedures will be required.

The District Court found each of the suspensions involved here to have occurred without a hearing, either before or after the suspension, and that each suspension was therefore invalid and the statute unconstitutional insofar as it permits such suspensions without notice or hearing. Accordingly, the judgment is

Affirmed.

*Procedural Due Process Is
a Flexible Concept*

McCLAIN v. LAFAYETTE COUNTY BOARD OF EDUCATION

United States Court of Appeals,
Fifth Circuit, 1982.
673 F.2d 106, rehearing denied
687 F.2d 121 (1982).

COLEMAN, Circuit Judge.

On September 23, 1980, Michael carried a switchblade knife to school. The physical education teacher saw the knife in the student's possession and took him forthwith to the principal's office where . . . . Michael admitted that he had the knife. He also admitted that he knew that it was against the rule. His explanation was that he had found the knife, forgot that he had it in his pocket, and unintentionally had brought it to school.

The principal sent Michael back to class and later the same day directed him to appear in his office the following morning with his mother.

On September 24, 1980, Michael and his mother met with Mr. Bigham in his office where they were informed that Michael would be indefinitely suspended for his possession of the knife. At that time the principal gave Mrs. McClain a letter informing her that Michael was "indefinitely suspended" because of his possession and display of a switchblade knife and that she had a right to attend the Lafayette County School Board meeting which was to be held on September 30, 1980 to "request re-admittance" for Michael.

Mrs. McClain arranged an appointment in accordance with the third paragraph of the letter. She, along with Michael, attended the meeting of the Lafayette County School Board on the night of September 30, 1980. The principal and the physical education teacher attended the meeting and related their accounts of the switchblade knife event leading to Michael's suspension. Tape recordings of statements taken from other students during the course of the investigation which followed Michael's September 24 suspension were played. Mrs. McClain and Michael were given the opportunity to question anyone present, and they were also afforded the opportunity to explain any facts or circumstances which might have a bearing on the Board's decision regarding Michael's reinstatement.

Lafayette County High School provides each of its students with a *Student Handbook* at the start of the school year. . . . the *Student Handbook* was read aloud to Michael and other members of his class on the first day of classes. In addition, Mrs. McClain testified that she had read the *Handbook.*

The School Board voted to change Michael's indefinite suspension to a suspension for the remainder of the school year. Mrs. McClain was notified later on the night of the meeting of the Board's actions.

This suit for injunctive relief soon followed and the District Court held an evidentiary hearing, filed findings of fact, and denied injunctive relief.

On appeal, the McClains contend that Michael's procedural due process rights were violated when he was suspended for an indefinite period of time from the high school without first being given a hearing. They argue that this indefinite suspension was in fact a long-range suspension, which should have been preceded by a fair, impartial and meaningful hearing on both the charges and the appropriate punishment. Furthermore, they contend even if the suspension by Mr. Bigham were viewed as a short-range suspension, Michael's procedural due process rights were violated during the School Board meeting because he was not given adequate notice of the type of hearing and the charges, the names of his accusers and a summary of their expected testimonies, the right to retain and to be represented by counsel, nor the right to confront and cross-examine the witnesses.

> [T]he State is constrained to recognize a student's legitimate entitlement to a public education as a property interest which is protected by the Due Process Clause and which may not be taken away for misconduct without adherence to the minimum procedures required by the Clause. Goss v. Lopez, 419 U.S. 565, 574 [95 S.Ct. 729, 736, 42 L.Ed.2d 725] (1975).
>
> Once it is determined that due process applies, the question remains what process is due. Morrissey v. Brewer, 408 U.S. 471, 481 [92 S.Ct. 2593, 2600, 33 L.Ed.2d 484] (1972).

At the very minimum . . . students facing suspension and the consequent interference with a protected property interest must be given *some* kind
of notice and afforded *some* kind of hearing . . . .

[D]ue process requires, in connection with a suspension of ten days or less,
that the student be given oral or written notice of the charges against him
and, if he denies them, an explanation of the evidence the authorities have
and an opportunity to present his side of the story . . . . There need be no
delay between the time "notice" is given and the time of the hearing. In the
great majority of the cases the disciplinarian may informally discuss the
alleged misconduct with the student minutes after it has occurred. We hold
only that, in being given an opportunity to explain his version of the facts at
this discussion, the student first be told what he is accused of doing and what
the basis of the accusation is. 419 U.S. at 579, 581, 582 [95 S.Ct. at 738, 739,
740.]

The Supreme Court has cautioned that "suspensions or expulsions for the
remainder of the school term, or permanently, may require more formal
procedures." Id. at 584, 95 S.Ct. at 741.

The District Court held that the standards of *Goss* v. *Lopez,* supra, were
met. Michael admitted the possession of the knife when first taken to the
principal. Indeed, he could hardly have done otherwise because the physical
education teacher saw him in possession of it and took it from him. Never
at any time or place, including the hearing in the District Court, did Michael
deny it. He did say that he forgot about having this large jackknife, and a
switchblade at that, in his pocket. This is not the kind of defense to
carrying a deadly weapon that a jury or other factfinder must accept.

Relying upon Dixon v. Alabama State Board of Education, 294 F.2d 150,
159 (5th Cir., 1961), plaintiff argues that he should have been given the
names of the witnesses against him and an oral or written report of their
testimonies. Plaintiff contends that the taped testimony denied him a right
of confrontation. Though the *Dixon* Court did find that the students in that
case should have been given the list of witnesses against them, the Court
noted, "The nature of the hearing should vary depending upon the circumstances of the particular case." Id. at 158.

We can conceive of situations in which the playing of the tapes as done
here might be a denial of due process. Not in this instance, however. The
issue was whether Michael had carried a switchblade knife to school. There
is no representation that the tapes presented any untruths or dealt with any
other issue. Therefore, they were merely cumulative on an issue in which
Michael had conceded his guilt and has never afterward denied it.

The nub of the matter is that the student was given an opportunity to
present his side of the case, including anything by way of denial or mitigation. He and his mother appeared and participated. There has never been
any doubt of Michael's guilt in carrying this deadly weapon to school. There
was nothing fundamentally unfair or legally prejudicial in the proceedings.

The judgment of the District Court denying injunctive relief is
Affirmed.

NOTES

1. Is hearsay admissible in student hearings? When a high school principal
   read statements made by teachers in an expulsion hearing, the students

challenged, claiming that hearsay evidence could not be used in such hearings. The United States Court of Appeals, Fifth Circuit, stated:

> There is a seductive quality to the argument—advanced here to justify the importation of technical rules of evidence into administrative hearings conducted by laymen—that, since a free public education is a thing of great value, comparable to that of welfare sustenance or the curtailed liberty of a parolee, the safeguards applicable to these should apply to it. . . . In this view we stand but a step away from the application of the *strictissimi juris* due process requirements of criminal trials to high school disciplinary processes. And if to high school, why not to elementary school? It will not do. Basic fairness and integrity of the fact-finding process are the guiding stars. Important as they are, the rights at stake in a school disciplinary hearing may be fairly determined upon the "hearsay" evidence of school administrators charged with the duty of investigating the incidents. We decline to place upon a board of laymen the duty of observing and applying the common-law rules of evidence. Boykins v. Fairfield Board of Education, 492 F.2d 697 (5th Cir.1974) *cert. denied,* 420 U.S. 962, 92 S.Ct. 1350 (1975).

Although *Boykins* predates *Goss* v. *Lopez,* the hearsay principle was reaffirmed by the Fifth Circuit in Tasby v. Estes, 643 F.2d 1103 (5th Cir. 1981). Other courts' opinions have been somewhat mixed concerning hearsay evidence. *Tasby* v. *Estes* (hearsay may be allowed in hearings for serious student offenses); *Boykins* v. *Fairfield Board of Education* (hearsay may be allowed in suspension/expulsion); Linwood v. Board of Education, 463 F.2d 763 (7th Cir.), *cert. denied* 409 U.S. 1027, 93 S.Ct. 475 (1972) (hearsay may be allowed by implication in expulsion hearing); Whiteside v. Kay, 446 F.Supp. 716 (D.La.1978) (hearsay may be allowed by implication at expulsion hearing); Racine Unified School District v. Thompson, 107 Wis.2d 657, 321 N.W.2d 334 (1982) (hearsay evidence may be allowed from school teachers or staff); Fielder v. Board of Education, 346 F.Supp. 722 (D.Neb.1972) (hearsay may not be allowed by implication at expulsion hearing); DeJesus v. Penberthy, 344 F.Supp. 70 (Conn.1972) (hearsay may not be allowed in hearing for thirty-day suspension).

2. When faced with both a criminal and school disciplinary punishments, students have claimed that constitutional prohibition against double jeopardy comes into play. In Paine v. Board of Regents of University of Texas System, 355 F.Supp. 199 (W.D.Tex.1972), affirmed 474 F.2d 1397 (5th Cir.1973), a group of students faced criminal prosecution for drug use and suspension from the university. The court rejected their double jeopardy claims stating:

> Through two separate governmental organs, the *legislative branch* and the *Board of Regents,* the State does indeed impose two successive sanctions for the same offense: judicially imposed punishment and automatic suspension from the University of Texas System. However, the state laws defining criminal conduct and authorizing its punishment are intended to vindicate public justice in regard to the individual offender while . . . the Regents' Rule mandating . . . suspension of student drug or narcotic offenders is intended to protect the university community and the educational goals of the institution from such adverse influence as the offender may wield if he is allowed to remain a student. Thus the two sanctions imposed by the state upon plaintiffs have *sufficiently different underlying purposes* to permit characterization of the first as "criminal" or "punitive" and the second as "civil,"

"remedial" or "administrative." Since the Double Jeopardy Clause operates only upon sanctions of the first type successively imposed for the same offense, plaintiffs may not avail themselves of its protection here. See also Clements v. Board of Trustees of Sheridan County, 585 P.2d 197 (Wyo.1978).

3. A student is not entitled to a *Miranda* warning prior to being questioned by school authorities. Boynton v. Casey, 543 F.Supp. 995 (D.Me.1982); see: Baxter v. Palmigiano, 425 U.S. 308, 96 S.Ct. 1551 (1976).

FREEDOM OF SPEECH AND EXPRESSION

There are few areas of the law more misunderstood by lay people than those connected with First Amendment rights, especially as they relate to freedom of speech and expression. While it is true that the right to speak one's mind carries with it at least the moral obligation to mind one's speech, this rule of thumb is not the prevailing yardstick or standard used by the courts in resolving issues in this area.

The Supreme Court has relied primarily on two tests to determine whether the state can control freedom of speech or expression. These are: (1) clear and present danger and (2) material and substantial disruption. In 1919, the Court [21] said that the question to be asked is whether the words used are used in such circumstances and are of such a nature as to create a "clear and present danger" that they will bring about the substantial evils . . . which may harm the state. In subsequent decisions [22] the Court further defined the concept. Justice Brandeis said

> no danger flowing from speech can be deemed clear and present, unless the incidence of the evil apprehended is so imminent that it may befall before there is opportunity for full discussion. If there be time to expose through discussion the falsehood and fallacies, to avert the evil by the processes of education, the remedy to be applied is more speech, not enforced silence.[23]

Government cannot limit speech where the dangers are merely perceived or are not "present" or "imminent." Justice Black observed that "What finally emerges from the 'clear and present danger' cases is a working principle that the substantive evil must be extremely serious and the degree of imminence extremely high before utterances can be punished." [24]

The second rationale, "material and substantial disruption," is the standard applied to public education by the Supreme Court in the famous *Tinker* case. The Court in this case made it clear that school authorities would not be permitted to deny a student his fundamental right simply because of "a mere desire to avoid discomfort and unpleasantness that always accompany an unpopular viewpoint." [25]

The great weight of judicial authority supports the proposition that a board of education possesses the authority to regulate pupil dress and personal appearance if they become so extreme as to interrupt the school's decorum and favorable learning atmosphere. An illustration of this judicial position was provided several years ago when the Arkansas Appellate Court [26] upheld a school regulation that forbade the wearing of low-necked dresses, any immodest dress, or the use of face paints or cosmetics. Of somewhat more recent vintage an application is the right of a school district to require pupils to participate in physical education programs and to wear clothing suitable for these occasions. The majority rule in these instances is that the pupils must participate in physical education programs, but they may not be required to wear "immodest" attire.[27]

Students and parents have relied on several legal issues in contesting student appearance regulations, including freedom of speech of the First Amendment, the due process and equal protection clauses of the Fourteenth Amendment, the Ninth Amendment, which provides for retention of rights by the people, and even the Civil Rights Acts. The cases convey a lack of agreement by the courts in the application of these rights to students in public schools. From the numerous cases that exist on this subject, it is quite difficult to identify a prevailing view of the courts. The courts, from the United States Courts of Appeals down, appear to be about evenly split on the application of constitutional rights and haircuts. The courts are in general agreement in keeping with *Tinker*, that any hair style or dress that is disruptive of classroom decorum may be prevented, but it is quite difficult for many of the courts to see precisely how an untidy haircut can be so destructive to a favorable learning environment.

Denial of Freedom of Expression
Must be Justified by a Reasonable
Forecast of Substantial Disruption

TINKER v. DES MOINES INDEPENDENT COMMUNITY SCHOOL DISTRICT

Supreme Court of the United States, 1969.
393 U.S. 503, 89 S.Ct. 733.

Mr. Justice FORTAS delivered the opinion of the Court.

Petitioner John F. Tinker, fifteen years old, and petitioner Christopher Eckhardt, sixteen years old, attended high schools in Des Moines, Iowa. Petitioner Mary Beth Tinker, John's sister, was a thirteen-year-old student in junior high school.

In December 1965, a group of adults and students in Des Moines held a meeting at the Eckhardt home. The group determined to publicize their objections to the hostilities in Vietnam and their support for a truce by wearing black armbands during the holiday season and by fasting on December 16 and New Year's Eve. Petitioners and their parents had previously engaged in similar activities, and they decided to participate in the program.

The principals of the Des Moines schools became aware of the plan to wear armbands. On December 14, 1965, they met and adopted a policy that any student wearing an armband to school would be asked to remove it, and if he refused he would be suspended until he returned without the armband. Petitioners were aware of the regulation that the school authorities adopted.

On December 16, Mary Beth and Christopher wore black armbands to their schools. John Tinker wore his armband the next day. They were all sent home and suspended from school until they would come back without their armbands. They did not return to school until after the planned period for wearing armbands had expired—that is, until after New Year's Day.

This complaint was filed in the United States District Court by petitioners, through their fathers, under § 1983 of Title 42 of the United States Code. It prayed for an injunction restraining the respondent school officials and the respondent members of the board of directors of the school district from disciplining the petitioners, and it sought nominal damages. After an evidentiary hearing the District Court dismissed the complaint. It upheld the constitutionality of the school authorities' action on the ground that it was reasonable in order to prevent disturbance of school discipline. 258 F.Supp. 971 (1966). The court referred to but expressly declined to follow the Fifth Circuit's holding in a similar case that the wearing of symbols like the armbands cannot be prohibited unless it "materially and substantially interfere[s] with the requirements of appropriate discipline in the operation of the school." Burnside v. Byars, 363 F.2d 744, 749 (1966).

On appeal, the Court of Appeals for the Eighth Circuit considered the case *en banc*. The court was equally divided, and the District Court's decision was accordingly affirmed, without opinion. 383 F.2d 988 (1967). We granted certiorari. 390 U.S. 942, 88 S.Ct. 1050, 19 L.Ed.2d 1130 (1968).

The District Court recognized that the wearing of an armband for the purpose of expressing certain views is the type of symbolic act that is within the Free Speech Clause of the First Amendment. . . . As we shall discuss, the wearing of armbands in the circumstances of this case was entirely divorced from actually or potentially disruptive conduct by those participating in it. It was closely akin to "pure speech" which, we have repeatedly held, is entitled to comprehensive protection under the First Amendment. . . .

First Amendment rights, applied in light of the special characteristics of the school environment, are available to teachers and students. It can hardly be argued that either students or teachers shed their constitutional rights to freedom of speech or expression at the schoolhouse gate. This has been the unmistakable holding of this Court for almost fifty years. . . . The school officials banned and sought to punish petitioners for a silent, passive expression of opinion, unaccompanied by any disorder or disturbance on the part of petitioners. There is here no evidence whatever of petitioners' interference, actual or nascent, with the schools' work or of collision with the rights of other students to be secure and to be let alone. Accordingly, this case does not concern speech or action that intrudes upon the work of the schools or the rights of other students.

Only a few of the 18,000 students in the school system wore the black armbands. Only five students were suspended for wearing them. There is no indication that the work of the schools or any class was disrupted. Outside the classrooms, a few students made hostile remarks to the children wearing armbands, but there were no threats or acts of violence on school premises.

The District Court concluded that the action of the school authorities was reasonable because it was based upon their fear of a disturbance from the wearing of the armbands. But, in our system, undifferentiated fear or apprehension of disturbance is not enough to overcome the right to freedom of expression. Any departure from absolute regimentation may cause trouble. Any variation from the majority's opinion may inspire fear. Any word spoken, in class, in the lunchroom, or on the campus, that deviates from the views of another person may start an argument or cause a disturbance. But our Constitution says we must take this risk, Terminiello v. Chicago, 337 U.S. 1, 69 S.Ct. 894, 93 L.Ed.1131 (1949); and our history says that it is this sort of hazardous freedom—this kind of openness—that is the basis of our national strength and of the independence and vigor of Americans who grow up and live in this relatively permissive, often disputatious, society.

In order for the State in the person of school officials to justify prohibition of a particular expression of opinion, it must be able to show that its action was caused by something more than a mere desire to avoid the discomfort and unpleasantness that always accompany an unpopular viewpoint. Certainly where there is no finding and no showing that engaging in the forbidden conduct would "materially and substantially interfere with the requirements of appropriate discipline in the operation of the school," the prohibition cannot be sustained. Burnside v. Byars, supra, 363 F.2d at 749.

In the present case, the District Court made no such finding, and our independent examination of the record fails to yield evidence that the school authorities had reason to anticipate that the wearing of the armbands would substantially interfere with the work of the school or impinge upon the rights of other students. Even an official memorandum prepared after the suspension that listed the reasons for the ban on wearing the armbands made no reference to the anticipation of such disruption.

On the contrary, the action of the school authorities appears to have been based upon an urgent wish to avoid the controversy which might result from the expression, even by the silent symbol of armbands, of opposition to this Nation's part in the conflagration in Vietnam. It is revealing, in this respect, that the meeting at which the school principals decided to issue the contested regulation was called in response to a student's statement to the journalism teacher in one of the schools that he wanted to write an article on Vietnam and have it published in the school paper. (The student was dissuaded.)

It is also relevant that the school authorities did not purport to prohibit the wearing of all symbols of political or controversial significance. The record shows that students in some of the schools wore buttons relating to national political campaigns, and some even wore the Iron Cross, traditionally a symbol of Nazism. The order prohibiting the wearing of armbands did not extend to these. Instead, a particular symbol—black armbands worn to exhibit opposition to this Nation's involvement in Vietnam—was singled out for prohibition. Clearly, the prohibition of expression of one particular opinion, at least without evidence that it is necessary to avoid material and substantial interference with schoolwork or discipline, is not constitutionally permissible.

In our system, state-operated schools may not be enclaves of totalitarianism. School officials do not possess absolute authority over their students. Students in school as well as out of school are "persons" under our Constitution. They are possessed of fundamental rights which the State must respect, just as they themselves must respect their obligations to the State.

In our system, students may not be regarded as closed-circuit recipients of only that which the State chooses to communicate. They may not be confined to the expression of those sentiments that are officially approved. In the absence of a specific showing of constitutionally valid reasons to regulate their speech, students are entitled to freedom of expression of their views. As Judge Gewin, speaking for the Fifth Circuit, said, school officials cannot suppress "expressions of feelings with which they do not wish to contend." Burnside v. Byars, supra, 363 F.2d at 749. . . .

If a regulation were adopted by school officials forbidding discussion of the Vietnam conflict, or the expression by any student of opposition to it anywhere on school property except as part of a prescribed classroom exercise, it would be obvious that the regulation would violate the constitutional rights of students, at least if it could not be justified by a showing that the students' activities would materially and substantially disrupt the work and discipline of the school. . . . In the circumstances of the present case, the prohibition of the silent, passive "witness of the armbands," as one of the children called it, is no less offensive to the constitution's guarantees.

As we have discussed, the record does not demonstrate any facts which might reasonably have led school authorities to forecast substantial disruption of or material interference with school activities, and no disturbances or disorders on the school premises in fact occurred. These petitioners merely went about their ordained rounds in school. Their deviation consisted only in wearing on their sleeve a band of black cloth, not more than two inches wide. They wore it to exhibit their disapproval of the Vietnam hostilities and their advocacy of a truce, to make their views known, and, by their example, to influence others to adopt them. They neither interrupted school activities nor sought to intrude in the school affairs or the lives of others. They caused discussion outside of the classrooms, but no interference with work and no disorder. In the circumstances, our Constitution does not permit officials of the State to deny their form of expression.

We express no opinion as to the form of relief which should be granted, this being a matter for the lower courts to determine. We reverse and remand for further proceedings consistent with this opinion.

Reversed and remanded.

Rule Banning Buttons Is Not
Unconstitutional If It Is Reasonably
Related to Prevention of
Disruptive Conduct

GUZICK v. DREBUS

United States Court of Appeals,
Sixth Circuit, 1970.
431 F.2d 594.

MEMORANDUM OPINION AND ORDER

LAMBROS, District Judge. This is an action arising under the provisions of Title 42 U.S.C.A. § 1983. This section provides as follows:

Every person who, under color of any statute, ordinance, regulation, custom, or usage, of any State or Territory, subjects, or causes to be subjected, any

citizen of the United States or other person within the jurisdiction thereof to
the deprivation of any rights, privileges, or immunities secured by the Constitution and laws, shall be liable to the party injured in an action at law, suit in
equity, or other proper proceeding for redress.

The complaint, in summary, alleges the following: Thomas Guzick, Jr., is
seventeen years of age and is a student at Shaw High School in East
Cleveland, Ohio. Defendant, Donald L. Drebus, is the principal of Shaw
High School. The other defendants are: Nelson F. Leist, Superintendent of
the East Cleveland School District; and Robert Henderson, Charles Hamilton, Leslie Reardon, Erwin Schrader, and George Beasley, who are members
of the East Cleveland Board of Education. Plaintiff desires to wear a button
on his lapel while attending school at Shaw High. The button reads:

April 5 Chicago
G.I.Civilian
Anti-War
Demonstration
Student Mobilization Committee

He wore this button to school on March 11, 1969. The school principal, Mr.
Drebus, ordered the plaintiff to remove the button. Upon the plaintiff's
refusal to remove the button, Mr. Drebus suspended him from Shaw High
School until such time as he returned to school without the button. The
complaint alleges that the acts of Mr. Drebus in suspending the plaintiff
have been ratified, approved, or encouraged by the other defendants in their
official capacities. Plaintiff alleges that his right to wear this button is
protected by the First Amendment to the Constitution, and that his suspension deprives him of rights guaranteed by the Constitution; and, further,
that his suspension was without just cause, without a hearing, and without
due process of law. The complaint alleges that similar buttons are being
worn in other high schools in the Cleveland area, and that the acts of the
defendants denying the plaintiff his right to wear a similar button deprives
him of the equal protection of the law as guaranteed by the Fourteenth
Amendment. The complaint seeks a temporary restraining order enjoining
the defendants from interfering with the plaintiff's right to wear the button
while attending school and from refusing to reinstate the plaintiff. It also
seeks a preliminary and permanent injunction directed toward securing the
same relief. The complaint further seeks a declaratory judgment that any
rule or regulation of the East Cleveland Board of Education proscribing the
wearing of such buttons is unconstitutional, and the complaint further seeks
damages in the amount of $1000.00 per day for every day the plaintiff is
compelled to miss school and for costs and attorneys' fees. . . .

In a case where there are substantial factual disputes raised by the
testimony of the various witnesses, their demeanor on the stand and their
relative degree of knowledge are particularly important. The court has,
therefore, reviewed the evidence and its impressions of the various witnesses
and has reached its considered judgment as to the actual facts in this case.

The city of East Cleveland, Ohio, is a suburb located east of Cleveland.
At one time, it was an almost exclusively white community. In the last few
years, however, many Negroes have moved into the community from Cleve-

land, which is immediately adjoining; and East Cleveland now is a racially mixed community. . . .

Approximately 70 percent of the students at Shaw High School are black. Approximately 30 percent are white. There has been considerable friction between the students of the two races. There has also been friction among students of the same race. Nonetheless, Shaw High School has not, as yet, had a serious racial disturbance.

At the same time, many other high schools in the area have had such disturbances. At John Hay High, a predominately black school approximately one mile to the west, there have been repeated disturbances; and, in fact, John Hay High School was forced to close for a number of days as a result of these. East High School and Glenville High School have also had serious disturbances. East High was also required to close. Both of these high schools have a high percentage of black students.

Collinwood High School, which is racially mixed, has had serious disturbances. Indeed, these required the closing of the school at one time this year.

So far there have been no crippling disruptions at Shaw High. The situation, however, is not peaceful.

Although there have been no crippling disruptions of school activities, Shaw High has a significant, perhaps serious, discipline problem. Students have been threatened in both the men's rooms and locker rooms, among other places. These threats have often been accompanied by violence. Money has been extorted from students under these circumstances. The problem has been of such significance that the P.T.A. and other groups in the community have become concerned. There have been numerous fights at Shaw, both between blacks and whites and among students of the same race. These fights have occurred both during school hours and in the evening.

Tension at Shaw High is at an incendiary point. The school officials spend a great portion of their time disciplining students in an attempt to control this situation. In January of this year, black students attempted to organize a walkout. Such walkouts have occurred in a number of the other schools in the area. Shaw High officials were forced to call police to the school. The walkout was aborted, and only one student actually left the school.

These are but a few of the incidents described to the Court. It appears that the principal reason why more such incidents have not occurred is the extensive effort by school officials to avert such situations by maintaining discipline and discussing these problems with the students and their parents.

For many years Shaw High has had an informal rule with respect to the wearing of emblems and other insignia. The rule has never been published; nevertheless, it has been applied uniformly and consistently for at least forty years at both Shaw High School and Kirk Junior High. To summarize the rule, it provides that students will not be permitted to wear buttons, emblems, or other insignia on school property during school hours unless these emblems or insignia are related to a school activity.

This informal rule has been applied in a wide variety of situations. School officials have applied it against the high school fraternities and sororities which existed at Shaw in the 1940s. Emblems signifying or indicating membership in any of these fraternities were prohibited. Students wearing them were asked to remove them or leave school.

Subsequently, informal clubs replaced the outlawed high school fraternities. The rule was applied to these clubs. Pins, emblems, lavalieres, lettering on clothing, and other insignia have not been permitted at Shaw High School. . . . The problem again exists as a result of the racial mixture at Shaw. Buttons, pins, and other emblems have been used as identifying "badges." They have portrayed and defined the divisions among students in the school. They have fostered an undesirable form of competition, division and dislike. The presence of these emblems, badges and buttons are taken to represent, define and depict the actual division of the students in various groups. . . .

The rule has acquired a particular importance in recent years. Students have attempted to wear buttons and badges expressing inflammatory messages, which, if permitted, and as the evidence indicates, would lead to substantial racial disorders at Shaw. Students have attempted to wear buttons with the following messages inscribed thereon. "White is right"; "Say it loud, Black and Proud"; "Black Power." Other buttons have depicted a mailed black fist, commonly taken to be the symbol for black power.

There have been occasions when the wearing of such insignia has led to disruptions at Shaw and at Kirk Junior High. A fight resulted in the cafeteria when a white student wore a button which read "Happy Easter, Dr. King." (Dr. Martin Luther King was assassinated in the Easter season.) On another occasion, students at Kirk Junior High entered the corridors wearing a distinctive headdress. They proceeded down the corridors striking and attacking certain other students whom they had expected would join them in wearing the headdress, but who had not done so.

School authorities have attempted to eliminate the wearing of buttons, emblems, other insignia, and distinctive forms of dress characteristic of a particular club or group. The evidence discloses a number of instances in which various individuals and groups attempted to wear such insignia or clothing and in which the school officials prohibited it. . . .

On March 11, 1969, the plaintiff, Thomas Guzick, Jr., in the company of Hunter Havens, went to the office of the principal of Shaw High, Mr. Donald Drebus. Both the plaintiff and Mr. Havens wore a button on their clothing inscribed with the message:

April 5 Chicago
G.I. Civilian
Anti-War
Demonstration
Student Mobilization Committee

Plaintiff also carried certain leaflets which he and Mr. Havens desired to distribute at Shaw High School.

The conversation had that morning between the two students and Mr. Drebus is in dispute. It appears, however, that the students requested permission to pass out the leaflets at the school. Mr. Drebus refused permission, stating that Shaw High had a policy against distribution of leaflets. Mr. Drebus demanded that the students remove the buttons which they were wearing. The students asserted that they had a constitutional right to wear such buttons. Hunter Havens removed his. The plaintiff, however, refused to remove his button, even after a warning by Mr. Drebus that he would suspend the plaintiff from school if he refused to remove it. Upon the plaintiff's further refusal to remove the button, he was suspended from school until such time as he returned without the button. Subsequently, the plaintiff filed suit with this Court seeking a legal determination whether he is entitled under the Constitution to wear this button at Shaw High School.

As outlined above, the Court has concluded that Shaw High School has had a long-standing and consistently-applied rule prohibiting the wearing of buttons and other insignia on school grounds during school hours, unless these are related to a school-sponsored activity. The Court finds that this rule has been a significant factor in preserving peace and good order at Shaw High School and in preventing provocations, distractions, and disruptive conduct. The Court finds that if this policy of excluding buttons and other insignia is not retained, some student will attempt to wear provocative or inciting buttons and other emblems. If these provocative buttons and insignia are permitted to be worn, they will further amplify an already serious discipline problem, they will exacerbate an already tense racial situation, and they will inevitably cause substantial disruptions in the educational process at Shaw High.

The Court further finds that if students are permitted to wear *some* buttons but not others, similar disruptions of the educational process will occur. Many students will not understand the justification for any rule that prohibits the wearing of certain buttons while permitting others. Many will not accept the distinction. . . .

The Court finds that the prohibition of buttons and other insignia at Shaw High significantly contributes to the preservation of peace and order, and that the blanket prohibition of buttons and other insignia is reasonably related to the prevention of the distractions and disruptive and violent conduct at Shaw High. The Court finds that if all buttons are permitted or if any buttons are permitted, a serious discipline problem will result, racial tensions will be exacerbated, and the educational process will be significantly and substantially disrupted.

CONCLUSIONS OF LAW

On February 24, 1969, the United States Supreme Court decided Tinker v. Des Moines Independent Community School District, 393 U.S. 503, 89 S.Ct. 733. This is the landmark case in the area of the student's rights to free speech in the public schools, and it has formed the basis of this litigation. . . .

The Court noted that the wearing of an expressive arm band is "closely akin" to "pure speech." It was, in substance, the silent expression of an idea. . . .

The regulation in the *Tinker* case was not applied in an even-handed manner. Other buttons and symbols of political and controversial significance were permitted to be worn in the school. The Court concluded that the regulation was directed at the principle expressed in this particular demonstration—that is, opposition to the Vietnam War. The school authorities, the Court concluded, wanted not to introduce the Vietnam controversy into the school.

Certain factors present in the *Tinker* case, and upon which the Court rested its decision, are not present here. The rule prohibiting the wearing of emblems at Shaw High School is one of long standing. It has been applied evenhandedly both in politically controversial and noncontroversial areas. . . . They have applied this rule consistently; they have applied it equally. The rule is applied (and it is applied in this case) without regard to the content and the ideas sought to be expressed in the emblem. It is applied without regard to the status of the wearer or to the message, inflammatory or innocuous, sought to be expressed.

Furthermore, there is in the present case much more than an "undifferentiated fear or apprehension" of disturbances likely to result from the wearing of buttons at Shaw High School. The wearing of buttons and other emblems and insignia has occasioned substantial disruptive conduct in the past at Shaw High. It is likely to occasion such conduct if permitted henceforth. The wearing of buttons and other insignia will serve to exacerbate an already tense situation, to promote divisions and disputes, including physical violence among the students, and to disrupt and interfere with the normal operation of the school and with appropriate discipline by the school authorities. . . .

The school authorities have adopted the policy of excluding all insignia and emblems, in view of the explosive situation and the likelihood of substantial disruption if provocative emblems are permitted. This Court is unprepared to say that the rule excluding all buttons is unreasonable, in view of the difficulty in applying a selective rule and in view of the real likelihood that such a rule would itself contribute to disruption. This Court is also unprepared to say that the school authorities were unreasonable in rejecting such a selective rule. . . . This Court concludes that such a rule is reasonably related to the prevention of disruptive conduct at Shaw High School.

The wearing of buttons or, as in the *Tinker* case, wearing of arm bands is itself and without accompanying conduct "closely akin" to "pure speech." Nevertheless, wearing of such insignia has other characteristics different from pure speech. A button is not merely a statement; it is an identification tag. It identifies the wearer as an adherent or member of one group or class. It identifies him as not being a member of other groups or classes. This identification aspect exists independent of the nature of the message contained in the button. Thus, for example, a button on which appears a mailed black fist certainly identifies the wearer with a particular political persuasion. This is apart from any message sought to be conveyed by the button.

The button also demonstrates that the wearer has a particular and keen interest in the goals and outlook of the group with which the button identifies him. It marks the wearer as a proponent; it also may mark him as someone's opponent. In so doing, buttons have an inherent tendency to divide a body of individuals into separate sub-groups, each identified by its own insignia, each declaring by a particular decoration its position in relation to other individuals. Such an effect may not be significant in the context of many high schools in this country. But because of the "peculiar situation" at Shaw High, this divisive influence is likely and, indeed, almost certain to lead to disruptive conduct. When there is added the fact that many of these expressive buttons are likely to convey that expression in a most inflammatory and, perhaps, insulting manner, it is apparent that a most dangerous situation will result.

Free speech is the single most important element upon which this nation has thrived. Wherever reasonably possible, it must be upheld, cherished, and nurtured. There are, however, situations in which free speech, or manifestations which are "closely akin" to free speech, must be exercised with care and restraint; and there are situations in which the manifestations of speech may even be prohibited altogether. It has been demonstrated that the identifying aspects of buttons and other insignia have led to considerable disruption at Shaw High in the past. It has also been demonstrated that such insignia would be likely and, indeed, more likely to lead to such disruptions if permitted now.

We bear in mind that the buttons and other insignia are not speech themselves. Rather, they are a pictorial manifestation of speech. As such, they acquire other characteristics which would not be possessed by the spoken word itself. Buttons and other insignia have an inherently identifying nature. They are in a sense "badges." It is this aspect of emblems and other insignia that has caused difficulty at Shaw High. It is this aspect, and not the actual speech of any of the students, which has been prohibited and which is at issue here. . . .

The prohibition of buttons and other insignia at Shaw High is the result of a history of problems which the Shaw High authorities have encountered as a result of this activity. The prohibition against buttons is reasonably related in preventing the occurrence of disruptive conduct. It is also reasonably related to what is administratively possible at Shaw High School. If any buttons are permitted to be worn at Shaw High, it is likely that students will require that all buttons be permitted. In any event, the wearing of any buttons will lead to disruptive, even violent, activities, will materially and substantially affect the normal educational processes at Shaw High, and will diminish significantly the ability of the school officials to maintain proper discipline.

In this case, it is relevant that the school authorities *did* prohibit the wearing of all symbols and applied the rule uniformly and consistently. This was not the case in *Tinker*.

It is also relevant that the wearing of a button by the plaintiff in this case was associated with a distribution of leaflets. This was not the case in *Tinker*.

An evidentiary pattern has developed in this case which specifically shows to this Court that the school authorities had a constitutionally valid reason to regulate student conduct regarding the wearing of buttons and other emblems and symbols. This was not the case in *Tinker*. . . .

It is also relevant that leaflets of all kinds are being distributed and circulated throughout the public schools, and specifically at Shaw High School, and finding their way on the bulletin boards. Many of these are of a harmless nature, but many of these are downright immoral and sinister, such as, defendants' Exhibit B distributed by SDS, which was posted on the Shaw High School bulletin board. It encouraged a demonstration in Washington opposing our political leaders and, among other things, contained this phrase: "Don't let the bastards grind you down!"

It is also relevant in the instant case that one of the pamphlets which was circulated at Shaw High School by the Student Mobilization Committee advertised a city-wide meeting to consider a possible high school strike.

The regulation prohibiting the wearing of the button is an appropriate standard of behavioral conduct which is reasonably relevant to the mission and function of Shaw High School.

The regulation is not discriminatory nor unreasonable, arbitrary or capricious. The rule does not deny a federally protected constitutional right.

Upholding the Shaw High School rule prohibiting buttons or other symbols does not sound the death knell for student freedom of speech.

The evidence in this case has made it abundantly clear that the school authorities have a factual basis upon which to forecast substantial disruption of, or material interference with, school activities if student behavioral conduct regarding the wearing of buttons is not regulated.

Therefore, the Court finds the issues in this case in favor of the defendants; and the plaintiff's claim for injunctive relief and damages is denied.

It is, therefore, ordered that this cause be and is hereby dismissed and terminated.

NOTES

1. In a corollary case, a United States District Court in California upheld the suspension of high school pupils for ten days for use of profanity and/ or vulgarity appearing in an off campus newspaper "Oink." The more damaging portions of the publication appeared to be a "vulgar retouching of what appears to be a photograph of President Nixon. . . ." Baker v. Downey City Board of Education, 307 F.Supp. 517 (D.Cal.1969).

2. A clear case of disruptive school activities by non-students arose when twelve youths entered the office of the secretary of the school principal and told her "they were going to interrupt us that day," locked the secretary out of her office, moved furniture about, scattered papers, and dumped some books on the floor, all of which resulted in the dismissal of school. The conviction of the defendants was affirmed in State v. Midgett, 8 N.C.App. 230, 174 S.E.2d 124 (1970).

3. Suspension of black students for disrupting a student assembly because the tune "Dixie" was played was upheld by the United States Court of Appeals, Eighth Circuit. The Court said that "On the record we cannot say that the tune 'Dixie' constitutes a badge of slavery or that the playing of the tune under the facts as presented constituted officially sanctioned

racial abuse. Such a ruling would lead to the prohibition of the playing of many of our most famous tunes." Tate v. Board of Education of Jonesboro, Arkansas, 453 F.2d 975 (8th Cir.1972).

4. Students can be temporarily suspended from school for disrupting school by engaging in a sit-in and not attending classes. Gebert v. Hoffman, 336 F.Supp. 694 (E.D.Pa.1972).

5. Symbols and insignia such as the Confederate flag, indicating the desire to maintain a segregated school must be removed. Smith v. St. Tammany Parish School Board, 448 F.2d 414 (5th Cir.1971).

6. The Federal Circuit Courts of Appeals are divided as to whether and under what conditions schools may regulate student hairstyles. The following circuits, Third, Fifth, Sixth, Ninth, Tenth, and Eleventh have upheld school regulation while the First, Second, Fourth, Seventh, and Eighth have ruled that grooming has attendant constitutional rights. In King v. Saddleback, 445 F.2d 932 (9th Cir.1971) the court ruled long hair was not protected by the constitutional right of privacy. The Sixth Circuit in Jackson v. Dorrier, 424 F.2d 213 (6th Cir.1970) cert. denied 400 U.S. 850, 91 S.Ct. 55 (1970) ruled that hair that was a distracting influence could be regulated. In Richards v. Thurston, 424 F.2d 1281 (1st Cir.1970) the court found the students' hair was protected by the Due Process Clause of the Fourteenth Amendment, this Amendment "establishes a sphere of personal liberty. . . ."

7. The case of Ferrell v. Dallas Independent School District, 392 F.2d 697 (1968), involved a suit to enjoin school officials from refusing to enroll male pupils who had failed to comply with a school regulation banning long hair. The United States District Court for the Northern District of Texas denied any injunctive relief and the pupils appealed. The Court of Appeals held that the regulation promulgated by the principal was valid.

8. The Fifth Circuit ruled against three male pupils who refused to shave in compliance with a good grooming rule of their school. The Fifth Circuit noted, with approval, the sentiment of the District Court that "the Court felt somewhat put upon by having to fit a controversy over shaving into an inordinately busy schedule. It was viewed as a problem for school administrators . . .. The entire problem seems miniscule in light of other matters involving the school system . . .." Stevenson v. Board of Education of Wheeler County, Georgia, 426 F.2d 1154 (5th Cir.1970).

9. See Breen v. Kahl, 419 F.2d 1034 (7th Cir.1969), where 7th Circuit held hair regulation unconstitutional.

10. The United States Court of Appeals, Fourth Circuit, in reviewing all the relevant appellate haircut decisions concluded that the state interest may overcome the student's constitutional interest if the evidence supports that the health and safety of the student or students are jeopardized, but the court found that proof that "jest, disgust, and amusement were evoked" by the long hair was insufficient to restrain the students' constitutional interest. In so saying, the court did hold that hair style is a constitutionally protected right, "to be secure in one's person" as

guaranteed by substantive due process. Massie v. Henry, 455 F.2d 779
(4th Cir.1972).

STUDENT PUBLICATIONS

Freedom of the press is a cornerstone of the basic freedoms of the Constitution. In settling the Pentagon papers dispute between the New York Times
and the United States Government, the Supreme Court said:

> In the First Amendment the Founding Fathers gave the free press the
> protection it must have to fulfill its essential role in our democracy. The
> press was to serve the governed, not the governors. The Government's power
> to censor the press was abolished so that the press would remain forever free
> to censure the Government.[28]

While the Supreme Court has not ruled on the subject of restraint of
student publications, the position taken by the court in *Tinker* v. *Des
Moines* [29] suggests that the standard of "reasonable forecast of material and
substantial interference" is a standard that may be applied to freedom of the
press as well as to freedom of speech and expression. In *Dickey* v. *Alabama
State Board of Education* [30] the United States District Court in Alabama
made it clear that First Amendment protections are extended to students
and that the school or university can only restrict those rights through
reasonable regulation.

According to the United States Court of Appeals, Sixth Circuit, however,
the requirement of a showing of "reasonable forecast of material and
substantial" disruption does not mandate that the school officials "delay
action against the inciters until after the riot has started and the buildings
have been taken over and damaged." [31] This court upheld the suspension of
university students for distribution on campus of an underground newspaper
that berated the student body for apathy and urged them to "stand up and
fight" the school administration by seizing campus buildings. The language,
the court held, was "an open exhortation to the students to engage in
disorderly and destructive activity." [32]

Freedom of speech protection does not apply equally to high school
students and adults alike. In determining the extent of its application, the
court may properly consider the age or maturity of those addressed. Therefore, publications may be protected when directed to adults but may not be
appropriate for minors. A different set of judicial standards may validly
apply to prior restraint when exercised at the high school level as opposed to
the college level of education. First Amendment rights of children are not
co-extensive with those of adults.[33]

Restraint of student publications in the absence of reasonable forecast of
disruption, however, is generally not justified. The United States Court of
Appeals, Seventh Circuit, has held that punishment of students was constitutionally unjustifiable where the board of education failed to produce evidence showing imminence of disruption.[34] The Court said:

> We conclude that absent an evidentiary showing, and an appropriate balanc-
> ing of the evidence by the district court to determine whether the Board was
> justified in a "forecast" of the disruption and interference, as required under

Tinker, plaintiffs are entitled to the declaratory judgment, injunctive and damage relief sought.

Public school officials may promulgate student newspaper regulations that prohibit distribution of material that will cause interference with school operation and discipline, but according to *Eisner* v. *Stamford Board of Education,* the school policy cannot be overbroad and unconstitutionally vague and where prior approval is required the policy must prescribe a definite brief period within which review of the submitted material is to be approved and by whom.[35]

*School Newspaper Is Entitled to the
Same First Amendment Protection
Afforded a Public Forum*

GAMBINO v. FAIRFAX COUNTY SCHOOL BOARD

United States District Court, Eastern
District of Virginia, 1977.
429 F.Supp. 731.
United States Court of Appeals,
Fourth Circuit, 1977.
564 F.2d 157.

ALBERT V. BRYAN, Jr., District Judge.

This action was brought to enjoin the defendant from prohibiting the publication of an article entitled "Sexually Active Students Fail to Use Contraception" in *The Farm News,* a newspaper published in the Hayfield Secondary School (Hayfield). . . .

Hayfield is governed by the Fairfax County School Board (the School Board), an agency of the Commonwealth of Virginia. On August 11, 1976, the School Board issued notice 6130 which prohibited the schools from offering sex education until a decision was reached on a proposed program. The article in question here was submitted for publication on November 22, 1976 while the School Board's notice was in effect. Pursuant to a prior agreement regarding potentially controversial material, this article was submitted to the principal, Doris Torrice, for review. Perceiving that portions of the submission containing information on contraceptives, apparently viewed apart from those portions incorporating results obtained from a canvass of Hayfield student attitudes toward birth control, violated notice 6130, she ordered plaintiffs not to publish it as written. Although plaintiffs were given the option of publishing the article with the objectionable passages excised, they chose to insist on printing all or none of the piece.

Ms. Torrice's decision was reviewed and upheld by the Advisory Board on Student Expression . . . .

The action of the Advisory Board was sustained by the Division Superintendent of the Fairfax County Public Schools and by the School Board. A few days before hearing plaintiffs' appeal, the School Board adopted Regulation 6131 approving a sex education program but specifically proscribing birth control as a subject of that program.

As noted above, *The Farm News* is a student activity. Some staff members are enrolled in Journalism and receive academic credit for their work on the paper. Other staff members work on the paper as an extracurricular activity. The paper is written and edited in the school during school hours and at the homes of the participants. Revenues are generated from advertising, allocations by the School Board, sales of individual issues, and student subscriptions. . . . the faculty advisor provided to supervise the paper was paid a salary supplement of $1,225.00. Copies of the newspaper usually are distributed to student subscribers in homeroom.

As the Court views it, this case turns upon one issue—whether *The Farm News* is a publication protected by the First Amendment. The authority of the School Board to determine course content in the school curriculum is not questioned. Nor is there any contention that the content of the article would fall outside the limits of First Amendment freedom if the newspaper otherwise is protected. In fact, upon an actual reading of the article, the Court is surprised at its innocuousness and that it could spawn the controversy at hand. Nevertheless, the defendants have perceived sufficient danger in the publication to warrant judicial resolution of the problem. Defendants also recognize that if the newspaper is found to be a First Amendment forum the regulations pursuant to which this suppression was undertaken are open to serious question. . . .

The defendants rely on the contention that *The Farm News* is not a public forum entitled to First Amendment protection. They argue that the newspaper is essentially an "in-house" organ of the school system, or alternatively that the students in Hayfield are a "captive audience," rendering the publication subject to reasonable regulation.

While the state may have a particular proprietary interest in a publication that legitimately precludes it from being a vehicle for First Amendment expression, it may not foreclose constitutional scrutiny by mere labelling. Once a publication is determined to be in substance a free speech forum, constitutional protections attach and the state may restrict the content of that instrument only in accordance with First Amendment dictates.

The extent of state involvement in providing funding and facilities for *The Farm News* does not determine whether First Amendment rights are applicable. The language of *Antonelli* v. *Hammond* is persuasive.

> We are well beyond the belief that any manner of state regulation is permissible simply because it involves an activity which is a part of the university structure and is financed with funds controlled by the administration. The state is not necessarily the unrestrained master of what it creates and fosters.

The defendants urge that this principle is inapposite because . . . decisions have arisen out of the college environment. They point out, and the Court does not dispute, that the "First Amendment rights of children are not 'co-extensive with those of adults.' " Further, the defendants assert the illogic of applying the First Amendment to a high school newspaper, conjuring up visions of irresponsible and uncontrollable publication.

There are, however, two distinctions that invalidate these objections. While the scope of constitutional freedom may vary with the nature of the environment and the maturity of the individuals affected, the considerations governing the applicability of First Amendment analysis in the first instance do not change. Either the First Amendment is operative, or it is not. And if it is applicable, only then does the distinction between the *extent* to which speech is protected in colleges and in high schools become significant.

Defendants' fears of irresponsible journalism are met first by the fact that no evidence of it has surfaced in the past or in the article here in question, nor has there been any demonstrated likelihood of it in the future. More significantly, defendants have failed to appreciate the very real distinction between what a private citizen and the state constitutionally may do with regard to limiting otherwise protected speech. The First Amendment mandate is directed toward state action, not private. As no contention has been made that the student editorial board of *The Farm News* acts as an agent of the state, the argument that the newspaper is powerless to control the content of its own publication is without merit. Irresponsible journalism may occur at some point in the future, but speculation is not a proper consideration in the decision of the case presently before the Court.

Turning to the substantive question of whether *The Farm News* was established as a vehicle for expression, the Court finds . . . that this instrument was conceived, established, and operated as a conduit for student expression on a wide variety of topics. It falls clearly within the parameters of the First Amendment.

The defendants have suggested, however, that the circumstances under which the newspaper is produced require an application of the "captive audience" principle, . . . application of the "captive audience" concept appears untenable.

The defendants have asserted, however, that the subscription tie-in with the yearbook, the distribution in home rooms, the official status of the newspaper, and peer pressure, coupled with mandatory attendance all combine to compel the student body's exposure to the contents of *The Farm News*. The Court is not persuaded . . . . No substantive distinction can be drawn betweeen the relative lack of choice in exposure to the communication in this case and that in *Tinker*. If anything, the students of Hayfield are less captive because they must act affirmatively to pick up the newspaper. In *Tinker* the non-protesting students were required to avert their eyes to avoid the message.

Katz v. *McAulay*, 438 F.2d 1058 (2d Cir.1971), cert. denied, 405 U.S. 933, 92 S.Ct. 930, 30 L.Ed.2d 809 (1972), which the defendants cite as an application of the captive audience principle to the high school milieu, is not to the contrary. There the court was considering an interlocutory appeal from a denial of a preliminary injunction. The rules under which the school authorities acted appeared sufficiently precise to render plaintiffs' probability of success short of the threshold beyond which denial of a preliminary injunction becomes an abuse of discretion. The significance of the captive nature of the student audience to the Court was its tendency to amplify conduct to a level of material and substantial disruption. The Court did not hold, nor could it have held consistent with *Tinker*, that First Amendment rights in the school were extinguished by the mere fact of compulsory attendance.

Finally defendants argue that to allow the students to publish this article would permit them to override the decision of the School Board not to include birth control in the sex education curriculum. As noted above, the Court does not question the authority of the School Board to prescribe course content. Further, while even under principles of liberal construction a considerable effort is required to find the questioned portions of the article instructional, the Court assumes that the article does contain information which, if it appeared in material used in a sex education course, would contravene the School Board's policy.

A corollary of the finding that *The Farm News* was established as a vehicle for First Amendment expression and not as an official publication is that the newspaper cannot be construed objectively as an integral part of the curriculum offered at Hayfield. . . . Rather, it occupies a position more akin to the school library where more extensive and explicit information on birth control philosophy and methodology is available. In either place, the material is not suppressible by reason of its objectionability to the sensibilities of the School Board or its constituents. . . . Therefore, because the newspaper is not in reality a part of the curriculum of the school, and because it is entitled to First Amendment protection, the power of the School Board to regulate course content will not support its action in this case.

Having determined that *The Farm News* is entitled to the First Amendment protection afforded a public forum, that the circumstances at Hayfield do not justify application of the "captive audience" theory, and that publication of the proposed article cannot be suppressed solely because its subject matter does not accord with the School Board's notion of appropriate course content, the Court finds that the application of the regulations under which the defendants acted in this instance was constitutionally invalid. The RR–SSS [Rights and Responsibilities—Secondary School Students] lacks the detailed criteria required by the line of Fourth Circuit decisions defining the permissible regulation of protected speech in high schools. . . . The Court declines, however, to declare the regulations facially invalid and limits its holding solely to the application of those regulations to prohibit publication in *The Farm News* of any portion of the article "Sexually Active Students Fail to Use Contraception."

Accordingly the plaintiffs are entitled to an injunction prohibiting the defendants, or those acting in concert with them, from banning the publication in *The Farm News* of those portions of the article which were found objectionable.

It is so ordered.

PER CURIAM:

The Fairfax County School Board appeals the district court's order enjoining it from banning the publication of portions of an article about birth control in a school newspaper, *The Farm News.* The Board's major contentions are that (1) the first amendment does not apply to *The Farm News* because it is an in-house organ of the school system, funded and sponsored by the Board, and therefore cannot be viewed as a public forum; (2) the school's students are a captive audience because the newspaper is solicited for and distributed during school hours, and students cannot avoid exposure to the controverted article—therefore the public forum doctrine does not apply; and (3) even if the newspaper itself is subject to the first amendment protection, the article is not protected because its publication would undermine a valid school policy which prohibits the teaching of birth control as part of the curriculum.

Upon considering the Board's general policy toward student publications, as well as past articles in *The Farm News,* the district court found that the newspaper was established as a public forum for student expression, and therefore is subject to First Amendment protection. It also concluded that the students are not a captive audience merely because of their compulsory attendance at the school. Finally, the court concluded that because the newspaper was established as a public forum and not as an official publication, it cannot be viewed as part of the curriculum; accordingly, the general power of the Board to regulate course content does not apply.

Because we conclude that the district court's findings are substantially supported by both the evidence and the law, we affirm for the reasons stated in its opinion.

Affirmed.

School Officials May Prohibit
Distribution of Underground
Newspaper on School Grounds If
Health and Safety of Students
Are Endangered

WILLIAMS v. SPENCER

United States Court of Appeals,
Fourth Circuit, 1980.
622 F.2d 1200.

WIDENER, Circuit Judge. . . .

During the 1976–77 school term, the plaintiffs published and distributed the first issue of the *Joint Effort,* a self-styled underground newspaper designed as an alternative for student expression. This issue was distributed on school grounds with the express permission of the principal.

Following the success of that first issue, the plaintiffs published a second issue of the paper the following school year. The second issue contained various literary contributions, cartoons, and advertisements.

The plaintiffs printed approximately 350 copies of the *Joint Effort,* and acquired advance approval of the school officials for the distribution of the paper on February 17, 1978. The plaintiffs were not, however, required to seek prepublication or predistribution approval of the contents of the publication. In fact, the school officials were not even aware of the contents of the publication prior to the commencement of distribution.

Ten to twenty minutes after the sale of the paper began, the building monitor, Mr. Austin Patterson, halted the sale of the paper, confiscated the remaining copies, and took them to the school principal, Dr. Thomas P. Marshall. Patterson was the subject of a cartoon on the back cover of the paper that depicted him in cowboy clothing and speaking in dialect. The students had distributed approximately eighty copies of the paper before the distribution was halted.

Marshall upheld Patterson's seizure of the paper and banned any further distribution of Issue 2 on school property. The principal did, however, return the confiscated papers to the plaintiffs at the conclusion of the same day on which the papers were confiscated. The ban on distribution applied only to distribution on school property.

As required by the Student Rights and Responsibilities Policy, the school principal, within two school days of halting distribution, stated in writing his reasons for the action. In his letter, Marshall stated:

1. A copy of the *Joint Effort* was reviewed and the publication was found to be in violation of Section 4C, titled "Publications." A member of the staff was depicted in derogatory terms with clear indications of racial overtones.

2. A second violation occurs in the promotion of drug paraphernalia. This is a violation of Section 2–C(c)(5), which prohibits the distribution of material which encourages actions which endanger the health and safety of students.

The first reason referred to the cartoon depicting the building monitor in western clothing. The second reason for halting the distribution of the *Joint Effort* referred to an advertisement for the Earthworks Headshop, a store that specializes in the sale of drug paraphernalia. The advertisement primarily promoted the sale of a waterpipe used to smoke marijuana and hashish. The ad also advertised paraphernalia used in connection with cocaine.

Following the principal's decision to ban any further distribution of that issue of the *Joint Effort,* the students followed the appeals procedure provided . . . . The students first appealed to the area assistant superintendent, Dr. George B. Thomas, and obtained an informal hearing on March 15, 1978. In an undated memorandum . . . Thomas upheld the decision of the principal.

The students then appealed to the superintendent of schools, Dr. Charles M. Bernardo, who rendered his decision in writing on April 14, 1978. . . . Bernardo supported the decision of the principal and upheld the ban on further distribution on school property of that issue of the *Joint Effort*. The superintendent expressly noted that the ban did not apply to any future issue of the publication that did not violate the guidelines.

Following their unsuccessful administrative appeals, the students filed this suit against members of the school board, the superintendent, the area assistant superintendent, the principal, and the building monitor. The plaintiffs claimed that the seizure and continued restraint against distribution of the *Joint Effort* violated their First Amendment rights, and that the school system's regulatory scheme was facially invalid. The students sought damages for the restraint on distribution of the *Joint Effort,* and declaratory relief and an injunction to prohibit the school officials from further preventing its distribution. Additionally, the plaintiffs sought to enjoin the enforcement of the publication guidelines of Montgomery County.

Regarding the alleged First Amendment violation from the prohibition against distribution, the district court considered only whether the presence of the advertisement for the head shop provided the school with the right to halt the distribution of the *Joint Effort*, and held that the school was justified in halting and prohibiting further distribution of the paper. As to the alleged facial invalidity of the guidelines, the court held that the health and safety regulation was not so vague as to violate First Amendment standards, and that the time involved in the school administrative appeal procedure was not unconstitutional. . . . We must determine whether the school officials violated the plaintiffs' First Amendment rights when the copies of the *Joint Effort* were seized and distribution on school property prohibited. The question is whether the publication guidelines involved in the stoppage of distribution and subsequent administrative appeal violate the First Amendment.

While secondary school students do not "shed their constitutional rights to freedom of speech or expression at the schoolhouse gate" . . . neither are their First Amendment rights necessarily "co-extensive with those of adults." . . . "It is generally held that the constitutional right to free speech of public secondary school students may be modified or curtailed by school regulations 'reasonably designed to adjust these rights to the needs of the school environment.' "

In this case . . . "Distribution may be halted, and disciplinary action taken by the principal after the distribution has begun, if the publication: . . . Encourages actions which endanger the health or safety of students." The school principal, under this regulation, halted and prohibited the further distribution of the student publication that contained an advertisement for drug paraphernalia.

Plaintiffs challenge this regulation as being impermissibly vague and thus violative of the First Amendment. We disagree. In *Baughman* v. *Freienmuth*, we held that a prior restraint regulation "must contain precise criteria sufficiently spelling out what is forbidden so that a reasonably intelligent student will know what he may write and what he may not write." We find no merit to the argument that a reasonably intelligent high school student would not know that an advertisement promoting the sale of drug paraphernalia encourages actions that endanger the health or safety of students. The district court took judicial notice of the problem of drugs in today's society and their danger to the health and safety of those who use them. We find no error in that determination by the district court. Because of the infinite variety of materials that might be found to encourage actions which endanger the health or safety of students, we conclude that the regulation describes as explicitly as is required the type of material of which the principal may halt distribution. . . . The First Amendment rights of the students must yield to the superior interest of the school in seeing that materials that encourage actions which endanger the health or safety of students are not distributed on school property. Because the only type of material regulated by the guideline is material that must yield to the school's superior interest, we think the guideline does not prohibit constitutionally protected conduct of the students. Thus, the guideline is not unconstitutional on its face.

Nor can it be disputed that an advertisement encouraging the use of drugs encourages actions which in fact endanger the health or safety of students. The district court took judicial notice of this, and we agree with

that determination. Indeed, the plaintiffs themselves as much as concede
that drug use is a harmful activity endangering health and safety.

We also find no merit to the argument of plaintiffs that the school
officials had to demonstrate that the material would substantially disrupt
school activities. We note that the Supreme Court in *Tinker* v. *Des Moines
Independent Community School District,* and this court in *Quarterman,
Baughman,* and *Nitzberg* v. *Parks,* indicated that "school authorities may by
appropriate regulation, exercise prior restraint upon publications distributed
on school premises during school hours in those special circumstances where
they can 'reasonably "forecast substantial disruption . . ."' on account of
such printed material." Such disruption, however, is merely one justification for school authorities to restrain the distribution of a publication;
nowhere has it been held to be the sole justification. . . .

We hold therefore that the regulation which allows the principal to halt
the distribution of materials that encourage "actions which endanger the
health or safety of students" is not violative of the First Amendment. The
school officials thus acted within their constitutional authority in halting
and banning the further distribution of the *Joint Effort* on school property.

Plaintiffs also claim that the appeals procedure fails to meet minimum
constitutional guarantees, alleging that the length of the appeal in this
instance was excessive. We find no merit to that contention. . . if the
principal decides to halt distribution of a non-school sponsored publication,
he shall state his reasons in writing within two school days and provide the
students with a copy of his reasons. . . . The aggrieved student may,
within ten school days, appeal the decision to the area assistant superintendent who must issue a written decision within ten school days after receiving
the appeal. If the student requests an informal hearing, the hearing must
be held within ten school days, and the assistant superintendent then must
render his decision within five school days of the hearing. The student may
then appeal an adverse decision to the superintendent of schools who must
render his decision in writing within five school days. The guidelines do not
provide for an appeal to the School Board. The record in this case indicates
that only eight weeks, including holidays, elapsed from the time the distribution was first halted until the superintendent rendered his decision.

We hold that the appeals procedure provided for meets the requirement
of this court that there be an "adequate and prompt appeals procedure."
First, the time limits are on their face quite reasonable, two days for the
principal to state reasons, and ten days for the area assistant superintendent
(five if after a hearing), and five days for the superintendent to decide. Ten
day limits to appeal decisions of the principal and assistant superintendent
discourage delay. Nor was the duration of the administrative appeal in this
case unduly long. There is no indication that there was any undue delay in
handing down the various decisions required. Also, the record does not
disclose what portion of the eight week period was expended by plaintiffs in
exercising the various appeals. And we again emphasize that the students
were not required to submit a copy of the publication for prior approval, and
they were free to distribute the papers off school property the same day
distribution on school property was halted, thus lessening the impact from

the duration of the administrative appeals process. Therefore, we find no infirmity in the length of the appeals process.

In deciding this case, although there was no prior restraint in the sense of previous approval of content of the printed matter, we have, to give the plaintiffs the benefit of the doubt, considered that the regulations complained of come with a presumption of invalidity, although, without deciding the question, it may be doubtful that such heavy burden should exist on the facts of this case. In all events, we are of opinion any such burden to establish validity as may exist has been successfully borne by defendants.

Were injunctive relief all that plaintiffs prayed for, we would remand for the dismissal of those claims as moot. Because we decide the substantive merits of the controversy, however, without considering the availability of injunctive relief because the question is moot, and, of course, not deciding that question, we simply affirm the order of the district court appealed from which entered judgment for the defendants.

Affirmed.

NOTES

1. The United States Court of Appeals for the Fourth Circuit has provided propositions of law that must be followed in order for a school's prior restraint regulation to be constitutionally valid. These are:

   a. Secondary school children are within the protection of the First Amendment, although their rights are not coextensive with those of adults.
   b. Secondary school authorities may exercise reasonable prior restraint upon the exercise of students' First Amendment rights.
   c. Such prior restraints must contain precise criteria sufficiently spelling out what is forbidden so that a reasonably intelligent student will know what he may write and what he may not write.
   d. A prior restraint system, even though precisely defining what may not be written, is nevertheless invalid unless it provides for:
      1. A definition of "Distribution" and its application to different kinds of material;
      2. Prompt approval or disapproval of what is submitted;
      3. Specification of the effect of failure to act promptly; and
      4. An adequate and prompt appeals procedure.

   Baughman v. Freienmuth, 478 F.2d 1345 (4th Cir.1973).

2. A few "earthy words" relating to bodily functions and sexual intercourse are not obscene in the legal sense. Jacobs v. Board of School Commissioners, 490 F.2d 601 (1973), cert. granted 417 U.S. 929, 94 S.Ct. 2638. The Supreme Court limited the scope of the obscenity exception of First Amendment protection to: "works which depict or describe sexual conduct" and which, taken as a whole, appeal to the prurient interest in sex, which portray sexual conduct in a patently offensive way, and which, taken as a whole, do not have serious literary, artistic, political, or scientific value. Miller v. California, 413 U.S. 15, 93 S.Ct. 2607 (1973).

3. First Amendment protection does not prohibit a school's regulation of student's off-campus sale of underground newspaper where prior submission rule was the product of an extensive and good faith effort to formulate a valid student conduct code. Sullivan v. Houston Independent School District, 475 F.2d 1071 (5th Cir.1973), rehearing denied 475 F.2d 1404 (5th Cir.1973), cert. denied 414 U.S. 1032, 94 S.Ct. 461 (1973).

4. The United States Court of Appeals for the Seventh Circuit held that school board provisos between two distributions of literature were invalid and that occasional presence of "earthy" words in an unofficial student newspaper did not render their newspaper obscene. See Jacobs v. Board of School Commissioners, 490 F.2d 601 (7th Cir.1973).

5. In Trachtman v. Anker, the U.S. Court of Appeals for the 2nd Circuit held that the school could prevent a sex survey being distributed to students for the purpose of gathering information about attitudes, knowledge and preferences toward sex. The Court agreed with the school board the survey could cause psychological damage. 563 F.2d 512 (2d Cir. 1977).

SEARCH AND SEIZURE

The Fourth Amendment of the United States Constitution provides: "The right of people to be secure in their persons, houses, papers, and effects, against unreasonable searches and seizures shall not be violated, and no warrants shall issue, but upon probable cause . . .."

To search or not to search a pupil's desk, locker, pockets, purses, book-bags, coats, shoes, and socks and his automobile is a question frequently confronting school administrators. Oftentimes, the issue must be decided forthwith because of the gravity of the situation—bomb threats, dangerous weapons, illegal drugs—which could result in serious injury to school pupils.[36]

The issue of search and seizure in the public schools balances primarily on whether or not the court views the school teacher or administrator as a parent or a police officer. To assume that the school administrator or teacher represents the state and seeks to obtain seized goods for purposes of criminal prosecution would require a warrant.

On January 15, 1985, the Supreme Court of the United States, in New Jersey v. T.L.O., held that the Fourth Amendment applies to schools and that searches in schools must be based on "reasonable suspicion." The Court rejected the argument of the plaintiff that school officials should be required to have "probable cause" and obtain warrants to search students. In differentiating between searches by school officials and police officers or other public officials, the Court pointed out that in balancing the interests, substantial weight must be given to the importance of maintaining discipline in the classroom and on school grounds. Justice White, writing for the majority, held that the legality of the search should depend "simply on the reasonableness, under all circumstances, of the search."[37]

The opinion of the Supreme Court in T.L.O. reflected the prevailing view of lower court decisions rendered during the last several years as school authorities sought to stem the use and possession of drugs in the schools.

A New York court was also restrictive in its application of *in loco parentis*, holding that the student had constitutional rights against illegal search and seizure and this right had to be weighed against the school authorities' power of *in loco parentis*.[38] Without unlimited right to search, school authorities can search only if they have "reasonable suspicion" that something of an illegal nature is in the possession of a student. The court commented that *in loco parentis* could not stand alone without reasonable suspicion, saying:

> a school teacher, to a limited extent at least, stands *in loco parentis* to pupils under his charge. . . .
> The *in loco parentis* doctrine is so compelling in light of public necessity and as a social concept antedating the Fourth Amendment, that any action, including a search, taken thereunder upon *reasonable suspicion* should be accepted as necessary and reasonable. (emphasis added)

In reaching a similar conclusion, a Delaware court held that a vice-principal's search of a student's jacket did not violate the Constitution since the vice-principal stood *in loco parentis*.[39] But the court was careful to point out that the search, as in T.L.O., was accompanied by a reasonable suspicion that contraband was secreted in the student's pockets. This court rejected the argument that a principal was a private individual, to whom search and seizure prohibitions do not apply, and concluded that his actions were those of a state official. For a state official to conduct a search without a warrant in the absence of the power of *in loco parentis* or other extenuating circumstances would, of course, offend the Constitution.

Although the standard of "reasonable suspicion" is a lower standard than that of the "probable cause" required for police to obtain a warrant, it is not so unrestrictive as to place no restraint on school personnel.[40] A New York court held that school personnel conducting a strip search of fifth-grade students after classroom thefts violated the children's Fourth Amendment rights because there were no acts that allowed school officials to particularize which student might have actually taken the money. The court maintained that there must be some available facts that together provide reasonable grounds to search and the search must be conducted in order to further a legitimate school purpose, such as the maintenance of discipline in the school.

A student's freedom from unreasonable search and seizure must be balanced against the need for school officials to maintain order and discipline and to protect the health and welfare of all the students. Where an assistant principal threatened to call a student's parents, forcing the student to reluctantly, but voluntarily, empty his pockets producing a pipe and marijuana, the court held that such a search was legitimate. Where the scope of intrusion is slight and there is no police involvement, school officials are held only to a "reasonable cause to believe" standard.[41]

With regard to searching school lockers, the Supreme Court of Kansas [42] has held that the student does not have exclusive possession of the school locker against the school and its officials. The school locker does not possess the same attributes of sole possession that is found in one's dwelling, motor vehicle, or private locker.

The Kansas court was careful to indicate that the locker was opened on the principal's "own judgment" even though requested to do so by police. The court appeared to imply that the school principal must instigate the search of his own volition with reasonable suspicion on behalf of the school. But without the intervention of the principal, the police cannot search the locker for the primary purpose of obtaining evidence for criminal prosecution.

It may be permissible for a school principal to search a student's car if he has reason to believe that something harmful to students is hidden there.[43] A federal district court's decision in Maine held constitutional a search of a "corpsman" bag at a Job Corp Center, producing marijuana. The search was conducted without a warrant and not incident to arrest. The search, according to the court, was a constitutional exercise of the administrator's authority "to maintain proper standards of conduct and discipline at the Center. . . . Quite plainly the investigation was conducted solely for the purpose of ensuring proper moral and disciplinary conditions of the Center, an obligation mandated by federal statute."[44]

A warrantless search of a student's automobile by police officers violates the Fourth Amendment if the police officers received information in sufficient time to obtain a warrant and there is no danger that the goods will be removed or transported away.[45]

Canine Searches

In recent years, because of the use of drugs in public schools, officials have used dogs to sniff out contraband. These canine searches have been viewed by the courts with mixed reactions.

The Tenth Circuit Court of Appeals in *Zamora* v. *Pomeroy*[46] upheld the use of dogs in the exploratory sniffing of lockers. The court noted that since the schools gave notice at the beginning of the year that the lockers might be periodically opened, the lockers were jointly possessed by both student and school. The court further stated that since the school officials had a duty to maintain a proper educational environment it was necessary for them to inspect lockers, and, even though there might be a slight Fourth Amendment infringement, it was not significant.

The Seventh Circuit Court in *Doe* v. *Renfrow*[47] held that school officials stood *in loco parentis* and had a right to use dogs to seek out drugs, especially because of the diminished expectations of privacy inherent in the public schools. School officials had a duty to maintain an educational environment that was conducive to learning. This decision may be contrary to New Jersey v. T.L.O. in which the Supreme Court expressly limited the application of *in loco parentis*.

In a federal district court case *Jones* v. *Latexo Independent School District*[48] the decision was different from that in *Doe* and *Zamora*. The school district in *Jones* used dogs to sniff both students and automobiles.

The court ruled, in the absence of individual suspicion, that the sniffing of the students was too intrusive and not reasonable. Since the students did not have access to their automobiles during the school day, the school's interest in sniffing the cars was minimal, and therefore also unreasonable.

In *Horton* v. *Goose Creek Independent School District* [49] the court stated, "The problem presented in this case is convergence of two troubling questions. First, is the sniff of a drug-detecting dog a 'search' within the purview of the Fourth Amendment? Second, to what extent does the Fourth Amendment protect students against searches by school administrators seeking to maintain a safe environment conducive to education?"[50] In response to the first question the court stated, "We accordingly hold that the sniff of the lockers and cars did not constitute a search and, therefore, we need make no inquiry into the reasonableness of the sniffing of the lockers and automobiles."[51] Concerning the second question the court ruled that school officials may search students if they have "reasonable cause" but "the instrusion on dignity and personal security that goes with the type of canine inspection of the student's person involved in this case cannot be justified by the need to prevent abuse of drugs and alcohol when there is no individualized suspicion; and we hold it unconstitutional."[52]

Strip Searches

The courts have allowed school officials to search students if they have reasonable suspicion that the student is in possession of something that is illegal, against school regulation, or may be harmful to the health and safety of other students. But the courts have determined that the reasonable suspicion standard does not always apply when a strip search is conducted. As one court stated, "We are also of the view that as the intrusiveness of the search intensifies, the standard of Fourth Amendment 'reasonableness' approaches probable cause, even in the school context. Thus, when a teacher conducts a highly intrusive invasion such as a strip search in this case, it is reasonable to require that probable cause be present."[53] In *Bellnier* v. *Lund,*[54] the court ruled that a teacher who strip searched the class trying to locate a missing three dollars violated the Fourth Amendment. However, in *Bellnier* the court noted that the relative slight danger of the missing money had to be considered and if something more dangerous were present, it might be different. In *Rone* [55] school officials were specific in knowing the facts surrounding the student's drug activity before searching. In *Renfrow* school officials used dogs "unsupported by particularized facts, reasonable suspicion, or probable cause" [56] to detect drug odors and then strip searched a student.

Here the court said:

> It does not require a constitutional scholar to conclude that a nude search of a thirteen-year-old child is an invasion of constitutional rights of some magnitude. More than that: It is a violation of any known principal of human decency. Apart from any constitutional readings and rulings, simple common sense would indicate that the conduct of the school officials in permitting such a nude search was not only unlawful but outrageous under settled indisputable principles of law.[57]

Exclusionary Rule

School officials should be concerned with removing contraband from the school environment for the betterment of other students and not for use in the criminal prosecution of students. Because materials frequently seized in public schools are illegal and turned over to law enforcement officials, the Exclusionary Rule has been frequently raised. Can illegal materials seized by school officials be used in criminal prosecutions?

In 1914, in *Weeks* v. *United States* [58] the Supreme Court established that evidence, in this instance lottery tickets, private letters, and papers, seized without a warrant could not be used in federal courts for federal prosecution. This doctrine, the *Weeks Doctrine,* thereafter excluded evidence obtained illegally by federal officials from use in federal trials.

In *Wolf* v. *People of the State of Colorado,* 1949 [59] the question arose concerning the issue of whether materials illegally seized could be used in state courts. The question was:

> Does a conviction by a state court for a state offense deny the "due process of law" required by the Fourteenth Amendment, solely because evidence that was admitted at the trial was obtained under circumstances which would have rendered it inadmissible in a prosecution for violation of a federal law in a court of the United States because there deemed to be an infraction of the Fourth Amendment as applied in *Weeks* v. *United States.* . . . [60]

The court reasoned that the *Weeks Doctrine* did not apply to states because other remedies could be used to negate arbitrary police actions in conducting illegal searches.[61]

In *Mapp* v. *Ohio* in 1961 [62] the Supreme Court reversed the *Wolf Doctrine* and expanded the *Weeks Doctrine* or Exclusionary Rule to ban illegally seized evidence in state courts. This extension of the Exclusionary Rule has been litigated numerous times in public education cases. The courts generally have allowed materials seized by school officials to be used in a criminal prosecution. Therefore the Exclusionary Rule has not been applied.

School Officials May Be Obligated to
Inspect School Lockers

PEOPLE v. OVERTON

Court of Appeals of New York, 1967.
20 N.Y.2d 360, 283 N.Y.S.2d 22, 229
N.E.2d 596, affirmed on reargument 24
N.Y.2d 522, 301 N.Y.S.2d 479,
249 N.E.2d 366 (1969).

KEATING, Judge. Three detectives of the Mount Vernon Police Department having obtained a search warrant went to the Mount Vernon High School. The warrant directed a search of the persons of two students and, also, of their lockers.

The detectives presented the warrant to the vice-principal, Dr. Panitz, who sent for the two students, one of whom was the defendant, Carlos Overton. The detectives searched them and found nothing. A subsequent search of Overton's locker, however, revealed four marijuana cigarettes.

The defendant moved to invalidate that portion of the search warrant which directed a search of his locker, on the ground that the papers were defective upon which it was based. This motion was granted. The court denied the motion to suppress, however, on the grounds that the vice-principal had consented to the search and that he had a right to do so. The Appellate Term reversed and dismissed the information, holding that the consent of the vice-principal could not justify an otherwise illegal search. The People have appealed from this order of the Appellate Term.

It is axiomatic that the protection of the Fourth Amendment is not restricted to dwellings. A depository such as a locker or even a desk is safeguarded from unreasonable searches for evidence of a crime (*United States* v. *Blok,* 88 U.S.App.D.C. 326, 188 F.2d 1019).

There are situations, however, where someone other than the defendant in possession of a depository may consent to what otherwise would have been an illegal search. Such a case was *United States* v. *Botsch,* 364 F.2d 542 [2d Cir. 1966], cert. den. 386 U.S. 937, 87 S.Ct. 959, 17 L.Ed.2d 810. In that case, the defendant had rented a shed from one Stein. Stein retained a key to the shed and accepted deliveries on behalf of the defendant. When the police approached Stein and informed him of their suspicion that the defendant was receiving goods obtained through fraud, Stein consented to a search of the shed.

In upholding the search, the court noted two significant factors. First, Stein had a key to the shed and, second, more than a mere landlord-tenant relationship existed, since Stein was empowered to take deliveries on behalf of the defendant. The court also noted that Stein had a right to exculpate himself from implication in the defendant's scheme.

Considering all these factors cumulatively, the court concluded that, in this situation, Stein could give consent to the search. Thus, the search was not unreasonable in contravention of the Fourth Amendment.

Dr. Panitz, in this case, gave his consent to the search of Overton's locker. The dissenting opinion suggests, however, that Dr. Panitz' consent was not freely given, because he acted under compulsion of the invalid search warrant. If this were the case, his consent might be rendered somewhat questionable. However, Dr. Panitz testified that: "Being responsible for the order, assignment, and maintenance of the physical facilities, if *any* report were given to me by *anyone* of an article or item of the nature that does not belong there, or of an illegal nature, I would inspect the locker." (Italics supplied.)

This testimony demonstrates beyond doubt that Dr. Panitz would have consented as he did regardless of the presence of the invalid search warrant.

The power of Dr. Panitz to give his consent to this search arises out of the distinct relationship between school authorities and students.

The school authorities have an obligation to maintain discipline over the students. It is recognized that when large numbers of teenagers are gathered together in such an environment, their inexperience and lack of mature judgment can often create hazards to each other. Parents, who surrender their children to this type of environment, in order that they may continue developing both intellectually and socially, have a right to expect certain safeguards.

It is in the high school years particularly that parents are justifiably concerned that their children not become accustomed to antisocial behavior, such as the use of illegal drugs. The susceptibility to suggestion of students of high school age increases the danger. Thus, it is the affirmative obligation of the school authorities to investigate any charge that a student is using or possessing narcotics and to take appropriate steps, if the charge is substantiated.

When Overton was assigned his locker, he, like all the other students at Mount Vernon High School, gave the combination to his home room teacher who, in turn, returned it to an office where it was kept on file. The students at Mount Vernon are well aware that the school authorities possess the combinations of their lockers. It appears understood that the lock and the combination are provided in order that each student may have exclusive possession of the locker vis-à-vis other students, but the student does not have such exclusivity over the locker as against the school authorities. In fact, the school issues regulations regarding what may and may not be kept in the lockers and presumably can spot check to insure compliance. The vice-principal testified that he had, on occasion, inspected the lockers of students.

Indeed, it is doubtful if a school would be properly discharging its duty of supervision over the students, if it failed to retain control over the lockers. Not only have the school authorities a right to inspect but this right becomes a duty when suspicion arises that something of an illegal nature may be secreted there. When Dr. Panitz learned of the detectives' suspicion, he was obligated to inspect the locker. This interest, together with the nonexclusive nature of the locker, empowered him to consent to the search by the officers.

Accordingly, the order of the Appellate Term should be reversed and the matter remitted to that court for consideration of the other points raised by the defendant which were not decided on the prior appeal. . . .

*Search of Students By School
Officials Is Constitutionally
Permissible if Reasonable and Not
Excessively Intrusive*

NEW JERSEY v. T. L. O.

Supreme Court of the United States, 1985.
No. 83–712, ___ U.S. ___, 105 S.Ct. 733.

JUSTICE WHITE delivered the opinion of the Court.

We granted certiorari in this case to examine the appropriateness of the exclusionary rule as a remedy for searches carried out in violation of the Fourth Amendment by public school authorities. Our consideration of the proper application of the Fourth Amendment to the public schools, however, has led us to conclude that the search that gave rise to the case now before us did not violate the Fourth Amendment. Accordingly, we here address only the questions of the proper standard for assessing the legality of searches conducted by public school officials and the application of that standard to the facts of this case.

On March 7, 1980, a teacher at Piscataway High School in Middlesex County, N.J., discovered two girls smoking in a lavatory. One of the two girls was the respondent T. L. O., who at that time was a 14-year-old high school freshman. Because smoking in the lavatory was a violation of a school rule, the teacher took the two girls to the Principal's office, where they met with Assistant Vice Principal Theodore Choplick. In response to questioning by Mr. Choplick, T. L. O.'s companion admitted that she had violated the rule. T. L. O., however, denied that she had been smoking in the lavatory and claimed that she did not smoke at all.

Mr. Choplick asked T. L. O. to come into his private office and demanded to see her purse. Opening the purse, he found a pack of cigarettes, which he removed from the purse and held before T. L. O. as he accused her of having lied to him. As he reached into the purse for the cigarettes, Mr. Choplick also noticed a package of cigarette rolling papers. In his experience, possession of rolling papers by high school students was closely associated with the use of marihuana. Suspecting that a closer examination of the purse might yield further evidence of drug use, Mr. Choplick proceeded to search the purse thoroughly. The search revealed a small amount of marihuana, a pipe, a number of empty plastic bags, a substantial quantity of money in one-dollar bills, an index card that appeared to be a list of students who owed T. L. O. money, and two letters that implicated T. L. O. in marihuana dealing.

Mr. Choplick notified T. L. O.'s mother and the police, and turned the evidence of drug dealing over to the police. At the request of the police, T. L. O.'s mother took her daughter to police headquarters, where T. L. O. confessed that she had been selling marihuana at the high school. On the basis of the confession and the evidence seized by Mr. Choplick, the State brought delinquency charges against T. L. O. in the Juvenile and Domestic Relations Court of Middlesex County. Contending that Mr. Choplick's search of her purse violated the Fourth Amendment, T. L. O. moved to suppress the evidence found in her purse as well as her confession, which, she argued, was tainted by the allegedly unlawful search. . . .

The New Jersey Supreme Court agreed with the lower courts that the Fourth Amendment applies to searches conducted by school officials. The court also rejected the State of New Jersey's argument that the exclusionary rule should not be employed to prevent the use in juvenile proceedings of evidence unlawfully seized by school officials. Declining to consider whether applying the rule to the fruits of searches by school officials would have any deterrent value, the court held simply that the precedents of this Court establish that "if an official search violates constitutional rights, the evidence is not admissible in criminal proceedings."

With respect to the question of the legality of the search before it, the court agreed with the Juvenile Court that a warrantless search by a school official does not violate the Fourth Amendment so long as the official "has reasonable grounds to believe that a student possesses evidence of illegal activity or activity that would interfere with school discipline and order." However, the court, with two justices dissenting, sharply disagreed with the Juvenile Court's conclusion that the search of the purse was reasonable. According to the majority, the contents of T. L. O.'s purse had no bearing on the accusation against T. L. O., for possession of cigarettes (as opposed to smoking them in the lavatory) did not violate school rules, and a mere desire for evidence that would impeach T. L. O.'s claim that she did not smoke cigarettes could not justify the search. Moreover, even if a reasonable suspicion that T. L. O. had cigarettes in her purse would justify a search, Mr. Choplick had no such suspicion, as no one had furnished him with any specific information that there were cigarettes in the purse. Finally, leaving aside the question whether Mr. Choplick was justified in opening the purse, the court held that the evidence of drug use that he saw inside did not justify the extensive "rummaging" through T. L. O.'s papers and effects that followed.

In determining whether the search at issue in this case violated the Fourth Amendment, we are faced initially with the question whether that Amendment's prohibition on unreasonable searches and seizures applies to searches conducted by public school officials. We hold that it does.

It is now beyond dispute that "the Federal Constitution, by virtue of the Fourteenth Amendment, prohibits unreasonable searches and seizures by state officers." Equally indisputable is the proposition that the Fourteenth Amendment protects the rights of students against encroachment by public school officials:

> "The Fourteenth Amendment, as now applied to the States, protects the citizen against the State itself and all of its creatures—Boards of Education not excepted. These have, of course, delicate, and highly discretionary functions, but none that they may not perform within the limits of the Bill of Rights. That they are educating the young for citizenship is reason for scrupulous protection of constitutional freedoms of the individual, if we are not to strangle the free mind at its source and teach youth to discount important principles of our government as mere platitudes." *West Virginia State Bd. of Ed. v. Barnette*, 319 U.S. 624, 637 (1943). . . .

It may well be true that the evil toward which the Fourth Amendment was primarily directed was the resurrection of the pre-Revolutionary practice of using general warrants or "writs of assistance" to authorize searches for contraband by officers of the Crown. But this Court has never limited the Amendment's prohibition on unreasonable searches and seizures to operations conducted by the police. Rather, the Court has long spoken of the Fourth Amendment's strictures as restraints imposed upon "governmental action"—that is, "upon the activities of sovereign authority.". . .

Notwithstanding the general applicability of the Fourth Amendment to the activities of civil authorities, a few courts have concluded that school officials are exempt from the dictates of the Fourth Amendment by virtue of the special nature of their authority over schoolchildren. Teachers and school administrators, it is said, act *in loco parentis* in their dealings with students: their authority is that of the parent, not the State, and is therefore not subject to the limits of the Fourth Amendment.

Such reasoning is in tension with contemporary reality and the teachings of this Court. We have held school officials subject to the commands of the First Amendment, . . . and the Due Process Clause of the Fourteenth Amendment, . . . If school authorities are state actors for purposes of the constitutional guarantees of freedom of expression and due process, it is difficult to understand why they should be deemed to be exercising parental rather than public authority when conducting searches of their students. More generally, the Court has recognized that "the concept of parental delegation" as a source of school authority is not entirely "consonant with compulsory education laws." Today's public school officials do not merely exercise authority voluntarily conferred on them by individual parents; rather, they act in furtherance of publicly mandated educational and disciplinary policies. . . . In carrying out searches and other disciplinary functions pursuant to such policies, school officials act as representatives of the State, not merely as surrogates for the parents, and they cannot claim the parents' immunity from the strictures of the Fourth Amendment.

To hold that the Fourth Amendment applies to searches conducted by school authorities is only to begin the inquiry into the standards governing such searches. Although the underlying command of the Fourth Amendment is always that searches and seizures be reasonable, what is reasonable depends on the context within which a search takes place. The determination of the standard of reasonableness governing any specific class of searches requires "balancing the need to search against the invasion which the search entails." On one side of the balance are arrayed the individual's legitimate expectations of privacy and personal security; on the other, the government's need for effective methods to deal with breaches of public order. . . .

The State of New Jersey has argued that because of the pervasive supervision to which children in the schools are necessarily subject, a child has virtually no legitimate expectation of privacy in articles of personal property "unnecessarily" carried into a school. This argument has two factual premises: (1) the fundamental incompatibility of expectations of privacy with the maintenance of a sound educational environment; and (2) the minimal interest of the child in bringing any items of personal property into the school. Both premises are severely flawed.

Although this Court may take notice of the difficulty of maintaining discipline in the public schools today, the situation is not so dire that students in the schools may claim no legitimate expectations of privacy. We have recently recognized that the need to maintain order in a prison is such that prisoners retain no legitimate expectations of privacy in their cells, but it goes almost without saying that "[t]he prisoner and the schoolchild stand in wholly different circumstances, separated by the harsh facts of criminal conviction and incarceration." We are not yet ready to hold that the schools and the prisons need be equated for purposes of the Fourth Amendment.

Nor does the State's suggestion that children have no legitimate need to bring personal property into the schools seem well anchored in reality. Students at a minimum must bring to school not only the supplies needed for their studies, but also keys, money, and the necessaries of personal hygiene and grooming. In addition, students may carry on their persons or in purses or wallets such nondisruptive yet highly personal items as photographs, letters, and diaries. Finally, students may have perfectly legitimate reasons to carry with them articles of property needed in connection with extracurricular or recreational activities. In short, schoolchildren may find it necessary to carry with them a variety of legitimate, noncontraband items, and there is no reason to conclude that they have necessarily waived all rights to privacy in such items merely by bringing them onto school grounds.

Against the child's interest in privacy must be set the substantial interest of teachers and administrators in maintaining discipline in the classroom and on school grounds. Maintaining order in the classroom has never been easy, but in recent years, school disorder has often taken particularly ugly forms: drug use and violent crime in the schools have become major social problems. . . . Accordingly, we have recognized that maintaining security and order in the schools requires a certain degree of flexibility in school disciplinary procedures, and we have respected the value of preserving the informality of the student-teacher relationship.

How, then, should we strike the balance between the schoolchild's legitimate expectations of privacy and the school's equally legitimate need to maintain an environment in which learning can take place? It is evident that the school setting requires some easing of the restrictions to which searches by public authorities are ordinarily subject. The warrant requirement, in particular, is unsuited to the school environment: requiring a teacher to obtain a warrant before searching a child suspected of an infraction of school rules (or of the criminal law) would unduly interfere with the maintenance of the swift and informal disciplinary procedures needed in the schools. Just as we have in other cases dispensed with the warrant requirement when "the burden of obtaining a warrant is likely to frustrate the governmental purpose behind the search," we hold today that school officials need not obtain a warrant before searching a student who is under their authority.

The school setting also requires some modification of the level of suspicion of illicit activity needed to justify a search. Ordinarily, a search—even one that may permissibly be carried out without a warrant—must be based upon "probable cause" to believe that a violation of the law has occurred. However, "probable cause" is not an irreducible requirement of a valid search. The fundamental command of the Fourth Amendment is that searches and seizures be reasonable, and although "both the concept of probable cause and the requirement of a warrant bear on the reasonableness of a search, . . . in certain limited circumstances neither is required." . . . .

We join the majority of courts that have examined this issue in concluding that the accommodation of the privacy interests of schoolchildren with the substantial need of teachers and administrators for freedom to maintain order in the schools does not require strict adherence to the requirement that searches be based on probable cause to believe that the subject of the search has violated or is violating the law. Rather, the legality of a search of a student should depend simply on the reasonableness, under all the circumstances, of the search. Determining the reasonableness of any search involves a twofold inquiry: first, one must consider "whether the . . . action was justified at its inception," second, one must determine whether the search as actually conducted "was reasonably related in scope to the circumstances which justified the interference in the first place,". Under ordinary circumstances, a search of a student by a teacher or other school official will be "justified at its inception" when there are reasonable grounds for suspecting that the search will turn up evidence that the student has violated or is violating either the law or the rules of the school. Such a search will be permissible in its scope when the measures adopted are reasonably related to the objectives of the search and not excessively intrusive in light of the age and sex of the student and the nature of the infraction.

This standard will, we trust, neither unduly burden the efforts of school authorities to maintain order in their schools nor authorize unrestrained intrusions upon the privacy of schoolchildren. By focusing attention on the question of reasonableness, the standard will spare teachers and school administrators the necessity of schooling themselves in the niceties of probable cause and permit them to regulate their conduct according to the dictates of reason and common sense. At the same time, the reasonableness standard should ensure that the interests of students will be invaded no more than is necessary to achieve the legitimate end of preserving order in the schools.

There remains the question of the legality of the search in this case. We recognize that the "reasonable grounds" standard applied by the New Jersey Supreme Court in its consideration of this question is not substantially different from the standard that we have adopted today. Nonetheless, we believe that the New Jersey court's application of that standard to strike down the search of T. L. O.'s purse reflects a somewhat crabbed notion of reasonableness. Our review of the facts surrounding the search leads us to conclude that the search was in no sense unreasonable for Fourth Amendment purposes.

The incident that gave rise to this case actually involved two separate searches, with the first—the search for cigarettes—providing the suspicion that gave rise to the second—the search for marihuana. Although it is the fruits of the second search that are at issue here, the validity of the search for marihuana must depend on the reasonableness of the initial search for cigarettes, as there would have been no reason to suspect that T. L. O. possessed marihuana had the first search not taken place. Accordingly, it is to the search for cigarettes that we first turn our attention.

The New Jersey Supreme Court pointed to two grounds for its holding that the search for cigarettes was unreasonable. First, the court observed that possession of cigarettes was not in itself illegal or a violation of school rules. Because the contents of T. L. O.'s purse would therefore have "no direct bearing on the infraction" of which she was accused (smoking in a lavatory where smoking was prohibited), there was no reason to search her purse. Second, even assuming that a search of T. L. O.'s purse might under some circumstances be reasonable in light of the accusation made against T. L. O., the New Jersey court concluded that Mr. Choplick in this particular case had no reasonable grounds to suspect that T. L. O. had cigarettes in her purse. At best, according to the court, Mr. Choplick had "a good hunch."

Both these conclusions are implausible. T. L. O. had been accused of smoking, and had denied the accusation in the strongest possible terms when she stated that she did not smoke at all. Surely it cannot be said that under these circumstances, T. L. O.'s possession of cigarettes would be irrelevant to the charges against her or to her response to those charges. T. L. O.'s possession of cigarettes, once it was discovered, would both corroborate the report that she had been smoking and undermine the credibility of her defense to the charge of smoking. To be sure, the discovery of the cigarettes would not prove that T. L. O. had been smoking in the lavatory; nor would it, strictly speaking, necessarily be inconsistent with her claim that she did not smoke at all. But it is universally recognized that evidence, to be relevant to an inquiry, need not conclusively prove the ultimate fact in issue, but only have "any tendency to make the existence of any fact that is of consequence to the determination of the action more probable or less probable than it would be without the evidence." The relevance of T. L. O.'s possession of cigarettes to the question whether she had been smoking and to the credibility of her denial that she smoked supplied the necessary "nexus" between the item searched for and the infraction under investigation. Thus, if Mr. Choplick in fact had a reasonable suspicion that T. L. O. had cigarettes in her purse, the search was justified despite the fact that the cigarettes, if found, would constitute "mere evidence" of a violation.

Of course, the New Jersey Supreme Court also held that Mr. Choplick had no reasonable suspicion that the purse would contain cigarettes. This conclusion is puzzling. A teacher had reported that T. L. O. was smoking in the lavatory. Certainly this report gave Mr. Choplick reason to suspect that T. L. O. was carrying cigarettes with her; and if she did have cigarettes, her purse was the obvious place in which to find them. Mr. Choplick's suspicion that there were cigarettes in the purse was not an "inchoate and unparticularized suspicion or 'hunch,'" rather, it was the sort of "common-sense conclusio[n] about human behavior" upon which "practical people"—including government officials—are entitled to rely. Of course, even if the teacher's report were true, T. L. O. *might* not have had a pack of cigarettes with her; she might have borrowed a cigarette from someone else or have been sharing a cigarette with another student. But the requirement of reasonable suspicion is not a requirement of absolute certainty: "sufficient probability, not certainty, is the touchstone of reasonableness under the Fourth Amendment. . . ." Because the hypothesis that T. L. O. was carrying cigarettes in her purse was itself not unreasonable, it is irrelevant that other hypotheses were also consistent with the teacher's accusation. Accordingly, it cannot be said that Mr. Choplick acted unreasonably when he examined T. L. O.'s purse to see if it contained cigarettes.

Our conclusion that Mr. Choplick's decision to open T. L. O.'s purse was reasonable brings us to the question of the further search for marihuana once the pack of cigarettes was located. The suspicion upon which the search for marihuana was founded was provided when Mr. Choplick observed a package of rolling papers in the purse as he removed the pack of cigarettes. Although T. L. O. does not dispute the reasonableness of Mr. Choplick's belief that the rolling papers indicated the presence of marihuana, she does contend that the scope of the search Mr. Choplick conducted exceeded permissible bounds when he seized and read certain letters that implicated T. L. O. in drug dealing. This argument, too, is unpersuasive. The discovery of the rolling papers concededly gave rise to a reasonable suspicion that T. L. O. was carrying marihuana as well as cigarettes in her purse. This suspicion justified further exploration of T. L. O.'s purse, which turned up more evidence of drug-related activities: a pipe, a number of plastic bags of the type commonly used to store marihuana, a small quantity of marihuana, and a fairly substantial amount of money. Under these circumstances, it was not unreasonable to extend the search to a separate zippered compartment of the purse; and when a search of that compartment revealed an index card containing a list of "people who owe me money" as well as to letters, the inference that T. L. O. was involved in marihuana trafficking was substantial enough to justify Mr. Choplick in examining the letters to determine whether they contained any further evidence. In short, we cannot conclude that the search for marihuana was unreasonable in any respect.

Because the search resulting in the discovery of the evidence of marihuana dealing by T. L. O. was reasonable, the New Jersey Supreme Court's decision to exclude that evidence from T. L. O.'s juvenile delinquency proceedings on Fourth Amendment grounds was erroneous. Accordingly, the judgment of the Supreme Court of New Jersey is

Reversed.

NOTES

1. Where the primary purpose of the school official's search was not to obtain convictions, but to secure evidence of student misconduct, the fact that evidence of crime is uncovered and prosecution results therefrom should not itself make the search and seizure illegal. In re Donaldson, 269 Cal.App.2d 509, 75 Cal.Rptr. 220 (1969).

2. A search of a student's automobile by officials of a nonpublic quasi-military academy has been upheld by a federal district court in Maine. Plaintiff student was dismissed from the academy following a search of his car at the direction of the school disciplinary officer. The search produced a quantity of marijuana and a can of beer. Such a search, according to the court, was a reasonable exercise of supervisory authority of the school. The court pointed out that the search was not conducted by a police officer. It should also be observed that this case has limited utility for public schools since the Fourth Amendment protects an individual from unwarranted search by government and does not protect against search by a private person or private school. Keene v. Rodgers, 316 F.Supp. 217 (D.Me.1970).

3. Search of a student's locker and briefcase in a private university without a search warrant was upheld by the Supreme Court of California. Marijuana was found in the locker after other students reported an offensive odor coming from the locker. The court said:

Even if [the] University were a "public" rather than a "private" institution, the search here challenged would be reasonable within the meaning of the Fourth Amendment. It is true the search was conducted without a warrant, and the burden therefore rested upon the People to show justification. . . . But that burden was sustained in the case at bar by a compelling showing of facts bringing the search within the "emergency" exception to the warrant requirement. In the case at bar . . . a "compelling urgency" was clearly shown . . . inasmuch as the students entitled to use the room had already been disturbed by this offensive odor throughout the preceding day, further delay in suppressing it would have been unjustifiable. Once the defendant's briefcase was discovered and opened, its contents were in plain sight. An observation from a lawful vantage point of contraband in plain sight is not a "search" in the constitutional sense. People v. Lanthier, 5 Cal.3d 751, 97 Cal. Rptr. 297, 488 P.2d 625 (1971).

Footnotes

1. State ex rel. Burpee v. Burton, 45 Wis. 150, 30 Am.Rep. 706 (1878).

2. People v. Ball, 58 Ill.2d 36, 317 N.E.2d 54 (1974).

3. Fletcher v. People, 52 Ill. 395 (1869); People v. Parris, 130 Ill.App.2d 933, 267 N.E.2d 39 (1971).

4. Fox v. People, 84 Ill.App. 270 (1899); People v. Ball, supra.

5. Ingraham v. Wright, 430 U.S. 651, 97 S.Ct. 1401 (1977).

6. 430 U.S. 651, 97 S.Ct. 1401 (1977).

7. Hurtado v. California, 110 U.S. 516, 4 S.Ct. 111 (1884).

8. Adkins v. Children's Hospital, 261 U.S. 525, 43 S.Ct. 394 (1923).

9. Valley National Bank of Phoenix v. Glover, 62 Ariz. 538, 159 P.2d 292 (1945).

10. 262 U.S. 390, 43 S.Ct. 625 (1923); See Pierce v. Society of Sisters, 268 U.S. 510, 45 S.Ct. 571 (1925).

11. Id.

12. Meyer v. Nebraska, supra; Pierce v. Society of Sisters, supra.

13. Ken v. Dulles, 357 U.S. 116, 78 S.Ct. 1113 (1958); United States v. Guest, 383 U.S. 745, 86 S.Ct. 1170 (1966); Shapiro v. Thompson, 394 U.S. 618, 89 S.Ct. 1322 (1969).

14. Richards v. Thurston, 424 F.2d 1281 (1st Cir.1970); Breen v. Kahl, 296 F.Supp. 702 (Wis. 1969), affirmed 419 F.2d 1034 (7th Cir.1969), cert. denied 398 U.S. 937, 90 S.Ct. 1836 (1970).

15. 295 F.Supp. 978 (W.D.Wis.1968), affirmed 418 F.2d 163 (7th Cir.1968).

16. Hobson v. Bailey, 309 F.Supp. 1393 (D.C.Tenn.1970); Zanders v. Louisiana State Board of Education, 281 F.Supp. 747 (D.C.La.1968).

17. Joint Anti-Fascist Refugee Comm. v. McGrath, 341 U.S. 123, 71 S.Ct. 624 (1951) (concurring opinion of Justice Frankfurter).

18. Dixon v. Alabama State Board of Education, 294 F.2d 150 (5th Cir.1961), cert. denied 368 U.S. 930, 82 S.Ct. 368 (1961). For an excellent discussion of procedural due process, see William G. Buss, "Procedural Due Process for School Discipline: Probing the Constitutional Outline," *University of Pennsylvania Law Review*, vol. 119 (1971): 545–641.

19. Due v. Florida A. & M. University, 233 F.Supp. 396 (D.Fla.1963).

20. Goss v. Lopez, 419 U.S. 565, 95 S.Ct. 729 (1975).

21. Schenck v. United States, 249 U.S. 47, 39 S.Ct. 247 (1919).

22. Whitney v. California, 274 U.S. 357, 47 S.Ct. 641 (1927); Bridges v. California, 314 U.S. 252, 62 S.Ct. 190 (1941).

23. Whitney v. California, supra.

24. Bridges v. California, supra.

25. Tinker v. Des Moines Independent Community School District, 393 U.S. 503, 89 S.Ct. 733 (1969).

26. Pugsley v. Sellmeyer, 158 Ark. 247, 250 S.W. 538 (1923).

27. Mitchell v. McCall, 273 Ala. 604, 143 So.2d 629 (1962).

28. New York Times Co. v. United States, 403 U.S. 713, 91 S.Ct. 2140 (1971).

29. 393 U.S. 503, 89 S.Ct. 733 (1969).

30. 273 F.Supp. 613 (1967), vacated 402 F.2d 515 (5th Cir.1968).

31. Norton v. East Tennessee State University Disciplinary Committee, 419 F.2d 195 (6th Cir. 1969), certiorari denied 399 U.S. 906, 90 S.Ct. 2191 (1970).

32. Id.

33. Quarterman v. Byrd, 453 F.2d 54 (4th Cir.1971).

34. Scoville v. Board of Education of Joliet Township High School District 204, 286 F.Supp. 988 (N.D.Ill.1968), affirmed 415 F.2d 860 (6th Cir.1969) reversed on rehearing 425 F.2d 10 (7th Cir. 1970), certiorari denied 400 U.S. 826, 91 S.Ct. 51 (1970).

35. Eisner v. Stamford Board of Education, 440 F.2d 803 (2d Cir.1971).

36. See Search and Seizure in Education, Mary Jane Connelly, unpublished doctoral dissertation, Virginia Tech University, 1982.

37. New Jersey v. T.L.O., ___ U.S. ___, 105 S.Ct. 733, No. 83–712, January 15, 1985.

38. People v. Jackson, 65 Misc.2d 909, 319 N.Y.S.2d 731 (1971).

39. State v. Baccino, 282 A.2d 869 (Del.Super.1971).

40. Bellnier v. Lund, 438 F.Supp. 47 (N.D.N.Y.1977).

41. M. v. Board of Education Ball—Chatham Community School District No. 5, 429 F.Supp. 288 (S.D.Ill.1977).

42. State v. Stein, 203 Kan. 638, 456 P.2d 1 (1969), cert. denied 397 U.S. 947, 90 S.Ct. 966 (1970).

43. People v. Jackson, supra. (*In loco parentis* does not end at the school door.)

44. United States v. Coles, 302 F.Supp. 99 (D.Me.1969).

45. Caldwell v. Cannady, 340 F.Supp. 835 (D.Tex.1972).

46. 639 F.2d 662 (10th Cir.1981).

47. 475 F.Supp. 1012 (N.D.Ind.1979), opinion adopted on this issue and reversed on another issue 631 F.2d 91 (7th Cir.1980), 635 F.2d 582 (7th Cir.1980), cert. denied, 451 U.S. 1022, 101 S.Ct. 3015 (1981).

48. 499 F.Supp. 223 (E.D.Tex.1980).

49. 690 F.2d 470 (5th Cir.1982).

50. Id. at 475.

51. Id. at 477.

52. Id. at 481–82.

53. M.M. v. Anker, 607 F.2d 588 (2d Cir.1979).

54. 438 F.Supp. 47 (N.D.N.Y.1977).

55. Rone v. Daviess County Board of Education, 655 S.W.2d 28 (Ky.1983).

56. Renfrow, supra.

57. Doe v. Renfrow, 631 F.2d 91 (7th Cir.1980), cert. denied 451 U.S. 1022, 101 S.Ct. 3015 (1981).

58. 232 U.S. 383, 34 S.Ct. 341 (1914).

59. 338 U.S. 25, 69 S.Ct. 1359 (1949).

60. Wolf at 1360.

61. Wolf at 1361.

62. 367 U.S. 643, 81 S.Ct. 1684 (1961).

9

Rights of Handicapped Children

Programs for handicapped children developed slowly in public schools. Meager financial resources and public apathy combined to prevent significant efforts to extend an equal educational opportunity to the handicapped until relatively recently.

During the 1940s through 1960s several states distributed categorical funds to local school districts for handicapped programs, and a few states required local school districts to establish programs for the handicapped in order to receive state foundation program allocations, but such efforts were not comprehensive and failed to address the special needs of most handicapped children, particularly those who were severely handicapped.

It was not until the latter part of the 1960s and early 1970s that pervasive concern for the equality of educational opportunity that swept the nation during the Johnson presidency expanded to touch the handicapped. The watershed in development of handicapped programs in public schools came with a few key court decisions and the federal government's landmark legislation in 1975 entitled Education for All Handicapped Children Act. From that point, comprehensive educational programs were rapidly developed in virtually all states.

In order to better understand the recent court cases involving this federal legislation, it is instructive to first briefly review the early antecedents of provision of educational opportunity for the handicapped.

NINETEENTH CENTURY

Special education programs in the United States originated during the early nineteenth century when isolated advocates of handicapped children established educational programs for specific handicaps or pressured state legisla-

The authors wish to express appreciation to Patricia Anthony, Ph.D., for preparation of this chapter.

tures to pass legislation to achieve this purpose. The earliest known school
for handicapped students was established in Hartford, Connecticut, in 1817.
Thomas Hopkins Gallaudet founded the American Asylum for the Education
of the Deaf and Dumb (now the American School for the Deaf) two years
after returning from France, where he was newly trained in the French
method of manual communication for the deaf. Gallaudet brought with him
a deaf teacher, Laurent Clerc, and together the two men traveled to various
American cities soliciting money from private sources to establish their
school.[1]

The Connecticut legislature appropriated $5,000 for the school in 1816
and by April 15, 1817, it opened its doors to seven students. In 1819, the
school's future was assured when the federal government turned over 23,000
acres of land to the school, which the school in turn sold, accruing over
$300,000. During the same year, other states began providing the tuition
moneys necessary to send deaf children to The American School.[2]

A second school, the New York Institution for the Education of the Deaf
and Dumb, was opened in New York in 1818. This school was funded by
private donations but, in 1821, the State of New York appropriated funds for
its support. The New York school was the first day school for deaf students
but soon evolved into a residential school program.

Pennsylvania was the site of the third school founded in this country for
deaf students. Initially established in 1820, also as a private school, the
state began supporting it in 1821 with funds to provide an education for fifty
students. From 1823 to 1844, three new state schools were built for deaf
students in Kentucky, Ohio, and Virginia. From 1844 to 1860, seventeen
new schools for deaf students were established, and in 1864 the National
Deaf Mute College was founded in Washington, D.C. The name later was
changed to Gallaudet College in honor of the man who first began deaf
education in the United States.

The need for educational services for other handicaps was not ignored.
In 1830, due to the tireless efforts of Horace Mann, the Massachusetts State
Legislature passed into law, "Resolve for Erecting a Lunatic Hospital,"[3] and
the first state hospital for the mentally ill was founded in the city of
Worcester, Massachusetts. Mann, of course, was best known for his labors
in establishing free compulsory public education for all children.

Elected in 1827 by the town of Dedham, Massachusetts, to the Massachusetts State Legislature, Mann sought legislative support in abolishing the
deplorable living conditions of the insane.[4] Forming a committee to study
the plight of the insane, Mann toured poorhouses and gaols (jails) throughout Massachusetts, gathering evidence to encourage legislative action. In
1830, Mann's bill was passed by both the Massachusetts House and Senate.

Other states were not idle in efforts to aid handicapped children. In
1832, New York established a school for blind students, and by 1852, New
York, Pennsylvania, and Massachusetts all had appropriated money for
programs for mentally retarded children.[5] In 1869, day programs for deaf
students were started in Boston and in 1896, programs for mentally retarded
students were started in Providence, Rhode Island. Public school classes for
physically handicapped and blind students were begun in Chicago in 1900.

Consequently, by the early twentieth century, handicapped children had gained entry into the public schools in several states.

Severely handicapped students had a difficult time conforming to the structure and expectations of public school systems. Schools were ill-equipped to handle students who exhibited aberrant characteristics. In 1893, a Massachusetts court ruled that student behavior resulting from "imbecility" was grounds for expulsion, thereby barring many mentally retarded students from public schools.[6] A later decision[7] ruled that a handicapped student, although academically capable, could be excluded from regular public school classes because his handicap had "a depressing and nauseating effect on the teachers and school children."[8]

This ruling prevented severely handicapped children suffering from cerebral palsy or poliomyelitis from attending regular public school day classes. Since special classes for these severely handicapped students had not yet been created in many cities, parents of such children had to resort to residential schools, private tutors, or forego formal education completely.

TWENTIETH CENTURY

Despite these earlier judicial setbacks, social conditions of the twentieth century impacted favorably upon the growth of education services for the handicapped. The return home of disabled World War I veterans focused national attention upon the need for handicapped educational programs.

In 1918, The Soldiers' Rehabilitation Act was passed by Congress, followed in 1920 by the Smith-Bankhead Act.[9] Both pieces of legislation offered vocational rehabilitation services in the form of job training and counseling. By 1944, these acts were amended to include services for mentally ill individuals and the mentally retarded, as well as to provide additional funds for research and training programs.[10]

Another condition significantly affecting handicapped children's quest for equal educational opportunity was the court-ordered desegregation of the public schools.[11] While specifically referring to the rights of black children, the legal mandate of *Brown* set a precedent for the extension of educational access to all children, including the handicapped.[12]

A turning point for handicapped children's rights occurred in 1971, when a federal district court ruled that retarded children in Pennsylvania were entitled to a free public education.[13] The ruling stipulated that whenever possible, retarded children must be educated in regular classrooms rather than be segregated from the normal school population. The court said a

> free, public program of education and training appropriate to the child's capacity, within the context of a presumption that, among the alternative programs of education and training required by statute to be available, placement in a regular public school class is preferable to placement in a special public school class [i.e., a class for "handicapped" children] and placement in a special public school class is preferable to placement in any other type of program of education and training . . ..[14]

Procedural due process and periodic reevaluations of retarded children were also part of the court's consent agreement.

In 1972, *Mills* v. *Board of Education of the District of Columbia* [15] expanded the Pennsylvania (PARC) decision to include all handicapped children. Emphasizing the need for appropriate educational services in the District of Columbia, the court pointed out that there are "22,000 retarded, emotionally disturbed, blind, deaf, and speech, or learning disabled children, and perhaps as many as 18,000 of these children are not being furnished with programs of specialized education."[16] In granting summary judgment in favor of the plaintiffs, the court adopted a comprehensive plan that had been formulated by the District of Columbia Board of Education. Included in the plan were provisions for: (1) a free appropriate education, (2) an Individualized Educational Plan, and (3) due process procedures. The groundwork for future federal legislation in the area of handicapped children's rights to an education had been laid.

VOCATIONAL REHABILITATION ACT OF 1973

Following the *PARC* and *Mills* decisions, federal legislation was introduced in both chambers of Congress during the early 1970s seeking to eliminate discrimination against the handicapped in both the work and education environment. These measures eventually culminated in the passage of the Vocational Rehabilitation Act in 1973. Section 504 of the Act states:

> No otherwise qualified handicapped individual in the United States . . . shall, solely by reason of his handicap, be excluded from the participation in, be denied the benefits of, or be subjected to discrimination under any program or activity receiving Federal financial assistance.[17]

Although Section 504 is concerned with the discrimination of handicapped individuals in work situations, it also addresses the problems encountered by handicapped children in seeking equal educational opportunity. There are five mandates encompassed in Section 504 that pertain directly to the educational needs of handicapped children:

> (a) location and notification, (b) free appropriate public education, (c) educational setting, (d) evaluation and placement, and (e) procedural safeguards.[18]

These provisions of Section 504 have been used successfully in obtaining desirable school programs and services for individual handicapped students. Specifically, the provisions for a free appropriate public education and educational setting [19] enabled a child with cystic fibrosis to attend regular classes while receiving supportive services for a daily suctioning procedure.[20]

PUBLIC LAW 94–142

In 1975, federal legislation in the form of the Education for All Handicapped Children Act, P.L. 94–142, was enacted. Incorporating many provisions of earlier litigation and legislation, P.L. 94–142 assured the right of all handicapped children to a public school education.

The need for P.L. 94–142 was expressed by Congress:

(1) there are more than eight million handicapped children in the United States today;

(2) the special educational needs of such children are not being fully met;

(3) more than half of the handicapped children in the United States do not receive appropriate educational services which would enable them to have full equality of opportunity;

(4) one million of the handicapped children in the United States are excluded entirely from the public school system and will not go through the educational process with their peers;

(5) there are many handicapped children throughout the United States participating in regular school programs whose handicaps prevent them from having a successful educational experience because their handicaps are undetected.[21]

To ensure handicapped children basic educational rights, P.L. 94–142 incorporated certain tenets: (1) a free appropriate public education, (2) an individualized education program, (3) special education services, (4) related services, (5) due process procedures, and (6) the least restrictive environment (LRE) in which to learn.[22]

Congress authorized immediate implementation of all sections of the Education for All Handicapped Children Act on a priority basis: first, addressing the needs of handicapped children who were currently receiving no educational services at all and, second, upgrading the inadequately served needs of the most severely handicapped children. The Act further required that all handicapped children between the ages of three and eighteen receive an appropriate education by September 1, 1978; by September 1, 1980, all handicapped children from age three to twenty-one were to receive appropriate educational services.[23]

From 1976 to 1981, the number of children receiving special education services rose 13 percent. During the 1981–82 school year, 4,233,282 handicapped children were served, the majority of whom attended regular public schools. This increase in the number of school-aged children requiring special education services created a surge of litigation, as parents, school administrators, and teachers turned to the courts for answers to complex questions regarding appropriate educational placement of handicapped children.

FREE APPROPRIATE PUBLIC EDUCATION

On June 28, 1982, the United States Supreme Court reversed a lower federal court decision and ruled that, pursuant to P.L. 94–142's provision of free and appropriate education for handicapped children, a school district was not required to provide interpreter services for a deaf student.[24] The central issue was the definition of "free and appropriate education," the underlying tenet of the Education for All Handicapped Children Act of 1975.

According to P.L. 94–142, free appropriate education is defined as special education and related services that (1) have been provided at public expense, under public supervision and direction, and without charge; (2) meet the standards of the state educational agency; (3) include an appropriate preschool, elementary, or secondary school education; and (4) are provided in conformity with the individualized education program.[25]

In ruling against Rowley, the Supreme Court refuted the district court's definition of appropriate education maintaining that Congress[26] intended only to provide handicapped students with a "basic floor of opportunity," not a specific quality of education.

To further define the meaning of "appropriate," the majority in *Rowley* asserted that access should result in educational benefit for the handicapped child. In a vigorous dissent, Justice White took issue with the use of the term "benefit," pointing out that in the case of a deaf student, instruction by "a teacher with a loud voice" could be viewed as an educational placement providing some benefit.[27]

PRIVATE SCHOOL PLACEMENT

The use of private schools for appropriate educational placement has been the subject of bitter dispute between parents of handicapped children and local school administrators.[28] Increasingly, courts have had to decide whether "parents have the right under the law to write a prescription for an ideal education for their child and to have the prescription filled at public expense."[29]

Results of such court intervention are mixed. However, in most cases, if a public school program is available, and judged to be appropriate for the child's needs, the courts have tended to favor local district administrative decisions. An exception to this was made in *Grkman* v. *Scanlon,*[30] where it was determined to be in the best interests of the child to continue private school placement even when a public school program was available. This case, however, was later drawn into question by the results of the *Rowley* decision and was remanded back to state officials for reconsideration and an update on the facts.

When no appropriate placement can be provided within the local public schools, "special education and related services . . . including nonmedical care and room and board must be [provided] at no cost to the parents of the child."[31] This holds true even when it has been contended that twenty-four hour residential care is necessary for noneducational reasons, i.e., emotional problems or custodial care.

RELATED SERVICES

Under P.L. 94–142, supportive services that enable handicapped children to benefit from special education must be made available without cost to the parents. Related services mandated by the Act are: transportation, psychological services, physical and occupational therapy, speech pathology, audiology, recreation, counseling, and medical services.[32]

Confusion has arisen regarding which medical services fall within P.L. 94–142's domain. The courts have generally taken a broad interpretation of allowable medical services. In *Irving Independent School District* v. *Tatro*[33] clean intermittent catheterization (CIC) was required by the Supreme Court in spite of the fact that the school district had claimed the service was impermissible under P.L. 94–142 guidelines,[34] which exempt medical services except those for diagnostic and evaluation purposes.[35]

DISCIPLINE OF HANDICAPPED STUDENTS

The mainstreaming of handicapped children has underscored the need for guidelines governing the disciplining of handicapped students. Neither Section 504 nor P.L. 94–142 addresses this issue, leaving it to the courts to decipher the legal ramifications involved.

Two provisions of the Education for All Handicapped Children Act must be considered when disciplinary action is taken with a handicapped student: appropriate education and least restrictive environment. P.L. 94–142 mandates that a handicapped student must be provided a free appropriate education in the least restrictive environment. Acceptable environments for the placement of a handicapped child range from least restrictive (a regular classroom) to highly restrictive (an institution). However, each environment can be termed "least restrictive" depending upon the seriousness of a particular handicap, and the student's ability to cope within a specific environment.

Courts have consistently ruled that handicapped students must be given special consideration in disciplinary proceedings.[36] Earlier court decisions prohibited expulsion, noting that, under P.L. 94–142, services must be provided through alternative placement in one of the other educational environments offered.[37]

In 1981, expulsion again surfaced as an issue, when nine mentally retarded students in the state of Florida sued local districts and the state, claiming that they had been denied an appropriate education due to expulsion.[38] The court upheld expulsion in *S–1* v. *Turlington* [39] as a viable form of discipline to be used with handicapped students. The court, however, pointed out that cessation of all educational programs violated the rights of handicapped students, consequently even after expelling a student, services must be provided.

Suspension, on the other hand, has been viewed favorably by the courts as an appropriate disciplinary action for handicapped students, when it has been determined that misconduct is not related to the student's handicap. If it is related to the handicapping condition, an alternate or more restrictive placement should be considered, rather than suspension or expulsion.[40]

Procedural Due Process Is Required to
Reassign Handicapped Children

MILLS v. BOARD OF
EDUCATION OF DISTRICT OF
COLUMBIA

United States District Court, District of
Columbia, 1972.
348 F.Supp. 866.

WADDY, District Judge. This is a civil action brought on behalf of seven children of school age by their next friends in which they seek a declaration of rights and to enjoin the defendants from excluding them from the District of Columbia Public Schools and/or denying them publicly supported education and to compel the defendants to provide them with immediate and adequate education and educational facilities in the public schools or alternative placement at public expense. They also seek additional and ancillary relief to effectuate the primary relief. They allege that although they can profit from an education either in regular classrooms with supportive services or in special classes adapted to their needs, they have been labeled as behavioral problems, mentally retarded, emotionally disturbed or hyperactive, and denied admission to the public schools or excluded therefrom after admission, with no provision for alternative educational placement or periodic review. . . .

The genesis of this case is found (1) in the failure of the District of Columbia to provide publicly supported education and training to plaintiffs and other "exceptional" children, members of their class, and (2) the excluding, suspending, expelling, reassigning and transferring of "exceptional" children from regular public school classes without affording them due process of law.

The problem of providing special education for "exceptional" children (mentally retarded, emotionally disturbed, physically handicapped, hyperactive and other children with behavioral problems) is one of major proportions in the District of Columbia. The precise number of such children cannot be stated because the District has continuously failed to comply with Section 31–208 of the District of Columbia Code which requires a census of all children aged three to eighteen in the District to be taken. Plaintiffs estimate that there are "22,000 retarded, emotionally disturbed, blind, deaf, and speech or learning disabled children, and perhaps as many as 18,000 of these children are not being furnished with programs of specialized education." According to data prepared by the Board of Education, Division of Planning, Research and Evaluation, the District of Columbia provides publicly supported special education programs of various descriptions to at least 3,880 school-age children. However, in a 1971 report to the Department of Health, Education and Welfare, the District of Columbia Public Schools admitted that an estimated 12,340 handicapped children were not to be served in the 1971–72 school year.

Each of the minor plaintiffs in this case qualifies as an "exceptional" child. . . .

Although all of the named minor plaintiffs are identified as Negroes the class they represent is not limited by their race. They sue on behalf of and represent all other District of Columbia residents of school age who are eligible for a free public education and who have been, or may be, excluded from such education or otherwise deprived by defendants of access to publicly supported education. . . .

Plaintiffs' entitlement to relief in this case is clear. The applicable statutes and regulations and the Constitution of the United States require it.

Statutes and Regulations Section 31–201 of the District of Columbia Code requires that:

> Every parent, guardian, or other person residing [permanently or temporarily] in the District of Columbia who has custody or control of a child between the ages of seven and sixteen years shall cause said child to be regularly instructed in a public school or in a private or parochial school or instructed privately during the period of each year in which the public schools of the District of Columbia are in session. . . .

Under Section 31–203, a child may be "excused" from attendance only when

> upon examination ordered by . . . [the Board of Education of the District of Columbia, the child] is found to be unable mentally or physically to profit from attendance at shcool: Provided, however, That if such examination shows that such child may benefit from specialized instruction adapted to his needs, he shall attend upon such instruction."

Failure of a parent to comply with Section 31–201 constitutes a criminal offense. D.C.Code 31–207. The Court need not belabor the fact that requiring parents to see that their children attend school under pain of criminal penalties presupposes that an educational opportunity will be made available to the children. The Board of Education is required to make such opportunity available. . . .

The Constitution—Equal Protection and Due Process . . . In Hobson v. Hansen, 269 F.Supp. 401 (D.C.D.C.1967) Circuit Judge J. Skelly Wright considered the pronouncements of the Supreme Court in the intervening years and stated that "the Court has found the due process clause of the Fourteenth Amendment elastic enough to embrace not only the First and Fourth Amendments, but the self-incrimination clause of the Fifth, the speedy trial, confrontation and assistance of counsel clauses of the Sixth, and the cruel and unusal clause of the Eighth." (269 F.Supp. 401 at 493, citations omitted). Judge Wright concluded "[F]rom these considerations the court draws the conclusion that the doctrine of equal educational opportunity—the equal protection clause in its application to public school education—is in its full sweep a component of due process binding on the District under the due process clause of the Fifth Amendment."

In *Hobson* v. *Hansen,* supra, Judge Wright found that denying poor public school children educational opportunities equal to that available to more affluent public school children was violative of the Due Process Clause of the Fifth Amendment. *A fortiori,* the defendants' conduct here, denying plaintiffs and their class not just an equal publicly supported education but all publicly supported education while providing such education to other children, is violative of the Due Process Clause.

Not only are plaintiffs and their class denied the publicly supported education to which they are entitled, many are suspended or expelled from regular schooling or specialized instruction or reassigned without any prior hearing and are given no periodic review thereafter. Due process of law requires a hearing prior to exclusion, termination of classification into a special program. . . .

The Defense The Answer of the defendants to the Complaint contains the following:

> These defendants say that it is impossible to afford plaintiffs the relief they request unless:
> (a) The Congress of the United States appropriates millions of dollars to improve special education services in the District of Columbia; or
> (b) These defendants divert millions of dollars from funds already specifically appropriated for other educational services in order to improve special educational services. These defendants suggest that to do so would violate an Act of Congress and would be inequitable to children outside the alleged plaintiff class.

This Court is not persuaded by that contention.

The defendants are required by the Constitution of the United States, the District of Columbia Code, and their own regulations to provide a publicly supported education for these "exceptional" children. Their failure to fulfill this clear duty to include and retain these children in the public school system, or otherwise provide them with publicly-supported education, and their failure to afford them due process hearing and periodic review, cannot be excused by the claim that there are insufficient funds. In Goldberg v. Kelly, 397 U.S. 254, 90 S.Ct. 1011, 25 L.Ed.2d 287 (1969) the Supreme Court, in a case that involved the right of a welfare recipient to a hearing before termination of his benefits, held that constitutional rights must be afforded citizens despite the greater expense involved. The Court stated at page 266, 90 S.Ct. at page 1019, that "the State's interest that his [welfare recipient's] payments not be erroneously terminated, clearly outweighs the State's competing concern to prevent any increase in its fiscal and administrative burdens." Similarly the District of Columbia's interest in educating the excluded children clearly must outweigh its interest in preserving its financial resources. If sufficient funds are not available to finance all of the services and programs that are needed and desirable in the system then the available funds must be expended equitably in such a manner that no child is entirely excluded from a publicly supported education consistent with his needs and ability to benefit therefrom. The inadequacies of the District of Columbia Public School System whether occasioned by insufficient funding or administrative inefficiency, certainly cannot be permitted to bear more heavily on the "exceptional" or handicapped child than on the normal child. . . .

Inasmuch as the Board of Education has presented for adoption by the Court a proposed "Order and Decree" embodying its present plans for the identification of "exceptional" children and providing for their publicly supported education, including a time table, and further requiring the Board to formulate and file with the Court a more comprehensive plan, the Court will not now appoint a special master as was requested by plaintiffs. . . .

Judgment and Decree . . . it is hereby ordered, adjudged and decreed that summary judgment in favor of plaintiffs and against defendants be, and hereby is, granted, and judgment is entered in this action as follows:

1. That no child eligible for a publicly supported education in the District of Columbia public schools shall be excluded from a regular public school assignment by a rule, policy, or practice of the Board of Education of the District of Columbia or its agents unless such child is provided (a) adequate alternative educational services suited to the child's needs, which may include special education or tuition grants, and (b) a consitutionally adequate prior hearing and periodic review of the child's status, progress, and the adequacy of any educational alternative.

2. The defendants, their officers, agents, servants, employees, and attorneys and all those in active concert or participation with them are hereby enjoined from maintaining, enforcing or otherwise continuing in effect any and all rules, policies and practices which exclude plaintiffs and the members of the class they represent from a regular public school assignment without providing them at public expense (a) adequate and immediate alternative education or tuition grants, consistent with their needs, and (b) a constitutionally adequate prior hearing and periodic review of their status, progress and the adequacy of any educational alternatives; and it is further ORDERED that:

3. The District of Columbia shall provide to each child of school age a free and suitable publicly supported education regardless of the degree of the child's mental, physical or emotional disability or impairment. Furthermore, defendants shall not exclude any child resident in the District of Columbia from such publicly supported education on the basis of a claim of insufficient resources.

4. Defendants shall not suspend a child from the public schools for disciplinary reasons for any period in excess of two days without affording him a hearing pursuant to the provisions of Paragraph 13.f., below, and without providing for his education during the period of any such suspension.

5. Defendants shall provide each identified member of plaintiff class with a publicly-supported education suited to his needs within thirty (30) days of the entry of this order. . . .

9. (a) Defendants shall utilize public or private agencies to evaluate the educational needs of all identified "exceptional" children and, within twenty (20) days of the entry of this order, shall file with the Clerk of this Court their proposal for each individual placement in a suitable educational program, including the provision of compensatory educational services where required. . . .

10. (a) Within forty-five (45) days of the entry of this order, defendants shall file with the Clerk of the Court, with copy to plaintiffs' counsel, a

comprehensive plan which provides for the identification, notification, assessment, and placement of class members. Such plan shall state the nature and extent of efforts which defendants have undertaken or propose to undertake to

1. describe the curriculum, educational objectives, teacher qualifications, and ancillary services for the publicly supported educational programs to be provided to class members; and,

2. formulate general plans of compensatory education suitable to class members in order to overcome the present effects of prior educational deprivations. . . .

. . .

12. Within forty-five (45) days of the entry of this order, defendants shall file with this Court a report showing the expunction from or correction of all official records of any plaintiff with regard to past expulsions, suspensions, or exclusions effected in violation of the procedural rights . . . .

13. Hearing Procedures.

   a. Each member of the plaintiff class is to be provided with a publicly supported educational program suited to his needs, within the context of a presumption that among the alternative programs of education, placement in a regular public school class with appropriate ancillary services is preferable to placement in a special school class.

   b. Before placing a member of the class in such a program, defendants shall notify his parent or guardian of the proposed educational placement, the reasons therefore, and the right to a hearing before a Hearing Officer if there is an objection to the placement proposed. . . .

   e. Whenever defendants take action regarding a child's placement, denial of placement, or transfer . . . the following procedures shall be followed.

      1. Notice required hereinbefore shall be given in writing by registered mail to the parent or guardian of the child.

      2. Such notice shall:

         a. describe the proposed action in detail;

         b. clearly state the specific and complete reasons for the proposed action, including the specification of any tests or reports upon which such action is proposed;

         c. describe any alternative educational opportunities available on a permanent or temporary basis;

         d. inform the parent or guardian of the right to object to the proposed action at a hearing before the Hearing Officer;

         e. inform the parent or guardian that the child is eligible to receive, at no charge, the services of a federally or locally funded diagnostic center for an independent medical, psychological and educational evaluation and shall specify the name, address and telephone number of an appropriate local diagnostic center;

         f. inform the parent or guardian of the right to be represented at the hearing by legal counsel; to examine the child's school records before the hearing, including any tests or reports upon which the proposed action may be based; to present evidence, including expert medical, psychological and educational testimony; and to confront and cross-examine any school official, employee, or agent of the school district or public department who may have evidence upon which the proposed action was based.

3. The hearing shall be at a time and place reasonably convenient to such parent or guardian. . . .

5. The hearing shall be a closed hearing unless the parent or guardian requests an open hearing.

6. The child shall have the right to a representative of his own choosing, including legal counsel.

7. The decision of the Hearing Officer shall be based solely upon the evidence presented at the hearing.

8. Defendants shall bear the burden of proof as to all facts and as to the appropriateness of any placement, denial of placement or transfer.

9. A tape recording or other record of the hearing shall be made and transcribed and, upon request, made available to the parent or guardian or his representative.

10. At a reasonable time prior to the hearing, the parent or guardian, or his counsel, shall be given access to all public school system and other public office records pertaining to the child, including any tests or reports upon which the proposed action may be based.

11. The independent Hearing Officer shall be an employee of the District of Columbia, but shall not be an officer, employee or agent of the Public School System. . . .

13. The parent or guardian, or his representative, shall have the right to present evidence and testimony, including expert medical, psychological or educational testimony.

14. Within thirty (30) days after the hearing, the Hearing Officer shall render a decision in writing. . . .

The "Free Appropriate Public Education" Clause of the Education of the Handicapped Act Does Not Require a State to Maximize the Potential of Each Handicapped Child

HENDRICK HUDSON DISTRICT BOARD OF EDUCATION v. ROWLEY

United States Supreme Court, 1982.
458 U.S. 176, 102 S.Ct. 3034.

JUSTICE REHNQUIST delivered the opinion of the Court.

This case presents a question of statutory interpretation. Petitioners contend that the Court of Appeals and the District Court misconstrued the requirements imposed by Congress upon States which receive federal funds under the Education of the Handicapped Act. We agree and reverse the judgment of the Court of Appeals.

The Education of the Handicapped Act provides federal money to assist state and local agencies in educating handicapped children, and conditions such funding upon a State's compliance with extensive goals and procedures. . . .

This case arose in connection with the education of Amy Rowley, a deaf student at the Furnace Woods School in the Hendrick Hudson Central School District, Peekskill, N.Y. Amy has minimal residual hearing and is an excellent lipreader. During the year before she began attending Furnace Woods, a meeting between her parents and school administrators resulted in a decision to place her in a regular kindergarten class in order to determine what supplemental services would be necessary to her education. Several members of the school administration prepared for Amy's arrival by attending a course in sign-language interpretation, and a teletype machine was installed in the principal's office to facilitate communication with her parents who are also deaf. At the end of the trial period it was determined that Amy should remain in the kindergarten class, but that she should be provided with an FM hearing aid which would amplify words spoken into a wireless receiver by the teacher or fellow students during certain classroom activities. Amy successfully completed her kindergarten year.

As required by the Act, an IEP was prepared for Amy during the fall of her first-grade year. The IEP provided that Amy should be educated in a regular classroom at Furnace Woods, should continue to use the FM hearing aid, and should receive instruction from a tutor for the deaf for one hour each day and from a speech therapist for three hours each week. The Rowleys agreed with parts of the IEP but insisted that Amy also be provided a qualified sign-language interpreter in all her academic classes in lieu of the assistance proposed in other parts of the IEP. Such an interpreter had been placed in Amy's kindergarten class for a two-week experimental period, but the interpreter had reported that Amy did not need his services at that time. The school administrators likewise concluded that Amy did not need such an interpreter in her first-grade classroom. They reached this conclusion after consulting the school district's Committee on the Handicapped, which had received expert evidence from Amy's parents on the importance of a sign-language interpreter, received testimony from Amy's teacher and other persons familiar with her academic and social progress, and visited a class for the deaf.

When their request for an interpreter was denied, the Rowleys demanded and received a hearing before an independent examiner. After receiving evidence from both sides, the examiner agreed with the administrators' determination that an interpreter was not necessary because "Amy was achieving educationally, academically, and socially" without such assistance. The examiner's decision was affirmed on appeal by the New York Commissioner of Education on the basis of substantial evidence in the record. Pursuant to the Act's provision for judicial review, the Rowleys then brought an action in the United States District Court for the Southern District of New York, claiming that the administrators' denial of the sign-language interpreter constituted a denial of the "free appropriate public education" guaranteed by the Act. . . .

We granted certiorari to review . . . . Such review requires us to consider two questions: What is meant by the Act's requirement of a "free appropriate public education"? And what is the role of state and federal courts in exercising the review granted by 20 U.S.C. § 1415? We consider these questions separately.

This is the first case in which this Court has been called upon to interpret any provision of the Act. . . . "(t)he Act itself does not define 'appropriate education,' " but leaves "to the courts and the hearing officers" the responsibility of "giv(ing) content to the requirement of an 'appropriate education.' " Petitioners contend that the definition of the phrase "free appropriate public education," used by the courts below overlooks the definition of that phrase actually found in the Act. Respondents agree that the Act defines "free appropriate public education," but contend that the statutory definition is not "functional" and thus "offers judges no guidance in their consideration of controversies involving 'the identification, evaluation, or educational placement of the child or the provision of a free appropriate public education.' " . . .

We are loath to conclude that Congress failed to offer any assistance in defining the meaning of the principal substantive phrase used in the Act. It is beyond dispute that, contrary to the conclusions of the courts below, the Act does expressly define "free appropriate public education":

> The term "free appropriate public education" means *special education* and *related services* which (A) have been provided at public expense, under public supervision and direction, and without charge, (B) meet the standards of the State educational agency, (C) include an appropriate preschool, elementary, or secondary school education in the State involved, and (D) are provided in conformity with the individualized education program required under section 1414(a)(5) of this title. § 1401(18) (emphasis added).

"Special education," as referred to in this definition, means "specially designed instruction, at no cost to parents or guardians, to meet the unique needs of a handicapped child, including classroom instruction, instruction in physical education, home instruction, and instruction in hospitals and institutions." § 1401(16). "Related services" are defined as "transportation, and such developmental, corrective, and other supportive services . . . as may be required to assist a handicapped child to benefit from special education." § 1401(17).

Like many statutory definitions, this one tends toward the cryptic rather than the comprehensive, but that is scarcely a reason for abandoning the quest for legislative intent. . . .

According to the definitions contained in the Act, a "free appropriate public education" consists of educational instruction specially designed to meet the unique needs of the handicapped child, supported by such services as are necessary to permit the child "to benefit" from the instruction. . . .

Noticeably absent from the language of the statute is any substantive standard prescribing the level of education to be accorded handicapped children. Certainly the language of the statute contains no requirement like the one imposed by the lower courts—that States maximize the potential of handicapped children "commensurate with the opportunity provided to other children." That standard was expounded by the District Court without reference to the statutory definitions or even to the legislative history of the Act. Although we find the statutory definition of "free appropriate public education" to be helpful in our interpretation of the Act, there remains the question of whether the legislative history indicates a congressional intent that such education meet some additional substantive standard. For an answer, we turn to that history.

That the Act imposes no clear obligation upon recipient States beyond the requirement that handicapped children receive some form of specialized education is perhaps best demonstrated by the fact that Congress, in explaining the need for the Act, equated an "appropriate education" to the receipt of some specialized educational services. The Senate Report states: "[T]he most recent statistics provided by the Bureau of Education for the Handicapped estimate that of the more than eight million children . . . with handicapping conditions requiring special education and related services, only 3.9 million such children are receiving an appropriate education." This statement, which reveals Congress' view that 3.9 million handicapped children were "receiving an appropriate education" in 1975, is followed immediately in the Senate Report by a table showing that 3.9 million handicapped children were "served" in 1975 and a slightly larger number were "unserved." A similar statement and table appear in the House Report.

It is evident from the legislative history that the characterization of handicapped children as "served" referred to children who were receiving some form of specialized educational services from the States, and that the characterization of children as "unserved" referred to those who were receiving no specialized educational services. . . .

Respondents contend that "the goal of the Act is to provide each handicapped child with an equal educational opportunity." We think, however, that the requirement that a State provide specialized educational services to handicapped children generates no additional requirement that the services so provided be sufficient to maximize each child's potential "commensurate with the opportunity provided other children." Respondents and the United States correctly note that Congress sought "to provide assistance to the States in carrying out their responsibilities under . . . the Constitution of the United States to provide equal protection of the laws." But we do not think that such statements imply a congressional intent to achieve strict equality of opportunity or services.

The educational opportunities provided by our public school systems undoubtedly differ from student to student, depending upon a myriad of factors that might affect a particular student's ability to assimilate information presented in the classroom. The requirement that States provide "equal" educational opportunities would thus seem to present an entirely unworkable standard requiring impossible measurements and comparisons. Similarly, furnishing handicapped children with only such services as are available to nonhandicapped children would in all probability fall short of the statutory requirement of "free appropriate public education"; to require, on the other hand, the furnishing of every special service necessary to maximize each handicapped child's potential is, we think, further than

Congress intended to go. Thus to speak in terms of "equal" services in one instance gives less than what is required by the Act and in another instance more. The theme of the Act is "free appropriate public education," a phrase which is too complex to be captured by the word "equal" whether one is speaking of opportunities or services. . . .

In explaining the need for federal legislation, the House Report noted that "no congressional legislation has required a precise guarantee for handicapped children, i.e., a basic floor of opportunity that would bring into compliance all school districts with the constitutional right of equal protection with respect to handicapped children."

Assuming that the Act was designed to fill the need identified in the House Report—that is, to provide a "basic floor of opportunity" consistent with equal protection—neither the Act nor its history persuasively demonstrates that Congress though that equal protection required anything more than equal access. Therefore, Congress' desire to provide specialized educational services, even in furtherance of "equality," cannot be read as imposing any particular substantive educational standard upon the States.

The District Court and the Court of Appeals thus erred when they held that the Act requires New York to maximize the potential of each handicapped child commensurate with the opportunity provided nonhandicapped children. Desirable though that goal might be, it is not the standard that Congress imposed upon States which receive funding under the Act. Rather, Congress sought primarily to identify and evaluate handicapped children, and to provide them with access to a free public education.

Implicit in the congressional purpose of providing access to a "free appropriate public education" is the requirement that the education to which access is provided be sufficient to confer some educational benefit upon the handicapped child. It would do little good for Congress to spend millions of dollars in providing access to a public education only to have the handicapped child receive no benefit from that education. The statutory definition of "free appropriate public education," in addition to requiring that States provide each child with "specially designed instruction," expressly requires the provision of "such . . . supportive services . . . as may be required to assist a handicapped child *to benefit* from special education." (Emphasis added.) We therefore conclude that the "basic floor of opportunity" provided by the Act consists of access to specialized instruction and related services which are individually designed to provide educational benefit to the handicapped child.

The determination of when handicapped children are receiving sufficient educational benefits to satisfy the requirements of the Act presents a more difficult problem. The Act requires participating States to educate a wide spectrum of handicapped children, from the marginally hearing-impaired to the profoundly retarded and palsied. It is clear that the benefits obtainable by children at one end of the spectrum will differ dramatically from those obtainable by children at the other end, with infinite variations in between. One child may have little difficulty competing successfully in an academic setting with nonhandicapped children while another child may encounter great difficulty in acquiring even the most basic of self-maintenance skills. We do not attempt today to establish any one test for determining the adequacy of educational benefits conferred upon all children covered by the Act. Because in this case we are presented with a handicapped child who is receiving substantial specialized instruction and related services, and who is performing above average in the regular classrooms of a public school system, we confine our analysis to that situation.

The Act requires participating States to educate handicapped children with nonhandicapped children whenever possible. When that "mainstreaming" preference of the Act has been met and a child is being educated in the regular classrooms of a public school system, the system itself monitors the educational progress of the child. Regular examinations are administered, grades are awarded, and yearly advancement to higher grade levels is permitted for those children who attain an adequate knowledge of the course material. The grading and advancement system thus constitutes an important factor in determining educational benefit. Children who graduate from our public school systems are considered by our society to have been "educated" at least to the grade level they have completed, and access to an "education" for handicapped children is precisely what Congress sought to provide in the Act.

When the language of the Act and its legislative history are considered together, the requirements imposed by Congress become tolerably clear. Insofar as a State is required to provide a handicapped child with a "free appropriate public education," we hold that it satisfies this requirement by providing personalized instruction with sufficient support services to permit the child to benefit educationally from that instruction. Such instruction and services must be provided at public expense, must meet the State's educational standards, must approximate the grade levels used in the State's regular education, and must comport with the child's IEP. In addition, the IEP, and therefore the personalized instruction, should be formulated in accordance with the requirements of the Act and, if the child is being educated in the regular classrooms of the public education system, should be reasonably calculated to enable the child to achieve passing marks and advance from grade to grade. . . .

In assuring that the requirements of the Act have been met, courts must be careful to avoid imposing their view of preferable educational methods upon the States. The primary responsibility for formulating the education to be accorded a handicapped child, and for choosing the educational method most suitable to the child's needs, was left by the Act to state and local educational agencies in cooperation with the parents or guardian of the child. The Act expressly charges States with the responsibility of "acquiring and disseminating to teachers and administrators of programs for handicapped children significant information derived from educational research, demonstration, and similar projects, and [of] adopting, where appropriate, promising educational practices and materials." § 1413(a)(3). In the face of such a clear statutory directive, it seems highly unlikely that Congress intended courts to overturn a State's choice of appropriate educational theories in a proceeding conducted pursuant to § 1415(e)(2).

We previously have cautioned that courts lack the "specialized knowledge and experience" necessary to resolve "persistent and difficult questions of educational policy." San Antonio Independent School Dist. v. Rodriguez, 411

U.S. 1, 42, 93 S.Ct. 1278, 1301, 36 L.Ed.2d 16 (1973). We think that Congress shared that view when it passed the Act. As already demonstrated, Congress' intention was not that the Act displace the primacy of States in the field of education, but that States receive funds to assist them in extending their educational systems to the handicapped. Therefore, once a court determines that the requirements of the Act have been met, questions of methodology are for resolution by the States.

Entrusting a child's education to state and local agencies does not leave the child without protection. Congress sought to protect individual children by providing for parental involvement in the development of state plans and policies, and in the formulation of the child's individual educational program. As the Senate Report states:

> The Committee recognizes that in many instances the process of providing special education and related services to handicapped children is not guaranteed to produce any particular outcome. By changing the language [of the provision relating to individualized educational programs] to emphasize the process of parent and child involvement and to provide a written record of reasonable expectations, the Committee intends to clarify that such individualized planning conferences are a way to provide parent involvement and protection to assure that appropriate services are provided to a handicapped child.

As this very case demonstrates, parents and guardians will not lack ardor in seeking to ensure that handicapped children receive all of the benefits to which they are entitled by the Act.

Applying these principles to the facts of this case, we conclude that Court of Appeals erred in affirming the decision of the District Court. Neither the District Court nor the Court of Appeals found that petitioners had failed to comply with the procedures of the Act, and the findings of neither court would support a conclusion that Amy's educational program failed to comply with the substantive requirements of the Act. On the contrary, the District Court found that the "evidence firmly establishes that Amy is receiving an 'adequate' education, since she performs better than the average child in her class and is advancing easily from grade to grade." In light of this finding, and of the fact that Amy was receiving personalized instruction and related services calculated by the Furnace Woods school administrators to meet her educational needs, the lower courts should not have concluded that the Act requires the provision of a sign-language interpreter. Accordingly, the decision of the Court of Appeals is reversed, and the case is remanded for further proceedings consistent with this opinion.

So ordered.

NOTE

Decision by school district to transfer handicapped student to another school where the instructor was better qualified to train student with that particular hardship was not unreasonable. Wilson v. Marana Unified School Dist. No. 6, 735 F.2d 1178 (9th Cir. 1984).

Expulsion of Handicapped Student
Must Be Accompanied By
Determination as to Whether His
Misconduct Bears Relationship to
His Handicap

S–1 v. TURLINGTON

United States Court of Appeals,
Fifth Circuit, 1981.
635 F.2d 342.

HATCHETT, Circuit Judge.

In this appeal, we are called upon to decide whether nine handicapped students were denied their rights under the provisions of the Education for All Handicapped Children Act, 20 U.S.C. §§ 1401–1415, or section 504 of the Rehabilitation Act of 1973, codified at 29 U.S.C. § 794, and their implementing regulations. The trial court found a denial of rights and entered a preliminary injunction against the state and local officials. Defendants attack the trial court's entry of a preliminary injunction as an abuse of discretion. Because we find that the trial court did not abuse its discretion in entering the preliminary injunction, we affirm.

Plaintiffs . . . were expelled from Clewiston High School, Hendry County, Florida, in the early part of the 1977–78 school year for alleged misconduct.[41] Each was expelled for the remainder of the 1977–78 school year and for the entire 1978–79 school year, the maximum time permitted by state law. All of the plaintiffs were classified as either educable mentally retarded (EMR), mildly mentally retarded, or EMR/dull normal. It is undisputed that the expelled plaintiffs were accorded the procedural protections required by Goss v. Lopez, 419 U.S. 565, 95 S.Ct. 729, 42 L.Ed.2d 725 (1975). Except for S–1, they were not given, nor did they request, hearings to determine whether their misconduct was a manfestation of their handicap. Regarding S–1, the superintendent of Hendry County Schools determined that because S–1 was not classified as seriously emotionally disturbed, his misconduct, as a matter of law, could not be a manifestation of his handicap.

At all material times, plaintiffs S–7 and S–9 were not under expulsion orders. S–7 was not enrolled in high school by his own choice. In October 1978, he requested a due process hearing to determine if he had been evaluated or if he had an individualized educational program. S–9 made a similar request in October, 1978. Shortly before her request, S–9's guardian had consented to the individualized educational program being offered her during that school year. The superintendent denied both students' requests, but offered to hold conferences in order to discuss the appropriateness of their individualized educational programs.

Plaintiffs initiated this case alleging violations of their rights under the Education for all Handicapped Children Act, (EHA) 20 U.S.C. §§ 1401–1415, and section 504 of the Rehabilitation Act of 1973, 29 U.S.C. § 794. Plaintiffs sought preliminary and permanent injunctive relief compelling state and local officials to provide them with the educational services and procedural rights required by the EHA, section 504, and their implementing regulations.

The trial court found that the EHA, effective in Florida on September 1, 1978, provided all handicapped children the right to a free and appropriate public education. The court further found that the expelled students were denied this right in violation of the EHA. In addition, the trial court decided that under section 504 and the EHA, no handicapped student could be expelled for misconduct related to the handicap. That in the case of S–2, S–3, S–4, S–5, S–6, and S–8, no determination was ever made of the relationship between their handicaps and their behavioral problems. With regard to S–1, the trial court found that the superintendent's determination was insufficient under section 504 and the EHA. The court reasoned that an expulsion is a change in educational placement. That under the educational placement procedures of section 504 and the EHA, only a trained and specialized group could make this decision. For these reasons, the trial court concluded that a likelihood of success on the merits had been shown with respect to the expelled plaintiffs.

With regard to S–7 and S–9, the trial court stated that under 20 U.S.C. § 1415(b)(1)(E), students and their parents or guardians must be provided "an opportunity to present complaints with respect to any matter relating to the identification, evaluation, or educational placement of the child, or the provision of a free appropriate education to such child." That under 20 U.S.C. § 1415(b)(2), "whenever such a complaint has been received, the parents or guardians shall have an opportunity for an impartial due process hearing." The trial court found that the superintendent's failure to grant S–7 and S–9 impartial due process hearings contravened the express provisions of the EHA. The court therefore concluded that S–7 and S–9 had shown a likelihood of success on the merits of their claim.

Finally, the trial court found that the plaintiffs had suffered irreparable harm in that two years of education had been irretrievably lost. The court further determined that an injunction was necessary to ensure that plaintiffs would be provided their rights, even though the expulsions had expired at the time the injunction was entered.

In an appeal from an order granting preliminary relief, the applicable standard of review is whether the issuance of the injunction, in light of the applicable standard, constitutes an abuse of discretion. Therefore, in order to decide whether the trial court abused its discretion in entering the preliminary injunction, we must resolve the following issues: (1) whether an expulsion is a change in educational placement thereby invoking the procedural protections of the EHA and section 504; (2) whether the EHA, section 504, and their implementing regulations contemplate a dual system of discipline for handicapped and nonhandicapped students; (3) whether the burden of raising the question, whether a student's misconduct is a manifestation of the student's handicap, is on the state and local officials or on the student; (4) whether the EHA and its implementing regulations required the local defendants to grant S–7 and S–9 due process hearings; and, (5) whether the trial judge properly entered the preliminary injunction against the state defendants.

Section 504 of the Rehabilitation Act and the EHA have been the subject of infrequent litigation. No reported appellate cases deal with these acts and the issues presented in the instant case. Therefore, a review of these statutes and their pertinent regulations is necessary to the disposition of this controversy.

Section 504, effective in Florida four months prior to the expulsions in question, provides:

> No otherwise qualified handicapped individual in the United States, as defined in section 706(7) of this title, shall, solely by reason of his handicap, be excluded from the participation in, be denied the benefits of, or be subjected to discrimination under any program or activity receiving federal financial assistance. . . .

Under 29 U.S.C. § 706(7)(B), a handicapped individual is defined as "any person who (1) has a physical or mental impairment which substantially limits one or more of such person's major life activities . . . ."

Under the EHA, 20 U.S.C. § 1412(1) and (5)(B), effective in Florida on September 1, 1978, a state receiving financial assistance under this Act is required to provide all handicapped children a free and appropriate education in the least restrictive environment. The definition of handicapped children under the EHA is similar to the definition under section 504.

Florida, and the Hendry County School Board, are recipients of federal funds under both section 504 and the EHA. The children in this suit are clearly handicapped within the meaning of both section 504 and the EHA. The parties agree that a handicapped student may not be expelled for misconduct which results from the handicap itself. It follows that an expulsion must be accompanied by a determination as to whether the handicapped student's misconduct bears a relationship to his handicap. From a practical standpoint, this is the only logical approach. How else would a school board know whether it is violating section 504?

Defendant local officials argue that they complied with section 504. As support for their position, they state that they determined, in the expulsion proceedings, that the plaintiffs were capable of understanding rules and regulations or right from wrong. They also assert that they found, based upon a psychological evaluation, that plaintiffs' handicaps were not behavioral handicaps (as it would be if plaintiffs were classified as seriously emotionally disturbed), thereby precluding any relationship between the misconduct and the applicable handicap. We cannot agree that consideration of the above factors satisfies the requirement of section 504. A determination that a handicapped student knew the difference between right and wrong is not tantamount to a determination that his misconduct was or was not a manifestation of his handicap. The second prong of the school officials' argument is unacceptable. Essentially, what the school officials assert is that a handicapped student's misconduct can never be a symptom of his handicap, unless he is classified as seriously emotionally disturbed. With regard to this argument, the trial court stated:

> The defendants concede that a handicapped student cannot be expelled for misconduct which is a manifestation of the handicap itself. However, they would limit application of this principle to those students classified as "seriously emotionally disturbed." In the Court's view such a generalization is contrary to the emphasis which Congress has placed on individualized evaluation and consideration of the problems and needs of handicapped students.

We agree. In addition, the uncontradicted testimony elicited at the preliminary injunction hearing suggests otherwise. At the hearing, a psychologist testified that a connection between the misconduct upon which the expulsions were based and the plaintiffs' handicaps may have existed. She reasoned that "a child with low intellectual functions and perhaps the lessening of control would respond to stress or respond to a threat in the only way that they feel adequate, which may be verbal aggressive behavior." She further testified that an orthopedically handicapped child, whom she had consulted,

> [w]ould behave in an extremely aggressive way towards other children and provoke fights despite the fact that he was likely to come out very much on the short end of the stick. That this was his way of dealing with stress and dealing with a feeling of physical vulnerability. He would be both aggressive and hope that he would turn off people and as a result provoke an attack on him.

The record clearly belies the school officials' contention.

With regard to plaintiff S–1, the trial court found that the school officials entrusted with the expulsion decision determined at the disciplinary proceedings that S–1's misconduct was unrelated to his handicap. The trial court, however, held that this determination was made by school board officials who lacked the necessary expertise to make such a determination. The trial court arrived at this conclusion by holding that an expulsion is a change in educational placement. Under 45 CFR § 121a.533(a)(3) and 45 CFR § 84.35(c)(3), evaluations and placement decisions must be made by a specialized and knowledgeable group of persons.

The trial court's finding presents the novel issue in this circuit whether an expulsion is a change in educational placement, thereby invoking the procedural protections of both the EHA and section 504 of the Rehabilitation Act. In deciding this issue, the EHA and section 504, as remedial statutes, should be broadly applied and liberally construed in favor of providing a free and appropriate education to handicapped students.

The EHA, section 504, and their implementing regulations do not provide this court any direction on this issue. We find the reasoning of the district court in Stuart v. Nappi, 443 F.Supp. 1235 (D.Conn.1978), persuasive. In Stuart, a child was diagnosed as having a major learning disability caused by either a brain disfunction or a perceptual disorder. She challenged the use of disciplinary proceedings which, if completed, would have resulted in her expulsion for participating in a schoolwide disturbance. The trial court held that the proposed expulsion constituted a change in educational placement, thus requiring the school officials to adhere to the procedural protections of the EHA. In so holding the court stated:

> The right to an education in the least restrictive environment may be circumvented if schools are permitted to expel handicapped children [without following the procedures prescribed by the EHA] . . . . An expulsion has the effect not only of changing a student's placement, but also of restricting the availability of alternative placements. For example, plaintiff's expulsion may well exclude her from a placement that is appropriate for her academic and social development. This result flies in the face of the explicit mandate of the handicapped act which requires that all placement decisions be made in

conformity with a child's right to an education in the least restrictive environment. [Citation omitted.]

We agree with the district court in *Stuart,* and therefore hold that a termination of educational services, occasioned by an expulsion, is a change in educational placement, thereby invoking the procedural protections of the EHA.

The proposition that an expulsion is a change in educational placement has been cited with approval in Sherry v. New York State Education Department, 479 F.Supp. 1328 (W.D.N.Y.1979). . . . and Doe v. Koger, 480 F.Supp. 225 (N.D.Ind.1979). . . . As stated by the district court in *Doe* v. *Koger,* our holding that expulsion of a handicapped student constitutes a change in educational placement distinguishes the handicapped student in that, "unlike any other disruptive child, before a disruptive handicapped child can be expelled, it must be determined whether the handicap is the cause of the child's propensity to disrupt. This issue must be determined through the change of placement procedures required by the handicapped act."

The school officials point out that a group of persons entrusted with the educational placement decision could never decide that expulsion is the correct placement for a handicapped student, thus insulating a handicapped student from expulsion as a disciplinary tool. They further state that Florida law does not contemplate this result because expulsion is specifically provided for under Florida law as a disciplinary tool for all students. While the trial court declined to decide the issue whether a handicapped student can ever be expelled, we cannot ignore the gray areas that may result if we do not decide this question. We therefore find that expulsion is still a proper disciplinary tool under the EHA and section 504 when proper procedures are utilized and under proper circumstances. We cannot, however, authorize the complete cessation of educational services during an expulsion period.

State defendants focus their attention on the fact that, with the exception of S–1, none of the expelled plaintiffs raised the argument, until eleven months after expulsion, that they could not be expelled unless the proper persons determined that their handicap did not bear a causal connection to their misconduct. By this assertion, we assume that state defendants contend that the handicapped students waived their right to this determination. The issue is therefore squarely presented whether the burden of raising the question whether a student's misconduct is a manifestation of the student's handicap is on the state and local officials or on the student. The EHA, section 504, and their implementing regulations do not prescribe who must raise this issue. In light of the remedial purposes of these statutes, we find that the burden is on the local and state defendants to make this determination. Our conclusion is buttressed by the fact that in most cases, the handicapped students and their parents lack the wherewithal either to know or to assert their rights under the EHA and section 504.

The next issue is whether the EHA and its implementing regulations required the local defendants to grant S–7 and S–9 due process hearings. The school officials suggest that because S–7 had voluntarily withdrawn from school, he was not entitled to a due process hearing. With regard to S–9, the school officials assert that because she had previously agreed to the educational program being offered her during the school year, she was not entitled to a due process hearing. They also suggest that the conference offered by the superintendent was an adequate substitute for the due process hearings. They cite 45 CFR § 121a.506 as support for their argument. Under this regulation, the Department of Health, Education and Welfare (HEW, now Health and Human Services), states in a comment that mediation can be used to resolve differences between parents and agencies without the development of an adversarial relationship.

The Justice Department, as amicus curiae, and the trial court, point out that under 20 U.S.C. § 1415(b)(1), parents and guardians of handicapped children must have "an opportunity to present complaints with respect *to any matter* relating to the identification, evaluation, or educational placement of the child, or the provision of a free appropriate public education to such child." (Emphasis added.) The statute also states, in section 1415(b), that "whenever a complaint has been received under paragraph (1) of this subsection, the parents or guardian shall have an opportunity for an impartial due process hearing . . . ." No exception is made for handicapped students who voluntarily withdraw from school or previously agree to an educational placement. With regard to defendants' argument under 45 CFR § 121a.506, HEW states in the same comment that mediation may not be used to deny or delay a parent's rights under this subpart. In the circumstances, the trial judge correctly found that plaintiffs S–7 and S–9 were entitled to due process hearings.

State defendants advance three arguments that deserve comment. First, they assert that the trial judge erred in analyzing section 504 in light of the Supreme Court's decision in Southeastern Community College v. Davis, 442 U.S. 397, 99 S.Ct. 2361, 60 L.Ed.2d 980 (1979). In that case, the issue was whether section 504, which prohibits discrimination against an otherwise qualified handicapped individual enrolled in a federally funded program, solely by reason of his handicap, forbids professional schools from imposing physical qualifications for admission to their clinical training program. The Supreme Court held that section 504 did not forbid professional schools from imposing physical qualifications for admission. Without discussing *Southeastern* any further, it is clear that it does not apply to this case. Physical qualifications are not at issue in this case. Furthermore, we do not deal here with a professional school.

Secondly, state defendants argue that the trial court erred in imposing the EHA as a requirement at the time of the expulsions because the EHA was not effective in Florida until September 1, 1978. The trial court did not impose the EHA as a requirement at the time of the expulsion. The court found that the expelled plaintiffs became entitled to the protections of the EHA on September 1, 1978. As such, the expelled plaintiffs became entitled to a free and appropriate education in the least restrictive environment. In fact, under 20 U.S.C. § 1412(3), because plaintiffs were not receiving educational services on September 1, 1978, they fell within a special class of handicapped students entitled to priority regarding the provision of a free and appropriate education. The only way in which the expulsions could have continued as of September 1, 1978, is if a qualified group of individuals determined that no relationship existed between the plaintiffs' handicap and their misconduct. Furthermore, section 504, effective at the time of the expulsions, provides protections and procedures similar to those of the EHA.

Finally, the state officials argue that the trial court improperly entered the injunction against them. They assert that they lacked the authority to intervene in the expulsion proceedings because disciplinary matters are exclusively local. While this argument may be true regarding non-handicapped students, it is inapplicable to handicapped students. Expulsion proceedings are of the type that may serve to deny an education to those entitled to it under the EHA. Under 20 U.S.C. § 1412(6), the state educational agency is:

> Responsible for assuring that the requirements of this sub-chapter be carried out and that all educational programs for handicapped children within the state, including all such programs administered by any other state or local agency, will be under the general supervision of the persons responsible for educational programs for handicapped children in the state educational agency and shall meet educational standards of the state educational agency.

Clearly, the state officials were empowered to intervene in the expulsion proceedings under 20 U.S.C. § 1412(6).

Accordingly, we hold that under the EHA, section 504, and their implementing regulations: (1) before a handicapped student can be expelled, a trained and knowledgeable group of persons must determine whether the student's misconduct bears a relationship to his handicapping condition; (2) an expulsion is a change in educational placement thereby invoking the procedural protections of the EHA and section 504; (3) expulsion is a proper disciplinary tool under the EHA and section 504, but a complete cessation of educational services is not; (4) S-7 and S-9 were entitled to due process hearings; and (5) the trial judge properly entered the preliminary injunction against the state defendants. In the circumstances, the trial judge did not abuse his discretion in entering the injunction.

Affirmed.

NOTES

1. The Sixth Circuit Court of Appeals concurred with the decision rendered in *S-1* v. *Turlington,* and held that the expulsion of a mentally retarded student must be considered a change in educational placement and thus could not occur without affording the student procedural protections as outlined in P.L. 94–142, Kaelin v. Grubbs, 682 F.2d 595 (6th Cir.1982).

2. In Mayson v. Teague, 749 F.2d 652, December 1984, the U.S. Court of Appeals, 11th Circuit, ruled that officers and employees of local school boards and certain university personnel were not eligible to serve on due process hearing panels under P.L. 94–142.

*School Is Required to Provide
Catheterization for a Handicapped
Child*

IRVING INDEPENDENT
SCHOOL DISTRICT v. TATRO

Supreme Court of the United States.
— U.S. —, 104 S.Ct. 3371.

CHIEF JUSTICE BURGER delivered the opinion of the Court.

We granted certiorari to determine whether the Education of the Handicapped Act or the Rehabilitation Act of 1973 requires a school district to provide a handicapped child with clean intermittent catheterization during school hours.

Amber Tatro is an eight-year-old girl born with a defect known as spina bifida. As a result, she suffers from orthopedic and speech impairments and a neurogenic bladder, which prevents her from emptying her bladder voluntarily. Consequently, she must be catheterized every three or four hours to avoid injury to her kidneys. In accordance with accepted medical practice, clean intermittent catheterization (CIC), a procedure involving the insertion of a catheter into the urethra to drain the bladder, has been prescribed. The procedure is a simple one that may be performed in a few minutes by a layperson with less than an hour's training. Amber's parents, babysitter, and teenage brother are all qualified to administer CIC, and Amber soon will be able to perform this procedure herself.

In 1979 petitioner Irving Independent School District agreed to provide special education for Amber, who was then three and one-half years old. In consultation with her parents, who are respondents here, petitioner developed an individualized education program for Amber under the requirements of the Education of the Handicapped Act, 84 Stat. 175, as amended significantly by the Education for All Handicapped Children Act of 1975, 89 Stat. 773, 20 U.S.C. §§ 1401(19), 1414(a)(5). The individualized education program provided that Amber would attend early childhood development classes and receive special services such as physical and occupational therapy. That program, however, made no provision for school personnel to administer CIC. . . .

This case poses two separate issues. The first is whether the Education of the Handicapped Act requires petitioner to provide CIC services to Amber. The second is whether § 504 of the Rehabilitation Act creates such an obligation. We first turn to the claim presented under the Education of the Handicapped Act.

States receiving funds under the Act are obliged to satisfy certain conditions. A primary condition is that the state implement a policy "that assures all handicapped children the right to a free appropriate public education." 20 U.S.C. § 1412(1). Each educational agency applying to a state for funding must provide assurances in turn that its program aims to provide "a free appropriate public education to all handicapped children." § 1414(a)(1)(C)(ii).

A "free appropriate public education" is explicitly defined as "special education and related services." § 1401(18). The term "special education" means

> specially designed instruction, at no cost to parents or guardians, to meet the unique needs of a handicapped child, including classroom instruction, instruction in physical education, home instruction, and instruction in hospitals and institutions. § 1401(16).

"Related services" are defined as

> transportation, and such developmental, corrective, and other *supportive services (including* speech pathology and audiology, psychological services, physical and occupational therapy, recreation, and *medical* and counseling *services, except that such medical services shall be for diagnostic and evaluation purposes only) as may be required to assist a handicapped child to benefit from special education,* and includes the early identification and assessment of handicapping conditions in children. § 1401(17) (emphasis added).

The issue in this case is whether CIC is a "related service" that petitioner is obliged to provide to Amber. We must answer two questions: first, whether CIC is a "supportive servic[e] . . . required to assist a handicapped child to benefit from special education"; and second, whether CIC is excluded from this definition as a "medical servic[e]" serving purposes other than diagnosis or evaluation.

The Court of Appeals was clearly correct in holding that CIC is a "supportive servic[e] . . . required to assist a handicapped child to benefit from special education." It is clear on this record that, without having CIC services available during the school day, Amber cannot attend school and thereby "benefit from special education." CIC services therefore fall squarely within the definition of a "supportive service."

As we have stated before, "Congress sought primarily to make public education available to handicapped children" and "to make such access meaningful." Board of Education of Hendrick Hudson Central School District v. Rowley, 458 U.S. 176, 192 (1982). A service that enables a handicapped child to remain at school during the day is an important means of providing the child with the meaningful access to education that Congress envisioned. The Act makes specific provision for services, like transportation, for example, that do no more than enable a child to be physically present in class, see 20 U.S.C. § 1401(17); and the Act specifically authorizes grants for schools to alter buildings and equipment to make them accessible to the handicapped, § 1406; see S.Rep. No. 94–168, p. 38 (1975); 121 Cong. Rec. 19483–19484 (1975) (remarks of Sen. Stafford). Services like CIC that permit a child to remain at school during the day are no less related to the effort to educate than are services that enable the child to reach, enter, or exit the school.

We hold that CIC services in this case qualify as a "supportive servic[e] . . . required to assist a handicapped child to benefit from special education."

We also agree with the Court of Appeals that provision of CIC is not a "medical servic[e]," which a school is required to provide only for purposes of diagnosis or evaluation. See 20 U.S.C. § 1401(17). We begin with the regulations of the Department of Education, which are entitled to deference. See, e.g., *Blum* v. *Bacon,* 457 U.S. 132, 141 (1982). The regulations define "related services" for handicapped children to include "school health services," 34 CFR § 300.13(a) (1983), which are defined in turn as "services provided by a qualified school nurse or other qualified person," § 300.13(b)(10). "Medical services" are defined as "services provided by a licensed physician." § 300.13(b)(4). Thus, the Secretary has determined that the services of a school nurse otherwise qualifying as a "related service" are not subject to exclusion as a "medical service," but that the services of a physician are excludable as such.

This definition of "medical services" is a reasonable interpretation of congressional intent. Although Congress devoted little discussion to the "medical services" exclusion, the Secretary could reasonably have concluded that it was designed to spare schools from an obligation to provide a service that might well prove unduly expensive and beyond the range of their competence. From this understanding of congressional purpose, the Secretary could reasonably have concluded that Congress intended to impose the obligation to provide school nursing services.

Congress plainly required schools to hire various specially trained personnel to help handicapped children, such as "trained occupational therapists, speech therapists, psychologists, social workers and other appropriately trained personnel." S.Rep. No. 94–168, supra, at 33. School nurses have long been a part of the educational system, and the Secretary could therefore reasonably conclude that school nursing services are not the sort of burden that Congress intended to exclude as a "medical service." By limiting the "medical services" exclusion to the services of a physician or hospital, both far more expensive, the Secretary has given a permissible construction to the provision.

Petitioner's contrary interpretation of the "medical services" exclusion is unconvincing. In petitioner's view, CIC is a "medical service," even though it may be provided by a nurse or trained layperson; that conclusion rests on its reading of Texas law that confines CIC to uses in accordance with a physician's prescription and under a physician's ultimate supervision. Aside from conflicting with the Secretary's reasonable interpretation of congressional intent, however, such a rule would be anomalous. Nurses in petitioner's school district are authorized to dispense oral medications and administer emergency injections in accordance with a physician's prescription. This kind of service for nonhandicapped children is difficult to distinguish from the provision of CIC to the handicapped. It would be strange indeed if Congress, in attempting to extend special services to handicapped children, were unwilling to guarantee them services of a kind that are routinely provided to the nonhandicapped.

To keep in perspective the obligation to provide services that relate to both the health and educational needs of handicapped students, we note several limitations that should minimize the burden petitioner fears. First, to be entitled to related services, a child must be handicapped so as to require special education. See 20 U.S.C. § 1401(1); 34 CFR § 300.5 (1983). In the absence of a handicap that requires special education, the need for what otherwise might qualify as a related service does not create an obligation under the Act. See 34 CFR § 300.14, Comment (1) (1983).

Second, only those services necessary to aid a handicapped child to benefit from special education must be provided, regardless how easily a school nurse or layperson could furnish them. For example, if a particular medication or treatment may appropriately be administered to a handicapped child other than during the school day, a school is not required to provide nursing services to administer it.

Third, the regulations state that school nursing services must be provided only if they can be performed by a nurse or other qualified person, not if they must be performed by a physician. See 34 CFR §§ 300.13(a), (b)(4), (b) (10) (1983). It bears mentioning that here not even the services of a nurse are required; as is conceded, a layperson with minimal training is qualified to provide CIC. . . .

Finally, we note that respondents are not asking petitioner to provide *equipment* that Amber needs for CIC. Tr. of Oral Arg. 18–19. They seek only the *services* of a qualified person at the school.

We conclude that provision of CIC to Amber is not subject to exclusion as a "medical service," and we affirm the Court of Appeals' holding that CIC is a "related service" under the Education of the Handicapped Act.

Respondents sought relief not only under the Education of the Handicapped Act but under § 504 of the Rehabilitation Act as well. After finding petitioner liable to provide CIC under the former, the District Court proceeded to hold that petitioner was similarly liable under § 504 and that respondents were therefore entitled to attorney's fees under § 505 of the Rehabilitation Act, 29 U.S.C. § 794a. [We hold today, in *Smith* v. *Robinson*, ___ U.S. ___, 104 S.Ct. 3457 (1984), that § 504 is inapplicable when relief is available under the Education of the Handicapped Act to remedy a denial of educational services. Respondents are therefore not entitled to relief under § 504, and we reverse the Court of Appeals' holding that respondents are entitled to recover attorney's fees.] In all other respects, the judgment of the Court of Appeals is affirmed.

It is so ordered.

NOTE

In Rose v. Nebraska, 748 F.2d 1258 (1984), the U.S. Court of Appeals, 8th Circuit, allowed attorney's fees for a due process challenge of the impartiality of a hearing officer. The court distinguished Smith v. Robinson, above, because *Rose* was a due process case.

*Before Ordering Residential Placement
for a Handicapped Child, the Court
Should Weigh the Mainstreaming
Policy in Education for All
Handicapped Children Act, Which
Encourages the Placement of the
Child in the Least Restrictive
Environment*

KRUELLE v. NEW CASTLE COUNTY SCHOOL DISTRICT

United States Court of Appeals, Third
Circuit, 1981.
642 F.2d 687.

ADAMS, Circuit Judge.

. . . did the district court err in determining that Paul Kruelle is entitled to residential placement under the Education Act?

Appellee is profoundly retarded and is also afflicted with cerebral palsy. At age thirteen he has the social skills of a six-month-old child and his I.Q. is well below thirty. As found by the district court, "he cannot walk, dress himself, or eat unaided. He is not toilet trained. He does not speak, and his receptive communication level is extremely low. In addition to his physical problems, he has had a history of emotional problems which result in choking and self-induced vomiting when experiencing stress."

The chronicle of Paul's educational placements begins in 1973, when he entered the Barber Center Preschool Program in Pennsylvania, where the Kruelle family then resided. Paul next spent three years in the public school system in a mixed class with the trainable mentally retarded. By 1977 Paul's behavior had significantly deteriorated. He was vomiting food in school and having frequent temper tantrums. That summer Paul received in-home instruction to compensate for his rejection of the school environment.

In September 1977, at the behest of the public educational authorities, Paul was placed in the private day program at the Barber Center. Admission was based on the local school agencies' certification that "an appropriate education for this child cannot be met in a special education program operated either by the school district or Intermediate Unit" in Pennsylvania. Despite initial improvement, by early 1978 Paul again manifested the vomiting and choking that apparently is caused by emotional stress. Because of the severity and increased frequency of the vomiting, both the school authorities and Paul's parents concluded that twenty-four-hour residential placement was needed.

After a short period in respite care, Paul was admitted in June 1978 to the Barber Center's New Community Living Arrangement Program for multiply-handicapped children. Although not a "residential" placement in the sense of having the living environment and school facilities on the same premises, this combination school program and group home did provide around-the-clock training by skilled caretakers. The local and state educational agencies, Department of Public Welfare and Social Security Administration provided funding for the program. Most importantly, except for a brief hospital stay for pneumonia, Paul appears to have adjusted well to this joint CLA residence-school program.

The Kruelle family then moved to Delaware. Paul was immediately enrolled in the Meadowood School and placed in respite care at the home of Mrs. Albanese. Mrs. Albanese had extensive experience in the care and training of handicapped children. Although the teachers at Meadowood indicated that Paul made observable progress at the school and Mrs. Albanese noted some improvements from her continuation of Paul's day-time training, after two weeks the Kruelles withdrew Paul from Meadowood. Having objected from the start to the lack of a residential placement in Delaware, as well as to Paul's assignment to a mixed class of trainable mentally retarded, which had previously failed, the Kruelles next began through the administrative process, an unsuccessful quest for a residential program.

Parents or guardians challenging a child's educational placement are offered an impartial hearing under the Education Act. 20 U.S.C. § 1415(b) (2). In states such as Delaware, where the hearing is conducted by a local or an intermediate educational unit, the party may appeal to the state educational agency. 20 U.S.C. § 1415(c). Both the district hearing officer and the state-level review officer determined that the individual educational program (IEP) proposed by the Meadowood staff was "appropriate" within the meaning of the Education Act. The district hearing officer found that residential placement was "too restrictive," while the state review officer asserted that the full-time services sought "were more in the nature of parenting than education." The Kruelle's request for Paul's placement in a residential setting was therefore denied.

In October, 1979, Paul's parents, pro se, sought review of the administrative decision by filing a civil suit in district court. The multiple defendants included the local New Castle County School District (NCCSD), the supervisory State Board of Education, the Superintendent of the Division of Public Instruction, Dr. Kenneth Madden as well as the state authorities with general jurisdiction over programs for handicapped children in Delaware— the Division of Health and Social Services and the Division of Mental Retardation. Both sides requested the opportunity to present additional evidence at the court hearing.

Dr. Angert, who had previously served as a consultant for the NCCSD but who had no firsthand knowledge of Paul's experience at Meadowood, was the principal witness for the Kruelles. Although he generally was inclined against residential placement, he recommended such a program for Paul, because of Paul's need for a consistent environment. Dr. Angert believed, in light of Paul's history, that "inconsistency of approach, environment or caretakers typically led to stress and self-destructive behaviors such as vomiting." Accordingly, he urged a twenty-four-hour placement "with programming by people who know how to do it" in order to maximize Paul's chances of learning. Kruelle v. Biggs, 489 F.Supp. at 173. The defendant school and state authorities continued to maintain that the day program at Meadowood satisfied Paul's educational needs, and any necessity for residential placement arose from social and emotional problems clearly beyond the competency and responsibility of school officials.

Much like Dr. Angert, the district court concluded that Paul required a greater degree of consistency than many other profoundly retarded children. Specifically, it held that the present educational program provided by the NCCSD was not a free appropriate public education within the meaning of the Act. Then, in a supplemental order, the district court directed the State Education Board to provide Paul with a full-time residential program. The local and state school authorities now appeal this decision challenging both the residential placement and the imposition of the order against the state agency as erroneous interpretations of the requirements of the Education Act. We affirm. . . .

The Education Act, however, is not silent on what qualifies as a free appropriate public education (FAPE). In fact, the 1975 statute and regulations promulgated thereunder, for the first time, give definitional content to the term "appropriate education" and its component parts, "special education" and "related services."

Theoretically, the scope and details of an appropriate education which the local educational agencies are obligated to provide as a condition to receiving federal grants under the statute, are left primarily to state definition. But the term "special education" is given specific content:

> The term "special education" means specially designed instruction, at no cost to parents or guardians, to meet the unique needs of a handicapped child, including classroom instruction, instruction in physical education, home instruction, and instruction in hospitals and institutions. 20 U.S.C. § 1401(16).

Similarly, "related services" is extensively defined:

> The term "related services" means transportation, and such developmental corrective, and other supportive services (including speech pathology and audiology, psychological services, physical and occupational therapy, recreation, and medical and counseling services, except that such medical services shall be for diagnostic and evaluation purposes only) as may be required to assist a handicapped child to benefit from special education, and includes the early identification and assessment of handicapping conditions in children. 20 U.S.C. § 1401(17).

Moreover, the regulations promulgated under the Act explicitly contemplate residential placement:

> If placement in a public or private residential program is necessary to provide special education and related services to a handicapped child, the program, including nonmedical care and room and board, must be at no cost to the parents of the child.

> Comment. This requirement applies to placements which are made by public agencies for educational purposes, and includes placements in State-operated schools for the handicapped, such as a State school for the deaf or blind. 45 C.F.R. § 121a.302.

In light of these provisions, a court is not without guidance in determinig whether a residential setting is consistent with the purpose and directives of the Education Act. And most courts confronted with the question whether residential placement is necessary to meet the goals of an individual education plan have answered in the affirmative.

Another salient feature of the Education Act, for our purposes, is the congressional rejection of court deference to agency determinations. The statute contemplates a *de novo* review role by the district courts, including the hearing of additional evidence and an independent decision by the district courts based on the preponderance of the evidence. 20 U.S.C. § 1415(e)(2). Thus, in evaluating the ruling by the district court here, what is critical is not whether the judge reversed the conclusions of the state agencies, but whether he properly applied the preponderance of the evidence standard prescribed by Congress.

Significantly, all parties concede that Paul needs full-time assistance from the state of Delaware beyond that available in any day school program. It is also uncontroverted that the Education Act specifically provides for residential placement in certain instances. The question, then, is whether the trial judge correctly construed the Education Act as requiring more continuous supervision for Paul than he was receiving under the Meadowood Program in order to meet the standard of a free appropriate education.

Based on our careful review of the record, we cannot find that the district court erred in holding that the six-hour day provided by the Meadowood program was an inappropriate education given the terms of the Act. . . .

Analysis must focus, then, on whether full-time placement may be considered necessary for educational purposes, or whether the residential placement is a response to medical, social or emotional problems that are segregable from the learning process. . . .

The relevant question in the present case is whether residential placement is part and parcel of a "specially designed instruction . . . to meet to the unique needs of a handicapped child," in conformity with § 1401(16). And we cannot conclude that the district judge misapplied the statutory standard in determining that "because of his combination of physical and mental handicaps, [Paul] requires a greater degree of consistency of programming than many other profoundly retarded children" and that "it would appear that full-time care is necessary in order to allow Paul to learn." Indeed, it would be difficult to conceive of a more apt case than Paul's for which the unique needs of a child required residential placement. . . .

Of course, before ordering residential placement, a court should weigh the mainstreaming policy embodied in the Education Act which encourages placement of the child in the least restrictive environment. The district judge here, however, carefully undertook such a calculation. He noted that in the past attempts to provide in-home care and after-school instruction had been singularly unsuccessful; all had occasioned regression for Paul. . . . once a court concludes that residential placement is the only realistic option for learning inprovement, the question of "least restrictive" environment is also resolved. "Only when alternatives exist must the court reach the issue of which is the least restrictive." If day school cannot provide an appropriate education it is, by definition, not a possible alternative.

Admittedly, the unequivocal congressional directive to provide an appropriate education for all children regardless of the severity of the handicap,

20 U.S.C. § 1412(2)(C), places a substantial burden on states in certain instances. The language and the legislative history of the Act simply do not entertain the possibility that some children may be untrainable. Consequently, the present situation is distinguishable from cases such as Southeastern Community College v. Davis, 442 U.S. 397, 99 S.Ct. 2361, 60 L.Ed.2d 980 (1979), arising under the Rehabilitation Act of 1973, for the Rehabilitation Act stops short of mandating "substantial adjustments in existing programs beyond those necessary to eliminate discrimination against otherwise qualified individuals." In *Davis* a handicapped person with a serious hearing disability challenged the denial of her admission to a nursing program as a violation of the Rehabilitation Act. That legislation prohibits discrimination against an otherwise qualified handicapped individual in a federally funded program solely by reason of his handicap, but does not require more than evenhanded treatment of handicapped and nonhandicapped by state agencies. As the court explained, "neither the language, purpose, nor history of § 504 [of the Rehabilitation Act] reveals an intent to impose an affirmative action obligation on all recipients of federal funds." Thus, a court's interpretation of the regulations that required extensive modifications in the school program in order to accommodate a handicapped individual would constitute an unauthorized extension of the obligations imposed by that statute. The court, therefore, upheld the rejection by the state college of the applicant. Under the Education Act, in contradistinction, schools are required to provide a comprehensive range of services to accommodate a handicapped child's educational needs, regardless of financial and administrative burdens, and if necessary, to resort to residential placement. The district court's order, consequently, did not impose a duty beyond the contemplation of the Education Act; rather it carried out the implications of an undeniably broad statutory intent. . . .

*Public School Placement for Hearing-
Impaired Child Is the Least
Restrictive Placement*

SILVIO v. COMMONWEALTH, DEPARTMENT OF EDUCATION

Commonwealth Court of Pennsylvania,
1982.
439 A.2d 893.

ROGERS, Judge.

Melissa Silvio, an eight-year-old hearing-impaired person, who resides with her parents in the School District of Pittsburgh, had been attending DePaul Institute, an approved private school for hearing-impaired children, from the time her impairment was discovered when she was about three years old. Her attendance at DePaul has been publicly funded. When Melissa attained the school attendance age of six years, the school district, after a review of her case records kept by DePaul, determined that an appropriate program would be her attendance at the district's Beechwood

School, an elementary school having special programs for hearing-impaired children. Melissa's parents, the appellants here, objected to the proposed placement, believing that Melissa was making good progress in her ability to speak and understand speech at DePaul and that the district should so provide. They asked for and were accorded the due process hearing provided for at 24 Pa.Code § 13.31. After five days of hearings which produced almost eight hundred pages of testimony, the hearing officer filed a report containing findings and a recommendation to the Commonwealth Secretary of Education that the program proposed by the district for Melissa, her placement at Beechwood, was appropriate. On appeal, the Secretary of Education agreed with the hearing officer's recommendation but by imposing upon the district the duty to provide Melissa with a program which would concentrate on her oral development. . . .

In this category of complaint is the appellants' contention that the school district should have made its own evaluations instead of relying on records obtained from DePaul . . . . In the same stead is the appellants' argument that the records on which the placement determination was made were outdated. The State Board of Education regulations at 22 Pa.Code § 13.31(c) requires that an exceptional person must be evaluated not less than every two years or annually at the request of the parents. No request for an annual evaluation was made by Melissa's parents . . . the evaluations here used were more than two years old. The school district relied on the psychological, audiological and educational tests made at DePaul in March and November of 1977. Since the placement at Beechwood was made in May, 1978, the evaluation was conducted within two years and therefore was not outdated. . . .

The appellants also complain that they were denied an impartial hearing because the hearing officer was a professor at Slippery Rock State College and therefore, as they term it, an employee of the Secretary of Education. . . . We reject the appellants' thesis on the merits of this case. The only regulation on the subject is that found at 22 Pa.Code § 13.32(12) which states that the hearing officer should not be an officer, employee or agent of the school district or intermediate unit in which the exceptional child resides. . . . The hearing officer in this class of case does not have final adjudicatory authority; he simply hears the evidence and makes recommendations to the Secretary. Furthermore, the hearing officer here, a professor at Slippery Rock State Teachers College, could hardly be said to be subject to the influence of the Secretary of Education merely because both are functionaries of the Department of Education. Finally, on this subject, a fair reading of this record reveals that the hearing officer's rulings were if anything overly favorable to the appellants. For instance, on the motion of their counsel, the hearing officer sequestered the witnesses although most of the testimony was of a highly technical nature based upon special competence of the witnesses in teaching the hearing-impaired. Also, the examiner patiently considered the appellants' counsel's numerous objections to evidence proffered by the school district and in close rulings seems to us to have inclined toward exclusion rather than admission. There was neither bias nor the appearance of bias in the conduct of the hearing.

The appellants' principal contention is that the Secretary's conclusion that Beechwood is an appropriate place for Melissa to attend school is not supported by the evidence. The appellants' counsel writes in his brief that the issue before us is whether there was a preponderance of evidence to support the determination that the Beechwood School had an appropriate program for Melissa. This is much wide of the mark. It is true that the school district had the burden to show the appropriateness of the proposed placement of Melissa at Beechwood. 22 Pa.Code § 13.32(15). Our review of this appeal from the Secretary's order, as in every agency appeal, is not to determine whether the order in favor of the party having the burden below is supported by a preponderance of the evidence but whether the agency's findings upon which its order was based are supported by substantial evidence. Our careful examination of this long record convinces us that the evidence supporting the findings and the decision below are amply supported by the record.

The Director of the Division for Exceptional Children of the School District of Pittsburgh testified that upon Melissa's attaining school age, he and his staff reviewed the Individualized Educational Program developed for her at DePaul and concluded that the program at the district's Beechwood Elementary School would be appropriate, and would further have the advantage of being less restrictive than the program at DePaul.

The supervisor of the program for hearing-impaired children in the Pittsburgh schools, formerly a classroom teacher of the hearing-impaired at Beechwood, testified that there are two classrooms set aside at Beechwood exclusively for the education of hearing-impaired children; that there are seven hearing-impaired children in the Beechwood program; that there are two teachers who work on an individual basis with the seven pupils, one full time, the other more than half time; that there are available to serve the seven hearing-impaired students a speech therapist, a person trained in sign language, and other specialists; and that the hearing-impaired children are partially mainstreamed, that is, that they attend classes with nonexceptional children in art, gym, library, and mathematics.

The speech and language specialist for the hearing-impaired, whose duty for the school district is that of visiting schools attended by hearing-impaired students and to help its children with their speech and language, testified that he spent some 25 to 30 percent of his week at Beechwood working individually with the seven students there attending.

An audiologist employed by the school district testified that she calls on the students at Beechwood regularly and there inspects the amplification of each of their personal hearing aids and of the classroom amplification system, consults with the children's parents and performs periodic ear testing of her charges.

The full-time teacher of the hearing-impaired children at Beechwood described her daily regime in the classroom and during her charges' attendance at other classes. She recounted her responsibility for preparing education programs for each of the children and for consulting with the parents, an event that sometimes happens daily. As we have mentioned, this evidence, of which the foregoing is a very sketchy description, since each of the witnesses was minutely cross-examined by the appellants' counsel, clearly provides ample evidence for the findings upon which the conclusion that Beechwood's program was appropriate was based.

Consideration of the appellants' evidence brings us to the nub of this case, the appellants' no doubt sincere belief that the school district's basic method of teaching the hearing-impaired is wrong, at least for their daughter, and that a different basic method used by DePaul and espoused by DePaul instructors is the only proper means of teaching the hearing-impaired. Their support for this thesis consisted principally of the testimony of DePaul instructors that their system was better generally for Melissa than any other.

There are in fact three recognized basic methods of teaching the hearing-impaired: verbal-tonal, oral-aural and total communication. Of the three, only the oral-aural method used at DePaul eschews signing, that is, manual communication. Both the verbal-tonal and total communication methods use signing. The Beachwood School employs the total communication method which uses all methods including, but not to the exclusion of any other means, the use of signing. For instance, at Beechwood, when the hearing-impaired children are placed in classrooms with nonexceptional children, a manualist stands at the front of the room and signs what transpires in speech between the teacher and the students. The appellants, supported by their expert witness, believe that Melissa's progress in understanding and speaking which she has achieved at DePaul will be impeded by her being exposed to signing. On the other hand, the experts produced by the school district are of the belief that signing will not impede Melissa's speaking and further that her association with nonexceptional children, not available at DePaul, will improve her ability to communicate with others, including orally. The case therefore presents to some degree a clash of philosophies among experts in the field, with respect to which we have no disposition, if we had the power, to overturn the conclusions, based on ample evidence, reached by the school district and upheld by the Secretary of Education. We add in this aspect of the case that the Secretary's decision is consistent with the order of preference for educational placement for handicapped school age persons set forth in 22 Pa.Code § 13.11(d) which accords a special educational program conducted in a regular school second in order of preference only to attendance in a regular class in a regular school. Attendance at an approved private school indeed is ranked sixth of the nine categories thus evaluated.

Order affirmed.

NOTE

In Clevenger v. Oak Ridge School Board, 744 F.2d 514, 1984, the U.S. Court of Appeals, 6th Circuit, stated:

> ". . . cost can be a legitimate consideration when devising an appropriate program . . . . Nevertheless, cost considerations are only relevant when choosing between several options, all of which offer an appropriate education."

Footnotes

1. Donald F. Moores, *Educating the Deaf, Psychology, Principles and Practices*, (Boston: Houghton Mifflin, 1978).

2. Id.

3. Resolve for Erecting a Lunatic Hospital (1831), Resolves of the General Court of the Commonwealth of Massachusetts.

4. Jonathan Messerli, *Horace Mann* (New York: Alfred A. Knopf, 1972).

5. Samuel A. Kirk and James J. Gallagher, *Educating Exceptional Children*, 4th ed. (Boston: Houghton Mifflin, 1983).

6. Watson v. City of Cambridge, 157 Mass. 561, 32 N.E. 864 (1893).

7. State ex rel. Beattie v. Board of Education, 169 Wis. 231, 172 N.W. 153 (1919).

8. Id. p. 154.

9. Ralph B. Kimbrough and Michael Y. Nunnery, *Educational Administration*, (New York: Macmillan Publishing Company, Inc., 1976).

10. Id.

11. Brown v. Board of Education, 347 U.S. 483, 74 S.Ct. 686 (1954).

12. Id.

13. Pennsylvania Association for Retarded Children v. Commonwealth, 334 F.Supp. 1257 (E.D. Pa.1971), 343 F.Supp. 279 (E.D.Pa.1972).

14. Id.

15. 348 F.Supp. 866 (D.D.C.1972).

16. Id.

17. Rehabilitation Act of 1973, Section 504, 29 U.S.C.A. § 794.

18. Id. Section 84.32–84.36.

19. Id. Section 84.33, 84.34.

20. DOE, State of Hawaii v. Katherine D., 531 F.Supp. 517 (1982).

21. The Education for All Handicapped Children Act, 20 U.S.C.A. § 1400(b), (1976).

22. Id. § 1401(16–91).

23. Id.

24. Board of Education v. Rowley, 458 U.S. 176, 102 S.Ct. 3034 (1982).

25. Id.

26. Education for All Handicapped Children Act, supra, § 1401(18).

27. Board of Education v. Rowley, supra, p. 3055.

28. Grkman v. Scanlon, 528 F.Supp. 1032 (D.Pa.1981), vacated and remanded 707 F.2d 1388 (3d Cir.1982), rehearing 563 F.Supp. 793 (1983); Silvio v. Commonwealth, 62 Pa.Cmwlth. 192, 439 A.2d 893 (1982); Bales v. Clark, 523 F.Supp. 1366 (D.Va.1981).

29. Bales v. Clark, 523 F.Supp. 1366, 1370 (D.Va.1981).

30. 528 F.Supp. 1032 (D.Pa.1981).

31. Education for All Handicapped Children Act, 34 C.F.R. § 300.302.

32. Education for All Handicapped Children Act, 20 U.S.C.A. § 1401(17).

33. ___ U.S. ___, 104 S.Ct. 3371 (1984).

34. Education for All Handicapped Children Act, supra.

35. Irving Independent School District v. Tatro, supra.

36. Stuart v. Nappi, 443 F.Supp. 1235 (D.Conn.1978); Doe v. Koger, 480 F.Supp. 225 (N.D.Ind. 1979).

37. Stuart v. Nappi, 443 F.Supp. 1235 (D.Conn. 1978).

38. S–1 v. Turlington, 635 F.2d 342 (5th Cir.1981), cert. denied 454 U.S. 1030, 102 S.Ct. 566 (1981).

39. Id.

40. Doe v. Koger, 480 F.Supp. 225 (N.D.Ind.1979).

41. The misconduct upon which the expulsions were based ranged from masturbation or sexual acts against fellow students to willful defiance of authority, insubordination, vandalism, and the use of profane language.

10

Desegregation

No one could have predicted that the pre-1850 education of a five-year-old child by the name of Sarah Roberts would have had such a profound effect on the historical development of the public schools. Sarah left home each day and walked through the streets of the City of Boston past five elementary schools for white children to reach the Smith Grammar School, which had been established in 1820 for blacks.

Not only was the school remote from the child's home, but an evaluation committee had reported that the school was in poor condition—"the school rooms are too small, the paint is much defaced" and the equipment needed repair. Sarah's father tried repeatedly to place her in the better nearby schools for whites, but each time his efforts had failed. After persistent rebuffs, Mr. Roberts sought the most able lawyer, civil rights enthusiast, and later United States Senator, Charles Sumner, to represent his child and challenge the unequal treatment. From the ensuing legal conflict, the now infamous doctrine of separate-but-equal was born.

Citing passages from the Massachusetts Constitution, which would later be likened to the Equal Protection Clause of the Fourteenth Amendment, Sumner maintained that compelling black children to attend separate schools was to effectively "brand a whole race with the stigma of inferiority and degradation." [1] Eloquently, Sumner pointed out that segregated schools could not be considered equivalent to white schools because of the stigma of caste that mandatory attendance attached thereto. Sumner effectively expounded the same constitutional position that was to be the heart of the plaintiff's successful contention over 100 years later in *Brown* v. *Board of Education,* that a separate school "exclusively devoted to one class must differ essentially, in its spirit and character, from that public school known to the law, where all classes meet together in equality." [2]

Justice Shaw of the Massachusetts Court was, however, unconvinced and in his historical opinion set forth the "separate-but-equal" doctrine that was to prevail for so long. In theory, he agreed with "the great principle" advanced by Sumner that all persons ought to stand equal before the law, but he went on to contrarily conclude that the standard of equality did not imply that all men and women were legally clothed with the same civil and political powers but that all were merely entitled to equal consideration and protection for their maintenance and security. What exactly the protected rights were was dependent on the laws adapted to their "respective relations and conditions." As one of these conditions, race was seen to be a legitimate rationale for classification. Judge Shaw failed to show, however, that there was any reasonable relationship between racial classification and legitimate objectives of the school system; he merely asserted that school segregation was for the good of both races. With this decision, "separate-but-equal" was born into education and it would not expire for over one hundred years. During the intervening years a Civil War would be fought, civil rights laws would be enacted by the United States Congress to little or no avail, and the United States Supreme Court itself would transplant the unfortunate standard from the Massachusetts Constitution to the Constitution of the United States.

In 1868, the Fourteenth Amendment was ratified to assure the constitutionality of reconstruction statutes that had been enacted to proscribe racial discrimination. The third clause of the critical second sentence of the Amendment stated: "Nor shall any State . . . deny to any person within its jurisdiction the equal protection of the laws." In spite of the strength of the wording, the Amendment was to have little immediate effect as was evidenced by the Civil Rights Cases wherein the Supreme Court held that no application could be made to private enterprise discrimination such as occurred in inns, conveyances, restaurants, and places of entertainment.[3]

The move from private discrimination to state-sanctioned discrimination came about through interplay of an educationally irrelevant issue concerning interstate commerce by which a Mississippi statute requiring segregated train cars was upheld because it pertained solely to transportation within the state.[4] The Equal Protection Clause was thereby circumvented and state-enforced classification of citizens by race was made possible. In the South, state action began transforming the private custom of discrimination into state law. Jim Crow laws began in Florida in 1887, and soon engulfed the South.[5] Justice Powell, commenting much later, said "the Equal Protection Clause was virtually strangled in its infancy by post-Civil War judicial reactionism."[6]

The capstone of segregation, though, came in 1896 with *Plessy* v. *Ferguson*[7] in which the separate-but-equal rationale of the Roberts Court was implanted as a national standard applying to the Fourteenth Amendment. In *Plessy*, the Supreme Court maintained that an 1890 Louisiana law entitled "An Act to Promote the Comfort of Passengers" providing that "all railway companies carrying passengers in their coaches in this State, shall provide equal but separate accommodations for the white and colored races, by providing two or more passenger coaches for each passenger train, or by dividing the passenger coaches by a partition so as to secure separate accommodations" was not unconstitutional because state legislatures have wide discretion in promoting public peace and good order, and such actions will be upheld so long as they are reasonable. In a now infamous passage Justice Brown said: "In determining the question of reasonableness it (legislature) is at liberty to act with reference to the established usages, customs and traditions of the people, and with a view to the promotion of their comfort, and the preservation of the public peace and good order. Gauged by this standard, we cannot say that a law which authorizes or even requires the separation of the two races in public conveyances is unreasonable. . . . " [8] In essence, the Court made the Equal Protection Clause subject to custom and tradition in accordance with legislative interpretation, no matter how blatantly and objectionably the law affected a particular classification of people.

In a lonely dissent in *Plessy*, Justice Harlan attacked the majority opinion and enunciated the law that would eventually become the prevailing view over fifty years later. He maintained, "Our constitution is color-blind, and neither knows nor tolerates classes among its citizens. In respect to civil rights, all citizens are equal before the law." [9] He maintained that separation of the races was a "badge of servitude."

After *Plessy*, the precedent of separation of the races was quickly transferred to education and further extended. In Richmond County, Georgia, the school board discovering that it needed more facilities at the grade school level to accommodate black children discontinued the black high school and turned the building into a black elementary school. [10] The board advised the black high school students to seek their education in church-affiliated schools. Upon challenge, the United States Supreme Court held that in this matter the only interest of the federal judiciary was to see that all citizens share equitably in the tax burden, but that the matter of education and how it was conducted, supported by that taxation, was solely a state concern.

Further expansion of segregation in education was justified in 1908 in *Berea College* v. *Kentucky* [11] wherein the Supreme Court upheld a state law that forbade any institution as a corporation to provide instruction to both races at the same time unless the classes were conducted at least twenty-five miles apart. The law, the "Day Law" as it was named after its author, [12] was enacted specifically to prohibit integration at Berea College, a small private college that had been founded in 1859 to provide nondiscriminatory education for needy students, both black and white. In upholding the law and sidestepping the direct issue of state-enforced racial discrimination in the private sector, the Court simply asserted that the College, as a corporation of Kentucky, was subject to state regulation and was not entitled to all the immunities to which individuals were entitled. Since the College was the plaintiff and not black students, the Court was free to say that "a state may withhold from its corporations privileges and powers of which it cannot constitutionally deprive individuals." [13]

The *Plessy, Cumming,* and *Berea College* cases had not only fully established that the state could constitutionally maintain a separate system of education for blacks and whites, but that the arm of the state could reach into private education and require that it be segregated as well. Beyond this, *Cumming* laid the groundwork for almost unlimited state discretion in defining what constituted separate-but-equal. The federal courts would not intervene. Separation of the races in education was subsequently expanded to include not only black and white, but also yellow, brown, and red as well. In *Gong Lum* v. *Rice,* [14] in 1927, the Supreme Court held that states could segregate a Mongolian child from the Caucasian schools and compel her to attend a school for black children. Segregation of the *Gong Lum* type was practiced in many states both North and South.

EROSION OF SEPARATE–BUT–EQUAL

As long as state legislatures had plenary power to define the limits of separate-but-equal, the concept was accepted with little or no argument. By the 1930s, however, the National Association for the Advancement of Colored People (NAACP) initiated a movement that was to pursue racial abuse and seek judicial clarification of the limits of separate-but-equal as a legal basis for segregation. At first, the intention was to attack segregation where equal facilities were obviously inadequate or nonexistent. As a result of these efforts, in 1938 a landmark desegregation case, *Missouri ex rel. Gaines* v. *Canada,* was handed down by the Supreme Court.[15] By a vote of seven to one, the Supreme Court held a Missouri law prohibiting blacks from entering the University of Missouri Law School unconstitutional because there were no other public law schools in the state to which blacks could go as an alternative. The ruling was singularly important because it not only placed some outward boundaries on implementation of separate-but-equal but more significantly it represented a reassertion of judicial authority in construing the Equal Protection Clause as a limitation on previously unfettered state action in education.

With the World War II years intervening, little was accomplished during the next decade, but slowly a public attitude against separate-but-equal began to materialize that would set the stage for more direct judicial action. The foundation of separate-but-equal was shaken by the Supreme Court in 1950, in another case involving a law school, this time the University of Texas.[16] Law schools were good targets for desegregation attorneys because judges and lawyers could more readily see the disparate condition in the legal field. In this case, a black Houston mail carrier by the name of Sweatt sought admission to the University of Texas Law School. Since the state had no law school for blacks, under the precedent of *Gaines,* a lower Texas Court ordered that the state set up a law school for blacks. The school that was established was woefully inadequate and Sweatt further challenged reasserting his claim to be admitted to the University of Texas Law School. Here, the Supreme Court was presented with a rather different dilemma of comparing two schools and rendering a judgment as to their comparability. Thus, the high Court found itself in the uneasy role of a super accreditation agency. In ordering Sweatt admitted to the all-white law school, Chief Justice Fred Vinson pointed out that the new law school "could never hope to be equal in reputation of the faculty, experience of the administration, position and influence of the alumni, standing in the community, tradition and prestige." [17]

Vinson virtually eliminated the use of separate law schools for blacks by further observing that "The law school to which Texas is willing to admit [Sweatt] excludes from its student body members of the racial groups which number 85 percent of the population of the State and include most of the lawyers, witnesses, jurors, judges, and other officials with whom [he] will inevitably be dealing when he becomes a member of the Texas Bar. With such a substantial and significant segment of society excluded, we cannot conclude that the education offered [Sweatt] is substantially equal to that which he would receive if admitted to the University of Texas Law School." [18]

The obvious educational infirmity of the separate-but-equal doctrine emerged with litigation in this case. Limitations on curriculum, faculty, educational atmosphere, and professional development combined to draw into serious constitutional question the further maintenance of separate higher education facilities for both blacks and whites. On the same day that *Sweatt* was handed down, the Supreme Court ruled that if a state chose not to establish separate and substantially equal facilities for blacks, it could not segregate them within the white school.[19] McLaurin, a black, doctoral student in the College of Education at the University of Oklahoma, was allowed to enroll in the white school but was compelled to sit and study in designated sections for blacks while in the classrooms, library, and dining hall. The Court held this treatment unconstitutional as well.

Even though these cases served to expound the frailties of separate-but-equal, they did little to help the black elementary and secondary school children who were denied equal opportunity with no relief in sight. With *Cumming* as the precedent, the black child attended school in ramshackled facilities, had poor instructors, and in most cases attended schools that were in session for only a minor portion of the year. This circumstance could not be corrected so long as the separate-but-equal doctrine stood.

BROWN AND THE DEMISE OF SEGREGATED SCHOOLS

Several cases began making their way through the lower courts, each of which held potential for challenging the separate-but-equal doctrine head-on. Eventually five cases from Kansas, South Carolina, Virginia, Delaware, and Washington, D.C. reached the Supreme Court,[20] and were first argued in December, 1952.

Lower courts in each case, with the exception of the Delaware case, had denied relief to black children. In Delaware, a decision by the Delaware Court of Chancery holding for the plaintiffs, requiring that black children be admitted to schools previously attended only by white children, was affirmed by the Supreme Court of Delaware. The defendants in this case applied for certiorari to the United States Supreme Court challenging the immediate admission of black children to the white schools. In *Brown* v. *Board of Education,* the plaintiffs were black children of elementary age residing in Topeka. They brought action to enjoin a state statute that permitted, but did not require cities in Kansas of more than 15,000 population to maintain separate facilities for black and white students. Under that authority, the Topeka Board of Education chose to establish segregated elementary schools. The lower federal court held that segregation in public education had a detrimental effect on black children but denied plaintiffs relief because the facilities were substantially equal. In both the South Carolina and Virginia cases, the lower courts had found the black schools to be inferior and had ordered improvements for equalization, but had not required admission of the black children to the schools for white children during the transition period. In the Washington, D.C. case, black children directly challenged school segregation in the nation's capital alleging that segregation deprived them of due process of law under the Fifth Amendment. It was necessary to couch this latter claim in the Fifth Amendment since the Fourteenth Amendment did not apply to Congress.

These cases combined presented a range of situations by which the Supreme Court could comprehensively view the segregation issue. The Kansas case involved permissive segregation legislation in a northern state for elementary children; in the Virginia case a compulsory segregation law was used to segregate high school students in an upper southern state; South Carolina represented the Deep South, and Delaware a border state.[21] The District of Columbia case drew due process and congressional power into question. The differing circumstances and the wide geographical distribution gave the decision more importance and imbued it with a national flavor and aura.

The importance of the case was reflected in the Court's hesitancy to rush to judgment. Though the case was first argued on December 9, 1952, the Court reached no decision and on June 8, 1953, the court issued an order setting the case for reargument that fall and submitted a series of questions for litigants to address. The first question asked what evidence there was to indicate that Congress and the states contemplated that the Fourteenth Amendment, when ratified, was intended to abolish school segregation. Second, the Court asked whether Congress had the power to abolish school segregation and what the limits of the Court's own powers were. Third, the Court sought opinions on the extent of its own powers to resolve the issue, should the answer to the first two questions be inconclusive. Fourth, the Court asked whether, in the event of a decision in favor of plaintiffs, desegregation should be immediate or gradual and whether the plaintiff children's grievance was personal and present. The fifth question concerned the procedural form the final decree should take.[22]

Within the parameters of these issues, several alternatives were open to the Court. Ashmore [23] listed those that appeared to be within the realm of possibility.

1. That there was no need to rule on the constitutionality of segregation per se, since each case might be disposed of on other grounds. (The Supreme Court had repeatedly declared that it would not rule on questions of a constitutional nature if a case could be decided by any other means.)

2. That the separate-but-equal doctrine was still the law, and when the separate facilities were unequal the Court would allow a reasonable period for the facilities to be made equal in fact.

3. That the separate-but-equal doctrine was still the law, but when separate facilities were unequal the Court would require immediate admission of blacks to the white schools pending the achievement of actual equality of facilities.

4. That the separate-but-equal doctrine was still the law, but the Court might require nonsegregation in certain phases of public education that it deemed impossible of equality within the separate framework. (In other words, the Court might conceivably hold that a particular course of activity could not be provided equally under segregation, as it had at least implied in the higher education cases.)

5. That whether segregation in a given case was a denial of equal protection of the laws was a question of fact, to be decided as are other questions of fact in the lower trial court.

6. That segregation was unconstitutional; the Court recognized the need for orderly progress of transition to nonsegregation; but the Court would limit itself to minimum personal relief of the plaintiffs, leaving to Congress the job of legislating detailed rules for implementing desegregation in the schools generally. (This would be in keeping with the idea that the administration of local school systems involves a "political question.")

7. That separate-but-equal was a clear denial of equal protection of the laws and thus unconstitutional; but the Court would permit a gradual change-over to a nonsegregated system under the supervision of the District Courts, or under the direction of a master appointed by the Supreme Court itself.

8. That separate-but-equal was unconstitutional and must be ended immediately; black plaintiffs in the case before the Court must be admitted at once to the white schools.

Realistically, the major point of the case could only have been decided one way, that separate-but-equal was unconstitutional. When asked how the Court would decide, the Solicitor General of the United States responded that the court "properly could find only one answer." [24] The final judgment came in a unanimous decision written by Chief Justice Earl Warren. The Court ruled: "We conclude that in the field of public education the doctrine of separate but equal has no place. Separate educational facilities are inherently unequal." [25] For directness and finality, the decision was a model. In overturning separate-but-equal, Warren did not dwell on other judicial precedents because the precise issue before the Court had not been presented before. The validity of separate-but-equal, since *Roberts,* had been assumed but had never been argued and validly established.

The case was not only a watershed in American education, but was one of the most important decisions ever rendered by the Supreme Court. For sheer impact on society, it undoubtedly had the most far-reaching impact. Pollak commented: "Except for waging and winning the Civil War and World Wars I and II, the decision in the *School Segregation Cases* was probably the most important American governmental act of any kind since the Emancipation Proclamation." [26]

Separate-but-Equal Facilities Are
Inherently Unequal

BROWN v. BOARD OF EDUCATION OF TOPEKA

Supreme Court of the United States, 1954.
347 U.S. 483, 74 S.Ct. 686.

Mr. Chief Justice WARREN delivered the opinion of the Court.

These cases come to us from the States of Kansas, South Carolina, Virginia, and Delaware. They are premised on different facts and different local conditions, but a common legal question justifies their consideration together in this consolidated opinion.

In each of the cases, minors of the Negro race, through their legal representatives, seek the aid of the courts in obtaining admission to the public schools of their community on a nonsegregated basis. In each instance, they have been denied admission to schools attended by white children under laws requiring or permitting segregation according to race. This segregation was alleged to deprive the plaintiffs of the equal protection of the laws under the Fourteenth Amendment. In each of the cases other than the Delaware case, a three-judge federal district court denied relief to the plaintiffs on the so-called "separate but equal" doctrine announced by this Court in Plessy v. Ferguson, 163 U.S. 537, 16 S.Ct. 1138, 41 L.Ed. 256. Under that doctrine, equality of treatment is accorded when the races are provided substantially equal facilities, even though these facilities be separate. In the Delaware case, the Supreme Court of Delaware adhered to that doctrine, but ordered that the plaintiffs be admitted to the white schools because of their superiority to the Negro schools.

The plaintiffs contend that segregated public schools are not "equal" and cannot be made "equal," and that hence they are deprived of the equal protection of the laws. Because of the obvious importance of the question presented, the Court took jurisdiction. Argument was heard in the 1952 Term, and reargument was heard this Term on certain questions propounded by the Court. . . .

In the first cases in this Court construing the Fourteenth Amendment, decided shortly after its adoption, the Court interpreted it as proscribing all state-imposed discriminations against the Negro race. The doctrine of "separate but equal" did not make its appearance in this Court until 1896 in the case of *Plessy* v. *Ferguson,* supra, involving not education but transportation. American courts have since labored with the doctrine for over half a century. In this Court, there have been six cases involving the "separate but equal" doctrine in the field of public education. In Cumming v. Board of Education of Richmond County, 175 U.S. 528, 20 S.Ct. 197, 44 L.Ed. 262, and Gong Lum v. Rice, 275 U.S. 78, 48 S.Ct. 91, 72 L.Ed. 172, the validity of the doctrine itself was not challenged. In more recent cases, all on the graduate school level, inequality was found in that specific benefits enjoyed by white students were denied to Negro students of the same educational qualifications. . . . In none of these cases was it necessary to re-examine the doctrine to grant relief to the Negro plaintiff. And in *Sweatt* v. *Painter,* the Court expressly reserved decision on the question whether *Plessy* v. *Ferguson* should be held inapplicable to public education.

In the instant cases, that question is directly presented. Here, unlike *Sweatt* v. *Painter,* there are findings below that the Negro and white schools involved have been equalized, or are being equalized, with respect to buildings, curricula, qualifications and salaries of teachers, and other "tangible" factors. Our decision, therefore, cannot turn on merely a comparison of these tangible factors in the Negro and white schools involved in each of the cases. We must look instead to the effect of segregation itself on public education.

In approaching this problem, we cannot turn the clock back to 1868 when the Amendment was adopted, or even to 1896 when *Plessy* v. *Ferguson* was written. We must consider public education in the light of its full development and its present place in American life throughout the Nation. Only in this way can it be determined if segregation in public schools deprives these plaintiffs of the equal protection of the laws.

Today, education is perhaps the most important function of state and local governments. Compulsory school attendance laws and the great expenditures for education both demonstrate our recognition of the importance of education to our democratic society. It is required in the performance of our most basic public responsibilities, even service in the armed forces. It is the very foundation of good citizenship. Today it is a principal instrument in awakening the child to cultural values, in preparing him for later professional training, and in helping him to adjust normally to his environment. In these days, it is doubtful that any child may reasonably be expected to succeed in life if he is denied the opportunity of an education. Such an opportunity, where the state has undertaken to provide it, is a right which must be made available to all on equal terms.

We come then to the question presented: Does segregation of children in public schools solely on the basis of race, even though the physical facilities and other "tangible" factors may be equal, deprive the children of the minority group of equal educational opportunities? We believe that it does.

In *Sweatt* v. *Painter,* in finding that a segregated law school for Negroes could not provide them equal educational opportunities, this Court relied in large part on "those qualities which are incapable of objective measurement but which make for greatness in a law school." In *McLaurin* v. *Oklahoma State Regents,* the Court, in requiring that a Negro admitted to a white graduate school be treated like all other students, again resorted to intangible considerations: "his ability to study, to engage in discussions and exchange views with other students, and, in general, to learn his profession." Such considerations apply with added force to children in grade and high schools. To separate them from others of similar age and qualifications solely because of their race generates a feeling of inferiority as to their status in the community that may affect their hearts and minds in a way unlikely ever to be undone. The effect of this separation on their educational opportunities was well stated by a finding in the Kansas case by a court which nevertheless felt compelled to rule against the Negro plaintiffs:

> Segregation of white and colored children in public schools has a detrimental effect upon the colored children. The impact is greater when it has the sanction of the law; for the policy of separating the races is usually interpreted as denoting the inferiority of the Negro group. A sense of inferiority affects the motivation of a child to learn. Segregation with the sanction of law, therefore, has a tendency to [retard] the educational and mental development of Negro children and to deprive them of some of the benefits they would receive in a racial[ly] integrated school system.

Whatever may have been the extent of psychological knowledge at the time of *Plessy* v. *Ferguson,* this finding is amply supported by modern authority. Any language in *Plessy* v. *Ferguson* contrary to this finding is rejected.

We conclude that in the field of public education the doctrine of "separate but equal" has no place. Separate educational facilities are inherently unequal. Therefore, we hold that the plaintiffs and others similarly situated for whom the actions have been brought are, by reason of the segregation complained of, deprived of the equal protection of the laws guaranteed by the Fourteenth Amendment. This disposition makes unnecessary any discussion whether such segregation also violates the Due Process Clause of the Fourteenth Amendment.

Because these are class actions, because of the wide applicability of this decision, and because of the great variety of local conditions, the formulation of decrees in these cases presents problems of considerable complexity. On reargument, the consideration of appropriate relief was necessarily subordinated to the primary question—the constitutionality of segregation in public education. We have now announced that such segregation is a denial of the equal protection of the laws. In order that we may have the full assistance of the parties in formulating decrees, the cases will be restored to the docket, and the parties are requested to present further argument on Questions 4 and 5 previously propounded by the Court for the reargument this Term. The Attorney General of the United States is again invited to participate. The Attorney General of the states requiring or permitting segregation of public education will also be permitted to appear as *amici curiae* upon request to do so by September 15, 1954, and submission of briefs by October 1, 1954.

It is so ordered.

NOTES

1. On the same day as *Brown,* the Court also announced a decision stating that "racial segregation in the public schools of the District of Columbia is a denial of the due process of law guaranteed by the Fifth Amendment to the Constitution." The Fourteenth Amendment applies to the States, but not to the District of Columbia. It found racial segregation of the District schools a denial of due process under the Fifth Amendment. The Court stated: "Classifications based solely on race must be scrutinized with particular care, since they are contrary to our traditions and hence constitutionally suspect . . . ." Bolling v. Sharpe, 347 U.S. 497, 74 S.Ct. 693 (1954).

2. One commentator has written as follows about the second *Brown* decision:

   The admission of a few dozen children to a few dozen schools would have presented no very grave difficulties calling for a study of means of gradual adjustment. Seen in its totality, however, as involving some 5,000 school districts, nearly nine million white children and nearly three million colored, the situation exhibited great variety and complexity. To begin with, a vast number of statutes and regulations incorporating centrally or marginally the rule of segregation, would require change in order to conform to the new principle. Bickel, A., *The Least Dangerous Branch* (Bobbs-Merrill, New York, 1962), p. 248.

INTERPRETING BROWN

Over a generation after *Brown,* judicial decisions are still required to settle social and legal issues emanating from the circumstances surrounding desegregation. Full realization of the complexities brought on by the decision were probably, to a degree, foreseen by the Supreme Court when it first rendered its decision in 1954. Because of this awareness the Court delayed granting specific relief and invited the United States Attorney General and Attorneys General of all the States to submit their views regarding the ultimate order of the Court.

After due consideration of courses of action for implementation, the Court, with Chief Justice Warren again delivering the opinion, said that consideration should be given to "the public interest," as well as the "personal interest of the plaintiffs." In viewing this dichotomy, the Court directed lower courts to fashion remedies that would permit desegregation "with all deliberate speed." [27] In retrospect, the wisdom of the decision in *Brown II* has been called into question. Today, some maintain that the implementation decision, *Brown II,* allowed too much flexibility, others claimed not enough. But from the Supreme Court's perspective, the wisest course was to allow the local federal district courts to settle the individual complaints on a case-by-case basis with due regard for equity for all concerned, and, during the periods of transition, the lower courts were to retain jurisdiction to see that desegregation was properly implemented. The Supreme Court sought to avoid unreasonable delays by requiring specifically that the lower courts "require that the defendants make a prompt and reasonable start toward full compliance with our May 17, 1954, ruling." [28]

Considerable conflict followed the *Brown* decisions. Perhaps one of the most dramatic episodes occurred in Little Rock, Arkansas, where at first the National Guard was used to prevent black children from entering school and later federal troops and the National Guard were used to protect the entrance of black children into the formerly white public schools.[29] Ultimately, the Supreme Court was called on to render a judgment in the Little Rock case. The question of nullification and interposition, the Civil War question, was again raised by the Governor and the Legislature of Arkansas asserting that they had no duty to obey federal court orders directed to them to effectuate desegregation.[30] The Court's response was direct and unambiguous, it said:

> In short, the constitutional rights of children not to be discriminated against in school admission on grounds of race or color declared by this Court in the *Brown* case can neither be nullified openly and directly by state legislators or state executive or judicial officers, nor nullified indirectly by them through evasive schemes for segregation whether attempted "ingeniously or ingenuously." [31]

During the years immediately after *Brown,* school districts experimented with various devices to avoid desegregation. Initially, some states sought to provide funding for private schools through tuition or voucher type arrangements. The most blatant example of this transpired in Virginia where, in Prince Edward County, the public schools were closed and private schools were operated with state and county assistance. In holding this scheme to be unconstitutional, the Supreme Court said that, "the record in the present case could not be clearer that Prince Edward's public schools were closed and private schools operated in their place . . . for one reason, and one reason only: to ensure . . . that white and colored children in Prince Edward County would not, under any circumstances, go to the same school." [32]

Brown definitely proscribed government action that compelled or encouraged segregation, but did it require government intervention to integrate or mix the races in the schools?

When the *Briggs* case, a companion to *Brown,* was remanded to a federal district court in South Carolina, the lower court judge discussed desegregation versus integration and defined the situation thusly:

> [A]ll that is decided, is that a state may not deny to any person on account of race the right to attend any school that it maintains. . . . The Constitution, in other words, does not require integration. It merely forbids segregation.[33]

The difference between desegregation and integration was also emphasized later by northern courts, which held that:

> there is no constitutional duty on the part of the board to bus Negro or white children out of their neighborhoods or to transfer classes for the sole purpose of alleviating racial imbalance. . . .[34]

Contrarily, in another case in the South, the United States Court of Appeals for the Fifth Circuit held that there was indeed an affirmative duty on the part of government to integrate the schools where *de jure* segregation had existed prior to *Brown.*[35] This court distinguished *de facto* segregation, caused by housing patterns, from *de jure* segregation that had governmentally promulgated and enforced discrimination in the South.

These cases taken together enunciated a rule of law that required affirmative action by school boards in the South, *de jure* states, but did not compel school boards in the North, *de facto* states, to act affirmatively to move children about to assure that black children attended school with white children.

This issue was not treated by the United States Supreme Court until 1968 when it held that "freedom of choice" was an acceptable plan for desegregation only if it did in fact erase the vestiges of the past dual system of education. The Court said, "The school officials have the continuing duty to take whatever action may be necessary to create a unitary, nonracial system."[36] The constitutionality of an "open door" or "freedom of choice" policy could be judged only in light of its utility in bringing about desegregation. Effectively, the courts dismissed the distinction between integration and desegregation. The standard required that school districts be unitary and not dual. Where *de jure* segregation existed before, the state had an obligation to affirmatively assert itself to remove barriers to desegregation.

After waiting for fifteen years for the lower courts to effectuate the desegregation mandate of *Brown II,* the Supreme Court acted in 1969 to require that all school districts operating in states that had legal segregation in 1954 immediately become unitary.[37] The standard "with all deliberate speed" was replaced with an "immediately" standard. Whether this was accomplished through rezoning, busing, or other devices was not of concern to the Court; it simply required that all districts become unitary without further delay.

*State's Closing of Public Schools and
Contributing to the Support of Private
Segregated Schools Is Unconstitutional*

GRIFFIN v. COUNTY SCHOOL BOARD OF PRINCE EDWARD COUNTY

Supreme Court of the United States, 1964.
377 U.S. 218, 84 S.Ct. 1226.

Mr. Justice BLACK delivered the opinion of the Court.

This litigation began in 1951 when a group of Negro school children living in Prince Edward County, Virginia, filed a complaint in the United States District Court for the Eastern District of Virginia alleging that they had been denied admission to public schools attended by white children and charging that Virginia laws requiring such school segregation denied complainants the equal protection of the laws in violation of the Fourteenth Amendment. On May 17, 1954, ten years ago, we held that the Virginia segregation laws did deny equal protection. Brown v. Board of Education, 347 U.S. 483, 74 S.Ct. 686, 98 L.Ed. 873 (1954). On May 31, 1955, after reargument on the nature of relief, we remanded this case, along with others heard with it, to the District Courts to enter such orders as "necessary and proper to admit [complainants] to public schools on a racially nondiscriminatory basis with all deliberate speed . . .." Brown v. Board of Education, 349 U.S. 294, 301, 75 S.Ct. 753, 757, 99 L.Ed. 1083 (1955).

Efforts to desegregate Prince Edward County's schools met with resistance. In 1956, Section 141 of the Virginia Constitution was amended to authorize the General Assembly and local governing bodies to appropriate funds to assist students to go to public or to nonsectarian private schools. In addition to those owned by the State or by the locality. The General Assembly met in special session and enacted legislation to close any public schools where white and colored children were enrolled together, to cut off state funds to such schools, to pay tuition grants to children in nonsectarian private schools, and to extend state retirement benefits to teachers in newly created private schools. The legislation closing mixed schools and cutting off state funds was later invalidated by the Supreme Court of Appeals of Virginia, which held that these laws violated the Virginia Constitution. Harrison v. Day, 200 Va. 439, 106 S.E.2d 636 (1959). In April 1959, the General Assembly abandoned "massive resistance" to desegregation and turned instead to what was called a "freedom of choice" program. The Assembly repealed the rest of the 1956 legislation, as well as a tuition grant law of January 1959, and enacted a new tuition grant program. At the same time the Assembly repealed Virginia's compulsory attendance laws and instead made school attendance a matter of local option.

In June 1959, the United States Court of Appeals for the Fourth Circuit directed the Federal District Court (1) to enjoin discriminatory practices in Prince Edward County schools, (2) to require the County School Board to take "immediate steps" toward admitting students without regard to race to the white high school "in the school term beginning September 1959," and

(3) to require the Board to make plans for admissions to elementary schools without regard to race. Allen v. County School Board of Prince Edward County, 266 F.2d 507, 511 (C.A.4th Cir.1959). Having as early as 1956 resolved that they would not operate public schools "wherein white and colored children are taught together," the Supervisors of Prince Edward County refused to levy any school taxes for the 1959–1960 school year, explaining that they were "confronted with a court decree which requires the admission of white and colored children to all the schools of the county without regard to race or color." As a result, the county's public schools did not reopen in the fall of 1959 and have remained closed ever since, although the public schools of every other county in Virginia have continued to operate under laws governing the State's public school system and to draw funds provided by the State for that purpose. A private group, the Prince Edward School Foundation, was formed to operate private schools for white children in Prince Edward County and, having built its own school plant, has been in operation ever since the closing of the public schools. An offer to set up private schools for colored children in the county was rejected, the Negroes of Prince Edward preferring to continue the legal battle for desegregated public schools, and colored children were without formal education from 1959 to 1963, when federal, state, and county authorities cooperated to have classes conducted for Negroes and whites in school buildings owned by the county. During the 1959–1960 school year the Foundation's schools for white children were supported entirely by private contributions, but in 1960 the General Assembly adopted a new tuition grant program making every child, regardless of race, eligible for tuition grants of $125, or $150 to attend a nonsectarian private school or a public school outside his locality, and also authorizing localities to provide their own grants. The Prince Edward Board of Supervisors then passed an ordinance providing tuition grants of $100, so that each child attending the Prince Edward School Foundation's schools received a total of $225 if in elementary school or $250 if in high school. In the 1960–1961 session, the major source of financial support for the Foundation was in the indirect form of these state and county tuition grants, paid to children attending Foundation schools. At the same time, the County Board of Supervisors passed an ordinance allowing property tax credits up to 25 percent for contributions to any "nonprofit, nonsectarian private school" in the county.

In 1961 petitioners here filed a supplemental complaint, adding new parties and seeking to enjoin the respondents from refusing to operate an efficient system of public free schools in Prince Edward County and to enjoin payment of public funds to help support private schools which excluded students on account of race. The District Court, finding that "the end result of every action taken by that body [Board of Supervisors] was designed to preserve separation of the races in the schools of Prince Edward County," enjoined the county from paying tuition grants or giving tax credits so long as public schools remained closed. . . . At this time the District Court did not pass on whether the public schools of the county could be closed but abstained pending determination by the Virginia courts of whether the constitution and laws of Virginia required the public schools to be kept open. Later, however, without waiting for the Virginia courts to decide the question,[38] the District Court held that "the public schools of Prince Edward County may not be closed to avoid the effect of the law of the land as interpreted by the Supreme Court, while the Commonwealth of Virginia permits other public schools to remain open at the expense of the taxpayers." . . . Soon thereafter, a declaratory judgment suit was brought by the County Board of Supervisors and the County School Board in a Virginia Circuit Court. Having done this, these parties asked the Federal District Court to abstain from further proceedings until the suit in the state courts had run its course, but the District Court declined; it repeated its order that Prince Edward's public schools might not be closed to avoid desegregation while the other public schools in Virginia remained open. The Court of Appeals reversed, Judge Bell dissenting, holding that the District Court should have abstained to await state court determination of the validity of the tuition grants and the tax credits, as well as the validity of the closing of the public schools. Griffin v. Board of Supervisors of Prince Edward County, 322 F.2d 332 (C.A.4th Cir.1963). We granted certiorari, stating:

> In view of the long delay in the case since our decision in the *Brown* case and the importance of the questions presented, we grant certiorari and put the case down for argument March 30, 1964, on the merits, as we have done in other comparable situations without waiting for final action by the Court of Appeals. 375 U.S. 391.

For reasons to be stated, we agree with the District Court that, under the circumstances here, closing the Prince Edward County schools while public schools in all the other counties of Virginia were being maintained denied the petitioners and the class of Negro students they represent the equal protection of the laws guaranteed by the Fourteenth Amendment. . . . The case has been delayed since 1951 by resistance at the state and county level, by legislation, and by lawsuits. The original plaintiffs have doubtless all passed high school age. There has been entirely too much deliberation and not enough speed in enforcing the constitutional rights which we held in *Brown* v. *Board of Education,* supra, had been denied Prince Edward County Negro children. We accordingly reverse the Court of Appeals' judgment remanding the case to the District Court for abstention, and we proceed to the merits.

In County School Board of Prince Edward County v. Griffin, 204 Va. 650, 133 S.E.2d 565 (1963), the Supreme Court of Appeals of Virginia upheld as valid under state law the closing of the Prince Edward County public schools, the state and county tuition grants for children who attend private schools, and the county's tax concessions for those who make contributions to private schools. The same opinion also held that each county had "an option to operate or not to operate public schools," 204 Va., at 671, 133 S.E.2d, at 580. We accept this case as a definitive and authoritative holding of Virginia law, binding on us, but we cannot accept the Virginia court's further holding, based largely on the Court of Appeals' opinion in this case, 322 F.2d 332, that closing the county's public schools under the circumstances of the case did not deny the colored school children of Prince Edward County equal protection of the laws guaranteed by the Federal Constitution.

Since 1959, all Virginia counties have had the benefits of public schools but one: Prince Edward. However, there is no rule that counties, as counties, must be treated alike; the Equal Protection Clause relates to equal protection of the laws "between persons as such rather than between areas." Salsburg v. Maryland, 346 U.S. 545, 551, 74 S.Ct. 280, 283, 98 L.Ed. 281 (1954). Indeed, showing that different persons are treated differently is not enough, without more, to show a denial of equal protection. . . .

Virginia law, as here applied, unquestionably treats the school children of Prince Edward differently from the way it treats the school children of all other Virginia counties. Prince Edward children must go to a private school or none at all; all other Virginia children can go to public schools. Closing Prince Edward's schools bears more heavily on Negro children in Prince Edward County since white children there have accredited private schools which they can attend, while colored children until very recently have had no available private schools, and even the school they now attend is a temporary expedient. Apart from this expedient, the result is that Prince Edward County school children, if they go to school in their own county, must go to racially segregated schools which, although designated as private, are beneficiaries of county and state support.

A State, of course, has a wide discretion in deciding whether laws shall operate statewide or shall operate only in certain counties, the legislature "having in mind the needs and desires of each." Salsburg v. Maryland, supra, 346 U.S., at 552, 74 S.Ct., at 284. A State may wish to suggest, as Maryland did in *Salsburg*, that there are reasons why one county ought not to be treated like another. But the record in the present case could not be clearer that Prince Edward's public schools were closed and private schools operated in their place with state and county assistance, for one reason, and one reason only: to ensure, through measures taken by the county and the State, that white and colored children in Prince Edward County would not, under any circumstances, go to the same school. Whatever nonracial grounds might support a State's allowing a county to abandon public schools, the object must be a constitutional one, and grounds of race and opposition to desegregation do not qualify as constitutional.

. . . Accordingly, we agree with the District Court that closing the Prince Edward schools and meanwhile contributing to the support of the private segregated white schools that took their place denied petitioners the equal protection of the laws. . . .

The District Court held that "the public schools of Prince Edward County may not be closed to avoid the effect of the law of the land as interpreted by the Supreme Court, while the Commonwealth of Virginia permits other public schools to remain open at the expense of the taxpayers." . . . At the same time the court gave notice that it would later consider an order to accomplish this purpose if the public schools were not reopened by September 7, 1962. That day has long passed, and the schools are still closed. On remand, therefore, the court may find it necessary to consider further such an order. An order of this kind is within the court's power if required to assure these petitioners that their constitutional rights will no longer be denied them. The time for mere "deliberate speed" has run out, and that phrase can no longer justify denying these Prince Edward County school children their constitutional rights to an education equal to that afforded by the public schools in the other parts of Virginia.

The judgment of the Court of Appeals is reversed, the judgment of the District Court is affirmed, and the cause is remanded to the District Court with directions to enter a decree which will guarantee that these petitioners will get the kind of education that is given in the State's public schools. And, if it becomes necessary to add new parties to accomplish this end, the District Court is free to do so. It is so ordered.

Judgment of Court of Appeals reversed, judgment of the District Court affirmed and cause remanded with directions.

Mr. Justice CLARK and Mr. Justice HARLAN disagree with the holding that the federal courts are empowered to order the reopening of the public schools in Prince Edward County, but otherwise join in the Court's opinion.

*State Must Institute Affirmative
Action Where "Freedom of Choice"
Fails to Create Unitary System*

GREEN v. COUNTY SCHOOL OF BOARD OF NEW KENT COUNTY, VIRGINIA

Supreme Court of the United States, 1968.
391 U.S. 430, 88 S.Ct. 1689.

Mr. Justice BRENNAN delivered the opinion of the Court.

The question for decision is whether, under all the circumstances here, respondent School Board's adoption of a "freedom-of-choice" plan which allows a pupil to choose his own public school constitutes adequate compliance with the Board's responsibility "to achieve a system of determining admission to the public schools on a nonracial basis . . . ." Brown v. Board of Education of Topeka, Kan., 349 U.S. 294, 300–301, 75 S.Ct. 753, 756, 99 L.Ed. 1083 (*Brown II*).

Petitioners brought this action in March 1965 seeking injunctive relief against respondent's continued maintenance of an alleged racially segregated school system. . . .

The pattern of separate "white" and "Negro" schools in the New Kent County school system established under compulsion of state laws is precisely the pattern of segregation to which *Brown I* and *Brown II* were particularly addressed, and which *Brown I* declared unconstitutionally denied Negro school children equal protection of the laws. Racial identification of the system's schools was complete, extending not just to the composition of student bodies at the two schools but to every facet of school operations— faculty, staff, transportation, extracurricular activities and facilities. In short, the State, acting through the local school board and school officials, organized and operated a dual system, part "white" and part "Negro."

It was such dual systems that fourteen years ago *Brown I* held unconstitutional and a year later *Brown II* held must be abolished; school boards operating such school systems were *required* by *Brown II* "to effectuate a transition to a racially nondiscriminatory school system." 349 U.S., at 301,

75 S.Ct. at 756. It is of course true that for the time immediately after *Brown II* the concern was with making an initial break in a long-established pattern of excluding Negro children from schools attended by white children. The principal focus was on obtaining for those Negro children courageous enough to break with tradition a place in the "white" schools. See, e.g., Cooper v. Aaron, 358 U.S. 1, 78 S.Ct. 1401, 3 L.Ed.2d 5. Under *Brown II* that immediate goal was only the first step, however. The transition to a unitary, nonracial system of public education was and is the ultimate end to be brought about; it was because of the "complexities arising from the transition to a system of public education freed of racial discrimination" that we provided for "all deliberate speed" in the implementation of the principles of *Brown I*. 349 U.S., at 299–301, 75 S.Ct. at 755. Thus we recognized the task would necessarily involve solution of "varied local school problems." Id., at 299, 75 S.Ct. at 756. . . .

It is against this background that thirteen years after *Brown II* commanded the abolition of dual systems we must measure the effectiveness of respondent School Board's "freedom-of-choice" plan to achieve that end. The School Board contends that it has fully discharged its obligation by adopting a plan by which every student, regardless of race, may "freely" choose the school he will attend. The Board attempts to cast the issue in its broadest form by arguing that its "freedom-of-choice" plan may be faulted only by reading the Fourteenth Amendment as universally requiring "compulsory integration," a reading it insists the wording of the Amendment will not support. But that argument ignores the thrust of *Brown II*. In the light of the command of that case, what is involved here is the question whether the Board has achieved the "racially nondiscriminatory school system" *Brown II* held must be effectuated in order to remedy the established unconstitutional deficiencies of its segregated system. In the context of the state-imposed segregated pattern of long standing, the fact that in 1965 the Board opened the doors of the former "white" school to Negro children and of the "Negro" school to white children merely begins, not ends, our inquiry whether the Board has taken steps adequate to abolish its dual, segregated system. *Brown II* was a call for the dismantling of well-entrenched dual systems tempered by an awareness that complex and multifaceted problems would arise which would require time and flexibility for a successful resolution. School boards such as the respondent then operating state-compelled dual systems were nevertheless clearly charged with the affirmative duty to take whatever steps might be necessary to convert to a unitary system in which racial discrimination would be eliminated root and branch. . . . The constitutional rights of Negro school children articulated in *Brown I* permit no less than this; and it was to this end that *Brown II* commanded school boards to bend their efforts.

In determining whether respondent School Board met that command by adopting its "freedom-of-choice" plan, it is relevant that this first step did not come until some eleven years after *Brown I* was decided and ten years after *Brown II* directed the making of a "prompt and reasonable start." This deliberate perpetuation of the unconstitutional dual system can only have compounded the harm of such a system. Such delays are no longer tolerable, for "the governing constitutional principles no longer bear the imprint of newly enunciated doctrine." . . . The burden on a school board today is to come forward with a plan that promises realistically to work, and promises realistically to work *now*.

The obligation of the district courts, as it always has been, is to assess the effectiveness of a proposed plan in achieving desegregation. There is no universal answer to complex problems of desegregation; there is obviously no one plan that will do the job in every case. The matter must be assessed in light of the circumstances present and the options available in each instance. It is incumbent upon the school board to establish that its proposed plan promises meaningful and immediate progress toward disestablishing state-imposed segregation. It is incumbent upon the district court to weigh that claim in light of the facts at hand and in light of any alternatives which may be shown as feasible and more promising in their effectiveness. Where the court finds the board to be acting in good faith and the proposed plan to have real prospects for dismantling the state-imposed dual system "at the earliest practicable date," then the plan may be said to provide effective relief. Of course, the availability to the board of other more promising courses of action may indicate a lack of good faith; and at the least it places a heavy burden upon the board to explain its preference for an apparently less effective method. Moreover, whatever plan is adopted will require evaluation in practice, and the court should retain jurisdiction until it is clear that state-imposed segregation has been completely removed. . . .

We do not hold that "freedom of choice" can have no place in such a plan. We do not hold that a "freedom-of-choice" plan might of itself be unconstitutional, although that argument has been urged upon us. Rather, all we decide today is that in desegregating a dual system a plan utilizing "freedom of choice" is not an end in itself. . . .

The New Kent School Board's "freedom-of-choice" plan cannot be accepted as a sufficient step to "effectuate a transition" to a unitary system. In three years of operation not a single white child has chosen to attend Watkins school and although 115 Negro children enrolled in New Kent school in 1967 (up from 35 in 1965 and 111 in 1966) 85 percent of the Negro children in the system still attend the all-Negro Watkins school. In other words, the school system remains a dual system. Rather than further the dismantling of the dual system, the plan has operated simply to burden children and their parents with a responsibility which *Brown II* placed squarely on the School Board. The Board must be required to formulate a new plan and, in light of other courses which appear open to the Board, such as zoning, fashion steps which promise realistically to convert promptly to a system without a "white" school and a "Negro" school, but just schools.

The judgment of the Court of Appeals is vacated insofar as it affirmed the District Court and the case is remanded to the District Court for further proceedings consistent with this opinion. It is so ordered.

Dual School Systems Are to Be
Terminated at Once and Unitary
Systems Are to Begin Immediately

ALEXANDER v. HOLMES

Supreme Court of the United States, 1969.
396 U.S. 19, 90 S.Ct. 29, reh. denied 396
U.S. 976, 90 S.Ct. 437, 1970.

PER CURIAM. This case comes to the Court on a petition for certiorari to the Court of Appeals for the Fifth Circuit. The petition was granted on October 9, 1969, and the case set down for early argument. The question presented is one of paramount importance, involving as it does the denial of fundamental rights to many thousands of school children, who are presently attending Mississippi schools under segregated conditions contrary to the applicable decisions of this Court. Against this background the Court of Appeals should have denied all motions for additional time because continued operation of segregated schools under a standard of allowing "all deliberate speed" for desegregation is no longer constitutionally permissible. Under explicit holdings of this Court the obligation of every school district is to terminate dual school systems at once and to operate now and hereafter only unitary schools. . . .

It is hereby adjudged, ordered, and decreed:

The Court of Appeals' order of August 28, 1969, is vacated, and the case is remanded to that court to issue its decree and order, effective immediately, declaring that each of the school districts here involved may no longer operate a dual school system based on race or color, and directing that they begin immediately to operate as unitary school systems within which no person is to be effectively excluded from any school because of race or color. . . .

The Court of Appeals shall retain jurisdiction to insure prompt and faithful compliance with its order, and may modify or amend the same as may be deemed necessary or desirable for the operation of a unitary school system. . . .

DE FACTO SEGREGATION

De facto segregation is not unconstitutional whether it occurs in the South or in the North. President Nixon summarized the law in this regard in 1969. He said: "There is a fundamental distinction between so-called 'de jure' and 'de facto' segregation: de jure segregation arises by law or by the deliberate act of school officials and is unconstitutional; de facto segregation results from residential housing patterns and does not violate the Constitution."

This legal position concerning *de facto* segregation has been reiterated several times by the courts in various decisions. A notable early example was the *Bell* decision in which the United States Court of Appeals for the Seventh Circuit said: "there is no affirmative United States constitutional duty to change innocently arrived at school attendance districts by the mere fact that shifts in population either increase or decrease the percentage of either Negro or white pupils." [39]   Similarly, the Court of Appeals for the Fifth Circuit held that boards of education have no constitutional obligation to relieve racial imbalance that they do not cause or create.   These are both decisions from northern states but fundamentally the law is the same whether the segregation occurs in the North or in the South.   If segregation is created by law or official act, then an affirmative duty is required to integrate the schools.   The Supreme Court summarized the constitutional standard in a Denver, Colorado, case: "we have held that where plaintiffs prove that a current condition of segregated schooling exists within a school district where a dual system was compelled or authorized by statute at the time of our decision in *Brown* . . . the State automatically assumes an affirmative duty to 'effectuate a transition to a racially nondiscriminatory school system.' " [40]   In this case, the Supreme Court emphasized that the differentiating factor between *de jure* segregation and so-called *de facto* segregation is *purpose* or *intent*.

If school authorities practice purposeful segregation, then a *de jure* condition exists and the school district will be required to take affirmative measures to correct racial imbalance in the schools.

School Board Actions May Have
Effect of Creating Unconstitutional De
Jure Segregation

KEYES v. SCHOOL DISTRICT
NO. 1, DENVER

Supreme Court of the United States, 1973.
413 U.S. 189, 93 S.Ct. 2686.

Mr. Justice BRENNAN delivered the opinion of the Court.

This school desegregation case concerns the Denver, Colorado, school system.   That system has never been operated under a constitutional or statutory provision that mandated or permitted racial segregation in public education.   Rather, the gravamen of this action, brought in June 1969 in the District Court for the District of Colorado by parents of Denver schoolchildren, is that respondent School Board alone, by use of various techniques such as the manipulation of student attendance zones, schoolsite selection and a neighborhood school policy, created or maintained racially or ethnically (or both racially and ethnically) segregated schools throughout the school district, entitling petitioners to a decree directing desegregation of the entire school district.

  .   .   .   The District Court found that by the construction of a new, relatively small elementary school, Barrett, in the middle of the Negro community west of Park Hill, by the gerrymandering of student attendance zones, by the use of so-called "optional zones," and by the excessive use of mobile classroom units, among other things, the respondent School Board had engaged over almost a decade after 1960 in an unconstitutional policy of deliberate racial segregation with respect to the Park Hill schools.   The court therefore ordered the Board to desegregate those schools through the implementation of the three rescinded resolutions. D.C., 303 F.Supp. 279 and 289 (1969).

Segregation in Denver schools is not limited, however, to the schools in the Park Hill area, and not satisfied with their success in obtaining relief for Park Hill, petitioners pressed their prayer that the District Court order desegregation of all segregated schools in the city of Denver, particularly the heavily segregated schools in the core city area. But that court concluded that its finding of a purposeful and systematic program of racial segregation affecting thousands of students in the Park Hill area did not, in itself, impose on the School Board an affirmative duty to eliminate segregation throughout the school district. Instead, the court fractionated the district and held that petitioners had to make a fresh showing of *de jure* segregation in each area of the city for which they sought relief. Moreover, the District Court held that its finding of intentional segregation in Park Hill was not in any sense material to the question of segregative intent in other areas of the city. . . .

Before turning to the primary question we decide today, a word must be said about the District Court's method of defining a "segregated" school. Denver is a tri-ethnic, as distinguished from a bi-racial, community. The overall racial and ethnic composition of the Denver public schools is 66 percent Anglo, 14 percent Negro, and 20 percent Hispano. . . . What is or is not a segregated school will necessarily depend on the facts of each particular case. In addition to the racial and ethnic composition of a school's student body, other factors, such as the racial and ethnic composition of faculty and staff and the community and administration attitudes toward the school, must be taken into consideration. The District Court has recognized these specific factors as elements of the definition of a "segregated" school and we may therefore infer that the court will consider them again on remand.

We conclude, however, that the District Court erred in separating Negroes and Hispanos for purposes of defining a "segregated" school. We have held that Hispanos constitute an identifiable class for purposes of the Fourteenth Amendment. Hernandez v. Texas, 347 U.S. 475, 74 S.Ct. 667, 98 L.Ed. 866 (1954). . . . Indeed the District Court recognized this in classifying predominantly Hispano schools as "segregated" schools in their own right. But there is also much evidence that in the Southwest Hispanos and Negroes have a great many things in common. The United States Commission on Civil Rights has recently published two Reports on Hispano education in the Southwest. Focusing on students in the States of Arizona, California, Colorado, New Mexico, and Texas, the Commission concluded that Hispanos suffer from the same educational inequities as Negroes and American Indians. In fact, the District Court itself recognized that "[o]ne of the things which the Hispano has in common with the Negro is economic and cultural deprivation and discrimination." 313 F.Supp., at 69. This is agreement that, though of different origins, Negroes and Hispanos in Denver suffer identical discrimination in treatment when compared with the treatment afforded Anglo students. In that circumstance, we think petitioners are entitled to have schools with a combined predominance of Negroes and Hispanos included in the category of "segregated" schools.

In our view, the only other question that requires our decision at this time is that subsumed in Question 2 of the questions presented by petitioners, namely whether the District Court and the Court of Appeals applied an incorrect legal standard in addressing petitioners' contention that respondent School Board engaged in an unconstitutional policy of deliberate segregation in the core city schools. Our conclusion is that those courts did not apply the correct standard in addressing that contention.

Petitioners apparently concede for the purposes of this case that in the case of a school system like Denver's, where no statutory dual system has ever existed, plaintiffs must prove not only that segregated schooling exists but also that it was brought about or maintained by intentional state action. Petitioners proved that for almost a decade after 1960 respondent School Board had engaged in an unconstitutional policy of deliberate racial segregation in the Park Hill schools. . . . This finding did not relate to an insubstantial or trivial fragment of the school system. On the contrary, respondent School Board was found guilty of following a deliberate segregation policy at schools attended, in 1969, by 37.69 percent of Denver's total Negro school population . . . . Respondent argues, however, that a finding of state-imposed segregation as to a substantial portion of the school system can be viewed in isolation from the rest of the district, and that even if state-imposed segregation does exist in a substantial part of the Denver school system, it does not follow that the District Court could predicate on that fact a finding that the entire school system is a dual system. We do not agree. We have never suggested that plaintiffs in school desegregation cases must bear the burden of proving the elements of *de jure* segregation as to each and every school or each and every student within the school system. Rather, we have held that where plaintiffs prove that a current condition of segregated schooling exists within a school district where a dual system was compelled or authorized by statute at the time of our decision in Brown v. Board of Education, 347 U.S. 483, 74 S.Ct. 686, 98 L.Ed. 873 (1954) (*Brown I*), the State automatically assumes an affirmative duty "to effectuate a transition to a racially nondiscriminatory school system," Brown v. Board of Education, 349 U.S. 294, 301, 75 S.Ct. 753, 756, 99 L.Ed. 1083 (1955) (*Brown II*), see also Green v. County School Board, 391 U.S. 430, 437–438, 88 S.Ct. 1689, 1693–1694, 20 L.Ed.2d 716 (1968), that is, to eliminate from the public schools within their school system all "vestiges of state-imposed segregation." Swann v. Charlotte-Mecklenburg Board of Education, 402 U.S. 1, 15, 91 S.Ct. 1267, 1275, 28 L.Ed.2d 554 (1971).

This is not a case, however, where a statutory dual system has ever existed. Nevertheless, where plaintiffs prove that the school authorities have carried out a systematic program of segregation affecting a substantial portion of the students, schools, teachers, and facilities within the school system, it is only common sense to conclude that there exists a predicate for a finding of the existence of a dual school system. Several considerations support this conclusion. First, it is obvious that a practice of concentrating Negroes in certain schools by structuring attendance zones or designating "feeder" schools on the basis of race has the reciprocal effect of keeping other nearby schools predominantly white. Similarly, the practice of building a school—such as the Barrett Elementary School in this case—to a certain size and in a certain location, "with conscious knowledge that it would be a segregated school," 303 F.Supp., at 285, has a substantial reciprocal effect on the racial composition of other nearby schools. So also, the use of mobile classrooms, the drafting of student transfer policies, the transportation of students, and the assignment of faculty and staff on racially identifiable bases, have the clear effect of earmarking schools according to their racial composition, and this, in turn, together with the elements of student assignment and school construction, may have a profound reciprocal effect on the racial composition of residential neighborhoods, within a metropolitan area, thereby causing further racial concentration within the schools. We recognized this in *Swann* . . . .

In short, common sense dictates the conclusion that racially inspired school board actions have an impact beyond the particular schools that are subjects of those actions. This is not to say, of course, that there can never be a case in which the geographical structure of, or the natural boundaries within, a school district may have the effect of dividing the district into separate, identifiable and unrelated units. Such a determination is essentially a question of fact to be resolved by the trial court in the first instance, but such cases must be rare. In the absence of such a determination, proof of state-imposed segregation in a substantial portion of the district will suffice to support a finding by the trial court of the existence of a dual system. Of course, where that finding is made, as in cases involving statutory dual systems, the school authorities have an affirmative duty "to effectuate a transition to a racially nondiscriminatory school system." *Brown II,* supra, 394 U.S., at 301, 75 S.Ct. at 756.

On remand, therefore, the District Court should decide in the first instance whether respondent School Board's deliberate racial segregation policy with respect to the Park Hill schools constitutes the entire Denver school system a dual school system. We observe that on the record now before us there is indication that Denver is not a school district which might be divided into separate, identifiable, and unrelated units. . . . In any event, inquiry whether the District Court and the Court of Appeals applied the correct legal standards in addressing petitioners' contention of deliberate segregation in the core city schools is not at an end even if it be true that Park Hill may be separated from the rest of the Denver school district as a separate, identifiable, and unrelated unit.

The District Court proceeded on the premise that the finding as to the Park Hill schools was irrelevant to the consideration of the rest of the district, and began its examination of the core city schools by requiring that petitioners prove all of the essential elements of *de jure* segregation—that is, stated simply, a current condition of segregation resulting from intentional state action directed specifically to the core city schools. The segregated character of the core city schools could not be and is not denied. Petitioners' proof showed that at the time of trial twenty-two of the schools in the core city area were less than 30 percent in Anglo enrollment and eleven of the schools were less than 10 percent Anglo. Petitioners also introduced substantial evidence demonstrating the existence of a disproportionate racial and ethnic composition of faculty and staff at these schools.

On the question of segregative intent, petitioners presented evidence tending to show that the Board, through its actions over a period of years, intentionally created and maintained the segregated character of the core city schools. Respondents countered this evidence by arguing that the segregation in these schools is the result of a racially neutral "neighborhood school policy" and that the acts of which petitioners complain are explicable within the bounds of that policy. Accepting the School Board's explanation, the District Court and the Court of Appeals agree that a finding of *de jure* segregation as to the core city schools was not permissible since petitioners had failed to prove "(1) a racially discriminatory purpose and (2) a causal relationship between the acts complained of and the racial imbalance admittedly existing in those schools." 445 F.2d at 1006. This assessment of petitioners' proof was clearly incorrect.

Although petitioners had already proved the existence of intentional school segregation in the Park Hill schools, this crucial finding was totally ignored when attention turned to the core city schools. Plainly, a finding of intentional segregation as to a portion of a school system is not devoid of probative value in assessing the school authorities' intent with respect to other parts of the same school system. On the contrary where, as here, the case involves one school board, a finding of intentional segregation on its part in one portion of a school system is highly relevant to the issue of the board's intent with respect to the other segregated schools in the system. This is merely an application of the well-settled evidentiary principle that "the prior doing of other similar acts, whether clearly a part of a scheme or not, is useful as reducing the possibility that the act in question was done with innocent intent." 2 J. Wigmore, Evidence 200 (3d ed. 1940). . . .

Applying these principles in the special context of school desegregation cases, we hold that a finding of intentionally segregative school board actions in a meaningful portion of a school system, as in this case, creates a presumption that other segregated schooling within the system is not adventitious. It establishes, in other words, a prima facie case of unlawful segregative design on the part of school authorities, and shifts to those authorities the burden of proving that other segregated schools within the system are not also the result of intentionally segregative actions. This is true even if it is determined that different areas of the school district should be viewed independently of each other because, even in that situation, there is high probability that where school authorities have effectuated an intentionally segregative policy in a meaningful portion of the school system, similar impermissible considerations have motivated their actions in other areas of the system. We emphasize that the differentiating factor between *de jure* segregation and so-called *de facto* segregation to which we referred in *Swann* is *purpose* or *intent* to segregate. Where school authorities have been found to have practiced purposeful segregation in part of a school system, they may be expected to oppose system-wide desegregation, as did the respondents in this case, on the ground that their purposefully segregative actions were isolated and individual events, thus leaving plaintiffs with the burden of proving otherwise. But at that point where an intentionally segregative policy is practiced in a meaningful or significant segment of a school system, as in this case, the school authorities cannot be heard to argue that plaintiffs have proved only "isolated and individual" unlawfully segregative actions. In that circumstance, it is both fair and reasonable to require that the school authorities bear the burden of showing that their actions as to other segregated schools within the system were not also motivated by segregative intent. . . .

In discharging that burden, it is not enough, of course, that the school authorities rely upon some allegedly logical, racially neutral explanation for their actions. Their burden is to adduce proof sufficient to support a finding that segregative intent was not among the factors that motivated their actions. The courts below attributed much significance to the fact that many of the Board's actions in the core city area antedated our decision in *Brown.* We reject any suggestion that remoteness in time has any relevance to the issue of intent. If the actions of school authorities were to any degree motivated by segregative intent and the segregation resulting from those actions continues to exist, the fact of remoteness in time certainly does not make those actions any less "intentional." . . .

The respondent School Board invoked at trial its "neighborhood school policy" as explaining racial and ethnic concentrations within the core city schools, arguing that since the core city area population had long been Negro and Hispano, the concentrations were necessarily the result of residential patterns and not of purposefully segregative policies. We have no occasion to consider in this case whether a "neighborhood school policy" of itself will justify racial or ethnic concentrations in the absence of a finding that school authorities have committed acts constituting *de jure* segregation. It is enough that we hold that the mere assertion of such a policy is not dispositive where, as in this case, the school authorities have been found to have practiced *de jure* segregation in a meaningful portion of the school system by techniques that indicate that the "neighborhood school" concept has not been maintained free of manipulation. . . .

In summary, the District Court on remand, *first,* will afford respondent School Board the opportunity to prove its contention that the Park Hill area is a separate, identifiable, and unrelated section of the school district that should be treated as isolated from the rest of the district. If respondent School Board fails to prove that contention, the District Court, *second,* will determine whether respondent School Board's conduct over almost a decade after 1960 in carrying out a policy of deliberate racial segregation in the Park Hill schools constitutes the entire school system a dual school system. If the District Court determines that the Denver school system is a dual school system, respondent School Board has the affirmative duty to desegregate the entire system "root and branch." Green v. County School Board, 391 U.S., at 438, 88 S.Ct. at 1694. If the District Court determines, however, that the Denver school system is not a dual school system by reason of the Board's actions in Park Hill, the court, *third,* will afford respondent School Board the opportunity to rebut petitioners' prima facie case of intentional segregation in the core city schools raised by the finding of intentional segregation in the Park Hill schools. There, the Board's burden is to show that its policies and practices with respect to schoolsite location, school size, school renovations and additions, student-attendance zones, student assignment and transfer options, mobile classroom units, transportation of students, assignment of faculty and staff, etc., considered together and premised on the Board's so-called "neighborhood school" concept, either were not taken in effectuation of a policy to create or maintain segregation in the core city schools, or, if unsuccessful in that effort, were not factors in causing the existing condition of segregation in these schools. Considerations of "fairness" and "policy" demand no less in light of the Board's intentionally segregative actions. If respondent Board fails to rebut petitioners' prima facie case, the District Court must, as in the case of Park Hill, decree all-out desegregation of the core city schools.

The judgment of the Court of Appeals is modified to vacate instead of reverse the parts of the Final Decree that concern the core city schools, and the case is remanded to the District Court for further proceedings consistent with this opinion. . . .

It is so ordered.

NOTES

1. In taking the position that there is no affirmative duty to integrate where *de facto* segregation exists, one commentator had this to say. "Revolutionary as was the decision in *Brown* in its rendition and subsequent application, the Court has not sought to overturn the established principle of constitutional law that 'the unlawful administration by state officers of a state statute fair on its face, resulting in its unequal application to those who are entitled to be treated alike, is not a denial of equal protection unless there is shown to be present in it an element of intentional or purposeful discrimination.'" Snowden v. Hughes, 321 U.S. 1, 64 S.Ct. 397 (1944). In one of its first cases, Virginia v. Rives, 100 U.S. 313 (1879), construing the Equal Protection Clause of the Fourteenth Amendment, the Court held that a mere showing that blacks were not included in a particular jury was not enough, there must be a showing of actual discrimination because of race. Down through the years, this has been the law of the land: "The purpose of the Equal Protection Clause of the Fourteenth Amendment is to secure every person within the State's jurisdiction against intentional and arbitrary discrimination, whether occasioned by express terms of a statute or by its improper execution through duly constituted agents." Sunday Lake Iron Co. v. Township of Wakefield, 247 U.S. 350, 38 S.Ct. 495 (1918). "No different purpose was attributed to the amendment by the Court either in *Brown* or any case since decided." Charles J. Bloch, "Does the Fourteenth Amendment Forbid De Facto Segregation?" 16 Western Reserve L.Rev. 542 (1965). Permission to quote granted by Wm. S. Hein and Company, Inc., Buffalo, New York.

2. A minority view regarding *de facto* segregation was expounded in a case in Washington, D.C. in 1967. The court, in this case, held that racially and socially homogeneous schools damage the mind and spirit of the child and whether segregation occurs by law or by fact, there is an affirmative duty to overcome the segregation. The court said further that aptitude and achievement tests used for placing children in separate learning tracks were middle-class oriented and served to perpetuate segregation in the schools. Based on these conclusions, the court handed down a decree ordering the busing of volunteering children from predominantly black schools to predominantly white schools and also mandated the abolition

of ability grouping of children by the "tracking" procedures that were being used at that time in Washington, D.C. Hobson v. Hansen, 269 F.Supp. 401 (1967). Affirmed on Appeal by United States Court of Appeals for the District of Columbia.

3. The Court of Appeals for the Fifth Circuit said in United States v. Jefferson County Board of Education 372 F.2d 836 (1970) that:

> The Constitution is both color blind and color conscious.
> To avoid a conflict with the equal protection clause, a classification that denies a benefit, causes harm, or imposes a burden must not be based on race. But the Constitution is color conscious to prevent discrimination being perpetuated and to undo the effects of past discrimination. The criterion is the relevancy of color to a legitimate governmental purpose.

QUOTAS AND BUSING

If the vestiges of past state-sanctioned segregation remain, then the courts may do whatever is reasonably necessary to desegregate the schools. What constitute legitimate remedies to overcome past segregation to bring into effect a unitary school system has been the subject of controversy since the days of "freedom of choice." Beyond freedom of choice though, the state is required to assert a positive policy of placement of either students or facilities to bring about integration.

The problem really has two aspects: The measurement of inequality and the physical process used by the courts to effectuate integration. In determining the degree of inequality, the lower courts have tended to rely on quotas as a primary yardstick. In this regard, the Supreme Court has held that racial percentages of each school do not have to reflect the racial composition of the school system as a whole.[41] A fixed mathematical racial balance is not required and according to the Court should not be the sole criterion to determine appropriate movement toward a unitary state. The Supreme Court is consistent in this position in higher education as well as in elementary and secondary. In the celebrated *Bakke* decision,[42] the Supreme Court rejected the University of California's quota system for admission to medical school that specified a percentage of the student body be set aside for selected classifications of persons. The Court said that

> it is evident that the Davis special admission program involves the use of an explicit racial classification never before countenanced by this court. It tells applicants who are not Negro, Asian, or "Chicano" that they are totally excluded from a specific percentage of the seats in an entering class . . . .
> The fatal flaw in petitioner's preferential program is its disregard of individual rights as guaranteed by the Fourteenth Amendment.[43]

In both higher education and the public schools, the court has been consistent in allowing the use of quotas or percentage as one criterion or as a starting point, but has never required nor permitted it to be used as the sole determinant.

Several alternatives have been approved by the Supreme Court in overcoming *de jure* racial imbalances, and transportation is one such acceptable remedy. Significantly, in *Swann* v. *Charlotte-Mecklenburg,* the court observed, "Desegregation plans cannot be limited to walk-in schools."

Busing to Overcome Racial
Segregation Is a Judicially Acceptable
Alternative Where De Jure
Segregation Has Existed

SWANN v. CHARLOTTE-MECKLENBURG BOARD OF EDUCATION

Supreme Court of the United States, 1971.
402 U.S. 1, 91 S.Ct. 1267.

Mr. Chief Justice BURGER delivered the opinion of the Court. . . .

This case and those argued with it arose in States having a long history of maintaining two sets of schools in a single school system deliberately operated to carry out a governmental policy to separate pupils in schools solely on the basis of race. That was what *Brown* v. *Board of Education* was all about. . . .

The Charlotte-Mecklenburg school system, the forty-third largest in the Nation, encompasses the city of Charlotte and surrounding Mecklenburg County, North Carolina. The area is large—550 square miles—spanning roughly twenty-two miles east-west and thirty-six miles north-south. During the 1968–1969 school year the system served more than 84,000 pupils in 107 schools. Approximately 71 percent of the pupils were found to be white and 29 percent Negro. As of June 1969 there were approximately 24,000 Negro students in the system, of whom 21,000 attended schools within the city of Charlotte. Two-thirds of those 21,000—approximately 14,000 Negro students—attended twenty-one schools which were either totally Negro or more than 99 percent Negro. . . .

In April 1969 the District Court ordered the school board to come forward with a plan for both faculty and student desegregation. Proposed plans were accepted by the court in June and August 1969 on an interim basis only, and the board was ordered to file a third plan by November 1969. In November the board moved for an extension of time until February 1970, but when that was denied the board submitted a partially completed plan. In December 1969 the District Court held that the board's submission was unacceptable and appointed an expert in education administration, Dr. John Finger, to prepare a desegregation plan. Thereafter, in February 1970, the District Court was presented with two alternative pupil assignment plans—the finalized "board plan" and the "Finger plan."

The Board Plan. As finally submitted, the school board plan closed seven schools and reassigned their pupils. It restructured school attendance zones to achieve greater racial balance but maintained existing grade structures and rejected techniques such as pairing and clustering as part of a desegregation effort. The plan created a single athletic league, eliminated the previously racial basis of the school bus system, provided racially mixed faculties and administrative staffs, and modified its free-transfer plan into an optional majority-to-minority transfer system.

The board plan proposed substantial assignment of Negroes to nine of the system's ten high schools, producing 17 percent to 36 percent Negro population in each. The projected Negro attendance at the tenth school, Independence, was 2 percent. The proposed attendance zones for the high schools were typically shaped like wedges of a pie, extending outward from the center of the city to the suburban and rural areas of the county in order to afford residents of the center city area access to outlying schools.

As for junior high schools, the board plan rezoned the twenty-one school areas so that in twenty the Negro attendance would range from 0 percent to 38 percent. The other school, located in the heart of the Negro residential area, was left with an enrollment of 90 percent Negro.

The board plan with respect to elementary schools relied entirely upon gerrymandering of geographic zones. More than half of the Negro elementary pupils were left in nine schools that were 86 percent to 100 percent Negro; approximately half of the white elementary pupils were assigned to schools 86 percent to 100 percent white.

The Finger Plan. The plan submitted by the court-appointed expert, Dr. Finger, adopted the school board zoning plan for senior high schools with one modification: it required that an additional 300 Negro students be transported from the Negro residential area of the city to the nearly all-white Independence High School.

The Finger plan for the junior high schools employed much of the rezoning plan of the board, combined with the creation of nine "satellite" zones. Under the satellite plan, inner-city Negro students were assigned by attendance zones to nine outlying predominately white junior high schools, thereby substantially desegregating every junior high school in the system.

The Finger plan departed from the board plan chiefly in its handling of the system's seventy-six elementary schools. Rather than relying solely upon geographic zoning, Dr. Finger proposed use of zoning, pairing, and grouping techniques, with the result that student bodies throughout the system would range from 9 percent to 38 percent Negro. . . .

On February 5, 1970, the District Court adopted the board plan, as modified by Dr. Finger, for the junior and senior high schools. The court rejected the board elementary school plan and adopted the Finger plan as presented. Implementation was partially stayed by the Court of Appeals for the Fourth Circuit on March 5, and this Court declined to disturb the Fourth Circuit's order, 397 U.S. 978, 90 S.Ct. 1099, 25 L.Ed.2d 389 (1970).

On appeal the Court of Appeals affirmed the District Court's order as to faculty desegregation and the secondary school plans, but vacated the order respecting elementary schools. . . .

Nearly seventeen years ago this Court held, in explicit terms, that state-imposed segregation by race in public schools denies equal protection of the laws. At no time has the Court deviated in the slightest degree from that holding or its constitutional underpinnings. None of the parties before us challenges the Court's decision of May 17, 1954, that

> in the field of public education the doctrine of "separate but equal" has no place. Separate educational facilities are inherently unequal. Therefore, we hold that the plaintiffs and others similarly situated . . . are, by reason of the segregation complained of, deprived of the equal protection of the laws guaranteed by the Fourteenth Amendment. . . .

. . . . The central issue in this case is that of student assignment, and there are essentially four problem areas:

1. to what extent racial balance or racial quotas may be used as an implement in a remedial order to correct a previously segregated system;

2. whether every all-Negro and all-white school must be eliminated as an indispensable part of a remedial process of desegregation;

3. what the limits are, if any, on the rearrangement of school districts and attendance zones, as a remedial measure; and

4. what the limits are, if any, on the use of transportation facilities to correct state-enforced racial school segregation.

Racial Balances or Racial Quotas The constant theme and thrust of every holding from *Brown I* to date is that state-enforced separation of races in public schools is discrimination that violates the Equal Protection Clause. The remedy commanded was to dismantle dual school systems. . . .

Our objective in dealing with the issues presented by these cases is to see that school authorities exclude no pupil of a racial minority from any school, directly or indirectly, on account of race; it does not and cannot embrace all the problems of racial prejudice, even when those problems contribute to disproportionate racial concentrations in some schools.

In this case it is urged that the District Court has imposed a racial balance requirement of 71 percent–29 percent on individual schools. The fact that no such objective was actually achieved—and would appear to be impossible—tends to blunt that claim, yet in the opinion and order of the District Court of December 1, 1969, we find that court directing

> that efforts should be made to reach a 71–29 ratio in the various schools so that there will be no basis for contending that one school is racially different from the others . . . [t]hat no school [should] be operated with an all-black or predominantly black student body, [and] [t]hat pupils of all grades [should] be assigned in such a way that as nearly as practicable the various schools at various grade levels have about the same proportion of black and white students.

The District Judge went on to acknowledge that variation "from that norm may be unavoidable." This contains intimations that the "norm" is a fixed mathematical racial balance reflecting the pupil constituency of the system. If we were to read the holding of the District Court to require, as a matter of substantive constitutional right, any particular degree of racial balance or mixing, that approach would be disapproved and we would be obliged to reverse. The constitutional command to desegregate schools does not mean that every school in every community must always reflect the racial composition of the school system as a whole.

As the voluminous record in this case shows, the predicate for the District Court's use of the 71 percent–29 percent ratio was twofold: first, its express finding, approved by the Court of Appeals and not challenged here, that a dual school system had been maintained by the school authorities at least until 1969; second, its finding, also approved by the Court of Appeals, that the school board had totally defaulted in its acknowledged duty to come forward with an acceptable plan of its own, notwithstanding the patient efforts of the District Judge who, on at least three occasions, urged the board to submit plans. . . .

We see therefore that the use made of mathematical ratios was no more than a starting point in the process of shaping a remedy, rather than an inflexible requirement. From that starting point the District Court proceeded to frame a decree that was within its discretionary powers, as an equitable remedy for the particular circumstances. As we said in *Green,* a school authority's remedial plan or a district court's remedial decree is to be judged by its effectiveness. Awareness of the racial composition of the whole school system is likely to be a useful starting point in shaping a remedy to correct past constitutional violations. In sum, the very limited use made of mathematical ratios was within the equitable remedial discretion of the District Court.

One-race Schools The record in this case reveals the familiar phenomenon that in metropolitan areas minority groups are often found concentrated in one part of the city. In some circumstances certain schools may remain all or largely of one race until new schools can be provided or neighborhood patterns change. Schools all or predominantly of one race in a district of mixed population will require close scrutiny to determine that school assignments are not part of state-enforced segregation.

In light of the above, it should be clear that the existence of some small number of one-race, or virtually one-race, schools within a district is not in and of itself the mark of a system that still practices segregation by law. The district judge or school authorities should make every effort to achieve the greatest possible degree of actual desegregation and will thus necessarily be concerned with the elimination of one-race schools. . . . Where the school authority's proposed plan for conversion from a dual to a unitary system contemplates the continued existence of some schools that are all or predominately of one race, they have the burden of showing that such school assignments are genuinely nondiscriminatory. The court should scrutinize such schools, and the burden upon the school authorities will be to satisfy the court that their racial composition is not the result of present or past discriminatory action on their part.

An optional majority-to-minority transfer provision has long been recognized as a useful part of every desegregation plan. Provision for optional transfer of those in the majority racial group of a particular school to other schools where they will be in the minority is an indispensable remedy for those students willing to transfer to other schools in order to lessen the impact on them of the state-imposed stigma of segregation. In order to be effective, such a transfer arrangement must grant the transferring student free transportation and space must be made available in the school to which he desires to move. . . . The court orders in this and the companion *Davis* case now provide such an option.

Remedial Altering of Attendance Zones The maps submitted in these cases graphically demonstrate that one of the principal tools employed by school planners and by courts to break up the dual school system has been a frank—and sometimes drastic—gerrymandering of school districts and attendance zones. An additional step was pairing, "clustering," or "grouping" of schools with attendance assignments made deliberately to accomplish the transfer of Negro students out of formerly segregated Negro schools and transfer of white students to formerly all-Negro schools. More often than not, these zones are neither compact nor contiguous; indeed they may be on opposite ends of the city. As an interim corrective measure, this cannot be said to be beyond the broad remedial powers of a court.

Absent a constitutional violation there would be no basis for judicially ordering assignment of students on a racial basis. All things being equal, with no history of discrimination, it might well be desirable to assign pupils to schools nearest their homes. But all things are not equal in a system that has been deliberately constructed and maintained to enforce racial segregation. The remedy for such segregation may be administratively awkward, inconvenient, and even bizarre in some situations and may impose burdens on some; but all awkwardness and inconvenience cannot be avoided in the interim period when remedial adjustments are being made to eliminate the dual school systems. . . .

We hold that the pairing and grouping of noncontiguous school zones is a permissible tool and such action is to be considered in light of the objectives sought. . . . Maps do not tell the whole story since noncontiguous school zones may be more accessible to each other in terms of the critical travel time, because of traffic patterns and good highways, than schools geographically closer together. Conditions in different localities will vary so widely that no rigid rules can be laid down to govern all situations.

Transportation of Students The scope of permissible transportation of students as an implement of a remedial decree has never been defined by this Court and by the very nature of the problem it cannot be defined with precision. No rigid guidelines as to student transportation can be given for application to the infinite variety of problems presented in thousands of situations. Bus transportation has been an integral part of the public education system for years, and was perhaps the single most important factor in the transition from the one-room schoolhouse to the consolidated school. . . .

The importance of bus transportation as a normal and accepted tool of educational policy is readily discernible in this and the companion case *Davis*. The Charlotte school authorities did not purport to assign students on the basis of geographically drawn zones until 1965 and then they allowed almost unlimited transfer privileges. . . .

Thus the remedial techniques used in the District Court's order were within that court's power to provide equitable relief; implementation of the decree is well within the capacity of the school authority.

The decree provided that the buses used to implement the plan would operate on direct routes. Students would be picked up at schools near their homes and transported to the schools they were to attend. The trips for elementary school pupils average about seven miles and the District Court found that they would take "not over thirty-five minutes at the most." This system compares favorably with the transportation plan previously operated in Charlotte under which each day 23,600 students on all grade levels were transported an average of fifteen miles one way for an average trip requiring over an hour. In these circumstances, we find no basis for holding that the local school authorities may not be required to employ bus transportation as one tool of school desegregation. Desegregation plans cannot be limited to the walk-in school.

An objection to transportation of students may have validity when the time or distance of travel is so great as to either risk the health of the children or significantly impinge on the educational process. . . . It hardly needs stating that the limits on time of travel will vary with many factors, but probably with none more than the age of the students. The reconciliation of competing values in a desegregation case is, of course, a difficult task with many sensitive facets but fundamentally no more so than remedial measures courts of equity have traditionally employed.

The Court of Appeals, searching for a term to define the equitable remedial power of the district courts, used the term "reasonableness." In *Green,* this Court used the term "feasible" and by implication, "workable," "effective," and "realistic" in the mandate to develop "a plan that promises realistically to work, and . . . to work *now.*" On the facts of this case, we are unable to conclude that the order of the District Court is not reasonable, feasible, and workable. However, in seeking to define the scope of remedial power or the limits on remedial power of courts in an area as sensitive as we deal with here, words are poor instruments to convey the sense of basic fairness inherent in equity. Substance, not semantics, must govern, and we have sought to suggest the nature of limitations without frustrating the appropriate scope of equity.

At some point, these school authorities and others like them should have achieved full compliance with this Court's decision in *Brown I.* The systems would then be "unitary" in the sense required by our decisions in *Green* and *Alexander.*

It does not follow that the communities served by such systems will remain demographically stable, for in a growing, mobile society, few will do so. Neither school authorities nor district courts are constitutionally required to make year-by-year adjustments of the racial composition of student bodies once the affirmative duty to desegregate has been accomplished and racial discrimination through official action is eliminated from the system. This does not mean that federal courts are without power to deal with future problems; but in the absence of a showing that either the school authorities or some other agency of the State has deliberately attempted to fix or alter demographic patterns to affect the racial composition of the schools, further intervention by a district court should not be necessary.

For the reasons herein set forth, the judgment of the Court of Appeals is affirmed as to those parts in which it affirmed the judgment of the District Court. The order of the District Court, dated August 7, 1970, is also affirmed.

It is so ordered. . . .

INTERDISTRICT DESEGREGATION

Since school districts in the South are generally quite large, geographically, most of the litigation has involved intradistrict desegregation. The courts found that much integration could be accomplished without going beyond the school district boundaries. Few instances are extant where it has been necessary to question the boundaries of the basic school district unit in order to effectuate a unitary educational system. Some cases have, however, been initiated in the South when it appeared that the school district boundaries were actually being used to thwart effective desegregation. In one such instance, a town in Virginia exercised its discretion under Virginia municipal law and withdrew from the county, forming an independent municipality.[44] At the time of withdrawal of municipal functions, the newly independent city decided to continue to operate the school system as a part of the overall county school system. Later, however, it was decided to also separate the independent city's school system from the countywide school district. This decision came about shortly after a federal district court had required a new desegregation plan for the entire county replacing the older freedom of choice plan. The new reorganization resulted in an increase in the proportion of blacks in the county schools and a decrease in the city schools, although both systems retained a majority of blacks. The United States Supreme Court enjoined the reorganization saying that the Court must look to the effect of such action on the segregation of the schools. When the effect is to exacerbate the problem of racial imbalance the Court will frown on changing school district boundaries. The Supreme Court listed three factors supporting the conclusion under which such reorganizations may be judged constitutionally impermissible: first, the likelihood of increased segregation as white parents shifted their children to the new school district from private schools and the county system was apparent; second, the fact that the independent city schools in the state had traditionally been predominately white suggested that the same pattern might ensue here; third, the timing of the city's decision was psychologically poor since it made it appear that the rationale for separating the school system was based on the lower court's prohibition of the use of a freedom of choice plan for the entire school system. Effectively, then, the Supreme Court said that where segregation is perpetuated as a result of *de jure* governmental action, the Court will not be deterred from intervening even though the remedy goes beyond school district boundaries.[45]

In another case rendered on the same day as the above decision, the Supreme Court refused to permit severance of Scotland Neck schools from those of surrounding Halifax County, North Carolina.[46] The Court reasoned that the motivation of Scotland Neck's departure from the county school system was prompted solely for purposes of segregation and the effect of the action would weld the two systems into a segregated pattern, the new city district being predominately white and the county schools being basically black.

An entirely different situation was presented in the notable Richmond, Virginia case.[47] Here, a federal district court required the merger of three large and separate school districts to bring about desegregation. Chesterfield and Henrico County school districts are the suburban school district surrounding Richmond and, as in most large urban areas, the city school district had become progressively segregated over the years as white families moved beyond the city limits. Effectively, the federal district judge's decision would have made one large administrative unit of the three systems with a complex system of rezoning and busing among the school centers. On appeal, the United States Court of Appeals for the Fourth Circuit reversed the lower court decision holding that there was no evidence to indicate that there was ever any state action taken to keep blacks confined to a particular school district. The court said:

> This court believes that the root causes of the concentration of blacks in inner cities of America are simply not known and that the district court could not realistically place on the counties the responsibility for the effect that inner city decay has had on the public schools of Richmond . . .. The facts of this case do not show that state establishment and maintenance of school districts coterminous with the political subdivision of the city of Richmond and the counties of Chesterfield and Henrico have been intended to circumvent any federally protected right.[48]

In review of this decision by the United States Supreme Court, eight justices were unable to render a decision, deadlocking four to four. Justice Powell had removed himself from the case because he had formerly been a member of the Richmond school board. Thus, the decision by the Court of Appeals stood.

A similar but more complicated situation arose in Michigan where the school district pattern around Detroit was found by a lower federal district court to be so constituted as to create school segregation in the central city of Detroit.[49] Both the federal district court and the federal Court of Appeals concluded that desegregation of the Detroit schools was impossible, unless the racial composition of the entire metropolitan area was taken into account. Dismantling of segregation, therefore, according to these federal courts, required interdistrict busing between the Detroit core city and several suburban school districts. On appeal, the United States Supreme Court in reversing the decision held that there was no evidence in the record to show that the original boundaries of the Detroit School District or any other school districts in Michigan were established for the purpose of segregation of the races.

Subsequent to the Supreme Court's decision in *Milliken,* the United States Court of Appeals for the Sixth Circuit upheld a federal district court decision that effectively merged the Louisville and Jefferson County, Kentucky, school districts.[50] The court did not depart from the *Milliken* rationale but reached a different result because of the special circumstances that were attendant to the Louisville situation. The court found that there still remained vestiges of past *de jure* discrimination in the two large school districts, which was not true in *Milliken.* The Court of Appeals found the crucial difference between the Louisville and Detroit cases to lie in the fact that in the past school district boundaries in Louisville had been ignored in order to segregate the schools. For example, it was shown that in pre-*Brown* days black high school students in the Jefferson County school district were sent to Central High School located in the Louisville school district. This was done because the Jefferson County system had no black high school. It was also shown that another city high school was actually located geographically in the county, and students of both systems had attended school there. No such interplay was present or had ever transpired between the suburban school districts of Detroit and the central city. Further, school districts in

Kentucky had been legally segregated in pre-*Brown* days and, as such, evinced a record of a segregated past that was not present in Michigan.

The Detroit and Louisville cases, although reaching different results, continued a consistent legal rationale enunciating a rule of law that states essentially that school district integration will be required, by busing or other means, either within or among school districts, where it can be shown that segregation is the result of governmental action that tends to create, maintain, or perpetuate segregation of the races. The rule applies to northern as well as to southern states. In the North, although schools were not segregated by statute before *Brown* in 1954, it is quite possible for subsequent government acts, whether patent or latent, to discriminate in such a way as to create patterns of racial imbalance in the schools. In such instances, the segregation will not be viewed as *de facto* by the courts but as *de jure* and, therefore, unconstitutional.

Interdistrict Integration May Be an Improper Remedy to Overcome Single-district Segregation

MILLIKEN v. BRADLEY

Supreme Court of the United States, 1974.
418 U.S. 717, 94 S.Ct. 3112.

Mr. Chief Justice BURGER delivered the opinion of the Court.

We granted certiorari in these consolidated cases to determine whether a federal court may impose a multidistrict, areawide remedy to a single-district *de jure* segregation problem absent any finding that the other included school districts have failed to operate unitary school systems within their districts, absent any claim or finding that the boundary lines of any affected school district were established with the purpose of fostering racial segregation in public schools, absent any finding that the included districts committed acts which effected segregation within the other districts, and absent a meaningful opportunity for the included neighboring school districts to present evidence or be heard on the propriety of a multidistrict remedy or on the question of constitutional violations by those neighboring districts. . . . In Brown v. Board of Education, 349 U.S. 294, 75 S.Ct. 753, 99 L.Ed. 1083 (1955) (*Brown II*), the Court's first encounter with the problem of remedies in school desegregation cases, the Court noted:

> In fashioning and effectuating the decrees, the courts will be guided by equitable principles. Traditionally, equity has been characterized by a practical flexibility in shaping its remedies and by a facility for adjusting and reconciling public and private needs. Id., at 300, 75 S.Ct., at 756.

In further refining the remedial process, *Swann* held, the task is to correct, by a balancing of the individual and collective interests, "the condition that offends the Constitution." A federal remedial power may be exercised "only on the basis of a constitutional violation" and, "[a]s with any equity case, the nature of the violation determines the scope of the remedy." 402 U.S., at 16, 91 S.Ct., at 1276.

Proceeding from these basic principles, we first note that in the District Court the complainants sought a remedy aimed at the *condition* alleged to offend the Constitution—the segregation within the Detroit City School District. The court acted on this theory of the case and in its initial ruling on the "Desegregation Area" stated:

> The task before this court, therefore, is now, and . . . . has always been, how to desegregate the Detroit public schools. 345 F.Supp., at 921.

Thereafter, however, the District Court abruptly rejected the proposed Detroit-only plans on the ground that "while [they] would provide a racial mix more in keeping with the black-white proportions of the student population [they] would accentuate the racial identifiability of the [Detroit] district as a black school system, and would not accomplish desegregation." Pet. App., 56a. "[T]he racial composition of the student body is such," said the court, "that the plan's implementation would clearly make the entire Detroit public school system racially identifiable" (Id., at 54a), "leav[ing] many of its schools 75 to 90 percent black." Id., at 55a. Consequently, the court reasoned, it was imperative to "look beyond the limits of the Detroit school district for a solution to the problem of segregation in the Detroit public schools . . . " since "[s]chool district lines are simply matters of political convenience and may not be used to deny constitutional rights." Id., at 57a. Accordingly, the District Court proceeded to redefine the relevant area to include areas of predominantly white pupil population in order to ensure that "upon implementation, no school, grade or classroom [would be] substantially disproportionate to the overall pupil racial composition" of the entire metropolitan area. . . .

Viewing the record as a whole, it seems clear that the District Court and the Court of Appeals shifted the primary focus from a Detroit remedy to the metropolitan area only because of their conclusion that total desegregation of Detroit would not produce the racial balance which they perceived as desirable. Both courts proceeded on an assumption that the Detroit schools could not be truly desegregated—in their view of what constituted desegregation—unless the racial composition of the student body of each school substantially reflected the racial composition of the population of the metropolitan area as a whole. The metropolitan area was then defined as Detroit plus fifty-three of the outlying school districts. . . .

In *Swann,* which arose in the context of a single independent school district, the Court held:

> If we were to read the holding of the District Court to require, as a matter of substantive constitutional right, any particular degree of racial balance or mixing, that approach would be disapproved and we would be obliged to reverse. 402 U.S., at 24, 91 S.Ct., at 1280.

The clear import of this language from *Swann* is that desegregation, in the sense of dismantling a dual school system, does not require any particular racial balance in each "school, grade or classroom." See Spencer v. Kugler, 404 U.S. 1027, 92 S.Ct. 707, 30 L.Ed.2d 723 (1972).

Here the District Court's approach to what constituted "actual desegregation" raises the fundamental question, not presented in *Swann*, as to the circumstances in which a federal court may order desegregation relief that embraces more than a single school district. The court's analytical starting point was its conclusion that school district lines are no more than arbitrary lines on a map drawn "for political convenience." Boundary lines may be bridged where there has been a constitutional violation calling for interdistrict relief but the notion that school district lines may be casually ignored or treated as a mere administrative convenience is contrary to the history of public education in our country. No single tradition in public education is more deeply rooted than local control over the operation of schools; local autonomy has long been thought essential both to the maintenance of community concern and support for public schools and to quality of the educational process. . . .

The Michigan educational structure involved in this case, in common with most States, provides for a large measure of local control, and a review of the scope and character of these local powers indicates the extent to which the interdistrict remedy approved by the two courts could disrupt and alter the structure of public education in Michigan. The metropolitan remedy would require, in effect, consolidation of fifty-four independent school districts historically administered as separate units into a vast new super school district. Entirely apart from the logistical and other serious problems attending large-scale transportation of students, the consolidation would give rise to an array of other problems in financing and operating this new school system. Some of the more obvious questions would be: What would be the status and authority of the present popularly elected school boards? Would the children of Detroit be within the jurisdiction and operating control of a school board elected by the parents and residents of other districts? What board or boards would levy taxes for school operations in these fifty-four districts constituting the consolidated metropolitan area? What provisions could be made for assuring substantial equality in tax levies among the fifty-four districts, if this were deemed requisite? What provisions would be made for financing? Would the validity of long-term bonds be jeopardized unless approved by all of the component districts as well as the State? What body would determine that portion of the curricula now left to the discretion of local school boards? Who would establish attendance zones, purchase school equipment, locate and construct new schools, and indeed attend to all the myriad day-to-day decisions that are necessary to school operations affecting potentially more than three-quarters of a million pupils?

It may be suggested that all of these vital operational problems are yet to be resolved by the District Court, and that this is the purpose of the Court of Appeals' proposed remand. But it is obvious from the scope of the interdistrict remedy itself that absent a complete restructuring of the laws of Michigan relating to school districts the District Court will become first, a *de facto* "legislative authority" to resolve these complex questions, and then the "school superintendent" for the entire area. This is a task which few, if any, judges are qualified to perform and one which would deprive the people of control of schools through their elected representatives.

Of course, no state law is above the Constitution. School district lines and the present laws with respect to local control, are not sacrosanct and if they conflict with the Fourteenth Amendment federal courts have a duty to prescribe appropriate remedies. . . . But our prior holdings have been confined to violations and remedies within a single school district. We therefore turn to address, for the first time, the validity of a remedy mandating cross-district or interdistrict consolidation to remedy a condition of segregation found to exist in only one district.

The controlling principle consistently expounded in our holdings is that the scope of the remedy is determined by the nature and extent of the constitutional violation. Swann, 402 U.S., at 16, 91 S.Ct., at 1276. Before the boundaries of separate and autonomous school districts may be set aside by consolidating the separate units for remedial purposes or by imposing a cross-district remedy, it must first be shown that there has been a constitutional violation within one district that produces a significant segregative effect in another district. Specifically, it must be shown that racially discriminatory acts of the state or local school districts, or of a single school district have been a substantial cause of interdistrict segregation. Thus an interdistrict remedy might be in order where the racially discriminatory acts of one or more school districts caused racial segregation in an adjacent district, or where district lines have been deliberately drawn on the basis of race. In such circumstances an interdistrict remedy would be appropriate to eliminate the interdistrict segregation directly caused by the constitutional violation. Conversely, without an interdistrict violation and interdistrict effect, there is no constitutional wrong calling for an interdistrict remedy.

The record before us, voluminous as it is, contains evidence of *de jure* segregated conditions only in the Detroit schools; indeed, that was the theory on which the litigation was initially based and on which the District Court took evidence. With no showing of significant violation by the fifty-three outlying school districts and no evidence of any interdistrict violation or effect, the court went beyond the original theory of the case as framed by the pleadings and mandated a metropolitan area remedy. To approve the remedy ordered by the court would impose on the outlying districts, not shown to have committed any constitutional violation, a wholly impermissible remedy based on a standard not hinted at in *Brown I* and *II* or any holding of this Court.

In dissent, Mr. Justice WHITE and Mr. Justice MARSHALL undertake to demonstrate that agencies having statewide authority participated in maintaining the dual school system found to exist in Detroit. They are apparently of the view that once such participation is shown, the District Court should have a relatively free hand to reconstruct school districts outside of Detroit in fashioning relief. Our assumption, *arguendo*, that state agencies did participate in the maintenance of the Detroit system, should make it clear that it is not on this point that we part company. The difference between us arises instead from established doctrine laid down by our cases. *Brown, Green, Swann, Scotland Neck* and *Emporia*, each addressed the issue of constitutional wrong in terms of an established geographic and administrative school system populated by both Negro and white children. In such a context, terms such as "unitary" and "dual" systems and "racially identifiable schools," have meaning, and the necessary federal authority to remedy the constitutional wrong is firmly established. But the remedy is necessarily designed, as all remedies are, to restore the victims of discriminatory conduct to the position they would have occupied in the absence of such conduct. Disparate treatment of white and Negro students occurred within the Detroit school system, and not elsewhere, and on this record the remedy must be limited to that system. Swann, supra, 402 U.S., at 16, 91 S.Ct., at 1276.

The constitutional right of the Negro respondents residing in Detroit is to attend a unitary school system in that district. Unless petitioners drew the district lines in a discriminatory fashion, or arranged for white students residing in the Detroit district to attend schools in Oakland and Macomb Counties, they were under no constitutional duty to make provisions for Negro students to do so. The view of the dissenters, that the existence of a dual system in *Detroit* can be made the basis for a decree requiring cross-district transportation of pupils, cannot be supported on the grounds that it represents merely the devising of a suitably flexible remedy for the violation of rights already established by our prior decisions. It can be supported only by drastic expansion of the constitutional right itself, an expansion without any support in either constitutional principle or precedent.

.   .   .   The Court of Appeals .   .   . held the State derivatively responsible for the Detroit Board's violations on the theory that actions of Detroit as a political subdivision of the State were attributable to the State. Accepting, *arguendo,* the correctness of this finding of state responsibility for the segregated conditions within the city of Detroit, it does not follow that an interdistrict remedy is constitutionally justified or required. With a single exception, discussed later, there has been no showing that either the State or any of the eighty-five outlying districts engaged in activity that had a cross-district effect. The boundaries of the Detroit School District, which are coterminous with the boundaries of the city of Detroit, were established over a century ago by neutral legislation when the city was incorporated; there is no evidence in the record, nor is there any suggestion by the respondents, that either the original boundaries of the Detroit School District, or any other school district in Michigan, were established for the purpose of creating, maintaining, or perpetuating segregation of races. There is no claim and there is no evidence hinting that petitioner outlying school districts and their predecessors, or the thirty-odd other school districts in the tricounty area—but outside the District Court's "desegregation area"—have ever maintained or operated anything but unitary school systems. Unitary school systems have been required for more than a century by the Michigan Constitution as implemented by state law. Where the schools of only one district have been affected, there is no constitutional power in the courts to decree relief balancing the racial composition of that district's schools with those of the surrounding district.   .   .   .

We conclude that the relief ordered by the District Court and affirmed by the Court of Appeals was based upon an erroneous standard and was unsupported by record evidence that acts of the outlying districts effected the discrimination found to exist in the schools of Detroit. Accordingly, the judgment of the Court of Appeals is reversed and the case is remanded for further proceedings consistent with this opinion leading to prompt formulation of a decree directed to eliminating the segregation found to exist in Detroit city schools, a remedy which has been delayed since 1970.

Reversed and remanded.

NOTE

In a suit seeking desegregation of the Indianapolis public schools, the litigation followed a course similar to that of *Milliken*. In its first opinion, the District Court held that the Indianapolis City public schools were de jure segregated; the Court of Appeals affirmed and the United States Supreme Court denied certiorari. 332 F.Supp. 655 (S.D.Ind.1971), affirmed 474 F.2d 81, certiorari denied, 413 U.S. 920, 93 S.Ct. 3066. In subsequent proceedings to select a remedy, the District Court concluded that Indianapolis' only desegregation plans were inadequate and ordered the preparation of a metropolitan desegregation plan. 368 F.Supp. 1191 (S.D.Ind.1973). In 1969, after the filing of the suit, the Indiana Legislature had enacted a law consolidating the governments of Indianapolis and surrounding Marion County, but specifically excluding the area school districts from consolidation. The Court of Appeals for the Seventh Circuit vacated those portions of the District Court's opinion ordering a metropolitan remedy, citing *Milliken* 503 F.2d 68 (7th Cir.1974).

Federal Officials Cannot Permit
Funding Assistance to School Districts
Not in Compliance with the Civil
Rights Act of 1964

ADAMS v. RICHARDSON

United States District Court, District of
Columbia, 1972.
351 F.Supp. 636.

MEMORANDUM OPINION

JOHN H. PRATT, District Judge. This is a suit for declaratory and injunctive relief against the Secretary of Health, Education and Welfare and the Director of the Office for Civil Rights (OCR) of the Department of Health, Education and Welfare (HEW), complaining of alleged defaults on the part of defendants in the administration of their responsibilities under Title VI of the Civil Rights Act of 1964, as amended, 42 U.S.C.A. § 2000d et seq. (1970).

The responsibilities of the OCR include the administration and enforcement of HEW's regulation issued pursuant to Title VI and published at 45 C.F.R. Part 80. In addition, the OCR through agreement with other departments and agencies of the Executive Branch, had been assigned responsibility for Title VI enforcement with respect to most federal financial assistance to elementary, secondary and higher education and for health and social welfare activities, including such assistance as is granted and administered by those departments and agencies. . . .

FINDINGS OF FACT

A. Higher Education. . . .

B. Elementary and Secondary School Districts—1970–71

1. HEW has reported that as of the school year 1970–71, 113 school districts had reneged on prior approved plans and were out of compliance with Title VI. Some seventy-four of these districts are still out of compliance with Title VI.

2. Although HEW has known of the noncompliance of most of these districts since early in the 1970–71 school year, HEW has commenced administrative enforcement actions against only seven such districts, and of the eight cases referred to the Justice Department, only three have been sued.

3. HEW has attempted to excuse its administrative inaction on the grounds that it is still seeking voluntary compliance through negotiation and conciliation.

4. These noncomplying districts have received and continue to receive substantial federal assistance from HEW.

C. Compliance with Supreme Court Decisions

1. In Alexander v. Holmes County Board of Education, 396 U.S. 19, 90 S.Ct. 29, 24 L.Ed.2d 19 (1969), the Supreme Court required desegregation "at once" of dual school systems in thirty Mississippi school districts. At the time of this decision (October 29, 1969), eighty-seven school districts had HEW-approved desegregation plans which permitted segregation to be postponed until September, 1970. Despite the Supreme Court's directive, HEW took no steps to compel immediate desegregation in these eighty-seven districts.

2. Following the decision of the Supreme Court in Swann v. Charlotte-Mecklenburg Board of Education, 402 U.S. 1, 91 S.Ct. 1267, 28 L.Ed.2d 554 (1971), which enunciated "a presumption against schools that are substantially disproportionate in their racial composition" HEW identified 300 non-court order school districts with one or more schools composed mostly of local minority students.

3. Initially, HEW eliminated seventy-five of the 300 districts from further consideration without any on-site investigation or communication with the districts because in HEW's judgment the racial disproportion of the schools in these districts was too small to constitute a violation of Swann. HEW then eliminated 134 of the remaining 225 districts from further consideration still without any on-site investigation or communication with the districts. Although at least eighty-five of these districts have one or more schools substantially disproportionate in their racial composition, none was required to justify the substantial racial disproportion in its schools. HEW mailed letters to the remaining ninety-one districts in the summer of 1971, notifying them that additional desegregation steps may be required under the Swann decision. Of these ninety-one districts, HEW received desegregation plans acceptable to HEW from thirty-seven districts, noticed three for administrative hearing, and found Swann "not applicable" to nine.

4. Thus, forty-two districts which HEW deemed to be in presumptive violation of *Swann* remained so approximately a year later while HEW continues to review them.

5. These forty-two school districts have been receiving federal funds from HEW throughout this period of over one year.

D. Vocational and Other Schools. . . .

E. Districts Subject to Court Orders

1. Some 640 school districts which receive HEW aid, including many of the largest school districts, are subject to school desegregation court orders in the seventeen southern and border states.

2. Shortly after the passage of the statute in 1964, HEW issued a regulation which, in effect, deemed a district in compliance if it were subject to a final desegregation order and provided assurance that it will comply with said order including any subsequent modification thereof.

3. In 1968, Congress in amending § 2000d–5 of the statute, adopted the HEW regulation in part by providing that, for the purpose of determining whether an educational agency is in compliance with Title VI, compliance by such agency with a final court desegregation order shall be deemed to be compliance with said Title.

4. Once a school district has been placed under a court desegregation order and gives assurance "on paper" that it is in compliance with such order, it is the practice of HEW to regard such school district as in compliance with Title VI. HEW does not monitor said school districts to determine whether or not the court order is being obeyed.

5. HEW's justification for failure to monitor school districts under court order is allegedly based upon possible conflicts with the courts, possible conflicts with the Justice Department, and HEW's alleged lack of resources to provide systematic monitoring.

6. HEW has advanced and continues to advance substantial federal funds to school districts under court order.

F. HEW's Record of Administrative Enforcement Proceedings

1. Between the passage of the Civil Rights Act in 1964 and March 1970, HEW initiated approximately 600 administrative proceedings against noncomplying school districts. In 1968 alone, HEW initiated about 100 enforcement proceedings. In 1969 HEW initiated nearly the same number of proceedings.

2. From March 1970, the month in which defendant Pottinger assumed the position as director of HEW's OCR, until February 1971, no enforcement proceedings were initiated, and since February 1971, only a small, token number of such proceedings have been commenced.

3. As a result of such enforcement proceedings, forty-four school districts were subject to fund terminations in 1968–69. Only two cutoffs occurred in 1969–70. No termination of funds have occurred since the summer of 1970.

4. Upon initiating an administrative enforcement proceeding, it is the practice of HEW to defer the school district's application for "new"

programs funds only. HEW does not defer its advancement of funds under "continuing" and previously-approved programs.

5. HEW makes no attempt subsequently to recapture funds distributed to a district between the notice of hearing and the formal determination of its Title VI ineligibility.

6. Since administrative enforcement proceedings generally consume one or more years, HEW's limited deferral practice allows the continued flow of large federal aid to the respondent school districts.

7. Despite defendants' reluctance or failure to employ enforcement proceedings terminating funds, substantial progress toward compliance with Title VI has been made. Since 1968 the number of Negro pupils in 100 percent minority schools or mostly minority schools in eleven southern states has greatly declined, decreasing from 68 percent of the total Negro pupils in the region in 1968 to 9.2 percent in 1971–72. On the other hand, the number of said pupils in 51 percent or more majority white schools has substantially increased, rising from 18 percent in 1968 to 43 percent in 1971–72.

The basic issue presented for determination is whether defendants' exercise of discretion in relying largely on voluntary compliance to accomplish the progress achieved and to obtain compliance in the areas still unresolved meets their full responsibilities under the mandate of Title VI.

CONCLUSIONS OF LAW

3. In its enactment of Title VI of the Civil Rights Act of 1964, Congress clearly indicated its intent and purpose by providing in § 2000d that:

> No person in the United States shall, on the ground of race, color, or national origin, be excluded from participation in, be denied the benefits of, or be subjected to discrimination *under any program or activity receiving Federal financial assistance.* (Emphasis supplied)

4. HEW and all other federal agencies empowered to grant federal assistance to any program or activity are directed by § 2000d–1 of Title VI to effectuate the provisions of § 2000d by the issuance of rules, regulations and orders of general applicability consistent with the objectives of the statute authorizing financial assistance. Agencies granting federal assistance are authorized to enforce compliance with such requirements (1) by termination of or by refusal to grant or continue such assistance after opportunity for hearing and an express finding on the record of a failure to comply with such requirement, or (2) by any other means authorized by law. Prior to such enforcement action, notice of failure to comply with the requirement must be given by the agency concerned and there must be a determination by the agency that compliance cannot be secured by voluntary means. After the enforcement action terminating or refusing to grant or continue assistance has been concluded, the agency is required to make a report to the appropriate committee of the House and Senate of the circumstances and grounds for such action, which shall not take effect until thirty days after the filing of such report.

5. The underlying thrust of the statute requires that the agency involved, i.e., in this case HEW, attempt at the outset to secure compliance by voluntary means, if such method is reasonably possible. This course involves negotiation, and negotiation takes time. To such extent, the defendants have discretion but such discretion is not unlimited.

6. Where a substantial period of time has elapsed, during which period attempts toward voluntary compliance have been either not attempted or have been unsuccessful or have been rejected, defendants' limited discretion is ended and they have the duty to effectuate the provisions of § 2000d by either administrative determination, after a hearing on the record, that there has been a failure to comply and that funds should be terminated, or by any other means authorized by law, such as reference to the Department of Justice. Under such circumstances, defendants cannot rely on their alleged complete discretion as justification for permitting the mandate of the statute to be unenforced.

7. Title VI of the Civil Rights Act of 1964 is not a new statutory provision. The record is replete with instances occurring over long periods of time since 1964, where defendants' efforts seeking voluntary compliance has either not been attempted or have been unsuccessful or have met with rejection. In these cases, defendants cannot in their discretion permit further advances of federal assistance in violation of the statute, but have the duty of accomplishing the purposes of the statute through administrative enforcement proceedings or by other legal means.

8. After the initiation and during the pendency of an administrative enforcement proceeding HEW can only defer a school district's application for new program funds. After such initiation and during the pendency of administrative enforcement proceedings and until action by HEW terminating or refusing to grant or continue federal assistance, defendants have no authority to withhold federal payments to school systems or agencies under continuing and previously-approved programs. Under the statute, said termination action is not to become effective (a) until the agency head makes a report to the appropriate Committees of Congress, and (b) thirty days have elapsed after the filing of said report. Nor can HEW recapture funds distributed to a district between the notice of hearing and the final determination of Title VI ineligibility.

9. Compliance by school districts and other educational agencies under final order of a federal court for the desegregation of the school or school system operated by such agency is, by virtue of § 2000d-5, to be deemed compliance with the provisions of Title VI. Until there has been a finding by the court entering the order that its order has not been complied with, defendants are under no obligation to effectuate the provisions of Title VI through the means previously described. To the extent that their resources permit, defendants have the duty to monitor school districts under court order and to bring their findings to the attention of the court concerned. The responsibility for compliance by school districts and other educational agencies under court order rests upon the court issuing said order.

10. In summary, the discretion implicitly vested in defendants by statute exists solely for the purpose of achieving voluntary compliance with the requirements of Title VI. As the undisputed record demonstrates, defendants' efforts toward voluntary compliance have been unsuccessful in the case of many state and local educational agencies which continue to receive substantial federal funds in violation of the statute. Defendants now have no discretion to negate the purpose and intent of the statute by a policy described in another context as one of "benign neglect" but, on the contrary, have the duty, on a case-by-case basis, to employ the means set forth in § 2000d–1 to achieve compliance. . . .

Footnotes

1. Roberts v. City of Boston, 59 Mass. (5 Cush.) 198 (1850).

2. Id.

3. See: Jethro K. Lieberman, *Milestones, 200 Years of American Law* (New York: Oxford University Press and St. Paul, MN: West Publishing Company, 1976), pp. 256–257; Richard Kluger, *Simple Justice* (New York: Vintage Books, 1977), pp. 77–78.

4. Louisville, New Orleans and Texas Railway Co. v. Mississippi, 133 U.S. 587, 10 S.Ct. 348 (1890).

5. Lieberman, op. cit. p. 260.

6. Regents of University of Calif. v. Bakke, 438 U.S. 265, 98 S.Ct. 2733 (1978).

7. 163 U.S. 537, 16 S.Ct. 1138 (1896).

8. Id.

9. Id.

10. Cumming v. Richmond County Board of Education, 175 U.S. 528, 20 S.Ct. 197 (1899).

11. 211 U.S. 45, 29 S.Ct. 33 (1908).

12. See: Kern Alexander and Erwin Solomon, *College and University Law* (Charlottesville, VA: The Michie Company, 1972), p. 518.

13. Berea College v. Commonwealth of Kentucky, op. cit.

14. 275 U.S. 78, 48 S.Ct. 91 (1927).

15. 305 U.S. 337, 59 S.Ct. 232 (1938).

16. Sweatt v. Painter, 339 U.S. 629, 70 S.Ct. 848 (1950).

17. Id.

18. Id.

19. McLaurin v. Oklahoma State Regents for Higher Education, 339 U.S. 637, 70 S.Ct. 851 (1950).

20. Brown v. Board of Education, 98 F.Supp. 797 (D.C.Kan.1951); Briggs v. Elliott, 98 F.Supp. 529 (D.C.S.C.1951); Davis v. County School Board, 103 F.Supp. 337 (D.C.Va.1952); Belton v. Gebhart, 32 Del.Ch. 343, 87 A.2d 862 (1952); and Bolling v. Sharpe, cert. granted 344 U.S. 873, 73 S.Ct. 173 (1952).

21. Loren Miller, "The Petitioners," from Harold W. Horowitz and Kenneth L. Karst, *Law Lawyers and Social Change* (Indianapolis: Bobbs-Merrill, 1969), pp. 181–182.

22. Id.

23. Harry S. Ashmore, *The Negro and the Schools* (Chapel Hill: The University of North Carolina Press, 1954), pp. 42–43.

24. Lieberman, op. cit. p. 276.

25. Brown v. Board of Education, 347 U.S. 483, 74 S.Ct. 686 (1954).

26. Louis H. Pollak, *The Constitution and the Supreme Court, A Documentary History,* vol. II (The World Publishing Company, 1966), p. 266.

27. Brown v. Board of Education of Topeka, 349 U.S. 294, 75 S.Ct. 753 (1955).

28. Id.

29. Cooper v. Aaron, 358 U.S. 1, 78 S.Ct. 1401 (1958).

30. Id.

31. Id.

32. Griffin v. County School Board of Prince Edward County, 377 U.S. 218, 84 S.Ct. 1226 (1964).

33. Briggs v. Elliott, 132 F.Supp. 776 (E.D.S.C.1955).

34. Bell v. School City, 324 F.2d 209 (7th Cir.1964), cert. denied 377 U.S. 924, 84 S.Ct. 1223 (1964); Deal v. Cincinnati Board of Education, 369 F.2d 55 (6th Cir.1966), cert. denied 389 U.S. 847, 88 S.Ct. 39 (1967).

35. United States v. Jefferson County Board of Education, 372 F.2d 836 (1966).

36. Green v. County School Board of New Kent County, Virginia, 391 U.S. 430, 88 S.Ct. 1689 (1968).

37. Alexander v. Holmes, 396 U.S. 19, 90 S.Ct. 29, reh. denied 396 U.S. 976, 90 S.Ct. 437 (1970).

38. The Supreme Court of Appeals of Virginia had, in a mandamus proceeding instituted by petitioners, held that the State Constitution and statutes did not impose upon the County Board of Supervisors any mandatory duty to levy taxes and appropriate money to support free public schools. Griffin v. Board of Supervisors of Prince Edward County, 203 Va. 321, 124 S.E.2d 227 (1962).

39. Bell v. School City of Gary, 324 F.2d 209 (7th Cir.1963).

40. Keyes v. School District, No. 1, Denver, 413 U.S. 189, 93 S.Ct. 2686 (1973).

41. Swann v. Charlotte-Mecklenburg Bd. of Education, 402 U.S. 1, 91 S.Ct. 1267 (1971).

42. Regents of the University of Calif. v. Bakke, 438 U.S. 265, 98 S.Ct. 2733 (1978).

43. Id.

44. Wright v. Council of the City of Emporia, 107 U.S. 451, 92 S.Ct. 2196 (1972).

45. See also: Lee v. Macon County Bd. of Education, 448 F.2d 746 (1971); Stout v. Jefferson County Bd. of Education, 448 F.2d 403 (1971); Haney v. County Bd. of Education, 410 F.2d 920 (1969).

46. United States v. Scotland Neck City Board of Education, 407 U.S. 484, 92 S.Ct. 2214 (1972).

47. Bradley v. Richmond School Board, 456 F.2d 6 (4th Cir.1972); 416 U.S. 696, 94 S.Ct. 2006 (1974).

48. Id.

49. Milliken v. Bradley, 418 U.S. 717, 94 S.Ct. 3112 (1974).

50. Newburg Area Council, Inc. v. Gordon, 521 F.2d 578 (1975); Newburg Area Council, Inc. v. Board of Education, 510 F.2d 1358 (1974).

11

Torts

The law grants to each individual certain personal rights with regard to conduct that others must respect. Some of these rights arise through the execution of a contract between individuals, for breach of which financial liability may result. The law also grants to each individual certain personal rights not of a contractual nature, such as freedom from personal injury and security of life, liberty, and property. The law imposes corresponding duties and responsibilities on each individual to respect the rights of others. If, by speech or other conduct, one fails to respect these rights, thereby damaging another, a tort has been committed and the offending party may be held liable.

A tort is a civil wrong independent of contract. It may be malicious and intentional or it may be the result of negligence and disregard for the rights of others. An action in tort compensates private individuals for harm caused to them by the unreasonable conduct of others. Social norms have provided the basis for legal precedent in the determination of that which is considered unacceptable or unreasonable conduct.

The legally proper relationship between two persons may be breached by injury caused by either an act or an omission to act on the part of either party. The word tort is derived from the Latin word "*tortus*" or "twisted." [1] In personal relationships, the term "twisted" is applied to activity that in some way deviates from a normally acceptable pattern of behavior.

A tort is different from a crime and emanates from a separate and distinct body of law. A civil action for tort is initiated and maintained by the injured party for the purpose of obtaining compensation for the injury suffered, whereas in a criminal proceeding the action is brought by the state to protect the public from actions of a wrongdoer. In a criminal case the state prosecutes not to compensate the injured person, but rather to protect the public from further wrongful acts. Since criminal law does not, nor was ever intended to compensate an injured individual, social justice demanded the birth of the action in tort.

Grounds for actions in tort may be divided into three categories: (1) intentional interference, (2) strict liability, and (3) negligence. Each of these may, at times, be applied to cases in public schools where pupils are injured.

INTENTIONAL INTERFERENCE

An intentional tort may result from an intended act whether accompanied by enmity, antagonism, maliciousness, or by no more than a good-natured, practical joke.[2] With this type of tort, it is not necessary for the wrongdoer to be hostile or desire to do harm to the injured party. Even when a person does not plan to injure another but proceeds intentionally to act in a way that invades the rights of another, he commits an intentional tort. In order for intent to exist, the activity of an individual must, with substantial certainty, be the result of his act. If one does not know with substantial certainty the result of an act and injury results, then it is not an intentional tort but is negligence instead.

Assault. An intentional tort may be committed even if no physical "touching" takes place. To have assault there must be an "overt act or an attempt, or the unequivocal appearance of an attempt, to do some immediate physical injury to the person of another." The overt act must be a display of force or menace of violence of such a nature as to cause reasonable apprehension of immediate bodily harm.[3] It is assault when a person stands within striking distance of another and with sword drawn says, "I intend to run you through." Such words and acts may be sufficient to put the plaintiff in immediate apprehension of imminent harm and it is apparent that the offender has the present ability to effectuate the harm. Thus, an intentional tort may be consummated by an act that, while not involving physical contact, places a person in immediate fear that such action will transpire.

Battery. Technically, battery is an intentional tort that comes about through physical contact. Prosser points out that it is battery to injure a man in his sleep, even though he does not discover the injury until later, while it is an assault to shoot at him while he is awake, and frighten but miss him.[4] In both cases, a person's interests are invaded. If a wrongdoer swings a bottle intending to strike the plaintiff, and the plaintiff sees the movement and is apprehensive for his own safety, there is assault and if the attack is consummated and the blow is actually landed, both assault and battery are present.

Teachers accused of assault and battery for administering corporal punishment are usually given considerable leeway as to the reasonableness of their action. In one case, the court explained the rule of law this way: "To be guilty of an assault and battery, the teacher must not only inflict on the child immoderate chastisement, but he must do so with legal malice or wicked motives or he must inflict some permanent injury."[5]

Cases involving assault and battery by a teacher usually result from a teacher's attempt to discipline a child. The courts generally allow wide latitude for teachers in chastisement of pupils, presuming that the teacher is innocent, has acted reasonably, and has done his duty, until the contrary is proved.

The courts still uphold the ancient doctrine of *in loco parentis,* which holds that the teacher stands in place of the parent and in such capacity has the right to chastise a pupil. The teacher's prerogatives are, of course, limited to the jurisdiction of the school and are not unlimited. Within these boundaries, the teacher may require pupils to abide by all reasonable commands and may inflict reasonable corporal punishment to enforce compliance. One court stated the situation in this manner:

> In the school, as in the family, there exists on the part of the pupils the obligations of obedience to lawful commands, subordination, civil deportment, respect for the right of other pupils, and fidelity to duty. Those obligations are inherent in any proper school system, and constitute, so to speak, the common law of the school.[6]

Courts do, however, make it quite clear that a teacher may be guilty of assault and battery if chastisement is cruel, brutal,[7] excessive,[8] or if administered in anger or insolence.[9] In one interesting old case, the court said that a teacher was not justified in beating a scholar so severely as to wear out two whips, striking two blows to the head with fists, and kicking the scholar in the face, because he misspelled a word and refused to try again.[10]

A case illustrating extreme conduct on the part of a teacher, resulting in a charge of assault and battery, took place in 1967 in Louisiana. The pupil sustained a broken arm when a physical education teacher tried to remove him from the basketball court. According to the teacher's testimony, the teacher twice ordered the boy off the basketball court and the boy returned a third time and was this time escorted from the court by the teacher. During this final episode, the boy attempted to strike the teacher whereupon the teacher tried to restrain him with the resultant effect that the boy's arm was broken. This testimony was contradicted by the boy, who claimed he had not provoked the teacher other than by returning to the court, and further claimed that the teacher had menaced, chased, seized, lifted, and shaken him against the bleachers and suddenly let him fall on the floor fracturing his arm. The appellate court found that the teacher was five feet, eight inches tall and weighed 230 pounds, while the pupil was only five feet tall and weighed only 101 pounds. The court was unconvinced that the teacher actually believed that a blow from the pupil could harm him. The court in ruling for the pupil concluded that the lifting, shaking, and dropping of the pupil was force in excess of that required to either protect himself or to discipline the pupil.[11]

Chastisement of a pupil may become assault and battery if the teacher does not administer the punishment reasonably. Criteria used by courts to identify excessive punishment include: (1) proper and suitable weapon, (2) part of person to which it is applied, (3) manner and extent of chastisement, (4) nature and gravity of offense, (5) age of pupil, (6) temper and deportment of the teacher,[12] and (7) history of pupil's previous conduct.

Both assault and battery may be criminal wrongs as well as tort where statutes so require. Criminal statutes usually define assault as attempted battery, requiring present ability. However, the reasoning pertaining to individual statutes may or may not have application to tort law.

Interference with peace of mind. In keeping with the theory that every man who is injured should have recompense, modern courts have had a tendency to recognize as a separate tort interference with peace of mind, the infliction of mental or emotional anguish. In such cases, it is necessary and quite difficult to prove mental suffering. The courts have been unable to precisely delineate between actual tortious actions and what may be considered everyday rough language or immoderate personal behavior that hurts one's feelings yet is so severe as to create an action in tort. One cannot recover simply because of hurt feelings.[13]

Courts have held that where an act is malicious, as distinguished from being merely negligent, there may be recovery for mental anguish, even though no physical injury results.[14] However, cases involving actions for mental anguish and suffering are easier to prove before a jury if the emotional distress has produced some visible or identifiable physical harm.

Another intentional tort is false imprisonment, sometimes called false arrest. Relatively few cases have occurred in this area, but the general rule is that an unauthorized person cannot detain or physically restrain the movements of another. This type of tort is not applicable to the situation in which a teacher confines a child in his classroom since a teacher is charged with the responsibility for overseeing pupil activities in the school setting and is authorized to confine a pupil, if necessary, in order to discipline him.

STRICT LIABILITY

Generally, liability for tort has been imposed with regard to "fault" on the part of the defendant. Both intentional interference and negligence are based on the supposition that someone was injured at the fault of another party. However, cases have arisen in which a person has been injured through no actual, identifiable fault of anyone. Such cases have forced some courts to hand down damage awards based on strict liability of the defendant. In these instances, a person may be liable even though he is not strictly at fault for the other party's injury. This rule was adopted in order to place the damages on the person best able to bear the burden. In these cases, the defendant's acts are not so important as the injury and suffering of the injured person. Underlying this type of decision is the older social justice reasoning that requires that "he who breaks must pay" regardless of whether the injury is knowingly or negligently caused.[15]

While fault is not a prerequisite to liability in these cases, the courts do generally require that the defendant has caused some unusual hazard to exist. The defendant's activity must be one that involves abnormal danger to others.

Today in the United States, strict liability will not be imposed unless the activity or thing is classified as hazardous or even "ultrahazardous." [16] While strict liability cases reported by appellate courts involving activities in the public schools are scarce, the possibility of such actions, nevertheless, exist. For example, the hazards in schools caused by laboratory experiments, shop activity, or field trips present possibilities of actions involving strict liability. However, this area makes up such a small element of the total tort liability picture in schools that it is more important at this point to move to a discussion of the much more prevalent tort of negligence.

NEGLIGENCE

Negligence differs from an intentional tort in that negligent acts are neither expected nor intended while an intentional tort may be both anticipated and intended. With negligence [17] a reasonable man in the position of the actor could have anticipated the harmful results. A teacher, for example, could not have reasonably foreseen that a hidden can in an incinerator would explode and injure a child when the teacher had sent the child to empty the classroom wastebaskets.[18]

An accident that could not have been prevented by reasonable care does not constitute negligence. Many times what first appears to be an accident can be traced to someone's negligence; however, instances of pure accident do occur where someone is injured and no one is actually at fault. For example, when a child closed a music room door cutting off the tip of another student's finger the court found no negligence, merely an accident.[19]

A negligent act in one situation may not be negligence under a different set of circumstances. No definite rules as to what constitutes negligence apply. The standard of conduct of the actor is the key. The conditions embracing a negligent act have been described in this fashion:

> It is fundamental that the standard of conduct which is the basis of the law of negligence is determined by balancing the risk, in the light of the social value of the interest threatened, and the probability and extent of the harm, against the value of the interest which the actor is seeking to protect, and the expedience of the course pursued.[20]

In order for the court to strike a balance between the threatened harm and the actor's conduct,[21] the court must establish a standard by which such activity can be measured. In attempting to set boundaries for negligent acts committed in different factual situations, the courts have developed the reasonableness theory. For negligence to be present, someone must sustain an injury resulting from an "unreasonable risk" taken by another person. To determine unreasonableness the courts personify the test in the terms of the "reasonable man."

The reasonable man. The reasonable man has been described by different courts as a prudent man, a man of average prudence, a man of ordinary sense using ordinary care [22] and skill, and as a reasonably prudent man. He is an ideal, a model of conduct and a community standard. The model for the reasonable man, although a community ideal, varies in every case. His characteristics are: (1) the physical attributes of the defendant himself, (2) normal intelligence, (3) normal perception and memory with a minimum level of information and experience common to the community, and (4) such superior skill and knowledge as the actor has or holds himself out to the public as having.[23] While this standard of behavior provides a framework for the whole theory of negligence, the exact formula varies with attributes of the persons involved and with the circumstances.

The reasonable man then has the same physical characteristics as the actor himself and the acts in question are measured accordingly. Correspondingly, the man who is crippled is not held to the same standard as the man with no physical infirmities. The courts have also made allowances for the weaknesses or attributes connected with the sex [24] and age [25] of the individual. The courts have not, however, been so lenient with individuals who have mental deficiencies. The courts have traditionally held that a man with less mental ability than an average person must adjust and conform to the rules of society. He is not given an allowance by the courts for subnormal mentality, but, if a man is actually insane, a more convincing argument can be made for allowing for his particular incapacity.[26]

In this regard, courts have held that when a person is temporarily ill and loses control of his faculties, he may not be held strictly accountable for his actions. This is true, however, only when the illness is caused by circumstances beyond the control of the actor.

ELEMENTS OF NEGLIGENCE

To have a valid cause of action for negligence certain prerequisites must exist and are frequently summarized into four categories: (1) A *duty* on the part of the actor to protect others, (2) a failure on the part of the actor to exercise an appropriate *standard of care*, (3) the act must be the *proximate cause* or *legal cause* of the injury, and (4) an *injury*, causing damage or loss, must exist.

DUTY

The routine of everyday life creates situations where persons constantly create risks and incur obligations for the safety of others. In negligence cases, a person has a duty to abide by a standard of reasonable conduct in the face of apparent risks.[27]

The courts generally hold that no duty exists where the defendant could not have reasonably foreseen the danger of risk involved. A duty owed by one person to another may well intensify as the risk increases. In other words, the duty to protect another is proportional to the risk or hazard of a particular activity. In certain school functions where risks are greater to children, a teacher has an increased level of obligation or duty to the children. For example, whenever children perform a dangerous experiment, the teacher has a greater obligation for the children's safety than when he is merely supervising a study hall. One judge has explained the duty requirement in this way:

> Every person is negligent when, without intending any wrong, he does such an act or omits to take such a precaution that under the circumstances he, as an ordinary prudent person, ought reasonably to foresee that he will thereby expose the interest of another to an unreasonable risk of harm. A person is required to take into account such of the surrounding circumstances as would be taken into account by a reasonably prudent person and possess such knowledge as is possessed by an ordinary reasonable person and to use such judgment and discretion as is exercised by persons of reasonable intelligence under the same or similar circumstance.[28]

Therefore, the school district has no duty to protect a child who is injured when he leaves campus without permission. The district is not responsible for the student's welfare off school grounds unless the school assumes responsibility and has knowledge of the specific danger involved.[29]

Generally, the law holds that a person is not liable for an omission to act when there is not some definite relationship between the parties; no general duty exists to aid a person in danger. For example, even though a moral duty may be present, no legal duty mandates that a mere bystander aid a drowning person. If, however, a person acts affirmatively to assist a person in peril, he assumes a duty to the person and all his subsequent acts must be performed reasonably. Because of this requirement, passersby in many situations will not assist victims of auto wrecks or other mishaps. Some states, in order to encourage more humanitarian responses and to protect well meaning rescuers, have enacted laws that protect the "good Samaritan" from liability.

While a teacher has no more of a duty than anyone else to be a "good Samaritan" to the general public, he does have an obligation or duty to help a student under his jurisdiction when injured at school. Because of the teacher-student relationship, a teacher may be liable for an omission to act as well as for an affirmative act. In such a case, though, the teacher is required to provide only such assistance as a person with the same training and experience in similar circumstances could reasonably provide.

STANDARD OF CARE

A legally recognized duty requires the actor to conform to a certain standard of conduct or care. As the risk involved in an act increases, the standard of care required of the actor likewise increases.[30] The standard of care of a woodshop teacher is, of course, greater than that of the school librarian because the risk of injury involved in handling power tools is much greater than the risk of being injured while reading a book. Similarly, chemistry classes require a high standard of care.[31]

The standard of care required by the courts is not uniform among all persons. Children and aged persons have generally been given substantially more leeway in their activities than is allowed a normal adult. While both children and aged persons are liable for their torts, they are not held to the same standard as others without impairments of age. Although it is difficult to pinpoint precise standards to determine the reasonableness of a child because of the great variations in age, maturity, and capacity, the courts have nevertheless established as a subjective test that which is "reasonable to expect of children of like age, intelligence, and experience." [32]

While most courts appear to follow the above criteria for determination of negligence of children, some courts have applied criminal law standards that prescribe the following criteria:

a. Children between one and seven years cannot be liable for negligence. They theoretically have no capacity for negligence.[33]

b. Children between the ages of seven and fourteen have a *prima facie* case for incapacity but it can be rebutted. In other words, children in this age group are presumed not to be capable of negligence until proved to the contrary.

Authorities generally agree that while arbitrary age limits for negligence have been established by some courts, it is not a generally acceptable rule of law. One court has said that the rule providing for a specific age limit

> is arbitrary and open to the objection that one day's difference in age should not be the dividing line as to whether a child is capable of negligence or not. Under present-day circumstances, a child of six is permitted to assume many responsibilities. There is much opportunity for him to observe and thus become cognizant of the necessity for exercising some degree of care. Compulsory school attendance, the radio (television), the movies, and traffic conditions all tend to have this effect. Under the arbitrary cut-off rule, a child may be guilty of the most flagrant violation of duty and still be precluded from any presumption of negligence.

With regard to teachers or others in the teaching profession, the generally accepted standard of care would be that of a reasonably prudent teacher, not that of a reasonably prudent lay person. A New York court has put it this way:

> The standard of care required of an officer or employee of a public school is that which a person of ordinary prudence charged with his duties, would exercise under the same circumstances.[34]

A Vermont court has defined the "standard of care" owed to a pupil by a teacher in the following manner. A teacher's "relationship to the pupils under his care and custody differs from that generally existing between a public employee and a member of the general public. In a limited sense the teacher stands in the parents' place in his relationship to a pupil . . . and has such a portion of the powers of the parent over the pupil as is necessary to carry out his employment. In such relationship, he owes his pupils the duty of supervision . . . ."[35]

While the above is the prevailing view, some courts have held teachers to a lesser degree of care. These courts have said that a teacher may be charged only with reasonable care such as any person of ordinary prudence would exercise under comparable circumstances.

PROXIMATE OR LEGAL CAUSE

"Proximate cause" or "legal cause" is the connection between the act and the resultant injury. The question the court will ask is: "Was the injury a natural and probable consequence of the wrongful act, and ought it to have been foreseen in light of the attendant circumstances?"[36] The *Restatement of Torts* explains the necessity of adequate causal relation in this way:

> In order that a negligent actor shall be liable for another's harm, it is necessary not only that the actor's conduct be negligent toward the other, but also that the negligence of the actor be a legal cause of the other's harm.[37]

To establish proximate cause there must first be a duty or obligation on the part of the actor to maintain a reasonable standard of conduct. In most negligence cases, however, the courts will not refer to proximate cause but will rely solely on the duty or obligation of the defendant and the standard of conduct required to avoid liability. Proximate cause as a criterion of liability has been used most often where some doubt is present as to whether the injured person was within the zone of obvious danger.[38]

In these cases, the courts require that the negligence of the defendant must be the "substantial" cause of the harm to the plaintiff. In other words, the cause must be substantial enough to lead reasonable people to conclude it is indeed the cause of injury. If the negligence is not a substantial factor in producing the harm then no liability will follow.

The actor's negligent act must be in continuous and active force up to the actual harm, and the lapse of time must not be so great that contributing causes and intervening factors render the original negligent act to be an unsubstantial or insignificant force in the harm. Therefore, a teacher may be relieved of liability for negligent conduct if some intervening act is sufficient to break the causal connection between her act and a pupil's injury. For example, where a principal gave pupils permission to hold a race in a street and a "recklessly negligent" pupil ran into and injured a pedestrian, the court held that the causal relation was too remote to hold the principal liable.[39]

In order to break the chain of events causing injury, the intervening act must legally supersede the original negligent act. This rule is illustrated in a case in which a student was cleaning a power saw in shop class and another student turned on the switch starting the machine in violation of safety rules. In this instance, the court held that the board's negligence in not having a guard over the beltdrive was not the proximate or legal cause of the injury.[40]

A different result might have been reached, however, if the intervening act had been foreseeable and could have been prevented by reasonable care on the part of the defendant. For example, were a teacher to send a child on an errand across a busy street and a motorist, while driving carelessly, injures the child, both the teacher and the motorist may be liable. Here the intervening negligent act is not substantial enough to entirely overcome the original act. In an actual case demonstrating this point, a school bus driver was negligent when a student was struck by an automobile after alighting from the bus. The driver of the automobile was also negligent; however, the court held that the negligent bus driver had a continuing obligation that was not ended by the negligence of the driver of the automobile. The automobile driver's negligence did not constitute a sufficient break in the causal connection to be a defense for the bus driver and was not a superseding or intervening cause.[41]

INJURY OR ACTUAL LOSS

A plaintiff, of course, cannot recover unless actual injury is suffered and the plaintiff is able to show actual loss or damages resulting from the defendant's act. If the harm suffered is caused by more than one person, then damages may be apportioned among the tortfeasors. Sometimes both school district and teacher are joined together by a plaintiff student in a case wherein it is claimed that the injury was caused by acts of both parties.

DEFENSES FOR NEGLIGENCE

In all cases involving negligence, the defendant may attempt to show that he is not negligent because the injury was a mere accident, that his act was not the proximate or legal cause of injury, or that some other act intervened and was responsible for the injury. However, aside from these essentials of a tort claim there are other rejoinders against negligence that may be classified as defenses. The more common of these are: (1) contributory negligence, (2) comparative negligence, (3) assumption of risk, and (4) immunity.

Of these defenses, contributory negligence and assumption of risk are most often used in school law cases. Immunity is a defense found in both common and statutory law that derives from the state's sovereignty. Each of these concepts is briefly explained below.

Contributory negligence. Contributory negligence involves some fault or breach of duty on the part of the injured person, or failure to exercise the required standard of care for his or her own safety. One court explained contributory negligence as conduct on the part of the injured party that caused or contributed to the injury and that would not have been done by a person exercising ordinary prudence under the circumstances.[42] The *Restatement of Torts* defines contributory negligence in much the same manner:

> conduct on the part of the plaintiff which falls below the standard to which he should conform for his own protection, and which is legally contributing cause cooperating with the negligence of the defendant in bringing about the plaintiff's harm.[43]

As previously pointed out, a child is capable of negligence and his failure to conform to a required standard of conduct for a child of the same age, physical characteristics, sex, and training will result in the court assigning fault to his actions. Thus, if an injured child is negligent and his negligence contributes to the harm, then a defendant, who is also negligent, may be completely absolved from liability. If the student has superior knowledge that would be protective, the courts will take it into consideration in adjudging fault. In a case in which students knew that chemicals should not be held near a flame and the students intentionally set fire to the experiment and injury resulted, the court held the students were contributorily negligent because they should have known the consequences.[44]

However, since a child is not expected to act with the same standard of care as an adult, teachers have more difficulty in showing contributory negligence than if the plaintiff were an adult. A child is by nature careless and often negligent and, knowing this, a teacher should allow for an additional margin of safety. This is especially true with younger children. In fact, courts have said that where a child is concerned, the test to be employed is whether the child has committed a gross disregard of safety in the face of known, perceived, and understood dangers.[45]

In a case in which contributory negligence was found, a boy climbed on top of wire screening, fell through a hole, and was injured. The jury found the boy to be contributorily at fault because he did not exercise a reasonable degree of care for his own protection.[46]

Another court has held that a pupil who was injured when he mixed chemicals in a school laboratory was guilty of contributory negligence because he knew the chemicals were dangerous.[47]

If a plaintiff's negligence or fault contributes to the injury, the court will bar recovery of any damages at all. Some courts have held that complete barring of any damages because of contributory fault is perhaps a little drastic and have, therefore, endeavored to pro-rate damages based on the degree of fault. This results in what is known as comparative negligence.

Comparative negligence. When contributory negligence on the part of the plaintiff is shown, the defendant is usually completely absolved from all liability. This, some courts and legislatures have felt, works a hardship on the negligent plaintiff who suffers injury but can recover nothing from the negligent defendant. This concern for the injured party has led legislatures in some states to enact statutes to determine degrees of negligence and to allow recovery based on the relative degree of fault. While the specific provisions of "comparative negligence" statutes vary from state to state, the concept works this way: If the plaintiff's fault is found to be about equal to the defendant's, the plaintiff will recover one-half the damages and must bear the remainder of the loss himself. If the plaintiff's negligence amounted to one-third the fault and the defendant's two-thirds, the plaintiff could recover two-thirds of the damages.

Assumption of risk. Assumption of risk is another defense against negligence. Here the plaintiff acts in a manner that effectively relieves the defendant of his duty or obligation of conduct. The plaintiff by expressed or implied agreement recognizes the danger and assumes the risk. Defendant is thereby under no legal duty to protect the plaintiff. With knowledge of the danger, the plaintiff voluntarily enters into a relationship with the defendant, and by so doing agrees to take his chances.[48]

Plaintiff's knowledge and awareness of the danger is an important factor in this defense. For example, a boy playing basketball was injured when his arm went through a glass pane in a door immediately behind the basketball backboard. The court later said that the boy had not assumed the risk of such an injury. The boy did not know the glass in the door was not shatterproof.[49] However, another court held that a boy had assumed the risk when he suffered an injury by colliding with a doorjamb in a brick wall while playing as a voluntary member of a team in a school gymnasium. The boy had played in the gym previously and knew the location of the basket, the door, and the wall and, therefore, was aware of the danger involved in voluntarily playing in this particular gymnasium.[50] In a case in which a batter in a softball game struck a classmate with the bat who was sitting on the third base line, the court said the child who was struck either assumed the risk or was contributorily negligent.[51]

Courts have generally established that the participant in athletic events, whether intramural or interscholastic, assumes the risk of the normal hazards of the game. This rule also applies to spectators attending sports or amusement activities. Spectators assume all the obvious or normal risks of being hurt by flying balls,[52] fireworks,[53] or the struggles of combatants.[54]

Everyone has seen spectators knocked down along the sidelines of football games by players careening off the field. A high school girl was injured precisely in this fashion as she was standing by the sidelines and was run over by football players. The court found against the plaintiff in following prevailing precedent and said that a spectator at a sporting event assumes risks incident to the game. This is especially true when the spectator chooses to stay at an unsafe place despite the availability of protected seating.[55]

Essential to the doctrine of assumption of risk is that the plaintiff have knowledge of the risks; if he is ignorant of the conditions and dangers, he does not assume the risk. If reasonable precautions are not taken to determine the hazards involved, then he has not assumed the risk but may have been contributorily negligent instead. However, neither a participant nor a spectator assumes the risk for negligence or willful or wanton conduct of others. For example, a spectator at an athletic contest does not assume the risk of the stands falling at a football game nor does he assume that by attending a baseball game, a player will intentionally throw a bat into the stands.

Immunity. Immunity from tort liability is generally conferred on: (1) national and state governments, unless abrogated by statute; (2) public officials performing quasi-judicial or discretionary functions; (3) charitable organizations, granted immunity in some states; (4) infants, under certain conditions; and (5) in some cases, insane persons.

Where public schools are concerned, the defense of immunity is usually employed to protect the public school district against liability.[56] This governmental or sovereign immunity is an historical and common law precedent that protects a state agency against liability for its torts. Because of the importance of this concept and its frequent applicability in public school tort cases, governmental or sovereign immunity is treated separately below.

Intervening Causative Factor May
Absolve School from Liability

ALBERS v. INDEPENDENT
SCHOOL DISTRICT NO. 302
OF LEWIS COUNTY

Supreme Court of Idaho, 1971.
94 Idaho 342, 487 P.2d 936.

McFADDEN, Justice. This action was instituted by appellant Ray Albers, the father of Morris Albers, a minor, to recover damages from Independent School District No. 302 of Lewis County, respondent, for personal injuries suffered by his son Morris. A motion for summary judgment was made by the school district which the trial court granted. We affirm this judgment. . . .

The record discloses that on December 23, 1967, during the Christmas holiday, Morris Albers, with five other boys, drove to the high school gymnasium of the district with the intention of playing an informal basketball game. Upon arrival they found the entrance locked; however, the custodian was working on the premises and was persuaded, perhaps reluctantly, to open the door and let the youths use the basketball court. The custodian went about his cleaning duties after admitting the boys.

Morris undertook to clean the playing surface of the gymnasium, by sweeping the court with a wide dust mop or broom for five or ten minutes, while his friends changed clothes. The boys then engaged in warming up activities, shooting baskets, using two worn leather basketballs which they found lying about, the equipment room of the gymnasium being locked.

At the time Morris was wearing standard basketball shoes and slacks. He was a member of the high school basketball team, an accomplished high school athlete, and participated in several other team sports. At least one of the other five boys was a teammate of his on the basketball team.

After warming up the boys split into two teams and played a "half-court" basketball game. Morris' deposition reflects that "it was a real clean game" from the standpoint of fouls and close calls. Sometime into their play a shot came off the backboard and "headed out towards [the] out of bounds line on the east side of the gym." Morris and an opposing player ran for the loose ball. As Morris reached to pick it up the two boys collided, Morris hitting his head against his opponent's hip. Morris fell to the floor on his back in a semi-conscious state. Morris suffered a fracture in the cervical area of his spine necessitating surgical correction and prolonged hospitalization. . . .

Generally, schools owe a duty to supervise the activities of their students whether they be engaged in curricular activities or non-required but school sponsored extra-curricular activities. . . . Further, a school must exercise ordinary care to keep its premises and facilities in reasonably safe condition for the use of minors who foreseeably will make use of the premises and facilities. . . .

On the claim that the school district breached its duty to supervise the boys' game, the record lacks any evidence as to how the presence of a coach or teacher would have prevented the collision of the boys chasing the rebounding basketball. . . . Physical contact in such a situation in an athletic contest is foreseeable and expected. The general rule is that participants in an athletic contest accept the normal physical contact of the particular sport. . . . Nothing in the record would justify an exception to the rule here.

Regarding the allegation that the school district was negligent in allowing the youths to play on a dirty playing surface, the deposition of Morris Albers and his statements quoted above show there was no breach of any such duty. He had personally cleaned the floor and stated he saw no water spots or anything of that nature on the floor. . . .

The summary judgment of the trial court is affirmed. Costs to respondent.

Reasonable Supervision Does Not
Require Constant Unremitting
Scrutiny

FAGAN v. SUMMERS

Supreme Court of Wyoming, 1972.
498 P.2d 1227.

McINTYRE, Chief Justice. This case involves a suit for damages brought on behalf of seven-year-old George Fagan against a teacher's aide, Mrs. Lloyd Summers, and Park County School District No. 1.

During a noon recess a fellow student threw a small rock which hit a larger rock on the ground and then bounced up and struck George Fagan, causing him to lose the sight in his left eye. . . .

The trial court granted summary judgment for both Mrs. Summers and the school district. . . .

The Teacher Regarding defendant Summers, she has stated by affidavit that she walked past the plaintiff and five or six other boys twice prior to the accident, while they were sitting on the ground near the school building. The boys were laughing and talking and she saw nothing out of the ordinary. After Mrs. Summers strolled by this group of youngsters, she had walked approximately twenty-five feet (taking about thirty seconds) when she heard an outcry from plaintiff. The accident happened in that interval.

There is no evidence or indication that Mrs. Summers' explanation is not true. Also, it is claimed on behalf of defendants that Mrs. Summers was reliable, conscientious and capable in her work and a good playground supervisor. This does not appear to be challenged in any of the evidence.

There is no requirement for a teacher to have under constant and unremitting scrutiny all precise spots where every phase of play activities is being pursued; and there is no compulsion that general supervision be continuous and direct at all times and all places. . . .

In Butler v. District of Columbia, 135 U.S.App.D.C. 203, 417 F.2d 1150, 1152, the court considered it common knowledge, susceptible of judicial notice, that small boys may indulge in horseplay when a teacher's back is turned. . . .

A teacher cannot anticipate the varied and unexpected acts which occur daily in and about the school premises. Where the time between an act of a student and injury to a fellow student is so short that the teacher has no opportunity to prevent injury, it cannot be said that negligence of the teacher is a proximate cause of the injury. . . .

As far as the instant case is concerned, counsel for appellant was asked during oral argument what should have been done by Mrs. Summers which was not done. His answer was to the effect that she could really not have done more than she did do and she could probably be dismissed from the suit. We consider counsel's answer frank and honest. In view of it and in view of what we have said about the absence of proximate cause on the part of Mrs. Summers, we hold summary judgment for her was proper.

The District When counsel for appellant was asked during oral argument what the district should have done which was not done, his answer was that the district should have put the playground in better shape and should have provided more supervisors.

There is evidence that construction of a new school building was taking place. In connection with this construction, the blacktop of the playground had been torn up leaving clods of blacktop and a rough playground. It is also shown that this condition remained for approximately two years.

Although plaintiff alleged in his complaint that he had been hit with a piece of torn-up blacktop, counsel for appellant conceded in oral argument, as far as the record is concerned, plaintiff was hit with a rock. Counsel then advanced the theory that when the blacktop was torn up, it left rocks from beneath exposed.

There would be a possibility of this set of facts being proved if trial were had. Therefore, we will assume, for purposes of considering the propriety of summary judgment, that the playground was rough for a long period of time, with the blacktop torn up and rocks from beneath exposed. Although there appears to be no evidence as to where the rock which struck plaintiff came from, we will assume it was one which had been beneath the blacktop prior to ripping up of such blacktop.

We realize there are cases which hold a school district can be liable for injury resulting from a dangerous and defective condition of a playground. We have found no case, however, which holds rocks on the ground to be a dangerous and defective condition. Left on the ground, a rock will hurt no one.

Therefore, if we were to assume the school district was negligent for allowing rocks to be on the playground, we would have to hold the act of a third person who throws one of the rocks and injures the plaintiff an intervening cause of the accident. . . .

In the case before us, plaintiff was not injured by negligence, if any, from rocks being on the playground. The injury was clearly caused by the intervening act of a third person—the boy who picked up and threw the rock. Appellant cites no authority for the proposition that such a result was reasonably foreseeable.

It is apparent from all we have said that the proximate cause of George Fagan's injury was the act of his fellow student in throwing a rock. It was not the failure of the Park County School District No. 1 to maintain the playground in a safe condition.

Appellant has made no effort to show that supervision of the playground was inadequate or that the accident would have been prevented if more supervisors had been present. We need not discuss counsel's casual suggestion that there may have been negligence in this regard.

Summary judgment for Mrs. Summers and for the school district was justified and proper.

Affirmed.

Horseplay By Students Not Sufficient
to Maintain Contributory Negligence

WILKERSON v. HARTFORD ACCIDENT AND INDEMNITY CO.

Supreme Court of Louisiana, 1982.
411 So.2d 22.

MARCUS, Justice. . . .

The facts are generally not in dispute. On November 8, 1978, David Len Wilkinson, age twelve, attended his seventh-grade physical education class conducted by Joe Rivers, athletic coach, in the high school gymnasium. The gymnasium was originally constructed in 1965 with ordinary glass installed in all windows. When entering the gymnasium through the front doors, the first area encountered is a lobby or foyer extending from left (south) to right (north) about seventy feet with glass panels extending from the floor to the ceiling at each end of the lobby. A concession stand is located immediately in front of the entrance doors, about seven feet back, and rest room facilities are located on either side of the front doors. A water fountain is outside each rest room. To reach the spectator area from the front door of the gymnasium, it is necessary to walk into the lobby, turn left or right and walk about thirty feet in either direction to a door which leads from the lobby to the bleachers. Each door is about five feet from the glass panels at the end of the lobby. There is a wall immediately behind the concession stand with openings or doorless "portages" on either side which provide direct access between the lobby and the basketball court. The panel at the north end of the lobby was safety glass (the original plate glass panel having been replaced several years earlier following an incident in which a visiting coach walked through the glass) and the south panel was the original plate glass.

On the day of the accident, the physical education class was being conducted on the east half of the basketball court (side nearer to the lobby). Another class was being conducted on the other half. Coach Rivers had divided the boys into about six teams of five boys each. Relay races were being conducted between two teams at a time. At the conclusion of each race, the participants were instructed to sit along the inside east wall of the gymnasium and await their next turn. Coach Rivers was supervising the races at the time. While the boys had been instructed not to linger or engage in horseplay in the lobby, they were permitted to go into the lobby to get water from the fountains. Following one of the races, David Len and the other members of his team went into the lobby to get a drink of water from the north fountain. It was decided at that time to conduct a race of their own between David Len and another boy in order to determine the order they should be positioned in the next race. The race was to be from the north water fountain to the south glass panel and back again. The other boy reached the panel first and turned but when David Len reached the glass panel, running at his full speed, he pushed off the panel with both hands causing the glass to break. He fell through the glass onto the outside. He sustained multiple cuts on his arms and right leg and was bleeding profusely. Coach Rivers came immediately to the scene and administered first aid. David Len was then taken to the hospital for further treatment. After the accident, the school board replaced the south panel with safety glass.

The issues presented are the alleged negligence of Coach Rivers in failing to properly supervise the physical education class and/or that of the school board in maintaining a plate glass panel in the foyer of the gymnasium and if either or both was negligent, whether plaintiff's action is barred by the contributory negligence of David Len.

The trial judge found that Rivers exercised reasonable supervision over the physical education class commensurate with the age of the children and the attendant circumstances. The court of appeal agreed. Our review of the record supports the conclusion reached by the courts below. Hence, we conclude that Coach Rivers was not negligent.

The trial court found that the negligence of the school board was a cause of the accident. A school board is liable if it has actual knowledge or constructive knowledge of a condition unreasonably hazardous to the children under its supervision. The evidence in the record amply supports the conclusion that the school board had actual and constructive knowledge that the existence and maintenance of plate glass in the foyer of the gymnasium was dangerous. An identical panel at the north end of the foyer was broken when a visiting coach walked into the plate glass several years earlier. The panel had been replaced by safety glass. Moreover, we consider that the plate glass in the foyer of the gymnasium less than five feet from the traffic pattern of spectators of all ages and directly accessible to the basketball court was so inherently dangerous that the school authorities should have known of the hazard it created. The court of appeal agreed with the finding of the trial court that the school board was negligent. We agree. Accordingly, we conclude that the school board was negligent.

Having found that the school board was negligent, we must next consider whether David Len, age twelve, was contributorily negligent. While a child of twelve can be guilty of contributory negligence, such a child's caution must be judged by his maturity and capacity to evaluate circumstances in each particular case, and he must exercise only the care expected of his age, intelligence and experience. Defendant bears the burden of proving contributory negligence by a preponderance of the evidence.

The race in the lobby of the gymnasium was simply an unsupervised extension of the relay races being conducted on the basketball court in the main area of the gymnasium. We consider that it was normal behavior for twelve-year-old boys to do what David Len and his teammates did under the circumstances despite a previous warning to refrain from engaging in horseplay in the lobby. Moreover, David Len had no reason to be aware that the panel through which he fell was plate glass as opposed to safety glass or to anticipate that pushing against this panel would cause it to shatter. Hence, we do not find that defendants met their burden of proving contributory negligence on the part of David Len. . . .

In sum, we find that Joseph L. Rivers was not negligent. However, we do find that the Rapides Parish School Board was negligent but do not find that David Len Wilkinson was contributorily negligent. Hence, the negligence of the Rapides Parish School Board was the sole cause of the accident and the school board is responsible to plaintiff for damages sustained by David Len as a result of the accident. . . .

For the reasons assigned, the judgment of the court of appeal is reversed and the case is remanded to the court of appeal to consider the issue of the amount of damages not reached in its original opinion. . . .

NOTES

1. *Liability of Teacher Aide for Pupil Injury.* When teacher aides are assigned tasks involving supervision, they are placed in a position of potential liability for pupil injury. In such a situation, liability is likely to arise out of negligence on the part of the aide. Any persons assigned such responsibilities are ignorant at their own peril. If they are not qualified to supervise playgrounds, they should not attempt to perform the task.

   In cases involving pupil injury, the courts have traditionally held the teacher to a higher "standard of care" than that owed to the general public. Likewise, a teacher aide, when placed in a supervisory capacity, owes the pupils a greater "standard of care" than is normally required in other personal relationships.

2. *Liability of Administrator or Supervisor for Negligent Acts of Teacher Aide.* Where the administrator or supervisor appoints a well-qualified person to perform certain functions about the school and injury results, the administrator is not liable for negligence. The general rule of law is that in the public school situation the master is not liable for the commissions or omissions of his servant. In a Rhode Island case illustrating this principle, the court held that a school principal, who had authority over a school janitor, was not liable for injuries to a school teacher when the principal failed to warn her of a slippery floor in the school building. Gray v. Wood, 75 R.I. 123, 64 A.2d 191 (1949).

   Therefore, a teacher or a principal is not liable for the negligent acts of a properly appointed and qualified teacher aide. On the other hand, if a teacher or a principal assigns duties for which the teacher aide is not qualified and the purposes of which do not fall within the scope of the aide's employment, the teacher or the principal may be liable for negligent acts by the aide.

3. An Illinois court in relating tort liability to the *in loco parentis* standard found that teachers are not subject to any greater liability than parents for injury to their children. Parents are liable only for willful and wanton misconduct, but not for mere negligence. Montague v. School Board of the Thorton Fractional Township North High School District 215, 57 Ill.App.3d 828, 15 Ill.Dec. 373, 373 N.E.2d 719 (1978).

4. *Duty.* A Florida court has spoken about the duty owed by the school to the student:

   To sustain a cause of action in negligence, a complaint must allege ultimate facts which establish a relationship between the parties giving rise to a legal duty on the part of the defendant to protect the plaintiff from the injury of which he complains. It must also show that the defendant negligently breached that duty, and that the plaintiff's injury was proximately caused by the defendant's negligence. Ankers v. District School Board of Pasco County, 406 So.2d 72 (Fla.App.1981).

Reasonable Supervision Entails
General Supervision Unless Dangerous
Situations Require Specific
Supervision

MILLER v. YOSHIMOTO

Supreme Court of Hawaii, 1975.
56 Hawaii 333, 536 P.2d 1195.

KOBAYASHI, Justice.

This appeal by plaintiff (appellant) is against the State of Hawaii (appellee) only.

The appellant instituted this negligence action for damages for the total loss of her left eye caused by the willful action of defendant Richard Yoshimoto, a minor (defendant). Appellant brought this action against both Yoshimoto and the appellee and alleged, *inter alia*, that appellee failed to provide proper supervision of students in or around the school area in which appellant was injured. The trial court gave judgment to the appellee. We affirm. . . .

Aliamanu Intermediate School, hereinafter A.I.S., is a public school operated by the appellee. It is comprised of approximately 1,600 students in the seventh and eighth grades.

Of the 1,600 students approximately 80 percent use the buses to return home, while the other 20 percent walk home. Between sixty to ninety students walk home in the school campus area where the appellant was injured.

The principal of A.I.S., Mr. Harry Ono, had assigned various school personnel supervisory duties between 2:10 p.m. and 2:35 p.m.

On November 2, 1971, at about 2:10 p.m., Helen M. Miller, appellant, and her fellow students were dismissed from their classes at A.I.S. Accompanied by her friend, neighbor and classmate, Susan Colburn, appellant started walking home from her classroom in "B" Building at about 2:15 p.m. In order to reach home the girls had to walk between "F" Building and "B" Building and then across the school yard toward a flight of stairs which leads to Salt Lake Boulevard.

As appellant and Susan proceeded between "B" Building and "F" Building, Susan heard and appellant saw rocks being thrown from the end of "F" Building toward the area near "B" Building.

They recognized the two boys who were throwing the rocks as fellow students at A.I.S.

Appellant saw the boys throw three or four rocks; Susan saw the boys throw two or three rocks.

The girls then continued past the end of "F" Building and appellant asked the boys to stop throwing rocks as the rocks were going across the route where the girls would be walking. One of the boys then started to tease appellant.

As the girls continued walking the boys threw three or four rocks at the girls. Appellant again told the boys to stop throwing rocks, but the boys continued to throw rocks. These rocks came close enough to cause the girls to dodge them.

Appellant then told one of the boys that they "better not throw any more rocks" at her. Two more rocks were thrown at Susan and then appellant was struck in the eye by a rock.

Including the rock that injured appellant's eye, a total of between eight and twelve rocks were thrown by the boys at appellant and Susan.

The injury to appellant's eye required an enucleation of the left eye, an operation whereby the entire eye is removed from the socket. An artificial eye was later inserted. . . .

It is widely recognized that the public school systems have a duty of reasonable supervision of the students entrusted to them. . . .

We agree with the above view and conclude that the appellee has a duty of reasonably supervising the public school students of Hawaii during their required attendance and presence at school and while the students are leaving school immediately after the school day is over. And, in our opinion, the duty of reasonable supervision entails general supervision of the students, unless specific needs, or a dangerous or a likely to be dangerous situation, calls for specific supervision. . . .

The critical question is whether the record herein shows that the appellee fulfilled its duty of reasonable supervision under the circumstances of this case. . . .

Would the fact that there was no personnel assigned specifically to supervise the area in which appellant was injured be sufficient to show that appellee has breached its duty to provide reasonable supervision? We are of the opinion that that in itself is not sufficient to show a breach by the appellee of its duty of reasonable supervision.

The duty of reasonable supervision does not require the appellee to provide personnel to supervise every portion of the school buildings and campus area. However, if certain specific areas are known to the appellee as dangerous, or the appellee should have known that a specific area is dangerous, or the appellee knew or should have known that certain students would or may conduct themselves in a manner dangerous to the welfare of others, duty of reasonable supervision would require specific supervision of those situations.

The appellant, however, failed to adduce any evidence showing that the area in which appellant was injured was dangerous in character or likely to be dangerous because of known deviant conduct of students or of others, requiring specific supervision by the appellee. . . . [W]e are of the opinion that the evidence, in itself, is not sufficient to prove that the appellee failed to perform its duty herein. . . . The record does not show that the findings of fact of the trial court are clearly erroneous.

The other issues urged upon this court by the appellant are without merit.

NOTES

1. The Supreme Court of Florida has attempted to set out an objective standard for review for damage awards. In the case of Bould v. Touchette, 349 So.2d 1181 (Fla.1977) the court stated:

> Where recovery is sought for a personal tort, or where punitive damages are allowed, we cannot apply fixed rules to a given set of facts and say that a verdict is for more than would be allowable under a correct computation. In tort cases damages are to be measured by the jury's discretion. The court should never declare a verdict excessive merely because it is above the amount which the court itself considers the jury should have allowed. The verdict should not be disturbed unless it is so inordinately large as obviously to exceed the maximum limit of a reasonable range within which the jury may properly operate.

2. Presence of rocks on playground does not create an unreasonably hazardous condition. Hampton v. Orleans Parish School Board, 422 So.2d 202 (La.App.1982).

*Momentary Absence from Classroom
Does Not Constitute Negligence*

SIMONETTI

v.

SCHOOL DISTRICT OF PHILADELPHIA

Superior Court of Pennsylvania, 1982.
308 Pa.Super. 555, 454 A.2d 1038.

WIEAND, Judge:

Richard Simonetti, a fifth-grade student, returned to the classroom from recess and was struck in the left eye by a pencil which had been propelled from the hand of a classmate when he tripped. The teacher, an employee of the School District of Philadelphia, was outside the classroom, standing at the door, when Simonetti was injured. There she was engaged in monitoring the return of her students from recess and talking with another teacher. The student who dropped or threw the pencil and two other students had been required to remain in the classroom during recess as punishment for misbehavior at breakfast. They had been talking with the teacher during the recess period and were instructed to take their seats when the teacher stepped outside the classroom to supervise the return of the students from recess.

In an action against the School District, it was contended by Simonetti that the teacher had been negligent in failing to provide adequate classroom supervision. . . . The teacher, it may confidently be observed, could not have been at two places at the same time. With equal confidence, it can be said that it was not negligence for the teacher to give priority to an entire class of approximately thirty students returning from recess rather than to remain in the classroom to supervise three students who had been required to stay in the classroom during the recess period.

It is common knowledge that children may indulge in horseplay. They may throw a pencil, shoot a paper clip or snap a rubber band when a teacher is absent or turns his or her back. In the instant case, the teacher attempted to guard against any horseplay by instructing the three students who were in the classroom to return to their seats and remain there. While these students were capable of free spirits and were even being punished for unrelated misconduct at breakfast, there is no evidence that they were hellions who required constant custody.

To require the teacher to anticipate the events which occurred while she was outside the classroom door would be to hold that a teacher is required to anticipate the myriad of unexpected acts which occur daily in classrooms in every school in the land. This is not the law, and we perceive no good reason for imposing such an absolute standard on teachers and school districts.

The judgment is reversed and is now entered for the appellant.

NOTES

1. *Proximate Cause.* In Holler v. Lowery, a Maryland case, the court said:

> There is no mystery in the doctrine of proximate cause. It rests upon common sense rather than legal formula. Expressed in the simplest terms it means that negligence is not actionable unless it, without the intervention of any independent factor causes the harm complained of. It involves of course the idea of continuity, that the negligent act continuously extends through every event, fact, act and occurrence related to the tortious conduct of the defendant and is itself the logical and natural cause of the injury complained of. In the statement of the doctrine an intervening cause means not a concurrent and contributing cause, but a superseding cause, which is itself the natural and logical cause of the harm. 175 Md. 149, 161, 200 A. 353, 358 (1938).

2. *Proper Supervision.* If a rule can be developed from the teacher liability cases, it is this: a teacher's absence from the classroom, or failure properly to supervise students' activities, is not likely to give rise to a cause of action for injury to a student, unless under all the circumstances the possibility of injury is reasonably foreseeable. In Carroll v. Fitzsimmons, 153 Colo. 1, 3, 384 P.2d 81, 82 (1963), the Supreme Court of Colorado had before it the question whether an allegation "that the plaintiff was struck in the eye by a rock thrown by a fellow student" and "that the defendant teacher permitted the rock to be thrown" stated a cause of action. In affirming the dismissal of the complaint, the court quoted from Nestor v. City of New York, supra, 28 Misc.2d 70 at 71, 211 N.Y.S.2d 975 at 977:

> There is no requirement that the teacher have under constant and unremitting scrutiny the precise spots wherein every phase of play activity is being pursued; nor is there compulsion that the general supervision be continuous and direct.

3. *Foreseeability.* The test of foreseeability was well stated in McLeod v. Grant County School Dist. No. 128, 42 Wash.2d 316, 255 P.2d 360 (1953), a case that held the school district answerable in damages to a girl who was attacked in an unlighted room adjacent to the school gymnasium. There the court said:

> Whether foreseeability is being considered from the standpoint of negligence or proximate cause, the pertinent inquiry is not whether the actual harm was of a particular kind which was expectable. Rather, the question is whether the actual harm fell within a general field of danger which should have been anticipated. 42 Wash.2d at 321, 255 P.2d at 363.

having previously said:

> The harm which came to appellant was not caused by the direct act or omission of the school district, but by the intervening act of third persons. The fact that the danger stems from such an intervening act, however, does not of itself exonerate a defendant from negligence. If, under the assumed facts, such intervening force is reasonably foreseeable, a finding of negligence may be predicated thereon. 42 Wash.2d at 320, 255 P.2d at 362.

4. The Supreme Court of California has held that the fact that another student's misconduct was the immediate precipitating cause of injury does not compel a conclusion that negligent supervision by the teacher was not the proximate cause of a student's death. The mere involvement of a third party nor the party's own wrongful conduct is sufficient in itself to absolve the defendants of liability, once a negligent failure to provide adequate supervision is shown. Dailey v. Los Angeles Unified School Dist., 2 Cal.3d 741, 87 Cal.Rptr. 376, 470 P.2d 360 (1970).

5. Adequate supervision did not require a physical education teacher to provide a spotter for a student performing a forward roll when the student had been given proper instruction and had performed the routine on many occasions before without the assistance of a spotter. Lueck v. City of Janesville, 57 Wis.2d 254, 204 N.W.2d 6 (1973).

6. The intervening act of a student throwing a bamboo high-jump cross bar, after school hours, and striking another student in the eye was the sole proximate cause of injury. High jumping equipment is not an "inherently dangerous" instrumentality that imposes a duty on teacher or school to provide supervision during nonschool hours. Bush v. Smith, 154 Ind.App. 382, 289 N.E.2d 800 (1973).

7. Requiring students to run to the dressing room, when time between classes is short, does not create an unreasonable risk. Driscol v. Delphi Community School Corp., 155 Ind.App. 56, 290 N.E.2d 769 (1973).

8. In preparation of a project for a science fair, a girl was burned when students attempted to light a defective burner that had gone out and alcohol exploded after the teacher had set the experiment up, checked that it worked correctly, and returned to his regular class. The court, in holding the teacher liable for negligence, said: "where one creates, deals in, handles or distributes an inherently dangerous object or substance . . . an extraordinary degree of care is required of those responsible . . .. The duty is particularly heavy where children are exposed to a dangerous condition which they may not appreciate." The duty was to either positively warn the students not to try to light the burner or to personally supervise; the teacher did neither. Station v. Travelers Insurance Co., 292 So.2d 289 (La.App.1974).

School Bus Driver's Negligence Is
Proximate Cause of Injury

BLAIR

v.

BOARD OF EDUCATION OF SHERBURNE–EARLVILLE CENTRAL SCHOOL

Supreme Court, Appellate Division, Third
Department, 1982.
86 A.D.2d 933, 448 N.Y.S.2d 566.

MEMORANDUM BY THE COURT. . . . Bobby Wayne Blair allegedly sustained permanent serious injuries to his right eye when he was struck in that eye by an object thrown by one of the other passengers on the bus, and plaintiffs assert that these injuries were caused by defendants' negligence in failing to properly supervise and control the activities on the bus. Following a jury trial, a verdict was returned in the amounts of $100,000 in favor of Bobby Wayne Blair and $10,000 in favor of Richard C. Blair, and the trial court set aside the $10,000 verdict as excessive and ordered a new trial unless Richard C. Blair stipulated to accept $2,602.73. . . .

Seeking a reversal of the judgment at Trial Term, defendants basically argue that plaintiffs failed to prove at trial the existence of any culpable negligence on the part of defendants. We find their arguments unpersuasive. In his testimony, defendant Brown conceded that his duties as a school bus driver included the maintenance of order on the bus by the prevention of, *inter alia,* tomfoolery and the throwing of things around the bus. Significantly, there is also testimony from several of the passengers on this bus that this kind of activity had been occurring for fifteen minutes prior to Bobby Wayne Blair's injury and that defendant Brown took no action to stop it. One witness even testified that she told the bus driver of the unruly activity prior to the injury, but that he paid no attention to her. Under these circumstances, defendants' arguments that the disruptive and dangerous actions of some of the pupils were unanticipated and that defendant Brown could not have foreseen the danger to his passengers arising from such activity ring hollow, and the jury could reasonably conclude that defendants' negligent supervision of the activity on bus No. 72 was a proximate cause of Bobby Wayne Blair's injuries. . . .

Judgment affirmed, with costs.

NOTE

Intervening negligence of third party does not break proximate cause relieving original tort-feasor of his negligence if intervening negligence is foreseeable. Leahy v. School Board of Hernando Co., 450 So.2d 883 (Fla.App. 1984).

*Injured Student with Knowledge of
Risk Involved Is Contributorily
Negligent*

HUTCHISON v. TOEWS

Court of Appeals of Oregon,
Department 2, 1970.
4 Or.App. 19, 476 P.2d 811.

LANGTRY Judge. Plaintiff appeals from a judgment of involuntary nonsuit, entered on motion of both defendants at the conclusion of the plaintiff's case.

Plaintiff and his friend, Phillip Brown, both fifteen years old, attempted to shoot a homemade pipe cannon which exploded, injuring plaintiff's hands. They had made the explosive charge by mixing potassium chlorate and powdered sugar.

Brown, as plaintiff's witness, testified that he and the plaintiff had "badgered" defendant Toews, the chemistry teacher at Phoenix High School, for potassium chlorate to use in fireworks experimentation. He said they had asked Mr. Toews for the material about a dozen times. The plaintiff said five or six times. Finally, Mr. Toews had given them some powdered potassium chlorate, which they put in a baby food jar. A day or two later, when Mr. Toews left the separate chemical storage room unattended while he stepped into the adjoining chemistry classroom, Brown took, without Mr. Toews' knowledge or permission, some crystalline potassium chlorate also stored there. Brown positively identified this crystalline potassium chlorate as the substance used in the explosion. He was the one who mixed the ingredients. The plaintiff equivocated, first indicating that the powdered substance was what was used, but on cross-examination he said, "It looked like crystal." Brown waited approximately two years after the accident before he revealed to anyone that he had taken the crystalline substance and that it had caused the explosion. The plaintiff did not reveal that he knew the crystalline substance had been taken until after Brown's disclosure of the true facts. The injury occurred in November 1965. Plaintiff commenced this action for damages against defendant Toews only in June 1966, and filed an amended complaint in August 1967. In these complaints, plaintiff alleged that defendant Toews "supplied" the potassium chlorate to him. . . .

Prosser says:

> [T]he kind of contributory negligence which consists of voluntary exposure to a known danger, and so amounts to assumption of risk, is ordinarily a defense . . . . Prosser, Torts 539, § 78 (3rd ed.1964).

We think the evidence construed in the light most favorable to plaintiff . . . justifies the judgment of the court. The boys had purchased from a mail order firm in Michigan a pamphlet which gave 100 formulas for explosives. Together, they built the cannon and conducted their experiments. They admitted that they had looked at the warnings in the pamphlet. They had shown the pamphlet to defendant Toews, and he had cautioned them, and told them they should have supervision. He had declined their invitation to supervise them because of another commitment. Among other things, the pamphlet warned:

> Some of the formulas listed in this booklet are very dangerous to make. Therefore, it is strongly suggested that the making of fireworks be left in the hands of the experienced.

. . . They had previously experimented with homemade gunpowder in the cannon and in doing so had used up all of their fuses. When they mixed and placed the charge of potassium chlorate and powdered sugar in the cannon, they put the head of a paper match into the fuse hole and tried to light the paper end of the match in order to have time to take over before the explosion. When Brown tried to light the paper match, wind impeded him. On Brown's request, plaintiff held his hands around the fuse hole to shield it from the wind. The charge exploded, and the closed pipe end "peeled like a banana." Plaintiff's hands were severely injured. The evidence is lengthy, but it is replete with statements from both of the boys that they knew the experiment conducted was dangerous. Plaintiff testified on cross-examiantion he knew "That you might get burned if you held onto it, or if you stood too close to it when it did shoot . . . that it might fly up or hit you in the face . . . ."

Plaintiff testified he knew that the pamphlet said the formula was very powerful. . . .

There are many cases involving tort liability of suppliers of explosives to children. No purpose is served by a detailed discussion of them here. We note that they usually turn on whether the plaintiff had or should have had knowledge and understanding so that he could have avoided the explosion. . . .

In the case at bar, the only reasonable conclusion from the evidence was that plaintiff had knowledge of the risk involved, and that he was contributorily negligent as a matter of law.

Affirmed.

NOTES

1. Trade school welding student was not contributorily negligent when injured by exploding freon cylinder. Danos v. Foret, 354 So.2d 667 (La. App.1977).

2. A chemistry experiment in an introductory high school course, requiring students to use materials that could explode, should be conducted under strictest supervison and personal attention of the teacher. Mastrangelo v. West Side Union High School District of Merced County, 2 Cal.2d 540, 42 P.2d 634 (1935).

3. Father of student may be required to pay actual damages assessed when his son struck and injured a teacher. Garrett v. Olsen, 691 P.2d 123 (Or. App.1984).

*Lack of Supervision in School
Bathroom Is Gross Negligence*

CARSON v. ORLEANS
PARISH SCHOOL BOARD

Court of Appeal of Louisiana, Fourth
Circuit, 1983.
432 So.2d 956.

BYRNES, Judge.

Plaintiffs' daughter was injured by another student on December 21, 1979, while attending Stuart R. Bradley Elementary School. . . .

Tiffany Carson was a third-grade student at the time of the accident. At approximately noon, immediately following the lunch recess, she entered the girls' restroom. In the breezeway adjacent to the bathroom, several children were engaged in playing with apples which had apparently been wrongfully removed from the cafeteria. One of the apples fell near Sam Hall who picked it up and instructed Erskine Walker to hold the door of the girls' restroom ajar while he hurled the apple into the bathroom, striking Tiffany in the right eye. . . .

Two issues are presented on appeal. First, appellant contends that there was no negligence on the part of Bradley Elementary School and thus, the School Board cannot be held liable. The second is a quantum question, raised by appellees, who urge that the award for general damages should be increased from $3,000.00 to $10,000.00. . . .

The trial court found that the breezeway area near the bathrooms was inadequately supervised at the time of the accident. The court held that this lack of supervision amounted to "gross negligence" on the part of the School Board and further found that the injury suffered may have been prevented had there been greater supervision of the area. We agree.

Officials at Bradley Elementary School are aware of the propensity of small children to get into mischief, particularly during recess. Therefore, certain teachers are assigned to supervise student activities. Two of the teachers at the school, Amanda McMurray and Daisy Palmer, testified that a teacher is assigned to the area between the breezeway and the lunchroom. It is apparently this person's responsibility to control the lunch line and to supervise the entrance into the school, the breezeway area, and the boys' and girls' restrooms. The record clearly establishes that it was common for boys and girls to play in the breezeway during recess and that girls often stuck their heads out of the restroom to see if the "coast was clear" of any young male pursuers. Testimony reflects that it was the responsibility of the teacher on duty to keep the area around the girls' restroom clear of boys and not to allow the children to run around or play games in the breezeway. Hence, the school was aware of the possibility of injury resulting from the children's games.

It was established at trial that at the time of the accident, the teacher assigned to be on duty, Mrs. Valero, was not at her post and apparently was not aware of the children playing outside the restrooms or the resulting accident. The record reflects that it was often very difficult to watch the lunchroom, the entrance from the yard and the breezeway simultaneously.

While we agree with appellant's contention that accidents such as this could happen in a split second, we find the accident in question herein did not. The record reflects that the situation developed over a period of a few minutes. There were several points along the chain of events beginning with the removal of the apples from the lunchroom where proper supervison could have prevented the accident. . . .

We find that the holding of the trial court is clearly supported by the evidence presented at trial. . . .

In the instant case the record reflects that Tiffany Carson suffered an intraocular hemorrhage in the right eye. The doctor's report states that Tiffany's eye healed quite well and that there was no permanent residual disability. Further, there is no indication that in the four-month period during which Tiffany was treated that there was any question that the eye would not heal completely. In our opinion the trial court did not abuse its discretion in awarding $3,000.00 general damages and $969.55 special damages to plaintiffs.

For the foregoing reasons the decision of the trial court is affirmed. All costs of this appeal are to be borne by the appellant.

Affirmed.

NOTES

1. A third-grade pupil was directed by the teacher to water a plant located on the window ledge. The pupil used a chair to stand on while watering the plant with water poured from a glass milk bottle. The child fell off the chair, broke the bottle, and she sustained a severe wrist laceration. Was judgment rendered for or against the teacher? Why? See Gaincott v. Davis, 281 Mich. 515, 275 N.W. 229 (1937).

2. Suppose a teacher in inclement weather raised a window in the room in such a way as to cause a draft upon the pupils and the teacher did not permit the pupils to escape the effects of the draft and a child became ill as a direct result. Would the teacher be liable for the consequential damages? See Guyten v. Rhodes, 65 Ohio App. 163, 18 O.O. 356, 29 N.E.2d 444 (1940).

3. May a teacher be held accountable for injuries sustained by a pupil who lost his sight in one eye because of a pencil thrown by another pupil during the teacher's absence from the room? See Ohman v. Board of Education, 275 App.Div. 840, 88 N.Y.S.2d 273 (1949).

4. School bus driver was found not to be negligent for the death of a five-year-old child who had gotten off the school bus, crossed the street in front of the bus, and then ran back under the rear wheels of the bus while chasing a blowing piece of paper. The bus driver was attentive, watched the child cross the street originally, but had not seen the child return. Johnson v. Svoboda, 260 N.W.2d 530 (Iowa 1978).

EDUCATIONAL MALPRACTICE

Several courts in recent years have issued opinions on cases that fall under a general classification of educational malpractice. Such cases are not a separate area of law, but, instead represent an expansion of the traditional tort law concept as applied to the educational setting. Basically, educational malpractice is an attempt to apply tort law to educational outcomes in such a way as to redress a student for knowledge deficiencies allegedly created by some substandard treatment visited upon that student during the educational process.

Evidence to support an allegation of intentional tort would seem to be very difficult to support unless one could show that an educator, for some malicious purpose, set out to prevent a child from obtaining an education. The possibility of maintaining an action for intentional tort was recognized by a Maryland court when it stated: "It is our view that where an individual engaged in the education process is shown to have willfully and maliciously injured a child entrusted to his educational care, such outrageous conduct greatly outweighs any public policy considerations which would otherwise preclude liability so as to authorize recovery."[57]

The more common application of tort to redress a student's educational deficiencies is found in negligence. Here it is maintained that educators failed to act reasonably in administering to a student's educational needs. Such actions, though, have met with little or no success as the courts have established an imposing array of precedents denying students damages. The courts have generally denied redress for three reasons: "the absence of a workable rule of care against which defendant's conduct may be measured, the inherent uncertainty in determining the cause and nature of any damages, and the extreme burden which would be imposed on the already strained resources of the public school system to say nothing of the judiciary."[58]

The first reason given is, of course, related directly to the negligence question. How can a court enunciate a standard of care without a clear determination of the actual duty owed to the student? Does the educator have a duty to fill the vessel of the student's mind with a given amount of knowledge and if the vessel remains half-full, does the educator, student, parent, or society bear the blame?

The problem of delineating an actionable duty was recognized by a California court in *Peter W.*[59] when it explained:

> The "injury" claimed here is plaintiff's inability to read and write. Substantial professional authority attests that the achievement of literacy in the schools, or its failure, is influenced by a host of factors which affect the pupil subjectively, from outside the formal teaching process, and beyond the control of its ministers. They may be physical, neurological, emotional, cultural, environmental; they may be present but not perceived, recognized but not identified.

In such a situation, the court could not find that the student had suffered injury within the meaning of negligence law, nor could it identify a workable "rule of care" that could be applied. Neither could the court find a causal relationship between any perceived injury and the alleged negligent commission or omission by the defendant. A New York court had drawn a conclusion similar to that in *Peter W.* and further maintained that judicial interference in this area would constitute a "blatant interference" with the administration of the public school system.[60] In agreement with these courts, the court in *Hunter* said that "to allow petitioners asserted negligence claims to proceed would in effect position the courts of this state as overseers of both the day-to-day operation of our educational process as well as the formulation of its governing policies. This responsibility we are loath to impose on our courts." [61]

Other courts have likewise rejected plaintiffs' claims in negligence actions.[62]

Educational Malpractice Is Not a
Cognizable Cause of Action
in Tort Law

DONOHUE v. COPIAGUE UNION FREE SCHOOL DISTRICT

Court of Appeals of New York, 1979.
47 N.Y.2d 440, 418 N.Y.S.2d 375, 391
N.E.2d 1352.

JASEN, Judge.

This appeal poses the question whether a complaint seeking monetary damages for "educational malpractice" states a cause of action cognizable in the courts.

Appellant entered Copiague Senior High School in September, 1972, and graduated in June, 1976. The thrust of appellant's claim is that notwithstanding his receipt of a certificate of graduation he lacks even the rudimentary ability to comprehend written English on a level sufficient to enable him to complete applications for employment. His complaint attributes this deficiency to the failure of respondent to perform its duties and obligations to educate appellant. To be more specific, appellant alleges in his complaint that respondent through its employees "gave to [appellant] passing grades and/or minimal or failing grades in various subjects; failed to evaluate [appellant's] mental ability and capacity to comprehend the subjects being taught to him at said school; failed to take proper means and precautions that they reasonably should have taken under the circumstances; failed to interview, discuss, evaluate and/or psychologically test [appellant] in order to ascertain his ability to comprehend and understand such matter; failed to provide adequate school facilities, teachers, administrators, psychologists, and other personnel trained to take the necessary steps in testing and evaluation processes insofar as [appellant] is concerned in order to ascertain the learning capacity, intelligence and intellectual absorption on the part of [appellant]."

Based upon these acts of commission and omission, appellant frames two causes of action, the first of which sounds in "educational malpractice" and the second of which alleges the negligent breach of a constitutionally imposed duty to educate. To redress his injury, appellant seeks the sum of $5,000,000. Upon respondent's motion, Special Term dismissed appellant's complaint for failure to state a cause of action. The Appellate Division affirmed, with one Justice dissenting. There should be an affirmance.

The second cause of action need not detain us long. The State Constitution (art. XI, § 1) commands that "[t]he legislature shall provide for the maintenance and support of a system of free common schools, wherein all the children of this state may be educated." Even a terse reading of this provision reveals that the Constitution places the obligation of *maintaining and supporting* a system of public schools upon the *Legislature*. To be sure, this general directive was never intended to impose a duty flowing directly from a local school district to individual pupils to ensure that each pupil receives a minimum level of education, the breach of which duty would entitle a pupil to compensatory damages. . . .

Appellant's first cause of action bears closer scrutiny. It may very well be that even within the strictures of a traditional negligence or malpractice action, a complaint sounding in "educational malpractice" may be formally pleaded. Thus, the imagination need not be overly taxed to envision allegations of a legal duty of care flowing from educators, if viewed as professionals, to their students. If doctors, lawyers, architects, engineers and other professionals are charged with a duty owing to the public whom they serve, it could be said that nothing in the law precludes similar treatment of professional educators. Nor would creation of a standard with which to judge an educator's performance of that duty necessarily pose an insurmountable obstacle. . . . As for proximate causation, while this element might indeed be difficult, if not impossible to prove in view of the many collateral factors involved in the learning process, it perhaps assumes too much to conclude that it could never be established. This would leave only the element of injury and who can in good faith deny that a student who upon graduation from high school cannot comprehend simple English—a deficiency allegedly attributable to the negligence of his educators—has not in some fashion been "injured."

The fact that a complaint alleging "educational malpractice" might on the pleadings state a cause of action within traditional notions of tort law does not, however, require that it be sustained. The heart of the matter is whether, assuming that such a cause of action may be stated, the courts should, as a matter of public policy, entertain such claims. We believe they should not. . . .

To entertain a cause of action for "educational malpractice" would require the courts not merely to make judgments as to the validity of broad educational policies—a course we have unalteringly eschewed in the past—but, more importantly, to sit in review of the day-to-day implementation of these policies. Recognition in the courts of this cause of action would constitute blatant interference with the responsibility for the administration of the public school system lodged by Constitution and statute in school administrative agencies. . . . Of course, "[t]his is not to say that there may never be gross violations of defined public policy which the courts would be obliged to recognize and correct." . . .

Finally, not to be overlooked in today's holding is the right of students presently enrolled in public schools, and their parents, to take advantage of the administrative processes provided by statute to enlist the aid of the Commissioner of Education in ensuring that such students receive a proper education. The Education Law (§ 310, subd. 7) permits any person aggrieved by an "official act or decision of any officer, school authorities, or meetings concerning any other matter under this chapter, or any other act pertaining to common schools" to seek review of such act or decision by the commissioner.

Accordingly, the order of the Appellate Division should be affirmed, with costs.

WACHTLER, Judge (concurring).

I agree that complaints of "educational malpractice" are for school administrative agencies, rather than the courts, to resolve.

There is, however, another even more fundamental objection to entertaining plaintiff's cause of action alleging educational malpractice. It is a basic principle that the law does not provide a remedy for every injury. . . . As the majority notes, the decision of whether a new cause of action should be recognized at law is largely a question of policy. Critical to such a determination is whether the cause of action sought to be pleaded would be reasonably manageable within our legal system. The practical problems raised by a cause of action sounding in educational malpractice are so formidable that I would conclude that such a legal theory should not be cognizable in our courts. These problems, clearly articulated at the Appellate Division, include the practical impossibility of proving that the alleged malpractice of the teacher proximately caused the learning deficiency of the plaintiff student.

Factors such as the student's attitude, motivation, temperament, past experience and home environment may all play an essential and immeasurable role in learning. Indeed as the majority observes proximate cause might "be difficult, if not impossible, to prove."

I would, therefore, affirm the order of the Appellate Division on the ground that educational malpractice, as here pleaded, is not a cognizable cause of action. . . .

Order affirmed.

GOVERNMENTAL IMMUNITY

Governmental agencies have historically been immune from tort liability. As a general rule, common law asserts that government is inherently immune unless the legislature specifically abrogates the privilege. The immunity concept evolved to this country from England where the King could, theoretically, do no wrong. Various legal scholars maintain the concept was a product of the dark ages where custom established that the lord of the fief was also the lawmaker and judge. As such, the lord was singly responsible for all laws and justice and since he made and implemented the laws, he could not be sued without his permission.[63] As the feudal system drew to a close and fiefdoms became consolidated into larger governmental units, immunity became enmeshed with the "divine right of Kings" placing the King in a superior and preferred legal position.[64] Sovereign immunity became formalized in English law at least as early as the thirteenth century at which time the King could not be sued in his own courts.[65] Sovereign immunity apparently reached its zenith in fifteenth-century England where it stabilized as a prerogative of the monarch. Judicial recognition of this power was taken when an English court held in 1607 that the King was not liable for damages to private property caused by the government's digging for saltpeter that was to be used in the manufacture of gunpowder.[66] In spite of his judicial sanction affirming sovereign immunity, the great jurist Coke held in the same year that the King could not sit as a judge in his own case.[67] Effectively, this began a whittling away process of the sovereign immunity that was not to culminate until over 250 years later when the House of Lords held that a public entity was liable for the damages caused by acts of its employees.[68] Later, this rationale was applied to schools in England when a court held that if negligence occurred resulting in student injury either the teacher or the school could be liable.[69]

The sovereign immunity doctrine may have been transported across the Atlantic to the United States directly under the precedent of *Russell* v. *The Men Dwelling in the County of Devon* [70] as relied upon by a Massachusetts court in *Mower* v. *The Inhabitants of Leicester* in 1812.[71] It is unlikely, however, that the concept did traverse the Atlantic through a single precedent, especially since the court in *Russell* attributed its holding of nonliability to (1) the lack of a public treasury, (2) general judicial apprehension that imposing liability would encourage a flow of such actions, (3) the belief that public inconvenience should be avoided, and (4) that no legislation existed imposing such liability. No direct judicial notice was taken of the doctrine of Crown Prerogative or the "King can do no wrong" doctrine. It seems more likely that sovereign immunity came to be commonly accepted in this country through the use by early lawyers and judges of English legal books and materials such as Blackstone's Commentaries, which were used as standard references, and, of course, many of the notable jurists of early America received their legal training in the Inns of Court in London. Regardless of its origin, however, the United States Supreme Court and state courts adopted the principle that the sovereign could not be sued without its permission. The Supreme Court in 1869 commented that "It is a familiar doctrine of the common law, that the sovereign cannot be sued in his own courts without his consent . . ." [72] and, in the same year in another case, the court stated that "Every government has an inherent right to protect itself against suits . . . . The principle is fundamental [and] applies to every sovereign power."[73] The federal government abrogated immunity to a statutorily prescribed extent in the *Federal Tort Claims Act of 1946*.

Beginning from the point of nearly universal adherence to the immunity doctrine, state courts have in recent years tended to move away from the doctrine in several notable examples. Most significant is the *Molitor* case, which abolished immunity in Illinois and directly refuted the legal rationale that supported sovereign immunity.[74] In *Muskopf*, the California Supreme Court observed the trend away from immunity saying:

> Only the vestigial remains of such governmental immunity have survived; its requiem has long been foreshadowed. For years the process of erosion of governmental immunity has gone on unabated. The Legislature has contributed mightily to that erosion. The courts, by distinction and extension, have removed much of the force of the rule. Thus, in holding that the doctrine of governmental immunity for torts for which its agents are liable has no place in our law we make no startling break with the past but merely take the final step that carries to its conclusion an established legislative and judicial trend.[75]

Since *Molitor* the gradual trend away from immunity has carried to the point that today at least thirty states have case law precedents that place limits on sovereign immunity.[76] Of these, eighteen of the states have established by legislation types of tort claims acts. Six states substantially abrogate immunity by statute while three state legislatures specifically reinforce the immunity doctrine.[77]

*Sovereign Immunity May Be
Abrogated By the Courts*

MOLITOR v. KANELAND COMMUNITY UNIT DISTRICT NO. 302

Supreme Court of Illinois, 1959.
18 Ill.2d 11, 163 N.E.2d 89.

KLINGBIEL, Justice. Plaintiff, Thomas Molitor, a minor, by Peter his father and next friend, brought this action against Kaneland Community Unit School District for personal injuries sustained by plaintiff when the school bus in which he was riding left the road, allegedly as a result of the driver's negligence, hit a culvert, exploded and burned.

The complaint alleged, in substance, the negligence of the School District, through its agent and servant, the driver of the school bus; that plaintiff was in the exercise of such ordinary care for his own safety as could be reasonably expected of a boy of his age, intelligence, mental capacity and experience; that plaintiff sustained permanent and severe burns and injuries as a proximate result of defendant's negligence, and prayed for judgment in the amount of $56,000. Plaintiff further alleged that defendant is a voluntary unit school district organized and existing under the provisions of sections 8–9 to 8–13 of the School Code and operates school buses within the district pursuant to section 29–5. Ill.Rev.Stat.1957, Chap. 122, pars. 8–9 to 8–13 and par. 29–5.

The complaint contained no allegation of the existence of insurance or other nonpublic funds out of which a judgment against defendant could be satisfied. Although plaintiff's abstract of the record shows that defendant school district did carry public liability insurance with limits of $20,000 for each person injured and $100,000 for each occurrence, plaintiff states that he purposely omitted such an allegation from his complaint.

Defendant's motion to dismiss the complaint on the ground that a school district is immune from liability for tort was sustained by the trial court, and a judgment was entered in favor of defendant. Plaintiff elected to stand on his complaint and sought a direct appeal to this court on the ground that the dismissal of his action would violate his constitutional rights. At that time we held that no fairly debatable constitutional question was presented so as to give this court jurisdiction on direct appeal, and accordingly the cause was transferred to the Appellate Court for the Second District. The Appellate Court affirmed the decision of the trial court and the case is now before us again on a certificate of importance.

In his brief, plaintiff recognizes the rule, established by this court in 1898, that a school district is immune from tort liability, and frankly asks this court to abolish the rule *in toto* . . . .

Thus we are squarely faced with the highly important question—in the light of modern developments—should a school district be immune from liability for tortiously inflicted personal injury to a pupil thereof arising out of the operation of a school bus owned and operated by said district?

It appears that while adhering to the old immunity rule, this court has not reconsidered and re-evaluated the doctrine of immunity of school districts for over fifty years. During these years, however, this subject has received exhaustive consideration by legal writers and scholars in articles and texts, almost unanimously condemning the immunity doctrine. . . .

Historically we find that the doctrine of the sovereign immunity of the state, the theory that "the King can do no wrong," was first extended to a subdivision of the state in 1788 in Russell v. Men of Devon, 2 Term Rep. 671, 100 Eng.Rep. 359. As pointed out by Dean Prosser (*Prosser on Torts,* p. 1066), the idea of the municipal corporate entity was still in a nebulous state at that time. The action was brought against the entire population of the county and the decision that the county was immune was based chiefly on the fact that there were no corporate funds in Devonshire out of which satisfaction could be obtained, plus a fear of multiplicity of suits and resulting inconvenience to the public.

It should be noted that the *Russell* case was later overruled by the English courts, and that in 1890 it was definitely established that in England a school board or school district is subject to suit in tort for personal injuries on the same basis as a private individual or corporation. . . .

The immunity doctrine of *Russell* v. *Men of Devon* was adopted in Illinois with reference to towns and counties in 1870 in Town of Waltham v. Kemper, 55 Ill. 346. Then, in 1898, eight years after the English courts had refused to apply the *Russell* doctrine to schools, the Illinois court extended the immunity rule to school districts in the leading case of Kinnare v. City of Chicago, 171 Ill. 332, 49 N.E. 536, where it was held that the Chicago Board of Education was immune from liability for the death of a laborer resulting from a fall from the roof of a school building, allegedly due to the negligence of the Board in failing to provide scaffolding and safeguards. That opinion reasoned that since the State is not subject to suit nor liable for the torts or negligence of its agents, likewise a school district, as a governmental agency of the State, is also "exempted from the obligation to respond in damages, as master, for negligent acts of its servants to the same extent as is the State itself." Later decisions following the *Kinnare* doctrine have sought to advance additional explanations such as the protection of public funds and public property, and to prevent the diversion of tax moneys to the payment of damage claims. . . .

Of all of the anomalies that have resulted from legislative and judicial efforts to alleviate the injustice of the results that have flowed from the doctrine of sovereign immunity, the one most immediately pertinent to this case is the following provision of the Illinois School Code: "Any school district, including any non-high school district, which provides transportation for pupils may insure against any loss or liability of such district, its agents or employees, resulting from or incident to the ownership maintenance or use of any school bus. Such insurance shall be carried only in companies duly licensed and authorized to write such coverage in this state. Every policy for such insurance coverage issued to a school district shall provide, or be endorsed to provide, that the company issuing such policy waives any right to refuse payment or to deny liability thereunder within the limits of said policy, by reason of the non-liability of the insured school district for the wrongful or negligent acts of its agents and employees, and, its immunity from suit as an agency of the state performing governmental functions." Ill.Rev.Stat.1957, c. 122, § 29–11a.

Thus, under this statute, a person injured by an insured school district bus may recover to the extent of such insurance, whereas, under the *Kinnare* doctrine, a person injured by an uninsured school district bus can recover nothing at all.

Defendant contends that the quoted provision of the School Code constitutes a legislative determination that the public policy of this State requires that school districts be immune from tort liability. We can read no such legislative intent into the statute. Rather, we interpret that section as expressing dissatisfaction with the court-created doctrine of governmental immunity and an attempt to cut down that immunity where insurance is involved. The difficulty with this legislative effort to curtail the judicial doctrine is that it allows each school district to determine for itself whether, and to what extent, it will be financially responsible for the wrongs inflicted by it.

Coming down to the precise issue at hand, it is clear that if the above rules and precedents are strictly applied to the instant case, plaintiff's complaint, containing no allegation as to the existence of insurance, was properly dismissed. On the other hand, the complaint may be held to state a good cause of action on either one of two theories: (1) application of the doctrine of Moore v. Moyle, 405 Ill. 555, 92 N.E.2d 81, or (2) abolition of the rule that a school district is immune from tort liability.

As to the doctrine of *Moore* v. *Moyle,* that case involved an action for personal injuries against Bradley University, a charitable education institution. Traditionally, charitable and educational institutions have enjoyed the same immunity from tort liability as have governmental agencies in Illinois. . . . The trial court dismissed the complaint on the ground that Bradley was immune to tort liability. The Supreme Court reversed, holding that the complaint should not have been dismissed since it alleged that Bradley was fully insured. Unfortunately, we must admit that the opinion in that case does not make the basis of the result entirely clear. However, the court there said, 405 Ill. at page 564, 92 N.E.2d at page 86: "the question of insurance in no way affects the liability of the institution, but would only go to the question of the manner of collecting any judgment which might be obtained, without interfering with, or subjecting the trust funds or trust-held property to, the judgment. The question as to whether or not the institution is insured in no way affects its liability any more than whether a charitable institution holding private nontrust property or funds would affect its liability. These questions would only be of importance at the proper time, when the question arose as to the collection of any judgment out of nontrust property or assets. . . . Judgments may be obtained, but the question of collection of the judgment is a different matter." If we were to literally apply this reasoning to the present school district case, we would conclude that it was unnecessary that the complaint contain an allegation of the existence of insurance or other nonpublic funds. Plaintiff's complaint was sufficient as it stood without any reference to insurance, and plaintiff would be entitled to prosecute his action to judgment. Only at that time, in case of a judgment for plaintiff, would the question of insurance arise, the possession of nonpublic funds being an execution rather than a liability question. It cannot be overlooked, however, that some doubt is cast on this approach by the last paragraph of the *Moore* opinion, where the court said: "It appears that the trust funds of Bradley will not be impaired or depleted by the prosecution of the complaint, and therefore it was error to dismiss it." These words imply that if from the complaint it did not appear that the trust funds would not be impaired, the complaint should have been dismissed. If that is the true holding in the case, then liability itself, not merely the collectability of the judgment, depends on the presence of nontrust assets, as was pointed out by Justice Crampton in his dissenting opinion. The doctrine of *Moore* v. *Moyle* does not, in our opinion, offer a satisfactory solution. Like the provision of the School Code above quoted, it would allow the wrongdoer to determine its own liability.

It is a basic concept underlying the whole law of torts today that liability follows negligence, and that individuals and corporations are responsible for the negligence of their agents and employees acting in the course of their employment. The doctrine of governmental immunity runs directly counter to that basic concept. What reasons, then, are so impelling as to allow a school district, as a quasi-municipal corporation, to commit wrongdoing without any responsibility to its victims, while any individual or private corporation would be called to task in court for such tortious conduct?

The original basis of the immunity rule has been called a "survival of the medieval idea that the sovereign can do no wrong," or that "the King can do no wrong." (38 Am.Jur., Mun.Corps., sec. 573, p. 266.) In Kinnare v. City of Chicago, 171 Ill. 332, 49 N.E. 536, 537, the first Illinois case announcing the tort immunity of school districts, the court said: "The state acts in its sovereign capacity, and does not submit its action to the judgment of courts, and is not liable for the torts or negligence of its agents, and a corporation created by the state as a mere agency for the more efficient exercise of governmental functions is likewise exempted from the obligation to respond in damages, as master, for negligent acts of its servants to the same extent as is the state itself, unless such liability is expressly provided by the statute creating such agency." This was nothing more nor less than an extension of the theory of sovereign immunity. Professor Borchard has said that how immunity ever came to be applied in the United States of America is one of the mysteries of legal evolution. (Borchard, Governmental Liability in Tort, 34 Yale L.J. 1, 6.) And how it was then infiltrated into the law controlling the liability of local governmental units has been described as one of the amazing chapters of American common-law jurisprudence. . . .

We are of the opinion that school district immunity cannot be justified on this theory. As was stated by one court, "The whole doctrine of governmental immunity from liability for tort rests upon a rotten foundation. It is almost incredible that in this modern age of comparative sociological enlightenment, and in a republic, the medieval absolutism supposed to be implicit in the maxim, 'the King can do no wrong,' should exempt the various branches of the government from liability for their torts, and that the entire burden of damage resulting from the wrongful acts of the government should be imposed upon the single individual who suffers the injury, rather than distributed among the entire community constituting the government, where it could be borne without hardship upon any individual, and where it justly belongs." Barker v. City of Santa Fe, 47 N.M. 85, 136 P.2d 480, 482. Likewise, we agree with the Supreme Court of Florida that in preserving the sovereign immunity theory, courts have overlooked the fact that the Revolutionary War was fought to abolish that "divine right of Kings" on which the theory is based.

The other chief reason advanced in support of the immunity rule in the more recent cases is the protection of public funds and public property. This corresponds to the "no fund" or "trust fund" theory upon which charitable immunity is based. This rationale was relied on in Thomas v. Broadlands Community Consolidated School Dist., 348 Ill.App. 567, 109 N.E.2d 636, 640, where the court stated that the reason for the immunity rule is "that it is the public policy to protect public funds and public property, to prevent the diversion of tax moneys, in this case school funds, to the payment of damage claims." This reasoning seems to follow the line that it is better for the individual to suffer than for the public to be inconvenienced. From it proceeds defendant's argument that school districts would be bankrupted and education impeded if said districts were called upon to compensate children tortiously injured by the negligence of those districts' agents and employees.

We do not believe that in this present day and age, when public education constitutes one of the biggest businesses in the country, that school immunity can be justified on the protection-of-public-funds theory.

In the first place, analysis of the theory shows that it is based on the idea that payment of damage claims is a diversion of educational funds to an improper purpose. As many writers have pointed out, the fallacy in this argument is that it assumes the very point which is sought to be proved, i.e., that payment of damage claims is not a proper purpose. "Logically, the 'No-fund' or 'trust fund' theory is without merit because it is of value only after a determination of what is a proper school expenditure. To predicate immunity upon the theory of a trust fund is merely to argue in a circle, since it assumes an answer to the very question at issue, to wit, what is an educational purpose? Many disagree with the 'no-fund' doctrine to the extent of ruling that the payment of funds for judgments resulting from accidents or injuries in schools is an educational purpose. Nor can it be properly argued that as a result of the abandonment of the common-law rule the district would be completely bankrupt. California, Tennessee, New York, Washington and other states have not been compelled to shut down their schools." (Rosenfield, Governmental Immunity from Liability for Tort in School Accidents, 5 Legal Notes on Local Government, 376–377.) Moreover, this argument is even more fallacious when viewed in the light of the Illinois School Code, which authorizes appropriations for "transportation purposes" . . . and authorizes expenditures of school tax funds for liability insurance covering school bus operations . . . . It seems to us that the payment of damage claims incurred as an adjunct to transportation is as much a "transportation purpose" and therefore a proper authorized purpose as are payments of other expenses involved in operating school buses. If tax funds can properly be spent to pay premiums on liability insurance, there seems to be no good reason why they cannot be spent to pay the liability itself in the absence of insurance.

Neither are we impressed with defendant's plea that the abolition of immunity would create grave and unpredictable problems of school finance and administration. We are in accord with Dean Green when he disposed of this problem as follows: "There is considerable talk in the opinions about the tremendous financial burdens tort liability would cast upon the taxpayer. In some opinions it is stated that this factor is sufficient to warrant the courts in protecting the taxpayer through the immunity which they have thrown around municipal corporations. While this factor may have had compulsion on some of the earlier courts, I seriously doubt that it has any great weight with the courts in recent years. In the first place, taxation is not the subject matter of judicial concern where justice to the individual citizen is involved. It is the business of other departments of government to provide the funds required to pay the damages assessed against them by the courts. Moreover, the same policy that would protect governmental corporations from the payment of damages for the injuries they bring upon others would be equally pertinent to a like immunity to protect private corporations, for conceivably many essential private concerns could also be put out of business by the damages they could incur under tort liability. But as a matter of fact, this argument has no practical basis. Private concerns have rarely been greatly embarrassed, and in no instance, even where immunity is not recognized, has a municipality been seriously handicapped by tort liability. This argument is like so many of the horribles paraded in the early tort cases when courts were fashioning the boundaries of tort law. It has been thrown in simply because there was nothing better at hand. The public's willingness to stand up and pay the cost of its enterprises carried out through municipal corporations is no less than its insistence that individuals and groups pay the cost of their enterprises. Tort liability is in fact a very small item in the budget of any well organized enterprise." Green, Freedom of Litigation, 38 Ill.L.Rev. 355, 378.

We are of the opinion that none of the reasons advanced in support of school district immunity have any true validity today. Further we believe that abolition of such immunity may tend to decrease the frequency of school bus accidents by coupling the power to transport pupils with the responsibility of exercising care in the selection and supervision of the drivers. As Dean Harno said: "A municipal corporation today is an active and virile creature capable of inflicting much harm. Its civil responsibility should be co-extensive. The municipal corporation looms up definitely and emphatically in our law, and what is more, it can and does commit wrongs. This being so, it must assume the responsibilities of the position it occupies in society." (Harno, Tort Immunity of Municipal Corporations, 4 Ill.L.Q. 28, 42.) School districts will be encouraged to exercise greater care in the matter of transporting pupils and also to carry adequate insurance covering that transportation, thus spreading the risk of accident, just as the other costs of education are spread over the entire district. At least some school authorities themselves have recognized the need for the vital change which we are making. See Editorial, 100 American School Board Journal 55, Issue No. 6, June, 1940.

> The nation's largest business is operating on a blueprint prepared a hundred, if not a thousand, years ago. The public school system in the United States, which constitutes the largest single business in the country, is still under the domination of a legal principle which in great measure continued unchanged since the Middle Ages, to the effect that a person has no financial recourse for injuries sustained as a result of the performance of the State's functions . . . . That such a gigantic system, involving so large an appropriation of public funds and so tremendous a proportion of the people of the United States, should operate under the principles of a rule of law so old and so outmoded would seem impossible were it not actually true. Rosenfield, Governmental Immunity from Liability for Tort in School Accidents, 9 Law and Contemporary Problems 358, 359.

We conclude that the rule of school district tort immunity is unjust, unsupported by any valid reason, and has no rightful place in modern day society.

Defendant strongly urges that if said immunity is to be abolished, it should be done by the legislature, not by this court. With this contention we must disagree. The doctrine of school district immunity was created by this court alone. Having found that doctrine to be unsound and unjust under present conditions, we consider that we have not only the power, but the duty, to abolish that immunity. "We closed our courtroom doors without legislative help, and we can likewise open them." Pierce v. Yakima Valley Memorial Hospital Ass'n, 43 Wash.2d 162, 260 P.2d 765, 774.

PROPRIETARY FUNCTIONS

Some courts, being reluctant to totally abrogate immunity, have sought ways to avoid direct confrontation with the issue. In order to sidestep the overall problem, courts have settled tort actions in several states on the basis of the activity or function that was being performed by the school district when the injury occurred. In this regard, we should note that school districts operate in a dual capacity: performing functions that are strictly governmental the majority of the time they also, on some occasions, perform proprietary functions or functions that may be performed by a private corporation.

Proprietary functions have been defined as things not normally required by law or things not governmental in nature. If a function is within the scope of the public school operation, as expressed or implied by statute, then the function is governmental and not proprietary. Courts have generally held that school athletic contests are governmental functions.[78] While the courts have rather consistently held that municipalities are liable for injuries arising out of functions for which admission is charged or some financial gain is realized, they have been reluctant to generally apply this standard to school districts.

Thus, if a spectator or participant is injured at an athletic contest, the courts will not usually impose liability on the school district even when a fee is charged and the school has realized a profit. Of course, exceptions exist to all general rules, and in regard to this question, one court held that when a school district leased its football stadium to another for a fee, the lessor was held to have been engaged in a proprietary activity and was liable for injury to a spectator who was injured when a railing broke.

In following the rule that school districts are immune from liability for incidents arising during functions that charge fees, a Tennessee court said:

> The mere fact that an admission fee was charged by the high school does not make the transaction an enterprise for profit. . . . The duties of a County Board of Education are limited to the operation of the schools. This is a governmental function. Therefore, in legal contemplation, there is no such thing as such a Board acting in a proprietary capacity for private gain.[79]

Texas[80] and Kansas[81] courts have said, *in dicta*, that if a school district can and does perform proprietary activities, then it must answer in damages when guilty in tort for injuries resulting from such functions. The Supreme Court of Oregon has laid down a test for distinguishing proprietary from governmental functions. "The underlying test is whether the act is for the common good of all without the element of special corporate benefit or pecuniary profit."[82]

The rule, therefore, may probably be summarized: as long as the purpose of the activity is educational and for the common good and the profit accrued is only incidental, the activity is governmental in nature.

*Holder of a Free Pass to a Football
Game Was an Invitee to Whom the
School District Owed a Duty of
Reasonable Care*

TANARI v. SCHOOL
DIRECTORS OF DISTRICT
NO. 502

Supreme Court of Illinois, 1977.
69 Ill.2d 630, 14 Ill.Dec. 874,
373 N.E.2d 5.

UNDERWOOD, Justice: Plaintiff, Flora Tanari, brought an action . . .
seeking damages for injuries she sustained when she allegedly was knocked
to the ground by a group of children engaged in horseplay at a high school
football game sponsored by defendant on its premises. The complaint
alleged ordinary negligence on the part of defendant in failing to provide
adequate supervision and control of children at the game. At the close of
the evidence, the trial court granted the defendant's motion for a directed
verdict on the ground that plaintiff was a licensee on defendant's premises;
that defendant therefore only owed her the duty to refrain from wilful and
wanton misconduct; and that breach of such duty had neither been alleged
nor proved at trial. . . .

Plaintiff, age 64, was employed as a bus driver by an individual who had
a contract with the defendant school district to transport students to and
from school. She had been so employed for twenty-seven years and had
attended all of the local high school football games for the last twenty-five
years. On October 13, 1972, plaintiff attended the Hall Township High
School homecoming football game with her daughter, son-in-law and
grandchildren. The game was held on defendant's premises at a sports
stadium under defendant's supervision and control. Plaintiff entered the
stadium using a complimentary season pass issued by the defendant. As she
was walking toward her seat, she noticed a crowd of boys and girls playing
near the northwest end of the stadium, and the next thing she knew she had
been knocked to the ground by a "big" boy who fell on top of her. The boy,
who was never identified, got up, apologized and hurried away. . . .

The athletic director of Hall Township High School testified that he had
hired off-duty policemen and teachers to keep order at all high school
football games conducted by the defendant. . . . He responded in the
affirmative when asked if he had seen boys and girls at almost every game
"playing tag, or horseplaying and roughing it up" in the area in question.
However, when he was later asked if there was "rowdiness and horseplaying
by these kids in that area," he responded that he did not know whether it
should be called rowdiness and horseplay but the children were definitely
there. He further testified that on previous occasions he had tried to
"correct" the children but that, as soon as he left, they were back at it again.
He knew from his personal observation that a policeman was in the area of
the accident on the night in question.

The trial court allowed the defendant's motion for a directed verdict on
the sole ground that plaintiff was a licensee on the defendant's premises and

that there was no proof whatsoever that defendant had breached its duty to refrain from willful and wanton misconduct. . . . Considering the state of the record before us, we are unable to concur with the appellate court's conclusions regarding defendant's immunity under the above-referred-to statutes and are likewise unable to agree with the court's further determination that "irrespective of the standard of care which might have been required in this case, no verdict in favor of the plaintiff could stand as against the defendant school directors."

The Local Governmental and Governmental Employees Tort Immunity Act (hereafter referred to as the Tort Immunity Act) provides, *inter alia,* that "a public employee serving in a position involving the determination of policy or the exercise of discretion is not liable for an injury resulting from his act or omission in determining policy when acting in the exercise of such discretion even though abused." Section 2–109 of the Act also provides that "[a] local public entity is not liable for an injury resulting from an act or omission of its employee where the employee is not liable." . . .

At the time of plaintiff's injury section 24–24 of the School Code provided in pertinent part:

> Teachers and other certificated educational employees shall maintain discipline in the schools. In all matters relating to the discipline in and conduct of the schools and the school children, they stand in the relation of parents and guardians to the pupils. This relationship shall extend to all activities connected with the school program and may be exercised at any time for the safety and supervision of the pupils in the absence of their parents or guardians.

Since the foregoing statute specifically confers upon educators the status of parent or guardian to the students, and since a parent is not liable for injuries to his child absent willful and wanton misconduct . . . it therefore follows that the same standard applies as between educator and student. . . . We [have] held that section 24–24 of the School Code was intended to confer *in loco parentis* status in nondisciplinary as well as disciplinary matters. . . .

In our view, section 24–24 of the School Code is not applicable here in view of the absence of any *in loco parentis* relationship between the injured plaintiff and the certificated employees of the defendant school district who allegedly failed to exercise proper supervision. . . . [S]ection 24–24 reflects "a legislative determination that educators should stand in the place of a parent or guardian in matters relating to discipline, the conduct of the schools and the school children. It is this status as parent or guardian which requires a plaintiff to prove willful and wanton misconduct in order to impose liability upon educators." That status is clearly lacking here, and it seems evident that the purpose of the immunity which arises from such status would not be served by extending it to immunize school districts from liability to third parties for ordinary negligence in situations such as that now before us. We accordingly hold that section 24–24 of the School Code does not provide any basis for affirmance of the trial court's decision in this case.

It is unnecessary to dwell at length on the common law distinctions between invitees and licensees which have evolved over the years. It suffices to observe that the general definition of an invitee is a visitor who comes upon premises at the invitation of the owner in connection with the owner's business or related activity. . . . Licensees are persons who have not been invited to enter upon the owner's premises and who come there for their own purposes and not those of the owner. . . . However, their presence is condoned by the owner, which distinguishes them from trespassers. The trial court concluded in the case at bar that since the plaintiff had not purchased a ticket but rather had attended the football game using a complimentary season pass, there was an absence of "commercial benefit" to the defendant school district, and she must therefore be considered a licensee. For the reasons hereafter stated, we must disagree with that conclusion.

In determining whether or not a person is an invitee or a licensee in a given situation, appellate courts in this State have often looked at the surrounding circumstances to determine whether, as between the visitor and the owner, there was a "mutuality of interest in the subject to which the visitor's business relates" . . . "a mutually beneficial interest" . . . a "mutuality of interest" . . . a "mutuality of benefit or a benefit to the owner" . . . or whether the visitor had come to "transact business in which he and the owner have a mutual interest or to promote some real or fancied material, financial, or economic interest of the owner". . . . Such inquiries into the purpose and nature of the visit were deemed relevant, particularly in cases involving implied invitations, to ascertain whether the visitor was upon the owner's premises within the scope and purpose of the invitation or for some other reason.

That type of analysis is not necessary here. In our opinion, the complimentary pass issued to plaintiff was tantamount to an express invitation to attend Hall Township High School football games, and there can be no question about the fact that at the time of her injury, plaintiff was acting within the scope of that invitation. Unlike a person who comes upon an owner's premises for his own purposes rather than those of the owner and whose presence is merely condoned by the owner, plaintiff in this case was expressly invited and encouraged to come to the defendant's football stadium to swell the crowd in support of its team. In this type of situation, it would be entirely illogical to conclude that a person attending the game using a complimentary pass provided by the school district should be owed a lesser duty of care than a person otherwise similarly situated who had purchased a ticket. In our view, both persons should be owed the same duty of reasonable care, and we so hold.

Upon application of a reasonable care standard to the case at bar, we cannot conclude that all of the evidence, when viewed in its aspect most favorable to the plaintiff, so overwhelmingly favors the defendant that no verdict for the plaintiff could ever stand. . . . The question of whether defendant failed to exercise reasonable care in supervising children attending the football game and whether such failure, if found to exist, was the proximate cause of plaintiff's injuries, should have been submitted to the jury. . . .

Reversed and remanded.

*School District Not Immune
Regardless of Whether It Was
Performing a Governmental or
Proprietary Function*

BOARD OF SCHOOL
COMMISSIONERS OF MOBILE
COUNTY v. CAVER

Supreme Court of Alabama, 1978.
355 So.2d 712.

BLOODWORTH, Justice. . . .

Plaintiff, Caver, a student who was allegedly injured by a Mobile County School Board bus while she was standing in the school yard, brought suit for negligence, and the Board moved to dismiss her complaint because of sovereign immunity. . . .

Defendant, Board, contends that the issue of sovereign immunity was decided in its favor in Sims v. Etowah County Board of Education, 337 So.2d 1310 (Ala.1976), which held in a plurality decision, (based upon an interpretation of Tit. 52, § 99, Code of Alabama 1940) that a school board is immune from suit in tort.

Although at first blush, the Board's argument seems an appealing one, for *Sims* appears to foreclose further inquiry into this question, a close reading of *Sims* and an examination of Act No. 480, Acts of Alabama, Regular Session 1969, as well as § 270 of the Constitution of 1901, convinces us that the Mobile County School Board is amenable to suit in tort.

Mr. Justice Stakely, in Morgan v. Board of School Commissioners of Mobile County, 248 Ala. 22, 26 So.2d 108 (1946), gave the history of the Mobile County Board of School Commissioners. In that opinion, he pointed out that the Mobile County School Board has been exempted, in large part, from the general scheme of public school legislation ever since 1854 when the State of Alabama set up its first comprehensive school system.

That legislative policy, which is based upon the fact that Mobile County established its school system before the State did so, continues to this date, as evidenced by Section 270 of Article XIV of the Alabama Constitution. . . .

This limitation on legislative power is restrictive in its scope and purpose and is to be strictly construed. . . .

Act Number 480 (the latest amendatory act regulating the public schools in Mobile County) falls within neither one of these two exceptions. That act provides, *inter alia,* that, "The said Board shall be a body corporate; and may have a common seal; *may sue and be sued* . . . ." (Emphasis supplied.) Clearly, the authority to "sue and be sued" is not one of those educational areas in which the legislature may not act concerning the Mobile County School Board.

We stressed in *Sims* v. *Etowah County Board of Education,* supra, as well as in Enterprise City Board of Education v. Miller, 348 So.2d 782 (1977), that the sovereign immunity we held was due to be accorded those boards of education flowed directly from the statutes. In both cases, the pertinent statutes stated that the county and city boards of education, respectively, "may sue." There was no corresponding provision in those statutes that the respective boards could "be sued." For that reason, we said in each case, *inter alia*, that the respective boards of education were immune from suit in tort.

In the case at bar, by contrast, Act Number 480 clearly states that the Mobile County School Board "may sue and be sued." We hold, therefore, as we said in *Sims* and *Enterprise City Board*, that the statute must be given effect, and, therefore, the Mobile County School Board may be sued in tort.

Defendant Board argues, however, that the phrase "sue and be sued" is not an all-encompassing term, and that if the county school board may be sued, it may only be sued for acts performed in its corporate or proprietary capacity as opposed to acts performed in its governmental capacity. In other words, defendant Board would have us resort to determining whether the act is governmental or corporate. As we held in Jackson v. City of Florence, 294 Ala. 592, 320 So.2d 68 (1975) . . . however, these distinctions are tenuous, at best, and our continued reliance upon them, in the context of sovereign immunity cases, would serve no useful purpose.

For the foregoing reasons, we hold that the trial judge's order is due to be affirmed.

Affirmed.

NOTES

Nuisance. Another device used by the courts to partially skirt the boundaries of immunity is the nuisance doctrine. A "nuisance" has been defined as "the existence or creation of a dangerous, unsafe, or offensive condition which is likely to cause injury, harm, or inconvenience to others." A more complete definition has been given by a Connecticut Court:

> to constitute a nuisance there must have arisen a condition, the natural tendency of which is to create danger or inflict injury upon person or property . . . there must be more than an act or failure to act on the part of the defendant . . . the danger created must have been a continuing one . . . . Bush v. City of Norwalk, 122 Conn. 426, 189 A. 608 (1937).

A leading case in which a school district was held to have created a nuisance was one in which snow had fallen from the roof of a school building onto adjacent property, damaging the property. The owner was also injured when he fell on the ice. The court held that in this case there was both nuisance and trespass. The court said:

> The plaintiff had the right to the exclusive use and enjoyment of his property, and the defendant had no more right to erect a building in such a manner that the ice and snow would inevitably slide from the roof, and be precipitated upon the plaintiff's premises, than it would have to accumulate water upon its own premises, and then permit it to flow in a body upon his premises. Ferris v. Board of Education of Detroit, 122 Mich. 315, 81 N.W. 98 (1899).

In keeping with the legal definition, a dangerous condition must be created by the school district for nuisance to exist. In Kansas, an action was brought to recover damages for injury sustained by a nine-year-old pupil who slipped and fell on a wet lavatory floor. Pupils had made the floor wet and slippery by throwing wet paper towels and splashing water. The plaintiff claimed the district was maintaining a nuisance and was therefore liable. In response, the court held that the school did not create the nuisance since pupils could be expected to splash water and throw wet towels on the floor while using the lavatory and that wash basins were a necessary part of the school building equipment. Jones v. Kansas City, 176 Kan. 406, 271 P.2d 803 (1954). The adequacy of supervision on the part of school personnel was another matter. Adequacy of supervision is not a question to be dealt with in a nuisance action, since to constitute nuisance there must be a continuing hazard and there must be more than a mere failure to act on the part of the defendant. Rose v. Board of Education, 184 Kan. 486, 337 P.2d 652 (1959). It seems safe to conclude that while the "nuisance" theory is a viable method of averting direct confrontation with the governmental immunity issue, the courts in other jurisdictions will not plunge headlong toward its use as piecemeal abrogation. This, of course, does not mean courts will never employ the device since it is an acceptable legal doctrine, but it does indicate a reluctance on the part of the courts to tamper with the doctrine of governmental immunity in this limited fashion.

DEFAMATION

Defamation is constituted of the twin torts of libel and slander. On their face a distinction between libel as written and slander as oral communication are easily distinguishable. However, other forms of communication such as acts or gestures, motion pictures, radio or television complicate the dichotomy. Some courts simply maintain that defamation designed for visual perception is libel and all other forms of communication are slander.[83] General acceptance by the courts is found in the following definitions: libel is a malicious publication, expressed in either printing or writing, or by signs and pictures, while slander is personal imputation effected by writings, pictures, or signs, both of which tend to injure a party's situation in society.[84]

Teachers and school administrators are particularly susceptible to actions in defamation because of the sensitivity of personal information with which they come into contact each day. Teachers, as a matter of routine, process and communicate information that relates to pupil performance, the misuse of which could potentially harm the student's reputation and stigmatize his or her future. The problem of the administrator is even more complex in communication of information concerning teacher performance to other administrators or to school board members. Public interest in education, though, makes it absolutely essential that proper pupil and teacher evaluations are made and that public school officials and employees not be subjected to constant fear of personal liability. Because of this important public interest, the courts have generally recognized that statements regarding school matters are qualifiedly privileged if made by persons having a common duty or interest in the information and acting in good faith.[85] "In the absence of malice, a school official is not liable to a teacher for performing the duties of his office."[86] A teacher likewise has a qualified or conditional privilege when acting in good faith in school matters but the qualified privilege is not unlimited and no privilege attaches to a teacher's entry in a school register to the effect that a certain pupil "was ruined by tobacco and whisky."[87] Absolute privileges are only afforded those individuals who perform vital governmental functions that the courts have defined as judicial proceedings, legislative proceedings, and certain executive proceedings. With the judiciary, absolute privilege extends only to the particular statements that are relevant or pertinent to the case at bar.[88] In the legislature, complete privilege extends to statements made in the course of debate, voting, or reports on work performed in committees.[89] Public officers holding executive positions also have absolute immunity for communications made in connection with the performance of their official duties.

While courts generally hold that school superintendents have a conditional or qualified privilege, some courts have maintained that public policy requires that superintendents be given an absolute privilege in evaluating teacher activities before a school board. Similarly, school board members have been held to have absolute privilege in imputing inefficiency and lack of qualification in evaluating a school superintendent's performance.[90]

The more common precedent to follow, though, is that officials, teachers and others dealing in the public interest context have at least a qualified privilege. This conditional immunity can even extend to parents presenting a petition before a school board to the effect that a teacher was "incompetent."[91]

A qualified privilege requires that the statements be made in good faith and without malice. One court explained such privileges in this way:

> If a communication comes within the class denominated absolute privileged or qualifiedly privileged, no recovery can be had. Privileged communications are divided and defined as follows: (1) that the communication was made by the defendant in good faith, without malice, not voluntarily but in answer to an inquiry, and in the reasonable protection of his own interest or performance of a duty to society; (2) that the defendant must honestly believe the communication to be true; (3) there must have been reasonable or probable grounds known to him for the suspicion; (4) that the communication, if made in answer to an inquiry, must not go further than to truly state the facts upon which the suspicion was founded, and to satisfy the inquirer that these were reasons for the suspicion.[92]

Under this definition, it is clear that the communication must be made in good faith, without malice, upon reasonable grounds, in answer to inquiry, and, importantly, it must be made with regard to assisting or protecting the interests of either of the parties involved or in performing a duty to society. The school official or employee's communication is qualifiedly privileged if it is prompted by a duty owed to either the public or a third party and is made in good faith and without malice.

In some states, truth is a defense for a defamation action. In these jurisdictions it is not necessary to show that the statement is the literal truth, but it is adequate to show that the imputation is only substantially true. In a Texas case, the president of a commercial college was asked for information concerning a former student. He replied that the man had been a student at the institution but had not graduated. He related that, in fact, the student had been dismissed from school for stealing a typewriter and had been placed in jail. Consequently, the student sued for damages and was able to show that the statement was untrue. The president could not show that the statement was even substantially true; therefore, the case was decided in favor of the student.[93]

While some states still use truth as a defense, the more modern concept is that even if an utterance is the truth, it must be made with good intentions and for justifiable reasons. To volunteer damaging information when the interests of the school or children are not at stake may well be considered by the courts to constitute malice. Further, if an unintentionally erroneous report is made conveying information potentially harmful to a child's reputation, failure to correct the error may constitute malice sufficient to destroy a conditional privilege.[94]

PUPIL RECORDS AND INFORMATION

Teachers, guidance counselors, and principals are generally involved in the release of pupil information and records to other teachers, professional personnel within the school, prospective employers outside the school, or other educational institutions to which pupils may be applying for entrance. Considering these areas of pupil information flow, common law suggests the following rules be followed. First, information should not be related to other teachers or administrators unless the motive and purpose is to assist and enhance the educational opportunities of the pupil. Transmittal should be made in the proper channels and to persons assigned the responsibility for the relevant educational function. Gossip or careless talk among teachers, which is not calculated to help the student, is not protected by the cloak of qualified privilege. Second, pupil information should be transmitted to prospective employers only upon request. This protects the teacher from the presumption that the transmittal was made with malice.[95] A qualified privilege has been upheld when a communicator responded to a questionnaire and only gave answers to specific questions.[96] It is a good practice not to release information over a telephone unless the identity of the caller is absolutely certain. Third, records should be released to colleges and other institutions only if there is statutory or regulatory requirement for the transmittals or if the pupil requests the conveyance. Most states have laws or regulations that require the transfer of elementary and secondary school pupils' records when they change schools. This, of course, facilitates the transition for the pupil as well as for the school and provides needed data for placement and is, therefore, proper.

Beyond the common law, federal statute intervenes to further protect the student. The Family Educational Rights and Privacy Act was passed in August, 1974, as an amendment to the Omnibus Education Bill.[97] The act establishes standards to which school districts must adhere in handling student records. Failure to abide by the law can result in the withdrawal of federal education funds.

Essentially, the amendment provides that parents and emancipated students shall have the right to review and inspect all official records, files, and data concerning the student. Information routinely gathered and shared by school personnel are included. The data to which access is given are not limited to completed grade reports, achievement test scores, attendance data, health data, but also includes behavior reports and teacher and counselor ratings. Personal notes kept by teachers or counselors that are not communicated or routinely shared are probably exempt.[98]

The school cannot release individual student information unless written consent has been given by the student or the student's legal guardian or the school is under court order or subpoena. School officials, including all teachers with a "legitimate educational interest" and school officials of other schools and school systems to which the student is transferred or intends to transfer have the right to see the student's records. In the event that records are transferred, the parent or emancipated student must be notified of the record transfer, receive a copy if requested, and have the opportunity to have a hearing to challenge the contents.

Negative Recommendation Is Protected
by a Conditional Privilege

HETT v. PLOETZ

Supreme Court of Wisconsin, 1963.
20 Wis.2d 55, 121 N.W.2d 270.

Hett brought this action to recover damages for injury to his professional reputation from an allegedly libelous publication by Ploetz. . . .

From 1956 to 1959 Hett had been employed as a speech therapist in the school system of the city of Cudahy, Wisconsin. His schedule required that he travel to six different schools and teach those pupils who were in need of his specialty. . . .

Based upon their analysis of Hett's qualifications, the principals of the six schools in which Hett taught reported to Ploetz that they did not recommend renewal of Hett's contract for the 1959–1960 school year.

While the principals did not recommend Hett's retention for that year, Ploetz decided that because he had been the superintendent for only six months it would be unfair to Hett to recommend his dismissal.

Ploetz informed Hett that his contract was not going to be renewed and told him that it would be in his best interest to resign so that a dismissal would not appear on his record. Hett resigned. . . .

On November 9, 1959, Hett applied for a position as a speech therapist at the Southern Wisconsin Colony and Training School, Union Grove, Wisconsin. In his application he stated that the reason he left the Cudahy school system was that there was a lack of advancement opportunities. He listed Ploetz as a reference and gave permission to the Southern Colony officials to communicate with Ploetz. . . .

GORDON, Justice. The plaintiff contends that he was libeled by the defendant's response to an inquiry from a prospective employer of the plaintiff. Hett had not only given Ploetz's name as a reference but had also given express permission to the prospective employer to communicate with Ploetz.

We must resolve two questions. The first is whether any privilege insulates the defendant's letter; the second is whether an issue of malice exists for trial.

Conditional Privilege It is clear that Ploetz's allegedly defamatory letter was entitled to a conditional privilege. Ploetz was privileged to give a critical appraisal concerning his former employee so long as such appraisal was made for the valid purpose of enabling a prospective employer to evaluate the employee's qualifications. The privilege is said to be "conditional" because of the requirements that the declaration be reasonably calculated to accomplish the privileged purpose and that it be made without malice. . . . Lord Blackburn has said:

> Where a person is so situated that it becomes right in the interests of society that he should tell to a third person facts, then, if he *bona fide* and without malice does tell them, it is a privileged communication. See Rude v. Mass, supra, p. 329, 48 N.W. p. 557.

The public school official who expresses an opinion as to the qualifications of a person who has submitted an application for employment as a school teacher should enjoy the benefits of a conditional privilege.

The Absence of Malice As previously noted, the employee had given Ploetz's name as a reference and had authorized that an inquiry be made of him. The letter contains certain factual matters as well as expressions of opinion. The factual portions are not contradicted by any pleading before this court. Thus, the following statement contained in the letter written by Ploetz stands unchallenged:

> Last year, our six Principals and Elementary Coordinator unanimously recommended that he be no longer retained in our system as a speech correctionist. He, therefore, was not offered a contract to return this year.

The expression of opinion of which Hett complains is contained in the following portion of the defendant's letter:

> We feel that Mr. Hett is not getting the results that we expected in this very important field. I, personally, feel that Mr. Hett does not belong in the teaching field. He has a rather odd personality, and it is rather difficult for him to gain the confidence of his fellow workers and the boys and girls with whom he works.

In our opinion, the record before us establishes that this expression of opinion is not founded in malice. The background of the relationship of Hett and Ploetz satisfactorily demonstrates that the latter's negative recommendation was grounded on the record and not upon malice. Ploetz was not an intermeddler; he had a proper interest in connection with the letter he wrote. . . .

The plaintiff has failed to recite any evidentiary facts which are sufficient to raise questions for trial. His allegations that the letter contains defamatory material are mere conclusions. No presumption of malice has arisen; no showing of express malice has been presented.

In Otten v. Schutt (1962), 15 Wis.2d 497, 503, 113 N.W.2d 152, 155, this court stated:

> The law relating to defamatory communications is based on public policy. The law will impute malice where a defamatory publication is made without sufficient cause or excuse, or where necessary to protect the interests of society and the security of character and reputation; but where the welfare of society is better promoted by a freedom of expression, malice will not be imputed. . . .

Public policy requires that malice not be imputed in cases such as this, for otherwise one who enjoys a conditional privilege might be reluctant to give a sincere, yet critical, response to a request for an appraisal of a prospective employee's qualifications.

. . . A thorough examination of the entire record compels our conclusion that the respondent is entitled to the benefit of a conditional privilege.

Judgment affirmed.

NOTES

1. If a statement is made by defendant in response to an inquiry by the plaintiff, then a conditional privilege may be elevated to the status of an absolute privilege. An "absolute privilege is confined to relatively few situations. It is accorded, judicial proceedings, legislative proceedings, proceedings of executive officers charged with responsibility of importance, publications made *with consent of the plaintiff* and communications between husband and wife." Prosser, *Law of Torts*, 2nd ed., West Publishing Company, Walker v. D'Alesandro, 212 Md. 163, 129 A.2d 148 (1957).

   The Supreme Court of Missouri invoked this rule when a superintendent responded to a question by a teacher in a hearing before the school board.

   > When plaintiff asked the defendant at the board meeting why she was not going to be re-employed the following school year the superintendent should be at liberty to say to her, "Miss Williams, you have disobeyed school rules and regulations, you are insubordinate and are insufficient and inadequate with your students." In that situation he (superintendent) is absolutely protected in his explanation to plaintiff. Williams v. School District of Springfield R–12, 447 S.W.2d 256 (Mo.1969).

2. Would a school superintendent be protected by an absolute privilege in responding to a similar teacher inquiry at a teachers' meeting rather than at a school board meeting?

3. In the case of De Bolt v. McBrien, 96 Neb. 237, 147 N.W. 462 (1914), the court applied the absolute privilege rule to a state superintendent of public instruction's statement to the county supervisor accusing the plaintiff of poker-playing and being under the influence of liquor.

4. The Oklahoma Appellate Court found that defamatory statements about the school librarian made by the president and dean of the medical school at a session of the board of regents were absolutely privileged. See Hughes v. Bizzel, 189 Okl. 472, 117 P.2d 763 (1941).

5. In other related cases see Haskell v. Perkins, 165 Ill.App. 144 (1911); Forsythe v. Durham, 270 N.Y. 141, 200 N.E. 674 (1936); and Maurice v. Worden, 54 Md. 233 (1880).

6. Parents and patrons of the school have a qualified privilege in disclosing information at a school board meeting. Where school patrons presented the school trustees with a letter charging that the teacher failed to keep proper order and discipline and allowed older boys to take improper privileges with her and girl students, the court held that if the defendants believed that the school was conducted as stated then it was their right to complain to the trustees since they were the only ones authorized to remedy it. According to the court, the central issue was whether the letter was presented with malicious intent. In reversing a judgment in favor of the teacher, the court remanded the case for jury determination of whether malice existed. According to the court, the jury should be instructed to find that malice was present if the publication by defendants was not made in good faith and had actually intended to injure the teacher, not merely to correct the school situation. Malone v. Carrico, 16 Ky.Law Rev. 155 (1894).

7. Residents and patrons of a school district were held to be protected by a qualified privilege when they presented a petition to the school board stating that "we do not think she (plaintiff teacher) is a competent teacher and has but little control over the school." The court said that if the occasion, the motive, and the cause be proper, the publication or communication does not imply malice. To overcome a qualified privilege, malice must be proved by the person claiming to have been defamed, and the mere falsity of the alleged defamatory matter is not sufficient. Hoover v. Jordan, 27 Colo.App. 515, 150 P. 333 (1915); see also, 40 A.L.R.3d 490.

8. Where a tenured teacher and assistant principal were responsible for investigating suspected drug involvement of students and counseling with students and their parents, their communications to parent of high school student concerning the sale of drugs in plaintiffs' place of business were qualifiedly privileged. Comments were made in good faith and on an occasion that properly served their duty and under circumstances that were fairly warranted by the occasion. The teacher and assistant principal were not liable to plaintiffs for defamation in the absence of a showing of express malice. The court defined *qualified privilege* as: "A communication, although it contains criminating matter, is privileged when made in good faith upon any subject in which the party communicating has an interest, or in reference to which he has a right or duty, if made to a person having a corresponding interest, right, or duty, and made upon an occasion to properly serve such right, interest, or duty, and in a manner and under circumstances fairly warranted by the occasion and the duty, right, or interest, and not so made as to unnecessarily or unduly injure another, or to show express malice." Chapman v. Furlough, 334 So.2d 293.

In defining *good faith* the court quoted an older Florida case saying: "Good faith, a right, duty, or interest in a proper subject, a proper occasion, and a proper communication to those having a like right, duty, or interest, are all essential to constitute words spoken, that are actionable per se, a privileged communication, so as to make the proof by the Plaintiff of express malice essential to liability. In determining whether or not a communication is privileged, the nature of the subject, the right, duty, or interest of the parties in such subject, the time, place and circumstances of the occasion, and the manner, character, and extent of the communication, should all be considered. When all these facts and circumstances are conceded, a court may decide whether a communication is a privileged one, so as to require the Plaintiff to prove express malice . . . ." Abraham v. Baldwin, 52 Fla. 151, 42 So. 591 (1906).

Qualified Privilege Protects Parents
Who Convey Information About
Teachers

DESSELLE v. GUILLORY

Court of Appeal of Louisiana, Third
Circuit, 1981.
407 So.2d 79.

SWIFT, Judge. . . .

In July of 1979, Mrs. Jane Guillory was a counselor at a summer church camp for girls. She participated in a conversation with several of the girls who told her about incidents which they had heard or witnessed concerning certain teachers, including the plaintiffs, at Bordelonville High School. When Mrs. Guillory discussed with one of her church deacons the information, which included allegations that the teachers were fondling students, he advised her to inform the school principal.

The following month Mrs. Guillory took up the matter with Mr. Jimmy Bordelon, the principal of the high school, who assured her that he would observe the teachers' behavior.

On March 6, 1980, Mrs. Guillory visited with Mr. Bordelon to discuss a poor grade on a test given to her daughter by Maxwell Desselle. Mr. Desselle was called in to talk to Mrs. Guillory about it. They had a heated discussion concerning the test and the defendant also made a comment to the effect that she had something else on Desselle. After he returned to his classroom Mrs. Guillory told the principal that the teachers had continued to molest the children. She testified that prior to this visit Abigail Farbes had informed her that it was still going on. The principal told Mrs. Guillory he did not believe such rumors and had not observed any such behavior. Mrs. Guillory then informed the principal she would take her information to the superintendent.

That same afternoon Mrs. Guillory had a conversation with Mrs. Jeannette Huffmaster. When Mrs. Guillory informed her of what she had heard, Mrs. Huffmaster told her that she had seen Maxwell Desselle pat a girl on the buttocks in the presence of Mr. Bordelon.

On March 7, 1980, Mr. Bordelon met with the plaintiffs and informed them of what Mrs. Guillory had said. The four then went to the Guillory home to discuss the matter. At this meeting an argument ensued and at least one of the plaintiffs threatened to sue the Guillorys for defamation.

Later that night Mrs. Guillory called her attorney who advised her to obtain written statements from the girls who had given her the information about the teachers. Mrs. Guillory went to the homes of Abigail Farbes, Joan Hess, Tammy Lemoine, Beverly Martin and Terry Bringold to obtain such statements. She said she explained the situation and alleged incidents to their parents and got their permission before asking the girls to write "letters" as to what they saw or heard about the matter. Three of these persons and her daughter did so.

On March 10, 1980, Mrs. Guillory and Mrs. Huffmaster drew up a petition calling for an investigation by the Evangeline Parish School Board into wrongdoings at Bordelonville High School. The petition did not contain the names of the plaintiffs or of any specific facts concerning the alleged wrongdoings. These ladies then visited five or six homes in an attempt to obtain signatures on the petition. The school board directed a representative to make an investigation. Upon his failure to obtain any testimony of wrongdoing, the board concluded there was no basis for action against any teacher and closed the case. The recorded statements taken by the representative were destroyed and the interested parties were notified in writing of the board's decision. . . .

Beverly Martin testified she had told Mrs. Guillory that she had heard students say that some of the teachers played with the students. In particular, she had heard Kenneth Maillet would take girls in the bathroom after practice, but they wouldn't tell her what they did. She also told her that Garland Desselle was friendly with the girls and would allow them to sit in his lap and that he felt one girl during P.E. In addition she told Mrs. Guillory of an incident when Maxwell Desselle kissed her under the mistletoe. Abigail Farbes testified she had told Mrs. Guillory that Maxwell and Kenneth Maillet would flirt around with girls and that Beverly had told her that Maxwell Desselle once had grabbed Beverly and gave her a passionate kiss.

Joan Hess testified that before the Mardi Gras trip she had her majorette uniform on under her jeans and part of the uniform was showing. She stated Mr. Maillet tugged at the jeans and a button came undone from the jeans. Joan further testified she told Kaye Guillory, the defendant's daughter, that Kenneth Maillet tugged at her jeans pulling a button off.

Tammy Lemoine testified that in the written statement given Mrs. Guillory she said she heard that Kenneth Maillet and another girl "had something going on" and that Garland Desselle said "he was going to get some meat" from two girls "one of these days."

The testimony as to the content of the statements Mrs. Guillory made to the principal and the parents of high school students is in dispute. Mr. Bordelon, the principal, said Mrs. Guillory told him the teachers were fondling and molesting girls, although she never used the word "intercourse." Clara Laborde and Peggy Hess stated Mrs. Guillory had told them that one of the plaintiffs, Kenneth Maillet, had unzipped Mrs. Hess' daughter's pants before a Mardi Gras band trip and that the plaintiffs were molesting the girls. She also said some teachers were starting this in the elementary grades and taking them to bed by the time they reached the high school grades.

Mrs. Guillory testified that she did not accuse the plaintiffs of anything, but merely told Mrs. Hess and Mrs. Laborde what she had heard from the girls and said she felt the plaintiffs might be having sexual relations with the students. Having heard things about these men, such as one girl having seen Kenneth Maillet with his pants down in the bathroom one night after basketball practice, she was trying to determine if they were true. She also stated at trial that she thought the parents had a right to know and she never intended to do any harm to the men allegedly involved.

The plaintiffs emphatically denied ever molesting or having intercourse with any high school students. Kenneth Maillet did not recall any incident where he unbuttoned a girl's jeans or did anything improper. Maxwell Desselle said he had harmlessly kissed Beverly Martin at a Christmas dinner. Mr. Bordelon and Maxwell Desselle denied the occurrence of Mr. Desselle patting a girl on the buttocks.

Concerning the statement Mr. Guillory made to James Armand, Mr. Armand stated Mr. Guillory told him certain teachers were molesting girls on a school trip and named the three plaintiffs. Mr. Guillory disputed this by saying he told him some of the girls had stated to his wife that some of the teachers were "messing around." He testified he did not intend any harm.

The issues presented by this appeal are: (1) whether or not the jury erred in rendering a verdict in favor of the defendants and (2) whether or not the jury erred in awarding the defendants attorney's fees under LSA–C.C. Article 2315.1.

In order to maintain an action in defamation, the plaintiff must establish the following elements: (1) defamatory words; (2) publication; (3) falsity; (4) malice, actual or implied; and (5) resulting injury.

The available defenses against an action in defamation are: (1) privilege and (2) truth.

The appellants argue that the evidence presented sufficiently proved the elements necessary for an action in defamation and the defendants failed to bear their burden of proving privilege or truth. Assuming the evidence was sufficient to prove the first three elements of defamation, we find that a qualified privilege existed between Mrs. Guillory and each person she discussed the rumors with.

A qualified privilege exists as to a communication, even if false, between parties sharing an interest or duty. However, to be a good defense such communication must be made in good faith and without malice.

In the present case Mrs. Guillory had discussions with the school principal and with several parents of girls attending Bordelonville High School concerning the alleged actions of certain teachers. The interests shared by each of these persons were to protect the welfare of their children at school and to provide good teachers in the public schools.

There was sufficient evidence for the jury to have found that Mrs. Guillory was in good faith and without malice in her communications to the principal and the parents. Several high school girls told her that certain teachers were playing with the female students. She had heard that one of the plaintiffs was taking girls into the bathroom after practice for an unmentioned purpose; that a teacher was allowing a girl to sit on his lap while he felt her body; that a teacher had unbuttoned the jeans of a girl; and that a teacher had kissed a student and he also had patted a girl on the buttocks. Hearing these things from the girls and a parent, it was not unreasonable for Mrs. Guillory to have believed that improprieties were occurring at the school. From these facts the jury could have concluded that Mrs. Guillory had reasonable grounds to believe her statements were true and were made in good faith and without malice. In such case they were privileged. . . .

From our review of the record we are unable to say that the verdict of the jury favoring the defendants on the plaintiffs' demands is clearly wrong. . . .

We do not believe the filing of these suits was frivolous. Our decision is based on the defense of qualified privilege and the record contains no indication of any lack of sincerity on the part of plaintiffs as to their legal position. Therefore the jury award of $3,000 to the Guillorys for attorney's fees was in error and must be set aside. Boyd v. Community Center Credit Corporation, 359 So.2d 1048 (La.App. 4 Cir.1978).

For these reasons the judgment of the district court is reversed and set aside insofar as it awarded $3,000.00 at attorney's fees to the plaintiffs-in-reconvention. Otherwise, it is affirmed. The costs of this appeal are assessed one-half to plaintiffs and one-half to the defendants.

Affirmed in part and reversed in part.

CIVIL RIGHTS TORTS

An individual's constitutional rights may be protected through application of the Civil Rights Act of 1871, Title 42 U.S.C. § 1983. Under this law denial of an individual's constitutional rights can result in damages assessed by the court against the school board or against an individual school board member, administrator, or teacher or against the individual responsible for the constitutional denial. This act had been virtually dormant for almost 100 years when it was revived in the early 1960s in the famous Supreme Court case of *Monroe* v. *Pape* [99] at which time the Court opened the courts to actions against public officials. The law itself states:

> Every person who, under color of any statute, ordinance, regulation, custom, or usage, of any State or Territory, subjects, or causes to be subjected, any citizen of the United States or other person within the jurisdiction thereof to the deprivation of any rights, privileges or immunities secured by the Constitution and laws, shall be liable to the party injured in an action at law, suit in equity, or other proper proceeding for redress.[100]

This law was enacted by the Congress on April 20, 1871, after a month of debate during which time it became clear that there was great sentiment toward providing legal redress against those Southerners who repressed individual rights of southern blacks. The press at that time called the legislation the Southern-outrage Repression bill.[101]

As written, the law provides for both injunctive and monetary relief to be awarded by the federal courts. Offenders against whom action may be instituted are statutory persons—"persons" as the law is written. The United States Supreme Court has had difficulty in deciding exactly who a "person" is, whether it is a public board or an individual official or employee. In *Monroe* the Court first held that Congress did not intend the word "person" to include municipalities or agencies of the government. Therefore, suits seeking relief under the Act were filed only against school officials and not school districts as entities. The result was that from 1961 to 1978 school districts insured the school officials against damages that may have been incurred by lawsuit in such cases and the municipality was immune. On June 6, 1978, in *Monell* v. *New York City*,[102] this all changed when the Supreme Court voted 7 to 2 to overrule *Monroe* insofar as it provided immunity for municipalities. The Court, in so ruling, did not upset the interpretation of the *respondeat superior* doctrine, that a public school district is not responsible for the wrongdoing of its employees, but it did say that the school district could be held liable under Section 1983 if it adopts an unconstitutional policy or acquiesces in an unconstitutional custom. Justice Brennan stated:

> We conclude, therefore, that a local government may not be sued for an injury inflicted solely by its employees or agents. Instead, it is when execution of a government's policy or custom, whether made by its lawmakers or by those whose edicts or acts may fairly be said to represent official policy, inflicts the injury that the government as an entity is responsible under Section 1983.

Monell, therefore, taken in context with two other cases, *Wood* v. *Strickland* [103] and *Carey* v. *Piphus*,[104] clearly permits courts to assess damages against either the governmental agency or an individual official of government if it or they suppress one's civil rights, whether it be a student, teacher, or some other party. *Wood* established the potential liability of school board members for denial of students due process rights, while *Carey* clarified the nature and extent of the damages that could be levied by the courts. In *Carey,* Justice Powell writing for the Court explained that there was a limitation to the damages that were possible under this kind of action. According to Powell, Section 1983 was not intended to provide purely punitive relief whereby the court would punish the wrongdoer for ill deeds, but instead the Act was designed to compensate the victim for detriment and damage caused by the denial. Compensatory damages of this nature are quite difficult to prove and the Supreme Court places this burden squarely on the shoulders of the plaintiff. In the absence of such proof the individual is entitled to collect only nominal damages, which the Supreme Court set at one dollar.

*School Board Members May Be
Liable, as Individuals, for Damages
Under Section 1983 of the Civil
Rights Act of 1871*

WOOD v. STRICKLAND

Supreme Court of the United States, 1975.
420 U.S. 308, 95 S.Ct. 992.

Mr. Justice WHITE delivered the opinion of the Court.

Respondents Peggy Strickland and Virginia Crain brought this lawsuit against petitioners, who were members of the school board at the time in question, two school administrators, and the Special School District of Mena, Ark., purporting to assert a cause of action under 42 U.S.C.A. § 1983, and claiming that their federal constitutional rights to due process were infringed under color of state law by their expulsion from the Mena Public High School on the grounds of their violation of a school regulation prohibiting the use or possession of intoxicating beverages at school or school activities. The complaint as amended prayed for compensatory and punitive damages against all petitioners, injunctive relief allowing respondents to resume attendance, preventing petitioners from imposing any sanctions as a result of the expulsion, and restraining enforcement of the challenged regulation, declaratory relief as to the constitutional invalidity of the regulation, and expunction of any record of their expulsion. . . .

The violation of the school regulation prohibiting the use or possession of intoxicating beverages at school or school activities with which respondents were charged concerned their "spiking" of the punch served at a meeting of an extracurricular school organization attended by parents and students. At the time in question, respondents were sixteen years old and were in the tenth grade. The relevant facts begin with their discovery that the punch had not been prepared for the meeting as previously planned. The girls then agreed to "spike" it. Since the county in which the school is located is "dry," respondents and a third girl drove across the state border into Oklahoma and purchased two twelve-ounce bottles of "Right Time," a malt liquor. They then bought six ten-ounce bottles of a soft drink, and after having mixed the contents of the eight bottles in an empty milk carton, returned to school. Prior to the meeting, the girls experienced second thoughts about the wisdom of their prank, but by then they were caught up in the force of events and the intervention of other girls prevented them from disposing of the illicit punch. The punch was served at the meeting, without apparent effect. . . . the board voted to expel the girls from school for the remainder of the semester, a period of approximately three months.

The board subsequently agreed to hold another meeting on the matter, and one was held approximately two weeks after the first meeting. The girls, their parents, and their counsel attended this session. The board began with a reading of a written statement of facts as it had found them. The girls admitted mixing the malt liquor into the punch with the intent of "spiking" it, but asked the board to forgo its rule punishing such violations by such substantial suspensions. . . . The board voted not to change its policy and, as before, to expel the girls for the remainder of the semester.

The District Court instructed the jury that a decision for respondents had to be premised upon a finding that petitioners acted with malice in expelling them and defined "malice" as meaning "ill will against a person—a wrongful act done intentionally without just cause or excuse." In ruling for petitioners after the jury had been unable to agree, the District Court found "as a matter of law" that there was no evidence from which malice could be inferred.

The Court of Appeals, however, viewed both the instruction and the decision of the District Court as being erroneous. Specific intent to harm wrongfully, it held, was not a requirement for the recovery of damages. Instead, "[i]t need only be established that the defendants did not, in the light of all the circumstances, act in good faith. The test is an objective, rather than a subjective one."

Petitioners as members of the school board assert here, as they did below, an absolute immunity from liability under § 1983 and at the very least seek to reinstate the judgment of the District Court. If they are correct and the District Court's dismissal should be sustained, we need go no further in this case. Moreover, the immunity question involves the construction of a federal statute, and our practice is to deal with possibly dispositive statutory issues before reaching questions turning on the construction of the Constitution. . . . We essentially sustain the position of the Court of Appeals with respect to the immunity issue.

The nature of the immunity from awards of damages under § 1983 available to school administrators and school board members is not a question which the lower federal courts have answered with a single voice. There is general agreement on the existence of a "good faith" immunity, but the courts have either emphasized different factors as elements of good faith or have not given specific content to the good-faith standard. . . .

Common-law tradition, recognized in our prior decisions, and strong public-policy reasons also lead to a construction of § 1983 extending a qualified good-faith immunity to school board members from liability for damages under that section. Although there have been differing emphases and formulations of the common-law immunity of public school officials in cases of student expulsion or suspension, state courts have generally recognized that such officers should be protected from tort liability under state law for all good-faith nonmalicious action taken to fulfill their official duties.

As the facts of this case reveal, school board members function at different times in the nature of legislators and adjudicators in the school disciplinary process. Each of these functions necessarily involves the exercise of discretion, the weighing of many factors, and the formulation of long-term policy. "Like legislators and judges, these officers are entitled to rely on traditional sources for the factual information on which they decide and act." . . . As with executive officers faced with instances of civil disorder, school officials, confronted with student behavior causing or threatening disruption, also have an "obvious need for prompt action, and decisions must be made in reliance on factual information supplied by others."

Liability for damages for every action which is found subsequently to have been violative of a student's constitutional rights and to have caused compensable injury would unfairly impose upon the school decisionmaker the burden of mistakes made in good faith in the course of exercising his discretion within the scope of his official duties. School board members, among other duties, must judge whether there have been violations of school regulations and, if so, the appropriate sanctions for the violations. Denying any measure of immunity in these circumstances "would contribute not to principled and fearless decision-making but to intimidation." . . . The imposition of monetary costs for mistakes which were not unreasonable in the light of all the circumstances would undoubtedly deter even the most conscientious school decision-maker from exercising his judgment independently, forcefully, and in a manner best serving the long-term interest of the school and the students. The most capable candidates for school board positions might be deterred from seeking office if heavy burdens upon their private resources from monetary liability were a likely prospect during their tenure.

These considerations have undoubtedly played a prime role in the development by state courts of a qualified immunity protecting school officials from liability for damages in lawsuits claiming improper suspensions or expulsions. But at the same time, the judgment implicit in this common-law development is that absolute immunity would not be justified since it would not sufficiently increase the ability of school officials to exercise their discretion in a forthright manner to warrant the absence of a remedy for students subjected to intentional or otherwise inexcusable deprivations.

. . . We think there must be a degree of immunity if the work of the schools is to go forward; and, however worded, the immunity must be such that public school officials understand that action taken in the good-faith fulfillment of their responsibilities and within the bounds of reason under all the circumstances will not be punished and that they need not exercise their discretion with undue timidity. . . .

The disagreement between the Court of Appeals and the District Court over the immunity standard in this case has been put in terms of an "objective" versus a "subjective" test of good faith. As we see it, the appropriate standard necessarily contains elements of both. The official himself must be acting sincerely and with a belief that he is doing right, but an act violating a student's constitutional rights can be no more justified by ignorance or disregard of settled, indisputable law on the part of one entrusted with supervision of students' daily lives than by the presence of actual malice. To be entitled to a special exemption from the categorical remedial language of § 1983 in a case in which his action violated a student's constitutional rights, a school board member, who has voluntarily undertaken the task of supervising the operation of the school and the activities of the students, must be held to a standard of conduct based not only on permissible intentions, but also on knowledge of the basic, unquestioned constitutional rights of his charges. Such a standard imposes neither an unfair burden upon a person assuming a responsible public office requiring a high degree of intelligence and judgment for the proper fulfillment of its duties, nor an unwarranted burden in light of the value which civil rights have in our legal system. Any lesser standard would deny much of the promise of § 1983. Therefore, in the specific context of school discipline, we hold that a school board member is not immune from liability for damages under § 1983 if he knew or reasonably should have known that the action he took within his sphere of official responsibility would violate the constitutional rights of the student affected, or if he took the action with the malicious intention to cause a deprivation of constitutional rights or other injury to the student. That is not to say that school board members are "charged with predicting the future course of constitutional law." . . . A compensatory award will be appropriate only if the school board member has acted with such an impermissible motivation or with such disregard of the student's clearly established constitutional rights that his action cannot reasonably be characterized as being in good faith.

The Court of Appeals based upon its review of the facts but without the benefit of the transcript of the testimony given at the four-day trial to the jury in the District Court, found that the board had made its decision to expel the girls on the basis of *no* evidence that the school regulation had been violated:

> To justify the suspension, it was necessary for the Board to establish that the students possessed or used an "intoxicating" beverage at a school-sponsored activity. No evidence was presented at either meeting to establish the alcoholic content of the liquid brought to the campus. Moreover, the Board made no finding that the liquid was intoxicating. The only evidence as to the nature of the drink was that supplied by the girls, and it is clear that they did not know whether the beverage was intoxicating or not. 485 F.2d, at 190.

. . . In its statement of facts issued prior to the onset of this litigation, the school board expressed its construction of the regulation by finding that the girls had brought an "alcoholic beverage" onto school premises. The girls themselves admitted knowing at the time of the incident that they were doing something wrong which might be punished. In light of this evidence, the Court of Appeals was ill advised to supplant the interpretation of the regulation of those officers who adopted it and are entrusted with its enforcement. . . .

When the regulation is construed to prohibit the use and possession of beverages containing alcohol, there was no absence of evidence before the school board to prove the charge against respondents. The girls had admitted that they intended to "spike" the punch and that they had mixed malt liquor into the punch that was served. . . .

Given the fact that there *was* evidence supporting the charge against respondents, the contrary judgment of the Court of Appeals is improvident. It is not the role of the federal courts to set aside decisions of school administrators which the court may view as lacking a basis in wisdom or compassion. Public high school students do have substantive and procedural rights while at school. . . . But § 1983 does not extend the right to relitigate in federal court evidentiary questions arising in school disciplinary proceedings or the proper construction of school regulations. The system of public education that has evolved in this Nation relies necessarily upon the discretion and judgment of school administrators and school board members and § 1983 was not intended to be a vehicle for federal-court correction of errors in the exercise of that discretion which do not rise to the level of violations of specific constitutional guarantees. . . .

Respondents have argued here that there was a procedural due process violation which also supports the result reached by the Court of Appeals. . . . But because the District Court did not discuss it, and the Court of Appeals did not decide it, it would be preferable to have the Court of Appeals consider the issue in the first instance.

The judgment of the Court of Appeals is vacated and the case remanded for further proceedings consistent with this opinion.

So ordered.

*Students Are Entitled to Recover Only
Nominal Damages Unless They Can
Prove Actual Injury*

CAREY v. PIPHUS

Supreme Court of the United States, 1978.
435 U.S. 247, 98 S.Ct. 1042.

Mr. Justice POWELL delivered the opinion of the Court.

In this case, brought under 42 U.S.C.A. § 1983, we consider the elements and prerequisites for recovery of damages by students who were suspended from public elementary and secondary schools without procedural due process. The Court of Appeals for the Seventh Circuit held that the students are entitled to recover substantial nonpunitive damages even if their suspensions were justified, and even if they do not prove that any other actual injury was caused by the denial of procedural due process. We disagree, and hold that in the absence of proof of actual injury, the students are entitled to recover only nominal damages.

Respondent Jarius Piphus was a freshman at Chicago Vocational High School during the 1973–1974 school year. On January 23, 1974, during school hours, the school principal saw Piphus and another student standing outdoors on school property passing back and forth what the principal described as an irregularly shaped cigarette. The prinicpal approached the students unnoticed and smelled what he believed was the strong odor of burning marijuana. He also saw Piphus try to pass a packet of cigarette papers to the other student. When the students became aware of the principal's presence, they threw the cigarette into a nearby hedge.

The principal took the students to the school's disciplinary office and directed the assistant principal to impose the "usual" twenty-day suspension for violation of the school rule against the use of drugs. The students protested that they had not been smoking marijuana, but to no avail. Piphus was allowed to remain at school, although not in class, for the remainder of the school day while the assistant principal tried, without success, to reach his mother.

A suspension notice was sent to Piphus' mother, and a few days later two meetings were arranged among Piphus, his mother, his sister, school officials, and representatives from a Legal Aid Clinic. The purpose of the meetings was not to determine whether Piphus had been smoking marijuana, but rather to explain the reasons for the suspension. Following an unfruitful exchange of views, Piphus and his mother, as guardian *ad litem,* filed suit against petitioners in Federal District Court . . . charging that Piphus had been suspended without due process of law in violation of the Fourteenth Amendment. The complaint sought declaratory and injunctive relief, together with actual and punitive damages in the amount of $3,000. Piphus was readmitted to school under a temporary restraining order after eight days of his suspension.

Respondent Silas Brisco was in the sixth grade at Clara Barton Elementary School in Chicago during the 1973–1974 school year. On September 11, 1973, Brisco came to school wearing one small earring. The previous school year the school prinicpal had issued a rule against the wearing of earrings by male students because he believed that this practice denoted membership in certain street gangs and increased the likelihood that gang members would terrorize other students. Brisco was reminded of this rule, but he refused to remove the earring, asserting that it was a symbol of black pride, not of gang membership.

The assistant principal talked to Brisco's mother, advising her that her son would be suspended for twenty days if he did not remove the earring. Brisco's mother supported her son's position, and a twenty-day suspension was imposed. Brisco and his mother, as guardian *ad litem,* filed suit in Federal District Court . . . charging that Brisco had been suspended without due process of law in violation of the Fourteenth Amendment. The complaint sought declaratory and injunctive relief, together with actual and punitive damages in the amount of $5,000. Brisco was readmitted to school during the pendency of proceedings for a preliminary injunction after seventeen days of his suspension. . . . We granted certiorari to consider whether, in an action under § 1983 for the deprivation of procedural due process, a plaintiff must prove that he actually was injured by the deprivation before he may recover substantial "nonpunitive" damages.

42 U.S.C.A. § 1983, enacted as § 1 of the Civil Rights Act of 1871, 17 Stat. 13, provides:

> Every person who, under color of any statute, ordinance, regulation, custom, or usage, of any State or Territory, subjects, or causes to be subjected, any citizen of the United States or other person within the jurisdiction thereof to the deprivation of any rights, privileges, or immunities secured by the Constitution and laws, shall be liable to the party injured in an action at law, suit in equity, or other proper proceeding for redress.

The legislative history of § 1983 . . . demonstrates that it was intended to "create a species of tort liability" in favor of persons who are deprived of "rights, privileges, or immunities secured" to them by the Constitution. . . .

Insofar as petitioners contend that the basic purpose of a § 1983 damages award should be to compensate persons for injuries caused by the deprivation of constitutional rights, they have the better of the argument. Rights, constitutional and otherwise, do not exist in a vacuum. Their purpose is to protect persons from injuries to particular interests, and their contours are shaped by the interests they protect.

Our legal system's concept of damages reflects this view of legal rights. "The cardinal principle of damages in Anglo-American law is that of *compensation* for the injury caused to plaintiff by defendant's breach of duty." . . . The Court implicitly has recognized the applicability of this principle to actions under § 1983 by stating that damages are available under that section for actions "found . . . to have been violative of . . . constitutional rights *and to have caused compensable injury . . ..*" Wood v. Strickland, 420 U.S. 308, 319 (1975) (emphasis supplied). . . .

The members of the Congress that enacted § 1983 did not address directly the question of damages, but the principle that damages are designed to compensate persons for injuries caused by the deprivation of rights hardly could have been foreign to the many lawyers in Congress in 1871. Two other sections of the Civil Rights Act of 1871 appear to incorporate this principle, and no reason suggests itself for reading § 1983 differently. To the extent that Congress intended that awards under § 1983 should deter the deprivation of constitutional rights, there is no evidence that it meant to establish a deterrent more formidable than that inherent in the award of compensatory damages. . . .

It is less difficult to conclude that damages awards under § 1983 should be governed by the principle of compensation than it is to apply this principle to concrete cases. But over the centuries the common law of torts has developed a set of rules to implement the principle that a person should be compensated fairly for injuries caused by the violation of his legal rights. These rules, defining the elements of damages and the prerequisites for their recovery, provide the appropriate starting point for the inquiry under § 1983 as well.

It is not clear, however, that common-law tort rules of damages will provide a complete solution to the damages issue in every § 1983 case. In some cases, the interests protected by a particular branch of the common law of torts may parallel closely the interests protected by a particular constitutional right. In such cases, it may be appropriate to apply the tort rules of damages directly to the § 1983 action. . . . In other cases, the interests protected by a particular constitutional right may not also be protected by an analogous branch of the common law of torts. . . . In those cases, the task will be the more difficult one of adapting common-law rules of damages to provide fair compensation for injuries casued by the deprivation of a constitutional right.

Although this task of adaptation will be one of some delicacy—as this case demonstrates—it must be undertaken. The purpose of § 1983 would be defeated if injuries caused by the deprivation of constitutional rights went uncompensated simply because the common law does not recognize an analogous cause of action. . . . In order to further the purpose of § 1983, the rules governing compensation for injuries caused by the deprivation of constitutional rights should be tailored to the interests protected by the particular right in question—just as the common-law rules of damages themselves were defined by the interests protected in the various branches of tort law. We agree with Mr. Justice Harlan that "the experience of judges in dealing with private [tort] claims supports the conclusion that courts of law are capable of making the types of judgment concerning causation and magnitude of injury necessary to accord meaningful compensation for invasion of [constitutional] rights." . . . With these principles in mind, we now turn to the problem of compensation in the case at hand.

The Due Process Clause of the Fourteenth Amendment provides:

> nor shall any State deprive any person of life, liberty, or property, without due process of law . . ..

This clause "raises no impenetrable barrier to the taking of a person's possessions," or liberty, or life. . . . Procedural due process rules are meant to protect persons not from the deprivation, but from the mistaken or unjustified deprivation of life, liberty, or property. Thus, in deciding what process constitutionally is due in various contexts, the Court repeatedly has emphasized that "procedural due process rules are shaped by the risk of error inherent in the truth-finding process . . .." . . . Such rules "minimize substantively unfair or mistaken deprivations of" life, liberty, or property by enabling persons to contest the basis upon which the State proposes to deprive them of protected interests. . . .

The parties . . . disagree as to the . . . holding of the Court of Appeals that respondents are entitled to recover substantial—although unspecified—damages to compensate them for "the injury which is 'inherent in the nature of the wrong,'" even if their suspensions were justified and even if they fail to prove that the denial of procedural due process actually caused them some real, if intangible, injury. Respondents, elaborating on this theme, submit that the holding is correct because injury fairly may be "presumed" to flow from every denial of procedural due process. Their argument is that in addition to protecting against unjustified deprivations, the Due Process Clause also guarantees the "feeling of just treatment" by the government. . . . They contend that the deprivation of protected interests without procedural due process, even where the premise for the deprivation is not erroneous, inevitably arouses strong feelings of mental and emotional distress in the individual who is denied this "feeling of just treatment." They analogize their case to that of defamation *per se*, in which "the plaintiff is relieved from the necessity of producing any proof whatsoever that he has been injured" in order to recover substantial compensatory damages.

Petitioners do not deny that a purpose of procedural due process is to convey to the individual a feeling that the government has dealt with him fairly, as well as to minimize the risk of mistaken deprivations of protected interests. They go so far as to concede that, in a proper case, persons in respondents' positions might well recover damages for mental and emotional distress caused by the denial of procedural due process. Petitioners' argument is the more limited one that such injury cannot be presumed to occur, and that plaintiffs at least should be put to their proof on the issue, as plaintiffs are in most tort actions.

We agree with petitioners in this respect. As we have observed in another context, the doctrine of presumed damages in the common law of defamation *per se* "is an oddity of tort law, for it allows recovery of purportedly compensatory damages without evidence of actual loss." . . . The doctrine has been defended on the grounds that those forms of defamation that are actionable *per se* are virtually certain to cause serious injury to reputation, and that this kind of injury is extremely difficult to prove. Moreover, statements that are defamatory *per se* by their very nature are likely to cause mental and emotional distress, as well as injury to reputation, so there arguably is little reason to require proof of this kind of injury either. But these considerations do not support respondents' contention that damages should be presumed to flow from every deprivation of procedural due process.

First, it is not reasonable to assume that every departure from procedural due process, no matter what the circumstances or how minor, inherently is as likely to cause distress as the publication of defamation *per se* is to cause injury to reputation and distress. Where the deprivation of a protected interest is substantively justified but procedures are deficient in some respect, there may well be those who suffer no distress over the procedural irregularities. Indeed, in contrast to the immediately distressing effect of defamation *per se*, a person may not even know that procedures *were* deficient until he enlists the aid of counsel to challenge a perceived substantive deprivation.

Moreover, where a deprivation is justified but procedures are deficient, whatever distress a person feels may be attributable to the justified deprivation rather than to deficiencies in procedure. But as the Court of Appeals held, the injury caused by a justified deprivation, including distress, is not properly compensable under § 1983. This ambiguity in causation, which is absent in the case of defamation *per se*, provides additional need for requiring the plaintiff to convince the trier of fact that he actually suffered distress because of the denial of procedural due process itself.

Finally, we foresee no particular difficulty in producing evidence that mental and emotional distress actually was caused by the denial of procedural due process itself. Distress is a personal injury familiar to the law, customarily proved by showing the nature and circumstances of the wrong and its effect on the plaintiff. In sum, then, although mental and emotional distress caused by the denial of procedural due process itself is compensable under § 1983, we hold that neither the likelihood of such injury nor the difficulty of proving it is so great as to justify awarding compensatory damages without proof that such injury actually was caused. . . .

Even if respondents' suspensions were justified, and even if they did not suffer any other actual injury, the fact remains that they were deprived of their right to procedural due process. "It is enough to invoke the procedural safeguards of the Fourteenth Amendment that a significant property interest is at stake, whatever the ultimate outcome of a hearing." . . .

Common-law courts traditionally have vindicated deprivations of certain "absolute" rights that are not shown to have caused actual injury through the award of a nominal sum of money. By making the deprivation of such rights actionable for nominal damages without proof of actual injury, the law recognizes the importance to organized society that those rights be scrupulously observed; but at the same time, it remains true to the principle that substantial damages should be awarded only to compensate actual injury or, in the case of exemplary or punitive damages, to deter or punish malicious deprivations of rights.

Because the right to procedural due process is "absolute" in the sense that it does not depend upon the merits of a claimant's substantive assertions, and because of the importance to organized society that procedural due process be observed . . . we believe that the denial of procedural due process should be actionable for nominal damages without proof of actual injury. We therefore hold that if, upon remand, the District Court determines that respondents' suspensions were justified, respondents nevertheless will be entitled to recover nominal damages not to exceed one dollar from petitioners. . . .

Municipalities and Other Local
Governmental Units Are Included
Among Those "Persons" to Whom the
Civil Rights Act of 1871, 42 U.S.C.
§ 1983, Applies

MONELL v. DEPARTMENT OF SOCIAL SERVICES OF THE CITY OF NEW YORK

Supreme Court of the United States, 1978.
436 U.S. 658, 98 S.Ct. 2018.

Mr. Justice BRENNAN delivered the opinion of the Court.

We granted certiorari in this case, 429 U.S. 1071, 97 S.Ct. 807, 50 L.Ed.2d 789, to consider

Whether local governmental officials and/or local independent school boards are "persons" within the meaning of 42 U.S.C. § 1983 when equitable relief in the nature of back pay is sought against them in their official capacities? Pet. for Cert. 8.

Although, after plenary consideration, we have decided the merits of over a score of cases brought under § 1983 in which the principal defendant was a school board . . . we indicated in Mt. Healthy City Board of Education v. Doyle, 429 U.S. 274, 279, 97 S.Ct. 568, 573, 50 L.Ed.2d 471 (1977), last Term that the question presented here was open and would be decided "another day." That other day has come and we now overrule *Monroe* v. *Pape,* insofar as it holds that local governments are wholly immune from suit under § 1983.

In *Monroe* v. *Pape,* we held that "Congress did not undertake to bring municipal corporations within the ambit of [§ 1983]." The sole basis for this conclusion was an inference drawn from Congress' rejection of the "Sherman amendment" to the bill which became the Civil Rights Act of 1871. The Amendment would have held a municipal corporation liable for damage done to the person or property of its inhabitants by *private* persons "riotously and tumultuously assembled." Although the Sherman amendment did not seek to amend § 1 of the Act, which is now § 1983, and although the nature of the obligation created by that amendment was vastly different from that created by § 1, the Court nonetheless concluded in *Monroe* that Congress must have meant to exclude municipal corporations from the coverage of § 1 because " 'the House [in voting against the Sherman amendment] had solemnly decided that in their judgment Congress had no constitutional power to impose any *obligation* upon county and town organizations, the mere instrumentality for the administration of state law.'" 365 U.S., at 190, 81 S.Ct. at 485 (emphasis added), quoting Globe 804 (Rep. Poland). This statement, we thought, showed that Congress doubted its "constitutional power . . . to impose *civil liability* on municipalities," and that such doubt would have extended to any type of civil liability.

A fresh analysis of the debate on the Civil Rights Act of 1871, and particularly of the case law which each side mustered in its support, shows, however, that *Monroe* incorrectly equated the "obligation" of which Representative Poland spoke with "civil liability." . . .

The meaning of the legislative history . . . can most readily be developed by first considering the debate on the report of the first conference committee. This debate shows conclusively that the constitutional objections raised against the Sherman amendment—on which our holding in *Monroe* was based, . . . would not have prohibited congressional creation of a civil remedy against state municipal corporations that infringed federal rights. Because § 1 of the Civil Rights Act does not state expressly that municipal corporations come within its ambit, it is finally necessary to interpret § 1 to confirm that such corporations were indeed intended to be included within the "persons" to whom that section applies. . . .

Our analysis of the legislative history of the Civil Rights Act of 1871 compels the conclusion that Congress *did* intend municipalities and other local government units to be included among those persons to whom § 1983 applies. Local governing bodies, therefore, can be sued directly under § 1983 for monetary, declaratory, or injunctive relief where, as here, the action that is alleged to be unconstitutional implements or executes a policy statement, ordinance, regulation, or decision officially adopted and promulgated by that body's officers. Moreover, although the touchstone of the § 1983 action against a government body is an allegation that official policy is responsible for a deprivation of rights protected by the Constitution, local governments, like every other § 1983 "person," by the very terms of the statute, may be sued for constitutional deprivations visited pursuant to governmental "custom" even though such a custom has not received formal approval through the body's official decision-making channels. As Mr. Justice Harlan, writing for the Court, said in Adickes v. S.H. Kress & Co., 398 U.S. 144, 167–168, 90 S.Ct. 1598, 1613, 26 L.Ed.2d 142 (1970): "Congress included customs and usages [in § 1983] because of the persistent and widespread discriminatory practices of state officials . . . . Although not authorized by written law, such practices of state officials could well be so permanent and well settled as to constitute a 'custom or usage' with the force of law."

On the other hand, the language of § 1983, read against the background of the same legislative history, compels the conclusion that Congress did not intend municipalities to be held liable unless action pursuant to official municipal policy of some nature caused a constitutional tort. In particular, we conclude that a municipality cannot be held liable *solely* because it employs a tortfeasor—or, in other words, a municipality cannot be held liable under § 1983 on a *respondeat superior* theory.

We begin with the language of § 1983 as originally passed:

> *"[A]ny person who,* under color of any law, statute ordinance, regulation, custom, or usage of any State, *shall subject or cause to be subjected,* any person . . . to the deprivation of any rights, privileges, or immunities secured by the Constitution of the United States, shall, any such law, statute, ordinance, regulation, custom, or usage of the State to the contrary notwithstanding, be liable to the party injured in any action at law, suit in equity, or other proper proceeding for redress . . . . (emphasis added)

The italicized language plainly imposes liability on a government that, under color of some official policy, "causes" an employee to violate another's constitutional rights. At the same time, that language cannot be easily read to impose liability vicariously on governing bodies solely on the basis of the existence of an employer-employee relationship with a tortfeasor. Indeed, the fact that Congress did specifically provide that A's tort became B's liability if B "caused" A to subject another to a tort suggests that Congress did not intend § 1983 liability to attach where such causation was absent.

Equally important, creation of a federal law of *respondeat superior* would have raised all the constitutional problems associated with the obligation to keep the peace, an obligation Congress chose not to impose because it thought imposition of such an obligation unconstitutional. To this day, there is disagreement about the basis for imposing liability on an employer for the torts of an employee when the sole nexus between the employer and the tort is the fact of the employer-employee relationship. Nonetheless, two justifications tend to stand out. First is the common-sense notion that no matter how blameless an employer appears to be in an individual case, accidents might nonetheless be reduced if employers had to bear the cost of accidents. Second is the argument that the cost of accidents should be spread to the community as a whole on an insurance theory.

The first justification is of the same sort that was offered for statutes like the Sherman amendment: "The obligation to make compensation for injury resulting from riot is, by arbitrary enactment of statutes, affirmatory law, and the reason of passing the statute is to secure a more perfect police regulation." This justification was obviously insufficient to sustain the amendment against perceived constitutional difficulties and there is no reason to suppose that a more general liability imposed for a similar reason would have been thought less constitutionally objectionable. The second justification was similarly put forward as a justification for the Sherman amendment: "we do not look upon [the Sherman amendment] as a punishment . . . . It is a mutual insurance." Again, this justification was insufficient to sustain the amendment.

We conclude, therefore, that a local government may not be sued under § 1983 for an injury inflicted solely by its employees or agents. Instead, it is when execution of a government's policy or custom, whether made by its lawmakers or by those whose edicts or acts may fairly be said to represent official policy, inflicts the injury that the government as an entity is responsible under § 1983. Since this case unquestionably involves official policy as the moving force of the constitutional violation found by the District Court . . . we must reverse the judgment below. In so doing, we have no occasion to address, and do not address, what the full contours of municipal liability under § 1983 may be. We have attempted only to sketch so much of the § 1983 cause of action against a local government as is apparent from the history of the 1871 Act and our prior cases, and we expressly leave further development of this action to another day.

Although we have stated that *stare decisis* has more force in statutory analysis than in constitutional adjudication because, in the former situation, Congress can correct our mistakes through legislation, we have never applied *stare decisis* mechanically to prohibit overruling our earlier decisions determining the meaning of statutes. . . . Nor is this a case where we should "place on the shoulders of Congress the burden of the Court's own error."

First, *Monroe* v. *Pape,* insofar as it completely immunizes municipalities from suit under § 1983, was a departure from prior practice. . . . Moreover, the constitutional defect that led to the rejection of the Sherman amendment would not have distinguished between municipalities and school boards, each of which is an instrumentality of state administration. For this reason, our cases—decided both before and after *Monroe*—holding school boards liable in § 1983 actions are inconsistent with *Monroe*, especially as *Monroe's* immunizing principle was extended to suits for injunctive relief in City of Kenosha v. Bruno, 412 U.S. 507, 93 S.Ct. 2222, 37 L.Ed.2d 109 (1973). And although in many of these cases jurisdiction was not questioned, we ought not "disregard the implications of an exercise of judicial authority assumed to be proper for [100] years." . . . Thus, while we have reaffirmed *Monroe* without further examination on three occasions, it can scarcely be said that *Monroe* is so consistent with the warp and woof of civil rights law as to be beyond question.

Second, the principle of blanket immunity established in *Monroe* cannot be cabined short of school boards. Yet such an extension would itself be inconsistent with recent expressions of congressional intent. In the wake of our decisions, Congress not only has shown no hostility to federal-court decisions against school boards, but it has indeed rejected efforts to strip the federal courts of jurisdiction over school boards. Moreover, recognizing that school boards are often defendants in school desegregation suits, which have almost without exception been § 1983 suits, Congress has twice passed legislation authorizing grants to school boards to assist them in complying with federal-court decrees. Finally, in the Civil Rights Attorney's Fees Awards Act of 1976, 90 Stat. 2641, 42 U.S.C. § 1988 (1976 ed.), which allows prevailing parties (in the discretion of the court) in § 1983 suits to obtain attorney's fees from the losing parties, the Senate stated:

> [D]efendants in these cases are often State or local *bodies* or State or local officials. In such cases it is intended that the attorneys' fees, like other items of costs, will be collected either directly from the official, *in his official capacity,* from funds of his agency or under his control, or *from the State or local government (whether or not the agency or government is a named party).* (Emphasis added.)

Far from showing that Congress has relied on *Monroe,* therefore, events since 1961 show that Congress has refused to extend the benefits of *Monroe* to school boards and has attempted to allow awards of attorney's fees against local governments even though *Monroe, City of Kenosha* v. *Bruno,* and *Aldinger* v. Howard, 427 U.S. 1, 96 S.Ct. 2413, 49 L.Ed.2d 276 (1976), have made the joinder of such governments impossible.

Third, municipalities can assert no reliance claim which can support an absolute immunity. As Mr. Justice Frankfurter said in *Monroe,* "[t]his is not an area of commercial law in which, presumably, individuals may have arranged their affairs in reliance on the expected stability of decision." Indeed, municipalities simply cannot "arrange their affairs" on an assumption that they can violate constitutional rights indefinitely since injunctive suits against local officials under § 1983 would prohibit any such arrangement. And it scarcely need be mentioned that nothing in *Monroe* encourages municipalities to violate constitutional rights or even suggests that such violations are anything other than completely wrong.

Finally, even under the most stringent test for the propriety of overruling a statutory decision proposed by Mr. Justice Harlan in *Monroe*—"that it appear[s] beyond doubt from the legislative history of the 1871 statute that [*Monroe*] misapprehended the meaning of the [section]," the overruling of *Monroe* insofar as it holds that local governments are not "persons" who may be defendants in § 1983 suits is clearly proper. It is simply beyond doubt that, under the 1871 Congress' view of the law, were § 1983 liability unconstitutional as to local governments, it would have been equally unconstitutional as to state officers. Yet everyone—proponents and opponents alike—knew § 1983 would be applied to state officers and nonetheless stated that § 1983 was constitutional. And, moreover, there can be no doubt that § 1 of the Civil Rights Act was intended to provide a remedy, to be broadly construed, against all forms of official violation of federally protected rights. Therefore, absent a clear statement in the legislative history supporting the conclusion that § 1 was not to apply to the official acts of a municipal corporation—which simply is not present—there is no justification for excluding municipalities from the "persons" covered by § 1.

For reasons stated above, therefore, we hold that *stare decisis* does not bar our overruling of *Monroe* . . . .

Since the question whether local government bodies should be afforded some form of official immunity was not presented as a question to be decided on this petition and was not briefed by the parties or addressed by the courts below, we express no views on the scope of any municipal immunity beyond holding that municipal bodies sued under § 1983 cannot be entitled to an absolute immunity, lest our decision that such bodies are subject to suit under § 1983 "be drained of meaning," Scheuer v. Rhodes, 416 U.S. 232, 248, 94 S.Ct. 1683, 40 L.Ed.2d 90 (1974). . . .

For the reasons stated above, the judgment of the Court of Appeals is Reversed.

NOTES

1. *Absolute Immunity.* The Supreme Court, in a series of cases, determined that absolute immunity was available as a defense for prosecutors in initiating and presenting the state's case, Imbler v. Pachtman, 424 U.S. 409, 96 S.Ct. 984 (1976), and state legislators. Tenney v. Brandhove, 341 U.S. 367, 71 S.Ct. 783 (1951).

2. *Qualified or Conditional Immunity.* Prosecutors and legislators have absolute immunity; therefore it may appear that other state officials have absolute immunity. But in Scheuer v. Rhodes, 416 U.S. 232, 94 S.Ct. 1683 (1974), the Supreme Court declared the Governor of Ohio and other state officials have only qualified or conditional immunity. Qualified or conditional immunity from civil liability means individuals would not be liable as long as they are acting clearly within the scope of their authority for the betterment of those they serve. If they venture outside the scope of their authority, and, in doing so, violate someone's rights, then they may be personally liable. Qualified immunity has been established by Supreme Court decision for superintendents of state hospitals, O'Connor v. Donaldson, 422 U.S. 563, 95 S.Ct. 2486 (1975), and for local school board members, Wood v. Strickland, 420 U.S. 308, 95 S.Ct. 992 (1975).

3. *Good Faith Immunity.* Although individuals may assert good faith as a defense in a constitutional tort action, a municipality has no immunity and may not assert a good faith defense. Owen v. City of Independence, 445 U.S. 622, 100 S.Ct. 1398 (1980).

4. *Punitive Damages.* A municipality is immune from punitive damages. The Supreme Court of the United States in concluding that punitive damages should not be assessed against municipalities (or school districts) has said:

> Punitive damages by definition are not intended to compensate the injured party, but rather to punish the tortfeasor whose wrongful action was intentional or malicious, and to deter him and others from similar extreme conduct. . . . Regarding retribution, it remains true that an award of punitive damages against a municipality "punishes" only the taxpayers, who took no part in the commission of the tort. These damages are assessed over and above the amount necessary to compensate the injured party. Thus, there is no question here of equitably distributing the losses resulting from official misconduct. . . . Indeed, punitive damages imposed on a municipality are in effect a windfall to a fully compensated plaintiff, and are likely accompanied by an increase in taxes or a reduction of public services for the citizens footing the bill. Neither reason nor justice suggests that such retribution should be visited upon the shoulders of blameless or unknowing taxpayers.
>
> Under ordinary principles of retribution, it is the wrongdoer himself who is made to suffer for his unlawful conduct. If a government official acts knowingly and maliciously to deprive others of their civil rights, he may become the appropriate object of the community's vindictive sentiments. . . . A municipality, however, can have no malice independent of the malice of its officials. Damages awarded for *punitive* purposes, therefore, are not sensibly assessed against the governmental entity itself. City of Newport v. Fact Concerts, Inc., 453 U.S. 247, 101 S.Ct. 2748 (1981).

Footnotes

1. William L. Prosser, *Law of Torts* (St. Paul, MN: West Publishing Co., 1971), p. 1.

2. Reynolds v. Pierson, 29 Ind.App. 273, 64 N.E. 484 (1902); State v. Monroe, 121 N.C. 677, 28 S.E. 547 (1897).

3. State v. Ingram, 237 N.C. 197, 74 S.E.2d 532 (1953).

4. Prosser, supra, p. 37.

5. Suits v. Gover, 260 Ala. 449, 71 So.2d 49 (1949).

6. State ex rel. Burpee v. Burton, 45 Wis. 150 (1878).

7. Gardner v. State, 4 Ind. 632 (1853).

8. Vanvactor v. State, 113 Ind. 276, 15 N.E. 341 (1888).

9. Cooper v. McJunkin, 4 Ind. 290 (1853).

10. Gardner v. State, supra.

11. Frank v. Orleans Parish School Bd., 195 So.2d 451 (La.App.1967).

12. Cooper v. McJunkin, 4 Ind. 290 (1853); Danenhoffer v. State, 69 Ind. 295 (1879).

13. Wallace v. Shoreham Hotel Corp., 49 A.2d 81 (D.C.Mun.App.1946).

14. Barnett v. Collection Service Co., 214 Iowa 1303, 242 N.W. 25 (1932).

15. Prosser, supra, p. 315.

16. Restatement of Torts, pp. 519–520.

17. See Kern Alexander and Erwin Solomon, *College and University Law* (Charlottesville, VA: The Michie Co., 1972), pp. 590–602.

18. Prier v. Horace Mann Insurance Co., 351 So.2d 265 (La.App.1977).

19. Lewis v. St. Bernard Parish School Board, 350 So.2d 1256 (La.App.1977).

20. Terry, "Negligence," 29 Harv.L.Rev. 40 (1915); See also The Restatement of Torts, pp. 291–293.

21. William L. Prosser, supra, p. 123.

22. Id. p. 124.

23. Lehmuth v. Long Beach Unified School District, 53 Cal.2d 544, 2 Cal.Rptr. 279, 348 P.2d 887 (1960).

24. Hassenyer v. Michigan Central Railway Co., 48 Mich. 205, 12 N.W. 155 (1882).

25. Johnson v. St. Paul City Railway Co., 67 Minn. 260, 69 N.W. 900 (1887); Kitsap County Transportation Co. v. Harvey, 15 F.2d 166 (9th Cir.1927).

26. In criminal law the courts have applied the rule as established in M'Naghten's Case, 10 Ct. & F. 200, 8 E.R. 718 (1843) which holds the defense of insanity can only be established by showing that the accused was "laboring under such a defect of reason, from disease of the mind, as not to know the nature and quality of the act he was doing; or, if he did know it, that he did not know what he was doing was wrong."

27. Morris v. Douglas County School District, 241 Or. 23, 403 P.2d 775 (1965).

28. Osborne v. Montgomery, 203 Wis. 223, 234 N.W. 372 (1931).

29. Hoyem v. Manhattan Beach City School District, 71 Cal.App.3d 866, 139 Cal.Rptr. 769 (1977).

30. Cirillo v. Milwaukee, 34 Wis.2d 705, 150 N.W.2d 460 (1967).

31. Connett v. Freemont County School District No. 6, 581 P.2d 1097 (Wyo.1978).

32. Prosser, supra, p. 127.

33. *The Restatement of Torts* § 464 states that: "Age is only one of the elements to be considered, along with experience and judgment, the latter involving discretion and power of self control, being predominant."

34. Ohman v. Board of Education of City of New York, 300 N.Y. 306, 90 N.E.2d 474 (1949), reargument denied 301 N.Y. 662, 93 N.E.2d 927.

35. Eastman v. Williams, 124 Vt. 445, 207 A.2d 146 (1965).

36. Scott v. Greenville Pharmacy, 212 S.C. 485, 48 S.E.2d 324 (1948).

37. Restatement, Second, Torts, § 430.

38. Prosser, supra, p. 252. See: Woodsmall v. Mt. Diablo Unified School District, 188 Cal.App. 2d 262, 10 Cal.Rptr. 447 (1961); Munson v. Board of Education, 17 A.D.2d 687, 230 N.Y.S.2d 919, affirmed 13 N.Y.2d 854, 242 N.Y.S.2d 492, 192 N.E.2d 272 (1962).

39. McDonell v. Brozo, 285 Mich. 38, 280 N.W. 100 (1938).

40. Meyer v. Board of Education, 9 N.J. 46, 86 A.2d 761 (1952).

41. Mikes v. Baumgartner, 277 Minn. 423, 152 N.W.2d 732 (1967).

42. Walsh v. West Coast Mines, 31 Wash.2d 396, 197 P.2d 233 (1948).

43. Restatement, Second, Torts, § 463.

44. Rixmann v. Somerset Public Schools, 83 Wis.2d 571, 266 N.W.2d 326 (1978). See also: Lemelle v. State, Through Board of Elm. and Secondary Education, 435 So.2d 1162 (La.App. 3 Cir.1983).

45. Cormier v. Sinegal, 180 So.2d 567 (La.App.1965).

46. Basmajian v. Board of Education, 211 App.Div. 347, 207 N.Y.S. 298 (1925).

47. Wilhelm v. Board of Education of City of New York, 16 A.D.2d 707, 227 N.Y.S.2d 791 (1962).

48. Prosser, supra, p. 303. See: Passantino v. Board of Education of City of New York, 41 N.Y.2d 1022, 395 N.Y.S.2d 628, 363 N.E.2d 1373 (1977).

49. Stevens v. Central School District No. 1, 25 A.D.2d 871, 270 N.Y.S.2d 23 (1966).

50. Maltz v. Board of Education of New York City, 32 Misc.2d 492, 114 N.Y.S.2d 856 (1952).

51. Benedetto v. Travelers Insurance Co., 172 So.2d 354 (La.App.1965).

52. Brisson v. Minneapolis Baseball and Athletic Association, 185 Minn. 507, 240 N.W. 903 (1932); Kavafiam v. Seattle Baseball Club Association, 105 Wash. 215, 177 P. 776 (1919).

53. Scanlon v. Wedger, 156 Mass. 462, 31 N.E. 642 (1891).

54. Dusckiewicz v. Carter, 115 Vt. 122, 52 A.2d 788 (1947).

55. Cadieux v. Board of Education of the City School Dist. for the City of Schenectady, 25 A.D.2d 579, 266 N.Y.S.2d 895 (1966).

56. Barr v. Bernhard, 562 S.W.2d 844 (Tex.1978).

57. Hunter v. Board of Education of Montgomery County, 439 A.2d 582 (Md.1982).

58. Id.

59. Peter W. v. San Francisco Unified School District, 60 Cal.App.3d 814, 131 Cal.Rptr. 854 (1976).

60. Donohue v. Copiague Union Free School District, 47 N.Y.2d 440, 418 N.Y.S.2d 375, 391 N.E.2d 1352 (1979).

61. Supra, 439 A.2d at 585.

62. See, D.S.W. v. Fairbanks No. Star School District, 628 P.2d 554 (Alaska 1981); Smith v. Alameda County Social Service Agency, 90 Cal.App.3d 929, 153 Cal.Rptr. 712 (1979); Hoffman v. Board of Education of City of New York, 49 N.Y.2d 121, 424 N.Y.S.2d 376, 400 N.E.2d 317 (1979); Aubrey v. School District of Philadelphia, 63 Pa.Cmwlth. 330, 437 A.2d 1306 (1981).

63. F. Pollock and F.W. Maitland, *The History of English Law Before the Time of Edward I* (Cambridge University Press, Boston: Little, Brown & Co., 1905).

64. Eugene T. Conners, "Governmental Immunity: Legal Basis and Implications for Public Education," Ph.D. dissertation, University of Florida, 1977.

65. Id.

66. *The Case of the King's Prerogative in Saltpetre,* 12 Co.Rep. 12 (1607).

67. *Prohibitions del Roy,* 12 Rep. 63 (1607).

68. Mersey Trustees v. Gibbs, L.R. 1 H.L. 93 (1866).

69. Crisp v. Thomas, 63 LINS 756 (1890).

70. 100 Eng.Rep. 359, 2 T.R. 667 (1788).

71. 9 Mass. 247 (1812).

72. The Siren, 74 U.S. (7 Wall.) 152 (1869).

73. Nichols v. United States, 74 U.S. (7 Wall.) 122 (1869).

74. Molitor v. Kaneland Community Unit District No. 302, 18 Ill.2d 11, 163 N.E.2d 89 (1959).

75. Muskopf v. Corning Hospital District, 55 Cal.2d 211, 11 Cal.Rptr. 89, 359 P.2d 457 (1961).

76. Conners, supra, p. 72.

77. Id.

78. Sawaya v. Tucson High School District No. 1, 78 Ariz. 389, 281 P.2d 105 (1955).

79. Reed v. Rhea County, 189 Tenn. 247, 225 S.W.2d 49 (1949).

80. Braun v. Trustees of Victoria Ind. School District, 114 S.W.2d 947 (Tex.Civ.App.1938).

81. Koehn v. Board of Education of City of Newton, 193 Kan. 263, 392 P.2d 949 (1964).

82. Rankin v. School District No. 9, 143 Or. 449, 23 P.2d 132 (1933).

83. 50 Am.Jur.2d 516.

84. Id.

85. *Restatement of Torts,* § 596; 12 A.L.R. 147; 50 A.L.R. 339.

86. Barton v. Rogers, 21 Idaho 609, 123 P. 478 (1912).

87. Dawkins v. Billingsley, 69 Okl. 259, 172 P. 69 (1918).

88. Prosser, supra, p. 609.

89. Coffin v. Coffin, 4 Mass. 1, 3 Am.Dec. 189 (1808).

90. Smith v. Helbraun, 21 A.D.2d 830, 251 N.Y.S.2d 533 (1964).

91. Ottinger v. Ferrell, 171 Ark. 1085, 287 S.W. 391 (1926).

92. Baskett v. Crossfield, 190 Ky. 751, 228 S.W. 673 (1921).

93. Tyler Commercial College v. Lattimore, 24 S.W.2d 361 (Tex.1930).

94. Vigil v. Rice, 74 N.M. 693, 397 P.2d 719 (1964).

95. Solow v. General Motors Truck Co., 64 F.2d 105 (2nd Cir.1933).

96. Hoff v. Pure Oil, 147 Minn. 195, 179 N.W. 891 (1920).

97. Education Amendments of 1974, Public Law No. 93–380, 20 U.S.C.A. § 1232g. (Sometimes referred to as the Buckley Amendment). See Appendix.

98. David G. Carter, J. John Harris III, and Frank Brown, "Privacy in Education: Legal Implications for Educational Researchers." *Journal of Law and Education,* vol. 5, no. 4 (October 1976), p. 470.

99. 365 U.S. 167, 81 S.Ct. 473 (1961).

100. 42 U.S.C.A. § 1983 enacted 1871.

101. Ernest W. Williams, *Liability of Public Schools and Public School Officials for Damages Under 42 U.S.C. 1983,* unpublished thesis for Juris Doctor, Harvard Law School, 1975, p. 1.

102. 436 U.S. 658, 98 S.Ct. 2018 (1978).

103. 420 U.S. 308, 95 S.Ct. 992 (1975).

104. 435 U.S. 247, 98 S.Ct. 1042 (1978).

12

Terms and Conditions of Teacher Employment

The terms and conditions of employment of educators vary from state to state. All states require teachers be certified or licensed to qualify for employment as a public school teacher. Besides state certification requirements, local school boards may establish additional requirements that employees must satisfy before they are eligible for employment. These requirements may be residency requirements, health and safety qualifications, plus others. Basic terms of employment are created by the teacher's contract with the school board and the tenure laws of the respective states.

CERTIFICATION

All state legislatures have enacted laws relating to the certification of teachers, and when such laws are properly promulgated with no intent to discriminate, and are not arbitrary, they will be upheld by the courts. These laws run the gamut from great particularity to gross generality. Hence, it is necessary to consider the specific laws of each state individually to determine specific certification requirements.

The general rule is that if a teacher satisfies all the requirements set forth in the statutes and regulations relative to the issuance of a certificate, the certifying body may not arbitrarily refuse to issue the certificate. However, in most cases, the certificate-issuing body is vested with discretionary authority. Also, the issuing agency may, in many instances, prescribe higher standards for certification than are contained in laws enacted by a state legislature.

Most states require that an applicant for a teacher's certificate be of good moral character. In order to remain eligible for either continued certification or renewal of an existing certificate, the teacher must continue to evidence good moral character.

Besides good moral character, state law generally requires that applicants have successfully completed a predetermined number of college credits in the subject that the individual plans to teach (i.e., English). Also, states generally require the individual to be of a specified age (usually eighteen or older) and a citizen of the United States. Some states require the pledging of loyalty to the state and/or federal constitution and, in recent years, have required the completion of an examination, such as the National Teacher Examination.

Teacher certification does not guarantee employment. State legislatures have delegated the authority for employment of teachers to local school boards. Local boards have been given wide latitude and may place additional requirements or restrictions on employment as long as these rules do not contradict or reduce the effect of state requirements. Neither can such rules violate one's constitutional or statutory rights. Local boards may not impose requirements that are arbitrary, capricious, or enacted in bad faith.

Some additional requirements that have been upheld are mandating greater academic credentials than those established by the state or having employees take additional academic courses after employment.[1] School boards have been upheld in requiring teachers to establish residency within the boundaries of the school district,[2] restricting outside employment, adopting reasonable health and physical requirements (within federal and state provisions for the handicapped), assigning (within state statutes) teachers to teaching positions, and the supervision of extracurricular activities.

State Board of Education Will Not
Be Deprived of Discretion in
Granting Certificates

METCALF v. COOK

Court of Appeals of Maryland, 1935.
168 Md. 475, 178 A. 219.

BOND, Chief Judge. The question here is one of statutory construction, raised by a demand of the appellant for a writ of mandamus to compel the superintendent of schools to grant him a certificate authorizing him to teach in a high school of the state, notwithstanding a by-law of the state board of education limiting the issue of such certificates to those who have attained a higher rank in their own training. The appeal is from a denial of the writ upon an agreed statement of the facts supplemented by testimony.

The Code, art. 77, §§ 87 and 88, provides generally for the issue of teachers' certificates by the state superintendent, and section 83 limits employment as a teacher to a person holding a certificate. Section 85, subsec. 5, of the article provides that a high school teacher's certificate "may be granted to persons who are graduates of a standard college or university, or who have had the equivalent in scholastic preparation." Section 11 of the same article directs and empowers the state board of education to "determine the educational policies of the State," and "enact by-laws for the administration of the public school system, which when enacted and published shall have the force of law." And in pursuance of this authority the board, on September 19, 1930, enacted a by-law that "only such graduates as rank academically in the upper four-fifths of the Class and who make a grade of 'C' or better in practical teaching, shall be issued Maryland Teachers' Certificates." The appellant ranked only in the lowest fifth of his class, and for that reason was denied the certificate which he now seeks through the courts. He contends that the passage of the by-law was not within the authority vested in the board by the statutes.

In 1927 he was awarded a scholarship to Western Maryland College, under the provision in article 77, section 243, which required that the winner of such a scholarship should give a bond to the state "that he will teach school within this State for not less than two years after leaving college." And having complied and attended the college, the appellant considers himself assured a teaching position by that provision of the statute. But we are unable to see in the requirement of a bond anything more than a measure to assure the state that it may derive so much benefit in return for its grant to the student. It secures the benefit in case the state should want it. No assurance is given the student, and no obligation assumed by the state toward him.

The provision in section 85, subsec. 5, that a high school teacher's certificate "may be granted," to persons of the specified experience, is construed by the appellant as the equivalent of "shall be granted," and therefore as prohibiting a choice among such persons by the board, limiting eligibility to those in the upper four-fifths of the classes. With this construction, too, the court is in disagreement. There seems to the court to be no intention manifested other than that of setting a minimum requirement for the board's selection of teachers. That seems to be a reasonable construction, in accord with the evident plan of the whole statute that the board shall be depended upon largely to make the educational system work properly. Discretion in selection from eligibles, whose fitness must differ greatly, would seem to be a very likely intention. And if the discretion is given, as we think it is, then when exercised it acquires by the express terms of the statute the force of law, not to be interfered with by the courts. . . .

. . . the appellant argues that exercise of the authority retroactively could not be intended, so that after a student has started on his preparation a higher test than that with which he was faced at the start could be imposed. The by-law makes no change in courses of study and preparation; it concerns only the diligence and ability of the student in it, and the contention seems to be that the student had a right to take his work more easily. We see no vested rights in the standards of work which might restrict retroactive by-laws. Before the student is selected as a teacher he has no contract with the state, and no vested rights. He is only the recipient of the state's bounty, with the state left unrestrained in adopting requirements it might find desirable at any time.

A further objection, that no notice was given the appellant of the adoption of this by-law, is subject to the same criticisms. There is no requirement of notice to individuals. Publication of the by-law is required by the statute, and it is not denied that there was publication; and in that the full measure of the statutory requirements was met. Upon publication, the by-law acquired the force of law.

Order affirmed, with costs.

Certificate May Be Denied When
Board Has Evidence to Question Good
Moral Character of Applicant

APPLICATION OF BAY

Supreme Court of Oregon, 1963.
233 Or. 601, 378 P.2d 558.

PERRY, Justice. Dean Norman Bay petitioned the circuit court of Union County for judicial review of the decision of appellant State Board of Education denying him issuance of a five-year elementary teacher's certificate. From the decree of the circuit court reversing the Board's decision for lack of competent evidence, appeal is made to this court.

In December of 1953, petitioner was tried and convicted in the state of Washington for his acts of breaking, entering, and grand larceny of several stores, the American Legion Club, and the local high school, committed while employed as a night policeman. At the time these acts were perpetrated, petitioner was twenty-four years old. After serving eighteen months of a two-year sentence, he was paroled. He moved to La Grande, Oregon, where, in the fall of 1956 he enrolled at the Eastern Oregon College of Education. In 1958 the state of Washington restored to him his full civil rights.

In 1960 petitioner was granted a one-year elementary teacher's emergency certificate by the Superintendent of Public Instruction, and taught elementary school while completing his fourth year at the college. Following graduation he applied for a five-year elementary teacher's certificate, but his application was denied on June 14, 1961.

On September 13, 1961, a hearing was conducted before the Board, the primary purpose of which was to determine whether petitioner had furnished the evidence of good moral character which ORS 342.060(2) authorizes the superintendent to require of an applicant. Whereas numerous witnesses appeared at the hearing to testify of petitioner's good character and over-all reputation in the community, the sole evidence of bad character introduced was the record of the prior conviction. The Board concluded that petitioner had not met his burden of furnishing satisfactory evidence of good moral character and he thereupon petitioned the circuit court of Union County for review of the administrative order pursuant to ORS 183.480. The court held that evidence as to a prior conviction was irrelevant and immaterial in determining present character where not accompanied by other evidence which related the prior act to the present, and therefore adjudged there was no competent evidence to support the Board's findings. The Board was ordered to issue petitioner the certificate, from which order this appeal is taken. . . .

In order to properly discuss the issues presented it is first necessary to discuss the powers of the trial court in reviewing the Board's determination.

While the statute uses the language "as a suit in equity," it is quite clear that this language refers only to the fact that the review shall be made by the court, not a jury, and does not grant to a trial court the right on appeal to try the cause de novo. That is, the reviewing court is not granted the power to weigh the evidence and substitute its judgment as to the preponderance thereof for that of the agency. The extent to which a reviewing court should review the action of an administrative agency has been expressed by this court as follows:

> Generally, they go no further than to determine whether the agency (1) acted impartially; (2) performed faithfully the duties delineated in the legislative acts which conferred jurisdiction upon it; (3) stayed within its jurisdiction; (4) committed no error of law; (5) exercised discretion judiciously and not capriciously; and (6) arrived at no conclusion which was clearly wrong. Richardson v. Neuner, 183 Or. 558, 564, 194 P.2d 989, 991.

The learned trial court recognized these guideposts and reached the conclusion that the finding of the Board as to lack of good moral character could not be sustained by the record. This conclusion of the court is based upon a finding that there was no evidence of bad moral character at the time of application and therefore the Board's conclusion was clearly wrong.

Whether or not the Board arrived at a conclusion which was clearly wrong depends upon whether a review of the entire record discloses any facts from which the conclusion drawn by the Board could be reached by reasonable minds. . . .

The Board made the following findings of fact which are pertinent to this appeal:

1. That the applicant on December 9, 1953, was convicted of grand larceny of four counts in the Superior Court for Klickitat County, State of Washington and received a one- to fifteen-year sentence by the said Court. That thereafter this sentence was fixed at a term of two years by the State Board of Terms and Parole of the State of Washington, and the applicant served an eighteen-month term at the Monroe Reformatory in the State of Washington.

2. Thereafter upon his release he was placed on parole for approximately a year and moved to the City of LaGrande, Oregon, and in the fall of 1956 entered the Eastern Oregon College of Education and enrolled in a teacher education course.

3. That by act of the Governor of the State of Washington full civil rights were restored to him on July 3, 1958. . . .

8. The Board further finds the offenses committed by Mr. Bay consisted of breaking and entering various stores in Goldendale, Washington, and grand larceny, and included safe burglaries at the American Legion Club, and Goldendale High School. That at the time he committed the offenses for which he was imprisoned he had reached the age of twenty-four years; that his offenses numbered not one but several; that he was a man of superior intelligence as evidenced by his scores on intelligence tests in his subsequent college record.

9. The Board further finds that at the time of the thefts he occupied a position of trust as a night policeman in the community and that while so engaged he committed the acts resulting in his conviction.

10. That a teacher in a public school is the key factor in teaching by precept and example the subjects of honesty, morality, courtesy, obedience to law, and other lessons of a steadying influence which tend to promote and develop an upright and desirable citizenry, as required by ORS 336.240 and related statutes.

11. That there has been no evidence submitted to the Board of any violations of law or deviations from normally considered moral conduct from the time of his release from the Monroe Reformatory to the present time.

The Board then made the following conclusions of law:

1. That the applicant has not furnished evidence of good moral character deemed satisfactory and necessary by the Board to establish the applicant's fitness to serve as a teacher.

In resolving the question of moral character there must be kept in mind the distinction between character and reputation. "Character is what a man or woman is morally, while reputation is what he or she is reputed to be." Leverich v. Frank, 6 Or. 212; State v. Charlie Sing, 114 Or. 267, 229 P. 921.

A person's "character" is usually thought to embrace all his qualities and deficiencies regarding traits of personality, behavior, integrity, temperament, consideration, sportsmanship, altruism, etc. which distinguish him as a human being from his fellow men. His disposition toward criminal acts is only one of the qualities which constitute his character. . . .

Since the crux of the question before the Board was good moral character, the fact that he had been guilty of burglarizing properties while he held a position of trust was most pertinent. These actions of petitioner clearly evidenced a lack of the moral fiber to resist temptation. The trial court therefore erred in holding there was no evidence of lack of good moral character.

The petitioner offered numerous witnesses from which a conclusion might properly be reached that this lack of moral fiber no longer exists. However, this condition having been shown to have existed, it became a matter of judgment as to whether it had been overcome.

The power to decide such an issue was delegated by the legislature to the Board of Education, therefore, as previously pointed out, the courts are not permitted to substitute their judgment for that of the Board where there is substantial evidence to support the agency.

The judgment of the trial court is reversed with instructions to enter findings of fact and conclusions of law sustaining the action of the Board of Education.

NOTES

1. Under what circumstances and when would applicant Bay be eligible for a certificate?

2. One of the basic purposes of the certification laws is that a capable and competent instructor will be provided in every classroom. Consequently, a teacher's certificate is a prerequisite not only to employment and reemployment, but is necessary for schools to qualify for state aid. It is a common practice in several states to permit student teachers to assume complete control of a class in the absence of the regular teacher. This violates not only the spirit but also the letter of the law of many states because a student teacher is not a qualified teacher, but is seeking to become a qualified teacher. If a teacher teaches without a certificate, she is considered to be a volunteer and is entitled to no compensation for

services rendered. See: Floyd County Board of Education v. Stone, 307 S.W.2d 912 (Ky.1957).

3. A teacher who has no certificate when entering into an employment contract with a school board could not recover salary for services rendered, even though he had obtained the license prior to actually beginning work. McCloskey v. School District, 134 Mich. 235, 96 N.W. 18 (1903); O'Conner v. Francis, 42 App.Div. 375, 59 N.Y.S. 28 (1899); Lee v. Mitchell, 108 Ark. 1, 156 S.W. 450 (1913).

4. A state board of education was held entitled to conclude that a teacher was unfit to teach and her teaching credentials could be revoked where the teacher had joined a "swingers" club, engaged in sexual acts with men other than her husband, and had appeared disguised on television to discuss nonconventional sexual behavior even though the teacher's school principal found her teaching satisfactory. Pettit v. State Board of Education, 10 Cal.3d 29, 109 Cal.Rptr. 665, 513 P.2d 889 (1973).

*Statute Forbidding Certification to
Persons Who Are Not Citizens and
Have Manifested No Intent to Become
Citizens Is Not Violative of
Equal Protection*

AMBACH v. NORWICK

Supreme Court of the United States, 1979.
441 U.S. 68, 99 S.Ct. 1589.

Mr. Justice POWELL delivered the opinion of the Court.

This case presents the question whether a State, consistently with the Equal Protection Clause of the Fourteenth Amendment, may refuse to employ as elementary and secondary school teachers aliens who are eligible for United States citizenship but who refuse to seek naturalization.

New York Education Law § 3001(3) forbids certification as a public school teacher of any person who is not a citizen of the United States, unless that person has manifested an intention to apply for citizenship. The Commissioner of Education is authorized to create exemptions from this prohibition, and has done so with respect to aliens who are not yet eligible for citizenship. Unless a teacher obtains certification, he may not work in a public elementary or secondary school in New York.

Appellee Norwick was born in Scotland and is a subject of Great Britain. She has resided in this country since 1965 and is married to a United States citizen. Appellee Dachinger is a Finnish subject who came to this country in 1966 and also is married to a United States citizen. Both Norwick and Dachinger currently meet all of the educational requirements New York has set for certification as a public school teacher, but they consistently have refused to seek citizenship in spite of their eligibility to do so. Norwick applied in 1973 for a teaching certificate covering nursery school through sixth grade, and Dachinger sought a certificate covering the same grades in 1975. Both applications were denied because of appellees' failure to meet the requirements of § 3001(3). Norwick then filed this suit seeking to enjoin the enforcement of § 3001(3), and Dachinger obtained leave to intervene as a plaintiff. . . .

Applying the rational basis standard, we held last term that New York could exclude aliens from the ranks of its police force. Foley v. Connelie, 435 U.S. 291 (1978). Because the police function fulfilled "a most fundamental obligation of government to its constituency" and by necessity cloaked policemen with substantial discretionary powers, we viewed the police force as being one of those appropriately defined classes of positions for which a citizenship requirement could be imposed. Accordingly, the State was required to justify its classification only "by a showing of some rational relationship between the interest sought to be protected and the limiting classification."

The rule for governmental functions, which is an exception to the general standard applicable to classifications based on alienage, rests on important principles inherent in the Constitution. The distinction between citizens and aliens, though ordinarily irrelevant to private activity, is fundamental to the definition and government of a State. The Constitution itself refers to the distinction no less than eleven times, see Sugarman v. Dougall (Rehnquist, J., dissenting), indicating that the status of citizenship was meant to have significance in the structure of our government. The assumption of that status, whether by birth or naturalization, denotes an association with the polity which, in a democratic republic, exercises the powers of governance. The form of this association is important: an oath of allegiance or similar ceremony cannot substitute for the unequivocal legal bond citizenship represents. It is because of this special significance of citizenship that governmental entities, when exercising the functions of government, have wider latitude in limiting the participation of noncitizens.

In determining whether, for purposes of equal protection analysis, teaching in public schools constitutes a governmental function, we look to the role of public education and to the degree of responsibility and discretion teachers possess in fulfilling that role. Each of these considerations supports the conclusion that public school teachers may be regarded as performing a task "that go[es] to the heart of representative government."

Public education, like the police function, "fulfills a most fundamental obligation of government to its constituency." The importance of public schools in the preparation of individuals for participation as citizens, and in the preservation of the values on which our society rests, long has been recognized by our decisions:

> Today, education is perhaps the most important function of state and local governments. Compulsory school attendance laws and the great expenditures for education both demonstrate our recognition of the importance of education to our democratic society. It is required in the performance of our most basic public responsibilities, even service in the armed forces. It is the very foundation of good citizenship. Today it is a principal instrument in awakening the child to cultural values, in preparing him for later professional training, and in helping him to adjust normally to his environment. Brown v. Board of Education, 347 U.S. 483, 493 (1954).

. . . Other authorities have perceived public schools as an "assimilative force" by which diverse and conflicting elements in our society are brought together on a broad but common ground. . . . These perceptions of the public schools as inculcating fundamental values necessary to the maintenance of a democratic political system have been confirmed by the observations of social scientists. . . .

Within the public school system, teachers play a critical part in developing students' attitude toward government and understanding the role of citizens in our society. Alone among employees of the system, teachers are in direct, day-to-day contact with students both in the classrooms and in the other varied activities of a modern school. In shaping the students' experience to achieve educational goals, teachers by necessity have wide discretion over the way the course material is communicated to students. They are responsible for presenting and explaining the subject matter in a way that is both comprehensible and inspiring. No amount of standardization of teaching materials or lesson plans can eliminate the personal qualities a teacher brings to bear in achieving these goals. Further, a teacher serves as a role model for his students, exerting a subtle but important influence over their perceptions and values. Thus, through both the presentation of course materials and the example he sets, a teacher has an opportunity to influence the attitudes of students toward government, the political process, and a citizen's social responsibilities. This influence is crucial to the continued good health of a democracy.

Furthermore, it is clear that all public school teachers, and not just those responsible for teaching the courses most directly related to government, history, and civic duties, should help fulfill the broader function of the public school system. Teachers, regardless of their specialty, may be called upon to teach other subjects, including those expressly dedicated to political and social subjects. More importantly, a State properly may regard all teachers as having an obligation to promote civic virtues and understanding in their classes, regardless of the subject taught. Certainly a State also may take account of a teacher's function as an example for students, which exists independently of particular classroom subjects. In light of the foregoing considerations, we think it clear that public school teachers come well within the "governmental function" principle recognized in *Sugarman* and *Foley*. Accordingly, the Constitution requires only that a citizenship requirement applicable to teaching in the public schools bears a rational relationship to a legitimate state interest. . . .

As the legitimacy of the State's interest in furthering the educational goals outlined above is undoubted, it remains only to consider whether § 3001(3) bears a rational relationship to this interest. The restriction is carefully framed to serve its purpose, as it bars from teaching only those aliens who have demonstrated their unwillingness to obtain United States citizenship. Appellees, and aliens similarly situated, in effect have chosen to classify themselves. They prefer to retain citizenship in a foreign country with the obligations it entails of primary duty and loyalty. They have rejected the open invitation extended to qualify for eligibility to teach by applying for citizenship in this country. The people of New York, acting through their elected representatives, have made a judgment that citizenship should be a qualification for teaching the young of the State in the public schools, and § 3001(3) furthers that judgment.

Reversed.

Employee Residency Requirements Are
Constitutional

WARDWELL v. BOARD OF EDUCATION OF THE CITY SCHOOL DISTRICT OF THE CITY OF CINCINNATI ET AL.

United States Court of Appeals,
Sixth Circuit, 1976.
529 F.2d 528.

WILLIAM E. MILLER, Circuit Judge.

In December, 1972, plaintiff, Terry Wardwell, was hired to teach in the Cincinnati schools. As a condition of employment he agreed to move into the city school district pursuant to a rule announced by the school superintendent in November, 1972, that all newly employed teachers must establish residence within the district within thirty days after employment. In January, 1973, the Board adopted the following resolution, essentially ratifying the superintendent's rule:

> RESOLVED, That any employee hired by the Cincinnati Schools after November 13, 1972, must either reside within the Cincinnati School District, or agree, as a condition of employment, to establish residency within the district within ninety days of employment. Employees who live in the district must continue to reside therein as long as they are so employed. This policy does not affect in any way personnel hired before the above date.

Plaintiff Wardwell lived outside the district but within the State of Ohio. Despite the requirement he failed to change his residence. He filed the present action in July, 1973, under 28 U.S.C. § 1343 and 42 U.S.C. § 1983, challenging the residency requirement on equal protection grounds and seeking injunctive relief and attorney's fees. No preliminary injunction was requested because enforcement of the rule had been stayed by a preliminary injunction issued by a state court. Since being hired, plaintiff Wardwell has taught at one time in a predominantly white school located within a ten-minute drive from his home and later at a predominantly black school about twenty minutes from his home outside the district.

The district court denied the request for an injunction and upheld the validity of the rule, relying heavily on the Fifth Circuit's reasoning in Wright v. City of Jackson, 506 F.2d 900 (5th Cir.1975).

Plaintiff argues that the Board's residency requirement infringes his constitutionally protected right to travel as defined in Shapiro v. Thompson, 394 U.S. 618, 89 S.Ct. 1322, 22 L.Ed.2d 600 (1969), and in Dunn v. Blumstein, 405 U.S. 330, 92 S.Ct. 995, 31 L.Ed.2d 274 (1972), extending the protection, as he contends, to both intrastate and interstate travel and embracing as a necessary corollary the right to remain in one place.

We find no support for plaintiff's theory that the right to intrastate travel has been afforded federal constitutional protection. An examination of *Shapiro,* supra, *Dunn,* supra, and the Supreme Court's more recent opinion in Memorial Hospital v. Maricopa County, 415 U.S. 250, 94 S.Ct. 1076, 39 L.Ed.2d 306 (1974), convinces us that the aspect of the right to travel with which the Court was concerned in thoses cases is not involved here. It is clear that the Court was dealing with the validity of durational residency requirements which penalized recent interstate travel. Such *durational* residency requirements or restrictions affecting the interstate aspect of travel will not pass constitutional muster "absent a compelling state interest."

In *Memorial Hospital,* supra . . . the Court at some length emphasized that *Shapiro* and the later cases were not to be construed as applying to bona fide *continuing,* as distinguished from *durational,* residency requirements when it said:

> The right of interstate travel has repeatedly been recognized as a basic constitutional freedom. Whatever its ultimate scope, however, the right to travel was involved in only a limited sense in *Shapiro.* The Court was there concerned only with the right to migrate, "with intent to settle and abide" or, as the Court put it, "to migrate, resettle, find a new job, and start a new life." Even a bona fide residence requirement would burden the right to travel, if travel meant merely movement. But, in *Shapiro,* the Court explained that "[t]he residence requirement and the one-year waiting-period requirement are distinct and independent prerequisites" for assistance and only the latter was held to be unconstitutional. Later, in invalidating a durational residence requirement for voter registration on the basis of *Shapiro,* we cautioned that our decision was not intended to "cast doubt on the validity of appropriately defined and uniformly applied bona fide residence requirements."

Our conclusion that *Shapiro* and the other right-to-travel cases are not applicable to intrastate travel and *continuing* employee residency requirements is supported by Detroit Police Officers Association v. City of Detroit, 405 U.S. 950, 92 S.Ct. 1173, 31 L.Ed.2d 227 (1972), on which the district court in this case and the Fifth Circuit in *Wright,* supra, relied. The case involved a Detroit residency requirement for policemen. The Michigan Supreme Court, applying the "rational basis test," determined that the classification bore a reasonable relationship to the object of the legislation and was therefore valid. Detroit Police Officers Association v. City of Detroit, 385 Mich. 519, 190 N.W.2d 97 (1971). The Supreme Court in a brief order dismissed the appeal "for want of a substantial federal question." While we do not consider it necessary to base the result in the present case primarily on *Detroit Police Officers,* we recognize that the Supreme Court's dismissal of the appeal "for want of a substantial federal question" is a decision on the merits of the case appealed. We conclude that the "compelling state interest" test is the applicable test in cases involving infringement of the right to interstate travel by *durational* residency requirements. On the other hand, where, as in the present case, a *continuing* employee residency requirement affecting at most the right of intrastate travel is involved, the "rational basis" test is the touchstone to determine its validity.

We find a number of rational bases for the residency requirement of the Cincinnati School Board. The Cincinnati school superintendent testified that promulgation of the rule was based on the following conclusions: (1) such a requirement aids in hiring teachers who are highly motivated and deeply committed to an urban educational system, (2) teachers who live in the district are more likely to vote for district taxes, less likely to engage in illegal strikes, and more likely to help obtain passage of school tax levies, (3) teachers living in the district are more likely to be involved in school and community activities bringing them in contact with parents and community leaders and are more likely to be committed to the future of the district and its schools, (4) teachers who live in the district are more likely to gain sympathy and understanding for the racial, social, economic, and urban problems of the children they teach and are thus less likely to be considered isolated from the communities in which they teach, (5) the requirement is in keeping with the goal of encouraging integration in society and in the schools. These conclusions appear to us clearly to establish rational bases for the residency requirement imposed by the Cincinnati Board.

Appellant insists that the basic purpose of the residency rule is to advance "quality integrated" education and to help in eliminating racial segregation in the community and school system. The rule is not rationally related to this objective, appellant claims, because school and community integration would only be promoted by requiring teachers to live in the attendance districts of the schools at which they teach. Integration is not encouraged, it is argued, by a regulation such as the present one which requires teachers to live somewhere in the district at large when the district itself contains many segregated areas. This argument overlooks the various other convincing and rational bases for adoption of the rule. Although it is possible that the rule will not materially contribute to racial integration, we consider that the numerous other legitimate objectives of the rule are wholly adequate to demonstrate that the residency classification fully comports with the rational basis test. Many other courts have recognized the importance of employees being highly committed to the area in which they work and motivated to find solutions for its problems. . . . Such commitment and motivation, it is not unreasonable to suppose, may best be fostered by requiring teachers to live and pay taxes in the place in which they are employed to work.

Other arguments against the validity of this residency requirement are advanced. First, it is said that the right to teach, which in Ohio is controlled by state law through the issuance of a teaching certificate, entitles a teacher to be considered for employment only on his merits as prescribed by statute. This right may not be withheld on constitutionally impermissible grounds. The state certification of teachers distinguishes teachers as a group from municipal employees performing other functions. We agree with appellee, however, that the possession of an Ohio certificate establishes only that a teacher has met certain minimum standards. It does not entitle him to a teaching position with any particular local school board. Local boards are free to impose additional qualifications and conditions of employment or to adopt higher standards.

Finally, appellant argues that the residency requirements is invalid because it requires newly hired teachers to move into and remain in the district and permits those already hired to remain or move outside the district. Appellee replies that distinguishing between new teachers and teachers with experience who may have tenure and who did not know of the requirment when they accepted employment, is a reasonable distinction which the state is free to make. While we recognize that the limited applicability of the rule may be its most questionable feature, we do not believe that the residency requirement must fail because it does not apply to all teachers employed by the Cincinnati schools. The Supreme Court has pointed out that there is no constitutional requirement that regulations must cover every class to which they might be applied. It has further stated that "if the classification has some reasonable basis, it does not offend the constitution simply because the classification 'is not made with mathematical nicety or because in practice it results in some inequality.'"

Affirmed.

Teacher's Adultery Insufficient to
Support Revocation of Certificate

ERB v. IOWA STATE BOARD OF PUBLIC INSTRUCTION

Supreme Court of Iowa, 1974.
216 N.W.2d 339.

McCORMICK, Justice.

In this appeal plaintiff Richard Arlan Erb challenges the revocation of his teaching certificate. The certificate was revoked by defendant Board of Educational Examiners after a hearing on July 16, 1971. Erb brought an action in certiorari alleging the board's action was illegal. After trial the writ of certiorari was annulled. Erb appealed. We reverse.

Under Code § 260.1, the State Board of Public Instruction constitutes the Board of Educational Examiners. Code § 260.2 empowers the examining board to issue teaching certificates "to applicants who are eighteen years of age or over, physically competent and morally fit to teach, and who have the [required] qualifications and training . . .."

Erb, a native Iowan, military veteran, and holder of a master's degree in fine arts, received his Iowa teaching certificate in 1963. Since then he has taught art in the Nishna Valley Community School which serves an area including the towns of Strahn, Emerson, Hastings, and Stanton. He resides in Emerson, is married and has two young sons. In addition to teaching he has coached wrestling, assisted with football, and acted as senior class sponsor.

The complaint against Erb was made by Robert M. Johnson, a farmer whose wife Margaret taught home economics in the Nishna Valley School. Johnson told the board his goal was removal of Erb from the school and not revocation of his teaching certificate. He read an extensive statement in which he detailed his observations relating to an adulterous liaison between Erb and Johnson's wife which began and ended in spring 1970.

Margaret planned to quit teaching and open a boutique in Red Oak. Her association with Erb began in early spring when he agreed to assist her with design of the store. They saw each other often. By May, Johnson became suspicious of Margaret's frequent late-night absences from home. He suspected Margaret and Erb were meeting secretly and engaging in illicit activity in the Johnson automobile. One night in May he hid in the trunk of the car. Margaret drove the car to school, worked there for some time, and later drove to a secluded area in the country where she met Erb. Margaret and Erb had sexual intercourse in the back seat of the car while Johnson remained hidden in the trunk. Johnson did not disclose his presence or his knowledge of the incident.

Instead he consulted a lawyer with a view toward divorcing Margaret. He told the board he was advised his interests in a divorce action would be better served if he had other witnesses to his wife's misconduct. After several days of fruitless effort to catch Margaret and Erb in a compromising situation, he and his "raiding party" eventually located them one night in June parked in a remote area. Johnson and the others surrounded the car and took photographs of Margaret and Erb who were partially disrobed in the back seat. Johnson told Margaret not to come home and that further communication would be through lawyers. He told Erb to disclose the affair to his wife.

Erb did so. He and Margaret terminated their affair. Erb offered to resign his teaching position, but the local school board unanimously decided not to accept his resignation. The board president testified Erb's teaching was highly rated by his principal and superintendent, he had been forgiven by his wife and the student body, and he had maintained the respect of the community. Erb was retained for the ensuing school year and continued to teach in the Nishna Valley School.

Witnesses before the board included Erb's past and present high school principals, his minister, a parent of children in the school, and a substitute teacher. All vouched for his character and fitness to teach. His superintendent gave essentially the same testimony in district court. . . . Trial court ruled in its pretrial order that under the admitted record Erb's teacher-student relationship had not been impaired by his conduct.

The [state] board voted five to four to revoke Erb's teaching certificate and, without making any findings of fact or conclusions of law, ordered it revoked. Revocation was stayed by trial court and then by this court pending outcome of the certiorari action and appeal. Trial court held Erb's admitted adulterous conduct was sufficient basis for revocation of his certificate and annulled the writ. . . . In this appeal Erb contends the board acted illegally . . . in revoking his teaching certificate without substantial evidence that he is not morally fit to teach. . . .

Since the board made no findings there is no intelligible way to determine what interpretation the board gave to its statutory authorization to revoke the certificate of one not "morally fit to teach." But nothing prevents us from determining whether there is substantial evidence in the record which would have supported revocation if the proper standard had been applied. Erb contends there is not. We agree. We will first examine the standard and then the sufficiency of the evidence.

This court has not previously been called upon to decide what constitutes moral unfitness to teach. . . .

A teacher occupies a sensitive position. Since students are taught by example as well as lecture, the teacher's out-of-school conduct may affect his classroom fitness. . . .

> The private conduct of a man, who is also a teacher, is a proper concern to those who employ him only to the extent it mars him as a teacher, who is also

a man. Where his professional achievement is unaffected, where the school community is placed in no jeopardy, his private acts are his own business and may not be the basis of discipline.

The board contends the fact Erb admitted adultery is sufficient in itself to establish his unfitness to teach. This assumes such conduct automatically and invariably makes a person unfit to teach. We are unwilling to make that assumption. It would vest the board with unfettered power to revoke the certificate of any teacher whose personal, private conduct incurred its disapproval regardless of its likely or actual effect upon his teaching. . . . ("Where the courts have been presented with the question whether or not specific conduct of a teacher constitutes moral unfitness which would justify revocation, they have apparently required that the conduct must adversely affect the teacher-student relationship before revocation will be approved."). . . .

> Surely incidents of extramarital heterosexual conduct against a background of years of satisfactory teaching would not constitute "immoral conduct" sufficient to justify revocation of a life diploma without any showing of an adverse effect on fitness to teach.

We emphasize the board's power to revoke teaching certificates is neither punitive nor intended to permit exercise of personal moral judgment by members of the board. Punishment is left to the criminal law, and the personal moral views of board members cannot be relevant. A subjective standard is impermissible and contrary to obvious legislative intent. . . .

In *Morrison* the California court discussed factors relevant to application of the standard:

> In determining whether the teacher's conduct thus indicates unfitness to teach the board may consider such matters as the likelihood that the conduct may have adversely affected students or fellow teachers, the degree of such adversity anticipated, the proximity or remoteness in time of the conduct, the type of teaching certificate held by the party involved, the extenuating or aggravating circumstances, if any, surrounding the conduct, the praiseworthiness or blameworthiness of the motives resulting in the conduct, the likelihood of the recurrence of the questioned conduct, and the extent to which disciplinary action may inflict an adverse impact or chilling effect upon the constitutional rights of the teacher involved or other teachers. 82 Cal.Rptr. at 186, 461 P.2d at 386.

These factors have relevance in deciding whether a teacher is morally fit to teach under Code § 260.2. Since the same standard is applicable in determining whether a certificate should be revoked under Code § 260.23, a certificate can be revoked only upon a showing before the board of a reasonable likelihood that the teacher's retention in the profession will adversely affect the school community.

There was no evidence of such adverse effect in the present case. No one even asserted such an effect. The complainant himself acknowledged his purpose was to remove Erb from the school rather than from teaching. The evidence showed Erb to be a teacher of exceptional merit. He is dedicated, hardworking and effective. There was no evidence to show his affair with Margaret Johnson had or is likely to have an adverse effect upon his relationship with the school administration, fellow teachers, the student body, or the community. Overwhelming and uncontroverted evidence of local regard and support for Erb is a remarkable testament to the ability of a community to understand, forgive and reconcile.

There was no evidence other than that Erb's misconduct was an isolated occurrence in an otherwise unblemished past and is not likely to recur. The conduct itself was not an open or public affront to community mores; it became public only because it was discovered with considerable effort and made public by others. Erb made no effort to justify it; instead he sought to show he regretted it, it did not reflect his true character, and it would not be repeated. . . .

The board acted illegally in revoking his certificate. Trial court erred in annulling the writ of certiorari.

Reversed.

SCOPE OF TEACHER'S DUTIES

There are many attendant duties outside the classroom that teachers are called upon to perform. These may include supervision of athletic events and field excursions, selling of tickets at student activities, loading of school buses, and other related non-academic duties too numerous to mention.

The court cases to date on this subject indicate that a teacher may be required to perform tasks incidental to regular classroom work. Teachers may not be required to render such services as janitorial duties, traffic duty, school bus driving, and similar activities not coming within the implied duties of a teacher's contract. All such common-law legal principles may be altered, of course, by a collective bargaining contract.

Assignment of Teacher to Supervise
Athletic Events of School Is Not
Unreasonable and Is Within Scope of
Teaching Duties

McGRATH v. BURKHARD

California District Court of Appeal,
Third District, 1955.
131 Cal.App.2d 367, 280 P.2d 864.

SCHOTTKY, Justice. Plaintiff, a teacher in the Sacramento Senior High School, commenced an action for declaratory relief against defendant Superintendent of Sacramento City Unified School District, the Board of Education of said district and the individual members of said board, and the principal of the Sacramento Senior High School. Plaintiff sought declaratory relief on the ground that the non-classroom assignments, as hereinafter detailed, did not fall within the scope of his duties as a teacher under the terms of his contract of employment, and that such duties were unprofessional in nature. Plaintiff asked the court to declare the rights and duties under the contract of employment; that the non-classroom work was not within the scope of employment; that plaintiff should not be assigned duties on a teaching day which required more than eight hours per day to perform competently; that if more than eight hours may be assigned the court should declare the number of hours per day plaintiff is obligated to perform under the contract; that no duties be assigned on days for which he is not paid, i.e., Saturdays, holidays and most non-teaching days. . . . Before discussing the contentions made by plaintiff and appellant we shall summarize the factual situation which is not in substantial dispute.

Appellant is a teacher in the Sacramento Senior High School. From 1942 to 1945 he was employed as a long term substitute teacher; from July, 1945, to July, 1948, he was employed as a probationary teacher and from July, 1948, to the date of this action he was employed as a permanent teacher. He achieved the status of tenure in 1948.

At all times appellant has been employed under a written contract, which incorporates the rules of the respondent Board of Education.

During his course of employment by respondents, appellant and other male teachers have been required to attend certain non-classroom activities and act in a supervisory capacity. The activities are school football and basketball games, which are under the auspices and control of the school authorities. These games may be held at places other than on the school grounds. Six of these athletic assignments are made to each male member of the faculty during each school year, three football games and three basketball games. At the beginning of the school year each male teacher selects the three football games at which he would prefer to supervise; at the end of such season he then selects the three basketball games at which he would prefer to attend in a supervisory capacity. To the extent possible the requests of the teachers are complied with in the scheduling of these assignments, but at times a teacher receives an assignment on a date other than the one he had selected. The teachers are selected impartially and without discrimination. For many years past this administrative practice of assigning the male teachers to supervise at the school athletic contests in football and basketball has been carried out to protect the welfare of the students. The teachers have no authority to act as police officers, but policemen are present at the games to handle any situation in which their authority is needed. Appellant testified that the teacher's duties at these games consisted of maintaining order in the student section of the stands . . . controlling conduct of the students, preventing smoking in the gymnasium by students or adults and preventing spectators from entering the gymnasium with soft drinks, candy or other food. The female teachers of the school are given assignments to supervision of nonclassroom activities, but of a different nature, as supervising in the cafeteria, variety shows and dances. . . .

Appellant first contends that he is under no contractual obligation in regard to the athletic assignments and that if so obligated, the required duties are unreasonable and not within the scope of teaching duties. He states that such obligation is nowhere set forth in the contract, the rules of the Board of Education, nor in the laws of the state of California. While it is true that this specific duty is not set forth, a study of the evidence and the provisions set forth in the Education Code and the Administrative Code reveals that the assignment complained of by appellant is and was within the contemplation of the parties when the contract of employment was entered into. Relevant portions of each are set out below:

> Education Code, section 2204. The governing board of any school district shall: (a) Prescribe and enforce rules not inconsistent with law or with the rules prescribed by the State Board of Education, for its own government, and for the government of the schools under its jurisdiction.
> Education Code, section 13201. The governing board of each school district shall fix and prescribe the duties to be performed by all persons in public school service in the school district.

These sections provide for the delegation of rule making authority, so that the correct body can prescribe exactly what the duties are. In connection with this, certain rules promulgated by the State Board of Education must be considered. The following excerpts are taken from the California Administrative Code, Title 5, Article 3, which is entitled "Duties of Principals and Teachers."

> Section 16. Responsibility of Principal. The principal is responsible for the supervision and administration of his school.
> Section 18. Playground supervision. Where playground supervision is not otherwise provided, the principal of each school shall provide for the supervision, by teachers, of the conduct and direction of the play of the pupils of the school or on the school grounds during recesses and other intermissions and before and after school. All athletic or social activities, wherever held, when conducted under the name or auspices of any public school, or any class or organization thereof, shall be under the direct supervision of the authorities of the district. . . .

. . . These provisions relate to all teachers in the public school system. Of course, the State Board of Education has expressed other duties which are required of teachers, as shown in the above excerpts from the Administrative Code. The local governing board has power delegated to it to make the necessary rules and regulations which its district requires. Ed. Code, secs. 2204, 13201. And finally, the principal has the necessary power which is inherent in his office to properly administer and supervise his school.

Appellant's contract expressly set forth that it was subject to the laws of California, the rules of the State Board of Education and of the local governing board. The trial court found that the rule of the Sacramento City Unified School District with reference to the athletic assignments was a part of appellant's contract. The code provisions relating to the duties of teachers do not set forth the particular duty which is the subject of this controversy. The rules promulgated by the State Board of Education do not set forth such specific duty. However, the rules in Article 3 of Title 5 of the Administrative Code do show that the principals and teachers are charged with certain duties . . ..

Appellant . . . asserts that the trial court should be reversed since the duties at the athletic contests were (1) in the nature of police work, (2) unprofessional, (3) foreign to the field of instruction, and (4) imposed unreasonable hours, and therefore were not within the scope of the teaching duties required by the contract. However, the record does not sustain appellant's contention in this regard. The teachers have no authority to act as police officers; in fact, they are expressly informed that their duties are supervisory only. At no time is a teacher to exert police powers. The teachers are to act in a supervisory capacity, much as they do at school assembly meetings, etc. They are acting to protect the welfare of the students. Appellant asserts that he has received no training for this type of work and that the evidence suggests, since women are not assigned this type of duty, that physical strength is a requisite and that the motivating reason for the assignments is to quell and put down disturbances, which is in the nature of police duty. The record refutes appellant's statement. From the deposition of Dr. Murphy, the principal at Sacramento Senior High School, it appears that he was asked questions directly on this point and he replied that the duties did not relate to physical strength or power . . .. Appellant states that the duties were degrading, humiliating and unprofessional. Certain instances are cited. Dr. Murphy admitted that the duty was disagreeable to some, but he felt that it was the same with some women with the cafeteria assignments, or with anyone when they have to perform a task which they do not like, and apparently this is especially so with some teachers when they are faced with these types of supervisory duties. All public school teachers have general duties as expressed by the Education Code, sections 13228, 13229 and 13230, supra, relating to the control of the conduct of pupils, endorsement of rules and the training of them to be good American citizens. Coupled with these are the rules of the State Board of Education in Article 3 of Title 5 of the Administrative Code, which relate to certain duties, and section 24 in particular, quoted supra, which requires principals and teachers to exercise careful supervision of moral conditions in the schools and not to tolerate participation by students in gambling, profanity, the use of intoxicating liquors, etc., on or off the schoolgrounds. Teachers are expected to perform these obligations. It is of great importance that the association of teacher and pupil should tend to inculcate in the latter principles of justice, fair-play, good sportsmanship, good citizenship and respect for rules and authority. Viewing the duties at the games in light of the above, it is apparent that they are not of an unprofessional nature. For as stated in the case of *Parrish* v. *Moss,* so strongly relied upon by appellant, "The day in which the concept was held that teaching duty was limited to classroom instruction has long since passed."

Appellant's final contention is that the duties here involved impose unreasonable hours. The record shows that six of these assignments are made in a school year from September to the following June. Generally, the hours are evening ones, from about six or seven o'clock to ten o'clock. Some assignments fall on Saturday evenings or on Thanksgiving Day. Appellant also claims that the Saturday or legal holiday on which an assignment occasionally occurs is a day of duty for which he is not paid. However, appellant is not paid on a basis of so much per hour worked. Teachers are engaged in a professional employment. Their salaries and hours of employment are fixed with due regard to their professional status and are not fixed upon the same basis as those of day laborers. The worth of a teacher is not measured in terms of a specific sum of money per hour. A teacher expects to and does perform a service. If that service from time to time requires additional hours of work, a teacher expects to and does perform it. If that service from time to time requires additional hours of work, a teacher expects to and does put in the extra hours, without thought of measuring his or her compensation in terms of a given sum of money per hour. A teacher's duties and obligations to students and the community are not satisfied by closing the classroom door at the conclusion of a class. The direction and supervision of extracurricular activities are an important part of his duties. All of his duties are taken into consideration in his contract for employment at the annual salary. All of this is, of course, subject to the test of reasonableness. It does not appear that six of these athletic assignments in an entire school year are unreasonable, nor that the hours of such assignments are unreasonable, under the circumstances. What is reasonable must necessarily depend upon the facts of the situation and the teachers are protected in that regard by the appropriate administrative and judicial procedure. Supervising the students and being present to protect their welfare at school athletic and social activities, conducted under the name and auspices of the school, is within the scope of the contract and such assignments are proper so long as they are distributed impartially, they are reasonable in number and hours of duty and each teacher has his share of such duty. . . .

We believe that respondent school authorities had the right under the law and the contract with appellant to assign appellant to attend and assist in supervising these athletic contests. We believe that the presence of teachers at such contests should be helpful not only to the students but should be of benefit to the teachers themselves. We believe that the school authorities had the right to determine that such duties should be performed by the teachers assigned thereto. As stated by the learned trial judge in his memorandum opinion, "Have the parents not the right to expect, and, indeed, to demand, that all such school activities be under the supervision of the school authorities? If not, then who is to be in control? The answers to these questions seem obvious." . . .

The judgment is affirmed.

NOTES

1. In the case of Parrish v. Moss, 200 Misc. 375, 160 N.Y.S.2d 577 (1951), New York teachers contested the right of a school board to assign incidental duties. The court held that teachers could be assigned only those duties related to their respective subject fields. English teachers could be required to coach plays and assist debate teams; band leaders would have to go with the band on field excursions; and physical education instructors could be required to coach intramural and inter school athletic teams.

2. Considering the decision in the California and New York cases, what criteria may be established to determine what outside assignments come within the "implied duties" portion of a teacher's contract?

3. A school board may assign reasonable non-academic duties to teachers. An Illinois court has stated: "it has been held that school authorities may assign teachers to supervise non-academic school activities outside of school hours. As long as such assignments are reasonably related to teaching duties and not unduly time-consuming or burdensome, school

authorities may, in the exercise of their sound discretion, require teachers to perform them . . . . A broad spectrum of implied incidental powers is to be inferred from the general power of boards of education to adopt all necessary rules for the management and government of the schools." Littrell v. Board of Education, etc., 45 Ill.App.3d 690, 4 Ill.Dec. 355, 360 N.E.2d 102 (1977).

4. A school board has broad powers in assignment of teachers' duties. Incidental to the board's powers is the right to assign non-classroom duties. Teaching duties are not solely confined to the classroom and additional responsibilities may be properly imposed so long as they are within the scope of the license held by the teacher. Extra duty requirements do not need to be specified in school board rules in order to be valid. Courts generally maintain that duties that are not onerous, demeaning, unusually time consuming or assigned in a discriminatory manner may be assigned even though the teacher considers them an inconvenience. Thomas v. Board of Education of Community Unit School District, 117 Ill.App.3d 374, 72 Ill. Dec. 845, 453 N.E.2d 150 (1983).

5. The Supreme Court of Iowa citing *McGrath* v. *Burkhard,* supra, upheld the reassignment of a school principal to extra duties. An elementary school principal who administered two small elementary schools was given the assignment of coordinator of the outdoor educational program and attendance officer. The reason for the reassignment was that one of his small schools was closed because of declining enrollment. The court found the assignment to be within the school board's discretion. "The assignments objected to do not appear to have been onerous in nature or unreasonably time consuming and are not demeaning to the professional status . . . ." Gere v. Council Bluffs Community School District, 334 N.W.2d 307 (Iowa 1983).

6. Guidance counselors may also be assigned extra duties. In a case in which a counselor refused to supervise the school campus before school began each day and also refused to obey other directives from the assistant principal, the court upheld dismissal, observing that the major issue for dismissal was the failure to supervise the students and when placed in concert with the other acts "[t]here is sufficient evidence in the record to support his dismissal." Jones v. Alabama State Tenure Commission, 408 So.2d 145 (Ala.1981).

In another Alabama case, a teacher was dismissed for insubordination for refusal to participate in an enrichment program designed to improve classroom management and control student behavior. The court upheld the dismissal. Howell v. Alabama State Tenure Commission, 402 So.2d 1041 (Ala.1981).

CONTRACTS

The framers of the Constitution realized the importance of contracts. Provision for protecting the obligation of contracts was included in Article I, Section 10 of the United States Constitution.

The Supreme Court, in the famous *Dartmouth College* case,[3] interpreted Article I, Section 10 of the Constitution, declaring that states could not enact legislation that impairs the obligation of a contract. In this case, the English crown had granted a charter to Dartmouth College, which had been established in the colony of New Hampshire as a private college. The college was governed by a self-perpetuating board of twelve members. A conflict developed between the college president and the board members, which had political ramifications. Reacting to this controversy, the legislature of New Hampshire in 1816, enacted legislation that materially altered the charter, making the college a state institution. The college trustees brought an action and claimed, in part, that the act of the legislature was unconstitutional and impaired the obligation of their contract, the original charter. The opinion of the Court delivered by Justice Marshall, stated:

> The points for consideration are: 1. Is this contract protected by the Constitution of the United States? 2. Is it impaired by the acts under which the defendant holds?
>
> 1. On the first point, it has been argued, that the word "contract" in its broadest sense would comprehend the political relations between the government and its citizens, would extend to offices held within a state, for state purposes, and to many of those laws concerning civil institutions, which must change with circumstances, and be modified by ordinary legislation; which deeply concern the public, and which, to preserve good government, the public judgment must control . . . .
> This (charter) is plainly a contract to which the donors, the trustees and the crown (to whose rights and obligation New Hampshire succeeds) were the original parties. It is a contract made on a valuable consideration. It is a contract for the security and disposition of property. It is a contract, on the faith of which, real and personal estate has been conveyed to the corporation. It is, then, a contract within the letter of the Constitution, and within its spirit also unless the fact that the property is invested by the donors in trustees, for the promotion of religion and education, for the benefit of persons who are perpetually changing, though the objects remain the same, shall create a particular exception, taking this case out of the prohibition contained in the Constitution. . . .
> The opinion of the court, after mature deliberation, is, that this is a contract, the obligation of which cannot be impaired, without violating the Constitution of the United States. This opinion appears to us to be equally supported by reason, and by the former decisions of this court.
>
> 2. We next proceed to the inquiry, whether its obligation has been impaired by those acts of the legislature of New Hampshire, to which the special verdict refers?
> From the review of this charter, which has been taken, it appears that the whole power of governing the college, of appointing and removing tutors, of fixing salaries, of directing the course of study to be pursued by the students, and of filling up vacancies created in their own body, was vested in the trustees. On the part of the crown it was expressly stipulated, that this corporation, thus constituted, should continue forever; and that the number of trustees should forever consist of twelve, and no more. By this contract the crown was bound, and could have made no violent alteration in its essential terms, without impairing its obligation.
> By the Revolution the duties, as well as the powers, of government devolved on the people of New Hampshire. It is admitted, that among the latter was comprehended the transcendent power of parliament, as well as that of the executive department. It is too clear, to require the support of

argument, that all contracts and rights respecting property, remained unchanged by the Revolution. The obligations, then, which were created by the charter to Dartmouth College, were the same in the new, that they had been in the old government . . . But the Constitution of the United States has imposed this additional limitation, that the legislature of a state shall pass no act "impairing the obligation of contracts." . . .

It results from this opinion, that the acts of the legislature of New Hampshire, which are stated in the special verdict found in this cause, are repugnant to the Constitution of the United States; and that the judgment on this special verdict ought to have been for the plaintiffs. The judgment of the state court must, therefore, be reversed.

In an Indiana case, Article I, Section 10 of the Constitution of the United States is directly applied as a limitation on state legislative actions pertaining to public education. The Indiana legislature passed an act that repealed a 1927 law granting tenure to teachers. The teacher sought a writ of mandamus to compel her continued employment. She claimed the original act had granted her a continuing contract that could not be impaired nor breached by subsequent legislation. The original act provided:

It is further agreed by the contracting parties that all of the Teachers' Tenure Law, approved March 8, 1927, shall be in full force and effect in this contract.

The Supreme Court of Indiana ruled in favor of the defendant board of education and the teacher appealed. The Supreme Court of the United States reversed the Indiana Court.[4]

Both of these decisions illustrate the constitutional requirements within which a state legislature must operate when dealing with contracts. Particular application may be noted where legislation such as tenure and retirement statutes may create a contract between the state and an individual.

There is a fine line between the constitutional rights of one individual and the rights of the people as exercised through the elected authority of the legislature to provide for the welfare of the state. This is demonstrated by the dissent of Justice Black in the *Anderson* v. *Brand* case when he said that the Supreme Court should not interfere with the determination of educational policy by the Indiana legislature because the legislature of a state cannot make and be held to a contract "with a few citizens, that would take from all the citizens, the continuing power to alter the educational policy for the best interests of Indiana school children . . . ."

A teacher's contract must satisfy the same requirements applicable to contracts in general. A school district is a legal entity, a corporate body with the power to sue and be sued; purchase, receive, hold, and sell real and personal property, make contracts and be contracted with; and do all other things necessary to accomplish the purposes for which it is created.

Contracts of school districts must conform not only to the requirements of general contract law, but must satisfy other statutory and case law demands as well. A contract may be defined as an agreement between two or more competent persons for a legal consideration on a legal subject matter in the form required by law. This definition includes the five basic elements inherent in every valid contract, to-wit: offer and acceptance, competent persons, consideration, Legal subject matter, and proper form.

We shall discuss these elements in the order set out above.

All contracts are agreements, but not all agreements are contracts. An agreement is an offer and an acceptance. Every valid contract contains an offer and acceptance. For example, a board of education offers a fifth-grade teaching position in a particular school to an individual. There is no agreement unless and until the individual accepts the offer.

Several significant factors concerning agreements should be kept in mind. An offer can be accepted only by the individual or individuals to whom it is made. Unless otherwise stated, an offer must be accepted within a reasonable time after it is made or it will be terminated automatically. Newspaper advertisements are usually considered to be invitations for offers and not offers. That is, the board of education is soliciting offers. Also, an offer cannot be accepted unless at the time the individual performed the act necessary to accept the offer he knew of the existence of the offer. By way of illustration, let us assume that vandals broke into a school building and the board of education offered a reward for information leading to the arrest and conviction of the vandals. The information was provided to the police by an individual who was unaware of the reward offer. A majority of the States hold that the individual is not entitled to the reward because he could not have accepted the offer since he was unaware of its existence—there was no meeting of the minds.

Each valid contract must be entered into between two or more competent persons—persons who have the legal capacity to contract. As already indicated, a board of education is considered a competent person under the law with full capacity to enter into contracts. However, there are certain classes of people who have limited capacity to contract. These include minors, married women, insane persons, drunken persons, and corporations.

A minor has the right to disaffirm his contract until a reasonable time after he reaches his majority, i.e., becomes an adult. If a board of education contracts with a minor, the minor has the prerogative of electing to avoid the contract within a reasonable time after he becomes an adult and no penalties for a contractual breach will be imposed against the minor. A board of education would have no right or option to avoid its contract with the minor.

If an individual is so insane or drunk at the time he enters into a contract that he does not know what he is doing, he may have the contract set aside because there was no meeting of the minds, which is always essential in every valid contractual situation.

At the common law, married women did not possess the legal capacity to contract. This was premised on the age-old concept that when a man and woman married, the two became one and the man was that one. This contractual limitation has been removed by statutes in all states and women now possess the power to enter into contracts on the same basis as men.

Before entering into a contract with a corporation, a board of education should ascertain that the corporation has the power, by statute or under its articles of incorporation, to perform the services agreed upon.

Valid contracts must be supported by consideration—something of value. Consideration is divided into three types. These are good, valuable, and a promise for an act.

Good consideration is love and affection. For example, a mother may convey property to a child for good consideration. This notion is seldom invoked by courts today.

Valuable consideration is cash or its equivalent. Most deeds will recite that the property is being conveyed for good and valuable consideration.

The third type of consideration is that found in a unilateral contract—a promise for an act. For example, a board of education promises a reward of $500 for information leading to the arrest and conviction of vandals who damaged school property. An individual, knowing of the offer, provides the information that leads to the arrest and conviction of the vandals; he is entitled to the reward. His consideration was the doing of the act requested.

All contracts, to be valid, must involve a legal subject matter. Most, if not all, states prohibit the holding of various types of assemblies, such as rooster fighting. If a board of education entered into a contract to lease school premises for the purposes of staging a rooster fighting conclave, such a contract would involve an illegal subject matter and would be declared void.

Contracts, to be enforceable, must be in the form required by law. For example, all agreements, with respect to the sale or leasing of real estate, must be in writing to be enforceable. An oral agreement to sell real property, even if made in the town square before ten thousand people, is unenforceable in the courts. This is but one example of the requirement that contracts must be in the proper form to be enforceable. Most states require that teacher's contracts be in writing.

*Tenure Contracts Between the State
and Teacher Cannot Be Unilaterally
Cancelled by the State*

STATE OF INDIANA EX REL. ANDERSON v. BRAND

Supreme Court of the United States, 1938.
303 U.S. 95, 58 S.Ct. 443.

Mr. Justice ROBERTS delivered the opinion of the Court.

The petitioner sought a writ of mandate to compel the respondent to continue her in employment as a public school teacher. Her complaint alleged that as a duly licensed teacher she entered into a contract in September, 1924, to teach in the township schools and, pursuant to successive contracts, taught continuously to and including the school year 1932–1933; that her contracts for the school years 1931–1932 and 1932–1933 contained this clause: "It is further agreed by the contracting parties that all of the provisions of the Teachers' Tenure Law, approved March 8, 1927, shall be in full force and effect in this contract"; and that by force of that act she had a contract, indefinite in duration, which could be canceled by the respondent only in the manner and for the causes specified in the act. She charged that in July, 1933, the respondent notified her he proposed to cancel her contract for cause; that, after a hearing, he adhered to his decision and the county superintendent affirmed his action; that, despite what occurred in July, 1933, the petitioner was permitted to teach during the school year 1933–1934 and the respondent was presently threatening to terminate her employment at the end of that year. The complaint alleged the termination of her employment would be a breach of her contract with the school corporation. The respondent demurred on the grounds that (1) the complaint disclosed the matters pleaded had been submitted to the respondent and the county superintendent who were authorized to try the issues and had lawfully determined them in favor of the respondent; and (2) the Teachers' Tenure Law, Acts Ind.1927, c. 97, had been repealed in respect of teachers in township schools. The demurrer was sustained and the petitioner appealed to the state Supreme Court which affirmed the judgment. The court did not discuss the first ground of demurrer relating to the action taken in the school year 1932–1933, but rested its decision upon the second, that, by an act of 1933, Acts Ind.1933, c. 116, the Teachers' Tenure Law had been repealed as respects teachers in township schools; and held that the repeal did not deprive the petitioner of a vested property right and did not impair her contract within the meaning of the Constitution. . . .

As in most cases brought to this court under the contract clause of the Constitution, the question is as to the existence and nature of the contract and not as to the construction of the law which is supposed to impair it. The principal function of a legislative body is not to make contracts but to make laws which declare the policy of the state and are subject to repeal when a subsequent Legislature shall determine to alter that policy. Nevertheless, it is established that a legislative enactment may contain provisions which, when accepted as the basis of action by individuals, become contracts between them and the State or its subdivisions within the protection of article 1, § 10. If the people's representatives deem it in the public interest they may adopt a policy of contracting in respect of public business for a term longer than the life of the current session of the Legislature. This the petitioner claims has been done with respect to permanent teachers. . . .

The courts of Indiana have long recognized that the employment of school teachers was contractual and have afforded relief in actions upon teachers' contracts. An act adopted in 1899 required all contracts between teachers and school corporations to be in writing, signed by the parties to be charged, and to be made a matter of public record. A statute of 1921 enacted that every such contract should be in writing and should state the date of the beginning of the school term, the number of months therein, the amount of the salary for the term, and the number of payments to be made during the school year.

In 1927 the State adopted the Teachers' Tenure Act under which the present controversy arises. . . . By this act it was provided that a teacher who has served under contract for five or more successive years, and thereafter enters into a contract for further service with the school corporation, shall become a permanent teacher and the contract, upon the expiration of its stated term, shall be deemed to continue in effect for an indefinite period, shall be known as an indefinite contract, and shall remain in force unless succeeded by a new contract or canceled as provided in the act. The corporation may cancel the contract, after notice and hearing, for incompetency, insubordination, neglect of duty, immorality, justifiable decrease in the number of teaching positions, or other good or just cause, but not for political or personal reasons. The teacher may not cancel the contract during the school term nor for a period thirty days previous to the beginning of any term (unless by mutual agreement) and may cancel only upon five days' notice.

By an amendatory act of 1933 township school corporations were omitted from the provisions of the act of 1927. The court below construed this act as repealing the act of 1927 so far as township schools and teachers are concerned and as leaving the respondent free to terminate the petitioner's employment. But we are of the opinion that the petitioner had a valid contract with the respondent, the obligation of which would be impaired by the termination of her employment.

Where the claim is that the state's policy embodied in a statute is to bind its instrumentalities by contract, the cardinal inquiry is as to the terms of the statute supposed to create such a contract. The State long prior to the adoption of the act of 1927 required the execution of written contracts between teachers and school corporations, specified certain subjects with which such contracts must deal, and required that they be made a matter of public record. These were annual contracts, covering a single school term. The act of 1927 announced a new policy that a teacher who had served for five years under successive contracts, upon the execution of another was to become a permanent teacher and the last contract was to be indefinite as to duration and terminable by either party only upon compliance with the conditions set out in the statute. The policy which induced the legislation evidently was that the teacher should have protection against the exercise of the right, which would otherwise inhere in the employer, of terminating the employment at the end of any school term without assigned reasons and solely at the employer's pleasure. The state courts in earlier cases so declared.

The title of the act is couched in terms of contract. It speaks of the making and canceling of indefinite contracts. In the body the word "contract" appears ten times in section 1, defining the relationship; eleven times in section 2, relating to the termination of the employment by the employer; and four times in section 4, stating the conditions of termination by the teacher.

The tenor of the act indicates that the word "contract" was not used inadvertently or in other than its usual legal meaning. By section 6 it is expressly provided that the act is a supplement to that of March 7, 1921, supra, requiring teachers' employment contracts to be in writing. By section 1 it is provided that the written contract of a permanent teacher "shall be deemed to continue in effect for an indefinite period and shall be known as an indefinite contract." Such an indefinite contract is to remain in force unless succeeded by a new contract signed by both parties or canceled as provided in section 2. No more apt language could be employed to define a contractual relationship. By section 2 it is enacted that such indefinite contracts may be canceled by the school corporation only in the manner specified. The admissible grounds of cancellation, and the method by which the existence of such grounds shall be ascertained and made a matter of record, are carefully set out. Section 4 permits cancellation by the teacher only at certain times consistent with the convenient administration of the school system and imposes a sanction for violation of its requirements. Examination of the entire act convinces us that the teacher was by it assured of the possession of a binding and enforceable contract against school districts. . . .

Our decisions recognize that every contract is made subject to the implied condition that its fulfillment may be frustrated by a proper exercise of the police power but we have repeatedly said that, in order to have this effect, the exercise of the power must be for an end which is in fact public and the means adopted must be reasonably adapted to that end, and the Supreme Court of Indiana has taken the same view in respect of legislation impairing the obligation of the contract of a state instrumentality. The causes of cancellation provided in the act of 1927 and the retention of the system of indefinite contracts in all municipalities except townships by the act of 1933 are persuasive that the repeal of the earlier act by the later was not an exercise of the police power for the attainment of ends to which its exercise may properly be directed.

As the court below has not passed upon one of the grounds of demurrer which appears to involve no federal question, and may present a defense still open to the respondent, we reverse the judgment and remand the cause for further proceedings not inconsistent with this opinion.

So ordered.

A Contract Between a School Trustee
and a Teacher to Pay "Good Wages"
Is Too Indefinite to Enforce

FAIRPLAY SCHOOL
TOWNSHIP v. O'NEAL

Supreme Court of Indiana, 1891.
127 Ind. 95, 26 N.E. 686.

ELLIOTT, J. The complaint of the appellee alleges that she was duly licensed to teach school, and that her license was in force on the 31st day of March, 1888; that she entered into a verbal contract with the school trustee on that day, wherein she undertook to teach school for the term to be held in the school year 1888; that the school trustee promised in said oral contract to pay her "good wages;" that she has been ready and willing to teach, but the trustee refused to permit her to do so. The question presented is whether there was such a contract as bound the school township, and made it liable for damages for a breach. Our opinion is that there was no such contract. The trustee is an officer clothed with statutory power, and all who deal with him are bound to take notice of the nature and extent of his authority. . . . The authority of the trustee respecting schools is vested in him for a public purpose, in which all the citizens of the township have an interest, and upon many phases of which they have a right to be heard by petition or remonstrance. This is especially so with regard to the employment of teachers. It is necessary, for the information of the citizens, that contracts made with teachers should be certain and definite in their terms; otherwise the citizens cannot guard their interests, nor observe the conduct of their officer. It is necessary that the contract should be definite and certain, in order that when the time comes for the teacher to enter upon duty there may be no misunderstanding as to what his rights are. Any other rule would put in peril the school interests. Suppose, for illustration, that a contract providing for "good wages," "reasonable wages," "fair wages," or the like, is made, and when the time comes for opening the schools there arises a dispute as to what the compensation shall be. How shall it be determined, and in what mode can the teacher be compelled to go on with the duty he has agreed to perform? Until there is a definite contract, it can hardly be said that a teacher has been employed, and the public interest demands that there should be a definite agreement before the time arrives for the schools to open; otherwise the school corporation may be at the mercy of the teacher, or else there be no school. We think that a teacher cannot recover from the school corporation for the breach of an executory agreement, unless it is so full and definite as to be capable of specific enforcement. . . . There is much reason for scrutinizing with care contracts made so far in advance of the opening of the school year as was that here sued on, and sound policy requires that the terms should be so definitely fixed and made known that all interested may have full and reliable information. It is, we may say in passing, not altogether clear that the statute does not require that all contracts shall be in writing and be recorded; but we do not deem it necessary to decide that question. Judgment reversed.

NOTES

1. Would the outcome of this case have been different if the contract had been written?

2. Teachers' general relationships with school boards are created by contract and governed by general principles of contract law. Kirk v. Miller, 83 Wash.2d 777, 522 P.2d 843 (1974).

3. Power to employ or discharge teachers is exclusively vested in the school board and cannot be delegated to any other body or official, such as a school superintendent. Snider v. Kit Carson School District R–1, in Cheyenne County, 166 Colo. 180, 442 P.2d 429 (1968).

4. In order to have a valid teacher employment contract, as in other discretionary matters, the school board must act as a board and not as individuals. Landers v. Board of Education of Town of Hot Springs, 45 N.M. 446, 116 P.2d 690 (1941).

5. If a statute provides for nonrenewal of a teacher's contract for "cause," such cause cannot be found in constitutionally protected reasons; even nontenured teachers cannot be dismissed for exercising constitutional rights. Board of Trustees, Laramie County School District No. 1 v. Spiegel, 549 P.2d 1161 (Wyo.1976).

TENURE

After meeting designated academic requirements and teaching within a school district for a prescribed number of years, if a teacher is recommended for re-employment, she acquires tenure in most states. This usually means that the teacher has a right of re-employment in the school district but no right to a particular school or position.

Once a teacher acquires tenure, she must be re-employed in that school district until she dies, resigns, or retires. The only way a tenured teacher's contract can be terminated is for the board to prefer charges against the teacher and remove her for cause. The statutes usually specify what constitutes "cause" or, as sometimes stated, "good cause."

Many court cases have arisen concerning the transferring of a tenured teacher from one class or school to another class or school. Generally, a tenured teacher, like a teacher on a limited contract, may be assigned to any class or school in the district if she is qualified to teach in that position. The courts frown, however, upon any attempt of a school board or administrator to use "undesirable reassignment" as a means of getting at a teacher who has achieved continuing contract status. If a teacher has committed an act for which her contract may be terminated, the proper legal procedure should be followed to terminate her contract, rather than using "undesirable reassignment" as a substitute.

*Reassignment of Teacher from
Secondary Grade to Elementary Grade
Is Not an Impermissible Demotion*

IN RE SANTEE APPEAL

Supreme Court of Pennsylvania, 1959.
397 Pa. 601, 156 A.2d 830.

PER CURIAM. The decree appealed from is affirmed on the following opinion of Judge Flannery for the court en banc.

Miss Clara N. Santee has been a professional employee of the School District of the City of Hazleton where, since 1925, she has held the status of a teacher.

For the school year 1956–1957 she was assigned to the D.A. Harman, Jr. High School teaching English and Mathematics in the ninth grade.

On August 22, 1957, she was assigned to teach a sixth-grade class in the Arthur Street School, which assignment she regarded as a demotion and accepted under protest. Her salary was not affected by the transfer and is not here involved.

Exercising her rights under the School Code she demanded restoration of her previous status and requested a hearing before the School Board. That was granted and her petition was denied. She appealed to the Superintendent of Public Instruction of the Commonwealth of Pennsylvania who, by decision dated June 11, 1958, dismissed her appeal. From that decision she appealed to this court, and on October 3, 1958, we affirmed the decision and order of the Superintendent of Public Instruction. . . .

The question is narrow. Does an assignment from the ninth to the sixth grade constitute a demotion in type of position as contemplated by the Code? We believe it does not.

The statute provides:

> but there shall be no demotion of any professional employe either in salary or in type of position without the consent of the employe, or, if such consent is not received, then such demotion shall be subject to the right to a hearing before the board of school directors and an appeal in the same manner as hereinbefore provided in the case of the dismissal of a professional employe.

. . . There was a salary distinction between "elementary and secondary schools" under the Act of May 18, 1911, P.L. 309, as amended and revised. . . . But this distinction was swept away in the amendment of July 5, 1947, P.L. 1266, which provided for minimum salaries based on certification and academic qualifications and not on assignment and this system has been retained under the amendments to the Code. . . .

Thus the Legislature has abolished the legal distinction between elementary and secondary schools and unless we can find in the law some differences between the two in importance, dignity, responsibility, authority and/or prestige—some distinguishing difference—the appellant cannot prevail.

The definition of professional employee, as mandated in the Code, must be kept in mind. It provides:

> The term "professional employe" shall include teachers, supervisors, supervising principals, directors of vocational education, dental hygienists, visiting teachers, school secretaries the selection of whom is on the basis of merit as determined by eligibility lists, school nurses who are certified as teachers and any regular full-time employe of a school district who is duly certified as a teacher.

. . . We construe these to be the "type of position" referred to in Art. XI, Sec. 1151, which prohibits demotion of any professional employee either in salary or in type of position without the consent of the employee, as we have quoted above. Under this construction the appellant has not been demoted.

There is no less importance, dignity, responsibility, authority, prestige or compensation in the elementary grades than in secondary. Here the young student still pliant, still susceptible, still in the formative stage, receives his earlier impressions, his inspiration, his direction. Here personality traits are brought out and developed, tastes are instilled, habit patterns are established, character is formed. This is perhaps the most important period of life, the most crucial, the period which may determine a child's ultimate moral, ethical and intellectual stature. To be charged with the responsibility for children in this critical time of their lives is no demotion.

Decree affirmed at appellant's costs.

NOTES

1. Tenure laws are enacted to provide job security to experienced teachers and to ensure that they will not be discharged for insufficient and inadequate reasons. A system of tenure has as its objective the maintenance of an able teaching force who have undergone a period of probation with the concomitant result that because of such protections more talented personnel will be attracted to the teaching profession. State v.

Redman, 491 P.2d 157 (1971), appeal after remand Redman v. Department of Education, 519 P.2d 760 (Alaska 1974).

2. The broad purpose of teacher tenure is to protect worthy instructors from enforced yielding to political preferences and to guarantee employment regardless of the vicissitudes of politics. School District No. 8, Pinal County v. Superior Court of Pinal County, 102 Ariz. 478, 433 P.2d 28 (1967).

3. A continuing contract has as one of its central purposes the elimination of uncertainty in the employment plans of both teacher and school district. Peters v. South Kitsap School District No. 402, 8 Wn.App. 809, 509 P.2d 67 (1973).

4. Tenure laws are not grants of power to school districts, but rather constitute a limitation on the power of the school district to freely contract with teachers. Carlson v. School District No. 6 of Maricopa County, 12 Ariz.App. 179, 468 P.2d 944 (1970).

5. Teaching of one-half days during school term does not prevent counting that term toward tenure. Independent School District No. 10 of Seminole County v. Lollar, 547 P.2d 1324 (Okl.App.1976).

6. The Teacher Tenure Act of Colorado creates a contract by law between the school board and its teachers. Sedgewick County v. Ebke, 193 Colo. 40, 562 P.2d 419 (1977).

7. A transfer involving a reduction in salary may be a violation of a teacher's tenure rights if such protection is expressly provided by statute. Such was the case in People ex rel. Callahan v. Board of Education, 174 N.Y. 169, 66 N.E. 674 (1903).

8. Some courts construe the term "removal" as used in tenure laws to include a demotion in office by assigning the employee to a lower position with a reduction of compensation. See State v. Avoyelles, 199 La. 859, 7 So.2d 165 (1942).

9. Courts may hold that transfers that involve no salary reduction may violate tenure rights if the new position is of less dignity and prestige. See Smith v. School District No. 18, Pondera County, 115 Mont. 102, 139 P.2d 518 (1943), and State v. Tangipahoa Parish School Board, 12 So.2d 496 (La.App.1943).

10. The case of Board of School Trustees v. Moore, 218 Ind. 386, 33 N.E.2d 114 (1941), involved the legality of a salary schedule that provided a separate classification for inefficient, uncooperative, and uninterested teachers. In approving this schedule the Court said:

> In all walks of life it is expected that those who serve best will be appreciated most and will be best remunerated. There is no expression in the law which denies the school authorities the right to weigh such considerations in classifying teachers and fixing their compensation. But, on the contrary, the vesting of discretion in school officers to maintain the school system for the good of the community would seem to command a consideration of such matters. Teachers' contracts may be canceled by the school authorities for incompetency, insubordination, or neglect of duty, but the statute does not

command that contracts be canceled. There are no doubt degrees of incompetency, and insubordination and neglect of duty.

It is argued by the (district) that if teachers become lethargical in professional attitude, manifest defects in practical service, and fail to make progressive development in their qualification for work, and to manifest a seemly interest in the welfare of the schools, the board is confronted with a perplexing problem. It is said that teachers of this type are not essentially bad; that they may be potentially good; that the board may not desire to cancel their contracts, but may feel that something should be done to stimulate a desire upon the part of these teachers to improve their professional ability and service.

REDUCTION IN FORCE

In recent years, many school districts have been faced with declining student enrollments and, as a result, there has been a corresponding reduction in the number of professional employees. Reductions in force may be brought about through enrollment declines, financial exigencies, reorganization, or the elimination of programs. Therefore, even a tenured teacher may be removed from the work force if justification is substantiated. (See Chapter 14)

Local school boards may, within their discretion, establish a reduction in force policy, absent contractual obligations created by statutory or collective bargaining agreements. Such policy should consider: (1) the necessity of reduction in force; (2) the positions eliminated; (3) the bad faith actions of school boards; and (4) seniority.[5]

Reduction in Force Must Be in Good
Faith and for Constitutional Reasons

ZOLL v. EASTERN ALLAMAKEE COMMUNITY SCHOOL DISTRICT

United States Court of Appeals, Eighth
Circuit, 1978.
588 F.2d 246.

Action was brought by former school teacher for reinstatement and back pay following nonrenewal of her contract. The United States District Court for the Northern District of Iowa . . . entered judgment in favor of teacher against superintendent and elementary principal, and superintendent and principal appealed and teacher cross-appealed. The Court of Appeals . . . held that: (1) there was sufficient evidence of illicit motive for nonrenewal of teacher's contract to support jury verdict of liability; (2) no reversible error was committed in charging jury on elements of teacher's case, but (3) district court failed to comply with requisite guidelines for attorney fee awards and decided back pay claims against school district without benefit of the Supreme Court's recent *Monell* decision, which foreclosed absolute immunity for local governing bodies.

Mrs. Zoll holds a Masters Degree in Elementary Administration and is certified by the State of Iowa as both a teacher and an administrator. Prior to the nonrenewal of her contract, she had been employed as a first-grade teacher in Allamakee County for twenty-nine years. The last fifteen years of her teaching career were with the Eastern Allamakee Community School District which was organized after she began teaching. She was promoted to elementary school principal in the Eastern Allamakee Community School District but resigned after two years to devote her full time to teaching.

In September 1973, Mr. Harold Pronga succeeded Mrs. Zoll as the elementary school principal. In June and July 1974, Mrs. Zoll wrote two letters to the editor of a local newspaper sharply criticizing Mr. Pronga, School Superintendent Duane Fuhrman, and school board members Lawrence Protsman, Hugh Conway, James Mettille and Roy Renk for a decline in administrative concern with academic excellence.

Mrs. Zoll complained that athletics were stressed over academics in the high school and that the quality of the elementary school was also in jeopardy. Her fears were based in part upon Mr. Pronga's refusal to authorize her requisition for work books and his suggestion that Mrs. Zoll teach her students to play "Fish" and "Concentration."

In August, 1974, on her second day at school following the summer vacation, Mrs. Zoll was summoned to Mr. Pronga's office to discuss the letters. Mr. Pronga had informed Superintendent Fuhrman of the planned meeting. At the outset of their discussion, Mr. Pronga read to Mrs. Zoll from his prepared notes: "I am very concerned and equally puzzled by your letters to the editor." Mr. Pronga accused Mrs. Zoll of misrepresenting facts and chastised her for failing to express her feelings through proper channels.

In December 1974, the school board followed the suggestion of the Iowa Department of Public Instruction in adopting a contingency plan for staff reduction in the event of a decline in enrollment. The plan included rules for determining the pool of teachers from which layoffs would be made. Selection from the pool would be by a 100-point system. A maximum of 40 points could be awarded for experience and training. The principal, superintendent and school board could award up to 20 points each, based on their subjective evaluations.

At the February 1975 school board meeting, the board was informed of a projected enrollment decline of first-grade students for the 1975–76 school year which would warrant a staff reduction. The board treated as a pool from which a lay-off would be made the three first-grade teachers: Mrs. Zoll, Mrs. Rebecca Okerlund and Mrs. Jane Meyer. The official decision of which teacher to terminate was postponed until the March board meeting. Mrs. Zoll was advised by a colleague of the school board president that the decision to terminate her was actually made at the closed executive session of the February board meeting.

Out of the potential 100 points, Mrs. Zoll received 57, Mrs. Okerlund 62½, and Mrs. Meyer 72. Mrs. Zoll was erroneously awarded 17 points for experience, although she was entitled to 20 points under the objective scale. Thus, she was actually awarded 54 points, although entitled to 57 points. Mrs. Zoll received the highest point totals on the objective evaluation of experience and training. Out of a possible 40 points, Mrs. Zoll received 40, Mrs. Okerlund 4½ and Mrs. Meyer 16. Mrs. Zoll received the lowest point totals on the subjective evaluations by Mr. Pronga, Mr. Fuhrman and the school board. Out of a possible 60 points, Mrs. Zoll received 17, Mrs. Okerlund 58, and Mrs. Meyer 56.

On April 8, 1975, the school board notified Mrs. Zoll that her contract would not be renewed for the 1975–76 school year. A public hearing was convened by the school board at Mrs. Zoll's request on June 9, 1975, pursuant to Iowa Code § 279.13 (1975). At the conclusion of the hearing, the board voted four to one not to renew her contract.

On December 15, 1975, Mrs. Zoll filed suit against Mr. Pronga, Mr. Fuhrman, and the four board members who voted not to renew her contract, alleging that they had refused to renew her teaching contract in retaliation for her exercise of First Amendment rights in violation of 42 U.S.C. § 1983 (1970). . . .

There is sufficient evidence of a retaliatory motive for the nonrenewal of Mrs. Zoll's contract to support the jury verdict. Mrs. Zoll's letters to the editor criticizing the school administration were published in the summer of 1974. On the second day of the 1974–75 school year, Mr. Pronga called Mrs. Zoll to his office to express his displeasure with the letters. Mr. Fuhrman had foreknowledge of the meeting. There was testimony that the decision to terminate Mrs. Zoll was made before the statistical evaluation. Mrs. Zoll's expert witness testified to inconsistencies between the points assigned Mrs. Zoll and the notes and testimony of Mr. Pronga and Mr. Fuhrman.

Under the staff reduction policy which the board had adopted in December 1974, teachers laid off pursuant to the policy were granted certain "recall rights" for a three-year period: "Any staff member laid off due to reduction of staff policy may be recalled if a vacancy exists within three years." Three vacancies arose during the year following Mrs. Zoll's termination. The vacancies were at the first grade, sixth grade and seventh-eighth grade levels. Mrs. Zoll applied for but was not offered any of these positions. Instead, two new teachers were hired and one teacher was transferred to fill the vacancies. The jury could reasonably have believed that the subjective rating of Mrs. Zoll by Mr. Pronga and Mr. Fuhrman was a pretext for discharging her for exercising her First Amendment rights. See Mt. Healthy City Board of Education v. Doyle, 429 U.S. 274, 97 S.Ct. 568, 50 L.Ed.2d 471 (1977). . . .

Accordingly, we affirm the entry of judgment of liability on the jury verdict, vacate the attorney's fee award and remand to the district court for reconsideration of the post-trial back pay issue and the attorney's fee award and for further proceedings consistent with this opinion.

Affirmed in part, vacated and remanded in part.

Footnotes

1. Harrah Independent School District v. Martin, 440 U.S. 194, 99 S.Ct. 1062 (1979).

2. Wardwell v. Board of Education, 529 F.2d 625 (6th Cir.1976). See McCarthy v. Philadelphia Civil Service Commission, 424 U.S. 645, 96 S.Ct. 1154 (1976).

3. Trustees of Dartmouth College v. Woodward, 17 U.S. (4 Wheat) 518 (1819).

4. State ex rel. Anderson v. Brand, 303 U.S. 95, 58 S.Ct. 433 (1938).

5. Phay, Robert, *Reduction in Force: Legal Issues and Recommended Policy* (Topeka: National Organization on Legal Problems of Education, 1980).

13

Teacher Freedoms

The law relating to teacher personnel administration has many legal ramifications including issues pertaining to the many aspects of constitutional and federal statutory law as they affect teachers' freedoms. Particularly in recent years, the federal Constitution has had a profound impact on teacher employment practices. Federal civil rights legislation has further created new standards that have caused a substantial amount of litigation. This chapter attempts to summarize the prevailing view of the courts in each situation bearing on freedom of speech and expression, religion, loyalty, self-incrimination, discrimination, and due process as well as the cases discussed in Chapter 12, that are based on obligation of contracts and the strictures of tenure statutes.

FREEDOM OF SPEECH AND EXPRESSION

At an earlier point in our nation's constitutional development, public employment was viewed as a privilege and not a right.[1] This privilege-right dichotomy is no longer controlling; today public employees are not expected to shed their rights on taking positions in public institutions.

In search of a new standard, the courts have developed a flexible rule that provides for balancing the public's interests against the private interest of the employee in each circumstance. This balancing, however, does not remove all vestiges of state restraint from teacher activities; on the contrary, the courts have reflected a strong belief that because of their sensitive position in the classroom, the teacher must be held accountable for certain activities both internal and external to the school.[2] The interest of the public is, to a great extent, dependent on the teachers' status, appearance, and stature in the community. The school board must preserve the integrity of the learning processes of the school. Because a teacher enters the school setting with the constitutional freedoms of speech and association, the school must have a compelling reason to overcome the teacher's interest. Valid rationale has been used by boards of education in dismissing teachers for activities ranging from in-school issues such as insubordination and incompetency to out-of-school activities that tend to reflect on the welfare of the school such as alcoholism, sexual misconduct, and gambling.

Teachers' freedoms have been given a high degree of protection by the courts. In the leading case, *Pickering* v. *Board of Education*,[3] the United States Supreme Court found that even though free speech is not an "absolute right" it is nevertheless sufficiently strong to require a "compelling state interest" on the part of the state to overcome a teacher's right to speak out against a school board's handling of school fiscal matters. The Court equated the teacher's right of free speech with that of other members of the general public to criticize public policies and actions.

Extramural speech and association of the teacher may be questioned by a school board if the teacher's exercise of these rights raises issues pertaining to competence to teach. Extramural activities may indicate that a teacher will inculcate in students values that are inconsistent with those formally espoused by the public educational system as required by society.

Teachers have always served as role models for pupils, and school boards expect high moral standards consistent with this status. The courts have generally upheld school boards in regulating the personal conduct of teachers within reasonable limits. Litigation usually results when teachers allege school rules invade their privacy. Although the right of privacy is not specifically found in the Constitution, it is afforded individuals through the Fourth Amendment and, under certain conditions, through the First Amendment.[4]

Most of the litigation concerning a teacher's right of privacy involves issues of morality or fitness to teach, and have included such issues as homosexual activities, heterosexual improprieties, and use of marijuana and other drugs. (See Chapter 15). The courts attempt to determine a rational nexus between the conduct in question and the professional duties being performed. In order to sustain their case against a teacher, the school board must establish whether the outside activity has a detrimental impact on the teacher's effectiveness to teach. "No person can be denied government employment because of factors unconnected with the responsibilities of that employment."[5]

At what point does the teacher's right of privacy end and the school and community's interest begin? The answer to this question has been answered by the courts with two tests: (1) Does the conduct directly affect the performance of the occupational responsibilities of the teacher? or (2) Has the conduct become the subject of such notoriety as to significantly and reasonably impair the capability of the particular teacher to discharge the responsibilities of the teaching position?[6]

FREEDOM OF RELIGION

All persons in this country have the right of religious freedom as guaranteed by the First Amendment. However, religion, as with other freedoms is not without certain limits. For example, in *Palmer* v. *Board of Education of the City of Chicago*, a teacher refused to carry out certain aspects of the approved curriculum because of religious beliefs. The court acknowledged the teacher's right to freedom of belief, but also recognized a compelling state interest in the proper education of all its children. The court stated that education "cannot be left to individual teachers to teach the way they please." Teachers have "no constitutional right to require others to submit to [their] views and to forego a portion of their education they would otherwise be entitled to enjoy." [7]

A teacher's religious freedom may extend into several aspects of the educational program. For example, if the tenets of a teacher's religion are violated by the Pledge of Allegiance to the American Flag, the teacher cannot be compelled to recite the pledge, but, the teacher, in accordance with school board rules, must hold the pledge ceremony for student participation. [8] Religious freedom of teachers will be sustained by the courts so long as the exercise of the freedom does not encroach on the rights of students or is not deleterious to the good conduct of the school.

The right of religious freedom, where employment is concerned, has been expanded by the 1972 Amendments to the Civil Rights Act of 1964, Title VII. The original act prohibited an employer from discriminating against an employee because of race, color, or sex, but did not specify religion. The 1972 Amendments incorporated religion and states, "It shall be an unlawful employment practice for an employment agency to fail or refuse for employment, or otherwise to discriminate against, any individual because of his race, color, religion, sex, or national origin, or to classify or refer for employment any individual on the basis of his race, color, religion, sex, or national origin." The act further states that "[t]he term religion includes all aspects of religious observances and practice, as well as belief, unless an employer demonstrates that he is unable to reasonably accommodate an employee's or prospective employee's religious observance or practice without undue hardship on the conduct of the employer's business." [9]

Teachers Have a Constitutional Right
to Speak Out Freely on Matters of
Public Concern

PICKERING v. BOARD OF EDUCATION

Supreme Court of the United States, 1968.
391 U.S. 563, 88 S.Ct. 1731.

Mr. Justice MARSHALL delivered the opinion of the Court.

Appellant Marvin L. Pickering, a teacher in Township High School District 205, Will County, Illinois, was dismissed from his position by the appellee Board of Education for sending a letter to a local newspaper in connection with a recently proposed tax increase that was critical of the way in which the Board and the district superintendent of schools had handled past proposals to raise new revenue for the schools. Appellant's dismissal resulted from a determination by the Board, after a full hearing, that the publication of the letter was "detrimental to the efficient operation and administration of the schools of the district" and hence, under the relevant Illinois statute, Ill.Rev.Stat., c. 122, § 10–22.4 (1963), that "interests of the schools require[d] [his dismissal]." . . .

The letter constituted, basically, an attack on the School Board's handling of the 1961 bond issue proposals and its subsequent allocation of financial resources between the schools' educational and athletic programs. It also charged the superintendent of schools with attempting to prevent teachers in the district from opposing or criticizing the proposed bond issue.

The Board dismissed Pickering for writing and publishing the letter. Pursuant to Illinois law, the Board was then required to hold a hearing on the dismissal. At the hearing the Board charged that numerous statements in the letter were false and that the publication of the statements unjustifiably impugned the "motives, honesty, integrity, truthfulness, responsibility and competence" of both the Board and the school administration. The Board also charged that the false statements damaged the professional reputations of its members and of the school administrators, would be disruptive of faculty discipline, and would tend to foment "controversy, conflict and dissension" among teachers, administrators, the Board of Education, and the residents of the district. Testimony was introduced from a variety of witnesses on the truth or falsity of the particular statements in the letter with which the Board took issue. The Board found the statements to be false as charged. No evidence was introduced at any point in the proceedings as to the effect of the publication of the letter on the community as a whole or on the administration of the school system in particular, and no specific findings along these lines were made.

. . . It is not altogether clear whether the Illinois Supreme Court held that the First Amendment had no applicability to appellant's dismissal for writing the letter in question or whether it determined that the particular statements made in the letter were not entitled to First Amendment protection. In any event, it clearly rejected Pickering's claim that, on the facts of this case, he could not constitutionally be dismissed from his teaching position.

To the extent that the Illinois Supreme Court's opinion may be read to suggest that teachers may constitutionally be compelled to relinquish the First Amendment rights they would otherwise enjoy as citizens to comment on matters of public interest in connection with the operation of the public schools in which they work, it proceeds on a premise that has been unequivocally rejected in numerous prior decisions of this Court. . . . "[T]he theory that public employment which may be denied altogether may be subjected to any conditions, regardless of how unreasonable, has been uniformly rejected." Keyishian v. Board of Regents, supra, 385 U.S. at 605–606, 87 S.Ct. at 685. At the same time it cannot be gainsaid that the State has interests as an employer in regulating the speech of its employees that differ significantly from those it possesses in connection with regulation of the speech of the citizenry in general. The problem in any case is to arrive at a balance between the interests of the teacher, as a citizen, in commenting upon matters of public concern and the interest of the State, as an employer, in promoting the efficiency of the public services it performs through its employees.

The Board contends that "the teacher by virtue of his public employment has a duty of loyalty to support his superiors in attaining the generally accepted goals of education and that, if he must speak out publicly, he should do so factually and accurately, commensurate with his education and experience." Appellant, on the other hand, argues that the test applicable to defamatory statements directed against public officials by persons having no occupational relationship with them, namely, that statements to be legally actionable must be made "with knowledge that [they were] . . . false or with reckless disregard of whether [they were] . . . false or not" . . . should also be applied to public statements made by teachers. . . .

An examination of the statements in appellant's letter objected to by the Board reveals that they, like the letter as a whole, consist essentially of criticism of the Board's allocation of school funds between educational and athletic programs, and of both the Board's and the superintendent's methods of informing, or preventing the informing of, the district's taxpayers of the real reasons why additional tax revenues were being sought for the schools. The statements are in no way directed towards any person with whom appellant would normally be in contact in the course of his daily work as a teacher. Thus no question of maintaining either discipline by immediate superiors or harmony among coworkers is presented here. Appellant's employment relationships with the Board and, to a somewhat lesser extent, with the superintendent are not the kind of close working relationships for which it can persuasively be claimed that personal loyalty and confidence are necessary to their proper functioning. Accordingly, to the extent that the Board's position here can be taken to suggest that even comments on matters of public concern that are substantially correct . . . may furnish grounds for dismissal if they are sufficiently critical in tone, we unequivocally reject it.

We next consider the statements in appellant's letter which we agree to be false. The Board's original charges included allegations that the publication of the letter damaged the professional reputations of the Board and the superintendent and would foment controversy and conflict among the Board, teachers, administrators, and the residents of the district. However, no evidence to support these allegations was introduced at the hearing. So far as the record reveals, Pickering's letter was greeted by everyone but its main target, the Board, with massive apathy and total disbelief. . . .

In addition, the fact that particular illustrations of the Board's claimed undesirable emphasis on athletic programs are false would not normally have any necessary impact on the actual operation of the schools, beyond its tendency to anger the Board. For example, Pickering's letter was written after the defeat at the polls of the second proposed tax increase. It could, therefore, have had no effect on the ability of the school district to raise necessary revenue, since there was no showing that there was any proposal to increase taxes pending when the letter was written.

More importantly, the question whether a school system requires additional funds is a matter of legitimate public concern on which the judgment of the school administration, including the School Board, cannot, in a society that leaves such questions to popular vote, be taken as conclusive. On such a question free and open debate is vital to informed decision-making by the electorate. Teachers are, as a class, the members of a community most likely to have informed and definite opinions as to how funds allotted to the operation of the schools should be spent. Accordingly, it is essential that they be able to speak out freely on such questions without fear of retaliatory dismissal. . . .

What we do have before us is a case in which a teacher has made erroneous public statements upon issues then currently the subject of public attention, which are critical of his ultimate employer but which are neither shown nor can be presumed to have in any way either impeded the teacher's proper performance of his daily duties in the classroom or to have interfered with the regular operation of the schools generally. In these circumstances we conclude that the interest of the school administration in limiting teachers' opportunities to contribute to public debate is not significantly greater than its interest in limiting a similar contribution by any member of the general public.

The public interest in having free and unhindered debate on matters of pubic importance—the core value of the Free Speech Clause of the First Amendment—is so great that it has been held that a State cannot authorize the recovery of damages by a public official for defamatory statements directed at him except when such statements are shown to have been made either with knowledge of their falsity or with reckless disregard for their truth or falsity. . . . It is therefore perfectly clear that, were appellant a member of the general public, the State's power to afford the appellee Board of Education or its members any legal right to sue him for writing the letter at issue here would be limited by the requirement that the letter be judged by the standard laid down in New York Times.

This Court has also indicated, in more general terms, that statements by public officials on matters of public concern must be accorded First Amendment protection despite the fact that the statements are directed at their nominal superiors. . . .

While criminal sanctions and damage awards have a somewhat different impact on the exercise of the right to freedom of speech from dismissal from employment, it is apparent that the threat of dismissal from public employment is nonetheless a potent means of inhibiting speech. We have already noted our disinclination to make an across-the-board equation of dismissal from public employment for remarks critical of superiors with awarding damages in a libel suit by a public official for similar criticism. However, in a case such as the present one, in which the fact of employment is only tangentially and insubstantially involved in the subject matter of the public communication made by a teacher, we conclude that it is necessary to regard the teacher as the member of the general public he seeks to be.

In sum, we hold that, in a case such as this, absent proof of false statements knowingly or recklessly made by him, a teacher's exercise of his right to speak on issues of public importance may not furnish the basis for his dismissal from public employment. Since no such showing has been made in this case regarding appellant's letter, his dismissal for writing it cannot be upheld and the judgment of the Illinois Supreme Court must, accordingly, be reversed and the case remanded for further proceedings not inconsistent with this opinion. It is so ordered.

Judgment reversed and case remanded with directions.

NOTES

1. Free speech protection does not entitle a teacher to be excessively critical and derisive of duly constituted school authority and to personally denounce and abuse other teachers. Amburgey v. Cassady, 370 F.Supp. 571 (E.D.Ky.1974).

2. Can a superintendent move a teacher to another school in the school system if the motivation for the transfer is based on the teacher's exercise of a constitutionally protected right? See: Adcock v. Board of Education of San Diego Unified School District, 10 Cal.3d 60, 109 Cal.Rptr. 676, 513 P.2d 900 (1973).

3. What political statements may a teacher make in the classroom?

4. A tenured teacher announced his candidacy for state representative. On the same day, the board of education adopted a rule requiring any candidate for public office to take a leave without pay beginning on the day the teacher becomes a candidate. Did the court uphold this regulation, which was made applicable to all teachers currently employed? See School City of East Chicago v. Sigler, 219 Ind. 9, 36 N.E.2d 760 and Adams v. State, 69 So.2d 309 (Fla.1954).

5. In a case in which a tenured teacher, who was also president of the local teachers' union, made a speech attacking the administration in general and the superintendent in particular, called the district a snake pit, and alleged the district had burned books and failed to hire black teachers, the court said that the teacher had a right to speak out on hiring minorities, but had exceeded permissible bounds in choosing to distort issues and bring scorn and abuse on the school district and the superintendent. Pietrunti v. Board of Education of Brick Township, 128 N.J. Super. 149, 319 A.2d 262 (N.J.1974).

6. It is well settled that a teacher, as a citizen, may run for political office, but there is a difference between the right to run for public office and the right to continued public employment after being elected. Common law provides that a teacher or other public employee may not hold positions simultaneously that are incompatible and, therefore, present a conflict of interest. Whether or not a teacher may hold political office and serve as a teacher is dependent upon statutes of the particular state. Some states have statutes that provide the teacher may not serve as a state legislator and teacher at the same time. But if a state does not have a statute prohibiting serving, then the courts generally have allowed them to serve. A board can reasonably request the teacher to take an unpaid leave of absence while serving in a public position.

7. Some states have passed legislation modeled after the Federal Hatch Act, which prohibits participation in partisan politics. The United States Supreme Court in Broadrick v. Oklahoma, 413 U.S. 601, 93 S.Ct. 2908 (1973), upheld an Oklahoma statute prohibiting public employees from participating in partisan politics. These statutes usually limit activities such as direct fundraising for candidates, becoming a candidate, starting a political party, or actively managing a campaign. See: United States

Civil Service Commission v. National Association of Letter Carriers, 413 U.S. 548, 93 S.Ct. 2880 (1973).

8. School boards have attempted to dismiss unwed pregnant teachers on charges of immorality. The teachers have countered claiming that the dismissals are an invasion of their privacy rights, denial of due process and equal protection, violation of Title VII of the Civil Rights Act of 1964 and Title IX of the Education Amendment Act of 1972. The courts have upheld the teachers unless it can be shown that the education environment has been disrupted. Drake v. Covington County Board of Education, 371 F.Supp. 974 (M.D.Ala.1974); see also: Avery v. Homewood City Board of Education, 674 F.2d 337 (5th Cir.1982).

9. In a case involving the religious rights of teachers, a member of the World Wide Church of God requested seven days off, without pay, to attend a religious festival. When the request was denied, he attended the festival and was subsequently discharged. The teacher filed suit under Title VII, claiming his religious rights had been violated and the board should have "reasonably accommodated" him. The board claimed a qualified teacher could not be found to serve as a substitute. A guidance counselor had to substitute and, according to the board, this placed an undue hardship on the employer. Before the teacher went to the religious festival, he prepared lesson plans and models and consulted with the counselor about his classes. The court determined the classes ran very smoothly and therefore upheld the teacher's action saying the board had violated Title VII. Wangsness v. Watertown School District No. 14–4, etc., 541 F.Supp. 332 (D.S.D.1982); see also: Pinsker v. Joint District No. 28J, etc., 554 F.Supp. 1049 (D.Colo.1983), Hunterdon Central High School Board of Education v. Hunterdon Central High Teachers' Association, 174 N.J.Super. 468, 416 A.2d 980 (1980).

Evidence Must Show That Teacher's
Exercise of Constitutional Right Was
the Motivating Factor Not to Rehire
Before Judicial Action Is Justified

MT. HEALTHY CITY SCHOOL DISTRICT BOARD OF EDUCATION v. DOYLE

Supreme Court of the United States, 1977.
429 U.S. 274, 97 S.Ct. 568.

Mr. Justice REHNQUIST delivered the opinion of the Court.

Respondent Doyle sued petitioner Mt. Healthy Board of Education in the United States District Court for the Southern District of Ohio. Doyle claimed that the Board's refusal to renew his contract in 1971 violated his rights under the First and Fourteenth Amendments to the United States Constitution. After a bench trial the District Court held that Doyle was entitled to reinstatement with back pay. The Court of Appeals for the Sixth Circuit affirmed the judgment. . . .

Doyle was first employed by the Board in 1966. He worked under one-year contracts for the first three years, and under a two-year contract from 1969 to 1971. In 1969 he was elected president of the Teachers' Association, in which position he worked to expand the subjects of direct negotiation between the Association and the Board of Education. During Doyle's one-year term as president of the Association, and during the succeeding year when he served on its executive committee, there was apparently some tension in relations between the Board and the Association.

Beginning early in 1970, Doyle was involved in several incidents not directly connected with his role in the Teachers' Association. In one instance, he engaged in an argument with another teacher which culminated in the other teacher's slapping him. Doyle subsequently refused to accept an apology and insisted upon some punishment for the other teacher. His persistence in the matter resulted in the suspension of both teachers for one day, which was followed by a walkout by a number of other teachers, which in turn resulted in the lifting of the suspensions.

On other occasions, Doyle got into an argument with employees of the school cafeteria over the amount of spaghetti which had been served him; referred to students, in connection with a disciplinary complaint, as "sons of bitches"; and made an obscene gesture to two girls in connection with their failure to obey commands made in his capacity as cafeteria supervisor. Chronologically the last in the series of incidents which respondent was involved in during his employment by the Board was a telephone call by him to a local radio station. It was the Board's consideration of this incident which the court below found to be a violation of the First and Fourteenth Amendments.

In February of 1971, the principal circulated to various teachers a memorandum relating to teacher dress and appearance, which was apparently prompted by the view of some in the administration that there was a relationship between teacher appearance and public support for bond issues. Doyle's response to the receipt of the memorandum—on a subject which he apparently understood was to be settled by joint teacher-administration action—was to convey the substance of the memorandum to a disc jockey at WSAI, a Cincinnati radio station, who promptly announced the adoption of the dress code as a news item. Doyle subsequently apologized to the principal, conceding that he should have made some prior communication of his criticism to the school administration.

Approximately one month later the superintendent made his customary annual recommendations to the Board as to the rehiring of nontenured teachers. He recommended that Doyle not be rehired. The same recommendation was made with respect to nine other teachers in the district, and in all instances, including Doyle's, the recommendation was adopted by the Board. Shortly after being notified of this decision, respondent requested a statement of reasons for the Board's actions. He received a statement citing "a notable lack of tact in handling professional matters which leaves much doubt as to your sincerity in establishing good school relationships." That general statement was followed by references to the radio station incident and to the obscene gesture incident.

The District Court found that all of these incidents had in fact occurred. It concluded that respondent Doyle's telephone call to the radio station was "clearly protected by the First Amendment," and that because it had played a "substantial part" in the decision of the Board not to renew Doyle's employment, he was entitled to reinstatement with backpay. App. to pet., at 12a–13a. The District Court did not expressly state what test it was applying in determining that the incident in question involved conduct protected by the First Amendment, but simply held that the communication to the radio station was such conduct. The Court of Appeals affirmed in a brief *per curiam* opinion.

Doyle's claims under the First and Fourteenth Amendments are not defeated by the fact that he did not have tenure. Even though he could have been discharged for no reason whatever, and had no constitutional right to a hearing prior to the decision not to rehire him, Board of Regents v. Roth, 408 U.S. 564, 92 S.Ct. 2701, 33 L.Ed.2d 548 (1972), he may nonetheless establish a claim to reinstatement if the decision not to rehire him was made by reason of his exercise of constitutionally protected First Amendment freedoms. Perry v. Sindermann.

That question of whether speech of a government employee is constitutionally protected expression necessarily entails striking "a balance between the interests of the teacher, as a citizen, in commenting upon matters of public concern and the interest of the State as an employer, in promoting the efficiency of the public services it performs through its employees." Pickering v. Board of Education. There is no suggestion by the Board that Doyle violated any established policy, or that its reaction to his communication to the radio station was anything more than an ad hoc response to Doyle's action in making the memorandum public. We therefore accept the District Court's finding that the communication was protected by the First and Fourteenth Amendments. We are not, however, entirely in agreement with that court's manner of reasoning from this finding to the conclusion that Doyle is entitled to reinstatement with backpay.

The District Court made the following "conclusions" on this aspect of the case:

> (1) If a non-permissible reason, e.g., exercise of First Amendment rights, played a substantial part in the decision not to renew—even in the face of other permissible grounds—the decision may not stand (citations omitted).
>
> (2) A non-permissible reason did play a substantial part. That is clear from the letter of the Superintendent immediately following the Board's decision, which stated two reasons—the one, the conversation with the radio station clearly protected by the First Amendment. A court may not engage in any limitation of First Amendment rights based on "tact"—that is not to say that "tactfulness" is irrelevant to other issues in this case.
> At the same time, though, it stated that "in fact, as this Court sees it and finds, both the Board and the Superintendent were faced with a situation in which there did exist in fact reason . . . independent of any First Amendment rights or exercise thereof, to not extend tenure."

Since respondent Doyle had no tenure, and there was therefore not even a state law requirement of "cause" or "reason" before a decision could be made not to renew his employment, it is not clear what the District Court meant by this latter statement. Clearly the Board legally *could* have dismissed respondent had the radio station incident never come to its attention. One plausible meaning of the court's statement is that the Board and the Superintendent not only could, but in fact *would* have reached that decision had not the constitutionally protected incident of the telephone call to the radio station occurred. We are thus brought to the issue whether, even if that were the case, the fact that the protected conduct played a "substantial part" in the actual decision not to renew would necessarily amount to a constitutional violation justifying remedial action. We think that it would not.

A rule of causation which focuses solely on whether protected conduct played a part, "substantial" or otherwise, in a decision not to rehire, could place an employee in a better position as a result of the exercise of constitutionally protected conduct than he would have occupied had he done nothing. The difficulty with the rule enunciated by the District Court is that it would require reinstatement in cases where a dramatic and perhaps abrasive incident is inevitably on the minds of those responsible for the decision to rehire, and does indeed play a part in that decision—even if the same decision would have been reached had the incident not occurred. The constitutional principle at stake is sufficiently vindicated if such an employee is placed in no worse a position than if he had not engaged in the conduct. A borderline or marginal candidate should not have the employment question resolved against him because of constitutionally protected conduct. But that same candidate ought not to be able, by engaging in such conduct, to prevent his employer from assessing his performance record and reaching a decision not to rehire on the basis of that record, simply because the protected conduct makes the employer more certain of the correctness of its decision.

This is especially true where, as the District Court observed was the case here, the current decision to rehire will accord "tenure." The long term consequences of an award of tenure are of great moment both to the employee and to the employer. They are too significant for us to hold that the Board in this case would be precluded, because it considered constitutionally protected conduct in deciding not to rehire Doyle, from attempting to prove to a trier of fact that quite apart from such conduct Doyle's record was such that he would not have been rehired in any event.   . . .

Initially, in this case, the burden was properly placed upon respondent to show that his conduct was constitutionally protected, and that this conduct was a "substantial factor"—or to put it in other words, that it was a "motivating factor" in the Board's decision not to rehire him. Respondent having carried that burden, however, the District Court should have gone on to determine whether the Board had shown by a preponderance of the evidence that it would have reached the same decision as to respondent's reemployment even in the absence of the protected conduct.

We cannot tell from the District Court opinion and conclusions, nor from the opinion of the Court of Appeals affirming the judgment of the District Court, what conclusion those courts would have reached had they applied this test. The judgment of the Court of Appeals is therefore vacated, and the case remanded for further proceedings consistent with this opinion.

NOTE

The burden of proof is on the teacher to show that he or she was not rehired after engaging in constitutionally protected conduct. The teacher must also show that this conduct was the "motivating factor" in the school board's decision not to rehire. From this point the burden shifts to the defendant school board, which must show by a preponderance of evidence that it would have reached the same decision regardless of whether the teacher had engaged in the constitutionally protected conduct. McGee v. South Pemiscot School District R–V, 712 F.2d 339 (8th Cir.1983).

Freedom of Speech Is Guaranteed to
Teacher in Private Communication
with Employer

GIVHAN v. WESTERN LINE CONSOLIDATED SCHOOL DISTRICT

Supreme Court of the United States, 1979.
439 U.S. 410, 99 S.Ct. 693.

Mr. Justice REHNQUIST delivered the opinion of the Court.

Petitioner Bessie Givhan was dismissed from her employment as a junior high English teacher at the end of the 1970–1971 school year. At the time of petitioner's termination, respondent Western Line Consolidated School District was the subject of a desegregation order entered by the United States District Court for the Northern District of Mississippi. Petitioner filed a complaint . . . seeking reinstatement on the ground that nonrenewal of her contract . . . infringed her right of free speech secured by the First and Fourteenth Amendments of the United States Constitution. In an effort to show that its decision was justified, respondent school district introduced evidence of, among other things, a series of private encounters between petitioner and the school principal in which petitioner allegedly made "petty and unreasonable demands" in a manner variously described by the principal as "insulting," "hostile," "loud," and "arrogant." After a two-day bench trial, the District Court held that petitioner's termination had violated the First Amendment. Finding that petitioner had made "demands" on but two occasions and that those demands "were neither 'petty' nor 'unreasonable,' insomuch as all of the complaints in question involved employment policies and practices at [the] school which [petitioner] conceived to be racially discriminatory in purpose or effect," the District Court concluded that "the primary reason for the school district's failure to renew [petitioner's] contract was her criticism of the policies and practices of the school district, especially the school to which she was assigned to teach." . . .

The Court of Appeals for the Fifth Circuit reversed. Although it found the District Court's findings not clearly erroneous, the Court of Appeals concluded that because petitioner had privately expressed her complaints and opinions to the principal, her expression was not protected under the First Amendment. . . .

This Court's decisions in *Pickering, Perry,* and *Mt. Healthy* do not support the conclusion that a public employee forfeits his protection against governmental abridgment of freedom of speech if he decides to express his views privately rather than publicly. While those cases each arose in the context of a public employee's public expression, the rule to be derived from them is not dependent on that largely coincidental fact.

In *Pickering* a teacher was discharged for publicly criticizing, in a letter published in a local newspaper, the school board's handling of prior bond issue proposals and its subsequent allocation of financial resources between the schools' educational and athletic programs. Noting that the free speech rights of public employees are not absolute, the Court held that in determining whether a government employee's speech is constitutionally protected, "the interests of the [employee], as a citizen, in commenting upon matters of public concern" must be balanced against "the interest of the State, as an employer, in promoting the efficiency of the public services it performs through its employees." . . . The Court concluded that under the circumstances of that case "the interest of the school administration in limiting teachers' opportunities to contribute to public debate [was] not significantly greater than its interest in limiting a similar contribution by any member of the general public." Here the opinion of the Court of Appeals may be read to turn in part on its view that the working relationship between principal and teacher is significantly different from the relationship between the parties in *Pickering* . . . . But we do not feel confident that the Court of Appeals' decision would have been placed on that ground notwithstanding its view that the First Amendment does not require the same sort of *Pickering* balancing for the private expression of a public employee as it does for public expression.

Perry and *Mt. Healthy* arose out of similar disputes between teachers and their public employers. As we have noted, however, the fact that each of these cases involved public expression by the employee was not critical to the decision. Nor is the Court of Appeals' view supported by the "captive audience" rationale. Having opened his office door to petitioner, the principal was hardly in a position to argue that he was the "*unwilling* recipient" of her views.

The First Amendment forbids abridgment of the "freedom of speech." Neither the Amendment itself nor our decisions indicate that this freedom is lost to the public employee who arranges to communicate privately with his employer rather than to spread his views before the public. We decline to adopt such a view of the First Amendment.

While this case was pending on appeal to the Court of Appeals, *Mt. Healthy City Board of Education* v. *Doyle* was decided. In that case this Court rejected the view that a public employee must be reinstated whenever constitutionally protected conduct plays a "substantial" part in the employer's decision to terminate. Such a rule would require reinstatement of employees that the public employer would have dismissed even if the constitutionally protected conduct had not occurred and, consequently "could place an employee in a better position as a result of the exercise of constitutionally protected conduct than he would have occupied had he done nothing." Thus, the Court held that once the employee has shown that his constitutionally protected conduct played a "substantial" role in the employer's decision not to rehire him, the employer is entitled to show "by a preponderance of the evidence that it would have reached the same decision as to [the employee's] reemployment even in the absence of the protected conduct." Id., at 287, 97 S.Ct., at 576.

The Court of Appeals in the instant case rejected respondents' *Mt. Healthy* claim that the decision to terminate petitioner would have been made even if her encounters with the principal had never occurred:

> The [trial] court did not make an express finding as to whether the same decision would have been made, but on this record the [respondents] do not, and seriously cannot, argue that the same decision would have been made without regard to the "demands." Appellants seem to argue that the preponderance of the evidence shows that the same decision would have been justified, but that is not the same as proving that the same decision would have been made. . . . Therefore [respondents] failed to make a successful "same decision anyway" defense.

Since this case was tried before *Mt. Healthy* was decided, it is not surprising that respondents did not attempt to prove in the District Court that the decision not to rehire petitioner would have been made even absent consideration of her "demands." Thus, the case came to the Court of Appeals in very much the same posture as *Mt. Healthy* was presented in this Court. And while the District Court found that petitioner's "criticism" was the "primary" reason for the school district's failure to rehire her, it did not find that she would have been rehired *but for* her criticism. Respondents' *Mt. Healthy* claim called for a factual determination which could not, on this record, be resolved by the Court of Appeals.

Accordingly, the judgment of the Court of Appeals is vacated and the case remanded for further proceedings consistent with this opinion.

So ordered.

Teacher Dress Policy Ruled
Constitutional

EAST HARTFORD
EDUCATION ASSOCIATION v.
BOARD OF EDUCATION

United States Court of Appeals,
Second Circuit, 1977.
562 F.2d 838.

MESKILL, Circuit Judge:

Although this case may at first appear too trivial to command the attention of a busy court, it raises important issues concerning the proper scope of judicial oversight of local affairs. The appellant here, Richard Brimley, is a public school teacher reprimanded for failing to wear a necktie while teaching his English class. Joined by the teachers union, he sued the East Hartford Board of Education, claiming that the reprimand for violating the dress code deprived him of his rights of free speech and privacy. . . .

In the vast majority of communities, the control of public schools is vested in locally-elected bodies. This commitment to local political bodies requires significant public control over what is said and done in school. It is not the federal courts, but local democratic processes, that are primarily responsible for the many routine decisions that are made in public school systems. Accordingly, it is settled that "[c]ourts do not and cannot intervene in the resolution of conflicts which arise in the daily operation of school systems and which do not directly and sharply implicate basic constitutional values." Epperson v. Arkansas, 393 U.S. 97, 104, 89 S.Ct. 266, 270, 21 L.Ed. 2d 228 (1968).

Federal courts must refrain, in most instances, from interfering with the decisions of school authorities. Even though decisions may appear foolish or unwise, a federal court may not overturn them unless the standards set forth in *Epperson* is met. . . .

Mr. Brimley claims that by refusing to wear a necktie he makes a statement on current affairs which assists him in his teaching. In his brief, he argues that the following benefits flow from his tielessness:

> (a) He wishes to present himself to his students as a person who is not tied to "establishment conformity."
> (b) He wishes to symbolically indicate to his students his association with the ideas of the generation to which those students belong, including the rejection of many of the customs and values, and of the social outlook, of the older generation.
> (c) He feels that dress of this type enables him to achieve closer rapport with his students, and thus enhances his ability to teach.

Appellant's claim, therefore, is that his refusal to wear a tie is "symbolic speech," and, as such, is protected against governmental interference by the First Amendment.

We are required here to balance the alleged interest in free expression against the goals of the school board in requiring its teachers to dress somewhat more formally than they might like. When this test is applied, the school board's position must prevail.

Obviously, a great range of conduct has the symbolic, "speech-like" aspect claimed by Mr. Brimley. To state that activity is "symbolic" is only the beginning, and not the end, of constitutional inquiry. . . . Even though intended as expression, symbolic speech remains conduct, subject to regulation by the state. As the Supreme Court has stated in discussing the difference between conduct and "speech in its pristine form":

> We emphatically reject the notion urged by appellant that the First and Fourteenth Amendments afford the same kind of freedom to those who would communicate ideas by conduct such as patrolling, marching, and picketing on streets and highways, as these amendments afford to those who communicate ideas by pure speech. . . . We reaffirm . . . that "it has never been deemed an abridgement of freedom of speech or press to make a course of conduct illegal merely because the conduct was in part initiated, evidenced, or carried out by means of language, either spoken, written, or printed."

. . . As conduct becomes less and less like "pure speech" the showing of governmental interest required for its regulation is progressively lessened. In those cases where governmental regulation of expressive conduct has been struck down, the communicative intent of the actor was clear and "closely akin to 'pure speech.'" Tinker v. Des Moines School District, 393 U.S. 503, 505, 89 S.Ct. 733, 21 L.Ed.2d 731 (1969). Thus, the First Amendment has been held to protect wearing a black armband to protest the Vietnam War, *Tinker* v. *Des Moines School District,* supra, burning an American Flag to highlight a speech denouncing the government's failure to protect a civil rights leader, Street v. New York, 394 U.S. 576, 89 S.Ct. 1354, 22 L.Ed.2d 572 (1969), or quietly refusing to recite the Pledge of Allegiance, Russo v. Central School District, 469 F.2d 623 (2d Cir.1972), cert. denied, 411 U.S. 932, 93 S.Ct. 1899, 36 L.Ed.2d 391 (1973).

In contrast, the claims of symbolic speech made here are vague and unfocused. Through the simple refusal to wear a tie, Mr. Brimley claims that he communicates a comprehensive view of life and society. It may well be, in an age increasingly conscious of fashion, that a significant portion of the population seeks to make a statement of some kind through its clothes. However, Mr. Brimley's message is sufficiently vague to place it close to the "conduct" end of the "speech-conduct" continuum described above. While the regulation of the school board must still pass constitutional muster, the showing required to uphold it is significantly less than if Mr. Brimley had been punished, for example, for publicly speaking out on an issue concerning school administration.

At the outset, Mr. Brimley had other, more effective means of communicating his social views to his students. He could, for example, simply have told them his views on contemporary America; if he had done this in a temperate way, without interfering with his teaching duties, we would be confronted with a very different First Amendment case. The existence of alternative, effective means of communication, while not conclusive, is a factor to be considered in assessing the validity of a regulation of expressive conduct.

Balanced against appellant's claim of free expression is the school board's interest in promoting respect for authority and traditional values, as well as discipline in the classroom, by requiring teachers to dress in a professional manner. A dress code is a rational means of promoting these goals. As to the legitimacy of the goals themselves, there can be no doubt. In *James* v. *Board of Education,* Chief Judge Kaufman stated:

> The interest of the state in promoting the efficient operation of its schools extends beyond merely securing an orderly classroom. Although the pros and cons of progressive education are debated heatedly, a principal function of all elementary and secondary education is indoctrinative—whether it be to teach the ABCs or multiplication tables or to transmit the basic values of the community. 461 F.2d 566 (2d Cir.), cert. denied, 409 U.S. 1042, 93 S.Ct. 529 (1972).

This balancing test is primarily a matter for the school board. Were we local officials, and not appellate judges, we might find Mr. Brimley's arguments persuasive. However, our role is not to choose the better educational policy. We may intervene in the decisions of school authorities only when it has been shown that they have strayed outside the area committed to their discretion. If Mr. Brimley's argument were to prevail, this policy would be completely eroded. Because teaching is by definition an expressive activity, virtually every decision made by school authorities would raise First Amendment issues calling for federal court intervention.. . .

Mr. Brimley also claims that the "liberty" interest grounded in the due process clause of the Fourteenth Amendment protects his choice of attire. . . .

The Supreme Court dealt with a similar claim in Kelley v. Johnson, 425 U.S. 238, 96 S.Ct. 1440, 47 L.Ed.2d 708 (1976). That case involved a challenge to the hair-grooming regulations of a police department. The Court was careful to distinguish privacy claims made by government employees from those made by members of the public:

> Respondent has sought the protection of the Fourteenth Amendment, not as a member of the citizenry at large, but on the contrary as an employee of the police force of Suffolk County, a subdivision of the State of New York. While the Court of Appeals made passing reference to this distinction, it was thereafter apparently ignored. We think, however, it is highly significant. In Pickering v. Board of Education, 391 U.S. 563, 568[, 88 S.Ct. 1731, 20 L.Ed.2d 811] (1968), after noting that state employment may not be conditioned on the relinquishment of First Amendment rights, the Court stated that "[a]t the same time it cannot be gainsaid that the State has interests as an employer in regulating the speech of its employees that differ significantly from those it possesses in connection with regulation of the speech of the citizenry in general." More recently, we have sustained comprehensive and substantial restrictions upon activities of both federal and state employees lying at the core of the First Amendment. If such state regulations may survive challenges based on the explicit language of the First Amendment, there is surely even more room for restrictive regulations of state employees where the claim implicates only the more general contours of the substantive liberty interest protected by the Fourteenth Amendment.

The same distinction applies here. The regulation involved in this case affects Mr. Brimley in his capacity as a public school teacher. Of course, as he points out, the functions of policemen and teachers differ widely. Regulations well within constitutional bounds for one occupation might prove invalid for another. Nonetheless, we can see no reason why the same constitutional test should not apply, no matter how different the results of their constitutional challenges.

Kelley goes on to set forth the standard to be applied in such cases:

> We think the answer here is so clear that the District Court was quite right in the first instance to have dismissed respondent's complaint. Neither this Court, the Court of Appeals, nor the District Court is in a position to weigh the policy arguments in favor of and against a rule regulating hairstyles as a part of regulations governing a uniformed civilian service. The constitutional issue to be decided by these courts is whether petitioner's determination that such regulations should be enacted is so irrational that it may be branded "arbitrary," and therefore a deprivation of respondent's "liberty" interest in freedom to choose his own hairstyle.

If Mr. Brimley has any protected interest in his neckwear, it does not weigh very heavily on the constitutional scales. As with most legislative choices, the board's dress code is presumptively constitutional. It is justified by the same concerns for respect, discipline and traditional values described in our discussion of the First Amendment claim. Accordingly, appellant has failed to carry the burden set out in *Kelley* of demonstrating that the dress code is "so irrational that it may be branded 'arbitrary,'" and the regulation must stand. . . .

Each claim of substantive liberty must be judged in the light of that case's special circumstances. In view of the uniquely influential role of the public school teacher in the classroom, the board is justified in imposing this regulation. As public servants in a special position of trust, teachers may properly be subjected to many restrictions in their professional lives which would be invalid if generally applied. We join the sound views of the First and Seventh Circuits, and follow *Kelley* by holding that a school board may, if it wishes, impose reasonable regulations governing the appearance of the teachers it employs. . . . There being no material factual issue to be decided, the grant of summary judgment is affirmed.

NOTE

A Louisiana school board expanded its student dress code to prohibit employees from wearing beards. The Fifth Circuit Court of Appeals recognized the liberty interest of the individual in choosing how to wear one's hair, but ruled the school board had made a rational determination in establishing the rule as "a reasonable means of furthering the school board's undeniable interest in teaching hygiene, instilling discipline, asserting authority, and compelling uniformity." Domico v. Rapides Parish School Board, 675 F.2d 100 (5th Cir.1982).

LOYALTY

Teachers have also been subjected to government restraint when they have allegedly been involved in subversive activities or belonged to certain types of organizations. Oaths have been a favorite device of government in attempting to enforce allegiance of the citizenry. For example,[10] under Arizona law, one who was, or thereafter became, a knowing member of an organization that had as "one of its purposes" the violent overthrow of the government was subject to discharge and criminal penalties. The United States Supreme Court held this particular statute unconstitutionally vague, violating the freedom of association protected by the First Amendment, because nothing in the state's oath purported to exclude association by one who does not subscribe to the organization's unlawful ends. The court explained that a person could be a knowing member of an organization but yet not subscribe to its goal of violent overthrow of the government.[11]

The United States Supreme Court in viewing loyalty statutes has said that "we do not question the power of a State to take proper measures safeguarding the public service from disloyal conduct. But measures which purport to define disloyalty must allow public servants to know what is and is not disloyal." [12] An oath cannot be lacking in "terms susceptible of objective measurement." [13]

The state does, of course, have justifiable reason in attempting to prevent the overthrow of government but whether the loyalty oath route is desirable in preventing belief in overthrow is another question. Mr. Justice Marshall, in *Connell* v. *Higginbotham*,[14] indicated that he believes the entire notion of oaths is obnoxious to the Constitution because the state uses the oath as a mechanism to punish one for his beliefs:

> But in my view it simply does not matter what kind of evidence a State can muster to show that a job applicant "believes in overthrow." For state action injurious to an individual cannot be justified on account of the nature of the individual's beliefs, whether he "believes in the overthrow" or has any other sort of belief. If there is any fixed star in our constitutional constellation, it is that no official, high or petty, can prescribe what shall be orthodox in politics, nationalism, religion, or other matters of opinion . . . .[15]

The majority of the United States Supreme Court in *Connell* struck down the disclaimer portions of a Florida loyalty oath preserving only the portion of the oath that required a teacher to swear: "I will support the Constitution of the United States and of the State of Florida . . . ." [16]

The Court's decisions seem to indicate that any oath disclaiming association will be viewed with strict scrutiny; vagueness and overbreadth in oath construction will render it unconstitutional. *Keyishian* makes clear that the state in administering its loyalty program must rely on overt acts or direct evidence of illegal intent and not merely on beliefs or knowing membership in a subversive organization.[17]

Merely Knowing Membership Without
Specific Intent to Further Unlawful
Aims Is Not a Constitutionally
Adequate Basis for Imposing
Sanctions

KEYISHIAN v. BOARD OF REGENTS OF UNIVERSITY OF STATE OF NEW YORK

Supreme Court of the United States, 1967.
385 U.S. 589, 87 S.Ct. 675.

MR. JUSTICE BRENNAN delivered the opinion of the Court.

Appellants were members of the faculty of the privately owned and operated University of Buffalo, and became state employees when the University was merged in 1962 into the State University of New York, an institution of higher education owned and operated by the State of New York. As faculty members of the State University their continued employment was conditioned upon their compliance with a New York plan, formulated partly in statutes and partly in administrative regulations, which the State utilizes to prevent the appointment or retention of "subversive" persons in state employment.

Appellants Hochfield and Maud were Assistant Professors of English, appellant Keyishian, an instructor in English, and appellant Garver, a lecturer in philosophy. Each of them refused to sign, as regulations then in effect required, a certificate that he was not a Communist, and that if he had ever been a Communist, he had communicated that fact to the President of the State University of New York. Each was notified that his failure to sign the certificate would require his dismissal. Keyishian's one-year-term contract was not renewed because of his failure to sign the certificate. . . .

We considered some aspects of the constitutionality of the New York plan 15 years ago in Adler v. Board of Education, 342 U.S. 485, 72 S.Ct. 380, 96 L.Ed. 517. That litigation arose after New York passed the Feinberg Law which added § 3022 to the Education Law, McKinney's Consol.Laws, c. 16. The Feinberg Law was enacted to implement and enforce two earlier statutes. The first was a 1917 law, now § 3021 of the Education Law, under which "the utterance of any treasonable or seditious word or words or the doing of any treasonable or seditious act" is a ground for dismissal from the public school system. The second was a 1939 law which was § 12–a of the Civil Service Law when *Adler* was decided and, as amended, is now § 105 of that law, McKinney's Consol.Laws, c. 7. This law disqualifies from the civil service and from employment in the educational system any person who advocates the overthrow of government by force, violence, or any unlawful means, or publishes material advocating such overthrow or organizes or joins any society or group of persons advocating such doctrine.

The Feinberg Law charged the State Board of Regents with the duty of promulgating rules and regulations providing procedures for the disqualification or removal of persons in the public school system who violate the 1917 law or who are ineligible for appointment to or retention in the public school system under the 1939 law. The Board of Regents was further directed to make a list, after notice and hearing, of "subversive" organizations, defined as organizations which advocate the doctrine of overthrow of government by force, violence, or any unlawful means. Finally, the Board was directed to provide in its rules and regulations that membership in any listed organization should constitute prima facie evidence of disqualification for appointment to or retention in any office or position in the public schools of the State.

The Board of Regents thereupon promulgated rules and regulations containing procedures to be followed by appointing authorities to discover persons ineligible for appointment or retention under the 1939 law, or because of violation of the 1917 law. The Board also announced its intention to list "subversive" organizations after requisite notice and hearing, and provided that membership in a listed organization after the date of its listing should be regarded as constituting prima facie evidence of disqualification, and that membership prior to listing should be presumptive evidence that membership has continued, in the absence of a showing that such membership was terminated in good faith. Under the regulations, an appointing official is forbidden to make an appointment until after he has first inquired of an applicant's former employers and other persons to ascertain whether the applicant is disqualified or ineligible for appointment. In addition, an annual inquiry must be made to determine whether an appointed employee has ceased to be qualified for retention, and a report of findings must be filed.

Adler was a declaratory judgment suit in which the Court held, in effect, that there was no constitutional infirmity in former § 12–a or in the Feinberg Law on their faces and that they were capable of constitutional application. But the contention urged in this case that both § 3021 and § 105 are unconstitutionally vague was not heard or decided. Section 3021 of the Education Law was challenged in *Adler* as unconstitutionally vague, but because the challenge had not been made in the pleadings or in the proceedings in the lower courts, this Court refused to consider it. . . . Appellants in this case timely asserted below the unconstitutionality of all these sections on grounds of vagueness and that question is now properly before us for decision. Moreover, to the extent that *Adler* sustained the provision of the Feinberg Law constituting membership in an organization advocating forceful overthrow of government a ground for disqualification, pertinent constitutional doctrines have since rejected the premises upon which that conclusion rested. *Adler* is therefore not dispositive of the constitutional issues we must decide in this case.

A 1953 amendment extended the application of the Feinberg Law to personnel of any college or other institution of higher education owned and operated by the State or its subdivisions. In the same year, the Board of Regents, after notice and hearing, listed the Communist Party of the United States and of the State of New York as "subversive organizations." In 1956 each applicant for an appointment or the renewal of an appointment was required to sign the so-called "Feinberg Certificate" declaring that he had read the Regents Rules and understood that the Rules and the statutes constituted terms of employment, and declaring further that he was not a member of the Communist Party, and that if he had ever been a member he had communicated that fact to the President of the State University. This was the certificate that appellants Hochfield, Maud, Keyishian, and Garver refused to sign.

In June 1965, shortly before the trial of this case, the Feinberg Certificate was rescinded and it was announced that no person then employed would be deemed ineligible for continued employment "solely" because he refused to sign the certificate. In lieu of the certificate, it was provided that each applicant be informed before assuming his duties that the statutes, §§ 3021 and 3022 of the Education Law and § 105 of the Civil Service Law, constituted part of his contract. He was particularly to be informed of the disqualification which flowed from membership in a listed "subversive" organization. The 1965 announcement further provides: "Should any question arise in the course of such inquiry such candidate may request . . . a personal interview. Refusal of a candidate to answer any question relevant to such inquiry by such officer shall be sufficient ground to refuse to make or recommend appointment." A brochure is also given new applicants. It outlines and explains briefly the legal effect of the statutes and invites any applicant who may have any question about possible disqualification to request an interview. The covering announcement concludes that "a prospective appointee who does not believe himself disqualified need take no affirmative action. No disclaimer oath is required."

The change in procedure in no wise moots appellants' constitutional questions raised in the context of their refusal to sign the now abandoned Feinberg Certificate. The substance of the statutory and regulatory complex remains and from the outset appellants' basic claim has been that they are aggrieved by its application.

Section 3021 requires removal for "treasonable or seditious" utterances or acts. . . .

. . . . We cannot gainsay the potential effect of this obscure wording on "those with a conscientious and scrupulous regard for such undertakings." . . . The teacher cannot know the extent, if any, to which a "seditious" utterance must transcend mere statement about abstract doctrine, the extent to which it must be intended to and tend to indoctrinate or incite to action in furtherance of the defined doctrine. The crucial consideration is that no teacher can know just where the line is drawn between "seditious" and nonseditious utterances and acts.

Other provisions of § 105 also have the same defect of vagueness. Subdivision 1(a) of § 105 bars employment of any person who "by word of mouth or writing wilfully and deliberately advocates, advises or teaches the doctrine" of forceful overthrow of government. This provision is plainly susceptible of sweeping and improper application. It may well prohibit the employment of one who merely advocates the doctrine in the abstract without any attempt to indoctrinate others, or incite others to action in furtherance of unlawful aims. . . . And in prohibiting "advising" the "doctrine" of unlawful overthrow does the statute prohibit mere "advising" of the existence of the doctrine, or advising another to support the doctrine? Since "advocacy" of the doctrine of forceful overthrow is separately prohibited, need the person "teaching" or "advising" this doctrine himself "advocate" it? Does the teacher who informs his class about the precepts of Marxism or the Declaration of Independence violate the prohibition?

Similar uncertainty arises as to the application of subdivision 1(b) of § 105. That subsection requires the disqualification of an employee involved with the distribution of written material "containing or advocating, advising or teaching the doctrine" of forceful overthrow, and who himself "advocates, advises, teaches, or embraces the duty, necessity or propriety of adopting the doctrine contained therein." Here again, mere advocacy of abstract doctrine is apparently included. And does the prohibition of distribution of matter "containing" the doctrine bar histories of the evolution of Marxist doctrine or tracing the background of the French, American, or Russian revolutions? The additional requirement, that the person participating in distribution of the material be one who "advocates, advises, teaches, or embraces the duty, necessity or propriety of adopting the doctrine" of forceful overthrow, does not alleviate the uncertainty in the scope of the section, but exacerbates it. Like the language of § 105, subd. 1(a), this language may reasonably be construed to cover mere expression of belief. For example, does the university librarian who recommends the reading of such materials thereby "advocate . . . the . . . propriety of adopting the doctrine contained therein"?

We do not have the benefit of a judicial gloss by the New York courts enlightening us as to the scope of this complicated plan. In light of the intricate administrative machinery for its enforcement, this is not surprising. The very intricacy of the plan and the uncertainty as to the scope of its proscriptions make it a highly efficient *in terrorem* mechanism. It would be a bold teacher who would not stay as far as possible from utterances or acts which might jeopardize his living by enmeshing him in this intricate machinery. The uncertainty as to the utterances and acts proscribed increases that caution in "those who believe the written law means what it says."

. . . The result must be to stifle "that free play of the spirit which all teachers ought especially to cultivate and practice . .) . ." That probability is enhanced by the provisions requiring an annual review of every teacher to determine whether any utterance or act of his, inside the classroom or out, came within the sanctions of the laws. . . .

There can be no doubt of the legitimacy of New York's interest in protecting its education system from subversion. But "even though the governmental purpose be legitimate and substantial, that purpose cannot be pursued by means that broadly stifle fundamental personal liberties when the end can be more narrowly achieved." . . . The principle is not inapplicable because the legislation is aimed at keeping subversives out of the teaching ranks. . . .

Our Nation is deeply committed to safeguarding academic freedom, which is of transcendent value to all of us and not merely to the teachers concerned. That freedom is therefore a special concern of the First Amendment, which does not tolerate laws that cast a pall of orthodoxy over the classroom. "The vigilant protection of constitutional freedoms is nowhere more vital than in the community of American schools." . . . The classroom is peculiarly the "marketplace of ideas." The Nation's future depends upon leaders trained through wide exposure to that robust exchange of ideas which discovers truth "out of a multitude of tongues, [rather] than through any kind of authoritative selection." . . .

The regulatory maze created by New York is wholly lacking in "terms acceptable of objective measurement." . . . Vagueness of wording is aggravated by prolixity and profusion of statutes, regulations, and administrative machinery, and by manifold cross-references to interrelated enactments and rules.

We therefore hold that § 3021 of the Education Law and subdivisions 1(a), 1(b) and 3 of § 105 of the Civil Service Law as implemented by the machinery created pursuant to § 3022 of the Education Law are unconstitutional.

Appellants have also challenged the constitutionality of the discrete provisions of subdivision 1(c) of § 105 and subdivision 2 of the Feinberg Law, which make Communist Party membership, as such, prima facie evidence of disqualification. The provision was added to subdivision 1(c) of § 105 in 1958 after the Board of Regents, following notice and hearing, listed the Communist Party of the United States and the Communist Party of the State of New York as "subversive" organizations. Subdivision 2 of the Feinberg Law was, however, before the Court in *Adler* and its constitutionality was sustained. But constitutional doctrine which has emerged since that decision has rejected its major premise. That premise was that public employment, including academic employment, may be conditioned upon the surrender of constitutional rights which could not be abridged by direct government action. . . .

We proceed then to the question of the validity of the provisions of subdivision 1 of § 105 and subdivision 2 of § 3022, barring employment to members of listed organizations. Here again constitutional doctrine has developed since *Adler.* Mere knowing membership without a specific intent to further the unlawful aims of an organization is not a constitutionally adequate basis for exclusion from such positions as those held by appellants.

In Elfbrandt v. Russell, 384 U.S. 11, 86 S.Ct. 1238, 16 L.Ed.2d 321, we said, "Those who join an organization but do not share its unlawful purposes and who do not participate in its unlawful activities surely pose no threat, either as citizens or as public employees." Id., at 17, 86 S.Ct. at 1241. We there struck down a statutorily required oath binding the state employee not to become a member of the Communist Party with knowledge of its unlawful purpose, on threat of discharge and perjury prosecution if the oath were violated. We found that "[a]ny lingering doubt that proscription of mere knowing membership, without any showing of 'specific intent,' would run afoul of the Constitution was set at rest by our decision in Aptheker v. Secretary of State . . . ."

These limitations clearly apply to a provision, like § 105, subd. 1(c), which blankets all state employees, regardless of the "sensitivity" of their positions. But even the Feinberg Law provision, applicable primarily to activities of teachers, who have captive audiences of young minds, are subject to these limitations in favor of freedom of expression and association; the stifling effect on the academic mind from curtailing freedom of association in such manner is manifest, and has been documented in recent studies. Elfbrandt and Aptheker state the governing standard: legislation which sanctions membership unaccompanied by specific intent to further the unlawful goals of the organization or which is not active membership violates constitutional limitations. . . .

We therefore hold that Civil Service Law § 105, subd. 1(c), and Education Law § 3022, subd. 2, are invalid insofar as they proscribe mere knowing membership without any showing of specific intent to further the unlawful aims of the Communist Party of the United States or of the State of New York. . . .

Disclaimer Provisions of Loyalty Oath
Are Unconstitutional

CONNELL v. HIGGINBOTHAM

Supreme Court of the United States, 1971.
403 U.S. 207, 91 S.Ct. 1772.

PER CURIAM. This is an appeal from an action commenced in the United States District Court for the Middle District of Florida challenging the constitutionality of §§ 876.05–876.10 of Fla.Stat. (1965), and the various loyalty oaths upon which appellant's employment as a school teacher was conditioned. The three-judge U.S. District Court declared three of the five clauses contained in the oaths to be unconstitutional, and enjoined the State from conditioning employment on the taking of an oath including the language declared unconstitutional. The appeal is from that portion of the District Court decision, 305 F.Supp. 445, which upheld the remaining two clauses in the oath: I do hereby solemnly swear or affirm (1) "that I will support the Constitution of the United States and of the State of Florida"; and (2) "that I do not believe in the overthrow of the Government of the

United States or of the State of Florida by force or violence." [The clauses declared unconstitutional by the court below required the employee to swear: (a) "that I am not a member of the Communist Party"; (b) "that I have not and will not lend my aid, support, advice, counsel or influence to the Communist Party"; and (c) "that I am not a member of any organization or party which believes in or teaches, directly or indirectly, the overthrow of the Government of the United States or of Florida by force or violence."]

On January 16, 1969, appellant made application for a teaching position with the Orange County school system. She was interviewed by the principal of Callahan Elementary School, and on January 27, 1969, appellant was employed as a substitute classroom teacher in the fourth grade of that school. Appellant was dismissed from her teaching position on March 18, 1969, for refusing to sign the loyalty oath required of all Florida public employees, Fla.Stat. § 876.05.

The first section of the oath upheld by the District Court, requiring all applicants to pledge to support the Constitution of the United States and of the State of Florida, demands no more of Florida public employees than is required of all state and federal officers. U.S. Const., Art. VI, cl. 3. The validity of this section of the oath would appear settled. . . .

The second portion of the oath, approved by the District Court, falls within the ambit of decisions of this Court proscribing summary dismissal from public employment without hearing or inquiry required by due process. . . . That portion of the oath, therefore, cannot stand.

Affirmed in part, and reversed in part.

NOTES

1. With the *Connell* v. *Higginbotham* precedent it appeared that the Supreme Court was on the verge of striking down all loyalty oaths for public employment, yet only one year later the Court reaffirmed the right of the state to require properly worded oaths. In a Massachusetts case in 1972, the Court upheld the termination of employment of an employee of the Boston State Hospital when she refused to take the following oath required of all public employees in Massachusetts: "I do solemnly swear (or affirm) that I will uphold and defend the Constitution of the United States of America and the Constitution of the Commonwealth of Massachusetts and that I will oppose the overthrow of the government of the United States of America or of this Commonwealth by force, violence, or by any illegal or unconstitutional method." Appellee challenged the constitutionality of the oath statute. A three-judge District Court concluded that the attack on the "uphold and defend" clause was foreclosed by Knight v. Board of Regents, 390 U.S. 36, 88 S.Ct. 816 but found the "oppose the overthrow" clause "fatally vague and unspecific" and thus violative of the First Amendment. In response to a remand, the District Court concluded that the case was not moot, and reinstated its earlier judgment. The Massachusetts oath is held constitutionally permissible.

   (a) The oath provisions of the United States Constitution are not inconsistent with the First Amendment.

   (b) The District Court properly held that the "uphold and defend" clause, a paraphrase of the constitutional oath, is permissible.

(c) The "oppose the overthrow" clause was not designed to require specific action to be taken in some hypothetical or actual situation but was to assure that those in positions of public trust were willing to commit themselves to live by the constitutional processes of our government.

(d) The oath is not void for vagueness. Perjury, the sole punishment, requires a knowing and willful falsehood, which removes the danger of punishment without fair notice; and there is no problem of punishment inflicted by mere prosecution, as there has been no prosecution under the statute since its enactment nor has any been planned.

(e) There is no constitutionally protected right to overthrow a government by force, violence, or illegal or unconstitutional means, and therefore there is no requirement that one who refuses to take Massachusetts' oath be granted a hearing for the determination of some other fact before being discharged.

Reversed and remanded.

Cole v. Richardson, 405 U.S. 676, 92 S.Ct. 1332 (1972).

2. Constitutional guarantees of free speech and free press do not permit a state to forbid or proscribe "advocacy" of overthrow of government in the abstract unless such advocacy is directed to inciting or producing imminent lawless action and is likely to incite or produce such action. Scales v. United States, 367 U.S. 203, 81 S.Ct. 1469 (1961), rehearing denied 366 U.S. 978, 81 S.Ct. 1912; Communist Party of Indiana v. Whitcomb, 414 U.S. 441, 94 S.Ct. 656 (1974).

PRIVILEGE AGAINST SELF–INCRIMINATION

Teachers may, as may anyone else, invoke the Fifth Amendment privilege against self-incrimination. Refusing to provide information to the state because it may tend to incriminate cannot be interpreted as an admission of guilt. No presumption can be inferred from the act. In *Slochower* v. *Board of Education*,[18] the Supreme Court held that the dismissal of a Brooklyn College professor for invoking the Fifth Amendment before a congressional committee was unconstitutional. This principle cannot, however, be too broadly interpreted, for only a short time later the Supreme Court held in *Beilan* v. *Board of Education* [19] that a teacher could be dismissed for refusing to answer questions posed by the school superintendent about alleged past subversive activities. The Court found that the dismissal was not predicated on an impermissible inference of guilt drawn from refusal to answer, but instead on a finding of insubordination emanating from the fact that the teacher refused to answer.[20] *Slochower* was distinguished from *Beilan* in that the refusal to answer in *Beilan* was directed toward questions posed by a superior in specific regard to fitness to teach and incompetency was specifically cited as the reason for dismissal.

The rationale of *Beilan*, though, comes under a shadow as the Court has ruled subsequently that disbarment of a lawyer for refusing to produce evidence in an ethical practices proceeding was unconstitutional.[21] Also, the dismissal of a policeman for invoking the Fifth Amendment privilege in refusing to answer questions regarding his fitness and concerning conduct that could open him to criminal prosecution was held to be unconstitutional.[22] Although these cases can be distinguished in that the former involved disbarment and complete denial of future employment and the latter related to criminal evidence, the strength of the *Beilan* decision is somewhat diminished if the fitness of a teacher is viewed in the broader constitutional light of both *Pickering* and *Keyishian*.

Failure of Teacher to Answer
Questions Posed by Superintendent
Concerning Loyalty May Be
Incompetency

BEILAN v. BOARD OF PUBLIC EDUCATION OF PHILADELPHIA

Supreme Court of the United States, 1958.
357 U.S. 399, 78 S.Ct. 1317.

Mr. Justice BURTON delivered the opinion of the Court.

The question before us is whether the Board of Public Education for the School District of Philadelphia, Pennsylvania, violated the Due Process Clause of the Fourteenth Amendment to the Constitution of the United States when the Board, purporting to act under the Pennsylvania Public School Code, discharged a public school teacher on the ground of "incompetency," evidenced by the teacher's refusal of his Superintendent's request to confirm or refute information as to the teacher's loyalty and his activities in certain allegedly subversive organizations. For the reasons hereafter stated, we hold that it did not.

On June 25, 1952, Herman A. Beilan, the petitioner, who had been a teacher for about twenty-two years in the Philadelphia Public School System, presented himself at his Superintendent's office in response to the latter's request. The Superintendent said he had information which reflected adversely on petitioner's loyalty and he wanted to determine its truth or falsity. In response to petitioner's suggestion that the Superintendent do the questioning, the latter said he would ask one question and petitioner could then determine whether he would answer it and others of that type. The Superintendent, accordingly, asked petitioner whether or not he had been the Press Director of the Professional Section of the Communist Political Association in 1944. Petitioner asked permission to consult counsel before answering and the Superintendent granted his request.

On October 14, 1952, in response to a similar request, petitioner again presented himself at the Superintendent's office. Petitioner stated that he had consulted counsel and that he declined to answer the question as to his activities in 1944. He announced he would also decline to answer any other "questions similar to it," "questions of this type," or "questions about political and religious beliefs . . . ." The Superintendent warned petitioner that this "was a very serious and a very important matter and that failure to answer the questions might lead to his dismissal." The Superintendent made it clear that he was investigating "a real question of fitness for [petitioner] to be a teacher or to continue in the teaching work." These interviews were given no publicity and were attended only by petitioner, his Superintendent and the Assistant Solicitor of the Board. . . . The only question before us is whether the federal Constitution prohibits petitioner's discharge for statutory "incompetency" based on his refusal to answer the Superintendent's questions.

By engaging in teaching in the public schools, petitioner did not give up his right to freedom of belief, speech or association. He did, however, undertake obligations of frankness, candor and cooperation in answering inquiries made of him by his employing Board examining his fitness to serve it as a public school teacher.

> A teacher works in a sensitive area in a schoolroom. There he shapes the attitude of young minds towards the society in which they live. In this, the state has a vital concern. It must preserve the integrity of the schools. That the school authorities have the right and the duty to screen the officials, teachers, and employees as to their fitness to maintain the integrity of the schools as a part of ordered society, cannot be doubted. Adler v. Board of Education, 342 U.S. 485, 493, 72 S.Ct. 380, 385.

As this Court stated in Garner v. Board of Public Works, 341 U.S. 716, 720, 71 S.Ct. 909, 912, "We think that a municipal employer is not disabled because it is an agency of the State from inquiring of its employees as to matters that may prove relevant to their fitness and suitability for the public service."

The question asked of petitioner by his Superintendent was relevant to the issue of petitioner's fitness and suitability to serve as a teacher. Petitioner is not in a position to challenge his dismissal merely because of the remoteness in time of the 1944 activities. It was apparent from the circumstances of the two interviews that the Superintendent had other questions to ask. Petitioner's refusal to answer was not based on the remoteness of his 1944 activities. He made it clear that he would not answer any question of the same type as the one asked. Petitioner blocked from the beginning any inquiry into his Communist activities, however relevant to his present loyalty. The Board based its dismissal upon petitioner's refusal to answer any inquiry about his relevant activities—not upon those activities themselves. It took care to charge petitioner with incompetency, and not with disloyalty. It found him insubordinate and lacking in frankness and candor—it made no finding as to his loyalty.

We find no requirement in the federal Constitution that a teacher's classroom conduct be the sole basis for determining his fitness. Fitness for teaching depends on a broad range of factors. The Pennsylvania tenure provision specifies several disqualifying grounds, including immorality, intemperance, cruelty, mental derangement and persistent and willful violation of the school laws, as well as "incompetency." However, the Pennsylvania statute, unlike those of many other States, contains no catch-all phrase, such as "conduct unbecoming a teacher," to cover disqualifying conduct not included within the more specific provisions. Consequently, the

Pennsylvania courts have given "incompetency" a broad interpretation. . . .

> The term "incompetency" has a "common and approved usage." The context does not limit the meaning of the word to lack of substantive knowledge of the subjects to be taught. Common and approved usage give a much wider meaning. For example, in 31 C.J., with reference to a number of supporting decisions, it is defined: "A relative term without technical meaning. It may be employed as meaning disqualification; inability; incapacity; lack of ability, legal qualifications, or fitness to discharge the required duty". . . .

In the instant case, the Pennsylvania Supreme Court has held that "incompetency" includes petitioner's "deliberate and insubordinate refusal to answer the questions of his administrative superior in a vitally important matter pertaining to his fitness." 386 Pa. at page 91, 125 A.2d at page 331. This interpretation is not inconsistent with the federal Constitution.

Petitioner complains that he was denied due process because he was not sufficiently warned of the consequences of his refusal to answer his Superintendent. The record, however, shows that the Superintendent, in his second interview, specifically warned petitioner that his refusal to answer "was a very serious and a very important matter and that failure to answer the questions might lead to his dismissal." That was sufficient warning to petitioner that his refusal to answer might jeopardize his employment. Furthermore, at petitioner's request, his Superintendent gave him ample opportunity to consult counsel. There was no element of surprise.

Our recent decisions in Slochower v. Board of Higher Education, 350 U.S. 551, 76 S.Ct. 637, 100 L.Ed. 692, and Konigsberg v. State Bar of California, 353 U.S. 252, 77 S.Ct. 722, 1 L.Ed.2d 810, are distinguishable. In each we envisioned and distinguished the situation now before us. In the *Slochower* case, 350 U.S. at page 558, 76 S.Ct. at page 641, the Court said:

> It is one thing for the city authorities themselves to inquire into Slochower's fitness, but quite another for his discharge to be based entirely on events occurring before a federal committee whose inquiry was announced as not directed at "the property, affairs, or government of the city, or . . . official conduct of city employees." In this respect the present case differs materially from *Garner* [Garner v. Board of Public Works, 341 U.S. 716, 71 S.Ct. 909, 95 L.Ed. 1317], where the city was attempting to elicit information necessary to determine the qualifications of its employees. Here, the Board had possessed the pertinent information for twelve years, and the questions which Professor Slochower refused to answer were admittedly asked for a purpose wholly unrelated to his college functions. On such a record the Board cannot claim that its action was part of a bona fide attempt to gain needed and relevant information.

. . . In the instant case, no inferences at all were drawn from petitioner's refusal to answer. The Pennsylvania Supreme Court merely equated refusal to answer the employing Board's relevant questions with statutory "incompetency."

Inasmuch as petitioner's dismissal did not violate the federal Constitution, the judgment of the Supreme Court of Pennsylvania is affirmed.

Plea of Constitutional Privilege
Against Self-incrimination Bears No
Presumption of Unfitness

BOARD OF PUBLIC
EDUCATION SCHOOL
DISTRICT OF PHILADELPHIA
v. INTILLE

Supreme Court of Pennsylvania, 1960.
401 Pa. 1, 163 A.2d 420.

CHARLES ALVIN JONES, Chief Justice.

The three appellants (Angelina Intille, Thomas Deacon and Sadie T. Atkinson) were teachers in the public schools of Philadelphia until the Spring of 1954 when they were dismissed by the Board of Public Education of the School District on a charge of "incompetency," preferred by Dr. Louis P. Hoyer, Superintendent of the Philadelphia public schools. In each case, the dismissal was based *solely* on the teacher's refusal to answer certain questions propounded by a Subcommittee (also known as the Velde Committee) of the Un-American Activities Committee of the House of Representatives concerning the witness' alleged membership in and association with the Communist Party. In refusing to testify in such regard, each of the appellants expressly relied upon the privilege against self-incrimination guaranteed by the Fifth Amendment of the federal Constitution.

All of the proceedings below, which resulted in the final orders of dismissal, now before us, were conducted separately throughout but, since the basic legal questions raised (both federal and state), are the same in all three appeals, they will be disposed of in this one opinion.

The appellants contend that their dismissals as teachers (1) violated the due process clause of the Fourteenth Amendment and (2) abridged their privilege against self-incrimination under the Fifth Amendment in further violation of the Fourteenth Amendment and of Article VI of the federal Constitution.

There is also an additional question raised by the Board's contention that the appellants' plea of privilege against self-incrimination under the Fifth Amendment constituted incompetency within the intent of Pennsylvania's Public School Code of 1949.

As teachers under contract prescribed by the Public School Code of 1949, the appellants were entitled to tenure as professional employees and, by virtue of the same statutory authority, were subject to dismissal from their teaching positions *only* for cause upon notice, hearing and right of appeal. One of the specified causes for removal, as prescribed by the School Code, is incompetency, which is the charge upon which Superintendent Hoyer suspended these teachers and recommended their dismissal to the Board of Education. The Superintendent based his finding of incompetency solely upon the fact that the appellants had refused to answer questions asked them by the Congressional Committee in reliance on their pleas of privilege under the Fifth Amendment against self-incrimination. . . .

It follows from what we have said that the appellants' dismissals by the Board of Education, because they refused to answer certain questions of the

Congressional Committee on a plea of the Fifth Amendment's protection against self-incrimination, deprived them of liberty and property without due process of law and, at the same time, worked abridgment by State action of the same constitutional privilege, all in violation of the Fourteenth Amendment.   .   .   .

For a public school teacher to plead a constitutional privilege, in appropriate circumstances, does not prove the teacher's incompetency within the intended scope of that term as used in our Public School Code; the plea is not even relevant as evidence of incompetency. Just as remaining mute, upon a plea of the Fifth Amendment, carries no implication of guilt of the matter inquired about in the unanswered questions .   .   . so also does the plea not carry an implication of the pleader's *incompetency.* Nor is it of any materiality to a question of the pleader's competency whether or not the propriety of the plea against self-incrimination is conceded or rejected by the inquiring body so long as the plea is made in good faith and is not plainly frivolous. There is no prerequisite to the exercise of the privilege against self-incrimination that the pleader must first establish affirmatively his good faith and lack of frivolity in entering the plea. The appellants' pleas of the Fifth Amendment did not prove their incompetency within the meaning of the Public School Code and, since their refusal to answer the Committee's questions, in reliance on the Fifth Amendment privilege, was all that was proven against them, the Board failed to make out a case for their dismissal.

But, the Board presently advances the idea that a teacher who refuses to answer a Congressional Committee's questions, implying possible subversive affiliations on the part of the witness, is incompetent within the meaning of the tenure provisions of our Public School Code. Such a contention transgresses what was thought to have been decided in *Beilan,* where we were assured that no question of loyalty was in any way involved. If the refusal to answer a particular question is to be made a basis for the discharge of a professional employee, the question should, obviously, have for its purpose the eliciting of information concerning some matter material to the fitness of the employee to continue at work. This is so whether the question propounded be by a Congressional Committee or by the Board of Education itself. And, if the only material matter to which the question relates is possible disloyalty or subversion on the part of the employee, then any proceeding looking to his dismissal for refusal to answer questions relating to his possible disloyal or subversive activities or affiliations must be brought under the Pennsylvania Loyalty Act of December 22, 1951, P.L. 1726, 65 P.S. § 211 et seq. In a proceeding under that statute a teacher may be discharged if it is determined "by a fair preponderance of the evidence" that he is a disloyal or subversive person; and "If the appointing authority shall be comprised of three or more members, a vote of two-thirds of the members shall be necessary in order to discharge a person." See Section 7 of the Act (65 P.S. § 217). What the Board of Education has attempted to do in these cases is to avoid the requirement of the Pennsylvania Loyalty Act that disloyalty or subversion, as a ground for the discharge of a public school teacher, must be proven "by a fair preponderance of the evidence." The Board's action evidences a belief that it has found a way to dismiss, without any evidence at all, teachers whom it suspects of disloyalty or subversion.

Anything in the *Beilan* case to the contrary is herewith overruled for the future. In searching out and eliminating disloyalty or subversion among teachers in public schools the procedures of the applicable statute enacted for that purpose must be faithfully pursued, and violence must no longer be done the meaning of the word "incompetency" in order to circumvent the procedures of the Loyalty Act.

The orders of the courts below, now here on appeal at Numbers 331, 332 and 352, are severally reversed, and the records remanded for further proceedings not inconsistent with this opinion.   . . .

FOOTNOTES

1. Justice Holmes' often-quoted statement in McAuliffe v. New Bedford, 155 Mass. 216, 29 N.E. 517 (1892) is thought to be the first reference to this idea: "The petitioner may have a constitutional right to talk politics, but he has no constitutional right to be a policeman."

2. See: "Developments in the Law—Academic Freedom," Harvard Law Review, vol. 81, pp. 1045–1159 (1968).

3. 391 U.S. 563, 88 S.Ct. 1731 (1968).

4. Griswold v. Connecticut, 381 U.S. 479, 85 S.Ct. 1678 (1965).

5. Morrison v. State Board of Education, 1 Cal.3d 214, 82 Cal.Rptr. 175, 461 P.2d 375 at 391 (1969).

6. Golden v. Board of Education of County of Harrison, 285 S.E.2d 665 (W.Va.1982).

7. Palmer v. Board of Education of the City of Chicago, 603 F.2d 1271 at 1274 (7th Cir.1979), *cert. denied* 444 U.S. 1026, 100 S.Ct. 689 (1980).

8. Russo v. Central School District No. 1, 469 F.2d 623 (2d Cir.1972) *cert. denied* 411 U.S. 932, 93 S.Ct. 1899 (1973).

9. 42 U.S.C.A. Section 2000e–2, The Civil Rights Act of 1964, Title VII as amended in 1972.

10. Elfbrandt v. Russell, 384 U.S. 11, 86 S.Ct. 1238 (1966).

11. Id.

12. Baggett v. Bullitt, 377 U.S. 360, 84 S.Ct. 1316 (1964).

13. Cramp v. Board of Public Instruction, 368 U.S. 278, 82 S.Ct. 275 (1961).

14. 403 U.S. 207, 91 S.Ct. 1772 (1971).

15. Id.

16. Id. See also: Cole v. Richardson, 405 U.S. 676, 92 S.Ct. 1332 (1972).

17. Keyishian v. Board of Regents of University of State of New York, 385 U.S. 589, 87 S.Ct. 675 (1967).

18. 350 U.S. 551, 76 S.Ct. 637 (1956).

19. 357 U.S. 399, 78 S.Ct. 1317 (1958).

20. "Developments in the Law—Academic Freedom," op. cit. p. 1076.

21. Spevack v. Klein, 385 U.S. 511, 87 S.Ct. 625 (1967).

22. Garrity v. New Jersey, 385 U.S. 493, 87 S.Ct. 616 (1967).

14

Teacher Dismissal: Procedural Due Process and Tenure

Statutory language defines whether a teacher is a probationary teacher, a permanent employee, tenured, or on a continuing contract. Statutes also prescribe procedures for the nonrenewal of a probationary teacher's contract or for the dismissal of a teacher who is a permanent employee, tenured, or on continuing contract.

A legal distinction exists between nonrenewals and dismissals. Nonrenewal comes about when a probationary teacher who has received a contract for a specified period of time, usually one year, is notified that a new contract will not be forthcoming for the succeeding school year. State statute specifies the date when a school board must notify the teacher of nonrenewal.

A dismissal is the removal of a teacher who has served a probationary period and has been granted tenure, continuing contract, or status as a permanent teacher. The school board may dismiss the tenured teacher only for good cause, and the teacher must be offered the opportunity to rebut the charges preferred by the school board. Dismissal requires full procedural due process, whereas nonrenewal generally requires only notice by a specified date, unless a constitutional right or freedom is involved.

PROCEDURAL DUE PROCESS

Teachers have certain liberty and property interests guaranteed by the United States Constitution, and the extent of these rights has been widely discussed and interpreted by the courts.[1] When liberty or property interests are involved, procedural due process must be afforded before that right can be taken away. Teacher tenure or a permanent contract, as established by the legislature, has been recognized as a property right. Such a property right is created if the teacher has a legitimate claim or entitlement to continued employment as created by state law or by the policies of school boards.

Liberty issues arise if the employer stigmatizes the employee and jeopardizes the person's opportunities for future employment or diminishes the individual's good name or reputation.

Until recently it was generally assumed that teachers without tenure were not entitled to a hearing if they were not rehired at the end of their employment period. In several landmark cases, teachers have maintained that they have a right to procedural due process whether they have statutory tenure or not. In *Roth,* later reversed,[2] a federal district court in Wisconsin concluded that pretermination procedural due process required the following minimum rights:

1. A statement of the reasons why the university intends not to retain him, to be furnished upon his request;

2. Notice of a hearing at which he may respond to the stated reasons, to be provided upon his request.[3]

At such a hearing the professor must have a reasonable opportunity to submit evidence relevant to the stated reasons. The burden of going forward and the burden of proof rest with the professor. Only if he makes a reasonable showing that the stated reasons are wholly inappropriate as a basis for decision or that they are wholly without basis in fact would the university administration become obliged to show that the stated reasons are not inappropriate or that they have a basis in fact.[4]

The assumption on the part of this court was that a dependency or expectation of continued employment may be established between teacher and institution to such a degree that the termination may constitute a "grievous loss" within the scope of the United States Supreme Court's rulings in welfare cases. In welfare cases, the Supreme Court has held that whether and to what extent procedural due process is afforded the individual is influenced by (a) the extent to which he may be "condemned to suffer grievous loss" and (b) whether the recipient's interest in avoiding that loss outweighs the governmental interest that involves a determination of the "precise nature of the governmental function involved as well as of the private interest that has been affected by government action."[5]

In keeping with this standard, the United States Court of Appeals, Fifth Circuit, found that a teacher's "expectancy of reemployment" could be of sufficient import to cause the court to invoke due process requirements.[6] The *Ferguson* court said:

[A] college can create an obligation as between itself and an instructor where none might otherwise exist under the legal standards for the interpretation of contract relationships regularly applied to transactions in the market place if it adopts regulations and standards of practice governing nontenured employees which create an expectation of reemployment.[7]

These college cases are equally applicable to teachers in elementary and secondary schools, the test being a balancing of the public school's interest against the private interest that has been affected by governmental action.[8] The public school's interest is the desirability of selecting and retaining an effective and competent teaching staff, while on the other side the teacher's interest is his future employability, professional reputation, and other career

interests.[9] In *Shrick* v. *Thomas,* the court found after weighing the teacher's interest against the school's that due process required that she was entitled not only to a statement of reasons for dismissal, but also to notice of a hearing at which she could respond to accusations. The court, however, would not go so far as to say that the teacher had to be furnished in advance with specifications of standards of teacher competence.

Coupled with the "expectancy of reemployment" doctrine, courts require procedural due process when a teacher can show that his termination emanates from an exercise of one of his fundamental freedoms such as free speech, expression, and press. The state must show a compelling interest in order to suspend a fundamental right. "Simply because teachers are on the public payroll does not make them second-class citizens in regard to their constitutional rights." [10] Courts will invalidate denial of reemployment when the denial rests on an unconstitutional restriction of a fundamental liberty. In *Pred,* the court said the determination must rest on facts showing whether the denial of a continuing contract was "(a) a reprisal for these actions in expression of ideas, thoughts, or associations rather than permissable nondiscriminatory professional evaluations, and, if so, (b) whether under the circumstances in relation to the reasonable demands of a system of organized responsible learning these actions were protected." [11]

In 1972, the Supreme Court of the United States clarified the rights of nontenured teachers in *Board of Regents* v. *Roth* holding that the terms of a nontenured teacher's employment afford no "property" interest in the teaching position. Therefore, to deny it did not require procedural due process. To simply hold a nontenured position does not give a teacher "expectancy of reemployment" requiring procedural due process in order to dismiss. This is true so long as no stigma is attached to his dismissal that would permanently impair his employment opportunities. "The nonretention of respondent, absent any charges against him or stigma or disability foreclosing other employment, is not tantamount to a deprivation of 'liberty' and the terms of respondent's employment accorded him no 'property' interest protected by procedural due process." [12]

The Supreme Court did say, however, in *Perry* v. *Sindermann,*[13] that a lower federal district court erred in foreclosing determination of a teacher's claim when he alleged that nonrenewal of his contract violated his freedom of speech. In this case, the Court said that although subjective "expectancy" of tenure is not protected by the due process clause, that it is possible for a college [or school] to have a *de facto* tenure policy that entitled a teacher to a legitimate claim of job tenure that can be terminated only through a hearing process. Although upholding its denial of the validity of "expectancy of reemployment" in *Roth,* the Supreme Court here found an unusual situation in which the college had implied a tenure arrangement. In fact, the faculty guide prepared by the college itself stated that "the College wishes the faculty member to feel that he has permanent tenure as long as his teaching services are satisfactory . . . ." [14] The Court concluded that "there may be an unwritten 'common law' in a particular university that certain employees shall have the equivalent of tenure." [15]

Procedural Due Process Is Not
Required When Teacher Is Not
Deprived of Constitutional Right

BOARD OF REGENTS OF
STATE COLLEGES v. ROTH
Supreme Court of the United States, 1972.
408 U.S. 564, 92 S.Ct. 2701.

Mr. Justice STEWART delivered the opinion of the Court.

In 1968 the respondent, David Roth, was hired for his first teaching job as assistant professor of political science at Wisconsin State University-Oshkosh. He was hired for a fixed term of one academic year. The notice of his faculty appointment specified that his employment would begin on September 1, 1968, and would end on June 30, 1969. The respondent completed that term. But he was informed that he would not be rehired for the next academic year.

The respondent had no tenure rights to continued employment. Under Wisconsin statutory law a state university teacher can acquire tenure as a "permanent" employee only after four years of year-to-year employment. Having acquired tenure, a teacher is entitled to continued employment "during efficiency and good behavior." A relatively new teacher without tenure, however, is under Wisconsin law entitled to nothing beyond his one-year appointment. There are no statutory or administrative standards defining eligibility for reemployment. State law thus clearly leaves the decision whether to rehire a nontenured teacher for another year to the unfettered discretion of university officials.

The procedural protection afforded a Wisconsin State University teacher before he is separated from the University corresponds to his job security. As a matter of statutory law, a tenured teacher cannot be "discharged except for cause upon written charges" and pursuant to certain procedures. A nontenured teacher, similarly, is protected to some extent *during* his one-year term. Rules promulgated by the Board of Regents provide that a nontenured teacher "dismissed" before the end of the year may have some opportunity for review of the "dismissal." But the Rules provide no real protection for a nontenured teacher who simply is not reemployed for the next year. He must be informed by February 1 "concerning retention or nonretention for the ensuing year." But "no reason for nonretention need be given. No review or appeal is provided in such case."

In conformance with these Rules, the President of Wisconsin State University-Oshkosh informed the respondent before February 1, 1969, that he would not be rehired for the 1969–1970 academic year. He gave the respondent no reason for the decision and no opportunity to challenge it at any sort of hearing.

The respondent then brought this action in Federal District Court alleging that the decision not to rehire him for the next year infringed his Fourteenth Amendment rights. (He attacked the decision both in substance and procedure. First, he alleged that the true reason for the decision was to punish him for certain statements critical of the University administration, and that it therefore violated his right to freedom of speech. Second, he alleged that the failure of University officials to give him notice of any reason for nonretention and an opportunity for a hearing violated his right to procedural due process of law.)

The District Court granted summary judgment for the respondent on the procedural issue, ordering the University officials to provide him with reasons and a hearing. 310 F.Supp. 972. The Court of Appeals, with one judge dissenting, affirmed this partial summary judgment. 446 F.2d 806. We granted certiorari. 404 U.S. 909, 92 S.Ct. 227, 30 L.Ed.2d 181. The only question presented to us at this stage in the case is whether the respondent had a constitutional right to a statement of reasons and a hearing on the University's decision not to rehire him for another year. We hold that he did not.

The requirements of procedural due process apply only to the deprivation of interests encompassed by the Fourteenth Amendment's protection of liberty and property. When protected interests are implicated, the right to some kind of prior hearing is paramount. But the range of interests protected by procedural due process is not infinite.

The District Court decided that procedural due process guarantees apply in this case by assessing and balancing the weights of the particular interests involved. It concluded that the respondent's interest in reemployment at Wisconsin State University-Oshkosh outweighed the University's interest in denying him reemployment summarily. 310 F.Supp., at 977–979. Undeniably, the respondent's reemployment prospects were of major concern to him—concern that we surely cannot say was insignificant. And a weighing process has long been a part of any determination of the *form* of hearing required in particular situations by procedural due process. But, to determine whether due process requirements apply in the first place, we must look not to the "weight" but to the *nature* of the interest at stake. . . . We must look to see if the interest is within the Fourteenth Amendment's protection of liberty and property.

"Liberty" and "property" are broad and majestic terms. They are among the "[g]reat [constitutional] concepts . . . purposely left to gather meaning from experience. . . . [T]hey relate to the whole domain of social and economic fact, and the statesmen who founded this Nation knew too well that only a stagnant society remains unchanged." National Mutual Ins. Co. v. Tidewater Transfer Co., 337 U.S. 582, 646, 69 S.Ct. 1173, 1195, 93 L.Ed. 1556 (Frankfurter, J., dissenting). For that reason, the Court has fully and finally rejected the wooden distinction between "rights" and "privileges" that once seemed to govern the applicability of procedural due process rights. The Court has also made clear that the property interests protected by procedural due process extend well beyond actual ownership of real estate, chattels, or money. By the same token, the Court has required due process protection for deprivations of liberty beyond the sort of formal constraints imposed by the criminal process.

Yet, while the Court has eschewed rigid or formalistic limitations on the protection of procedural due process, it has at the same time observed certain boundaries. For the words "liberty" and "property" in the Due Process Clause of the Fourteenth Amendment must be given some meaning.

> While this court has not attempted to define with exactness the liberty . . . guaranteed [by the Fourteenth Amendment], the term has received much consideration and some of the included things have been definitely stated. Without doubt, it denotes not merely freedom from bodily restraint but also the right of the individual to contract, to engage in any of the common occupations of life, to acquire useful knowledge, to marry, establish a home and bring up children, to worship God according to the dictates of his own conscience, and generally to enjoy those privileges long recognized . . . as essential to the orderly pursuit of happiness by free men. Meyer v. Nebraska, 262 U.S. 390, 399, 43 S.Ct. 625, 626, 67 L.Ed. 1042.

In a Constitution for a free people, there can be no doubt that the meaning of "liberty" must be broad indeed. See e.g., Bolling v. Sharpe, 347 U.S. 497, 499–500, 74 S.Ct. 693, 694, 98 L.Ed. 884; Stanley v. Illinois, 405 U.S. 645, 92 S.Ct. 1208, 31 L.Ed.2d 551.

There might be cases in which a State refused to reemploy a person under such circumstances that interests in liberty would be implicated. But this is not such a case.

The State, in declining to rehire the respondent, did not make any charge against him that might seriously damage his standing and associations in his community. It did not base the nonrenewal of his contract on a charge, for example, that he had been guilty of dishonesty, or immorality. Had it done so, this would be a different case. For "[w]here a person's good name, reputation, honor, or integrity is at stake because of what the government is doing to him, notice and an opportunity to be heard are essential." . . . In such a case, due process would accord an opportunity to refute the charge before University officials. In the present case, however, there is no suggestion whatever that the respondent's "good name, reputation, honor, or integrity" is at stake.

Similarly, there is no suggestion that the State, in declining to reemploy the respondent, imposed on him a stigma or other disability that foreclosed his freedom to take advantage of other employment opportunities. The State, for example, did not invoke any regulations to bar the respondent from all other public employment in state universities. Had it done so, this, again, would be a different case. For "[t]o be deprived not only of present government employment but of future opportunity for it certainly is no small injury . . . ."

To be sure, the respondent has alleged that the nonrenewal of his contract was based on his exercise of his right to freedom of speech. But this allegation is not now before us. The District Court stayed proceedings on this issue, and the respondent has yet to prove that the decision not to rehire him was in fact based on his free speech activities.

Hence, on the record before us, all that clearly appears is that the respondent was not rehired for one year at one university. It stretches the concept too far to suggest that a person is deprived of "liberty" when he simply is not rehired in one job but remains as free as before to seek another. . . .

The Fourteenth Amendment's procedural protection of property is a safeguard of the security of interests that a person has already acquired in specific benefits. These interests—property interests—may take many forms.

Thus, the Court has held that a person receiving welfare benefits under statutory and administrative standards defining eligibility for them has an interest in continued receipt of those benefits that is safeguarded by procedural due process. Goldberg v. Kelly, 397 U.S. 254, 90 S.Ct. 1011, 25 L.Ed.2d 287. . . . Similarly, in the area of public employment, the Court has held that a public college professor dismissed from an office held under tenure provisions, Slochower v. Board of Education, 350 U.S. 551, 76 S.Ct. 637, 100 L.Ed. 692, and college professors and staff members dismissed during the terms of their contracts, Wieman v. Updegraff, 344 U.S. 183, 73 S.Ct. 215, 97 L.Ed. 216, have interests in continued employment that are safeguarded by due process. Only last year, the Court held that this principle "proscribing summary dismissal from public employment without hearing or inquiry required by due process" also applied to a teacher recently hired without tenure or a formal contract, but nonetheless with a clearly implied promise of continued employment. Connell v. Higginbotham, 403 U.S. 207, 208, 91 S.Ct. 1772, 1773, 29 L.Ed.2d 418.

Certain attributes of "property" interests protected by procedural due process emerge from these decisions. To have a property interest in a benefit, a person clearly must have more than an abstract need or desire for it. He must have more than a unilateral expectation of it. He must, instead, have a legitimate claim of entitlement to it. It is a purpose of the ancient institution of property to protect those claims upon which people rely in their daily lives, reliance that must not be arbitrarily undermined. It is a purpose of the constitutional right to a hearing to provide an opportunity for a person to vindicate those claims.

Property interests, of course, are not created by the Constitution. Rather they are created and their dimensions are defined by existing rules or understandings that stem from an independent source such as state law—rules or understandings that secure certain benefits and that support claims of entitlement to those benefits. Thus, the welfare recipients in *Goldberg* v. *Kelly,* supra, had a claim of entitlement to welfare payments that was grounded in the statute defining eligibility for them. The recipients had not yet shown that they were, in fact, within the statutory terms of eligibility. But we held that they had a right to a hearing at which they might attempt to do so.

Just as the welfare recipients' "property" interest in welfare payments was created and defined by statutory terms, so the respondent's "property" interest in employment at Wisconsin State University-Oshkosh was created and defined by the terms of his appointment. Those terms secured his interest in employment up to June 30, 1969. But the important fact in this case is that they specifically provided that the respondent's employment was to terminate on June 30. They did not provide for contract renewal absent "sufficient cause." Indeed, they made no provision for renewal whatsoever.

Thus, the terms of the respondent's appointment secured absolutely no interest in reemployment for the next year. They supported absolutely no possible claim of entitlement to reemployment. Nor, significantly, was there any state statute or University rule or policy that secured his interest in reemployment or that created any legitimate claim to it. In these circumstances, the respondent surely had an abstract concern in being rehired, but he did not have a *property* interest sufficient to require the University authorities to give him a hearing when they declined to renew his contract of employment.

Our analysis of the respondent's constitutional rights in this case in no way indicates a view that an opportunity for a hearing or a statement of reasons for nonretention would, or would not, be appropriate or wise in public colleges and universities. For it is a written Constitution that we apply. Our role is confined to interpretation of that Constitution.

We must conclude that the summary judgment for the respondent should not have been granted, since the respondent has not shown that he was deprived of liberty or property protected by the Fourteenth Amendment. The judgment of the Court of Appeals, accordingly, is reversed and the case is remanded for further proceedings consistent with this opinion. It is so ordered.

Teacher with De Facto Tenure Is
Entitled to a Hearing Before
Termination of Employment

PERRY v. SINDERMANN

Supreme Court of the United States, 1972.
408 U.S. 593, 92 S.Ct. 2694.

Mr. Justice STEWART delivered the opinion of the Court.

From 1959 to 1969 the respondent, Robert Sindermann, was a teacher in the state college system of the State of Texas. After teaching for two years at the University of Texas and for four years at San Antonio Junior College, he became a professor of Government and Social Science at Odessa Junior College in 1965. He was employed at the college for four successive years, under a series of one-year contracts. He was successful enough to be appointed, for a time, the cochairman of his department.

During the 1968–1969 academic year, however, controversy arose between the respondent and the college administration. The respondent was elected president of the Texas Junior College Teachers Association. In this capacity, he left his teaching duties on several occasions to testify before committees of the Texas Legislature, and he became involved in public disagreements with the policies of the college's Board of Regents. In particular, he aligned himself with a group advocating the elevation of the college to four-year status—a change opposed by the Regents. And, on one occasion, a newspaper advertisement appeared over his name that was highly critical of the Regents.

Finally, in May 1969, the respondent's one-year employment contract terminated and the Board of Regents voted not to offer him a new contract for the next academic year. The Regents issued a press release setting forth allegations of the respondent's insubordination. But they provided him no official statement of the reasons for the nonrenewal of his contract. And they allowed him no opportunity for a hearing to challenge the basis of the nonrenewal.

The respondent then brought this action in Federal District Court. He alleged primarily that the Regents' decision not to rehire him was based on his public criticism of the policies of the college administration and thus infringed his right to freedom of speech. He also alleged that their failure to provide him an opportunity for a hearing violated the Fourteenth Amendment's guarantee of procedural due process. The petitioners—members of the Board of Regents and the president of the college—denied that their decision was made in retaliation for the respondent's public criticism and argued that they had no obligation to provide a hearing. On the basis of these bare pleadings and three brief affidavits filed by the respondent, the District Court granted summary judgment for the petitioners. It concluded that the respondent had "no cause of action against the [petitioners] since his contract of employment terminated May 31, 1969, and Odessa Junior College has not adopted the tenure system."

The Court of Appeals reversed the judgment of the District Court. 430 F.2d 939. First, it held that, despite the respondent's lack of tenure, the nonrenewal of his contract would violate the Fourteenth Amendment if it in fact was based on his protected free speech. Since the actual reason for the Regents' decision was "in total dispute" in the pleadings, the court remanded the case for a full hearing on this contested issue of fact. Id. at 942–943. Second, the Court of Appeals held that, despite the respondent's lack of tenure, the failure to allow him an opportunity for a hearing would violate the constitutional guarantee of procedural due process if the respondent could show that he had an "expectancy" of reemployment. It, therefore, ordered that this issue of fact also be aired upon remand. Id. at 943–944. We granted a writ of certiorari, 403 U.S. 917, 91 S.Ct. 2226, 29 L.Ed.2d 694, and we have considered this case along with Board of Regents v. Roth, 408 U.S. 564, 92 S.Ct. 2701, 33 L.Ed.2d 548.

The first question presented is whether the respondent's lack of a contractual or tenure right to reemployment, taken alone, defeats his claim that the nonrenewal of his contract violated the First and Fourteenth Amendments. We hold that it does not.

For at least a quarter-century, this Court has made clear that even though a person has no "right" to a valuable governmental benefit and even though the government may deny him the benefit for any number of reasons, there are some reasons upon which the government may not rely. It may not deny a benefit to a person on a basis that infringes his constitutionally protected interests—especially his interest in freedom of speech. For if the government could deny a benefit to a person because of his constitutionally protected speech or associations, his exercise of those freedoms would in effect be penalized and inhibited. This would allow the government to "produce a result which [it] could not command directly." Speiser v. Randall, 357 U.S. 513, 526, 78 S.Ct. 1332, 1342, 2 L.Ed.2d 1460. Such interference with constitutional rights is impermissible. . . .

Thus, the respondent's lack of a contractual or tenure "right" to reemployment for the 1969–1970 academic year is immaterial to his free speech

claim. Indeed, twice before, this Court has specifically held that the nonrenewal of a nontenured public school teacher's one-year contract may not be
predicated on his exercise of First and Fourteenth Amendment rights.
. . . We reaffirm those holdings here.

In this case, of course, the respondent has yet to show that the decision
not to renew his contract was, in fact, made in retaliation for his exercise of
the constitutional right of free speech. The District Court foreclosed any
opportunity to make this showing when it granted summary judgment.
Hence, we cannot now hold that the Board of Regents' action was invalid.

But we agree with the Court of Appeals that there is a genuine dispute as
to "whether the college refused to renew the teaching contract on an
impermissible basis—as a reprisal for the exercise of constitutionally protected rights." 430 F.2d, at 943. The respondent has alleged that his nonretention was based on his testimony before legislative committees and his other
public statements critical of the Regents' policies. And he has alleged that
this public criticism was within the First and Fourteenth Amendments'
protection of freedom of speech. Plainly, these allegations present a bona
fide constitutional claim. For this Court has held that a teacher's public
criticism of his superiors on matters of public concern may be constitutionally protected and may, therefore, be an impermissible basis for termination of
his employment. *Pickering* v. *Board of Education*, supra.

For this reason we hold that the grant of summary judgment against the
respondent, without full exploration of this issue, was improper.

The respondent's lack of formal contractual or tenure security in continued employment at Odessa Junior College, though irrelevant to his free
speech claim, is highly relevant to his procedural due process claim. But it
may not be entirely dispositive.

We have held today in Board of Regents v. Roth, 408 U.S. 564, 92 S.Ct.
2701, that the Constitution does not require opportunity for a hearing before
the nonrenewal of a nontenured teacher's contract, unless he can show that
the decision not to rehire him somehow deprived him of an interest in
"liberty" or that he had a "property" interest in continued employment,
despite the lack of tenure or a formal contract. In *Roth* the teacher had not
made a showing on either point to justify summary judgment in his favor.

Similarly, the respondent here has yet to show that he has been deprived
of an interest that could invoke procedural due process protection. As in
Roth, the mere showing that he was not rehired in one particular job,
without more, did not amount to a showing of a loss of liberty. Nor did it
amount to a showing of a loss of property.

But the respondent's allegations—which we must construe most favorably to the respondent at this stage of the litigation—do raise a genuine issue
as to his interest in continued employment at Odessa Junior College. He
alleged that this interest, though not secured by a formal contractual tenure
provision, was secured by a no less binding understanding fostered by the
college administration. In particular, the respondent alleged that the college had a *de facto* tenure program, and that he had tenure under that
program. He claimed that he and others legitimately relied upon an

unusual provision that had been in the college's official Faculty Guide for many years:

> *Teacher Tenure:* Odessa College has no tenure system. The Administration of the College wishes the faculty member to feel that he has permanent tenure as long as his teaching services are satisfactory and as long as he displays a cooperative attitude toward his co-workers and his superiors, and as long as he is happy in his work.

Moreover, the respondent claimed legitimate reliance upon guidelines promulgated by the Coordinating Board of the Texas College and University System that provided that a person, like himself, who had been employed as a teacher in the state college and university system for seven years or more has some form of job tenure. Thus, the respondent offered to prove that a teacher with his long period of service at this particular State College had no less a "property" interest in continued employment than a formally tenured teacher at other colleges, and had no less a procedural due process right to a statement of reasons and a hearing before college officials upon their decision not to retain him.

We have made clear in *Roth* . . . that "property" interests subject to procedural due process protection are not limited by a few rigid, technical forms. Rather, "property" denotes a broad range of interests that are secured by "existing rules or understandings." . . . A person's interest in a benefit is a "property" interest for due process purposes if there are such rules or mutually explicit understandings that support his claim of entitlement to the benefit and that he may invoke at a hearing.

A written contract with an explicit tenure provision clearly is evidence of a formal understanding that supports a teacher's claim of entitlement to continued employment unless sufficient "cause" is shown. Yet absence of such an explicit contractual provision may not always foreclose the possibility that a teacher has a "property" interest in reemployment. For example, the law of contracts in most, if not all, jurisdictions long has employed a process by which agreements, though not formalized in writing, may be "implied." 3 A. Corbin on Contracts §§ 561–572A. Explicit contractual provisions may be supplemented by other agreements implied from "the promisor's words and conduct in the light of the surrounding circumstances." Id., at § 562. And, "[t]he meaning of [the promisor's] words and acts is found by relating them to the usage of the past."

A teacher, like the respondent, who has held his position for a number of years, might be able to show from the circumstances of this service—and from other relevant facts—that he has a legitimate claim of entitlement to job tenure. Just as this Court has found there to be a "common law of a particular industry or of a particular plant" that may supplement a collective-bargaining agreement, United Steelworkers v. Warrior & Gulf Nav. Co., 363 U.S. 574, 579 . . . so there may be an unwritten "common law" in a particular university that certain employees shall have the equivalent of tenure. This is particularly likely in a college or university, like Odessa Junior College, that has no explicit tenure system even for senior members of its faculty, but that nonetheless may have created such a system in practice. . . .

In this case, the respondent has alleged the existence of rules and understandings, promulgated and fostered by state officials, that may justify his legitimate claim of entitlement to continued employment absent "sufficient cause." We disagree with the Court of Appeals insofar as it held that a mere subjective "expectancy" is protected by procedural due process, but we agree that the respondent must be given an opportunity to prove the legitimacy of his claim of such entitlement in light of "the policies and practices of the institution." 430 F.2d, at 943. Proof of such a property interest would not, of course, entitle him to reinstatement. But such proof would obligate college officials to grant a hearing at his request, where he could be informed of the grounds for his nonretention and challenge their sufficiency.

Therefore, while we do not wholly agree with the opinion of the Court of Appeals, its judgment remanding this case to the District Court is affirmed.

Affirmed.

Mr. Justice POWELL took no part in the decision of this case.

NOTES

1. Nonreemployment without a hearing of a nontenured teacher because of general ineffectiveness as a teacher does not violate the First and Fourteenth Amendments. Robinson v. Jefferson County Board of Education, 485 F.2d 1381 (5th Cir.1973), rehearing denied 488 F.2d 1055 (5th Cir.1974).

2. When a nontenured teacher had taught for ten years in a state with no tenure law and was not rehired, the court held that no substantive due process rights existed on behalf of the teacher that would invoke a cause of action under the Civil Rights Act § 1983, even though the only rationale used by the school board for dismissal was that the students of the teacher scored below expected levels on achievement tests. Scheelhaase v. Woodbury Central Community School District, 488 F.2d 237 (8th Cir.1973).

3. A nontenured teacher's claim of entitlement to a position was, under the Illinois Tenure Act, insufficient to constitute a property interest within the Fourteenth Amendment. Appellant was unable to show that the tenure law limited in any way the authority of the school board to terminate employment prior to acquiring tenure status. Miller v. School District Number 167, Cook County, Illinois, 500 F.2d 711 (7th Cir.1974).

4. A probationary teacher had no expectancy of reemployment vesting him with a property interest. McCullough v. Lohn, 483 F.2d 34 (5th Cir. 1973).

5. When a nontenured teacher was indicted for alleged sexual misconduct with students, the court held that, should he be convicted, the school board was not obligated to provide him with a hearing; however, in the event that he was exonerated by the court, the school board must provide a hearing in order for him to clear his name. The court found, in referring to *Roth*, though, that when a teacher is indicted it is not the

obligation of the school board to hold a hearing prior to his trial in order to determine his guilt or innocence. To do so, according to the court, would have placed the board in the untenable position of dispensing findings that "in one direction would have injured the interests of the state, and in another direction would have damaged those of the teacher." Moore v. Knowles, 482 F.2d 1069 (5th Cir.1973).

6. Notice of nonrenewal of a nontenured teacher that is not posted or published does not create a "stigma" upon the teacher's good name, reputation, honor, or integrity sufficient to deprive her of "liberty" under the Fourteenth Amendment. Shrick v. Thomas, 486 F.2d 691 (7th Cir.1973).

7. When nontenured elementary teachers distributed a poem to students imploring them to throw off the dull discipline of the moral environment of their home life and enter into a new world of love and freedom— freedom to use acid and grass, freedom to engage in sexual activities, and freedom to use vulgarities, the court denied the teachers recovery under the Civil Rights Act. In so doing the court commented:

> We do not believe that however much the reach of the First Amendment has been extended and however eager today's courts have been to protect the many varieties of claims to civil rights, the appellee school board had to put up with the described conduct of appellants.

Brubaker v. Board of Education, School District 149, Cook County, Illinois, 502 F.2d 973 (7th Cir.1974).

8. A United States District Court in Minnesota listed five occasions when *Roth* and *Sindermann* dictated a hearing on nonrenewal:

a. When the contract nonrenewal is related to the teacher's exercise of freedom of speech under the First Amendment.

b. When the teacher is confronted with a charge that might seriously damage his or her standing and associations in the community.

c. When the failure to reemploy the teacher imposes a stigma or other disability on him or her that forecloses future freedom to take advantage of other employment opportunities.

d. When the teacher, by virtue of existing state policies, the contract terms, or similar understandings, has a reasonable expectancy of reemployment.

e. When the adverse reports on which action is taken are prepared by the school's superiors or plaintiffs' compatriots and are fabricated, without any foundation or basis in fact whatsoever, or are maliciously designed so as to use the freedom of the probationary period for reasons of personal calumny, hatred, vindication, or dislike thus using the probationary period as a sword rather than a shield. Ferris v. Special School District No. 1, 367 F.Supp. 459 (D.Minn.1973).

9. When there was evidence that teachers' contracts had not been renewed in retaliation for their public comments regarding teacher's salaries and affiliation with a teacher's association, the court held that the nonrenewal of their contracts violated their First Amendment rights of freedom of

speech and association. Greminger v. Seaborne, 584 F.2d 275 (8th Cir. 1978).

10. An allegation by a teacher that nonrenewal of his contract was due to the failure to shave his beard was held by the court to be unfounded and wholly insubstantial. Ball v. Board of Trustees of Kerrville, 584 F.2d 684 (5th Cir.1978). See also: Carmichael v. Chambers County Board of Education, 581 F.2d 95 (5th Cir.1978); Cain v. McQueen, 580 F.2d 1001 (9th Cir.1978); Graves v. Duganne, 581 F.2d 222 (9th Cir.1978).

11. *Stigmatizing Reasons.* The Supreme Court established in *Perry* v. *Sindermann* and in *Roth* v. *Board of Regents* that a nontenured teacher has a liberty interest not to be stigmatized or to have anything be said that damages his or her good name or reputation. Although the Court established this as a standard, it did not define specifically what stigmatizing means. Case law has defined these liberty interests as presented below.

   a. Allegations of incompetence, inadequacy, and insubordination have not been determined to be stigmatizing. "These allegations certainly are not complimentary and suggest that (the teacher) may have problems . . . but do not import serious character defects . . . as contemplated by *Roth*." Gray v. Union County Intermediate Education District, 520 F.2d 803 (9th Cir.1975).

   b. Charges of racism have been determined to be a deprivation of a liberty interest, reflecting on a professor's reputation and good name, and therefore required due process to be afforded to prove the charges. Wellner v. Minnesota State Junior College Board, 487 F.2d 153 (8th Cir.1973).

   c. A school board's charges of "apparent emotional instability" stigmatizes a teacher because it goes beyond job-related comments. Bomhoff v. White, 526 F.Supp. 488 (D.Ariz.1981).

DISMISSAL OF TENURED TEACHERS

As indicated in Chapter 12, most states have enacted legislation specifying the grounds for and the manner in which a teacher's employment may be terminated. These laws may apply in instances of dismissal during the period of an annual contract or to termination of teachers who have either continuing contracts or tenure. The usual grounds for dismissal are incompetency and insubordination.

Incompetency has been construed by the courts to mean any physical or mental condition that tends to incapacitate a teacher to perform effectively. This rather broad definition generally concerns a fitness to teach that contains a range of factors and has been used by many boards as a catch-all for teacher dismissal. Insubordination, on the other hand, is narrower and imports a willful disregard for express or implied directions of the employer and repeated refusal to obey reasonable regulations.[16]

Other grounds for dismissal include immorality, misconduct, neglect of duty, and other good or just cause. Every teacher is charged with the responsibility of setting a good example. Not only must teachers be of good moral character, but their general reputation must attest to this fact. This is somewhat akin to the statement made so often in the trial of criminal cases that not only is a defendant entitled to a fair trial, but the trial should be conducted so fairly that the defendant believes he or she had a fair trial. Teachers must be not only moral persons, but must conduct themselves in such a manner that others will know of their virtue.

Although court opinions are not uniform on the subject, it may generally be concluded that misconduct is a broader term than immorality and that different standards of proof are required for each.

Incompetency and Immorality May Be Interpreted By the Courts to Broadly Mean a General Lack of Fitness

HOROSKO v. SCHOOL DISTRICT OF MOUNT PLEASANT

Supreme Court of Pennsylvania, 1939.
335 Pa. 369, 6 A.2d 866.

LINN, Justice. This appeal is from an order of the Superior Court reversing an order of the Common Pleas which had affirmed the action of a school board in discharging a teacher. . . .

The difference of view between the two learned courts which have considered the case arises from a different construction of the following provision in section 1205(a), 24 P.S. § 1126(a): "(a) The only valid causes for termination of a contract in accordance with the provisions of this section shall be—Immorality, incompetency, intemperance, cruelty, willful and persistent negligence, mental derangement, persistent and willful violation of the school laws of this Commonwealth on the part of the professional employe. . . .

All the members of this court agree that the Superior Court's construction is much narrower than was apparently intended by the legislature; we also think the case calls for the application of the rule that findings of fact supported by competent evidence must be accepted on appeal. In the opinion of the Superior Court it is said—"It may be true, as counsel for appellee [the school board] argues, that appellant [teacher] now commands neither the respect nor the good will of the community, but these are not matters which the statute now recognizes as causes for dismissal." If the fact be that she "now commands neither the respect nor the good will of the community" and if the record shows that effect to be the result of her conduct within the clause quoted, it will be conclusive evidence of incompetency. It has always been the recognized duty of the teacher to conduct himself in such way as to command the respect and good will of the community, though one result of the choice of a teacher's vocation may be to deprive him of the same freedom of action enjoyed by persons in other vocations. Educators have always regarded the example set by the teacher as of great importance, particularly in the education of the children in the lower grades such as those attending the school in which this teacher had been employed; it was a country school with eighteen pupils classified into eight grades.

Difficulties between this teacher and the board had been existing some time and grew out of her conduct with respect to a restaurant maintained by a man whom she married in August 1936, during the course of the period involved. In this restaurant beer was sold and a pinball and a slot machine were maintained and dice were played. The restaurant was across the road and about one hundred and twenty five feet from the school. In the opinion filed by the learned trial judge, he said:

> The evidence in the case is that: (1) While Miss Horosko used and was known by the name of Evelyn Horosko she was in fact married to one William Connors and lived with him as his wife; (2) That the said Connors was the proprietor of a lunch room and beer garden in which Evelyn Horosko acted as waitress and, on occasion, as bartender, such services being performed after school hours and during the summer vacation; (3) That in this beer garden and in the presence of several of her pupils whom she was tutoring, she (a) took an occasional drink of beer; (b) served beer to customers; (c) shook dice with customers for drinks; (d) played, and showed customers how to play, a pinball machine on the premises. And further, that she was rated by A.H. Howell, County Superintendent of Schools, under the rating card provided by the Department of Education, as 43 percent competent, a rating of 50 percent being the "passing" or average rating.
>
> Is such a course of conduct immoral or intemperate, and does it—in connection with her scholastic and efficiency rating—amount to incompetency? We hold it to be self evident that, under the intent and meaning of the act, immorality is not essentially confined to a deviation from sex morality; it may be such a course of conduct as offends the morals of the community and is a bad example to the youth whose ideals a teacher is supposed to foster and to elevate. Nor need intemperance be confined strictly to overindulgence in alcoholic liquors—temperance implies moderation, and a person may be intemperate in conduct without being an alcoholic addict. And so as to incompetency; as we take it, this means under the Act incompetency as a teacher—but does this mean that competency is merely the ability to teach the "Three R's"?

He concluded that it would be "just" (the word used in clause (j) of section 1205) to affirm the action of the school board in dismissing the teacher.

The opinion of the Superior Court is based, as we understand it, on a narrower construction of the word "incompetency" than that adopted by the trial court. The Statutory Construction Act of 1937, P.L. 1019, in section 33, 46 P.S. § 533, provides:

> Words and phrases shall be construed according to rules of grammar and according to their common and approved usage; but technical words and phrases and such others as have acquired a peculiar and appropriate meaning or are defined in this act, shall be construed according to such peculiar and appropriate meaning or definition.
>
> General words shall be construed to take their meanings and be restricted by preceding particular words.

The provisions of clause (a), which include the words "incompetency" and "immorality," are therefore to be construed "according to their common and approved usage," having regard, of course, to the context in which the legislature used them.

Among the definitions of "immorality" is "conduct inconsistent with moral rectitude." A large body of public opinion regards gambling as immoral. Gambling with a pinball or a slot machine or with dice is prohibited by law. We are not prepared to say the learned judge erred in concluding that the teacher's shaking "dice with customers for drinks" and showing them how to play a pinball machine in the presence of school children supported the finding of incompetency in the circumstances shown.

The term "incompetency" has a "common and approved usage." The context does not limit the meaning of the word to lack of substantive knowledge of the subjects to be taught. Common and approved usage give a much wider meaning. For example, in 31 C.J., with reference to a number of supporting decisions, it is defined: "A relative term without technical meaning. It may be employed as meaning disqualification; inability; incapacity; lack of ability, legal qualifications, or fitness to discharge the required duty." In Black's Law Dictionary, 3rd edition, page 945, and in 1 Bouv.Law Dict., Rawle's Third Revision, p. 1528, it is defined as "Lack of ability or fitness to discharge the required duty." Cases construing the word to the same effect are found in 4 Words and Phrases, First Series, page 3510, and 2 Words and Phrases, Second Series, page 1013. Webster's New International Dictionary defines it as "want of physical, intellectual, or moral ability; insufficiency; inadequacy; specif., want of legal qualifications or fitness." Funk & Wagnalls Standard Dictionary defines it as "General lack of capacity of fitness, or lack of the special qualities required for a particular purpose."

In the circumstances, therefore, we must conclude that the order made in the Common Pleas was "just."

The order of the Superior Court is reversed and that of the Common Pleas is reinstated; each party to bear its own costs.

NOTES

1. Failure to maintain discipline, excessive discipline, or lack of knowledge of subject matter have all been reasons for dismissing tenured teachers for incompetency. Generally, when incompetency is involved, other charges are also presented. In one case, the dismissal notification listed fourteen specific charges and included inadequate maintenance of discipline during class, excessive and ineffective use of films, ineffective classroom teaching, and failure to cooperate with school administrators. The school presented a preponderance of evidence that children were disruptive, daydreamed in class, and left the room without permission. Therefore the court upheld the dismissal. Board of Directors of Sioux City v. Mroz, 295 N.W.2d 447 (Iowa 1980).

2. A New York court upheld the dismissal of a tenured teacher when the board gave evidence that the teacher administered excessive punishment on three separate occasions. Kinsella v. Board of Education, etc., 64 A.D.2d 738, 407 N.Y.S.2d 78 (1978).

3. The dismissal of a tenured teacher, who had been teaching for twenty-five years, was upheld because the teacher used poor grammar and made spelling errors. The teacher also attempted to teach spelling before the

children mastered the alphabet. Blunt v. Marion County School Board, 515 F.2d 951 (5th Cir.1975).

4. Some states, through statute, require that teachers be given an opportunity to improve or to remediate themselves. If state statute requires remediation, the school board must show that remediation was attempted or that the actions were irremediable. When a teacher was charged with incompetency based on a number of items, such as lacking rapport with pupils, giving irregular homework assignments, and grabbing children's hair, arms, and shoulders in a cruel manner, the teacher claimed the acts were remediable but the court disagreed and stated "many causes, when standing alone, may be remediable, whereas those same causes in combination with others may well be irremediable. Here, we think it clear that the combination of a number of causes plus the continuous nature of the conduct were sufficient bases for a finding of irremediability." Gilliland v. Board of Education of Pleasant View, 67 Ill.2d 143, 8 Ill.Dec. 84, 365 N.W.2d 322 (1977).

5. Charges of insubordination are generally not supportable if: "(1) the alleged misconduct was not proved; (2) the existence of a pertinent school rule or a superior's order was not proved; (3) the pertinent rule or order was not violated; (4) the teacher tried, although unsuccessfully, to comply with the rule or order; (5) the teacher's motive for violating the rule or order was admirable; (6) no harm resulted from the violation; (7) the rule or order was unreasonable; (8) the rule or order was invalid as beyond the authority of the maker; (9) the enforcement of the rule or order revealed possible bias or discrimination against the teacher; or (10) the enforcement of the rule or order violated the First Amendment rights to free speech or academic freedom." 78 A.L.R.3d 83, 87.

6. When a tenured teacher made statements to an unauthorized assembly of students contradicting statements of the principal and superintendent and encouraging the students not to return to classes, the court held that the teacher's dismissal was valid as constituting insubordination and that he was not effectively denied freedom of speech. Whitsell v. Southeast Local School District, 484 F.2d 1222 (6th Cir.1973).

7. As grounds for dismissal, "immorality" must generally be shown to have an adverse effect upon fitness to teach. When a teacher had sexual relations with a female minor student, the court held that such conduct was inherently detrimental to the teacher-student relation and was thus injurious to the welfare of the school. Denton v. South Kitsap School District, 10 Wn.App. 69, 516 P.2d 1080 (1973).

8. The conclusion of a board of education that a teacher is unable "to establish rapport with the students," without supporting evidence, is insufficient, standing alone, to establish "good or just cause" for dismissal. Powell v. Board of Trustees of Crook County School District No. 1, 550 P.2d 1112 (Wyo.1976).

*Board's Inference That Teacher's
Activities Constituted Social
Misbehavior Was Arbitrary and
Capricious*

FISHER v. SNYDER

United States Court of Appeals,
Eighth Circuit, 1973.
476 F.2d 375.

BRIGHT, Circuit Judge. Appellants, as members of the school board of a rural Nebraska county district, dismissed appellee, Frances Fisher, as a high school teacher at the close of the 1972 school year, giving as a reason her "unbecoming conduct" outside the classroom. Mrs. Fisher thereafter brought an action against the members of the board under 42 U.S.C.A. § 1983, alleging that constitutionally impermissible reasons underlay their dismissal action. The district court ordered her reinstatement, and the board members bring this appeal. We affirm the district court.

The relevant facts are not in dispute. Mrs. Fisher, a middle-aged divorcee, was employed at the high school in Tryon, Nebraska, from 1970 to 1972. Her married son, then twenty-six years old, lived and taught in the neighboring town of Stapleton, Nebraska. Mrs. Fisher lived alone in a one-bedroom apartment. On several occasions, young ladies, married couples, and young men, who were friends of her son, visited Tryon. Because hotel and motel accommodations were generally sparse and unavailable in Tryon, Mrs. Fisher followed the advice of the secretary of the school board and allowed these guests to stay overnight at her apartment. Cliff Rowan, age twenty-six, was a particularly frequent visitor. Rowan's parents lived in California. He, therefore, regularly visited Mrs. Fisher during his school vacations and at other times, and she referred to him as her second son. In the spring of 1972, Rowan spent about a week in Tryon visiting school classes as a means of fulfilling certain of his college requirements. Mrs. Fisher made arrangements with school administrators for this visitation and it was reported in the local newspaper.

Following Rowan's visit, the school board notified Mrs. Fisher that her contract would not be renewed at the end of the 1972 school year. At her request, pursuant to provisions of Nebraska law, the board afforded Mrs. Fisher a hearing relating to the notice of dismissal. . . .

Nebraska by statute requires that notice and a hearing be given nontenured teachers who are to be terminated. Neb.Rev.Stat. § 79–1254. The appellees concede that the school board, in dismissing Fisher, complied with the statute, and its judgment, therefore, must be afforded judicial deference "so long as the board does not act unreasonably, arbitrarily, capriciously, or unlawfully." Smith v. Board of Educ., 365 F.2d 770, 782 (8th Cir. 1966) . . . .

However, a high school teacher may successfully argue that his dismissal was arbitrary and capricious if he can prove:

> . . . that each of the stated reasons [underlying his dismissal] is trivial, or is unrelated to the educational process or to working relationships within the educational institution, or is wholly unsupported by a basis in fact. [McEnteg-

gart v. Cataldo, 451 F.2d 1109, 1111 (1st Cir.1971), cert. denied, 408 U.S. 943, 92 S.Ct. 2878, 33 L.Ed.2d 767 (1972).]

Thus, while a school board may legitimately inquire into the character and integrity of its teachers . . . it must be certain that it does not arbitrarily or capriciously dismiss a teacher based on unsupported conclusions drawn from such inquiries.

In seeking to justify the dismissal in this case, the school board argues that the evidence developed at the board hearing supported its finding Mrs. Fisher guilty of conduct unbecoming a teacher. In the board's view, "the inferences from her social behavior are that there was a strong potential of sexual misconduct." The board does not actually accuse Mrs. Fisher of immoral conduct but "of social misbehavior that is not conducive to the maintenance of the integrity of the public school system." . . .

But here there is no proof of improper conduct. The only whit of evidence offered as support for the board's conclusion that Mrs. Fisher was guilty of unbecoming conduct was the fact that she had overnight guests. But the presence of these guests in her home provides no inkling beyond subtle implication and innuendo which would impugn Mrs. Fisher's morality. Idle speculation certainly does not provide a basis in fact for the board's conclusory inference that "there was strong potential of sexual misconduct" and that, therefore, Mrs. Fisher's activity was "social misbehavior that is not conducive to the maintenance of the integrity of the public school system." We agree with the district court that "At most, the evidence may be said to raise a question of Mrs. Fisher's good judgment in her personal affairs, when measured against an undefined standard which someone could suppose exists in a small town in Nebraska." . . .

The record, furthermore, contains considerable evidence tending to negate any inference of improper or immoral conduct by Mrs. Fisher. She did not attempt to conceal the presence of her house guests but instead openly inquired of the school board's secretary about motel accommodations in Tryon for these guests. She was advised to keep them in her home because other accommodations were so limited. She formally introduced one of her guests at school so that he might observe classes to satisfy college requirements. The local Avon lady, wife of the pastor of a church in Tryon, called at Mrs. Fisher's residence on a Saturday morning during the 1970–1971 school year. Although Mrs. Fisher was apparently awakened by the visit, she invited the pastor's wife into her apartment. A young man who had been an overnight guest was also present in the apartment, and the three drank coffee together.

Two citizens of Tryon called as witnesses for the school board were subpoenaed. Their testimony cast no aspersions upon Mrs. Fisher's character or her fitness as a teacher. No evidence of a community reaction against Mrs. Fisher has been presented . . . nor has she been shown incapable of maintaining discipline in her classes because of any inferences of impropriety drawn by her students or their parents.

This evidence, in the context of our review of the entire record, convinces us of the correctness of the district court's determination. The openness of the association, and the age differential between Mrs. Fisher and her guests, would seem to belie any inference of impropriety. The school board's inference of misconduct was arbitrary and capricious and therefore constituted an impermissible reason for terminating her employment, since the inference lacked any valid basis in fact.

Accordingly, we affirm the judgment of the district court.

*Homosexuality of Teacher Is
Immorality Justifying Dismissal*

GAYLORD v. TACOMA
SCHOOL DISTRICT NO. 10

Supreme Court of Washington, 1977.
88 Wash.2d 286, 559 P.2d 1340.

HOROWITZ, Associate Justice. Plaintiff-appellant, James Gaylord, appeals a judgment of the trial court upholding Gaylord's discharge from employment as a high school teacher by defendant school district. . . .

Defendant school district discharged Gaylord—who held a teacher's certificate—from his teaching position at the Wilson High School in Tacoma on the ground of "immorality" because he was a known homosexual. . . .

We need consider only the assignments of error which raise two basic issues: (1) whether substantial evidence supports the trial court's conclusion plaintiff-appellant Gaylord was guilty of immorality; (2) whether substantial evidence supports the findings, that as a known homosexual, Gaylord's fitness as a teacher was impaired to the injury of the Wilson High School, justifying his discharge by the defendant school district's board of directors. The relevant findings of the trial court may be summarized as follows.

Gaylord knew of his homosexuality for twenty years prior to his trial, actively sought homosexual company for the past several years, and participated in homosexual acts. He knew his status as a homosexual, if known, would jeopardize his employment, damage his reputation and hurt his parents.

Gaylord's school superior first became aware of his sexual status on October 24, 1972, when a former Wilson High student told the school's vice-principal he thought Gaylord was a homosexual. The vice-principal confronted Gaylord at his home that same day with a written copy of the student's statement. Gaylord admitted he was a homosexual and attempted unsuccessfully to have the vice-principal drop the matter.

On November 21, 1972, Gaylord was notified the board of directors of the Tacoma School Board had found probable cause for his discharge due to his status as a publicly known homosexual. This status was contrary to school district policy No. 4119(5), which provides for discharge of school employees for "immorality." After hearing, the defendant board of directors discharged Gaylord effective December 21, 1972.

The court found an admission of homosexuality connotes illegal as well as immoral acts, because "sexual gratification with a member of one's own sex is implicit in the term 'homosexual.'" These acts were proscribed by RCW 9.79.120 (lewdness) and RCW 9.79.100 (sodomy).

After Gaylords' homosexual status became publicly known, it would and did impair his teaching efficiency. A teacher's efficiency is determined by his relationship with his students, their parents, the school administration and fellow teachers. If Gaylord had not been discharged after he became known as a homosexual, the result would be fear, confusion, suspicion, parental concern and pressure on the administration by students, parents and other teachers.

The court concluded "appellant was properly discharged by respondent upon a charge of immorality upon his admission and disclosure that he was a homosexual" and that relief sought should be denied.

Was Gaylord guilty of immorality?

Our concern here is with the meaning of immorality in the sense intended by school board policy No. 4119(5). School boards have broad management powers. RCW 28A.58. Under RCW 28A.58.100(1) the school board may discharge teachers for "sufficient cause." Policy No. 4119(5) adopted by the school board and in effect during the term of Gaylord's teaching contract with defendant school district permits the Tacoma School Board of Directors to treat "immorality" as sufficient cause for discharge.

"Immorality" as used in policy No. 4119(5) does not stand alone. RCW 28A.67.110 makes it the duty of all teachers to "endeavor to impress on the minds of their pupils the principles of morality, truth, justice, temperance, humanity, and patriotism. . . . " RCW 28A.70.140 requires that an applicant for a teacher's certificate be "a person of good moral character." RCW 28A.70.160 makes "immorality" a ground for revoking a teacher's certificate. Other grounds include the commission of "crimes against the laws of the state." The moral conduct of a teacher is relevant to a consideration of that person's fitness or ability to function adequately as a teacher of the students he is expected to teach—in this case high school students. . . .

"Immorality" as a ground of teacher discharge would be unconstitutionally vague if not coupled with resulting actual or prospective adverse performance as a teacher. . . . The basic statute permitting discharge for "sufficient cause" (RCW 28A.58.100(1)) has been construed to require the cause must adversely affect the teacher's performance before it can be invoked as a ground for discharge. . . .

The next question is whether the plaintiff's performance as a teacher was sufficiently impaired by his known homosexuality to be the basis for discharge. The court found that Gaylord, prior to his discharge on December 21, 1972, had been a teacher at the Wilson High School in the Tacoma School District No. 10 for over twelve years, and had received favorable evaluations of his teaching throughout this time. (Findings of fact Nos. 1 and 2.) The court further found that "while plaintiff's status as a homosexual [was] unknown to others in the school," his teaching efficiency was not affected nor did his status injure the school. When, however, it became publicly known that Gaylord was a homosexual "the knowledge thereof would and did impair his efficiency as a teacher with resulting injury to the school had he not been discharged." (Finding of fact No. 9.)

The court further found:

> A teacher's efficiency is determined by his relationship with students, their parents, fellow teachers and school administrators. In all of these areas the continued employment of appellant after he became known as a homosexual would result, had he not been discharged, in confusion, suspicion, fear, expressed parental concern and pressure upon the administration from students, parents and fellow teachers, all of which would impair appellant's efficiency as a teacher and injure the school. (Finding of fact No. 10.)

Gaylord assigns error to findings of fact numbers 9 and 10, contending there is no substantial evidence to support either. We do not agree.

First, he argues his homosexuality became known at the school only after the school made it known and that he should not be responsible therefor so as to justify his discharge as a homosexual. The difficulty with this argument is twofold. First, by seeking out homosexual company he took the risk his homosexuality would be discovered. It was he who granted an interview to the boy who talked to him about his homosexual problems. The boy had been referred to Gaylord for that purpose by the homosexual friend to whom Gaylord had responded favorably in answering his advertisement in the paper of the Dorian Society. As a result of that interview the boy came away with the impression plaintiff was a homosexual and later told the assistant high school principal about the matter. The latter in turn conferred with plaintiff for the purpose of verifying the charge that had been made. It was the vice-principal's duty to report the information to his superiors because it involved the performance capabilities of Gaylord. The school cannot be charged with making plaintiff's condition known so as to defeat the school board's duty to protect the school and the students against the impairment of the learning process in all aspects involved.

Second, there is evidence that at least one student expressly objected to Gaylord teaching at the high school because of his homosexuality. Three fellow teachers testified against Gaylord remaining on the teaching staff, testifying it was objectionable to them both as teachers and parents. The vice-principal and the principal, as well as the retired superintendent of instruction, testified his presence on the faculty would create problems. There is conflicting evidence on the issue of impairment but the court had the power to accept the testimony it did on which to base complained of findings. . . . The testimony of the school teachers and administrative personnel constituted substantial evidence sufficient to support the findings as to the impairment of the teacher's efficiency.

It is important to remember that Gaylord's homosexual conduct must be considered in the context of his position of teaching high school students. Such students could treat the retention of the high school teacher by the school board as indicating adult approval of his homosexuality. It would be unreasonable to assume as a matter of law a teacher's ability to perform as a teacher required to teach principles of morality (RCW 28A.67.110) is not impaired and creates no danger of encouraging expression of approval and of imitation. Likewise to say that school directors must wait for prior specific overt expression of homosexual conduct before they act to prevent harm from one who chooses to remain "erotically attracted to a notable degree towards persons of his own sex and is psychologically, if not actually, disposed to engage in sexual activity prompted by this attraction" is to ask the school directors to take an unacceptable risk in discharging their fiduciary responsibility of managing the affairs of the school district.

We do not deal here with homosexuality which does not impair or cannot reasonably be said to impair his ability to perform the duties of an occupation in which the homosexual engages and which does not impair the effectiveness of the institution which employs him. However, even the federal civil service regulations on which Gaylord relies to show a change in attitude towards homosexuals provides:

> [W]hile a person may not be found unsuitable based on unsubstantiated conclusions concerning possible embarrassment to the Federal service, a person may be dismissed or found unsuitable for Federal employment where the evidence establishes that such person's sexual conduct affects job fitness. 2 CCH Employment Practice's Guide ¶ 5339 (1975).

It must be shown that "the conduct of the individual may reasonably be expected to interfere with the ability of the person's fitness in the job or against the ability to discharge its responsibility." 2 CCH, supra. These principles are similar to those applicable here. The challenged findings and conclusions are supported by substantial evidence.

Affirmed.

NOTES

1. Dismissal of a homosexual for immorality by a board of education must demonstrate a rational nexus between the conduct of the teacher and fitness to teach. A showing of potential rather than actual harm to students will suffice. Factors such as adverse effect on students or fellow teachers, adversity anticipated within school system, surrounding circumstances, and possible chilling effects on discipline may be used to establish unfitness. Morrison v. State Board of Education, 1 Cal.3d 214, 82 Cal.Rptr. 175, 461 P.2d 375 (1969).

2. The dismissal of a teacher who underwent a change of sex has been held to constitute incapacity. The tenured teacher changed his external anatomy to that of a female and was subsequently dismissed by the board, which reasoned that the situation would cause emotional harm to students. The teacher's proficiency in the classroom was not in question. According to the court, a teacher's fitness to teach is not based entirely upon academic proficiency but depends on a broad range of factors. One of those factors the court said, was the "teacher's impact and effect upon his or her students" and the impact in this case would be harmful to the children. In re Grossman, 127 N.J. Super. 13, 316 A.2d 39 (1974).

3. Arrest for a homosexual act by a teacher was held to be sufficient grounds for board to dismiss him. Although the teacher was later acquitted the court held that the difference in burden of proof in

criminal and civil cases precludes application of the doctrine of res judicata. The court said:

> Our legislature properly intended by the enactment of the pertinent sections of the Education Code to permit school boards to shield children of tender years from the possible detrimental influence of teachers who commit acts described therein even though they are not found guilty beyond a reasonable doubt . . . the criminal charge between defendant and the state was penal in nature while the case between defendant and the board is remedial, for the protection of young children. Board of Education v. Calderon, 35 Cal.App.3d 490, 110 Cal. Rptr. 916 (1973); See also Pettit v. State Board of Education, 10 Cal.3d 29, 109 Cal.Rptr. 665, 513 P.2d 889 (1973).

4. Although illegally obtained evidence cannot be used against a defendant teacher for alleged homosexual activity in a criminal proceeding, the same evidence is admissible in an administrative hearing by the school board to determine the teacher's fitness and moral character. Governing Bd. v. Metcalf, 36 Cal.App.3d 546, 111 Cal.Rptr. 724 (1974).

5. In a dismissal proceeding for immorality, the school board must relate the immoral conduct to the teacher's fitness. In so doing the board may consider such matters as the age and maturity of the teacher's students, the likelihood that the conduct will adversely affect students, the degree of adversity, proximity or remoteness of the conduct, the likelihood that the conduct would be repeated, and the underlying motives for the conduct. Weissman v. Board of Education of Jefferson County School District No. R–1, 190 Colo. 414, 547 P.2d 1267 (1976).

6. Teachers are role models and because of the exemplary nature of teaching, the courts have left little question about the seriousness of sexual involvement with students. A tenured teacher was dismissed for immorality when he tickled and touched female students while on a field trip. He also made sexual remarks and innuendos. The teacher, who had a reputation as a good teacher, contended there was no nexus between his conduct and his classroom performance. The court determined his activities constituted unfitness to teach. Weissman v. Board of Education of Jefferson County School District, 190 Colo. 414, 547 P.2d 1267 (1976).

7. Two teachers had their teaching certificates revoked for growing fifty-two marijuana plants in a greenhouse. The court determined that since teachers are in leadership positions they are obligated to maintain high moral standards in the community. The possession of the plants impaired their effectiveness as teachers. Adams v. State Professional Practices Council, 406 So.2d 1170 (Fla.App.1981) petition denied 412 So. 2d 463.

8. An unmarried pregnant teacher was dismissed for immorality. The school district argued that "unwed parenthood is per se proof of immorality and that a parent of an illegitimate child is an unfit role model." But the school district could offer no support of either assertion. "Therefore, we hold that Avery's discharge was in violation of her rights under the equal protection clause of the Fourteenth Amendment." Avery v. Homewood City Board of Education, 674 F.2d 337 (5th Cir.1982).

9. A permanent teacher was dismissed for immorality because, in a racially mixed class, he told some disruptive students, "How many times a day do I have to ask you dumb niggers to stop playing around, stop talking, and get to work." The teacher maintained that immorality involved only physical sexual behavior but the court stated "(t)he term 'immoral' has been defined generally as that which is hostile to the welfare of the general public and contrary to good morals. Immorality has not been confined to sexual matters. . . ." The court went on to say "(t)he question . . . is whether it is immoral for a teacher to teach white students that it is all right to engage in conduct which is humiliating, painful, and harmful to individuals, which subjects a class of people to public disdain and ridicule, and which is in violation of rules and regulations adopted by the Board for the purpose of putting an end to racial discrimination. Of necessity, such action must be considered to be immoral, just as if Clarke had instructed the students how to cheat on an examination." Clarke v. Board of Education of School District of Omaha, 215 Neb. 250, 338 N.W.2d 272 (1983). See also Bovino v. Board of School Directors of Indiana Area, 32 Pa. Cmwlth. 105, 377 A.2d 1284 (1977). It was immoral to refer to a student as a "slut" or "prostitute."

10. "(W)e note that statutes from colonial days forward recognize the unique position of teachers as examples to our youth and charge them to 'exert their best endeavors to impress on the minds of children and youth committed to their care and instruction' the values basic to our society . . . requiring school committees to have full and satisfactory evidence of a teacher's moral character. This special role of teachers on impressionable and not fully tutored minds distinguished them from other public officials." Dupree v. School Committee of Boston, 15 Mass.App. Ct. 535, 446 N.E.2d 1099 (1983).

11. Off-campus conduct obstensibly involving consensual sexual conduct between a teacher and an adult of the opposite sex cannot, alone, constitute "good cause" for school board's rejection of superintendent's nomination of the teacher for reemployment. Sherbourne v. School Board of Suwannee County, 455 So.2d 1057 (Fla.App., 1984).

12. Evidence given at a school board hearing in which student testified, corroborated by a polygraph test, that she and teacher had engaged in sexual intercourse was sufficient to support termination for "just cause" of the teacher's contract. Libe v. Board of Education of Twin Cedars, 350 N.W.2d 748 (Iowa App. 1984).

FOOTNOTES

1. Due Process Clause, Fourteenth Amendment, United States Constitution.

2. Board of Regents of State Colleges v. Roth, 408 U.S. 564, 92 S.Ct. 2701 (1972).

3. William Van Alstyne, "The Constitutional Rights of Teachers and Professors," Duke Law Journal, Vol. 1970, No. 5, p. 851. Copyright © 1970 by Duke Law Journal. Reprinted with permission. Originally published at 1970 Duke L.J. 841.

4. Board of Regents of State Colleges v. Roth, supra.

5. Goldberg v. Kelly, 397 U.S. 254, 90 S.Ct. 1011 (1970).

6. Ferguson v. Thomas, 430 F.2d 852, 430 F.2d 945 (1st Cir.1970).

7. Id.

8. Shrick v. Thomas, 447 F.2d 1025 (7th Cir.1971). See also: Gouge v. Joint School District No. 1, 310 F.Supp. 984 (1970); Lucas v. Chapman, 430 F.2d 945 (1st Cir.1970).

9. Shrick, supra.

10. Pred v. Board of Public Instruction of Dade County, 415 F.2d 851 (5th Cir.1969).

11. Id.

12. Board of Regents of State Colleges v. Roth, supra.

13. 408 U.S. 593, 92 S.Ct. 2694 (1972).

14. Id.

15. Id. See: Soni v. Board of Trustees of University of Tennessee, 513 F.2d 347 (6th Cir.1975) *cert. denied* 426 U.S. 919, 96 S.Ct. 2623, where the Circuit Court of Appeals explained some conditions of objective expectancy for reemployment.

16. School District No. 8, Pinal County v. Superior Court of Pinal County, 102 Ariz. 478, 433 P.2d 28 (1967).

15

Discrimination in Employment

The social and political upheavals experienced in the United States after World War II have brought about tremendous changes in employment practices. These movements have spawned both federal and state legislation that has attempted to overcome the effects of past discrimination against minorities and to ensure against reemergence of discrimination in the future. Legislation, such as the Civil Rights Act of 1964, the Equal Pay Act, the Age Discrimination in Employment Act, the Pregnancy Discrimination Act, and the Rehabilitation Act have all addressed issues of employment discrimination. This chapter discusses precedents bearing on race, sex, age, and handicap discrimination emanating from statutes, court decisions, and regulations that have impacted on employment practices in public education.

The Equal Protection Clause is a general protection against invidious discrimination while Title VII is a broad-based legislative prohibition specifically against discrimination due to race, color, religion, sex, or national origin. Other statutes such as the Equal Pay Act and the Age Discrimination Act prohibit practices that classify persons according to sex or age. (See Appendix.) Discrimination against the handicapped is prohibited in the Rehabilitation Act of 1973.

RACE DISCRIMINATION

Since *Brown* v. *Board of Education,* numerous employment practices have been litigated regarding discrimination in public employment. Many cases have challenged hiring and testing practices, reduction of staff resulting in nonretention of minority employees, and reverse discrimination. Most of these cases have been brought under the Equal Protection Clause of the Fourteenth Amendment and Title VII of the Civil Rights Act of 1964. Title VI of the Civil Rights Act allows a federal agency to withhold funds if discrimination has been proven.

Equal Protection

The standards under the Equal Protection Clause are not precisely the same as under the various statutory provisions that have been designed by Congress to eradicate discrimination. The equal protection standard as developed in the school desegregation cases prohibits discrimination that can be ultimately traced to a racially motivated purpose.[1] As discussed in the chapter on desegregation, remedial action to overcome segregation will not be required by the courts under the Equal Protection Clause unless it can be shown that the segregation was caused by official actions, the purpose and intent of which was to discriminate.[2] To show merely that the effect of a neutral policy results in segregation is not sufficient to prove violation of the equal protection of employment opportunity.

If plaintiffs cannot show that segregation was a result of discriminatory purpose or intent the state need only show that its actions were not irrational. On the other hand, if discriminatory intent is shown, the state must bear the burden of showing that it had a compelling reason to act as it did.

In contrast, Title VII imposes a more rigorous standard on the state. Under Title VII, Congress provided that where employment practices are concerned, discriminatory purpose need not be proved, and it is insufficient for the state to show merely a rational basis to justify its challenged practice.[3]

The Supreme Court has set out evidentiary guidelines that plaintiffs must sustain in supporting claims of a discriminatory purpose. Topically, these are: (1) historical background, (2) specific sequence of events leading to the passage or implementation of the practice, (3) departure from accepted practices and normal procedures, (4) substantial departures, and (5) legislative and administrative history. In commenting further, the Supreme Court has said that: "Determining whether invidious discriminatory purpose was a motivating factor demands a sensitive inquiry into such circumstances and direct evidence of intent as may be available. The impact of the official action . . . may provide an important starting point."[4]

Title VI

Title VI of the Civil Rights Act prohibits discrimination based on race, color, or national origin. (See Appendix for exact wording of the statute.) With Title VI Congress provided a statutory remedy against discrimination that could be administered by federal agencies in their regulatory capacity. The ultimate enforcement weapon given the federal agencies under this law is the denial of federal funds. It was under Title VI that the *Adams* v. *Richardson* case [5] (presented in the chapter on student rights) originated because plaintiffs felt that the Department of Health, Education and Welfare had been derelict in its enforcement responsibilities. In that case, the federal court assumed the responsibility for monitoring enforcement of federal regulations promulgated pursuant to Title VI. The regulations require desegregation of faculty, administration, and other personnel positions in public schools and universities (43 F.R. 6658, Feb. 15, 1978).

Recently, the Supreme Court has exhibited some uncertainty as to the application of Title VI. The problem lies in whether officials are required to redress *de jure* segregation only or whether they have a corresponding statutory obligation to correct racial imbalance caused by *de facto* segregation as well. In the *Bakke* case Justice Powell, writing for a splintered majority, said that Title VI requirements were coterminous with those of the Equal Protection Clause, that neither required school officials to correct unintended racial imbalances.[6] On the other hand, four justices, while agreeing with Powell's general disposition of the case, disagreed with his interpretation of Title VI, maintaining that congressional intent was to prohibit discrimination, regardless of intent. Writing for these four judges, Justice Stevens said that "the meaning of the Title VI ban on exclusion is crystal clear: Race cannot be the basis of excluding anyone from participation in a federally funded program." He further maintained that it was not necessary to liken Title VI to the Equal Protection Clause since Title VI's origins emanated from its own legislative intent and history. Having said this, however, the Court did not resolve the fundamental issue of whether Title VI requires affirmative administrative response for unintended segregation.

Some clarification of the intent questions under Title VI did come forth in 1983 in the case of *Guardians* v. *Civil Service Commission of New York*[7] wherein the Court held that a private person may be compensated for a state agency's violation of his Title VI rights, but only if the person is able to show intent to discriminate. In other words, as now written, intent must be shown to exist before Title VI is violated and federal funds can be withheld.

Title VII

When first enacted in 1970,[8] Title VII did not extend to discriminatory employment practices in educational institutions, but in 1972 the law was amended, eliminating this exemption.[9] As a result, it is Title VII that has been used most often to challenge discrimination in teacher and administrator employment.

An area of important concern in applying Title VII has been employee testing for purposes of hiring and promotion. The position of the United States Supreme Court on employee testing was enunciated in 1971 in *Griggs* v. *Duke Power Co.*[10] In this case, the Court found that Title VII of the Civil Rights Act prevented an employer from rejecting black job applicants on the basis of lack of completion of high school or on the results of a general intelligence test. Duke Power Company was unable to show that the general standards it had established were related to job performance. The Court said:

> The facts of this case demonstrate the inadequacy of broad and general testing devices as well as the infirmity of using diplomas or degrees as fixed measures of capability. Nothing in the Act precludes the use of testing or measuring procedures; obviously they are useful. What Congress has forbidden is giving

these devices and mechanisms controlling force unless they are demonstrably a reasonable measure of job performance.[11]

After *Griggs* several lower courts invalidated the use of the Graduate Record Examination and the National Teachers Examination as violative of due process and equal protection because the examinations were not job related. School districts, in these instances, were unable to shoulder the burden of showing job relatedness in the face of the high percentage of black teachers who were disqualified.[12]

According to *Griggs,* after the plaintiff successfully shows that the effect of a particular employment practice is to create a racial imbalance the burden then shifts to the defendant to justify the practice by showing that the imbalance is related to job performance. The Supreme Court has attempted to further clarify the issues by creating a distinction between *disparate treatment* and *disparate impact* cases and has explained the two terms in this way:

> "Disparate treatment" . . . is the most easily understood type of discrimination. The employer simply treats some people less favorably than others because of their race, color, religion, sex, or national origin. Proof of discriminatory motive is critical, although it can in some situations be inferred from the mere fact of differences in treatment . . . . Undoubtedly disparate treatment was the most obvious and Congress had it in mind when it enacted Title VII . . . . Claims of disparate treatment may be distinguished from claims that stress "disparate impact." The latter involves employment practices that are facially neutral in their treatment of different groups but in fact fall more heavily on one group than another and cannot be justified by business necessity . . . .. Proof of discriminatory motive, we have held, is not required under a disparate impact theory.[13]

Disparate treatment cases generally occur when a single plaintiff challenges a particular practice that is detrimental to him or her personally. For example, a faculty member's claim that her promotion in a particular academic department was denied because of bias must be brought as a disparate treatment issue. The nature of the facts do not lend themselves to a showing of impact. On the other hand, disparate impact may be more easily shown in cases involving a number of persons who are affected by a particular employment practice, such as a requirement that all employees pass a test.

When a plaintiff shows evidence to substantiate a claim of disparate impact the employer must then bear the burden of showing that the particular employment practice was justified as a "business necessity" or that it was "related to job performance." For example, a written examination indicating one's level of verbal skills has been held a valid device to select recruits for a police department.[14] Similarly, the use of the National Teacher Examination has been found to be a valid "job related" instrument to determine teacher qualifications for employment and pay.[15]

Thus the Supreme Court has enunciated two routes for plaintiffs to pursue discrimination under Title VII, disparate treatment and disparate impact. Under the former, the initial burden of proof is difficult to bear because the plaintiff must show a discriminatory motive. Under the latter, the initial burden of the plaintiff is less difficult to sustain, but this is offset because the courts have allowed substantial leeway to defendants in showing "business necessity" or "job relatedness." In either instance, taking into account trends and philosophy of the current Supreme Court, plaintiffs may have an increasingly difficult burden in supporting claims of discrimination in the future.

Reverse Discrimination

The term reverse discrimination has surfaced in recent years when referring to the use of remedial legislation as under Titles VI and VII. In *Furnco Construction Corp.* v. *Waters*,[16] the Supreme Court stated that Title VII "does not impose a duty to adopt a hiring procedure that maximizes hiring of minority employees"; the act only prohibits an employer from discriminating against an employee. Job requirements must be neutral. In *McDonald* v. *Santa Fe Train Transportation Co.*,[17] the Court said, "Title VI, whose terms are not limited to discrimination against members of any particular race, prohibits racial discrimination in private employment against white persons upon the same standards as racial discrimination against nonwhites."

In the aforementioned case of the *University of California* v. *Bakke*,[18] the University's medical school admissions program was challenged by a student applicant named Bakke. The school had established two admission programs, the first, the regular admission program, considered the applicant's grade point average, scores on the Medical College Admissions Test, and other requirements, such as recommendations. Under this plan applicants could be either minority or nonminority, and each year a few minorities were accepted into the medical school through this regular applicant process. The second admissions program was designated for blacks, Chicanos, Asians, and American Indians. These candidates were screened on similar standards as those in the regular admissions process but were given special consideration because of their disadvantaged backgrounds. Minority candidates who did not qualify for the regular program were eligible for admission under the special admission program.

The plaintiff, Bakke, a white applicant, challenged the admission process, charging reverse discrimination based on the Equal Protection Clause of the Fourteenth Amendment and Title VI of the Civil Rights Act of 1964. Mr. Bakke stated that he was only allowed to apply for one of eighty-four positions, while a minority candidate could apply for one of the regular eighty-four slots and, if not successful in the regular process, could apply for one of the sixteen reserved positions.

The Supreme Court decided the case on Title VI grounds and did not address the Fourteenth Amendment issue of equal protection. The Court held that the use of "quotas" was not allowable and that the admission system was quota based. It also determined that race may be used as a factor in admission programs and it may even be "weighted" more heavily, but it cannot be the sole and decisive factor.

In 1979, in the case of *United Steelworkers, etc.* v. *Weber*[19] an employee of a steel company claimed reverse discrimination. The United Steelworkers and Kaiser Aluminum had negotiated an agreement that included a provision for the elimination of racial imbalance at the Kaiser Aluminum Plant. The agreement provided that craft-training positions would be reserved for minorities until the percentage of blacks in the craft workforce equaled the percentage of blacks in the local labor market. In the first year of the agreement, thirteen individuals were selected for craft training, seven blacks and six whites. The most senior black of the group had less seniority than a number of white workers who were not selected. The white workers who were not selected filed suit claiming reverse discrimination based on Title VII of the Civil Rights Act of 1964. The Supreme Court ruled that the mutually agreed-upon contract did not violate Title VII because not all private, voluntary, race-conscious, affirmative action plans instituted by companies are prohibited. The Court left open the question of what kind of a voluntary, private, affirmative action program actually does violate Title VII. "We need not today define in detail the line of demarcation between permissible and impermissible affirmative action plans. It suffices to hold that the challenged Kaiser-USWA affirmative action plan falls on the permissible side of the line."[20]

*Employment Standards and Tests
That Are Not Significantly Related to
Job Performance Violate the Civil
Rights Act of 1964*

GRIGGS v. DUKE POWER CO.

Supreme Court of the United States, 1971.
401 U.S. 424, 91 S.Ct. 849.

Mr. Chief Justice BURGER delivered the opinion of the Court.

We granted the writ in this case to resolve the question whether an employer is prohibited by the Civil Rights Act of 1964, Title VII, from requiring a high school education or passing of a standardized general intelligence test as a condition of employment in or transfer to jobs when (a) neither standard is shown to be significantly related to successful job performance, (b) both requirements operate to disqualify Negroes at a substantially higher rate than white applicants, and (c) the jobs in question formerly had been filled only by white employees as part of a longstanding practice of giving preference to whites. . . . .

The objective of Congress in the enactment of Title VII is plain from the language of the statute. It was to achieve equality of employment opportunities and remove barriers that have operated in the past to favor an identifiable group of white employees over other employees. Under the Act, practices, procedures, or tests neutral on their face, and even neutral in terms of intent, cannot be maintained if they operate to "freeze" the status quo of prior discriminatory employment practices.

The Court of Appeals' opinion, and the partial dissent, agreed that, on the record in the present case, "whites register far better on the Company's alternative requirements" than Negroes. . . . . Because they are Negroes, petitioners have long received inferior education in segregated schools and this court expressly recognized these differences in Gaston County v. United States, 395 U.S. 285, 89 S.Ct. 1720 (1969). . . . Congress did not intend by Title VII, however, to guarantee a job to every person regardless of qualifications. In short, the Act does not command that any person be hired simply because he was formerly the subject of discrimination, or because he is a member of a minority group. Discriminatory preference for any group, minority or majority, is precisely and only what Congress has proscribed. What is required by Congress is the removal of artificial, arbitrary, and unnecessary barriers to employment when the barriers operate invidiously to discriminate on the basis of racial or other impermissible classification.

. . . The Act proscribes not only overt discrimination but also practices that are fair in form, but discriminatory in operation. The touchstone is business necessity. If an employment practice that operates to exclude Negroes cannot be shown to be related to job performance, the practice is prohibited.

On the record before us, neither the high school completion requirement nor the general intelligence test is shown to bear a demonstrable relationship to successful performance of the jobs for which it was used. Both were adopted, as the Court of Appeals noted, without meaningful study of their relationship to job-performance ability. . . .

The evidence, however, shows that employees who have not completed high school or taken the tests have continued to perform satisfactorily and make progress in departments for which the high school and test criteria are not used. The promotion record of present employees who would not be able to meet the new criteria thus suggests the possibility that the requirements may not be needed even for the limited purpose of preserving the avowed policy of advancement within the Company. . . .

The Court of Appeals held that the Company had adopted the diploma and test requirements without any "intention to discriminate against Negro employees." . . . But Congress directed the thrust of the Act to the *consequences* of employment practices, not simply the motivation. More than that, Congress has placed on the employer the burden of showing that any given requirement must have a manifest relationship to the employment in question.

The facts of this case demonstrate the inadequacy of broad and general testing devices as well as the infirmity of using diplomas or degrees as fixed measures of capability. . . .

Nothing in the Act precludes the use of testing or measuring procedures; obviously they are useful. What Congress has forbidden is giving these devices and mechanisms controlling force unless they are demonstrably a reasonable measure of job performance. Congress has not commanded that the less qualified be preferred over the better qualified simply because of minority origins. Far from disparaging job qualifications as such, Congress has made such qualifications the controlling factor, so that race, religion, nationality, and sex become irrelevant. What Congress has commanded is that any tests used must measure the person for the job and not the person in the abstract.

*State Use of Test Scores for Both
Certification Purposes and as a
Salary Factor Does Not Violate Equal
Protection Clause or Title VII of Civil
Rights Act*

UNITED STATES OF
AMERICA v. STATE OF
SOUTH CAROLINA

United States District Court, District of
South Carolina, Columbia Div., 1977.
445 F.Supp. 1094, aff'd 434 U.S. 1026, 98
S.Ct. 756, 1978.

Before HAYNSWORTH and RUSSELL, Circuit Judges and SIMONS, District Judge. . . . The defendants are charged with violations of the Fourteenth Amendment to the Constitution of the United States and Title VII of the Civil Rights Act of 1964, as amended, 42 U.S.C. § 2000e, et seq., (1970), through the use of minimum score requirements on the National Teacher Examinations (hereinafter "NTE") to certify and determine the pay levels of teachers within the State. . . .

For over thirty years the State of South Carolina and its agencies have used scores on the NTE to make decisions with respect to the certification of teachers and the amount of state aid payable to local school districts. Local school boards within the State use scores on the NTE for selection and compensation of teachers. From 1969 to 1976, a minimum score of 975 was required by the State for its certification and state aid decisions. In June, 1976, after an exhaustive validation study by Educational Testing Service (ETS), and after a critical review and evaluation of this study by the Board of Education's Committee on Teacher Recruitment, Training and Compensation and the Department Staff, the State established new certification requirements involving different minimum scores in various areas of teaching specialization that range from 940 to 1198. . . .

Plaintiffs challenge each of the uses of the NTE. They contend that more blacks than whites historically have failed to achieve the required minimum score, and that this result creates a racial classification in violation of the constitutional and statutory provisions cited in their complaints. . . .

I. CONSTITUTIONAL ISSUES

We first consider whether the use by the State and its Board of Education of a minimum score requirement on the NTE violates the equal protection clause of the Fourteenth Amendment. . . .

In disposing of the remaining constitutional claims, separate consideration must be given to the State's use of the test scores to certify teachers and to determine the amount of state aid for local school districts. Plaintiffs allege that the disparate racial impact of defendants' certification and compensation systems creates a racial classification in violation of the Fourteenth Amendment. In order to sustain that allegation, the Supreme Court's decision in Washington v. Davis, 426 U.S. 229, 96 S.Ct. 2040, 48 L.Ed.

2d 597 (1976), requires plaintiffs to prove that the State intended to create and use a racial classification. If plaintiffs fail to prove intent (or defendants adequately rebut that proof), then we must evaluate this classification under the rational relationship standard required by the Fourteenth Amendment as to all such classifications.

A. Discriminatory Intent Because of its paramount importance under *Washington* v. *Davis,* we look first at whether the plaintiffs have proved that any of the challenged decisions of defendants were motivated by an intent to discriminate. The purpose or intent that we must assess is the purpose or intent that underlies the particular act or acts under review. . . .

1. Certification South Carolina requires persons who teach in the public schools to hold a certificate issued by the State Board of Education. S.C. Code § 21–354. From 1945 to the present the State has had four certification systems, each requiring prospective teachers to take the NTE. Candidates are able to take the NTE an unlimited number of times. (The tests are given by the State three or four times each year).

The record before us indicates that during this period, the racial composition of the South Carolina teacher force has closely paralleled the racial composition of the State's population. . . .

From 1945 through 1968, the State issued four grades of certificates: A, B, C and D. From 1945 through 1956, candidates were awarded certificates based on their relative standing with respect to test scores of all candidates in the State for the year. . . .

In 1957, a new system of absolute, rather than relative, requirements was instituted. Under this system, a score of 500 or more on the Common Examinations portion of the NTE was required for an *A* certificate; a score of 425 to 499 for a *B* certificate; a score of 375 to 424 for a *C* certificate; and a score of 332 to 374 for a *D* certificate. . . .

In 1969, the certification system was further revised by replacing the four-tiered system with two types of certificates: the professional certificate and the warrant. . . . Those who attained scores below 400 were not licensed. In the academic year 1969–70, the maximum score requirement of 400 on the Common Examinations eliminated approximately 41 percent of the graduates of predominantly black colleges and less than 1 percent of the graduates of predominantly white colleges. Similar results were obtained in succeeding years, despite the fact that a score of 400 is usually below the 11th percentile nationally, and almost 90 percent of the candidates who take these tests get a higher score.

In 1976, the certification system was again revised, the two-tiered sytem being replaced with a single certificate with separate minimum score requirements in each of the eighteen fields of teaching specialty replacing the single minimum score requirement. These combined scores on both Common Examinations and Area Examinations ranged from 940 in Agriculture to 1178 in Library and Media Specialties; and are set forth in detail hereinafter. There are no statistics in the record indicating the impact of the new score requirements because they will be applied first to the class of 1977; however, plaintiffs predict that, under these requirements the disparate impact may be even greater. . . .

With respect to the constitutional challenge to South Carolina's use of the NTE for certification purposes, we conclude that the plaintiffs have not demonstrated the required discriminatory intent with respect to any of the specific decisions setting certification standards based on NTE scores. This is especially true in connection with the State's 1976 change in requirements where there is no indication whatsoever that the State and its officers were motivated by anything more than a desire to use an accepted and racially neutral standardized test to evaluate the teacher applicants competing for relatively few jobs in South Carolina.

The NTE are developed and administered by ETS, an independent non-profit organization of recognized professional reputation. ETS recommends that minimum score requirements not be used as a sole determinant of certification decisions where other appropriate information or criteria are available.

In this case, the plaintiffs have come forth with no other reasonably appropriate criteria upon which certification may be properly based.

Neither have plaintiffs been able to establish any defect in the NTE indicating that the examinations themselves discriminate on the basis of race. The choices as to subject matter and question format are reasonable and well-documented on the record, and although other subject matters or other examination forms might be possible or even preferable, there is no proof of any inherent discrimination. The inference that plaintiffs would have us draw from the statistics which indicate that blacks as a group have lower average scores than whites is rebutted by the evidence with respect to the construction of the tests and their content validity. Since we find that the NTE create classifications only on permissible bases (presence or absence of knowledge or skill and ability in applying knowledge), and that they are not used pursuant to any intent to discriminate, their use in making certification decisions by the State is proper and legal.

2. *Pay scales* Plaintiffs raise a separate constitutional challenge to South Carolina's use of the NTE as a partial determinant of the salaries paid to public school teachers. The use of the NTE for salary purposes is distinct from, and, in significant ways, unrelated to the use of the NTE for certification purposes. Accordingly, we must again examine plaintiffs' proof with respect to intent.   .   .   .

We are unable to find a discriminatory intent from these facts, even though the historical background of a dual pay system and a delay in implementing a unitary system after the Fourth Circuit struck down a similar system in another state provide some support for such an inference. Such inference is adequately rebutted by the evidence with respect to what the Legislature actually did. The unitary pay system was based in part on the amount of educational training and years of teaching experience possessed by each teacher. Plaintiffs make no claim that the use of either of these factors was motivated by discriminatory intent, and it is evident that the monetary rewards available through these avenues alone, without regard to the grade of certificate, were significant. The link between the new unitary pay system and the new certification system is not without a reasoned basis. It was important to the State to use its limited resources to improve the quality of the teacher force and to put whatever monetary incentives were available in the salary schedule to that task. As before stated, we have found that no discriminatory intent has been established with respect to the decision in 1945 to adopt a certification system based in part on NTE scores; and, therefore, without independent proof, there is no associated discriminatory intent in linking the certification and salary systems. . . .

Plaintiffs urge that the Legislature was motivated by an intent to discriminate because the state aid schedule provided fewer benefits and incentives for two classifications of teachers in which there were relatively more blacks than whites; the classifications continued to be based, if only in part, on examination scores; and the developer of the tests was later opposed to their use for this purpose. In the absence of any competent or persuasive direct evidence of intent, plaintiffs would have us draw an inference from the facts that are available. But such an inference can stand only if there is no equally persuasive explanation consistent with a legitimate intent. Here the reordering of priorities with respect to the limited resources available for teacher salaries appears entirely consistent with an intent to obtain the maximum incentive for improvement that could be accomplished with a fixed number of dollars. We are unable to find an intent to discriminate.

B. *Application of Rational Relationship Standard* In the absence of discriminatory intent, the classifications of teachers for both certification and pay purposes may be assessed under the "rational relationship" standard required by the Fourteenth Amendment of all classifications.

The Supreme Court has defined this standard in the following terms:

> Although no precise formula has been developed, the Court has held that the Fourteenth Amendment permits the States a wide scope of discretion in enacting laws which affect some groups of citizens differently than others. The constitutional safeguard is offended only if the classification rests on grounds wholly irrelevant to the achievement of the State's objective. State legislatures are presumed to have acted within their constitutional power despite the fact that, in practice, their laws result in some inequality. A statutory discrimination will not be set aside if any state of facts reasonably may be conceived to justify it. McGowan v. Maryland, 366 U.S. 420, 425–26, 81 S.Ct. 1101, 1105, 6 L.Ed.2d 393 (1961).

We conclude that the State's use of the NTE for both certification and pay purposes meets the "rational relationship" standard of *McGowan* v. *Maryland,* supra, and consequently does not violate the equal protection clause of the Fourteenth Amendment. . . .

. . . we find that the defendants have offered a legitimate and important governmental objective for their use of the NTE. The State has the right to adopt academic requirements and to use written achievement tests designed and validated to disclose the minimum amount of knowledge necessary to effective teaching. . . . The evidence in the record supports a finding that South Carolina officials were concerned with improving the quality of public school teaching, certifying only those applicants possessed of the minimum knowledge necessary to teach effectively, utilizing an objective measure of applicants coming from widely disparate teacher training programs, and providing appropriate financial incentives for teachers to improve their academic qualifications and thereby their ability to teach. We conclude that these are entirely legitimate and clearly important governmental objectives.

In considering whether defendants' use of the NTE bears a fair and substantial relationship to these governmental objectives, we conclude that it does.

The record supports the conclusion that the NTE are professionally and carefully prepared to measure the critical mass of knowledge in academic subject matter. The NTE do not measure teaching skills, but do measure the content of the academic preparation of prospective teachers. . . . the NTE program "is neutral on its face and rationally may be said to serve a purpose the Government is constitutionally empowered to pursue." . . . Plaintiffs have not contended nor proved that the NTE are racially biased or otherwise deficient when measured against the applicable professional and legal standards.

Furthermore, there is ample evidence in the record of the content validity of the NTE. The NTE have been demonstrated to provide a useful measure of the extent to which prospective teachers have mastered the content of their teacher training programs. In a similar challenge to a bar examination the Fourth Circuit has held that proof of such content validity is persuasive evidence that the equal protection clause has not been violated. Richardson v. McFadden, 540 F.2d 744 (4th Cir.1976). The Supreme Court has held that a substantial relationship between a test and a training program—such as is found here—is sufficient to withstand challenge on constitutional grounds. Washington v. Davis, 426 U.S. at 248–52, 96 S.Ct. 2040. State officials surely have the right to require graduation from approved teacher training programs as a prerequisite to being certified to teach in South Carolina. Plaintiffs have acknowledged the substantial relationship between the academic training program and the job of teaching by advocating that a requirement of graduation from an approved program *alone* is sufficient to protect the public interest. . . .

We also conclude that defendants' use of the NTE for salary purposes bears the necessary relationship to South Carolina's objectives with respect to its public school teaching force. Although the NTE were not designed to evaluate experienced teachers, the State could reasonably conclude that the NTE provided a reliable and economical means for measuring one element of effective teaching—the degree of knowledge possessed by the teacher. . . .

II. TITLE VII ISSUES

We turn now to the question whether defendants' uses of the NTE violate Title VII, 42 U.S.C.A. § 2000e, et seq.   . . .

The remaining claims under Title VII must be tested under statutory standards. In Washington v. Davis, 426 U.S. 229, 96 S.Ct. 2040, 48 L.Ed.2d 597 (1976), the Supreme Court summarized the order of proof:

> Under Title VII, Congress provided that when hiring and promotion practices disqualifying substantially disproportionate numbers of blacks are challenged, discriminatory purpose need not be proved, and that it is an insufficient response to demonstrate some rational basis for the challenged practices. It is necessary, in addition, that they be "validated" in terms of job performance in

any one of several ways, perhaps by ascertaining the minimum skill, ability or potential necessary for the position at issue and determining whether the qualifying tests are appropriate for the selection of qualified applicants for the job in question. (Id. at 246, 96 S.Ct. at 2051).

Thus, it was held not sufficient for the governmental entity to prove that the classification resulting from the test scores had a rational basis, that is, that it differentiated between persons who did and did not have some minimum verbal and communication skill. It was necessary, in addition, for the governmental entity to demonstrate that the minimum verbal and communication skill, in turn, had some rational relationship to the legitimate employment objectives of the employer . . . that the employment practice must be a "business necessity." Id. at 431, 91 S.Ct. 849.

A. *Certification* Plaintiffs have proved that the use of NTE scores by the State in its certification decisions disqualifies substantially disproportionate numbers of blacks. The burden of proof was thereby shifted to the defendants, and in an effort to meet this burden the State commissioned an extensive validity study by ETS. The design of this study is novel, but consistent with the basic requirements enunciated by the Supreme Court, and we accordingly hold such study sufficient to meet the burden placed on defendants under Title VII.

The study seeks to demonstrate content validity by measuring the degree to which the content of the tests matches the content of the teacher training programs in South Carolina. It also seeks to establish a minimum score requirement by estimating the amount of knowledge (measured by the ability to answer correctly test questions that have been content-validated) that a minimally qualified teacher candidate in South Carolina would have. . . .

We find that the results of the validity study are sufficiently trustworthy to sustain defendants' burden under Title VII. . . . Plaintiffs misconceive their burden once defendants have made a reasonable showing that the study was executed in a responsible, professional manner designed to produce trustworthy results. In order to rebut the presumption that trustworthy results were indeed produced, plaintiffs must not only show that the study was not executed as intended, but also that the results were adversely affected. . . .

There remains, however, the question whether the State has satisfied the "business necessity" requirement set out in Griggs v. Duke Power Co., 401 U.S. 424, 91 S.Ct. 849, 28 L.Ed.2d 158 (1971). This "business necessity" doctrine appears neither in the explicit language nor the legislative history of Title VII. The Court in *Griggs* and subsequent Title VII cases did not establish judicial standards for determining whether a particular practice is a business necessity. The EEOC Guidelines are of little assistance because they were published before *Griggs* and have not been updated since that time.

We think that *Griggs* did not import into Title VII law the concept of "compelling interest" developed as a part of the "strict scrutiny" standard for assessing certain classifications under the Fourteenth Amendment. Under this concept, the Court would balance the disparate impact on blacks against the business purpose of the employer and uphold the business practice only if it were sufficiently "compelling" to overcome the disparate impact. It is our view that the Supreme Court intended an examination of the alternatives available with respect to the legitimate employment objective identified by the employer to determine whether there is available to the employer an alternative practice that would achieve his business purpose equally well but with a lesser disparate impact by race. In examining alternatives, the risk and cost to the employer are relevant.

Here, plaintiffs have suggested only one alternative to the use of the NTE for certification purposes. Plaintiffs contend that mere graduation from an approved program should be sufficient and would have a lesser disparate impact on blacks. We cannot find that this alternative will achieve the State's purpose in certifying minimally competent persons equally well as the use of a content-validated standardized test. The record amply demonstrates that there are variations in admissions requirements, academic standards and grading practices at the various teacher training institutions within the State. The approval that the State gives to the teacher training program is to general subject matter areas covered by the program, not to the actual course content of the program, and not to the means used within the program to measure whether individual students have actually mastered the course content to which they have been exposed. The standardized test scores do reflect individual achievement with respect to specific subject matter content, which is directly relevant to (although not sufficient in itself to assure) competence to teach, and thus the use of these scores for certification purposes survives the business necessity test under Title VII.

B. Pay scales There remains, finally, the question whether the uses of the NTE for salary purposes are a violation of Title VII. . . .

We believe that a distinction for pay purposes between those who are qualified as well as between those who are not qualified survives the business necessity test. There appears to be no alternative available to the State, within reasonable limits of risk and cost, for providing the incentive necessary to motivate thousands of persons to acquire, generally on their own time and at their own expense, the necessary additional academic training so that they will be minimally competent teachers. Having made the investment of four years in an undergraduate education, it seems reasonable to try to upgrade the talent of unqualified teachers where possible, rather than rejecting them altogether.

In accordance with the foregoing findings and conclusions, we conclude that plaintiff and plaintiff-intervenors have failed to establish their right to any of the relief sought in their respective complaints. It is, therefore,

Ordered that judgment be entered in favor of the defendants.

NOTE

Because of the difficulties of proving intent, most litigation has been concerned with disparate impact under Title VII. The plaintiff, in establishing a prima facie case must show that four basic factors are true: "(i) that he belongs to a racial minority; (ii) that he applied and was qualified for a job for which the employer was seeking applicants; (iii) that, despite his qualifications, he was rejected; and (iv) that, after his rejection, the position remained open and the employer continued to seek applicants from persons of complainant's qualifications." McDonnell Douglas Corp. v. Green, 411 U.S. 792, 93 S.Ct. 1817 (1973).

The *McDonnell Douglas* standards for establishing a prima facie case are flexible. Facts will vary from case to case and specifications for prima facie proof will not necessarily be the same in every aspect. "A prima facie case under *McDonnell Douglas* raises an inference of discrimination only because we [the Courts] presume these acts, if otherwise unexplained, are more likely than not based on the consideration of impermissible factors." Furnco Construction Corp. v. Waters, 438 U.S. 567, 98 S.Ct. 2943 (1978).

Therefore, to dispel the adverse inference from a prima facie showing, all the employer needs to do is "articulate some legitimate, nondiscriminatory reason for the employee's rejection." McDonnell Douglas v. Green, 411 U.S. 792, 93 S.Ct. 1817 (1973). After the employer has articulated some legitimate reason, the plaintiff must be afforded the opportunity to present evidence that this is no more than a pretext for discrimination.

A female teacher established a prima facie case of discrimination in Board of Trustees of Keene State College v. Sweeney, 439 U.S. 25, 99 S.Ct. 295 (1978). The Appeals Court required the defendant university "to prove [the] absence of [a] discriminatory motive." The Supreme Court reaffirmed *Furnco* and distinguished between "articulate," "show," and "prove." "[W]e think that there is a significant distinction between merely 'articulating some legitimate, nondiscriminatory reason' and 'proving absence of discriminatory motive.'" The case was remanded to the lower court to allow the university to articulate a legitimate reason as established and defined by the Supreme Court. *Source: Kern Alexander and M. David Alexander, The Law of School, Students and Teachers. (West Publishing Company, St. Paul, Minn., 1984).*

Percentage of Black Teachers in the School District Compared to Percentage of Blacks in the School Teacher Population in the Relevant Labor Market Is a Statistical Criterion of Discrimination

HAZELWOOD SCHOOL DISTRICT v. UNITED STATES

Supreme Court of the United States, 1977.
433 U.S. 299, 97 S.Ct. 2736.

Mr. Justice STEWART delivered the opinion of the Court.

The petitioner Hazelwood School District covers seventy-eight square miles in the northern part of St. Louis County, Mo. In 1973 the Attorney General brought this lawsuit against Hazelwood and various of its officials, alleging that they were engaged in a "pattern or practice" of employment discrimination in violation of Title VII of the Civil Rights Act of 1964, as amended, 42 U.S.C.A. § 2000e et seq. The complaint asked for an injunction requiring Hazelwood to cease its discriminatory practices, to take affirmative steps to obtain qualified Negro faculty members, and to offer employment and give backpay to victims of past illegal discrimination.

Hazelwood was formed from thirteen rural school districts between 1949 and 1951 by a process of annexation. By the 1967–1968 school year, 17,550 students were enrolled in the district, of whom only 59 were Negro; the number of Negro pupils increased to 576 of 25,166 in 1972–1973, a total of just over 2 percent.

From the beginning, Hazelwood followed relatively unstructured procedures in hiring its teachers. . . . Generally, those who had most recently submitted applications were most likely to be chosen for interviews.

Interviews were conducted by a department chairman, program coordinator, or the principal at the school where the teaching vacancy existed. Although those conducting the interviews did fill out forms rating the applicants in a number of respects, it is undisputed that each school principal possessed virtually unlimited discretion in hiring teachers for his school. The only general guidance given to the principals was to hire the "most competent" person available, and such intangibles as "personality, disposition, appearance, poise, voice, articulation, and ability to deal with people" counted heavily. The principal's choice was routinely honored by Hazelwood's superintendent and Board of Education.

. . . As a buyer's market began to develop for public school teachers, Hazelwood curtailed its recruiting efforts. For the 1971–1972 school year, 3,127 persons applied for only 234 teaching vacancies; for the 1972–1973 school year, there were 2,373 applications for 282 vacancies. A number of the applicants who were not hired were Negroes.

Hazelwood hired its first Negro teacher in 1969. The number of Negro faculty members gradually increased in successive years: six of 957 in the 1970 school year; 16 of 1,107 by the end of the 1972 school year; 22 of 1,231 in the 1973 school year. By comparison, according to 1970 census figures, of more than 19,000 teachers employed in that year in the St. Louis area, 15.4 percent were Negro. That percentage figure included the St. Louis City School District, which in recent years has followed a policy of attempting to maintain a 50 percent Negro teaching staff. Apart from that school district, 5.7 percent of the teachers in the county were Negro in 1970.

Drawing upon these historic facts the Government mounted its "pattern or practice" attack in the District Court upon four different fronts. It adduced evidence of (1) a history of alleged racially discriminatory practices, (2) statistical disparities in hiring, (3) the standardless and largely subjective hiring procedures, and (4) specific instances of alleged discrimination against fifty-five unsuccessful Negro applicants for teaching jobs. Hazelwood offered virtually no additional evidence in response, relying instead on evidence introduced by the Government, perceived deficiencies in the Government's case, and its own officially promulgated policy "to hire all teachers on the basis of training, preparation and recommendations, regardless of race, color or creed."

The District Court ruled that the Government had failed to establish a pattern or practice of discrimination. The court was unpersuaded by the alleged history of discrimination, noting that no dual school system had ever existed in Hazelwood. . . .

The Court of Appeals for the Eighth Circuit reversed. After suggesting that the District Court had assigned inadequate weight to evidence of discriminatory conduct on the part of Hazelwood before the effective date of Title VII, the Court of Appeals rejected the trial court's analysis of the statistical data as resting on an irrelevant comparison of Negro teachers to Negro pupils in Hazelwood. The proper comparison, in the appellate court's view, was one between Negro teachers in Hazelwood and Negro teachers in the relevant labor market area. Selecting St. Louis County and St. Louis City as the relevant area the Court of Appeals compared the 1970 census figures, showing that 15.4 percent of teachers in that area were Negro, to the racial composition of Hazelwood's teaching staff. In the 1972–1973 and 1973–1974 school years, only 1.4 percent and 1.8 percent, respectively, of Hazelwood's teachers were Negroes. This statistical disparity, particularly when viewed against the background of the teacher hiring procedures that Hazelwood had followed, was held to constitute a prima facie case of a pattern or practice of racial discrimination.

. . . Applying that standard, the appellate court found sixteen cases of individual discrimination, which "buttressed" the statistical proof. Because Hazelwood had not rebutted the Government's prima facie case of a pattern or practice of racial discrimination, the Court of Appeals directed judgment for the Government and prescribed the remedial order to be entered. . . .

This Court's recent consideration, in *International Brotherhood of Teamsters* v. *United States,* of the role of statistics in pattern or practice suits under Title VII provides substantial guidance in evaluating the arguments advanced by the petitioners. In that case we stated that it is the Government's burden to "establish by a preponderance of the evidence that racial discrimination was the [employer's] standard operating procedure—the regular rather than the unusual practice." We also noted that statistics can be an important source of proof in employment discrimination cases . . . . Where gross statistical disparities can be shown, they alone may in a proper case constitute prima facie proof of a pattern or practice of discrimination.

There can be no doubt, in light of the *Teamsters* case, that the District Court's comparison of Hazelwood's teacher work force to its student population fundamentally misconceived the role of statistics in employment discrimination cases. The Court of Appeals was correct in the view that a proper comparison was between the racial composition of Hazelwood's teaching staff and the racial composition of the qualified public school teacher population in the relevant labor market. The percentage of Negroes on Hazelwood's teaching staff in 1972–1973 was 1.4 percent and in 1973–1974 it was 1.8 percent. By contrast, the percentage of qualified Negro teachers in the area was, according to the 1970 census, at least 5.7 percent. Although these differences were on their face substantial, the Court of Appeals erred in substituting its judgment for that of the District Court and holding that the Government had conclusively proved its "pattern or practice" lawsuit.

The Court of Appeals totally disregarded the possibility that this prima facie statistical proof in the record might at the trial court level be rebutted by statistics dealing with Hazelwood's hiring after it became subject to Title VII. Racial discrimination by public employers was not made illegal under Title VII until March 24, 1972. A public employer who from that date forward made all its employment decisions in a wholly nondiscriminatory way would not violate Title VII even if it had formerly maintained an all-white work force by purposefully excluding Negroes. For this reason, the Court cautioned in the *Teamsters* opinion that once a prima facie case has been established by statistical work force disparities, the employer must be given an opportunity to show "that the claimed discriminatory pattern is a product of pre-Act hiring rather than unlawful post-Act discrimination."

The record in this case showed that for the 1972–1973 school year, Hazelwood hired 282 new teachers, ten of whom (3.5%) were Negroes; for the following school year it hired 123 new teachers, five of whom (4.1%) were Negroes. Over the two-year period, Negroes constituted a total of fifteen of the 405 new teachers hired (3.7%). Although the Court of Appeals briefly mentioned these data in reciting the facts, it wholly ignored them in discussing whether the Government had shown a pattern or practice of discrimination. And it gave no consideration at all to the possibility that post-Act data as to the number of Negroes hired compared to the total number of Negro applicants might tell a totally different story.

What the hiring figures prove obviously depends upon the figures to which they are compared. The Court of Appeals accepted the Government's argument that the relevant comparison was to the labor market area of St. Louis County and St. Louis City, in which, according to the 1970 census, 15.4 percent of all teachers were Negro. The propriety of that comparison was vigorously disputed by the petitioners, who urged that because the City of St. Louis has made special attempts to maintain a 50 percent Negro teaching staff, inclusion of that school district in the relevant market area distorts the comparison. Were that argument accepted, the percentage of Negro teachers in the relevant labor market area (St. Louis County alone) as shown in the 1970 census would be 5.7 percent rather than 15.4 percent.

The difference between these figures may well be important; the disparity between 3.7 percent (the percentage of Negro teachers hired by Hazelwood in 1972–1973 and 1973–1974) and 5.7 percent may be sufficiently small to weaken the Government's other proof, while the disparity between 3.7 percent and 15.4 percent may be sufficiently large to reinforce it. In determining which of the two figures—or very possibly, what intermediate figure—provides the most accurate basis for comparison to the hiring figures at Hazelwood, it will be necessary to evaluate such considerations as (i) whether the racially based hiring policies of the St. Louis City School District were in effect as far back as 1970, the year in which the census figures were taken; (ii) to what extent those policies have changed the racial composition of that district's teaching staff from what it would otherwise have been; (iii) to what extent St. Louis' recruitment policies have diverted to the city teachers who might otherwise have applied to Hazelwood; (iv) to what extent Negro teachers employed by the city would prefer employment in other districts such as Hazelwood; and (v) what the experience in other school districts in St. Louis County indicates about the validity of excluding the City School District from the relevant labor market.

It is thus clear that a determination of the appropriate comparative figures in this case will depend upon further evaluation by the trial court. As this Court admonished in *Teamsters*, "statistics . . . come in infinite variety . . .. [T]heir usefulness depends on all of the surrounding facts and circumstances." Only the trial court is in a position to make the appropriate determination after further findings. And only after such a determination is made can a foundation be established for deciding whether or not Hazelwood engaged in a pattern or practice of racial discrimination in its employment practices in violation of the law.

We hold, therefore, that the Court of Appeals erred in disregarding the post-Act hiring statistics in the record, and that it should have remanded the case to the District Court for further findings as to the relevant labor market area and for an ultimate determination of whether Hazelwood engaged in a pattern or practice of employment discrimination after March 24, 1972. Accordingly, the judgment is vacated, and the case is remanded to the District Court for further proceedings consistent with this opinion.

It is so ordered.

SEX DISCRIMINATION

The unequal treatment of employees based on sex was condoned by society for many years. Sex-based discrimination in working conditions, compensation, prerequisites for employment, and work-related benefits came under criticism during the early 1960s and Congress responded by passing legislation to prohibit such discrimination. In recent years lawsuits have been filed under the Equal Protection Clause of the Fourteenth Amendment, the Equal Pay Act of 1963, Title VII of the Civil Rights Act of 1964, and Title IX of the Education Amendments of 1972 [21] challenging discriminatory practices based on sex.

Equal Pay Act

In 1963, the Fair Labor Standards Act of 1938 was amended to include what is commonly referred to as the Equal Pay Act. The Equal Pay Act was designed to eliminate discrimination regarding pay or wages based on sex, where equal work, equal skills, and equal effort are performed under the same working conditions.[22] The Act specified that differential pay may be appropriate if the decision is based on: (1) a seniority system, (2) a merit system, (3) a situation in which quantity and quality of production is a factor, and (4) situations in which pay differences are based on any factor other than sex.

The Equal Pay Act was incorporated into Title VII of the Civil Rights Act of 1964. Title VII and the Equal Pay Act have almost identical language except that Title VII covers not only sex, but also race, color, religion, and national origin. Title VII states that the employer may provide different compensation, "or different terms, conditions, or privileges of employment pursuant to a bona fide seniority or merit system, or a system which measures earnings by quantity or quality of production or to employees who work in different locations, provided that such differences are not the result of an intention to discriminate because of race, color, religion, sex, or national origin." [23]

Not only are the reasons for differential pay the same under both the Equal Pay Act and Title VII, but the standard used to determine unequal pay for equal work is basically the same for both Acts. This standard is stated: "To establish a claim of unequal pay for equal work a plaintiff has the burden of proof that the employer pays different wages to employees of opposite sexes for equal work on jobs the performance of which requires equal skill, effort, and responsibility, and which are performed under similar working conditions." [24] Congress did not intend jobs to be exactly equal but intended to require substantial equality of skills, effort, responsibility, and working conditions. Each case must be reviewed on a case-by-case basis to see if the remedial remedies of Equal Pay or Title VII may be invoked. Once the employee has established that the pay is unequal for the same work, the burden shifts to the employer to show that the differential (pay scale) is justified under one of the Act's four exceptions listed above.[25]

Title IX

Title IX of the Education Amendments of 1972 was enacted to protect the rights of individuals and to prohibit discrimination based on gender in educational programs or activities receiving federal funds. Title IX is closely patterned after Title VI of the Civil Rights Act of 1974. Title IX states:

> No person in the United States shall, on the basis of sex, be excluded from participating in, be denied the benefits of, or be subjected to discrimination under any education program or activity receiving Federal financial assistance . . ..

Since Title IX is patterned after Title VI, and covers students in educational institutions, some courts have ruled that Title IX did not cover employees. But the Supreme Court, in *North Haven Board of Education* v. *Bell*, stated, "while section 901(a) does not expressly include or exclude employees within its scope, its broad directive that 'no person' may be discriminated against on the basis of gender includes employees as well as students." [26]

Pregnancy

Sex discrimination has been charged as a result of a wide range of employment practices involving leave policies, seniority, and medical benefits.

Such challenges have met with only moderate success, as illustrated by a number of cases. Pregnancy has been a popular area of such litigation. The state of California implemented an Unemployment Compensation Disability Fund to pay individuals who are temporarily unable to work and were not covered by the regular workman's compensation plan. The plan allowed for compensation for pregnancies when complications occurred, but excluded payment for normal pregnancies. The act was challenged by female employees as discriminatory against those who experienced normal pregnancies.

The United States Supreme Court, in *Geduldig* v. *Aiello,* found that no evidence was produced establishing that the program discriminated against any definable group and, therefore, was not violative of the Equal Protection Clause. The Court said: "the program divides potential recipients into two groups—pregnant women and non-pregnant persons. While the first group is exclusively female, the second includes members of both sexes. The fiscal and actuarial benefits of the programs thus accrue to members of both sexes." [27]

In *Gilbert* v. *General Electric,* another disability plan was challenged as discriminatory under Title VII. This plan paid for non-occupation sickness and accidents but excluded payment for those arising from pregnancy. The lower court found for the women but the Supreme Court disagreed and stated, "We think therefore that our decision in *Geduldig* v. *Aiello* . . . dealing with a strikingly similar disability plan, is quite relevant in determining whether or not the pregnancy exclusion did discriminate on the basis of sex." [28] The Court mentioned that the classification was not gender related, but only a classification between pregnant and non-pregnant persons. In the *Gilbert* case, the Supreme Court said that no clear definition for sex existed under Title VII and that this lack of clarity was compounded by conflicting federal regulations published by the EEOC and the Wage and Hour Administration. [29] Since no clear definition existed and federal regulations were in conflict, the Supreme Court queried whether Congress meant to cover pregnancy under the term sex.

Because of the Court's apparent confusion about whether pregnancy was intended to be covered under Title VII, as evidenced by *Geduldig,* and especially *Gilbert,* Congress amended Title VII to specifically cover pregnancy. [30] "Congress decided to overrule [the United States Supreme Court] decision in *General Electric Co.* v. *Gilbert* . . . by amending Title VII of the Civil Rights Act of 1964 to prohibit sex discrimination on the basis of pregnancy. [31] The Act prohibits discrimination based on pregnancy, childbirth, or related medical conditions. Pregnancy, childbirth, or related medical conditions must be treated the same for fringe benefit purposes as other medical conditions. The Act does not mandate that the employer's health insurance program cover abortions unless the life of the mother would be endangered, or if medical complications arise. The employer may provide abortion programs; the Act does not preclude such programs.

Mandatory leave policies have also been challenged by pregnant teachers. The Supreme Court resolved some of the issues concerning pregnancy policies in *Cleveland Board of Education* v. *LaFleur* and *Cohen* v. *Chesterfield.* [32] Here the Court acknowledged that rules that required teachers to give notice of their pregnancy to their employer were rational in that they provided for continuity of school instruction. However, arbitrary cut-off dates, at which time pregnant teachers were forced to stop teaching, were not rationally related to preserving continuity of instruction and could even work to the detriment of that goal. Cut-off dates were held to be unconstitutional because they created an *irrebuttable presumption,* in violation of the Due Process Clause, that all women who are pregnant become physically incompetent at a specified date.

Benefits

Insurance companies and others use actuarial tables in calculating payments and benefits for insurance and other types of benefit plans. The actuarial tables indicate, on average, that females live longer than males; therefore, females have been charged more at the initial pay-in stage or receive smaller monthly payments at the pay-out stage. These types of programs have been challenged as a form of sex discrimination under Title VII.

The Supreme Court held in the *Manhart* case in 1978 that a pension plan that required female employees to make larger contributions than males for equivalent benefits violated Title VII because the difference in treatment was based strictly on sex.[33]

The State of Arizona[34] developed a different approach with the differential at the pay-out as opposed to the pay-in stage. Employees were offered a deferred annuity plan and could select from three options: (1) a single lump-sum payment upon retirement, (2) payments at a specified amount for a fixed period of time, or (3) monthly annuity payments for the remainder of the employee's life. The first two options treated males and females equally and were not in dispute. But option three, the monthly annuity plan, was set up in accordance with sex-based mortality tables. If males and females retired at the same age, with the same contributions, males received a greater payment per month. Sex was thus the only factor used to classify the individuals. Citing *Manhart,* the Court ruled the system violated Title VII.

Mandatory Leave Rules and Arbitrary
Cutoff Dates for Pregnant Teachers
Violate Due Process

CLEVELAND BOARD OF EDUCATION v. LaFLEUR

Supreme Court of the United States, 1974.
414 U.S. 632, 94 S.Ct. 791.

Mr. Justice STEWART delivered the opinion of the Court.

The respondents in No. 72–777 and the petitioner in No. 72–1129 are female public school teachers. During the 1970–1971 school year, each informed her local school board that she was pregnant; each was compelled by a mandatory maternity leave rule to quit her job without pay several months before the expected birth of her child. These cases call upon us to decide the constitutionality of the school boards' rules.

Jo Carol LaFleur and Ann Elizabeth Nelson, the respondents in No. 72–777, are junior high school teachers employed by the Board of Education of Cleveland, Ohio. Pursuant to a rule first adopted in 1952, the school board requires every pregnant school teacher to take maternity leave without pay, beginning five months before the expected birth of her child. Application for such leave must be made no later than two weeks prior to the date of departure. A teacher on maternity leave is not allowed to return to work until the beginning of the next regular school semester which follows the date when her child attains the age of three months. A doctor's certificate attesting to the health of the teacher is a prerequisite to return; an additional physical examination may be required. The teacher on maternity leave is not promised reemployment after the birth of the child; she is merely given priority in reassignment to a position for which she is qualified. Failure to comply with the mandatory maternity leave provisions is ground for dismissal. . . .

The petitioner in No. 72–1129, Susan Cohen, was employed by the School Board of Chesterfield County, Virginia. That school board's maternity leave regulation requires that a pregnant teacher leave work at least four months prior to the expected birth of her child. Notice in writing must be given to the school board at least six months prior to the expected birth date. A teacher on maternity leave is declared reeligible for employment when she submits written notice from a physician that she is physically fit for reemployment, and when she can give assurance that care of the child will cause only minimal interference with her job responsibilities. . . .

This Court has long recognized that freedom of personal choice in matters of marriage and family life is one of the liberties protected by the Due Process Clause of the Fourteenth Amendment. . . . There is a right "to be free from unwarranted governmental intrusion into matters so fundamentally affecting a person as the decision whether to bear or beget a child."

By acting to penalize the pregnant teacher for deciding to bear a child, overly restrictive maternity leave regulations can constitute a heavy burden on the exercise of these protected freedoms. Because public school maternity leave rules directly affect "one of the basic civil rights of man," Skinner v. Oklahoma, supra, 316 U.S., at 541, 62 S.Ct., at 1113, the Due Process Clause of the Fourteenth Amendment requires that such rules must not needlessly, arbitrarily, or capriciously impinge upon this vital area of a teacher's constitutional liberty. The question before us in these cases is whether the interests advanced in support of the rules of the Cleveland and Chesterfield County School Boards can justify the particular procedures they have adopted.

The school boards in these cases have offered two essentially overlapping explanations for their mandatory maternity leave rules. First, they contend that the firm cutoff dates are necessary to maintain continuity of classroom instruction, since advance knowledge of when a pregnant teacher must leave facilitates the finding and hiring of a qualified substitute. Secondly, the school boards seek to justify their maternity rules by arguing that at least some teachers become physically incapable of adequately performing certain of their duties during the latter part of pregnancy. By keeping the pregnant teacher out of the classroom during these final months, the maternity leave rules are said to protect the health of the teacher and her unborn child, while at the same time assuring that students have a physically capable instructor in the classroom at all times.

It cannot be denied that continuity of instruction is a significant and legitimate educational goal. Regulations requiring pregnant teachers to provide early notice of their condition to school authorities undoubtedly facilitate administrative planning toward the important objective of continuity. But, as the Court of Appeals for the Second Circuit noted in *Green v. Waterford Board of Education*, 473 F.2d 629, 635:

Where a pregnant teacher provides the Board with a date certain for commencement of leave . . . . that value [continuity] is preserved; an arbitrary leave date set at the end of the fifth month is no more calculated to facilitate a planned and orderly transition between the teacher and a substitute than is a date fixed closer to confinement. Indeed, the latter . . . would afford the Board more, not less, time to procure a satisfactory long-term substitute. (Footnote omitted.)

Thus, while the advance-notice provisions in the Cleveland and Chester-field County rules are wholly rational and may well be necessary to serve the objective of continuity of instruction, the absolute requirements of termination at the end of the fourth or fifth month of pregnancy are not. Were continuity the only goal, cutoff dates much later during pregnancy would serve as well as or better than the challenged rules, providing that ample advance notice requirements were retained. Indeed, continuity would seem just as well attained if the teacher herself were allowed to choose the date upon which to commence her leave, at least so long as the decision were required to be made and notice given of it well in advance of the date selected.

In fact, since the fifth or sixth month of pregnancy will obviously begin at different times in the school year for different teachers, the present Cleve-land and Chesterfield County rules may serve to hinder attainment of the very continuity objectives that they are purportedly designed to promote. For example, the beginning of the fifth month of pregnancy for both Mrs. LaFleur and Mrs. Nelson occurred during March of 1971. Both were thus required to leave work with only a few months left in the school year, even though both were fully willing to serve through the end of the term. Similarly, if continuity were the only goal, it seems ironic that the Chester-field County rule forced Mrs. Cohen to leave work in mid-December 1970 rather than at the end of the semester in January as she requested.

We thus conclude that the arbitrary cutoff dates embodied in the mandatory leave rules before us have no rational relationship to the valid state interest of preserving continuity of instruction. As long as the teach-ers are required to give substantial advance notice of their condition, the choice of firm dates later in pregnancy would serve the boards' objectives just as well, while imposing a far lesser burden on the women's exercise of constitutionally protected freedom.

The question remains as to whether the cutoff dates at the beginning of the fifth and sixth months can be justified on the other ground advanced by the school boards—the necessity of keeping physically unfit teachers out of the classroom. There can be no doubt that such an objective is perfectly legitimate, both on educational and safety grounds. And, despite the pletho-ra of conflicting medical testimony in these cases, we can assume, *arguendo,* that at least some teachers become physically disabled from effectively performing their duties during the latter stages of pregnancy.

The mandatory termination provisions of the Cleveland and Chesterfield County rules surely operate to insulate the classroom from the presence of potentially incapacitated pregnant teachers. But the question is whether the rules sweep too broadly. . . .

That question must be answered in the affirmative, for the provisions amount to a conclusive presumption that every pregnant teacher who reaches the fifth or sixth month of pregnancy is physically incapable of continuing. There is no individualized determination by the teacher's doctor—or the school board's—as to any particular teacher's ability to continue at her job. The rules contain an irrebuttable presumption of physical incompetency, and that presumption applies even when the medical evidence as to an individual woman's physical status might be wholly to the contrary.

. . . While the medical experts in these cases differed on many points, they unanimously agreed on one—the ability of any particular pregnant woman to continue at work past any fixed time in her pregnancy is very much an individual matter. Even assuming, *arguendo*, that there are some women who would be physically unable to work past the particular cutoff dates embodied in the challenged rules, it is evident that there are large numbers of teachers who are fully capable of continuing work for longer than the Cleveland and Chesterfield County regulations will allow. Thus, the conclusive presumption embodied in these rules . . . is neither "necessarily [nor] universally true," and is violative of the Due Process Clause.

. . . While the regulations no doubt represent a good-faith attempt to achieve a laudable goal, they cannot pass muster under the Due Process Clause of the Fourteenth Amendment, because they employ irrebuttable presumptions that unduly penalize a female teacher for deciding to bear a child.

In addition to the mandatory termination provisions, both the Cleveland and Chesterfield County rules contain limitations upon a teacher's eligibility to return to work after giving birth. Again, the school boards offer two justifications for the return rules—continuity of instruction and the desire to be certain that the teacher is physically competent when she returns to work. As is the case with the leave provisions, the question is not whether the school board's goals are legitimate, but rather whether the particular means chosen to achieve those objectives unduly infringe upon the teacher's constitutional liberty.

Under the Cleveland rule, the teacher is not eligible to return to work until the beginning of the next regular school semester following the time when her child attains the age of three months. A doctor's certificate attesting to the teacher's health is required before return; an additional physical examination may be required at the option of the school board.

The respondents in No. 72–777 do not seriously challenge either the medical requirements of the Cleveland rule or the policy of limiting eligibility to return to the next semester following birth. The provisions concerning a medical certificate or supplemental physical examination are narrowly drawn methods of protecting the school board's interest in teacher fitness; these requirments allow an individualized decision as to the teacher's condition, and thus avoid the pitfalls of the presumptions inherent in the leave rules. Similarly, the provision limiting eligibility to return to the semester following delivery is a precisely drawn means of serving the school board's interest in avoiding unnecessary changes in classroom personnel during any one school term.

The Cleveland rule, however, does not simply contain these reasonable medical and next-semester eligibility provisions. In addition, the school board requires the mother to wait until her child reaches the age of three months before the return rules begin to operate. The school board has offered no reasonable justification for this supplemental limitation, and we can perceive none. To the extent that the three-month provision reflects the school board's thinking that no mother is fit to return until that point in time, it suffers from the same constitutional deficiencies that plague the irrebuttable presumption in the termination rules. The presumption, moreover, is patently unnecessary, since the requirement of a physician's certificate or a medical examination fully protects the school's interests in this regard. And finally, the three-month provision simply has nothing to do with continuity of instruction, since the precise point at which the child will reach the relevant age will obviously occur at a different point throughout the school year for each teacher.

Thus, we conclude that the Cleveland return rule, insofar as it embodies the three-month age provision, is wholly arbitrary and irrational, and hence violates the Due Process Clause of the Fourteenth Amendment. The age limitation serves no legitimate state interest, and unnecessarily penalizes the female teacher for asserting her right to bear children.

We perceive no such constitutional infirmities in the Chesterfield County rule. In that school system, the teacher becomes eligible for reemployment upon submission of a medical certificate from her physician; return to work is guaranteed no later than the beginning of the next school year following the eligibility determination. The medical certificate is both a reasonable and narrow method of protecting the school board's interest in teacher fitness, while the possible deferring of return until the next school year serves the goal of preserving continuity of instruction. In short, the Chesterfield County rule manages to serve the legitimate state interests here without employing unnecessary presumptions that broadly burden the exercise of protected constitutional liberty.

For the reasons stated, we hold that the mandatory termination provisions of the Cleveland and Chesterfield County maternity regulations violate the Due Process Clause of the Fourteenth Amendment, because of their use of unwarranted conclusive presumptions that seriously burden the exercise of protected constitutional liberty. For similar reasons, we hold the three-month provision of the Cleveland return rule unconstitutional.

*Title IX of the Education
Amendments of 1972 Protects
Employees Against Gender
Discrimination in Educational
Institutions*

NORTH HAVEN BOARD OF EDUCATION v. BELL

Supreme Court of the United States, 1982.
456 U.S. 512, 102 S.Ct. 1912.

Justice BLACKMUN delivered the opinion of the Court.

At issue here is the validity of regulations promulgated by the Department of Education pursuant to Title IX of the Education Amendments of 1972, Pub.L. 92–318, 86 Stat. 373, 20 U.S.C. § 1681 et seq. These regulations prohibit federally funded education programs from discriminating on the basis of gender with respect to employment.

Title IX proscribes gender discrimination in education programs or activities receiving federal financial assistance. Patterned after Title VI of the Civil Rights Act of 1964, Pub.L. 88–352, 78 Stat. 252, 42 U.S.C. § 2000d et seq., Title IX, as amended, contains two core provisions. The first is a "program-specific" prohibition of gender discrimination:

> No person in the United States shall, on the basis of sex, be excluded from participation in, be denied the benefits of, or be subjected to discrimination under any education program or activity receiving Federal financial assistance . . . ." § 901(a).

Nine statutory exceptions to § 901(a)'s coverage follow. See §§ 901(a)(1)–(9).[35]

The second core provision relates to enforcement. Section 902 authorizes each agency awarding federal financial assistance to any education program to promulgate regulations ensuring that aid recipients adhere to § 901(a)'s mandate. The ultimate sanction for noncompliance is termination of federal funds or denial of future grants.

In 1975, the Department of Health, Education, and Welfare (HEW) invoked its § 902 authority to issue regulations governing the operation of federally funded education programs. These regulations extend, for example, to policies involving admissions, textbooks, and athletics. Interpreting the term "person" in § 901(a) to encompass employees as well as students, HEW included among the regulations a series entitled "Subpart E," which deals with employment practices, ranging from job classifications to pregnancy leave. . . .

Petitioners are two Connecticut public school boards that brought separate suits challenging HEW's authority to issue the Subpart E regulations. Petitioners contend that Title IX was not meant to reach the employment practices of educational institutions.

A. *The North Haven case.* The North Haven Board of Education (North Haven) receives federal funds for its education programs and activities and is therefore subject to Title IX's prohibition of gender discrimination. Since the 1975–1976 school year, North Haven has devoted between 46.8 percent and 66.9 percent of its federal assistance to the salaries of its employees; this practice is expected to continue.

In January 1978, Elaine Dove, a tenured teacher in the North Haven public school system, filed a complaint with HEW, alleging that North Haven had violated Title IX by refusing to rehire her after a one-year maternity leave. In response to this complaint, HEW began to investigate the school board's employment practices and sought from petitioner information concerning its policies on hiring, leaves of absence, seniority, and tenure. Asserting that HEW lacked authority to regulate employment practices under Title IX, North Haven refused to comply with the request. . . .

B. *The Trumbull case.* The Trumbull Board of Education (Trumbull) likewise receives financial support from the federal government and must therefore adhere to the requirements of Title IX and appropriate implementing regulations. In October 1977, HEW began investigating a complaint filed by respondent Linda Potz, a former guidance counselor in the Trumbull school district. Potz alleged that Trumbull had discriminated against her on the basis of gender with respect to job assignments, working conditions, and the failure to renew her contract. In September 1978, HEW notified Trumbull that it had violated Title IX and warned that corrective action, including respondent's reinstatement, must be taken.

Trumbull then filed suit in the United States District Court for the District of Connecticut, contending that HEW's Title IX employment regulations were invalid . . ..

Our starting point in determining the scope of Title IX is, of course, the statutory language. Section 901(a)'s broad directive that "no person" may be discriminated against on the basis of gender appears, on its face, to include employees as well as students. Under that provision, employees, like other "persons," may not be "excluded from participation in," "denied the benefits of," or "subjected to discrimination under" education programs receiving federal financial support.

Employees who directly participate in federal programs or who directly benefit from federal grants, loans, or contracts clearly fall within the first two protective categories described in § 901(a). In addition, a female employee who works in a federally funded education program is "subjected to discrimination under" that program if she is paid a lower salary for like work, given less opportunity for promotion, or forced to work under more adverse conditions than are her male colleagues.

There is no doubt that "if we are to give [Title IX] the scope that its origins dictate, we must accord it a sweep as broad as its language." Because § 901(a) neither expressly nor impliedly excludes employees from its reach, we should interpret the provision as covering and protecting these "persons" unless other considerations counsel to the contrary. After all, Congress easily could have substituted "student" or "beneficiary" for the word "person" if it had wished to restrict the scope of § 901(a).

Petitioners, however, point to the nine exceptions to § 901(a)'s coverage set forth in §§ 901(a)(1)–(9). . . . The exceptions, the school boards argue, are directed only at students, and thus indicate that § 901(a) similarly applies only to students. But the exceptions are not concerned solely with students and student activities: two of them exempt an entire class of institutions—religious and military schools—and are not limited to student-related activities at such schools. See §§ 901(a)(3), (4). Moreover, petitioners' argument rests on an inference that is by no means compelled; in fact, the absence of a specific exclusion for employment among the list of exceptions tends to support the Court of Appeals' conclusion that Title IX's broad protection of "person[s]" does extend to employees of educational institutions.

Although the statutory language thus seems to favor inclusion of employees, nevertheless, because Title IX does not expressly include or exclude employees from its scope, we turn to the Act's legislative history for evidence as to whether Congress meant somehow to limit the expansive language of § 901. . . .

In our view, the legislative history thus corroborates our reading of the statutory language and verifies the Court of Appeals' conclusion that employment discrimination comes within the prohibition of Title IX. . . .

Whether termination of petitioners' federal funds is permissible under Title IX is a question that must be answered by the District Court in the first instance. Similarly, we do not undertake to define "program" in this opinion. Neither of the cases before us advanced beyond a motion for summary judgment, and the record therefore does not reflect whether petitioners' employment practices actually discriminated on the basis of gender or whether any such discrimination comes within the prohibition of Title IX. Neither school board opposed HEW's investigation into its employment practices on the grounds that the complaining employees' salaries were not funded by federal money, that the employees did not work in an education program that received federal assistance, or that the discrimination they allegedly suffered did not affect a federally funded program. Instead, petitioners disputed the Department's authority to regulate any employment practices whatsoever, and the District Court adopted that view, which we find to be error. Accordingly, we affirm the judgment of the Court of Appeals but remand the case for further proceedings consistent with this opinion.

It is so ordered.

NOTE

Section 601 of the Civil Rights Act of 1964, 42 U.S.C.A. § 2000d, and Section 901(a) of Title IX of the Education Amendments of 1972, §§ 901–903, are virtually the same as § 504 of the Rehabilitation Act, 29 U.S.C.A. § 794. Section 601 is framed the same way except that it refers to race, color, or national origin. Section 901(a) has the same qualities, although it refers to discrimination based on sex, whereas in § 504 the reference is to otherwise qualified handicapped individuals.

School District Did Not Violate Title VII Prohibition Against Disparate Treatment In Not Hiring Female For School Principalship

DANZL v. NORTH ST. PAUL— MAPLEWOOD—OAKDALE INDEPENDENT SCHOOL DISTRICT NO. 622

United States Court of Appeals,
Eighth Circuit, 1983.
706 F.2d 813.

FAGG, Circuit Judge.

Once again we are asked to determine whether the North St. Paul-Maplewood-Oakdale Independent School District discriminated on the basis of sex, in violation of Title VII of the Civil Rights Act of 1964, when it did not hire Agnes Danzl to fill a one-year high school principal position. The district court found that the school district's articulated nondiscriminatory reasons for not hiring Danzl were pretextual, and held that the school district intentionally discriminated against Danzl solely on the basis of her sex. Because we believe the district court's findings of pretext and intentional discrimination are clearly erroneous, we reverse.

In late July 1979, a vacancy arose for a high school principalship in the school district for the 1979–80 school year. Twelve individuals—ten male and two female—applied for the position. Director of Secondary Education Richard St. Germain selected four finalists—two male and two female—based upon his review of the papers submitted, phone conversations with the applicants and reference checks. Several male applicants with prior principal experience were eliminated by this investigatory process. Between August 15 and August 20, St. Germain interviewed the four finalists.

On August 21, a committee of male and female teachers from the high school interviewed the candidates. Following the interviews, the teachers discussed and rated the candidates, and then met with St. Germain. The teachers agreed that Agnes Danzl, a female, and Jack Edling, a male, were the two leading candidates, but favored Danzl slightly based on the interviews. St. Germain told the teachers committee that he favored Edling; he had contacted various persons regarding Edling, including both administrators and teachers, and the references were very positive. His two reference checks on Danzl, he said, were not as positive. St. Germain had contacted an administrator who knew both candidates and he stated that he would hire Edling over Danzl. Also, one of Danzl's supervisors had stated that he would hesitate to hire Danzl for a high school as large as Burnsville, where she was currently teaching. The teachers, concerned that only administrators had been contacted for Danzl, while both administrators and teachers had been contacted for Edling, asked for time to conduct their own investigation of Danzl. St. Germain was amenable to this procedure.

Three male and female committee members, independent of St. Germain and of one another, contacted three teachers at Burnsville. Each of the references were considered, on balance, unfavorable to Danzl and were similar in content. The references indicated that Danzl was inflexible, had certain staff relations problems, and was insensitive to student needs. After the teachers informed the other committee members of the reference checks, St. Germain polled each member of the committee by phone. Their unanimous choice for the interim principal position was Edling. St. Germain cross-checked the references from the teachers with a Burnsville administrator, who did not disagree, in general, with the unfavorable comments about Danzl. Edling was recommended to the school board which in turn appointed him to the principal position.

On May 28, 1980, Danzl filed a complaint in federal district court, alleging that the school district had declined to hire her as a high school principal for the 1979–80 school year because of her sex, in violation of Title VII of the Civil Rights Act of 1964, 42 U.S.C. § 2000e et seq. and 42 U.S.C. § 1983. The district court held that the defendants had discriminated against Danzl on the basis of her sex, in violation of Title VII, and ordered the school district to make available to Danzl for at least one school year either a secondary school principalship or a comparable position. . . .
We held that the district court had erred in shifting to the school district the burden of proving that it had not hired Danzl because of nondiscriminatory reasons and remanded for further proceedings on whether the nondiscriminatory reasons articulated for not hiring Danzl were pretextual.

The district court held a remand hearing but heard no additional evidence on the pretext issue. Based on the original trial record, the district court concluded that the school district's reasons for not hiring Danzl were "nothing more than pretexts and that the real motive underlying Dr. Danzl not being hired was due to sex-based discrimination." The school district appeals, urging that the district court erred in its findings of pretext and intentional discrimination.

There is a three-step allocation of burdens and order of presentation of proof in a Title VII disparate treatment case. The initial burden is on the plaintiff to establish a prima facie case of discrimination. If the plaintiff succeeds, the burden then shifts to the defendant to rebut the inference of discrimination by producing evidence that the plaintiff was rejected, or someone else was preferred, for some legitimate nondiscriminatory reason. The defendant's evidence is sufficient if it raises a genuine issue of fact as to whether it discriminated against the plaintiff. In addition, the reasons given must be legally sufficient to justify a judgment for the defendant. Finally, should the defendant carry this burden of production, the plaintiff must demonstrate by a preponderance of the evidence that the proffered reasons were not the true reason for the challenged employment decision. The plaintiff may prove this either by means of affirmative evidence that a discriminatory reason played an impermissible role in the decision or by showing that the proffered nondiscriminatory reasons are unworthy of credence. At all times the ultimate burden of persuasion that the defendant committed intentional discrimination remains with the plaintiff. In discharging this burden, Danzl need not prove that her sex was the sole reason for the challenged employment decision, but need only prove that sex was a factor in the decision.

There is no dispute that plaintiff has established a prima facie case of disparate treatment. Similarly, there is no dispute that the school district has met its burden of articulating reasons for not hiring Danzl that are legitimate and nondiscriminatory: (1) the candidate who was hired, Jack Edling, was better qualified because he had experience as a high school principal; and (2) Agnes Danzl had received unfavorable reference checks. Thus, the sole issue before this court concerns the district court's finding that the school district's articulated reasons for not hiring Danzl were a pretext for intentional sexual discrimination. We may not set aside the district court's findings of fact unless they are clearly erroneous. A finding is clearly erroneous if it is not supported by substantial evidence, if it evolves from an erroneous conception of the applicable law, or if the reviewing court on the entire record is left with the definite and firm conviction that a mistake has been made. Moreover, it is now the law that we may reverse a finding of intentional discrimination only if the finding is clearly erroneous.

The first reason the school district proffered for not hiring Danzl was that Edling was better qualified, due to his experience as a high school principal. Rejecting this explanation, the district court first found that Danzl and Edling were equally qualified for the position. This finding is clearly erroneous. We have no doubt that both candidates were qualified for the position. Nevertheless, an employer could distinguish between Edling, who had seven years' experience as a principal and one year's experience as a school superintendent, and Danzl, who had only five years' experience as an associate principal. The district court implied that Danzl made up for any lack of experience with her superior educational qualifications. Danzl had a Ph.D. awarded by an unaccredited school for certain courses and papers, including a dissertation, conducted by correspondence. Edling had a master's degree. Unlike principal experience, an advanced degree was not listed as a qualification for the position. The district court cannot substitute its judgment for the employer's by saying that Danzl's advanced degree compensates for Edling's superior experience. . . .

The district court's alternative rationale for its finding of pretext was that several of the original twelve applicants had experience as a high school principal, but of the final four applicants only Edling possessed such experience. Hence, the district court concluded that if past experience as a secondary school principal was so important, then "Dr. St. Germain had already decided to hire Mr. Edling as of the date the finalists were chosen, and all subsequent selection activities were mere window dressing designed to obscure the true intent of the defendant to hire a male."

This finding is simply without support in the record. When St. Germain selected the four finalists, an extensive and real selection process remained, involving interviews, reference checks, and numerous meetings with administrators, teachers and school district members. It just does not follow that by considering experience as a factor, the school district had therefore preselected Edling among the four finalists. The school district has never contended that experience was an absolute requirement for the job; the vacancy notice stated only that it was a desirable qualification to be considered. Although the issue is not before us, the district court conceded that principal experience could have been a legitimate requirement for the job of interim principal under the disparate impact test of Griggs v. Duke Power Co., 401 U.S. 424, 91 S.Ct. 849, 28 L.Ed.2d 158 (1971).

Because we find no evidence in the record to contradict the school district's first legitimate nondiscriminatory reason for not hiring Danzl, her lack of principal experience, we conclude that the district court's finding of pretext was clearly erroneous.

The school district's second articulated reason for not hiring Danzl was that it had received several negative references concerning Danzl. The references for Edling, in contrast, were very positive. The district court found this reason pretextual because the references "were not received by the defendants until after the decision to hire Mr. Edling had already been made." There is nothing in the record to support this finding. . . .

We have thoroughly searched the record in this case and have found nothing that supports the district court's finding of intentional discrimination. Both Danzl and Edling, as well as several others, were qualified candidates. Unremarkably, the school district hired the candidate with superior experience and superior references. Although this may not comport with the district court's view of how hiring practices should compensate for years of underrepresentation of women in educational administration, it does not violate Title VII. The employer is free to choose the best candidate for the position without regard to sex. Nothing more than that occurred in this case.

The judgment of the district court is reversed.

NOTE

Sexual Harassment. Regulations by the Equal Employment Opportunity Commission (EEOC) implementing Title VII of the Civil Rights Act clearly prohibit sexual harassment. The regulation provides in part:

> (a) Harassment on the basis of sex is a violation of Section 703 of Title VII. Unwelcome sexual advances, requests for sexual favors, or other verbal or physical conduct of a sexual nature constitute sexual harassment when (1) submission to such conduct is made either explicitly or implicitly a term or condition of an individual's employment, (2) submission to or rejection of such conduct by an individual is used as the basis for employment decisions affecting such individual, or (3) such conduct has the purpose or effect of unreasonably interfering with an individual's work performance or creating an intimidating, hostile, or offensive working environment. 29 C.F.R. 1604.11(a). See also: Nashville Gas Co. v. Satty, 434 U.S. 136, 98 S.Ct. 347 (1977); Bundy v. Jackson, 641 F.2d 934 (D.C.Cir.1981); Tompkins v. Public Service Electric & Gas Co., 568 F.2d 1044 (3rd Cir.1977); Berg v. LaCrosse Cooler Co., 612 F.2d 1041 (7th Cir.1980).

AGE DISCRIMINATION

The federal government passed the Age Discrimination in Employment Act in 1967,[36] which prohibits discrimination against individuals who are at least forty, but less than seventy years of age. The Act prohibits discrimination with respect to: hiring, discharging, compensation, terms and conditions, privileges, retirement, and demotion. The Act was not intended to increase the number of elderly in the workforce, but only to prevent discrimination against them. The Act is intended to supplement the protections provided under the Equal Protection Clause.

Two cases decided by the Supreme Court are important in understanding mandatory retirement statutes and age discriminations. In the first case, the Court upheld a Massachusetts statute requiring uniformed state police to retire at age fifty.[37] The Court held that government employment was not a fundamental constitutional right, nor age a suspect classification. Therefore, the court required that the government show a rational interest to support its policy, but did not require it to bear the burden of showing a compelling interest in creating the policy. Because the purpose of the statute was to assure physical preparedness by having younger troopers patrolling the highways, the policy was not unconstitutional. The rationale that younger policemen are more physically capable and can provide better protection to all of society was held to be a proper and reasonable societal objective.

In another case, again using the rational interest test, the Supreme Court upheld a statute requiring Foreign Service employees to retire at age sixty. The Court said: "Congress . . . was legitimately intent on stimulating the highest performance in the Foreign Service by assuring that opportunities for promotion would be available despite [the] limits on [the] number of personnel in the Service, and plainly intended to create [a] relatively small, homogeneous and particularly able corps of foreign service officers . . . ."[38] This the Court found to be an acceptable objective.

In *Palmer* v. *Ticcione*,[39] a federal circuit court held that teachers could be required to retire at a specific age. Also, since school bus drivers over sixty-five have a higher accident rate, a New York court determined that it was reasonable to establish retirement for bus drivers at age sixty-five for health and safety reasons.[40]

The courts have held that the party claiming age discrimination will be evaluated under the same factors as established for race discrimination. If the action is a private, nonclass action, "the complainant has the burden of establishing a *prima facie* case, which he can satisfy by showing that (i) he belongs to a special minority; (ii) he applied and was qualified for a job the employer was trying to fill; (iii) though qualified, he was rejected; and (iv) therefore, the employer continued to seek applicants with complainant's qualifications."[41] After establishing a *prima facie* case, the burden shifts to the employer, who must articulate legitimate, nondiscriminatory reasons for not employing the individual or individuals.

Equal Protection and Due Process
Guarantees Were Not Violated When
Teacher Was Forced to Retire
at Age 70

PALMER v. TICCIONE

United States Court of Appeals,
Second Circuit, 1978.
576 F.2d 459.

HAYS, Circuit Judge:

Appellant, Lois Palmer, commenced this action under 42 U.S.C. § 1983 (1970) for age discrimination in violation of the equal protection and due process guarantees of the Fourteenth Amendment. The district court granted the defendants' motion to dismiss for want of a substantial federal question. For the reasons stated below, we affirm the dismissal of the complaint.

The facts are undisputed. Appellant has been a teacher since 1943. She has been employed by the defendant Copiague Union Free District #5 as a kindergarten teacher since the 1961–62 school year. She received tenure at the end of the 1963–64 school year. In February 1975, she reached the age of 70. On May 15, 1975, she met with defendant N. Paul Buscemi, the Copiague superintendent of schools. He informed her that she was to be retired at the end of the school year because she had reached the retirement age of 70. This decision was subsequently ratified by the Copiague school board, and the New York State Retirement System was directed to place Mrs. Palmer on retirement status as of August 25, 1975.

It is not disputed that appellant is willing and able to teach. Her performance as a teacher was rated satisfactory in each year of her employment. In the last evaluation, made just before she was retired in 1975, her principal recommended that she be rehired, "[s]ubject to review of compulsory retirement under New York State Education Law."

Appellant contends that retirement solely on the basis of her age violates her constitutional and state law rights. Essentially, she claims: that compulsory retirement at age 70 violates the equal protection clause; that it creates an irrebuttable presumption of incompetency based on age; that, as a tenured teacher, she is entitled to a hearing before termination; and that, in the alternative, the New York Education Law should be read to prohibit compulsory retirement or, if not, to require a hearing before termination.

Compulsory retirement systems have come under constitutional attack in several contexts. These equal protection and due process challenges have been rejected by this and other courts. The only exception is Gault v. Garrison, 569 F.2d 993 (7th Cir.1977). In that case, the Seventh Circuit ruled that a retired teacher is entitled to a trial on her age discrimination claim. Because *Gault* involves a factual situation very similar to that of the instant case—the major difference is that the retirement age in *Gault* was 65, not 70—and because we disagree with the *Gault* holding, we think it appropriate to focus on this issue once again.

The ruling in *Gault* is premised on the implications of the Supreme Court's most recent decision in this area. In Massachusetts Board of Retirement v. Murgia, 427 U.S. 307, 96 S.Ct. 2562, 49 L.Ed.2d 520 (1976), the Court upheld a state law requiring the mandatory retirement of uniformed police at age 50. First *Murgia* established that the proper standard for equal protection review in a case challenging a compulsory retirement statute is the rational basis test. Applying this standard, the Court found that forced retirement at age 50 did foster the purpose identified by the state; it assured the continued physical preparedness of the state's uniformed police. In *Murgia*, there had been a trial, and there was evidence in the record to support the conclusion that physical preparedness is rationally related to age.

As in the instant case, but unlike *Murgia*, *Gault* involved an appeal from an order dismissing the complaint. The *Gault* court assumed that the strongest justification for a retirement law for teachers is to remove those who are unfit. Working from that premise, it held that, absent an evidentiary showing, there was no reason to assume that there is any relationship beween advancing age and fitness to teach. *Gault* distinguished *Murgia* as involving a question of whether physical fitness declines with age, and noted that there was evidence in the record to support the conclusion that it does. It contrasted this with the question whether teaching ability, which involves predominately mental skills, similarly declines with age. Absent an evidentiary showing, the court saw no reason to assume that it does; in fact, it speculated that the knowledge and experience necessary for teaching increases with age.[42] Accordingly, it remanded for further proceedings to determine whether compulsory retirement of teachers at age 65 is rationally based.

We decline to follow *Gault* for two reasons. First, while there is a valid distinction between the instant case and *Murgia*, we cannot distinguish the prior cases that have sustained compulsory retirement statutes for occupations that involve primarily mental skills. In *Johnson v. Lefkowitz*, we upheld the constitutionality of § 70 of the New York State Retirement and Social Security Law (McKinney's 1971), which requires tenured civil servants to retire at age 70. In *Johnson*, the plaintiff had been dismissed from his position as senior attorney in the Real Property Bureau of the state's law department. In *Rubino* v. *Ghezzi*, we upheld the constitutionality of the mandatory retirement of state judges at age 70. And, in *Weisbrod* v. *Lynn*, mandatory retirement of federal civil servants at age 70 was upheld as constitutional, even though the statute undoubtedly requires the retirement of some civil servants who are engaged in occupations that involve primarily mental skills. See also *Weiss* v. *Walsh*, (denial of state-endowed chair to college professor over 65 is not unconstitutional age discrimination).

Second, *Gault* too narrowly conceives the possible rational bases for a compulsory retirement statute. Unrelated to any notion of physical or mental fitness, a state might prescribe mandatory retirement for teachers in order to open up employment opportunities for young teachers—particularly in the last decade when supply has outpaced demand, or to open up more places for minorities, or to bring young people with fresh ideas and techniques in contact with school children, or to assure predictability and ease in establishing and administering pension plans. A compulsory retirement system is rationally related to the fulfillment of any or all of these legitimate state objectives.

Thus it would seem clear that *Gault* notwithstanding, the New York State compulsory retirement system for teachers is immune from constitutional attack. However, appellant seeks to distinguish the instant case on two grounds. First, she argues that, since the statute must "rationally [further] the purpose *identified* by the State . . . ," *Murgia*, we may only look to the purpose of the compulsory retirement law as evidenced by the statutory scheme. Section 510(1)(b) of the New York Education Law (McKinney's 1969), which provides for compulsory retirement at the employer's discretion, is part of a statute governing retirement benefits. Thus, appellant contends that the only possible purpose of the statute is to further the efficient distribution of retirement benefits. She argues that compulsory retirement is not rationally related to this purpose because the statute provides for compulsory retirement at the discretion of the employer. This encourages unpredictability in the administration of the pension program. Also, she contends that, to the extent that able teachers are forced to retire at age 70, compulsory retirement defeats the purpose of the statute by adding unnecessarily to the retirement rolls. Second, appellant argues that because this case involves a statute that provides for discretionary rather than mandatory compulsory retirement, the precedents are inapposite.

Closer scrutiny of the statute provides the answer to the first argument. Section 510(1)(b) is permissive; it allows individual school boards to implement compulsory retirement policies. Thus, if an individual school board adopts a compulsory retirement policy, whether mandatory or discretionary, it may be to further any of the purposes suggested above, without regard to the narrow context of the empowering statute. Since such a board-adopted policy would be supportable as rationally based, we would be constrained to uphold it as a legitimate exercise of a statutorily authorized power.

With regard to the second argument, we fail to see its relevance. The record is inconclusive on whether Copiague has adopted a mandatory or discretionary retirement policy. There is nothing in the record to indicate that the appellant was discharged under anything other than an across-the-board, mandatory retirement policy. If so, then, as noted above, the board's action is clearly immune from constitutional attack. However, even if appellant was retired under a discretionary policy, the result would be the same. First, a discretionary retirement policy would still be rationally related to a legitimate state goal; it would further any of the purposes noted above, with the exception of those related to the maintenance of pension plans. Second, the *Johnson* case would still be on point. *Johnson* involved § 70 of the New York Retirement and Social Security Law (McKinney's 1971), a statute that is functionally equivalent to discretionary retirement. Subsection (c) provides that a civil servant may be retained beyond age 70 under certain conditions. If he or she is retained, however, he or she is subject to termination upon sixty days' notice. Johnson had been given two extensions and was then summarily retired. The court found no constitutional infirmity with that system. We find none in the instant case either.

We reach the same conclusion with regard to the due process attack on compulsory retirement as establishing an irrebuttable presumption. That claim is analytically very similar to the equal protection one. If the statutory classification is sustainable as rationally based, then it should not fall because it might also be labeled a presumption. . . .

Appellant also claims that she was entitled to a due process hearing before being retired. However, we can see no purpose for a hearing if appellant was retired under an across-the-board, mandatory retirement system. And even if a discretionary system was employed, we would be constrained to follow *Johnson*, supra, and deny this claim. In *Johnson*, we held that a hearing is not required because the benefits of holding such a hearing are outweighed by the burdens imposed upon the state by requiring a hearing in every case. 566 F.2d at 869.

Today's decision is not intended as an endorsement of compulsory retirement for teachers or compulsory retirement in general. Rather, we are aware of the many older Americans who continue to be able and eager to work beyond age seventy. We are also aware of the debilitating effects that compulsory retirement has on many such individuals, with regard to their economic situation, their health, their outlook on life, and the continuing opportunities for fulfillment. However, in determining the desirability of compulsory retirement, these considerations must be weighed against the social goals that compulsory retirement furthers. This is precisely the type of clash of competing social goals that is best resolved by the legislative process. The federal courts should not second guess the wisdom or propriety of such legislative resolutions as long as they are rationally based.

Congress has recently considered this issue and, after extensive hearings, has amended the Age Discrimination in Employment Act of 1967. The amendments prohibit, with some exceptions, the compulsory retirement of people under seventy, and of federal employees at any age. The original Act requires the Secretary of Labor to make annual reports concerning the effects of the Act, taking into account demographic changes. The 1978 amendments impose on the Secretary the further duty of reporting, by 1981, on the effects of the amendments and the feasibility of extending their coverage. We note these developments because we are persuaded that they reinforce today's decision. There is no question but that the passage of the 1978 amendments to the Age Discrimination in Employment Act was the result of a process that was fair, deliberate, and well informed. Moreover, Congress has provided a mechanism for continually reassessing the effects and the wisdom of its actions on this issue. The superior ability of Congress to collect data and to resolve competing social goals, as well as the flexibility resulting from its ability to monitor the effects of its actions and to make adjustments accordingly, mark this issue as one which the Constitution has appropriately left to the legislative processes, both state and federal.

Affirmed.

DISCRIMINATION AGAINST THE HANDICAPPED

The Rehabilitation Act of 1973, Section 504, is violated if a handicapped person is denied a position "solely by reason of his handicap." [43] The Act also specifies that the employer must "reasonably accommodate" an individual, but this standard applies only if the individual is "otherwise qualified" for the position. "The standards for determining the merits of a case under Section 504 are contained in the statute. First, the statute provides that the individual in question must be an 'otherwise qualified handicapped individual;' second, the statute provides that a qualified handicapped individual may not be denied admission to any program or activity or denied the benefits of any program or activity . . . solely on the basis of handicap." [44] The two factors are interrelated. If the individual is not otherwise qualified, he cannot be said to have been rejected solely because of his handicap.

In a case in which a blind woman, who was certified by the Philadelphia Department of Education, attempted to obtain employment in the Philadelphia School District, the school district offered her several jobs that she refused because seniority was not to be granted from the date of her original application. The teacher had applied some four years earlier and was not allowed to take an examination and was therefore, not employed. The teacher filed suit seeking retroactive seniority and tenure. The court awarded the teacher retroactive seniority, but not tenure. [45] Tenure was denied because the bestowing of tenure must be preceded by subjective evaluation of the teacher's performance and the courts will not take this responsibility upon themselves unless absolutely necessary. Also, in this case the Court held that a handicap would not be considered by the courts to be a suspect classification for equal protection purposes.

In another equal protection case a blind teacher sued because school policies and procedures prevented him from obtaining an administrative position. [46] The policies required that an oral and written examination be completed by each prospective administrator. The plaintiff completed the written section of the test, with the aid of a reader, and performed very poorly. A committee also rated the plaintiff very low on the oral part of the examination. The court held that physical handicaps were not to be treated as a suspect classification and, therefore, the school district needed only to show a rational interest in the practice in question. Using this test, the court determined that the plaintiff did not possess the skills and qualifications to be an administrator. It was a legitimate rational purpose for the school district to seek competent individuals, and the oral and written tests were reasonable devices to assure such competence.

*Rehabilitation Act of 1973 Requires
That School Board Articulate
Genuine Nondiscriminatory Reasons
For Failure to Hire a Handicapped
Person*

NORCROSS v. SNEED

United States District Court, W.D.
Arkansas, Harrison Division, 1983.
573 F.Supp. 533.

H. FRANKLIN WATERS, Chief Judge.

I. *Introduction*

Plaintiff, Rebecca Norcross, brought this action pursuant to 28 U.S.C. § 1343, 29 U.S.C. § 794 (the Rehabilitation Act of 1973), and 28 U.S.C. § 1331 against defendants, Wallace Sneed, *et al.* . . .

Plaintiff contends that she was denied employment as a school librarian because of her being "legally blind" and seeks injunctive relief in the form of instatement, back pay and retroactive benefits. Plaintiff also seeks compensatory damages for mental distress, punitive damages and attorney's fees.

Factual Summary

Plaintiff was born with a congenital visual impairment which renders her legally blind. Plaintiff's vision in her right eye can be corrected to 20/200 visual acuity. The vision in plaintiff's left eye is unmeasurable, and what little vision there is in this eye is of a nature which causes double vision and distortion of the corrected vision in the right eye. Plaintiff has no night vision at all.

. . . Plaintiff has been certified "legally blind" by her ophthamologist and by the federal government for purposes of receiving federal benefits accorded to blind persons. In any event, defendants do not assert that plaintiff is not "legally blind," and, considering the evidence adduced, the Court specifically finds that plaintiff is "legally blind" and is a "handicapped individual" within the meaning of 29 U.S.C. § 706(7)(B).

Plaintiff is capable of reading some print, however, and received a B.S. degree in library science from Sam Houston State University, Huntsville, Texas, in January, 1966, notwithstanding her disability.

After her graduation, she was employed for three years as assistant librarian at F.M. Black Junior High School in Houston, Texas. Because of pregnancy and family commitments, she quit her employment at F.M. Black Junior High School in January, 1969.

From 1969 to 1978, plaintiff remained outside of the work force. She again sought employment in June, 1978, at which time she inquired as to employment opportunities at the Flippin school system. At the time plaintiff made this initial inquiry, she resided in Houston, Texas. Plaintiff met with defendant, Wallace Sneed, in early June of 1978, the meeting having been arranged by defendant, Jimmie French.

At the meeting plaintiff described her education and experience in the field of library science, and advised defendant, Wallace Sneed, that she was legally blind. Mr. Sneed asked plaintiff to read aloud from a letter from his desk and plaintiff did so.

At the time of this initial meeting, there were no positions available with the Flippin system, plaintiff was a citizen and resident of Texas, and plaintiff was not certified in the state of Arkansas.

Defendant Sneed told plaintiff she could fill out an application form and further advised her that she would need to obtain certification in Arkansas. Plaintiff filled out the application provided. . . .

In January, 1979, plaintiff was certified by the Arkansas Department of Education as Librarian, K–12 (Kindergarten through Grade 12), and soon thereafter again contacted defendant Sneed by telephone, informing Mr. Sneed of her certification and her further interest in a position as librarian if one became available. Plaintiff testified that Mr. Sneed replied that if such a position became available, he would hire the most qualified applicant.

In July, 1979, plaintiff submitted another application to defendant Sneed requesting consideration for any available position. . . .

During this school year plaintiff worked as a kindergarten aide and instructed small groups under supervision. She received no criticism of her performance, although there was a controversy concerning her responsibility for playground duties. Plaintiff's supervisor, Meg Hanna, counseled her as to methods of better instructing the students.

The controversy arose from resentment from other teachers of plaintiff's failure to perform playground duties during her first semester as an aide. . . .

During this first year, Mr. Bryant (school principal) received some reports that plaintiff was cross and irritable on occasion with the children. . . .

Plaintiff was not re-employed as a teacher's aide for the following year because of a cutback in federal funding.

Near the end of the 1979–80 school year, plaintiff learned that the high school librarian, Geneva Hurst, had decided not to return in the 1980–81 year. She called Mr. Sneed's office in May, 1980, to confirm that her applications were still on file.

On June 2, 1980, plaintiff visited Mr. Sneed at his office to reiterate her interest in the library position. At that meeting Mr. Sneed told plaintiff that he would not recommend her for the job as librarian. Plaintiff contends that Mr. Sneed also said that he would refuse to recommend her because of her visual handicap. Mr. Sneed testified that he told plaintiff that he would not recommend her to the board because of problems she encountered as a teacher's aide: crossness, supervision, discipline and problems with playground duty.

Plaintiff testified that Mr. Sneed further told her that he would not submit her application for consideration. Defendant Sneed denied having made any such statement. . . .

After Mr. Sneed learned of Mrs. Hurst's intention not to return as librarian in the 1980–81 school year, Mr. Sneed was advised by the Superintendent of Schools in Eureka Springs, at a superintendents' meeting, that Mrs. Frolkey, a fourth grade teacher at the Flippin schools, had been an excellent librarian while employed at the Eureka Springs schools.

Mr. Sneed called Mrs. Frolkey advising her of Mrs. Hurst's resignation and requested that she submit an application for the position if she was interested. On June 7, 1980, Mrs. Frolkey's application was received.

Mrs. Frolkey was well known to everyone in the Flippin school community. She possessed a double Arkansas certificate as Librarian/K–12 (Kindergarten through Twelfth Grade/Elementary).

Mrs. Frolkey had taught fourth grade at Flippin since 1977. Although her application reflected only one year as a librarian at the Eureka Springs high school because of space limitations on the application, she had a total of six years' experience employed as a school librarian in two Iowa schools similar in size to Flippin prior to her position in Eureka Springs. . . .

A board meeting was held on June 23, 1980. At the meeting were the board members, Mr. Sneed, plaintiff and her husband, Rev. Sam Williams and his wife, and a newspaper reporter, Linda Leicht.

After the board decided to convene an executive session, plaintiff expressed her desire to make a presentation concerning her application. Plaintiff did so for five to ten minutes, at which time the board convened in executive session.

For approximately two hours the board deliberated. When the public was re-admitted, the board announced that it had unanimously selected Mrs. Frolkey for the librarian position. . . .

All of the board members testified that Mrs. Frolkey was chosen because they felt she was the most qualified. They noted that plaintiff had served ten years earlier as an "assistant librarian," while on the face of the application Mrs. Frolkey had served within the past six years as a "librarian" in a similar sized school. Plaintiff's total teaching experience comprised three years as an assistant librarian at F.M. Black Junior High School in Houston, Texas, and one year as a teacher's aide in Flippin, while Mrs. Frolkey had 22 years' teaching experience, five years as head librarian in a high school similar to Flippin, and had taught three years in the Flippin school district with a double certification.

The board members regarded both Mrs. Frolkey and plaintiff as qualified and indicated that plaintiff would have been chosen had Mrs. Frolkey not been. . . .

As a result of the foregoing events, plaintiff instituted this action, contending that the actions of Mr. Sneed and the board had violated her rights to due process and equal protection and denied her rights secured by 29 U.S.C. § 794 (§ 504 of the Rehabilitation Act of 1973).

II. *Applicable Law*

Section 504 of the Rehabilitation Act of 1973 provides in pertinent part:

No otherwise qualified handicapped individual in the United States, as defined in [29 U.S.C. § 706(7)], shall, solely by reason of his handicap, be excluded from the participation in, be denied the benefits of, or be subjected to discrimination under any program or activity receiving Federal financial assistance or under any program or activity conducted by any Executive agency or by the United States Postal Service.

29 U.S.C. § 794 (as amended by section 119 of the Rehabilitation, Comprehensive Services, and Developmental Disabilities Amendments of 1978, Pub.L. No. 95–602, 92 Stat. 2955, 2982) (hereinafter "1978 amendments"). . . .

Section 504 provides coverage for any "otherwise qualified handicapped individual." . . .

It is conceded that plaintiff . . . is a "handicapped individual" within the meaning of section 504. Thus, our initial inquiry is whether plaintiff is an "otherwise qualified" handicapped individual.

In *Davis,* [Southeastern Community College v. Davis, 442 U.S. 397, 99 S.Ct. 2361 (1979)], the Supreme Court held that an "otherwise qualified" individual is "one who is able to meet all of a program's requirements in spite of his handicap." In *Davis,* the Court held that the plaintiff was not entitled to relief because her handicap, *i.e.,* deafness, would prevent her from performing the duties imposed by the nursing program which had refused to admit her. . . .

The Court believes that the burden of proof in the instant case should be as follows: First, plaintiff must show that she is an "otherwise qualified handicapped" individual, that she applied for the position as librarian, and that she was rejected. If plaintiff satisfies this requirement, defendant must articulate legitimate, non-discriminatory reasons for rejecting the plaintiff's application for the position. Having satisfied this requirement, the burden shifts to the plaintiff to show that the reasons offered are pretextual and that plaintiff was rejected solely because of her handicap. Plaintiff retains the ultimate burden of persuasion on the case as a whole to prove that she is an "otherwise qualified handicapped individual" and that she was rejected solely because of her handicap.

III. *Discussion*

The Court concludes that plaintiff is an "otherwise qualified handicapped individual." Although plaintiff may have some difficulty in performing hall duty and playground duty due to her limited vision, both Mrs. Hurst and Mrs. Frolkey testified that full-time librarians had never been required to perform these duties. The job description required by the Office of Civil Rights requires only that the librarian perform these duties "as requested." . . .

As the school board members uniformly testified that plaintiff would have been hired had Mrs. Frolkey not been hired instead, defendants implicitly concede that plaintiff was at least minimally qualified for the library position. Further, plaintiff's experience in this area further demonstrates that she was at least minimally qualified for such a position.

Thus, the burden shifts to the defendants to articulate genuine non-discriminatory reasons for the failure to hire her.

We believe that defendants have met this burden. Plaintiff had not been personally involved in any school system since 1969 while Mrs. Frolkey was currently teaching at Flippin. Although Mrs. Frolkey had not served as a librarian in six years, plaintiff had not done so in ten years. Mrs. Frolkey was regarded as an excellent teacher and librarian while plaintiff was virtually unknown and suffered various problems in her role as a teacher's aide. Mrs. Frolkey was double-certified and had more experience both as a librarian and as a teacher than did the plaintiff. Mrs. Frolkey had lived in the area longer than had the plaintiff and had past work experience in the area and in schools of the same general size as Flippin's. Mrs. Frolkey had served as a head librarian while plaintiff's only experience in the library field was as an assistant librarian, although it is true that the duties were similar.

Simply stated, the Court believes that there is ample evidence in the record of legitimate, non-discriminatory reasons for the board's action in hiring Mrs. Frolkey. Thus, plaintiff must come forward with evidence that these reasons are mere "pretext" and that plaintiff was denied employment solely because of her handicap.

Defendants do not contend that plaintiff is not qualified for the position and admitted that plaintiff would have been hired had Mrs. Frolkey not been.

As evidence of pretext, plaintiff argues that Mr. Sneed's requiring plaintiff to submit to two "employment tests" which were not required of the other candidates shows that it was bias against her rather than Mrs. Frolkey's qualifications which was dispositive. These two "tests" were allegedly comprised of Mr. Sneed's asking plaintiff to read and plaintiff's employment as an aide.

However, Mr. Sneed did not ask plaintiff to read until plaintiff advised him of her blindness. Although the regulations prohibit tests that simply measure the degree of impairment, this rule is inapplicable where the test measures job-related skills. The ability to read is a legitimate job-related skill, as plaintiff concedes. Thus, although the situation could probably have been handled more tactfully, the Court does not believe that the incident can reasonably lead to an inference that plaintiff was not hired solely because of her handicap.

Plaintiff asserts that she was employed as an aide solely to "test" her ability to function in an academic environment, and that her performance as an aide is wholly unrelated to plaintiff's skills as a librarian.

The Court does not agree that the two jobs are so completely different as to render plaintiff's performance in one wholly irrelevant to ability in the other. Acceptability in the areas of supervision, discipline and temperament would appear to be a prerequisite for any teaching assignment just as dependability is a legitimate concern of any employer for any position. . . .

Plaintiff correctly notes that the burden of proving that an employer's reasons are a pretext for discrimination is essentially a burden of persuasion.

Although there was evidence in the record to the effect that Mr. Sneed acted somewhat less than tactfully toward plaintiff, and perhaps that Mr. Sneed was not particularly fond of plaintiff, the Court believes that Mr. Sneed's attitude toward plaintiff was purely personal and did not result in plaintiff's rejection solely because of her handicap.

Although the board could hardly have been unaware of plaintiff's perception of Mr. Sneed's attitude, it was plaintiff who repeatedly brought this knowledge to the attention of the board, however proper her motives. . . . .

Having carefully considered and scrutinized the testimony, conduct and demeanor of the witnesses, weighed the facts and all legitimate inferences that may be drawn therefrom, the Court concludes that plaintiff has failed to demonstrate that the reasons offered for not hiring plaintiff are pretextual and thus has failed to demonstrate that she was refused employment solely by reason of her handicap. . . .

However, because plaintiff did not prevail in her private action under section 504, it follows that section 1983 is not available to plaintiff to remedy a section 504 violation. Section 1983 cannot breathe new life into an unsuccessful section 504 claim. Thus, we need not decide whether, under appropriate facts, section 1983 provides a remedy for a violation of section 504.

Plaintiff also advances claims under the Fourteenth Amendment for alleged deprivations of equal protection and due process. . . .

Because the Court does not believe that plaintiff was denied employment because of her handicap and finds that the board had a rational basis for its actions, plaintiff's equal protection claim is unavailing.

As to plaintiff's due process claim, it is clear that plaintiff has no protected "property" interest. . . .

Nor does plaintiff have a protected "liberty" interest. . . .

Plaintiff was not stigmatized in any manner by not being hired as a librarian by the Flippin schools.

With respect to the procedural aspect of due process, assuming without deciding that plaintiff was entitled to some sort of hearing, it is beyond question that plaintiff has had ample opportunity to present and argue her qualifications for the job, as well as to air her grievance. . . . Thus, any hearing to which plaintiff was entitled was sufficiently provided. Therefore, the Court finds plaintiff's constitutional claims to be without merit. . . .

The Court specifically wishes to commend the plaintiff for her perseverance, tenacity, and accomplishments in life and this Memorandum Opinion in no way is intended to reflect negatively upon plaintiff's abilities as a wife, mother, employee, or as an individual. However, in light of the foregoing findings of fact and conclusions of law, the Court has no alternative but to dismiss plaintiff's complaint and to enter judgment in favor of defendants.

Judgment in accordance with this Memorandum Opinion will be concurrently entered.

NOTE

Prohibition by the Rehabilitation Act of 1973 against discrimination applies to recruitment and to processing of applications for employment as well as to job assignments, job description, and any term or condition of employment. Fitzgerald v. Green Valley Area Education Agency, 589 F.Supp. 1130 (D.C.Iowa 1984).

Footnotes

1. Keyes v. School District No. 1, 413 U.S. 189, 93 S.Ct. 2686 (1973).
2. Swann v. Charlotte-Mecklenburg Board of Education, 402 U.S. 1, 91 S.Ct. 1267 (1971).
3. Washington v. Davis, 426 U.S. 229, 96 S.Ct. 2040 (1976).
4. Village of Arlington Heights v. Metropolitan Housing Development Corp., 429 U.S. 252, 97 S.Ct. 555 (1977).
5. 480 F.2d 1159 (D.C. Cir.1973).
6. Regents of the University of California v. Bakke, 438 U.S. 265, 98 S.Ct. 2733 (1978).
7. 463 U.S. 582, 103 S.Ct. 3221 (1983).
8. 42 U.S.C. § 2000e-1 (1970).
9. Equal Employment Opportunities Act of 1972, Public Law 92–261.
10. 401 U.S. 424, 91 S.Ct. 849 (1971).
11. Id.
12. Armstead v. Starkville Municipal Separate School District, 325 F.Supp. 560 (N.D.Miss.1971), affirmed in part and reversed in part 461 F.2d 276 (5th Cir.1972); Chance v. Board of Examiners, 458 F.2d 1167 (2d Cir.1972); Baker v. Columbus Municipal Separate School District, 462 F.2d 1112 (5th Cir.1972); United States v. Chesterfield County School District, 484 F.2d 70 (4th Cir.1972); United States v. North Carolina, 400 F.Supp. 343 (E.D.N.C.1975), vacated 425 F.Supp. 789 (E.D.N.C.1977).
13. Teamsters v. United States, 431 U.S. 324, 97 S.Ct. 1843 (1977).
14. Washington v. Davis, 426 U.S. 229, 96 S.Ct. 2040 (1976).
15. United States v. South Carolina, 445 F.Supp. 1094 (D.S.C.1977), *affirmed* 434 U.S. 1026, 98 S.Ct. 756 (1978).
16. 438 U.S. 567, 98 S.Ct. 2943 at 2950 (1978).
17. 427 U.S. 273, 96 S.Ct. 2574 at 2576 (1976).
18. 438 U.S. 265, 98 S.Ct. 2733 (1978).
19. 443 U.S. 193, 99 S.Ct. 2721 (1979).
20. Id. at 2729–2730.
21. Kern Alexander and M. David Alexander, *The Law of Schools, Students and Teachers* (St. Paul, MN: West Publishing Company, 1984).
22. 29 U.S.C.A. Section 206(d)(1).
23. 42 U.S.C.A. Section 2000e-2.
24. Odomes v. Nucare, Inc., 653 F.2d 246 at 250 (6th Cir.1981). See: Corning Glass Works v. Brennan, 417 U.S. 188, 94 S.Ct. 2223 (1974).
25. Corning Glass Works v. Brennan, 417 U.S. 188, 94 S.Ct. 2223 (1974).
26. 456 U.S. 512, 102 S.Ct. 1912 at 1913 (1982).
27. Geduldig v. Aiello, 417 U.S. 484, 94 S.Ct. 2485 (1974).
28. Gilbert v. General Electric Co., 429 U.S. 125, 97 S.Ct. 401 at 407 (1976).
29. Id. at 412.
30. P.L. 95–535, Amended Section 701 of Title VII.
31. Newport News Shipbuilding & Dry Dock Co. v. EEOC, 462 U.S. 669, 103 S.Ct. 2622, at 2624 (1983).
32. 414 U.S. 632, 94 S.Ct. 791 (1974).
33. City of Los Angeles, Department of Water v. Manhart, 435 U.S. 702, 98 S.Ct. 1370 (1978).
34. Arizona Governing Committee v. Norris, 463 U.S. 1073, 103 S.Ct. 3492 (1983).
35. Section 901(a)(1) provides that, with respect to admissions, § 901(a) applies only to institutions of vocational education, professional education, and graduate higher education, and to public institutions of undergraduate higher education. Specific exceptions are made for the admissions policies of schools that begin admitting students of both sexes for the first time, § 901(a)(2); religious schools, § 901(a)(3); military schools, § 901(a)(4); the admissions policies of public institutions of undergraduate higher education that traditionally and continually have admitted students of only one gender, § 901(a)(5); social fraternities and sororities, and voluntary youth service organizations, § 901(a)(6); Boys/Girls State/Nation conferences, § 901(a)(7); father-son and mother-daughter activities at educational institutions, § 901(a)(8); and scholarships awarded in "beauty" pageants by institutions of higher education, § 901(a)(9).
36. 29 U.S.C.A. Section 621, as amended in 1978, Age Discrimination in Employment Act Amendments of 1978, 92 Stat. 191.

37. Massachusetts Board of Retirement v. Murgia, 427 U.S. 307, 96 S.Ct. 2562 (1976).

38. Vance v. Bradley, 440 U.S. 93, 99 S.Ct. 939 at 939 (1979).

39. 576 F.2d 459 (2 Cir.1978).

40. Kerwick v. New York State Board of Equalization & Assessment, 114 Misc.2d 928, 453 N.Y.S.2d 151 (1982).

41. McDonnell Douglas Corp. v. Green, 411 U.S. 792, 93 S.Ct. 1817 at 1824 (1973). See also: Schwager v. Sun Oil Co. of Pennsylvania, 591 F.2d 58 at 61 (10th Cir.1979); Loeb v. Textron, Inc., 600 F.2d 1003 at 1014–1015 (1st Cir.1979); Stanojeu v. Ebasco Services, Inc., 643 F.2d 914 (2d Cir.1981).

42. *Gault* also distinguished *Murgia* on another ground. It noted that, as between teachers and policemen, the consequences of lack of fitness differ substantially. If a police officer is not fit, his inability to perform could become a matter of life or death. Thus, a general, perhaps overly broad rule is justified to prevent such occurrences. If a teacher becomes unfit, however, the consequences are not so immediate. There is adequate time to effect his or her removal via appropriate procedural means. While this distinction has merit, we do not find it sufficiently persuasive in view of the considerations expressed below.

43. Section 504 of Rehabilitation Act, 29 U.S.C.A. Section 794.

44. Pushkin v. Regents of University of Colorado, 658 F.2d 1372 at 1384 (10th Cir.1981).

45. Gurmankin v. Costanzo, 556 F.2d 184 (3d Cir.1977).

46. Upshur v. Love, 474 F.Supp. 332 (D.Cal.1979).

16

Collective Bargaining

Labor law in public education encompasses collective bargaining, strikes, wages, hours, and working conditions. With such broad import for the operation of the schools, it is little wonder that the movement toward unionism has had such a profound effect on school administration. This has manifested itself at all levels, from statutory provisions down to the day-to-day contract administration by the school building principal. The result has been that the administrative role has, to a great extent, shifted from discretionary activities to duties that are ministerial in nature. Public school labor relations is the story of this legal transition.

Developments of today in public school labor relations closely track the precedents of the private sector of the 1930s. Differences do exist, however, between the public and private sectors that cannot be ignored, thus preventing direct transference of private sector legal precedents into public practice. Both common law and statutory law that govern public school labor relations are, effectively, a modification of the well-established private sector view of labor relations.

HISTORICAL DEVELOPMENT

"Labor Relations in the Public Sector,"
Charles M. Rehmus, Paper prepared for
the 3rd World Congress, International
Industrial Relations Association, London,
England (September 3–7, 1973)

Background of Public Employee Labor Relations Workers in the industrial private sector in the United States were given the statutory right to organize and bargain collectively in the 1930s. By 1960, approximately 30 percent of all nonagricultural private sector employees were represented by unions. Yet by this same date, there was practically no unionization in the public sector other than in the traditionally organized postal service and in a few other isolated situations.

The reasons for the delay in union organization of employees in the public sector in the United States are complex. In part, they stem from certain philosophical ideas long prevalent in the nation. Traditional concepts of sovereignty asserted that government is and should be supreme, hence immune from contravening forces and pressures such as that of collective bargaining. Related to this concept was that of the illegality of delegation of sovereign power. This assertion was that public decision-making could be done only by elected or appointed public officials, whose unilateral and complete discretion was therefore unchallengeable.

More practical considerations also delayed the advent of public employee unionism in the United States. The private sector unions and their international federations were fully occupied in trying to increase the extent of organization in the private sector. They had neither the money nor energy to turn to the public sector until the 1960s. Equally or more importantly, public employees were not generally dissatisfied with their terms and conditions of employment and, therefore, except in isolated cases, did not press for collective bargaining rights. Though the wages and salaries of public employees in the United States had traditionally lagged slightly behind comparable private sector salaries, the greater fringe benefits and job security associated with public employment were traditionally thought to be adequate compensation.

By the late 1950s and early 1960s, several of these practical considerations that had delayed public employee unionism had disappeared. Moreover, new factors came into play that are difficult to assess as to sequence or relative importance, but in total added to a new militancy. Change increasingly became endemic in American society as more and more groups, including public employees, found it commonplace to challenge the established order. Some public employees were made less secure by organizational and technological changes as government came under pressure to reduce tax increases and, therefore, turned to devices to increase efficiency and lower unit labor costs. Public employee wages and salaries began to lag further behind those in the unionized private sector as the post-war inflationary spiral continued. The private sector international unions saw the large and growing employment in the non-union public sector as a fertile alternative that might substitute for their failure after 1956 to increase membership steadily in the private sector. Finally, many observers of public employment, both in and out of government, began strongly and publicly to question the logic behind governmentally protected collective bargaining in the private sector and government's complete failure to grant similar privileges and protections in the public sector.

By the 1960s, these practical challenges to the traditional arguments of sovereignty and illegal delegation of powers came to be seen as overriding in a number of government jurisdictions. The City of New York, the school board of that same city, and the State of Wisconsin gave modified collective bargaining rights to their public employees. Most importantly, in 1962 President Kennedy by executive order gave federal employees a limited version of the rights that private employees had received thirty years before. These seminal breakthroughs in granting some form of bargaining right to public employees led increasingly to similar kinds of state legislation, particularly in the more industrialized states. Today, over thirty American states have granted some form of collective bargaining rights to some or all of their public employees. President Nixon in two subsequent executive orders expanded and clarified the bargaining rights of federal employees. . . .

PRIVATE VERSUS PUBLIC SECTOR

Before 1932, labor relations in the United States was a product of common law. In our laissez faire economic system, the courts tended to favor industrial management since the damage done by work stoppages was both social and economic. In the period extending from about 1870 to 1930, business interests held hegemony in labor relations and the courts backed it up by liberal use of the injunction to suppress strikes, picketing, and boycotts. Further, neither the courts nor the legislatures fashioned remedies for the employee to prevent employers from discriminating against union members. Consequently, by 1930, labor unions were quite weak and had relatively little influence on the American economic system.[1]

Aware of the onesidedness of the legal precedents and the suppressive nature of the injunction and its overuse by the courts, the Congress enacted the Norris-LaGuardia Act in 1932 which had as its primary purpose preventing federal courts from issuing injunctions against union activities occurring as a result of labor disputes. Several states followed suit and, within a few years, the scales were tipped in favor of unions making the use of the injunction almost impossible. Anti-injunction legislation was the seed that allowed labor to develop strength and to secure the favorable position it now holds in the country. Modern labor statutes have largely carried forth the anti-injunction theory allowing injunctions only if union activities violate the law or place the national health and safety in peril.[2]

Following the anti-injunction statute of 1932, the first broad labor relations act was the National Labor Relations Act of 1935 (The Wagner Act). Its purpose was to encourage collective bargaining as a means of promoting industrial peace. The Act established the National Labor Relations Board as a regulatory body to prosecute and remedy unfair labor practice. Additionally, the law created procedures for determining employee representation and placed a duty on both parties to bargain in good faith.

In 1947, the National Labor Relations Act was amended by the Labor Management Relations Act of 1947, more popularly known as the Taft-Hartley Act. With this law, more limitations were placed on union activities through more definitive regulation of unfair labor practices by the union. Later in 1959, the Taft-Hartley Act itself was amended by the Labor Management Reporting and Disclosure Act. This act was necessitated by widespread union mismanagement and corruption. A Senate investigating committee had found that unions in many cases had misused funds, had been infiltrated by gangsters, and had failed to conduct union business in a democratic manner. Designed to curb these abuses, the 1959 Act specifically delineated employee rights as protection against union abuse, prescribed union election procedures, and established criminal penalties for misappropriation of union funds.[3]

The experience of private sector labor relations laid the groundwork for present statutory and judicial regulation of union activity. State statutes governing public employee collective bargaining reflect this in many ways; for example, scope of bargaining, representation procedures, impasse redress, etc., all have earmarks of the private experience.

Private and public sectors are, however, substantially different and the application of private labor relations to the public schools has proceeded slowly. Some contend, as did Franklin D. Roosevelt in 1937, that "The process of collective bargaining as usually understood cannot be transplanted into the public service."[4] This view maintains that decision-making in education is a sovereign prerogative that cannot be shared. Those who are elected and speak with the voice of the citizenry as a whole must exercise their discretion in such matters and the decision process that reflects this public will cannot be impaired or delegated. Public employees reject this rationale arguing that the sovereign, legislature, or public agency is merely another employer with the power to delegate labor-management issues to the decision-making process of the bargaining table.

Most commentators admit, however, that the theoretical differences between the private and public sectors are probably of less practical importance than the more pragmatic distinctions relating to the strike, the process of governmental decision-making, existing civil service systems, and the different economic forces and motivations that bear on government as opposed to industry.[5]

At the heart of collective bargaining is the right to strike. From the viewpoint of the employee, if employees cannot strike, effective negotiations may be a hollow exercise. Labor's position is simply that "One cannot negotiate without ability to reject the proffered terms. The only way in which employees can reject an employer's offer is to stop work. Consequently, collective bargaining can hardly exist without preserving the right to strike."[6] With few exceptions, though, the people through their state legislature have rejected the right of public school teachers to strike. Where collective bargaining is permitted by statute, legislation usually falls short of allowing strikes and, in most instances, provides express prohibition. No such restraint, of course, exists in the private sector.

Another essential difference is that in the public sector, especially where school teachers are concerned, statutory budget deadlines and taxing restrictions make the bargaining process dependent on direct legislative action. In states in which local school district taxing leeway is limited, much of the new money for education is derived each year from state tax revenues. In such a situation, the bargaining agreement for increased wages is usually subject to legislative appropriation regardless of the bargaining agreement. As state systems of school finance become more centralized this situation can only be expected to intensify.

A further very practical difference between the private and public sectors is that private employees have fewer inherent protections that public employees enjoy. In our system of government, as reviewed in other sections of this book, public school teachers have constitutional rights of equal protection and due process against arbitrary state action, a benefit not enjoyed by employees in the private sector. These constitutional protections coupled with statutory prohibitions of discrimination, state salary schedules, fringe benefits of teacher retirement systems, sick leave, vacation leave, et cetera, are examples of a public response to public employee needs that would probably not be found in the private sector in the absence of collective bargaining.

Finally, the normal market pressures of the private sector do not exist in the public schools. Public schools cannot lock out employees, go out of business, or raise prices. Beyond this, when the legislature of a state becomes involved, laws can be enacted that quickly change the rules of the game, possibly entirely redefining the criteria or certification for the teacher work force or unilaterally altering the nature of the public service in its entirety.

These distinctions, though, are held by many union leaders to be more apparent than real and it is certainly true that over the past decade a substantial erosion of the differences between private and public bargaining has transpired. To a large extent, some of the traditional points of departure have become irrelevant, but throughout any discussion of this issue, one cannot help but observe that essential differences remain. The employee in the public sector as a citizen, taxpayer, and human being has greater potential influence over his employment destiny than can be found in the private sector.

As Werne points out, "The employee in the private sector, except for the very devious method of shareholder voting, has no control over his management, unless by union contract. In the public sector, the employee can remove his employer from office and in not a few cases has effected such removal. In short, the strict dichotomy between employer and employee in the private sector has no exact counterpart in the public sector."[7]

Thus, the law pertaining to labor relations in the public schools may, to a great extent, be characterized as an adaptation of the private sector experience to the differing circumstances of the public schools.

THE RIGHT TO BARGAIN COLLECTIVELY

The right of public employees to engage in collective bargaining entails important legal aspects, such as the employees right to organize, the authority of the school board to bargain, the right to strike, and the authority of the school board to submit to compulsory arbitration. Employees have a right to organize and join labor unions. A North Carolina law forbidding public employees from joining unions was held unconstitutional on its face as violative of the First and Fourteenth Amendments.[8] In *AFSCME* v. *Woodward*[9] the court held that employees not only have a right to join labor unions but may file suit for damages and injunctive relief under the Civil Rights Act of 1871 if this freedom is denied. In *Woodward* the court stated:

> The First Amendment protects the right of one citizen to associate with other citizens for any lawful purpose free from government interference. The guarantee of the "right of assembly" protects more than the "right to attend a meeting; it includes the right to express one's attitudes or philosophies by membership in a group or by affiliation with it or by other lawful means . . . ." Griswold v. Connecticut, 381 U.S. 479, 85 S.Ct. 1678 (1965); N.A. A.C.P. v. Alabama, 357 U.S. 449, 78 S.Ct. 1163 (1958).[10]

In the absence of statute, authority to bargain may[11] be within the discretion of the local school board,[12] but there is no constitutional duty to bargain collectively with an exclusive bargaining agent.

> The refusal of [the School Board] to bargain in good faith does not equal a constitutional violation of plaintiffs-appellees' positive rights of association, free speech, petition, equal protection, or due process. Nor does the fact that the agreement to collectively bargain may be enforceable against a state elevate a contractual right to a constitutional right.[13]

Statutes prohibiting public employees' right to strike do not violate the state or federal constitutional mandates of equal protection. This issue was settled in a New York case contesting the Taylor Law's prohibition against strikes. The New York Court of Appeals held:

> In view of the strong policy considerations which led to the enactment of the Taylor Law, it is our conclusion that the statutory prohibition against strikes by public employees is reasonably designed to effectuate a valid state policy in an area where it has authority to act. . . .[14]

Similarly, the Supreme Court has ruled that public school teachers have no inherent right to strike[15] and these judgments have been reinforced at the federal level where, following a strike by the United States postal workers in 1970, a three-judge panel held that government employees do not have a right to strike. The Court held that neither public nor private employees have an absolute right to strike without statutory authorization. The opinion stated:

> Given the fact that there is no constitutional right to strike, it is not irrational or arbitrary for the Government to condition employment on a promise to withhold labor collectively, and to prohibit strikes by those in public employment, whether because of the prerogative of the sovereign, some sense of higher obligation associated with public service, to assure the continuing functioning of the Government without interruption, to protect public health and safety or for other reasons.[16]

The public attitude against public employee strikes has become more moderate in recent years and even the courts, albeit usually in dissents, are tending to view the strike situation more liberally. In a dissent in an Indiana case involving teachers in the City of Anderson, Justice DeBruler summarized arguments in favor of public employee strikes.

1. State sovereignty is not necessarily infringed upon if collective bargaining and a limited right to strike are extended to public sector employees.

2. The difference between public and private sector employees is in many instances negligible.

3. The impact of a private sector strike might be more crippling than a strike by public employees.

4. Public employees are guaranteed the same irrevocable rights by the Constitution as employees working in the private sector.

5. Public employees must have some means to assert their rights, especially when such rights are not ensured through legislation.[17]

Compulsory interest arbitration has been used in the private sector as an alternative to the strike and may become more common in public education. Impasse resolution in this manner provides that either party may request arbitration of the dispute and that the decision of the arbitrator is binding on both parties. Compulsory arbitration has been extended to firefighters in Wyoming, Rhode Island, Massachusetts, and New York. A statute in Oregon requires binding arbitration in the field of public education and Minnesota law provides for the Director of Mediation to resolve impasses by sending the dispute to arbitration.[18]

Without authorization from statute, however, school boards cannot generally submit to binding arbitration. The Virginia Supreme Court has held that binding rights arbitration imposed by State Board Regulation constitutes an unlawful denial of local school board power and an unwarranted delegation of authority and as such violates the Virginia Constitution, which makes management of the teaching staff an essential function of the local school board.[19]

In Michigan, however, the courts have upheld a state statute that provided for compulsory arbitration. The city had maintained that the act violated the prerogative of city government as delineated in the Michigan Constitution. The court held that validity of the statute should be upheld "unless the contrary clearly appears."[20] Although this case was later reversed on other grounds it clearly enunciated that a state statute imposing arbitration on local government will be presumed to be valid unless in direct conflict with the state constitution. In the absence of such statute, however, local agencies are not required to delegate their authority to an arbitrator.

Teachers May Organize and Bargain
Collectively but Cannot Strike

NORWALK TEACHERS ASSOCIATION v. BOARD OF EDUCATION OF CITY OF NORWALK

Supreme Court of Errors of Connecticut,
1951.
138 Conn. 269, 83 A.2d 482.

JENNINGS, Justice. This is a suit between the Norwalk Teachers' Association as plaintiff and the Norwalk board of education as defendant for a declaratory judgment. . . . The plaintiff is a voluntary association and an independent labor union to which all but two of the teaching personnel of approximately 300 in the Norwalk school system belong. In April, 1946, there was a dispute between the parties over salary rates. The board of estimate and taxation was also involved. After long negotiations, 230 members of the association rejected the individual contracts of employment tendered them and refused to return to their teaching duties. . . . The contracts, subject to conditions precedent therein set forth, recognize the plaintiff as the bargaining agent for all of its members, defined working conditions and set up a grievance procedure and salary schedule. Similar contracts were entered into for the succeeding school years, including 1950–1951. From September, 1946, to the present and particularly with reference to the contract for 1950–1951, much doubt and uncertainty have arisen concerning the rights and duties of the respective parties, the interpretation of the contract and the construction of the state statutes relating to schools, education and boards of education. "In addition," the complaint states, "there has been the possibility of strikes, work stoppage or collective refusals to return to work by the teachers through their organization and the possibility of discharges or suspensions by the defendant by reason of difficult personnel relations, all of which tends to disharmony in the operation of the school system and to the ever present possibility that either, or both, the parties may be unwittingly violating statutes by reason of mistaken or erroneous interpretation thereon." The parties agreed that the contract for the school year 1949–1950 would govern their relations for the school year 1950–1951, that they would join in this action, and "that whatever contractual obligations exist will be forthwith modified so soon as they shall have received from the Court judgments and orders declaring their respective rights, privileges, duties and immunities." The specific points of dispute are stated in the questions reserved, printed in the footnote.* . . .

Under our system, the government is established by and run for all of the people, not for the benefit of any person or group. The profit motive, inherent in the principle of free enterprise, is absent. It should be the aim of every employee of the government to do his or her part to make it function as efficiently and economically as possible. The drastic remedy of the organized strike to enforce the demands of unions of government employees is in direct contravention of this principle. It has been so regarded by the heads of the executive departments of the states and the

---

* The plaintiff claimed a declaratory judgment answering and adjudicating the following questions:

"(a) Is it permitted to the plaintiff under our laws to organize itself as a labor union for the purpose of demanding and receiving recognition and collective bargaining?

"(b) Is it permitted to the plaintiff organized as a labor union to demand recognition as such and collective bargaining?

"(c) Is it permissible under Connecticut law for the defendant to recognize the plaintiff for the purpose of collective bargaining?

"(d) Is collective bargaining to establish salaries and working conditions permissible between the plaintiff and the defendant?

"(e) May the plaintiff engage in concerted action such as strike, work stoppage, or collective refusal to enter upon duties?

"(f) Is arbitration a permissible method under Connecticut law to settle or adjust disputes between the plaintiff and the defendant?

"(g) Is mediation a permissible method under Connecticut law to settle or adjust disputes between the plaintiff and the defendant?

"(h) If the answer to the previous questions is yes, are the State's established administrative facilities, such as the State Board of Mediation and Arbitration and the State Labor Relations Board, available, as they are available in industrial disputes, to the plaintiff and the defendant?

"(i) Does the continuing contract law, so-called, create a status of employment within which the plaintiff may claim employment subject to the right to bargain salaries and working conditions?

"(j) Has the plaintiff the right to establish rules, working conditions and grievance resolution procedures by collective bargaining?"

nation. Most of the text writers refer to one or more of the following statements by three of our recent presidents. They are quoted, for example, in 1 Labor Law Journal 612 (May, 1950): "There is no right to strike against public safety by anybody anywhere at any time" (Calvin Coolidge on the Boston police strike). This same strike was characterized by President Wilson as "an intolerable crime against civilization." President Franklin D. Roosevelt said in a letter to the president of the National Federation of Federal Employees on August 16, 1937: "Particularly, I want to emphasize my conviction that militant tactics have no place in the functions of any organization of Government employees. . . . [A] strike of public employees manifests nothing less than an intent on their part to prevent or obstruct the operations of Government until their demands are satisfied. Such action, looking toward the paralysis of Government by those who have sworn to support it, is unthinkable and intolerable." As the author of the article cited says, "The above statement by President Roosevelt, who certainly was no enemy of labor unions, epitomizes the answer to the problem. It seems to be axiomatic." . . .

Few cases involving the right of unions of government employees to strike to enforce their demands have reached courts of last resort. That right has usually been tested by an application for an injunction forbidding the strike. The right of the governmental body to this relief has been uniformly upheld. It has been put on various grounds: public policy; interference with governmental function; illegal discrimination against the right of any citizen to apply for government employment (where the union sought a closed shop). . . .

The plaintiff, recognizing the unreasonableness of its claims in the case of such employees as the militia and the judiciary, seeks to place teachers in a class with employees employed by the municipality in its proprietary capacity. No authority is cited in support of this proposition. "A town board of education is an agency of the state in charge of education in the town . . . ." . . . In fulfilling its duties as such an agency, it is acting in a governmental, not a proprietary, capacity. . . .

In the American system, sovereignty is inherent in the people. They can delegate it to a government which they create and operate by law. They can give to that government the power and authority to perform certain duties and furnish certain services. The government so created and empowered must employ people to carry on its task. Those people are agents of the government. They exercise some part of the sovereignty entrusted to it. They occupy a status entirely different from those who carry on a private enterprise. They serve the public welfare and not a private purpose. To say that they can strike is the equivalent of saying that they can deny the authority of government and contravene the public welfare. The answer to question (e) is "No."

Questions (a) and (b) relate to the right of the plaintiff to organize itself as a labor union and to demand recognition and collective bargaining. The right to organize is sometimes accorded by statute or ordinance. See, for example, the Bridgeport ordinance adopted June 17, 1946 (Bridgeport Munic. Reg. [1947] p. 15), discussed in National Institute of Municipal Law Officers Report No. 129, p. 51. The right to organize has also been forbidden by statute or regulation. Perez v. Board of Police Commissioners, 78 Cal.App. 2d 638, 178 P.2d 537. In Connecticut the statutes are silent on the subject. Union organization in industry is now the rule rather than the exception. In the absence of prohibitory statute or regulation, no good reason appears why public employees should not organize as a labor union. Springfield v. Clouse, 356 Mo. 1239, 1246, 206 S.W.2d 539. It is the second part of the question (a) that causes difficulty. The question reads: "Is it permitted to the plaintiff under our laws to organize itself as a labor union for the purpose of demanding and receiving recognition and collective bargaining?" The question is phrased in a very peremptory form. The common method of enforcing recognition and collective bargaining is the strike. It appears that this method has already been used by the plaintiff and that the threat of its use again is one of the reasons for the present suit. As has been said, the strike is not a permissible method of enforcing the plaintiff's demands. The answer to questions (a) and (b) is a qualified "Yes." There is no objection to the organization of the plaintiff as a labor union, but if its organization is for the purpose of "demanding" recognition and collective bargaining the demands must be kept within legal bounds. What we have said does not mean that the plaintiff has the right to organize for all of the purposes for which employees in private enterprise may unite, as those are defined in § 7391 of the General Statutes. Nor does it mean that, having organized, it is necessarily protected against unfair labor practices as specified in § 7392 or that it shall be the exclusive bargaining agent for all employees of the unit, as provided in § 7393. It means nothing more than that the plaintiff may organize and bargain collectively for the pay and working conditions which it may be in the power of the board of education to grant.

Questions (c) and (d) in effect ask whether collective bargaining between the plaintiff and the defendant is permissible. The statutes and private acts give broad powers to the defendant with reference to educational matters and school management in Norwalk. If it chooses to negotiate with the plaintiff with regard to the employment, salaries, grievance procedure and working conditions of its members, there is no statute, public or private, which forbids such negotiations. It is a matter of common knowledge that this is the method pursued in most school systems large enough to support a teachers' association in some form. It would seem to make no difference theoretically whether the negotiations are with a committee of the whole association or with individuals or small related groups, so long as any agreement made with the committee is confined to members of the association. If the strike threat is absent and the defendant prefers to handle the matter through negotiation with the plaintiff, no reason exists why it should not do so. The claim of the defendant that this would be an illegal delegation of authority is without merit. The authority is and remains in the board. This statement is not to be construed as approval of the existing contracts attached to the complaint. Their validity is not in issue.

As in the case of questions (a) and (b), (c) and (d) are in too general a form to permit a categorical answer. The qualified "Yes" which we give to them should not be construed as authority to negotiate a contract which involves the surrender of the board's legal discretion, is contrary to law or is otherwise ultra vires. For example, an agreement by the board to hire only union members would clearly be an illegal discrimination. Mugford v. Baltimore, 185 Md. 266, 270, 44 A.2d 745; Rhyne, Labor Unions & Municipal Employee Law, pp. 34, 137, 157. Any salary schedule must be subject to the powers of the board of estimate and taxation. "The salaries of all persons appointed by the board of education . . . shall be as fixed by said board, but the aggregate amount of such salaries . . . shall not exceed the amount determined by the board of estimate and taxation . . . ." 21 Spec. Laws, p. 285, No. 315, § 3; Board of Education of Stamford v. Board of Finance, 127 Conn. 345, 349, 16 A.2d 601. One of the allegations of the complaint is that the solution of the parties' difficulties by the posing of specific issues is not satisfactory. Whether or not this is so, that course will be necessary if this discussion of general principles is an insufficient guide.

Question (f) reads, "Is arbitration a permissible method under Connecticut law to settle or adjust disputes between the plaintiff and the defendant?" The power of a town to enter into an agreement of arbitration was originally denied on the ground that it was an unlawful delegation of authority. Griswold v. North Stonington, 5 Conn. 367, 371. It was later held that not only the amount of damages but liability could be submitted to arbitration. Hine v. Stephens, 33 Conn. 497, 504; Mallory v. Huntington, 64 Conn. 88, 96, 29 A. 245. The principle applies to the parties to the case at bar. If it is borne in mind that arbitration is the result of mutual agreement, there is no reason to deny the power of the defendant to enter voluntarily into a contract to arbitrate a specific dispute. On a proposal for a submission, the defendant would have the opportunity of deciding whether it would arbitrate as to any question within its power. Its power to submit to arbitration would not extend to questions of policy but might extend to question of liability. Arbitration as a method of settling disputes is growing in importance and, in a proper case, "deserves the enthusiastic support of the courts." International Brotherhood of Teamsters v. Shapiro, 138 Conn. 57, 69, 82 A.2d 345. Agreements to submit all disputes to arbitration, commonly found in ordinary union contracts, are in a different category. If the defendant entered into a general agreement of that kind, it might find itself committed to surrender the broad discretion and responsibility reposed in it by law. For example, it could not commit to an arbitrator the decision of a proceeding to discharge a teacher for cause. So, the matter of certification of teachers is committed to the state board of education. General Statutes, §§ 1432, 1433, 1435. The best answer we can give to question (f) is, "Yes, arbitration may be a permissible method as to certain specific, arbitrable disputes."

From what has been said, it is obvious that, within the same limitations, mediation to settle or adjust disputes is not only permissible but desirable. The answer to question (g) is "Yes." The state board of mediation and arbitration and the state labor relations board, however, are set up to handle disputes in private industry and are not available to the plaintiff and defendant for reasons given in the opinion of the attorney general dated July 6, 1948. 25 Conn.Atty.Gen.Rep. 270. This was confirmed as to Norwalk teachers by an opinion dated June 12, 1950, not yet published. See also United States v. United Mine Workers, 330 U.S. 258, 269, 67 S.Ct. 677, 91 L.Ed. 884. The answer to question (h) is "No."

General Statutes, Sup.1949, § 160a, provides in part: "The contract of employment of a teacher shall be renewed for the following school year unless such teacher has been notified in writing prior to March first of that year that such contract will not be renewed." Question (i) asks whether this law creates "a status of employment within which the plaintiff may claim employment subject to the right to bargain salaries and working conditions?" The meaning of this is not clear and the briefs do not clarify it. It is the type of question that should be related to a specific state of facts. It cannot be answered in vacuo.

As to question (j), the plaintiff has no right to establish rules. As stated above, the right is and remains in the board.

Question (g) is answered, "Yes, but not under chapter 369 of the General Statutes as amended." Questions (e), (h) and (j) are answered "No." Question (i) is not answered. No purpose would be served by answering the other questions categorically. Questions (a) and (b) are answered, "Yes, with relation to the plaintiff's own members, provided its demands are kept within legal bounds." Questions (c) and (d) are answered, "Yes, with relation to the plaintiff's own members, provided that this answer shall not be construed as approval of any specific contract which has been or may be entered into between the parties." Question (f) is answered, "Yes, arbitration may be a permissible method as to certain specific, arbitrable disputes." In answering some of these questions we have gone beyond the requirements of the specific questions asked in order to render such assistance as we properly may in helping to solve the difficulties of the parties.

No costs will be taxed in this court to either party.

In this opinion the other judges concurred.

Public Employees Must Have Express
Legislative Permission to Strike

ANDERSON FEDERATION OF TEACHERS, LOCAL 519 v. SCHOOL CITY OF ANDERSON

Supreme Court of Indiana, 1969.
252 Ind. 558, 251 N.E.2d 15, reh. denied
254 N.E.2d 329, cert. denied 399 U.S. 928,
90 S.Ct. 2243.

GIVEN, Judge. On May 6, 1968, the Superior Court of Madison County found the appellant, Anderson Federation of Teachers, Local 519, in contempt of court for the violation of a restraining order which had been issued without notice on the 2nd day of May, 1968, directing the appellant, teachers' union, and its members to refrain from picketing and striking against the appellee school corporation. It is from this judgment of contempt that this appeal is taken.

The appellant is an organization of public school teachers employed by the appellee.

The appellee is a municipal corporation organized under the statutes of this state for the purpose of operating the public schools within the boundaries of the School City of Anderson, Indiana.

In the spring of 1968 the appellant and the appellees entered into negotiations concerning salary schedules for the following year. These negotiations apparently were not satisfactory to the appellant for on May 1, 1968, the appellant instituted a strike against the school corporation and established picket lines at the various schools operated by appellee. Evidence discloses that school children were unloaded in the public streets because of the presence of the picket lines. It was this action of picketing by the appellant which precipitated the temporary restraining order issued on May 2, 1968, and it was the continuation of this activity without regard for the restraining order upon which the trial court based its judgment after a hearing on May 6, 1968, that the appellant was in contempt of court for violating the restraining order.

The trial court was in all things correct in its finding and judgment of contempt of court.

It is the contention of the appellant that Indiana's "Little Norris-LaGuardia Act," also known as the anti-injunction statute, the same being Burns' Ind.Stat.Ann. § 40–501 et seq., is applicable in this case. This act prohibits the issuance of restraining orders and injunctions in matters involving labor disputes between unions and private employers. We do not agree with the appellant that this act is applicable to disputes concerning public employees. The overwhelming weight of authority in the United States is that government employees may not engage in a strike for any purpose.

The Supreme Court of the United States clearly enunciated the proposition that public employees did not have a right to strike and that the injunctive processes might properly be used to prevent or halt such strikes in the case of United States v. United Mine Workers (1947), 330 U.S. 258, 67 S.Ct. 677, 91 L.Ed. 884. This case has never been overruled or modified. . . .

This same proposition has been followed generally in most of the other state jurisidictions where it has been repeatedly held that strikes by public employees are or should be prohibited and that injunctions should be granted to halt or prevent them. . . .

We find only one case where an injuction to prevent a pending strike of public employees was denied. That case was Board of Education of City of Minneapolis v. Public School Employees Union (1951), 233 Minn. 141, 45 N.W.2d 797, 29 A.L.R.2d 424. That case, however was overruled in 1966 by the Supreme Court of Minnesota in Minneapolis Federation of Teachers Local 59, AFL-CIO v. Obermeyer, supra. . . .

We thus see that both the federal and state jurisdictions and men both liberal and conservative in their political philosophies have uniformly recognized that to allow a strike by public employees is not merely a matter of choice of political philosophies, but is a thing which cannot and must not be permitted if the orderly function of our society is to be preserved. This is not a matter for debate in the political arena for it appears fundamental, as stated by Governor Dewey, public strikes would lead to anarchy, and, as stated by President Roosevelt, the public strike "is unthinkable and intolerable."

The Madison Superior Court, is, therefore, in all things affirmed.

Teachers' Sanctions Against Board Is
Concerted Action Toward Illegal End

BOARD OF EDUCATION v.
NEW JERSEY EDUCATION
ASSOCIATION

Supreme Court of New Jersey, 1968.
53 N.J. 29, 247 A.2d 867.

WEINTRAUB, C.J. . . . In February 1967 a dispute arose between the secretary of the Board and defendant Haller, president of UBTA. Haller was a teacher in plaintiff's system but had not yet acquired tenure. On March 14, 1967 the Board met to consider teacher contracts for the following school year and decided not to offer one to Haller and two other nontenure teachers who were active in UBTA. Haller was so notified on March 29. UBTA held a special meeting of its membership on March 31 at which a lengthy resolution was adopted listing seventeen grievances. . . .

Meanwhile, on April 12 UBTA resolved that "sanctions be imposed" against the Board and requested NJEA to follow suit. On April 21 the NJEA resolved to "impose sanctions" on the Board, and gave wide circulation to its resolution. . . .

NJEA proclaimed through the local press that it would be "a violation of the professional code of ethics for any teacher to accept employment in Union Beach or for any administrator to offer employment in Union Beach as long as the sanctions which had been invoked were in effect."

[1] It has long been the rule in our State that public employees may not strike. . . .

Defendants deny there was a "strike." They seek to distinguish the usual concerted refusal to work from what transpired here. As to the teachers employed by the Board, defendants say they merely resigned as of a future date, and with respect to the interference with the Board's recruitment of replacements, defendants, as we understand them, say a refusal to accept employment is inherently different from a quit. But the subject is the public service, and the distinctions defendants advance are irrelevant to it, however arguable they may be in the context of private employment. Unlike the private employer, a public agency may not retire. The public demand for services which makes illegal a strike against government inveighs against any other concerted action designed to deny government the necessary manpower, whether by terminating existing employments in any mode or by obstructing access to the labor market. Government may not be brought to a halt. So our criminal statute, N.J.S. 2A:98–1, N.J.S.A., provides in simple but pervasive terms that any two or more persons who conspire "to commit any act" for the "obstruction of . . . the due administration of the laws" are guilty of a misdemeanor.

Hence, although the right of an individual to resign or to refuse public employment is undeniable, yet two or more may not agree to follow a common course to the end that an agency of government shall be unable to function. Here there was such collective action by agreement both as to the quitting and as to new employment. As to the mass resignations, an agreement to that end must be inferred from the very adoption by the members through their teachers union of the program of sanctions which, despite some verbal obscurity in this regard, quite plainly imports an understanding to withdraw services when the union officialdom "imposes sanctions" upon a school district. The use of "unethical" in condemning new employment because of working conditions must mean it is also "unethical" to continue an existing employment under the same conditions. The full understanding must be that upon the imposition of sanctions, all services will be withdrawn. We have no doubt that the agreement to strike was not articulated because of the established illegality of that course. In any event, if it should be thought the plan did not include the obligation to quit in connection with the imposition of sanctions, we think it clear that the teachers entered into an agreement to quit when they voted in favor of mass resignations and then executed thirty-six of them. Although the Board accepted the resignations and hence does not ask that that work stoppage be ended, we are satisfied the stoppage was concerted action to an illegal end.

And with respect to blacklisting of the school district and the scheme of "sanctions" upon teachers who offer or take employment with a "sanctioned" school board, it can escape no one that the purpose is to back up a refusal of others to continue to work. At a minimum the object is to withhold additional services a school district may need to discharge its public duty, which, as we have said, is no less illegal. Such an illegal agreement may come into being at the time of the strike or may antedate it. If individuals enter into a union or association on terms that upon the occurrence of some stipulated event or signal they will impede government in its recruitment of services, that very arrangement constitutes an agreement the law denounces. An agreement not to seek, accept, or solicit employment in government whenever the upper echelon of the union makes a prescribed pronouncement is, no less than an accomplished shutdown, a thrust at the vitality of government, and comes within the same policy which denounces a concerted strike or quit or slowdown or other obstruction of the performance of official duties.

. . . That the conventional terminology of a "strike" nowhere appears is of no moment. The substance of a situation and not its shape must control. A doctrine designed to protect the public interest is equal to any demand upon it. It does not yield to guise or ingenuity.

. . . The trial court expressly added that "There is no intention, however, of restraining defendants from exercising the right of free speech concerning what they think the conditions are in the Union Beach school system."

What reappears in defendants' argument is a protest that "sanctions" are no more than an expression of disapproval of conditions in the school district and of the conduct of the Board. It is difficult, even in the abstract, to take that view of the terms used. Far from importing a mere denunciation of men and their work, the "imposition of sanctions" imports the imposition of a penalty. . . .

The imposition of "sanctions" was the stipulated signal for unlawful activity. The right to utter even a pleasantry may be lost if it is the agreed call for lawlessness. It need hardly be said that freedom of speech does not include the right to use speech as an instrument to an unlawful end. . . .

The judgment is affirmed (for Board).

NOTE

Refusal to perform extracurricular duties constitutes a strike. "Extracurricular activities are a fundamental part of a child's education, making the supervision of such activities an integral part of a teacher's duty toward his or her students." Board of Educ. of City of Asbury Park v. Asbury Park Educ. Ass'n, 145 N.J. Super. 495, 368 A.2d 396 (1976).

*Teachers Who Strike in Violation of
Law May be Disciplined Without a
Prior Hearing*

ROCKWELL v. THE BOARD OF EDUCATION OF THE SCHOOL DISTRICT OF CRESTWOOD

Supreme Court of Michigan, 1975.
393 Mich. 616, 227 N.W.2d 736.

LEVIN, Justice. The issue is whether school teachers who strike may be discharged without a prior hearing.

Resolution requires construction of the Public Employment Relations Act (the PERA) in relation to the Teachers' Tenure Act and consideration of the teachers' claim that the PERA is violative of the Due Process Clause unless construed to require a prior hearing.

Section 6 of the PERA provides that public employees who, in concerted action with others, in support of efforts to obtain a change in compensation or other conditions of employment, fail to render services shall be deemed on strike. If the employee is disciplined by his employer for striking, he is entitled, on request, to a determination whether he violated the provisions of the act. The request is to be made "within ten days *after* regular compensation of such employee has ceased or other discipline has been imposed." (Emphasis added.) If the employee is found to have violated the act, he may seek review by the circuit court.

In contrast, the Teachers' Tenure Act requires a hearing *before* discharge. That act provides that a teacher on continuing tenure may be discharged or demoted "only for reasonable and just cause, and only *after* such charges, notice, hearing and determination thereof." (Emphasis supplied.)

The circuit court found that the failure of the school board to proceed in accordance with the Teacher's Tenure Act required reinstatement of the teachers who were discharged. The Court of Appeals affirmed.

We conclude that a teacher, including a teacher on continuing tenure, who strikes in violation of the PERA may be disciplined without a prior hearing, and we reverse the circuit court and the Court of Appeals.

The Crestwood Education Association (the union) and the Board of Education of the School District of Crestwood (the school board) have been involved in a prolonged labor dispute. There has been no collective bargaining agreement since August, 1973.

When the school year commenced on September 3, 1974, the teachers, members of the union, did not report for work. This action was brought against the union and the school board on September 30, 1974, by the plaintiffs as homeowners, taxpayers and parents. By subsequent stipulation, the plaintiffs were dismissed and the litigation has continued on the cross-complaint of the school board.

Injunctive orders were issued in October and classes resumed. In December the teachers again did not report for work and classes were suspended. Contempt proceedings followed. Thereafter the school board adopted a resolution requiring the teachers either to report for work or to submit a letter of resignation by December 27, 1974, failing which their employment would be terminated. Thirty-eight teachers reported for work, one submitted a letter of resignation and the remaining 184 were, by school board resolution of December 30, 1974, deemed to have terminated their employment.

The school board hired substitute teachers and attempted to operate the schools.

The union had theretofore filed unfair labor practice charges with the Michigan Employment Relations Commission (MERC). The union then filed an amended charge complaining that the school board had not bargained in good faith and was attempting to destroy and interfere with the union. The teachers sought individual Section 6 hearings on January 6, 1975. On January 10 the circuit court set aside the school board's resolution of December 30, 1974, and directed reinstatement of the teachers and the resumption of classes. The Court of Appeals affirmed. The teachers returned to work.

The PERA defines "strike," prohibits strikes by public employees, and interdicts any public employee from authorizing a strike.

Section 6 of the PERA empowers the officer or body generally having disciplinary authority over an employee to terminate the employment of or impose other discipline on an employee who strikes in violation of the PERA. In providing that an employee's request for a hearing to determine whether he did violate the PERA be filed within ten days *after* regular compensation has ceased or other discipline has been imposed, the Legislature manifested an intention that the officer or body may impose discipline without a prior hearing.

Section 6 begins with the words "[n]otwithstanding the provisions of any other law." . . .

This court has consistently construed the PERA as the dominant law regulating public employee labor relations. . . . The supremacy of the provisions of the PERA is predicated on the constitution (Const.1963, art. 4, § 48) and the apparent legislative intent that the PERA be the governing law for public employee labor relations.

The Teachers' Tenure Act was not intended, either in contemplation or design, to cover labor disputes between school boards and their employees. The 1937 Legislature in enacting the Teachers' Tenure Act could not have anticipated collective bargaining or meant to provide for the resolution of labor relations disputes in public employment. . . .

All teachers do not have rights of continuing tenure. Yet both tenured and nontenured teachers are in a single public employee bargaining unit and have the same rights and obligations under Michigan's labor relations statutes.

A construction of the statutes providing uniform treatment of all public employee labor relations questions is more likely to effect a sound and expeditious resolution of labor disputes. Requiring hearings under both the Teachers' Tenure Act and the Michigan labor relations statutes, with review of the former by the circuit court and of the latter by the Court of Appeals, could result in competing claims and conflicting adjudications with untoward and costly delay.

Public employees may be disciplined under Section 6 of the PERA only for engaging in *concerted* strike action, while most disciplinary actions subject to the jurisdiction of the State Tenure Commission concern individual teachers. It should therefore be a rare case where the line separating disputes subject to the jurisdiction of the State Tenure Commission from those subject to the jurisdiction of the MERC will be unclear. . . .

This construction of the two acts will not enable MERC to circumvent, at the request of school boards, the protection provided tenured teachers by the Teachers' Tenure Act. If the school board claims that a teacher was discharged for striking, the appeal is to the circuit court, not to MERC. If the school board claims that the teacher was discharged for a reason other than striking, MERC's jurisdiction is invoked only if the teacher claims he was discharged for activity protected under the PERA and the teacher himself files an unfair labor practice charge with the MERC; such a charge would not preclude the teacher from also defending against the discharge at a Teachers' Tenure Act hearing on the ground that it was not supported by reasonable and just cause.

Whether a teacher's employment can be terminated, consistent with the Due Process Clause, without a hearing need not be decided. The PERA provides for a hearing.

The claim that the Due Process Clause requires a *prior* hearing in every case of deprivation of a property right has been rejected by the United States Supreme Court. . . .

In its most recent expression on the subject, the Supreme Court in *Arnett v. Kennedy,* rejected a due process challenge to a statute allowing the discharge of a federal employee without a predisciplinary evidentiary hearing. A variety of rationales were espoused, but the uniform thrust of each opinion, including the dissents, is that the constitutional necessity of a predisciplinary hearing must be determined by balancing the competing interests of the government and employee. . . .

When public employees strike, the public employer must, like a private employer, be able to hire substitute employees so that the public business is not interrupted. In order to hire competent replacements, it may be necessary for the public employer to offer permanent employment and thus displace strikers. Where essential services have been suspended, the hiring of replacements often cannot await time-consuming adjudicatory processes.

The predominant interest secured by pre-disciplinary hearings, as advanced in *Arnett,* is protection against removal of the wrong person and, assuming ultimate employee vindication, protection against interim financial deprivation.

The possibility of removal of a nonstriker is minimized when, as here, the school board gives each striking teacher personal notice of the opportunity to return to the classroom before disciplinary action is taken. While on strike, a teacher receives no compensation; striking teachers do not suffer additional interim financial deprivation when disciplined.

.   .   . Although a strike begins as an economic strike, if it is determined that the employer engaged in an unfair labor practice, the strike may be held to be an unfair labor practice strike and the striking employees entitled to reinstatement.

Since an economic strike is protected concerted activity under the NLRA and the Michigan labor mediation act, it is an unfair labor practice for a private employer to discharge an employee for engaging in an economic strike before the employee has been replaced. The Crestwood school board discharged the school teachers before hiring replacements. However, in contrast with the NLRA and the Michigan labor mediation act, the PERA prohibits strikes in public employment; public employee strikes, therefore, are not protected "lawful concerted [activity] for the purpose of collective negotiation or bargaining or other mutual aid and protection" within the meaning of Section 9 of the PERA, modeled on Section 8 of the Michigan labor mediation act and Section 7 of the National Labor Relations Act.

The federal courts have held that a strike may be unlawful either because it has an unlawful purpose or unlawful means are used to accomplish a lawful purpose and strikers who engage in unlawful strike activity may be discharged.

The action of the Crestwood school board in discharging teachers for striking in violation of the provisions of the PERA prior to the hiring of replacements was not violative of that act. It does not necessarily follow, however, that these teachers may not be entitled to reinstatement should MERC determine that the school board engaged in an unfair labor practice.

.   .   . If MERC should determine that the employing school district committed an unfair labor practice, MERC *may,* despite the illegality of the teachers' strike, order reinstatement.   .   .   .

Reversed. No costs, a public question.

NOTES

1. An injunction against a teacher work stoppage was upheld where the teachers refused to work unless the school board reinstated certain provisions in a previously expired contract. The board refused to extend the terms of the old contract, and during the period when no contract was in existence, imposed interim operating regulations that eliminated protections of the old contract. The court said that the work stoppage was an illegal strike within the meaning of state statute prohibiting such stoppages for the purpose of inducing a "change in the conditions" of employment. Warren Education Association v. Adams, 57 Mich.App. 496, 226 N.W.2d 536 (1975).

2. No civil action in tort can lie against teachers union for striking when employee relations act provides other remedies. The court reasoned that "public policy considerations interdict the creation of a new cause of action, which would unsettle an already precarious labor-management balance in the public labor relations sector." Lamphere Schools v. Lamphere Federation of Teachers, 400 Mich. 104, 252 N.W.2d 818 (1977).

Binding Arbitration Is an Unlawful
Delegation of Power Violating State
Constitution

SCHOOL BOARD OF THE
CITY OF RICHMOND v.
PARHAM

Supreme Court of Virginia, 1978.
218 Va. 950, 243 S.E.2d 468.

CARRICO, Justice. This is an appeal from the final order of the trial court awarding Margaret W. Parham (hereinafter, Parham), a Richmond public schoolteacher, a writ of mandamus against the School Board of the City of Richmond (hereinafter, the School Board). The order compelled the School Board to submit to arbitration a grievance Parham had brought pursuant to the "Procedure for Adjusting Grievances," adopted by the State Board of Education (hereinafter, the State Board). The same order awarded the State Board, an intervenor in the proceeding, a declaratory judgment upholding the constitutionality of a provision of the Procedure which requires binding arbitration of certain disputes between local school boards and their nonsupervisory employees. The sole question for decision is whether the provision for binding arbitration is constitutionally valid.

Adopted in 1973 and subsequently amended, the Procedure prescribes the method for settling employee grievances. . . .

In the present case, Parham unsuccessfully processed her grievance through the several administrative levels prescribed by the Procedure and ultimately presented the dispute to the School Board, where she received an adverse decision. When she called for arbitration, the School Board refused to arbitrate, stating that it questioned the constitutionality of the Procedure "insofar as it compels arbitration binding on school boards in Virginia." Parham then filed her petition for a writ of mandamus to compel the School Board to submit the matter to arbitration.

At the heart of the present controversy are the provisions of Article VIII of the Virginia Constitution, which article relates to education. In pertinent part, the article reads:

. . . § 2. *Standards of quality; State and local support of public schools.*—Standards of quality for the several school divisions shall be determined and prescribed from time to time by the Board of Education, subject to revision only by the General Assembly. . . .

§ 4. *Board of Education.*—The general supervision of the public school system shall be vested in a Board of Education . . . .

§ 5. *Powers and duties of the Board of Education.*—The powers and duties of the Board of Education shall be as follows. . . .

(e) Subject to the ultimate authority of the General Assembly, the Board shall have primary responsibility and authority for effectuating the educational policy set forth in this Article, and it shall have such other powers and duties as may be prescribed by law. . . .

§ 7. *School boards.*—The supervision of schools in each school division shall be vested in a school board . . . .

The School Board recognizes that § 4 of Article VIII places "general supervision" of the public school system in the hands of the State Board. The School Board notes, however, that, under § 7 of Article VIII, the "supervision" of schools is vested in local school boards and that, implementing this constitutional mandate, the General Assembly has conferred upon such local boards extensive authority to execute their supervisory duties. . . .

The School Board argues, however, that "management of a school board's teaching staff and other employees is . . . an essential function of supervision" and that neither the General Assembly nor the State Board can divest local school boards of this function and place it "in an authority other than the local boards." Yet, the School Board asserts, the effect of the binding arbitration provision of the Procedure is to permit "an outside agency, in the form of an arbitration panel . . . to divest the local board of its essential function by the substitution of [the panel's] judgment for that of the board." As a result of the panel's action, the School Board maintains, a local school board's policies, rules, and regulations relating to the work activity of employees could be altered or rendered meaningless. This, the School Board concludes, is constitutionally impermissible under § 7 of Article VIII. . . .

In analyzing the arguments of Parham and the State Board, it is interesting to note that neither of these parties specifically defends the binding arbitration provision of the Procedure; the arguments merely assert the validity of the Procedure in general. The closest approach to a defense of the provision is a statement that "the arbitration panel has no authority whatsoever to make or enforce any decisions as to how the local school is to be operated." This merely evades, rather than answers, the School Board's contention that the arbitration provision permits "an outside agency, in the form of an arbitration panel . . . to divest the local board of its essential function [of managing its teaching staff] by the substitution of [the panel's] judgment for that of the board."

This contention of the School Board presents the real question in the case, viz., whether the binding arbitration provision of the Procedure produces an unlawful delegation of power. . . .

There can be no doubt that a delegation of power is involved in the binding arbitration provision. Indeed, the very section of the Procedure which provides that an arbitration panel shall have authority to make a final and binding decision also states that the local school board "hereby delegates such authority to the Panel."

Whether, however, the arbitration provision results in an *unlawful* delegation of authority is a more difficult question. . . .

Although not involving binding arbitration provisions, Howard v. School Board of Alleghany County, 203 Va. 55, 122 S.E.2d 891 (1961), is pertinent to resolution of the present case. There, a state statute required the sale of school property if such disposition was favored by a majority of voters in a referendum. Ruling the statute invalid, we said that it was an "essential function" of a local school board's power of supervision, granted by what is now § 7 of Article VIII of the Constitution, "to determine whether a particular property is needed for school purposes and the manner in which it shall be used." The effect of the disputed statute, we stated, was "to divest the board of the exercise of that function and lodge it in the electorate," thus stripping the board "of any or all authority to exercise its judgment in the matter." 203 Va. at 58, 122 S.E.2d at 894. This is but another way of saying that the statute produced an unlawful delegation of power.

We believe the binding arbitration provision involved in the present case has the same effect as the offending statute in *Howard*, viz., to remove from a local school board and transfer to others a function essential and indispensable to the exercise of the power of supervision vested by § 7 of Article VIII. . . .

Equally clear, the function of *applying* local policies, rules, and regulations, adopted for the management of a teaching staff, is a function essential and indispensable to exercise of the power of supervision vested by § 7 of Article VIII. This power of supervision would be an empty one, indeed, if a local school board, once having adopted a valid policy, rule, or regulation, found itself powerless to enforce what it had promulgated. . . .

We conclude, therefore, that the binding arbitration provision of the Procedure produces an unlawful delegation of power, violative of § 7 of Article VIII of the Constitution. . . .

Reversed and final judgment.

Binding Arbitration Is Not an Illegal
Delegation of School Board Power

CITY OF BIDDEFORD v. BIDDEFORD TEACHERS ASSOCIATION

Supreme Judicial Court of Maine, 1973.
304 A.2d 387.

WEATHERBEE, Justice. These two complaints necessitate our first examination of the provisions of the Municipal Employees Labor Relations Law, 26 M.R.S.A. Chap. 9–A, which was enacted by the Maine Legislature in 1969. The complaints direct our attention only to the application of the statute to teachers in the public schools.

In the fall of 1970 the Board of Education of the City of Biddeford and the representatives of the Biddeford Teachers Association entered into negotiations in an attempt to effect a contract for the professional services of teachers in the Biddeford public schools for the school year 1971–1972. When the Board and the Association were unable to reach an agreement, the fact-finding procedures provided in section 965(3) were called into play but they proved unsuccessful. Finally, in August of 1971 the parties resorted to the arbitration process found in section 965(4). . . .

The purpose of the Municipal Public Employees Labor Relations Law is stated by 26 M.R.S.A. § 961 as follows:

> It is declared to be the public policy of this State and it is the purpose of this chapter to promote the improvement of the relationship between public employers and their employees by providing a uniform basis for recognizing the right of public employees to join labor organizations of their own choosing and to be represented by such organizations in collective bargaining for terms and conditions of employment.

. . . The Act makes it the obligation of the public employer and the bargaining agent to meet and bargain collectively and provides a four-step procedure consisting of negotiation, mediation (when jointly requested), fact finding and arbitration. The parties are first obligated to negotiate in good faith concerning "wages, hours, working conditions and contract grievance arbitration"—with the exception—

> [T]hat public employers of teachers shall meet and consult but not negotiate with respect to educational policies . . . .

Secondly, if the parties are unable to agree after negotiation they may jointly agree upon mediation procedures. Thirdly, if mediation procedures are omitted or are unsuccessful, either one or both may request fact-finding and the parties are then obligated to present their contending positions to the fact-finding board which will, after hearing, submit its findings to the parties. If a thirty-day period of further effort to resolve the controversy is unsuccessful either party may make the findings public. Fifteen more days are then allowed to permit a further good faith effort to resolve the controversy. Fourth, and lastly, if, after another ten days they have not agreed as to an arbitration procedure, either party may request in writing that their differences shall be arbitrated in accordance with the procedure described in subsection 4.

In brief, this procedure requires each party to choose an arbitrator and the two so chosen shall name a "neutral" arbitrator. The three arbitrators shall then proceed to hear the matter. If the subject of the controversy has been salaries, pensions or insurance, the arbitrator shall *recommend* terms of settlement which are advisory only and may make findings of fact. As to other matters in dispute the arbitrators shall make determinations which are binding upon the parties and "the parties will enter into an agreement or take whatever other action that may be appropriate to carry out and effectuate such binding determinations." The determinations are subject to review in accordance with M.R.C.P., Rule 80B but, in the absence of fraud, the arbitrators' decisions upon questions of fact are final.

The Act obviously represents a fresh approach to municipal public employee labor relations problems and enters an area as yet unexplored here. In the field of education, particularly, it appears to clash with traditional concepts of school control and management. As a result, members of the Board here—as several school boards in other jurisdictions have done—protest that if the members entered into the proposed contract, as the arbitration award has ordered them to do—they would be surrendering their authority as public officers to persons who are in no way responsible to the electorate. . . .

While the present actions present many issues concerning various areas of the arbitrators' award, we must first consider the constitutionality of the Act in so far as it requires local school boards, at the request of the teaching employees, to submit to binding arbitration disputes arising both out of the making of the labor contract and out of later employment under the contract. Can the superintending school committees constitutionally delegate this authority to arbitrators? In requiring them to do so, can the Legislature constitutionally take away the authority which local officials had traditionally exercised and repose it in persons who compose ad hoc boards of arbitration? If so, has there been such a valid delegation of authority here? . . .

It appears that most of the cases holding that agreements to submit public employee labor disputes to binding arbitration are invalid attempts to delegate official responsibility come from states that had no legislation authorizing such agreements. On the other hand, serious concern over the problem is apparent in all the decisions and several of those often spoken of as favorable to the position urged here by the Association limit their holdings to grievance arbitration of contracts which municipalities have already entered into. It may be that the Rhode Island statute is the only one imposing upon the municipalities binding arbitration in the areas of both interest and grievance, without specific constitutional authorization, which has been finally upheld. We consider that decisions involving arbitration in essential industries in the private sector such as hospitals and public utilities give us little assistance as to this problem.

With scant solid precedent to guide us, we return to our own situation. We find that our Constitution gave the Legislature full responsibility over the subject matter of public schools and education and empowered it to make all reasonable laws in reference to schools and education for the "benefit of the people of this state." Opinions of the Justices, 68 Me. 582 (1876). Except for the areas where the Legislature has from time to time seen fit to impose its own requirements and except for the authority later given to the Commissioner of Education, the responsibilities for operating the public schools have remained in the local school boards.

The Legislature has now decided to take from the school boards the ultimate authority they have exercised in certain areas of school management—that is, as to "hours, and working conditions" and contract grievance arbitration—and to give it to ad hoc boards of arbitration.

It is settled beyond question that the Legislature may properly conclude that the purposes of its legislation may best be carried out through agents and that it may delegate to the agents a portion of its power to facilitate the functioning of the legislative program.

There can be no doubt but that the Legislature, which is the source of all municipal authority, Squires v. Inhabitants of City of Augusta, 155 Me. 151, 153 A.2d 80 (1959), has also the power to take back from municipal officers portions of the authority it has earlier given them.

It is clear that the Legislature has recognized that the maintenance of a satisfactory quality of public education requires harmonious relations between school officials and the teaching staffs and that disagreements inevitably arise during the carrying out of their respective responsibilities. The abrasive effect of the existence of unresolved grievances is one of the threats to harmonious relations which the Legislature considers should be removed.

The lawmakers have recognized that policy-making decisions should remain in the local officials, responsible to the public, and that while the citizens may properly be subjected to moral suasion as to such matters as wages and pensions, the ultimate determination of such matters with such heavy impact upon—and so limited by—municipal appropriations should be made by local officials.

The Legislature has apparently concluded, on the other hand, that experience has taught that certain aspects of this dynamic and complicated municipal employer-employee relationship no longer need remain subject to arbitrary decision by the employer and that in the area of working conditions and hours and of contract grievances the interests of the employees must in fairness be examined by impartial persons. The Legislature appears to believe that this much can be done without serious disruption of the balancing of operating costs against municipal appropriations.

We realize that in providing that the contract-making process itself (as it affects working conditions and hours) is subject to binding arbitration, our Legislature has moved into an area forbidden by many courts. The Legislature must have concluded that the benefits which are sought by the statute can never be achieved if an impasse occurs at the very beginning of the relationship. This conclusion is not unreasonable.

True, the statute does not contemplate the delegation of authority to public administrative boards or agencies but instead gives it to ad hoc panels whose memberships are not to be controlled by governmental action. Here we are of the opinion that the Legislature, mindful of the denial to municipal employees of such economic weapons as strikes amd work stoppages which are available to employees in private employment, has sought to avoid the disruptive feelings of resentment and bitterness which may result if the governmental employee may look only to the government for redress of his grievances.

Where the ultimate arbiter of the dispute is a representative of one side of the dispute, adverse decisions will be hard to accept and the tendency toward alienation will be strong.

We consider that there is a rational reason for the Legislature's decision that its purposes would be best effectuated if the parties are left to choose their own arbitrators in the limited non-policy areas which are subject to arbitration.

NOTE

Issues regarding adherence to proper grievance procedures, union's standing to file grievance as well as substantive issues may be subject to reasonable debate and therefore may be submitted to arbitrator for resolution. Mora Federation of Teachers, Local 1802 v. Independent School Dist. No. 332, 352 N.W.2d 489 (Minn.App.1984).

*Agency Shop Does Not Violate First
Amendment Rights*

ABOOD v. DETROIT BOARD
OF EDUCATION

Supreme Court of the United States, 1977.
431 U.S. 209, 97 S.Ct. 1782.

Mr. Justice STEWART delivered the opinion of the Court.

The State of Michigan has enacted legislation authorizing a system for union representation of local governmental employees. A union and a local government employer are specifically permitted to agree to an "agency shop" arrangement, whereby every employee represented by a union—even though not a union member—must pay to the union, as a condition of employment, a service fee equal in amount to union dues. The issue before us is whether this arrangement violates the constitutional rights of government employees who object to public sector unions as such or to various union activities financed by the compulsory service fees. . . .

On November 7, 1969—more than two months before the agency-shop clause was to become effective—Christine Warczak and a number of other named teachers filed a class action in a state court, naming as defendants the Board, the Union, and several Union officials. Their complaint, as amended, alleged that they were unwilling or had refused to pay dues and that they opposed collective bargaining in the public sector. . . .

Consideration of the question whether an agency shop provision in a collective-bargaining agreement covering governmental employees is, as such, constitutionally valid must begin with two cases in this Court that on their face go far towards resolving the issue. The cases are *Railway Employes' Department v. Hanson* . . . and International Association of Machinists v. Street, 367 U.S. 740, 81 S.Ct. 1784, 6 L.Ed.2d 1141.

In the *Hanson* case a group of railroad employees brought an action in a Nebraska court to enjoin enforcement of a union-shop agreement. The challenged clause was authorized, and indeed shielded from any attempt by a State to prohibit it, by the Railway Labor Act, 45 U.S.C.A. § 152, Eleventh. . . .

The record in *Hanson* contained no evidence that union dues were used to force ideological conformity or otherwise to impair the free expression of employees, and the Court noted that "[i]f 'assessments' are in fact imposed for purposes not germane to collective bargaining, a different problem would be presented." Id., at 235, 76 S.Ct., at 720. (footnote omitted). But the Court squarely held that "the requirement for financial support of the collective-bargaining agency by all who receive the benefits of its work . . . does not violate . . . the First Amendment." Id., at 238, 76 S.Ct., at 721.

The Court faced a similar question several years later in the *Street* case, which also involved a challenge to the constitutionality of a union shop authorized by the Railway Labor Act. In *Street*, however, the record contained findings that the union treasury to which all employees were required to contribute had been used "to finance the campaigns of candidates for federal and state offices whom [the plaintiffs] opposed, and to promote the propagation of political and economic doctrines, concepts and ideologies with which [they] disagreed." 367 U.S., at 744, 81 S.Ct., at 1787.

The Court recognized that these findings presented constitutional "questions of the utmost gravity" not decided in *Hanson,* id., at 749, 81 S.Ct., at 1789, and therefore considered whether the Act could fairly be construed to avoid these constitutional issues. Id., at 749–750, 81 S.Ct., at 1789–90. The Court concluded that the Act could be so construed, since only expenditures related to the union's functions in negotiating and administering the collective bargaining agreement and adjusting grievances and disputes fell within "the reasons . . . accepted by Congress why authority to make union-shop agreements was justified," id., at 768, 81 S.Ct. at 1800. The Court rule, therefore, that the use of compulsory union dues for political purposes violated the Act itself. Nonetheless, it found that an injunction against enforcement of the union-shop agreement as such was impermissible under *Hanson,* and remanded the case to the Supreme Court of Georgia so that a more limited remedy could be devised.

. . . A union-shop arrangement has been thought to distribute fairly the cost of these activities among those who benefit, and it counteracts the incentive that employees might otherwise have to become "free riders"—to refuse to contribute to the union while obtaining benefits of union representation that necessarily accrue to all employees. . . .

To compel employees financially to support their collective bargaining representative has an impact upon their First Amendment interests. An employee may very well have ideological objections to a wide variety of activities undertaken by the union in its role as exclusive representative. His moral or religious views about the desirability of abortion may not square with the union's policy in negotiating a medical benefits plan. One individual might disagree with a union policy of negotiating limits on the right to strike, believing that to be the road to serfdom for the working class, while another might have economic or political objections to unionism itself. An employee might object to the union's wage policy because it violates guidelines designed to limit inflation, or might object to the union's seeking a clause in the collective-bargaining agreement proscribing racial discrimination. The examples could be multiplied. To be required to help finance the union as a collective-bargaining agent might well be thought, therefore, to interfere in some way with an employee's freedom to associate for the advancement of ideas, or to refrain from doing so, as he sees fit. But the judgment clearly made in *Hanson* and *Street* is that such interference as exists is constitutionally justified by the legislative assessment of the important contribution of the union shop to the system of labor relations established by Congress. "The furtherance of the common cause leaves some leeway for the leadership of the group. As long as they act to promote the cause which justified bringing the group together, the individual cannot withdraw his financial support merely because he disagrees with the group's strategy. If that were allowed, we would be reversing the *Hanson* case, *sub silentio.*" . . .

The governmental interests advanced by the agency shop provision in the Michigan statute are much the same as those promoted by similar provisions in federal labor law. The confusion and conflict that could arise if rival teachers' unions, holding quite different views as to the proper class hours, class sizes, holidays, tenure provisions, and grievance procedures, each sought to obtain the employer's agreement are no different in kind from the evils that the exclusivity rule in the Railway Labor Act was designed to avoid. . . . The desirability of labor peace is no less important in the public sector, nor is the risk of "free riders" any smaller. . . .

While recognizing the apparent precedential weight of the *Hanson* and *Street* cases, the appellants advance two reasons why those decisions should not control decision of the present case. First, the appellants note that it is *government* employment that is involved here, thus directly implicating constitutional guarantees, in contrast to the private employment that was the subject of the *Hanson* and *Street* decisions. Second, the appellants say that in the public sector collective bargaining itself is inherently "political," and that to require them to give financial support to it is to require the "ideological conformity" that the Court expressly found absent in the *Hanson* case. 351 U.S., at 238, 76 S.Ct., at 721. We find neither argument persuasive. . . .

The distinctive nature of public-sector bargaining has led to widespread discussion about the extent to which the law governing labor relations in the private sector provides an appropriate model. To take but one example, there has been considerable debate about the desirability of prohibiting public employee unions from striking, a step that the State of Michigan itself has taken, Mich.Comp.Laws § 423.202. But although Michigan has not adopted the federal model of labor relations in every respect, it has determined that labor stability will be served by a system of exclusive representation and the permissive use of an agency shop in public employment. As already stated, there can be no principled basis for according that decision less weight in the constitutional balance than was given in *Hanson* to the congressional judgment reflected in the Railway Labor Act. The only remaining constitutional inquiry evoked by the appellants' argument, therefore, is whether a public employee has a weightier First Amendment interest than a private employee in not being compelled to contribute to the costs of exclusive union representation. We think he does not.

Public employees are not basically different from private employees; on the whole, they have the same sort of skills, the same needs, and seek the same advantages. "The uniqueness of public employment is *not in the employees* nor in the work performed; the uniqueness is in the special character of the employer." . . . The very real differences between exclusive agent collective bargaining in the public and private sectors are not such as to work any greater infringement upon the First Amendment interests of public employees. A public employee who believes that a union representing him is urging a course that is unwise as a matter of public policy is not barred from expressing his viewpoint. Besides voting in accordance with his convictions, every public employee is largely free to express his views, in public or private orally or in writing. With some exceptions not pertinent here, public employees are free to participate in the full range of political activities open to other citizens. Indeed, just this Term we have held that the First and Fourteenth Amendments protect the right of a public school teacher to oppose, at a public school board meeting, a position advanced by the teacher's union. . . . In so ruling we recognized that the principle of exclusivity cannot constitutionally be used to muzzle a public employee who, like any other citizen, might wish to express his view about governmental decisions concerning labor relations, id., 97 S.Ct. at 426.

There can be no quarrel with the truism that because public employee unions attempt to influence governmental policy-making, their activities—and the views of members who disagree with them—may be properly termed political. But that characterization does not raise the ideas and beliefs of public employees onto a higher plane than the ideas and beliefs of private employees. It is no doubt true that a central purpose of the First Amendment "was to protect the free discussion of governmental affairs." . . . But our cases have never suggested that expression about philosophical social, artistic, economic, literary, or ethical matters—to take a nonexhaustive list of labels—is not entitled to full First Amendment protection. Union members in both the public and private sector may find that a variety of union activities conflict with their beliefs. . . . Nothing in the First Amendment or our cases discussing its meaning makes the question whether the adjective "political" can properly be attached to those beliefs of the critical constitutional inquiry.

The differences between public and private sector collective bargaining simply do not translate into differences in First Amendment rights. Even those commentators most acutely aware of the distinctive nature of public-sector bargaining and most seriously concerned with its policy implications agree that "[t]he union security issue in the public sector . . . is fundamentally the same issue . . . as in the private sector. . . . No special dimension results from the fact that a union represents public rather than private employees." . . . We conclude that the Michigan Court of Appeals was correct in viewing this Court's decisions in *Hanson* and *Street* as controlling in the present case insofar as the service charges are applied to collective bargaining, contract administration, and grievance adjustment purposes.

. . . Our decisions establish with unmistakable clarity that the freedom of an individual to associate for the purpose of advancing beliefs and ideas is protected by the First and Fourteenth Amendments. . . . Equally clear is the proposition that a government may not require an individual to relinquish rights guaranteed him by the First Amendment as a condition of public employment. . . . The appellants argue that they fall within the protection of these cases because they have been prohibited not from actively associating, but rather from refusing to associate. They specifically argue that they may constitutionally prevent the Union's spending a part of their required service fees to contribute to political candidates and to express political views unrelated to its duties as exclusive bargaining representative. We have concluded that this argument is a meritorious one.

One of the principles underlying the Court's decision in Buckley v. Valeo, 424 U.S. 1, 96 S.Ct. 612, 46 L.Ed.2d 659, was that contributing to an organization for the purpose of spreading a political message is protected by the First Amendment. Because "[m]aking a contribution . . . enables like-minded persons to pool their resources in furtherance of common political goals," id., at 22, 96 S.Ct. at 636, the Court reasoned that limitations upon the freedom to contribute "implicate fundamental First Amendment interests," id., at 23, 96 S.Ct. at 636.

The fact that the appellants are compelled to make, rather than prohibited from making, contributions for political purposes works no less an infringement of their constitutional rights. For at the heart of the First Amendment is the notion that an individual should be free to believe as he will, and that in a free society one's beliefs should be shaped by his mind and his conscience rather than coerced by the State. . . . They are no less applicable to the case at bar, and they thus prohibit the appellees from requiring any of the appellants to contribute to the support of an ideological cause he may oppose as a condition of holding a job as a public school teacher.

We do not hold that a union cannot constitutionally spend funds for the expression of political views, on behalf of political candidates, or towards the advancement of other ideological causes not germane to its duties as collective bargaining representative. Rather, the Constitution requires only that such expenditures be financed from charges, dues, or assessments paid by employees who do not object to advancing those ideas and who are not coerced into doing so against their will by the threat of loss of governmental employment.

There will, of course, be difficult problems in drawing lines between collective bargaining activities, for which contributions may be compelled, and ideological activities unrelated to collective bargaining, for which such compulsion is prohibited. . . . All that we decide is that the general allegations in the complaint, if proven, establish a cause of action under the First and Fourteenth Amendments. . . .

The judgment is vacated, and the case is remanded for further proceedings not inconsistent with this opinion.

It is so ordered.

NOTES

1. An agency shop fee or a "fair share fee" provided for in statute does not deny an individual teacher due process. In this case, decided by the Minnesota Supreme Court, the primary question was whether the fair share statute was constitutional since it did not provide for a hearing for individual nonunion teachers before imposition of the fair share fee. The court concluded that the governmental interest in securing the financial stability of the exclusive union representation was sufficiently strong to override the individual's interest in obtaining a prior determination of the fee's validity. Robbinsdale Education Association v. Robbinsdale Federation of Teachers, 307 Minn. 96, 239 N.W.2d 437 (1976).

2. An agency shop provision in a contract was held invalid in face of a statute that granted public employees the right to voluntarily join, form, and participate in organizations of their own choosing. The court found that the statute assured the "right not to join," and the forced payment of dues or their equivalent "is tantamount to coercion or, at the very least, toward participation" in the labor organization as expressly forbidden by

statute. Churchill v. SAD No. 49 Teachers Association, 380 A.2d 186 (Me.1977).

3. The United States Supreme Court has upheld a collective bargaining agreement between a board of education and a teacher union giving the union exclusive access to the interschool mail system and teacher mailboxes of the school system. Plaintiffs, a competing union, had claimed that the preferential access to the internal mail system violated the First Amendment and the Equal Protection Clause of the Fourteenth Amendment. With regard to the First Amendment, the Court pointed out that equivalent access to all parts of a school building is not guaranteed. "Nowhere [have we] suggested that students, teachers, or anyone else has an absolute constitutional right to use all parts of a school building or its immediate environs for . . . unlimited expressive purposes." See Grayned v. City of Rockford, 408 U.S. 104, 92 S.Ct. 2294 (1972). According to the Court, persons do not have the right of access to all types of public property; access depends on the character of the property at issue. The Court delineated three types of public property: (1) streets and parks are types of public property that have "Immemorially been held in trust for public use for communication and assembly"; (2) facilities and meeting places where open forums have traditionally existed as on a university, Widmar v. Vincent, 454 U.S. 263, 102 S.Ct. 269 (1981); and (3) public property that has not traditionally been an open forum for public communication. Public school mail facilities fall into this third category. School officials may decide what type of selective access will be given to such facilities. The fact that school mail facilities had been opened to such groups as the Girl Scouts and Boys Clubs does not make them an open forum; instead, the Court said that such facilities remain a "limited" public forum that can be regulated by the school board. Hence, the incumbent union may be allowed access while another union is denied. Perry Education Association v. Perry Local Educator's Association, 460 U.S. 37, 103 S.Ct. 948 (1983).

Scope of Negotiations Is Essentially a Question for Legislative Guidance

KENAI PENINSULA BOROUGH SCHOOL DISTRICT v. KENAI PENINSULA EDUCATION ASSOCIATION

Supreme Court of State of Alaska, 1977.
572 P.2d 416.

CONNOR, Justice. These cases present important questions of labor law and constitutional law concerning the collective bargaining requirements for teachers in the public schools. . . .

Introduction To facilitate the understanding of our more detailed legal discussion later in this opinion, we will summarize at the outset the contentions of the parties. The statutes at issue in this litigation are AS 14.20.550 and .610, which provide:

> Sec. 14.20.550. *Negotiation with certificated employees.* Each city, borough and regional school board shall negotiate with its certificated employees in good faith on matters pertaining to their employment and the fulfillment of their professional duties. (§ 1 ch 18 SLA 1970; am § 3 ch 71 SLA 1972; am § 21 ch 124 SLA 1975).

> Sec. 14.20.610. *Legal responsibilities of boards.* Nothing in §§ 550–600 of this chapter may be construed as an abrogation or delegation of the legal responsibilities, powers, and duties of the school board including its right to make final decisions on policies. (§ 21 ch 18 SLA 1970).

. . . The school boards contend that the submission of educational policies to a good faith collective bargaining requirement would remove the final decisions on such matters from the boards, contrary to the intent of the legislature expressed in AS 14.20.610. The boards contend that to require bargaining on questions of educational policy would also contravene the Alaska Constitution, art. VII, § 1, which makes education the exclusive domain of the legislature. See Macauley v. Hildebrand, 491 P.2d 120 (Alaska 1971). Delegation of part of the decision-making power on educational policy to labor unions is unconstitutional, they urge, because the union is a private organization, unaccountable to the public. The union can use the power for its own ends, and is under no duty to foster educational policies which are in the general public interest.

The unions argue that such delegation is perfectly proper, and that there is no delegation of decision-making power inherent in a labor negotiations requirement. They further argue that they represent professional employees, and that their participation in good faith collective bargaining labor negotiations is an attempt by the legislature to provide professional advice to school boards on the management of the schools. . . .

Scope of the Duty to Bargain   If we were to look to the law concerning bargaining between labor unions and private employers, we would conclude that the scope of negotiable issues is broad. The law relating to the private sector has always contained, and still does contain, uncertainties. But the general trend has been to require that employers bargain in good faith on a wide range of items with respect to wages, hours, and other conditions of employment, without regard to whether the employers consider the items bargained for to be within the prerogatives of management. . . .

When we turn to employment in the public sector, and particularly in education, the question of what is properly bargainable is thrown into more doubt. If teachers' unions are permitted to bargain on matters of educational policy, it is conceivable that through successive contracts the autonomy of the school boards could be severely eroded, and the effective control of educational policy shifted from the school boards to the teachers' unions. Such a result could threaten the ability of elective government officials and appointive officers subject to their authority, in this case the school boards and administrators, to perform their functions in the broad public interest. . . .

The school boards initially argue that to make matters of school operation and educational policy subject to collective bargaining amounts to an unconstitutional delegation of governmental power to the unions.

. . . courts in an earlier era often held laws unconstitutional on the ground that they delegated legislative power to private persons or groups. . . .

Furthermore, the statute merely requires the school board to negotiate with the union. It does not require the board to accept any particular proposal the union might offer. It does not require, and probably does not permit, the board to delegate to the union the sole power to make any decision. Therefore, cited cases invalidating outright grants of governmental power to private groups . . . are not apposite.

The cases in other states rejecting the argument that collective bargaining with teachers' unions is an unconstitutional delegation of power, all involve statutes which fairly narrowly constrict either the scope of bargainable issues, or the school boards' duty to accede to union proposals, or both. . . . In this opinion, we similarly construe the Alaska statute. A statute defining the scope of collective bargaining as broadly as the union would have us do, might well present a more troubling constitutional question. But we find no constitutional infirmity in AS 14.20.550 and .610. The delegation of power problem still bears upon our task of statutory interpretation, however, for in interpreting the relevant statutes we will not readily assume that the legislature intended to divest the school boards of their power to determine matters of educational policy and school system management. . . .

Put another way, a matter is more susceptible to bargaining the more it deals with the economic interests of employees and the less it concerns professional goals and methods. Bargaining over the latter topics presents particular problems because there is less likely to be any politically organized interest group other than the union concerned with these issues. The salaries of public employees have a direct financial effect on the taxpayers; on the other hand, a question such as teacher evaluation of administrators is unlikely to have any impact sufficiently direct to be discernible by laymen. Furthermore, it is such an abstract and abstruse subject that it is unlikely that any appreciable portion of the public will either understand it or care greatly about it. In such circumstances, the risk that effective power over the governmental decision will come to rest with the union is significantly greater. Moreover, it is more likely that there will be disagreements among union members on questions of this nature than on "bread and butter" issues; the risk that minority viewpoints within the union will not be meaningfully represented in the bargaining is a real one. . . .

Specific Issues We will now consider the Alaska situation in more detail. At the outset it appears to us that questions concerning salaries, the number of hours to be worked, and amount of leave time are all so closely connected with the economic well-being of the individual teacher that they must be held negotiable under our statutes. The troubling question is what other items are bargainable.

The various trial courts in these cases considered such items as (1) relief from nonprofessional chores, (2) elementary planning time, (3) para-professional tutors, (4) teacher specialist, (5) teacher's aides, (6) class size, (7) pupil-teacher ratio, (8) a teacher ombudsman, (9) teacher evaluation of administrators, (10) school calendar, (11) selection of instructional materials, (12) the use of secondary department heads, (13) secondary teacher preparation and planning time, and (14) teacher representation on school board advisory committees.

The testimony adduced in the trial courts does not provide us with much enlightenment as to why any of these items should fall on one side of the line or another. Realistically the two areas, i.e., (1) educational policy and (2) matters pertaining to employment and professional duties, merge into and blend with each other at many points. Logically and semantically it is nearly impossible to assign specific items to one category and not the other. . . . We are confronted, then, with a situation in which the legislature has not spoken with clarity and concerning which we possess no expertise. We can only conclude that salaries, fringe benefits, the number of hours worked, and the amount of leave time are negotiable . . . we conclude that the other specific items . . . are, under the existing statutory language, non-negotiable.

It would be helpful if the legislature, through future enactments, provided more specific guidance on a number of the items which the unions seek to negotiate. Lacking that guidance, however, we cannot confidently say that the legislature intended any of these items to be bargainable. We cannot, therefore, read the statutes expansively as to the scope of what is negotiable.

As to matters which affect educational policy and are, therefore not negotiable, we believe that there is nevertheless implicit in our statutes the intention that the school boards meet and confer with the unions. It is desirable that the boards consider teacher proposals on such questions. This will encourage teachers to give the boards the benefit of their expertise, and to make their positions known for the board's use in establishing educational policy. . . .

Affirmed in part, reversed in part.

NOTES

1. When teachers voluntarily surrender their individual academic freedom in exchange for protectionism of collective action and a group contract, they cannot later avoid their contractual commitments by recalling their constitutional freedoms. Where teachers maintained that school board policy unduly restricted use of certain books, thus violating their First and Fourteenth Amendment rights, the court found that they had no redress since they had submitted themselves to an employer-employee contractual model that gave the school board the authority to control communication through the assignment of reading material. Cary v. Board of Education of Adams-Arapahoe School District, 427 F.Supp. 945 (D.Colo.1977).

2. Agreement by a school board to confine itself in hiring to those applicants within the system is beyond the scope of bargaining and is therefore unenforceable. Board of Education of Township of North Bergen v.

North Bergen Federation of Teachers, 141 N.J.Super. 97, 357 A.2d 302 (1976).

Freedom of Nonunion Teacher to
Speak at Open Meeting Cannot
Be Curtailed

CITY OF MADISON v. WISCONSIN EMPLOYMENT RELATIONS COMMISSION

Supreme Court of the United States, 1976.
429 U.S. 167, 97 S.Ct. 421.

Mr. Chief Justice BURGER delivered the opinion of the Court.

The question presented on this appeal from the Supreme Court of Wisconsin is whether a State may constitutionally require that an elected Board of Education prohibit teachers, other than union representatives, to speak at open meetings, at which public participation is permitted, if such speech is addressed to the subject of pending collective-bargaining negotiations.

The Madison Board of Education and Madison Teachers, Inc. (MTI), a labor union, were parties to a collective-bargaining agreement during the calendar year of 1971. In January 1971 negotiations commenced for renewal of the agreement and MTI submitted a number of proposals. One among them called for the inclusion of a so-called "fair-share" clause, which would require all teachers, whether members of MTI or not, to pay union dues to defray the costs of collective bargaining. . . .

During the same month, two teachers, Holmquist and Reed, who were members of the bargaining unit, but not members of the union, mailed a letter to all teachers in the district expressing opposition to the "fair share" proposal. Two hundred teachers replied, most commenting favorably on Holmquist and Reed's position. Thereupon a petition was drafted calling for a one-year delay in the implementation of "fair share" while the proposal was more closely analyzed by an impartial committee. The petition was circulated to all teachers in the district on December 6, 1971. Holmquist and Reed intended to present the results of their petition effort to the school board and to MTI at the school board's public meeting that same evening.

. . . During a portion of the meeting devoted to expression of opinion by the public, the president of MTI took the floor and spoke on the subject of the ongoing negotiations. He concluded his remarks by presenting to the board a petition signed by 1,300–1,400 teachers calling for the expeditious resolution of the negotiations. Holmquist was next given the floor, after John Matthews, the business representative of MTI, unsuccessfully attempted to dissuade him from speaking. Matthews had also spoken to a member of the school board before the meeting and requested that the board refuse to permit Holmquist to speak. Holmquist stated that he represented "an informal committee of seventy-two teachers in forty-nine schools" and that he desired to inform the Board of Education, as he had already informed the union, of the results of an informal survey concerning the "fair share" clause. He then read the petition which had been circulated to the teachers in the district that morning and stated that in the thirty-one schools from which reports had been received 53 percent of the teachers had already signed the petition.

Holmquist stated that neither side had adequately addressed the issue of "fair share" and that teachers were confused about the meaning of the proposal. He concluded by saying: "Due to this confusion, we wish to take no stand on the proposal itself, but ask only that all alternatives be presented clearly to all teachers and more importantly to the general public to whom we are all responsible. We ask simply for communication, not confrontation." The sole response from the school board was a question by the president inquiring whether Holmquist intended to present the board with the petition. Holmquist answered that he would. Holmquist's presentation had lasted approximately two and one-half minutes.

Later that evening, the board met in executive session and voted a proposal acceding to all of the union's demands with the exception of "fair share." During a negotiating session the following morning, MTI accepted the proposal and a contract was signed on December 14, 1976.

In January 1972 MTI filed a complaint with the Wisconsin Employment Relations Commission (WERC) claiming that the board had committed a prohibited labor practice by permitting Holmquist to speak at the December 6 meeting. . . .

The Wisconsin court perceived "clear and present danger" based upon its conclusion that Holmquist's speech before the school board constituted "negotiation" with the board. Permitting such "negotiation," the court reasoned, would undermine the bargaining exclusivity guaranteed the majority union under Wis.Stat. § 111.70(3)(a)4. From that premise it concluded that teachers' First Amendment rights could be limited. Assuming, *arguendo*, that such a "danger" might in some circumstances justify some limitation of First Amendment rights, we are unable to read this record as presenting such danger as would justify curtailing speech.

The Wisconsin Supreme Court's conclusion that Holmquist's terse statement during the public meeting constituted negotiation with the board was based upon its adoption of the lower court's determination that, "[e]ven though Holmquist's statement superficially appears to be merely a 'position statement,' the court deems from the total circumstances that it constituted 'negotiating.'" This cryptic conclusion seems to ignore the ancient wisdom that calling a thing by a name does not make it so. Holmquist did not seek to bargain or offer to enter into any bargain with the board, nor does it appear that he was authorized by any other teachers to enter into any agreement on their behalf. Although his views were not consistent with those of MTI, communicating such views to the employer could not change the fact that MTI alone was authorized to negotiate and to enter into a contract with the board.

Moreover, the school board meeting at which Holmquist was permitted to speak was open to the public. He addressed the school board not merely as one of its employees but also as a concerned citizen, seeking to express his views on an important decision of his government. We have held that teachers may not be "compelled to relinquish the First Amendment rights they would otherwise enjoy as citizens to comment on matters of public interest in connection with the operation of the public school in which they work." . . . Where the State has opened a forum for direct citizen involvement, it is difficult to find justification for excluding teachers who make up the overwhelming proportion of school employees and are most vitally concerned with the proceedings. It is conceded that any citizen could have presented precisely the same points and provided the board with the same information as did Holmquist. . . .

The Employment Relations Commission's order was not limited to a determination that a prohibited labor practice had taken place in the past; it also restrains future conduct. By prohibiting the school board from "permitting employees to appear and speak at meetings of the Board of Education" the order constitutes an indirect, but effective, prohibition on persons such as Holmquist from communicating with their government. The order would have a substantial impact upon virtually all communication between teachers and the school board. The order prohibits speech by teachers "on matters subject to collective bargaining." As the dissenting opinion below noted, however, there is virtually no subject concerning the operation of the school system that could not also be characterized as a potential subject of collective bargaining. Teachers not only constitute the overwhelming bulk of employees of the school system, but they are the very core of that system; restraining teachers' expressions to the board on matters involving the operation of the schools would seriously impair the board's ability to govern the district. . . . The challenged portion of the order is designed to govern speech and conduct in the future, not to punish past conduct and as such it is the essence of prior restraint.

The judgment of the Wisconsin Supreme Court is reversed and the case is remanded to that court for further proceedings not inconsistent with this opinion.

Reversed and remanded.

Footnotes

1. *1975 Guidebook to Labor Relations* (Chicago: Commerce Clearing House, Inc., 1975), pp. 8–9.
2. Id.
3. Id., p. 11.
4. See: Benjamin Werne, *Public Employment Labor Relations* (The Michie Company, 1974), p. 5.
5. Id., p. 6.
6. Speech by Jerry Wurf, International President of American Federation of State, County, and Municipal Employees, AFL–CIO, United States Conference of Mayors, Honolulu, Hawaii, 1967.
7. Werne, supra, p. 11; see also: *Collective Bargaining and Politics in Public Employment,* 19 U.C.L.A.L.Rev. 887 (1972).
8. Atkins v. City of Charlotte, 296 F.Supp. 1068 (D.N.C.1969).
9. 406 F.2d 137 (8th Cir.1969).
10. Id.
11. This rule can vary among jurisdictions. For example, the Virginia Supreme Court has held that school boards do not have either statutory or constitutional authority to enter into collective bargaining agreements. Commonwealth v. Arlington County Board, 217 Va. 558, 232 S.E.2d 30 (1977).
12. Chief of Police v. Town of Dracut, 357 Mass. 492, 258 N.E.2d 531 (1970).

13. 48 Am.Jur.2d, § 1027–1043.

14. City of New York v. DeLury, 23 N.Y.2d 175, 295 N.Y.S.2d 901, 243 N.E.2d 128 (1968).

15. Anderson Federation of Teachers v. School City of Anderson, 252 Ind. 558, 251 N.E.2d 15 (1969).

16. United Federation of Postal Clerks v. Blount, 325 F.Supp. 879, aff'd 404 U.S. 805, 92 S.Ct. 80 (1971).

17. Anderson, supra.

18. Hugh D. Jascourt, "Can Compulsory Arbitration Work in Education Collective Bargaining: An Introduction," *Journal of Law and Education* vol. 4, no. 4 (October 1975).

19. School Board of the City of Richmond v. Parham, 218 Va. 950, 243 S.E.2d 468 (1978).

20. Dearborn Fire Fighters Union v. City of Dearborn, 42 Mich. App. 51, 201 N.W.2d 650 (1972).

17

Finance

The state legislature, in the absence of contrary constitutional restraints, has plenary power over state and local financing of schools. State constitutional provisions empowering the legislature to provide for a system of public schools expressly or impliedly confer on the legislature the authority to tax and distribute funds for public schools. Where litigation does arise it usually involves the methods used by the legislature to regulate and control revenues and expenditures in the exercise of this authority. A substantial amount of litigation is devoted to the legal requirements for taxation and taxpayers remedies for payment of illegal taxes as well as legal requirements for budgeting and accounting for school funds. Many cases question the legal authority of school districts to issue bonds, hold bond elections, and impose certain fees and charges on children and parents. Although the volume of cases is relatively small compared to other fiscal matters, the issue of constitutional rights of students and the resulting impact on state school finance has probably been the most widely publicized area of school finance litigation.

Recent court actions challenging the constitutionality of state school aid formulas under specific state constitutional provisions and the Equal Protection Clause of the Fourteenth Amendment represent an evolutionary step in judicial expansion of constitutional protections of individual rights. Constitutional rights of students have been extended, placing new limitations and restrictions on the police power of the state to regulate and control education. Courts once obliquely mantained that education was a privilege bestowed upon the individual by the good will of the state and that it could be altered or even taken away at state discretion. Today, however, this attitude has been changed and now the concept is that the student possesses a constitutional interest in an education. Under Due Process, the litigation continues to test various provisions of state constitutions and their attendant ramifications. The theory that education is a protected interest has manifested itself in constitutional protections for students in both the substantive and procedural aspects of constitutional law.

The Equal Protection Clause of the Fourteenth Amendment has been a primary vehicle by which plaintiffs have sought to expand individual rights. With the desegregation cases as the basic source of precedent, some lower courts initially invoked equal protection rights as a means of forcing redistribution of state fund sources for education. In subsequent cases, state consitutional provisions were used to contest the legitimacy of certain methods of school fund allocation. These cases harbored pervasive legal implications not the least of which was their impact on the traditional role of the legislature in setting governmental finance policy. Of all of the powers possessed by the legislative branch of government, the discretionary power to tax and distribute resources has been the most fundamental and jealously guarded. The courts, in treading on this hallowed ground, entered a "political thicket" as formidable as reapportionment and desegregation.

The school finance cases, therefore, represent an important step in legal precedents not only because they involve limitations on the police power of the state to regulate and control education but because they also restrict a state's power to devise and implement its own system of taxation. Each of these issues has traditionally formed almost entirely separate precedents.

TAXATION FOR EDUCATION

The power of taxation is an inherent power of the state, limited only by the Fourteenth Amendment of the federal Constitution and the constitution of the state. The states are not prevented by the Equal Protection Clause from taxing according to reasonable classification. For example, a state may impose a heavier tax on nonresidents than on residents because of difficulties and expense of tax collection. However, a state may not impose an arbitrary or discriminatory tax burden upon a segment of the population.

The courts have held that school districts have no inherent power to levy taxes. This power must be expressly conferred upon the school district by the legislature. In the levy and collection of taxes, school districts must adhere strictly to the language of the statutory authority; the courts are hesitant to extend powers of taxation by statutory implication. The power of a local school district to tax for education funds is not implied by a statutory mandate to establish and operate a local school system. In the absence of contrary constitutional provisions, the legislature may choose to finance education entirely from a tax levied at the state level and redistributed to the school districts.

School districts must construe statutes strictly and expend the moneys for the specific purposes as set out by the legislature. If a school tax levy is illegal because of failure to follow the prescribed procedure, the courts will make a determination depending on whether the statutory provision is mandatory or directory. If the provision is mandatory, the tax is invalid. However, the courts have established no clear guidelines for determining if a provision is mandatory or directory. In these situations, courts are generally faced with the perplexing problem of finding a tax levy invalid and thereby harming the educational program. Because of this, the courts are usually very liberal in this regard and are hesitant to call a tax invalid. If a procedural error is relatively minor and does not deprive the taxpayers of a substantial or fundamental right, the courts will allow the tax to stand.

THE DEVELOPMENT OF THE
AMERICAN STATE AND
LOCAL TAX SYSTEM

With permission of Jerome R. Hellerstein,
Third Ed., West Publishing Company, St.
Paul, Minn pp. 1–2 & pp. 70–72.

Colonial Taxation. The colonial governments in their early days subsisted on voluntary payments, subsidies and allowances abroad, quit-rents, and occasional fees and fines of early justice. When compulsory levies developed, the tax systems followed the pattern of the local economies. In the democratic New England communities almost everyone owned land; and the distribution of property was fairly equal. Consequently, in New England, in addition to the poll tax, the colonies levied a tax on the gross produce of land, either actual or computed, according to the extent and quality of the land held. Gradually, this levy grew into a real property tax, which was soon expanded into a general property tax. The town artisans and other townsmen who subsisted on the fruit of their labor, instead of property, were not adequately taxed by the property levy. The "faculty tax" was added to reach these persons. The faculty tax was not an income tax, but instead a levy in a fixed amount, imposed rather arbitrarily, according to occupations and callings.[1]

An entirely different development took place in the Southern colonies, dominated by an aristocratic landed gentry with large holdings. There, the land tax played an insignificant role. After slavery was introduced, it became difficult to retain even the poll tax, which became in a sense a property tax on slaves. Consequently, the Southern colonies turned to excise taxes, particularly on imports and exports, which bore heavily on poorer consumers.

The middle colonies, particularly the New Netherlands, reflected the dominance of the moneyed interests and trading classes, who brought with them a Dutch tradition. Here, there was neither the more or less equal distribution of wealth characteristic of New England, nor the preponderance of the landed interests typified by Virginia. Instead of a system of poll and property levies or of excises primarily on imports and exports, the fundamental characteristic of the tax structure was an excise system of taxation of trade, borrowed from Holland.

> Each section, therefore, had a fiscal system more or less in harmony with its economic conditions. It was not until these conditions changed during the eighteenth century that the fiscal systems began somewhat to approach each other; and it was not until much later that we find throughout the country a general property tax based not on the produce, but on the market value of property.[2]

The outstanding development in State and local taxation during the nineteenth century was the rise of the property tax. As stated by Professor Ely, during the period from 1796 to the Civil War "the distinguishing feature of the system of state and local taxation in America may be described in one sentence. It is the taxation of all property, movable or immovable, visible or invisible, or real or personal . . . at one uniform rate.[3]

Nevertheless, the divergence of economic systems was reflected in the development of the State fiscal systems. In the Southern States, with imports and exports as a source of revenue cut off by the federal Constitution, land had to bear a large part of the tax burden. As increased revenues were needed, these States, dominated by landed proprietors at least until the Civil War, turned primarily to license and privilege taxes on peddlers, auctioneers, saloon keepers, traders in slaves and horses, keepers of ferries, toll bridges and turnpikes, and indeed virtually all occupations carried on outside the farms.

In the Northern States, where business interests were dominant, the license or privilege tax system did not take hold. To supplement property tax yields, banks, insurance companies, canals, railroads, and other businesses were taxed; and as corporations came to play a more important role in the economy, general corporate franchise taxes were enacted. These levies were the precursors of the present day corporate taxes on or measured by net income. The newer States adopted the current tax philosophy of the older States, making the property tax the cornerstone of their tax structures. . . .

Early property taxation. Although property taxes were regarded as an extraordinary source of revenue in early history, they, nevertheless, have ancient origins. In Athens, the land tax was originally levied on gross produce, but it gradually developed into a property tax imposed not only on land and houses but also on slaves, cattle, furniture and money. Rome taxed many forms of personalty as well as realty. In Europe, the early property taxes were levied on land but were gradually extended to buildings and cattle, until they became general property taxes. As new types of movable and intangible property developed, evasion became prevalent and assessment difficult. The principle of the general property tax broke down and personal property taxes were gradually abandoned. By 1800, the base of European property taxes had largely dwindled down to land alone or land and buildings.

The development of the general property tax in the United States. . . . the general property tax became formally established in this country for the States and localities during the nineteenth century.

At first the property tax was really a tax on land at a fixed sum per acre of different types of land—cleared and uncleared, cultivated and cleared, and so forth. It soon was expanded to include livestock, buildings, and personal property. Each item of taxable property was listed and taxed at a fixed sum for each cow, each barn, and so on. The increasing complexity of this taxable list led finally to (1) the general property tax—general taxation of all properties, instead of the growing lists of taxable specified properties; (2) appraisal of property—the tax rates were imposed as percentages of per millages of the property valuation, rather than as a fixed sum of money per unit of property; (3) the adoption of the principle of uniformity—whereas earlier laws provided for varying rates for different classes of property, the uniformity concept adopted by State constitutions required real and personal property to be taxed at a uniform proportion of value.

*Authority to Levy Taxes Must Be
Found in Express Legislative
Provision*

MARION & McPHERSON
RAILWAY CO. v. ALEXANDER

Supreme Court of Kansas, 1901.
63 Kan. 72, 64 P. 978.

CUNNINGHAM, J. The plaintiff in error in this action seeks to enjoin the collection of all taxes levied for school purposes in school district No. 79, Marion county, Kan., in excess of 2 percent on the taxable property owned by it in said district. A graded school district, No. 79, had been organized, identical in boundaries and inhabitants with school district No. 79; such organization being authorized by article 7, c. 92, of the General Statutes of 1889. That article generally provided for the organization of union or graded schools, its principal sections being as follows: Section 107 provides for the selection of a board of directors by the graded school district, and that such board shall consist of a director, clerk, and treasurer. Section 108 directs that such board of directors shall, in all matters relating to the graded schools, possess all the powers and discharge all the like duties of boards of directors in other districts. Section 109 provides that the union districts thus formed shall be entitled to an equitable share of the school funds, to be drawn from the treasurer of each district so uniting, in proportion to the number of children attending the said graded school for each district. Section 110: "The said union district may levy taxes for the purpose of purchasing a building or furnishing proper buildings, for the accommodation of the school or for the purpose of defraying necessary expenses and paying teachers, but shall be governed in all respects by the law herein provided for levying and collecting district taxes." Section 111 provides certain duties for the clerk of the union district in relation to reports, and that the district treasurer shall apportion the amount of school moneys due the union district, and pay the same over to the treasurer of the union district on order of the clerk and director thereof. Section 112, that the clerk of the union district shall make report to the county superintendent, and discharge all the duties of clerk in like manner as the clerk of the district. Section 113, that the treasurer of the district shall perform all the duties of treasurer as prescribed in the act in like manner as the district treasurer. Section 115, that any single district shall possess power to establish graded schools in like manner and subject to the same provisions as two or more districts united. Section 28 of the same chapter (being the section which gives the general power for levying district taxes) provides: "The inhabitants qualified to vote at a school meeting, lawfully assembled, shall have power: . . . To vote a tax annually not exceeding 2 percent on the taxable property in the district, as the meeting shall deem sufficient for the various school purposes, and distribute the amount as the meeting shall deem proper in the payment of teachers' wages, and to purchase or lease a site."

These are all the sections which afford light for the solution of the question involved. From these, it is contended by plaintiff in error that while the inhabitants of one or more school districts may form a union or graded district, and create the machinery to run the same and to maintain any and all schools therein, the total levy "for the various school purposes" cannot exceed 2 percent on the taxable property in any one district annually. It is contended by the defendants in error that the various sections quoted, conferring as they do upon the various members of the graded school district board all the powers of like officers of ordinary district boards, and erecting a separate entity for the purpose of managing a separate school, and conferring upon that entity the power to levy taxes as found in section 110, give the power to such graded school district to make within its bounds an additional levy not to exceed 2 percent; that is, that it may levy as much as the original school district may, and this in addition to what the original district levies, and not that the total of both levies must be the limit fixed in section 28. The court below took this view of the question. In this we do not agree. We think that by section 28 the entire levy may not exceed 2 percent; and we are strengthened in this conclusion by the language of section 109, which says that a union district shall be entitled to "an equitable share of the school funds," and also by that in section 111—"the district treasurer shall apportion the amount of school money due the union district and pay the same over to the union district." The law fixes the time for holding the annual meetings of the union or graded districts in June, while the annual meetings of school districts occur in July. All these provisions, taken together, indicate that it was the purpose of the legislature that, while the first meeting—that of the graded district—could suggest the levy desired for graded school purposes, the last one only possessed the power to vote the tax which for "the various school purposes" could not in any one year exceed 2 percent. Or, at least, there must be such harmony in the action of both bodies that the aggregate levy may not exceed the limit found in section 28. We may say that the question is not one entirely free from doubt, but can hardly believe that the legislature would have left it in that condition, had its purpose been to confer the right to so largely increase the burden of taxation. The authority to levy taxes is an extraordinary one. It is never left to implication, unless it is a necessary implication. Its warrant must be clearly found in the act of the legislature. Any other rule might lead to great wrong and oppression, and when there is a reasonable doubt as to its existence the right must be denied. Therefore to say that the right is in doubt is to deny its existence. . . .

The levies sought to be enjoined are those for the years 1894 and 1895, and our conclusion is that the judgment of the district court must be reversed, and it be directed to make the injunction perpetual, enjoining all of the defendants from collecting all of said school taxes in excess of 2 percent. All the justices concurring.

NOTES

1. "Neither municipalities nor school districts are sovereigns, and they have no original or fundamental power of legislation or taxation, but have only the right and power to enact those legislative and tax ordi-

nances or resolutions which are authorized by act of the legislature."
Appeal of School District of City of Allentown, 370 Pa. 161, 87 A.2d 480
(1952).

2. Taxes levied and collected for school purposes are state taxes whether
they are collected by the school district or a municipality. In an
Alabama case, the court said: "If the Constitution raises the fund and
directs its use in furthering a state function, it continues to be such a
state fund regardless of the sort of agency designated to administer it."
City Board of Education of Athens v. Williams, 231 Ala. 137, 163 So. 802
(1935).

3. In relating legislative provisions for taxation to constitutional requirements, the courts have held that revenue statutes must be given a
reasonable construction, and no statute can circumvent positively stated
constitutional provisions. Mathews v. Board of Education of City of
Chicago, 342 Ill. 120, 174 N.E. 35 (1930).

4. "The authority to levy taxes is an extraordinary one. It is never left to
implication, unless it is a necessary implication. Its warrant must be
clearly found in the act of the legislature. Any other rule might lead to
great wrong and oppression, and when there is a reasonable doubt as to
its existence the right must be denied . . .." Marion and M. Ry. Co. v.
Alexander, County Treasurer, 63 Kan. 72, 64 P. 978 (1901).

5. "The power of the board of education of a non-high school district to levy
taxes is statutory. The language granting the power is to be strictly
construed and will not be extended beyond the plain import of the words
used." People ex rel. Smith, Co. Collector v. Wabash Railway Co. et al.,
374 Ill. 165, 28 N.E.2d 119 (1940).

6. The intent of the legislature in enacting taxation statutes is often
difficult to interpret. A Pennsylvania court in determining that a
statute prescribing taxation for "amusements" included admissions to
"fair grounds" had this to say about statutory interpretation:

The language of a statute must be read in a sense which harmonizes with the
subject matter and its general purpose and object. The general design and
purpose of the law is to be kept in view . . . . School Dist. of Cambria
Township v. Cambria Co. Legion Recreation Association, 201 Pa.Super. 163, 192
A.2d 149 (1963).

7. Courts will not interfere with the exercise of sound business judgment on
the part of taxing authorities, but will intervene only to prevent a clear
abuse by such officers of their discretionary powers. People v. Baltimore
& Ohio Southwestern Railway Co., 353 Ill. 492, 187 N.E. 463 (1933).

8. Where a wrongful tax is collected, the taxpayer may recover only on
such remedies as are authorized by law, such as an appeal to set aside or
cancel a tax deed and a tax protest. Wall v. M. & R. Sheep Co., 33 Cal.
2d 768, 205 P.2d 14.

9. A person who pays tax voluntarily and not under duress cannot recover
the tax. Harding v. Wiley, 219 Ill.App. 1. A mere protest by a taxpayer
is not sufficient to constitute payment under compulsion or duress.

10. A person may not question the legality of school funds unless he has a requisite interest in such funds. Chalupnik v. Savall, 219 Wis. 442, 263 N.W. 352 (1935).

11. Some states have statutory provisions for a taxpayer protest in a court or board of tax review. The findings of fact or judgment by this court or board will not be disturbed unless clearly arbitrary or against the weight of evidence.

12. Taxpayers may not sit idly by and allow illegal systems of taxation to be installed without protesting and then take advantage of the illegality of the system by collaterally attacking the system when they are sued. In such a case, the Court of Civil Appeals of Texas held that, although a scheme of taxation is illegal, the burden is on the taxpayers to show that they have suffered substantial financial loss as a result of the failure of the city and school district to assess property legally. City of Houston v. McCarthy, 371 S.W.2d 587 (1963).

13. Tangible personal property that is located in a state other than that in which the owner is domiciled may be taxed at the place of its location. Fennell v. Pauley, 83 N.W. 799 (1900). The "domicile" of a person is the place where he has his principal, true, fixed, permanent home, and to which he has, whenever he is absent, the intention of returning, and it also means the habitation, fixed in any place, from which a person does not have any present intention of removing. State v. Benny, 20 N.J. 238, 119 A.2d 155.

14. Intangible personal property is generally taxable at the domicile of the owner. Scripps v. Board of Review of Fulton Co., 55 N.E. 700 (1899). However, courts have upheld cases in which the state legislature provides that intangible personal property shall be taxed when located other than where the owner is domiciled. In arriving at this conclusion a Minnesota court stated:

For many purposes the domicile of the owner is deemed the situs of his personal property. This, however, is only a fiction, from motives of convenience, and is not of universal application, by yields to the actual situs of the property when justice requires that it should. It is not allowed to be controlling in matters of taxation. Thus, corporeal personal property is conceded to be taxable at the place where it is actually situated. A credit which cannot be regarded as situated in a place merely because the debtor resides there, must usually be considered as having its situs where it is owned, at the domicile of the creditor. The creditor, however, may give it a business situs elsewhere; as where he places it in the hands of an agent for collection or renewal, with a view to reloaning the money and keeping it invested as a permanent business . . ..
The allegation to pay taxes on property for the support of the government arises from the fact that it is under the protection of the government. In re Washington County v. Estate of Jefferson, 35 Minn. 215, 28 N.W. 256 (1886).

15. In a case in which property was assessed in the wrong district and the owner had means of knowing the mistake, he could not recover as having paid under a mistake of fact. A mistake of fact is one "not caused by the neglect of a legal duty on the part of the person making the mistake." Civ.Code, § 1577, San Diego Land & Town Co. v. La Presa School District, 122 Cal. 98, 54 P. 528 (1898).

Distribution of State School Funds

This discussion is adapted from a chapter by Kern Alexander and K. Forbis Jordan in *Financing Education; Fiscal and Legal Alternatives,* edited by R.L. Johns, Kern Alexander and K. Forbis Jordan (Charles Merrill Company, 1972).

Where constitutionality of a statute is questioned, all reasonable doubt will be resolved in favor of the questioned authority and the act will be declared constitutional unless it can be clearly demonstrated that the legislature did not have the power or authority exercised or that its authority was exercised arbitrarily and capriciously, for instance, as to classification or delegation of authority, to the prejudice of the rights of some of the citizens. Particularly, is this true where the act in question is . . . of great public concern involving the performance of an absolute duty imposed on the legislature by the basic law of the state.[4]

This statement describes the traditional position of the courts toward the judicial regulation of such important legislative functions as taxation for public education. Nonintervention has been the watchword for decades when courts have been asked to examine the constitutionality of legislatively prescribed methods of taxation for financing of education.

The courts have steadfastly adhered to the philosophy that an act of the legislature will not be rendered invalid unless the act obviously violates certain prescribed constitutional standards. With regard to the constitutionality of state school finance programs, the courts have traditionally only been asked to determine whether such programs created unconstitutional classifications or violated equality and uniformity of taxation requirements. The Equal Protection Clause of the Fourteenth Amendment encompasses, but is not limited to, the same protections as the equality and uniformity of taxation provisions of most state constitutions. Even though the federal Equal Protection Clause encompasses much more than mere equality and uniformity of taxation, its broader aspects were not successfully invoked in challenging state school finance programs until recently.

The Equal Protection Clause was first described as a limitation on state revenue legislation by the Supreme Court of the United States in 1890. The "test" devised by the Supreme Court to determine constitutionality of state taxation has been restated by Justice Jackson:

Equal protection does not require identity of treatment. It only requires that classification rest on real and not feigned differences, that the distinction have some relevance to the purpose for which the classification is made, and the different treatment be not so disparate, relative to the difference in classification, as to be wholly arbitrary.[5]

The Equal Protection Clause establishes a minimum standard of uniformity to which state tax legislation must conform in addition to and over and beyond similar limitations imposed by state constitutional requirements.[6]

In practically all cases, state constitutions have the equivalent of an "equal protection" provision—that is, some constitutional restriction against "unreasonable classifications." While the United States Supreme Court has the ultimate interpretative power regarding "reasonableness" under the federal Equal Protection Clause, state courts have the last word as to the meaning of reasonableness under their respective state constitutions.[7] The primary problem is, of course, the definition of reasonableness with regard to appropriate classification. There are apparently no universally applicable tests by which to determine the reasonableness or unreasonableness of a classification. The cases merely indicate a vague outline of reasonableness and, in some instances, a given basis may be valid with respect to one tax and invalid with another.[8] Justice Bradley, in *dictum* in the *Bell's Gap* case,[9] however, did give this explanation.

> [The Equal Protection Clause] was not intended to prevent a state from adjusting its system of taxation in all proper and reasonable ways. It may, if it chooses, exempt certain classes of property from any taxation at all, such as churches, libraries, and the property of charitable institutions. . . . We think we are safe in saying that the Fourteenth Amendment was not intended to compel the state to adopt an iron rule of equal taxation. If that were its proper construction it would not only supersede all those constitutional provisions and laws of some of the states, whose object is to secure equality of taxation, and which are usually accompanied with qualifications deemed material; but it would render nugatory those discriminations which the best interests of society require. . . .[10]

The Equal Protection Clause of the Fourteenth Amendment is no stranger to disputes over the distribution of school funds. As early as 1912, the Supreme Court of Maine in *Sawyer* v. *Gilmore* handed down an opinion that examined constitutional equality under both the Maine and United States Constitutions as applied to both taxation and distribution of funds by the state.[11] The court in this case maintained that the equality of taxation provision of the state constitution required only equality of assessment, not equality of distribution.

The logic in this case reflected a judicial philosophy that was relied upon for over half a century. The courts steadfastly refused to apply state constitutional uniformity and equality of taxing provisions to school fund distribution formulas. In fairness to the courts, however, seldom, if ever, was a statute challenged when the legislature was not seeking to move toward greater equity in distribution of resources among school districts. Plaintiffs were typically attempting to retard such process. Indeed, in most cases, state equality of taxation and the federal Constitution were invoked in an attempt to prevent the equalization of resources among school districts.

As state legislatures have attempted to provide greater equalization of resources among school districts through various taxing and funding techniques, disputes have arisen over the constitutionality of these methods. Many states have constitutional provisions that require that state school funds be distributed in a particular manner, usually a flat amount per school census or population count.[12] Such constitutional provisions have been an impediment to legislatures seeking to equalize resources for poorer school districts. In the earlier cases, these constitutional provisions were invoked by taxpayers from the wealthier school districts that sought to prevent state equalization of resources. A case in point is a 1924 Oklahoma case[13] in which the legislature enacted a law providing additional money from the state general fund to support school districts which could raise enough resources from a fifteen-mill levy to operate an eight-month school term. The plaintiff maintained such legislation was unconstitutional because the state constitution mandated that moneys from the state permanent school fund must be allocated on the basis of school population to all common school districts and also complained that state aid provided to only financially weak districts was special legislation constituting an unconstitutional classification. With regard to the first argument, the court held that the equalization moneys were to be paid out of the state general fund and not out of the constitutionally restricted permanent school fund, thereby allowing the legislature flexibility in its method of allocation. The court dismissed the latter argument saying that the state aid to weak school districts applied to all districts alike, extending aid to those that were similarly situated in privation of resources.

This court also pointed out that the Oklahoma constitution placed the duty on the legislature to "establish and maintain a *system* [emphasis added] of free public schools wherein all children of the state may be educated.[14] Significantly, the court maintained that such wording meant that the legislature was to provide an "efficient and sufficient system, with competent teachers, necessary general facilities" and adequate length of school terms. The word "system," the court said, indicates a degree of uniformity and equality of opportunity, and by assuming the responsibility to provide for public education the state had the duty to provide "insofar as it is practical, equal rights and privileges to its youth, to obtain such mental and moral training as will make them useful citizens. . . ." This equality of treatment, the court said, was an "imperative governmental duty." [15]

Courts have been hesitant to invalidate legislative acts on the basis of unconstitutional classification because the source of taxation is often tightly interwoven with the government's plan for distribution of funds to local districts. The essence of an illegal constitutional classification is to arbitrarily classify local districts or persons with no regard for their actual conditions or needs. The United States Court of Appeals for the Ninth Circuit speaks of this as fitting tax programs to needs:

> Traditionally classification has been a device for fitting tax programs to local needs and usages in order to achieve an equitable distribution of the tax burden. It has, because of this, been pointed out that in taxation, even more than in other fields, legislatures possess the greatest freedom in classification. Since the members of a legislature necessarily enjoy a familiarity with local conditions which this court cannot have, the presumption of constitutionality can be overcome only by the most explicit demonstration that a classification is a hostile and oppressive discrimination against particular persons and classes. The burden is on the one attacking the legislative arrangement to negate every conceivable basis which might support it.[16]

Even though the court denied that equality and uniformity of taxation requirements of both state and federal constitutions applied to the distribution of funds, it proceeded nevertheless to lay down "guiding principles" that govern the legislatures' distribution of tax funds. Quoting *Corpus Juris Secundum,* the court said:

> In the absence of constitutional regulation the method of apportioning and distributing a school fund, accruing from taxes or other revenue, rests in the wise discretion of the state legislature, which method, in the absence of abuse of discretion or violation of some constitutional provision, cannot be interfered with by the courts . . . the fact that the fund is distributed unequally among the different districts or political subdivisions does not render it invalid.[17]

In other words, the needs of the various types of school districts and the resulting impact of methods of taxation is a matter that is to be determined by the legislature.

In 1965, however, the theory was advanced that education was a constitutionally protected right and must be provided to all on equal terms. Thus a state that gives fewer dollars for the child in a poorer school district may be held to deny equal protection rights.[18] It was argued that the state had no reasonable equal protection basis on which to justify making a child's education dependent on the wealth of the school district. The United States Supreme Court had laid the groundwork for this conclusion by previously holding that to classify persons on either the basis of poverty [19] or according to their location, homesite, or occupation was unreasonable.[20] Therefore, it was concluded, the quality of a child's education could not be contingent upon a state and local taxing and fund distribution system that is based on the property wealth of the local school district.

By 1968, several suits had been filed, each seeking to have state school finance programs rendered unconstitutional through the application of this logic. A three-judge federal district court in Florida [21] was apparently the first court to hold that a state school finance mechanism was unconstitutional as violative of the equal protection rights of a child. This court, relying largely on precedent by the United States Supreme Court in *Reynolds* v. *Sims,*[22] reasoned that the Equal Protection Clause requires "the uniform treatment of persons standing in the same relation to the governmental action." The court then departed from the traditional line of thought of the courts that had held that so long as the act in question applies uniformly there is no violation of equal protection, reasoning to the contrary that a uniform act of the legislature may indeed violate the Equal Protection Clause if its effect is discriminatory. The court adopted the "rational basis" standard and concluded that a state must show a rational basis for its act or the act will be held unconstitutional. This decision was later vacated and remanded on other grounds by the United States Supreme Court.

Educators for some time have recognized that all children cannot be educated equally with equal resources. Some children with special learning deficiencies caused by cultural deprivation or mental or physical incapacities must be given special educational services. Today, some state aid programs partially take into account the differences in educational needs of children but most state finance programs do not adequately measure or compensate such educational needs by providing proportionately greater funds to school districts with high incidences of high cost children. Is a child denied a constitutional right of an equal education if he cannot hear the teacher, cannot enunciate clearly enough to progress normally in school, or has a cultural background placing him at such a learning deficit that he will be unable to ever catch up or compete? In such cases, equal expenditures or regular programs for all children may provide equal learning opportunity for normal, middle-class children, but attendance in such regular middle-class educational programs by the phsyically, mentally, or culturally deprived provides for less than equal educational opportunity.

A fundamental legal question is whether a state's responsibility to provide a child with an opportunity for equal education is successfully discharged when no recognition was given to individual needs and deficiencies. It was this issue that was addressed in two 1968 cases that ultimately reached the Supreme Court.

In *McInnis* v. *Shapiro*,[23] the plaintiffs claimed that the Illinois finance system created large variations in expenditures per student from district to district, thereby providing some students with a good education and depriving others who have equal or greater educational need. The court concluded that equal educational expenditures are not required by the Fourteenth Amendment and that variations created by taxation of property in the school districts do not discriminate. The court said:

> Unequal educational expenditures per student, based upon the variable property values and tax rates of local school districts, do not amount to an invidious discrimination. Moreover, the statutes which permit these unequal expenditures on a district to district basis are neither arbitrary nor unreasonable.[24]

The *McInnis* court declined to establish judicial standards for determining legislative allocations based on educational needs. Since *McInnis* was summarily affirmed by the Supreme Court of the United States,[25] this statement represented precedent and had substantial impact on legal thought at that time.

The position in *McInnis* was summed by saying that there were no "discoverable and manageable standards by which a court can determine when the Constitution is satisfied and when it is violated."[26]

McInnis was closely followed by a second "educational need" case in Virginia.[27] In *Burruss*, plaintiffs relied more directly on the educational need argument than did the plaintiffs in *McInnis*. Specifically, plaintiffs claimed the state formula created and perpetuated substantial disparities in educational opportunities throughout the state of Virginia and failed to relate to any of the variety of educational needs present in the several counties and cities of Virginia.

To the former allegation, the court found that the system of finance was not discriminatory as it operated under a uniform and consistent state plan. With regard to educational needs, the court praised the equalization of educational opportunity as a worthy and commendable goal, but refused to interject the wisdom of the court in ascertaining what constituted educational need disparities. In following the hands-off course of *McInnis*, the court said:

> the courts have neither the knowledge, nor the means, nor the power to tailor the public moneys to fit the varying needs of these students throughout the

state. We can only see to it that the outlays on one group are not invidiously greater or less than that of another. No such arbitrariness is manifest here.[28]

Accordingly, *Burruss* denied relief to plaintiffs under either the "efficiency" provision of the Virginia Constitution or the Equal Protection Clause of the Fourteenth Amendment. The United States Supreme Court summarily affirmed this decision.

Only a short time elapsed between *McInnis* and the now famous decision by the California Supreme Court in *Serrano* v. *Priest*.[29] In *Serrano*, the court handed down a well-reasoned decision that strongly documents the establishment of a new equal protection application to school finance. The court here spoke of equalization only in terms of the relative wealth of the local school districts as measured in terms of property valuation. It did not attempt to define the equal protection argument in terms of educational needs of children or educational programs.

According to this court, in order to answer the primary constitutional question, does the California public school financing scheme violate the Equal Protection Clause, it was first necessary to determine whether (1) education is a fundamental interest protected by the constitution, (2) wealth is a "suspect classification," and (3) the state has a "compelling interest" in creating a system of school finance that makes a child's education dependent on the wealth of his local school district. In a short treatise on constitutional law, the court pointed out that the United States Supreme Court had employed two tests for determining the constitutionality of state legislation under the Equal Protection Clause. In the first and more lenient test, the Supreme Court presumed that state legislation is constitutional and merely required the state to show that the distinctions drawn or classifications created by the challenged statute had some "rational relationship to a conceivable legitimate state purpose." On the other hand, if the state legislation touched on a "fundamental interest" of the individual or involved a "suspect classification," then the court would subject the challenged statute to "strict scrutiny" or active and critical analysis. If a fundamental interest or suspect classification is involved, the presumption of constitutionality is not with the state; on the contrary, the burden of establishing the necessity of the classification is with the state.

In critically analyzing the present California finance system, the court pointed out that, although the basic state aid program in California tends to equalize among school districts, the total system, including state and local funds combined, created great disparities in school revenues and the system as a whole generated school revenue proportional to the wealth of the individual school. After concluding that education was a "fundamental interest" and property wealth was a "suspect classification," the court then applied the "strict scrutiny" standard and found the system of finance unconstitutional.

Closely following *Serrano*, a United States District Court in Minnesota entertained a class action suit[30] wherein plaintiffs alleged denial of equal protection and violation of the Civil Rights Act.[31] Plaintiffs showed that rich districts in Minnesota enjoy both lower tax rates and higher spending. The court, in viewing the facts, arrived at the inescapable conclusion that, "the level of spending for publicly financed education in Minnesota is profoundly affected by the wealth of each school district." Education was considered to be a "fundamental interest" and wealth to be a "suspect classification" as held in *Serrano*. *Van Dusartz* though had limited utility as precedent because the court's comments were made merely in support of an order denying the defendant's motion to dismiss the action and the court deferred further action until after the 1972 Minnesota legislative session.

A significant decision by a federal three-judge court in Texas [32] followed both the California and Minnesota cases and reached the same conclusion. Here is was held that plaintiffs had been denied equal protection of the law by the Texas system of financing its public schools. Plaintiffs contended that the educational finance system of the state makes education a function of the local property tax base. The court observed that the school finance system of Texas erroneously assumes that the value of property in the various districts will be sufficiently equal to maintain comparable expenditures among districts. This inequality is not corrected to any substantial degree by state funds because when all state and local funds were combined to correct this unconstitutional inequality, *Rodriguez* established a standard of "fiscal neutrality." As was the case in both *Serrano* and *Van Dusartz*, the court maintained that fiscal neutrality did not require that all educational expenditures be equal for each child. The standard simply required that "the quality of public education may not be a function of wealth, other than the wealth of the state as a whole."

The rationale and precedents of the lower courts in *Serrano* and *Rodriguez*, that a child's education could not be contingent on the wealth of the local school district, were to no avail, however, for in 1973 the Supreme Court of the United States handed down a reversal of *Rodriguez*,[33] effectively terminating such state school finance litigation under the Equal Protection Clause. On rehearing *Serrano*, the California Supreme Court was forced to abandon the Fourteenth Amendment as the constitutional basis for overturning the state school aid formula and thereafter relied solely on an equal protection provision in the California constitution.

Justice Powell in upholding the constitutionality of the Texas method of financing its schools maintained that education was not a "fundamental" constitutional right under the Equal Protection Clause, as had been presumed from reading *Brown*, and as such education could not be viewed in special favor by the court so as to justify strict judicial scrutiny. In so holding, the Court reverted to the traditional judicial position of leaving such matters to the wisdom of the legislature. In this regard Justice Powell concluded:

> Education, perhaps even more than welfare assistance, presents a myriad of "intractable economic, social, and even philosophical problems." The very complexity of the problems of financing and managing a statewide public school system suggests that "there will be more than one constitutionally permissible method of solving them," and that, within the limits of rationality, "the legislature's efforts to tackle the problems" should be entitled to respect.[34]

Immediately after this decision most if not all such litigation in the federal courts was abandoned. From the Supreme Court's position it was quite clear that any future actions, if they were to be successful in attacking methods of state school financing, would have to be pursued in reliance on state constitutional grounds rather than on the Fourteenth Amendment. Subsequent to and in accordance with the Supreme Court's decision in *Rodriguez*, the Supreme Courts of Michigan [35] and Arizona [36] reversed previous precedent and upheld the constitutionality of their own state school finance programs. The Michigan Supreme Court had previously held that the Michigan school finance system violated the equal protection provision of the state constitution [37] but on rehearing found no violation of either the state or federal equal protection clauses. Similarly, the Supreme Court of Arizona in upholding that state's method of financing schools followed *Rodriguez* in finding that education was not a fundamental right deserving of strict judicial scrutiny.

Litigation in the realm of state school aid distribution has returned to state courts, and since *Rodriguez*, the actions now test state formulas in light of only state constitutional provisions. Bases for such litigation may be found in equal protection, uniformity, equality, thorough and efficient, or other provisions of state constitutions. State equal protection was, as mentioned previously, the ultimate basis on which the California Supreme Court relied to hold the method of financing in that state unconstitutional after the United States Supreme Court in *Rodriguez* removed equal protection of the Fourteenth Amendment from contention.[38]

Rodriguez continues, though, to have substantial influence in shaping state courts' view of their own constitutions. In a Louisiana case the court held that the method of school financing in that state did not differ significantly from that of Texas litigated in *Rodriguez* and that, as such, it was not unconstitutionally discriminatory against the poor people in poor school districts. The Supreme Court of Idaho held, in a 3–2 decision, that the education finance law of that state did not violate the "uniform system" requirement of that state's constitution.[39] In so doing, the court refused to recognize education as a "fundamental interest" under the Idaho Constitution and, in the same vein, turned back the plaintiff's equal protection claim. Decisions in Illinois,[40] Kansas,[41] Montana,[42] Oregon,[43] New York,[44] and Georgia [45] have likewise denied relief to plaintiffs where challenges to the school finance law were predicated on state constitutional provisions. In the Oregon case, the Oregon Supreme Court observed that it could interpret the equal protection clause of the Oregon Constitution more broadly than that placed on the federal Constitution in *Rodriguez*, but it declined to do so. The court refused to acknowledge that education was a fundamental right and the fact that education was mentioned in the Oregon Constitution was not sufficient to establish its fundamentality. Further, the court found that the word "uniform" in the constitution merely required that the legislature provide a minimum program of educational opportunity throughout the state. Complete uniformity, the court decided, would infringe on the state's reasonable objective to maintain local control of education.

In an important case that departed from the influence of *Rodriguez*, the New Jersey Supreme Court relied on that state's "thorough and efficient" clause to invalidate the state school aid formula.[46] This court made it quite clear that the state had an obligation to correct the fiscal imbalances created by local school district organization and fiscal ability variations. It further found that the "thorough and efficient" requirement required equal educational opportunity and that if local government fails to so provide then the state must act to either compel local school districts to meet the constitutional mandate or the state must meet the obligation itself. In broadly defining the "thorough and efficient" standard, the court said:

> The Constitution's guarantee must be understood to embrace that educational opportunity which is needed in the contemporary setting to equip a child for his role as a citizen and as a competitor in the labor market.[47]

Because of the variation in state constitutional provisions, and the diversity in state school finance formulas, one can expect little consistency in state court views on school finance equalization. While several aforementioned courts have declined to intervene in school finance issues, others, as in *Robinson,* have held that methods of financing the schools are unconstitutional. Noteworthy among those cases are decisions in Connecticut,[48] West Virginia,[49] Wyoming,[50] and Arkansas.[51] These cases, along with the original *Serrano* v. *Priest*[52] decision, have required a greater equalization of educational resources.

In Connecticut, the court held the equal protection provision of the state constitution was violated by the state educational finance formula which allocated money to local school districts on a flat grant basis, not taking into consideration the fiscal ability of local school districts.[53] The court reasoned that, under the Connecticut Constitution, education was a fundamental right because it was explicitly recognized in Article VIII, Section I, and the history and tradition of the state demonstrated a commitment to the education of children. In holding the system unconstitutional and mandating that the legislature redress the faults, the court observed that absolute equality was not required and that cost differences due to variations in educational needs and economic conditions may be taken into account.

In 1983, the Supreme Court of Arkansas held that state's system of financing public schools was unconstitutional. The court noted that minimal educational programs are not enough to satisfy the equal opportunity demanded by equal protection. It said that "[b]are and minimal sufficiency does not translate into equal educational opportunity."[54]

These cases suggest that, in spite of *Rodriguez,* there will be continuing judicial tests challenging school finance systems in state courts. The final resolution of these cases will depend on the circumstances in each particular state. It is reasonable to assume that the plaintiffs will prevail in several instances because of continuing disequalization among school districts and the tendency of many legislatures not to be responsive.

State School Finance System that
Results in Revenue Disparities Based
on Fiscal Ability of School Districts
Does Not Violate the Equal Protection
Clause of the Fourteenth Amendment

SAN ANTONIO
INDEPENDENT SCHOOL
DISTRICT v. RODRIGUEZ

Supreme Court of the United States, 1973.
411 U.S. 1, 93 S.Ct. 1278, rehearing
denied 411 U.S. 959, 93 S.Ct. 1919.

Mr. Justice POWELL delivered the opinion of the Court.

This suit attacking the Texas system of financing public education was initiated by Mexican-American parents whose children attend the elementary and secondary schools in the Edgewood Independent School District, an urban school district in San Antonio, Texas. They brought a class action on behalf of schoolchildren throughout the State who are members of minority groups or who are poor and reside in school districts having a low property tax base. Named as defendants were the State Board of Education, the Commissioner of Education, the State Attorney General, and the Bexar County (San Antonio) Board of Trustees. The complaint was filed in the summer of 1968 and a three-judge court was impaneled in January 1969. In December 1971 the panel rendered its judgment in a *per curiam* opinion holding the Texas school finance system unconstitutional under the Equal Protection Clause of the Fourteenth Amendment. The State appealed, and we noted probable jurisdiction to consider the far-reaching constitutional questions presented. . . . For the reasons stated in this opinion, we reverse the decision of the District Court. . . .

The school district in which appellees reside, the Edgewood Independent School District, has been compared throughout this litigation with the Alamo Heights Independent School District. This comparison between the least and most affluent districts in the San Antonio area serves to illustrate the manner in which the dual system of finance operates and to indicate the extent to which substantial disparities exist despite the State's impressive progress in recent years. Edgewood is one of seven public school districts in the metropolitan area. Approximately 22,000 students are enrolled in its twenty-five elementary and secondary schools. The district is situated in the core-city sector of San Antonio in a residential neighborhood that has little commercial or industrial property. The residents are predominantly of Mexican-American descent: approximately 90 percent of the student population is Mexican-American and over 6 percent is Negro. The average assessed property value per pupil is $5,960—the lowest in the metropolitan area—and the median family income ($4,686) is also the lowest. At an equalized tax rate of $1.05 per $100 of assessed property—the highest in the metropolitan area—the district contributed $26 to the education of each child for the 1967–1968 school year above its Local Fund Assignment for the Minimum Foundation Program. The Foundation Program contributed $222 per pupil for a state-local total of $248. Federal funds added another $108 for a total of $356 per pupil.

Alamo Heights is the most affluent school district in San Antonio. Its six schools, housing approximately 5,000 students, are situated in a residential community quite unlike the Edgewood District. The school population is predominantly "Anglo," having only 18 percent Mexican-Americans and less than 1 percent Negroes. The assessed property value per pupil exceeds $49,000, and the median family income is $8,001. In 1967–1968 the local tax rate of $.85 per $100 of valuation yielded $333 per pupil over and above its contribution to the Foundation Program. Coupled with the $225 provided from that Program, the district was able to supply $558 per student. Supplemented by a $36 per-pupil grant from federal sources, Alamo Heights spent $594 per pupil. . . .

Despite recent increases, substantial interdistrict disparities in school expenditures found by the District Court to prevail in San Antonio and in varying degrees throughout the State still exist. And it was these disparities, largely attributable to differences in the amounts of money collected through local property taxation, that led the District Court to conclude that Texas' dual system of public school financing violated the Equal Protection Clause. The District Court held that the Texas system discriminates on the basis of wealth in the manner in which education is provided for its people. 337 F.Supp., at 282. Finding that wealth is a "suspect" classification and that education is a "fundamental" interest, the District Court held that the Texas system could be sustained only if the State could show that it was premised upon some compelling state interest. Id., at 282–284. On this issue the court concluded that "[n]ot only are defendants unable to demonstrate compelling state interests . . . they fail even to establish a reasonable basis for these classifications." Id., at 284.

Texas virtually concedes that its historically rooted dual system of financing education could not withstand the strict judicial scrutiny that this Court has found appropriate in reviewing legislative judgments that interfere with fundamental constitutional rights or that involve suspect classifications. If, as previous decisions have indicated, strict scrutiny means that the State's system is not entitled to the usual presumption of validity, that the State rather than the complainants must carry a "heavy burden of justification," that the State must demonstrate that its educational system has been structured with "precision," and is "tailored" narrowly to serve legitimate objectives and that it has selected the "less drastic means" for effectuating its objectives, the Texas financing system and its counterpart in virtually every other State will not pass muster. The State candidly admits that "[n]o one familiar with the Texas system would contend that it has yet achieved perfection." Apart from its concession that educational financing in Texas has "defects" and "imperfections," the State defends the system's rationality with vigor and disputes the District Court's finding that it lacks a "reasonable basis."

This, then, establishes the framework for our analysis. We must decide, first, whether the Texas system of financing public education operates to the disadvantage of some suspect class or impinges upon a fundamental right explicitly or implicitly protected by the Constitution, thereby requiring strict judicial scrutiny. If so, the judgment of the District Court should be affirmed. If not, the Texas scheme must still be examined to determine whether it rationally furthers some legitimate, articulated state purpose and therefore does not constitute an invidious discrimination in violation of the Equal Protection Clause of the Fourteenth Amendment.

The District Court's opinion does not reflect the novelty and complexity of the constitutional questions posed by appellees' challenge to Texas' system of school financing. In concluding that strict judicial scrutiny was required, that court relied on decisions dealing with the rights of indigents to equal treatment in the criminal trial and appellate processes, and on cases disapproving wealth restrictions on the right to vote. Those cases, the District Court concluded, established wealth as a suspect classification. Finding that the local property tax system discriminated on the basis of wealth, it regarded those precedents as controlling. It then reasoned, based on decisions of this Court affirming the undeniable importance of education, that there is a fundamental right to education and that, absent some compelling state justification, the Texas system could not stand.

We are unable to agree that this case, which in significant aspects is *sui generis,* may be so neatly fitted into the conventional mosaic of constitutional analysis under the Equal Protection Clause. Indeed, for the several reasons that follow, we find neither the suspect-classification nor the fundamental-interest analysis persuasive.

The wealth discrimination discovered by the District Court in this case, and by several other courts that have recently struck down school-financing laws in other States, is quite unlike any of the forms of wealth discrimination heretofore reviewed by this Court. . . .

The case comes to us with no definitive description of the classifying facts or delineation of the disfavored class. Examination of the District Court's opinion and of appellees' complaint, briefs, and contentions at oral argument suggests, however, at least three ways in which the discrimination claimed here might be described. The Texas system of school financing might be regarded as discriminating (1) against "poor" persons whose incomes fall below some identifiable level of poverty or who might be characterized as functionally "indigent," or (2) against those who are relatively poorer than others, or (3) against all those who, irrespective of their personal incomes, happen to reside in relatively poorer school districts. Our task must be to ascertain whether, in fact, the Texas system has been shown to discriminate on any of these possible bases and, if so, whether the resulting classification may be regarded as suspect.

The precedents of this Court provide the proper starting point. The individuals, or groups of individuals, who constituted the class discriminated against in our prior cases shared two distinguishing characteristics: because of their impecunity they were completely unable to pay for some desired benefit, and as a consequence, they sustained an absolute deprivation of a meaningful opportunity to enjoy that benefit. . . .

Only appellees' first possible basis for describing the class disadvantaged by the Texas school-financing system—discrimination against a class of definably "poor" persons—might arguably meet the criteria established in . . . prior cases. Even a cursory examination, however, demonstrates that neither of the two distinguishing characteristics of wealth classifications can be found here. First, in support of their charge that the system discriminates against the "poor," appellees have made no effort to demonstrate that it operates to the peculiar disadvantage of any class fairly definable as indigent, or as composed of persons whose incomes are beneath any designated poverty level. Indeed, there is reason to believe that the poorest families are not necessarily clustered in the poorest property districts. A recent and exhaustive study of school districts in Connecticut concluded that "[i]t is clearly incorrect . . . to contend that the 'poor' live in 'poor' districts . . . . Thus, the major factual assumption of *Serrano*—that the educational financing system discriminates against the 'poor'—is simply false in Connecticut." Defining "poor" families as those below the Bureau of the Census "poverty level," the Connecticut study found, not surprisingly, that the poor were clustered around commercial and industrial areas—those same areas that provide the most attractive sources of property tax income for school districts. Whether a similar pattern would be discovered in Texas is not known, but there is no basis on the record in this case for assuming that the poorest people—defined by reference to any level of absolute impecunity—are concentrated in the poorest districts.

Second, neither appellees nor the District Court addressed the fact that, unlike each of the foregoing cases, lack of personal resources has not occasioned an absolute deprivation of the desired benefit. The argument here is not that the children in districts having relatively low assessable property values are receiving no public education; rather, it is that they are receiving a poorer quality education than that available to children in districts having more assessable wealth. Apart from the unsettled and disputed question whether the quality of education may be determined by the amount of money expended for it, a sufficient answer to appellees' argument is that, at least where wealth is involved, the Equal Protection Clause does not require absolute equality or precisely equal advantages. Nor indeed, in view of the infinite variables affecting the educational process, can any system assure equal quality of education except in the most relative sense. . . .

For these two reasons—the absence of any evidence that the financing system discriminates against any definable category of "poor" people or that it results in the absolute deprivation of education—the disadvantaged class is not susceptible of identification in traditional terms.

As suggested above, appellees and the District Court may have embraced a second or third approach, the second of which might be characterized as a theory of relative or comparative discrimination based on family income. Appellees sought to prove that a direct correlation exists between the wealth of families within each district and the expenditures therein for education. That is, along a continuum, the poorer the family the lower the dollar amount of education received by the family's children. . . . These questions need not be addressed in this case, however, since appellees' proof fails to support their allegations or the District Court's conclusions. . . .

This brings us, then, to the third way in which the classification scheme might be defined—*district* wealth discrimination. Since the only correlation indicated by the evidence is between district property wealth and expenditures, it may be argued that discrimination might be found without regard to the individual income characteristics of district residents. . . . Alternatively, as suggested in Mr. Justice MARSHALL's dissenting opinion, the class might be defined more restrictively to include children in districts with assessable property which falls below the statewide average, or median, or below some other artifically defined level.

However described, it is clear that appellees' suit asks this Court to extend its most exacting scrutiny to review a system that allegedly discriminates against a large, diverse, and amorphous class, unified only by the common factor of residence in districts that happen to have less taxable wealth than other districts. The system of alleged discrimination and the class it defines have none of the traditional indicia of suspectness: the class is not saddled with such disabilities, or subjected to such a history of purposeful unequal treatment, or relegated to such a position of political powerlessness as to command extraordinary protection from the majoritarian political process.

We thus conclude that the Texas system does not operate to the peculiar disadvantage of any suspect class. But in recognition of the fact that this Court has never heretofore held that wealth discrimination alone provides an adequate basis for invoking strict scrutiny, appellees have not relied solely on this contention. They also assert that the State's system impermissibly interferes with the exercise of a "fundamental" right and that accordingly the prior decisions of this Court require the application of the strict standard of judicial review. . . . It is this question—whether education is a fundamental right, in the sense that it is among the rights and liberties protected by the Constitution—which has so consumed the attention of courts and commentators in recent years. . . .

Nothing this Court holds today in any way detracts from our historic dedication to public education. We are in complete agreement with the conclusion of the three-judge panel below that "the grave significance of education both to the individual and to our society" cannot be doubted. But the importance of a service performed by the State does not determine whether it must be regarded as fundamental for purposes of examination under the Equal Protection Clause. . . . It is not the province of this Court to create substantive constitutional rights in the name of guaranteeing equal protection of the laws. Thus, the key to discovering whether education is "fundamental" is not to be found in comparisons of the relative societal significance of education as opposed to subsistence or housing. Nor is it to be found by weighing whether education is as important as the right to travel. Rather, the answer lies in assessing whether there is a right to education explicitly or implicitly guaranteed by the Constitution. . . .

Education, of course, is not among the rights afforded explicit protection under our federal Constitution. Nor do we find any basis for saying it is implicitly so protected. As we have said, the undisputed importance of education will not alone cause this Court to depart from the usual standard for reviewing a State's social and economic legislation. It is appellees' contention, however, that education is distinguishable from other services and benefits provided by the State because it bears a peculiarly close relationship to other rights and liberties accorded protection under the Constitution. Specifically, they insist that education is itself a fundamental personal right because it is essential to the effective exercise of First

Amendment freedoms and to intelligent utilization of the right to vote. . . .

. . . We need not dispute any of these propositions. The Court has long afforded zealous protection against unjustifiable governmental interference with the individual's rights to speak and to vote. Yet we have never presumed to possess either the ability or the authority to guarantee to the citizenry the most *effective* speech or the most *informed* electoral choice. That these may be desirable goals of a system of freedom of expression and of a representative form of government is not to be doubted. These are indeed goals to be pursued by a people whose thoughts and beliefs are freed from governmental interference. But they are not values to be implemented by judicial intrusion into otherwise legitimate state activities.

Even if it were conceded that some identifiable quantum of education is a constitutionally protected prerequisite to the meaningful exercise of either right, we have no indication that the present levels of educational expenditures in Texas provide an education that falls short. Whatever merit appellees' argument might have if a State's financing system occasioned an absolute denial of educational opportunities to any of its children, that argument provides no basis for finding an interference with fundamental rights where only relative differences in spending levels are involved and where—as is true in the present case—no charge fairly could be made that the system fails to provide each child with an opportunity to acquire the basic minimal skills necessary for the enjoyment of the rights of speech and of full participation in the political process. . . .

We have carefully considered each of the arguments supportive of the District Court's finding that education is a fundamental right or liberty and have found those arguments unpersuasive. In one further respect we find this a particularly inappropriate case in which to subject state action to strict judicial scrutiny. The present case, in another basic sense, is significantly different from any of the cases in which the Court has applied strict scrutiny to state or federal legislation touching upon constitutionally protected rights. Each of our prior cases involved legislation which "deprived," "infringed," or "interfered" with the free exercise of some such fundamental personal right or liberty. . . . A critical distinction between those cases and the one now before us lies in what Texas is endeavoring to do with respect to education. . . .

Every step leading to the establishment of the system Texas utilizes today—including the decisions permitting localities to tax and expend locally, and creating and continuously expanding the state aid—was implemented in an effort to *extend* public education and to improve its quality. Of course, every reform that benefits some more than others may be criticized for what it fails to accomplish. But we think it plain that, in substance, the thrust of the Texas system is affirmative and reformatory and, therefore, should be scrutinized under judicial principles sensitive to the nature of the State's efforts and to the rights reserved to the States under the Constitution.

It should be clear, for the reasons stated above and in accord with the prior decisions of this Court, that this is not a case in which the challenged state action must be subjected to the searching judicial scrutiny reserved for laws that create suspect classifications or impinge upon constitutionally protected rights.

We need not rest our decision, however, solely on the inappropriateness of the strict-scrutiny test. A century of Supreme Court adjudication under the Equal Protection Clause affirmatively supports the application of the traditional standard of review, which requires only that the State's system be shown to bear some rational relationship to legitimate state purposes. This case represents far more than a challenge to the manner in which Texas provides for the education of its children. We have here nothing less than a direct attack on the way in which Texas has chosen to raise and disburse state and local tax revenues. We are asked to condemn the State's judgment in conferring on political subdivisions the power to tax local property to supply revenues for local interests. In so doing, appellees would have the Court intrude in an area in which it has traditionally deferred to state legislatures. This Court has often admonished against such interferences with the State's fiscal policies under the Equal Protection Clause. . . .

Thus, we stand on familiar grounds when we continue to acknowledge that the Justices of this Court lack both the expertise and the familiarity with local problems so necessary to the making of wise decisions with respect to the raising and disposition of public revenues. Yet, we are urged to direct the States either to alter drastically the present system or to throw out the property tax altogether in favor of some other form of taxation. No scheme of taxation, whether the tax is imposed on property, income, or purchases of goods and services, has yet been devised which is free of all discriminatory impact. In such a complex arena in which no perfect alternatives exist, the Court does well not to impose too rigorous a standard of scrutiny lest all local fiscal schemes become subjects of criticism under the Equal Protection Clause.

In addition to matters of fiscal policy, this case also involves the most persistent and difficult questions of educational policy, another area in which this Court's lack of specialized knowledge and experience counsels against premature interference with the informed judgments made at the state and local levels. Education, perhaps even more than welfare assistance, presents a myriad of "intractable economic, social, and even philosophical problems." . . . The very complexity of the problems of financing and managing a statewide public school system suggests that "there will be more than one constitutionally permissible method of solving them," and that, within the limits of rationality, "the legislature's efforts to tackle the problems" should be entitled to respect. . . . On even the most basic questions in this area the scholars and educational experts are divided. Indeed, one of the major sources of controversy concerns the extent to which there is a demonstrable correlation between educational expenditures and the quality of education—and assumed correlation underlying virtually every legal conclusion drawn by the District Court in this case. Related to the questioned relationship between cost and quality is the equally unsettled controversy as to the proper goals of a system of public education. And the question regarding the most effective relationship between state boards of education and local school boards, in terms of their respective responsibilities and degrees of control, is now undergoing searching reexamination. The ultimate wisdom as to these and related problems of education is not likely to be divined for all time even by the scholars who now so earnestly debate the issues. In such circumstances, the judiciary is well advised to refrain from imposing on the States inflexible constitutional restraints that could circumscribe or handicap the continued research and experimentation so vital to finding even partial solutions to educational problems and to keeping abreast of ever-changing conditions.

It must be remembered, also, that every claim arising under the Equal Protection Clause has implications for the relationship between national and state power under our federal system. Questions of federalism are always inherent in the process of determining whether a State's laws are to be accorded the traditional presumption of constitutionality or are to be subjected instead to rigorous judicial scrutiny. While "[t]he maintenance of the principles of federalism is a foremost consideration in interpreting any of the pertinent constitutional provisions under which this Court examines state action," it would be difficult to imagine a case having a greater potential impact on our federal system than the one now before us, in which we are urged to abrogate systems of financing public education presently in existence in virtually every State.

The foregoing considerations buttress our conclusion that Texas' system of public school finance is an inappropriate candidate for strict judicial scrutiny. . . .

Apart from federal assistance, each Texas school receives its funds from the State and from its local school district. On a statewide average, a roughly comparable amount of funds is derived from each source. The State's contribution, under the Minimum Foundation Program, was designed to provide an adequate minimum educational offering in every school in the State. . . .

By virtue of the obligation to fulfill its Local Fund Assignment, every district must impose an ad valorem tax on property located within its borders. The Fund Assignment was designed to remain sufficiently low to assure that each district would have some ability to provide a more enriched educational program. Every district supplements its Foundation grant in this manner. In some districts, the local property tax contribution is insubstantial, as in Edgewood where the supplement was only $26 per pupil in 1967. In other districts, the local share may far exceed even the total Foundation grant. In part, local differences are attributable to differences in the rates of taxation or in the degree to which the market value for any category of property varies from its assessed value. The greatest interdistrict disparities, however, are attributable to differences in the amount of assessable property available within any district. Those districts that have more property, or more valuable property, have a greater capability for supplementing state funds. . . .

The "foundation grant" theory upon which Texas legislators and educators based the Gilmer-Aikin bills, was a product of the pioneering work of two New York Educational reformers in the 1920s, George D. Strayer and Robert M. Haig. Their efforts were devoted to establishing a means of guaranteeing a minimum statewide educational program without sacrificing the vital element of local participation. The Strayer-Haig thesis represented an accommodation between these two competing forces. . . .

The Texas system of school finance is responsive to these two forces. While assuring a basic education for every child in the State, it permits and encourages a large measure of participation in and control of each district's schools at the local level. In an era that has witnessed a consistent trend toward centralization of the functions of government, local sharing of responsibility for public education has survived. . . .

The persistence of attachment to government at the lowest level where education is concerned reflects the depth of commitment of its supporters. In part, local control means, as Professor Coleman suggests, the freedom to devote more money to the education of one's children. Equally important, however, is the opportunity it offers for participation in the decision-making process that determines how those local tax dollars will be spent. Each locality is free to tailor local programs to local needs. . . . No area of social concern stands to profit more from a multiplicity of viewpoints and from a diversity of approaches than does public education.

. . . Appellees suggest that local control could be preserved and promoted under other financing systems that resulted in more equality in educational expenditures. While it is no doubt true that reliance on local property taxation for school revenues provides less freedom of choice with respect to expenditures for some districts than for others, the existence of "some inequality" in the manner in which the State's rationale is achieved is not alone a sufficient basis for striking down the entire system. . . . It may not be condemned simply because it imperfectly effectuates the State's goals. . . . Nor must the financing system fail because, as appellees suggest, other methods of satisfying the State's interest, which occasion "less drastic" disparities in expenditures, might be conceived. Only where state action impinges on the exercise of fundamental constitutional rights or liberties must it be found to have chosen the least restrictive alternative. . . . The people of Texas may be justified in believing that other systems of school financing, which place more of the financial responsibility in the hands of the State, will result in a comparable lessening of desired local autonomy. . . .

Appellees further urge that the Texas system is unconstitutionally arbitrary because it allows the availability of local taxable resources to turn on "happenstance." . . . But any scheme of local taxation—indeed the very existence of idientifiable local governmental units—requires the establishment of jurisdictional boundaries that are inevitably arbitrary. It is equally inevitable that some localities are going to be blessed with more taxable assets than others. . . .

Moreover, if local taxation for local expenditures were an unconstitutional method of providing for education then it might be an equally impermissible means of providing other necessary services customarily financed largely from local property taxes, including local police and fire protection, public health and hospitals, and public utility facilities of various kinds. We perceive no justification for such a severe denigration of local property taxation and control as would follow from appellees' contentions. It has simply never been within the constitutional prerogative of this Court to nullify statewide measures for financing public services merely because the burdens or benefits thereof fall unevenly depending upon the relative wealth of the political subdivisions in which citizens live.

In sum, to the extent that the Texas system of school financing results in unequal expenditures between children who happen to reside in different districts, we cannot say that such disparities are the product of a system that is so irrational as to be invidiously discriminatory. . . . In its essential characteristics, the Texas plan for financing public education reflects what many educators for a half century have thought was an enlightened approach to a problem for which there is no perfect solution. We are unwilling to assume for ourselves a level of wisdom superior to that of legislators, scholars, and educational authorities in fifty States, especially where the alternatives proposed are only recently conceived and nowhere yet tested. The constitutional standard under the Equal Protection Clause is whether the challenged state action rationally furthers a legitimate state purpose or interest. . . . We hold that the Texas plan abundantly satisfies this standard.

. . . The consideration and initiation of fundamental reforms with respect to state taxation and education are matters reserved for the legislative processes of the various States, and we do no violence to the values of federalism and separation of powers by staying our hand. We hardly need add that this Court's action today is not to be viewed as placing its judicial imprimatur on the status quo. The need is apparent for reform in tax systems which may well have relied too long and too heavily on the local property tax. And certainly innovative thinking as to public education, its methods, and its funding is necessary to assure both a higher level of quality and greater uniformity of opportunity. These matters merit the continued attention of the scholars who already have contributed much by their challenges. But the ultimate solutions must come from the lawmakers and from the democratic pressures of those who elect them.

Reversed.

NOTES

The Supreme Court of Arizona held that the Arizona Constitution does establish education as a fundamental right, but went on to say that a school financing system that meets the mandates of that State's Constitution, that education be free, uniform, open a minimal number of months per year, and be open to all of the particular age group, needs to be only rational and reasonable and not discriminatory or capricious. In so finding, the Court upheld the constitutionality of Arizona's school financing system. Shofstall v. Hollins, 110 Ariz. 88, 515 P.2d 590 (1973).

Students rights under Equal Protection Clause of the Fourteenth Amendment are not violated by a Michigan State School Aid Act which provides for a reduction in state funding for districts receiving federal impact aid. Such reduction was permissible under amendments to P.L. 874 Impact Aid Law. (See Shepheard v. Godwin, Chapter 3, this book). Gwinn Area Schools v. State of Mich., 741 F.2d 840 (6th Cir. 1984).

School Finance System Producing
Wide Disparities in Expenditures Per
Pupil Violates Equal Protection of
State Constitution

DUPREE v. ALMA SCHOOL DISTRICT NO. 30 OF CRAWFORD COUNTY

Supreme Court of Arkansas, 1983.
279 Ark. 340, 651 S.W.2d 90.

HAYS, Justice.

The issue presented on appeal is the constitutionality of the current statutory method of financing public schools in Arkansas under Act 1100 of 1979, the Minimum Foundation Program and vocational funding . . . . Appellees, eleven school districts, brought this class action suit against appellants, Jim DuPree and other members of the Arkansas State Board of Education . . . charging that the present system violates the state constitution's guarantee of equal protection and its requirement that the state provide a general, suitable and efficient system of education. The appellees' basic contention is that the great disparity in funds available for education to school districts throughout the state is due primarily to the fact that the major determinative of revenue for school districts is the local tax base, a basis unrelated to the educational needs of any given district; that the current state financing system is inadequate to rectify the inequalities inherent in a financing system based on widely varying local tax bases, and actually widens the gap between the property poor and property wealthy districts in providing educational opportunities. The trial court found the present system to be in violation of the constitutional provisions in question, which decision we affirm. We will first comment on the trial court's finding and then address the points raised on appeal.

The funding for Arkansas schools comes from three sources: state revenues provide 51.6 percent, local revenues 38.1 percent, and federal revenues 10.3 percent. The majority of state aid is distributed under the Minimum Foundation Program (MFP). In 1978–79 MFP constituted 77.1 percent of all state aid. Act 1100 of 1979, the current MFP program, is similar to prior MFP programs and consists of two major elements: base aid and equalization aid. The base aid program originated under the Minimum School Budget Law of 1951. The formula was based on a calculation of teacher and student population per district. The base aid program contained a "hold-harmless" provision which guaranteed that no district would receive less aid in any year than it received the previous year. As a result, a district with declining enrollment would over the years get continually higher aid per pupil. While Act 1100 eliminates the district "hold-harmless" provision, it still contains a pupil "hold-harmless" provision which has no bearing on educational needs or property wealth; the base aid year is permanently held at the 1978–79 level, and the inequities resulting from thirty years of the district "hold-harmless" provision are being carried forward without compensating adjustments.

The funds remaining after allocation for base aid are distributed under "equalization aid." Under this section of the act, *half* of the remaining funds are distributed under a flat grant on a per pupil basis. Districts receive the same amount of aid under this provision irrespective of local property wealth and revenue raised. The remaining funds under the equalization provision are then distributed under a formula directed at equalizing the disparity between the poor and wealthy districts. Of the total allocated under this program in 1979–80, this accounted for only 6.8 percent of MFP aid.

The other area of contention is the distribution of funds for vocational education. In order for a school district to institute a program of vocational education approved for state funding, it must first establish a program with local funds. The state will consider funding a portion of the program only if the program is already operational. Obviously, this requirement works to the advantage of the wealthier school districts which can raise the funds and to the disadvantage of the poorer districts which lack the resources for such programs.

Against this backdrop of funding is the undisputed evidence that there are sharp disparities among school districts in the expenditures per pupil and the education opportunities available as reflected by staff, class size, curriculum, remedial services, facilities, materials and equipment. In dollar terms the highest and lowest revenues per pupil in 1978–79 respectively were $2,378 and $873. Disregarding the extremes, the difference at the 95th and 5th percentiles was $1,576 and $937. It is also undisputed that there is a substantial variation in property wealth among districts. The distribution of property wealth, measured as equalized assessed valuation per pupil in average daily attendance (ADA) in 1978–79, ranged from $73,773 to $1,853. These wealth disparities are prevalent among both large and small districts. As the system is currently operating, the major determinative of local revenues is district property wealth and the amount a school district can raise is directly related to its property wealth.

The range in revenues among school districts in Arkansas is not limited to the extremes. There are a substantial number of children affected by the revenue disparities. In 1978–79, only 7 percent of the pupils resided in school districts with over $1,500 per pupil in state-local revenues, while over 21 percent resided in districts with less than $1000 in state-local revenues, and 55 percent of the districts were below the state mean. This great disparity among the districts' property wealth and the current state funding system as it is now applied does not equalize the educational revenues available to the school districts, but only widens the gap.

The appellants devote little attention to the constitutional provisions in question, but contend that there is no requirement of uniformity of educational opportunities throughout the state, that the constitution only requires that all children receive a "general, suitable and efficient" education. . . .

There is no sound basis for holding the equal protection clause inapplicable to the facts in this case. The constitutional mandate for a general, suitable and efficient education in no way precludes us from applying the equal protection clause to the present financing system . . . .

We can find no legitimate state purpose to support the system. It bears no rational relationship to the educational needs of the individual districts, rather it is determined primarily by the tax base of each district. The trial court found the educational opportunity of the children in this state should not be controlled by the fortuitous circumstance of residence, and we concur in that view. Such a system only promotes greater opportunities for the advantaged while diminishing the opportunities for the disadvantaged. . . .

Consequently, even without deciding whether the right to a public education is fundamental, we can find no constitutional basis for the present system, as it has no rational bearing on the educational needs of the districts.

We come to this conclusion in part because we believe the right to equal educational opportunity is basic to our society. "It is the very essence and foundation of a civilized culture: it is the cohesive element that binds the fabric of our society together." Education becomes the essential prerequisite that allows our citizens to be able to appreciate, claim and effectively realize their established rights. . . .

The appellants' arguments are wide of the mark in this case. They concede the disparities that exist among the school districts, but they offer no legitimate state purpose to support it. Rather, their attack comes from an oblique standpoint. They assert that the constitution only requires a suitable, effective education and that the appellees have failed to prove that is not true in their districts. The evidence offered may have shown that the appellee districts offered the bare rudiments of educational opportunities, but we are in genuine doubt that they were proved to be suitable and efficient. However, even were the complaining districts shown to meet the bare requirements of educational offerings, that is not what the constitutional demands. For some districts to supply the barest necessities and others to have programs generously endowed does not meet the requirements of the constitution. Bare and minimal sufficiency does not translate into equal educational opportunity. "Equal protection is not addressed to minimal sufficiency but rather to the unjustifiable inequalities of state action." . . .

We have discussed the two major problems faced in financing our state's educational system. The first is the obvious disparity in property wealth among districts. That wealth is what primarily dictates the amount of revenue each district receives and the quality of education in that district. The second problem is the manner in which the state determines how the state funds are distributed, and as we have said, the current system is not a rational one. The end result is a violation of the mandates of our constitution. Ultimately, the responsibility for maintaining a general, suitable and efficient school system falls upon the state. "Whether the state acts directly or imposes the role upon the local government, the end product must be what the constitution commands. [When a district falls short of the constitutional requirements] whatever the reason for the violation, the obligation is the state's to rectify it. If local government fails, the state government must compel it to act, and if the local government cannot carry the burden, the state must itself meet its continuing obligation." . . .

The trial judge was assigned specially to this case. . . . His conclusions of fact and law were extensive and detailed, and obvious time and study went into the final decision. . . . After our own review of the trial court's findings, the arguments presented by both sides and the decisions of other jurisdictions, we conclude that the findings are not clearly erroneous . . . the decree is affirmed.

Appellees' motion to tax costs against appellants pursuant to Rule 9(e) is denied. We concede the abstract is abbreviated, to say the least, but this is an exceptional case, involving issues and concepts of the broadest possible scope, and we are satisfied appellants have made a good faith effort to give an adequate, if concise, abridgement of the record.

BUDGETING AND ACCOUNTING FOR SCHOOL FUNDS

In order that the school district can effectively plan for educational activities and account for the expenditure of tax funds, provisions must be made for budgetary and accounting procedures. School boards are generally given wide latitude in the determination of how educational funds will be expended. The attitude of the courts has been that a school district, being charged with the responsibility for operating the schools, should have as much freedom as possible to determine how and where the funds will be spent.

This broad budgetary authority, of course, extends to teachers salaries subject only to legislative or constitutional restraints against arbitrary, discriminatory or unreasonable classifications.

The exception to this rule is where the legislature has prescribed that school boards be fiscally dependent on city government. In such cases, the board must submit its budget for review and approval by the city government. However, where a city council has the authority to fix the amount of the school budget, it may not direct the itemized expenditure of the gross amount authorized; the board may spend the money for any purpose permitted by law. In instances where the law requires only the submission of the budget and does not specify control or approval authority, the courts have held that the reviewing agency cannot reduce the budget.

A school district must expend moneys for the purpose for which they are collected. If a statute requires fund accounting for special tax money, the school board must establish and deposit the money in such a fund. In such a case, a taxpayer may not require an accounting for the school funds beyond seeing that they are used for the purpose for which they were levied and collected.

*Funds Collected and Allocated for a
Particular Public Purpose Cannot Be
Lawfully Diverted to Another Purpose*

SAN BENITO INDEPENDENT
SCHOOL DISTRICT v.
FARMERS' STATE BANK

Court of Civil Appeals, Texas 1935.
78 S.W.2d 741.

SMITH, Justice. On May 16, 1932, Farmers' State Bank & Trust Company of San Benito was closed and its affairs were taken over by the state banking commissioner for administration, as provided by law. Up to that time San Benito Independent School District maintained four separate checking accounts in the bank, which was the district treasury, as follows:

First, an "interest and sinking fund account," from taxes assessed, collected, and deposited in said account for the purpose of paying interest and principal upon the district's bonded debt, in which account there was a balance, at the time the bank failed, of $12,942.68;

Second, a "local maintenance fund account," in which were deposited taxes assessed and collected for the specific purpose of local maintenance, exclusive of teachers' salaries, in which there was a balance of $318.25;

Third, an "interest and penalty refunding account," in which had been deposited interest and penalties unlawfully collected from the taxpayers, which under the law were required to be refunded to those paying them. In this account there was a balance, at the time the bank failed, of $124.16. The balances in the three foregoing accounts aggregated $13,385.09;

Fourth, a "state available warrant fund account," in which were deposited, as received, funds received from the state for the specific purpose of paying teachers' salaries. In this account, however, there was no balance on hand at the time the bank failed. Moreover, at that time the bank held unpaid district warrants drawn against that account in the aggregate amount of $3,409.18, which the bank carried, not as an overdraft, but as assets.

In this situation the district brought this action against the bank and banking commissioner to recover $13,385.09, being the amount of the balance of funds on deposit in the first three accounts mentioned, and prayed that the amount of the unpaid warrants held by the bank against the exhausted fourth, or "state available warrant fund account," be offset against the district's claim, leaving a balance of $9,975.91, for which net amount the district prayed judgment.

The bank and banking commissioner answered, setting up their claim of $3,409.18, represented by the unpaid district warrants held by them against the exhausted "state available warrant fund account," and, asserting that that claim against that fund could not lawfully be applied as an offset against the district's claim upon deposits in the other three specific fund accounts, prayed for direct judgment upon said warrants.

The trial court rendered judgment in favor of the district for the amount of its deposits in the bank, and in favor of the banking commissioner for the amount of the unpaid warrants held by him, but denied the district's prayer that the latter recovery be applied as an offset. The district has appealed. . . .

It is too well settled to require citation, or any extended discussion, that a public fund collected and allocated for a particular public purpose cannot be lawfully diverted to the use of another particular public purpose. Under that wise rule, when applied here, when the taxpayer pays a certain tax for the specific purpose of liquidating a particular public bonded indebtedness of his school district, the funds derived therefrom cannot lawfully be used for the purpose of paying teachers' salaries, chargeable under the law to a different public fund; when lawful interest and penalties have been collected from the taxpayers and segregated into a particular fund, and is required by law to be refunded to the taxpayer, as is the case here, that fund may not lawfully be diverted to the payment of teachers' salaries chargeable to another specific fund, as is sought to be done by appellant; when a specific tax has been levied and assessed by a school district and paid by the taxpayers, for the particular purpose of "local maintenance" (exclusive of teachers' salaries), and the fund so collected has been segregated and allocated to that purpose, as was done here, the district may not divert that fund to another for the purpose of paying teachers' salaries, as is sought to be done by the district in this case.

So when the bank acquired the warrants against the district's "state available fund" account, which was exhausted, at least for the time being, it could not lawfully collect them by charging the amounts thereof to the accounts of the interest and sinking fund, or the local maintenance fund, or the interest and penalty refunding fund; it could only hold the warrants until the account against which they were drawn was replenished, and it was so holding them, as among its assets, when it ceased to do business.

The corporate school district, as are all municipal corporations, is but a trustee of guardian of the public funds coming into its possession under the law, and may disburse those funds only in the manner and for the purposes prescribed by law. As the funds in question were gathered in, the district, in obedience to law, allocated them to the several purposes for which they were paid in, and deposited them with the bank in appropriate separate accounts kept for each specific fund. When so segregated into separate accounts, the district had no power or authority to transfer any part of the funds from either account and apply it to the purposes of any other account, any more than a trustee of several persons or estates could divert the funds of one cestui que trust to the use of another. Nor could the bank, in this case, lawfully pay the warrants drawn on one particular account out of the funds of another particular account, any more than it could charge the draft of one individual depositor to the account of another. The rights, capacities and interests of the respective parties are thus fixed by settled principles of law, and there being no mutuality of rights, interests and capacities between the district as trustee of the "available state" fund and account, and the same entity as trustee of the other three specific funds and accounts, it could not appropriate the one to the uses of the others.

The inevitable conclusion is, then, that in balancing the accounts between the district and the bank, the claim of the latter against the "state available fund" of the former could not be applied as an offset against the obligations of the bank to the other three separate fund accounts. The bank could not enforce such offset in an action thereon, nor may the district enforce it in this action.

The judgment is affirmed.

NOTES

1. The extent of budget itemization necessary to meet statutory requirements has been described in an Arizona case. Arizona statute requiring budgetary information divided the school budget into major general categories and then subdivided these categories into subitems. The operating expense category was broken down into two broad sections, Administration and Instruction. Each of these sections were divided into forty-one subitems. A controversy arose as to whether the forty-one subitems were merely explanatory of the major categories or were the expenditures of the board of education restricted to the amounts in the subitems making transfer of funds among subitems illegal. The statute governing this question stated:

> No expenditure shall be made for a purpose not particularly itemized and included in such budget, and no expenditure shall be made, and no debt, obligation or liability shall be incurred or created in any year for any purpose itemized in such budget in excess of the amount specified for such item.

The court in interpreting this statute defined the word "purpose" in light of judicial principle that where the language of a statute may be subject to more than one interpretation the court will adopt the one that is reasonable in view of the particular situation being litigated. The court said:

> Since the word "purpose" as used in (the statute) is susceptible of more than one interpretation, we are bound to declare as the intention of the legislature the alternative which is reasonable and convenient. It appears to us that to bind either the school district or the superintendent to a forty-one line operating expense budget, as advocated by the (treasurer), would be impractical, unduly restrictive, and lead to absurd results. Isley v. School District No. 2 of Maricopa County, 81 Ariz. 280, 305 P.2d 432 (1956).

2. An Oklahoma court upheld a state board of education directive requiring school districts to treat as a current expense certain items that taxpayers insisted should have been recorded as capital outlay expenditures. The state board of education had acted under a statute providing that the state board shall prescribe a list of appropriation accounts by which funds of school districts shall be budgeted. St Louis-San Francisco Railway v. McCurtain Co., Okl., 352 P.2d 896 (1960).

3. Where a school tax levy raises revenues in excess of the requested budgetary amount, the school board is entitled to the surplus. In Montgomery County, Maryland, where the county levies the tax rate requested by the school district, the county tax collector on many occasions received more from the school tax levy than was requested by the school board. The surplus remained in the county treasury and amounted to over one million dollars. The school board brought suit against

Montgomery County to obtain the funds. The court held that when the levy was actually and unconditionally made by the county, the statutes were explicit in declaring that no part of the sum levied for the use of the public schools be used for any other purpose, and that the amount so levied each year be paid by the county treasurer to the school board. Board of Education of Montgomery County v. Montgomery County, 237 Md. 191, 205 A.2d 202 (1964).

4. In the case of a fiscally dependent school district, a Connecticut court has held that where a school budget is submitted to a municipal reviewing agency and the expenditures are for purposes described by statute to be within the board of education's authority to effectuate, the finance board has no power to refuse to include an appropriation for such expenditure in its budget. This statement is qualified by the fact that the reviewing agency may refuse appropriation if the financial condition of the town does not permit such expenditures. This is, of course, an extremely important limitation, since in that state it is within the review board's authority to pronounce that the town is not in a financial position to support such expenditures for education and thereby cut the school budget. Board of Ed. of Town of Stamford v. Board of Finance of Town of Stamford, 127 Conn. 345, 16 A.2d 601 (1940).

5. In another case involving the authority of the town board of finance to control educational expenditures in Connecticut school districts, the court held that placement of certain funds to be used for school purposes in the general government budget contravened a statute permitting the board of education to transfer the unexpended or uncontracted-for portion of appropriations for school purposes to any other item, and this constituted an illegal restriction on the appropriation. Board of Ed. of Town of Ellington v. Town of Ellington, 151 Conn. 1, 193 A.2d 466 (1963).

6. A school district may not, in the absence of statute expressly permitting it, accumulate surpluses beyond that required to operate for the ensuing year. The theory is that a school district levying taxes sufficient to maintain a large surplus should reduce its tax levy. One court held that a tax levy that created a surplus of over 50 percent of the entire school district budget exceeded the amount reasonably contemplated for a contingency. The court went on to say:

A tax levy is required to be a reasonable approximation of the amount required. It has not been the policy of the law to permit the creation of funds by taxation in large amounts for future use, except where statutory authorization exists as in the case of building funds, sinking funds, and the like. Kissinger v. School District No. 49 of Clay County, 163 Neb. 33, 77 N.W.2d 767 (1956).

Money or Property Derived Under the
Auspices of the Public School Is
Accountable in Same Manner as
Other Tax Funds

PETITION OF AUDITORS OF
HATFIELD TOWNSHIP
SCHOOL DISTRICT

Superior Court of Pennsylvania, 1947.
161 Pa. 388, 54 A.2d 833.

ARNOLD, Judge.   This appeal is from an order of the court below directing the officers, directors and supervising principal of the Hatfield Joint Consolidated School District to comply with a duces tecum subpoena issued by the offical auditors calling for the production of various books, vouchers and papers.

The Hatfield Joint Consolidated School District was formed by the school districts of the borough of Hatfield and the township of Hatfield.   Its bank account is carried by its treasurer in the Hatfield National Bank under the name, "Hatfield Joint Consolidated School District," hereafter called the "official account."   The warrants or vouchers thereon are executed by the proper officers of the district.

In the same bank is an account called "Hatfield Joint School Accounts," and the sole right to withdraw funds therefrom is possessed by Elmer B. Laudenslager, the supervising principal.   This we will refer to as the "activities account."   The appellants challenge the right of the statutory auditors to examine this account. . . .

Appellants have asked us to determine whether the activities account is subject to official audit even though no tax moneys were in it, and state: "This question is a matter of interest to every district in the Commonwealth. The decision in this case will affect every school district . . . [and] . . . will decide once and for all the status of such funds . . . even as the legislature established the status of the cafeteria funds. Section 8 of Act of 1931, P.L. 243, and Act of 1945, P.L. 688, 24 P.S. § 331."   Indeed the evidence in this case disclosed four other nearby communities operating a similar system, and in fact the system is widespread.   It is fraught with great danger.   High school football and other athletics have achieved great popularity, and this means that almost any school district, depending in a degree upon the skill of the athletes, has athletic events the admission fees of which aggregate a large sum of money, probably in excess of $10,000.   It would be a great blow to the public school system if by embezzlement or lack of care such funds should be lost.   Not only has the school board a moral duty to perform but there is also a legislative imperative.   The public school system of this commonwealth is entirely statutory.   Within the constitutional limitations the legislature is supreme and there reposes in the courts no power to permit deviation from its commands; and neither the local school districts nor the State Department of Education may bypass the duties enjoined.

In the so-called activity accounts various situations obtain.   Of course if pupils of a class give money to a supervising principal to purchase for them class jewelry or similar things the school district has no official duty (although it may have a moral duty), for the supervising principal acts as agent of the pupils. This is the smaller end of the problem. At the other pole, a school district, acting under the express provisions of § 405 of the Code, 24 P.S. § 339, has athletic events. These activities produce large sums of money from paid admissions. Under the instant system these sums of money are not disbursed through the treasurer, nor through a resolution of the board, but are solely at the command of one individual, who has no statutory standing or duty. It is possible that some school district may neither *directly* nor *indirectly* furnish any money for the playing field or stadium; or for the coaching of the athletes, or for their uniforms or playing togs, or for the apparatus with which the sport is connected, or for the lighting of the field; although it is very doubtful whether such case exists. But it is certainly true that, if a school district operates and expends tax money for the acquisition, maintenance or lighting of the playing field, or for the payment of services of a coach, the admissions charged result from the use of public property and from the expenditure of tax moneys and are the property of the school district, must go into the official account of the treasurer thereof, and are subject to audit.

The moneys derived from the sale of admissions to witness the event in question come into being because of (1) the use and wear of the school building and grounds; (2) the use and wear of personal property owned by the district; (3) the payment to employes such as coaches for their services; (4) the payment by the district for light, heat and various maintenance charges, including janitor service. By reason of the use of these public funds the event takes place, and from it are reaped the admission fees paid to witness the performance. The pupils are not expected to and do not furnish any of the money. The admission fees could not belong to them, and indeed if taken they would be professionals instead of amateurs. The spectators are not to get their money back. No one has any investment except the school district. The money raised by admissions therefore belongs to the district, which by its property and funds made the admission fees possible.

Of lesser importance, but in the same category, are the admission fees charged for dramatic and musical enterprises held in the buildings of the district. These belong to the district for the same reasons and with the same results. For instance, the school districts usually and properly provide musical instruments, just as they provide equipment and uniforms for athletics. In the instant case admission fees were expended through the activities account for such instruments, but it was frankly admitted that when bought the instruments belonged to the district. So do the admission fees themselves.

We have not attempted to discuss each situation that may present itself, but where moneys or property are derived directly or indirectly through the use of school buildings, or from the expenditure of public funds of the district, the moneys thus derived are public property, must be handled exactly as tax moneys and be paid to the district treasurer. . . .

Order affirmed.

PUBLIC SCHOOL INDEBTEDNESS

The authority of school districts to issue bonds must be clearly and expressly conferred by statute. The failure of a school board to comply with the statutory conditions for school bond issuance will render the bonds illegal.

Bonds issued for a specific purpose must be used for that purpose and no other. It has been held that bonds approved by the voters for "erecting and constructing a new roof" for a school building were illegal when the statute provided for bonds to be issued for the purpose of "erecting and equipping, or purchasing and equipping" school houses.[55] In another case, a court held that a statute that authorized a bond election for the "erection and enlargement" of school buildings could not be construed to include the issuance of bonds for the purpose of equipping school buildings.[56]

While earlier cases generally held that statutory procedures for school bond elections were to be strictly followed and failure to do so would make the bonds illegal, more recent cases tend to allow some flexibility so long as irregularities do not affect the results of the election. It has been held that where the voters in a bond election authorize bonds for a greater amount than is consistent with the law, the voter authorization is not illegal, and the school board may issue bonds for the amount prescribed by law.

Generally the courts have held that a bondholder cannot recover on an illegal bond even if he is an innocent purchaser. This rule, however, has been modified in some states where it has been held that where illegal bonds have been sold and the funds applied to the improvement of the district, the bondholder may recover under the *quantum meruit*. Also, the courts will permit the holder of an illegal bond to recover if the money is identifiable and has not been commingled with other funds of the district. The courts, in some cases, have allowed the holder to recover property purchased with illegal bond proceeds if no other money of the district was used in payment for the property.

Constitutions of most states make provision for debt limitations, the maximum percentage of which a local school district may not exceed. Courts have held that the percentage of indebtedness is to be computed using the amount of bonds that actually has been issued and not the amount that was projected at the time of a bond election. While a state legislature must conform to prescribed constitutional requirements regarding indebtedness, some state legislatures have sought to avoid stringent constitutional debt restrictions that severely limit educational facility construction. One such device resorted to by a few states is the "holding company" or the "local school building authority." This method of financing school construction effectively increases the debt capacity of a local school district and has been upheld by the courts.[57]

Legislature Has Power to Direct Local
Authorities to Create Debt for Public
School Building

REVELL v. CITY OF
ANNAPOLIS

Court of Appeals of Maryland, 1895.
81 Md. 1, 31 A. 695.

ROBINSON, C.J. The act of 1894, c. 620, provides for the erection of a public school building in the city of Annapolis, and, to pay for the same, it authorizes and directs the school commissioners of Anne Arundel county to borrow money, not exceeding the sum of $20,000, on bonds to be indorsed by the county commissioners; and for the same purpose it directs that the city of Annapolis shall issue bonds to the amount of $10,000, and that said bonds shall be issued without submitting the question of their issue to the voters of said city. The city of Annapolis has refused to issue the bonds as thus directed by the act, and the question is whether the legislature has the power to direct that the city authorities shall issue bonds to raise money to be applied to the erection of a public school building in said city. This power is denied, on the broad ground that it is not competent for the legislature to compel a municipal corporation to create a debt or levy a tax for a local purpose, in which the state has no concern, or to assume a debt not within the corporate powers of a municipal government. If the correctness of this general proposition be conceded for the purposes of this case, we do not see how it affects in any manner the validity of the act now in question. We cannot agree that the erection of buildings necessary for the public schools is a matter of merely local concern, in which the state has no interest. In this country the people are not only in theory, but in practice, the source of all governmental power, and the stability of free institutions mainly rests upon an enlightened public opinion. Fully recognizing this, the constitution declares that it shall be the duty of the legislature "to establish throughout the state a thorough and efficient system of free public schools, and to provide by taxation or otherwise" for their maintenance and support. . . . And the legislature has accordingly established a public school system, and has provided for its support by state and local taxation. It cannot be said, therefore, that the erection of buildings for public school purposes is a matter in which the state has no concern; nor can we agree that the creation of a debt for such purposes is not within the ordinary functions of municipal government. What is a municipal corporation? It is but a subordinate part of the state government, incorporated for public purposes, and clothed with special and limited powers of legislation in regard to its own local affairs. It has no inherent legislative power, and can exercise such powers only as have been expressly or by fair implication delegated to it by the legislature. The control of highways and bridges within the corporate limits; the power to provide for an efficient police force; to pass all necessary laws and ordinances for the preservation of the health, safety, and welfare of its people; and the power to provide for the support of its public schools by local taxation,—are all among the ordinary powers delegated to municipal corporations. And the public schools in Baltimore city are not only under the control and supervision of the city authorities, but are mainly supported by municipal taxation. It is no answer to say that the public schools in Annapolis are under the control of the school commissioners of Anne Arundel county, and that under its charter it has no power to create a debt or levy taxes for their support. The legislature may, at its pleasure, alter, amend, and enlarge its powers. It may authorize the city authorities to establish public schools within the corporate limits, and direct that bonds shall be issued to raise money for their support, payable at intervals during a series of years. There is no difference in principle between issuing bonds and the levying of a tax in one year sufficient to meet the necessary expenditure. . . .

If the legislature has the power to direct the city authorities to create a debt for a public school building, the exercise of this power in no manner depends upon their consent or upon the consent of the qualified voters of the city. We recognize the force of the argument that the question whether a municipal debt is to be created ought to be left to the discretion and judgment of the people who are to bear the burden. We recognize the fact that the exercise of this power by the legislature may be liable to abuse. But this abuse of a power is no argument against its exercise. The remedy, however, in such cases, is with the people to whom the members of the legislature are responsible for the discharge of the trust committed to them. It is a matter over which the courts have no control. If the debt to be created was for a private purpose, that would present quite a different question, for it is a fundamental principle, inherent in the nature of taxation itself, that all burdens and taxes shall be levied for public, and not for private, purposes. Be that as it may, it is well settled in this state that the legislature has the power to compel a municipal corporation to levy a tax or incur a debt for a public purpose, and one within the ordinary functions of a municipal government. . . .

In closing his argument, the counsel for the appellees suggested that the act was invalid because it was in conflict with the Fourteenth Amendment of the federal Constitution which forbids the taking of "property without due process of law." . . . It is a sufficient answer to this objection to say that the act in question, which requires the city authorities to issue bonds to raise money to pay the cost of a public school building, is a lawful exercise of legislature power, and, this being so, taxes levied to pay such bonds are not open to the objection of taking property without due process of law. Nor can we agree that the act is in conflict with section 33, art. 3, of the constitution, which declares that the general assembly shall pass no special law for any case for which provision has been made by an existing general law. The general law provides, it is true, that the school commissioners of Anne Arundel county shall have the control and supervision of the public schools in said county, with power to build, repair, and furnish schoolhouses. But it does not authorize the commissioners to borrow money upon bonds to be indorsed by the county commissioners for such purposes, nor does it provide for the apportionment of the cost of a public school building to be erected in the city of Annapolis between the county and the city. This could only be done by special act, and, this being so, the special act is not in conflict with the constitution, which forbids the passing of a special act for any purpose for which provision has been made by an existing general law. It follows from what we have said that the judgment sustaining the demurrer in this case must be overruled. . . .

Issuance of Municipal Bonds Without
Statutory Authorization Is Ultra Vires

HEWITT v. BOARD OF EDUCATION
Supreme Court of Illinois, 1880.
94 Ill. 528.

Mr. Chief Justice WALKER delivered the opinion of the Court:

This was an action of assumpsit, brought by Hewitt in the circuit court of McLean county, against the "Board of Education of Normal School District," on a bond for $500, and two coupons of $25 each. The bond was dated the 1st of September, 1873, payable five years after its date, with ten percent interest, and it was payable to John Gregory or order. It was indorsed by him in blank, and he negotiated it to the Home Bank, of which appellant purchased, taking no further indorsement. . . .

The evidence tended to show that the bond was not issued to pay for a school house site, or to erect a building thereon. It also tended to prove that Gregory was, at the time the bond was issued to him, a member of the board, and that appellant was aware of the fact when he purchased the bond. As these were controverted facts, and were found by the circuit court against appellant, and as the Appellate Court has affirmed the judgment of the circuit court, we must take the affirmance as a finding of the facts as they were found by the circuit court, and we are precluded from reviewing these controverted facts, but are bound by the finding of the Appellate Court.

The fact, then, that the bond was not issued for an authorized purpose, undeniably rendered it void. Municipal corporations are not usually endowed with power to enter into traffic or general business, and are only created as auxiliaries to the government in carrying into effect some special governmental policy, or to aid in preserving the order and in promoting the well-being of the locality over which their authority extends. Where a corporation is created for business purposes, all persons may presume such bodies, when issuing their paper, are acting within the scope of their power. Not so with municipalities. Being created for governmental purposes, the borrowing of money, the purchase of property on time, and the giving of commercial paper, are not inherent, or even powers usually conferred; and unless endowed with such power in their charters, they have no authority to make and place on the market such paper, and persons dealing in it must see that the power exists. This has long been the rule of this court. . . . We might refer to other cases where it has been held that bonds issued without authority are void, even in the hands of purchasers before maturity and without actual notice.

A person taking bonds of a municipal corporation has access to the records of the body, and it is his duty to see that such instruments are issued in pursuance of authority, and when without power, they must be held void in whosesoever hands they are found. If, therefore, this bond was not issued to purchase a school house site, or for erecting a school building, as the Appellate Court seem to have found, the bond is void, as it was issued without power, and this, too, in the hands of a person taking without actual notice.

Again, this bond was issued without authority, and was void . . ..

The judgment of the Appellate Court is affirmed.

NOTES

1. The legislature, through its plenary power over public schools, may prescribe the conditions by which school bonds shall be issued. Failure to follow prescribed conditions will render the bonds illegal. Dupont v. Mills, 196 A. 168 (1937).

2. In an 1893 case, the Federal Circuit Court for the District of Nebraska held that a statute that provides that "any school district shall have power and authority to borrow money to pay for the sites of school-houses" does not confer authority on the school district to issue negotiable securities. Such securities issued by school districts are void even in the hands of an innocent purchaser. Ashuelot Bank v. School District No. 7, 56 F. 197 (1893).

3. Statutes relating to school bond elections frequently state that the notice of election or resolution shall relate to a single purpose only. The notice or resolution must state specifically the issues in order that the voter can make a clear choice. Such a statutory provision in Ohio provides for the notice of a bond election for "one purpose" but defines one purpose quite broadly as being

> in the case of a school district, any number of school buildings; and in any case, all expenditures, including the acquisition of a site and purchase of equipment, for any one utility building, or other structure, or group of buildings or structures for the same general purpose . . . included in the same resolution.

Pursuant to this statute an action was brought contesting a bond election for which the resolution had provided for (1) the acquisition of real estate, construction of fireproof school buildings and the provision of furniture and furnishing therefore and (2) improvement of non-fireproof school buildings and the provision of furniture and furnishings therefore. The court held that this resolution violated the statutory mandate for "one purpose" and stated:

> The purpose of the statute is to prevent the union in one act of diverse, incongruous and disconnected matters, having no relation to or connnection with each other . . . ; to give electors a choice to secure what they desire without the necessity of accepting something which they do not want . . . ; and to prevent double propositions being placed before a voter having but a single expression to answer all propositions, thus making logrolling impossible . . . .. In applying the rule, the courts invoke a test as to the existence of a natural relationship between the various structures or objects united in one proposition so that they form 'but one rounded whole'. . . . State ex rel. Board of Education v. Thompson, 167 Ohio St. 23, 145 N.E.2d 668 (1957).

4. One court has held that a statute authorizing the school district to issue bonds "for the purpose of raising funds to pay the cost of the equipping, enlarging, remodeling, repairing, and improving" the schoolhouse and "the purchase, repairing and installation of equipment thereof" did not authorize a rural high school district to issue bonds for the purpose of raising funds to pay the cost of removing a schoolhouse from one site to another. Byer v. Rural High School District No. 4 of Brown Co., 169 Kan. 351, 219 P.2d 382 (1950).

5. Courts have held that school district indebtedness, subject to legal limitations, extends only to voluntary indebtedness. A judgment against a school district for a sum of money is not considered the creation of a debt within the meaning of constitutional debt limitations. Such debt is not subject to collateral attack by a taxpayers' suit to avoid taxation. Edmundson v. Indiana School District, 98 Iowa 639, 67 N.W. 671.

6. It has generally been held that a school district whose boundaries overlap or are coterminous with a civil government has a separate computation in determining indebtedness. Vallelly v. Park Commissioners, 16 N.D. 25, 111 N.W. 615, 171 A.L.R. 732 (1907).

7. In determining whether an indebtedness limit has been exceeded, the amount of indebtedness is determined at the time the bonds are issued and not at the time the bonds are voted. Hebel v. School District R–1, Jefferson County, 131 Colo. 105, 279 P.2d 673 (1955).

8. Refunding bonds do not increase the indebtedness of a school district. Prohm v. Non-High School District, 130 N.E.2d 917 (1955).

9. The constitutions in Indiana and Kentucky limit the indebtedness of school districts and other political subdivisions to a mere 2 percent of the value of the taxable property in the district. These constitutional debt limitations are the lowest of any of the states in the nation. In order to bypass or avoid these uncommonly strict limitations, both states have enacted statutes that allow for the use of school building corporations in financing school construction. Such a procedure permits the formation of a holding company that is authorized to construct a school building and incur the indebtedness. The school building corporation contracts with the school district to lease the building to the district for a number of years and when the rental payments have paid off the bonded indebtedness the building becomes the property of the school district. This type of purchase on an installment arrangement does not increase the indebtedness of the school district. The Supreme Court of Indiana had this to say about the constitutionality of the procedure:

> The fact that the building company was willing to give the school building to the (school district) when the building company had been paid an amount equal to its investment . . . does not change the lease-contract into a contract to purchase. It is true that the (school district), through the device of a long term lease providing for annual rental payments, may become the owner of the school building which (under the constitutional limitation) it could not have acquired . . . by issuing bonds. But it does not follow that either the arrangement or the result constitutes an evasion of the limitations of the (Constitution). The lease-contract is not in contravention of (the

Constitution) unless it necessarily created a legally enforceable debt obligation for an amount in excess of the amount permitted by (the Constitution). Jefferson School Tp. v. Jefferson Tp., 212 Ind. 542, 10 N.E.2d 608 (1937); and Kees v. Smith, 235 Ind. 687, 137 N.E.2d 541 (1956).

Footnotes

1. For the details of American faculty taxes, see Seligman, *The Income Tax* 367 (2d ed. 1914).

2. See Seligman, *Essay in Taxation* 16–17 (10th ed. 1931), on which this section is based.

3. *Taxation in American States and Cities* 131 (1888).

4. School District No. 25 of Woods County v. Hodge, 199 Okl. 81, 183 P.2d 575 (1947).

5. Bell's Gap Railroad Co. v. Commonwealth of Pennsylvania, 134 U.S. 232, 10 S.Ct. 533 (1890).

6. Wade J. Newhouse, *Constitutional Uniformity and Equality in State Taxation* (Ann Arbor: University of Michigan Law School, 1959), p. 602.

7. Id., p. 608.

8. Id., p. 603.

9. Bell's Gap Railroad Co. v. Commonwealth of Pennsylvania, supra.

10. Id.

11. Sawyer v. Gilmore, 109 Me. 169, 83 A. 673 (1912).

12. See: Taylor v. School District of City of Lincoln, 128 Neb. 437, 259 N.W. 168 (1935).

13. Miller v. Childers, 107 Okl. 57, 238 P. 204 (1924).

14. Constitution of Oklahoma, Section 1, Art. 13. See also: Kennedy v. Miller, 97 Cal. 429, 32 P. 558 (1893); Piper v. Big Pine School Dist., 193 Cal. 664, 226 P. 926 (1924).

15. Miller v. Childers, supra.

16. Hess v. Mullaney, 15 Alaska 40, 213 F.2d 635 (9th Cir.1954), cert. denied Hess v. Dewey, 348 U.S. 836, 75 S.Ct. 50 (1954).

17. 79 C.J.S., Schools and School Districts, § 441.

18. "Is Denial of Equal Education Opportunity Constitutional?" *Administrator's Notebook,* no. 6. XIII (University of Chicago, Feb. 1965). See also: Arthur E. Wise, *Rich Schools Poor Schools* (Chicago: The University of Chicago Press, 1968).

19. Griffin v. Illinois, 351 U.S. 12, 76 S.Ct. 585 (1956).

20. Baker v. Carr, 369 U.S. 186, 82 S.Ct. 691 (1962); Gray v. Sanders, 372 U.S. 368, 83 S.Ct. 801 (1963).

21. Hargrave v. Kirk, 313 F.Supp. 944 (D.C.Fla.1970); vacated and remanded on other grounds sub nom., Askew v. Hargrave, 401 U.S. 476, 91 S.Ct. 856 (1971).

22. 377 U.S. 533, 84 S.Ct. 1362 (1964).

23. 293 F.Supp. 327, affirmed 394 U.S. 322, 89 S.Ct. 1197 (1969).

24. McInnis v. Shapiro, supra.

25. 394 U.S. 322, 89 S.Ct. 1197 (1969).

26. McInnis v. Shapiro, supra.

27. Burruss v. Wilkerson, 310 F.Supp. 572 (D.C.Va.1969) affirmed mem. 397 U.S. 44, 90 S.Ct. 812 (1970).

28. Id.

29. 96 Cal.Rptr. 601, 487 P.2d 1241 (1971).

30. Van Dusartz v. Hatfield, 334 F.Supp. 870 (D.C.Minn.1971).

31. Plaintiffs also raised the issue of discrimination under Civil Rights Act, 42 U.S.C.A. § 1983.

32. Rodriguez v. San Antonio Independent School District, 337 F.Supp. 280 (W.D.Texas 1971).

33. San Antonio Independent School District v. Rodriguez, 411 U.S. 1, 93 S.Ct. 1278, rehearing denied 411 U.S. 959, 93 S.Ct. 1919 (1973).

34. Id.

35. Milliken v. Green, 390 Mich. 389, 212 N.W.2d 711 (1973).

36. Shofstall v. Hollins, 110 Ariz. 88, 515 P.2d 590 (1973).

37. Governor v. State Treasurer, 389 Mich. 1, 203 N.W.2d 457 (1972).

38. Serrano v. Priest, supra.

39. Thompson v. Engelring, 96 Idaho 793, 537 P.2d 635 (1975).

40. Blase v. State of Illinois, 55 Ill.2d 94, 302 N.E.2d 46 (1973); People ex rel. Jones v. Adams, 40 Ill.App.3d 189, 350 N.E.2d 767 (1976).

41. Knowles v. State Board of Education, 219 Kan. 271, 547 P.2d 699 (1976).

42. State ex rel. Woodahl v. Straub, 164 Mont. 141, 520 P.2d 776 (1974).

43. Olsen v. State ex rel. Johnson, 276 Or. 9, 554 P.2d 139 (1976).

44. Board of Education v. Nyquist, 57 N.Y.2d 27, 453 N.Y.S.2d 643, 439 N.E.2d 359 (1982).

45. McDaniel v. Thomas, 248 Ga. 632, 285 S.E.2d 156 (1981).

46. Robinson v. Cahill, 62 N.J. 473, 303 A.2d 273 (1973).

47. Robinson v. Cahill, supra.

48. Horton v. Meskill, 172 Conn. 615, 376 A.2d 359 (1976).

49. Pauley v. Kelly, 255 S.E.2d 859 (W.Va.1979).

50. Washakie County School District, No. One v. Herschler, 606 P.2d 310 (Wyo.1980).

51. Dupree v. Alma School District No. 30 of Crawford Co., 279 Ark. 340, 651 S.W.2d 90 (1983).

52. Serrano v. Priest, supra.

53. Horton v. Meskill, supra.

54. Dupree v. Alma School District, supra.

55. School District No. 6, Chase County v. Robb, 150 Kan. 402, 93 P.2d 905 (1939).

56. Jewett v. School District No. 25 in Freemount County, 49 Wyo. 277, 54 P.2d 546 (1936).

57. Kees v. Smith, 235 Ind. 687, 137 N.E.2d 541 (1956); Waller v. Georgetown Board of Education, 209 Ky. 726, 273 S.W. 498 (1925).

18

Property

It goes without saying that property is of prime importance in operating a public school system just as it is to all individuals and corporations alike. School property is state property held in trust for public school purposes.[1] By vesting a local school district with the power to acquire and hold property, the legislature does not relinquish its control. School property remains the property of the state and the power of the local district may be expanded or abolished at the will of the legislature. For example, it is conceivable that a state legislature may decide to vest the control of school property in another agency, other than a school district, at the local level. In such a case, the school district would, abiding by the statute, relinquish control over the property in favor of the other agency.

The same reasoning prevails when the legislature decides to reorganize many small school districts into larger, more comprehensive district units. The property now owned by the smaller district becomes, by statute, the property of the new, larger, consolidated district. The state legislature in this case has merely changed the trustee in which control of school property is vested.

Absent Legislation to the Contrary, a
School District, as a State Agency, Is
Not Subject to Local Municipal
Zoning Ordinance

CITY OF BLOOMFIELD v. DAVIS COUNTY SCHOOL DISTRICT

Supreme Court of Iowa, 1963.
254 Iowa 900, 119 N.W.2d 909.

GARFIELD, Chief Justice. This is an action in equity by the City of Bloomfield to enjoin defendants, Davis County Community School District, and its contractor, Boatman, from installing in a restricted residence district in plaintiff city a bulk storage tank for gasoline and a pump to supply its school buses therewith. . . .

On September 19, 1933, the council of plaintiff city passed ordinance 84 designating and establishing a restricted residence district in the city.

Section 2 of the ordinance provides: "That no buildings or other structures, except residences, school houses, churches, and other similar structures shall hereafter be erected, reconstructed, altered, repaired or occupied within said district without first securing from the city council permit therefor . . . ."

Section 3 of the ordinance provides: "Any building or structure erected, altered, repaired or used in violation of any of the provisions of this ordinance, is hereby declared to be a nuisance . . . ." . . .

The only contention of defendants we find it necessary to consider is that ordinance 84 should not be held applicable to them to prevent installation on this school-owned site of this gasoline facility for servicing its school buses because the school district is an arm of the state and proposes to use its property for a governmental purpose. . . .

The law seems quite well settled that a municipal zoning ordinance is not applicable to the state or any of its agencies in the use of its property for a governmental purpose unless the legislature has clearly manifested a contrary intent. . . .

C.J.S. Zoning, § 135 says, "Ordinarily, a governmental body is not subject to zoning restrictions in its use of property for governmental purposes."

The underlying logic of some of these authorities is, in substance, that the legislature could not have intended, in the absence of clear expression to the contrary, to give municipalities authority to thwart the state, or any of its agencies in performing a duty imposed upon it by statute.

There can be no doubt the school district is an arm or agency of the state and that the maintenance of public schools, including providing transportation to the pupils entitled to it as required by statute, is a governmental function. Certainly it is not a proprietary one. . . .

Code section 297.1, I.C.A. states, "The board of each school corporation may fix the site for each schoolhouse . . . ." Section 297.3 says, "Any school corporation . . . may take and hold an area equal to two blocks . . . for a schoolhouse site, and not exceeding thirty acres for school playground, stadium, or field house, *or other purposes for each such site.*" (Emphasis added.)

Section 285.10, which requires local school boards to provide transportation for each pupil legally entitled thereto, states, in subsection 2, that local school boards "Establish, maintain and operate bus routes for the transportation of pupils so as to provide for the economical and efficient operation thereof . . . ." Section 285.10 also provides, in subsection 5, that local boards "Exercise any and all powers and duties relating to transportation of pupils enjoined upon them by law."

Section 285.11 provides that in the operation of bus routes and contracting for transportation, "The boards shall take advantage of all tax exemptions on fuel, equipment, *and of such other economies as are available.*" (Emphasis added.)

We think furnishing economical transportation to pupils entitled to it is as much a school matter, over which the district has exclusive jurisdiction, as maintenance of the school buildings or location of the high school football field. (Plaintiff concedes a football stadium is generally held to come within the meaning of a schoolhouse. See also Livingston v. Davis, 243 Iowa 21, 27, 50 N.W.2d 592, 596, 27 A.L.R.2d 1237.) . . .

No statute has come to our attention which indicates a clear legislative intent that the state or such of its agencies as defendant district, in the use of its property for a governmental purpose, must comply with a municipal zoning ordinance. Unless our decision is to be contrary to the uniform current of authority on the subject, we must hold defendant district, in the location of this tank and pump to supply fuel to its buses, is not subject to ordinance 84. . . .

We think this opinion does not conflict with our decision in Cedar Rapids Community School Dist. v. City of Cedar Rapids, supra, 252 Iowa 205, 106 N.W.2d 655, that the school district was subject to certain building ordinances of the city in renovating and constructing school buildings. No zoning ordinance or question as to the district's right to make use of its property in performing a duty enjoined on it by law—such as transportation of pupils—was there involved. The two cases are further to be distinguished on the ground that here the state appears to have taken over the field of legislation pertaining to transportation of pupils and therefore municipalities may not interfere in that field. See C.J.S. Zoning § 10.

Defendants are entitled to an injunction to restrain plaintiff from interfering with their installation of the gasoline tank and pump on the ground owned by the school district north of the high school football field. For decree accordingly the cause is—reversed and remanded.

All Justices concur.

*School District Is Obliged to Adhere
to Minimum Building Code
Standards*

EDMONDS SCHOOL DISTRICT v. CITY OF MOUNTLAKE TERRACE

Supreme Court of Washington, 1970.
77 Wash.2d 609, 465 P.2d 177.

HALE, Judge. A kind of sibling rivalry in governmental affairs brings the Edmonds School District and the City of Mountlake Terrace here on a declaratory judgment suit. The school district's claim of sovereign immunity from the city's building code is met by the city's equally vehement claim of sovereign authority to enforce the code. Failing to obtain in the superior court a declaratory judgment that it need not comply with the building code, the district now appeals from a judgment favoring its intergovernmental rival. . . .

The school district brings this suit for a declaratory judgment asking that ordinance No. 391, the building code of the City of Mountlake Terrace, be held inapplicable to and not binding upon the school district in the construction of its high school addition. From a summary judgment denying this relief and dismissing the complaint with prejudice, the district appeals.

Each party claims superior rights over the other deriving from their common source of governmental power, the sovereign state. They present two main questions: Has the state designated which of the two agencies should exercise its sovereign authority with respect to building permits and minimum setback requirements? Is there an irreconcilable dichotomy between the delegation to the school district of the sovereign's constitutional duty to educate the children of the state and the city's exercise of the police power in adopting and enforcing a building code?

Are the two sets of delegated powers in conflict? The school district says that the city, in forcing compliance with its building code, is transgressing and trespassing upon its powers and duties as an agency of the sovereign state, to build, operate and maintain public high schools. The district's function of providing the land, materials and designs for school buildings cannot, it contends, be lawfully preempted nor frustrated in any way by a municipality any more than a city could enforce its standards upon the sovereign state against its will.

Education is one of the paramount duties of the state. The duty and power to educate the people are not only inherent qualities of sovereignty but are expressly made an attribute of sovereignty in the State of Washington by the state constitution. Const. art. 9, §§ 1, 2. The state exercises its sovereign powers and fulfills its duties of providing education largely by means of a public school system under the direction and administration of the State Superintendent of Public Instruction, State Board of Education, school districts and county school boards.

School districts are, in law, municipal corporations with direct authority to establish, maintain and operate public schools and to erect and maintain buildings for that and allied purposes. RCW 28.58. In essence, a school district is a corporate arm of the state established as a means of carrying out the state's constitutional duties (RCW 28.57.135) and exercising the sovereign's powers in providing education. The state has thus made the local school district its corporate agency for the administration of a constitutionally required system of free public education. . . . The state now requires school districts to have the plans and specifications, including those features pertaining to heating, lighting, ventilating and safety, approved by the county superintendent of schools before entering into any school building construction contracts. RCW 28.58.301.

But in other spheres of governmental activity, the state has allocated some of its sovereign powers and responsibilities to cities, too. Under Const. art. 11, § 11, a city may make and enforce all police and sanitary regulations within its limits which do not conflict with general laws. By statute, cities are charged with the sovereign exercise of the police power to maintain peace and good government and to provide for the general welfare of their inhabitants through law not inconsistent with the constitution and statutes of the state. RCW 35.24.290(18). A city and other kinds of municipal corporations, too, are agencies of the state to accomplish these ends. Columbia Irrigation Dist. v. Benton County, 149 Wash. 234, 270 P. 813 (1928). Among these police powers, of course, is the capability of adopting and enforcing building codes. Just as the state has vested in the state superintendent, state board, and the school districts many of its attributes of sovereignty pertaining to education, it has done the same to incorporated cities with respect to the general police powers, among which are zoning and building regulations.

The City of Mountlake Terrace cannot, under existing statutes, supersede, set aside, invalidate or impair the educational processes of or limit the standards prescribed by the state for the operation of the public schools (State ex rel. School Dist. No. 37 of Clark County v. Clark County, 177 Wash. 314, 31 P.2d 897 (1934)), for that would be an infringement upon state sovereignty. But the state, in delegating to school districts power to build, maintain and operate public schools, has not prescribed minimum standards for street offsets, nor directed that building permits be waived in the construction of public school buildings or additions. It has left its subordinate municipalities free to regulate each other in those activities which traditionally are thought to lie within their particular competence and are more proximate to their respective functions. Fixing minimum offsets for streets, alleys, front, side and back yards would, unless the state has said otherwise, fit more relevantly into a city building code than into the general rules for the operation and maintenance of a high school. . . .

There is little doubt that the State of Washington . . . has the constitutional power to prescribe standards for and regulate school construction, and may, as an attribute of its sovereignty, deprive municipalities of any voice in these matters. But the state has not thus far exercised this power nor prohibited cities from exacting a building permit fee, nor relieved school districts within the corporate limits of a city from paying such fee or complying with the setback provisions of the municipal building code. Unless the state has, so to speak, preempted the field of building standards or specifically ousted the municipality of jurisdiction over school construction, we think the school district is obliged to comply with the minimum standards set forth in the city's building code.

Arguments of the district and amicus curiae convey a concern that, if the court holds a school district amenable to a municipal building code, the ruling will ultimately operate to permit cities—and counties—to interfere with or impinge upon the operation, management and control of the public schools. These fears, we think, are illusory. In the matter of education, a school district is deemed to be an arm of the state for the administration of the school system. . . . It follows that the school district exercises the paramount power of the state in providing education and carries out the will of the sovereign state as to all matters involved in the educational processes and in the conduct, operation and management of the schools. We find nothing in the constitution or existing law which would enable a city legislative body to trespass or impinge upon or interfere with the conduct and operation of the public schools. We do not apprehend that requiring the Edmonds School District to pay for a building permit and set back its new addition from the street or property lines in accordance with the city building code empowers the city to assume any responsibilities or control over the way the educational process is conducted. Such matters as curriculum, textbooks, teaching methods, grading, school hours and holidays, extracurricular school activities or those concerning the selection, tenure and compensation of school personnel—indeed, the thousand and one activities and facilities by which the school districts of the State of Washington afford an education to the children of the state, and adults, too—remain outside of the authority and control of the cities.

Affirmed.

NOTES

1. "A community unit school district, like any other school district established under enabling legislation, is entirely subject to the will of the legislature thereafter. With or without the consent of the inhabitants of a school district, over their protests, even without notice or hearing, the state may take the school facilities in the district, without giving compensation therefore, and vest them in other districts or agencies. The state may hold or manage the facilities directly or indirectly. The area of the district may be contracted or expanded, it may be divided, united in whole or in part with another district, and the district may be abolished. The 'property of the school district' is a phrase which is misleading. The district owns no property, all school facilities, such as grounds, buildings, equipment, etc., being in fact and law the property of the state and subject to the legislative will." People v. Deatherage, 401 Ill. 25, 81 N.E.2d 581 (1948).

   An Indiana court held: "Under the constitution and laws of this state, school property is held in trust for school purposes by the persons or corporations authorized for the time being by statute to control the same. It is in the power of the legislature, at any time, to change the trustee." Carson v. State, 27 Ind. 465 (1867).

2. The courts have consistently held that school property may be taken from one school district and vested in other agencies. In a school district organization case that has implications for the school district's control over property, an Illinois court held: "The state may, with or without the consent of the inhabitants or against their protest, and with or without notice or hearing, take their property [property of the district] without compensation and vest it in other agencies, or hold it itself, expand or contract the territorial area, divide it, unite our whole or part of it with another municipality, apportion the common property and the common burdens in accordance with the legislative will, and it may abolish the municipality [or school district] altogether." People ex rel. Taylor v. Camargo Community Consol. School District, 313 Ill. 321, 145 N.E. 154 (1924).

PURCHASE OF PROPERTY FOR SPECIAL PURPOSES

Taxpayers have, on many occasions, questioned a board of education's use of tax money for the purchase of property that does not fall strictly within the generally accepted definitions of a school or classroom instructional purpose. The purchase of property for such things as athletic fields, playgrounds, recreational centers, and camps have been litigated.

The weight of authority indicates that the courts tend to interpret the authority of a board of education in this area broadly and, especially in recent years, have expanded their interpretation of the purposes and objectives of public education. However, there are boundaries beyond which it may be questionable for a board of education to tread. For example, a "liberal minded" Florida court held that it was permissible for a board of education to purchase property in another county for a camp and recreational grounds.[2] On the other hand, a more cautious Kentucky court has held that there was no authorization for a board of education to purchase a recreation center in another county.[3]

School Board Has the Implied
Authority to Purchase Land Outside
Geographical Boundaries of
School District

IN RE BOARD OF PUBLIC INSTRUCTION OF ALACHUA COUNTY

Supreme Court of Florida, 1948.
160 Fla. 490, 35 So.2d 579.

TERRELL, Justice. . . .

The question for determination is whether or not the Board of Public Instruction of Alachua County is authorized to purchase and take title to lands outside the geographical limits of the county for the purpose of administering its public school program.

Appellants contend that this question should be answered in the negative. To support this contention they rely on certain provisions of Chapter 230, Florida Statutes 1941, F.S.A., particularly sections 230.22 and 230.23, defining the powers and duties of Boards of Public Instruction. . . . They contend that said statutes and decisions restrict the power of the Board of Public Instruction in the exercise of its school program to the county over which it exercises jurisdiction and that it is without authority to enter another county or to purchase lands beyond its borders for any purpose.

Prior to the enactment of Chapter 19,355, Acts of 1939, as amended by Chapter 23,726, Acts of 1947, F.S.A. § 227.01 et seq., hereafter referred to as the School Code, this contention might have been upheld, but as this Court pointed out in Taylor et al. v. Board of Public Instruction of Lafayette County, 157 Fla. 422, 26 So.2d 180, 181, the School Code "enlarged materially the scope of public school programs, public school plants, and public school activities." An adequate public school program is no longer limited to exploiting the three R's and acquiring such facilities as are necessary to do so. It contemplates the development of mental, manual and other skills that may not derive from academic training. It is predicated on the premise that a personality quotient is just as important as an intelligence quotient and that training the character and the emotions is just as important as training the mind if the product is to be a well balanced citizen.

. . . Section 230.23, among other things, authorizes the County Board of Public Instruction to assume such responsibilities as may be vested in it by law, or as may be required by the State Board of Education or as in the opinion of the County Board of Public Instruction are necessary to provide for the more efficient operation of the County school system in carrying out the purposes of the School Code. As to property ownership, the latter section provides that the County Board of Public Instruction shall retain possession of all property to which title is not held by the County Board and to attain possession of and accept and hold under proper title all property which may at any time be acquired by the County Board for educational purposes in the County.

. . . It is not at all clear that the legislature intended the words "in the county" to limit land purchase to lands in the county. It would be just as reasonable to conclude that the intent was to authorize the purchase of lands anywhere they might aid the county's school program.

The reason for purchasing the lands in question was to provide a camp and a recreational ground to aid the educational program of Alachua County. It was situated on a lake across the county line in Clay County but within easy reach of the schools of Alachua County. It is shown to be well adapted for that purpose and was being offered at a nominal price. Competitive sports are now a recognized part of the public school program. Eminent psychologists proclaim the doctrine that competitive sports contribute more to one's personality quotient and ability to work with people than any other school activity. Athletic coaches and physical directors tell us that the Olympic Games and other forms of physical competition have done more to put an end to class hatreds and promote international harmony than the United Nations Assembly, the reason being that they are conducted by a strict moral code that insures just treatment to all who participate in them.

This is a mere incident to the manner in which the public school program has been bounced out of its traditional groove and invaded by new experiments in education. An adequate school program is now as diversified as an experimental farm program and the very purpose of the School Code was to give sanction to such a program. The progenitors of the three R's would doubtless have "thrown a fit" if the School Board had talked about purchasing lands for a recreational center. The barn yard and the woodpile filled the need of a recreational center for them. It met the challenge of the time but its exponents, the three R's and the little red school house that symbolized it now repose in the museum of modern education. What we are concerned with is a system to cope with this machine age that we are in danger of becoming victims of if we do not become its masters.

We have learned that the public school program has a definite relation to the economy of our people, that the great majority of them must make their living with their hands and that those who do so must acquire different skills and trades from those who pursue the learned professions, various businesses and specialized activities. We have also learned that, while skill in the three R's was adequate for a rural democracy when the nearest neighbor was three miles away and it was sometimes three hundred yards from the front door to the front gate, it is entirely inadequate for an urban democracy where you speak to your neighbor through the window and sometimes live with a flock of them under the same roof. A democracy in which we cultivate our farms with machines, travel by automobile, send our mail by airplane and flip a gadget to warm the house, start breakfast and relieve much of the day's drudgery. Such is the social era that the public school program must prepare the citizen for and the School Code was designed to provide the wherewith for such a program. County lines may be treated as a fiction rather than a barrier to such a program.

It follows that the question confronting us impels an affirmative answer. To construe the School Code otherwise would render it impossible to bring about a public school program adequate for the needs contemplated by the legislature. So the fact that the lands in question were without the geographical limits of Alachua County is not material if they are essential to carry out its public school program.

Affirmed.

NOTES

1. In a ruling similar to the Alachua County case, the Kentucky Court of Appeals upheld a cooperative arrangement by which the Jefferson County Board of Education jointly with the Jefferson County Fiscal Court created a Jefferson County Board of Recreation. The activities of the recreation board were financed jointly by the cooperating agencies upon submission and approval of a budget by each agency. The primary legal question was, does a statute that provides that any school district may join with a city or county in "providing and conducting public playgrounds and recreational centers" extend sufficient authority for the school district to budget funds and purchase property for the establishment of playgrounds, parks and recreation centers? The court said it did and reasoned: "We think the statute is plain in extending the authority; it is subject to no other construction. It is true that there is no explicit provision for the expenditure by the board of such sum or sums as may appear to it in the exercise of reasonable discretion to further the intended purpose. The force of the argument is that while the school district may join in 'providing and conducting' the enterprise, the county must bear all incident expenses. The power and authority granted by a statute is not always limited to that which is specifically conferred, but includes that which is necessarily implied as incident to the accomplishment of those things which are expressly authorized." Dodge v. Jefferson County Board of Education, 298 Ky. 1, 181 S.W.2d 406 (1944).

2. The authority of a school district to purchase or construct teachers' homes has been upheld by the courts. One court had this to say: "An adequate public school system program now contemplates the development of skills that flow from the head, the hand, the heart . . . . Expenditures for facilities that aid these purposes may be lawfully made from the public school funds." Taylor v. Board of Education of Lafayette County, Fla., 26 So.2d 181 (1946). Evidently, the reasoning of this court was that homes for teachers would enhance the educational process to a sufficient degree to pay dividends through increased educational attainment of the pupils.

   Conversely, it has been held that public school funds may not be used to provide a house for the school superintendent. Fulk v. School Dist. No. 8 of Lancaster County, 155 Neb. 630, 53 N.W.2d 56 (1952). However, this view seems to be in the minority.

SCHOOL BUILDINGS

Since much of the educational dollar goes for capital outlay and by far the greatest portion of this money comes from local taxation, it is inevitable that people in the community will, from time to time, question the propriety of the expenditure of such money for certain capital construction purposes. In settling these disputes, the courts have found it necessary to define just what the legislature meant when it provided for local school boards to construct "school buildings" and "schoolhouses." Such an interpretation naturally reverts to a discussion of the parameters of educational purpose and the means by which to accomplish such purposes.

For example, in discussing educational purpose the courts have held both for and against the construction of football stadiums; however, the precedent seems to support the conclusion that stadiums do serve a school purpose and thereby constitute a schoolhouse within the meaning of statute. The rule seems to be that a schoolhouse is a place where instruction and training is given in any branch or branches of the educational endeavor regardless of whether such exercises are mental or physical.

*Term "Schoolhouse" Is Broad Enough
to Imply Authority to Build a
Stadium*

ALEXANDER v. PHILLIPS

Supreme Court of Arizona, 1927.
31 Ariz. 503, 254 P. 1056.

LOCKWOOD, J. Plaintiff brought this action for the purpose of restraining the issue of some $80,000 in bonds of the Phoenix union high school district of Maricopa County, Ariz. . . . The second question is the vital point in the case. In substance it is: May a high school district in Arizona issue bonds to build a "stadium"? The purpose for which school bonds may be issued is governed by the provisions of paragraph 2736, R.S.A.1913, Civil Code, as amended by chapter 24, Session Laws of 1925, which reads, so far as material to this feature of the case, as follows:

> 2736. The board of trustees of any school district may, whenever in their judgment it is advisable, and must, upon petition of fifteen per cent. of the school electors, as shown by the poll list at the last preceding annual school election, residing in the district, call an election for the following purposes: . . .

> (3) To decide whether the bonds of the district shall be issued and sold for the purpose of raising money for purchasing or leasing school lots, *for building schoolhouses,* and supplying same with furniture and apparatus, and improving grounds, or for the purpose of liquidating any indebtedness already incurred for such purposes. (Italics ours.)

The matter then for our determination is whether a stadium is a "schoolhouse" within the provision of paragraph 2736. The word "stadium" comes from the Greek, and was originally a measure of distance. From this, by easy transition, the term was applied first to a foot race of that distance, and then to the place where the race was run, usually an open area some 600 feet long, and flanked by terraced elevations providing seats for the spectators of the race. The modern definition follows the old one, but is somewhat broader in its scope and is technically given as:

> A similar modern structure with its enclosure used for athletic games . . . . Webster's New International Dictionary (1925 Ed.).

This is also the popular definition, and we may therefore assume that when the question was submitted to the electors of the district, it was understood by them that the proceeds of the bonds would be used to erect a structure where various forms of athletic games could be given by the students of the high school and spectators could be properly accommodated while watching them.

Is such a structure a "schoolhouse"? The terms "schoolhouse" and "school" are properly defined as follows:

> Schoolhouse—a building which is appropriated for the use of a school or schools, or as a place in which to give instruction.

> School—a place for instruction in any branch or branches of knowledge. Webster's New International Dictionary (1925 Ed.).

Was the stadium for which the bonds of the district were to be issued a "building which is appropriated for the use of a school or schools"? . . . No one would maintain that it was within the unfettered discretion of the pupils, the teachers, or any independent set of men or women to determine what should be taught in our public schools. Only the people, speaking through the proper authorities, can determine this question, and the law therefore provides in what branches of human knowledge instruction may be given. We therefore hold that the proper definition of a "schoolhouse" within the meaning of paragraph 2736, supra, is: Any building which is appropriated for a use prescribed or permitted by the law to public schools.

. . . The founders of our first public schools believed all that was necessary, or at least then advisable, was the most elementary mental training, and therefore for many years public school education was confined principally to the teaching of the "three R's." But as the world progressed, it was recognized more and more fully that man, using the language of the motto of one of our great philanthropic institutions, is composed of "body, mind, and spirit," and that the complete citizen must be trained in all three fields. . . . For this reason the new generation of educators has added to the mental education, which was all that was given by the public schools of the past, the proper training of the body, and a gymnasium is now accepted to be as properly a schoolhouse as is the chemical laboratory or the study hall. Not only is this true, but the public is realizing that, even on the mental side, the field is broadening, and, whereas fifty years ago such a thing as an auditorium with a stage was practically unheard of in connection with the public school, now even the rural school of three or four rooms is not considered to be properly equipped without such a structure, either separate or in combination with the ordinary lecture room.

We thus see that the branches of human knowledge taught in the public schools have been vastly expanded in the last few generations. Has this expansion been sufficient to bring within its scope a structure of the class in question? It is a well-known fact, of which this court properly takes judicial notice, that the large majority of the higher institutions of learning in the country are erecting stadiums differing from that proposed for the Phoenix union high school only in size, and it is commonly accepted that they are not only a proper but almost a necessary part of the modern college. This is true both of our privately endowed and our publicly maintained universities. That athletic games under proper supervision tend to the proper development of the body is a self-evident fact. It is not always realized, however, that they have a most powerful and beneficial effect upon the development of character and morale. To use the one game of football as an illustration, the boy who makes a successful football player must necessarily learn self-control under the most trying circumstances, courage, both physical and moral, in the face of strong opposition, sacrifice of individual ease for a community purpose, teamwork to the exclusion of individual glorification, and above all that "die in the last ditch" spirit which leads a man to do for a cause everything that is reasonably possible, and, when that is done, to achieve the impossible by sheer willpower. The same is true to a greater or lesser degree of practically every athletic sport which is exhibited in a stadium.

It seems to us that, to hold things of this kind are less fitted for the ultimate purpose of our public schools, to wit, the making of good citizens, physically, mentally, and morally, than the study of algebra and Latin, is an absurdity. Competitive athletic games therefore, from every standpoint, may properly be included in a public school curriculum. The question then is, Does the law of Arizona so include them?

The Eighth Legislature has specifically directed that all public school pupils not physically disabled must take, as part of the regular school work, a course in physical education, which is declared to include "athletic games and contests." So far as the instant case is concerned, this of course is merely illustrative of the present trend of thought along the lines of physical education. At the time the election referred to was held, paragraph 2733, R.S.A.1913, Civil Code, provided among other things, as follows:

> Under such conditions as are provided for by law, boards of trustees may employee such special teachers in drawing, music, domestic science, manual training, kindergarten, commercial work, agriculture and other special subjects as they shall deem advisable.

We think "other special subjects" reasonably includes physical education, and indeed, by virtue of this provision, not only practically all high schools in the state of Arizona, but many of the grammar schools, have for years employed physical and athletic directors, both men and women, and physical education for both boys and girls is a subject required in the courses of study adopted by a large majority of our high schools and approved by the state board of education in pursuance of paragraph 2778, R.S.A.1913; the Phoenix union high school being among this number.

If physical education be one of the special subjects permitted by law, it is a matter for the reasonable discretion of our school authorities as to how such subject should be taught and no parent who has ever had a child participate in any form of the athletic games and contests recognized and given by the various schools of this state, and who has noted the increased interest shown and effort put forth by the participants when such games and sports are open to the view of their schoolmates, friends, and parents, both in intra and inter mural competition, but will realize the educational value both of the games and of a suitable place for giving them.

For the foregoing reasons, we are of the opinion (1) that physical education is one of the branches of knowledge legally imparted in the Phoenix union high school; (2) that competitive athletic games and sports in both intra and inter mural games are legal and laudable methods of imparting such knowledge; and (3) that a structure whose chief purpose is to provide for the better giving of such competitive athletic games and sports as aforesaid is reasonably a schoolhouse within the true spirit and meaning of paragraph 2736, supra.

In view of the foregoing conclusions, it is not necessary to consider the other legal questions raised by plaintiff.

The judgment of the superior court of Maricopa county is affirmed.

NOTES

1. The Kentucky Court of Appeals has held that an auditorium-gymnasium is a "school building" within the meaning of statutes. Rainer v. Board of Education of Prestonsburg, 273 S.W.2d 577 (Ky.1954). The court in this case distinguished its reasoning from an earlier case in which it held that a football stadium did not constitute a "school building." Board of Education of Louisville v. Williams, 256 S.W.2d 29 (Ky.1953). The court reasoned that in the *Rainer* case the use of the auditorium-gymnasium constituted a useful educational purpose where use of the stadium did not.

   In the 1953 *Louisville* case, the court disagreed with the ruling in the case of *Alexander* v. *Phillips,* the principal case presented above, and said: "The case of *Alexander* v. *Phillips* [citation], apparently the leading case in point, differs in that the voters in that case specifically voted for construction of the stadium, where the Louisville voters only authorized an eight million dollar bond issue for school buildings." The Kentucky court further commented on the Arizona case saying: "The court apparently reasoned that, since a schoolhouse was a place for instruction, and since some athletic instruction took place in a stadium, a stadium was therefore a schoolhouse. This dubious logic was supported by a eulogy on the spiritual values of interscholastic athletic contests, of which the court took judicial notice. We think *Alexander* v. *Phillips* is not persuasive as to the intent of the Kentucky legislature in authorizing special taxes and special bond issues for "school buildings."

2. The Supreme Court of Oregon has ruled that a swimming pool falls within the statutory meaning of the term "school building." The court reasoned: "We believe that it was the legislative purpose to empower the issuance of bonds by school districts for the erection on school lands of any structure which the district was authorized to construct and which it deemed necessary or desirable in carrying out its educational program." In rejecting the criterion as to whether the pool was enclosed the court further stated: "The statute reflects the intent to make the function of the structure rather than its architectural design the criterion in deter-

mining whether the bonds may be issued." Petition of School Board, No. U2–20, Multnomah Co., 232 Or. 593, 377 P.2d 4 (1962).

3. Courts in other jurisdictions have upheld the authority of the school district to construct buildings for a gymnasium, Burlington ex rel. School Commissioners v. Burlington, 98 Vt. 388, 127 A. 892 (1925); building for dramatics and athletics Woodson v. School District, 127 Kan. 651, 274 P. 728 (1929); recreation field, Wilkinsburg v. School District, 298 Pa. 193, 148 A. 77 (1929); building for gymnasium, home economics and vocational training, Young v. Linwood School District, 193 Ark. 82, 97 S.W.2d 627 (1936).

4. In a case questioning whether a constitutional provision for taxes for "school purposes" included school buildings the court held that:

the unfettered term "school purpose" has an all-inclusive meaning including the erection of school buildings. In this case the court it seems used reverse implication in reasoning that: "If the General Assembly, [in redrafting the applicable constitutional amendment] had intended to limit the application of amendment to the usual and ordinary expenses of maintaining and operating schools or 'school district purposes excluding the erection of buildings,' it could have easily clarified the situation by the use of some such expression." Rathjen v. Reorganized School Dist. R–11 of Shelby County, 365 Mo. 518, 284 S.W.2d 516 (1955).

SCHOOL SITE SELECTION

A major responsibility of a school board is the location and selection of an appropriate property for the furtherance of the educational purposes of the school district. Many cases have arisen contesting the board's authority to select sites and the appropriateness of the selection. Usually such cases accrue from the efforts of a board to consolidate small schools into larger, more centralized schools that provide not only more efficient operation but also greater educational opportunities for the children.

The courts have uniformly held that it is within the discretion of a board of education to determine what school site will best meet the educational needs of the children and the mere fact that others do not agree is not grounds for interfering with the board's decision.

Courts Will Not Intervene Unless
Board's Decision Is Tainted with
Fraud or Abuse of Discretion

MULLINS v. BOARD OF EDUCATION OF ETOWAH COUNTY

Supreme Court of Alabama, 1947.
249 Ala. 44, 29 So.2d 339.

STAKELY, Justice. This is an appeal from a decree of the equity court sustaining the demurrer to the bill of complaint. . . . . The purpose of the bill is to enjoin the respondents from constructing a proposed school building in a particular community in Etowah County or in the alternative to declare legal rights of the Board of Education and Superintendent of Education of Etowah County.

The allegations of the bill in substance show the following. The respondents have requested and received bids for the proposed construction of a school building to consist of eighteen rooms or more, to be located in the Southside Community in Etowah County, Alabama. The building is to "consist of grammar school and high school grades, a vocational school and an agricultural school." . . .

The community now served by the John S. Jones Junior High School is more thickly populated and has more children of school age than the Southside Community. More students from the community served by the John S. Jones Junior High School would attend the proposed school than students of the Southside Community. The proposed plan would necessitate the transportation of a greater number of children for much greater distances and would remove the Junior High School grades from the John S. Jones Junior High School. . . .

The plan, if put into effect, will result in the construction in the Southside Community of a school building larger than needed by that community to care for the school children residing therein and a portion of the building so constructed would remain empty and unused. The respondents further propose to remove from neighboring communities, including the John S. Jones community, sufficient students to fill the proposed building, which will leave portions of the school facilities now being used in the John S. Jones community empty and unused. In either event the result will be a waste of funds and facilities held by respondents to the detriment of the taxpayers in the county and will prevent construction of much needed school buildings in other communities in Etowah County. The construction of a smaller and less expensive building for Southside High School will be adequate and sufficient to serve the needs of school children living in Southside Community.

It is further alleged that "the proposed action of the defendants . . . is a gross abuse of the discretion vested in them by the laws of the State of Alabama."

This court is committed to the view that the courts of this state will not ordinarily seek to control the exercise of the broad discretion given by the statutes to the county board of education since the powers vested in it are quasi-judicial as well as administrative. This principle prevails even though in the exercise of descretion there may have been error or bad judgment. The courts will act, however, if the acts of county boards of education are tainted with fraud or bad faith or gross abuse of discretion. . . .

It is conceded by appellants that there is nothing to show either fraud or bad faith in the present bill.

It is insisted, however, that the allegations of the bill present a case showing gross abuse of discretion. So far as we are aware this court has not attempted to define precisely "gross abuse of discretion," perhaps for the reason that it is best to allow the facts and circumstances peculiar to each case to determine its presence or absence. In a general way, however, we say that it means such an arbitrary and unreasonable act or conclusion as to shock the sense of justice and indicate lack of fair and careful consideration. . . .

The broad powers conferred on the county board of education to which we have referred include the power to consolidate schools and to arrange for transportation of pupils to and from such consolidated school (§ 76, Title 52, Code of 1940), the power to determine the "kind, grade and location of schools" (§ 113, Title 52, Code of 1940) and the power to adopt "a building program adequate to the present and future needs of the schools in the county" (§ 116, Title 52, Code of 1940). Do the allegations of the bill remove the case from within the discretion of the board to an arbitrary, unreasonable and unjustifiable misuse of power? Do the allegations of the bill overcome the presumption which is in favor of the reasonableness and propriety of the action of the board? It does not appear so to us.

The proposed school is to replace a school destroyed by fire in a community now without a school. Construing the bill against the pleader, it does not appear with sufficient certainty how much money is to be used to consummate the plan or how much empty or waste space will be created in the new school or be left in the John S. Jones Junior High School. There is nothing to show the dimensions, area or topography of the proposed site. There is nothing to show to what extent the proposed site is or is not a suitable school center or in a central location from the standpoint of other communities, not just the community in which one school, the John S. Jones Junior High School, is located. There is nothing to show a bad location from the standpoint of roads or the condition thereof.

Beyond all this there is nothing to show that the plan is out of step with the future needs of the schools of the county so far as they may be reasonably foreseen. § 116, Title 52, Code of 1940, supra. In the absence of a contrary showing it must be assumed that the authorities gave careful and due consideration to the growing and expanding needs of education in the county. The statutes as well as the high purposes of education contemplate that a plan should be adopted that has vision and foresight. A sparsely settled community today may well be a populous community tomorrow. Matters which may create irritations today because of inconvenience, etc., may be relatively unimportant in comparision with a long range plan.

The allegations of the bill will not be aided by the general allegation that "the proposed action of the defendants is a gross abuse of discretion" because this is "merely to apply an epithet without defining the act". . . . The court acted correctly in sustaining the demurrer to the bill.

Affirmed.

NOTES

1. In a later Alabama case contesting the school board's selection of a school site for a high school, it was alleged that (1) the population of the proposed site area was not sufficient to support a high school, and (2) the geographical conditions were not suitable for a high school. The court cited the principle case above, Mullins v. Board of Education of Etowah County, 249 Ala. 44, 29 So.2d 339 (1947) and said that it would not interfer unless the board's action constituted "gross abuse of discretion"

and in this case the selection of this particular school site did not demonstrate such gross abuse. The court further said that the complainants must show a "gross abuse of discretion" and the board's action must be "such an arbitrary and unreasonable act or conclusion as to shock the sense of justice and indicate lack of fair and careful consideration," and they had failed to do this. Board of Ed. of Blount County v. Phillips, 264 Ala. 603, 89 So.2d 96 (1956).

2. In an Indiana case, a taxpayer sought a writ of mandamus to compel the school trustee to build a school building at a specified site. The court denied the writ and held that mandamus does not lie to compel a school township trustee to provide for the construction of a school building—especially where it does not clearly appear that it is the trustee's duty to construct the building and that he has the means to do so. Good v. Howard, 174 Ind. 358, 92 N.E. 115 (1910). Of course, the authority of the old township trustee is of little relevance today except that the axiom holds true that a taxpayer cannot substitute his discretion for that of a school board or a trustee and compel the construction of a school building.

3. When a board of education selected a site for a school building and a large group of taxpayers objected, signed a petition, and brought an action to prevent purchase of the site, the court found that the evidence concerning the adequacy of the site was conflicting and said: "We do not deem it necessary to go into a detailed analysis of the proof. It is not the court's duty to select a site; it is only to determine whether the board of education abused a sound discretion in performing that duty. The weight of proof is largely with the board of education; and, if we had any doubt upon the question, it must be resolved in favor of the board of education . . .. Not only does the good faith of the board of education stand unimpeached; but, under the rule by which we will not set aside a finding of fact by the [board of education] where the proof is contradictory we will not disturb [its] judgment in the case." Spaulding v. Campbell County Board of Education, 239 Ky. 277, 39 S.W.2d 490 (1931).

EMINENT DOMAIN

Eminent domain is the power of the government to take private property for public use. Through the right of eminent domain the state can reassert, for reason of public exigency and for the public good, its dominion over any portion of the property of a state. Therefore, when statute so provides, a public board of education can condemn and take for public use property needed for public school purposes, but without legislative authorization, the right of eminent domain lies dormant and cannot be exercised.

Also, the power of eminent domain as exercised by local school boards must satisfy constitutional provisions of both the state and federal governments. Federal constitutional provisions that must be carefully observed are the Fifth Amendment, which prohibits depriving any person of life, liberty, or property without due process of law and from taking private property for public use without just compensation, and the Fourteenth

Amendment, which prohibits any state from depriving any person of life, liberty, or property without due process of law and from denying any person within its jurisdiction the equal protection of the laws. Comparable clauses are included in state constitutions. Such constitutional provisions make it necessary that owners are justly compensated for their property. The question of what is just compensation has been the impetus for much litigation. Generally, however, the fair market value or the value of the property between a willing buyer and a willing seller is the measure of compensation to be awarded the owner.

In taking private property for public use, the public agency must show a necessity for the land, and therefore, cannot condemn more property than public necessity dictates.

It is a general rule that a school board cannot take land that is already being used by another public agency; however, it has been held, in some cases, that where two public agencies need land the agency with the more necessary need will prevail.

Eminent Domain Can be Exercised to
Condemn Property for "Public Use"

OXFORD COUNTY
AGRICULTURAL SOCIETY v.
SCHOOL DISTRICT NO. 17
Supreme Judicial Court of Maine, 1965.
161 Me. 334, 211 A.2d 893.

WEBBER, Justice. On appeal. The defendant School Administrative District No. 17, a quasi-municipal corporation charged with the responsibility of providing public school education, seeks to take property of the plaintiff Oxford County Agricultural Society by eminent domain. The District requires the property for the location of a new high school. It has general statutory authority to take by eminent domain for its lawful purposes but it has never been given specific legislative authority to take the property of this plaintiff.

The . . . issue is whether or not the Society's property is devoted to public uses to such an extent and in such a manner as to provide it with an exemption from condemnation. The plaintiff conducts an annual fair on the property in question which has all the usual attributes of an agricultural fair with which Maine people have long been familiar. . . . The plaintiff is a private voluntary corporation chartered by the Legislature. It is not a political subdivision of the state nor is it invested with any political or governmental function. It was not created to assist in the conduct of government nor was it created by the sovereign will of the Legislature without the consent of the persons who constitute it. These persons may decline or refuse to execute powers granted by legislative charter. They may at any time dissolve and abandon it and are under no legal obligation to conduct an annual fair or to carry on or continue any of the activities which are said to benefit the public. The principles governing exemption from condemnation were well stated in Tuomey Hospital v. City of Sumter (1964) 134 S.E.2d (S.C.) 744, 747:

> We recognize that it is difficult to give an accurate and comprehensive definition of the term "public use." The distinction between public and private use lies in the character of the use and must to a large extent depend upon the facts of each case. There are, however, certain essential characteristics which must be present if the use is to be deemed public and not private within the meaning of the law of eminent domain. . . .
>
> The general rule, to which we adhere, was thus stated in the case of the President and Fellows of Middlebury College v. Central Power Corporation of Vermont, 101 Vt. 325, 143 A. 384, 388: "It is essential to a public use, as the term is used in proceedings involving the law of condemnation or eminent domain, that the public must, to some extent, be entitled to use or enjoy the property, not by favor, but as a matter of right. . . . The test whether a use is public or not is whether a public trust is imposed upon the property; whether the public has a legal right to the use, which cannot be gainsaid or denied, or withdrawn at the pleasure of the owner."

We are satisfied that the statement set forth in 18 Am.Jur. 720, Sec. 94, accurately summarizes the requirements for exemption:

> To exempt property from condemnation under a general grant of the power of eminent domain, it is not enough that it has been voluntarily devoted by its owner to a public or semipublic use. If the use by the public is permissive and may be abandoned at any time, the property is not so held as to be exempt. The test of whether or not property has been devoted to public use is what the owner must do, not what he may choose to do. It is immaterial how the property was acquired; if its owner has devoted it to a public use which he is under a legal obligation to maintain, it comes within the protection of the rule exempting it from condemnation.

We conclude, as did the justice below, that the property of the Society is not immune from condemnation by the District. . . .

Appeal denied.

NOTES

1. A Florida statute illustrates a typical right of eminent domain conferred upon a school district. "There is conferred upon the county board in each of the several counties in the state the authority and right to take private property for any public school purpose or use when, in the opinion of the county board, such property is needed in the operation of any or all of the public schools within the county, including property needed for any school purpose or use in any school district or districts within the county. The absolute fee simple title to all property so taken and acquired shall vest in the county board of such county unless the county board seeks to appropriate a particular right or estate in such property." F.S.A. § 235.05.

2. Where a school district takes property by condemnation, and the statutes do not require title to be taken in fee simple, the courts have held that a school district obtains only an easement or a qualified fee. The court in a Pennsylvania case held that under a condemnation proceeding: "whatever kind of right, estate, or easement, the school district acquired, terminated when it ceased to use it for the purpose for which the land was

appropriated, and the title reverted to the original owner or those who hold under him." Lazarus v. Morris, 212 Pa. 128, 61 A. 815 (1905).

3. In order to condemn property boards of education must show that the property will be used for a public school use. An Alabama court has held that an administrative building for the school superintendent and his staff constitutes a public use and falls within statutory provisions that provide for condemnation for "other public school purposes." Smith v. City Board of Education of Birmingham, 272 Ala. 227, 130 So.2d 29 (1961).

4. The prevailing view is that one public agency may condemn property belonging to another public agency if a "more necessary need" exists. In a case illustrating this view, the Supreme Court of North Dakota held that "the convenience to the public arising out of the use of certain property as a school site and grounds exceeded the convenience to the public arising from the use as a park." Board of Education of Minot v. Park District of Minot, N.D., 70 N.W.2d 899 (1955). A Massachusetts court held that school property could be taken for use as a public road. The court weighed the need for the road against the harm incurred and ruled that the road was the "more necessary need." The court said in part: "there is much greater freedom of choice as to where a schoolhouse shall be put than where roads shall run . . . ." Easthampton v. County Commissioners of Hampshire, 154 Mass. 424, 28 N.E. 298 (1891).

5. In a case illustrating the use of fair market value as the measure of damages, a school board in Louisiana contested a court's valuation of a condemned tract of land. The jury had assessed a value of $1,200 for a school site of 5.9 acres. On appeal, the board showed that similar land in the neighborhood was selling for from $5.00 to $25.00 per acre. Based on this evidence the total award was reduced to $300.00. Ouachita Parish School Board v. Clark, 197 La. 131, 1 So.2d 54 (1941).

6. Under condemnation procedures, the usual redress open to a landowner is an action to recover compensation and damages for the loss of property. The award to the owner is usually based on the appraised fair market value of property. However, some courts have used other measures such as the "substitute facility approach" in condemnation of special purpose property. For example, where a highway intersects a school campus, cutting growth potential or isolating a building, the courts may apply this alternative standard. Department of Highways v. City of Winchester, 431 S.W.2d 707 (Ky.1968). The United States Supreme Court has said: "we are not to make a fetish of market value 'since it may not be the best measure of value in some cases'. Where the highest and best use of the property is for municipal or governmental purposes, as to which no market value properly exists, some other method of arriving at just compensation must be adopted, and the cost of providing property in substitution for the property taken may reasonably be the basis of the award." United States v. Cors, 337 U.S. 325, 69 S.Ct. 1086 (1949).

ADVERSE POSSESSION

Adverse possession is a means of acquiring property that is of occasional concern to school district authorities. All states have statutes that limit the times during which certain actions may be brought. These are called statutes of limitation and apply not only to matters concerning property but to other areas of law such as actions for contracts under seal, actions for wrongful death, and actions for liability for torts. Statutes of limitation for recovery of property have particular significance because the running of the statutes has not only procedural but also proprietary significance. In other words, if the statute of limitation for recovery of possession of property is twenty years and the owner of the land does not initiate an action within this time against someone in actual open possession of the property, the owner loses his title to the land, his right of action is dead, and the person in possession of the property acquires title. However, in order to gain title to property by adverse possession the occupant must exercise dominion over the property in a manner that is actual, uninterrupted, open, notorious, hostile, and exclusive, with a claim of ownership such as will notify parties seeking information that the property is not held in subordination to any claim by others, but is held against all titles and claims.[4]

*Party Seeking to Acquire Property By
Adverse Possession Must Establish an
Open, Notorious, and Hostile Claim*

LOVEJOY v. SCHOOL DISTRICT NO. 46 OF SEDGWICK COUNTY

Supreme Court of Colorado, 1954.
129 Colo. 306, 269 P.2d 1067.

HOLLAND, Justice.   . . .

The sole question here involved is whether or not the district, by being in possession and holding school on the premises for a long period of time more than the statutory period of eighteen years, was entitled to possession and to have title quieted in it by adverse possession.

The fact that the district had established a school on the land involved about the year 1886, and that there had been continuously conducted a school thereon until the year 1947, is not disputed. The proof offered by the School District lacks any showing of a clear, positive and unequivocal act on the part of the district during any of the time involved that would disclose its claim or right to the land by adverse possession. Mere occupancy alone seems to be relied upon until after the spring of 1947, when a question arose between Phyllis Lovejoy, the fee owner of the quarter section, and District No. 68 as to the ownership of the building. Since the building was a permanent fixture, she authorized her attorney, on April 30, 1951, to write the president of School District No. 68, requesting the Board to remove the school building. This incident was notice to the District that she claimed ownership of the land, and there appears no denial of her claim at that time.

If the District then claimed ownership of the land, there then was an open opportunity for it to assert such claim of ownership; however, it consulted an attorney and then decided to claim ownership by adverse possession. By such action, a strong presumption follows that the School District, in effect, admitted that its claim was not open, hostile and notorious, as is necessary in reliance upon adverse possession.

Numerous witnesses, of the community, were called by plaintiff, some of whom had resided there for many years, and one in particular who attended the second term of school in 1887. None of the witnesses could recall any incident whereby it was known that the District claimed ownership to the land, but all were of the same positive impression that the District owned the building. . . .

The very essence of adverse possession is that the possession must be hostile, not only against the true owner, but against the world as well. An adverse claim must be hostile at its inception, because, if the original entry is not openly hostile or adverse, it does not become so, and the statute does not begin to run as against a rightful owner until the adverse claimant disavows the idea of holding for, or in subservience to another, it actually sets up an exclusive right in himself by some clear, positive and unequivocal act. The character of the possession must become hostile in order that it may be deemed to be adverse. And this hostility must continue for the full statutory period. 1 Am.Jur., p. 871, § 137. The statute begins to run at the time the possession of the claimant becomes adverse to that of the owner, and this occurs when the claimant sets up title in himself, by some clear, positive and unequivocal act.

No one representing School District No. 68 ever asserted that the District owned the land until immediately before the commencement of this action. The District, without color of title to possession, had to be in possession under an open and notorious claim of ownership. Under the circumstances here, mere occupancy was not sufficient to put any of the true owners on notice that the District claimed the land, and the burden of proof, as to open, notorious and hostile claim, is upon the District when it claims title by adverse possession without color of title. Every reasonable presumption is made in favor of the true owner as against adverse possession. Evans v. Welch, 29 Colo. 355, 68 P. 776.

In support of the general trend of the testimony that is was never known that the District claimed the land, only the building, it is to be noted that the District first claimed that it had a full acre after that time a right of way ditch cut across the corner of the section, which left an area of more than two acres, and the school land up to the ditch as a playground, and the fences along the ditch were not shown to have been placed there by the School District. Had the District been making a claim to the ground, it follows that there would have been no uncertainty as to the extent and boundaries thereof. The school board knew almost two years before this suit was commenced that Phyllis Lovejoy claimed ownership of the land when she asked them to remove the building. If originally this was a case of permission to use the ground, it would be in subordination to the title and here the burden was upon the District to prove that such notice was given, which it failed to meet.

There is no reason to discuss the question of the judgment for damages, since our determination of the rights of the parties involved necessitates a reversal of the judgment, and that the complaint be dismissed.

The judgment is reversed and the cause remanded with direction to the trial court to dismiss the complaint.

NOTES

1. Adverse possession must be open, visible, continuous, and exclusive, with a claim of ownership, such as will notify parties seeking information upon the subject that the premises are not held in subordination to any claim of others, but against all titles and claimants.

    The placing of a permanent school building and other necessary appendages on the land of another, and conducting school . . . thereon is evidence of adverse and hostile possession under which title may be claimed after fifteen years. Liles v. Smith, 206 Okl. 458, 244 P.2d 582 (1952).

2. A court in Wyoming had this to say about adverse possession and its relationship to title by the true owner: "the general rule in the United States is that possession will be presumed to be in subservience to the title of the true owner, and that the burden to prove adverse possession is upon the party who relies thereon. 2 C.J. 264. These rules, however, must be construed in the light of other rules, which have been adopted by our courts. Thus the intention to claim may be manifested either by words, or by acts . . . . Further, the term 'claim of right' has been treated as the equivalent of a hostile claim. (Citing authorities). The character of possession may give rise to a presumption, and it is generally held that the actual occupation, use, and improvement of the premises of the claimant as if he were in fact the owner thereof will, in the absence of explanatory circumstances showing the contrary, be sufficient to raise a presumption of his entry and holding as absolute owner, and, unless rebutted, will establish the fact of a claim of right. (Citing authorities). . . . Thus it is said in the last case cited:

    All reasonable presumptions are to be made in favor of the true owners, including the presumption that actual possession is subordinate to the right of the true owner, subject, however, to the limitation that actual, continuous, exclusive possession for the statutory period, unexplained, displaces a presumption in favor of the true owner and creates a presumption of fact that such possession, and the commencement of it, were characterized by all the requisites to title by adverse possession. (Emphasis added.)"

    City of Rock Springs v. Sturm, 39 Wyo. 494, 273 P. 908 (1929).

REVERSION OF SCHOOL PROPERTY

Conveyance of land may be made to school districts upon the same rules of future interests as a similar transaction between private persons. Under common law, the only way a fee simple estate could be created was by the use of the words, "and his heirs" or "and their heirs." However, under modern statutes, these words of inheritance are not necessary to create a fee simple estate. The name of the grantee only is sufficient to take a fee simple estate unless a lesser estate is described.[5]

When a school district acquires property and the words used in the conveyance are, "to X school district" or to "X school district and his heirs," and the grantor does not indicate a lesser estate, the school district obtains title in fee simple absolute. A fee simple absolute estate is the largest, exclusive, and most extensive interest that can be enjoyed in land. It is an estate when lands are given to a man or, in our case, a school district, and to his heirs absolutely without limit or end.[6]

However, many times grantors who convey property to school districts for school purposes desire that the land will sooner or later revert to them when it is no longer used for school purposes. In such cases, deeds making the conveyances of land must be unmistakably clear as to their intent; without sufficient clarity the courts will not permit a reversion. A New Jersey court had this to say about the interpretation of such deeds: "Conditions, when they tend to destroy estates, are stricti juris and to be construed strictly . . . . Conditions subsequent, especially when relied upon to work a forfeiture, must be created by express terms or clear implication, and are strictly construed . . . ."[7]

The condition subsequent of which the court speaks is a determinable fee the limitations of which are usually identified by the words "so long as," "until," "while," or "during." An example of such a condition is: A, fee simple owner, conveys Blackacre to school district for so long as said property is used for school purposes. In this case the school district has a determinable fee simple and A has a possibility of reverter.

In a case in which land was conveyed to a school district "for school purposes only," it was contended that the property should revert to the grantor when it was no longer used for school purposes. The court held that the words "for school purposes only" were neither preceded nor followed by words on condition such as those listed above. The court said: "The words upon which the appellant relies as debasing the fee are merely superfluous and not expressive of any intention of the parties to the conveyance as to the effect to be given to it."[8] In this case, the clause merely duplicated a limitation that was already imposed on school property anyway.

The following case discusses the relationship between the grantor and the school district when conditions subsequent exist or are alleged to exist.

*Reversionary Interest Does Not Come
into Play as Long as Property Is Used
for School Purposes*

WILLIAMS v. McKENZIE
Court of Appeals of Kentucky, 1924.
203 Ky. 376, 262 S.W. 598.

TURNER, C. On the 29th of August, 1895, appellee, W.H. McKenzie, and one Melvin Fyffe conveyed to the trustees of common school district No. 8 of Johnson county a tract of land of less than one acre, about one-half of which was from the property of appellee, and the other half from that of Fyffe.

The conveyance was made "in consideration of their respect for the system of common schools of Johnson county," and was absolute on its face except as hereinafter pointed out. The habendum clause is:

> To have and to hold the same, with all the appurtenances thereon, to the second party and their heirs and assigns forever, with covenants of general warranty.

However, after the description of the property there is appended the following:

> It is expressly understood that the aforesaid property is to belong to the aforesaid school district so long as it is used for common school purposes, but whenever the same is no longer so used it is to revert back to the parties of the first part, and the party of the second part is to have the right to remove the school building and fixtures on said premises.

As indicated in the face of the instrument, the property conveyed had been probably for some years before the conveyance used for school purposes; at any rate, a schoolhouse was erected on it, and it has been continuously used for school purposes at all times since that day, and is yet so used.

Thereafter by operation of law the title so held by the common school district became vested in the county board of education, and in November, 1920, the board of education, in consideration of $50 and the customary royalty, leased the same for oil and gas development to the appellant Junior Oil Company. Thereafter the latter under the lease drilled a well on that part of the school lot formerly belonging to appellee, McKenzie, and brought in thereon a producing oil well, whereupon, in December, 1921, McKenzie instituted this equitable action seeking to cancel the deed of August, 1895, and the lease so made by the board and to have it adjudged the title thereto was in him, and to enjoin the oil company from entering upon the same, or using or claiming the same, and asking for an accounting for the oil taken therefrom.

The original petition alleges, in substance, that the board of education had no right or authority to make the lease to the oil company for oil and gas development, and that the oil company had moved onto the property for the purpose of developing the same for such purposes, and asserting the right so to do, whereby a cloud was cast upon plaintiff's title. It is further alleged that the board of education had title to such lot only for the purpose of conducting thereon a common school for educational purposes, and that the conversion of same by it to commercial purposes was equivalent to an abandonment by it of the original purpose for which the grant was made, and by such acts it abandoned the property for the original purpose, whereby the title to same reverted to plaintiff. . . .

It will be observed that by the deed of August, 1895, appellee parted with his whole interest in the property. He made no reservation or exception, nor was there a condition or restriction of any nature upon the present title conveyed. He only provided that the title so conveyed should revert to him in the uncertain event that the property should ever cease to be used for common school purposes. He provided only for a mere possible reverter to himself if the property should ever cease to be used for such purposes. The questions, therefore, which it seems necessary to determine, are:

1. What estate did the grantees take in the deed of 1895, and what are their rights in the property while the same is still being used for common school purposes?

2. What estate, if any, remains in the grantor under that deed while the same continues to be used for common school purposes, and has he such a right or interest during that time as authorizes him to maintain an action for waste?

3. Have school authorities owning property in use for school purposes the right or power to lease the same for mineral development purposes, the funds, if any, derived therefrom to be used for schools?

Questions 1 and 2 are in effect one and the same, for, if the grantees in the deed took such estate as entitles them to the unrestricted use of the property before the reversion provided for takes place, then it is clear there is no such right or estate left in the grantor as entitles him to maintain an action for waste.

The grantor clearly parted with his whole present interest, and after parting with it engrafts upon the estate conveyed a possible reversionary interest in himself if the property should ever cease to be used for common school purposes, which is manifestly a thing which may or may never happen. The thing which will operate as a reversion in the grantor is and can be only the action of the grantees themselves or their successors in title.

A qualified or determinable fee is defined in 10 R.C.L. 652, as follows:

> A qualified or determinable fee is an estate limited to a person and his heirs, with a qualification annexed to it by which it is provided that it must determine whenever that qualification is at an end. Because the estate may last forever it is a fee; and because it may end on the happening of the event it is called a determinable or qualified fee.

Such an estate is defined in 21 C.J. 922, in the following way:

> Although distinctions have been made or discussed by some authorities, the terms "base fee," "qualified fee" and "determinable fee" are generally used interchangeably to denote a fee which has a qualification subjoined thereto, and which must be determined whenever the qualification annexed to it is at an end. This estate is a fee, because by possibility it may endure forever in a man and his heirs; yet as that duration depends upon the concurrence of collateral circumstances which qualify and debase the purity of the donation it is therefore a qualified or base fee.

Manifestly the estate passing under the deed in question is embraced by these definitions. The grantor parted with all present interest in the property, and conveyed it to the grantees without limitation or restriction of title, with the lone qualification that, if it should ever cease to be used for common school purposes, the title should revert to him. In conveying such a title, with no other limitation or restriction, the grantor not only divests himself of all present title, but places the unlimited and unrestricted use and occupation of the property in his grantee until such time, if ever, the event happens which will determine the estate conveyed. Such an estate, being one which may last forever, is from necessity such as carries with it the unlimited right to use and control the property at all times before the happening of the event which will end the estate.

As said by Mr. Washburn (4th Ed. vol. 1, p. 89) in discussing the incidents of a determinable fee:

> So long as the estate in fee remains the owner in possession has all the rights in respect to it which he would have if tenant in fee simple, unless it be so limited that there is properly a reversionary right in another—something more than a possibility of reverter belonging to a third person, when, perhaps, chancery might interpose to prevent waste of the premises.

This quotation from Mr. Washburn was approved by this court in the case of Landers v. Landers, 151 Ky. 206, 151 S.W. 386. Ann.Cas.1915A, 223, and the court in that case held there was no equitable waste where one only used the property in such way a prudent man would have used his own.

In 21 C.J. 923, in discussing the incidents of such an estate, it is said:

> Until its determination such an estate has all the incidents of a fee simple; and, while this estate continues, and until the qualification upon which it is limited is at an end, the grantee or proprietor had the same rights and privileges over his estate as if it was a fee simple. He has an absolute right to the exclusive possession, use, and enjoyment of the land, and has complete dominion over it all for purposes as though he held it in fee simple.

. . . the holder of a determinable fee before its determination has all the rights of a fee simple title holder, and that the holder of a mere possible estate in reversion has not sufficient right or interest in the property to authorize him to maintain an action for waste [citations].

The property in this case has been used for school purposes now for thirty years or more, and there is nothing in the pleadings or evidence to suggest any purpose upon the part of the school authorities to abandon its use for such purpose, and consequently there is nothing to indicate that the title conveyed to the school trustees will at any time in the near future be determined by the cessation of the use of the property for such purposes.

Appellee, however, relies upon a certain class of cases holding that, where property has been conveyed for school purposes and a reversionary clause is inserted, its use for other purposes works a forfeiture of the original grant, and the reversion takes place. But that class of cases has no application here whatsoever, for the very plain and sufficient reason that the property here is not being used for other than school purposes, or in any such way as to interfere with the efficient and orderly administration of the school. There is no allegation that the oil development has or will so interfere with the school; and, even if there was, appellee, who is not now a resident of the school district, is not in position to make that question.

But it is earnestly argued that, the county board of education being the creature of the statute for a specific purpose, its only duty and authority lies in the administration of educational affairs; that it is not authorized to go into the field of speculation and engage in hazardous industrial affairs, even though such activities might result profitably, and for that reason alone the oil lease given by the school board was invalid and properly cancelled. In the first place, the mere leasing of its property to others for development purposes is not engaging in a commercial venture, but is, properly speaking, only an effort to get from its property the real values therefrom, to the end that there may be a more efficient administration of school affairs.

In support of this argument reliance is had upon the case of Herald v. Board of Education, 65 W.Va. 765, 65 S.E. 102, 31 L.R.A. (N.S.) 588. In that case it was held by a majority of the Supreme Court of West Virginia that a school board under the statutes of that state had no power to lease a schoolhouse lot for oil and gas purposes, even though the school authorities had the absolute fee simple title thereto.

Under the provisions of section 4437, Ky.Stats., 1915 Ed., which was in effect at the time the deed was made from appellee to the school board, such school trustees were authorized to "take, hold and dispose of real and personal estate for the maintenance, use and benefit of the common school of their district." . . .

Oil and gas are fugitive minerals; they are connected by underground streams or crevices by which they may be drained from one property onto another, and there brought to the surface. There can be no sound or practical reason given that will deprive school authorities who own property under which there are valuable minerals from entering into contracts for its development, and particularly would this seem to be true when the character of the mineral is such that adjoining landowners may profit at the expense of the school property by the failure of the school authorities to enter into such contracts. It is shown in this record that there are on adjoining lands other producing oil wells very near to the property lines of the school lot, and it is perfectly apparent that if the well on the school lot had not been drilled the oil on the school lot would soon have been drained from it by such wells, and the school authorities would have thereby been deprived of the chief wealth on the property to which they had title for the benefit of the school. There was, however, in the West Virginia case referred to, a strong dissenting opinion, in which we fully concur. That opinion, after discussing the West Virginia statute, said:

> I think the statute not only expressly but impliedly gives this board ample power to lease this property. This ought especially to be so where the product, as in this case, is oil and gas, fugitive in nature and which will be drained and carried away by operations on adjoining lands.

We are of the opinion, therefore, that under the statute in existence at the time the title was conveyed to the school authorities the board of education had the right to execute the lease in question, and, having the right to do so, it was its duty to do so to prevent the valuable mineral product on the school property from being appropriated by others.

The views which we have here expressed make it unnecessary to discuss the other questions presented.

The judgment is reversed, with directions to set aside the judgment entered, to dismiss the plaintiff's petition, and on the counterclaim and cross-petition to quiet the present title of the school board and to enjoin appellee from further claiming any present right or interest in the school lot.

Whole court sitting.

NOTES

1. Whether a board of education by conveyance obtains a fee simple title or some type of defeasible fee is explained by the Kentucky Court of Appeals.

When a limitation merely states the purpose for which the land is conveyed, such limitation usually does not indicate an intent to create an estate in fee simple which is to expire automatically upon the cessation of use for the purpose named. Additional facts, however, can cause such an intent to be found. Among the facts sufficient to have this result are clauses in other parts of the same instrument, the relation between the consideration paid for the conveyance and the market value of the land in question, and the situation under which the conveyance was obtained. Scott County Board of Education v. Pepper, 311 S.W.2d 189 (Ky.1958).

2. Property obtained by a school district with a fee simple determinable provision in the deed providing that if the land is abandoned and "not used for school purposes" then property reverts was held sufficient to take the property from the school district when the property was no longer in use. School District No. Six in County of Weld v. Russell, 156 Colo. 75, 396 P.2d 929 (1964).

3. Can property with a reversionary interest be transferred from one school district to another in case of a merger of two or more school districts? See School District No. Six in County of Weld v. Russell, supra.

4. Does B have an estate in fee simple absolute or in fee simple determinable in the following situation? A, owning Blackacre in fee simple absolute, transfers Blackacre to B and his heirs to and for the use of C school district and for no other purpose. Scott County Board of Education v. Pepper, 311 S.W.2d 189 (Ky.1958).

Footnotes

1. Carson v. State, 27 Ind. 465 (1867).
2. In re Bd. of Public Inst. of Alachua County, 160 Fla. 490, 35 So.2d 579 (1948).
3. Wilson v. Graves County Board of Education, 307 Ky. 203, 210 S.W.2d 350 (1948).
4. Liles v. Smith, 206 Okl. 458, 244 P.2d 582 (1952).
5. Smith, Chester H., *Survey of the Law of Real Property*, (St. Paul, MN: West Pub. Co., 1956), p. 85.
6. *Black's Law Dictionary*, Revised Fourth Edition, (St. Paul, MN: West Pub. Co., 1968), p. 742.
7. Board of Education of Borough of West Paterson v. Brophy, 90 N.J. 57, 106 A. 32 (1919).
8. Phillips Gas and Oil Co. v. Lingenfelter, 262 Pa. 500, 105 A. 888 (1919).

Selected Constitutional Provisions

THE CONSTITUTION OF THE UNITED STATES

Amendment I

Congress shall make no law respecting an establishment of religion, or prohibiting the free exercise thereof; or abridging the freedom of speech, or of the press; or the right of the people peaceably to assemble, and to petition the Government for a redress of grievances.

Amendment IV

The right of the people to be secure in their persons, houses, papers, and effects, against unreasonable searches and seizures, shall not be violated, and no Warrants shall issue, but upon probable cause, supported by Oath or affirmation, and particularly describing the place to be searched, and the persons or things to be seized.

Amendment V

No person shall be held to answer for a capital or otherwise infamous crime, unless on a presentment of indictment of a Grand Jury, except in cases arising in the land or naval forces, or in the Militia, when in time of War or public danger; nor shall any person be subject to the same offense to be twice put in jeopardy of life or limb; nor shall be compelled in any criminal case to be a witness against himself, nor be deprived of life, liberty or property, without due process of law; nor shall private property be taken for public use, without just compensation.

Amendment VIII

Excessive bail shall not be required, nor excessive fines imposed, nor cruel and unusual punishments inflicted.

Amendment X

The powers not delegated to the United States by the Constitution, nor prohibited by it to the States, are reserved to the States respectively, or to the people.

Amendment XIV

Section 1. All persons born or naturalized in the United States, and subject to the jurisdiction thereof, are citizens of the United States and of the State wherein they reside. No state shall make or enforce any law which shall abridge the privileges or immunities of citizens of the United States; nor shall any State deprive any person of life, liberty, or property, without due process of law; nor deny to any person within its jurisdiction the equal protection of the laws.

Section 2. Representatives shall be apportioned among the several States according to their respective number, counting the whole number of persons in each state, excluding Indians not taxed. But when the right to vote at any election for the choice of electors for President and Vice President of the United States, Representatives in Congress, the Executive and Judicial officers of a State, or the members of the Legislature thereof, is denied any of the male inhabitants of such State, being twenty-one years of age, and citizens of the United States, or in any way abridged, except for participation in rebellion, or other crime, the basis of representation therein shall be reduced in the proportion which the number of such male citizens shall bear to the number of male citizens twenty-one years of age in such State. . . .

Section 5. The Congress shall have power to enforce, by appropriate legislation, the provisions of the article.

Selected Federal Statutes

CIVIL RIGHTS ACT OF 1964
TITLE VI (Selected Parts)
42 U.S.C.A. §§ 2000d—d-1

FEDERALLY ASSISTED PROGRAMS

§ 2000d. Prohibition against exclusion from participation in, denial of benefits of, and discrimination under Federally assisted programs on ground of race, color, or national origin

No person in the United States shall, on the ground of race, color, or national origin, be excluded from participation in, be denied the benefits of, or be subjected to discrimination under any program or activity receiving Federal financial assistance.

Pub.L. 88–352, Title VI, § 601, July 2, 1964, 78 Stat. 252.

§ 2000d–1. Federal authority and financial assistance to programs or activities by way of grant, loan, or contract other than contract of insurance or guaranty; rules and regulations; approval by President; compliance with requirements; reports to Congressional committees; effective date of administrative action

Each Federal department and agency which is empowered to extend Federal financial assistance to any program or activity, by way of grant, loan, or contract other than a contract of insurance or guaranty, is authorized and directed to effectuate the provisions of section 2000d of this title with respect to such program or activity by issuing rules, regulations, or orders of general applicability which shall be consistent with achievement of the objectives of the statute authorizing the financial assistance in connection with which the action is taken. No such rule, regulation, or order shall become effective unless and until approved by the President. Compliance with any requirement adopted pursuant to this section may be effected (1) by the termination of or refusal to grant or to continue assistance under such program or activity to any recipient as to whom there has been an express finding on the record, after opportunity for hearing, of a failure to comply with such requirement, but such termination or refusal shall be limited to the particular political entity, or part thereof, or other recipient as to whom such a finding has been made and, shall be limited in its effect to the particular program, or part thereof, in which such noncompliance has been so found, or (2) by any other means authorized by law: *Provided, however,* That no such action shall be taken until the department or agency concerned has advised the appropriate person or persons of the failure to comply with the requirement and has determined that compliance cannot be secured by voluntary means. In the case of any action terminating, or refusing to grant or continue, assistance because of failure to comply with a requirement imposed pursuant to this section, the head of the Federal department or agency shall file with the committees of the House and Senate having legislative jurisdiction over the program or activity involved a full written report of the circumstances and the grounds for such action. No such action shall become effective until thirty days have elapsed after the filing of such report.

Pub.L. 88–352, Title VI, § 602, July 2, 1964, 78 Stat. 252.

CIVIL RIGHTS ACT OF 1964
TITLE VII (Selected Parts)
42 U.S.C.A. § 2000e—e-2

EQUAL EMPLOYMENT OPPORTUNITIES

§ 2000e-2. Unlawful employment practices

Employer practices

(a) It shall be an unlawful employment practice for an employer—

(1) to fail or refuse to hire or to discharge any individual, or otherwise to discriminate against any individual with respect to his compensation, terms, conditions, or privileges of employment, because of such individual's race, color, religion, sex, or national origin; or

(2) to limit, segregate, or classify his employees or applicants for employment in any way which would deprive or tend to deprive any individual of employment opportunities or otherwise adversely affect his status as an employee, because of such individual's race, color, religion, sex, or national origin.

Employment agency practices

(b) It shall be an unlawful employment practice for an employment agency to fail or refuse to refer for employment, or otherwise to discriminate against, any individual because of his race, color, religion, sex, or national origin, or to classify or refer for employment any individual on the basis of his race, color, religion, sex, or national origin. . . .

Training programs

(d) It shall be an unlawful employment practice for any employer, labor organization, or joint labor-management committee controlling apprenticeship or other training or retraining, including on-the-job training programs to discriminate against any individual because of his race, color, religion, sex, or national origin in admission to, or employment in, any program established to provide apprenticeship or other training.

Businesses or enterprises with personnel qualified on basis of religion, sex, or national origin; educational institutions with personnel of particular religion

(e) Notwithstanding any other provision of this subchapter, (1) it shall not be an unlawful employment practice for an employer to hire and employ employees, for an employment agency to classify, or refer for employment any individual, for a labor organization to classify its membership or to classify or refer for employment any individual, or for an employer, labor organization, or joint labor-management committee controlling apprenticeship or other training or retraining programs to admit or employ any individual in any such program, on the basis of his religion, sex, or national origin in those certain instances where religion, sex, or national origin is a bona fide occupational qualification reasonably necessary to the normal operation of that particular business or enterprise, and (2) it shall not be an unlawful employment practice for a school, college, university, or other educational institution or institution of learning to hire and employ employees of a particular religion if such school, college, university, or other educational institution or institution of learning is, in whole or in substantial part, owned, supported, controlled, or managed by a particular religion or by a particular religious corporation, association, or society, or if the curriculum of such school, college, university, or other educational institution or institution of learning is directed toward the propagation of a particular religion. . . .

Seniority or merit system; quantity or quality of production; ability tests; compensation based on sex and authorized by minimum wage provisions

(h) Notwithstanding any other provision of this subchapter, it shall not be an unlawful employment practice for an employer to apply different standards of compensation, or different terms, conditions, or privileges of employment pursuant to a bona fide seniority or merit system, or a system which measures earnings by quantity or quality of production or to employees who work in different locations, provided that such differences are not the result of an intention to discriminate because of race, color, religion, sex, or national origin, nor shall it be an unlawful employment practice for an employer to give and to act upon the results of any professionally developed ability test provided that such test, its administration or action upon the results is not designed, intended or used to discriminate because of race, color, religion, sex or national origin. It shall not be an unlawful employment practice under this subchapter for any employer to differentiate upon the basis of sex in determining the amount of the wages or compensation paid or to be paid to employees of such employer if such differentiation is authorized by the provisions of section 206(d) of Title 29. . . .

Preferential treatment not to be granted on account of existing number or percentage imbalance

(j) Nothing contained in this subchapter shall be interpreted to require any employ-

er, employment agency, labor organization, or joint labor-management committee subject to this subchapter to grant preferential treatment to any individual or to any group because of the race, color, religion, sex, or national origin of such individual or group on account of an imbalance which may exist with respect to the total number or percentage of persons of any race, color, religion, sex, or national origin employed by any employer, referred or classified for employment by any employment agency or labor organization, admitted to membership or classified by any labor organization, or admitted to, or employed in, any apprenticeship or other training program, in comparison with the total number or percentage of persons of such race, color, religion, sex, or national origin in any community, State, section, or other area, or in the available work force in any community, State, section, or other area.

Pub.L. 88–352, Title VII, § 703, July 2, 1964, 78 Stat. 255; Pub.L. 92–261, § 8(a), (b), Mar. 24, 1972, 86 Stat. 109.

DISCRIMINATION BASED ON SEX TITLE IX (Selected Parts) 20 U.S.C.A. § 1681

§ 1681. Sex

Prohibition against discrimination; exceptions

(a) No person in the United States shall, on the basis of sex, be excluded from participation in, be denied the benefits of, or be subjected to discrimination under any education program or activity receiving Federal financial assistance, except that:

Classes of educational institutions subject to prohibition

(1) in regard to admissions to educational institutions, this section shall apply only to institutions of vocational education, professional education, and graduate higher education, and to public institutions of undergraduate higher education;

Educational institutions commencing planned change in admissions

(2) in regard to admissions to educational institutions, this section shall not apply (A) for one year from June 23, 1972, nor for six years after June 23, 1972, in the case of an educational institution which has begun the process of changing from being an institution which admits only students of one sex to being an institution which admits students of both sexes, but only if it is carrying out a plan for such a change which is approved by the Commissioner of Education or (B) for seven years from the date an educational institution begins the process of changing from being an institution which admits only students of only one sex to being an institution which admits students of both sexes, but only if it is carrying out a plan for such a change which is approved by the Commissioner of Education, whichever is the later;

Educational institutions of religious organizations with contrary religious tenets

(3) this section shall not apply to an educational institution which is controlled by a religious organization if the application of this subsection would not be consistent with the religious tenets of such organization;

Educational institutions training individuals for military services or merchant marine

(4) this section shall not apply to an educational institution whose primary purpose is the training of individuals for the military services of the United States, or the merchant marine;

Public educational institutions with traditional and continuing admissions policy

(5) in regard to admissions this section shall not apply to any public institution of undergraduate higher eduation which is an institution that traditionally and continual-ly from its establishment has had a policy of admitting only students of one sex;

Social fraternities or sororities; voluntary youth service organizations

(6) this section shall not apply to membership practices—

(A) of a social fraternity or social sorority which is exempt from taxation under section 501(a) of Title 26, the active membership of which consists primarily of students in attendance at an institution of higher education, or

(b) of the Young Men's Christian Association, Young Women's Christian Association, Girl Scouts, Boy Scouts, Camp Fire Girls, and voluntary youth service organizations which are so exempt, the membership of which has traditionally been limited to persons of one sex and principally to persons of less than nineteen years of age;

Boy or Girl conferences

(7) this section shall not apply to—

(A) any program or activity of the American Legion undertaken in connection with the organization or operation of any Boys State conference, Boys Nation conference, Girls State conference, or Girls Nation conference; or

(B) any program or activity of any secondary school or educational institution specifically for—

(i) the promotion of any Boys State conference, Boys Nation conference, Girls State conference, or Girls Nation conference; or

(ii) the selection of students to attend any such conference;

Father-son or mother-daughter activities at educational institutions

(8) this section shall not preclude father-son or mother-daughter activities at an educational institution, but if such activities are provided for students of one sex, opportunities for reasonably comparable

activities shall be provided for students of the other sex; and

Institution of higher education scholarship awards in "beauty" pageants

(9) this section shall not apply with respect to any scholarship or other financial assistance awarded by an institution of higher education to any individual because such individual has received such award in any pageant in which the attainment of such award is based upon a combination of factors related to the personal appearance, poise, and talent of such individual and in which participation is limited to individuals of one sex only, so long as such pageant is in compliance with other non-discrimination provisions of Federal law.

Preferential or disparate treatment because of imbalance in participation or receipt of Federal benefits; statistical evidence of imbalance

(b) Nothing contained in subsection (a) of this section shall be interpreted to require any educational institution to grant preferential or disparate treatment to the members of one sex on account of an imbalance which may exist with respect to the total number or percentage of persons of that sex participating in or receiving the benefits of any federally supported program or activity, in comparison with the total number or percentage of persons of that sex in any community, State, section, or other area: *Provided*, That this subsection shall not be construed to prevent the consideration in any hearing or proceeding under this chapter of statistical evidence tending to show that such an imbalance exists with respect to the participation in, or receipt of the benefits of, any such program or activity by the members of one sex.

Educational institution defined

(c) For purposes of this chapter an educational institution means any public or private preschool, elementary, or secondary school, or any institution of vocational, professional, or higher education, except that in the case of an educational institution composed of more than one school, college, or department which are administratively separate units, such term means each such school, college, or department.

Pub.L. 92–318, Title IX, § 901, June 23, 1972, 86 Stat. 373; Pub.L. 93–568, § 3(a), Dec. 31, 1974, 88 Stat. 1862; Pub.L. 94–482, Title IV, § 412(a), Oct. 12, 1976, 90 Stat. 2234.

EQUAL PAY ACT (Selected Parts) 29 U.S.C.A. § 206

§ 206. Minimum wage

Prohibition of sex discrimination

(d)(1) No employer having employees subject to any provisions of this section shall discriminate, within any establishment in which such employees are employed, between employees on the basis of sex by paying wages to employees in such establishment at a rate less than the rate at which he pays wages to employees of the opposite sex in such establishment for equal work on jobs the performance of which requires equal skill, effort, and responsibility, and which are performed under similar working conditions, except where such payment is made pursuant to (i) a seniority system; (ii) a merit system; (iii) a system which measures earnings by quantity or quality of production; or (iv) a differential based on any other factor other than sex: *Provided*, That an employer who is paying a wage rate differential in violation of this subsection shall not, in order to comply with the provisions of this subsection, reduce the wage rate of any employee.

(2) No labor organization, or its agents, representing employees of an employer having employees subject to any provisions of this section shall cause or attempt to cause such an employer to discriminate

against an employee in violation of paragraph (1) of this subsection.

(3) For purposes of administration and enforcement, any amounts owing to any employee which have been withheld in violation of this subsection shall be deemed to be unpaid minimum wages or unpaid overtime compensation under this chapter.

(4) As used in this subsection, the term "labor organization" means any organization of any kind, or any agency or employee representation committee or plan, in which employees participate and which exists for the purpose, in whole or in part, of dealing with employers concerning grievances, labor disputes, wages, rates of pay, hours of employment, or conditions of work.

June 25, 1938, c. 676, § 6, 52 Stat. 1062; June 26, 1940, c. 432, § 3(e), (f), 54 Stat. 616; Oct. 26, 1949, c. 736, § 6, 63 Stat. 912; Aug. 12, 1955, c. 867, § 3, 69 Stat. 711; Aug. 8, 1956, c. 1035, § 2, 70 Stat. 1118; May 5, 1961, Pub.L. 87–30, § 5, 75 Stat. 67; June 10, 1963, Pub.L. 88–38, § 3, 77 Stat. 56; Sept. 23, 1966, Pub.L. 89–601, Title III, §§ 301–305, 80 Stat. 838, 839, 841; Apr. 8, 1974, Pub.L. 93–259, §§ 2–4, 5(b), 7(b)(1), 88 Stat. 55, 56, 62; Nov. 1, 1977, Pub.L. 95–151, § 2(a)–(d)(2), 91 Stat. 1245, 1246.

FAMILY RIGHTS AND PRIVACY ACT (BUCKLEY AMENDMENT) (Selected Parts) 20 U.S.C.A. § 1232G

§ 1232G. Family educational and privacy rights

Conditions for availability of funds to educational agencies or institutions; inspection and review of education records; specific information to be made available; procedure for access to education records; reasonableness of time for such access; hearings; written explanations by parents; definitions

(a)(1)(A) No funds shall be made available under any applicable program to any educational agency or institution which has a policy of denying, or which effectively prevents, the parents of students who are or have been in attendance at a school of such agency or at such institution, as the case may be, the right to inspect and review the education records of their children. If any material or document in the education record of a student includes information on more than one student, the parents of one of such students shall have the right to inspect and review only such part of such material or document as relates to such student or to be informed of the specific information contained in such part of such material. Each educational agency or institution shall establish appropriate procedures for the granting of a request by parents for access to the education records of their children within a reasonable period of time, but in no case more than forty-five days after the request has been made. . . .

(2) No funds shall be made available under any applicable program to any educational agency or institution unless the parents of students who are or have been in attendance at a school of such agency or at such institution are provided an opportunity for a hearing by such agency or institution, in accordance with regulations of the Secretary, to challenge the content of such student's education records, in order to insure that the records are not inaccurate, misleading, or otherwise in violation of the privacy or other rights of students, and to provide an opportunity for the correction or deletion of any such inaccurate, misleading, or otherwise inappropriate data contained therein and to insert into such records a written explanation of the parents respecting the content of such records. . . .

Release of education records; parental consent requirement; exceptions; compliance with judicial orders and subpoenas; audit and evaluation of Federally-supported education programs; record-keeping

(b)(1) No funds shall be made available under any applicable program to any educational agency or institution which has a policy or practice of permitting the release of education records (or personally identifiable information contained therein other than directory information, as defined in paragraph (5) of subsection (a) of this section) of students without the written consent of their parents to any individual, agency, or organization, other than to the following—

(A) other school officials, including teachers within the educational institution or local educational agency who have been determined by such agency or institution to have legitimate educational interests;

(B) officials of other schools or school systems in which the student seeks or intends to enroll, upon condition that the student's parents be notified of the transfer, receive a copy of the record if desired, and have an opportunity for a hearing to challenge the content of the record;

(C) authorized representatives of (i) the Comptroller General of the United States, (ii) the Secretary, (iii) an administrative head of an education agency (as defined in section 1221e–3(c) of this title), or (iv) State educational authorities, under the conditions set forth in paragraph (3) of this subsection;

(D) in connection with a student's application for, or receipt of, financial aid;

(E) State and local officials or authorities to whom such information is specifically required to be reported or disclosed pursuant to State statute adopted prior to November 19, 1974;

(F) organizations conducting studies for, or on behalf of, educational agencies or institutions for the purpose of developing, validating, or administering predictive tests, administering student aid programs, and improving instruction, if such studies are conducted in such a manner as will not permit the personal identification of students and their parents by persons other than representatives of such organizations and such information will be destroyed when no longer needed for the purpose for which it is conducted;

(G) accrediting organizations in order to carry out their accrediting functions;

(H) parents of a dependent student of such parents, as defined in section 152 of Title 26; and

(I) subject to regulations of the Secretary, in connection with an emergency, appropriate persons if the knowledge of such information is necessary to protect the health or safety of the student or other persons.

Nothing in clause (E) of this paragraph shall prevent a State from further limiting the number or type of State or local officials who will continue to have access thereunder.

(2) No funds shall be made available under any applicable program to any educational agency or institution which has a policy or practice of releasing, or providing access to, any personally identifiable information in education records other than directory information, or as is permitted under paragraph (1) of this subsection unless—

(A) there is written consent from the student's parents specifying records to be released, the reasons for such release, and to whom, and with a copy of the records to be released to the student's parents and the student if desired by the parents, or

(B) such information is furnished in compliance with judicial order, or pursuant to any lawfully issued subpoena, upon condition that parents and the students are notified of all such orders or subpoenas in advance of the compliance therewith by the educational institution or agency. . . .

(C) With respect to this subsection, personal information shall only be transferred to a third party on the condition that such party will not permit any other party to have access to such information without the written consent of the parents of the student. . . .

Students' rather than parents' permission or consent

(d) For the purposes of this section, whenever a student has attained eighteen years of age, or is attending an institution of post-secondary education the permission or consent required of and the rights accorded to the parents of the student shall thereafter only be required of and accorded to the student. . . .

Pub.L. 90–247, Title IV, § 438, as added Pub.L. 93–380, Title V, § 513(a), Aug. 21, 1974, 88 Stat. 571, and amended Pub.L. 93–568, § 2(a), Dec. 31, 1974, 88 Stat. 1858.

§ 1232h.   Protection of pupil rights

Inspection by parents or guardians of instructional material

(a) All instructional material, including teacher's manuals, films, tapes, or other supplementary instructional material which will be used in connection with any research or experimentation program or project shall be available for inspection by the parents or guardians of the children engaged in such program or project. For the purpose of this section "research or experimentation program or project" means any program or project in any applicable program designed to explore or develop new or unproven teaching methods or techniques.

Psychiatric or psychological examinations, testing, or treatment

(b) No student shall be required, as part of any applicable program, to submit to psychiatric examination, testing, or treatment, or psychological examination, testing, or treatment, in which the primary purpose is to reveal information concerning:

(1) political affiliations;

(2) mental and psychological problems potentially embarrassing to the student or his family;

(3) sex behavior and attitudes;

(4) illegal, anti-social, self-incriminating, and demeaning behavior;

(5) critical appraisals of other individuals with whom respondents have close family relationships;

(6) legally recognized privileged and analogous relationships, such as those of lawyers, physicians, and ministers; or

(7) income (other than that required by law to determine eligibility for participation in a program or for receiving financial assistance under such program), without the prior consent of the student (if the student is an adult or emancipated minor), or in the case of unemancipated minor, without the prior written consent of the parent.

(Jan. 2, 1968, P.L. 90–247, Title IV, Part C, Subpart 2, § 439, as added Aug. 21, 1974, P.L. 93–380, Title V, § 514(a), 88 Stat. 574; Nov. 1, 1978, P.L. 95–561, Title XII, Part D, § 1250, 92 Stat. 2355.)

EDUCATION OF HANDICAPPED CHILDREN
(Selected Parts)
20 U.S.C.A. §§ 1400–1461

§ 1400.   Congressional statements and declarations . . .

§ 1401.   Definitions . . .

Purpose

(c) It is the purpose of this chapter to assure that all handicapped children have available to them, within the time periods specified in section 1412(2)(B) of this title, a free appropriate public education which emphasizes special education and related services designed to meet their unique needs, to assure that the rights of handicapped children and their parents or guardians are protected, to assist States and localities to provide for the education of all handicapped children, and to assess and assure the effectiveness of efforts to educate handicapped children.

Pub.L. 91–230, Title VI, § 601, Apr. 13, 1970, 84 Stat. 175, amended Pub.L. 94–142, § 3(a), Nov. 29, 1975, 89 Stat. 774.

As used in this chapter—. . .

(15) The term "children with specific learning disabilities" means those children who have a disorder in one or more of the basic psychological processes involved in understanding or in using language, spoken or written, which disorder may manifest itself in imperfect ability to listen, think, speak, read, write, spell, or do mathematical calculations. Such disorders include such conditions as perceptual handicaps, brain injury, minimal brain dysfunction, dyslexia, and developmental aphasia. Such term does not include children who have learning problems which are primarily the result of visual, hearing, or motor handicaps, of mental retardation, of emotional disturbance, or of environmental, cultural, or economic disadvantage.

(16) The term "special education" means specially designed instruction, at no cost to parents or guardians, to meet the unique needs of a handicapped child, including classroom instruction, instruction in physical education, home instruction, and instruction in hospitals and institutions.

(17) The term "related services" means transportation, and such developmental, corrective, and other supportive services (including speech pathology and audiology, psychological services, physical and occupational therapy, recreation, and medical and counseling services, except that such medical services shall be for diagnostic and eval-

uation purposes only) as may be required to assist a handicapped child to benefit from special education, and includes the early identification and assessment of handicapping conditions in children.

(18) The term "free appropriate public education" means special education and related services which (A) have been provided at public expense, under public supervision and direction, and without charge, (B) meet the standards of the State educational agency, (C) include an appropriate preschool, elementary, or secondary school education in the State involved, and (D) are provided in conformity with the individualized education program required under section 1414(a)(5) of this title.

(19) The term "individualized education program" means a written statement for each handicapped child developed in any meeting by a representative of the local educational agency or an intermediate educational unit who shall be qualified to provide, or supervise the provision of, specially designed instruction to meet the unique needs of handicapped children, the teacher, the parents or guardian of such child, and, whenever appropriate, such child, which statement shall include (A) a statement of the present levels of educational performance of such child, (B) a statement of annual goals, including short-term instructional objectives, (C) a statement of the specific educational services to be provided to such child, and the extent to which such child will be able to participate in regular educational programs, (D) the projected date for initiation and anticipated duration of such services, and (E) appropriate objective criteria and evaluation procedures and schedules for determining, on at least an annual basis, whether instructional objectives are being achieved.

(20) The term "excess costs" means those costs which are in excess of the average annual per student expenditure in a local educational agency during the preceding school year for an elementary or secondary school student, as may be appropriate, and which shall be computed after

deducting (A) amounts received under this subchapter or under title I or title VII of the Elementary and Secondary Education Act of 1965, and (B) any State or local funds expended for programs which would qualify for assistance under this subchapter or under such titles.

(21) The term "native language" has the meaning given that term by section 703(a)(2) of the Bilingual Education Act.

(22) The term "intermediate educational unit" means any public authority, other than a local educational agency, which is under the general supervision of a State educational agency, which is established by State law for the purpose of providing free public education on a regional basis, and which provides special education and related services to handicapped children within that State.

Pub.L. 91–230, Title VI, § 602, Apr. 13, 1970, 84 Stat. 175; Pub.L. 94–142, § 4(a), Nov. 29, 1975, 89 Stat. 775.

§ 1415. Procedural safeguards

Establishment and maintenance

(a) Any State educational agency, any local educational agency, and any intermediate educational unit which receives assistance under this subchapter shall establish and maintain procedures in accordance with subsection (b) through subsection (e) of this section to assure that handicapped children and their parents or guardians are guaranteed procedural safeguards with respect to the provision of free appropriate public education by such agencies and units.

Required procedures; hearing

(b)(1) The procedures required by this section shall include, but shall not be limited to—

(A) an opportunity for the parents or guardian of a handicapped child to examine all relevant records with respect to the identification, evaluation, and educational placement of the child, and the provision of a free appropriate public education to such child, and to obtain an independent educational evaluation of the child;

(B) procedures to protect the rights of the child whenever the parents or guardian of the child are not known, unavailable, or the child is a ward of the State, including the assignment of an individual (who shall not be an employee of the State educational agency, local educational agency, or intermediate educational unit involved in the education or care of the child) to act as a surrogate for the parents or guardian;

(C) written prior notice to the parents or guardian of the child whenever such agancy or unit—

(i) proposes to initiate or change, or

(ii) refuses to initiate or change, the identification, evaluation, or educational placement of the child or the provision of a free appropriate public education to the child;

(D) procedures designed to assure that the notice required by clause (C) fully inform the parents or guardian, in the parents' or guardian's native language, unless it clearly is not feasible to do so, of all procedures available pursuant to this section; and

(E) an opportunity to present complaints with respect to any matter relating to the identification, evaluation, or educational placement of the child, or the provision of a free appropriate public education to such child.

(2) Whenever a complaint has been received under paragraph (1) of this subsection, the parents or guardian shall have an opportunity for an impartial due process hearing which shall be conducted by the State educational agency or by the local educational agency or intermediate educational unit, as determined by State law or by the State educational agency. No hearing conducted pursuant to the requirements of this paragraph shall be conducted by an employee of such agency or unit involved in the education or care of the child.

Review of local decision by State educational agency

(c) If the hearing required in paragraph (2) of subsection (b) of this section is conducted by a local educational agency or an intermediate educational unit, any party aggrieved by the findings and decision rendered in such a hearing may appeal to the State educational agency which shall conduct an impartial review of such hearing. The officer conducting such review shall make an independent decision upon completion of such review.

Enumeration of rights accorded parties to hearings

(d) Any party to any hearing conducted pursuant to subsections (b) and (c) of this section shall be accorded (1) the right to be accompanied and advised by counsel and by individuals with special knowledge or training with respect to the problems of handicapped children, (2) the right to present evidence and confront, cross-examine, and compel the attendance of witnesses, (3) the right to a written or electronic verbatim record of such hearing, and (4) the right to written findings of fact and decisions (which findings and decisions shall also be transmitted to the advisory panel established pursuant to section 1413(a)(12) of this title).

PROTECTION OF PUPIL RIGHTS
20 U.S.Code § 1232h

Inspection by parents or guardians of instructional material

(a) All instructional material, including teacher's manuals, films, tapes, or other supplementary instructional material which will be used in connection with any research or experimentation program or project shall be available for inspection by the parents or guardians of the children engaged in such program or project. For the purpose of this section "research or experimentation program or project" means any program or project in any applicable program designed to explore or develop new or unproven teaching methods or techniques.

Psychiatric or psychological examinations, testing, or treatment

(b) No student shall be required, as part of any applicable program, to submit to psychiatric examination, testing, or treatment, or psychological examination, testing, or treatment, in which the primary purpose is to reveal information concerning:

(1) political affiliations;

(2) mental and psychological problems potentially embarrassing to the student or his family;

(3) sex behavior and attitudes;

(4) illegal, anti-social, self-incriminating and demeaning behavior;

(5) critical appraisals of other individuals with whom respondents have close family relationships;

(6) legally recognized privileged and analogous relationships, such as those of lawyers, physicians, and ministers; or

(7) income (other than that required by law to determine eligibility for participation in a program or for receiving financial assistance under such program), without the prior consent of the student (if the student is an adult or emancipated minor), or in the case of unemancipated minor, without the prior written consent of the parent.

Glossary of Terms *

Ab initio: From the beginning.

Ad valorem: According to the value, e.g., a duty or tax.

Adverse possession: A method of acquisition of title by possession for a statutory period under certain conditions.

Allegation: A statement of fact made in a legal proceeding.

Annotation: A remark, note, or commentary on some passage of a book, intended to illustrate its meaning.

Appeal: An application by an appellant to a higher court to rectify the order of the court below.

Appellant: One who appeals from a judicial decision.

Appellate court: A higher court which hears a case from a lower court on appeal.

Appellee: The person against whom an appeal is taken; the respondent to an appeal.

Arbitrary: Means in an "arbitrary" manner, as fixed or done capriciously or at pleasure, without adequate determining principle; not founded in the nature of things; nonrational; not done or acting according to reason or judgment; depending on the will alone; absolutely in power; capriciously; tyrannical; despotic.

Assault: Threatening to strike or harm.

Assumpsit: An early form of action in English law, later used in America, under which plaintiff seeks to recover damages for non-performance of a parol or simple contract.

Battery: Beating and wounding, including every touching or laying hold, however trifling, of another's person or clothes in an angry, insolent, or hostile manner.

Bill: A formal declaration, complaint, or statement of particular things in writing. As a legal term, this word has many meanings and applications, the more important of which are enumerated in *Black's Law Dictionary*.

Breach: A breaking; either the invasion of a right, or the violation of a duty.

Certiorari: (To be more fully informed) An original writ or action whereby a cause is removed from an inferior to a superior court for trial. The record of proceedings is then transmitted to the superior court. The term is most commonly used when requesting the U.S. Supreme Court to hear a case from a lower court.

---

* These definitions were selected from *Black's Law Dictionary* by Henry Campbell Black, West Publishing Company, St. Paul, Minn.

Citation: A writ issued out of a court of competent jurisdiction, commanding a person therein named to appear on a day named and do something therein mentioned, or show cause why he should not.

Civil action: An action which has for its object the recovery of private or civil rights, or compensation for their infraction.

Class bill or suit: One in which one or more members of a class sue either for themselves or for themselves and other members of a class.

Code: A compilation of statutes, scientifically analyzed into chapters, subheadings, and sections with a table of contents and an index. A collection or system of laws.

Collateral: By the side of; indirect. Not directly concerned with the issue.

Collateral attack: An attempt to avoid, defeat, or evade a judicial proceeding, or deny its force and effect, in some incidental proceeding not provided by law for the express purpose of attacking it.

Common law: Legal principles derived from usage and custom, or from court decisions affirming such usages and custom, or from the acts of Parliament in force at the time of the American Revolution, as distinguished from law created by enactment of American legislatures.

Concurring opinion: An opinion, separate from that which embodies the views and decision of the majority of the court, prepared and filed by a judge who agrees in the general result of the decision, and which either reinforces the majority opinion by the expression of the particular judge's own views or reasoning, or (more commonly) voices his disapproval of the grounds of the decision or the arguments on which it was based, though approving the final result.

Consideration in contracts: The inducement to a contract. The cause, motive, price, or impelling influence that induces a contracting party to enter into a contract.

Contract: A promissory agreement between two or more persons that creates, modifies, or destroys a legal relation.

Contributory negligence: Negligence of the plaintiff which, combined with the negligence of the defendant, was the proximate cause of the injury complained of.

Court of record: A court that keeps a permanent record of its proceedings. Frequently appellate courts are called courts of record since their proceedings are published.

Damages: A pecuniary compensation or indemnity, which may be recovered in the courts by any person who has suffered loss, detriment, or injury, whether to his person, property, or rights through the unlawful act or omission or negligence of another.

Declaratory relief: The opinion of a court on a question of law that, without ordering anything to be done, simply declares the rights of the parties.

Decree: The judgment of a court of equity or admiralty, answering for most purposes to the judgment of a court of common law.

De facto: (In fact) A *de facto* officer is in actual possession of an office without lawful title. A *de facto* corporation may be reorganized as legally effective even though defective in some particular.

Defamation: Scandalous words written or spoken concerning another, tending to the injury of his reputation, for which an action on the case for damages would lie.

Defendant: One required to make answer in a suit—the one against whom the suit is brought.

Defendant in error: The distinctive term appropriate to the party against whom a writ of error is sued out.

De jure: (By right) A *de jure* officer has just claim and rightful title to an office, though not necessarily in actual possession thereof; a legal or true corporation or officer as opposed to one that is *de facto*.

Demurrer: A plea by one of the parties to an action, who, while admitting for the sake of argument all the material facts properly pleaded by the opposing party, contends the existence of the facts does not constitute grounds for action.

Devise: A testamentary disposition of land or realty; a gift of real property by the last will and testament of the donor.

Dictum: The expression by a judge of an opinion on a point of law not necessary to the decision on the case; not binding on other judges.

Directory: A provision in a statute, rule of procedure, or the like, which is a mere direction or instruction of no obligatory force, and involves no invalidating consequence for its disregard, as opposed to an imperative or mandatory provision, which must be followed.

Discretionary power: Involves the exercise of judgment in reaching a decision; deciding whether to do something.

Dissenting opinion: An opinion disagreeing with that of the majority, handed down by one or more members of the court.

Due process: Law in the regular course of administration through courts of justice, according to those rules and forms that have been established for the protection of private rights.

Ejusdem generis: Of the same kind or nature.

Eminent domain: The power to take private property for public use.

Enjoin: To require, command, positively direct. To require a person, by writ of injunction from a court of equity, to perform, or to abstain or desist from, some act.

Equity: A system of law that affords a remedy where there is no complete or adequate remedy at law. A court of law assesses damages; a court of equity renders a decision in mandamus, injunction, or specific performance.

Estop: To stop, bar, or impede; to prevent, to preclude.

Estoppel: A man's own act or acceptance stops or closes his mouth to allege or plead the truth.

Ex officio: By virtue of his office.

Ex post facto: (After the fact) Act passed after another act that retroactively changes the legal consequences of that act. Federal Constitution prohibits passage of *ex post facto* criminal law.

Ex rel: (ex relatione) At the instance of; on behalf of; on relation of information.

Executory: That which is yet to be performed or accomplished.

Fee simple: A fee simple absolute is an estate limited absolutely to a man and his heirs and assigns forever without limitation or condition.

Governmental function: One imposed or required of a municipal corporation for the protection of the general public; a function relating to the corporation's purpose for existing.

Hearsay evidence: Evidence not proceeding from the personal knowledge of the witness, but from the mere repetition of what he has heard others say.

In loco parentis: In place of the parent; charged with some of the parents' rights, duties, and responsibilities.

In re: In the affair; in the matter of; concerning. This is the usual method of entitling a judicial proceeding in which there are no adversary parties.

Injunction: A prohibitive writ issued by a court of equity forbidding the defendant to do some act he is threatening, or forbidding him to continue doing some act that is injurious to the plaintiff and cannot be adequately redressed by an action at law.

Ipso facto: By the very act itself, i.e., as the necessary consequence of the act.

Ipso jure: By the mere operation of the law.

Laches: Negligence, or unreasonable delay in pursuing a legal remedy, whereby a person forfeits his right.

Legacy: A disposition of personalty by will.

Liability: The word is a broad legal term and has been referred to as of the most comprehensive significance, including almost every character of hazard or responsibility, absolute, contingent, or likely.

Libel: Defamation by printed or written communication.

Liquidated: Fixed, ascertained, e.g., damages, the exact amount of which must be paid, or may be collected, upon a default or breach of contract.

Liquidated damages: The term is applicable when the amount of the damages has been ascertained by the judgment in the action, or when a specific sum of money has been expressly stipulated by the parties to a bond or other contract as the amount of damages to be recovered by either party for a breach of the agreement by the other.

Mala in se (Malum in se): Acts wrong in themselves, whether prohibited by human law or not.

Mala prohibita (Malum prohibitum): Acts prohibited by human laws, but not necessarily wrong of themselves.

Malfeasance: The commission of an unlawful act.

Malice: Hatred, ill will; a formed design of doing an unlawful act.

Mandamus: A writ of mandamus is a command from a court of law directed to an inferior court, officer, corporate body, or person regarding him or them to do some particular thing.

Ministerial: Belonging to a minister or subordinate who is bound to follow instructions; opposed to judicial or discretionary.

Misfeasance: A wrongful act, negligence, or the improper performance of some lawful act.

Municipal corporation: A body politic created by the incorporation of the inhabitants as an agency of the state to regulate and administer the local affairs thereof; a voluntary corporation; a city, village, or borough. The term is sometimes used in a broader sense and includes all types of local governmental bodies including school districts.

Negligence: Want of care.

Nolens volens: Whether willing or unwilling; consenting or not.

Nuisance: Anything that unlawfully results in harm, inconvenience, or damage.

Original jurisdiction: The jurisdiction of a court to entertain a case in its inception, as contrasted with the appellate jurisdiction.

Parol: By word of mouth.

Per se: By itself, alone.

Petition: Written application or prayer to the court for the redress of a wrong or the grant of a privilege or license.

Plaintiff: Person who brings an action, the one who sues by filing a complaint.

Plenary: Full; conclusive.

Police power: Inherent or plenary legislative power to enact laws for the comfort, health, and prosperity of the state. The right to modify for the common good. In short, the right of the sovereign to govern.

Prayer: The request contained in a bill in equity that the court will grant the process, aid, or relief that the complainant desires.

Precedent: A decision considered as furnishing an example or authority for an identical or similar case afterward arising on a similar question of law.

Prima facie: At first view; on the first aspect. Prima facie evidence, presumptions, etc., are such as will prevail, if not rebutted, or disproved.

Privies of parties: Persons connected with mutual interest in the same action.

Proprietary functions: Those functions exercised by a municipality for the improvement of the territory within the corporate limits, or the doing of such things as inure to the benefit, pecuniarily or otherwise, of the municipality. Things not normally required by law or things not governmental in nature. Operation of an athletic contest where a fee is charged may be an example in some states.

Quantum meruit: (As much as he has earned) Action brought by a party to a contract against the other, not founded on the contract itself, but on an implied promise to pay for so much as the party suing has done, or as much as reasonably deserved for work or labor.

Quasi: As if; almost.

Quasi-municipal corporation (or quasi corporation): A political or civil subdivision of the state, created by law, to assist the state in administering the state's affairs—an involuntary corporation. Example: a school district.

Quid pro quo: "Something for something"; a consideration.

Quo warranto: (By what authority) A writ, or proceeding, by which the government inquires into the right of a person, or corporation, to hold an office, or exercise a franchise, which was never lawfully held, or which has been forfeited by neglect or abuse.

Ratification: In a broad sense, the confirmation of a previous act done either by the party himself or by another; confirmation of a voidable act.

Remand a case: An action by an appellate court to send the case back to the court from which it came for further proceedings there.

Res judicata: A matter judicially decided.

Respondeat superior: The responsibility of a master for the acts of his servants.

Respondent: The one making an answer—the defendant.

Restrain: To prohibit from action; to enjoin.

Restraining order: An injunction.

Reversion: The residue of an estate left by operation of law in the grantor or his heirs, or in the heirs, or in the heirs of a testator, commencing in possession on the determination of a particular estate granted or devised.

Slander: Defamation by spoken word.

Specific performance: A requirement by a court of equity that both parties go through with a contract.

Stare decisis: Adherence to precedent. When the court has made a declaration of legal principle it is the law until changed by a competent authority.

Statute: Law enacted by the legislative power of a country or state.

Subpoena duces tecum: A process by which a court commands a witness to produce some document or paper that is pertinent to the controversy being litigated.

Substantive law: The positive law of rights and duties.

Tenure: Right to perform duties and receive emoluments thereof.

Title to property: Title is the means whereby the owner of lands has the just possession of his property.

Tort: Legal injury or wrong committed upon the person or property of another independent of contract.

Trespass: The unauthorized entry upon, taking, or interfering with the property of another. Also, common law form of action brought to obtain damages for unlawful injury.

Ultra vires: An *ultra vires* contract is one beyond the powers of the corporation to make. In other words, it is one the corporation had no authority to make.

Void: Null; ineffectual; nugatory; having no legal force or binding effect; unable, in law, to support the purpose for which it was intended.

Voidable: That may be avoided, or declared void; not absolutely void, or void in itself.

Whereas: A word that introduces a recital of a fact.

Index

†